THE OXFORD HANDBOOK OF

THE BIBLE IN CHINA

THE OXFORD HANDBOOK OF

THE BIBLE IN CHINA

Edited by

K. K. YEO

OXFORD
UNIVERSITY PRESS

OXFORD
UNIVERSITY PRESS

Oxford University Press is a department of the University of Oxford. It furthers the University's objective of excellence in research, scholarship, and education by publishing worldwide. Oxford is a registered trade mark of Oxford University Press in the UK and certain other countries.

Published in the United States of America by Oxford University Press
198 Madison Avenue, New York, NY 10016, United States of America.

Library of Congress Cataloging-in-Publication Data

Names: Yeo, Khiok-Khng, editor.
Title: The Oxford handbook of the Bible in China / edited by K.K. Yeo.
Description: New York, NY : Oxford University Press, [2021]
Identifiers: LCCN 2020035038 (print) | LCCN 2020035039 (ebook) |
ISBN 9780190909796 (hardback) | ISBN 9780190909826 (ebook) |
ISBN 9780190909819 (epub)
Subjects: LCSH: Bible—History. | Bible—Criticism, interpretation, etc.—China. |
Bible—Influence. | Religion and culture—China—History.
Classification: LCC BS447.5.C6 O94 2021 (print) | LCC BS447.5.C6 (ebook) |
DDC 220.0951—dc23
LC record available at https://lccn.loc.gov/2020035038
LC ebook record available at https://lccn.loc.gov/2020035039

1 3 5 7 9 8 6 4 2

Printed by Sheridan Books, Inc., United States of America

Acknowledgments

This 400,000-word Handbook would not be possible without "a cloud of witnesses" and "good and faithful" supporters. Oxford University Press (OUP) Editor Dr. Steve Wiggins has been a joy to work with from the beginning to the end of this tedious project. He has answers to all my questions and replies to my emails instantly. He reads every essay and offers meticulously idiomatic expressions fitting for the genre of the academic handbook, and for a wider audience. I am grateful beyond words. His kind, patient, and encouraging spirit and acumen make this daunting task lighter. Other OUP teams worked behind the scenes and, despite their anonymity, I can count on them to deliver professionally, in areas of contract issuing, copyediting, printing, and publicity. The expertise and enthusiasm of Brad Rosenkrantz at OUP and Jayaprakash P. at SPi Global have ensured a smooth and timely production process.

Friends and colleagues have stepped up to the plate and committed to the research and writing on the assigned topics—all agreed to participate within a week of invitation, in the spring of 2018, with a ten-month submission deadline (though we waited for the last few to arrive in November 2019). I owe a great debt and appreciation to each and every contributor in this Handbook for journeying with me; together we form a community of scholars that accentuates this Handbook. It is a feat that forty-nine authors are able to complete forty-seven essays with such diligence and ahead of schedule.

A few authors under contracts, for various reasons understandably, were unable to complete the assignments. I am pleased that all the essential essays needed for the Handbook are completed with excellence. I lament the passing of my friend and colleague, Dr. Vincent T. Shen of Toronto University, on November 14, 2018, and the passing of Prof. Irene Eber of Hebrew University, on April 10, 2019; their essays would have graced this Handbook. Prof. Dr. Roman Malek S.V.D. passed away on November 29, 2019, and he was the second person to submit an essay to me in December of 2018, noting in his email "I am ill presently." Their lives of dedication, humility, and kindness have touched me.

I express my heartfelt gratitude to the following friends and institutions who have pitched in with consulting, proofreading, translating, and networking: Drs. Vincent T. Shen, Yang Naiqiao, Zhang Xin, Leopold Leeb, Chloë Starr, Terry Halliday, Li Zhengrong, the Academic Dean's office at Garrett-Evangelical Theological Seminary, and my colleagues there and at Northwestern University (Evanston), and those in China: Peking University, Tsinghua University, Beijing Normal University, Fudan University, Zhejiang University, and Minzu University of China. Special thanks are due to Dr. Melanie Baffes, who edited all essays in their first few drafts to make the manuscript more readable and raised helpful questions for me to work further with the authors. I appreciate also the help of Kungsiu Lau and Phoebe Yeo for putting together the index, a handy and necessary tool that will benefit readers.

The interpretation and view of each essay are solely that of its contributor(s), and insufficiency and errors especially in style and copyediting remain mine. I hope the conversations in the Handbook and outside will promote new knowledge and, as a result, enrich the world. The academic studies of the Bible in China have still to explore many uncharted territories, and I believe the better academic works we do the greater impact the Bible will have in China and the world. Many scholars studying Chinese cultures and/or the Bible in China are committed to realizing the task of building flourishing nations and civilizations of universal love and world peace. Perhaps, this Handbook can contribute towards that—stated eloquently in a verse from the Bible translated into Latin: *Gloria in excelsis Deo, et in terra pax hominibus bonae voluntatis* (Luke 1:14).

Contents

PART II EXPRESSION IN LITERARY AND RELIGIOUS CONTEXTS

PART III INTERPRETATION AND METHODS OF READING

List of Figures

List of Contributors

Zhaohui BAO 包兆會 Associate Professor in the School of Liberal Arts at Nanjing University (Nanjing, China). His recent research focuses on the relationship between literature and image, Christianity and Chinese literature, and the Daoist view of nature and life from the perspective of creation theology. He is the author of *Research on Zhuangzi's Existential Aesthetics* (2004) and *Zhuangzi* (Chinese and English version, *The Collection of Critical Biographies of Chinese Thinkers*) (2010). He is editor of the five-volume series of *Selecting Works of Chinese Christian Literature* (2019), and the *History of Chinese Literature and Image in Pre-Qin Period* (2020).

CAO Jian 曹堅 Associate Professor in the Philosophy department at Sun Yat-sen University (Guangzhou, China). His research focuses on the Hebrew Bible, with particular attention to its encounter with modern Chinese intellectuals. He is the author of *Chinese Biblical Anthropology* (2019).

CHAN Tak-Kwong 陳德光 Research Fellow in the Academia Catholica at Fu Jen Catholic University (New Taipei City, Taiwan). His research focuses on the Old Testament and Comparative Religion, with particular attention to mysticism in the East and West. He is the author of "Ex 3:14a—State of the Question and a Possible Chinese Mystical Interpretation (*Fu Jen International Religious Studies*, 2011)" and "The Essence of Faith and Paradigm Change: Catholicity and the Wisdom of the East" (*Lumen: A Journal of Catholic Studies*, 2017).

Daniel Kam-to CHOI 蔡錦圖 Missionary of Hong Kong Baptist Mission in Germany. Choi received his DTh degree from Lutheran Theological Seminary (Hong Kong). Choi's research focuses on Chinese church history and Chinese Bible translation. He is the author or editor of several books, including *Bible in China: With a Historical Catalogue of the Chinese Bible* (Chinese, 2018) and *In the Beginning Was the Word: Bible Translations into Chinese by the Baptists in the Nineteenth-Century* (Chinese, 2019).

Yanrong CHEN 陳妍蓉 Luce Post-Doctoral Research Fellow at the University of San Francisco (San Francisco, CA, USA). Having studied the reception of the Bible in China, she earned her PhD from the University of Leuven (KU Leuven), Belgium. Her new monograph entitled "The Diffused Story of the Footwashing in John 13: A Textual Study of Bible Reception in Late Imperial China" is forthcoming (2020).

Philip P. CHIA 謝品然 Professor of Hebrew Bible at the Chung Yuan Christian University (Taoyuan City, Taiwan). His research focuses on the Bible and public theology, with particular attention to critical biblical public theology. He is the author of "Occupy Central: Scribal Resistance in Daniel, the Long Road to Universal Suffrage" (in *Interested Readers: Essays on the Hebrew Bible in Honor of David J. A. Clines*, 2013) and "Biblical Studies in the Rising Asia: An Asian Perspective on the Future of the Biblical Past" (in *The Future of the Biblical Past*, 2012).

Christie Chui-Shan CHOW 周翠珊 PhD from Princeton Theological Seminary in 2015. Her forthcoming book, entitled "*Schism: How Adventism Is Reshaping Post-Denominational China*," reflects her interest in conversion and identity. Her articles have appeared in *Journal of the Royal Asiatic Society*, *Journal of World Christianity*, and *Social Sciences and Missions*.

Xiaobai CHU 褚瀟白 Professor at East China Normal University (Shanghai, China). Her main research interests lie in the areas of Christian literature and arts in China and Christology in cultural perspective. She is the author of *Jesus through the Centuries in China* (2011), *The Encounter of Chinese Folk Religions and Christianity in Modern History* (2016), and *A Narrative of Space and the Consciousness of Eschatology: A Study on Christian Literature in Late Antiquity* (2016).

Claudia von COLLANI Professor in the Department of Catholic Theology, University of Würzburg (Würzburg, Germany), a missiologist, and specialist in East Asian mission history of early modern times, the Chinese Rites Controversy, and Figurism, the figurist exchange of knowledge between Europe and China. Together with Paul Rule, she is co-editor of Kilian Stumpf S.J., *The Acta Pekinensia or Historical Records of the Maillard de Tournon Legation*, vol. 1 (2015), and vol. 2 (2019).

Terence C. HALLIDAY Research Professor at the American Bar Foundation, an independent and interdisciplinary institute of advanced studies on law and legal institutions; Honorary Professor in the School of Regulation and Global Governance, Australian National University (Canberra, Australia); and Adjunct Professor of Sociology, Northwestern University (Evanston, IL, USA). He has written extensively on law reform, law, and lawyers in China and their implications for China's legal and political futures, including *Fates of Political Liberalism in the British Post-Colony: The Politics of the Legal Complex* (2012), and *Criminal Defense in China: The Politics of Lawyers at Work* (2016), with Sida Liu.

Fang-Lan HSIEH 謝林芳蘭 Retired as the Associate Dean of libraries and music librarian at Southwestern Baptist Theological Seminary in Fort Worth, Texas. Her primary research areas are Chinese Christian hymnody and music bibliography. She is the author of *An Annotated Bibliography of Church Music* (2003) and *A History of Chinese Christian Hymnody: From Its Missionary Origins to Contemporary Indigenous Productions* (2009). In addition, she has translated nine church-music books into Chinese, including her own 2009 publication.

Paulos HUANG 黃保羅 Distinguished Professor at Shanghai University (Shanghai, China), and Adjunct Professor in the faculty of Humanities at the University of Helsinki (Helsinki, Finland). His research focuses on Sino-Christian academic theology, the Great National Studies of China, and the dialogue between the West and China. He is the author of *No. 1 Chu Tomb and the Earliest Bamboo Slip Versions of Laozi and Taiyi sheng shui* (2000), *Sino-Christian Academic Theology* (2008), *Confronting Confucian Understandings of Christian Doctrine of Salvation* (2010), *Sino-Christian Academic Biblical Studies in the Light of the Great National Studies* (2012). He also is the Chinese translator of eight books of Martin Luther (2018) and chief editor for *International Journal of Sino-Western Studies* (www.SinoWesternStudies.com) and *Brill Yearbook of Chinese Theology* (www.brill.com/yct).

John T. P. LAI 黎子鵬 Professor in the Department of Cultural and Religious Studies and Associate Dean of Arts, The Chinese University of Hong Kong (Hong Kong). His research focuses on the interdisciplinary study of religion, literature, and translation. He has published four monographs, including *Negotiating Religious Gaps: The Enterprise of Translating Christian Tracts by Protestant Missionaries in Nineteenth-Century China* (2012), and *Literary Representations of Christianity in Late Qing and Republican China* (2019).

Pan-chiu LAI 賴品超 Professor in the Department of Cultural and Religious Studies, The Chinese University of Hong Kong (Hong Kong). His primary research areas include Chinese Christian theology and inter-religious dialogue. He is the author of *Towards a Trinitarian Theology of Religions* (1994), *Mahayana Christian Theology* (2011), and *Sino-Christian Theology in Public Square* (2014).

Archie C. C. LEE 李熾昌 Professor of the Hebrew Bible in the Department of Cultural and Religious Studies of The Chinese University of Hong Kong (Hong Kong) before his retirement in 2014. He was then appointed as University Distinguished Professor of Humanities and Social Sciences, Center for Judaic and Inter-Religious Studies, and Director, Jao Tsung-I Institute of Religion and Chinese Studies, Shandong University (Jinan, China). He is the founding President of the Society of Asian Biblical Studies (SABS). His research interest is in cross-textual interpretation of the Bible and Chinese religious texts.

Joseph Tse-Hei LEE 李榭熙 Professor of History at Pace University (New York, NY, USA). His research focuses on faith and politics in China. He is the author of *The Bible and the Gun: Christianity in South China, 1860–1900* (2003) and co-author of *Context and Vision: Visualizing Chinese-Western Cultural Encounters in Chaoshan* (with Christie Chui-Shan Chow, 2017).

Leopold LEEB 雷立柏 Professor in the School of Liberal Arts at Renmin University of China (Beijing, China), where he has been teaching classical languages (Latin, Greek, Hebrew). His research area is the history of Christianity in China. He is the author of *Dictionary of Theological Terms* (Latin-English-Chinese, 2007) and *A Dictionary of the History of Christianity in China* (Chinese, 2013).

Sher-shiueh LI 李奭學 Research Fellow at the Institute of Chinese Literature and Philosophy, Academia Sinica (Taipei, Taiwan). His research focuses on translated literature from European languages in the transitional period between the Ming and the Qing dynasties. In this field, he has published several Chinese books, including *Late Ming China and European Literature* (2005), *Transwriting: Late Ming Jesuits and Translated Literature* (2012), *Jesuit Chreia in Late Ming China: Two Essays with an Annotated Translation of Alfonso Vagnone's "Illustrations of the Grand Dao"* (co-authored with Thierry Meynard, 2014), and *Western Learning in the Ming and the Qing: Six Studies* (2016).

LI Zhengrong 李正榮 Professor in the School of Chinese Language and Literature at Beijing Normal University (Beijing, China), a researcher at the Center for Russian Studies, Vice President of the College of Transcultural Studies, and Director of the Center for Study of Christian Literature and Art at the same university. His research focuses on Russian literature and culture, European literature and culture, Christian literature and culture, and intercultural chemistry and philology. He is the author of *The Enlightenment of Tolstoy and His Prose* [in Chinese] (2001) and series editor of *A·Ω* (2016–).

LIU Boyun 柳博贇 Assistant Professor of translation and interpreting at the School of Translation and Interpreting, Beijing Language and Culture University (Beijing, China). She was a visiting scholar at the Department of Religion, Baylor University. Her principal areas of research and writing are the history of Syriac Christianity and Chinese translations of Christian texts. Her works of Chinese translation include Origen of Alexandria's *Commentary on the Gospel According to John* (2 vols.) and *The Dead Sea Scrolls Today* by James VanderKam. She is also a professional simultaneous interpreter.

Evan LIU Executive Director of Servant Leadership Center of the US, an Adjunct Professor at Midwestern Baptist Theological Seminary (Kansas City, MO, USA), and East Asian Theological Seminary (Seoul, South Korea). His primary research areas are Pauline theology, 1–2 Corinthians, and modern studies of global Chinese churches. He is the author of *Temple Purity in 1–2 Corinthians* (2013).

George Kam Wah MAK 麥金華 Assistant Professor in the Department of Religion and Philosophy at Hong Kong Baptist University (Hong Kong). A historian of Chinese Bible translation, he is the author of *Protestant Bible Translation and Mandarin as the National Language of China* (2017) and *The British and Foreign Bible Society and the Translation of the Mandarin Chinese Union Version* (in Chinese, 2010).

Roman MALEK S.V.D. 馬雷凱 Professor of History of Religion in the theological faculty in Sankt Augustin (Sankt Augustin, Germany) and Sinology at the University of Bonn (Bonn, Germany) (b. 1951 in Bytow, Poland; d. November 29, 2019). He was the author and editor of *The Chinese Face of Jesus Christ*, and more than nine hundred pieces of works on the history of religion, Christianity in China, and the history of religion in China.

Kuo-Wei PENG 彭國瑋 Editor-in-chief and Translation Consultant of the *Chinese Union Study Bible Series* (forty-two units, once completed, and each unit will contain at least one volume); so far, twelve volumes have been published: *Galatians* (2009), *1–3 John* (2011), *1–2 Timothy & Titus* (2011), *Ruth* (2011), *Genesis* (2013), *Colossians & Philemon* (2014), *Acts* (2016), *2 Peter & Jude* (2017), *Sermon on the Mount* (2018), *James* (2018), *Ephesians* (2019), and *1-2 Thessalonians* (2020). He is the author of *Hate the Evil, Hold Fast to the Good: Structuring Romans 12:1–15:13* (2006) and *Witness to Jesus as Christ: An Introduction to Christian Biblical Interpretation* (in Chinese; 2011, 2013).

QU Yi 曲藝 Associate Professor at Nanjing University of the Arts (Nanjing, China). Her research focuses on Jesuit prints and the artistic and religious exchange between East Asia and Europe. Qu's publications include "Die Anweisung zur Rezitation des Rosenkranzes 誦念珠規程. Ein illustriertes christliches Buch aus China vom Anfang des 17. Jahrhundert" in Monumenta Serica, Bd. 60 (2012).

Guangqi RONG 榮光啟 Associate Professor in the College of Literature and Language at Wuhan University (Wuhan, China). His primary research area is new poetry study in modern Chinese literature, and he is acclaimed as an active contemporary poetry critic as well. He is the author of *The Emergence of Modern Chinese Poetry: From Late Qing Dynasty to the May 4th Period* (2015) and the editor of *Way Station: Haizi' First Anthology* (2009) and other collections of poems. In 2019, he completed *The History of Contemporary Christian Literature* and *The Studies on Contemporary Christian Poems.*

SHI Hengtan 石衡潭 Associate Researcher at the Institute of World Religions at the Chinese Academy of Social Sciences (Beijing, China). His main research areas are the relationship between Christianity and Chinese culture, Orthodox church, and film theology. He is author of a number of Chinese works, including *The Analects of Confucius Meets the Bible* (2014), *The Comparative Reading of Chinese and Western Scriptures* (2018), *A Freedom and Creation: Introduction to Berdyaev's Religious Philosophy* (2011); *Faith, Hope, and Love in Film* (2013).

SONG Gang 宋剛 Associate Professor of Chinese History at the University of Hong Kong (Hong Kong). His research focuses on Catholic Christianity in late imperial China. He is the author of *Giulio Aleni,* Kouduo richao, *and Christian-Confucian Dialogism in Late Ming Fujian* (2018), and editor of *Reshaping the Boundaries: The Christian Intersection of China and the West in the Modern Era* (2016) and *Transmission, Writing, and Imagination: The West in Late Imperial Chinese Culture* (2019).

SONG Jun 宋軍 Associate Professor of Theological Studies and Director of the Chinese Culture Research Centre at the China Graduate School of Theology (Hong Kong). His research areas are church history of China and folk religions in the Ming and Qing dynasties. He is the author of *Studies on Hong Yang Religion in Qing Dynasty* (2002) and *Making Choices in the Midst of Change: The End of National Christian Council of China (1949–1951)* (2017).

Nicolas STANDAERT 鐘鳴旦 Professor of Sinology at the University of Leuven (Leuven, Belgium). His research focuses on the intercultural contacts between China and Europe in the seventeenth and eighteenth centuries. He is the author of *An Illustrated Life of Christ Presented to the Chinese Emperor: The History of Jincheng shuxiang (1640)* (2007) and editor of *Handbook of Christianity in China*, Vol. 1: *(635–1800)* (2001).

Chloë STARR 司馬懿 Professor of Asian Christianity and Theology at Yale Divinity School (New Haven, CT, USA). Her research focuses on Chinese theology, especially its relationship to Chinese literature. She is the author of *Chinese Theology: Text and Context* (2016) and *Red-Light Novels of the Late Qing* (2007); editor of *Reading Christian Scripture in China* (2008); and co-editor of *China and the Quest for Gentility* (2007).

SUN Chenhui 孫晨薈 Associate Professor at the Music Institute of Chinese National Academy of Arts (Beijing, China.) Her research focuses on the Chinese Christian music culture and Chinese traditional music. She is the author of Chinese works including *Gregorian Chant in Tibet* (2010, 2015), *Catholic Music in North China* (2012, 2018), and *A Study on Protestant Music of Lisu and Huamiao* (2016).

Justin T. T. TAN 陳廷忠 Professor and former Vice-Principal at Melbourne School of Theology (Melbourne, Australia). He is the Director of Center for the Study of Chinese Christianity and Research Fellow of Australia College of Theology. His research areas are Patristic spirituality, especially the desert fathers and Gregory of Nyssa, and Old Testament theology. He has translated *The Sayings of the Desert Fathers* into Chinese (2013) and written on various traditions of early Christian spirituality. He is the Old Testament editor and contributor to the Chinese Shenzhou Biblical Commentaries and author of studies on the *Book of Job* (Chinese, 2011, 2016), and the Psalter (Chinese, 2019). He is the co-editor of *Spirit Wind: The Doctrine of the Holy Spirit in Global Theology—A Chinese Perspective* (2020).

Benoît VERMANDER 魏明德 Professor in the Department of Religious Studies at Fudan University (Shanghai, China). He is the author of *Shanghai Sacred* (2018, with Liz Hingley and Liang Zhang) and *Corporate Social Responsibility in China* (2014), among other publications. For the Oxford Handbooks series, he has authored contributions on "Jesuits in China" and "Jesuits in the 21st Century."

Lianming WANG Assistant Professor at the Centre for Asian and Transcultural Studies (CATS), Heidelberg University (Heidelberg, Germany). His research focuses on early modern Sino-European cultural exchanges, with special attention to Jesuit art and architecture in Asia. He is the author of "From Beijing to La Flèche: The Transcultural Moment of Jesuit Garden Spaces" (in *EurAsian Matters: China, Europe and the Transcultural Objects*, 2018) and *Jesuitenerbe in Peking: Sakralbauten und transkulturelle Räume, 1600–1800* (2020).

WANG Zi 王梓 Assistant Professor at Minzu University of China (Beijing, China). Her PhD from Peking University (Beijing, China) is on sociological study of Pauline theology in 1 Corinthians. Her primary research areas are the Pauline letters and the history of early Christianity. She has translated and published several books and various articles on biblical studies including co-edited (with K. K. Yeo) *Reading Scripture and World Civilizations* (Chinese, 2017).

Bernard K. WONG 黃國維 Associate Professor of Theological Studies and Associate Dean at the China Graduate School of Theology (Hong Kong). His research areas are theology of the family, bioethics, and technology and faith. He is the author of *Beginning from Man and Woman: Witnessing Christ's Love in the Family* (2017) and *Communio: A Biblical Reflection on Relationship and Community* (2018).

Jinghan XU 徐竟涵 Associate Professor of Photography in the School of Drama, TV and Cinematic Arts at the Communication University of China (Beijing, China). His research focuses on documentary photographic images and image aesthetics. He pays attention to Christian visual arts in contemporary life. Besides being a writer of books and essays, he is also a photographer, documentary filmmaker, and exhibition curator.

YANG Huilin 楊慧林 Professor at Renmin University of China (Beijing, China). His research focuses on religious studies and comparative literature, with particular attention to the interpretation and inculturation of Christianity in the Chinese context. He is the author of *China, Christianity and the Question of Culture* (2014) and *The Word of God and the Words of Man: Theological Hermeneutics* (2018 revised edition).

K. K. YEO 楊克勤 Harry R. Kendall Professor of New Testament at Garrett-Evangelical Theological Seminary and an Affiliate Professor in the Department of Asian Languages and Cultures, Northwestern University (Evanston, IL, USA). He is a Henry Luce III Scholar (2003) and series co-editor (with Melanie Baffes) of "Contrapuntal Readings of the Bible" (2018–). He has authored and edited more than forty books on critical engagement between Bible and cultures, including *Zhuangzi and James* (in Chinese, 2012), *Theologies of Land* (2020), and co-edited (with Gene Green and Steve Pardue) the Majority World Theology Series (2014–2019).

John Y. H. YIEH 葉約翰 Molly Laird Downs Professor of New Testament at Virginia Theological Seminary (Alexandria, VA, USA). His research focuses on the Gospel of Matthew and Johannine Literature, with particular interest in sociological inquiry and history of effects. He is the author of *One Teacher: Jesus' Teaching Role in Matthew's Gospel Report* (2004), *Conversations with Scripture: The Gospel of Matthew* (2012), and *The Lord's Prayer: Oxford Bibliographies in Biblical Studies* (2018).

YOU Bin 游斌 Professor of Religions at Minzu University of China (Beijing, China), where he directs the Academy of Religions and leads a research project on Comparative Scripture and Interreligious Dialogue. He is actively involved in interreligious dialogue between different religions in China. He is the founding editor of *Journal of Comparative Scripture* and the author of many books on Hebrew Bible, Christian Studies, etc.

YOU Rujie 游汝傑 Professor of Fudan University (Shanghai, China). His main research areas are Chinese dialectology with Wu dialects in particular and sociolinguistics, especially in the relationship between Chinese dialects and culture. He is the author of a number of Chinese works including: *An Introduction to Chinese Dialectology* (1992), *On Chinese Linguistic Works Written by Western Missionaries* (2002), *Selected Works on Chinese Dialects Contact* (2016), *Wu Dialectology* (2019).

Suee Yan YU 尤垂然 Global translation advisor with the United Bible Societies. He supervises several ethnic minority Bible-translation projects in China and elsewhere. His specialization is in the Old Testament. He conducts training workshops for translators and consultants and occasionally teaches intensive courses in China and Malaysia.

ZHA Changping 查常平 Professor of New Testament at the Institute of Daoism and Religious Culture's Center for Christianity Studies of Sichuan University (Chengdu, China). He is the chief editor of the *Journal for Humanities and Art* (*Renwen yishu*). His research areas are biblical studies, art criticism, and logic of world-picture. He is author of numerous Chinese works including: *History and Logic: The Cultural Logic of Humanitology* (2007), *Introduction to the Logic of World-Picture of the New Testament* (2011), *A History of Ideas in Pioneering Contemporary Chinese Art* (2 vols., 2017), and *Humanist Criticism of Contemporary Art* (2019).

ZHENG Haijuan 鄭海娟 Associate Professor in the Institute of Literature, Chinese Academy of Social Sciences (Beijing, China). Her research focuses on missionaries to China in the early modern period, particularly their Chinese writings and translations. She is co-editor of *GuXin ShengJing CanGao* with Li Sher-shiueh, 2014).

Clover Xuesong ZHOU 周雪松 Art journalist and art critic based in Los Angeles and Beijing. Her articles have been published in professional art journals such as *ArtForum China*, *Art Newspaper China*, *Randian*, and *Art World*. She specializes in reviewing contemporary art, especially Chinese contemporary art. Her recent research has focused on contemporary art and Christian theology.

Donghua ZHU 朱東華 Professor in the School of Humanities at Tsinghua University (Beijing, China). He specializes in phenomenology of religion, Chinese Christianity (Jingjiao) in the Tang and Yuan dynasties, and primitive Christianity, with Syrian Patristics as his particular focus. He is the author of *From Holiness to Numinous: On the Phenomenological Characteristics of Rudolf Otto's Numinology* (2007), *Reflections on the Disciplinary History of Religious Studies* (2016), and *A Comprehensive Study of Jingjiao in Tang and Yuan Dynasties* (2019).

Jeremiah ZHU Shuai 祝帥 Associate Professor in the School of Journalism and Communication at Peking University (Beijing, China). His research focuses on the history of Christianity in China and Chinese religious culture, especially paintings and calligraphy. He is the author of *From the Western Learning Spreading to the East and the Transformation of Chinese Calligraphy Studies* (2014) and the Chinese translation of *The Wisdom Literature* by Richard Clifford (2010).

CHAPTER 1

CREATIVE TRANSFORMATION, THE BIBLE, AND CHINA

K. K. YEO

FROM STOCKTAKING TO SENSE-MAKING

THE need for a reference text on the Bible in China is long overdue.[1] The research questions regarding the nature, the process, the purpose, and the influence of the Chinese Bible remain obscure and confusing to most Christian readers interested in how God has been at work in Chinese cultures and societies in "many and various ways" (Heb 1:1).[2] This Handbook showcases critical-descriptive evidence and the creative impact of the Bible's translation, expression, interpretation, and reception in China.

Ancient Times: Legend and Possibilities

The biblical paradigm of journey, be it of Abraham (Genesis 12–22), Moses (Exodus 1–40), Jonah (chaps. 1–4), Luke (chaps. 9–19), or Paul (his epistles) and the apostles (Acts), can be extended to the dissemination of the Bible to the Far East into China.[3] Legend has it that the apostle Thomas preached the gospel in China, converted some Chinese, and returned to southern India, where he founded a church and passed away. The Eastern Orthodox missionaries to China also could be one of the earliest attempts of early Christianity, but more research has yet to be done.

Distant Past: The Bible and Local Religious Language

The so-called "Nestorian Tablet" or "Jingjiao Stele" 景教碑 from the Tang dynasty (618–906) at Xi'an presents a solid marker of the transmission and expression of the Bible in China (along with Zoroastrianism, Manicheanism, and Islam). In Chinese, the stele is called "Daqin [Syria] Jingjiao." Because of Tang's open and tolerant foreign policy, the Church of the East in Persia sent missionaries to propagate its "illustrious religion" (jingjiao 景教), this appellation being the title of their religion that was inscribed on the stone slab. This ancient Christian group is actually called *Jing*jiao 經教 in Persia, literally meaning "religion of *scripture*," whose exegetical tradition can be traced back to the Antiochene school that used a mostly *literal* and sometimes typological method of exegesis. When Nestorian missionary Aluoben arrived in China, the imperial court allowed him to translate the Christian Scripture of Eastern Syriac Christianity using the religious language of Chinese Buddhism and Daoism. The cover image of this Handbook is the *Zun Jing* 尊經 (Sūtra of Veneration) from this religious group. This sūtra, found at the Dunhuang 敦煌 Buddhist library, has the earliest extant catalogue that renders some of the biblical book titles into Chinese (ca. 781 CE).[4]

Why was such a robust Antiochene exegetical tradition not able to sustain the Syrian Jingjiao's mission in China? Could it be that the principle of biblical translation is so enculturated that its message was unable to speak to the glorious Tang culture (literature, painting, poetry, china) that seemed to have no need for it at all? Or were the missionaries who came to China in fact diplomatic envoys, failing to thrive in the dominant political system of Tang?

The Last Five Hundred Years: The Bible and Indigenized Culture

From the thirteenth century, Catholic and Protestant missionaries came to China by means of different routes, commitments, and missions and, together with the contributions of Chinese Christians, they all played key roles in the way the Bible is read and used. Despite the threat of the Mongol-rule Yuan dynasty (1280–1367) in China, *Pax Mongolica* made it possible for the missionaries to preach the gospel via the silk route of international exchange. Kublai Khan requested that the Pope send a hundred men "wise in the Christian law and acquainted with the seven arts."[5] The first Catholic church was built in Beijing in 1299 and, by the year 1305, at least six thousand Chinese were baptized, but few biblical texts were translated. Chinese Christians were taught Greek and Latin rather than being invited to express biblical messages in the Chinese vernacular and understanding.

It was not until the Ming dynasty (1368–1643) that the Jesuits in China began to use the accommodation principle, adapting the biblical message to the Chinese audience. The Ming dynasty overthrew the Mongol rule and set up a Chinese empire; thus, sinocentrism rose in the form of Confucian orthodoxy. Matteo Ricci (1552–1610) strategized his mission to identify with the Confucian culture, as he studied the Chinese language and dressed like a Confucian scholar. He was able to translate the four canonical texts of Confucianism into Latin before attempting to render the Bible selectively into Chinese. He was so adept in Confucian ethics that the Confucian Academy of Wang Yangming welcomed him into dialogue with their eminent literati. Much of the successful Catholic missionary works since then have been on the translation and expression of the Bible in the cultural milieu of China, such as working with Chinese images, prints, and paintings, and offering exegesis of the Bible in the Confucian commentary method. Ricci, cross-cultural endeavor aimed to befriend the Confucian culture of "self-cultivation" as a form of Chinese Christian spirituality, was convinced that the earliest Confucian teaching about *Tian* 天 and *Shangdi* 上帝 referred to a personal supreme Being akin that of the Bible. Ricci believed that the fuller revelation of Christianity did not annul but supplemented and fulfilled the original Confucian teachings. However, he also was critical of the Confucian tradition as he interpreted the Christian doctrine of sin as humanity deformed by passion, which weakened the will's propensity for virtue and love. Some foreign biblical works were translated into Chinese, such as *Tianzhu Jiangsheng Yanxing Jilue* 天主降生言行紀略 (*Life of Jesus According to the Gospels*) by Guilio Aleni and *Shengjing Zhijie* 聖經直解 (*Literal Explanation of the Holy Scripture*) by Manuel Diaz Junior.

The early Ching dynasty (1644–1721) witnessed the rise of the Manchurian rule, which co-opted Confucian ethics for political power. Some Catholic missionaries disagreed with Ricci's view on the Rites of Confucius (to venerate Confucius and ancestors) and the Chinese naming of God (as *Tian* and *Shangdi*). Consequently, Chinese rulers since then were ready to excommunicate foreign missionaries and to persecute Chinese Christians, as the Chinese government often categorized Christianity as a "foreign religion" (*yangjiao* 洋教). To show that Christianity in China is not "foreign," Chinese Christians lived out "the prophetic call," an enactment of one's faith decision, as a way of transforming Chinese culture not through translation but by social action, such as getting involved in the works of education, medical services, and caring for orphans and the poor, among others. Their concern for "the welfare of the city" (Jer 29:7) would assure the continuing relevance and transforming impact of the Bible in Chinese society.

To make the Bible into a vernacular is another way to show that the Bible is part of the Chinese linguistic world. And Bible translation projects had been, and will continue to be, a collaboration of foreign and local scholars, employing interdisciplinary methods. The first Bible, in this case an incomplete New Testament [NT] (from Matthew to Hebrews 1), was translated into Chinese by French Jesuit Jean Bassett, with the help of a Chinese assistant, Johan Su, in 1704–1707. It is this incomplete NT that became the basis for the Protestant missionary Robert Morrison to translate his Bible version (*Shentian Shengshu* 神天聖書). Another French Jesuit, Louis Antoine de Poirot, eventually translated the first complete Chinese Bible (*Guxin Shengjing* 古新聖經) into the Mandarin language.

Translation of the Bible involves great hermeneutical sensitivity to the self-identity of the readers and their social context. In the modern era of China history (post-1911), Wang Mingdao and Watchman Nee grounded their faith in the Bible and focused on personal salvation, but were perhaps not fully aware of how much they were influenced respectively by the pietist tradition and dispensationalism (John Darby and the Plymouth Brethren). Is this a *Chinese* form of biblical interpretation or have they uncritically adopted a dualistic *Greek* anthropology? On the other side of the spectrum, Wu Leichuan, T. C. Chao, and Bishop Ting worked hard at their biblical interpretations of the "national salvation" of China, a socialist vision of God's kingdom, and "justification by love," exploring whether this is what Jesus's reign was and is about. The debates continue.

Today and Tomorrow: Sense-Making and Task-Finding

Today, with the rise of China's political, economic, and technological power, the field of Bible studies in modern China has taken on a life of its own, in addition to, and sometimes in spite of, what foreign and local missionaries, traders, explorers, educators, activists, artists, and translators have done. It is yet to be seen whether the expansive vision of the "Belt and Road Initiative"—its railroads, highways, seaways, and airways—will carry the Chinese Bible back out into the world, reversing the flow of centuries.

Therefore, the task of this Handbook is to gather accessible, especially primary, resources. It invites experts on Chinese interpretation of the Bible to collect memories and organize primary sources and narratives of pertinent topics for present and later generations to study. Essays in the Handbook highlight the strengths and weaknesses of Chinese biblical studies as they are put in conversation with the global academy and world Christianity. Yet, this Handbook faces some challenges. The information control and political firewall at the current moment, which resists academic freedom, presents challenges to biblical studies in China and its diaspora (Taiwan, Hong Kong). The Great Firewall will not ultimately bar the Chinese from contact with the outside world; thus, the lesson learned from a long history of self-protectionism that only leads to self-isolation is that the critical consciousness for overcoming ethnocentrism can happen only through global cultural and scholarly exchange, especially in biblical studies.

Direction-Finding and Agenda-Setting: Four Transformative Moves

The sheer vastness of primary material this Handbook seeks to address calls for selectivity. The four overarching parts of the Handbook, each made up of multiple essays, are outlined on the Contents page. The four parts can serve as four gates or entry points—translation, expression, interpretation, and reception—all leading to the center, the Bible. One can enter from any of them, reading the four parts in any order. Each essay consists of a synthetic treatment, often with a historical frame, on the given topic.

Four Synchronizing Moves

The four-quadrant structure is quite superficial. If one wants to have a more historical understanding of how the Bible emerged and developed into the present life-worlds in China, then the present order of translation, expression, interpretation, and reception is a natural route. The purpose, however, is to lead readers through the pilgrimage of studying each part linearly and then *begin* to do the cross-sectional analytical task and to raise synthetic, constructive questions straddling many fields. To assist readers in moving to this subsequent level, the Handbook has two useful features: (1) the primary sources of each essay are listed (and secondary sources are given in endnotes), as the bibliography aims to help serious students track down sources and investigate for themselves additional issues not fully addressed in the Handbook; (2) an index is provided to allow readers to observe key themes or intersectional material cutting across the four parts.[6]

Ancient texts are relics from the past that nevertheless continue to speak to the *new horizons* in Chinese history, demonstrating that various versions of the Chinese Bible are *living* texts.[7] Of course, it is not so much the text as script itself that has the ability to speak effectively across space and time, but more so how well *we* perform the four moves across the biblical texts. For example, it could be that the Greek word "*dragōn*" in Revelation was mistranslated into the Chinese "*long* 龍" (dragon) of prosperity, power, and wisdom, because the Chinese who received the translation understood the Bible to be prophesying about the Chinese dragon being evil and ultimately to be destroyed. A more critical translation would render the Greek word "*dragōn*" as "*e-long* 惡龍" (evil dragon) or simply "*shou* 獸" (beast), either of which involves interpretation that would give a more accurate meaning and better reception. Examples of the four moves illustrate how these four hermeneutical acts are considered sacred tasks of Bible readers. The four moves are synchronizing and mutually enriching of each other.

Translation

The Bible as a historical product was brought to China by traders, missionaries, travelers, officials, and nation-builders. And the first move, *translation*, in the essays of Part I, is to render the Bible into the languages and dialects of China. Language is the building-block of meaning and communication, just as furniture is in a room to make the space usable. Language is not simply a speaking and writing medium, but also part and parcel of any living culture—literary or otherwise—that serves to reorder and renew the world. Translation brings an exogenous concept to the unknown in China; it changes readers,

Table 1.1 Translation Involves Expression, Interpretation, and Reception

Translation Is:	Expression	Interpretation	Reception
Within the Bible Jesus is Lord (*kyrios*): though in the Chinese Union Version (CUV) the word "*kyrios*" is translated into "*zhu* 主" (Master/Main), the Greek word "*kyrios*" itself already involves expression, interpretation, and reception:	"Lord" in the NT is an expression of religious and cultural understanding in the first-century semantic domain, i.e., it refers to a religious leader and/or political ruler.	"Lord" is interpreted to be a political idiom (Caesar); thus, the interpreter understands "Lord of lords" (Rev 19:16) as saying that Jesus's lordship is above all religious leaders and political rulers; thus, the implication for Christians is to worship Jesus only but not the emperor.	Some of the audience in Acts 17:7 heard Paul and Sila's preaching of "Jesus as Lord" and received the message that Paul's preaching is "contrary to the decree of the emperor, saying that Jesus is another King." Is that reception not correct? Because if Jesus's kingdom is reigning over all, including politics, then the audience's reception has a certain truth to it. Of course, Paul's preaching is not about treason.
In the Chinese Union Version God (*theos*) is translated into the Chinese word "*Shangdi* 上帝" (God-Above) and this translation involves:	Expression—"*Shangdi*" is an archaic Chinese expression of supreme beings, such as powerful ancestor (*di* 帝) or emperor or god. So "*Shangdi*" literally is Emperor-Above or God-Above.	Interpretation—This translation results in two editions of Chinese Union Version: one uses the generic word "*shen* 神" (god) for *theos/Elohim* (God), and another version uses "*Shangdi*" for *theos/Elohim*; the former interprets God generally as a divine being, the latter interprets God as a Chinese understanding of the Supreme, All-Powerful Deity.	Reception—Depending on which Chinese cultural tradition the Chinese readers are familiar with, most Chinese receive the translation "*Shangdi*" as more endearing of God's attributes as having supreme power and care, more indigenous linguistically of ancient Chinese understanding of deity.

who in turn change future translations to further enrich them. Cycles of translation over time incorporate strands of Chinese culture into subsequent enriched translations. Thus, translation involves also expression, interpretation, and reception, and the mosaic of these synchronizing moves are found already in the Bible in, for example, the word "Lord" (Table 1.1).

Note that the translation of "*Shangdi*" is a cross-cultural *interpretation* between the biblical Greek and the Chinese words. Chinese Christians today prefer "*Shangdi*" over "*Shen*," citing *Shangdi*'s more distinctive meaning and, therefore, its differentiation of

God from other deities—though the original Chinese usage of the word "*Shangdi*" is not about the biblical God. This gets us to the crux of the matter: Is language's meaning determined and limited by the user? Or do language and meaning always exceed the users' intention? In other words, even though the word "*Shangdi*" is used in the original Chinese classical text *not specifically* to refer to the biblical God—but so are the original Greek word "*theos*" and the Hebrew word "*Elohim*"—can "*Shangdi*" not be used to refer to Yahweh? Does this mean that the God Jews worship can only be named in Hebrew (more accurately) and not in Chinese? Language is neither secular nor sacred, neither pagan nor revealed. That is why in the Bible God has many names, and ought to be rendered in many languages. The task of biblical translator then is to borrow and "baptize" a vernacular so that the interpretation is meaningful and the reception transformative. The question then is not why one cannot use "*Shen*" or "*Shangdi*" terms just because they are originally words outside the Bible. The question is rather how to make these idioms take on biblical content. The vernacular rendition of "*Shangdi*" is a Chinese linguistic *reception* that at the end impacts the Chinese language. An originally non-biblical word, "*Shangdi*," through this translation became an accepted Christian word to all Chinese Christians and most non-Christians today as referring to the God of the Bible.

The assumption of Part I on translation is that the Bible is shaping the life of the community of faith (the church) as much as the Bible version is shaped by the translation rendered by the community. The essays in Part I therefore explore the following critical questions: (1) What is the purpose of each Chinese version? (2) How intentional is a particular translator and his consciousness regarding the strength and limit of not only biblical language but, more importantly, of the Chinese vernacular? (3) How would a vernacular (a wineskin) shape the biblical message (wine) (cf. Mark 2:2), and how would the wine find a more fitting wineskin for its containment and presentation?

Expression

Part II essays encompass the second move of *expression*, which is akin to carvings on the furniture that highlight the homegrown religious and literary-changing cultures of China. Without this, expression and translation are only one-to-one sign correspondence and, subsequently, meaning is only the transmission of code without contextual decoding. Expression has to do with the cultural context of a translation; expression is like the face of a person that marks her presence and personality. A biblical word or concept needs to be expressed in a way meaningful for Chinese understanding. Translation and expression of the Bible have made use of Chinese semantics (Confucianist, Daoist, Buddhist, folklores, etc.) while, at the same time, influencing these semantics and their domains over time to have a now somewhat Christian gloss. Take, for example, the name, or rather *the naming*, of God as the "I am" (Table 1.2).

Essays on expression look at the relationship between the Bible and various cultural aspects of China, beginning with missionaries and foreign nations and continuing to

Table 1.2 The Name of God in Expression, Translation, Interpretation, and Reception

Expression Involves:	Translation	Interpretation	Reception
"I am who I am" is a Hebrew linguistic expression of God, who speaks to Moses (Exod 3:14; MT [Masoretic text]) regarding his name, implying God is: (1) the nameless One, i.e., no language can express God fully; (2) like no other, i.e., God cannot be controlled by anyone else:	A Chinese version does not translate this Hebrew naming of God literally (我是我所是 or 我是我是 or 我就是我); instead, it opts to translate either the meaning of MT or the LXX (Septuagint, Greek OT [Old Testament, or Hebrew Bible]) naming as "I am the self-existing and eternally existing" one (我是自有永有的).	Greek OT (LXX) does not translate the Hebrew literally; instead, its translation "I am the Being" is a philosophical interpretation of God as "the Being," i.e., the absolute, pure Being, the Ontology. The Chinese version is a paraphrase of both the MT (absolutely acting God) and the LXX (absolutely pure God).	The Gospel of John's reception of Jesus as the "I AM" echoes both the MT and LXX Exod 3:14 usage, for Jesus is both God in his perfect works (as seven signs/miracles indicate) and perfect being (fully human *and* fully divine). Chinese versions, like many English versions of John, unfortunately, are unable to hold to *both* the Hebrew and Greek cross-cultural expressions of naming God, so when the special self-naming of God (the "I AM") is misunderstood as the generic linguistic expression "I am the one…" (我就是) the result is a distorted reception. All seven unpredicated "I AM" namings of Jesus in John (4:26, 6:20, 8:24, 13:19, 18:5–8, and 18:8) were wrongly translated as "I am he." But Chinese readers in general appreciate the expression "I am the self-existing and eternally existing" one.[8]

mutual expressions or transpositions of language with biblical text, of culture and the biblical utterance. The assumption here is that the Bible is more than the possession and product of the church, but that of all cultures and languages. Readers might raise critical questions stimulated by the essays in Part II: (1) How can Chinese cultures read the Bible culturally (e.g., using the Daoist language of "*wuming* 無名" [Nameless One] to speak of the "I am who I am" God's like-no-other's attributes); and in turn, how can the Bible read Chinese cultures biblically (e.g., the Daoist "Nameless One" in *Daodejing* and the Confucianist "Tian" can be understood as taking on the biblical narrative and meaning)? (2) How is "Sinicization" (*Zhongguohua* 中國化) of Chinese Christianity done biblically rather than coopted politically? (3) If expression of the Bible involves accurate translation, meaningful interpretation, and purposeful reception, then what historical insights can we gain from the essays in Part II to inform the re-expression of biblical theology in the culture of China today—such as Chinese painting, calligraphy, and visual art as a form of illustrating biblical content, genre, and beauty?

Interpretation

We have seen in the previous two moves that a Chinese translation and expression of a biblical term or concept would in turn be reinscribed somewhat by a biblical concept; it is even more powerful in the next two moves of interpretation and reception because they are more prescriptive; i.e., in our engaging with the biblical text, the text all the more keeps engaging us—we are "read" by the text as we read it. Essays in Part III focus on the third move, *interpretation*, of Bible in China. Interpretation is similar to the shades of color painted on furniture; thus, interpretation is about meaningfulness in the nuanced unique existence of the text that is relevant to China *and beyond*. Ideally, translators want interpretation that is both contextual and global; contextual so that it is meaningful to the specific needs of China's peoples, and global so that blind spots of global parochial interpretation can be overcome. Creating a Handbook of the Bible in China in the English language in which some non-Chinese scholars write about Chinese topics is part of this glocal (global-local) intention and design. Readers may want to use this cross-cultural method in this Handbook, and progress toward a more accurate biblical interpretation; take, for example, the word Greek word "*agapē*" in Gal 5:6 (Table 1.3).

Table 1.3 Interpretation Involves Translation, Expression, and Reception

Interpretation Involves:	Translation	Expression	Reception
The Greek word "*agapē*" is interpreted as the Chinese word "*ren* 仁" to mean God's love, which is self-sacrificial and for the sake of others; the interpretation of "*ren*" can correspond to God's cruciform love more naturally.	The Chinese word "*ai* 愛" is used to translate "*agapē*" generally, but in Gal 5:6, "*ren-ai* 仁愛" is used to translate "*agapē*," meaning "*ren-ai*" is more specific than simply "*ai*."	The generic Chinese word "*ai*" expresses to everyone who knows the Chinese language (excepting the Buddhist semantic that views "*ai*" as negative passion) as love; but "*ren*" is predominantly a Confucianist expression that has rich meanings of relational integrity and self-sacrificial caring for others.	"*Ren-ai*" is more Chinese in expression (reading the Bible culturally) than "*ai*," and thus easily received by Chinese, but "*ren-ai*" received in the Chinese context will allow the biblical narrative of God's cruciform love to be part of the content of "*ren-ai*" (reading the culture biblically).
The Greek word "*logos*" is interpreted as the Chinese word "*dao* 道" to mean Jesus is (1) the Creator of the cosmos; (2) the personified/incarnated Wisdom; and (3) the God who speaks order from chaos, light from darkness, and meaning from void, and who speaks about himself ("I am….")	The Chinese word "*dao*" is used to translate "*logos*" in John's Gospel to mean Jesus is the eternal cosmic principle.	"*Dao*" is a Daoist term/expression that has rich meanings of (1) eternal principle; (2) wisdom; and (3) speech.	"*Dao*" is a polished Chinese expression (reading the Bible culturally) favored by Chinese, and using "*dao*" to speak of Jesus in John's Gospel makes its reception likely to transform the Chinese language (reading the culture biblically) as the word "*dao*" takes up a Christological meaning.

Interpretation involves a reader's linguistic- and life-worlds, which are "being read" by the biblical texts. While interpretation is rooted in exegesis, interpretation springs from exegesis and exudes surplus meaning from the biblical text to the translators' and interpreters' linguistic worlds. Because translation and interpretation done in one language is rather limited, multilingual translation and interpretation is more effective, and this calls for world Christianity to offer a corrective lens in studying the Bible not monolinguistically but multiculturally. For example, the Chinese translation of "*logos*" as "*dao*" gives an interpretation of Jesus that is far more robust and nuanced than the English translation "Word." On Jesus's teaching of "you are the salt of the earth," an English commentary will interpret "salt" as preservation and flavor addition. A Chinese preacher may interpret salt as "catalyst" because he explains that, in his village, farmers burn trash by adding salt to make it burn quicker into fertilizer. An African speaker, John Jusu, interprets "salt" as making people thirsty; thus, he interprets Jesus as teaching his followers to make people thirst for the kingdom of God.[9]

Versions of the Chinese Bible may be grounded contextually (incarnational in languages) but also globally so that (1) the Chinese Jesus can be visualized in painting, and at the same time; (2) the understanding of "Chinese" and "China" will eliminate nationalism or ethnocentrism—the Chinese Jesus is neither normative nor superior. The Handbook shows that, in the history of Chinese or global biblical interpretation, its trajectories are not single and linear (as if from Jews to Christians or from Hebrew to Greek to English to Chinese) but polyphonic and multiplex. That is, the biblical narrative often uses the "Adam" figure to suggest that God works with humanity *universally*, and the *diverse* representation of people groups God covenanted with in the OT and NT is polyphonic, such as all nations represented by Noah's three children, Melchidezek the gentile who worshipped *El Elyon* and Abraham who turned to worship Yahweh, Acts' multiple voices and languages, etc.[10] The ancient Silk Road could have provided cultural and religious exchange among Africa, Europe, and Asia, an exchange that promoted cross-pollination of the biblical influence on ancient civilizations, including China. The Chinese biblical interpretation also has multiple voices, neither singular in identity nor monolithic in propagation.

A biblical interpretation that is both contextual and global can check the idolatrous notion of a singular "Chinese Christian" and "China" identity. The global church can help China see its faulty thinking while China can help the global church see its blind spots as well. The essays in Part III raise critical questions: (1) What are the Chinese faces of Jesus, their commonalities and differences with understandings of Jesus elsewhere? (2) If these Chinese faces of Jesus share commonality with, say, Latinx or African or European faces of Jesus, what is so culturally unique about being Chinese? In other words, what does it mean to be a "Chinese Christian"? Do national and ethnic identities ground the Christian/biblical identity, or vice versa? (3) How can one construct biblical interpretations for China that are appropriate both for the Chinese church and the global church?

Reception

Essays in Part IV focus on the Bible's *reception*, which is akin to the actual *usage* of metaphorical furniture, insofar as the Bible in this Handbook is more than simple ornamentation or academic exercise. The reception of biblical utterance speaks of the impact of the Bible in the larger institutional life of China, including ethics, sciences, medicine, arts, and socio-political realities. Reception is not about passivity. Critical, creative, and purposeful reception is hard work because of change. Compared to the previous three moves, it is even more so in that the one constant in the lighting, color, and ambience of metaphorical furniture and its use in the room is change. Take the example of "communion" (the *eucharist*, the Lord's Supper, or the *agapē* meal), which can be expressed and received in the Chinese tea-drinking culture (Table 1.4).

Biblical readings are works in progress rather than static realities because languages, cultures, traditions, societies, behaviors, and civilizations are constantly changing. Yet, biblical readings can affect history, moving it closer to perceived truth, goodness, and beauty; or, if done ineffectively, moving history nearer to perceived deception, evil, and shame. Purposeful reception will want to extend the life-force of the ancient texts to its future neighbors (e.g., seventeenth-century China) and its seemingly "distant galaxies" such as the present China writ large, especially its institutional life of politics, ethics, law, architecture, films, and the arts.

The assumption is that the Bible is not simply the sacred scripture *of the church*; rather, it is a "sacred text" of all humanity in: (1) its power of *continuous utterance*;[11] and (2) its capacity to move and shake *every* civilization and society. Along these lines, Part IV provokes us to ask: (1) What is the impact of the Chinese Bible in Chinese aesthetics, rule of law, the film industry, painting, photography, calligraphy, the tea-ceremony, and ethics today (to name just a few)? (2) How can interdisciplinary study of the Chinese Bible be done not only in the seminary but also in schools of engineering, business and management, law, and medicine—for the impact of the Bible to Chinese society? In

Table 1.4 Purposeful Reception that needs Translation, Expression, and Interpretation

Purposeful Reception That Needs:	Correct Translation	Proper Expression	Meaningful Interpretation
Communion in the Chinese tea culture that has the twofold purpose of cultivating vertical and horizontal relationships for the church.	Translate tea-drinking as a form of Chinese Christian communion.	Use tea in Chinese culture to express the equivalence of wine in biblical times, a cultural practice that expresses properly a biblical concept in turn gets itself inscribed now with Christian significance and spirituality.	Interprets Chinese Christian tea-drinking, originally as social bonding, now as a Christian practice of spiritual communion with God *as well.*

what ways is the Bible relevant to speaking truth to power, justice to systematic brutality, dignity to dehumanization in our world?

Hope-Instilling and Culture-Transforming

How should readers use this Handbook? The Handbook encourages a critical and creative reading that brings about epistemic transformation as readers anticipate "new" issues or perspectives. There are three issues that emerge from the essays, discussed below.

The Identity and Making of China

This is an important issue, because the editorial inclusion or exclusion of essays and authors is to a large extent guided by my awareness of the complexity of "China," as it involves the interplay of identities, ethnicities and race, politics and empire, alongside ways that cultures embedded in the Bible engage with cultures embedded in the various territories of China.

"China" in the title of the Handbook means less political China than the land, people, and culture of the present-day, called by them the People's Republic of China. After 1949, the relationship among the People's Republic of China, Hong Kong, and Macau and Taiwan are complex and changing dramatically, but insofar as topics of the Bible are concerned, this Handbook includes these topics where their linguistic and historical connections to "this China" were evident.[12]

China's long history has no fewer than fifteen dynasties and is composed of a myriad of cultures; thus, China belongs neither to one people-group nor to one system. This Handbook recognizes that each ethnicity and China itself is a hybridized being and fluid entity. The Bible and biblical studies in the diaspora of Singapore, Malaysia, Canada, and the United States, though significant in their own right, are not covered in this Handbook, except when they are related substantially to the Bible and culture in China.

Though the official language "in China" at present is Mandarin, there have been and are dialects and "mother-tongues" of non-Han nationalities as well, and many of these fall within the scope of the Handbook. There are many "least of these" (cf. Matt 25:40), ethnic minorities who do not even make the nationality list because of their small numbers and lack of written languages, yet for the church to ignore "these little ones" (Matt 18:6) would be considered detrimental.

If China as a state and territory, present and past, is complex, China understood as language is even more complex, and China as culture the most complex. To demarcate the scope of "China" is a rather complex issue, but to include everything in the word "China" makes the task impossible to manage. So the Handbook has taken primarily the *cultural* and *theological* understanding of "China" by the Chinese and the Chinese

Christian themselves, including the following: linguistic, literary, philosophical, religious/theological, virtuous ethics, arts, common good, and civilizational components of cultures (*wenhua* 文化), or what it means to be "cultured" or cultivated in those components of culture.[13] Essays on translation of the Chinese Bible pay attention to the creative power of Chinese and non-Han languages and dialects in such versions as those by Jean Basset, De Poirot, Morrison, the Studium Biblicum, and minorities. Essays on the expression of the Bible look at mutual polishing of Bible and Chinese literary texts and genres, such as modern Chinese fiction, missionary novels, and Chinese Christian poetry. Essays in the interpretation of the Bible examine the cultivating science and art of biblical exegesis and theology as ways to transform Chinese institutions or movements, such as China's academia, Chinese patristic studies, printed illustrations of the Gospels, Sino-Christian theology, and Scriptural Reasoning. If China is complex, "the West" is even more so. The use of the words "China" and "the West" in this Handbook are often used in the generic sense (geographically), that is "the West" does not mean the political (ideological) colonizing powers of some countries in the "western" hemisphere. The contrast between "China" and "the West" is doubly an over-simplification.

We arrive at the dominant and longstanding question regarding the master-hybridity of "China": what does it mean to be a Chinese Christian? That is, can a Chinese become a *Chinese* Christian and/or a Chinese *Christian*? Can a Chinese person simultaneously be a citizen of the kingdom of God and of a nation-state? Not all essays in the Handbook are attuned to these questions, but those essays in the reception of the Bible are. These essays bear the tenor of theologizing for the authors themselves and for China, as their identities converse and engage with the Bible in areas such as: (1) popular Christianity as Chinese churches engage with social-political life in China; (2) the significant role of the Bible in the public square, ethics, and basic legal freedoms; (3) calligraphy, contemporary Christian arts, church architecture, and Chinese contemporary films. Overall, these essays imagine, implicitly or explicitly, a China that can be rehabilitated as styled, flourishing, and authentic (i.e., beautiful, good, and truthful; see Rom 12:1), thus overcoming what China's Christians observe in the destructive and seductive powers of pollution, utilitarianism, and brutality, or the intoxication of obscenity, objectification, and injustice.

Bible and Cultures in a "Dragon Dance"

How immersive and self-conscious are readers of the Chinese Bible in making a difference to the sinuous and undulating "river of life" (*lishi changhe* 歷史長河)? The forty-nine authors in this Handbook are like artists performing a "dragon dance" with intensity and long years of practice. Metaphorically displaying the potency and presence of the Chinese dragon, these scholars unleash creative power to simulate and maneuver among both historical and imagined meanings of the Chinese Bible, as they imitate and "play" with the biblical texts in order to display the power and dignity and auspiciousness that China's Christians have avowed can be observed of the Bible in China. A dominant hermeneutic theory[14] imagines writers as dancers, and readers as spectators, so caught up in the game that they become self-forgetful. The Handbook by contrast aims to evoke in readers the worlds of meanings, purposefulness, transformations, justice, and love, among others, that the Bible presents to its adherents as they see themselves encountering, recognizing, and reconstructing the historical and contemporary worlds of text, society, government, and power. For these Christians, the biblical mandate appropriates images of the lion lying down with the lamb or the little child leading wild animals (see Isa 11:6) in ways that would conform China to the spirit of trust, the virtue of mutual respect, the care of ecology, and the honoring of those outside the city gate who are distant from the seat of power.

All essays in the four parts of the Handbook demonstrate that the dialogue between the Bible and Chinese traditions constitutes an underlining "fabric" that joins the "hoops" to make a lively dragon dance. The relationship between versions of the Chinese Bible and cultures, such as church music or hymn-texts, Chinese poetry, church architecture, or paintings, is likely to continue a dialectical, spiral-movement of mutual reading, so that Bible and culture constitute a process of transfiguring each other.

Impacts of the Bible

One of the perennial questions, addressed especially in Part IV, asks: How does the Bible writ large feature in all facets of Chinese life? The Handbook points to eclectic forms of participation by China's Christians in their life-worlds.

First, texts, especially biblical texts, do not simply express reality, they create reality. The Handbook demonstrates that, in China's history, biblical texts have influenced culture in many ways. What enabled that to happen? Reading the Bible and cultures intertextually[15] seeks to observe the impact of the Bible on cultures. Numerous essays demonstrate ways that Chinese churches have appropriated the strong prophetic tradition in the Bible for their distinctive identity and purpose in life. They have seized upon passages such as let not "justice turn back... [let not] truth stumble in the *public square*" (Isa 59:14). They have identified themselves with NT images such as the salt of the earth and light of the world.

Second, the Handbook affirms the fact that the Bible and China's cultures have existed and continue to exist in an "intertextual" relationship. They are mutually transforming, in that the Bible "speaks" to China's cultures, and the cultures give new meanings to the Bible. The theory of intertextuality points to ways in which Chinese churches have understood themselves to be healing the malaise of their country, to be binding their rulers, to be releasing captives, to be empowering the weak, confounding the strong, and promoting flourishing. Some churches grasp tightly to the belief of "the crucified God" who demonstrated how the weak could confound the powerful, how the "foolishness of the cross" could confound the wisdom of the world. Intertextuality is both a descriptive skill and an imperative art. Thus, the four movements of hermeneutics in this Handbook muster the arguments and demonstrate the ways that readers might live into the experience of others. They take us well beyond conventional theological reasoning to reveal how diverse expressive forms, such as calligraphy or film, or social ideals, such as defense of basic legal freedoms, connect biblical content with everyday life in all its manifestations and richness.

Essays in Part III and especially Part IV link the Bible even more explicitly to society. Partly influenced by the Confucian organic relationship between sacred and secular, most Chinese Christians likewise believe that their commitment to Christianity should play a role in society. They call their task "public theology." For them, the Bible can "defamiliarize" conventional understandings and "sanctify" the public space.[16] For them, Chinese Christianity can deploy the Bible to make sense of their mundane, alienated, or even broken lives (e.g., essays that discuss calligraphy, films, pop culture), to reorder their meaningless and chaotic society (e.g., essays that discuss ethics, religions, minority cultures), to conform their institutions to what they champion as "Kingdom values" (e.g., essays that discuss government, church, the public square).

The Bible may be the original product of ancient Near Eastern and Mediterranean cultures, yet the Handbook demonstrates repeatedly that over the centuries China's Christians insist it is a gift for *all peoples*, including themselves. The Handbook observes and analyzes ways in which the Bible at once exhibits a staying power that is conveyed from other times and places and exhibits an adaptive capacity to reflect and shape this place, China. Thereby the Handbook displays the significant role of the Bible over thirteen centuries of Chinese history and Chinese cultures to a degree that cannot be erased. The Handbook might well provoke a twenty-first-century question: How will the ways that the world has invested the Bible in China come to be reciprocated through the export of a culturally enlivened Chinese Bible to invest in creative transformations across the world beyond the Middle Kingdom?

Notes

1. The history of *research* literature in this field is sparse; see Chloë Starr, *Reading Christian Scriptures in China* (London: Bloomsbury Publishing, 2008); Pan-chiu Lai and Jason Lam, eds., *Sino-Christian Theology* (Frankfurt: Peter Lang, 2010); K. K. Yeo, *Musing with Confucius and Paul* (Eugene: Cascade Books, Wipf & Stock, 2008); K. K. Yeo, *What Has Jerusalem to Do with Beijing?*, 2nd edition (Eugene: Pickwick, 2018), K. K. Yeo, *Zhuangzi and James* [in Chinese] 莊子與雅各 (Shanghai: Huadong Shifan Daxue VI Horae, 2012). There are dictionary articles, journals, or series on the Chinese Bible or Chinese biblical studies, but they seldom discuss the Bible in relationship to various Chinese cultural dimensions. *The Handbook of Christianity in China* [*HCC*], a substantial, two-volume work edited by Nicolas Standaert (Leiden: Brill, 2001–2009), is a significant resource; its scope is so large that the content as a whole does not appear to be user-friendly. See also "Chinese Christian Texts Database," n.d. https://www.arts.kuleuven.be/sinologie/english/cct (accessed May 1, 2020).
2. Unless otherwise stated, the Bible version used in this Handbook is New Revised Standard Version (NRSV).
3. On the following historical narrative, see K. K. Yeo, "Paul's Theological Ethic and the Chinese Morality of *Ren Ren*," in Charles Cosgrove et al., *Cross-Cultural Paul* (Grand Rapids: Eerdmans, 2005), 104–118.

4. The image of *Zun Jing* is taken from Bibliothèque nationale de France, Manuscrit Pelliot chinois 3847 (https://archivesetmanuscrits.bnf.fr/ark:/12148/cc120494m, accessed March 1, 2020). See Donghua Zhu and Liu Boyun's essays in this Handbook on Jingjiao.
5. Columbas Cary-Elwes, *China and the Cross* (London: Longman, 1957), 48.
6. All secondary sources are given in full bibliographical detail in their first appearance in the endnotes. All foreign words (Hebrew, Greek, Chinese) are transliterated. Chinese characters are used in the main text when it is necessary to show its meaning distinctively; the Handbook has both Chinese-foreign author names and subject indices for easy cross-reference. Scholars render Chinese terms into English differently, and the Handbook allows plural expressions (e.g., Nestorian Monument or Jingjiao Stele or Xi'an Stele). Consistency is observed only within a chapter on expression and style.
7. On the basic hermeneutical theories this Handbook follows, see K. K. Yeo, *Rhetorical Interactions in 1 Corinthians 8 and 10* (Leiden: E. J. Brill, 1995), 15–74; Anthony C. Thiselton, *New Horizons in Hermeneutics* (Grand Rapids: Zondervan, 1992), 1–30.
8. For more discussion on the "I AM" and Exod 3:14, see Yeo, *What Has Jerusalem to Do with Beijing?*, 76–86; also K. K. Yeo, "Chinese Christologies," in *The Oxford Handbook on Christology*, ed. Francesca Murphy (Oxford: Oxford University Press, 2015), 393–407.
9. See *Africa Study Bible*, ed. John Jusu (Wheaton: Oasis International Ltd., 2016); *African Bible Commentary*, ed. Tokunboh Adeyemo et al. (Nairobi: WordAlive, 2006).
10. For example, God works differently with Noah and his children Shem, Ham, and Japheth (Gen 5–10, Luke 3:36, Heb 11:7, 2 Pet 2:5), and with those in the table of nations in Genesis 10–11 (also 1 Chr 1). In counterpoint to the confusion of tongues in the Tower of Babel narrative (Gen 11:1–9), Acts 2, the Pentecost narrative, lists the various peoples receiving the Holy Spirit and therefore proclaim boldly and clearly in their own vernaculars "about God's deeds of power" (2:11).
11. This is Paul Ricoeur's definition of "sacred text"; see his "Epilogue: The Sacred Text and the Community," in *The Critical Study of Sacred Texts*, ed. W. D. O'Flaherty (Berkeley: Graduate Theological Union, 1979), 271–276.
12. For example, Ying Wa College 英華書院 in Malacca, Malay is studied, because of its connection to Robert Morrison's Bible translation and Christian literature printing. Yet, Bible translation works and commentaries done and published in Hong Kong and Taiwan in the last twenty years that are not accessible to those in mainland People's Republic of China will not be part of our study here.
13. See cultures and cultured in K. K. Yeo, *Musing with Confucius and Paul* (Eugene: Cascade Books 2008), 1–2, 23, 194–252, 424–431; K. K. Yeo, "Theology and the Future of Global Christianity," in *Theology and the Future*, ed. Trevor Cairney and David Starling (Edinburgh: T&T Clark, 2014), 56–60, on public theology and glocal theology.
14. As in Gadamer's understanding of play; see his *Truth and Method*, 102.
15. Jonathan Culler, *Structuralist Poetics* (London: Routledge & Kegan Paul, 1975), 113.
16. See "defamiliarization" in Hans Robert Jauss, "Literary History as a Challenge to Literary Theory," 18–19; Hans Robert Jauss, *Towards an Aesthetic of Reception*, tr. Timothy Bahti (Minneapolis: University of Minnesota Press, 1982), 25–26.

Primary Sources

Basset, Jean and Johan Su, *Testament Nouvm Sinice*, Bibilioteca Casanatense di Roma, Mss. 2024 (ca. 1705–1707).

Biblia Hebraica Stuttgartensia. Edited by K. Elliger and W. Rudolf. Stuttgart: Deutsche Bibelgesellschaft, 1977.

Novum Testamentum Graece: Nestle-Aland. 28th edition. Stuttgart: Deutsche Bibelgesellschaft, 2013.

Revised Chinese Union Version [in Chinese] 和合本修訂版. Hong Kong: Hong Kong Bible Society, 2010.

Septuaginta. Edited by Alfred Rahlfs. Stuttgart: Deutsche Biblegesellschaft, 2007.

Other online Bible resources

Society of Biblical Literature: https://www.sbl-site.org/educational/biblicalfonts.aspx.

Resource Page for Biblical Studies: http://torreys.org/bible/.

BibleAppWeb: http://biblewebapp.com/study/.

The Bible Tool: http://www2.crosswire.org/study/index.jsp.

FHL: http://rare.fhl.net/.

PART I

TRANSLATION THROUGH VERSIONS

CHAPTER 2

A HISTORY OF THE CHINESE BIBLE

DANIEL KAM-TO CHOI

INTRODUCTION

THE translation of the Chinese Bible is the mainstream of translation in Chinese Christianity, and it has had a long history and a profound influence. Protestant Christianity believes that the entire Bible, consisting of thirty-nine canonical books of the Old Testament (OT) and twenty-seven books of the New Testament (NT), are inspired by God. The Bible is the ultimate authority on faith and principles of living. For this reason, Bible translation is one of the main projects in Christian mission.

The Bible in China, including the different versions of the Chinese Bible that circulate in China and in the Chinese diaspora, is the result of a long historical preparation. The origin of Chinese Bible translation began in the early history of Christianity in China, but availability only became widespread in the nineteenth century, and new translation projects are still being undertaken.

This essay is a review of Chinese Bible translation history from the Nestorians of the seventh century and focuses on the Chinese Bible after the early nineteenth century until the present. It presents a historical review of the Bible editions translated by Catholic, Protestant, and Orthodox translators who worked on translating the whole or parts of the Bible into the common language and dialects of Chinese.

NESTORIANISM IN CHINA

Jewish or Christian traders probably had already visited China before the sixth century, but the earliest concrete evidence for the existence of Christianity in China comes from the early part of the Tang dynasty (618–907). According to different sources, Christianity was introduced by the Nestorian missionaries in the seventh and eighth centuries.

Nestorianism was the eastern branch of Syriac Christianity. It was attributed to Nestorius (ca. 386–450), patriarch of Constantinople from 428 to 431, whose view of Christ was condemned at the Council of Ephesus in 431. Nestorius was stripped of his position and exiled. His followers moved to the regions that were controlled by Persia. From the early seventh century, these first Christians to reach China came by way of the Silk Road. Nestorianism in China was named Jingjiao 景教, and it remained in China for more than two centuries under the Tang dynasty. Nestorians returned to China in the thirteenth century under the Mongol rulers but once again disappeared when the Mongolian dynasty fell to the Ming dynasty.

The earliest recorded translation of the Scriptures into Chinese was made by the Nestorian missionaries. The documents that exist, including the 781 Nestorian Monument, *Da-qin Jing-jiao Liu-xing Zhong-guo Bei* 大秦景教流行中國碑 (or named "Xi'an Stele"), in the city of Xi'an, which was discovered in the late Ming dynasty (between 1623 and 1625), suggest that some of the Scriptures were translated during this time.

The oldest of these Syrian Christian texts may be the *Xu-ting Mi-shi-suo Jing* 序聽迷斯所經 (*The Sūtra of Jesus the Messiah*, or *The Jesus Messiah Scripture*), which was dated between 635 and 638 or later and now held in Osaka by the Kyōu Shooku Library. It provided a basic outline of the fundamental teachings of Christianity. Another Nestorian manuscript was dated from 641 and was entitled *Shi-zun Bun-shi Lun Di Shan* 世尊布施論第三 (*Discourse of the Master of the World in Almsgiving, Part 3*). The text of this document spoke of the death and resurrection of Jesus. The above two earlier documents presented a comprehensive account of the Christian doctrine of salvation.

There were other documents still in existence. Some of them had the lists or selections of sacred books, such as *Zun Jing* 尊經 (*Let Us Praise* or *Venerable Books*). However, some others already had been lost, possibly including several biblical books that had been translated into Chinese, such as *Hun-yuan Jing* 渾元經 (*Genesis*), *Mou-shi Fa-wang Jing* 牟世法王經 (*Five Books of Moses*), *Duo-hui Sheng-wang Jing* 多惠聖王經 (*Psalms*), *Shan-he-lu Jing* 刪河律經 (*Book of Zechariah*) in the OT, and *A Si Qu-li-rong Jing* 阿思瞿利容經 (*Gospel*), *Chuan Hua Jing* 傳化經 (*Acts of the Apostles*), *Bao-lu Fa-wang Jing* 寶路法王經 (*Pauline epistles*), *Qu Zhen Jing* 啟真經 (*Apocalypse of John*) in the NT.

Although there is strong evidence in Nestorian writings that there was a translation of some books of the Bible into Chinese, no completely translated biblical book from this period has been found.

Jews in China

The existence of Jews in China may have started from the Tang dynasty or earlier, and the communities of Jews developed through the Tang and Song dynasties (960–1279).

The most important records of the Chinese Jews were in Kaifeng, the capital of China in the early Song dynasty. The Jewish community in Kaifeng was founded by immigrants, probably from the Middle East. In 1163, they built a synagogue there. In 1605, the prominent Italian Jesuit, Matteo Ricci (1552–1610), received a visit from a young Jew who came from the Jewish community in Kaifeng. Then, foreign missionaries, including Catholics and Protestants later, started to study the community of Chinese Jews in Kaifeng and contributed further to Chinese knowledge about them.

From the records of the Jesuit missionaries, the Jewish synagogue in Kaifeng had kept inscriptions, manuscripts, and books of the Bible in Hebrew. The drawings of this synagogue and the seat of Moses with the Torah scroll were made in 1722 by the Jesuit missionary Jean Domenge (1666–1735). However, when the Protestant missionaries arrived in Kaifeng in the middle of the nineteenth century, the synagogue already had disappeared. Much of the material of the synagogue had been sold. In 1851, George Smith (1815–1871), the Anglican bishop of Victoria (Hong Kong), published a book about the Jews in Kaifeng. He also brought back a selection of Hebrew manuscripts, including Torah scrolls and several books of the Pentateuch. The manuscripts in the Kaifeng synagogue were lost in the following years and partly recollected in the second half of the twentieth century. The primary holdings of the Kaifeng community are now held in Klau Library of Hebrew Union College in Ohio, the Vatican Library in Vatican City, and several other archives, as well as the Kaifeng Museum in Kaifeng.

Catholicism in China

Roman Catholic missionary priests from Europe were first recorded to have entered China in the thirteenth century and then re-entered in the sixteenth century. The missionary activities included cultural exchange, social welfare, education, and Bible translation.

Early Period

During the Yuan dynasty (1271–1368), Catholic missionaries from Western Europe came to China. Although there were several legends about the Bible in China, the most determined evidence came from Giovanni da Montecorvino (1247–1328), an Italian Franciscan in Beijing who worked as a missionary from 1294 until his death. It was said that all the NT and Psalms were translated into Chinese (or Mongolian, the official language of Yuan court) by Montecorvino, and the translated version was transcribed with fine Chinese (or Mongolian) calligraphy. Unfortunately, no copies exist today.

From the last years of the Ming dynasty (1368–1644) to the early years of the Qing dynasty (1644–1911), Catholic missionaries returned to China, including the Italian Jesuit priests Michele Ruggieri (1543–1607) and Matteo Ricci, as well as many others.

These missionaries wrote and translated Western works into Chinese. Some of them rewrote the texts of the Bible into Chinese, such as *Tianzhu Jiangsheng Yanxing Jilüe* 天主降生言行紀略 (*Life of Jesus According to the Gospels*) by Guilio Aleni (1582–1649) or *Shengjing Zhijie* 聖經直解 (*Explanation of the Holy Scripture*) by Manuel Dias the Younger (1574–1659). However, they did not translate the Bible in detail until the eighteenth century.

The earliest translation of the Bible into classical Chinese now in existence was translated by Jean Basset (1662–1707). Basset was the missionary of Missions Étrangères de Paris (M.E.P.) who was originally from Lyons in France. In 1689, Basset arrived at Canton (Guangzhou). From 1702, he worked in Sichuan, and planned to translate the NT into Chinese with his Chinese assistant John Xu 徐若翰 (or Johan Su, ?–1734) from 1704. Basset died in Canton before he could finish the work. He only just managed to translate the four Gospels, the Acts of the Apostles, the epistles of Paul, and up to Hebrews chapter one. This unfinished version had the Latin title *Novum Testamentum in Lingua Sinica*.

Basset's version was available only as manuscript copies. His translation located in the Biblioteca Casanatense of Rome was the earliest manuscript possible. This manuscript was discovered in 2006 at the Biblioteca Casanatense. It was apparently a translation from the Latin Vulgate into classical Chinese, and from the beauty of the writing style was judged to be the production of a native, possibly John Xu, who was the Chinese assistant of Jean Basset.

There also were two manuscripts of Basset's version, including a harmony of the Gospels, possibly edited later by John Xu or others, which were kept in the Bible Society's Library of Cambridge and the British Museum (today the "British Library"). The manuscript in Cambridge should be the earlier one, and the manuscript in the British Museum was copied from it. In 1737, Basset's manuscript was discovered by John Hodgson of the English East India Company in Canton. It was probably the manuscript in Cambridge mentioned above. Hodgson had a copy made, which he took to England in the following year. Hodgson presented this copy to Sir Hans Sloane (1660–1753) who, in turn, presented it to the British Museum; it was named "Sloane MS#3599" by the museum. In 1806, this manuscript was copied by Protestant missionary Robert Morrison (1782–1834), with the help of his Chinese assistant Yong Sam-tak in London. This copy became the basis of Morrison's NT translation later and, through Morrison, also was available to English Baptist missionary Joshua Marshman (1768–1837) in Serampore. Hence, Jean Basset's incomplete NT in the British Museum provided a link between Roman Catholic and Protestant Bible translations.

Another Chinese biblical work of Catholicism at that time was done by Père Francois Xavier d'Entrecolles (1664–1741), a French Jesuit who was the superior of the French Residence in Beijing from 1722 to 1732. In 1730, he translated the book of Tobit, a book of Scripture that was part of the Catholic and Orthodox biblical canons. His work was printed in Beijing and reprinted in 1872. This was not a word-by-word translation, but much more a paraphrase of the story of Tobit.

Half a century later, Louis Antoine de Poirot (1735–1813), a French Jesuit in Beijing, translated a Mandarin version of the NT and finished a substantial part of the OT in the 1790s. This was the first Mandarin Bible in history. Although the Rome Curia appreciated the work of Poirot in 1803, they forbade its publication. This translation had several manuscripts stored in different archives, but now only two known copies were in the Bibliotheca Zikawei 徐家匯藏書樓 in Shanghai and the Studium Biblicum Franciscanum 思高聖經學會 in Hong Kong. The first one was lost for many years and rediscovered only in 2011. The latter one was partly copied from the manuscript of the Pei-T'ang Library 北堂圖書館 in Beijing in 1936. The manuscript in Beijing was lost after 1949. There was also a manuscript of the Psalms, which was kept in Taiwan. Poirot also made a translation of the parts of OT, Apocrypha, and NT in the Manchu language.

In the meantime, there were several translation attempts by Catholic missionaries, mostly by Franciscans and Jesuits in China. The first was the translation of Genesis and parts of Exodus into colloquial Chinese by a Franciscan priest Antonio Laghi da Castrocaro (1668–1727). His work was revised by another Franciscan, Francesco Jovino (1677–1737), who had translated as far as the book of Judges (maybe including Tobit and Daniel), but no known published Bible of these works exist.

Chinese Jesuit priests also were involved in Bible translation later, such as Thomas Wang 王多默, who translated the Gospels and the Acts of the Apostles into Mandarin in 1875 and 1883, and Francis Xin 辛方濟, who translated the four Gospels into classical Chinese. Another Jesuit priest, Xu Bin 許彬, also translated four Gospels into classical Chinese, with an introduction for each Gospel and commentary, after 1884. Their manuscripts had been kept in the Bibliotheca Zikawei of Shanghai.

Late Nineteenth Century and Onwards

The first publication of the Bible by the Catholic Church in the late nineteenth century was the Acts of the Apostles by a Chinese Jesuit Laurent Li Wen-yu 李問漁 (1840–1911) in 1887. In 1897, he published his translation of the four Gospels into classical Chinese. In 1890, another Chinese Jesuit, Matthias Sen 沈則寬 (1838–1913), translated a Gospel harmony and selection of Acts into Mandarin and published in Shanghai. In 1892 and 1893, the first publication of the Gospels in classical Chinese was completed by Joseph Dejean M.E.P. (1834–1901).

Several Catholic versions were published in Hong Kong later. In 1918, Marie-Louis Félix Aubazac M.E.P. (1871–1919) published his translation of the Pauline epistles and the Catholic epistles in classical Chinese, and it was reprinted in 1927. In 1923, his colleague, Pierre Louis Bousquet M.E.P. (1874–1945), published his translation of the Catholic epistles and the Apocalypse of John.

In the early twentieth century, more Chinese Catholic scholars or priests were involved in Bible translation. In 1919, Chinese Catholic Ma Xiangbo 馬相伯 (1840–1939) translated a harmony of the Gospels. In 1937, he completed his translation of the four

Gospels into classical Chinese. This translation was not published until 1949, ten years after his death.

There was a more influenced work by a Chinese Jesuit. It was a NT version translated by Joseph Hsiao Ching-Shan 蕭靜山 (1855–1924). In 1918, Joseph Hsiao published his translation of the four Gospels in Mandarin, and his NT was published in 1922. This was the first complete NT done by a Catholic translator, and it was reprinted several times until the middle of the twentieth century.

From 1939 to 1943, another Chinese Jesuit, Hsiao Shun-hua 蕭舜華 (or Xiao Shun-hua), published several Gospels, the Acts of the Apostles, and the Pauline epistles in Mandarin. In 1949, Hsiao and several Western Jesuits, including György Litványi (1901–1983), René Archen (1901–?), and Édouard Petit (1897–1985), published an NT with emphasis on style rather than fidelity to the original text. In 1955, Édouard Petit also translated a Bible selection into Mandarin which was published in Hong Kong.

Another particularly interesting translation came from Catholic layman John Wu Ching-hsiung吳經熊 (1899–1986). He was a Catholic convert who served as the Republic of China's minister to the Vatican from 1940 to 1946. Wu translated the Psalms in this time and submitted his manuscript to Chiang Kai-shek 蔣介石 (1887–1975), head of the Chinese government in Chongqing. Chiang read the text through three times and wrote his comments on the manuscript. Wu translated the Psalms into classical Chinese and published in 1946. In 1949, he made a translation of the NT, as well as a separate edition of the Gospels and the Acts of the Apostles which were published in Hong Kong. Wu's translations were not literal and often noted to be florid.

In 1953, *First Draft of a New Translation of the Gospels* 新譯福音初稿 was published in Shanghai and Hong Kong. This was a Jesuit translation of the Gospels in Mandarin by the Theological Seminary of Xujiahui 徐匯總修院 in Shanghai.

Although the Roman Catholic NT had been translated, the full OT with Apocrypha was not completed until the middle of the twentieth century. The first complete Catholic Chinese Bible to be published was started by a young Italian Franciscan friar named Gabriel Maria Allegra (1907–1976) in China. In 1935, Allegra began translating the OT from the original Hebrew and Aramaic languages. From 1945, he organized a team of Chinese Franciscan friars in Beijing to work with him on the translation of the Bible. Allegra inaugurated the Studium Biblicum Franciscanum in Beijing and subsequently continued in Hong Kong. After twenty years of effort, they finished the first publication of the one-volume Catholic Chinese Bible in 1968. This version was called *Si-gao Sheng-jing* 思高聖經 (or *Si-gao Ben* 思高本) in Chinese, and called in English "Studium Biblicum version" (SBV). It contained seventy-three books, including the additional seven titles known as the Apocrypha. This is still the common Bible in the Chinese Catholic Church.

There were several Bible translation attempts after that. One of them was the book of Proverbs, Ecclesiastes, and the Song of Songs in Mandarin and classical Chinese by Kwok Xian-guang 郭先廣, a Catholic priest in Taiwan, in 1976. Several years later, there was a version prepared by the Chinese Catholic priests of Sheshan Xiuyuan 佘山修院 in mainland China. This NT version, with simplified Chinese characters in Mandarin, was prepared in 1983 and published from 1986 to 1994. It was revised in 2004.

After the publication of *Si-gao Sheng-jing*, another complete Bible translation project was *The Chinese Pastoral Bible* 牧靈聖經. It was the Chinese edition of the *Christian Community Bible*, which used easy-to-understand language and was published in 1998.

The last one was *Lectio Divina* 偕主讀經, with the Chinese translation of Luke and Acts in 2010, four Gospels in 2011, and the NT in 2014. This version was initiated by the Claretians in Macau. The NT was named *Claret Bible* 樂仁譯本, which memorialized Anthony Mary Claret (1807–1870), founder of Claretians. This version was published in Macau. It consists of scriptural readings and meditations.

Common Bible for Catholics and Protestants

In the second half of the twentieth century, Catholics cooperated with Protestants in two Bible translation projects. In 1968, the Secretariat for Promoting Christian Unity in the Vatican and the United Bible Societies (UBS) announced its "Guiding Principles for Interconfessional Cooperation in Translating the Bible" together and then started a cooperation project for Chinese Bible translation. The name of this project was "Interconfessional Version" 共同譯本. One of the results was the Catholic version of *The Today's Chinese Version* NT 新約全書現代中文譯本 in 1976 by the Protestant Bible Society in Taiwan. However, only two trial editions of Luke and John had been published in 2000 and a four Gospels version in 2015 by United Bible Societies (UBS) in Taiwan.

This Interconfessional Version was not the only translation project in which Catholics and Protestants cooperated. Another one was the *Ko-Tân* (Kerygma) Colloquial Taiwanese Version of the NT, also known as *the Red-Cover Bible* 紅皮聖經 (*Âng-phoê Sèng-keng* in Taiwanese). This work began in 1965 and continued until its completion in 1972 as an ecumenical effort between the Protestant Presbyterian Church in Taiwan and the Roman Catholic Mission Maryknoll. However, it was soon confiscated by the Kuomintang government (which objected to the use of Latin orthography) in 1975 and republished only after the 1990s.

Russian Orthodox Missionaries in China

Russian Orthodox missionaries arrived in China at the end of the seventeenth century, but the Bible translation into Chinese was not started until the middle of the nineteenth century.

The first Orthodox Chinese translation of the NT was completed by Archimandrite Grigory Platonovich Karpov (1814–1882, later bishop of Symferopol), head of the fourteenth Russian Ecclesiastical Mission in Beijing (1858–1864). While attending the academy, he received the name "Gury" in 1838, and this name became more famous. After his graduation, Gury was appointed a member of the Russian Orthodox Mission in Beijing in 1839. Gury commenced Bible translation work from the Slavonic in 1859. In 1864, he published the translation of NT in eleven volumes in Beijing. He also translated a Psalter and published volumes dealing with Orthodox services and church history.

Twenty years later, an updated version of the NT was prepared through the work of Archimandrite Flavian Gorodetsky (1840–1915, later Metropolitan of Kiev and Galicia), the head of the sixteenth Russian Ecclesiastical Mission (1879–1883). In 1879, Flavian had already translated the Psalms from the Russian Bible and published in Beijing. Flavian reexamined Gury's translation and, in 1884, published the *Gospel with Explanations*, with the help of the Protestant translation of the Bible done by Protestant missionary Samuel I. J. Schereschewsky (1831–1906, American Episcopal Church Mission, AECM) in China.

The last Orthodox translation of the NT was done as part of the eighteenth Russian Ecclesiastical Mission (1896–1931), led by its head, His Eminence Figurovsky Innokenty (1863–1931, bishop of Pereyaslav, later Metropolitan of Beijing and China). This was also the revised work of Gury but without the Apocalypse of John. It was published in 1910. Innokenty also translated and published Genesis and Matthew with commentaries in 1911.

Russian Orthodox missionaries had translated the NT and several OT books into Chinese. The above translations were all in classical Chinese. However, after the middle of the twentieth century, the Orthodox churches in China had not done anything more in Bible translation.

Protestant in China

Protestant missionaries came to China in the nineteenth century. Besides contributing to education and social services, they were dedicated in preaching and teaching the Bible, thus the task of translating the Bible.

Classical Chinese Translations in the Early Period

Before the publication of the Chinese Union Version (CUV), the common Chinese Bible translation project initiated by Protestant missionaries at the end of nineteenth century, Protestant missionaries already had translated the Bible into traditional classical Chinese (*wenyan* 文言; the Protestant missionaries called it "high *wenli*" 深文理), easy classical Chinese (淺文言, the simpler form of the literary style; the Protestant missionaries called it "easy *wenli*" 淺文理), Mandarin 官話, and local dialects in China.

The first print of the Chinese Bible was done by Protestant missionaries in the traditional classical Chinese. This was a written form of literary Chinese, which was used for almost all formal writing in China until the early twentieth century. Most of the Chinese Bibles at this time were translated into traditional classical Chinese. Early texts published in China or Malacca were in the literary form, and each page was hand-carved on wood blocks, but several editions from Serampore, a city of Hooghly district in the Indian state of West Bengal, were printed with moveable metal type.

The first known complete printed version of the Protestant Bible in Chinese was translated by English missionary Joshua Marshman (1768–1837). Marshman was a missionary of the Baptist Missionary Society and worked with William Carey (1761–1834) in Serampore. From 1805, Marshman and his son started translating the Bible into Chinese with his Armenian helper, Hovhannes Ghazarian (also known as Johannes Lassar, 1781–1835?), who was born in Macao. Lassar was acquainted with the Chinese language. He helped to translate Matthew's Gospel and Mark's Gospel into Chinese. In 1810, the above two Gospels were printed by the press in Serampore. The translation of the NT was completed in 1811, and the entire Bible was printed in 1822. This version was circulated among the Chinese outside of China. However, it had only limited influence partly because it was primarily used by the Baptists.

The Protestant work in China began with the arrival of Robert Morrison (1782–1834) of the London Missionary Society (LMS) in 1807. Under difficult, often hostile conditions, Morrison's major contribution was in the field of Bible translation. Morrison was accepted by the LMS in 1805. In 1806, he commenced the study of Chinese in London. Morrison copied a transcript of the Catholic Chinese Bible translation from the British Museum with the assistance of Yong Sam-tak, a Chinese who happened to be in England at that time. This was an incomplete NT translation of a volume by Catholic missionary Jean Basset mentioned above.

In 1807, Morrison embarked for China via America and reached Macao, whence he proceeded to Canton. He started to translate the NT. The Acts of the Apostles was revised from the above Catholic manuscript and first printed in Canton in 1810. The Gospel of Luke was printed in 1811. Most of the epistles were printed in 1812, with the Pauline epistles being merely revised by Morrison. The NT was completed in 1813. Later, his colleague William Milne (1785–1822), another LMS missionary, worked with him in the translation of the OT. Milne translated the books of Deuteronomy through Job, under the superintendence of Morrison. The remaining books were translated by Morrison. Morrison also had some Chinese assistants in Bible translation, such as a Cantonese Li 李 and his son Li Shi-gong 李十公, and other men with the names Yun Kwan-ming 袁光明, Gao 高, and Chen Lao-yi 陳老宜. The entire Bible version was completed in 1823 in twenty-one volumes with the title *Shen-tian Sheng-shu* 神天聖書 (literally, "God Heaven Holy Book"), which became the basis of many later Bible versions. It was presented by Morrison and his son, John Robert Morrison (1814–1843), to the British and Foreign Bible Society (BFBS) in London in 1824. In 1845, Morrison's Luke and Acts were revised by William C. Milne (1815–1863), son of William Milne, in London.

After Morrison died in 1834, the next new translation project was immediately made by Walter Henry Medhurst (1796–1857, LMS), Karl Friedrich August Gützlaff (1803–1851, German Lutheran missionary), Elijah Coleman Bridgman (1801–1861), missionary of the American Board of Commissioners for Foreign Missions (ABCFM) and Morrison's son, John Robert Morrison. The NT was chiefly made and revised by Medhurst and published in 1837. The OT was translated primarily by Gützlaff and published in 1838.

Medhurst also took part in the translation of the OT published by Gützlaff in the 1840s. Gützlaff modified the version of the NT that he and Medhurst had prepared jointly, and he printed several editions of his Bible translation, each edition being revised and improved. In 1853, Gützlaff's versions were adopted by Hong Xiuquan 洪秀全 (1814–1864) of the Taipei Heavenly Kingdom, an oppositional state in China from 1851 to 1864, and several editions of OT and NT books under their imprint appeared in the same year.

After the signing of the Treaty of Nanking (1842), which ended the First Opium War (1839–1842) in China, the missionaries were able to remain in Hong Kong and five other ports (Guangzhou, Xiamen, Fuzhou, Ningbo, and Shanghai). In August of 1843, fifteen Protestant missionaries from different countries and denominations gathered in Hong Kong. These missionaries decided to translate the Bible into Chinese with standardized terminologies for the names and terms in the Bible. The meeting appointed a translation committee, including several British missionaries and American missionaries, such as Walter H. Medhurst and Elijah C. Bridgman. Since the missionaries were called as the delegates of the conference, this version was therefore known as the Delegates' Version 委辦本, with the NT published in 1852 and the OT in 1854. This version was adopted by the British and Foreign Bible Society and most missionaries in China. It went through many printings and was still in use as late as the early twentieth century.

Term Question in the Chinese Bible

The Delegates' Version (DV) had remarkable significance in the history of Protestant in China. However, the DV translation project presented significant challenges and disputes, having failed to resolve completely the differences involved, which reflected the distinctions of various missionaries under common preaching.

The first controversy concerned the methods of translation, particularly the faithfulness to the original (Hebrew and Greek) texts versus the need to make the translation acceptable to Chinese readers. Another point of contention was over the best way to translate "God" (or transliterate "Elohim" in Hebrew and "Theos" in Greek) into Chinese. The latter controversy was the so-called "Term Question," which had to do with how to find a suitable Chinese term for "God."

From the seventeenth to the eighteenth century, the Chinese Rites controversy, the dispute among Roman Catholic missionaries about whether Chinese ritual practices of honoring family ancestors and other formal Confucius and Chinese imperial rites were too superstitious to be compatible with Catholic belief. In the early eighteenth century, the Roman Catholic Church decided to use *Tian-zhu* 天主 (literally, "Heavenly Lord" or "Lord of Heaven") as a translation for the "Supreme God." So, the word "Catholicism" is most commonly rendered *Tian-zhu Jiao* 天主教 (literally, "religion of Heavenly Lord") in Chinese.

In earlier versions of the Protestant Bible, there were different suggestions to translate "God." Joshua Marshman often translated "God" as *Shen* 神, but he also used *Tian-zhu* in his early Bible translations. Marshman used *Shen Hun* 神魂 (which means "Holy Ghost") to translate "Holy Spirit." Finally, in his 1822 edition of the Chinese Bible, Marshman translated "God" as *Shen* and "Holy Spirit" as *Sheng-shen-feng* 聖神風 (which means "Holy God wind" or "Holy Ghost wind").

In the Acts of the Apostles (1810), Robert Morrison took Jean Basset's translation as a point of reference and translated "God" as *Shen* and "Holy Spirit" as *Sheng Feng* 聖風 (which means "Holy wind"). In the first completed edition of the Holy Bible in 1823, he translated "God" as *Shen* and "Holy Spirit" as *Sheng-shen-feng*. However, William Milne, the LMS missionary colleague of Morrison, also used *Shangdi* 上帝 (which is the name of God in classical Chinese texts) sometimes in his commentary on Ephesians published in 1825. Obviously, in Milne's view, these two terms, "*Shen*" and "*Shangdi*," were interchangeable. In the 1830s, Walter H. Medhurst mainly used the term *Shangdi* for "God" and *Sheng-shen* 聖神 (which means "Holy God" or "Holy Ghost") for "Holy Spirit." His co-worker, Karl F. A. Gützlaff, used the same terms, but he sometimes used *Shangdi Zhi Shen* 上帝之神 (which means "God of God") for "Holy Spirit."

The Protestant missionaries in the process of translating the DV needed to make a final decision. They raised two suggestions on the "Term Question," whether to use *Shen* or *Shangdi*. For the missionaries from different sides, *Shen* was adapted as the term that had the meaning of the Christian God, while the term *Shangdi* was understood as the name of God rather than a generic term. The latter suggestion was mainly supported by Walter H. Medhurst. The translation committee of the DV broke down, as the Americans did not accept Medhurst's concepts of missionary indigenization, such as his adoption of the term "*Shangdi*" for God in the Bible translation and Medhurst's preference for a literary Bible translation. Finally, the team that translated God as "*Shangdi*" was mainly supported by the missionaries of LMS, while the Americans preferred another term, "*Shen*," for God. The two translating teams of the DV separated in 1851, and each translated it in their own way. Although the choice seemed to be narrowed down to "*Shen*" or "*Shangdi*," an agreement on the "Term Question" was never reached.

A similar problem was encountered in translating "YHWH" (transliteration of the Hebrew word, the Tetragrammaton) into Chinese. In the nineteenth century, two different approaches were adopted by the different missionaries. One was to translate "YHWH" as *Zhu* (主, which means "Lord"), *Shangzhu* 上主 (which means "Highly Lord"), or other alternatives with similar meaning. The other was to have the term transliterated into Chinese. In the end, most Protestant Chinese Bibles mainly used the transliterated term "*Ye-he-hua*" 耶和華 (a final transliteration of the English word "Jehovah") for "YHWH" in the OT, while the Catholic Bibles used "*Shangzhu*."

After the translating teams of the DV separated in 1851, another revision of the OT was completed by Elijah C. Bridgman, who worked independent of the missionaries of LMS. Bridgman later collaborated with Michael Simpson Culbertson (1819–1862, American Presbyterian Mission [APM]) in the translation of Bible. Their NT appeared in 1859 and the OT in 1863, in which the team translated "God" as *Shen*. This edition was issued by the American Bible Society (ABS) and continued to use the term *Shen*.

Until today, nearly all the Chinese Protestant churches believe the terms *Shen* and *Shangdi* can be used interchangeably. However, Chinese churches cannot decide which word is a better one. The Protestant Bible in Chinese church still has two editions for the term of "God": *Shen* and *Shangdi*, as well as *Tian-zhu* in the Bible of the Catholic churches. As for the term "Holy Spirit," Protestant churches referred to it as *Sheng-ling* 聖靈 (which means "Holy Spirit"), whereas the Catholic churches used *Sheng-shen* instead.

Classical Chinese Translations in the Latter Period

From the 1840s to the 1860s, revisions of Marshman's version by Baptist missionaries also appeared. Since most of the missionaries in China adopted the term "*xi* 洗" (wash) to denote "baptize," the Baptist missionaries insisted on "*jin* 浸" (immerse) or words with the same meaning. This term "*jin*" is still in common use in Chinese Baptist churches.

Since 1848, William Dean (1807–1895), an American Baptist missionary, began to translate the Bible books and add comments. About the same time, Josiah Goddard (1813–1854), another American Baptist missionary, revised the whole of Marshman's translation and published his NT in 1853. Goddard's version was the first Bible translation using "*jin*" to translate "baptize," while Marshman used another term, "*zhan* 蘸" (also means immerse but not popular) before. His labors were continued by William Dean and Edward Clemens Lord (1817–1887) of the same mission. In 1868, this translation work was completed and the whole Bible was published. This book is the only complete classical Chinese Bible published by Baptist missionaries in mainland China. Another further revision of Marshman's version was made by English Baptist missionary Thomas Hall Hudson (1800–1876), who published the NT in 1867.

The last traditional classical Chinese NT before the publication of the Chinese Union Version (CUV) in 1919, the most important Bible translation project by Protestant missionaries in China, was a translation by English missionary John Chalmers (1825–1899, LMS) and Swiss missionary Martin Schaub (1850–1900, Basler Mission). It was published with the help of German missionary Ernst Johann Eitel (1839–1908) in 1897.

There were several Bible selections in traditional classical Chinese during this time, including the Ten Commandments of Exodus by Jehu Lewis Shuck (1812–1863, American Southern Baptist Mission [ASBM]) in 1841, the Bible selection by John Stronach (1810–1888, LMS) in 1857, the Gospel of Luke with commentary by Issachar Jacox Roberts (1802–1871, an independent Baptist missionary from 1852) in 1860, the

Acts of the Apostles with commentary by Charles W. Gaillard (?–1862, ASBM) in 1860, the Psalms by William Muirhead (1822–1900, LMS) in 1860, the Gospel of Mark and the Acts of the Apostles with commentary by John Livingston Nevius (1829–1893, APM) in 1866 and 1868, the Epistle to Hebrews and several epistles by Samuel Dodd (1832–1894, APM) from 1875 to 1882, and the Epistle to the Galatians with commentary by Joseph Anderson Leyenberger (1834–1896, APM) in 1878.

Most of the Bible translators were Protestant or Catholic themselves, but some secular scholars also wanted to engage in such a task as Bible translation. For the literary translation in Chinese Bible, the famous one was the translation of the first four chapters of Mark's Gospel done by Yen Fu 嚴復 (1854–1921), one of the most distinguished Chinese scholars at the beginning of the twentieth century. Yen Fu's translation was full of literary recreation. This experimental translation was based on the English Revised Version (ERV; NT: 1881, OT: 1885). It was published in 1908 by the British and Foreign Bible Society. This unfinished Bible version was the first attempt by a non-Christian Chinese to translate a biblical segment from a literary perspective.

Easy Classical Chinese Translations

Most of the Chinese Bible in the late nineteenth century was translated into traditional classical Chinese, which was a written form of literary Chinese in China. However, after the publication of DV, there were several translation projects in easy classical Chinese, which was a simpler form of the literary style in the late nineteenth century.

The earliest publication in the easy classical Chinese style appears to be the Psalms of 1880 by Samuel Isaac Joseph Schereschewsky (1831–1906), a Jewish missionary bishop of the American Episcopal Church Mission appointed to China, who later completed the NT in 1898 and the entire Bible in 1902. Schereschewsky had translated the *Book of Common Prayer* into Chinese with John Shaw Burdon (1826–1907, Church Mission Society [CMS]) in 1872. He also translated the Bible in Mandarin later (see below).

Schereschewsky worked on the Bible translation under extremely difficult conditions. In 1881, Schereschewsky was paralyzed by sunstroke and was confined to a wheelchair. He served as bishop of Shanghai until 1883, when he resigned his bishopric for health reasons. However, he continued his translation work for twenty more years, with the assistance of an amanuensis in Chinese and later Japanese, sitting in the same chair to complete an easy classical Chinese translation of the whole Bible and a Mandarin translation of the OT. Since Schereschewsky's hands became paralyzed, he could write only by typing using one finger. His translation therefore is called the "one-finger Bible."

Another translator completing an easy classical Chinese translation was Griffith John (1831–1912, LMS) of Hankow (Hankou). John was the first missionary from Wales to China. He had extensive knowledge of the language and classics of China. John translated and published the Gospel of Mark in 1883, and after that he translated several books of NT in the easy classical Chinese. In these versions, John translated from the Greek *Textus Receptus*, with reference to the Mandarin version of the Beijing Committee (see below) and the traditional classical Chinese DV. John published the NT in 1885 and revised it in 1889, which was published by the National Bible Society of Scotland (NBSS) in Hankow. He also translated several books of the OT but did not complete the entire OT.

About the same time, John S. Burdon (CMS) and Henry Blodget (1825–1903, ABCFM) translated and published the Gospel of Matthew in 1886 based on the Mandarin version of the Beijing Committee (see below). Their NT was published in 1889.

The last translation in the easy classical Chinese was the Epistle of James by Calvin Lee 李啟榮 in 1928. Lee was a Chinese biblical scholar who taught in the Alliance Bible Seminary in Wuchow (Wuzhou). This version was published in Canton (Guangzhou) but not known to many people.

Mandarin Translations before the Chinese Union Version

Mandarin is the branch of Chinese language that includes the dialect of Beijing. It is the official language of China in the twentieth century.

Following the appearance in 1852 of DV of the NT, Walter H. Medhurst and John Stronach proceeded with the help of a Chinese scholar to translate the NT from that version into Nanking Mandarin, a Mandarin dialect spoken in Nanking (Nanjing). The earlier version of Nanking Mandarin was Matthew in 1854, as well as the Gospels and the Acts of the Apostles in 1856. The NT was published in 1857 and was funded by the Bible Society and became the first published NT translation not based on a classical and literary style. This version was printed in Chinese characters and reprinted several times.

In 1870, there also was a Gospel of Luke with Nanking Mandarin, which was printed in Romanized script and published in Zhenjiang. It was translated by Louise Desgraz (?–1907) of the China Inland Mission (CIM) and supervised by James Hudson Taylor (1832–1905), founder of the CIM.

In 1861, a committee was appointed by the British and Foreign Bible Society in Beijing to translate the NT into Beijing Mandarin. Later, this version was called the "Beijing Committee's version." The members of the committee were John S. Burdon, Joseph Edkins (1823–1905, LMS), Samuel I. J. Schereschewsky (AECM), William A. P. Martin (1827–1916, APM), and Henry Blodget (ABCFM). In the early stage, there were some trial versions of the Gospels by Alexander Williamson (1829–1890, LMS missionary, agent of the National Bible Society of Scotland in China after 1863) in 1867. There also were several editions for the Holy name, including *Shen*, *Shangdi*, *Tian-zhu*, and *Zhen Shen* 真神 (which means "True God"). The revised NT of the Beijing Committee's version was published in 1872. It was the most influential Mandarin translation before the Chinese Union Version (CUV) in 1919. Since 1869, several Roman phonetic Bible books of the Beijing Committee's version have been published. A Romanize NT edited by William Cooper (1858-1900) of the CIM was published by BFBS in London in 1888.

The Beijing Committee's version only had the NT. The OT in Mandarin was translated by Samuel I. J. Schereschewsky for the American Bible Society and published in 1874. From 1887, after his hands became paralyzed, Schereschewsky started to revise the

NT of the Beijing Committee's version, as well as his own Mandarin OT translation. He published the NT revised version in 1896 and the OT revised version in 1899. After his death, the whole revised edition with references and colored maps was published together in 1908.

Another Mandarin translation was prepared from his easy classical Chinese version by Griffith John. John published the Gospels in 1887 and the NT in 1889 by the National Bible Society of Scotland. This version differed to some extent in idiom from the Beijing Committee's version and was sometimes called the "Central Mandarin version." John also translated several books of the OT.

The Chinese Union Version

The above era represented an evolutionary process in which each translation built upon previous ones until the history reached its climax in the common version for the Protestant churches. This common Bible translation project of Protestant Churches in China was issued in the General Conference of Protestant Missionaries (GCPM) held at Shanghai in 1890. During the conference, plans were made for new Chinese Union Version (CUV, which was called "和合本" in Chinese) in three styles: the traditional classical Chinese (high *wenli*), the easy classical Chinese (easy *wenli*), and Mandarin. Three translation committees were appointed to prepare one Bible in three versions for the whole of China. The three Bible Societies in China, including the British and Foreign Bible Society (BFBS), the American Bible Society (ABS), and the National Bible Society of Scotland (NBSS), agreed to meet the expenses of the revision.

The first draft of Matthew and Mark in the easy classical Chinese appeared in 1897. After the publication of several tentative editions and the revised NT in 1904, it was increasingly clear that the future lay with Mandarin and that two classical Chinese versions were unnecessary. In the Centenary Conference of 1907 in Shanghai, the decision was made to stop further work in the easy classical Chinese and to proceed with one version only in the classical language.

The first edition of the NT in Mandarin came out in 1907, as well as the NT in the classical Chinese. The revised edition of the NT in the classical Chinese finished in the next year. The whole Bible with two versions, including the classical Chinese and Mandarin, finally appeared in 1919 and was published into both the "*Shen*" edition and the "*Shangdi*" edition, as well as a "*jin* 浸" (immerse) version later for Baptist churches.

The CUV was recognized as a great achievement, especially the Mandarin edition. It had gained wide acceptance into the Chinese church and become over the years the authorized, canonical version for Chinese Protestants. After nearly one century, this version still is widely used in China.

The CUV's appearance coincided with the breakout of the May Fourth Movement in 1919, so the Mandarin version of this Bible was regarded to have played a special role in the radical changes in language style at that time. However, the Chinese language has undergone tremendous changes over the past decades. In the twentieth century, standard Chinese, also referred to as *guoyu* 國語 (literally, "national language") or later *putonghua* 普通話 (literally, "common speech"), became the official language of China. Although the standard Chinese was based on Mandarin, it is a little different from Mandarin in the early twentieth century, when the CUV was translated. Certain words and expressions in the CUV that formerly sounded smooth and natural have since become unnatural and unintelligible in the second half of the twentieth century. In addition, different critical comments on the CUV still appeared from time to time. Furthermore, it was basically the work of Western scholars using a foreign medium.

In view of this, the United Bible Societies (UBS) started a revision project for the CUV in 1983. In 1988, the *Chinese Union Version with the New Punctuation* 新標點和合本 was published by the UBS in Hong Kong. It included the revision of punctuation, personal names, geographical names, and some Chinese characters.

More revisions were still going on. In 2010, almost one century after the publication of the CUV, the traditional Chinese version of the Revised Chinese Union Version 和合本修訂版 (RCUV), which is an update of the 1919 CUV, was published by the UBS and the Hong Kong Bible Society (HKBS) after twenty-seven years in the making. The RCUV provided numerous instances of modern, updated language while still retaining the biblical accuracy of the widely popular CUV. This new version also contained an introduction to each book of the Bible and well over two thousand footnotes. Since most of the Chinese church still used the CUV in their religious activities, the RCUV need some more time to gain public acceptance.

From the end of the 1980s, mainland China had started to publish the Bible in simplified Chinese. Around 1987, the Amity Printing Press in Nanjing was established as an independent commercial operation with ties to the Protestant churches in China. In cooperation with the UBS, it resumed printing of the CUV in simplified Chinese.

Mandarin Translations after the Chinese Union Version

There were several translation attempts after the publication of the CUV in 1919, and some of them co-translations by Chinese Christian scholars published in China, Hong Kong, Taiwan, and overseas.

From the 1910s, Absalom Sydenstricker (1852–1931, father of Pearl S. Buck, the winner of the Nobel Prize in Literature in 1938), an American Presbyterian missionary to China, started to revise the Bible from 1913 and published the NT in 1929. This NT was the earliest new version after the publication of the CUV. Unfortunately, Sydenstricker died in 1931 and did not finish the revision. His revision was continued by his Chinese student and colleague, Zhu Baohui 朱寶惠 (1889–1970). Zhu was a teacher of biblical Greek at Nanking Theological Seminary. He revised the NT with copious notes and cross-references. It was published in 1936.

The first complete Protestant NT version done by a Chinese was prepared by Wang Hsüan-ch'en 王宣忱 (or named Wang Yuen-det 王元德, 1879–1942), a former colleague of Calvin Wilson Mateer (1836–1908, APM), one of the translators of the CUV. Wang's NT was published in 1933 by the Church of Christ in China in Tsingtao (青島中華基督教會). Although this version may be understood as a revision of the CUV, it was memorialized as a milestone in Chinese Bible translation.

Another NT at this time was *The Bible Treasury New Testament* 國語新舊庫譯本新約全書 by German missionary Heinrich Ruck (1887–1972) and Chinese scholar Zheng Shou-lin 鄭壽麟 (1900–1990). The tentative version of the epistle to the Romans was published in 1933, the NT in 1939, and the Psalms in 1940. In 1941, the revised NT was published in Beijing. In 1958, their NT was revised again and published with the Psalms in Hong Kong.

Others were selections from the Bible, including the *Gospel according to Luke and Acts* by Gordon Poteat (1891–1986) in 1934; the English and Chinese versions of the *Gospels Harmony* by several scholars in West China Union University (華西協合大學) in 1936; a partial translation from *The New Testament in English* of John Bertram Phillips (1906–1982) published by Translation and Compilation Department of the Christian Life Society (基督教生活社編譯部) in 1956; the *Epistle of James* by a pseudonym which published by China Sunday School Association in Taiwan in 1958; the *Epistle to Philemon* and the Beatitudes by Frank Wilson Price (1895–1974) and Gu Dun Rou 顧敦鍒 which was printed in the journal *The Bible Translator* in 1960; the *Epistles of John* with commentary by Martin Armstrong Hopkins (1889–1964) in 1960; the *Gospel of John* by Liu Yi-ling 劉翼凌 (1901–1994) in 1964; the OT and NT selections by Di Shou Ren in 1965; the *Gospel of John* with commentary by Silas C. T. Hsu 許乾泰 in 1966; the *Gospel of John* in manuscript by Andrew Yu-Wang Hsieh 謝友王 (?–1994) in 1972.

After the 1950s, many Bible versions in Chinese were not translated and published in mainland China, but by the Christians in Taiwan, Hong Kong, and overseas. Among these Bible versions, the most important one was still the CUV, but there were several other Bible translations for different readers, including Christian and non-Christian, as discussed below.

The first complete Bible in Mandarin translated by Chinese biblical scholar Lü Chen-chung 呂振中 (1898–1988) appeared in this time. The first draft of his NT was published in Beijing in 1946. After Lü moved to Hong Kong, he revised and published his NT in 1952 and published the entire Bible in 1970. Lü was partially supported by the Bible society in Hong Kong but published the Bible in his name. Historical documents related to Lü's translation, including the OT autograph mimeograph draft, were kept in the Cambridge University Library.

In 1967, another NT was translated and published by Theodore E. Hsiao 蕭鐵笛 (1898–1984) in Hong Kong. This translation was validated by Timothy S. K. Dzao 趙世光 (1908–1973). A revised edition was published in 1986 in Japan.

Chinese Bibles until this time were mostly literal translations, which is the rendering of text from one language to another "word-for-word" (Latin: "*verbum pro verbo*") rather than conveying the sense of the original. From the 1970s, two Chinese Bible projects that used other translation principles appeared.

The first one was *The Chinese Living Bible* 當代聖經 (CLB). The NT was published in 1974; the whole Bible was published in 1979 and revised several times. CLB was a Chinese translation of *The Living Bible* in English (1971) of Kenneth N. Taylor (1917–2005), which was published by Living Bibles International; this was a simple translation and mostly used in gospel preaching. CLB was a "paraphrase," which means that it was taking ideas from a translation and putting them into the local vernacular for better understanding, especially for new Christians and younger people.

The Living Bible in English was revised as the *New Living Translation* (NLT) in 1996, 2004, and 2007. It was translated in Chinese as *The Chinese New Living Translation* 新普及譯本 (CNLT), the NT in 2006 and the whole Bible in 2012, by the Chinese Bible International (CBI, 漢語聖經協會).

Another one was The Today's Chinese Version 現代中文譯本 (TCV), which was a translation of the Bible into modern Chinese. The NT was first published in 1975, and the entire Bible was published in 1979. The revised version was published in 1995. TCV was published in two different editions to accommodate different translations used by Protestants and Catholics. It was published in several editions, and some of them were used in high schools of Hong Kong as a textbook for religious studies. In this situation, TCV was functioned as an evangelical tool to touch the world.

TCV was born out of the translation theories of linguist Eugene A. Nida (1914–2011), one of the founders of the modern discipline of translation studies and the executive secretary of the American Bible Society's translations department. Nida developed the "Dynamic Equivalence" Bible-translation theory in contrast to the traditional "Formal Equivalence" theory. "Formal Equivalence" focuses attention on the message itself, in both form and content, while "Dynamic Equivalence" aims at complete "naturalness" of expression. The literal principle, which was the basic of "Formal Equivalence," dominated Chinese Bible translation until the mid-twentieth century; the alternative principle of "Dynamic Equivalence" was present from this period on. TCV was the first Chinese Bible translation translated using the "Dynamic Equivalence" theory.

However, TCV was the only attempt that used the "Dynamic Equivalence" theory in Chinese Bible translation. The mainstream Bible versions in Chinese churches continues to be the literal translation and translated according to "Formal Equivalence."

The Chinese New Version 新譯本 (CNV) was one version in traditional literal translation used by many Chinese Christians in their private lives until today. This translation project was started in 1972, the NT was published in 1976, and the whole Bible was completed in 1992, by the Worldwide Bible Society (WBS, 環球聖經公會) with the assistance of the Lockman Foundation. From 2001, WBS had revised the CNV and started to publish a revised version named the Worldwide Chinese New Version (WCNV, 環球新譯本). The Gospels were published in 2011, and the NT was published in 2015. The revision is still in process.

There also was a Chinese Bible version used only by a small group of Christians: The Recovery Version 恢復本. The NT was published by the editorial section of Living Stream Ministry in 1987. The whole Bible was published in 2003 in Taiwan.

At the beginning of the twenty-first century, Chinese scholars of Bible translations from Taiwan, Hong Kong, and the United States have produced several works worthy of emulation by mainlanders. These versions included the *Chinese Holy Bible (Putonghua)* (CHB, also named "Easy-To-Read Version") by the World Bible

Translation Center in 1999 and 2015; the *Chinese Standard Bible* 中文標準譯本 (CSB) NT by Asia Bible Society and Holman Bible Publishers in 2008; the Contemporary Chinese Version 新漢語譯本 (CCV) NT in 2010 and Pentateuch in 2014 by the CBI; and *The Holy Bible: A Dynamic Chinese Translation* 新譯簡明聖經 (DCT) with NT and partial OT by Gene Hsiao 蕭慶松 of the Tucson Chinese Bible Society in 2012. Some of the above translations, such as the CHB, the CSB, and the DCT, were mainly focused on Chinese overseas who moved from mainland China. These translations were done according to the language of *Putonghua*, a standardized form of the language in mainland China.

In addition to the above versions, there were several Chinese translations that attempted to present the Bible in some of the most effective language of our day. The first were Chinese translations of *The Message*. *The Message* was a Bible translation by Eugene Peterson (1932–2018), a retired pastor in Montana. In *The Message*, Peterson's primary goal was to capture the tone of the text and the original conversational feel of the Greek in contemporary English. The Chinese edition in 2004, which was named "*Xin-xi-ben Sheng-jing*" 信息本聖經 in Chinese, was translated from the English version. Another was a Chinese version of the *New English Translation* (NET Bible), which was named the *Chinese NET Bible* or "NET *Sheng-jing*" NET 聖經 in Chinese. It was translated and published by Biblical Studies Press in 2011. The goal of these Bible versions was to engage people in the reading process and help them understand what they read.

Local Dialects

China has a large population spread over a vast geographical area, and the Chinese spoken there consists of several dialect continuums. Many Protestant missionaries, most of them working on the southeast coast of China, dedicated themselves to translating the Bible into various Chinese dialects from the middle of the nineteenth century to the early twentieth century. According to existing records and copies of Chinese Bibles, the Bible has been translated into more than twenty dialects. The translations mostly were single books but some of them were the entire NT or Bible. These products included Mandarin dialects 官話方言, Wu dialects 吳語, Min dialects 閩語, and Yue dialects 粵語. Some of the versions in these dialects were printed with Chinese characters, others in Pinyin Romanization script, National Phonetic script or Wang-Peill Phonetic script, and some in both.

Mandarin comprises the group of dialects spoken in northern and southwestern China and makes up the largest spoken language in China. There were several Mandarin dialects into which the Bible was translated, such as Shantung (Shandong) colloquial, Tientsin (Tianjin) colloquial, Kiaotung (Jiaodong) colloquial, and Chihli (Zhili, today "Hebei") colloquial.

In addition to the above dialects, there also was a version of Mark translated in the Hankow colloquial dialect according to Mandarin (so it was named "Hankow Mandarin") by LMS missionary James L. H. Paterson (1884–1952), a senior missionary doctor working in the Lester Chinese Hospital in Shanghai. It was printed in Mandarin

Wang-Peill Phonetic script and published in 1921. Hankow colloquial was spoken in Hankow, one of the Wuhan cities in East Hupeh province.

Wu dialects were spoken in the provinces of Jiangsu and Zhejiang, and the municipality of Shanghai. The first Bible in this language was the Gospel of John in Shanghai colloquial in 1847, which was also the earliest Bible version in Chinese dialect. The Bible in Shanghai colloquial was printed in Chinese characters and Romanized script, such as other dialects. In addition, it also had a special phonetic system. In 1859, Cleveland Keith (1827–1862), a missionary from American Protestant Episcopal Mission (APEM), translated and published the Gospel of Luke in Shanghai colloquial, which used Romanized script. In the same year, A. B. Cabaniss (1853–1859 in China), a missionary from ASBM in Shanghai, transcribed this version into a special phonetics system and gave it the title *Loo Ka Zen Foh Yung Zu* 路加真福音書 (pinyin in Mandarin was *Lu Jia Zhen Fu Yin Shu*). This phonetics system was designed by another ASBM missionary Tarleton Perry Crawford (1821–1902) and named *Shanghai Tu-yin-zi* 上海土音字 (which means "Local accent word of Shanghai"). It was the only Baptist version published in Shanghai colloquial. Other versions in Wu languages were Ningpo (Ningbo) colloquial, Kinhwa (Jinhua) colloquial, Hangchow (Hangzhou) colloquial, Soochow (Suzhou) colloquial, Taichow (Taizhou) colloquial, and Wenchow (Wenzhou) colloquial.

Min dialects were spoken in Fujian, Taiwan, and parts of Southeast Asia. The earliest Bible in these dialects was Amoy (Xiamen) colloquial, then Foochow (Fuzhou) colloquial, Shaowu colloquial, Hinghua (Xinghua) colloquial, Kienning (Jianning) colloquial, Kienyang (Jianyang) colloquial, and Tingchow (Tingzhou) colloquial.

Yue dialects is a group of similar Sinitic languages spoken in southern China, particularly the provinces of Guangdong and Guangxi. The main dialect in the Guangdong region was Cantonese (Canton colloquial). There were several other dialects circulating in the Guangdong region, and the earliest Bible was in Hakka colloquial. Hakka colloquial was spoken by the Hakka people, a cultural group of the Han Chinese, in several provinces across southern China. Other versions in the Guangdong region were Wukingfu colloquial (the Hakka colloquial usage of Wukingfu), Canton (Guangzhou) colloquial, Swatow (Shantou) colloquial, Hainan colloquial, and Sankiang (Sanjiang) colloquial.

After the publication of the CUV in the early twentieth century, most of the Bible dialect versions had disappeared in China. Today, there are only three Bible dialect versions still being published in Hong Kong and Taiwan, including Cantonese, Taiwanese (Amoy colloquial in Taiwan), and Hakka colloquial.

Overview of Protestant Chinese Bible in Common Languages and Local Dialects

Here is a chronological list of Chinese Bibles by Protestant translators in common languages, including the traditional classical Chinese, the easy classical Chinese and Mandarin, as well as local dialects (Table 2.1).

Table 2.1 Overview of Protestant Chinese Bible Versions in Common Languages and Local Dialects

Language/Dialect		Character	Books/NT/Bible with the Earliest Date of Publication
Traditional Classical (High *Wenli*) Chinese		Chinese Character	Matthew, Mark, and Acts (1810)/1814/1822
Lower Classical (Easy *Wenli*) Chinese		Chinese Character	Psalms (1880)/1885/1902
Mandarin and Mandarin Dialects	Southern Mandarin	Chinese Character	Matthew (1854)/1857
		Romanized Script	Luke (1870)
	Northern Mandarin (Beijing Mandarin)	Chinese Character	Mark (1862)/1872/1878
	Shantung (Shandong) colloquial	Romanized Script	Luke and John (1892)
	Tientsin (Tianjin) colloquial	Chinese Character with National Phonetic	Selections from NT (1917)
	Kiaotung (Jiaodong) colloquial	Wang-Peill Phonetic Script	Mark (1918)
		National Phonetic Script	Matthew (1920)
	Hankow (Hankou) colloquial	Wang-Peill Phonetic Script	Mark (1921)
	Chihli (Zhili) colloquial	Wang-Peill Phonetic Script	Luke (1925)
Wu Dialects	Shanghai colloquial	Chinese Character	John (1847)/1870/1908
		Romanized Script	John (1853)/1871
		Local Accent Word of Shanghai	Luke (1859)
	Ningpo (Ningbo) colloquial	Romanized Script	Luke (1852)/1868/1901
		Chinese Character	John (1894)
	Kinhwa (Jinhua) colloquial	Romanized Script	John (1866)
	Hangchow (Hangzhou) colloquial	Chinese Character	Selections from NT (1877)
		Romanized Script	John (1879)
	Soochow (Suzhou) colloquial	Chinese Character	Gospels and Acts (1879)/1881/1908
		Romanized Script	Mark (1891)
	Taichow (Taizhou) colloquial	Romanized Script	Matthew (1880)/1881/1914
	Wenchow (Wenzhou) colloquial	Romanized Script	Matthew (1892)/1902

(Continued)

Table 2.1 Continued

Language/Dialect		Character	Books/NT/Bible with the Earliest Date of Publication
Min Dialects	Amoy (Xiamen) colloquial	Romanized Script	John (1852)/1873/1884
	Foochow (Fuzhou) colloquial	Chinese Character	Matthew and Mark (1852)/1856/1891
		Romanized Script	John (1881)/1890/1905
		National Phonetic	Mark (1921)
	Shaowu colloquial	Romanized Script	James (1891)
	Hinghua (Xinghua) colloquial	Romanized Script	John (1892)/1900/1912
	Kienning (Jianning) colloquial	Romanized Script	Matthew (1896)/1896
	Kienyang (Jianyang) colloquial	Romanized Script	Mark (1898)
	Tingchow (Tingzhou) colloquial	Romanized Script	Matthew (1919)
Yue Dialects	Hakka colloquial	Romanized Script	Matthew (1860)
		Chinese Character	Luke (1881)/1883/1916
	Wukingfu colloquial	Romanized Script	Selections from Bible (1910)/1916
	Canton (Guangzhou) colloquial	Chinese Character	Matthew and John (1862)/1877/1894
		Romanized Script	Luke (1867)/1913/1915
	Swatow (Shantou) colloquial	Chinese Character	Ruth (1875)/1898/1922
		Romanized Script	Luke (1877)/1905
	Hainan colloquial	Romanized Script	Matthew (1891)
	Sankiang (Sanjiang) colloquial	Chinese Character	Matthew (1904)

Old Testament Apocrypha

The OT Apocrypha was a set of booklets that had been assembled between the completion of the OT and the first writings included in the NT, but generally not accepted by Protestant Christians as the Word of God. However, the Bible used by the Anglican Church included the OT Apocrypha. At the end of the nineteenth century, the English Revised Version (ERV; NT 1881; OT 1885) with the Apocrypha was used by the Anglican Church.

In 1898, the earliest edition with several Apocrypha selections in Chinese was published by the American Bible Society in Shanghai. This book was named *Sheng-jing Wai-zhuan* 聖經外傳 (which means "the Biblical Apocrypha"). In the following years, several books were translated and published by the *Chung Hwa Sheng Kung Hwei* 中華聖公會 (Chinese Anglican Church) in Shanghai. In 1933, the first completed translation of the Apocrypha, *Ci-jing Quan-shu* 次經全書 (which means "the Complete Apocrypha"), was published by *Chung Hwa Sheng Kung Hwei* in Beijing. It was translated into classical Chinese by Montgomery Hunt Throop (1885–1969) and a Chinese, Waung Yih-tsieu 黃葉秋, and re-translated into the Mandarin version by Rev. H. F. Lei 雷海峰 and others. The books included in *Ci-Jing Quan-shu* were the following: *Ma-ka-bi Chuan Shang-juan* 瑪喀比傳上卷 (*1 Maccabees*); *Ma-ka-bi Chuan Xia-juan* 瑪喀比傳下卷 (*2 Maccabees*); *Duo-bi Chuan*多比傳 (*Tobit*); *You-di Chuan* 猶滴傳 (*Judith*); *Bian-xi-la Zhi-xun* 便西拉智訓 (*Sirach*, or *Ecclesiasticus*); *Suo-luo-men Zhi-xun* 所羅門智訓 (*the Wisdom of Solomon*); *Yi-si-la Xu-bian Shang-juan* 以斯拉續編上卷 (*1 Esdras*); *Yi-si-la Xu-bian Xia-juan* 以斯拉續編下卷 (*2 Esdras*); *Ba-lu Shu* 巴錄書 (*Baruch*); *Ye-li-mi Shu-xin* 耶利米書信 (*Epistle of Jeremiah*); *Ma-na-xi Dao-yan* 瑪拿西禱言 (*Prayer of Manasses*); *San-tong Ge* 三童歌 (*Song of the Three Holy Children*); *Su-sa-na Chuan* 蘇撒拿傳 (*Susanna*); *Bi-le Yu Da-long* 彼勒與大龍 (*Bel and the Dragon*); and *Yi-si-tie Bu-pian* 以斯帖補篇 (*Additions to Esther*).

This Apocrypha was reprinted in 1949. The Holy Bible with Apocrypha was published as a commemorative edition for the tenth anniversary of Hong Kong Sheng Kung Hui (香港聖公會, Hong Kong Anglican Church) in 2008.

Chinese Bible in Literature

The Bible is a religious text, but it is also a work of literature. In fact, it is a literary masterpiece. Historically, most of the translations have aimed at accuracy of meaning in Bible text rather than literalness. However, some of the Protestant missionaries involved in the Bible translation translated according to a Chinese traditional literary style. They hoped this style would appeal to more Chinese people.

The earliest Bible selections in literature were the Psalms, with commentary in Mandarin by William Chalmers Burns (1815–1868, English Presbyterian Mission) in 1867. It was translated using the Western tetrameters poetic style. Another one was the Psalms in the traditional Chinese metrical style by Frederick William Baller (1852–1922, CIM) in 1908. The most special one may have come from John Chalmers of LMS. John Chalmers had rendered twenty of the Psalms with the free rhythmic style according to a chant from the *Chuci* 楚辭 (*Songs of the South*, an anthology of ancient Chinese poetry around 300 BCE), and published *A Specimen of Chinese Metrical Psalms* in 1890. This was an experimental translation in metrical form style, which was quite similar to the *Chuci*. John Chalmers had translated Psalms 1 to 19 and 23 in this book.

During the twentieth century, there also were other Bible selection translations in literature by several Chinese writers, such as the Song of Songs by the famous Chinese literary giants Xu Dishan 許地山 (1894–1941) in 1921, Chen Meng-jia 陳夢家 (1911–1966) in 1932, and Wang Fu-min 王福民 (or Wang Robert Gordis, 1908–?) in 1960 (in both classical Chinese and Mandarin), as well as the Lamentation of Jeremiah by Li Jung-fang 李榮芳 (1887–1965) in 1931 and Zhu Wei-zhi 朱維之 (or W. T. Chu, 1905–1999) in 1941. The above translations re-translated the Bible text in the Chinese poetic style.

After the publication of CUV, there were other works that re-edited the Bible text in the literary style. The first was titled *Shan-ren Zao-nan* 善人遭難 (means "Good people in suffering," editor unnamed) in 1922. It re-edited the Book of Job with the CUV in the Chinese opera style and was published in Wuxi. In 1930, Wu Shu-tian 吳曙天 (1903–1942), a female Chinese writer, also re-edited the Song of Songs in Chinese poetic style for a bilingual edition of the Chinese CUV and the English *King James Bible*. These were literary works rather than for religious use in the church.

At the end of the twentieth century, many editions of Chinese Bible stories had been published in widely differing formats. These Bible stories were published and distributed in secular bookstores, and they were read as a substitute for the Bible or for their literary and historical value. They seemed to be in favor with Chinese readers. Several writers in China, without any religious background, also translated certain books of Bible into modern Chinese. Many Bible stories were published by secular publishers and did not sell for religious purposes. However, they had a very large publication market so that the Bible, as least the stories of Bible, has been distributed in an unexpected way.

Conclusion

In the recent centuries, the Bible translation into Chinese was done in the common languages and more than twenty dialects in China. It was undertaken by the Catholic missionaries in the earlier stage and continued by the Protestant and Orthodox missionaries later. When the *Si-gao Sheng-jing* and the Chinese Union Version were translated and published by the Chinese Catholic and Protestant churches respectively, they became the predominant translations of the Bible into Chinese used by both sides. However, after the twentieth century, more Chinese Christian translators involved in this endeavor. New Bible translation plans still appear today.

In a review of the Bible in China, John Campbell Gibson (1849–1919), an English Presbyterian Mission missionary from Swatow (Shantou), pointed out in the General Conference of Protestant Missionaries (GCPM) of 1890 (quoted from *Records of the GCPM, May 2–20, 1890*, 62):

> A translation may be for either of two purposes:
>
> Either (1) To give a substantially faith presentation of the thoughts of Scripture to non-Christian readers, either with a direct view to their enlightenment and conversion, or for general apologetic purposes.

> Or (2) To supply Christian readers with as faithful a text as can possibly be given, to form the basis for a minute and loving study of the niceties of expression, and the minuitæ of distinctively Christian thought.

Gibson mentioned that the translation of Bible had two purposes, evangelical preaching and educational instruction. These two purposes still are the mission of the Chinese church today.

The goal of Bible translation is to transfer the meaning of a biblical text from its source languages to other receptor languages. During the past century, new studies in the biblical original language have appeared. Almost all the Bible translation projects recently emphasize that the entire Chinese Bible must be directly translated from the original Hebrew, Aramaic, and Greek texts. These newer versions are translated from the best available ancient manuscripts. Due to advances in computer technology, the revisions were aligned with the original language to facilitate cross-checking and consistency during the translation process. At the same time, Chinese churches believe that the purpose of the Bible translation is not only to be faithful to the original text but also to able to be read and known, including by people both in and outside of the church.

It is necessary for every Bible translation to be exceptionally accurate and readable. Communication is not just a matter of proclaiming something, but it requires that the message sent out be received so that the reader can understand it. It was difficult to find both accuracy and readability in such excellent balance in Chinese Bible translation. But this was the purpose of most Bible translations in China and will remain the ongoing work in the twenty-first century.

Primary Sources

The Chinese Bible versions mentioned in this article are mainly based on the collection in the Bible House Library of Cambridge University Library. It also is based on the holdings in the libraries of several archives, including Bodleian Library at Oxford, British Library, Library of American Bible Society, Library of National Bible Society of Scotland (now Scottish Bible Society), National Library of Australia, Yenching Library at Harvard University, and other collections.

For the catalogue of the Chinese Bible in the Cambridge University Library, see:

Darlow, Thomas H., and Horace F. Moule. *Historical Catalogue of the Printed Editions of Holy Scripture in the Library of the British and Foreign Bible Society*, 4 vols. London: Bible House, 1903–1911.

Falivene, M. Rosaria, compiled; edited by Alan F. Jesson. *Historical Catalogue of the Manuscripts of Bible House Library*. London: British and Foreign Bible Society, 1982.

Spillett, Hubert W. *A Catalogue of Scriptures in the Languages of China and the Republic of China*. London: British and Foreign Bible Society, 1975.

For the collection in the American Bible Society, see:

Nida, Eugene A. *The Book of a Thousand Tongues*. London: United Bible Societies, 1972.
North, Eric M. *The Book of a Thousand Tongues; Being Some Account of the Translation and Publication of All or Part of the Holy Scriptures into More Than a Thousand Languages and Dialects with Over 1100 Examples from the Text*. London: Pub. for the American Bible society [by] Harper & brothers, 1938.

For the collection in the National Bible Society of Scotland, see:

The National Bible Society of Scotland. *Catalogue of Scriptures in Chinese Published by the National Bible Society of Scotland*. Hankow: National Bible Society of Scotland Mission Press, 1902.

For the collection in Yenching Library, see:

Lai, John Yung-Hsiang, ed. *Catalogue of the Protestant Missionary Works in Chinese, Harvard-Yenching Library*. Boston: G.K. Hall, 1980.

For the history of Bible in China, see:

Choi, Daniel Kam-to 蔡錦圖. *Sheng-jing Zai Zhong-guo: Fu Zhong-wen Sheng-jing Li-shi Mu-lu* [in Chinese] 聖經在中國: 附中文聖經歷史目錄; *Bible in China: With a Historical Catalogue of the Chinese Bible*. Hong Kong: The Logos and Pneuma Press, 2018.
Choi, Daniel Kam-to. "The Baptist Endeavours in Biblical Translation in China before the Chinese Union Version." *Journal of the Royal Asiatic Society* 30 (2, 2020): 341–364.

CHAPTER 3

CHINESE JINGJIAO AND THE ANTIOCHENE EXEGESIS

DONGHUA ZHU

The Meaning of Chinese Jingjiao

Chinese Jingjiao 景教 had deep historical roots that can be traced back to one of the apostolic churches, that is: (1) the Church of the East whose patriarch (*catholicos*) had his see at the Persian capital, Seleucia-Ctesiphon; and (2) its exegetical and theological developments that had inherited richly the legacy of the Antiochene school, evident in its exegesis toward literary, literal, and historical interpretations. It is no wonder that the influence of the distinctive Antiochene emphasis can be seen in the strategic appropriation of the Chinese name of "Daqin Jingjiao 大秦景教" (literally, Daqin Illustrious Religion) instead of the so-called "Persian Jingjiao 波斯經教" ("*Jing* 經" here means scriptural, different from "*Jing* 景" meaning illustrious). When the Persian missionary Aluoben 阿羅本 arrived at the imperial court in 635 CE and was asked to translate the "true canon" (the Bible) into Chinese, the Chinese emperor subsequently commanded in an edict that the "Persian Jingjiao" should be granted freedom to preach throughout the empire.[1] What "*Jing*jiao 經教" means in Middle Chinese (ca. 420–1280 CE) reminds us of the religion of those who were called "*Ahl al-Kitāb*" ("People of the Book"), a Quranic term referring to Christians as possessors of Scriptures previously revealed by God. The Christian missionaries in Tang China, however, did not consistently use the appellation of "Jingjiao 經教." Nearly a century later, they finally gave it up, even though they, like Chinese people, attached great importance to classics and, as the inheritors of Antiochene tradition, they took pride in possessing sophistication in expounding Scriptures.

Because *Ahl al-Kitāb* sometimes was applied also to Zoroastrians and, therefore, Zoroastrianism also probably could be regarded as Persian Jingjiao, Persian Christian missionaries found it necessary to adopt a new name (i.e., Daqin Jingjiao 大秦景教) for people to distinguish Christianity from Zoroastrianism. A consideration of the change from Persian Jingjiao 波斯經教 to Daqin Jingjiao 大秦景教 shows two dimensions of understanding. First, from the perspective of the academic tradition of Eastern Syriac Christianity, it can be inferred that the authorities of the Tang dynasty had to know the fact that Persian Jingjiao 波斯經教 received its theological content and exegetical methods from the school of Nisibis and, finally, from the school of Edessa. Both Nisibis and Edessa—as central cities of Osrhoene and the Roman province of Syria, for which the ancient Chinese name "Daqin 大秦" is coined—were the gates through which theological and exegetical developments of the Antiochene school entered the Church of the East. So it is hardly surprising that the Chinese authorities could trace the origin of Persian Christianity back to the Eastern Church of Daqin after the Persian missionary Giwargis 佶和 told the whole story in 744.[2] Second, the change of the appellation pushes forward a deepening understanding in the Chinese Jingjiao documents that "Jingjiao 景教" is promoted as a category of self-understanding of connecting to the land of the great Christian intellectual heritage while also engaging with Persian Jingjiao in a subtle displacement of identity, especially in the name change. In the last centuries, many studies have been devoted to the meaning of Jingjiao 景教, and three main emphases are noteworthy:

First, the word "*jing* 景," used by writers in classical Chinese, almost had a connotation of "light" (*guang* 光), as we find it in Xu Shen's 許慎 dictionary titled *Shuowen Jiezi* 說文解字.[3] Albeit to a greater degree in emphasizing its meaning as a verb, this interpretation is also that of Li Zhizao 李之藻 (1565–1630), a prominent Christian leader in the late Ming dynasty. According to Li, "*jing* 景" means *zhao* 炤 (illuminating), *zhao* 照 (shining), or *guangming* 光明 (brightening).[4] There is obviously a robust analogy from the account of illumination as an aspect of the economic activities of the second Person of the Trinity. Providing the first Chinese commentary on the Jingjiao Stele (781 CE), Li's interpretation of "*jing*" enjoys a favorable reception. Modern scholars discuss frequently Christian traits of the Chinese word "*jing* 景," because they find that as early as Tang China this term already had taken on a religious connotation when Persian missionaries tried to articulate the divine action in the work of illumination. Pan Shen 潘紳, a scholar of the Republic of China, shed light on the religious connotation of *jing* 景 as it connects to the Gospel of John regarding divine light: "That was the true Light" (John 1:9), "I am the light of the world" (John 8:12), and "While I am in the world, I am the light of the world" (John 9:5).[5] As the light pertains to the Word in the Johannine Gospel, the narratives of light in Chinese Jingjiao documents implies, to a greater extent, intriguing christological and soteriological doctrines of illumination. With this speculation, the inscription of the Jingjiao Stele was the first to infer a raison d'être for the name of Jingjiao 景教:

> 開生滅死，懸景日以破暗府，魔妄於是乎悉摧。棹慈航以登明宮，含靈於是乎既濟...真常之道，妙而難名，功用昭彰，強稱景教。[6]

> He saved life and abolished death. He hung up a brilliant sun to break down the halls of darkness; the nebulous devils were then completely destroyed. He ferried the barge of mercy to go up to the Palace of Light; those who have souls were then completely liberated and succored.... The true and eternal Word is wonderful and difficult to name; its merits and benefits are manifest and splendid. Insufficiently, we call it Jingjiao (the Illustrious Religion). (Translation mine.)

Here we can see a gradual growth of Chinese Christian thought and language in an endeavor to find better names for "the One who admits to no name." As was the case with the Jingjiao Stele, so too with another Chinese Christian document, *Daqin Jingjiao Sanwei Mengduzan* 大秦景教三威蒙度讚 (*Hymn of the Angels*), which continues to follow and adopt both the better name of Jingjiao 景教 and the narrative of the economy of divine light:

> 慈父明子淨風王，於諸帝中為師帝，於諸世尊為法王。常居妙明無畔界，光威盡察有界疆。[7]
>
> Merciful Father, bright Son and King of *rūḥā ḏ-quḏšā* (pure Wind). Among all kings, He is the supreme King. Among all lords, He is the *Darma Raja* (Lord of law). He dwells for ever more in the unlimited Kingdom of wondrous brightness. With His mighty power of light, He patrols the limited world.

In the above verses of *Hymn of the Angels*, the original Syrian version reads "*aḇā wa-ḇrā w-rūḥā ḏ-quḏšā*" (Father, Son and Holy Spirit),[8] while the Chinese version interpolates "*ci* 慈" (merciful) before "*fu* 父" (Father), "*ming* 明" (bright) before "*zi* 子" (Son), and "*wang* 王" (King) after "*jing feng* 淨風" (pure Wind). Here, the interpolation of "*ming*" (bright) before "*zi*" (Son), together with the so-called "Kingdom of wondrous brightness" and "His mighty power of light" in the following verses, presumes a rhetoric of the economy of divine light and shows good agreement with the narrative style of the *Jingjiao Stele Text* 景教碑文. It is the consistency of rhetoric that manifests the profound influence of the doctrine of illumination upon Jingjing 景淨, both in his writing of the *Jingjiao Stele Text* and in his translating of *Hymn of the Angels*. Moreover, even more cryptically, the consistent rhetoric on the doctrine of illumination forms the basis for Jingjing and others to adopt the Chinese name "Jingjiao 景教."

Second, also noteworthy is the second meaning of "*jing* 景" invoked by Li Zhizao from the *Erya* 爾雅, a Chinese lexicography compiled in the second century. According to *Erya*, the character "*jing* 景" bears the same meaning of "*da* 大" (great or universal) as it does in its radical "*jing* 京."[9] Qian Nianqu 錢念劬, a Chinese diplomat and scholar in the Late Qing Dynasty, is the first to assert that Jingjiao 景教 is a good name for Christianity in Tang China, because what the character "*jing* 景" means is completely consistent with the original meaning of the word "catholic."[10] As a global form of world religions, Jingjiao 景教 lives in the full openness of universality. The *Jingjiao Stele Text* contains such vivid and accurate notions of the universal economy of Messiah the

Luminous Lord as *jingzun mi shihe* 景尊彌施訶: It is the Luminous Lord who can bring winds and rains in seasons (*fengyu shi* 風雨時), the empire to peace (*tianxia jing* 天下靜), the people to order and harmony (*ren neng li* 人能理), and all creatures to good condition (*wu neng qing* 物能清). It is the Luminous Lord who can give shelter to all the living and the dead (*da bi cunwang* 大庇存亡), who can relieve, with boundless mercy, the suffering of all (*guang ci jiu Zhong ku* 廣慈救眾苦). In one of Jingjing's translation works, *Hymn of the Angels*, the Luminous Lord *jingzun* 景尊 was called the "all respected *Mishihe* (Messiah), the great holy one" (*dasheng puzun mi shihe* 大聖普尊彌施訶) whose mighty power can save "millions of lives" from "all sufferings" (*guangdu kujie jiu wuyi* 廣度苦界救無億), and, therefore, "all shall venerate (Him)."[11]

Third, the Chinese character "*jing* 景" also can assume the meaning of "esteem" (*jingyang* 景仰) or "venerate" (*jingyang* 敬仰), which is deserving of special note. The *Pian Hai* 篇海, a dictionary that contains a far wider range of entries and meanings, remarkably includes in the entry of "*jing* 景" the special meaning of "admire" (*mu* 慕) and "venerate" (*yang* 仰).[12] Even though the *Pian Hai* was edited at a comparatively later time (Jin dynasty, 1115–1234 CE), the above meaning of "*jing*" often can be traced to metaphors of "lofty mountains and great roads" (*gaoshan yangzhi, jingxing xingzhi* 高山仰止, 景行行止) used by the earliest anthology of Chinese poetry called *Shijing* 詩經 in eulogizing exemplary figures and holding them in highest esteem.[13]

By the time of the Tang dynasty, cognate words such as "*jingmu* 景慕" (admire) and "*jingyang* 景仰" (hold in highest esteem) prevalently had been used among the literati, and thus most probably became a basis for Christians in Tang China to transplant the connotation of an affective response of reverent fear of God into the Chinese name of Jingjiao. As an interesting comparison study, we compare some transliterated words in Chinese documents of the Tang and Yuan Dynasties with the original Pahlavi (middle Persian) word "*tarsāk*." The designation for Christians in Pahlavi, *tarsāk* (literally meaning "fearer"),[14] is transliterated respectively as "*dasuo* 達娑" in the *Jingjiao Stele Text*, as "*dasuo* 怛索" in the Dunghuang document *Yishen Lun* 一神論 (*Discourse on God*), as "*diexie* 迭屑" in the *Changchun Zhenren Xiyouji* 長春真人西遊記 (*The Journey to the West of Daoist Master Changchun*).[15] These transliterated words, as well as the Pahlavi word *tarsāk*, derive ultimately from the famed "God-fearers," because "fear (of God)" may be the earliest term for religion in Semitic languages. For example, "fear of God" is a major theme in the Hebrew Bible (hereafter HB), and in almost 80 percent of the over four hundred instances of the HB "*yārē*," the object of fear is God. New Testament (hereafter NT) Greek terms for *phobeō* ("fear") were used earlier in the Septuagint to translate certain terms in the HB, while the Syrian NT Peshitta contributed even further to this semantic tendency by employing *deḥlta* ("fear") and its cognates to translate the word groups of *phobos* and *sebesthai* in such verses as Matt 15:9, Rom 3:18, 2 Cor 7:1, and Acts 18:13.[16] There is ample evidence in East Syrian texts of the use of "fear" terminology in Syriac, and especially the Syriac version of Theodore of Mopsuestia's *Catechetical Homilies*, which is shown more often to be derived from Peshitta usage and developments internal to the Syriac reception of "fear of God" in Hebrew and Greek texts.[17]

The brief overview of the Chinese transliterated words of Pahlavi *tarsāk* suggests Chinese acceptance of the idea of "God-fearers," and therefore it was no incidental evidence in support of highlighting the usage of "*jing* 景" as a subtle knowledge of Christian piety. As a broader category for religious practice and belief, "*jing*" should be holistically understood both from an objective perspective as "shining" or "universal," and from a subjective perspective as "venerating" or even "fearing (of God)." It is undoubtedly important to expound the meaning of "*jing* 景" in a dialectical relationship between the piety of believers with respect to the greatness of what is deemed the Sacred.

The Antiochene Exegetical Background and Jingjing's Chinese Translation of the Bible

Jingjing, who also bore the Syrian name Ādam, was a presbyter (*qaššišā*) and chorepiscopus famous for his Chinese translation works and his composition of the *Jingjiao Stele Text*. With an obvious style of *pianwen* 駢文, the *Stele Text* comprised a series of paired sentences that are rhymed with alternating tetrasyllabic and hexasyllabic lines. It abounded with quotations from various Chinese classics in many degrees and nuances for special occasions.[18] The *Stele Text* also made its special contributions to Chinese Christian theology and exegetics, most notably in connection with the Antiochene school. Scholarship usually assumes that the fundamental Antiochene concern is soteriological: salvation is attainable for humanity only by Christ's taking on a perfect human nature. In his detailed analysis of Christology in the early church, Aloys Grillmaeier has re-labelled the contrasting approaches as "frameworks" based on *Logos-sarx* and *Logos-anthropos* methodologies. Gerald O'Collins has described the Alexandrian *Logos-sarx* tendency as highlighting the Johannine theme of "the Word becoming flesh," and the Antiochene *Logos-anthropos* as "the eternal Word assuming the [hu]man Jesus."[19] Theodore of Mopsuestia, who stands as the formidable representative of the Antiochene exegetics and theology, demonstrated in an eminently clear-cut manner that the salvific role of the Messiah's humanity is more precisely indicated in His "inhumanation" (*hwa barnasa*) through his self-emptying. According to Theodore's interpretation of the central christological passages of Philippians 2:5–11—where the Syriac Peshitta renders the Greek *heauton ekenōsen* ("emptied oneself") with the Syriac *napšeh sareq*—there is a distinction between the One who is in the form of God and the One who is in the form of a servant, between the One who assumed and the One who was assumed. The One who assumed became in the fashion of a person in the One who was assumed. The One who was assumed was truly in the fashion of a person, in whom was found the One who assumed him; and the One who assumed, while not a person, became in his incorporeal and immaterial nature in the form of a servant, which by nature was corporeal and material. Moreover, Theodore provided further insight into the Pauline theme of "*napšeh sareq*" and showed how his personal exegetical characteristics can be accommodated within a fairly recognizably Antiochene account of "emptied Himself":

> w-hāḵanā napšeh taššī b-zaḇnā d-īṯayhi b-ālmā w-meṯhpak hwā̆ am bnaynāšā
>
> He thus hid Himself at the time in which He was in the world and conducted Himself with children of man....[20]

From the perspective of Theodore of Mopsuestia, the phrase "*napšeh taššī*" is meant to be the most properly expressed argument for Diphysitism or the two-nature doctrine. Aside from a zealous concern for the Messiah's self-hiding in this world, the logic of Theodore's Diphysitism drew heavily on the interpretation that the sentence, "He was in the likeness (*dmutā*) of human beings" (Phil 2:7), does not mean any other thing than that he became a human being or he assumed human nature (*kyānā nāšī*), both of the body and soul.[21] Thus, Theodore proceeded, after having taught about the divinity of the Word, to teach emphatically concerning the Messiah's self-hiding in order to leave room for the economy of his humanity, and to demonstrate the salvific significance of his "inhumanation." Indeed, according to Theresia Hainthaler and A. de Halleux, the expression "become a human being" is an "older formula" common to the early Syriac church.[22] This is especially the case for the Antiochene school, because as the chief rival of the Alexandrian school, it preferred the word "inhumanation" to "incarnation" on the grounds that the humanity of the God-man is more precisely indicated in it.

We can observe all the above characteristics in Chinese Jingjiao documents of the Tang Dynasty. The expression "*jiyin zhenwei, tongren chudai* 戢隱真威、同人出代" (hid His majesty and became a human being) in the *Stele Text* is obviously based on Theodore's interpretation of "hid" (*taššī*) and "inhumanation" (*hwa barnasa*). Jingjing, the author of the *Stele Text*, strategically called this salvific action "*tongren* 同人." Here, the Chinese word "*tongren*" means "become a human being," and it is really a sufficient reflection of its Syriac equivalent "*hwa barnasa*." It is this characteristic, which consists of Antiochene theological factors, that typifies the Antiochene style of Jingjing's exegetics and theology and indicates the ultimate source of the Chinese expression "*jiyin zhenwei, tongren chudai*."[23]

An exceptionally prolific translator, Jingjing is self-consciously following two traditions of Syriac-Chinese scholarship—that of the Antiochene biblical interpretation and that of the critical reading of the classical traditions of Confucianism, Daoism, and Buddhism. According to the Dunhuang document *Zunjing* 尊經, the Persian missionary Aluoben had brought five hundred and thirty Syriac sacred books to China when he first arrived in Chang'an 長安 in 635 CE, and nearly one and a half centuries later, Jingjing was asked to translate those books into Chinese; he finally finished the translation of thirty-five books, among which are such OT and NT books as *Moushi fawang jing* 牟世法王經 (*The Pentateuch*), *Duohui shengwang jing* 多惠聖王經 (*Davidic Psalms*), *A-enjulirong jing* 阿恩瞿利容經 (*Gospels*), *Shilihai jing* 師利海經 (*Acts of the Apostles*), and *Baolu fawang jing* 寶路法王經 (*Pauline Epistles*).[24] Regrettably, Jingjing's translation of the Bible, on which scholars would make increasingly strong conjectures about its high quality, has been lost. Nevertheless, a look in Jingjing's quotations in the *Stele Text* from various Chinese classics is sufficient to convince us that besides his training in Syriac as a translator, Jingjing had received a systematic education in Chinese classics. Most likely Jingjing could have read *Wujing Zhengyi* 五經正義 (*Corrected Meanings of the Five Classics*), because after the compilation of Kong Yingda 孔穎達 (574–648) and his team, this unified and systematized series of Confucian classics immediately became a standard of classical scholarship.[25] Moreover, the fact that Jingjing had a chance to co-operate with Kapisa monk Prajna in translating the *Satpâramitâ Sutra* (*Liuboluomi jing* 六波羅蜜經, 786) shows that he had developed some contacts with the circle of scholar-monks. It is possible Jingjing generated a comprehensive knowledge of Buddhism, and then effectively used a series of Buddhist terms to express Syriac biblical and theological ideas. Good examples of such translatioc—the first usage of which is a quotation from the first portion of Isaiah 6:3—now employed in Jingjing's extant translation works such as *Xuanyuan Zhiben Jing* 宣元至本經 and *Sanwei Mengduzan* 三威蒙度讚 (*Hymn of the Angels*). Based on such Buddhist terms as "*qingjing* 清淨," "*daweili* 大威力," and "*buzhuan* 不轉," *Xuanyuan Zhiben Jing* renders the Trisagion as follows:

> 清淨阿羅訶 清淨大威力 清淨…□□□[26]
> Holy Alaha, Holy Mighty, Holy…

The variant in *Sanwei Mengduzan* reads:

> 惟獨純凝清淨德 (He alone is Holy.)
> 惟獨神威無等力 (He alone is Mighty.)
> 惟獨不轉儼然存 (He alone is Immortal.)[27]

The Chinese versions of the Trisagion can be traced back to the Syriac original expression: *qudāšā Alāhā* (Holy God), *qudāšā ḥayltānā* (Holy Mighty), *qudāšā lā māyutā* (Holy Immortal).[28] The comparison shows that Jingjing had done well in translating the Trisagion (e.g. translating Syriac "*lā māyutā*" (immortal) into Chinese "*buzhuan yanrancun* 不轉儼然存"), and because of such an elegant, accurate, and extremely fluent translation, *Sanwei Mengduzan* (*Hymn of the Angels*) has been welcomed enthusiastically and circulated widely in the church of modern China.[29]

DUNHUANG DOCUMENT *XUTING MISHISUO JING* AND TATIAN'S *DIATESSARON*

It has long been recognized that the Dunhuang document *Xuting Mishisuo Jing* 序聽迷詩所經 (*Jesus Messiah Sūtra*, hereafter *XMJ*) is one of the Aluoben documents.[30] When examined closely, many Gospel quotations found in the *XMJ* display some unique characteristics of Diatessaronic readings. The Gospel quotations appear in the *XMJ* in ways completely different from the way they appear in other Aluoben documents, such as *Yishenlun*. Some variants in the *XMJ* seem to reflect specific liturgical practices of Tatian's time or his own particular Encratite views.

Tatian (ca. 120–ca. 180) is one of the important theologians and church fathers in the early history of Syriac Christianity. Furthermore, in the history of Bible versions, as well as in the early phase of textual development of the NT as a whole, there is no greater and more important name than Tatian.[31] According to Eusebius, Tatian "in his early life was trained in the learning of the Greeks and gained great distinction in it and has left many monuments of himself in writing."[32] Tatian's most famous and enduring legacy is the second-century Syriac Gospel harmony known as *Diatessaron*—a Greek loan word meaning "through [the] four [Gospels]." The Syrian name for *Diatessaron* is *Euangelion da-Meḥalleṭē* ("The Gospel of the Mixed"), a term in contrast to *Euangelion da-Mepharreshē* ("The Gospel of the Separated").

There are scattered passages in the *Diatessaron* which, when compared with the canonical text, appear to have been redacted by a hand sympathetic to Encratism.[33] An Encratite was used to rejecting marriage and practicing sexual continence, abhorring wine and other alcoholic drink, and was vegetarian. These performances constitute types of religious sources with which to study the Jingjiao ascetic traditions more broadly, and the *Diatessaron* witness in the Chinese *XMJ* in particular. The following are two examples of such Encratite features.

The first case is the diet of John the Baptist. According to Matt 3:4 and Mark 1:6, the diet of John consisted of locusts and wild honey. But modern scholars were surprised to find that the Chinese *XMJ* removed dramatically the words used by Matthew and Mark, substituting "raw vegetables" (*shengcai* 生菜) for "locusts" and explicitly stressing John's restriction against eating meat and drinking wine. The corresponding passage in the *XMJ* is as follows:

> 初時是彌師訶弟伏，聖在於硤中居住，生生已來，不喫酒肉，唯食生菜及蜜，蜜於地上。[34]
>
> At first, the *Mishihe* (Messiah) submitted to Yu-hun 谷昏 [i.e., John the Baptist] as a disciple. This sacred man dwelt in a gorge. Since his birth, he had never taken wine nor meat. He ate only raw vegetables and honey—honey on the field. (Translation mine.)

There can be little doubt as to the correct reading of the above passage, but here the Syriac Diatessaronic text comes to aid our understanding and solves the problem as to what had been puzzling modern scholars of Chinese Jingjiao. On the one hand, the words in Middle Chinese, "*mi yu dishang* 蜜於地上," were not in the proper order, and on the other hand, the Chinese words "*mi yu dishang*," and the Syriac words *dḇeš dḇarā* ("honey on the field"), are in agreement in the literal translation.

It is helpful to study the cross-lingual rhetorical features and focus on the influence of primitive Syriac Encratite readings. Although the original Syriac Diatessaronic text is not extant, it can be found, fortunately, in the commentaries of such Syriac writers as Isho'dad, Bar-Salibi, and Bar-Hebraeus. In the *Diatessaron*, it is written that the meat John ate was milk and honey on the field (*ḥalḇā w-ḏḇeš ḏḇarā*).[35] The substitution of "raw vegetables" for "locusts" in the Chinese *XMJ* enjoys a close relationship with Tatian's substitution of "milk" for "locusts." Even though the former substitution fits the context of farming-culture, while the latter one is consistent with a nomadic-culture, we have good reasons to suggest that the Chinese *XMJ* shares the same stance, argument, and logic Tatian once used to establish his Encratite claims. As an excellent and ascetical leader of Syriac Encratism, Tatian was surprised that an ascetic like John the Baptist should have eaten a non-vegetarian diet, and so he evidently sided with the Encratite readings. Besides Matthew 3:4, there are some other variants in the *Diatessaron* that can disclose traces of Tatian's dietetic rigor claims: (1) at Matthew 26:29, the thought of a renewed "drinking of fruit of the vine" in the future kingdom is suppressed, avoiding a possible reference to wine; (2) at Matthew 27:34, it reads that Jesus receives "vinegar and gall" on the cross, not the offending "wine mingled with gall"; and (3) at John 2:10, it omits the offending remark "when they have drunk freely."[36] The reservation toward wine-drinking in these texts also is reflected in the Chinese text. So, if the Chinese *XMJ* is taken as a Diatessaronic reading, it certainly adds weight to the influence of the particular Encratite views in the Chinese text.

A second, equally illustrative case is the Encratite view of marriage. According to Tatian, Christians must abandon sexual intercourse in marriage, because it is the clearest symptom of frailty and the most decisive obstacle to the indwelling of the Spirit. So, in the scattered variants in the *Diatessaron*, Tatian's antipathy to sexual activity can be perceived as characteristic of Encratism. In the narrative of the virgin birth, Mary had been engaged to Joseph, but it is stressed that they did not live together (Matt 1:18), and the function of the Holy Spirit is highlighted ("before they lived together, she was found to be with child from the Holy Spirit," 1:18, NRSV). Jesus's birth is described as a purely spiritual birth in the *Diatessaron*, whose attitude toward marriage is reflected.[37] Some variants in the *Diatessaron* have been identified as follows: (1) at Matt 1:19, three Diatessaronic witnesses refrain from calling Joseph the husband of Mary, "reflecting the Encratite bias against marriage"; (2) at Matt. 1:24, both the Armenian recension of Ephrem's *Commentary* and the Persian Harmony say that Joseph "guarded" Mary rather than "he took his wife," again avoiding the intimate marriage relationship between the two; (3) at Luke 14:26, the Persian Harmony changes the word "hate" (*misei*) to "abandon" one's wife when Jesus told those what to do if they wanted to be his disciple. This kind of antipathy to sexual activity also is evident in the Chinese *XMJ*, virtually in the same way as other Diatessaronic witnesses:

> 天尊當使涼風，向一童女，名為末艶。涼風即入末艶腹內，依天尊教，當即末艶懷身。為以天尊使涼風，伺童女邊，無男夫懷任。令一切眾生，見無男夫懷任，使世間人等見，即道：天尊有威力。[38]
>
> The Lord of Heaven sent the Holy Spirit toward a young virgin by the name of Maryam. The Holy Spirit entered the body of Mar-yam in accordance with the instruction

> of the Lord of Heaven, and immediately Mar-yam got pregnant. Because the Lord of Heaven sent the Holy Spirit to the virgin and she was conceived without a husband at her side, it taught all living beings to see that she conceived at the absence of a husband, and proclaim that the Lord of Heaven has mighty power. (Translation mine.)

Here we can trace such Chinese terms as "*liangfeng* 凉風," "*tongnu* 童女," "*moyan* 末艷," "*wunanfu* 無男夫," and "*huaishen* 懷身" respectively back to the Syriac terms *ruḥa d-qudša* (Holy Wind), *btultā* (virgin), *Mar-yam* (Mary), *layt lāh bålā* (has no husband), and *qabbel baṭnā* (got pregnant). By drawing on parallels in the Chinese *XMJ* of the sixth century and other early Syriac Diatessaronic witnesses, the *XMJ* narrative of the virgin birth is reflective of reproducing a discourse in which Mar-yam's (Mary's) pregnancy without a husband is very much stressed, and the function of the Holy Wind (Holy Spirit) is emphasized to show the "mighty power" (*wei li* 威力) of the Lord of Heaven. The *XMJ* carries a Diatessaronic attitude toward marriage.

The third Diatessaronic witness deserving our discussion is the report of the resurrection of the "dead" when Jesus died on the cross, and his appearance to many after the resurrection (Matt 27:52–53). Even though it is not directly related to Tatian's Encratism, this variant in the *Diatessaron* shows a more ancient form of the text than our present canonical manuscripts. Here a compare-contrast passage must be given first. According to the Peshitta, which agrees substantially with the Greek canonical text, when Jesus was crucified, "the curtain of the temple was torn in two, from top to bottom. The earth shook, and the rocks were split. The tombs also were opened, and many bodies of the saints who had fallen asleep were raised. After his resurrection they came out of the tombs and entered the holy city and appeared to many" (Matt 27:51–53, NRSV). Similarly, the Dunhuang document *Yishenlun* renders that:

> 執法上懸高。於彼時節，所以與命。地動、山崩、石磬，上氍毹蹋壁，彼處張設聖化，擘作兩段。彼處有墓自開，聞有福德死者，並從死得活，起向人處來。[39]
>
> He submitted himself to the law and was hanged (crucified) on a cross. At the moment when He gave His life, the earth shook, mountains collapsed, and the rocks split. At the place of the holiness, the tapestry was torn into two pieces from top to bottom. At another place, the tombs opened themselves, and the dead ones, who were blessed and virtuous, were heard to be raised to life from dead, and came up to the crowd. (Translation is mine.)

Yet, the Dunhuang document *Yishenlun* substitutes "blessed and virtuous" (*you fude* 有福德) for "saints" (*hagios*). Besides the substitution "the dead" (metaphor of "sleep" used in reference to the dead) for "saints," the Dunhuang document *XMJ* contains several unusual readings, such as giving a report that "all the dead were all raised to life." It reads as follows:

> 其日將彌師訶木上縛着，五時，是六日齋。平明縛着，及到日西，四方暗黑，地戰山崩，世間所有墓門並開，所有死人並悉得活。[40]

> Early in the morning of that day—it is the sixth day of fasting—they hanged Mishihe (Messiah) on the log. He was bound at dawn. Until the sunset, darkness came over all the land. The earth quaked and the mountains collapsed. All the gates of graves in the world broke open, and all the dead were all raised to life. (Translation is mine.)

The *XMJ* report reminds us of the *Hymn on the Ten Drachmas* (XLV. 17) of Romanos the Melodist (ca. 490–ca. 560), the preeminent religious poet of the Eastern church: "Then suddenly all the tombs were opened of themselves. And from them all the dead sprang out...."[41] Theologically absurd as it is to say that all the dead were raised to life when Jesus died on the cross, so it is reasonable for the canonical text to "correct the oversight" by qualifying the number: not *all* "dead" arose, only "*many*."[42] In the discipline of textual criticism, the less-theologically developed reading is assumed to be earlier; therefore, scholars such as Yao Zhihua argued, based on William L. Petersen's fourth characteristic of the Diatessaronic readings, that the Chinese *XMJ* is more primitive than the canonical text. In addition, *brevior lectio potior* (the shorter reading is earlier); thus, a single word "all" in the Chinese *XMJ* or in the Syriac *Hymn on the Ten Drachmas* (XLV. 17) is assumed to be earlier than the number raised ("many"), the form in which they are raised ("bodies"), and who is raised ("saints"). Considering such a close parallel between the Chinese text and the Diatessaronic readings in the East Syriac church, one cannot help but to assume their common source. Petersen and Yao have used this criterion to judge a Diatessaronic reading and shown the authenticity of this Chinese Diatessaronic text as well as its value to scriptural studies.

Conclusion

This study has several implications. First, the brief overview of modern studies of the meaning of "*jing* 景" suggests that the word originally had a sense of "*guang*" (light) or "*da*" (great or universal), and then, until the time of the Mid-Tang dynasty, took on the meaning of "*jingyang* 景仰" (to esteem; to venerate) or even "*jingwei* 敬畏" (fear [of God]). This kind of Jingjiao-hermeneutical lens shows up in Chinese Jingjiao authors as the legacy of the Antiochene School, evident in its exegesis toward literary, literal, and historical interpretations. The Antiochene influence also appears in Jingjing's theological expression of "*jiyin zhenwei, tongren chudai*" (hid His majesty and became a human being) in the *Jingjiao Stele Text*, which is obviously based on Theodore's interpretation of the central christological passages of Phil 2:5–11, where he creatively interpreted *napšeh sareq* (emptied Himself) as *napšeh tašši* (hid Himself). Generally speaking, the Antiochene approach has ultimately been the most central for the mainstream tradition of Jingjiao theology and exegetics.

Second, as the crucial undercurrent of Jingjiao theological and exegetical tradition, Tatian's *Diatessaron* and its particular ascetic views exerted profound influence upon the

Chinese Dunhuang document *XMJ*. When examined closely, many Gospel quotations in *XMJ*, such as the report of the diet of John the Baptist (Matt 3:4), the Encratite view of marriage (Matt 1:18–24), and the narrative of the resurrection of "all the dead" when Jesus died on the cross (Matt 27:52–53), display the unique characteristics of Diatessaronic readings. It makes Diatessaronic studies more exciting when new Diatessaronic witnesses appear in Jingjiao documents of Turfan and Dunhuang, especially in the Chinese *XMJ*. Moreover, the Diatessaronic points addressed in this essay serve to show the authenticity of this Chinese Diatessaronic text while at the same time to highlight its value to scriptural studies.

Notes

1. The edict reads: "The Persian Jingjiao originated in Daqin. Since its establishment in China, it has been there a long time. When the first monastery was built, we named it Persian Temple (because of their supposed origin). But in order that all men might know the (real and true) origin of this religion, the names of the 'Persian Monasteries' in the two Capitals should be henceforth changed to 'Daqin Monasteries.' All provinces and countries where such monasteries have been built, should follow suit by changing their names" (波斯經教，出自大秦，傳習而來，久行中國。爰初建寺，因以為名，將欲示人，必修其本。其兩京波斯寺，宜改為大秦寺。天下諸府郡置者，亦准此). See P. Y. Saeki, *The Nestorian Monument in China* (London: Society for Promoting Christian Knowledge, 1916), 288; Li Tang, *A Study of the History of Nestorian Christianity in China and Its Literature in Chinese* (Frankfurt am Main: Peter Lang, 2002), 23.
2. Wu Changxing, *Daqin Jingjiao Liuxing zhongguo Bei (the Xi'an Stele): Text Analyses with Commentary on Documents of Daqin Jingjiao* (Xinbei: Oliver Publishing Ltd., 2015), 29.
3. *Shuowen jiezi* (AD 100), written by Xu Shen of Eastern Han dynasty, is known as the first comprehensive dictionary on Chinese characters. Cf. Xu Shen, *Shuowen jiezi* 說文解字 (Beijing: Jiuzhou Press, 2001), 382.
4. Li Zhizao, "A Postscript on Jingjiao Stele Text," in *Collected Works of Li Zhizao*, ed. Zhen Cheng (Beijing: Zhonghua Shuju, 2018), 101.
5. Zhu Qianzhi, *Chinese Jingjiao: A Study on Ancient Chinese Christianity* (Beijing: Dongfang Press, 1993), 15.
6. Wu, *Daqin Jingjiao Liuxing zhongguo Bei (the Xi'an Stele)*, 15, 19.
7. Ibid. 203–204.
8. Cf. Paulus Bedjan, ed., *Breviarium iuxta ritum Syrorum Orientalium id est Chaldaeorum* (Paris, 1886–1887), 37–38.
9. Traditionally, the character "Jing 景" is written in the form of "景" which has "日" as the upper part, and "京" as the lower part. But in the Jingjiao documents of the Tang Dynasty, this character is written without exception in another way, i.e. it has "口" instead of "日" as the upper part. According to the prevailing view of Dunhuang studies, the addition or subtraction of strokes is popular in daily use, and it does not change the meaning of that character.
10. Zhu, *Chinese Jingjiao*, 15.
11. Zhu Donghua, "Ying /應 /Nirmāṇa: A Case Study on the Translatability of Buddhism into Jingjiao," in *Winds of Jingjiao: Studies on Syriac Christianity in China and Central Asia*, ed. Li Tang and Dietmar W. Winkler (Zürich: Lit Verlag, 2016), 427.

12. *Kangxi Zidian*, 496.
13. Gao Heng, ed., *Shijing Jinzhu* (Shanghai: Shanghai Guji Press, 1980), 341.
14. Cf. Francis Joseph Steingass, *A Comprehensive Persian-English Dictionary* (Ottawa: Laurier Books Ltd, 2003), 294.
15. Wu, *Daqin Jingjiao Liuxing zhongguo Bei (the Xi'an Stele)*, 36, 125. Li Zhichang, *Changchun Zhenren Xiyouji* (Hebei: Hebei Renmin Press, 2001), 36, 125.
16. Adam H. Becker, "Martyrdom, Religious Difference, and 'Fear' as a Category of Piety in the Sasanian Empire: The Case of the Martyrdom of Gregory and the Martyrdom of Yazdpaneh," *Journal of Late Antiquity* 2.2 (Fall): 312–315.
17. In 1932–1933, A. Mingana discovered and published a Syriac text of Theodore of Mopsuestia's *Catechetical Homilies*. Cf. *Commentary of Theodore of Mopsuestia on the Nicene Creed*, trans. A. Mingana (Cambridge: W. Heffer & Sons, 1932), 211.
18. Henri Havret, *La Stèle Chrétienne de Si-ngan-fou* (Shanghai: Imprimerie De La Mission Catholique, 1895), xv.
19. George Herring, *An Introduction to the History of Christianity: From the Early Church to the Enlightenment* (London: Continuum International, 2006), 95.
20. *Commentary of Theodore of Mopsuestia on the Nicene Creed*, 68, 181.
21. Ibid. 54–55, 164–165.
22. Theresia Hainthaler and A. de Halleux, *Christ in Christian Tradition*, Vol. 2 Part 3: *The Churches of Jerusalem and Antioch from 451 to 600* (Oxford: Oxford University Press, 2003), 482.
23. Zhu Donghua, "Person and Shen (身): An Ontological Encounter of 'Nestorian' Christianity with Confucianism in Tang China," in *Yearbook of Chinese Theology 2015* (Leiden: E. J. Brill, 2015), 205.
24. Wu, *Daqin Jingjiao Liuxing zhongguo Bei (the Xi'an Stele)*, 211–215.
25. Zhu, "Person and Shen (身)," 210.
26. Cf. Ge Chengyong, ed., *Precious Nestorian Relic* 景教遺珍: *Studies on the Nestorian Stone Pillar of the Tang Dynasty Recently Discovered in Luoyang* (Beijing: Wenwu Press, 2009), 62.
27. Wu, *Daqin Jingjiao Liuxing zhongguo Bei (the Xi'an Stele)*, 204.
28. Elizabeth A. Livingstone, ed., *Studia Patristica* (Leuven: Peeters, 1997), 336.
29. Cf. The United Hymnal Committee, ed., *Hymns of Universal Praise* 普天頌讚 (Music Edition) (Shanghai: Mei Hua Press, 1936/1943), 2.
30. Wang Lanping, *Tangdai Dunhuang Hanwen Jingjiao Xiejing Yanjiu* 唐代敦煌漢文景教寫經研究 (Beijing: Minzu Press, 2016), 124.
31. William L. Petersen, *Tatian's Diatessaron: Its Creation, Dissemination, Significance, and History in Scholarship* (Leiden: E. J. Brill, 1994), 1.
32. Cf. Li Tang, *A Study of the History of Nestorian Christianity in China and Its Literature in Chinese* (Frankfurt am Main: Peter Lang, 2002), 28.
33. Petersen, *Tatian's "Diatessaron,"* 79.
34. Kyouushooku, *Secret Documents of Dunhuang* 敦煌秘笈 (Osaka: Japanese Kyouushooku, 2012), 6: 86.
35. Cf. *Fragments of the Commentary of Ephrem Syrus upon the "Diatessaron,"* 17–18. John the Baptist lived off milk and honey, in other words, the food of the Promised Land (Deut. 6:3). Cf. Sebastian Brock, *The Bible in the Syriac Tradition* (Piscataway: Gorgias Press, 2006), 25.
36. From the Armenian recension of Saint Ephrem's *Commentary on the "Diatessaron"*. Cf. William L. Petersen, *Tatian's "Diatessaron"* (Leiden: E. J. Brill, 1994), 204–205.

37. Yao Zhihua, "A Diatessaronic Reading in the Chinese Nestorian Texts," in *Hidden Treasures and Intercultural Encounters: Studies on East Syriac Christianity in China and Central Asia*, ed. Dietmar W. Winkler and Li Tang (Münster–Vienna: Lit Verlag, 2009), 158–159.
38. Kyouushooku, *Secret Documents of Dunhuang*, 6:86.
39. Ibid. 94.
40. Ibid. 87.
41. Petersen, *Tatian's "Diatessaron,"* 407.
42. Ibid. 412.

Primary Sources

Daqin Jingjiao Sanwei Mengduzan 大秦景教三威蒙度讚 (*Hymn of the Angels*) and *Zunjing* 尊經 (Pelliot Chinois 3847). Collected by French National Library, see https://archivesetmanuscrits.bnf.fr/ark:/12148/cc8827v/cd0e49006.

Gao Heng, ed. *Shijing Jinzhu* [in Chinese] 詩經今注. Shanghai: Shanghai Guji, 1980.

Ge Chengyong, ed. *Precious Nestorian Relic: Studies on the Nestorian Stone Pillar of the Tang Dynasty Recently Discovered in Luoyang* [in Chinese] 景教遺珍. Beijing: Wenwu, 2009.

Jingjing 景淨. *Jingjiao Stele Text*, in *La Stèle Chrétienne de Si-ngan-fou*, ed. Henri Havret. Shanghai: Imprimerie De La Mission Catholique, 1895.

Kangxi Zidian [in Chinese] 康熙字典. Beijing: Zhonghua Book Company, 2007. http://tool.httpcn.com/Html/Kanghttp://tool.httpcn.com/KangXi/.

Liji Zhengyi [in Chinese] 禮記正義. Annotated by Zheng Xuan 鄭玄 with a commentary by Kong Yingda 孔穎達. Beijing: Peking University Press, 1999.

Li Zhichang, ed. *Changchun Zhenren Xiyouji* [in Chinese] 長春真人西遊記 (*The Journey to the West of Daoist Master Changchun*). Shijiazhuang: Hebei People's Publishing House, 2001.

Petersen, William L. *Tatian's "Diatessaron": Its Creation, Dissemination, Significance, and History in Scholarship*. Leiden: E. J. Brill, 1994.

Satpâramitâ Sutra (*Liuboluomi jing* 六波羅蜜經). Taishopitaka 大正藏, vol. 8, No. 0261.

Tetraevangelium Sanctum iuxta simplicem Syrorum versionem (Syriac Peshitta). Edited by P. E. Pusey and G. H. Gwilliam. Oxford: Oxford University Press, 1901.

Theodore of Mopsuestia. *Commentary of Theodore of Mopsuestia on the Nicene Creed*. Trans. A. Mingana. Cambridge: W. Heffer & Sons, 1932.

Xu Shen. *Shuowen jiezi* [in Chinese] 說文解字. Beijing: Jiuzhou Press, 2001.

Xuting Mishisuo Jing 序聽迷詩所經(羽 459), in *Secret Documents of Dunhuang* 敦煌秘笈, ed. Kyouushooku. Osaka: Japanese Kyouushooku, 2012, vol. 6, 83–87.

Yishen Lun 一神論 (*Discourse on God*) (羽 460). In Kyouushooku ed., *Secret Documents of Dunhuang* 敦煌秘笈. Osaka: Japanese Kyouushooku, 2012, vol. 6, 88–96.

Zhou Dewen and Li Yongfang, eds. *Erya* [in Chinese] 爾雅. Zhengzhou: Zhongzhou Guji, 2012.

Biblical Books Listed in *Zunjing* 尊經 but no longer extant:

A-enjulirong jing 阿恩瞿利容經 (*Gospels*)
Baolu fawang jing 寶路法王經 (*Pauline Epistles*)
Duohui shengwang jing 多惠聖王經 (*Davidic Psalms*)

Moushi fawang jing 牟世法王經 (*The Pentateuch*)
Shilihai jing 師利海經 (*Acts of the Apostles*)
Zun jing, Bibliothèque nationale de France, Manuscrit Pelliot chinois 3847, ca. 781 CE.
Soymié, Michel, ed. *Catalogue des manuscrits chinois de Touen-Houang. Fonds Pelliot chinois de la Bibliothèque nationale, Volume IV (n° 3501–4000)*. Paris: Publications hors série de l'École française d'Extrême-Orient, 1991. 332–3. b. Tsouen King, ff. 4 and 5.

CHAPTER 4

THE EASTERN ORTHODOX BIBLE IN CHINA

LI ZHENGRONG

Historical Consideration

THE concept of Orthodox Church[1] refers to one of three major sects of Christianity—Orthodox, Catholic, and Protestant. The birthplace of Christianity occurred at the beginning of the Common Era, at the eastern coast of the Mediterranean Sea, which is an area prevailingly using demotic Greek after three hundred years of Hellenization. The earliest text recording Christian narratives and doctrines is in Greek. Many Christian churches in the eastern Mediterranean can be called the "Eastern Orthodox Church." If the legend of the apostle St. Thomas coming to preach in China is true, the "Eastern Orthodox" would have entered China at that time. In the Tang dynasty, Nestorianism, which founds its beliefs in Saint Nestorius, the Patriarch of Constantinople, was introduced into China as "Jing religion" or "Jingjiao 景教," and Jing religion also could be regarded as one of the Eastern Orthodox Churches in the Middle Ages.[2]

To be more precise, when we say "the Orthodox" today, we are referring to the Eastern Christian Church that formally split from the Roman Catholic Church in 1054. However, in China, the Orthodox Church is primarily the result of the missionary work of the Russian Orthodox Church. In 988, Kievan Rus (the medieval political federation of East Slavic and Finnic peoples in Europe from the ninth to thirteenth centuries) joined the Constantinople Orthodox Church. After Constantinople (Constantine's "Oriental" capital) was destroyed by the Ottoman Empire in 1453, countries affiliated with the Orthodox Church successively submitted themselves to the rule of the Turks, while the Russian Orthodox Church undertook the mission of maintaining its own Orthodox polity. Since 1589, the Russian Orthodox Church has officially divorced from the jurisdiction of Constantinople's Patriarchal Diocese. From 1653 to 1665, Patriarch Nikon (1605–1681) carried out reforms and unified religious observances, resulting in the increasing power and growth of the church. In 1721, Czar Peter I (or Peter the Great, 1672–1725) reformed the church again and established the Holy Governing Synod.

Russian Orthodox Spreading into China

In the sixteenth century, Catholic and Protestant missionaries brought the gospel of Jesus Christ to China, and many of them engaged in translation of the Bible into Chinese. The expansion of the Orthodox Church in China began in 1685, when the Qing army occupied the Russian border town called "Jaxa" on the banks of Heilongjiang. After the war, the Qing army took Father Maxim Leontiev, the archpriest of the city's Resurrection Church, to Beijing. Leontiev brought church utensils and the icon of St. Nicholas to Beijing. Emperor Kangxi ordered captured Albazinians (Chinese of Russian descent) to be incorporated into the Yellow Banner of the Eight Banners, settled down at the Hujiaquan Hutong 胡家圈胡同 in Beijing, and gave the Albazinians a local Guan Yu temple as their worship place. Beijing people call this temple "Luosha Miao 羅刹廟," as "Luosha" is a transliteration of the word "Russia." In 1695, Metropolitan Bishop Ignati of Tobolsk and Siberian Orthodox parish sent priests and acolytes to Beijing, with sacred objects used in liturgical observances, including the Bible and prayer books. In 1696, Father Maksim and priests from Russia jointly held a consecration ceremony for the chapel in Beijing and named it St. Sophia Church. As there is a statue of Saint Nicholas in it, this church is also called "the Nicholas Church." In 1698, when Peter I learned that an Orthodox church had been established in Beijing, he ordered the strengthening of Tobolsk parish and charged the priests to pay attention to missionary work in Beijing, and appointed two or three young friars to study Chinese language in Beijing. In 1712, Metropolitan Bishop John of Tobolsk and Siberian Orthodox parish organized and dispatched the first mission to China, and they arrived in Beijing in 1715.

Eastern Orthodox Bible and Slavonic Bible in China

The biggest difference between the Orthodox Bible, the Catholic Bible, and the Protestant Bible in Europe lies in the source text and source language of the Orthodox Bible. While the New Testament (hereafter NT) was written in Greek, the extant manuscripts comprise thousands of Greek copies and at least three text-types (Alexandrian, Byzantine, and Western).[3] The authoritative version of the Western Christian Church Bible was Latin (old Latin Bible before Jerome), especially after Jerome's Vulgate translation probably from the Western text-type (such as *Codex Vaticanus* if available to him) to Latin. During the period of the Reformation, however, Erasmus's *Greek-Latin New Testament* (1516), based on the inferior minuscule Byzantine text-type (so-called *Koine* or the Majority Imperial text) of the fourteenth and fifteenth centuries, became an important reference for Bibles in many German, English, and other European Bible versions (before the more superior Alexandrian texts were used by biblical scholars). The Bible of the Russian Orthodox, however, is based on Slavonic, which has a very close connection with the early Greek of either the Byzantian text-type (Majority Text) or the Alexandrian text-type (such as *Codex Vaticanus* and *Codex Sinaiticus* if available to them).

In the ninth century, in order to preach in the Slavonic region, the Bulgarian clergymen Saints Cyril (Constantine, 826–869) and Methodius (815–885), both born in Thessalonica, created Glagolitic and Cyrillic scripts from ancient Greek writing symbols, and that began the history of Russian writing for liturgical church use. The first task of the created Cyrillic script was to translate the Bible from Greek into Slavonic, thus forming a writing system of "ancient Slavonic" (also called "Church Slavonic"). "Ancient Slavonic" is the language used by "South Yugoslavia" (Bulgaria and Moravia), quite different from the Eastern Slavonic used in the Russian region. However, because the documents of the Eastern Orthodox Church are written in Cyrillic script, the Orthodox Church has always used "ancient Slavonic" as its language carrier. As a result, the Russian Orthodox Bible also has maintained the "Greek" tradition. Likewise, "ancient Slavonic" exerted great influence upon the languages of the eastern Slavonic nations, such as the Russian language. The original translation of the Scriptures by the "Cyril Brothers" covered only the lectionary for liturgical usage. The earliest complete translation of the "ancient Slavonic" Bible in the Russian region was the Ostrog Bible (Острожская Библия) published in 1581. The source text for the NT of this Slavonic Bible version is likely to be the famous *Codex Alexandrinus* (the fifth century)[4] or the like. After the language reform of Peter the Great, the Bible was re-translated into the Church Slavonic used in Russia at that time, and the Bible was published in 1751. This Bible version is called the "Elizabeth Bible" (Елизаветинская Библия), which is still the official text of the Russian Orthodox to this day.

Eastern Orthodox Bible in China

Initially, the task of the Russian Ecclesiastical Mission (hereafter REM) sent to China was to serve the "Albazinians" and, unable to find a translator, they did not carry out the translation of the Orthodox Bible into Chinese. From the first REM sent to China in 1715 to 1861, the propagation of Orthodoxy in China developed slowly, absorbing Manchus and Han people under the rule of the Qing Dynasty into the Eastern Orthodox Church. In order to meet the needs of preaching to Manchus and Han people, the REM began to compile missionary books and translate the Bible.

The Initiation of the Chinese Orthodox Bible

The archimandrite Iakinf 雅金福 (Ya Jin Fu, Bichurin, 1777–1853), the head of the Ninth REM in China (1802–1821), was an outstanding scholar. He was gifted in learning Chinese and Mongolian. While working in Beijing, he compiled a Russian-Chinese dictionary. This dictionary had great influence on the later translation of the Chinese Orthodox Bible. In 1810, Iakinf published his first edited Chinese Orthodox catechism: *Tian Shen Hui Ke* 天神會課 (*Conversation of the Angels*). The content of this book is the Catholic catechism compiled earlier by the Jesuits in China in the seventeenth century. However, the Catholic Chinese vocabulary, which is widely used in this book, has since entered the Orthodox Chinese books.

The Tenth REM (1821–1830) was headed by Archimandrite Peter (Kamensky, 1765–1845). He encouraged missionaries in China to learn Chinese, Manchurian, and Mongolian, and advised them to translate the texts of Orthodox lectionary and liturgy into Chinese. Archimandrite Peter emphasized that the Orthodox Church should use the texts to distinguish its uniqueness from Catholicism and Protestantism. Subsequently, the Eleventh and Twelfth REM actively promoted the translation of Orthodox holy books into Chinese, Manchurian, and Mongolian.

In the early nineteenth century, the Albazinians captured by Beijing had been gradually integrated into Chinese culture, making it difficult for them to use the Russian language. In order to meet the needs of the converts, Orthodox priests in Beijing began to translate documents about liturgical observance and doctrine into Chinese, Manchurian, and Mongolian.

From 1822 to 1835, *The New Testament* in Manchurian translated by Stepan Vaciliyevich Lipovtsov (1770–1841) first appeared, and it was the first Eastern Orthodox Bible in China. In 1929, the Manchurian Bible was reprinted in Shanghai. Although Lipovtsov was a member of the Eighth REM, his translation work was commissioned by the British and Foreign Bible Society.

Creative Construction of the Chinese Orthodox Bible

The Twelfth REM in China (1840–1849) significantly promoted the translation and compilation of Orthodox books in China. Among the members of this mission was Hierodeacon Palladius 巴拉第 (Kafarov, 1817–1878), who was appointed head of the Thirteenth (1850–1858) and the Fifteenth (1865–1878) REM. Palladius energetically supported the Russian-Chinese translation of the Orthodox for more than forty years. During his second tenure as head of the REM in China, he actively promoted and personally participated in the compilation and publication of the Russian-Chinese dictionary. After his stepping down and passing, his edited *Han Er He Bi Yun Bian* 漢俄合璧韻編 (*Sino-Russian Dictionary*) was finally published in 1888. The dictionary introduced the Sino-Russian spelling system created in 1839 by Iakinf, the head of the Ninth REM in

China. This system was widely accepted later and named as the "Pallady system," according to the name of the dictionary's editor. This system is still in use today with only minor modifications.

The hieromonk Gury 固理 (Grigory Platonovich Karpov, 1814–1882), also member of the Twelfth REM, was a genius translator for the Orthodox Church. During his membership, Karpov already had begun his creative translation of Orthodox texts into Chinese. In 1858, Karpov was appointed head of the Fourteenth REM, ushering in the first peak of the publication of Chinese Orthodox literature in China. In 1860, the publication of *Dong Jiao Zong Jian* 東教宗鑑 (*Mirror of Orthodox Confession*) and *Sheng Shi Ti Yao* 聖史提要 (*The Summary of New Testament Salvation History: Life of Christ*), organized by Karpov, was an event of special significance in the history of Chinese Orthodox holy books. *Mirror of Orthodox Confession* was translated from the works of St. Dimitry of Rostov (1651–1709), who lived in the same period as Peter the Great and was made a saint in 1757. One of the purposes of Karpov in translating and publishing this book was evident in the preface to the second edition (1863): Christianity's "Eastern and Western churches sharing the same scripture, but having different comprehensions."[5]

The book focuses on the Orthodox viewpoints on the three virtues of faith, hope, and love. It was the first time for the Chinese Orthodox church to demonstrate its creed in *Xin Jing* 信經 (The Creed), *Tianzhu Jing* 天主經 (The Lord's Prayer), and *Tianzhu Shi Jie* 天主十誡 (The Ten Commandments). Most of the terms in the book follow the mature Chinese translation of Catholicism. The words "*You Huo* 誘惑" (temptation), for example, were translated into "*You Gan* 誘感," and a sentence "*Yin Fan Guo Ji Quan Neng Bing Guang Rong Jie Xi Yu Er Yu Shi Shi A Men* 因凡國及權能並光榮皆係於爾於世世阿民" (For thine is the kingdom, and the power, and the glory, forever. Amen), are rendered differently from Catholic translations.

The bigger difference lies in the fact that to show the discrepancy between Christianity's Eastern and Western churches sharing the same scripture, but having different comprehensions, Karpov was inventive in creating a set of unique Chinese translation methods for Russian Orthodox holy books when he translated important names of people. Obviously, Karpov took this translation method as a means to illustrate Russian Orthodox doctrines in line with ancient Greek tradition.

The first line on the left of page 1 in *Mirror of Orthodox Confession*: Grigory Karpov's treatment of the Chinese name for "Jesus Christ" in Article 2 of *the Creed* as *Yi-yi-su* 伊伊蘇. The fourth line on the right of page 2 in *Mirror of Orthodox Confession*: Grigory Karpov's treatment of the Chinese name for "Maria" in Article 3 in *The Creed* as *Ma-er-ya* 瑪爾利亞. The fifth line on the right of page 2 in *Mirror of Orthodox Confession*: Grigory Karpov's treatment of the Chinese name for "Pontius Pilate" in Article 4 in *The Creed* as *Peng-ti-pi-la-te* 彭提批拉特.

Sheng Shi Ti Yao 聖史提要 (*The Summary of New Testament Salvation History: Life of Christ*) was a compilation and translation of the first six books of the Old Testament (hereafter OT), namely the *Pentateuch* and *Joshua*. It is the first milestone in the translation of the Orthodox OT in China. Karpov chose the passages with stories in the first six books of the OT to be told in Chinese. Because the names of people and places involved in *The Summary of New Testament Salvation History: Life of Christ* are much more than those in *Mirror of Orthodox Confession*, Karpov used more techniques in the translation of the book to show the unique "Chinese translation methods for Russian Orthodox holy books" he invented. All Chinese names of people and places in the OT were translated differently from the customary Catholic translation.

The first method is to represent the syllables consisting of special consonant letters, such as the trill "p" in Russian, in original combining Chinese characters. The second method is to translate important names of people in accordance to the syllabic features of the Church Slavonic. The third method is to translate Scriptures and narrate biblical stories in proficient ancient Chinese. The fourth method is to use small-size characters to represent independent consonants of Church Slavonic.

In *The Exodus* in *The Summary of New Testament Salvation History: Life of Christ*, Karpov used "combining Chinese characters" and "small-size characters" to translate the names in Church Slavonic. These methods of Karpov were widely used in the translation of *Xin Yi Zhao Sheng Jing* 新遺詔聖經 (*The New Testament*) in 1864.

Grigory Karpov, the head of the Fourteenth REM in Beijing, published *Xin Yi Zhao Sheng Jing* in 1864, at the same time as the translation of *Mirror of Orthodox Confession* and *The Summary of New Testament Salvation History: Life of Christ* mentioned above. This time, the translator and publisher printed *Wu Zhu Yi Yi Su Si He Erli Si Tuo Si* 吾主伊伊蘇斯合爾利斯托斯 (*Our Lord Jesus Christ*) in longer form on the front cover—to publicize widely his original "Chinese translation methods for Russian Orthodox holy books" in a prominent position. This group of Chinese characters illustrated the four points of Karpov's method. And the purpose of this method was to emphasize that the translation strictly followed the Greek original, as he wrote, *Jin Zun Yuan Wen Yi Han Jing Juan Ban* 謹遵原文譯漢敬鐫板. This may be the earliest complete Eastern Orthodox NT in Chinese. This Bible was translated from Church Slavonic, consisting of two parts: *Fu Yin Jing Si Ce* 福音經四冊 (*The Gospels in Four Volumes*) and *Zong Tu Jing Er Shi Er Ce* 宗徒經七冊 (*The Apostles in Seven Volumes*).

Xin Yi Zhao Sheng Jing (*The New Testament*) was edited and published in full accordance to the conventions of ancient Chinese books. The format, printing, and binding of the Bible are all done in the styles of ancient Chinese books. The text is arranged vertically. In front of the text, there are two documents: *Xin Yi Zhao Sheng Jing Xu* 新遺詔聖經序 (Preface to the New Testament) and *Xin Yi Zhao Sheng Jing Zeng Yan* 新遺詔聖經贈言 (New Testament Dedication for Friends), with sixteen words per column and eight columns per page. After that is the main text of translation, with a changed format of twenty-two words per column, ten columns per page.

This NT has made a mark in the history of Chinese Bible translation. First, the sequence of the volumes in it is in accordance to the "ancient Greek church-ancient Slavonic Church." The first part is *Fu Yin Jing* 福音經 (The Gospels), which is arranged in sequence of *Jin An Zong Tu Ma Te Fei Shu* 謹按 宗徒瑪特斐述 (In strict accordance to the words of the Apostle Matthew), *Jin An Zong Tu Ma Er Ke Shu* 謹按 宗徒瑪爾克述 (In strict accordance to the words of the Apostle Mark), *Jin An Zong Tu Lu Ka Shu*

謹按 宗徒魯喀述 (In strict accordance to the words of the Apostle Luke), and *Jin An Zong Tu Yi Wang Shu* 謹按 宗徒伊望述 (In strict accordance to the words of the Apostle John). This sequence follows the catholic/universal Christian tradition,[6] but the names for the four *Gospels* have been translated into another set of names by Orthodox translators to stress the syllables of the original text as a deliberate way of differing from the Catholic rendition of names. Such a translation follows not only the original phonology of ancient Greek but also the tradition of Church Slavonic Bible translation: *Jin An Zong Tu…Shu* (*Yan Ge An Zong Tu…Suo Xu Shu De*) 謹按 宗徒…述 (嚴格按宗徒…所敘述的) (In strict accordance to the words of Apostle…).

The second part of this NT is *Zong Tu Jing* 宗徒經 (The Apostles). The first volume is *Shi Tu Xing Zhuan* 使徒行傳 (Acts of the Apostles). The Chinese title is *Zong Tu Xing Shi—Chuan Fu Yin Zong Tu Lu Ka Shu* 宗徒行實—傳福音宗徒魯喀述 (Acts of the Apostles—Words of Evangelist Luke), which is also the format of the "ancient Greek Church-ancient Slavonic Church," and in accordance with the Alexandrian text-type (e.g., four prohibitions in Acts 15:29).

Then follows *Zong Tu Shu Zha* 宗徒書札 (The Epistles of the Apostles), and finally *Mo Shi Lu* 默示錄 (The Revelation). The sequence of "The Epistles of the Apostles" represents the uniqueness of the Russian Orthodox NT in Church Slavonic, that is *Gong Shu* 公書 ("Catholic Epistles": James, Peter, John, Jude) come first, followed by *Si Ren Shu Xin* 私人書信 ("Personal Epistles," that is, Paul's fourteen epistles in this order: Romans, 1 and 2 Corinthians, Galatians, Ephesians, Philippians, Colossians, 1 and 2 Thessalonians, Hebrews, 1 and 2 Timothy, Titus, Philemon). This arrangement also may be a sign for the translator of this NT to emphasize the Greek tradition of the Orthodox Bible, the same with the sequence of the fifth-century *Codex Alexandrinus*.

Second, in this Orthodox NT translation, "*Ren Di Guan Wu Jian You Nan Yi Zhe Jie Huan Yin*" 人地官物閒有難譯者皆還音 admits that "Syllable/phonetic translation is used when it's difficult to translate the names of people, places, official positions and objects." The translator, Karpov, still adopted his Chinese translation methods from Russian Orthodox holy books, but we also find a new set of Chinese names of people and places in this NT.

Let me give two examples: (1) On page 2 of the catalogue of this NT (新遺詔聖經) is The Epistles of the Apostles. The first character in column 8 on the right is a combining character of "*Er* 爾" and "*Luo* 羅" making up a new Chinese word—referring to Romans. The second characters in Column 9 and Column 10 are the combination of "*Er* 爾" and "*Ling* 凌" making up a new Chinese word—referring to Corinthians. (2) The genealogy of Jesus in the Gospel of Matthew. Names for "Jesus Christ": Иисус Христос in Russian; ї҆и́съ хр҃то́съ in Church Slavonic; *Iēsous Christos* in Greek. The Russian phonetic syllable "ри" is translated as "*Erli* 爾利" in Chinese. The name for "St. Mary" is Мария in Russian.

Third, the typeface in this NT is intermingled large/small-size characters. In typesetting, the translator still used the small-size characters of "Chinese translation methods for Russian Orthodox holy books," to mark out single consonants in the original texts.

For example, on page 1 of the NT's table of contents, the small characters are translated from independent consonants that do not spell out with vowels. Such a treatment embodies the idea of the "syllable/phonetic" translation principle.

Yet another example, in the second chapter of Matthew, shows the feature of this NT. Matthew 2:1–2 in Church Slavonic reads: "2:1 Иисýсу же рóждшуся въ Виѳлеéмѣ Иудéйстѣмъ во дни́ Ирода царя́, сé, волсви́ от востóкъ пріидóша во Иерусали́мъ, глагóлюще: 2:2 гдѣ́ éсть рождéйся Цáрь Иудéйскій? ви́дѣхомъ бо звѣздý егó на востóцѣ и пріидóхомъ поклони́тися емý." ([1] In the time of King Herod, after Jesus was born in Bethlehem of Judea, wise men from the East came to Jerusalem, [2] asking, "Where is the child who has been born king of the Jews? For we observed his star at its rising and have come to pay him homage." [NRSV]) And look at the Orthodox Chinese translation:

> 伊伊穌斯 *Yi Yi Su Si* ("斯" is in small font) —Иисýс (Jesus)
>
> 微福 *Wei Fu* ("福" is in small font) 列耶木 *Lie Ye Mu* ("木" is in small font)—Church Slavonic: Виѳлеéмъ; ancient Greek: *Bēthleem* (Bethlehem).
>
> 伊屋疊亞 *Yi Wu Die Ya* (Four characters are in large font) clearly corresponds to "Иудея" in Russian and pointing to "*Ioudaia*" (Judaea) in ancient Greek.
>
> What is interesting is the translation of 黑落德 (Herod). 伊爾羅德 *Yi Er Luo De* ("爾羅" is a combining character and "德" is in small size) also corresponds to "И́род" in Church Slavonic, but this name does not correspond to ancient Greek "*Hērōidēs*."
>
> 耶爾魯 *Ye Er Lu* ("爾魯" is a combining character) 薩利木 *Sa Li Mu* ("木" is in small size) corresponds to Иерусали́мъ (Jerusalem) in Church Slavonic and pointing to *Hierousalēm* (Jerusalem) in ancient Greek.

All these special translation methods show the translator's "orthodox" pursuit of being "in full accordance to the original" of the Orthodox tradition, and the translator Karpov was proficient in Church Slavonic and ancient Chinese. Grigory Karpov was the archbishop of Tauria and Simferopol, later elected as the head of the Fourteenth REM in Beijing. Besides translating *Mirror of Orthodox Confession*, *The Summary of New Testament Salvation History: Life of Christ* (1860) and *The New Testament*, he also translated *Sheng Ti Gui Cheng* 聖體規程 (*Canon and Prayers for Holy Communion*, 1863), *Sheng Gong Si Yao* 神功四要 (*Four Principles of Spiritual Cultivation*, 1864), *Zao Wan Ke* 早晚課 (*Morning and Evening Prayers*, 1864), *Song Jing Jie Mu* 誦經節目 (*Lectionary Reading List*, 1865), and edited *Jiao Yi Wen Da* 教理問答 (*Catechesis*, 1865).[7]

Because these books are read daily by all Orthodox Christians, once the Chinese translation of Karpov was published, it established a unique "language image" for the Orthodox Church in Chinese. It creates a special legacy in the development history of the Chinese language and the Russian cross-cultural communication of the Orthodox Church to Chinese through the Slavonic Church language and biblical orthodoxy. Later translators employed his syllable/phonetic translation principle. In 1913, when the third edition of *Mirror of Orthodox Confession* was published, it was revised extensively. However, the names of people and places of the Bible still adopted "syllable translation" in accordance to the Church Slavonic phonetic system. Because Karpov's "Chinese translation methods for Russian Orthodox holy books," used in the hope of preserving more phonetic features of the original texts, did not work well with the Chinese character tradition, it was not used by later translators after Karpov's passing.

Inheritance and Adjustment of the Orthodox Bible Construction in China

Later in 1879, Nikolai Flavian (Gorodetsky, 1840–1915) was appointed the chief of the REM in Beijing. At the beginning of his tenure, he organized the translation and publication of *Sheng Yong Jing* 聖詠經 (*The Psalms*) in 1879 to meet the need of religious life of Chinese Orthodox Christians. The translator of *The Psalms* is uncertain. Some say Karpov may have been the translator, but Karpov's *Morning and Evening Prayers* (1864) and *The Psalms* are different, despite basic similarities. In any case, *The Psalms* was published by Flavian in 1879 and shows evidence of being translated from Russian—that is, neither from the Slavonic language of the ancient church nor from the Greek version of the Septuagint. It may be based on the new standard (popular) Russian translation of the OT published in Alexander II Era (1875). This is the first complete Chinese version of *The Psalms* from the Eastern Orthodox OT in China.

It is noteworthy that the OT published in St. Petersburg in 1875 is based on the ancient Jewish "Masoretic text" (seventh- to tenth-century manuscripts). Therefore, the 1879 Chinese version of *The Psalms* still bears a strong desire to be as close to the "original" text as possible (before the discovery of the Dead Sea Scrolls in 1947).

The 1879 Chinese version of *The Psalms* did not divide the 150 psalms into five volumes according to the Catholic and Protestant traditions, but divided them into twenty parts, with each part further divided into three sections, each of which was accompanied by "Praise of Glory" (*Rong Guang Zan Ci* 榮光讚詞). The author's information and thematic introduction preceding each psalm are deleted because they are not considered to be part of the biblical text. In addition to the 150 psalms, there was another *Sequel to The Psalms* (by King David). This edition shows its alignment with the "orthodoxy" of the Eastern Orthodox Church.

The Psalms was translated into classical Chinese, and names of people in the poems were all rendered phonetically, like the Russian pronunciation. For example, "King David" was translated into "*Da Wei De* 達微德." In typesetting, names of people and places basically adopted the Chinese syllables in Karpov's NT, but not his translation methods of combining characters and intermingled large and small fonts.

In 1884, Flavian also published *Zhan Li Zan Ci* 瞻禮讚詞 (*Festal Menaion*) and *Zhu Sheng Tian Zhan Li Zan Ci* 主升天瞻禮讚詞 (*Festal Menaion on Ascension*), and he revised *Zhu Fu Huo Zhan Li Zan Ci* 主復活瞻禮讚詞 (*Festal Menaion on Pascha*), which was translated by hieromonk Yi Sa Ya 伊薩亞 (Isaiah).

The publication of *Jiao Gui Lue Shu* 教規略述 (*Overview of the Commandments of the Church*) in 1882 by Flavian is of special significance. It is an overview of Orthodox regulations in vernacular Chinese. This shows that the Orthodox Church in China had begun to pay attention to the vernacular Chinese expression for Christians, such as:

> 第三、聖教的德行、頭一條是愛慕、是以奉教人、當常存愛人的心、行愛人的事、和遠避一切傷害人的、就如同拿言拿行拿資產施給幫助人、和眾人和睦、饒恕仇害自己的、不爭競、不嫉妒、不想念舊時的惡、不傷害人、不欺淩、不逼迫、不霸佔不竊取、不貪利等事。
>
> Third, regarding the virtues of the Faith: the first ones are to love, to teach sacrificially, and constantly having the heart of loving others. Then [one should] avoid hurting people, instead help others with word and action and fund, to keep the peace and harmony with all. [One needs] to forgive the enemy, not to compete; do not envy, do not remember any past evil, do not hurt people, do not bully, do not persecute others, neither dominate nor steal, not be greedy, and so on. (Handbook Editor's translation.)

The above sentences are very colloquial. *Overview of the Commandments of the Church*, which appeared before the May Fourth New Culture Movement in 1919, is important historical material for the development of Chinese language in the late Qing dynasty.

The Sixteenth REM in China, led by Archimandrite Flavian, has made fruitful achievements in translation and publication. Flavian's colleague, Nicolas Adoratsky (Peter Stepanovich, 1849–1896), was a genius missionary and scholar who was proficient in theology and foreign languages. Adoratsky joined the Beijing spiritual mission in 1881 and published *Dong Zheng Jiao Zai Hua Er Bai Nian Shi* 東正教在華 200 年史 (*The 200 Years' History of the Eastern Orthodox Church in China*) in 1887. Another Orthodox priest, Nikolai Aleksey (Sergeyevich Vinogradov, 1845–1919), came to Beijing from Russia and wrote many books, among which are very valuable material: *Sheng Jing Dong Fang Shi* 聖經東方史 (*Biblical History in the Orient*, 1889–1895) and *Li Ma Dou He Yi Ge Zhong Guo Xue Zhe Guan Yu Ji Du Jiao He Duo Shen Jiao De Dui Hua* 利瑪竇和一個中國學者關於基督教和多神教的對話 (*Dialogue between Matteo Ricci and a Chinese Scholar on Christianity and Polytheism*, 1889).

During the two years from 1883 to 1884, Flavian as the head of the mission, organized the entire group of monks to complete the translation of *Zhu Ri Ba Diao Zan Song Ci* 主日八調讚頌詞 (*Feast Rank Rubrical Signs*) and the like. By 1884, the Chinese translation of Orthodox books had exceeded 300,000 words. By the beginning of the twentieth century, the Orthodox Church may have had three Chinese versions of the NT (but this cannot be confirmed).

Most of the translation works of the mission in Beijing were sent to the Orthodox Church in Japan. After they were translated into Japanese, they were widely used in prayer activities. In the Russian Far East, Chinese translation texts are used to preach to local Chinese and Koreans.

The Turn of Biblical Construction in Chinese Orthodox Church

The tenure and the work of Innokenty (Figurovsky, 1863–1931), the head of the Eighteenth REM in China (1896–1931), also an archimandrite, plays a significant role in Orthodox ecclesiastical history in China.[8] Most importantly, during his tenure as head of the REM in China and as bishop of the Chinese Orthodox diocese, his Orthodox theological orientation began to turn to Protestantism; thus, the Chinese Orthodox Bible and sacred books began to adopt Protestant Chinese vocabulary.

Quan Gao Jie Wen 勸告解文 (*The Catechetical Instruction on Confession*), published in Beijing in 1904, is a two-page instruction document outlining two concepts: (1) The core concept of "*Tianzhu* 天主" (God) in Chinese has been replaced by "*Shangdi* 上帝" (God). Since then, the Chinese texts of Orthodox Scriptures basically use "*Shangdi*." (2) The Orthodox books of this period used Mandarin and vernacular.

Also in 1904, the Orthodox Church in China founded the journal, *Zhong Guo Dong Zheng Jiao Xie Hui Xiao Xi Bao* 中國東正教協會消息報 (*Orthodox Association News in China*), which was renamed *Zhong Guo Fu Yin Bao* 中國福音報 (*Gospel in China*) in 1907. Innokenty strongly advocated for producing a new Chinese translation of the Orthodox Bible and has achieved great results.

In 1910, *Xin Yue Sheng Jing* 新約聖經 (*The New Testament*), translated by Innokenty, was published. This Bible used the word "*Shangdi*," which showed Innokenty's concern about the attitude of Protestantism toward the Catholic Latin system. Innokenty sought to return to the Greek tradition by skipping over the Latin Bible. Because Church Slavonic was so close to Greek, it facilitated Innokenty in perusing the Greek tradition of the Orthodox. As a result, although he used "*Shangdi*" translation in the Protestant Bible, his translation of names of people and places in *The New Testament* was more Hellenistic, without adopting Karpov's translation method.

In 1911, Innokenty published a detailed annotated version of *Ma Te Fei Yi Sheng Fu Yin Jing* 瑪特斐乙聖福音經 (*The Gospel of Matthew*), which provided a detailed annotation in vernacular language to the "Mandarin" Scriptures. In the same year, Innokenty published a detailed annotated book, *Chuang Shi Ji Di Yi Shu* 創世紀第一書 (*Genesis the First Book*), a complete Chinese translation of the OT by the Orthodox Church after *Sheng Yong Jing* (*The Psalms*). Since then, due to the uneasy situation in Russia and China, the construction of the Chinese Orthodox Bible has basically stopped. Innokenty's work, *Genesis the First Book*, adopted the style of classical Chinese sentences, texts, and double-line notes (notes inserted in the texts) and *variorum* annotations. It was of primitive simplicity, but the notes and *variorum* annotations to the "Mandarin" language system in this book were in vernacular.

Another important historical marker was academic passages from *Sheng Jing Jie Yi* 聖經解義 (*Explanation of the Holy Bible*), *Jiu Yue Zong Lun* 舊約(總論) (*An Outline of the Old Testament*), *Wu Jing Zong Yao* 五經總要 (*A Summary of the Pentateuch*) being added to *Genesis the First Book*, which satisfied Innokenty's theoretical intention to make the interpretation of the Pentateuch more reflective for readers.

It is noteworthy that the theological ideas were expressed in *Explanation of the Holy Bible*. (1) The ideas expressed are Hellenistic, actually Church Slavonic. For example, under the first word "Bible" in the book, it added a note "*Yuan Yin Bi Bu Li Ya* 原音比布梨亞," that is, the Chinese phonetic rendition of the Greek pronunciation *bi-b-li-a*. The rest of the explanatory Chinese characters also represent their original Greek pronunciations. (2) The concepts of "canon," "apocrypha," "deuterocanon," and "pseudepigrapha," as understood by Protestantism, were used in *Explanation of the Holy Bible*, though in opposition to the Orthodox tradition. This reflects the reform of the Russian Orthodox Church in the late nineteenth and early twentieth centuries. Since that period, the translation of the Chinese Orthodox Bible has basically come to a standstill.

Chinese Orthodox Bible in the New Era

In the twenty-first century, the Chinese Orthodox Church began to revive itself. Upon the invitation of the Chinese government, Patriarch Kirill of Moscow and All Russia led the REM and officially visited China on May 10–15, 2013. Kirill declared the legitimacy of Russian Orthodox missionary work in China, seeking to open a new chapter for the Chinese Orthodox diocese in full communion with the Russian Orthodox Church.

However, the construction of the Chinese Orthodox Bible has remained in the age of Innokenty. Consequently, most of the Chinese Orthodox Bibles used now are Protestant Mandarin Chinese Union Version (國語聖經和合本, 1919) as well as the Catholic Studium Biblicum version (*Si Gao Ben* 思高本) for deuterocanonical texts that are missing in the Union Version. This is a challenge facing the Chinese Orthodox Church in the twenty-first century in terms of their *own* Bible translation.

Conclusion

The development of the Orthodox Church in China began in the eighteenth century with the missionary activities of the Russian Orthodox Church. It is in sync with Peter the Great's plan to revitalize Russia and, thus, to begin the first Orthodox mission in China. However, because the Jesuits and later Catholic missionary groups had a stronghold in China, the missionary activities of the Orthodox Church were difficult to develop, especially the challenging effort to translate and use the Orthodox Bible in China. On the one hand, they absorbed the translation results of the Catholic Bible and, on the other hand, they needed to show the uniqueness of the Orthodox distinctiveness of the "original," ancient Greek text.

In 1917 Russia changed dramatically; whereas politics and religion had previously been united, the Soviet socialist government separated religion from politics. The "freedom of belief" stated in the Soviet religious policy aimed to abolish the "state religion" status of the Russian Orthodox Church. Consequently, there was a lack of resources for missionary work in China. After the founding of the People's Republic of China in 1949, the Russian Orthodox Chinese ecclesial activities in Macao, Hong Kong, Taiwan, and other Southeast Asian countries did not have a solid development base. In terms of the Chinese Orthodox Bible, the Orthodox Church worldwide is paying attention to contributions the Chinese Orthodox Bible will make not only in areas of biblical literacy but also in biblical orthodoxy for both Christians and cultures in China.

NOTES

1. The international general term is Orthodox Church or Eastern Orthodox Church, and the official name is "Orthodox Catholic Church" (*Orthodoxē Katholikē ekklēsia*).
2. The invaluable documents such as the inscription on *Da Qin Jing Jiao Xuan Yuan Zhi Ben Jing Chuang* 大秦景教宣元至本經幢 (*The Stone Pillar Inscribed with Roman Nestorian Scripture* are evidence of the spreading of the early Eastern Orthodox Church in China. However, these documents are only a "summary" of the basic Christian doctrines, while the Nestorians' activities in the church and whether they used the Greek Bible, Latin Bible, Syrian Bible, or partly translated Chinese Bible in propagation need further investigation and archaeological data.
3. See Kurt Aland and Barbara Aland, *The Text of the New Testament*, tr. Erroll F. Rhodes (Grand Rapids: Eerdmans, 1987), Chap. II (48–71) and III (72–180) on the textual history of the NT. On the textual history of the OT, see Ernst Würthwein, *The Text of the Old Testament* (Grand Rapids: Eerdmans, 1979).
4. *Codex Alexandrinus* (sigla: A or 02) is a fifth-century manuscript of the Greek Bible, now kept in the British Library, London. It contains the LXX and the NT. Eastern Orthodox Patriarch Cyril Lucaris brought this codex from Alexandria to Constantinople.
5. Gregori Karpov, *Mirror of Orthodox Confession*, 2.
6. See for example the list of twenty-seven writings in Athanasius's (bishop of Alexandria, 296–373) *Thirty-Ninth Festal Letter* (in Nicene and Post-Nicene Fathers [Grand Rapids: Eerdmans, 1952–1957] 4:551–552) written in 367 CE.
7. Texts like *Canon and Prayers for Holy Communion* and *Morning and Evening Prayers* encompass a lot of biblical content, such as *The Lord's Prayer* and the *Psalms*.
8. Among his achievements are: (1) Innokenty suggested the establishment of a Standing Committee on Chinese Translation. (2) He expanded the Orthodox-administered area from Beijing to other places. (3) According to Order 1348 of 26 March 1901 of the Most Holy Synod of the Russian Orthodox Church, he was appointed bishop. On June 3, 1902, he was promoted to bishop of Periaslav and vicar general of Vladimir. He was responsible for the management of Orthodox Christians in China, which meant that the Orthodox Church in China became an Orthodox bishop diocese.
9. On the later, see: "*Ἡ Καινὴ Διαθήκη, ἐγκρίσει τῆς μεγάλης τοῦ Χρίστοῦ Ἐκκλησίας ἐν Κονσταντινουπόλει ἐκ τοῦ Πατριαρχικοῦ τυπογραφείου*, 1904"; cf. *The EOB New Testament* (2011), presented in memory of Archbishop Vsevolod of Scopelos (2007) of Ukrainian Orthodox Church of the USA and Ecumenical Patriarchate of Constantinople, and in honor of His Beatitude Metropolitan Jonah, Primate of the Orthodox Church in America.

Primary Sources

Adoratsky, Nicolas. *Dong Zheng Jiao Zai Hua Er Bai Nian Shi* [in Chinese] 東正教在華 200 年史 (*The 200 Years' History of the Eastern Orthodox Church in China*). Np., 1887. The first four chapters appeared as series of articles: "The Orthodox Mission in China for the Last 200 Years of its Existence: The History of the Beijing Spiritual Mission in the First and Second Period of Its Activity" in *Orthodox Dialogist* (February–November, 1887) and *Sojourner* (April–May, 1887); then printed as a whole book in 1887. See also: Guangzhou: Guangdong People's Publishing House, 2007.

Aleksey, Nikolai (1845–1919). "Li Ma Dou He Yi Ge Zhong Guo Xue Zhe Guan Yu Ji Du Jiao He Duo Shen Jiao De Dui Hua" [in Chinese] 利瑪竇和一個中國學者關於基督教和多神教的對話 ("Dialogue between Matteo Ricci and a Chinese Sscholar on Christianity and Polytheism." Np., 1889.

Aleksey, Nikolai. "Sheng Jing Dong Fang Shi" [in Chinese] 聖經東方史 ("Biblical History in the Orient"). Np., 1889–1895.

BHS "Masoretic text" (seventh- to tenth-century manuscripts). Stuttgart: Deutsche Bibelgesellschaft, 1968–1976.

Chuang Shi Ji Di Yi Shu 創世紀第一書 (*Genesis the First Book*), 1911. Innokenty (Figurovsky, 1863–1931), tr. Beijing: Beiguan, 1911. [The original copy is located in the library of Beijing Normal University.]

The Codex Sinaiticus and the Codex Alexandrinus. Edited by H. J. M. Milne and T. C. Skeat. London: Trustees of the British Museum, 1963.

Bibliorum Sacrorum Graecorum Codex Vaticanus. Rome: Istituto Poligrafico e Zecca dello Stato, 1999.

Da Qin Jing Jiao Xuan Yuan Zhi Ben Jing Chuang 大秦景教宣元至本經幢 (*The Stone Pillar Inscribed with Roman Nestorian Scripture*). *Xuanyuan zhiben jing dhāraṇī* pillar, 814 CE. [Kept in Luoyang Museum.] See: Ge Chengyong 葛承雍, ed. *Jingjiao yi zhen: Luoyang xin chu tangdai jingjiao jingchuang yanjiu* [in Chinese] 景教遺珍：洛陽新出唐代景教經幢研究 (*Precious Nestorian Relic: Studies on the Nestorian Stone Pillar of the Tang Dynasty Recently Discovered in Luoyang*). Beijing: Cultural Relics Press, 2009.

Dong Jiao Zong Jian 東教宗鑑 (*Mirror of Orthodox Confession,* 1860). Gury (Grigory Platonovich Karpov, 1814–1882), ed. There are three editions: (1) 1863 edition [kept in and made available by National Library of Australia]; (2) the second 1863 edition [in the China collection of the Scientific Library of Irkutsk State University and made available by Bp. Seraphim of Sendai. This edition has Japanese pronunciation marks. The Tōyō Bunko (or Oriental Library) also holds a copy]; (3) Beijing Orthodox Church reprinted (1913) "Shangdi" edition, distributed by Fr. Dionisy Pozdnyaev. [The original copy is at the Russian State Library in Moscow.]

Eastern Slavonic Bible (Cyrillic script), 1581, 1751, and other editions are inner circulation by Russian Orthodox Church. "Ancient Slavonic" (or "Church Slavonic") Bible, St. Petersburg: Alexander Nevsky Monastery, 1751. The standard Slavonic edition is the St. Petersburg revision of 1751, known also as the Bible of Elizabeth.

Eastern (Greek) Orthodox Bible (EOB) published in the United States in 2007. Its NT is based on 1904 *The Patriarchal Greek New Testament* (PATr). Istanbul: Ecumenical Patriarchate of Constantinople, 1904.[9]

Guo Yu Sheng Jing *He He Ben* 國語聖經和合本 (*Mandarin Chinese Union Version*, NT published in 1906; OT published in 1919). Complete Bible published in 1919. See *Chinese Union Version*. Nanjing: Amity Printing Co., 2000.

Han Er He Bi Yun Bian 漢俄合璧韻編 (*Sino-Russian Dictionary*). Palladius (Kafarov, 1817–1878), ed. Beijing: Tongwenguan, 1888.
Jerome, Vulgate: *Biblia Sacra Vulgatae Editionis Sixti Quinti Pont. Max. iussu recognita atque edita*. Rome: 1592. *Novum Testamentum Domini nostri Iesu Christi, vulgate editionis: juxta exemplar Vaticanum anni 1592*. Coloniae: Apud Jacobum Naulaeum, 1679.
Jiao Gui Lue Shu 教規略述 (*Overview of the Commandments of the Church*) in two editions: (1) "Tianzhu" edition. Kyoto: Dongjiaozong beiguan, 1882. (2) "Shangdi" edition. Shanghai: Chinese Orthodox Association, 1936.
Jiao Yi Wen Da 教理問答 (*Catechesis*, 1865). Gury, ed. Beijing: Np., 1865. [Now kept in Russian State Library in Moscow.]
Ma Te Fei Yi Sheng Fu Yin Jing 瑪特斐乙聖福音經 (*The Gospel of Matthew*). Innokenty, tr. Beijing: Beiguanshi, 1911. [The original kept in the Russian State Library in Moscow.]
Ostrog Bible (Острожская Библия), 1581. Ostroh (Polish-Lithuanian Commonwealth): (by the printer) Ivan Fyodorov, 1581 with the assistance of the Ruthenian Prince Konstantin Ostrogski. [See: https://rutracker.org/forum/viewtopic.php?p=77240353.]
Quan Gao Jie Wen 勸告解文 (*The Catechetical Instruction on Confession*) published in Beijing in 1904. Innokenty, ed. [The original is kept in Russian State Library in Moscow.]
Sheng Gong Si Yao 神功四要 (*Four Principles of Spiritual Cultivation*). Gury, ed. Beijing: Np., 1864. [This 1864 edition is in the China collection of the Scientific Library of Irkutsk State University.]
Sheng Shi Ti Yao 聖史提要 (*The Summary of New Testament Salvation History: Life of Christ*). Gury ed. Beijing: Np., 1860. [The original is kept in Australian National University Library and Tōyō Bunko (or Oriental Library) in Tokyo.]
Sheng Ti Gui Cheng 聖體規程 (*Canon and Prayers for Holy Communion*, 1863). Gury, ed. [The original copy is kept in the library of St. Petersburg Theological Academy.]
Sheng Yong Jing 聖詠經 (*The Psalms*). Flavian, ed. Beijing: Beiguan, 1879. [The original is kept in the library of Osaka Church (Dongjiaozong beiguan)].
Si Gao Ben 思高本 (Studium Biblicum version). Nanjing: Amity Printing Co., 2006.
Song Jing Jie Mu 誦經節目 (*Lectionary Reading List*). Gury, ed. Beijing: np., 1865. [The original is kept in the Russian State Library in Moscow.]
Tian Shen Hui Ke 天神會課 (*Conversation of the Angels*). Ya Jin Fu 雅金福 (Iakinf/Bichurin, 1777–1853). Beijing: Np., 1810. [The original copy is kept in Berlin State Library—Prussian Cultural Heritage Foundation, Germany.]
Xin Yi Zhao Sheng Jing 新遺詔聖經 (*The New Testament*). Guri, tr. from Slavonic. Beijing: Russian Ecclesiastical Mission in Beijing, 1864. [The original copy is kept in two volumes of the Gospels and the Apostles in the rare book department of the Harvard-Yenching Library. An eleven-volume copy is kept at the library of Peking University, Waseda University Library (in Tokyo), also in Russian State Library (in Moscow), as well as in the China collection of the Scientific Library of Irkutsk State University.]
Xin Yue Sheng Jing 新約聖經 (*The New Testament*). Bishop Innokenty, tr. Beijing: Beijing Eastern Orthodox Association, 1910 (first edition). [A copy is kept in the library of the Institute of World Religions at the Chinese Academy of Social Sciences in Beijing.]
Zao Wan Ke 早晚課 (*Morning and Evening Prayers*). Gury, ed. Beijing: np., 1864. [The original copy is kept in Tokyo Library, Japan.]
Zhan Li Zan Ci 瞻禮讚詞 (*Festal Menaion*). Flavian, ed. Beijing: Holy Virgin Church, 1884.
Zhong Guo Dong Zheng Jiao Xie *Hui Xiao Xi Bao* 中國東正教協會消息報 (*Orthodox Association News in China*). 1904–1907 (55 issues). Renamed as *Zhong Guo Fu Yin Bao* 中國福音報

(*Gospel in China*) since 1907. Innokenty, ed. Published by Russian Orthodox Mission in China, 1904–1947.

Zhu Fu Huo Zhan Li Zan Ci 主復活瞻禮讚詞 (*Festal Menaion on Pascha*), tr. Yi Sa Ya (Isaiah), rev. Flavian in 1884. [The original copy is kept in the library of St. Petersburg Theological Academy, Moscow.]

Zhu Ri Ba Diao Zan Song Ci 主日八调赞颂词 (*Feast Rank Rubrical Signs*). Flavian, ed. 1884.

Zhu Sheng Tian Zhan Li Zan Ci 主升天瞻禮讚詞 (*Festal Menaion on Ascension*). Flavian, ed. 1884. [The original copy is kept in the library of St. Petersburg Theological Academy, Moscow.]

CHAPTER 5

THE BASSET-SU CHINESE NEW TESTAMENT

SONG GANG

INTRODUCTION

CATHOLIC missionaries took the lead in spreading Christianity in China during the seventeenth and eighteenth centuries. Many of them, especially the Jesuits, promoted *Xixue* 西學 (Western Learning) or *Tianxue* 天學 (Learning from Heaven) and published Chinese works that covered a broad range of subjects in religion, science, philosophy, literature, art, and other fields. Nonetheless, there was not a full Chinese translation of the Bible over the long period of two centuries.

There were several reasons for the slow progress in Bible translation. The Jesuits published dozens of Chinese Christian works during the first few decades of their mission in China. Their priority, however, was given to translations of scientific, catechetical, and liturgical works instead of the Bible. Even when Pope Paul V (1550–1621) issued a decree in 1615 with permission to translate the holy Scriptures into the classical Chinese language, the Jesuits did not respond with any serious endeavor to produce a Chinese version of the Bible.[1]

Established in 1622, the Sacra Congregatio de Propaganda Fide set restrictive policies on publications and translations of the Bible.[2] Moreover, there was growing tension among the Catholic orders in China regarding Chinese ancestor worship. The controversy escalated into a confrontation between the Roman Catholic Church and the Qing empire. Emperor Kangxi (1654–1722) willfully changed his attitude about Christianity from tolerance to prohibition.[3] Chinese Christian works, including biblical texts, were banned by Qing authorities through the main course of the eighteenth century.

Despite the depression in the mid-Qing period, a small number of Catholic missionaries managed to break the restrictions imposed by religious and secular authorities and made the first attempts to translate the Bible into Chinese. Among these early endeavors, the New Testament (hereafter NT) translated by the missionary of the Paris Foreign

Missions Society (M.E.P.) Jean Basset (1662–1707) and Confucian convert Johan Su (?–1734) has drawn much attention in recent research. Some scholars examine the manuscripts and copies of the Basset-Su translation, some explore the life stories of Basset and Su, while others pay special attention to its later influence on Protestant Bible translations during the nineteenth century.[4]

TRANSLATION OF THE NEW TESTAMENT

The Basset-Su translation of the NT can be considered a breakthrough in the history of the Bible in China. Several factors, including the restrictions of the Propaganda Fide, the expanding Catholic missions in China, and the looming threat of anti-Christian suppressions, contributed to Basset's foresight on the need for a Chinese Bible. Some careful preparation had been made to launch the translation project. He developed sophisticated arguments on the important value of a Chinese Bible to the China mission. He acquired support from Johan Su, a capable scholar assistant. He also made efforts to search a set of Chinese equivalents of key biblical terms. No wonder the translation process was carried out in an efficient and organized manner. The immediate result met Basset's expectation—a Classical Chinese (*wenyan* 文言) version of the Bible that may not have been perfect at the early stage, but was still useful for the reading of Confucian converts and for the reference of later translators.

Basset's Vision of a Chinese Bible

In 1702, upon the invitation of Alexandre Pocquet (1655–1734), a director of the M.E.P. Seminary in Paris, Basset wrote a long and stimulating article titled *Avis sur la Mission de Chine* (Recommendations on the Mission of China, later as *Recommendations*). In the first two parts, he presented a study of the major problems in the China mission, such as apostasy, idol worship, errors and heresies in those translated Christian works, prejudices among the missionaries, and a lack of discipline. In the remaining two parts, Basset proposed three "remedies" to solve the problems: celebration of the sacraments in Chinese; translation of the Bible into Chinese; and ordination of Chinese priests. In other words, a further localization of Catholic mission work may yield more benefits and foster a sustainable development of the Chinese Church under the Qing regime.

In part two of his *Recommendations*, Basset highlighted several aspects of the "illness" in the China mission. He particularly directed his criticisms at Jesuit missionaries, who had achieved voluminous translations of Western scientific works yet without any substantial effort to translate the Bible into Chinese. Basset wrote:

> I am surprised that they [i.e., the Jesuits] took trouble to produce many translations, yet they did not translate the Bible, or at least some scriptures like the Four Gospels,

> into Chinese. They translated *Logic*, *Metaphysics* of Coimbra, mostly studies in physics taught in European schools, *Elements* of Euclid, various treatises on the sphere, astronomy, geography, geometry, arithmetic, and all of mathematics. They indeed have made some translations and works on religious and spiritual subjects, but the translation of the Bible should not be deemed unworthy of a place among these works, like we thought we would have had enough. As a result, the Chinese in the [imperial] court are now better trained in mathematics than in [the Christian] religion. Once the Europeans are expelled, their mathematics may remain with the books that they have prepared, but the [Christian] religion will perish for lack of any similar kind of support [from biblical works].[5]

The comments sounded very critical, but Basset clearly pointed out the defect and risk of the intellectual-oriented, top-down approach adopted by Matteo Ricci 利瑪竇 (1552–1610) and later Jesuits in their missions: They took too much effort in translating Western sciences, while the translation of the Bible, the most important Scripture of the Christian faith, was put aside. Moreover, they used their knowledge of Western sciences to serve the emperor and win over high-ranking officials in the imperial court, but without enough doctrinal teachings, their interests and support were not at all reliable. In Basset's eyes, the Christian religion in China was in a dangerous situation, just like "a tree without root and a building without foundation." If the emperor had any suspicions, all missionaries could be dismissed quietly and repatriated back to Europe, and the Christian religion could disappear in the Qing empire, like a candle being extinguished by just a breath.[6]

In another place, Basset discussed the possibility of a persecution of Christianity that may force European missionaries out of China. Considering the looming threat, he re-emphasized the urgent need for three things—a Chinese Bible, liturgies conducted in Chinese, and Chinese clergy—to save the Christian religion from being persecuted. He asked, "But who told us that we are far from the persecution? Should we wait till it comes before we take the measures? Would we, then, take the measures in time? Think about Japan where there was no time [for such measures], just like the doctor comes after the death [of the patient]. Why expose us here [in China] to the same misfortune?"[7] With great caution, Basset would call for every possible preparation, including a Chinese translation of the Bible. Indeed, about two decades after his death, a nation-wide persecution of Christianity became reality.

Basset further refuted the objection to a Chinese Bible with the reason that to translate the Bible into accurate, elegant Chinese was a very difficult, if not impossible, project. He argued that there had been innumerable Latin translations of the Bible since the time of St. Augustine (354–430), none of which was considered perfect, but with centuries of accumulative efforts of European translators, a standard version was finally made with endorsement of the Church authorities in the Council of Trent (1545–1563). Given this successful precedent, Basset would expect a similar process in Chinese translations of the Bible. He believed that, with the concerted efforts of missionaries, those early "imperfect" translations—his translation included—would contribute to the creation of an authoritative, perfect version of the Bible for all Chinese Christians.[8]

Translation Process

As Basset did not receive a response from Europe on his proposed "remedies," he decided to take actions on his own. The translation project was started soon after he recruited Johan Su. In a letter to Mgr. Artus de Lionne 梁弘任 (1655–1713) on September 17, 1704, Basset first mentioned his plan to translate the Bible.[9] He wrote another letter to de Lionne ten months later, saying that he had been busy with the translation of the NT and had already reached the end of St. John's Gospel.[10] Therefore, the Chinese translation of the Four Gospels had been completed within a year.

In his 1705 letter, Basset remarked on Su's great help in their translation work. Since Su returned to his hometown to address troubles with his family, Basset acknowledged that he had no other man who could help with the translation.[11] This indicated that Basset and Su must have worked together while translating the biblical texts. Considering the popular missionary-convert collaborations in translating Western religious, scientific, and philosophical works, it would be a similar process in which Basset first verbally translated Latin texts into colloquial or literary Chinese, then Su transcribed Basset's words and rendered the texts into classical Chinese.

Another M.E.P. missionary, Joachim de Martiliat 馬青山 (1706–1755), mentioned in his diary that Su had learned by heart the texts in the NT, and that he made a Gospel Harmony on his own after the death of Basset in 1707.[12] This valuable reference can be further verified by two extant original manuscripts of the Basset-Su translation, one at the Casanatense Library in Rome and the other at the Cambridge University Library, both bearing Su's own handwriting.[13]

De Martiliat also mentioned that Su helped Basset "translate the first part of the *Grand catéchisme historique* of Father Fleury, and to write a small treatise about the [Christian] religion where he uses an entire chapter to prove that *chîn* [i.e., *Shen*] has the same meaning as *Deus*."[14] According to Jean-François Martin de la Baluère 梁弘仁 (1668–1755), Basset's M.E.P. companion in Sichuan, Su had great love for Confucian learning and insisted that Confucianism and Christianity mostly resembled each other. It is not surprising that Su at times served as a tutor of Basset and explained to him "the difficult passages contained in Chinese works."[15] Though he had little knowledge of French or Latin, Su was able to share his expertise on Confucian classics and Chinese language. His support enabled Basset to adopt different Chinese words to translate key biblical terms and defend his views against other Catholic missionaries in China.

Source Text, Content, and Structure

The Vulgate Bible, officially endorsed as the standard version at the Council of Trent, must be the source text for the Basset-Su translation. In his *Recommendations*, Basset quoted many biblical passages from the *Vulgata Sixto-Clementina*, first printed in 1592 and later announced as the authoritative edition of the Bible for the Roman Catholic Church in the following centuries. Though Basset still hoped that a translator may have certain liberty to refer to other editions that do not contravene with the standard edition, the Vulgate Bible was his only option to carry out the Chinese translation project, with or without the approval from Rome.

Basset and Su translated eighteen books of the NT, including the Four Gospels, the Acts of the Apostles, and thirteen epistles (including the first chapter of the Epistle to the Hebrews). In the Casanatense manuscript, which contains the Four Gospels, the translated texts are arranged in the same order as in the 1592 standard edition. Each book is given the Chinese title rendered according to the Latin title, e.g., *Madou youbian Yesu Jidu sheng fuyin* 瑪竇攸編耶穌基督聖福音 for translation of *Sanctum Iesu Christi Evangelium secundum Matthæum*, and *Fu Baolu shitu yu Gelin bei diyi shu* 福保祿使徒與戈林輩第一書 for translation of *Epistola Beati Pauli Apostoli ad Corinthios Prima*.[16]

The Cambridge manuscript contains a Gospel Harmony, titled *Sishi youbian Yesu Jilisidu fuyin zhi huibian* 四史攸編耶穌基利斯督福音之會編 (literally *The Concordance of the Gospels of Jesus Christ Compiled by the Four Historians*), which replaces the Four Gospels in the Casanatense manuscript. There are twenty-eight chapters in this Gospel Harmony. The Gospel texts once translated by Basset and Su have been re-arranged into a chronology of events in the life of Jesus, while an index of the source—the shortened Gospel name with a chapter number—is provided at the end of each paragraph. Though Su gave no explanation on his motive to make this new version, he may have intended to compile a full biographical account of Jesus for reading by both Christians and non-Christians. As for the remaining parts of the Cambridge manuscript, they are mostly identical with the biblical texts from the Casanatense manuscript.

Translation Principle, Techniques, and Mistakes

Through the seventeenth century, the Jesuits had produced numerous biblical texts in Chinese, but all of them were abridged translations of the Bible. Giulio Aleni 艾儒略 (1582–1649), for example, presented paraphrases of Gospel texts in his *Tianzhu jiangsheng yanxing jilüe* 天主降生言行紀畧 (Brief Record on the Speeches and Conducts of the Incarnated Lord of Heaven, 1635), the first Chinese biography of Jesus.[17] Another well-circulated biblical text was Manoel Dias's 陽瑪諾 (1574–1659) abridged translation of Gospel episodes, with detailed annotations and commentaries, in his *Shengjing zhijie* 聖經直解 (Literal Explanations of the Sacred Scriptures, 1636).[18] As the Jesuits preferred a "transwriting" pattern (or *yishu* 譯述 in Chinese) rather than "translation" in a strict sense, their works did not make consistent use of the translation principle of truthfulness. The Basset-Su translation of the NT, though without official approval, was the first deliberate Catholic endeavor to put such a principle into practice.

Table 5.1 below presents a comparison between a section in the first chapter of the *Epistola Beati Pauli Apostoli ad Romanos* and the same section from the Basset-Su NT. The Chinese verses reflect an almost word-by-word rendering of the original Latin verses. Except for the unusual transliteration of "Græco" as *Jeza ren* 厄匝人 and the

Table 5.1 The Vulgate Bible Compared with the Basset-Su Translation of Romans 1:16–21

Biblia sacra vulgatae editionis (1592) *Epistola Beati Pauli Apostoli ad Romanos* 1:16–21	Basset-Su NT, *Fu Baolu shitu yu Luoma bei shu* 福保祿使徒與羅瑪輩書
16 Non enim erubesco Evangelium. Virtus enim Dei est in salutem omni credenti, Judæo primum, et Græco.	蓋余不羞福音，蓋為神之德以救凡信者，先如達及厄匝人。
17 Iustitia enim Dei in eo revelatur ex fide in fidem: sicut scriptum est: Iustus autem ex fide vivit.	蓋于之自信進信，而顯神之義。如經云：義者以信而活。
18 Revelatur enim ira Dei de cælo super omnem impietatem, et injustitiam hominum eorum, qui veritatem Dei in injustitia detinent:	蓋顯神之怒自天將討諸人無義拘神真理輩之悖逆。
19 quia, quod notum est Dei, manifestum est in illis. Deus enim illis manifestavit.	因神之明處伊等知之，蓋神示伊等。
20 Invisibilia enim ipsius, a creatura mundi, per ea, quæ facta sunt, intellecta, conspiciuntur: sempiterna quoque ejus virtus, et divinitas: ita ut sint inexcusabiles.	蓋神不可見之處，自天地之化成已顯著，即其永德與神明亦然，致伊等無諉。
21 quia cum cognovissent Deum non sicut Deum glorificaverunt aut gratias egerunt sed evanuerunt in cogitationibus suis et obscuratum est insipiens cor eorum.[19]	因伊等既認神，弗敬弗謝之如神，乃蕩散于諸思念，而其癲心為蒙昧。

awkward expression in verse 18 bearing non-Chinese syntax, Basset and Su managed to closely follow the source text. They also showed strong skills in rendering some faithful, fluent, and concise expressions, e.g., *Yizhe yi xin er huo* 義者以信而活 for "*Justus autem ex fide vivit*" (NRSV: "The one who is righteous will live by faith," Rom 1:17).

The principle of truthfulness also can be seen in the Basset-Su translation of two source texts of the *Pater Noster* in comparison with its two early Chinese versions translated by the Jesuits in China. Through the seventeenth century, the Jesuits made continuous efforts to create a standard translation of the *Pater Noster*. As Table 5.2 shows, when Basset and Su translated the source texts in Matt 6:9–13 and Luke 11:2–4, they used a few verses of the Jesuits' version, including "*Er guo lin ge* 爾國臨格" for "*Adveniat regnum tuum*" (NRSV: "Your kingdom come", Matt 6:10) and "*Jiu wo yu xiong'e* 救我于兇惡" for "*libera nos a malo*" (NRSV: "rescue us from the evil one", Matt 6:13). However, they followed the principle of truthfulness to render their own translation. The first verse "*Wo deng fu zai tian zhe* 我等父在天者" corresponded to the order of the Latin source text "*Pater noster, qui es in cælis*" (NRSV: "Our Father in heaven", Matt 6:9), while the order was reversed in the Jesuits' version. Moreover, Basset and Su made subtle changes in the Chinese expressions, especially "*zhicheng* 致成" in place of "*chengxing* 承行," "*yinyu* 引于" in place of "*daoyu* 蹈於," and "*Yameng* 亞孟" in place of "*Ameng* 阿孟." Though the meanings of these words were largely the same, Basset and Su tended to make a distinction between their literal translations of the source biblical texts and the Jesuits' translations of the *Pater Noster* as a para-biblical text.[20]

Table 5.2 ***Pater Noster*** **in the Translations of Matteo Ricci and Giulio Aleni, Compared with the Source Texts in the Vulgate Bible and the Basset-Su Translation**

Biblia sacra vulgatae editionis (1592)	Matteo Ricci's *Shenging yuelu* 聖經約錄 (Doctrina Christiana, ca. 1610)	Giulio Aleni's *Tianzhu jiangsheng yanxing jilüe* (1635)	Basset-Su NT
Pater noster, qui es in cælis: sanctificetur nomen tuum. Adveniat regnum tuum. Fiat voluntas tua, sicut in cælo et in terra. Panem nostrum supersubstantialem da nobis hodie, Et dimitte nobis debita nostra, sicut et nos dimittimus debitoribus nostris. Et ne nos inducas in tentationem. Sed libera nos a malo. Amen. (*Matthæum*, Cap. VI) Pater sanctificetur nomen tuum. Adveniat regnum tuum. Panem nostrum quotidianum da nobis hodie. Et dimitte nobis peccata nostra, siquidem et ipsi dimittimus omni debenti nobis. Et ne nos inducas in tentationem. (*Lvcum*, Cap. XI)[21]	在天我等父者， 我等願爾名成聖， 爾國臨格， 爾旨承行於地， 如於天焉。 我等望爾今日與我， 我日用糧。 而赦我債， 如我亦赦負我債者。 又不我許蹈於誘感， 乃救我於兇惡。 亞孟。[22]	在天我等父者， 我等願爾名見聖， 爾國臨格， 爾旨承行於地， 如於天焉。 我等望爾今日與我， 我日用糧。 而赦我債， 如我亦赦負我債者。 又不我許蹈於誘感， 乃救我於兇惡。 亞孟。[23]	我等父在天者， 我等願爾名致聖， 爾國臨格， 爾旨致成於地， 如于天焉。 今日與我， 養體之糧。 而免我債， 如我亦免負我債者。 又不我引于誘感， 乃救我于兇惡。 阿孟。 (《瑪竇福音》第六章) 父， 爾名致聖， 爾國臨格， 賜我等 以日用糧。 又免我等之罪， 蓋我等免凡負我債者 又勿引我于誘感。 (《路加福音》第十一章)

Another notable treatment was the translation of "supersubstantialem" and "quotidianum" in the two source texts of the *Pater Noster*. Both words had been indiscriminately interpreted as "daily" due to the identical contexts. No wonder Ricci and Aleni would use the same word "*riyong* 日用" in their Chinese translations of the *Pater Noster*. The Basset-Su translation, however, showed two different Chinese words—"*yangti* 養體" (literally "to nourish the body") and "*riyong*". While the latter kept the meaning of "daily," the former indicated a particular connotation in the Latin source text, which had been first made by St. Jerome (ca. 347–420) in his translation of the Greek word "*epiousios*" into "supersubstantialem" and "quotidianum" respectively.[24] In this case, "supersubstantialem" may be interpreted as "life-sustaining" to stress the eschatological dimension of the prayer. It therefore should be a purposeful decision of Basset and Su to adopt a different word, "*yangti*," to translate "supersubstantialem" in the Latin source text.

The revisions of the Basset-Su translation, made by Su after the death of Basset, deserve special attention. Some of the revisions could be justified, while others were inappropriate and even false, more or less the result of Su's own arbitrary decisions. For example, in the first chapter of the Acts of the Apostles in the Casanatense manuscript, there appeared two men with the same name, Ruda 茹荅, one referring to Iudas Iacobi (the brother of James) and the other referring to Iuda (or Iudæ) Simonis Iscariotæ (the son of Simon Iscariot) who betrayed Jesus.[25] In the Cambridge manuscript, Su changed the second Ruda 茹荅 to Ruda 儒達, apparently with a purpose to differentiate the two men and avoid possible confusion. Another revision can be found in the second chapter of this book in the Cambridge manuscript, where Su reversed the two sentences "*Ru lao jian meng; Ru you jian xiang* 汝老見夢, 汝幼見像" that appeared in the Casanatense manuscript. He switched the order with a common sense, as people normally talked about youth before old age. The change indeed corresponded to the order in the Latin source text, "*et iuvenes vestri visiones videbunt, et seniores vestri somnia somniabunt*"[26] (NRSV: "and your young men shall see visions, and your old men shall dream dreams," Acts 2:17).

However, as a Chinese who knew little Latin, Su did not realize that his revisions at times infringed on the principle of truthfulness with inappropriate or even false expressions. One of the mistakes appeared in the last three chapters of *Fu Baolu shitu yu Yalada bei shu* 福保祿使徒與雅辣達輩書 (*Epistola Beati Pauli Apostoli ad Galatas*), in which Su crossed out the word "*Feng* 風" in numerous places and changed to the word "*Shen* 神". Basset and Su have consistently translated "*Spiritus*" as *Feng* and "*Dominus*" as *Shen* in the Casanatense manuscript. When Su made the change, for instance, from "*Wubei huo yi **Feng**, bi xing yi **Feng** yi* 吾輩活以風，必行以風矣" to "*Wubei huo yi **Shen**, bi xing yi **Shen** yi*吾輩活以神，必行以神矣," he deviated from the earlier Basset-Su rendering of the original Latin text "*si spiritu vivimus, spiritu et ambulemus*" ("If we live by the Spirit, let us also live by the Spirit," Gal 5:25) in the Casanatense manuscript.[27] This revision mixed up these two words and presented a different translation at odds with the source text.

Similar mistakes appeared in other parts of the same book, though in a more nuanced manner. In chapter three, two sentences of the Latin source text read "*At ubi venit fides iam non sumus sub pædagogo. Omnes enim filii Dei estis per fidem, quæ est in Christo Iesu.*" (NRSV: "But now that faith has come, we are no longer subject to a disciplinarian, for in Christ Jesus you are all children of God through faith," Gal 3:25–26)[28] A faithful rendering was made in the Casanatense manuscript as "則信既來到，吾輩已弗屬開蒙師。尔等因耶穌基督所賜之信，皆為神之子也." But, Su removed the noun "*bei* 輩" (literally "a generation of people") and replaced the verb "*wei* 為" (to be) by "*you* 猶" (be like) in the Cambridge manuscript. These minor changes altered the original meanings presented in the source text: "*sumus*" refers to *we* (吾輩) instead of Paul himself (吾), while "*estis*" means that all people whom Paul talks with *are* (為), but not *are like* (猶), children of God.

The above examples can verify that the Casanatense manuscript was a result of the close collaboration of Basset and Su. By sharing knowledge and skills in Latin and Chinese, they managed to translate the Latin source texts as faithfully as they could. Unfortunately, their practical and efficient work stopped due to the sudden death of Basset. Su then made his own attempt to produce an "updated" version, featuring the Gospel Harmony and further revisions to the Cambridge manuscript. Despite his well-intended efforts, there appeared more mistakes than the necessary improvements. In this case, the quality of the Basset-Su translation has been compromised with Su's later revisions that no longer reflected the same standard of truthfulness.

Choice of Language, Style, and Terminology

In his *Recommendations*, Basset often mentioned that the target audience of a Chinese Bible should be Confucian scholars. These well-educated people loved to read and recite classical works. One may expect that upon conversion to Christianity they would devote themselves to the study of the Bible.[29] Basset firmly believed that, if given a Chinese Bible, Confucian converts could further help spread the authentic and orthodox doctrines among ordinary Chinese people. His view reflected a practical method somewhat similar to the top-down approach adopted by the Jesuits since the late Ming period, yet it should be interpreted differently at the turn of the eighteenth century. Unlike the Jesuits who actively searched for a harmony between Confucianism and Christianity, Basset was cautious about mainstream Confucian teachings, especially Neo-Confucianism and Chinese ancestor worship. His utmost concern was to utilize the intellectual skills of Confucian scholars as an effective aid for further spreading the Christian faith in China, but not to make compromises and adapt to a Confucian way of thinking.

Bearing the target audience in mind, Basset had to be careful at the choice of language for the ambitious translation project. In the early years of his mission in China, he may have already learned about the dominant status of classical Chinese (*weyan*) in most of the formal writings, as well as its distinction from vernacular Chinese (*baihua* 白話), which, despite a secondary status, had increasing influence on popular literature through the seventeenth and the eighteenth centuries. Basset would use classical Chinese in hope of more support for Confucian scholars, while Su proved himself as a well-versed scholar and a competent assistant in the collaborative translation. On the other hand, in response to the needs of a growing Catholic community in Sichuan, Basset decided to use vernacular Chinese to translate catechetical works, which were intended to be read by less educated neophytes and children.

The classical language in the Basset-Su translation can be compared with the vernacular language in *Jingdian jilüe wenda* 經典記略問答 (*Questions and Answers on the Summary of the Holy Scripture*), a major catechetical work that Basset translated, with

Table 5.3 Acts of the Apostles 1:1–4 in the Basset-Su Translation and in *Jingdian jilüe wenda*

Biblia sacra vulgatae editionis (1592) Actus Apostolorum, Cap. II	Basset-Su NT, Chapter 2, *Shitu xing* 使徒行	*Jingdian jilüe wenda*, Chap. 42, 聖神降臨	*Jingdian jilüe wenda*, Chap. 42, 問答
Et dum complerentur dies Pentecostes, erant omnes pariter in eodem loco: et factus est repente de cælo sonus, tamquam advenientis spiritus vehementis, et replevit totam domum ubi erant sedentes. Et apparuerunt illis dispertitæ linguæ tamquam ignis, seditque Ssupra singulos eorum: et repleti sunt omnes Spiritu Sancto, et cœperunt loqui variis linguis, prout Spiritus sanctus dabat eloqui illis.[30]	且五旬滿時，諸徒同在一所。忽自天響作，如烈風來，而盈伊等坐之全房。即散顯之以舌如火，而坐于各上。遂衆滿領聖風，而始講列音，隨聖風賜之語焉。	到五旬之日，衆齊一處時，自天忽響起，如猛風遍充房屋，遂現碎火形如舌，散住各人頂上。方皆滿領聖神，始講百方之音。	問：到了第十天有何變？ 答：到辰時，天轟響，烈風滿吹諸徒坐的房。忽舌火現各人頂，而皆滿聖神。

the help of Su, from the *Grand catéchisme historique* (1683) of church historian Claude Fleury (1640–1723).[31] Table 5.3 presents the Latin source text and three Chinese versions on the day of Pentecost in the second chapter of the Acts of the Apostles.

The Basset-Su translation showed almost word-for-word renderings of the Latin text, while the other two versions, one from the main text and one from the Q&A part in Chapter 42 of *Jingdian jilüe wenda*, presented the episode in the manner of paraphrasing. As far as language is concerned, the Basset-Su translation adopted expressions with typical lexical and grammatical features of classical Chinese, including, for example, "且...時," "自天響作," "盈...全房," "散顯," "以舌如火," and "賜之語焉." The expressions yielded a formal and elegant style in narration. In comparison, the versions from the *Jingdian jilüe wenda* adopted largely informal and colloquial expressions, such as "到...日/天/時," "天轟響," "滿吹...的房," "舌火," and "現各人頂." The style of narration looked more like a piece of vernacular literature. These differences suggest that Basset and Su indeed have taken language and style as a critical matter when translating different genres of Catholic works into Chinese.

Catholic missionaries in China in the late Ming and early Qing periods certainly were aware of many varieties within the category of classical Chinese, some bearing an archaic form of ancient texts while others taking a "modern" form close to the vernacular writings of the time. In this case, the language used in the Basset-Su translation looked more like a "modern" form than an archaic form of classical Chinese. Some characteristics of the classical style can be recognized, yet there was no sign of an acute interest in highly embellished expressions. Nor did the texts contain any special expressions alluding to ancient Chinese classics. More remarkably, in some parts of their translation, especially conversations between Jesus, the apostles, and people at different places, Basset and Su tended to use colloquial expressions. A good example can be seen in John 4:11, where Jesus was addressed by the woman of Samaria as "*Domine*" in the Latin source text.[32] Basset and Su translated this title as "*ye* 爺," a common colloquial form of Chinese salutation to a senior male, a master, or an official.[33]

The above special characteristics of the Basset-Su translation distinguished it from earlier biblical texts translated by the Jesuits. In his *Tianzhu jiangsheng yanxing jilüe*, Aleni provided an account on the same episode of Pentecost, but he used some more stylish phrases, such as "踰旬日," "倏聞," "烈風衝室," "被滿聖神," and "洞徹萬理," in the Chinese narration.[34] As for the salutation of the Samarian woman to Jesus, Aleni did not use the colloquial title "*ye*." He chose instead another word, "*zunzhe* 尊者," a formal honorific title that could match the Latin word "*Domine*." Due to his familiarity with Confucian classics and dedicated efforts to adopt a hybrid Christian-Confucian identity in the Fujian mission, Aleni presented a formal and embellished style in this first Chinese biography of Jesus, to an extent that it may be compared with the masterpieces among Chinese historical works, e.g., *Shiji* 史記 (*Records of the Grand Historian*, ca. 94 BCE) by the Western Han historian Sima Qian 司馬遷 (145–86 BCE).[35] The contrast in language and style between Aleni's translation and the Basset-Su translation re-affirmed the latter's "modern" form of classical Chinese. In other words, the Basset-Su NT reflected a middle style that mixed common linguistic features of classical Chinese and some components of vernacular Chinese.

Not only did the Basset-Su translation carry special characteristics in language and style but also it went through a controversy over terminology. Basset and Su particularly chose the Chinese words "*Shen* 神" and "*Sheng Feng* 聖風" in their translation of two essential Latin terms—"*Deus*" and "*Spiritus Sanctus*." For the term "*Deus*," though there had been debates on its Chinese equivalents among the Jesuits since the late Ming period, most Catholic missionaries in the early Qing era, including the friars and the members of the M.E.P., would abide by the officially endorsed translation of *Deus* as *Tianzhu* 天主, a term adopted by the first Jesuits in China.[36] It was unusual for Basset to openly reject such a translation. He once preferred another term, "*Shangdi*," that had been used since Matteo Ricci, but Bishop Charles Maigrot 顏璫 (1652–1730), the vicar apostolic of Fujian, gave a mandate in 1693 prohibiting the use of "*Shangdi*" for "*Deus*." Though he criticized the Jesuits' tolerance of Chinese ancestor worship, Maigrot would still accept the common use of "*Tianzhu*" for "*Deus*."[37] This, however, did not stop Basset from searching for alternative Chinese terms. In 1704, likely under the help of Su, he became determined to use "*Shen*" to translate "*Deus*." In the next few years, he engaged in heated discussions on the use of this term with other missionaries, including Maigrot and Franciscan missionary Basilio Brollo de Glemona 葉尊孝 (1648–1704).[38] In December 1707, only about two months before his death, Basset drafted a letter to papal legate Charles-Thomas Maillard de Tournon (1668–1710), asking for his help to have the new term "*Shen*" examined by the missionaries in Macao and to confirm his view that "*Chin* [i.e., *Shen*] is the true Chinese name that corresponds to the Latin word *Deus*."[39]

As to the second term, "*Spiritus Sanctus*," Basset also made long arguments on how the Latin word "*Spiritus*" incorporated the materialistic connotation of the Greek word "*pneuma*," how the Jesuits' rendering of "*Sheng Shen* 聖神" for "*Spiritus Sanctus*" was self-contradictory in their translations of biblical texts, and how the word "*Feng* 風" should be a more accurate Chinese equivalent to suggest both material and metaphorical connotations of "*Spiritus*." He further quoted the term "*Jing Feng* 淨風" (literally "Pure Wind"), inscribed on the Tang Nestorian Stele (781), as one historical precedent to reinforce his view.[40]

Basset's insistence should not be simply understood as a search for the best translations of *Deus* and *Spiritus Sanctus* in Chinese. By proposing different Chinese words for these Latin terms, he targeted the Jesuits' translations with the purpose of challenging their dominant role in the China mission. To him, a challenge in biblical terminology was both practical and strategic. In case the proposal to make a Chinese Bible could be endorsed finally by the authorities of the Roman Catholic Church, while his translation may become a pioneering work for later translations, the new set of *Deus-Shen* and *Spiritus Sanctus-Sheng Feng* would be among the most frequently read key terms in the Chinese Bible. Then, given the canonical nature of the Bible, these new terms could become authoritative expressions and finally replace the Jesuits' translations.

Unfortunately, the new Chinese terms did not gain much recognition among Catholic missionaries and Chinese converts of the time.[41] Su helped Basset find some relevant Chinese references, by which they managed to justify their claims. They also kept a consistent use of the terms in the Casanatense manuscript. However, Su could have developed a different view later, either with his own understanding or under the influence of mainstream translations. He intentionally changed "*Sheng Feng*" and "*Feng*" to "*Sheng Shen*" and "*Shen*" in various parts of the Cambridge manuscript.[42] As it turned out, Basset's insistence on terminology diminished. The terms have been largely ignored until Protestant missionaries started their translations in the early nineteenth century with a renewed interest in biblical terminology.

Catholic Legacy and Chinese Bible Translation

The Basset-Su NT should be considered an exemplary piece in the early stage of Chinese Bible translation. It is an undeniable fact that, ever since the later Ming period, Catholic missionaries and Chinese Christians have continued to make varied types of biblical texts. Some widely read texts have been circulated in multiple later editions, while other texts remained obscure over the later centuries. The above analysis in this research not only brings to light the special features of the Basset-Su NT but also uncovers a parallel of two trends—one visible and one invisible—in early Chinese biblical literature.

Those biblical texts in the visible trend were mostly abridged translations or paraphrases of scriptural texts. Many of them, bearing the official approval for publication (i.e., with *imprimatur* on the front page), became popular readings for Chinese converts. It is relatively easy to trace the circulation of these texts, as well as subsequent adaptations and revisions, over a long period of three centuries. However, this body of early Chinese biblical literature has been treated merely as a secondary category in recent research. Some scholars still hold a conventional view that these "non-translation" texts have been made solely for catechetical purpose and liturgical use, thereby having little value to the studies of the history of the Bible in China.

The fewer biblical texts in the invisible trend have been neglected as well. Though they represented endeavors for a direct translation of the Bible, these texts have never been published. Without official authorization, they were all circulated in the form of handwritten manuscripts and copies. Surprisingly, a few among these texts still attracted much attention at a later time. The Cambridge manuscript of the Basset-Su NT, which had multiple duplicates circulated by both Protestant and Catholic missionaries in China until the early twentieth century, can be considered a remarkable example in this respect.[43] The contributions of the Basset-Su translation and other Catholic endeavors still await further exploration, because they manifest in one way or another the dynamism of early Chinese biblical literature, as well as the multiformity and complexity of Bible translations with the spread of Christianity in global history.

Notes

1. Nicolas Standaert, *Handbook of Christianity in China*, Vol. 1: *635–1800* (Leiden: Brill, 2001), 621; Bernward H. Willeke, "Das Werden der chinesischen katholischen Bibel," in *Die Heilige Schrift in den katholischen Missionen*, ed. Johannes Beckmann, S.M.B., with P. Walbert Buhlmann, O.F.M., and Joh. Specker, S.M.B. (Schöneck-Beckenried: Neuen Zeitschrift für Missionswissenschaft, 1960), 284–285.
2. Nicolas Standaert, "The Bible in Early Seventeenth-Century China," in *Bible in Modern China: The Literary and Intellectual Impact*, ed. Irene Eber et al. (Sankt Augustin: Monumenta Serica Institute, 1999), 38–39, 52–53.
3. Jonathan D. Spence, "Claims and Counter-Claims: The Kangxi-Emperor and the Europeans (1661–1722)," in *The Chinese Rites Controversy: Its History and Meaning*, ed. D. E. Mungello (Nettetal: Steyler Verlag, 1994), 15–28.
4. For some early studies on the subject, see Marshall Broomhall, *The Bible in China* (London: British and Foreign Bible Society, 1934); Bernward H. Willeke, "The Chinese Bible Manuscript in the British Museum," *Catholic Biblical Quarterly* 7.4 (1945): 450–453; A. C. Moule, "A Manuscript Chinese Version of the New Testament (British Museum, Sloane 3599)," *Journal of the Royal Asiatic Society of Great Britain and Ireland*, no. 1 (April 1949): 23–33. For more recent studies, see François Barriquand, "First Comprehensive Translation of the New Testament in Chinese: Fr Jean Basset (1662–1707) and the Scholar John Xu," *Societas Verbi Divini: Verbum SVD* 49 (2008): 91–119; Uchida Keiichi 内田庆市, "白日昇漢譯聖經攷 (Jean Basset's Translation of the Bible into Chinese)," 東アジア文化交渉研究 (*Journal of East Asian Cultural Interaction Studies*) 5 (February 2012): 191–198; Song Gang 宋刚, "Small Figure, Big History: A Study on Johan Su, an Early Qing Sichuan

Catholic Convert" [in Chinese] 小人物的大歷史：清初四川天主教徒徐若翰個案研究的啟示, International Sinology [in Chinese] 國際漢學 10 (2017): 30–57; Choi Kam-to蔡錦圖, "Catholic Bible Translations in Late Ming and Early Qing China" [in Chinese] 晚明至清初天主教中文《聖經》翻譯, in *Transmission, Writing, and Imagination: The West in Late Imperial Chinese Culture* [in Chinese] 傳播、書寫與想像：明清文化視野中的西方, ed. Song Gang (Shanghai: Fudan University Press, 2019), 38–43.

5. Basset, "Avis sur la Mission de Chine (1702)," in *Jean Basset (1662–1707): Pionnier de l'Eglise au Sichuan, Précurseur d'une Eglise d'expression chinoise, Correspondance (Oct. 1701–Oct. 1707), Avis sur la Mission de Chine (1702)*, ed. François Barriquand and Joseph Ruellen (Paris: Éditions You Feng Libraire & Éditeur, 2012) 115–116, 219–220.
6. Ibid. 97, 207.
7. Ibid. 195–196, 276.
8. Ibid. 158, 186, 249, 269.
9. Basset, "Lettre à Mgr A. de Lionne (1655–1713, M.E.P.)" on September 17, 1704, in *Jean Basset (1662–1707): Pionnier de l'Eglise au Sichuan*," 553.
10. Basset, "Lettre à Mgr A. de Lionne (1655–1713, M.E.P.)" on July 13, 1705, in *Jean Basset (1662–1707): Pionnier de l'Eglise au Sichuan*," 564.
11. Ibid. 564.
12. The diary of de Martiliat was dated in October 1734, now being held in the Archives des Missions Etrangères de Paris [hereafter A.M.E.], 434: 508.
13. For a detailed examination of the four original texts handwritten by Su, including the Casanatense and the Cambridge manuscripts of the Basset-Su NT, see Song, "Small Figure, Big History," 30–39.
14. See A.M.E. 434: 509.
15. The description can be found in De la Baluère's letter dated on September 3, 1705. See A.M.E. 407: 582.
16. All original Latin biblical texts in this article are quoted from *Biblia Sacra vulgatae editionis (Roma 1592)*: http://bibbia.filosofia.sns.it/TOC15920000Vulgata15920000Vulgata.php. The Latin titles of the two books are on pages 961 and 1111 respectively.
17. For recent studies on Aleni's work, see, for example, Pan Feng-chuan 潘鳳娟, "Translation as Narration: Giulio Aleni's Cross-Language Narratives of 'A Brief Record of the Words and Deeds of the Incarnation'" [in Chinese] 述而不譯? 艾儒略《天主降生言行紀略》的跨語言敘事初探, *Academia Sinica* [in Chinese] 中國文哲研究集刊 3 (2009): 111–167; Song Gang, "From Sacred Scripture to Popular Narrative: *Tianzhu jiangsheng yanxing jilüe* and Its Later Adaptations in Qing China" [in Chinese] 從經典到通俗：《天主降生言行紀畧》及其清代改編本的流變, *Journal of Catholic Studies* [in Chinese] 天主教研究學報 2 (2011): 208–260.
18. For recent studies on this work, see, for example, Standaert, "The Bible in Early Seventeenth-Century China," 43–45; Chen Yanrong 陳妍蓉, "The 'Sheng jing zhi jie': A Chinese Text of Commented Gospel Readings in the Encounter between Europe and China in the Seventeenth Century," *Journal of Early Modern Christianity* 1.1 (2014): 165–193.
19. *Biblia Sacra vulgatae editionis (Roma 1592)*, 1099.
20. In the Casanatense manuscript, Basset and Su first used the word "*chengxing* 承行," but it was crossed out and a new word "*zhicheng* 致成" was added, both in Su's own handwriting. This change suggests that Basset and Su must have been aware of the Jesuits' earlier translations.
21. *Biblia Sacra vulgatae editionis (Roma 1592)*, 966, 1025.

22. Matteo Ricci, *Shengjing yuelu* 聖經約錄 [in Chinese], in *Chinese Christian Texts from the Roman Archives of the Society of Jesus* 耶穌會羅馬檔案館明清天主教文獻, ed. Nicolas Standaert and Adrian Dudink (Taipei: Ricci Institute, 2002), 1:90.
23. Giulio Aleni, *Brief Record on the Speeches and Conducts of the Incarnated Lord of Heaven*, in *Chinese Christian Texts from the Roman Archives of the Society of Jesus*, 4:115.
24. Nicholas Ayo, *The Lord's Prayer: A Survey Theological and Literary* (Lanham: Rowman & Littlefield Publishers, 2002), 59–62.
25. *Biblia Sacra vulgatae editionis (Roma 1592)*, 1067.
26. Ibid. 1068.
27. Ibid. 1137.
28. Ibid. 1136.
29. Basset, "Avis sur la Mission de Chine (1702)," 148.
30. *Biblia Sacra vulgatae editionis (Roma 1592)*, 1068.
31. Dudink, "Jean Basset MEP (1662–1707) and His Catechetical Writings in Chinese," 93.
32. Ibid. 1046.
33. For interpretations of the colloquial term *ye*, see Ji Changhong 吉常宏, et al., *Dictionary of Titles in Chinese* [in Chinese] 漢語稱謂大詞典 (Shijiazhuang: Hebei jiaoyu chubanshe, 2001), 1123, 1278.
34. Aleni, *Brief Record on the Speeches and Conducts of the Incarnated Lord of Heaven*, Vol. 4: 332.
35. For a detailed analysis of the formal style in Aleni's biography of Jesus, see Song, "From Sacred Scripture to Popular Narrative," 219–231.
36. Standaert, *Handbook of Christianity in China*, 1:683.
37. Rosso, *Apostolic Legations to China of the Eighteen Century* (South Pasadena: P.D. and Ione Perkins, 1948), 131–132.
38. Basset's arguments can be found in his letters to Maigrot and De Glemona in 1704 and 1707. See *Jean Basset (1662–1707): Pionnier de l'Eglise au Sichuan*, 402–502.
39. This draft letter was later copied by de Martiliat in 1743. See *Jean Basset (1662–1707): Pionnier de l'Eglise au Sichuan*, 507.
40. There are at least two places with the Chinese term "*Jing Feng*," A.M.E. 407: 425 and 425: 260, that appear to be handwritten by Su.
41. See de Martiliat's diary in A.M.E. 434: 509.
42. Song, "Small Figure, Big History," 46.
43. For recent studies of the influence of the Basset-Su NT on nineteenth-century Protestant translators, especially Robert Morrison (1782–1834) and Joshua Marshman (1768–1837), see Jost O. Zetzsche, *The Bible in China: The History of the Union Version or the Culmination of Protestant Missionary Bible Translation in China* (Sankt Augustin: Monumenta Serica Institute, 1999), 25–57; Zhou Yong 周永, "From Basset and Xu to Marshman and Morrison: Origin, Diffusion and Influence of Basset-Xu's New Testament Translation," [in Chinese] 从"白、徐譯本" 到 "二馬譯本"—簡論白、徐〈新約〉譯本的緣起、流傳及影響, *Journal of Catholic Studies* [in Chinese] 天主教研究學報2 (2011): 261–308.

Primary Sources

The following is a chronological list of extant original manuscripts and copies of the Basset-Su New Testament (Np.):

Basset, Jean and Johan Su, *Testament Nouvm Sinice*, Bibilioteca Casanatense di Roma, Mss. 2024, Np, ca. 1705–1707.

Basset, Jean and Johan Su, *Gospel Harmony, Acts, St. Paul's Epistles, Hebrews Chapter 1*, Bible Society's Library, Cambridge University Library, BFBS Mss. 127, Np, ca. 1707–1734.

John Hodgson's copy of the Cambridge manuscript of the Basset-Su New Testament, British Library, Sloane MS 3599, 1737.

Robert Morrison's copy of Sloane MS 3599, University of Hong Kong Library, Mor 226 M25, ca. 1806.

George H. Bondfield's copy of Robert Morrison's copy (through Elijah C. Bridgman's copy and then Jonathan Lee's copy), Cambridge University Library, BFBS Mss. 30, 1904.

Gabriele M. Allegra's copy of Sloane MS 3599, Studium Biblicum Franciscanum, Hong Kong, uncatalogued, ca. 1935.

CHAPTER 6

DE POIROT'S CHINESE BIBLE AND ITS INFLUENCE

ZHENG HAIJUAN

Introduction

THE translation of the Bible, together with some missionary translations of Western philosophy and Christian theology into Chinese, could be taken as the beginning of the translation of Western canons from early modern China until today. Before the nineteenth century, however, translation of the entire Bible had not been a major concern for most Catholic missionaries. For more than two hundred years since the arrival of the Jesuits in 1582, some selections of the Bible were rendered by different Catholic missionaries, including Matteo Ricci's (1552–1610) *Shengjing Yüelu* 聖經約錄 (selections from the Bible, 1605), Manuel Dias Jr.'s (1574–1659) *Shengjing Zhijie* 聖經直解 (translation and commentaries of the Gospel readings on Sunday and the major religious feast days, 1636), Giulio Aleni's (1582–1649) *Tianzhu Jiangsheng Yanxing Jilüe* 天主降生言行紀略 (the life of Christ, 1635), and the French Jesuit François-Xavier d'Entrecolles's (1664–1741) *Xunwei Shenbian* 訓慰神編 (the book of Tobit, 1730).[1]

Yet alongside these relatively fragmentary renditions were still a few Catholic missionaries' personal attempts to translate the entire Bible into Chinese during and before the mid-Qing dynasty. Among them was Jean Basset (1662–1707), a French priest of the Missions Etrangères de Paris, whose translation of the incomplete NT at the beginning of the eighteenth century is the oldest extant Chinese version of the NT. The other is Louis Antoine de Poirot 賀清泰 (1735–1813), a French Jesuit who translated the Vulgate into Manchu and vernacular Chinese. Basset's and de Poirot's versions were not published during their lifetimes. Basset's version has been much more noted by academia as its manuscripts were made available to famous pioneer Protestant biblical translators like Joshua Marshman (1768–1837) and Robert Morrison 馬禮遜 (1782–1834); in comparison, de Poirot's version, though more complete, has been hitherto largely ignored because its manuscripts had long remained obscure.

This essay provides a brief account of de Poirot's version, as well as the motivation behind his translation of the Bible into vernacular Chinese at a time when classical Chinese was still the dominant written language. Particular focus is given to textual features of this version, together with its direct and indirect influences on later translated versions, including Morrison's version and the Studium Biblicum version, called *Si-gao Sheng-jing* 思高聖經 in Chinese.

De Poirot and His Chinese Bible

De Poirot was born in 1735 in Lorraine, France and grew up in Italy. He joined the Society of Jesus in Florence in 1756.[2] After his arrival in China in 1770, he spent most of his years in Beijing while staying in Beitang 北堂 and serving as a court painter specializing in animal-and-bird paintings. He was the last of the Western painters who served Emperor Qianlong (1711–1799). Together with Giuseppe Panzi (1773–1812), he replaced previous famous court painters, including Giuseppe Castiglione (1688–1766). He was granted Liupin Dingdai 六品頂戴, an official title of nobility, by the court of the Qing dynasty for his services.[3]

Upon his arrival in China, de Poirot mastered the Chinese and Manchu languages in a short time. After that, he taught these two languages to several missionaries who came to Beijing later, including the Lazarist superior Nicolas-Joseph Raux (1754–1801).[4] While in court, de Poirot was in charge of translations of diplomatic correspondence between St. Petersburg and Beijing for a long period, before his replacement by Louis-François-Marie Lamiot (1767–1831) in his old age.[5] Besides translating the Bible into Manchu and Chinese, he also translated Emperor Kangxi's (1654–1722) admonitions to his children, "Tingxun Geyan" 庭訓格言, from Manchu language into Italian.[6] When George Macartney (1737–1806) led his embassy to China in 1792, de Poirot was able to meet with him together with other Jesuits who served in royal court at that time. Also, he was engaged in the translation of the second edict from Emperor Qianlong to King George III (1738–1820) to refuse to grant the requests of the embassy.[7]

According to the extant materials, it is difficult to date exactly when de Poirot started his translation of the Bible. However, in 1790, Panzi wrote in a letter that de Poirot was translating the Bible into "the language of the Tartar with commentaries."[8] And in 1803, de Poirot wrote to the Sacred Congregation de Propaganda Fide in Rome to inform them that he had translated most books of the OT and NT into Manchu and Chinese and to request permission to have his translation printed.[9] Based on these letters, we can conclude that de Poirot must have spent more than one decade on his biblical translation. And he probably started this impressive project by translating the

Bible into Manchu, the national language of the Qing dynasty, and then by translating it into Chinese.

De Poirot was commended for his zeal, yet, unfortunately, permission to publicize his versions was refused by the Sacred Congregation de Propaganda Fide.[10] Hence, his translations are largely unknown to the public except for certain scribed copies. The extant manuscripts are now seen in different libraries. For the Chinese version, which is named *Guxin Shengjing* 古新聖經 (the Holy Books of the OT and NT), the collections of the Bibliotheca Zi-ka-wei 徐家匯藏書樓, now Shanghai Library, is the most complete one, containing translations of the entire NT and of the OT except the Song of Songs and fifteen of the prophets (Jeremiah, Lamentations, Baruch, Ezekiel, Hosea, Joel, Amos, Obadiah, Micah, Nahum, Habakkuk, Zephaniah, Haggai, Zechariah, Malachi).[11] Beitang Library, now the National Library of China, hosts four volumes (including the Epistles and Revelation) and another fragmental volume (including part of the translator's preface and the beginning of Genesis).[12] Fusinian Library 傅斯年圖書館 in Academia Sinica keeps three volumes of *Dawei Shengyong* 達味聖詠 (Psalms).[13] And the Studium Biblicum Franciscanum Hong Kong 思高聖經學會 preserves more than three hundred photographed pages of fragmental parts from five books, including Exodus, Numbers, Deuteronomy, and 1 and 2 Kings.[14]

For the Manchu version, which is called "*Manwen Fuzhu Xinjiuyue Shengshu* 滿文附註新舊約全書," Tôyô Bunko hosts the most complete collections. Fragmental copies are found in the Institute of Oriental Manuscripts of the Russian Academy of Sciences in St. Petersburg (formerly the St. Petersburg Branch of the Institute of Oriental Studies of the Russian Academy of Sciences) and in the British and Foreign Bible Society in London. Furthermore, a fragmental copy with both Manchu and Chinese translations of 1 Chronicles also is found in the Russian Academy of Sciences.[15]

De Poirot's Bible is based on Jerome's (347–420) *Vulgate*, the late fourth-century Latin translation of the Bible recognized as the officially promulgated version by the Catholic Church. Though unpublished, this Chinese version comprises a large portion of the Bible. Altogether, de Poirot's Chinese Bible contains more than 1,400,000 characters, including the translator's two prefaces, the Scripture, and the translator's annotations that are annexed to each chapter, all in vernacular Chinese instead of classical Chinese—a rather unique choice of language that makes this version stand out in the historical and social context of that era.

A quick glance at the Chinese written language systems during Ming and Qing Dynasty clearly reveals the dominance of classical Chinese: the pedantic *baguwen* 八股文 remained the sole writing style required by the Imperial Examination, a selecting mechanism for the state bureaucracy; and an influential traditional-prose movement launched by the Tongcheng School 桐城派, a leading group of writers and scholars, revived the classical style in the Tang and Song dynasties, while written vernacular Chinese was allowed only in marginal literary genres like novels. The classical Chinese, extremely concise and compact, was at that time highly respected as the language of the ancient sages and, hence, the language to be followed in writing.

From the end of the Ming to the early Qing dynasty, the Jesuits in China employed the strategy of propagation and evangelization "from the top down," a strategy initiated by Francis Xavier (1506–1552) and Alessandro Valignano (1539–1606) and put into practice by Michele Ruggieri (1543–1607) and Matteo Ricci (1552–1610) and his followers. The Jesuits associated with the Chinese *literati* and tried to impress these social elite with their mastery of written classical Chinese.[16] For example, Ricci's *Jiaoyoulun* 交友論 (*Dell'amicizia*), was written in classical Chinese and received many compliments from distinguished mandarins and scholars.[17] Dias Jr. would be another example. He intentionally imitated the grand style of "*mogao* 謨誥" from *Shangshu* 尚書[18] in his translated works *Qingshi Jinshu* 輕世金書 (*De imitatione Christi*) and *Shengjing Zhijie*. These two Chinese versions, with their ancient grammar and profound rhetoric, were the best among all the Chinese Catholic texts in the grand style, which clearly reflected Dias Jr.'s efforts to re-canonize the two Christian canons as classics in the Chinese social context. As is known, in 1615, the Jesuits in Beijing were given permission to translate the sacred texts not into vernacular, but into the "erudite language proper to the literati."[19] Dias's method of translation no doubt was in accordance with that instruction.

However, as a consequence of the Chinese Rites Controversy, the Catholic missions were banned in China by Emperor Kangxi in 1721. And the anti-Christian policies were reinforced by his successors, Emperor Yongzheng, Emperor Qianlong, and Emperor Jiaqing (1760–1820). With all kinds of odds against the Society of Jesus in Europe (especially the Rites Controversy and the suppression of the Society of Jesus in 1773), de Poirot became one of the last few former Jesuits in Beijing, witnessing an increasingly stringent ban on missionary services,[20] especially after the legal case of Adeodato di Sant' Agostino (1760–1821) in 1805.[21]

As compared with the elite class of scholar-officials, who were naturally attached to the court, the common people were affected much less by the court's banning and were more in need of religious belief to help elevate their impoverished secular life. All these factors made the common people more susceptible than the social elites to the prospect of conversion to the Catholic faith. The mission, working underground in the provinces, tended to focus on the lower class and the illiterate, those who actually made up the largest group of Christians.[22] Undoubtedly, a plain vernacular style turned out much more valuable to the grand style in practical communication of biblical messages with the common people. Also, the missionaries had to rely upon Chinese catechists for contact with Christians. And, in contrast to classical Chinese, vernacular Chinese writings could be almost directly quoted verbatim in preaching. Therefore, it would be much easier for the Jesuits to write or translate in vernacular and let the Chinese catechists read among the common people.

Before de Poirot, missionaries' writings in China had witnessed a proportional growth of vernacular Chinese in order to meet the negative situation caused by the Chinese Rites Controversy.[23] *Shengshi Churao* 盛世芻蕘, a theological book by the French Jesuit Joseph-Francois-Marie-Anne de Moyriac de Mailla (1669–1748), is such an example. This book, written in Colloquial Chinese, was lauded by Fang Hao 方豪 (1894–1955) as representative of the missionary stylistic change from classical Chinese writing to vernacular Chinese writing, a herald for the Movement of Vernacular Chinese.[24] In its preface, the author elaborates on the rationale for utilizing vernacular Chinese by explicitly stating that "it is most inconvenient to orally transmit messages in hinterland regions"[25] and that the book is written in a form "even ignorant men or women could understand."[26]

Similarly, at the very beginning of de Poirot's Bible are two prefaces that try to explain his motivation for using vernacular Chinese instead of classical Chinese from the translator's perspective. In the second preface, de Poirot alludes to Jerome's *Vulgate* as a defense for his personal choice of plain vernacular Chinese in biblical translation, explicitly stating his aim of communicating divine providence to all people so that both "the clever and the ignorant" could easily understand Christian teachings and benefit from the Bible.[27] Jerome's famous dream, in which he was punished by the angels as he tried to translate the Bible modeling the grand style of Cicero's writing, is retold to support de Poirot's personal belief, that translating the Bible in vernacular language is truly and utterly following "God's will."[28] The illiterate, in de Poirot's mind, should not be deprived of the opportunity of knowing God because of their poor education.

Probably for this purpose of reaching out to all social sectors, de Poirot integrated colloquial expressions into his version—for example, "*tiwo qing'an* 替我請安"[29] as "*salutabitis eum ex nomine meo pacifice / greet him in my name*" (1 Sam 25:5)—to make the language more accessible to its potential targeted readers. He also employed a dialect of North China to reach the same goal, using in his translation expressions like "*yaozi* 腰子"[30] instead of "*shen* 腎" to translate "*renibus*/kidney" (Lev 3:4) and "*yanbianfu* 鹽蝙蝠"[31] rather than "*bianfu* 蝙蝠" to translate "*vespertilio*/bat" (Lev 11:19). *Erhua* 兒化is commonly used in his translated text, too, perfectly imitating the colloquial speech in North China, especially in the area of Beijing.[32]

Also, de Poirot tended to bring notions and conceptions from Chinese culture to his translation. To translate "*orare*/pray" (Matt 26:36; Luke 18:10), for example, he recycles the word "*qidao* 祈禱" (pray),[33] a word originating from Confucianism and then used often in Buddhist canons, and also "*songjing* 誦經" (chanting the scripture),[34] a term from Buddhism. Furthermore, to translate "*panis*/bread," the symbol of Christ's body in the Bible, de Poirot uses sometimes "*mantou* 饅頭" (the steamed bun) and sometimes "*bobo* 餑餑"[35] (a word from a dialect of North China designating the steamed bun). The reason is obvious: ancient Chinese people did not bake bread, but the steamed bun, an ordinary food in North China, is somehow an ancient Chinese equivalent to bread in Europe. But the problem is, the steamed bun carries no symbolic meaning as a sacramental food at all in Chinese culture, and hence neutralizes the sense of holiness of sacramental bread. Even when Jesus says: "*ego sum panis vitae*" (I am the bread of life; John 6:35), de Poirot, as before, translates it into "*wo shi shengming de mantou* 我是生命的饅頭."[36]

Such examples illustrate that domestication is widely used as a strategy of translation in de Poirot's version. Meanwhile, foreignization is used as an important strategy. De Poirot exhibits in his translation a tendency to introduce Latin grammar directly into the Chinese language. Europeanized words, as well as the frequent appearance of appositions, attributive clauses, and inverted sentences, which rarely occur in traditional written Chinese, are frequently found in the translated text. Transliteration is a usual way for de Poirot to translate names of persons and places. Throughout the OT, he transcribes "*Deus*," the one and the only God, into "*dousi* 陡斯," imitating the pronunciation of *deus* in Chinese while the combination of the two Chinese characters has no meaning in Chinese semantics. Actually, before de Poirot's translation, "*Dousi*" had been largely discarded by most Catholic translators—the favored translation was at that time "*Tianzhu*" 天主 (heavenly Lord),[37] but de Poirot was willing to use the disfavored "*dousi*." A similar example is the transliteration of "*Verbum*" (John 1:1) into "*wuerpeng* 物耳朋,"[38] which may confuse an ancient Chinese with its obscure meaning in the Chinese semantic domain. To clarify potential confusion on the part of readers, de Poirot explains such unusual words as "*dousi*" and "*wuerpeng*" in the annotations—in all, these annotations account for approximately 20 percent of the full contents and serve to bridge the source culture as embodied by the text and the targeted cultural context.[39] In this way, de Poirot tries to balance the need to follow the original meaning of the Bible and attain proper localization.

A combined usage of both strategies of foreignization and domestication in his version, which makes the language (or rather "languages") in de Poirot's version a hybridity of transliterated terms, Mandarin Chinese, dialect of North China, and classical Chinese expressions, sometimes with Latinized grammar. In other words, de Poirot's translation features a rather experimental style. Its language is a hybrid, an immature and translational form of vernacular Chinese writing, born at an early stage when two cultures from different origins encountered each other. Indeed, de Poirot's version bears the mark of transcultural communications. His efforts helped expand the expressive and stylistic range of vernacular Chinese, which facilitates the Chinese language's stylistic transformation, a change from classical into vernacular in the long run.

Chinese written language was undergoing a drastic transformation around the beginning of the twentieth century. Viewed against this cultural background, de Poirot's use of vernacular Chinese in his translation of the Bible seems a unique but wise choice. Although not allowed to be published, the manuscripts of de Poirot's version were still accessible to several later translators of the Bible. Its influence could be found in later Chinese biblical translations, in particular Morrison's Bible and the Studium Biblicum version.

Influence upon Morrison's Version

Unlike the Catholic missionaries, the first priority of Protestant missionaries to China was to translate the Bible. When Robert Morrison, the first Protestant missionary, arrived in China in 1807, mastering the Chinese language and translating the Bible immediately became his primary task. Shortly after his arrival, he initiated his biblical translation. By the end of the year 1813, he finished the NT translation and had it printed, claiming it was a version in the "middle style"[40] of Chinese; in 1822, he finished the translation of the OT, and it was in 1823 that the whole translated Bible was published in China.

Morrison had been able to make a copy of an earlier Chinese version of the NT by Jean Basset at the British Museum before he set out to China, which turned out to be a practical aid to his own translation project. As scholars pointed out, Morrison's rendition of the NT was based on Basset's version.[41] Besides Basset's version, however, Morrison also had consulted other texts from the Roman Catholic Church to support his translation. In a letter from Morrison to the British and Foreign Bible Society (BFBS) from Canton on June 8, 1816, he wrote that:

> an Italian clergyman of the Romish Church, and agent for the missionaries in Pekin, has liberally favored me with a translation of the Gospels, with notes, in MS. by a missionary still living at Pekin. His translation is in the colloquial style.[42]

This manuscript in question, according to Luo Xurong 羅旭榮, was part of de Poirot's version:[43] a point regarded "highly probable" by scholars like Jost Oliver Zetzsche.[44] Indeed, textual details in Morrison's record—a missionary "at Pekin" and a biblical translation "with notes" and "in colloquial style"—lead to the assumption that Morrison probably came across a manuscript of part of de Poirot's manuscript. Although de Poirot died at the end of 1813, a fact at variance with Morrison's record of a missionary "still living at Pekin," it might take a long time for the Catholic missionaries in Macau to know of de Poirot's death, which was announced in a letter by Lamiot in 1815.[45] As Christian missions were forbidden on the whole during that time, the correspondence between Beijing and Canton or Macau (where the "Italian clergyman"[46] mentioned by Morrison possibly resided) could be greatly belated.

Morrison's NT translation was first published in 1813, three years before he wrote the above letter about having obtained the "translation of Gospels" by a missionary in Beijing; and his complete translation, including both OT and NT, was published in 1823. It is to be noted that Morrison proceeded to publish a revised version in the year 1826. Interestingly, a textual comparison between the four Gospels from his original 1823 version and the counterpart in his 1826 version reveals certain unmistakable differences that may be ascribed to de Poirot's influence.

In his 1823 version, for instance, Morrison translated the text "*et procidentes adoraverunt eum et apertis thesauris suis obtulerunt ei munera aurum tus et murram*" ("and they knelt down and paid him homage. Then, opening their treasure chests, they offered him gifts of gold, frankincense, and myrrh," Matthew 2:11, NRSV) as follows:

> *Gu yideng fufu baizhi, you kaile he ji xianzhi yi jin yi xiangshui yi xiangyou ye.* 故伊等俯伏拜之，又開了盒即獻之以金以香水以香油也.[47]

While in his 1826 version, Morrison translated it as:

> *Gu yideng fufu baizhi, you kaile he ji xianzhi yi jin yi ruxiang yi moyao ye.* 故伊等俯伏拜之，又開了盒即獻之以金以乳香以沒藥也.[48]

The two specific revisions from "*xiangshu* 香水" to "*ruxiang* 乳香" and from "*xiangyou* 香油" to "*moyao* 沒藥" both coincide with de Poirot's translation:

> *Guitaqian koubai, kai shoubao de xia. Xian liwu: huangjin, ruxiang, moyao.*
> 跪他前叩拜，開收寶的匣。獻禮物：黃金、乳香、沒藥.[49]

Here, both Morrison's 1826 version and de Poirot's version adopt "*ruxiang* 乳香" and "*moyao* 沒藥" as the respective counterparts of "*tūs*" and "*murram*" from the Bible. In the Chinese language, "*ruxiang*" and "*moyao*" refer to two types of natural resins with a special aroma, introduced into China from abroad and later utilized in traditional Chinese medicine. Specifically, "*moyao*" is the Chinese transliteration of the Latin word "*murram/murra*". As compared with the "*xiangshui*" and "*xiangyou*" in the 1823 version (the two words are general terms for balm or fragrant oil in Chinese), "*ruxiang*" and "*moyao*" are doubtless better translations. It is likely that these revisions in Morrison's 1826 version can be attributed to the "translation of the Gospels" by "a missionary still living at Pekin," as he had mentioned in the 1816 letter to BFBS—which, as deduced from previous observations, is probably de Poirot's version. Apparently, it is also possible that Morrison revised his translation under the influence of Basset's translation—*Ji fudi chaobai, qiji xianli: huangjin, ruxiang, moyao* 即伏地朝拜，啟笈獻禮：黃金、乳香、沒藥[50]—but this possibility can be minimized by the fact that Robert Morrison had obtained Jean Basset's version much before his original 1813 translation of the New Testament.

There are, of course, other similarly revealing coincidences between Morrison's 1826 translation and de Poirot's translation. Take their respective translations of Matthew 24:3 as another example: Morrison translated in his 1823 version the Latin text "*et quod signum adventus tui et consummationis saeculi*" ("and what will be the sign of your coming and of the end of the age?") as:

> *You er lin yu shizhimo jiang you hehao ye.*
> 又爾臨與世之末將有何號也.[51]

While in his 1826 version, Morrison translated it as:

> *You er lin yu shizhimo jiang you hezhao ye.*
> 又爾臨與世之末將有何兆也.[52]

Here Morrsion revised "*hehao* 何號" into "*hezhao* 何兆" in his 1826 version, which coincides with de Poirot's translation:

> *Bing shijie qiong, ni you zailai, xian you hezhao?*
> 並世界窮，你有再來，現有何兆?[53]

As compared with "*hehao*," "*hezhao*" is a more proper rendering of "*signum*," because the Chinese word "*zhao* 兆" denotes a sign or foreboding of a certain event, while the word "*hao* 號" usually refers to an order or a sound accompanying an occurrence.

While it remains uncertain if parts of de Poirot's Chinese version of the Bible were included in the "several Roman Catholic works" listed by Morrison as references for his biblical translation,[54] a comparison of the versions translated by de Poirot and Morrison reveals another notable similarity in their use of the biblical term "*paradisus*."

"*Paradisus*," the original residence of Adam and Eve, was translated into "*jile zhiyuan* 極樂之園"[55] (the garden of bliss) by Michele Ruggieri in his Chinese Catechism, and "*fogou* 佛國"[56] (the Buddhist country) in Ruggieri and Ricci's *Dicionário Português-Chinês*. However, Ruggieri and Ricci's translations did not circulate to the public: the most popular translation of "*paradisus*" during the Ming and early Qing dynasties was "*ditang* 地堂"[57] (earthly paradise). In his translation, de Poirot retained the use of "*ditang*," but also innovatively translated "*paradisus*" into a new Chinese Christian term, "*leyuan* 樂園" (paradise)[58]—a rare word to be seen in classical Chinese writings, though it does exist in a few Buddhist Scriptures. Coincidentally, "leyuan" as the translation of "paradisus" also is found in Morrison's version.[59] Besides, Morrison's *A Dictionary of the Chinese Language*, which was published from 1815 to 1823, also took "*leyuan*" as a Chinese equivalent of "paradise."[60]

Intriguingly, this use of "*leyuan*" as Chinese translation of "*paradisus*," shared by de Poirot and Morrison, was later followed by a notable third missionary and gradually solidified into quite a textual convention. In 1839, German Lutheran missionary Karl Friedrich August Gützlaff (1803–1851) published his Chinese version of the NT and "*leyuan*" was found in it.[61] Gützlaff's version, translated in a style considered the most accessible to Chinese common readers, was later used in the Taiping Heavenly Kingdom. Three years before that, in 1836, Gützlaff was preparing to produce a revised version of Morrison's Bible with Medhurst (1796–1859) and John Morrison (1814–1843). Their proposal was rejected by BFBS, but it was clear that Gützlaff was conversant with Morrison's version.[62] Gützlaff's use of "*leyuan*" was probably an influence of the Morrison version.[63] Yet the influence also might have come from de Poirot's version. In 1849, Gützlaff planned to revise and publish de Poirot's Manchu version of the OT, and the BFBS tried to obtain a copy on his behalf; unfortunately, this plan finally was abandoned due to Gützlaff's death in 1851.[64] It would not be a random guess to assume that Gützlaff also might have read de Poiort's Chinese Bible.

When "*leyuan*" as "*paradisus*" was adopted by the Studium Biblicum version, it ultimately established itself as the norm in Chinese Catholicism, unlike "*yidianyuan* 伊甸園" (the garden of Eden), its Protestant counterpart in China authorized by the Chinese Union Version. Along with its widespread circulation, the word "*leyuan*" has metamorphosed from a Christian term into an everyday word in modern Chinese writing, a development that owes much to de Poirot's translation.

Historical record, together with textual specifics in their translations, suggests a lurking link between de Poirot and Morrison. Morrison initiated his missionary work in China in 1807, six years before de Poirot, the last survivor of all the former Jesuits in inland China, died in Beijing and unfortunately missed the restoration of the Society of Jesus in 1814. Through some "Italian clergyman," Morrison obtained de Poirot's translation of the Bible, and whether consciously or unwittingly, made the latter a textual influence in his own translation.

Viewed against a broader historical context, it has been established previously in academia that the earliest Protestant translations of the Bible—namely, Morrison's version and Marshman's version—owe much to the Catholic Basset's NT.[65] Now, another link between de Poirot and Morrison has also emerged, standing as an invitation to further explore the complex relationship between Catholic mission and Protestant mission in China.

Influence Upon Studium Biblicum Version

The Studium Biblicum version, published in 1968, is the first complete Chinese translation of the Catholic Bible and has remained the predominant version used by Chinese Catholics until today. Before the Studium Biblicum version, however, de Poirot's Chinese Bible had been recognized in academia as a most inclusive version of the Chinese Catholic Bible. A comparative view of these two versions leads to clear indications of their intimate associations.

A collective project in its final completed form, the Studium Biblicum version was originally initiated as a personal project: Gabriele Allegra (1907–1976), an Italian Franciscan friar, started the translation work in as early as 1935. Allegra's personal determination to translate the Bible into Chinese could be traced back to his encounter in Italy, in 1929, with Gao Siqian 高思謙 (John Baptist Se chien Kao, 1906–1983), a Franciscan priest from China, when Allegra learned from Gao about the many Chinese versions of the Bible, including the Union Version as the predominant version among Chinese Protestants.[66]

In 1931, Allegra arrived in China and started his missionary works in Hunan province; and in 1935, he travelled to Beijing to start his translation project. His first step in Beijing turned out to be a visit to Beitang, introduced by Mario Zanin (1890–1958); there, Allegra encountered, and cherished, de Poirot's version.[67] With an expense of around six hundred dollars, aided by a priest named Theo Ruehl, Allegra photographed the entire manuscript in a month. Back in Hunan province, Allegra replicated the photographed manuscript of de Poirot's version, with a cloth-cover design, and divided it into thirty books to be displayed in his library at Huangshawan.[68] This version was to become an influence for Allegra, and perhaps one greater than the influence from Basset's version, which Allegra obtained from the British Museum with the aid of Ying Qianli 英千里 (1900–1969).[69]

For the next thirty years, Allegra worked closely with his team of Chinese Franciscan friars, borrowing extensively from previous versions of the Bible,[70] and finally accomplished the complete Studium Biblicum version. As a most important reference for the Studium Biblicum version, a copy of de Poirot's version is still kept by the

Studium Biblicum Franciscanum (Hong Kong) in the form of over three hundred photographed pages.

A comparative reading of de Poirot's version and the Studium Biblicum version will immediately reveal a series of resemblances in translation. These similarities range from titles of the books in the Bible to religious terms and specific names of people and places.

Comparing titles of the biblical books in these two versions, readers can easily see that the Studium Biblicum version borrows from de Poirot's version. Both, for instance, use "*Shengyong* 聖詠" as the Chinese equivalent of "*Psalmi*/Psalms." In particular, the title "*Dawei Shengyong Ji* 達味聖詠集" (*Psalms of David*) is mentioned as a "conventional" name in the "Introduction to Psalms" of the Studium Biblicum version.[71] In fact, translating the *Psalms of David* as "*Dawei Shengyong* 達味聖詠" was probably a unique practice of de Poirot's version. Before de Poirot, the most conventional translation of "Psalms" in Chinese had been "*Shengshi* 聖詩" (i.e. "sacred poems"), which could be found in the works of Jesuits such as Aleni, Alfonso Vagnoni (1566–1640), and Martino Martini (1614–1661). That is to say, the Studium Biblicum version followed de Poirot's version in its translation of the "Psalms."

This preference for de Poirot's Version also is evident in the names adopted by the Studium Biblicum version, especially as revealed in the titles of the biblical books. *Tobias*, for instance, is translated as "*Duobiya Jing* 多俾亞經" in de Poirot's version and "*Duobiya Zhuan* 多俾亞傳" in the Studium Biblicum version; similarly, *Isaias* is translated respectively as "*Sheng Yisayiya Xianzhi Jing* 聖依撒依亞先知經" in de Poirot's version and "*Yisayiya* 依撒依亞" in the Studium Biblicum version. Such similarities also appear in the two translated versions of the NT: Matthew, Luke, and John are translated as "*Madou* 瑪竇," "*Lujia* 路加," "*Ruowang* 若望" exactly in both versions; and Mark is translated as "*Ma'ergu* 瑪爾谷" in de Poirot's version and "*Ma'ergu* 馬爾谷" in the Studium Biblicum version, with only a trivial difference in Chinese character writing.

Aside from titles of biblical books and names of important figures, the Studium Biblicum version also followed de Poirot's translation of some significant biblical terms and thoughts. Unique inventions coined by de Poirot, such as the above-mentioned "*leyuan* 樂園," and the translation of "*oculum pro oculo, dentem pro dente*" (Matt 5:38) as "*yiyanhuanyan, yiyahuanya* 以眼還眼，以牙還牙" ("an eye for an eye and a tooth for a tooth"),[72] also are adopted in the Studium Biblicum—and have already found their way into the everyday modern Chinese language. Even some idiosyncrasies of de Poirot's translation are retained. For instance, the Studium Biblicum version followed de Poirot's translation of "*lignum scientiae boni et mali*" ("the tree of the knowledge of good and evil") as "*zhi shan'e shu* 知善惡樹":[73] this noun phrase comprises a construction with a single-character verb and parallel objects, which is reminiscent of classical Chinese but quite an oddity for vernacular Chinese. This list of similarities in specifics between the two versions also includes, but is not limited to, the translation of "Satan" as "*sadan* 撒殫/撒旦." De Poirot followed earlier Jesuits in using "*sadan* 撒殫," which was adopted by the Studium Biblicum; he also innovatively used "*sadan* 撒旦," which has become a common word today.[74] Undoubtedly, de Poirot's Chinese Bible has exerted influence upon the Studium Biblicum and has contributed to the lexicon of modern Chinese vernacular.

Conclusion

Although de Poirot's version was not published in his lifetime and remained obscure for many years, it is historically the very first attempt to systematically translate the Bible into vernacular Chinese and features prominently among Chinese translations of the Bible. Viewed as an integral part of the tradition of Chinese translations of the Bible, de Poirot's version incorporated in itself traces of previous translations and etched diverse but unmistakable types of impressions onto later versions. Certain expressions from previous versions—to name a few, Dias Jr.'s *Shengjing Zhijie*, Aleni's *Tianzhu Jiangsheng Yanxing Jilüe*, and Basset's version—are directly preserved in de Poirot's version.[75]

As a historical fact, some Chinese versions of the Bible that appeared later than de Poirot's version—including Morrison's version, the Studium Biblicum version—were all one way or another shaped under its influence. Take Chinese translations of biblical texts since the late Ming Dynasty as a continuous course, de Poirot's version serves as a significant link bridging previous and later translations. And when viewed against the broad social-historical background, the ramifications of the cultural value of de Poirot's Bible may even extend from biblical translation and exegesis into diverse areas of humanities research.

Notes

1. Nicolas Standaert, *Handbook of Christianity in China* (Leiden, Boston, and Cologne: Brill, 2001), 1:620–624.
2. Louis Pfister, *Notices Biographiques et Bibliographiques sur les Jésuites de L'ancienne Mission de Chine, 1552–1773* (San Francisco: Chinese Materials Center, 1935), 966.
3. First Historical Archives of China [in Chinese], *Qing Zhongqianqi Xiyang Tianzhujiao Zaihua Huodong Dang'an Shiliao* 清中前期西洋天主教在華活動檔案史料 (Beijing: Zhonghua Book Company, 2003), 480.
4. Ibid. 480.
5. Josephe Dehergne榮振華, *Shiliu-Ershi Shiji Ruhua Tianzhujiao Chuanjiaoshi Liezhuan* [in Chinese] *16–20* 世紀入華天主教傳教士列傳, tr. Geng Sheng 耿昇 (Guilin: Guangxi University Press, 2010), 537.
6. Pfister, *Notices*, 969–970.
7. George Macartney, *An Embassy to China: Being the Journal Kept by Lord Macartney During His Embassy to the Emperor Chien-lung (1793–1794)* (London: Longmans, 1962), 92, 355, and 372. See also Pierre-Henri Durand 戴廷傑, "Jianting Zeming: Maga'erni Shihua Zaita" [in Chinese] 兼聽則明—馬戛爾尼使華再探 (De la confrontation naît la lumière: Nouvelles considérations sur l'ambassade Macartney), in *Yingshi Maga'erni Fanghua Dang'an Shiliao Huibian* 英使馬嘎爾尼訪華檔案史料, tr. Xu Minglong 許明龍, ed. First Historical Archives of China 中國第一歷史檔案館 (Beijing: China International Culture Press, 1996), 137.
8. Pfister, *Notices*, 969.

9. N. Kowalsky, "Die Sacra Congregatio 'de Propaganda Fida' und die Übersetzung der Hl. Schrift," in *Die Heilige schrift in den katholischen Missionen*, ed. J. Becknann (Schöneck-Beckenried: Neue Zeitschrift für Missiionswissenschaft, 1966), 31–32. See also Nicolas Standaert, "The Bible in Early Seventeenth-Century China," in *Bible in Modern China: The Literary and Intellectual Impact*, ed. Irene Eber et al. (Sankt Augustin: Monumenta Serica Monograph Series 43, Institut Monumenta Serica, 1999), 38.
10. Kowalsky, "Die Sacra Congregatio," 31–32.
11. See in bibliotheca Zi-ka-wei, Shanghai Library, no. 90908B–90924B, 92091B–92092B, 93600B–93605B, 93609B–93616B. See also in Louis Antoine de Poirot 賀清泰, "Guxin Shengjing" 古新聖經, in *Xujiahui Cang Mingqing Tianzhujiao Wenxian Xubian* [in Chinese] 徐家匯藏明清天主教文獻續編, ed. Nicolas standert, Ad Dudink, and Wang Renfang, vols. 28–34 (Taipei Ricci Institute, 2013); Louis Antoine de Poirot, *Guxin Shengjing Cangao* [in Chinese] 古新聖經殘稿, ed. Li Sher-shiueh 李奭學 and Zheng Haijuan 鄭海娟 (Beijing: Zhonghua Book Company, 2014).
12. The four volumes are [in Chinese]: (1) Sheng Baolu yu Luoma jiaoyou de shuzha 聖保祿諭羅馬教友的書札 (including Romans, and 1&2 Corinthians); (2) Sheng Baolu shuzha 聖保祿書札 (including Galatians, Ephesians, Philippians, Colossians, and 1&2 Thessalonians); (3) Sheng Baolu yu Dimode'a deng shu 聖保祿諭第莫得阿等書 (including 1&2 Timothy, Titus, Philemon, Hebrews, James, 1&2 Peter, and Jude); (4) Sheng Ruowang Mozhao Jing 聖若望默照經 (including 1, 2 & 3 John, and Revelation). All combined under the title "*Sheng Baolu Yu Luoma Jiaoyou de Shuzha*" 聖保祿諭羅馬教友的書札. See in National Library of China, no.138594. Aside from these four, there is another separate fragmental volume under the title "*Shengjing* 聖經," no. 138843.
13. See in Fusinian library, Academia Sinica, no. 109R.
14. See in Louis Antoine de Poirot, *Guxin Shengjing Cangao Waierzhong: Beitangben Yu Manhan Hebiben* [in Japanese and Chinese] 古新聖經殘稿外二種：北堂本與滿漢合璧本, ed. Li Sher-shiueh 李奭學 and Uchida Keiichi 內田慶市 (Osaka: Kansai University Press, 2018).
15. See in De Poirot, *Guxin Shengjing Cangao Waierzhong*. As for relevant researches on this Manchu version, see Hartmut Walravens, "Christliche Literatur in Mandschurischer Sprache," *China heute* 2 (2016): 110–120; Erling Mende, "Problems in Translating the Bible into Manchu: Observations on Louis Poirot's Old Testament," in *Sowing the Word: The Cultural Impact of the Bible and Foreign Bible Society, 1804–2004*, ed. Stephen Batalder, Kathleen Camn, and John Dean (Sheffield: Sheffield Phoenix Press, 2004), 154; Kim Dongso 金東昭, "The First Translator of the Bible into the Chinese and Manchu Languages, P. Louis de Poirot, S.J." [in Chinese] 最初中國語滿洲語聖書譯成者賀清泰神父, *Altai Hakpo* 13 (2003): 31.
16. Liam Brockey, *Journey to the East: The Jesuit Mission to China (1579–1724)* (Cambridge: Belknap Press of Harvard University Press, 2007), 265–268.
17. Zhu Weizheng 朱維錚, "Wanming Wangxue Yu Limadou Ruhua" 晚明王學與利瑪竇入華 [in Chinese], *Chinese Culture* 中國文化 21 (2004): 46–47.
18. Chen Yuan 陳垣, *The Complete Works of Chen Yuan* [in Chinese] 陳垣全集 (Hefei: Anhui University Press, 2009), 3:493.
19. This permission of Paul V (1615), a "missed opportunity" as Standaert called it, was soon replaced by the more restrictive policy towards biblical translation of the *Propaganda Fide*. See Standaert, "The Bible in Early Seventeenth-Century China," 36–38.

20. For the relevant edicts, see First Historical Archives, *Qing Zhongqianqi*, 104–105, 377, 403, 433–436, 545–546, 852–855, 925.
21. For the case of Adeodato di Sant' Agostino 德天賜, see First Historical Archives, *Qing Zhongqianqi*, 838. According to the Edict "Xiyang Shiwu Zhangcheng" 西洋事務章程 (Regulations on Foreign Affairs) announced after the case on May 16, 1805, the missionaries were not allowed to contact with Chinese people, and their range of activities were strictly limited to the churches and local authorities. See First Historical Archives, *Qing Zhongqianqi*, 930.
22. Standaert, *Handbook*, 390.
23. Fang Hao 方豪, *Biographical Accounts of Chinese Catholics* [in Chinese] 中國天主教史人物傳 (Beijing: Zhonghua Book Company, 1988), 2:310.
24. Ibid. 311.
25. Joseph de Moyriac de Mailla 馮秉正and Thomas Yang 楊多默, "Shengshi Churao" 盛世芻蕘 [in Chinese], in *Tianzhujiao Dongchuan Wenxian Xubian* 天主教東傳文獻續編, ed. Wu Xiangxiang 吳相湘 (Taipei: Student Book Company, 1966), 3:1423.
26. Ibid. 1424.
27. De Poirot, *Guxin Shengjing Cangao*, 3.
28. Ibid. 1.
29. Ibid. 876.
30. Ibid. 339.
31. Ibid. 360.
32. For research on de Poirot's localized translation, see also Song Gang 宋剛, "Between Original Meaning and Vernacular Language" [in Chinese] '本意'與 '土語' 之間：清代耶穌會士賀清泰的《聖經》漢譯及詮釋, *International Sinology* 國際漢學 5 (2015): 23–49.
33. De Poirot, *Guxin Shengjing Cangao*, 2878.
34. Ibid. 2745.
35. Ibid. 65, 69.
36. Ibid. 2924.
37. Brockey, *Journey*, 85–89.
38. De Poirot, *Guxin Shengjing Cangao*, 2903. For the explanation of "*dousi*" and "*wuerpeng*," see De Poirot, *Guxin Shengjing Cangao*, 5, 2906.
39. See Li Sher-shiueh, "Tantian Shuodi Lun Shenren: Cong Guxin Shengjing Huacheng Zhijing Qian Erpian Kan He Qingtai de Jiejingxue" [in Chinese] 談天說地論神人—從《古新聖經·化成之經》前二篇看賀清泰的解經學, in *Mingqing Xixue Liulun* 明清西學六論 (Hangzhou: Zhejiang University Press, 2016), 249–278. Song Gang, "Between Original Meaning and Vernacular Language," 43–48. Zheng Haijuan, "Xinchuan yu Xinquan: Guxin Shengjing de Jiejing Zhidao" [in Chinese] 薪傳與新詮：《古新聖經》的解經之道 (Annotating the Bible in Mid-Qing China: de Poirot's Efforts), in *Cowrie: Journal of Comparative Literature and Comparative Culture* (Shanghai: Fudan University Press, 2014), 11:55–84.
40. William Milne, *In a Retrospect of the First Ten Years of the Protestant Mission to China* (Malacca: the Anglo-Chinese Press, 1820), 89–90.
41. Jost Oliver Zetzsche, *The Bible in China: The History of the Union Version or The Culmination of Protestant Missionary Bible Translation in China* (Sankt Augustin: Monumenta Serica Institute, 1999), 35.

42. Robert Morrison, "Letter to the British and Foreign Bible Society, June 8, 1816," in *The Thirteenth Report of the British and Foreign Bible Society* (London: Tilling and Hughes, Grossnor-row, Chelsen, 1817), 15. Cited from Zetzsche, *The Bible in China*, 37.
43. Luo Xurong 羅旭榮, "'Shengjing' zai Zhongguo de Yiben" [in Chinese] '聖經' 在中國的譯本, *Nanjing Theological Review* 11 (1988): 36–38, 48–52.
44. Zetzsche, *The Bible in China*, 37.
45. Pfister, *Notices*, 968.
46. This "Italian clergyman" was probably one of the procurators of the *propaganda fide* residing at Macau, mostly Italians, who served as agents for the missionaries in China by sending money and solving problems. About the role of procurators, see Standaert, *Handbook*, 353–354.
47. Morrison, "Sheng Madou Chuan Fuyinshu" [in Chinese] 聖瑪竇傳福音書, in *Shentian Shengshu* 神天聖書 (Malacca: The Anglo-Chinese Press, 1823), 3b.
48. Robert Morrison, "Sheng Madou Chuan Fuyinshu" [in Chinese] 聖瑪竇傳福音書, in *Wodeng Jiushizhu Yesu Xinyizhaoshu* 我等救世主耶穌新遺詔書 (Malacca: The Anglo-Chinese Press, 1826), 3b.
49. De Poirot, *Guxin Shengjing Cangao*, 2643.
50. See in Morrison's copy of Jean Basset's version, http://bible.fhl.net/gbdoc/ob/nob.html?book=76, 12a.
51. Morrison, "Sheng Madou Chuan Fuyinshu," *in Shentian*, 55a.
52. Ibid. 55b.
53. De Poirot, *Guxin Shengjing Cangao*, 2734.
54. Marshall Broomhall, *Robert Morrison: A Master-Builder* (London: Student Christian Movement, 1927), 123.
55. Michele Ruggieri 羅明堅, "Tianzhu Shilu" [in Chinese] 天主實錄, in *Yesuhui Luoma Danganguan Mingqing Tianzhujiao Wenxian* 耶穌會羅馬檔案明清天主教文獻, ed. Nicolas Standaert and Ad Dudink (Taipei institute of Matteo Ricci, 2002), 1:31.
56. Michele Ruggieri and Matteo Ricci, *Dicionário Português-Chinês*, ed. John W. Witek, s.j., et al. (Lisbon and San Francisco: University of San Francisco, 2001), 127.
57. Interestingly, when Dias Jr., Gaspar Ferreira (1571–1649), and João Monteiro (1602–1648) revised Ruggieri's "*Tianzhu Shilu*" and had it published during 1637–1641, they deliberately replaced Ruggieri's translation of "*paradisus*" with the more favored translation "*ditang* 地堂." See Michele Ruggieri 羅明堅, "Tianzhu Shengjiao Shilu" [in Chinese] 天主聖教實錄, in *Tianzhujiao Dongchuan Wenxian Xubian*, ed. Wu Xiangxiang (Taipei: Student Book Company, 1966), 2:786.
58. De Poirot, *Guxin Shengjing Cangao*, 9, 10, 11, 15, et passim.
59. In his Chinese Bible, Morrison also translated the same word into "*xidan zhi yuan* 希但之園" (Gen 2:8) or "*baladishi* 巴拉底士" (Luke 23:44), varying according to the context. For the usage of "*leyuan*," see Morrison, "Ruohan Xianshi Shu" [in Chinese] 若翰現示書, in *Shentian*, 64a–64b.
60. Robert Morrison, *A Dictionary of the Chinese Language* (Macau: East India Company's Press, 1822), 6:309.
61. Karl Friedrich August Gützlaff, *Jiushizhu Xinyizhaoshu* [in Chinese] 救世主耶穌新遺詔書 (Singapore: American Mission Press, 1839), 3:43. Gützlaff introduced John Milton to the Chinese readers in his magazine and used "*leyuan*" to describe the lost paradise in Milton's poem. See Gützlaff, "Shi" [in Chinese] 詩, in *Dongxiyang Kao Meiyue Tongji*

Zhuan 東西洋考每月統計傳, ed. Aihanzhe 愛漢者 (Beijing: Zhonghua Book Company, 1997), 195.
62. Zetzsche, *The Bible in China*, 62–66.
63. Huang Heqing seems to generally support this opinion and thinks Gützlaff took the translation of "*leyuan*" from Morrison's dictionary. See Huang Heqing 黃河清, "Malixun Cidian Zhong de Xin Ciyu" [in Chinese] 馬禮遜辭典中的新詞語, in *Wakumon* 或問 15 (2008): 18.
64. Mende, "Problems in Translating the Bible into Manchu," 156.
65. Zetzsche, *The Bible in China*, 35, 49–51. Zhao Xiaoyang 趙曉陽, "Erma Yiben yu Bairisheng Yiben Guanxi Kaobian" [in Chinese] 二馬譯本餘白日陞聖經譯本關係考辨, *Modern Chinese History Studies* 近代史研究 4 (2009): 41–59.
66. Gabriele Allegra, *Lei Yongming Shenfu Huiyilu* [in Chinese] 雷永明神父回憶錄 (*Memoirs of Gabriele Maria Allegra*), tr. Han Chengliang 韓承良 (Hong Kong: Studium Biblicum OFM, 2001), 52.
67. Allegra, *Lei Yongming*, 92.
68. Ibid. 92–93.
69. The copy of Basset's version made by Ying is still kept today by the Studium Biblicum Hong Kong.
70. Arnulf Camps, "Father Gabriele M. Allegra, O.F.M. (1907–1976) and the *Studium Biblicum Franciscanum*: The First Complete Chinese Catholic Translation of the Bible," in *Bible in Modern China*, 55–76.
71. Studium Biblicum Franciscanum, "Introduction to Psalms" [in Chinese] 聖詠集引言, in *the Bible* 聖經 (Hong Kong: Studium Biblicum Franciscanum, 1976), 837.
72. Foley have established "*yiyanhuanyan, yiyahuanya*" a personal invention of de Poirot. See Toshikazu S. Foley, "Four-Character Set Phrases: A Study of Their Use in the Catholic and Eastern-Orthodox Version of the Chinese New Testament," *Hong Kong Journal of Catholic Studies* 2 (2001): 80. "*Yiyanhuanyan, yiyahuanya*" see in de Poirot, *Guxin Shengjing Cangao*, 2654.
73. De Poirot, *Guxin Shengjing Cangao*, 12.
74. Ibid. 2998.
75. About the influences of earlier Chinese biblical texts upon de Poirot's version, see Yu Yating, "Inheritance between *Shengjing Zhijie*, and *Guxin Shengjing*—Mainly a Part of the Matthew Gospels," *Journal of East Asian Cultural Interaction Studies* 9 (2016): 83–94; Yu Yating, "Chinese Translation of the Four Gospels—Inheritance between *Tianzhu Jiangsheng Yanxing Jilüe*, and *Guxin Shengjing*," *Journal of East Asian Cultural Interaction Studies* 10 (2017): 153–162. Zheng Haijuan, "Wenben Zhi Wang: *Guxin Shengjing* yu Qianhou Dai Shengjing Hanyiben Zhi Guanxi [in Chinese] 文本之網:《古新聖經》與前後代《聖經》漢譯本之關係," *Tsing Hua Journal of Chinese Literature* 11 (2014): 261–298.

Primary Sources

Chen, Yuan 陳垣. *The Complete Works of Chen Yuan* [in Chinese] 陳垣全集, vol. 2. Hefei: Anhui University Press, 2009.

De Poirot, Louis Antoine 賀清泰. *Guxin Shengjing Cangao* [in Chinese] 古新聖經殘稿. Ed. Li Sher-shiueh 李奭學 and Zheng Haijuan 鄭海娟. Beijing: Zhonghua Book Company, 2014.

De Poirot, Louis Antoine. *Guxin Shengjing Cangao Waierzhong: Beitangben Yu Manhan Hebiben* [in Japanese and Chinese] 古新聖經殘稿外二種: 北堂本與滿漢合璧本. Ed. Li Sher-shiueh 李奭學 and Uchida Keiichi 內田慶市. Osaka: Kansai University Press, 2018.

First Historical Archives of China. *Qing Zhongqianqi Xiyang Tianzhujiao Zaihua Huodong Dang'an Shiliao* [in Chinese] 清中前期西洋天主教在華活動檔案史料. Beijing: Zhonghua Book Company, 2003.

Gützlaff, Karl Friedrich August. *Jiushizhu Yesu Xinyizhaoshu* [in Chinese] 救世主耶穌新遺詔書, vol. 3. Singapore: American Mission Press, 1839.

Gützlaff, Karl Friedrich August. "Shi" [in Chinese] 詩. In *Dongxiyang Kao Meiyue Tongji Zhuan* 東西洋考每月統計傳. Edited by Aihanzhe 愛漢者, 195. Beijing: Zhonghua Book Company, 1997.

Miline, William 米憐. *In a Retrospect of the First Ten Years of the Protestant Mission to China.* Malacca: The Anglo-Chinese Press, 1820.

Morrison, Robert 馬禮遜. *A Dictionary of the Chinese Language*, vol. 6. Macau: East India Company's Press, 1822.

Morrison, Robert. *Shentian Shengshu* [in Chinese] 神天聖書. Malacca: The Anglo-Chinese Press, 1823.

Morrison, Robert. *Wodeng Jiushizhu Yesu Xinyizhaoshu* [in Chinese] 我等救世主耶穌新遺詔書. Malacca: The Anglo-Chinese Press, 1826.

CHAPTER 7

DEVELOPMENT OF CHINESE DIALECT BIBLES

YOU RUJIE

Introduction

FROM the Yongzheng period (1723–1735) of the Qing dynasty to the First Opium War (1840–1842), Christian mission was banned by Chinese law, but the government permitted Christian mission again after the War. Since then, a large number of Western missionaries rushed into China; in the early years, they could stay only in coastline cities, establish churches, and hold religious services in the "treaty ports," and mission work was still prohibited inland. After 1858, when the Tianjin Treaty was signed by the United States, England, France, and China, Western missionaries were allowed to hold religious services in all of China, they then penetrated into the inland rapidly. During the peak period, there were about two thousand missionaries living and working in China.

People in China, then and now, both in urban and rural areas, speak Chinese and dialects—besides the languages of the ethnic minorities. Thus, there were two basic groups of Western missionaries, Catholic and Protestant; the latter was fond of learning dialects and holding religious services in local dialects as their ideal way of disseminating the gospel among the common people. Thus, they were eager to do a linguistic survey and compile dialect dictionaries and textbooks. Their contribution to the translation of the Chinese dialects Bible and Chinese dialectology has its concentrated efforts in the years between the 1840s and the 1940s.

Chinese Language and Dialect Bible Versions

Chinese dialect Bibles are different in pronunciation, words, syntax, and characters from the Chinese Bible. Various Bible versions in China can be classified into five categories according to languages: the classical literary version (high *wenli* 深文理); the simpler literary version (easy *wenli* 淺文理); the Mandarin version; the dialects version; the national language version. The national language Bible published in 1919 was the distinguished Union Version 和合本. The Mandarin versions could be re-classified into Peking Mandarin, Nanjing Mandarin, Hankou Mandarin, and so on.

There are many kinds of Chinese dialects, and they are so different that some of them are not even intelligible to each other; in addition, oral language is different from written language. So, it is necessary to use dialects in conducting religious services, especially at a time when the national language was unpopular. Churches often were organized by dialects of Christians, such as one church for Mandarin speakers, and another for Suzhou dialect speakers. Moreover, the literacy rate of the common people was low; since many Christians could not read the classical Chinese or the Mandarin version, it was reasonable to publish dialect Bibles. Statistical Table 7.1 shows the earliest year of publication of the various Chinese Bible versions with different written systems.

Though Chinese has many dialects with a great deal of divergence, the writing system, i.e., Chinese characters with more than three thousand years of history, used by the dialects is identical. This means that people speak different dialects but use basically unified characters that could be read with local accents and understood by the literati. The first Chinese Bible translated by England missionaries J. Marshman 馬士文 and J. Lassas 拉撒 was published in 1822; the other translation by England missionary R. Morrison 馬禮遜 was published in 1823. Both versions were translated into the classical Chinese language, which was the standard written language used widely by the literati and in government documents before the early twentieth century. Meanwhile, Mandarin Chinese, which is the *lingua franca* (common language), is spoken by officials and northern and southwestern Chinese people with different accents locally, and many dialects in southern China have their own unique pronunciation, words, and even grammar. In a period when the Chinese language was evolving, American missionary Josiah T. Doddard 高德 corrected J. Marshman's version and turned it to a simpler form of classical language called plain *wenli*, which was published in 1853.

The first Mandarin version (using more plain Chinese in both grammar and expression) called *paihuawen* 白話文 or *guanhua dupai* 官話土白 was published in 1857 in Shanghai; many Mandarin versions were published one after another during the period between 1872 and 1916. One could ask the question if such a vernacular Mandarin is also a form of a Chinese dialect. In any case, the Presbyterian Mission decided to stop publishing the classical Chinese language Bible at the national conference in 1907 since it was too difficult for the common people to read. While many scholars argued that the

Table 7.1 The Earliest Year of Publication of Chinese Dialect Bibles

	Dialect	Portions	New Testament	Complete Bible
A	Mandarin 官話			
	high *wenli* 深文理	1810	1814	1822
	plain *wenli* 淺文理	1880	1885	1902
	Zhili 直隸	1862	1877	1894
	Peking 北京		1866	
	Jiaodong 膠東	1918		
	Hankou 漢口	1921		
	Nanjing 南京	1854	1857	
	Shandong 山東	1892		
B	Wu 吳 dialects			
	Shanghai	1847	1872	1908 (OT)
	Suzhou	1879	1881	1908 (OT)
	Ningbo	1852	1868	1901 (OT)
	Hangzhou	1890		
	Jinhua	1866		
	Taizhou	1880	1881	1914 (OT)
	Wenzhou	1892	1902	
C	Min 閩 dialects			
	Xiamen	1852	1856	1884 (OT)
	Fuzhou	1852	1856	1888 (OT)
	Shantou	1875	1898	1922
	Chaozhou	1888	1915	
	Xinghua	1892	1900	1912
	Jianyang	1898		
	Shaowu	1891		
	Hainan	1889		
D	Gan 贛 dialects			
	Jianning	1896	1896	
E	Hakka 客家話			
	Hakka	1860	1883	1916
	Wujingfu	1910	1919	
	Tingzhou	1919		
F	Yue 粵 dialects			
	Canton	1862	1873	1894
	Sanjiang	1904		

"writings in the more-plain vernacular movement" 白話文運動 was caused by the May Fourth Movement (1919),[1] yet the Mandarin Bible already had been translated before 1919. I think that the vernacular Bible 官話土白聖經 had not affected the "writings in the more-plain vernacular movement" since educational circles and Christian circles were quite separate at that time. On the contrary, the "writings in the more-plain vernacular movement" and the rise of the national language had a decisive and positive influence on the Chinese Bible, as various dialect versions were substituted gradually by the Union Version (1907 1st edition) and the national language Bible 國語譯本. Currently, only a few churches in Hong Kong and overseas still use the Cantonese Bible.

Generally speaking, portions of the Bible were translated into Chinese dialects first, and then full texts of the Bible followed. There were ten dialects that had complete Bibles translated: Shanghai, Suzhou, Ningbo, Taizhou, Fuzhou, Xiamen, Xinghua (Putian 莆田), Canton, Shantou, and Hakka. The following two had only the complete New Testament (hereafter NT) translated, Jianning and Wenzhou.

Brief History of Chinese Dialect Bibles

Below is a survey of the Bible translated into five major Chinese dialects: Wu, Min, Cantonese, Hakka, and Gan.

1. Wu dialects

Wu dialects are spoken in southern Jiangsu province, most parts of Zhejiang province, and adjacent areas of Fujian and Jiangxi provinces, including Shanghai Suzhou, Ningbo, Hangzhou, Jinhua, Taizhou, and Wenzhou with a combined population of 73.79 million.

The missionary who came to Shanghai first was Walter Henry Medhurst 麥都思 (1796–1857) of Foreign Mission, and the Shanghai dialect of the Gospel of John 約翰書 published in 1847 was translated mainly and finally revised by him. It was the earliest Chinese-script dialect Bible. The Gospel of Matthew, translated by W. C. Milane 小米憐, and the Gospel of Luke, translated by T. McClatchie, were published in 1848. Matthew also was translated by G. Owen and two of his colleagues, published in 1850 in Ningbo and reprinted in 1856. Since then, various portions of the NT were published in succession.[2]

The missionary who came to Ningbo first was D. J. MacGwan 馬高溫 of the Baptist Missionary; in the early years, he did mission hospital work and learned local Chinese. In 1847, he organized a church together with the pastor E. D. Lord 羅爾梯 and his wife; this was the first Baptist church established in East China. Most of the Ningbo dialect Bible was written in romanized script, and the translation work began in 1851. The Gospel of Luke, translated by William Armstrong Russel 祿賜悅理 and Divie Bethune MacCatee 麥嘉締, was published the following year. The spelling system used in this version was designed by W. A. P. Martin 丁韙良, R. E. Cobbold, and F. F. Gough 高夫, and this was the first romanized Chinese dialect Bible.[3]

The Suzhou dialect versions were written mostly in Chinese script. The Gospels and Acts, translated by J. W. Davis Gough, were published in 1879. The re-translated Gospels and Acts according to the Shanghai dialect versions, done by G. F. Fitch and A. P. Parker 潘慎文, were published by the American Bible Society in 1880. The two missionaries above completed the translation of the NT, and the revised version of the NT was published by a publishing committee made up of J. W. Davis, J. H. Hayes, D. N. Lyon, and A. P. Parker in 1892.[4]

Missionary A. E. Moule 慕阿德 (also translated as 慕爾) of Union Church and his wife, E. A. Moule, began missionary services in 1861 in Hangzhou where the China Inland Mission began its work in 1866. A. E. Moule spoke and wrote Chinese fluently, and his wife translated portions of the NT. They published the version in 1877 using their own funds.[5]

The Jinhua 金華 dialect had only one romanized portion of the Bible, i.e., The Gospel of John, published in 1966 in Shanghai with the financial support of American Bible Society. The translator was H. Jenkins 秦貞 (also rendered as 秦鏡) of American Baptist Mission.

All the Taizhou 台州 dialect versions were romanized. The Gospel of Matthew was published in the large style of Roman letters in 1880. The translator of the NT was distinguished missionary W. D. Rudland 路惠理 of China Inland Mission, and the full text of the NT was published by China Inland Mission in Taizhou in 1881.[6]

The Wenzhou dialect has only romanized versions. W. H. Soothill 蘇慧廉 (1861–1935) began mission work in 1878 in Wenzhou until 1935. He began to translate the Gospels and the Acts from the Greek original in 1888, but this version was finally corrected in 1894 in London. Before translating, W. H. Soothill had invited local Chinese scholars to design a Roman spelling system together for the Wenzhou dialect.[7]

2. Min dialects

Min dialects 閩語 are spoken mostly in Fujian province, Taiwan, and eastern Guangdong province, including Fuzhou, Xiamen, Putian, Jianyang, Shantou, and Hainan with a combined population of 75 million.

The Gospel of Mark was translated into the Fuzhou 福州 dialect by W. Welton 溫敦, and the Gospel of Matthew by M. C. White 懷德; both were published in 1852. W. Welton was a medical missionary of Church Mission in Fuzhou between 1850 and 1856 and, in 1852, he translated the NT from the Union classical Chinese version. His version was published by the British and Foreign Bible Society. Another version of the Fuzhou dialect of the NT translated by B. Peet 弼玆 of the American Board was published the following year. American Board and Methodist Episcopal Missions revised the OT together in 1864, and it was finally published in 1878. In 1874, Church Missionary, American Board, and Methodist Episcopal Mission began to translate the OT together with financial support from American Bible Society; the translation was completed in 1884 and published in 1888.[8]

All the Xiamen 廈門 versions were in Roman script. The earliest portion translated into the Xiamen dialect by Elihu Doty 羅啻 was the Gospel of John, printed by Wells William Press in 1852. The Gospel of Mark translated by Alvin Ostrom 胡理敏 was published before 1860. The above-mentioned Gospel of John and the Ningbo dialect Gospel of Luke both were the earliest romanized Bible of Chinese dialects. The NT was translated and printed in 1856. There were three Christian missionary societies in Xiamen in 1873: London Missionary Society, British Presbyterian, and American Reformed Dutch Church; together, they decided to translate the OT according to the high *wenli* Delegate's Version. The revised version of the OT was published in 1920.[9]

W. N. Brewster 蒲魯士 of American Episcopal undertook the job of translating the NT into the Xinghua 興化 (now Putian) dialect according to the original of the romanized Fuzhou dialect NT. The earliest portion was the Gospel of John, published in 1892 in Fuzhou. The full text of the Bible was published in 1912. All editions were in romanized script.

As Union Church began missionary work in 1891 in Jianyang 建陽, the Gospel of Mark was translated into the Jianning dialect version by H. T. Phillips 腓力, and it was published in 1898 in Fuzhou with funding from the translator himself.

American Congregational Church began Christian work in 1874 in Shaowu 邵武. The Shaowu dialect version of Acts was translated by its missionary, J. E. Walker, and published in 1891 in Fuzhou.

The first Scripture portion of the Shantou 汕頭 dialect was the book of Ruth, translated by S. B. Partridge 巴牧師 in 1875. He translated Acts of the Apostles in 1877. In the same year, the Gospel of Luke was translated into romanized script by W. Duffu 迪弗斯 of British Presbyterian Church and published in Glasgow. The OT in Chinese character script was published in 1898, and the Roman script version was published in 1905. The full text of the Bible was published in 1922.[10]

Presbyterian missionaries began Christian services in Hainan island in 1891. Jeremiassen, who was a customs staff member, translated the Gospel of Matthew, which was published in 1891 in Shanghai. All editions were in Roman script.[11]

3. Cantonese

Cantonese is mostly spoken in Guangdong and Guangxi provinces, Hong Kong, and overseas with a combined population of 58.82 million.

The Gospel of Matthew and the Gospel of John were translated into Cantonese and published in 1862. The Gospel of Luke was translated by W. Lews, and E. Faber turned it into the Lepsius Standard Alphabet version and published it in 1867. A revised and refined edition of the NT was finally published in 1886, and the OT was published by the American Bible Society in 1994. All editions were in Chinese characters except the Gospel of Luke (1867); however, there were bilingual versions (English and Cantonese), such as the 1911 NT version. There were no bilingual versions using other dialects.[12]

4. Hakka

Hakka is spoken in Northern Guangdong province and adjacent areas of Jiangxi and Fujian provinces with a combined population of 42.20 million.

Most of the Hakka dialect versions were in Roman script without special locations indicated except Wujingfu 五經富, Wuhua 五華, and Tingzhou 汀州. Most probably the early versions were rendered in Hong Kong Hakka dialect, and the others should be in Jiaying 嘉應 Hakka. Dispatched by Evangelische Missionsgesellschaft zu Basel, Theodore Hambergand 韓山文 and Rudolph Lechler 黎力基 were the earliest missionaries who came to the Hakka dialect-speaking area. The Gospel of Matthew translated by them was published by the Basel Church in 1860 in Berlin. It is the first Hakka dialect version with Richard Lepsius's spelling system (see the paragraph below on Lepsius). The romanized NT was published in 1883, and the revised NT was published in 1904. The full text of the Bible was translated and published by the British Bible Society in 1906.[13]

5. Gan dialects

Gan dialects are mostly spoken in Jiangxi province and adjacent areas of Hunan, Hubei, and Fujian provinces including Nanchang, Wuzhou, Yichun, and Jianning with a combined population of 48 million.

All of the Jianning dialect versions were in Roman script. The NT translated by L. J. Bryer of the Church of England Zenana Missionary Society was published in 1896 in London.[14]

Characteristics of the Dialect Versions in China

Since every dialect has its own lexicology and syntax, translation of the Bible into different dialects necessarily takes on different sentences, grammars, and renditions of meaning, thus giving various nuances. We will look at different translations of the first verse of the Gospel of John in different dialects, namely the English version (1996), Union Version (1919), the Shanghai dialect version (1847), the Ningbo dialect version (1868), Taizhou-tupai version 台州土白本 (1897), Wenzhou-tupai version 溫州土白本 (1894), the Cantonese dialect version, and the Hakka version (1823):

> In the beginning was the Word, and the Word was with God, and the Word was God. (English, NRSV)
>
> 太初有道, 道與神同在, 道就是神。(Union)
>
> 起頭道已經有拉個、第個道忒上帝兩一淘個、道就是上帝拉。(Shanghai)
>
> 道是起初有個, 道是等神明大家勒該, 並且道是神明。(Ningbo)
>
> 起初有道, 道搭上帝聚隊, 道就是上帝。(Taizhou)

起初有道，道與上帝同在。道就是上帝。(Wenzhou)
太初有道，道同埋上帝，道即係上帝。(Cantonese)
當初有道，道同上帝共在，道又係上帝。(Hakka)

Compared with the Union Version, the dialects versions have a prominent characteristic of translating "God" (*theos* in Greek) into three different Chinese words: "*Shangdi* 上帝," "*Shen* 神," and "*Shenming* 神明." For example, "*Shangdi*" was used in Xiamen, "*Shen*" was used in Fuzhou, and "*Shenming*" was used in Ningbo. While the Union Version, widely used in mainland China nowadays, just adopts "*Shen*," in early years one Union Version was printed with the word "*Shen*" for the term "God," and another Union Version was printed with the word "*Shangdi*." The Shanghai dialect NT and Hakka Bible published in 1923, persisted in using "*Shangdi*." There is a long history of debate about how to translate "God" (*theos, Elohim*) into "*Shen*" or "*Shangdi*." The debate was very acute from the beginning of the 1840s until 1852, when the Delegates' Version was published using "*Shangdi*" for the name of God; then American missionary E. C. Bridgman 俾治文 withdrew from the Delegates' Committee and translated and published a new version with "*Shen*" in 1863. The controversy continued, so that "*Shen*" or "*Shangdi*" appeared in different dialects versions.

As for the accuracy of the meaning rendered, generally speaking the dialect Bibles—the earlier editions in particular—were not as precise as the Union Version. Let us compare the different translations of the fourth verse of chapter 1 of the Gospel of John in the English version (1996), the Union Version, and the Shanghai dialect version (1847) as follows:

In him was life, and the life was the light of all people. (English, NRSV)
生命在他裏頭。這生命就是人的光。(Union Version)
勒拉道是活個、而且活拉個、是人個亮光拉。(Shanghai dialect)

The translation of the Shanghai dialect version was not accurate; the words failed to convey the original idea. In the Shanghai dialect, "活個" is an adjective that just means "alive" here, but in the original text, "life" is a noun that means a state of physical and mental existence as a human being.

The Chinese dialect Bibles can be classified into three categories according to writing systems: (1) Chinese character, (2) romanized system, (3) other spelling systems. The earliest Chinese character version was the Gospel of John in the Shanghai dialect published in 1847 in Shanghai; the earliest romanized version was St. Luke in the Ningbo dialect and St. John in Cantonese published in 1852. Few versions were translated using other phonetic systems; for example, there were five Fuzhou dialect versions translated using the national language phonetic system (國語注音符號), and there was one Shanghai dialect portion of Bible translated using the phonetic system designed by Tarleton P. Crawford; it also was used to translate novels such as *I soo boo kuh bi fong* 伊索寓言 (*The Fables of Aesop*) in the Shanghai dialect.

The Chinese dialect Bibles can be classified into five categories according to kinds of dialects: Wu dialects, Min dialects, Yue dialects, Hakka, and Gan dialects. The first two categories could be re-classified into a few sub-categories. See Table 7.2 below regarding the number of Chinese dialects Bibles according to kinds and writing systems.

From Table 7.2, we notice that Wu dialects had seven localities, Min dialects had eight localities, Yue dialects had two localities, Gan and Hakka each had only one locality with dialect versions. In total, there were nineteen Chinese vernaculars that had dialect versions. As for the number of dialect versions, the most numerous dialect was Cantonese, 153 altogether, followed by Fuzhou, Hakka, Shanghai, Xiamen, Shantou, Ningbo, Taizhou, Xinghua, Suzhou, Hainan, Jianning, Wenzhou, Lianzhou, Hangzhou, Chaozhou, and Jianyang. The fewest number of dialect versions was for Jinhua and Shaowu, which had only one and two respectively. In total, there were 708 Chinese dialects versions.

Table 7.3 shows the number of Chinese dialects versions and the percentage of the Bible translated.

From Table 7.3, we see that Chinese-character versions were little fewer than romanized versions. As for the percentage of the Bible translated for various dialects, Min dialects

Table 7.2 The Number of Chinese Dialect Bibles According to Kinds and Writing Systems

	Dialect	Chinese Character	Romanized	Other Phonetic Systems	Total
A	Wu dialects				
	Shanghai	44	18	2	64
	Suzhou	19	2	1	22
	Ningbo	14	39	0	53
	Hangzhou	2	2	0	4
	Jinhua	0	1	0	1
	Taizhou	2	22		24
	Wenzhou	0	5	0	5
B	Min dialects				
	Xiamen	6	58	0	64
	Fuzhou	45	77	5	127
	Shantou	16	44	0	60
	Chaozhou	0	3	0	3
	Xinghua	2	21	0	23
	Jianyang	0	2	0	2
	Shaowu	0	2	0	2
	Hainan	0	16	0	16
C	Gan dialects (Jianning)	1	9	0	10
D	Hakka	46	25	0	71
E	Yue dialects				
	Cantonese	139	14	0	153
	Lianzhou	4	0	0	4
amount		340	360	8	708

Table 7.3 The Number of Chinese Dialect Versions and Percentage of Bible Translated

	Dialect	Chinese Character	Romanized	Other	Total	Percentage
A	Wu	81	89	3	173	24.40%
B	Min	69	223	5	297	42.00%
C	Gan	1	9	0	10	0.01%
D	Hakka	46	25	0	71	10.00%
E	Yue	143	14	0	157	22.18%
amount		340	360	8	708	
%		48.02%	50.85%	0.01%		100%

Table 7.4 The Earliest Publication Year of Various Versions

	Dialect	Portion	NT	OT	Bible
A	Wu	1847/1853	1872/1868	1901/1901	1913/1914
B	Min	1852/1852	1856/1869	1888/1884	1884/1891
C	Gan	1896/1897	–/1896	–/–	–/–
D	Hakka	1881/1860	1883/1883	1916/–	1923/–
E	Yue	1862/1867	1873/1906	1907/–	1907/1907

had the most with 42 percent, followed by Wu, Yue, and Hakka, while the least was Gan, which had none. And Min dialects had the highest percentage of romanized versions.

Table 7.4 shows the earliest publication year of various versions.

The literacy percentage of the Chinese common people, especially among women, was very low in that era, so they did not know how to read the Bible in Chinese characters well. It is interesting that while the romanized spelling/phonetic system is a foreign import, most Chinese common people found it easier to read. Thus, if one wanted to evangelize among the common people, the Bible was translated into Chinese dialects using the romanized phonetic script.

The missionaries of Basel Church adopted Lepsius's phonetic system in translating the Bible into the Hakka dialect. This system was designed by Richard Lepsius (1810–1884), who was a well-known phonetician in the second half of the nineteenth century and published *Standard Alphabet for Reducing Languages and Foreign Graphic Systems to a Uniform Orthography in European Letters* in London in 1855. Before the creation of the International Phonetic Alphabet, the Lepsius phonetic system of writing was widely adopted in recording non-European languages. The system was set on the basis of twenty-six Latin letters, and the relation of symbols and phones was finally designed to refer to several main European languages.

The "standard letters" were created to meet the need of missionary works overseas. Union Church had already adopted Lepsius's system before the publication of his above-mentioned book. The first edition of this book (in 1855) had transcription samples of Mandarin Chinese, and the second edition (in 1863) had the Nanjing dialect, the Chaozhou Min dialect, and Hakka samples. All Hakka versions of the Bible published subsequently adopted this system; however, few other dialect versions adopted it. When these dialect versions designed their own spelling systems, their attitude was equally serious; for example, missionaries in Shanghai even organized the Shanghai Vernacular Society (滬語社) in order to study the Shanghai dialect in depth and to design their spelling/phonetic system.

At some localities, missionaries invited local scholars to design spelling/phonetic systems and translate the Bible together. They often consulted other dialect versions and seriously discussed over and over again before finalizing their manuscripts.

Punctuation marks in both traditional Chinese and Chinese dialects play a role in Bible translation. Chinese character versions could be categorized in two groups: one group used Western-style punctuation, and the other used traditional Chinese punctuation. The latter had only two marks, full stop (。) and comma (、) at most. Romanized versions adopting English punctuation marks was the pioneer of the new style of the modern Chinese punctuation mark.

Though the spelling/phonetic systems and translation of the Bible were not done perfectly, Bible translators put forth their best efforts. For example, the title of the fifteenth chapter (第十五章) of the Shanghai dialect Matthew (1895) was translated as "DI SO-NG TSANG," and the title of the sixteenth (第十六章) was translated as "DI SO-LOK TSANG." In fact, in the Shanghai dialect when the number "ten" ("十") was followed by other numbers, it read "*zeh*" with a voiced consonant z, except in "十五" (fifteen), which reads "*so ng*" with a voiceless *s* instead of "*zeh ng*." For more examples, in the old Shanghai dialect, there were two kinds of abrupt syllables. One ended with *h*, the other ended with *k*, and we can find the two kinds of abrupt syllables in romanized versions of the Shanghai dialect Matthew (1895), such as 讀 *dok*, 白 *bak*, 脚 *kyak*; 拔 *bah*, 吃 *chuh*, 物 *veh*. It is impossible to differentiate the two kinds without phonetic symbols.

Illiterate Chinese Christians preferred romanized spelling/phonetic systems, which were used not only in Christian missionary work but also in communication among common people, especially in the southern Min district and Taizhou district of Zhejiang province. For example, John C. Gibson wrote in 1890: "It is in constant use by a large number of readers in the prefectures of Chang-chow and Chin-chow, and the Island of Formosa."[15]

How many readers used the romanized versions? There is no statistical information, but we can guess from sales volume; more than 18,000 copies of the Bible and the OT and more than 15,000 of the NT were sold between 1890 and 1920. Incomplete Bible translations were excluded from sales volume, and the number of portions was far greater than the NT, OT, and complete Bible combined.

Most of the Chinese dialect Bibles were printed in the printing and publishing houses of various churches. There were twelve such publishing houses before 1899, and the most important was American Presbyterian Press (美華書館), which was established in

1844 in Macau, moved to Ningbo in 1945, and moved to Shanghai in 1960. In other cities, there were smaller publishing houses.

Most of the Chinese dialect Bibles were published in Shanghai, where there was a "sample books room" (樣書間), which kept five copies of every book printed there. It is a great pity that the "room" was ruined in the disaster of the so-called Cultural Revolution (1966–1976). Today, the following libraries have a good collection of Chinese-dialect versions:

1. British Bible Society. The British and Foreign Bible Society was its predecessor. It not only stores formally published dialect Bibles but also some original manuscripts. *A Catalogue of Scriptures in the Languages of China*, compiled by Hubert W. Spillett, was printed by this society in 1975. The catalogue lists mainly publications of the British and Foreign Bible Society, in addition to publications of the American Bible Society and Scottish Bible Society, including the impressive 315 Chinese dialect versions.
2. American Bible Society located at Broadway 1865, New York, which kept more than 140 Chinese dialect versions.
3. Basel Church in Switzerland. Because most missionaries in the Hakka area, including Hong Kong and the northern Guangdong province, came from Basel Church, it keeps the greatest number of Hakka versions and in perfect condition.
4. The library at the Northeast University of Japan. It stores more than thirty-five Cantonese Bibles, which were contributed by J. Dyer Ball (1919–1947) with his signature on every book. J. Dyer Ball did missionary work in Guangdong province and published various works related to the Cantonese and Hakka dialect.

Besides translating texts of the Holy Bible, missionaries also wrote or translated many books of Bible stories, hymns, Christian teaching, and instruction, such as *Hymns and Tunes* 贊神樂章附曲譜 in the Ningpo dialect with twenty-five hymns in 1856; *Biblical Histories in the Romanized Colloquial of the Hakka Chinese ŠIN*^{4} *ŠU1*^{1} *KAI*^{4} *S4* ŠIT^5; [16] *Prayer, Creed and Commandments* 禱文經誡 in the Hangzhou dialect (1867); *A Cup of Wine IH-PE TSIU* in the Ningbo dialect (1852) and so on. About one hundred such books in Chinese dialects were published then, and because they were useful as supplementary and guidance materials for reading and studying the Bible, they were welcomed not only by Christians but also by non-Christians.

Chinese Dialects Versions and Chinese Dialects

The Chinese dialect Bibles, with other missionary works on Chinese dialects, are the best literature for studying oral Chinese dialects in the second half of the nineteenth century and the first half of the twentieth century. The science of language originated in

Table 7.5 Comparison of Mandarin and Dialects Words and Expression

English	he	look	know	no	of	they	follow
Mandarin (1905)	他	看	認	不	的	他們	跟着
Cantonese (1927)	佢	睇	識	唔	嘅	佢哋	跟住
Shanghai (1923)	伊	看	認	勿	個	伊拉	跟拉
Hakka (1923)	佢	看	識	唔	個	佢等	跟緊
Suzhou (18??)	俚	看見	曉得	弗	個	俚篤	跟子

Europe in the early years of the nineteenth century. Western missionaries, who were mostly learned scholars, brought knowledge of the science of language and designed phonetic systems for many Chinese dialects, studying their phonology, lexicology, and grammar, and thus promoting the modernization of Chinese linguistics. In the meantime, Chinese scholars devoted themselves to traditional philology with attention to studying classic literature and written language; no phonetic signs were created to record dialects, while Chinese characters are impossible for describing dialect phonemes accurately. As a result, we were able to reconstruct the phonetic systems of the following nineteen dialects completely at least, such as: Shanghai, Suzhou, Ningbo, Taizhou, Wenzhou, Fuzhou, Xiamen, Putian, Shantou, Haikou, Guangzhou, Jiaying, and so on.

The Chinese dialect Bibles provide precious information for the synchronic study of every single dialect and, because it is best to have records of the same content recorded in different historical periods for synchronic study, the dialect Bibles are ideal literature for this purpose. It is possible to identify the historical evolution since the 1840s by comparing earlier and later published versions. Furthermore, Chinese dialects versions assist in the comparative study of different dialects in China.

There is no literature in China that could surpass the dialect Bibles in helping us to understand the differences of Chinese dialects by comparison. With the dialect versions placed in front of us, we can compare the biblical texts word by word and sentence by sentence according to the different dialects. For example, one can find differentiation among the four dialects and Mandarin on lexicology and syntax, as in Table 7.5 above; we note the lexical and syntactic differences among the four dialect versions of Luke 22:54–56:

The first three items are concerned solely with differences in words, and the remaining four items also are concerned with differences in grammar, such as negative forms, possession, the plural form of the personal pronoun, and tense of the verb.

Conclusion

More than seven hundred various Chinese dialect versions of the Bible, including portions of the biblical texts, have been published since 1847, and they have made tremendous contributions not only to the history of Chinese Christianity but also to Chinese linguistics.

These are invaluable literature for the study of phonetics, vocabulary, and grammar of Chinese dialects in modern times, as well as for the study of the evolution of Chinese dialects since the 1840s. Scholarly research values the importance of Chinese dialect Bibles in Chinese dialectology, and the following research agenda will further the field in the future: reconstruction of the phonology of different dialects; comparative studies of dialects including their phonology, vocabulary, grammar, and dialect characters; the evolution of some specific dialects, spelling systems created by missionaries, and so on.

Notes

1. See Hu Qiguang 胡奇光, "Volume Language and Written Language" [in Chinese] 白話文運動, in *Chinese Encyclopedia* 中國大百科全書: 語言文字卷 (Shanghai: Chinese Encyclopedia Press, 1988), 13.
2. About the spelling system used in this dialect, please refer to J. Edkins, *A Grammar of Colloquial Chinese, as Exhibited in the Shanghai Dialect* (Shanghai: London Mission Press, 1853; 2nd edition, 1868).
3. About the spelling system used in this dialect, please refer to *Nying-po Tu-wo Tsuoh* [in Chinese] 寧波土話初學 (Shanghai: np., 1868).
4. About the spelling system used in this translation, please refer to *A Syllabary of the Soochow Dialect* (Shanghai: Soochow Literary Society, 1892).
5. About the spelling system used here, please refer to G. E. Moule, *Hangchow Premier: Translation and Notes* (London: Society for Promoting Christian Knowledge, 1876).
6. About the spelling system here, please refer to W. D. Rudlang, "Táai-chow Romanization," *Chinese Recorder* 35 (1904): 89–91.
7. About the spelling system used here, please refer to Edward Harper Parker, "The Wenchow Dialect," *China Review* 12 (1884): 162–175, 377–389.
8. About the spelling system, please refer to Moses Clark White, *The Chinese Language Spoken at Fuh Chau* (Concord, NH: Missionary Society of the Methodist General Biblical Institute, 1956).
9. About the spelling system, please refer to E. Doty, *Anglo-Chinese Manual with Romanized Colloquial in the Amoy Dialect* [in Chinese] 翻譯英華廈腔語匯 (Canton: S. Wells Williams, 1853).
10. About the spelling system, please refer to Josiah Goddard, *A Chinese and English Vocabulary in the Tie Chiw Dialect* (Bangkok: Mission Press, 1847).
11. About the spelling system, please refer to S. Dyer, "Remarks on the Hainanese Dialect," *China Repository* 4 (1835): 172–176.
12. About the spelling system, please refer to Robert Morrison, *English and Chinese Vocabulary, the Letter in the Canton Dialect*, 2nd ed. (Calcutta: np., 1840).
13. About the spelling system, please refer to Edward Harper Parker, *Syllabary of the Hakka Language or Dialect*, *China Review* 8 (1880): 205–217.
14. About the spelling system, please refer to Hugh Stowell Phillips, "The Kien-Ning Romanised Dialects," *Chinese Recorder* 35 (1904): 517–519.
15. *Record of the General Conference of the Protestant Missionaries of China Held at Shanghai*, May 7–20, 1890 (Shanghai: Shanghai American Presbyterian Mission Press), 71.
16. This is pinyin in Hakka dialect, translated into Mandarin it is "聖經史實" (Basel: np., 1878).

Primary Sources

Acts of the Apostles [in Hakka] 使徒行傳. Np., 1883.

Biblical Histories in the Romanized Colloquial of the Hakka Chinese (*ŠIN⁴ ŠU1¹ KAI⁴ S4 ŠIT⁵*.) [in Hakka]. Basel: np., 1878.

C'Ih Yaeh-Gyi Kyi (*Exodus*) [in Chinese] 出埃及記. Shanghai: British Bible Society, 1899.

Chinese Bible: Revised Union Version [in Chinese] 聖經全書 (和合本修訂版). Hong Kong: Hong Kong Bible Societies, 2016.

Commentary on Dialect Catechism [in Chinese] 方言教理詳解, 3 volumes, 32 chapters. Shanghai: T-Usey Press, 1912.

Compendium Catechism [*in lingua vulgari* Chang-hai] 方言問答撮要. Edited by Miao Yangshan (苗仰山). Shanghai: T-Usey Press, 1926.

The Four Gospels and Acts in Wenchow [in Wenchow] 四福音帶使徒行傳. Translated by William Edward Soothill. London: British Bible Society, 1894.

The Gospel Aaccording to St. Mark in English and Cantonese [in Cantonese] 馬可福音(中西字). Shanghai: American Presbyterian Mission Press, 1899.

The Gospel According to St. Matthew in English & Cantonese [in English and Cantonese]. Shanghai: American Bible Society, 1910.

The Gospel of John [in Cantonese characters] 約翰傳福音書. Canton: British Bible Society, 1883.

The Gospel of John [in colloquial Shanghai] 約翰傳福音書. Shanghai: London Mission Press, 1847.

The Gospel of Luke [in Shuzhou] 路加傳福音書. Np., nd.

The Gospel of Mark in Wenchow Colloquial [in Wenchow colloquial]. London: British and Foreign Bible Society, 1902.

The Gospel of Matthew in Wenchow Colloquial [in colloquial Wenchow]. London: British and Foreign Bible Society, 1892.

The Gospel of Saint John in the Dialect of Shanghai [in Romanized script]. Edited by James Summers. London: W. M. Watts. Crown Court Temple Bar, 1853.

The Gospel of Saint Matthew in Ting-chow [in Fujian Tingzhou] 馬太福音. Shanghai: British Bible Society, 1919. Translated by L. R. Hughes and E. R. Rainey of London Missionary Society.

Hymns and Tunes [in colloquial Ningpo] 贊神樂章附曲譜. Compiled by E. C. Lord. Ningpo: np., 1856.

I soo boo kuh bi fong (*Selection from Aesop's and Other Fables*) [in colloquial Shanghai]. Shanghai: Np., 1856.

Iah Shü-Ùo Kyi (*Joshua*) [in colloquial Ningbo, romanized script] 約書亞記. London: British Bible Society, 1899.

Iah-'Aen Djün Foh-Ing Shü (*The Gospel of John*) [in colloquial Jinghua] 約翰傳福音書. Shanghai: Yangguo Shufang, 1966.

Iah-'En Djün Foh-Ing Shü (*The Gospel of John*) [in colloquial Ningpo] 約翰傳福音書. Ningpo: Np., 1853.

Lih-Wong Kyi-Liah [*Kings*] [in colloquial Ningbo, rRomanized script] 列王紀略. Shanghai: British and Foreign Bible Society, 1900.

Maxims Eternelles ou Preparation a la Mort, 2 volumes [in Shanghai dialect] 方言備終錄. Shanghai: T-Usey Press, 1907. [original author/translator is De Liguori (1696–1787)]

Ming-Su Ji-Liah (*Numbers*) [in colloquial Ningbo, romanized script] 民數紀略. Shanghai: American Presbyterian Press, 1895.

Mo K'o Djon Foh-Yin Sh (*The Gospel of Mark*) [in colloquial Shuzhou] 馬可傳福音書. Shanghai: American Presbyterian Press, 1891.

Mo-T'A Djü Foh-Ing Shü (*The Gospel of Matthew*) [in colloquial Taizhou] 馬太傳福音書. Taizhou: China Inland Mission, 1880.

Mo-T'A Dzen Foh-Ing Su (*The Gospel of Matthew*) [in Shanghai accent] 馬太傳福音書. Shanghai: American Presbyterian Press, 1895.

The New Testament [in colloquial Shuzhou] 新约全書. Shanghai: American Bible Society, 1922.

The New Testament in the Colloquial of the Hakka Dialect, 2nd edition [in Hakka]. Basel: L. Reinhardt, 1893.

Old Testament Prophets, 17 vols [in colloquial Shuzhou] 舊約先知十七卷. Shanghai: American Bible Society, 1908.

The Pilgrim Progress [in colloquial Shuzhou] 天路歷程. Shanghai: American Presbyterian Press, 1896.

Sah-Meo-R Kyi (*Samuel*) [in colloquial Ningbo, Romanized script] 撒母耳記. London: British Bible Society, 1900.

Shanghai Colloquial New Testament [in Shanghai colloquial] 新約全書. Shanghai: American Bible Society, 1923.

Sing Iah Shü (*New Testament*) [in colloquial Ningbo, Romanized script] 新約書. Translated by Frederick Foster Gough, et al. London: British and Foreign Bible Society, 1868.

Sing Iah Shü (*The New Testament*) [in colloquial Taizhou] 新約書. London: British Bible Society, 1897; revised in 1881, printed by China Inland Mission.

Sing-Saen-Yiae-Ko [*Holy Mountain Harmonious Songs*] 聖山諧歌 [in colloquial Ningbo]. Compiled by Filias B. Inslee. Ningpo: Huahua Shufang, 1858. [72 hymns, 80 pages.]

Taòu wăn king keaé 《禱文經誡》 [*Prayer, Creed and Commandments*], 6 leaves [in Hangzhou]. Hangzhou, 1867.

Ts'ong Shü Kyi (*Genesis*) [in colloquial Ningbo] 創世記. Shanghai: British Bible Society, 1899.

Z-S Kyi (*Judges*) [in colloquial Ningbo, Romanized script] 士師記. British Bible Society, 1900.

CHAPTER 8

BIBLE TRANSLATIONS FOR ETHNIC MINORITY GROUPS IN CHINA

SUEE YAN YU

INTRODUCTION

THERE are fifty-five officially recognized ethnic minority groups in China. The classification into groups is basically for administrative purposes and does not mean that there are only fifty-five ethnic minority languages in China. For instance, Miao is one of the fifty-five ethnic minority groups. Some linguists argue that there are about seventy languages and dialects within the Miao group. The languages are somewhat related but usually are not mutually intelligible. The same is true of the Yi ethnic minority group as well. The actual number of languages is far more than the fifty-five ethnic minority groups.

In the context of China, the term "minority" does not necessarily mean small. It simply means fewer in number compared to the dominant group, the Han Chinese, which has a population of 1,220,844,520, according to the 2010 census. Zhuang is an ethnic minority group in China, with a population of about 17 million, by no means a small number! In fact, according to the census carried out in 2010, the population of the ethnic minority groups in China totaled 114 million, about the same population as Japan, the eleventh most populous nation in the world.

The list of the fifty-five ethnic minority groups in China is given below (Table 8.1), based on population size, in descending order. The alternative name is included in brackets.[1]

Notice that ethnic minority groups like Mongol, Korean, Russian, Dai, Kazakh, Kyrgyz, and Uzbek are the dominant groups in their respective countries (Mongolia, Korea, Russia, Thailand, etc.). Mongols in China and Mongolia may be able to communicate with each other orally, to some extent, though the written scripts are different. Koreans in China and Korea use the same language, with the same script. Large populations of

Table 8.1 Fifty-Five Ethnic Minority Groups in China

Ethnic Minority Group	Traditional Chinese	Population (2010 Census)
Zhuang	壯族	16,926,381
Hui	回族	10,586,087
Manchu	滿族	10,387,958
Uyghur	維吾爾族	10,069,346
Miao	苗族	9,426,007
Yi	彝族	8,714,393
Tujia	土家族	8,353,912
Tibetan	藏族	6,282,187
Mongol	蒙古族	5,981,840
Dong (Kam)	侗族	2,879,974
Bouyei	布依族	2,870,034
Yao	瑤族	2,796,003
Bai	白族	1,933,510
Korean	朝鮮族	1,830,929
Hani	哈尼族	1,660,932
Li	黎族	1,463,064
Kazakh	哈薩克族	1,462,588
Dai	傣族	1,261,311
She	畲族	708,651
Lisu	傈僳族	702,839
Dongxiang	東鄉族	621,500
Gelao	仡佬族	550,746
Lahu	拉祜族	485,966
Wa	佤族	429,709
Sui	水族	411,847
Naxi (Nakhi)	納西族	326,295
Qiang	羌族	309,576
Tu	土族	289,565
Mulao	仫佬族	216,257
Xibe	錫伯族	190,481
Kyrgyz	柯爾克孜族	186,708
Jingpo	景頗族	147,828
Daur	達斡爾族	131,992
Salar	撒拉族	130,607
Blang	布朗族	119,639
Maonan	毛南族	101,192
Tajik	塔吉克族	51,069
Pumi	普米族	42,861
Achang	阿昌族	39,555
Nu	怒族	37,523
Evenki	鄂温克族	30,875
Gin	京族	28,199
Jino	基諾族	23,143
Deang	德昂族	20,556
Bonan	保安族	20,074
Russian	俄羅斯族	15,393
Yugur	裕固族	14,378

Uzbek	烏孜別克族	10,569
Monba	門巴族	10,561
Oroqen	鄂倫春族	8,659
Derung	獨龍族	6,930
Hezhen	赫哲族	5,354
Gaoshan	高山族	4,488
Lhoba	珞巴族	3,682
Tatars	塔塔爾族	3,556
Undistinguished[2]	未識別民族	640,101

other minority groups, e.g., Miao, Lisu, Lahu, Jingpo, Yao, Hani, and Wa, are found in countries neighboring China. Due to the spread of the same-people groups in different countries, this has implications for ethnic minority Bible translation in China, which is discussed later.

In this essay, Bibles for ethnic minority groups in Taiwan are not addressed. There are fourteen ethnic minority groups in Taiwan, with a great deal of ongoing Bible translation activities. This topic requires separate treatment.

Bible Translation Prior to the Nineteenth Century

There is a long history of translating the Bible into languages used in China. The Nestorian Stele recorded the arrival of Alopen in Chang'an (now Xi'an) in 635 CE, the capital of the Tang dynasty (618–907), and a church was established three years later. The Nestorian church canon, *Zunjing*, found in Dunhuang, indicated that dozens of books of the Bible had been translated. Unfortunately, we no longer have extant manuscripts of these translations.

When the Nestorians in China came under persecutions in 845 CE, they went to the northern parts of China and worked with the Mongol-Turkic people. Some of the people groups in northern China accepted Christianity. The city of Kashgar in Xinjiang, for instance, was once the site of a Nestorian Metropolitan, assisted by twelve bishops. In the late 1270s, Mark and Sauma, Uyghur Christians, left Khanbaliq (now Beijing) to visit the holy sites of the Nestorian faith in Persia. Through a series of circumstances, Mark became the Patriarch of the Nestorian church, under the name of Mar Yaballaha III.[3] From the ninth to the thirteenth centuries, Nestorian missionaries made inroads in northern China among the ethnic groups there. Unfortunately, we do not know if the Bible was translated into any of the local languages.

In the 1260s, Kublai Khan (1215–1294), arguably the most powerful emperor in the world at that time, sent a request via Niccolo and Matteo Polo to the Pope, asking for one hundred missionaries to come and teach Christianity in his court. When the letter arrived in 1271, Pope Gregory X (1210–1276) had just assumed office, and he could only afford to send two friars.[4] Unfortunately, they turned back halfway due to harsh weather and did not make it. By the time the first Roman Catholic missionary, John of Montecorvino (1247–1328), reached Khanbaliq in 1294, Kublai Khan had just died, and the Mongols had turned to Buddhism.[5] One wonders how history could have turned out if one hundred missionaries had been sent and arrived in Khanbaliq during Kublai Khan's reign to teach the Mongols about the Christian faith.

In any case, John of Montecorvino was successful in his work. He built churches and had about six thousand converts. In a letter sent to the Pope in 1305, he mentioned that he had mastered the Tartar language and script and had translated psalms and the NT. It is likely that the Tartar language he mentioned refers to the Mongol language used by the Mongol rulers of the Yuan dynasty in China (1271–1368). Benedict XIII (1328–1423) talks about a Mongolian Bible in China in one of his letters in 1335, but no manuscript has been found.[6] However, there is some debate on this issue. Some scholars argue that John of Montecorvino translated the Scriptures into Mandarin[7] or Old Uyghur, or both of these languages[8] instead of Mongolian.

Catholic missionaries reentered China in the sixteenth century. While most of them were working with the Han Chinese, some reached out to ethnic minority groups, but there was little sustained effort in translating the Bible into their languages.

Bible Translation from 1800 to 1949

Vernacular Bible translation work among ethnic minority groups in China began in earnest in the nineteenth century, which coincided with the onset of the Protestant missionary movements. Protestant missionaries were actively involved in translating the Scriptures into ethnic minority languages. In the early part of the nineteenth century, it was difficult for missionaries to enter China, so some of them, for instance, Robert Morrison, spent a significant amount of time in Macao as well as in Malacca, a port city in Malaya, trying to reach out to the Chinese who had migrated to South East Asia. Later, when China was forced to open her doors in the aftermath of the Opium Wars, Western missionaries went to China in droves. Most of them worked with the Han Chinese, but some reached out to minority groups as well. The work among ethnic minority groups was mostly concentrated in the northeastern and southwestern parts of China, population centers of these groups.

In the northern parts of China, missionaries concentrated their efforts on the Mongol and the Uyghur people groups. Attempts to reach the Mongols persisted through the centuries, though without any significant breakthrough. Large proportions of the Mongol subgroups, known as the Kalmyk (Kalmuk) and Buryat (Buriat), live in the former Soviet Union. Due to the difficulties for missionaries to enter China prior to the opening up in the 1840s, some missionaries, based in Soviet Union, tried to reach out to the Mongols living there.[9] They started translating the Bible into Kalmyk and Buryat, both

Mongol dialects. Mongol dialects are collectively known as the Mongolian language. Isaac Jacob Schmidt (1779–1847), a Moravian missionary from Amsterdam, an expert in Mongolian and Tibetan studies, translated the Gospel According to Matthew into Kalmyk and published it in 1815, which was well-received. Later, two learned Buryats, Badma and Nomtu, joined Schmidt in his translation work, and they completed the translation of the New Testament (NT) in Kalmyk, published in St. Petersburg in 1827, but this publication was apparently withheld from circulation.[10]

British missionaries, notably Edward Stallybrass (1793–1884), William Swan (1791–1866), and Robert Yuille (1786–1861), under the auspices of the London Missionary Society, worked among the Mongols in Soviet Union. Assisted by two Buryat nobles, they translated the Old Testament (OT) from the Hebrew text into classical Mongolian, also known as Literary Mongolian. The book of Genesis was printed in 1834, and the OT was completed in 1840, published by the British and Foreign Bible Society. Not satisfied with the NT produced by Schmidt and his colleagues, Stallybrass and Swan continued with the translation of the NT from the Greek text into classical Mongolian. The NT was published in 1846. This is known as the literary version, using a high form of the Mongolian language. A slight revision of this NT was carried out by Antoine Schiefner and Alexis Pozdneyeff and appeared in 1880.[11]

James Gilmour (1843–1891), a Scottish missionary working with the London Missionary Society, went to China and worked tirelessly among the Mongols. He is sometimes called "The Apostle to the Mongols." He analyzed the obstacles for the Mongols to accept the Christian faith and came up with new methods to reach out to them. He inspired many others to work with the Mongols. Missionaries from the Scandinavian countries showed a special interest in this work, in part due to the travel accounts of Sven Hedin, a Swedish explorer who traveled extensively in Mongol areas. Gilmour did not attach much importance to translating the Scriptures. He felt that the Bible contained too many things that are difficult for the Mongols to understand and preferred tracts instead.[12]

Uyghur is a Turkic language, used primarily by the Uyghur ethnic minority group in the Xinjiang Uyghur Autonomous Region, China. Sizable Uyghur communities also are located in Kazakhstan, Kyrgyzstan, and Uzbekistan. Johannes Avetaranian (1861–1919), a mullah in Turkey who later became a Christian and served as a missionary with the Swedish Missionary Society, went to Xinjiang, China, and translated the NT into Uyghur. The Gospels were published in 1898, and the NT was published in 1914. Other missionaries took part in the translation work as well. Due to political and religious sensitivities, the OT translation was carried out in India and the entire Bible was eventually published in 1950.[13]

There is some work among the Koreans in China as well. John Ross (1842–1915), a Scottish missionary, went to Manchuria and eventually settled down in Mukden (now Shenyang). He met some Koreans there and started translating the NT into Korean. The NT was published in 1887 in Mukden and shipped to Korea.[14]

The center of the outreach work, however, is located in the southwestern parts of China, notably in Yunnan, Guizhou, and Sichuan due to the high concentration of ethnic minority groups who settle in these provinces. For instance, out of the fifty-five ethnic minority groups, twenty-six groups have been living in Yunnan for centuries, and fifteen groups are uniquely found there. About 85 percent of the Christian population in Yunnan today are from the ethnic minority groups.

James Hudson Taylor (1832–1905), a British Protestant missionary, served for decades in China. He founded the China Inland Mission (CIM) in 1865, now known as Overseas Missionary Fellowship International.[15] Hundreds of missionaries went to China under CIM, and a number of them reached out to ethnic minority groups. George William Clarke (1848–1919), responding to a call from Hudson Taylor for workers in China, served in Hunan, Guizhou, and Sichuan provinces before moving on to Yunnan in 1881, being the first Protestant missionary to work in that province.[16]

From 1884 to 1888, several missionaries, namely Samuel Pollard (1864–1915), Francis John Dymond (1866–1932), and James R. Adam, set up preaching points in various parts of Yunnan and Guizhou. In 1903, James Adam befriended a few Big Flowery Miao who were out hunting near Anshun, Guizhou. He invited them to his house for a meal and to attend church service on Sunday. This encounter led to a breakthrough and later sparked an impressive people's movement to Christianity in Guizhou and Yunnan. Soon, scores of the Big Flowery Miao became Christians. News spread, and the Big Flowery Miao in Yunnan traveled for days on foot to Guizhou to listen to Adam. Out of consideration for the Miao in Yunnan, in 1904 Adam introduced a few Big Flowery Miao from Yunnan to Samuel Pollard, who worked in Yunnan at that time.[17]

Pollard and his coworkers befriended and ministered to the Miao in Zhaotong, Yunnan as well as in Shimenkan, Guizhou. In less than two decades, he and his coworkers saw thousands of Big Flowery Miao become Christians. It also has been estimated that the Big Flowery Miao population in China today is around 600,000, and about 60 percent are Christians.

The ethnic minority groups in southwestern parts of China have spoken languages without any written script. In order to translate the Bible into these languages, missionaries had to come up with written scripts. Pollard and his coworkers, including Chinese and Miao intellectuals, eventually came up with the Pollard script. They started translating the Bible. The Gospel according to Mark in Big Flowery Miao was published in 1906, followed by the Gospel according to John in 1908, and the NT was printed in 1917.

The Pollard script was adapted by various other groups (Small Flowery Miao, Sinicized Miao, Black Yi, Gan Yi, White Yi, and East Lisu) and used in their respective Bible translations. These scripts are still in use today. All these languages are tonal, with a large number of vowels. Gan Yi, for instance, has thirty-five vowels, besides various combinations of diphthongs. In addition, there are several vertical positions for each vowel or diphthong, depending on the tones. There are also significant linguistic variations within each language, which complicate matters.

The gospel reached the East Lisu, a subgroup listed under the Lisu ethnic minority, in 1903, and East Lisu churches were established in 1906. George Edgar Metcalf (1879–1956), a British missionary under CIM, left for China in 1906, arrived in Taogu, a remote village in Yunnan, and served as a missionary pastor. Working together with Arthur G. Nicholls, they translated the Gospel according to Matthew in 1912, later the

Gospel according to Luke in 1917. The translation of the NT was completed in 1947, published by the Hong Kong Bible Society in 1951. Due to the political changes that took place, the East Lisu Christians in Yunnan could not obtain copies of the printed NT.

Gladstone Charles Fletcher Porteous (1874–1944), an Australian missionary under CIM, arrived in Wuding county, Yunnan province, in 1915 and reached out to minority groups there. He adapted the Big Flowery Miao script and came up with a script for the Black Yi. He and his coworkers translated the NT into Black Yi, published posthumously in 1948.

James O. Fraser (1886–1938), under the auspices of CIM, arrived in China in 1910 and pioneered work among the West Lisu, a subgroup of the Lisu ethnic minority, in Yunnan. He worked with the same people group in Burma (now Myanmar) as well, since the West Lisu settled in China as well as in neighboring countries. A large number of Lisu became Christians. Fraser helped the West Lisu to come up with a script in 1913 known as the "Fraser script" and translated the Scriptures into West Lisu. He and his colleagues completed the NT in 1938. This Fraser script has been adopted by the West Lisu in Burma, Thailand, and elsewhere.

While the groups listed above were open to Christianity, others were not. F. B. Webb commenced Protestant mission work at Panghai, Guizhou, in 1896, followed by W. S. Fleming and Maurice and Stella Hutton. They labored for years but progress was slow, and only a handful of Black Miao responded. Maurice Hutton, assisted by Mr. Yang, translated the four Gospels in Black Miao in 1928 and completed the translation of the NT in 1934.[18] He had hoped that the translation would help further the spread of the Christian faith among the Black Miao. Unfortunately, the NT translation was hardly used, and the Black Miao continued to view Christianity as foreign. Maurice Hutton also translated the Gospels according to Mark and John in 1937 in Ge Miao. There are very few Christians among the Black Miao and Ge Miao today.

Missionaries reached out to other minority groups as well. Significant proportions of the Wa, Lahu, and Jingpo ethnic groups accepted the Christian faith, resulting in vibrant churches. Scriptures were translated into these languages, as can be seen in the table listed at the end of this essay.

Vernacular Bibles in ethnic minority languages often are produced at great cost. John Ross translated the first Korean NT. He and his wife, M. A. Stewart, arrived in Shenyang, China, in 1872. She died a year later after giving birth to a son. John Ross remarried, but lost four of his children in quick succession: Hugh in 1881, Findlay in 1884, John in 1888, and Catherine in 1889.[19] Many missionaries went to China but did not make it back to their home countries. Samuel Pollard translated the NT into Big Flowery Miao. Shortly after he translated the book of Revelation, he was infected with typhoid while tending to villagers who were struck with that disease. He died in 1915 and was buried in Shimenkan, Guizhou. James Fraser translated the NT into West Lisu. He died at the age of 52 and was buried in Baoshan, Yunnan. In the summer of 1900, 239 missionaries perished in China in what is known as the Boxer Rebellion (1899–1901).[20] Mission work and Bible translation activities were being carried out at great costs. Christians among ethnic minority groups were aware of this, and they treasured their Bibles.

Sociopolitical changes in the decades that followed the founding of the People's Republic of China (October 1, 1949) disrupted religious activities. Missionaries left China, and Bible translation activities were suspended. During the Cultural Revolution (1966–1976), Bibles were burned, and Christians went through difficult times.

Bible Translation from the 1980s

The late Deng Xiaoping ushered in a period of change when he assumed power. During the 11th Communist Party Congress held in 1978, the policy of internal reformation and opening up to the outside world was formulated. The following year, churches associated with the Three-Self Patriotic Movement resumed worship services, and the demand for Bibles, including ethnic minority Scriptures, increased. For instance, Yunnan Christian Council printed twenty thousand copies of the Big Flowery Miao NT in 1983, but the stock ran out quickly. During this early period of reform, the United Bible Societies, working together with the China Christian Council, set up the Amity Printing Company in Nanjing to print Bibles for local consumption. The facility expanded, and today, it has printed hundreds of millions of copies of the Bibles, including Bibles for other countries.

The comparatively more permissive environment since the 1980s, with greater religious tolerance, allows various ethnic minority groups to pursue their intentions of having the Scriptures translated into their own languages. Various ethnic minority groups, for instance, the Big Flowery Miao and the East Lisu churches in Yunnan, started assigning their own people to translate the Scriptures. This translation effort is entirely due to the initiatives of ethnic minority groups. They wanted to have the Bible in their own mother tongues.

In 1988, I-Jin Loh, a scholar from the United Bible Societies, visited Yunnan and taught a course on Bible translation at Yunnan Seminary. He encouraged leaders of various ethnic minority groups who attended his class to translate the Bible using their own language. This created further interest in Bible translation. Later, other ethnic minority groups in Yunnan such as Gan Yi, White Yi, and Wa started forming teams to translate the Bible. This trend took place among ethnic minority groups in other provinces as well, in Guizhou and later in Inner Mongolia, though Yunnan has by far the highest number of ethnic minority language Bible translation projects, largely due to the high concentration of ethnic minority groups living there as well as the openness of authorities in charge of religious affairs. Since 2001, leaders of the China Christian Council and the Three-Self Patriotic Movement invited translation consultants from the United Bible Societies to help train translators and supervise translation projects. By that time, some of these ethnic minority groups had completed translating the OT or NT by themselves. Translation consultants from the United Bible Societies checked the translations for accuracy, clarity, and naturalness of language usage, and the process took years. Eventually, the entire Bible in Big Flowery Miao and the East Lisu NT were published and distributed in 2007. This is a significant milestone, the first time since the formation of the Peoples Republic of China that Bibles were translated by local people and published in China.

Since then, the East Lisu Bible, Wa Bible, Black Yi Bible, West Lisu annotated Bible, White Yi NT, Dai Bible, Gan Yi OT (trial edition), and the Mongolian NT (trial edition) have been published, helping to meet the Scripture demands of these groups. In China, printing Scriptures can only be done at Amity Printing Company, with permission from the relevant central authorities, and the process takes time. Occasionally, provincial authorities allow parts of the Scriptures to be printed, as trial editions, to meet the needs of people groups.

Several Bible translation projects are still ongoing or waiting for publication, and a few ethnic minority groups are working on their own, translating the Bible into their mother tongues. In a few years, more ethnic minority groups in China will have access to the Scriptures in their heart language.

The major difference in Bible translations carried out over the last few decades is that the work is done essentially by mother-tongue speakers from local communities. Prior to the 1950s, Bible translation was carried out mostly by missionaries. They spent years learning the local tongue, translating the Scriptures using this acquired language, sometimes assisted by mother-tongue speakers who helped with language issues. This is often termed as "missionary" translations. At present, translation work is carried out by mother-tongue speakers from each ethnic minority group. They do the drafting, review the text, and make decisions about their translation. A translation consultant, an outsider who may or may not know the ethnic-minority language, helps translators understand the meanings in the Hebrew or Greek texts, for the purpose of quality assurance. The mother-tongue speakers assume the main role in the translation process, making decisions for their communities, for whom they have been entrusted to translate the Scriptures. Consultants are there to advise and provide assistance on technical matters.

Challenges in Ethnic-Minority Language Bible Translation

Those who are appointed by their communities to translate the Bible into their mother tongues are very dedicated to their work. It is common for translators of a particular ethnic minority group to leave their homes, stay at a translation center, and do their work collectively. This is partly due to the fact that often they are creating the first written literature in their culture, without any reference material. They need to consult with one another on the choice of words, grammar, sentence structures, etc. Some of them only go home during festive occasions, planting, and harvesting seasons. It has been a privilege for the present author to work with these dedicated translators. At the same time, there are challenges as well, and we will note five of them.

The first challenge has to do with training. The educational level of the translators varies from team to team. In general, most of them have lower secondary-school education. Some may have basic theological training as well. They have a reasonable command of Mandarin, though sometimes they misunderstand terms or sentences used in Chinese Bibles. Practically none of them has access to English and, therefore, they are unable to use the rich resources available in that language. In addition, they tend to produce a word-for-word type of translation, from a chosen Chinese Bible that serves as their model text. The result is a translation that lacks naturalness and therefore is not easy to understand. A great deal of training is needed so that they can produce a translation that is natural in terms of language and acceptable in terms of accuracy. A systematic long-term training program is needed to equip translators with the necessary skills so that they can produce reliable and good translations in their mother tongue.

The second challenge is about linguistic variations. There are significant linguistic variations within a particular language, especially among populations from the same ethnic group who live in isolation from each other. Take the Big Flowery Miao, for instance. It is a subgroup that belongs to the Miao ethnic minority. The Big Flowery Miao settled mostly in the remote mountainous regions of Yunnan and Guizhou. Due to geographical separation and isolation, the same language developed quite differently in different places. Translators of the Big Flowery Miao Bible adopted the pronunciation, tones, and words that are in common use in Wuding county, Yunnan province. The Big Flowery Miao who live in Guizhou have difficulties using this Bible due to "dialect" differences. In other words, the Big Flowery Miao Bible published in Yunnan may need to be adapted to the linguistic usage of the same people group who live in Guizhou. The White Yi group faced the same situation. Different White Yi communities in various parts of Yunnan use different tones for the same word; hence, some would like to have the vowel in the high tone position, while others want it to be placed in the middle or low tone positions. It is therefore not possible to produce a translation to satisfy the needs of all the White Yi communities. Unless language standardization takes place, each language may end up needing several editions of the same Bible. In the English-speaking world, the issue is less severe, but even then, some English versions have American, Australian, and British editions to deal with these linguistic variations.

The third challenge relates to script issue and computer technologies. Some of the scripts used by ethnic minority groups in China are complex, and it is not easy to input these characters into computer applications. Samuel Pollard and his colleagues developed the Pollard script for the Big Flowery Miao. This script has been adapted by several other groups. Each language has its own unique consonants and vowels; hence, each requires its own set of fonts. In earlier translations, translators used pen and paper for their work and resorted to woodblock printing when the translation was finished. Today, the computer is the usual tool for word processing. In order to key in the text using computers, missionaries developed hacked fonts and used keyman or other input method editors, at best a temporary solution. Professional typesetting and publishing software encountered problems in dealing with these hacked fonts. Fortunately, due to collaborative efforts of all parties, the characters or alphabets of these languages are now in Unicode. Experts are working to come up with Unicode fonts for these languages so that these texts can function properly on computers.

The fourth challenge concerns literacy of most minority groups. A large number of ethnic minority groups do not have any written literature in their languages. Often a Bible portion or a hymnal is the only written literature of their culture. They can speak using their mother tongue, but few can read or write in their own language. A literacy program goes hand in hand with Bible translation activities. Translators, being the few who can read and write, often have to teach literacy classes as well, using translated Bible verses as reading material. Some churches came up with creative ways to deal with this issue. They meet one evening a week in the church to read the Scriptures together in their own language in an effort to help those who have difficulty reading. Some churches have completed reading the Bible from Genesis to Revelation! This literacy program is bearing fruit, but there is still a sizable population who are illiterate. Some ethnic minority groups recorded their Bibles and made them available in audio format. This has helped to make Scripture more readily accessible to the intended audience.

The fifth challenge has to do with approvals from the relevant authorities. Each country has its own sets of limitations and opportunities, and China is no exception. It takes time to receive official permission from the relevant authorities for starting Bible translation projects, and for printing the Bibles when they are completed. Sometimes things move smoothly, and at other times progress is slow. Some agencies have tried to bypass this bureaucracy and have adopted different strategies, but it is practically impossible for them to have their translations printed for distribution in China. This is a local condition that confronts every agency operating in China.

Impact of the Bible on Ethnic Minority Groups

For some ethnic minority groups, having the NT or the whole Bible in their mother tongue is a very significant event for their communities. For centuries, cultures were transmitted orally from one generation to the next, but now they have a book written in their own language, and people can learn to read and write. Cultures and traditions could now be transmitted using the written script in addition to oral transmission. Often this leads to a social transformation in society. This can be clearly seen in the Big Flowery Miao, Lisu, and Yi communities who received the Bibles. Having a Bible in their own language gives them a sense of identity, and more and more people become interested in learning their own language. These Christians claim that, knowing and following the teachings of the Bible also has brought about significant changes in their lives. In the past, they lived in fear of the spirits, and offering sacrifices to the ancestors, to mountains, trees, and spirits added to their financial burden. They see their Christian faith sets them free from such practices and gives them a new sense of belonging. Among some ethnic minority communities, addiction to alcohol is a common problem, and drunkenness leads to all kinds of social problems. The vast majority of them stop drinking alcohol altogether once they become Christians. Commenting on the spread of Christianity among the West Lisu, some government officials attribute reduced crime and social problems in the communities to Christianity.

Meeting the Scripture Needs of Ethnic Minority Groups

There is a tightening of control on religious activities in China recently, and this poses some challenges for Bible translation. For ethnic minority groups that do not yet have any Scriptures in their language, it may be more difficult for them to embark on translating the Bible into their mother tongue.

As noted earlier, the same ethnic minority group may be living in different countries, and this is the situation with ethnic minority groups in China as well. Large populations of the Miao, West Lisu, Lahu, Wa, and Jingpo live in China, as well as in the neighboring countries, notably in Thailand and Burma; hence, it is not unusual for missionaries to work with the same ethnic group in several countries. These ethnic groups speak basically the same language and often use the same script. What this means is that Bibles translated in these countries could be used by ethnic minority groups in China. Thus far, permissions have been granted to print Jingpo, Lahu, and West Lisu Bibles, translated in Thailand and Burma in recent decades, for publication and distribution in China. Before the completion of the Wa Bible translation project in China, the Wa NT translated in Burma also was printed in China for local distribution. This avoids duplication of effort and is an effective way of meeting the Scripture needs of minority groups in China.

Some of the ethnic minority languages spoken in China are the national languages of sovereign nations. Kazakh, Korean, Kyrgyz, Mongolian, Russian, and Uzbek are notable examples. In some cases, Bibles translated in these countries could be used by ethnic minority groups in China. For instance, Korean Bibles printed in Korea are being used by Korean Christians in China. Others may need adaptations due to dialect or script differences.

Consider the case of the Mongolian language. Though the majority of the Mongols live in China, about three million live in Mongolia. The Mongols in China used the classical script, a modification of the Uyghur alphabets, which in turn is based on Syrian writing introduced into East Asia by the Nestorian missionaries during the sixth and seventh centuries CE.[21] Mongolia, on the other hand, uses the Cyrillic script, introduced in the 1940s under Soviet influence. The scripts are totally different. The vast majority of Mongols in China cannot read texts written in Cyrillic script, and vice versa. There are other linguistic differences as well. About 80 percent of the Mongols in Mongolia belong to the Khalka group, and this is the standard Mongolian language in Mongolia. In China, on the other hand, the linguistic diversity in the Mongol language is much more complex. The Mongol language spoken in eastern, central, and western parts of Inner Mongolia, China, varies greatly and often speakers have difficulty communicating with one another using the Mongol language. At the moment, there are different Mongol Bibles available in Mongolia. The Ariun Bible, a formal translation published by the Mongolian Union Bible Society, is used by most of the churches in Mongolia. Another Mongolian version, modeled on the Good News Bible, is also in circulation. The Mongolian Union Bible Society is working on the Mongolian Standard Version at the moment, focusing on accuracy as well as readability. If permissions are granted, perhaps the Mongolian biblical text could be converted to the classical script and the text adapted to fit linguistic usage in China for the use of Mongol churches there. Due to the differences noted above, the adaptation will involve a considerable amount of work. Mongol Christians have expressed their desire for different types of Bible translations; hence, there are still several ongoing Bible translation projects among the Mongols in China as well as in Mongolia.

There are about 6.3 million Tibetans in China, mostly in the Tibetan autonomous region. In addition, significant numbers of Tibetans settled in India and Nepal. Moravian Church missionaries translated and published the Gospel according to John in a Tibetan language in Kashmir in 1862. The NT in classical Tibetan appeared in 1885, and the whole Bible, using a dialect of Tibetan Gergen, was published in 1948. The translation work is done in India. At the moment, activities to translate the Bible into Tibetan are ongoing. The Tibetan language is complicated, with many variations. It is not clear how intelligible these Tibetan Bibles published in India and Nepal are to the Tibetans in China. More analyses and comparisons are needed. In any case, a NT in modern central Tibetan, meant for the Tibetans in China, is now available, published in Hong Kong in 2015.

Some subgroups of Miao live in Thailand, the United States, France, and Australia. The American Bible Society published the Hmong Daw Bible (White Miao) in the year 2000, and the Blue Hmong Bible in 2007. These Bibles are being used in Thailand and Vietnam. In China, the same people groups are listed as subgroups of Miao, but they use different scripts. At the moment, it is not clear how useful these translations are to Miao groups in China.

In light of the above, it is important to conduct linguistic surveys among ethnic minority languages used in China and their counterparts used elsewhere. This mapping provides clearer ideas about whether Bibles translated in other countries could be used in China, and what types of adaptations are needed. Also, duplication of efforts and wasting of resources will be avoided so that the Scripture needs of these people could be met in more efficient ways. The table provided at the end of the essay—summarizing the Scriptures in ethnic minority languages—serves as a starting point.

Some ethnic minority groups in China may not feel the need to have a Bible in their own mother tongue. For instance, Hui, the second-largest ethnic minority group in China, use Mandarin as their primary language; hence, they can read Chinese Bibles if they so desire. If some prefer to read in Arabic, they could access Arabic translations published elsewhere.

The printed Bible is still the most common way for ethnic minority Christians to access the text, but the situation is slowly changing. The Big Flowery Miao group made their Bible available in audio format. In addition, some ethnic-minority language Scriptures are now available in mobile apps, and users can download and read them using their mobile phones. This has helped promote the wider application of Scriptures. Attempts are being made to make the Scriptures available in various media and formats so that users can choose to access the Bible in ways that best suit them.

Conclusion

Many Christian scholars see the biblical warrant of missionary activity to express the Gospel to and in every culture, language, people, and nation (Rev 5:9, 7:9, 14, 13:7, 14:6) which serves as the foundation of Bible translation.[22] In the last few decades, there have been significant developments of Bible translation in China. Bibles in minority languages have been translated and published, and more minority groups can now access the Scriptures in their heart language. However, there are still many ethnic-minority languages in China whose speakers do not have any Scriptures, and some among these people are interested in the Bible.

This phenomenon is not unique to China. On the global scene, there are 7,350 languages, as of early 2019. The full Bible is now available in 692 languages. Another 1,547 languages have the NT, and a further 1,123 languages have at least a book of the Bible translated. The remaining 3,988 languages do not have any Scriptures translated.[23]

Bible-translation agencies are working hard to provide Scriptures for these groups. The hope of these agencies, as they work in partnership with one another, with funds provided by donors and churches, is that more and more people can access the Scriptures in their heart language, including ethnic-minority groups in China.

APPENDIX

Scriptures in Ethnic Minority Languages of China

The following list (Table 8.2) summarizes ethnic-minority languages in China for which there are Scriptures available. The order of the list is based on the descending size of the population. When a subgroup of an ethnic minority has Scriptures available, the language name is written first, followed by the forward slash and the name of the ethnic minority. The semicolon separating the years is meant to indicate different versions or translations.

Table 8.2 Ethnic-Minority Languages in China for Which are Scriptures Available

Language/Ethnic Group	Portions	NT	OT	Bible
Manchu	1822	1835		
Uyghur	1898–1995	1914; 2005		1950
Big Flowery Miao/Miao	1906–1915	1917; 1936		2007
Black Miao/Miao	1928–1932	1934		
White Miao/Miao	1922, 1938	1984		2000
Blue Miao/Miao				2007
Ge Miao/Miao	1937			
Small Flowery Miao/Miao		2010 (trial edition)		
Black Yi/Yi		1948		2016
Gan Yi/Yi			2015	
White Yi/Yi		2014		
Laka/Yi	1912, 1936			
Tibetan	1862–1935	1885; 1903; 1970; 2015		1948
Mongol[24]	1815–1948	1827; 1846; 1880; 1952; 2013	1840	
Dong		2006[25]		
Bouyei	1904			
Yao–Thai script[26]	1932			
Yao–Roman script	1959–1968			
Ban Yao/Yao[27]	1932–1996	1991		2008
Korean	1882–1961	1887; 1900		1911[28]
Akha/Hani[29]	1939–1991	1968; 1987		2001
Kazakh[30]	1818	1820		2010
Dai		1933		2019[31]
Tai Nua/Dai[32]	1931–1948			
West Lisu/Lisu	1921–1933	1938		1968; 1987[33]
East Lisu/Lisu	1912–1936	1951; 2007		2016
Gelao[34]	1864–1986	1981		1983
Lahu	1924–1951	1932; 1962		1959; 1989
Wa	1934–1935	1938		2012; 2016[35]
Naxi	1932			
Kyrgyz-Arabic[36]	1818	1820; 1880		
Kyrgyz-Cyrillic	1901–2016	1991; 2005		1995; 2004
Jingpo	1895–1912	1912; 2004		1927; 2016
Achang[37]		2005		2011
Gin[38]	1890–1963	1923; 1954; 1961		1916; 1925
Russian[39]	1815–1963	1821; 1906	1868; 1875	1876; 2000; 2015
Uzbek[40]	1891	1992		2016
Tatars[41]	1864–1893			

Notes

1. Adapted from Wikipedia, https://en.wikipedia.org/wiki/List_of_ethnic_groups_in_China [All websites on this essay accessed on May 1, 2020].
2. These peoples settled in China long ago but do not belong to any of the officially recognized ethnic groups.

3. Ralph R. Covell, *The Liberating Gospel in China: The Christian Faith among China's Minority Peoples* (Grand Rapids: Baker Books, 1995), 108–109.
4. Peter O. Koch, *To the Ends of the Earth: The Age of the European Explorers* (Jefferson, NC: McFarland & Company, 2003), 17–20.
5. https://www.christianexaminer.com/article/700-year-old-gospel-challenge-in-mongolia-is-answered/43038.htm.
6. Eugene A. Nida, ed., *The Book of a Thousand Tongues*, 2nd ed. (London: United Bible Societies, 1972), 303.
7. http://www.newadvent.org/cathen/08474a.htm.
8. https://www.newworldencyclopedia.org/entry/Giovanni_da_Montecorvino.
9. Covell, *The Liberating Gospel in China*, 115–118.
10. Nida, *The Book of a Thousand Tongues*, 303.
11. Ibid. See also Patrick Taveirne, *Han-Mongol Encounters and Missionary Endeavors: A History of Scheut in Ordos (Hetao) 1874–1911*, Leuven Chinese Studies XV (Leuven: Leuven University Press, 2004), 143–144.
12. Covell, *The Liberating Gospel in China*, 121–124.
13. Ibid. 168–71; See also https://joshuaproject.net/people_groups/15755/CH.
14. Sung Il Choi, "*John Ross (1842–1915) and the Korean Protestant Church: The First Korean Bible and its Relation to the Protestant Origins in Korea*," Ph.D. Diss., Edinburgh Univ., 1992.
15. https://omf.org/us/about/our-story/james-hudson-taylor/.
16. http://www.mundus.ac.uk/cats/3/9.htm.
17. Covell, *The Liberating Gospel in China*, 83–90.
18. Also known as Chuan Miao or Hmu. See Nida, *The Book of a Thousand Tongues*, 294–295.
19. Choi, *John Ross (1842–1915) and the Korean Protestant Church*, 64–67.
20. https://www.cmalliance.org/about/history/in-the-line-of-fire/boxer-rebellion.
21. Nida, *The Book of a Thousand Tongues*, 303.
22. See K. K. Yeo, "Beyond Chalcedon? Towards a Fully-Christian and Fully-Cultural Theology," in *Jesus without Borders*, ed. Gene Green et al. (Grand Rapids: Eerdmans, 2014), 162–179; K. K. Yeo, "Introduction: So Great a Salvation: Soteriology in the Majority World," in *So Great a Salvation*, Gene Green et al. (Grand Rapids: Eerdmans, 2017), 1–13.
23. United Bible Societies, "Key Facts about Bible Access," https://www.unitedbiblesocieties.org/key-facts-bible-access/.
24. Mongolian versions translated in Mongolia (using Cyrillic script) are not listed here.
25. https://rflr-bible.org/kam/.
26. Nida, *The Book of a Thousand Tongues*, 461. Translations using Thai and Romans scripts are for the Yao of Thailand.
27. https://joshuaproject.net/people_groups/18411/CH. The primary language used by Ban Yao is Lu Mien.
28. This is the first entire Bible in Korean. Several other Korean versions appeared subsequently, done in Korea. Today, Korean Christians in China are using the Korean Bible published in Korea.
29. The Akha translation is carried out mostly in Burma and Thailand. The NT has also been translated into the main Hani language but has not been published.
30. Translation work was being done mostly outside China.
31. This is trial edition, published in Xishuangbanna, Yunnan, China. The edition has not been properly checked by a translation consultant.

32. https://joshuaproject.net/people_groups/15193/CH.
33. After 1949, the translation of the Lisu Bible was carried out in Thailand and Burma. There are also annotated Lisu Bibles available in China as well as in Burma.
34. https://joshuaproject.net/people_groups/11857/CH.
35. The Wa Bible was published in Burma in 2012. Before that, trial editions were in circulation. Another Wa Bible was published in China in 2016.
36. Arabic script is used by the Kyrgyz in China. The bulk of Kyrgyz people live in Kyrgyzstan, and they use the Cyrillic script. The Kyrgyz Bible was translated and published outside China.
37. https://joshuaproject.net/people_groups/10146/CH.
38. Nida, *The Book of a Thousand Tongues*, 449–450. Gin people in China are descendants of ethnic Vietnamese. Translation work is done outside China.
39. The translation was carried out in Russia; see Nida, *The Book of a Thousand Tongues*, 374, http://www.russianbible.org.
40. The translation work was carried out mostly in Central Asia; see https://www.unitedbiblesocieties.org/the-bible-in-uzbek/.
41. The vast majority live in Russia and other post-Soviet countries. The translation work was done outside of China.

Primary Sources

See notes in the Appendix above.

Covell, Ralph R. *The Liberating Gospel in China: The Christian Faith among China's Minority Peoples*. Grand Rapids: Baker Books, 1995.

Nida, Eugene A., ed. *The Book of a Thousand Tongues*, 2nd ed. London: United Bible Societies, 1972.

CHAPTER 9

CLASSICAL LANGUAGES IN CHINESE BIBLICAL STUDIES

LEOPOLD LEEB

INTRODUCTION

THE three *linguae sacrae* (Hebrew, Greek, Latin) have been cultivated in Europe especially since the Renaissance era, when scholars like Reuchlin (1455–1522) and Melanchthon (1497–1560) produced textbooks for learning biblical Hebrew and Greek. In China, the study of these languages as a fruitful access to the Bible has not been prioritized for a long time for a number of reasons. In the period before 1900, there was little awareness within Chinese society of the necessity to learn foreign languages. However, since the seventeenth century, individual priests learned Latin, mainly abroad. Accompanying cultural changes since the early twentieth century was a quest for learning foreign languages, and the first textbooks for classical Greek and Latin were written by Chinese scholars. The spread of classical languages in China was somehow delayed during the Cold War era, but since the end of the twentieth century, a lasting quest for learning classical languages can be noticed, as reflected in the publication of textbooks, dictionaries, and polyglot Bible editions. A historical review might help to understand the special way the three classical languages have been slowly entering the hearts and minds of modern Chinese people.

BEFORE 1800: CHINESE PIONEERS LEARNING FOREIGN LANGUAGES

Latin was the theological language of Augustine, Thomas Aquinas, Erasmus, Luther, and it was the common liturgical language of the Catholic Church until the end of the twentieth century. Until the 1980s, Catholic Chinese clergymen were trained in this language, and they read the Bible in Latin.

According to his letters, Italian Franciscan Fr. Giovanni Montecorvino (1247–1328) started to teach Latin in Beijing and produced a (Mongolian) version of the New Testament (NT), based on the Vulgate. However, his effort to spread Latin in China was ephemeral.

In the 1580s, the first Western college in China was organized in Macau for students from China and Japan. In 1591, the first group of Chinese Jesuit candidates entered the novitiate, and began to learn Latin, among them Zhong Mingren 鐘鳴仁 (1562–1622), and Huang Mingsha 黃明沙 (1568–1606).[1]

In 1604, Chinese scholars ("literati") in Beijing saw for the first time the different textual versions (Hebrew, Latin, Greek, Syriac, Aramaic) of the Bible, namely the "Plantiniana" or "Biblia Polyglotta," an illustrated multilingual edition of the Bible, produced by Belgian printer C. Plantin in 1568. In response to M. Ricci's request, a set (eight volumes) of the polyglot Bible was sent to Beijing, which arrived in 1604. Ricci impressed some of the literati by showing them the Bible edition; however, the Jesuits did not set up language courses for the Chinese, nor did anyone try to introduce the Greek or Hebrew alphabet to China. The reluctance of early Jesuits to introduce Arabic numbers or Greek alphabetic symbols to China was certainly due to the fear of being accused of spreading obscure and dangerous knowledge, since all things foreign were viewed with suspicion. One sad example is Fr. Ricci's famous world map, the first of its kind in China, which was reprinted many times. This map contains numerous transliterations of geographical names into Chinese (e.g. "*Ou-luo-ba* 歐邏巴" for "Europe"), but Ricci did not keep one single word in the original alphabet, although this map would have been an excellent tool for spreading the ABC in China.[2]

In 1615, Fr. Nicholas Trigault obtained permission from Rome for the Chinese language to be used in the liturgy and for the Bible to be translated into the "erudite language proper to the literati," that is, into classical Chinese and not into the vernacular. The early Jesuits did not invest much energy in translation of the Bible, and Chinese theological books were rare before the translations of Fr. Ludovico Buglio (1606–1682). The translation of the whole Bible posed great problems, but quotations from the Bible soon appeared in Chinese works of the missionaries: Fr. Matteo Ricci introduced the Ten Commandments in his *Jiren shigui* 畸人十規. In 1636, Fr. Manoel Diaz (1574–1659) published *Shengjing zhijie* 聖經直解, a translation of about twenty-five percent of the Gospels into classical Chinese 文言文, adding explanations. This large work may be considered the first exegetical book in Chinese.[3] In the two years before his death, the French M.E.P. father, Jean Basset M.E.P. (1662–1707), produced a translation of most parts of the Vulgate version of the NT (the Gospels, Acts, and the letters of St. Paul), and this manuscript was later used by the first Protestant missionary to China, R. Morrison.

The huge challenge in translating theological terms into Chinese was whether to use transliterations ("*dou-lu-ri-ya* 陡祿日亞" for "*theologia*")[4] or translating the meaning of terms ("*chao-xing-xue*" for "theology," literally "transcend-nature-studies").[5] The translation of Hebrew, Greek, and Latin names into Chinese was and is another problem, although some biblical names have found universally accepted forms that have remained in use for centuries, such as "*Ye-su* 耶穌" for "Jesus" and "*Ya-dang* 亞當" for "Adam," "*Bao-lu* 保祿" for "Paul," "Ma-li-ya 馬利亞" for "Mary." These transliterations have been used already by L. Buglio in the 1650s and have remained constant within Catholic circles until today.[6]

It can safely be said that none of the famous scholar converts of the late Ming dynasty knew Latin, although some of them used Latin concepts. For example, the *Lingyan lishao* 靈言蠡勺, a Chinese work by the convert Xu Guangqi 徐光啟 (1562–1633) and Fr. Sambiasi, published in 1624, discussed the existence of the human soul, rendered as *ya-ni-ma* 亞尼瑪, a transliteration of Latin "*anima*." The book introduced Aristotelian concepts.

The first Chinese to know Latin very well were those sent overseas for studies, namely China's first native priest and bishop, Luo Wenzao 羅文藻 (1615–1691), who studied in the Philippines in the 1650s, Zheng Manuo 鄭瑪諾 (1633–1673), who returned from Italy in 1668, and Shen Fuzong 沈福宗 (1658–1691), who conversed (in Latin) with scholars in France and at Oxford University.

The first Chinese who assisted in the process of translating the Latin Bible was Xu Ruohan 徐若翰, also known as Xu Yingtian 徐應天 (ca. 1670–1740), a Chinese scholar from Jiading, Zhejiang. He did not succeed in the examination process. His wife died in 1704, whereupon he sought consolation in Buddhism and Daoism but could not find peace. He left his 9-year-old son with his parents and migrated to Chengdu, Sichuan. He heard about the Catholic Church and contacted Fr. Basset, who gave Xu Catholic literature to read. Basset needed someone to help him with his Bible translation, and since Xu had received good literary training, he became Basset's secretary. After Xu was baptized, the two men started the translation of the Bible in July 1705. After Basset's untimely death in 1707, Bp. Baluere (1668–1715) recommended Xu as secretary to Bp. Tournon; thus, from 1707 to 1710, Xu was in Macau, where he was probably an ordained priest. In 1710, he returned to Sichuan. Either in Macao, or after his return to Sichuan Xu on his own, he translated a Life of Jesus from Latin into Chinese (*Sishi youbian Yesu Jilisidu Fuyin zhi Hebian* 四史攸編耶穌基利斯督福音之合編), thus becoming the very first Chinese translator of Christian literature. Not much else is known about the life of Xu.[7] Needless to say, Xu probably had a very limited understanding of Greek and Hebrew.

Latin was useful as an international diplomatic language. Jesuit Fr. Parrenin (1665–1741) produced a small Latin dictionary, and Fr. Gaubil (1689–1759) taught some Manchu diplomats Latin. The Treaty of Nerchinsk (1689) was written in Latin, and Jesuit fathers Gerbillon, and Pereyra served as negotiators with the Russians. The early works of missionary sinologists and their translation of the Chinese classics were in Latin; most influential among these was the *Confucius, Sinarum Philosophus* (1687, published in Paris).

Fr. Matteo Ripa led a group of five seminarians to Italy in 1724 and set up a theological college in Naples, where Chinese priests were trained in Latin and Italian. Many of the 106 priests trained there between 1734 and 1880 secretly re-entered China and served as missionaries.[8] These men had certainly a good understanding of Christianity and the

Bible, but due to the lack of proper institutions, biblical studies could not develop in China in the eighteenth century.

An interesting example of a Chinese priest acting as translator using Latin is Li Zibiao 李自標 (1760–1828), a Chinese priest from Wuwei, Gansu. In 1773, at the age of 13, he traveled to the college in Naples, Italy, where he learned Latin, Italian, and theology. In 1784, he was ordained a priest. From 1792–1793, he accompanied the delegation of Lord Macartney to China, serving as translator. He was of crucial importance in Macartney's encounter with the Qianlong emperor. In 1794, he accompanied the British delegation to Macau but did not return to Europe. Li Zibiao stayed in China to secretly serve the Catholics in the provinces. However, he remained in contact with Macartney by writing letters until 1802.

The first Chinese to compile a bilingual Latin-Chinese dictionary was probably Zhu Wanhe 朱萬禾 (1770–1812), also known as Zhu Shouguan 朱壽官 and Antonius Ciu. He was a Catholic from Shanxi, who came to Italy in 1789 and studied at the Collegium Sinicum in Naples. He was ordained a priest in 1798 and elaborated a Latin-Chinese dictionary.[9] He died in Naples in 1812.

In the same period, one of the greatest translators of the Bible, Fr. Louis de Poirot S.J. (1735–1815), produced not only a translation of the Vulgate into colloquial Chinese, but another one into Manchu. Like Basset's work, Poirot's translation was not published and thus had very limited influence.[10]

From 1800–1918: The First Educational Institutions for Classical Languages in China

The period from 1800 to 1918 was marked by the renewed influx of foreign missionaries, this time also Protestants from the English-speaking world, who put much more emphasis on the translation of biblical texts than the Catholics, who primarily cared about the publication of catechetical books. The nineteenth century saw for the first time the printing of bilingual dictionaries, a good number of them Latin-Chinese or Chinese-Latin.[11]

Whereas the clandestine Catholic seminaries in Sichuan and Beijing in the late eighteenth century produced a group of Chinese Latinists, the educational level of these inland seminaries could not match the linguistic skills of the institutions in Naples and Macau. One outstanding man who educated many Chinese seminarians in the classical languages was Affonso Gonsalvez C.M. (1781–1841), a priest who joined the Lazarist seminary in Rihafoles, Portugal, in 1799. In 1801, he professed vows, and he came to Macau in 1813. He was appointed to go to Beijing but did not get permission due to the strict policies of the Jiaqing emperor. For many years, he taught at the Sao José Seminary in Macau, where he trained young priests. He compiled at least six bilingual dictionaries, among them a *Chinese-Portuguese Dictionary* 漢葡字典, a *Vocabularium Latino-Sinicum* 拉漢辭匯 (1836), a *Lexicon magnum Latino-Sinicum* 拉丁—漢語大詞典 (1841). He died in Macau on October 3, 1841. Chinese-Latin and Latin-Chinese dictionaries were compiled by several other missionaries. Among these the most important works were compiled by Bp. Brollo (1694), Fr. Petillon (1906), Fr. Boehm (1958).[12] However, most of the Latin students were seminarians, even up to the twentieth century.

The first Chinese Protestant biblical scholar was He Jinshan [Ho Chin-shan, Ho Tsun-sheen] 何進善, also He Futang 何福堂 and He Runyang 何潤養, sometimes called "the first modern Chinese theologian." His family was from Guangdong, his father a woodblock carver with the London Missionary Society (LMS) in Malacca. In 1837, he followed his father to Malacca and received baptism. In 1838, he learned from Evans at the Anglo-Chinese College in Malacca, then continued at Bishop's College in Calcutta. He had a personal conversion experience in 1839 and, from 1840–1843 was with Legge for a period of further schooling (in Malacca) "during which Jinshan achieved fluency in English and in reading Greek and Hebrew."[13] He helped Legge with translation projects and produced the translation of a Chinese novel (1843). He followed Legge to Hong Kong as a preacher. In 1846, he was ordained as pastor of the Union Chapel (Hop Yat Church). Following Legge's suggestion, he wrote commentaries for the Gospels of Matthew (*Matai Fuyin zhushi* 馬太福音注釋) and Mark (*Make Fuyin zhushi* 馬可福音注釋), also known as *Shengjing xiyi* 聖經析義 (first published 1855, completed 1868–1870), and a commentary on the Ten Commandments. He also penned *Shengjing Zhengju* 聖經証據 (printed in 1870), an introduction to the Bible. He died April 3, 1871. All his sons were educated abroad, and the most famous of them was Sir He Qi何啟 (1859–1914), who built Alice Memorial Hospital and co-founded Hong Kong College of Medicine.

Even before foreigners were permitted to enter the "treaty ports" (Shanghai, Ningbo, Amoy, and other ports opened to foreigners in 1842), seminaries that taught Latin (and sometimes other foreign languages) were established in these cities and in the inland provinces. In 1830, a seminary in Chengdu, Sichuan, was founded; in 1831 a Latin school was established in the area of Funing, Fujian. In 1843, the seminary of Zhangpuqiao 張朴橋, Shanghai, was founded; in 1844, a seminary in Nanchang, Jiangxi, was opened; in 1845, a Lazarist seminary opened in Zhoushan 舟山; and in 1852, a seminary in Guiyang (Guizhou), was started by French missionaries (M.E.P.).[14]

Among the Catholic schools, the most famous was the College of St. Ignace (Xuhui Gongxue), the first modern school in central China, which systematically taught foreign languages and the sciences. In 1849, the college was established by French Jesuit Fr. Gotteland (1803–1856) and directed by Italian Jesuit Fr. Zottoli (1826–1902). The school educated many future priests and translators and prepared students for university studies. In 1853, the school had thirty-one students and four teachers, and Fr. Zottoli was director of the institute. Many Jesuit novices were trained in this college. The students were given courses in Latin, French, and classical Chinese. In 1904, English was added. In 1953, the school was renamed Xuhui Middle School of Shanghai City. The directors of the school were: Gotteland (founder, 1850), Zottoli 晁德蒞 (1852–1866), Ma Xiangbo 馬相伯 (1871–1874), Huang Bolu 黃伯祿 (1874–1879), Jiang Yixu 蔣邑虛 (1880–1899), Pan Gusheng 潘谷聲 (1902–1903), Zhang Ruose 張若瑟 (1906–1907). All of these were priests with an excellent command of Latin and possibly even other Western languages, especially French.

Two of the early Chinese Catholic Bible translators are connected with this college, namely Ma Xiangbo 馬相伯 (1840–1939) and Li Wenyu 李問漁 (1840–1911). Both were well versed in Latin, and, according to some sources, they also had taken some courses of biblical Greek during their studies in Shanghai.

Joseph Ma Xiangbo, also known as Ma Liang 馬良, was a Catholic educator and reformer from Dantu (Zhenjiang), Jiangsu. In 1851, he entered the Xuhui College. In 1862, he entered the Jesuit novitiate and studied philosophy and theology, receiving outstanding language training from Fr. Zottoli (including Latin, French, Greek, and some Italian). Ma excelled in mathematics and astronomy. In 1869, he was ordained a priest, and in 1870, he obtained a PhD in theology. From 1872–1875, he served as principal of Xuhui College and as editor of Jesuit publications. Ma left the Jesuit order in 1876 and committed himself to social and political reform. In 1881, he served as minister to the Chinese ambassador in Japan and, in 1882, he was at the Chinese embassy in Korea. In the years 1902–1903, Aurora College was created, and Ma was rector of the college. He taught Latin in Shanghai, and among his students were influential reformers like Cai Yuanpei 蔡元培 and Liang Qichao 梁啟超. Ma also produced a textbook for Latin, the *Lading wentong* 拉丁文通 (1903), which was not as influential as the first modern Chinese grammar, the *Mashi wentong* 馬氏文通 (1897), which he wrote together with his brother. In 1919, Ma Xiangbo published *Xinshi hebian zhijiang* 新史合編直講, the translation of a life of Jesus by Mastai Ferretti and, by 1937, he had translated the four Gospels, which was published under the title *Fuyin jing* 福音經 in 1949. However, his lack of different text versions and the exaggerated use of elegant classical Chinese had the result that his translation sank into oblivion.

A classmate of Ma Xiangbo was Laurentius Li Wenyu 李問漁, also known as Li Duo 李杕, 1840–1911, from Chuansha, Jiangsu. In 1862, he entered the Jesuit novitiate, and in 1866 he was ordained a priest. From 1872–1878, he served as missionary in Songjiang, Nanhui, Anhui. Since he knew Latin, French, and other Western languages, he was appointed for teaching posts in Shanghai after 1878. In 1887, he created the *Yiwenlu* 益聞錄 (Useful Informations) magazine and the *Shengxin bao* 聖心報 (Sacred Heart Monthly), the first periodical in China to use colloquial language. In 1906, he was appointed president of Aurora College in Shanghai. He also taught at Nanyang Gongxue and translated some thirty-nine books, such as *Xixue guanjian* 西學關鍵 (eight vols.), *Zhexue tigang* 哲學提綱, etc. Li Wenyu produced a version of the NT, the *Xinjing yiyi* 新經譯義, but he only retold the four Gospels and the Acts of the Apostles in classical Chinese. Fr. Li counts as the most prolific Catholic Chinese writer of the late nineteenth century.

In the 1850s, the Jesuits also took over the region of Xianxian, Hebei, where they established schools and a seminary. There, the first Chinese Bible translator of that period, Fr. Xiao Jingshan 蕭靜山, or Joseph Xiao 蕭若瑟 (1855–1924), was teacher. He obtained a good education in the Chinese classics and passed the *xiucai* 秀才 examination at the age of 18. He went to the seminary of Zhangjiazhuang and was ordained a priest in 1886. He taught at the seminary and, from 1890–1893, he was teacher at the High School of Zhangjiazhuang. In 1893, he became a full member of the Society of Jesus. Since then he started to write and translate spiritual literature. The boxer year (1900) he spent in Xianxian. In 1913, he was ordered back from Hejian to the seminary in Zhangjiazhuang, and there he taught and continued to write his works. He translated the four Gospels in 1919 and finished the translation of the NT (according to the Vulgate) in 1922. His *Xinjing Quanji* 新經全集 (two volumes, together more than one thousand pages) was quite influential and counts as the first NT version ever translated by a Chinese scholar. In 1948, it was revised according to the Greek text. This revised version was used in China until the 1990s. It provided commentaries to certain passages. Fr. Xiao also wrote the substantial historical work *Shengjiao shilue* 聖教史略 (on the history of the Church in Europe and in China, more than one thousand pages, probably published in 1922) and the *Tianzhujiao chuanxing Zhongguo kao* 天主教傳行中國考 (1923, more than five hundred pages).

One of the early Chinese Bible translators was Wang Xuanchen 王宣忱 (also known as Wang Yuande 王元德), 1879–1942. He was born in Changle, Wutu zhen, Dengjiazhuang, Shandong. In 1895, he enrolled at the Presbyterian school in Weixian. In 1904, C. Mateer chose Wang to be his Chinese secretary for the translation of the Bible (1904–1908); thus, Wang made his contribution to the Mandarin Union Version (*Hehe yiben*) 官話和合譯本. In 1913, he edited the *Wenhuigan zhi* 文會館志. From 1918, he served at the YMCA in Ji'nan. In 1928, he moved to Qingdao, where he became director of the Shangde Elementary School. He also became founder of several companies; for example, "Laoshan Wine Company" 嶗山酒家 (1938). From 1930–1933, he translated the NT, based on the American Standard Version. In 1933, his translation was published by the Qingdao branch of the NCC 中華基督教會. In 1940, he produced a hymnal, the *Songzan shige* 頌讚詩歌, with 633 hymns. He died of hemorrhage in the brain in October of 1942. Wang Xuanchen had an exceptional command of foreign languages; he knew Hebrew, Greek, and Latin, but to what extent he grasped these languages is hard to know.

Although some individuals like Wang Xuanchen learned the languages of the Bible, the classical languages were not taught at the many emerging Protestant schools in China in the first decades of the twentieth century. Around the year 1915, "the curriculum of the American arts college had been transferred to China, with the elimination of Greek and Latin."[15] This stands in stark contrast to the Catholic Church in China, where all seminarians passed through an education course (five to eight years "minor seminary" and another five years "major seminary") that used Latin as a liturgical and academic language. However, the study of Greek and Hebrew had to wait until the following period.

From 1918–1950: The Way to Maturity

The years around 1918 mark the shift from classical Chinese to a modern language, promoted by the May Fourth Movement (1917–1919), which announced the advent of "Mr. Sai" ("Mr. Science") and "Mr. De" ("Mr. Democracy"). This popular expression implies a certain awareness that many concepts of modern Chinese are formed by Latin (*scientia*, science) and Greek (*demokratia*, democracy) ideas. At the same time, the outstanding American scholar, educator, and missionary, John Stuart Leighton (1876–1962), published his *New Testament Greek* 新約希臘文 (1917), the first textbook for students of classical Greek published in China, and his *Greek-Chinese-English Dictionary of the New Testament* (1919). For Chinese students of the biblical languages, the publication of these books in Shanghai marked a new era. Now it was possible to get a grasp of the original language of the NT; however, the precarious political situation, the Anti-Japanese War (1937–1945), and the Civil War (1945–1949) did not allow for the stable development of classical studies and exegetical research.

Outstanding Protestant scholars in the fields of Greek and Hebrew studies were concentrated at the two most well-known theological institutions of the period, the Jinling Theological College in Nanjing and the Department of Religion of Yanjing University in Beijing.

The first Chinese to produce a textbook for NT Greek was Zhu Baohui 朱寶惠 (1886–1970), a Chinese pastor from Shandong. He graduated from a Christian school in Xuzhou and, in 1912, he was among the first graduates of Jinling Theological College in Nanjing. He was a student of Stuart Leighton and Rev. Absalom Sydenstricker. From 1913–1917, he served as evangelizer and taught at a Christian school in Suqian, Jiangsu. In 1918, he taught at Jinling Theological Seminary and, at the same time (from 1918–1925), he continued his studies. He published the first Greek Grammar *Xinyue yuanwen leijie* 新約原文類解 (1925) written by a Chinese scholar. In 1929, he presented a revised version of the Chinese NT. From 1925, he taught courses on the Greek NT at Jinling Seminary, Nanjing and, at the same time, he served as pastor. In 1937, he and his family had to flee, passing through Anhui, Hubei, Hunan, and Sichuan. He taught at the combined theological seminary in Chengdu during the war, and at the end of 1945, he returned to Nanjing, where he continued to teach at Jinling Seminary and serve as pastor at Hanzhong Church. He retired in 1956 and died in Nanjing on February 22, 1970.

China's first internationally recognized Hebrew scholar was Li Rongfang 李榮芳, (1887–1965), a scholar from Hebei. He learned Greek and Hebrew from Stuart Leighton and, in 1913, he obtained an MA from Peking University. From 1914–1917, he continued Old Testament (OT) studies in Chicago. In 1919, he obtained a PhD degree in London, and from 1921–1928, he served as assistant professor at the Department of Religion of Yenching University, where he taught classical Hebrew. In 1928, he continued studies at King's College, London, and in 1929, he resumed work at Yenching University. He took part in archeological work in Israel and published articles on OT texts and apocryphal texts. He is considered the first qualified OT scholar from China, but unfortunately, he did not produce a good textbook for Hebrew. His handwritten Hebrew-Chinese dictionary (*Jiuyue Xibolaiwen Cidian* 舊約希伯來文辭典), a manuscript of 1,230 pages, was written in the 1950s but never printed. It was photocopied and bound by Jinling Seminary (Nanjing) in 2015.

Andrew Cheng Zhiyi 誠質怡 (or C. Y. Cheng, 1898–1977) was born in Beijing into a Manchu family. In 1906, he entered LMS elementary school in Beijing, and later the Union College in Tongzhou, Beijing. In 1918, he learned Hebrew and Greek from Stuart Leighton at Jinling Theological College, Nanjing. In 1927, he obtained a PhD in philosophy from Columbia University and was ordained a pastor. After his return to China, he taught Hebrew at Jenching (Yanjing) University, Beijing and, in 1934, he went to Jinling University, Nanjing, and became the head of the Department of Religion. In 1939, he served as teacher of NT at Jinling Theological Seminary, and from 1950–1952, he was rector of the seminary. Although Cheng Zhiyi counted as one of the leading experts on Greek and Hebrew, he did not produce any dictionary or textbook.

Another Chinese Hebraist was Zhu Weizhi 朱維之 (1905–1999) from Wenzhou, Zhejiang. He was born into a Christian family and studied in Japan from 1930 to 1932. He specialized in Hebrew literature and biblical literature. Starting in 1952, he was professor at Nankai University, Tianjin. After the Cultural Revolution, he resumed his work as teacher. Among his works are *Jidujiao yu wenxue* 基督教與文學 (*Christianity and Literature*, Shanghai 1941), *Yage he Jiuge* 雅歌和九歌 (*The Song of Songs and the Jiuge*), *Shipian Wenxue Jianshang* 詩篇文學鑒賞 (*Appraising the Literature of the Psalms*), *Yesu Jidu* 耶穌基督 (*Jesus Christ*, 1948). His *Wuchanzhe Yesu zhuan* 無產者耶穌傳 (*Jesus the Proletarian*, Shanghai, 1950) marks a turn in his worldview. In 1988, his *Xibolai wenhua* 希伯來文化 (*Hebrew Culture*) was published.

From 1950–1980: A Delay with Positive Side-Effects

The period from 1950–1980 was marked by the restructuring of China's society and by certain disastrous policies, which not only affected material living standards but also destroyed academic life. As the teaching of foreign languages was limited and contacts to the Western world were suppressed, it was hard for people with an interest in the biblical languages to develop their pursuits. However, following the example of Soviet Russia, Latin was universally taught at medical institutions in the 1950s and, for this purpose, a good number of textbooks for Latin were produced by a graduate from St. John's University, Xie Daren 谢大任 (1899–1994), whose efforts found their climax in the *Ladingyu Hanyu Cidian* 拉丁文漢語辭典 (*Latin-Chinese Dictionary*) published in 1988, the first medium-sized Latin dictionary to use modern vernacular language. Another medium-sized Latin-Chinese dictionary published by the Jesuit priest Wu

Jinrui (1891–1967) in Taiwan in 1965[16] still used classical Chinese and is less useful for modern readers.

For classical Greek, the situation was even worse. Only very few scholars were able to conduct studies or writing on Greek language or thought. All Catholic seminarians received good training in Latin, and some even in Greek during the 1940s; however, all Catholic seminaries were closed by 1954. Since the "anti-rightist movement" of 1957, the two remaining official Protestant theological schools in Beijing and Nanjing could not work properly, and university life was reduced to minimal standards. Only with the implementation of the "Opening and Reform" policies (after 1978) were classical studies and the study of the biblical languages slowly revived.

As many intellectuals left China in or after 1949, also the Catholic Bible study center founded by Fr. Allegra moved from Beijing to Hong Kong. Gabriele Stefano Allegra (1907–1976) was born in Sicily. He joined the Franciscans in 1923. In 1928, he had for the first time the idea to translate the Bible into Chinese. He was ordained a priest in 1930, served as missionary in Hengyang, Hunan from 1931–1939, and started with translations of biblical texts in 1935. He went to Beijing in 1941, started to establish a library and train local priests to help with the translation work. In 1945, he organized the "Studium Biblicum Franciscanum" (*Sigao Shengjing Xuehui* 思高聖經學會). In August 1948, the institution moved to Kowloon, Hong Kong. In 1968, the translation of the whole Bible was completed, and the publication in Hong Kong and Taiwan started. This Chinese version of the Bible is known as "*Sigao ben*" 思高本 (Studium Biblicum version) and is based on the original languages of the texts. In 1975, Allegra published a *Shengjing Cidian* 聖經辭典 (*Bible Dictionary*).

Comparing the most popular Protestant version (the Union Version of 1919) and the authoritative Catholic translation (the *Sigao ben* of 1968), it is obvious that in the question of Greek and Hebrew personal names, the Catholic Bible sometimes sticks to an old tradition dating back to the seventeenth century (examples: "*Mei-se* 梅瑟" for "Moses" and "*Ruo-wang* 若望" for "John"). Sometimes the Catholic transliteration is closer to the original pronunciation than the Union Version (for examples "*An-ti-yue-ji-ya* 安提約基亞" is closer to "Antiochia" than "*An-ti-a* 安提阿," "*Hei-luo-de* 黑落德" is closer to "Herod" than "*Xi-lü* 希律," and "*Fei-li-bo* 斐理伯" is closer to "Philippos" than "*Fei-li* 腓力").

The translation of central theological terms has remained a question of debate; thus, there are three names for "*theos*" (God): "*Tianzhu* 天主" (Catholic), "*Shangdi* 上帝" (Protestant), and "*Shen* 神" (Protestant).

Although the period from 1950 to 1980 did not produce many tools for the study of the biblical languages, it prepared the shift to the modern "vernacular" Chinese language, which standardized and unified academic terminology in the field of grammar. Thus, language textbooks published in China have unified grammar terms, and sometimes these terms are different from those used in books published in Taiwan and Hong Kong.[17]

Some scholars found time to devote themselves to the translation of Greek classics from the originals. One example is Zhou Zuoren 周作人 (1885–1967), one of the first to introduce Western literature to China. He acquired Greek language skills during his studies in Japan (1906–1911) and originally planned to translate the NT into Chinese, but in his later years (1945–1967) he translated the works of Euripides and other Greek poets. At the same time, scholars like Yan Qun 嚴群 (1907–1985), Luo Niansheng 羅念生 (1904–1990), and Shui Jianfu 水建馥 (1925–2008) laid foundations for further studies, especially by providing China with the first middle-sized Greek-Chinese dictionary (published in 2004).[18]

After 1980: Reaching Out toward New Horizons

The opening of Catholic seminaries and the re-opening of Protestant theological schools in the years from 1980–1985 implied that slowly more students were exposed to classical languages. On the Catholic side, Latin continued to be the liturgical language until the years 1990–1993, when Chinese became the main language used during masses. (This change had started in the 1960s in Taiwan and Hong Kong, and the liturgical books from those regions made a fast shift to Chinese possible in China mainland.) However, in some local churches a movement for the revival of Latin songs (Gregorian chant) was promoted by some Catholics who organized Latin choirs, as for example Li Yuzhang 李毓章 (1931–2013) at the Cathedral of Taiyuan, Shanxi.

The incipient tradition of teaching Hebrew in China was continued by a German Franciscan priest, Fr. Hubert Vogt, who taught Hebrew at Catholic seminaries in China after 1994. Fr. Vogt 傅和德 (1935–2005) joined the Franciscans in 1954, was ordained a priest in 1960, studied in Rome, and taught in the Philippines. In 1970, he learned Chinese in Taiwan, and from 1972–1994, he gave courses in Taiwan and Hong Kong. From 1994 until his death, he taught courses on the OT and classical Hebrew in Catholic seminaries in China, in Beijing, Shanghai, Shenyang, Xi'an, Wuhan, and Taiyuan. He died in Germany on May 31, 2005. Two of his Chinese books were published in Beijing in 2002: *Jiuyue Beijing* 舊約背景 (*Context of the Old Testament*) and *Jiuyue Quanshi* 舊約詮釋 (*Exegesis of the Old Testament*).

The role of foreigners and overseas Chinese who helped to raise the theological level of pastors and faithful in (Protestant) house churches in China since the 1980s is hard to ascertain. Likewise, it would be difficult to collect data about unofficial ("underground") theological schools in China that, since the late 1980s, have been training pastors, evangelizers, or priests and have offered courses in Greek, Latin, or Hebrew.

One of those who revived Greek studies at Jinling Seminary (Nanjing), was Luo Zhenfang 駱振芳 (1920–2000). He was born in Tianjin and, in 1931, he entered the Huiwen Elementary School, Beijing. He entered the English Department of Yanjing University in 1939. In 1946, he returned to Yanjing and studied in the Department of Religion. He produced a thesis on the *Parousia* in St. John's Gospel. After his graduation in 1949, he worked with the Methodists and the YMCA in Beijing and, in 1956, he was ordained a pastor. He was one of the few Greek experts in China and taught at Yanjing Union Seminary, Beijing, until 1961. He taught at Jinling Seminary, Nanjing, from 1961 to 1966 and again after 1981. He was important for the revival of Christian studies in the 1980s. In the early 1980s, he supervised English studies and theological studies at Nanjing University and at Jinling Seminary. In 1990, he traveled to the United States to take part in academic conferences, and he also participated in the common (Catholic and Protestant) Bible translation project. He died September 22, 2000.

Some Catholic priests who had received good training in languages in their youth in the seminary helped to build up institutions of higher learning in China. One example is Han Jingtao 韓井濤 (born 1921, ordained a priest in 1948, and consecrated a bishop in 1982), who taught English and classical Greek at North-East Normal University in Changchun, Jilin, from 1981 to 1997.

Judging from the quantity of dictionaries and textbooks, one can guess how many people (Christians and non-Christians) in China are studying Latin, Greek, or classical Hebrew. The Latin-Chinese dictionary by Xie Daren published in 1988 has not been reprinted; thus, the only available printed Latin-Chinese dictionary today is the one published in 2011 in Beijing.[19] It was reprinted twice by 2017 (with a total circulation of eighteen thousand copies). The only medium-sized Greek-Chinese dictionary available in China, published in 2004, had been reprinted four times by 2014 (each reprint was four thousand copies). One of the few textbooks for classical Hebrew is the one by Seow Choon-Leong (Xiao Junliang) 蕭俊良 (original in English, translated into Chinese in Taiwan, published in Shanghai in 2008, reprinted in 2016). The circulation of the paper version is probably fewer than six thousand copies, but electronic versions of the dictionaries and textbooks also are used.

Very few universities in China offer courses in Latin, classical Greek, and classical Hebrew. Most of these universities are in Beijing. Other centers of learning are Shanghai, Hangzhou, Canton, Xi'an, Kaifeng. It seems that there is a steady growth of the studies of the classical languages in China, both in numbers of students and in the study levels.

The Bible is not sold at public bookstores in China; it can only be purchased in churches. Likewise, courses on the Bible are offered as language training courses or introduction to Western culture. Exegesis and the study of biblical Greek and Hebrew are not established at Chinese universities, and even the only university that, since 2001, has had a Research Center for Biblical Literature (Henan University in Kaifeng) places the emphasis more on comparative literature than on exegesis and theology. The director of this center is Liang Gong 梁工 (born 1952), who studied with Zhu Weizhi 朱维之 in Tianjin from 1985 to 1988. Liang Gong published many translations and articles and, since 2007, he is the editor of the *Shengjing wenxue yanjiu* 聖經文學研究 (*Biblical Literature Studies*) magazine.

In the late 1980s, Liang Gong prepared a one-volume *Encyclopedia of the Bible* 聖經百科全書, which was published in 1990 and reprinted in 2015. However, the dictionary does not contain any words in Greek or Hebrew script. English and Chinese seem to be the only important entries; see for example, the entry "*Ai* 愛" (Love), which is purely

Chinese, yet at the beginning two English words are given: "Love, Charity." There is no mention of "*agapē*," "*ahaba*," or "*ruhama*." Professors from universities seldom teach at seminaries, and pastors or priests cannot teach at universities. This shows that biblical studies are "compartmentalized" in China: universities, seminaries, and the academia in Taiwan and Hong Kong form separate entities that do not interact much and use their own teaching materials. Books published in Hong Kong and Taiwan seldom make their way into China.

One notable exception is the "New Testament Hexapla" (*Xinyue Shengjing bingpaiban* 新約聖經並排版), which was published by the United Bible Societies in Hong Kong in 1997. In the year 2005, this book was published in Nanjing with simplified Chinese characters by the National Three-Self Patriotic Movement and the China Christian Council, and by 2015, the seventh reprint was made (with a total circulation of thirty-four thousand copies). It is sold at churches but not in official bookstores. This is the only NT version offering the Greek text, one English, and four Chinese translations. Although the printing quality is fine, the letters of the Greek text are too small for convenient reading. As of 2017, no Latin or Hebrew version of the Bible can be easily purchased within China.

The Greek-Chinese dictionaries of the NT published in Taiwan and Hong Kong do not have much impact in China, since it is difficult to purchase them. Also, the huge collection of Denzinger, which contains basic ecclesiastical documents in Greek, Latin, and their Chinese translations, published in Taiwan in 2013,[20] is virtually unknown in China mainland.

Books like *Shengjing Renmin Cidian* 聖經人名辭典 (*Dictionary of Biblical Names*)[21] only use the English and Chinese versions of biblical names.

Speaking from the author's experience as teacher of Latin, Greek, and Hebrew in Beijing since 2002, it can be observed that the primary obstacles impeding the spread of biblical languages in China are the same today as four hundred years ago: (1) the Chinese education and culture system favors Chinese characters and neglects ABC languages; (2) few teachers and few teaching institutions offer courses in classical biblical languages; (3) only a very limited quantity of polyglot Bibles, dictionaries, and teaching materials have been published in China.

First, since Chinese students usually grow up in a monolingual culture that emphasizes the use of Chinese characters, it is quite difficult for them to switch over to ABC languages. Most seminarians and students at theological colleges come from countryside regions, where the teaching of English or other foreign languages is not a priority; thus, they have great problems learning pronunciation, lexicon, and grammar of Greek, Latin, Hebrew, some of which are absent in the Chinese language such as "case" and "gender." The pronunciation of syllables like "*krat*," "*pro*," etc. poses problems, since the Chinese language has only four hundred syllables. If Chinese students have not been trained in English in their childhood, they will have problems pronouncing other European languages. Greek morphology and syntax are much more elaborate than Chinese. However, Chinese students who are used to analyzing English sentences have a better grasp of terms like "infinitive" or "participle" than native English speakers who never reflected on the structure of their mother tongue. Thus, in some sense, Chinese students with a good grasp of the English grammar are somehow prepared to tackle Greek or other classical languages.

Second, practically no high school in China offers Latin or Greek (or Hebrew), and even at universities, it is difficult to establish Greek or Hebrew courses. The author of this essay has offered courses like "basic Greek," "basic Latin," "basic Hebrew" for undergraduates at Renmin University (Beijing) since 2004, but the attendance has been limited (an average ten to twenty-five students out of twenty thousand come to these courses). If fewer than ten students sign up for a course, it is usually cancelled. Since I started to use the Chinese translation of the *Grammar for Biblical Hebrew*[22] by Choon-Leong Seow, the basic one-term course for classical Hebrew has never been cancelled since 2008. This grammar was published in Shanghai in 2008 and has been reprinted in 2016, which shows that several thousand Chinese have been using it.

In China, few academic teachers take the trouble to teach students the ABC and the basic grammar rules, and the administration of the university often does not see the value of learning classical Western languages.

Lastly, learning classical Western languages in China will require many more teaching materials that are attractive and useful. In the last years, a good number of Greek textbooks have been published in Shanghai, Beijing, and Hangzhou, by Liu Xiaofeng 劉小楓 (2005), Xin Delin 信德麟 (2007), Fu Yuehan 傅約翰 (2009), Zhou Zhan 周展 (2009), Sun Zhouxing 孫周興 (2010), Leopold Leeb 雷立柏 (a textbook in 2014; a grammar chart and dictionary in 2016), but many of these teaching materials are not very useful for beginners, due to small, unclear, irregular print, a too academic approach, or inferior binding quality. Some of these textbooks contain biblical texts, but the main emphasis is on Plato and Greek philosophy.

Also, a few textbooks for biblical Hebrew have been published, notably a textbook in three volumes published by Sichuan University in 2006.[23]

The future years will certainly see the publication of many more textbooks and dictionaries, probably also more Greek, Hebrew, and Latin versions of the Bible. However, because only a few publication houses have editors who can read classical languages, the editing process is usually long, the output is limited, and the prices are high. There are well-founded hopes that in the coming decade a new middle-sized Latin-Chinese dictionary, a concise Greek-Chinese dictionary, and at least a very small Hebrew-Chinese dictionary will be published in China.

Some Chinese students work hard to receive good training in the classical languages in China and abroad. They will be the future teachers and promoters of the Bible in China.

Notes

1. For their lives, see J. Dehergne, *Répertoire des Jésuites de Chine* (Rome, 1973); Chinese translation by Geng Sheng 耿升 [in Chinese] (Nanning: Guangxi Normal University Publications, 2010), 144, 232.

2. See the map in the appendix of Huang Shijian 黃時鑒, *Li Madou Shijie ditu yanjiu* [in Chinese] 利瑪竇世界地圖研究 *Research on Ricci's World Map* (Shanghai: Shanghai Guji Publications, 2004).
3. N. Standaert, ed., *Handbook of Christianity in China* (Leiden, Brill 2001), 1:623.
4. See Aleni's *Xixue fan* [in Chinese] 西學泛, where he used this term.
5. The term "*chaoxingxue*" 超性學 was used by Buglio in his translation of Thomas Aquinas's *Summa Theologiae*.
6. See Leopold Leeb, *Hanyu Shenxue Shuyu Cidian* [in Chinese] 漢語神學術語辭典 (Beijing: Religion and Culture Publications, 2007), 220.
7. Wang Shuofeng 王碩豐, *Zaoqi Hanyu Shengjing duikan yanjiu* [in Chinese] 早期漢語《聖經》對勘研究 (Beijing: Social Sciences Documentation Publications, 2017), 89–91.
8. See K. J. Rivinius, *Das Collegium Sinicum zu Neapel*, Monumenta Serica (Nettetal: St. Augustin, 2004).
9. See Rivinius, *Das Collegium Sinicum zu Neapel*, 101.
10. See H. Walravens, "Christliche Literatur in mandschurischer Sprache," *China heute* 2 (2016): 110–120.
11. See Yang Huiling 楊慧玲, *Shijiu Shiji Hanying cidian chuantong* [in Chinese] 十九世紀漢英辭典傳統 *The Tradition of English-Chinese Dictionaries in the 19th Century* (Beijing: The Commercial Press, 2012), 333–341.
12. See Fang Hao 方豪, "Ladingwen chuanru Zhongguo kao" [in Chinese] "拉丁文傳入中國考" "Research on the Spread of Latin in China," in Fang Hao, *Fang Hao Liushi ziding gao* [in Chinese] 方豪六十自定稿 (Taipei: Xuesheng, 1969), 1–38.
13. Quoted from R. Tiedemann, ed., *Handbook of Christianity in China* (Leiden: Brill, 2010), 2:268. It is hard to ascertain what level of Greek and Hebrew He Jinshan actually could achieve, and by what means.
14. See Fang Hao, "Ladingwen chuanru Zhongguo kao," 11–13.
15. K. S. Latourette, *A History of Christian Missions to China* (London: Gorgias Press, 1929), 634.
16. See Wu Jinrui, *Lading Hanwen Cidian* [in Chinese] 拉丁漢文辭典 (Taipei: Guangqi, 1965). This dictionary has more than 1,400 pages and some illustrations.
17. See, for example, the *Xinyue Xi-Han jianming Cidian* [in Chinese] 新約希漢簡明辭典 *A Concise Greek-Chinese Dictionary of the New Testament*, published by the United Bible Societies in Taiwan in 1989, which on p. 1 offers four different sets of Chinese grammar terms; for example, "accusative" is variously named "*zhijie shou ge* 直接受格," "*mudi ge* 目的格" or "*bin ge* 賓格." In China Mainland, the unified term is "*bin ge*."
18. Luo Niansheng and Shui Jianfu produced this *Guxilayu Hanyu Cidian* [in Chinese] 古希臘語漢語詞典, which was completed in 1983 but published only in 2004, which shows how difficult it was (is) for Chinese publication houses to process books in classical languages.
19. Lei Libo 雷立柏 (Leopold Leeb), *Ladingyu Hanyu jianming cidian* [in Chinese] 拉丁語漢語簡明詞典 (Beijing: Shijie dushu, 2011).
20. See Fu Jen Theological Publications Association, ed., *Gongjiaohui zhi xinyang yu lunli jiaoyi xuanji* [in Chinese] 公教會之信仰與倫理教義選集 *Enchiridion symbolorum definitionum et declarationum de rebus fidei et morum* (Taipei: Kuangchi Cultural Group, 2013).
21. Edited by Bai Yunxiao白雲曉 (Beijing: Zhongyang Bianyi, 2015).

22. This grammar book was published in the United States in 1996, the Chinese translation appeared in Taiwan in 2001, and in 2008 the version in simplified Chinese characters was released in Shanghai.
23. Xishui editorial, *Gu Xibolaiyu jiaocheng* [in Chinese] 古希伯來語教程 (Sichuan: Sichuan University Publications, 2006).

Primary Sources

Gongjiaohui zhi xinyang yu lunli jiaoyi xuanji [in Chinese] 公教會之信仰與倫理教義選集 (*Enchiridion symbolorum definitionum et declarationum de rebus fidei et morum*). Fu Jen Theological Publications Association edited. Taipei: Kuangchi Cultural Group, 2013.

Gu Xibolaiyu jiaocheng [in Chinese] 古希伯來語教程 (Classical Hebrew). Xishui editorial. Sichuan: Sichuan University Publications, 2006.

Leeb, Leopold 雷立柏. *Hanyu Shenxue Shuyu Cidian* [in Chinese] 漢語神學術語辭典 (*Dictionary of Chinese Theological Terms*). Beijing: Religion and Culture Publications, 2007.

Leeb, Leopold. *Ladingyu Hanyu jianming cidian* [in Chinese] 拉丁語漢語簡明詞典 (*A Concise Latin-Chinese Dictionary*. Beijing: Shijie dushu, 2011.

Luo Niansheng 羅念生and Shui Jianfu 水建馥. *Guxilayu Hanyu Cidian* [in Chinese] 古希臘語漢語詞典(*Classical Greek-Chinese Dictionary*). Jiangshu: Commercial Press, 2004.

Seow Choon-Leong 蕭俊良. *Shengjing yufa jiaocai* [in Chinese] 希伯來文聖經語法教材 (Biblical Hebrew). Shanghai: East China Normal University Press, 2008.

Shengjing Renmin Cidian [in Chinese] 聖經人名辭典 (*Dictionary of Biblical Names*). Ed. Bai Yunxiao 白雲曉. Beijing: Zhongyang Bianyi Publications, 2015.

Wu Jinrui 吴金瑞. *Lading Hanwen Cidian* [in Chinese] 拉丁漢文辭典 (*Latin-Chinese Dictionary*). Taipei: Guangqi, 1965.

Xinyue Xi-Han jianming Cidian [in Chinese] 新約希漢簡明辭典 (*A Concise Greek-Chinese Dictionary of the New Testament*). Taipei: United Bible Societies in Taiwan, 1989.

CHAPTER 10

CHINESE PROTESTANT BIBLE VERSIONS AND THE CHINESE LANGUAGE

GEORGE KAM WAH MAK

Introduction

THIS essay discusses the relationship between the Bible and the Chinese language. Although Protestant missionaries in China were not the first to engage in translating the Bible into Chinese, their efforts in this regard during the late Qing and Republican era (1800–1949) were marked by productivity and lasting influence on the Christian faith in China.[1] This essay focuses on the major Chinese Bible versions produced by Protestant missionaries during that period. It first introduces the varieties of the Chinese language adopted and linguistic techniques used in these Bible versions, so as to illustrate how Protestant Bible translators' understanding of the Chinese language informed their choices. It then explains how Protestant Bible translation was relevant to the evolution of the Chinese language with the example of the Mandarin Bible, which contributed to the development of Mandarin from a lingua franca into the national language of China. This essay concludes with a discussion of the value of Protestant Bible versions as materials for the historical study of the Chinese language.

Varieties of the Chinese Language Used in Protestant Bible Versions

Discussing the history of the Chinese Bible, John Yieh rightly pointed out that "the effort to translate the Bible motivated missionaries to study Chinese language and culture carefully."[2] On the other hand, missionaries' understanding of the Chinese language affected their choices in how to translate the Bible. An obvious example is the varieties of the Chinese language used in Protestant Bible versions. In late Qing and Republican China, the Protestant Bible was translated into *wenyan* 文言 (literary Chinese, also known as "*wenli* 文理," a term coined by Protestant missionaries),[3] simplified *wenyan* (also referred to as "easy *wenli*" or "*qian wenli* 淺文理" by Protestant missionaries), Mandarin (*guanhua* 官話), and regional dialects. The choice between these variants of the Chinese language depended on a variant's social prestige and functions in China and a Bible version's intended readership.

Protestant missionaries produced Bible versions in *wenyan* for several reasons. First of all, recognizing the diglossic situation in late Qing China—*wenyan* as the standard written language enjoyed unchallenged, prestigious status, whereas spoken languages only assumed a secondary position—they believed that writing in anything other than *wenyan* would be deemed vulgar and improper. To avoid the Bible being despised, *wenyan* was used in Bible translation by pioneering Protestant missionaries such as Robert Morrison (1782–1834) and Joshua Marshman (1768–1837), as well as subsequent translators such as those of the Delegates' Version (New Testament [NT]: 1852; Old Testament [OT]: 1854).[4] As explained by Walter Henry Medhurst (1796–1857), John Stronach (1810–1888), and William Charles Milne (1815–1863), who were British translators of the Delegates' Version, *wenyan* was used because it was "the chaste and correct style of language." If one's work was not written in *wenyan*, it would not be "fit for the public gaze and worthy of imitation."[5]

Moreover, inspired by the Jesuits' strategy of extending their influence in China through the literati class, Protestant missionaries in late Qing China were concerned about winning the respect of the literati. Since *wenyan* was the language of the literati, serving literary, scholarly, and official purposes, using *wenyan* as the target language of biblical translations was a means to gain recognition of the Bible by the literati. Also, as Chinese classics were written in *wenyan*, the Bible needed to be translated into *wenyan* in order to attain the same prominence and occupy the same position as Chinese classics, notably Confucian classics.[6]

The de facto spoken lingua franca in the Ming (1368–1644) and Qing (1644–1911) dynasties, Mandarin was another form of the Chinese language into which the Protestant Bible was translated. The "*koine* spoken by officials and educated people," Mandarin also was understood by the people in various regions of the Ming and Qing empires, since its major varieties encompassed local forms of Chinese spoken north of the Yangtze River, in China's northeast and northwest, as well as in the southwest.[7] The written form of Mandarin, often referred to as "*baihua* 白話," was a medium for vernacular novels, stories, and verses.

The earliest Mandarin translation of the Bible was produced by Louis Antoine de Poirot (1735–1813) in the late eighteenth and early nineteenth centuries. A French Jesuit, de Poirot translated almost all of the Latin Vulgate into Mandarin before his death. Known as *Gu xin Shengjing* in Chinese, de Poirot's translation was, however, not published.[8] Early Protestant missionaries in China were not ignorant of this form of the Chinese language. According to Morrison's co-worker, William Milne (1785–1822), Morrison once considered using Mandarin for his Chinese Bible version. However, he gave up, owing to the colloquial coarseness of Mandarin, although Jost Zetzsche argued that Morrison's reliance on Jean Basset's (1662–1707) *wenyan* NT translation was the determining factor.[9] It was not until the mid-1850s that the first Protestant Mandarin translation of the Bible came out. Published in 1856 or 1857, the Nanking Version, produced by Medhurst and Stronach with the help of a "young man, a native of Nanking," was a translation from the *wenyan* text of the NT of the Delegates' Version.[10]

For Medhurst and Stronach, the target audience of the Mandarin Bible was those who were illiterate in *wenyan* but could understand Mandarin because their own dialects were variants of Mandarin or linguistically close to Mandarin. Considering that these people could account for almost three-fourths of the Chinese population in nineteenth-century China,[11] producing a Mandarin Bible version could be regarded as a wise move in terms of efficiency and acceptability.

Moreover, the benefits of using the Mandarin Bible in preaching and public Scripture reading attracted Medhurst and Stronach. In *wenyan*, it was often the case that only one character was used to express an idea. However, it was not uncommon for several ideas to be contained in the same character. Also, there were many different Chinese characters of the same sound but of different meanings. These were among the reasons even the literati would find it difficult to understand the *wenyan* Bible immediately when it was read aloud. For preachers and Scripture readers, a Mandarin Bible could be a solution because of two features of Mandarin. First, the use of two characters for each idea in Mandarin allowed for preciseness and definiteness; second, the use of reduplication in word formation helped avoid ambiguity.[12]

The usefulness of the Mandarin Bible was unquestioned after the publication of the Nanking Version. Thanks to the Treaties of Tianjin (1858) and the Convention of Beijing (1860), starting in the 1860s, Protestant missionaries could conduct mission work and build churches not only in the five treaty ports but also in inland areas as well as Beijing and Tianjin. The growth of local churches and the expansion of itinerary evangelistic work meant that the Bible was increasingly read from the pulpit or preached in the open air. This further consolidated the view that Mandarin was a useful medium for spreading the gospel. It is thus not surprising that no later than the 1870s, the most circulated Protestant Bible versions were in Mandarin. Since Mandarin attained the status as modern standard Chinese in the first half of the twentieth century, it is the target language of contemporary Chinese Bible versions such as *Xiandai Zhongwen yiben* (Today's Chinese Version, 1979), *Shengjing xinyiben* (Chinese New Version, 1992), and *Xin Hanyu yiben* (Contemporary Chinese Version, NT: 2010; OT: translation work in progress).

Chinese Protestant Bible versions also were written in simplified *wenyan* or easy *wenli*, which was perceived as the "middle style" of the Chinese language by some Protestant missionaries in late nineteenth-century China.[13] Despite its success since the 1870s, the Mandarin Bible failed to gain popularity in southern provinces. The people there preferred reading the *wenyan* Bible to the Mandarin Bible, given the linguistic difference between southern dialects and Mandarin. Even in Mandarin-speaking areas, notably North China, it did not seem to many people dignified to use Mandarin as the medium for expressing sacred truths. Protestant missionaries also observed that in the Qing empire, there were people who ranked themselves in the educated class but were not as well-versed in *wenyan* as scholar-officials. To these people, it was a matter of pride not to read Mandarin works, although they had difficulty fully understanding *wenyan*, especially when it concerned matters with which they were unfamiliar.[14]

These gave rise within the late 1870s and the 1880s to the idea of producing Bible versions in easy *wenli*. According to Griffith John (1831–1912) of the London Missionary Society, whose Easy Wenli NT was published in 1885, this was a form of written Chinese that would be almost as easily comprehensible as Mandarin, while being better understood in non-Mandarin speaking areas and acceptable to scholarly tastes.[15] However, there was no consensus among Protestant missionaries on the definition of easy *wenli*. For example, at the 1877 General Conference of the Protestant Missionaries of China, Carstairs Douglas (1830–1877) of the English Presbyterian Mission, said that easy *wenli* was the language used in Chinese newspapers, whereas for Alexander Williamson (1829–1890) of the Scottish United Presbyterian Mission, it meant the language of Zhu Xi's 朱熹 (1130-1200) commentaries of the Four Books.[16] Samuel Isaac Joseph Schereschewsky (1831–1906) of the American Protestant Episcopal Mission, whose complete easy *wenli* translation of the Bible was published in 1902, described easy *wenli* at the 1890 General Conference of the Protestant Missionaries of China as "a style which should employ words in their primary sense and call a spade a spade; which should not strive after classicalities, and that should avoid ready-made phrases and expressions culled from poetical and rhetorical compositions."[17]

Despite being perceived in the late nineteenth century as the ideal language form for a Chinese Bible current nationwide in terms of intelligibility, easy *wenli* eventually failed to be *the* language of the Chinese Bible. The most important reason was the abolition in 1905 of the imperial civil service examination system, whereby scholars were selected for official positions. This led to gradual decline of the prestige of *wenyan* subsequently, as students and scholars were less motivated to stick to *wenyan*, which no longer helped enhance their career prospects.[18] The feature of easy *wenli* being a form of the Chinese language "as easily comprehensible as Mandarin and at the same time acceptable to scholarly tastes" was no longer seen as attractive. This, together with Chinese intellectuals' promotion of *baihua*, the written form of Mandarin, as the new standard written medium, helps explain why Protestant missionaries did not produce new easy *wenli* and *wenyan* Bible versions after the publication of Schereschewsky's Easy Wenli Bible (1902), the Easy Wenli (NT, 1902) and High Wenli (NT, 1907) Union Versions, and the Wenli Union Version (1919).

According to Daniel Kam-to Choi's Chinese Bible catalogue, there are more than twenty Chinese dialects into which at least one biblical book was translated. The dialects concerned are mostly non-Mandarin dialects, including Cantonese, Hakka, and members of the Min and Wu dialect groups. Of these dialects, only the following have a complete translated Bible: Amoy, Cantonese, Hakka, Shanghainese, Swatow, and the dialects of Fuzhou, Ningbo, Suzhou, Xinghua and Taizhou.[19]

The use of Chinese dialects in Protestant Bible translation responded to the socio-linguistic and political situation of nineteenth-century China. The *wenyan* Bible was useful for the educated class. The Mandarin Bible mainly served the Mandarin-speaking part of China. For those who were illiterate in *wenyan* but spoke non-Mandarin dialects, notably southern dialects, Bible versions in their own dialects would be a better option.

The publication dates of the earliest biblical translations in Chinese dialects indicate the close relationship between nineteenth-century Sino-foreign relations and the development of Protestant missions in China. The restrictions placed on foreigners' presence in the Qing Empire before 1860 meant that early Protestant missionaries did not have opportunities to learn regional dialects spoken outside the treaty ports. The linguistic distance between Mandarin and dialects spoken in the treaty ports and their vicinities suggested that biblical translations in those dialects instead of Mandarin Bible versions would better serve the mission fields there. This explains why the earliest editions of dialectal Bible versions were published in the dialects spoken in treaty ports opened after the Treaty of Nanjing (1842). Nevertheless, since Protestant missionaries could legally expand their work from treaty ports to inland areas after 1860, they were able not only to appreciate the merits of using Mandarin but also to be exposed to a variety of regional dialects. Hence, the number of dialects into which the Bible was translated increased greatly after 1860. Since the function of dialectal Bible versions was like that of Mandarin Bible versions, it is unsurprising that these dialects were mostly those having a considerable linguistic distance from Mandarin.

Linguistic Techniques Used in Chinese Protestant Bible Versions

Linguistic techniques adopted by Chinese Bible translators are among the aspects of Chinese Bible translation that have relatively been well-studied.[20] The scholarly efforts made in this area have shed light on how Protestant Bible translators painstakingly attempted to overcome linguistic differences between Chinese and biblical languages within the constraints imposed on them, so as to produce a faithful and intelligible translation of the Bible.

One of the major issues facing Chinese Protestant Bible translators in their translation work is the expression of definite reference of nouns. Whereas Hebrew and Greek have explicit means to mark definite reference, Chinese does not possess a similar means, as nouns in Chinese are neither inflected nor associated with articles. To solve this problem, a syntactic means was used. The translators made use of the position of a noun in relation to a verb in a Chinese sentence to mark definite reference, since as a rule, Chinese nouns appearing in preverbal positions are marked as having a definite reference, and vice versa. For example, Schereschewsky, whose Mandarin OT was published in 1874, and the translators of the Mandarin Union Version

(*Guanhua Heheben*, 1919), rendered the clause "*wayhi bime šᵉp̱ōṭ haššōp̱ṭim*" ("in the days when the judges ruled") in their Mandarin translations of Ruth 1:1 as "*dang shishi bingzheng de shihou* 當士師秉政的時候," instead of "*dang you shishi bingzheng de shihou* 當有士師秉政的時候." If the noun "*shishi*" were placed after the verb "*you*" ("there were"), the noun would mean "some judges" and the clause "in the days when there were some judges ruled."[21]

In addition, various lexical means in Chinese were used by Protestant Bible translators to convey semantic distinctions in the biblical text. For example, the emphatic particle "*qi* 豈" often was used as a rhetorical question marker in their *wenyan* and Mandarin OT translations, even though rhetorical questions in Hebrew are not marked formally as distinguished from regular questions. Also, the word "*yuan* 願" was added to express the optative mood of a Hebrew verb, which is indicated by its jussive form. As for NT translators, they would use a construction such as "*jiran . . . jiu* 既然 . . . 就" or "*ji . . . ze* 既 . . . 則" to render the causal use of a Greek adverbial participle, since such adverbial use could only be expressed lexically in Chinese. In the Mandarin Union Version, words like "*wanyi* 萬一" ("if by any chance," 2 Cor 9:4) and "*babude* 巴不得" ("to earnestly wish," Acts 20:16) were used to reflect the nuances of contingency in the Greek text that could not be expressed grammatically in Mandarin.[22]

Considering that frequent use of pronouns was not regarded as a good practice in Chinese, they were seldom used in Chinese Protestant Bible versions produced during the late Qing and Republican period. Schereschewsky stated it plainly at the 1890 General Conference of the Protestant Missionaries of China, that "particles and pronouns should be used sparingly as possible."[23] Also, the translators of the Easy Wenli, High Wenli and Mandarin Union Versions jointly adopted the principle that "where, according to Chinese idiom, pronouns would not be repeated, use them only when required for special emphasis or to prevent ambiguity."[24]

However, since the use of pronouns is common in Hebrew and Greek, Chinese Protestant Bible translators had to employ some techniques to render pronouns in the biblical text in their translations. One of them is to specify the number of people in a biblical verse where more than one actor is involved, instead of using the pronoun "*tamen* 他們." For example, in Schereschewsky's Mandarin OT, the Wenli Union Version, and the Mandarin Union Version, the Hebrew clauses "*wattiśśenâ qôlān wattiḇkênâ ʿôḏ*" ("and they raised their voice, and they wept again") in Ruth 1:14 were translated as "*liangge erfu you fangsheng daku* 兩個兒婦又放聲大哭," "*erxi fu fangsheng er ku* 二媳復發聲而哭," and "*liangge erxi you fangsheng er ku* 兩個兒媳又放聲而哭" respectively. Here the noun phrase "*liangge erfu* 兩個兒婦," "*erxi* 二媳," or "*liangge erxi* 兩個兒媳" ("two daughters-in-law") was used to render the third-person feminine plural pronominal suffixes attached to the two verbs in the Hebrew clauses. Another technique was to use Chinese nouns to translate pronouns in the biblical text. Instead of translating the third-person neuter singular pronoun "*auto*" in John 1:5 as "*ta* 它," the translators of the Mandarin Union Version, for instance, rendered it explicitly as "*guang* 光" ("light").[25]

As the use of pronouns has become more common in Chinese since the May Fourth era, their occurrence is much more frequent in Chinese Bible versions produced in the twenty-first century than those in the early twentieth century. It is unsurprising that in the biblical text of *Heheben xiudingban* (Revised Chinese Union Version), which is the revised version of the Mandarin Union Version published in 2010, the third person neuter singular pronoun "*ta* 它" and its plural form "*tamen* 它們" appear 706 times and 169 times respectively, compared with their non-existence in the Mandarin Union Version.

Protestant Bible translators in late Qing and Republican China did not avoid translating figurative expressions in biblical languages into Chinese literally.[26] As explained by Chauncey Goodrich, who was the chairman of the translation committee of the Mandarin Union Version from 1908 until the end of the translation work, translating figures of speech literally was to avoid losing "the beauty and poetry, and some of the precious meaning of the original."[27] Moreover, since Chinese was filled with figures of speech, it was possible that through the spread of the biblical translation, the figures of speech in biblical languages would "by and by" become familiar to the Chinese people.[28]

Nonetheless, figurative expressions in biblical languages sometimes were modified in their Chinese translations in order to ensure the translated biblical text's readability or communicability. This could occur in a Bible version featuring literal renderings of figurative expressions like the Mandarin Union Version. For example, the figurative expression "*hallaylâ hahûʾ yᵉhi galmûḏ*" ("let that night be barren") in Job 3:7 was rendered as "*heru shi xi bu dan yinghai* 何如是夕不誕嬰孩" ("It would be better not to have borne a child that night") by the translators of the Delegates' Version, who "avoided the awkwardness of a close translation, but at a certain cost in terms of figurative language."[29] Maybe the translators of the Mandarin Union Version considered that a literal translation of the figurative expression would jar the reader's sensibilities. They rendered the expression as "*yuan naye meiyou shengyu* 願那夜沒有生育" ("May no woman give birth that night"), instead of translating the expression more literally as something like "*que yuan biye wei jing* 却願彼夜為靜" ("May that night be silent") in Marshman's *wenyan* version (1822), which was produced with the assistance of Joannes Lassar (1781–ca. 1835), or "*naye buru xudu* 那夜不如虛度" ("That night had better be wasted") in the Peking Version (Mandarin NT, 1872).

The use of four-character idiomatic phrases, which are often called "*chengyu* 成語," was not unusual in Chinese Protestant Bible versions, since it helped Bible versions achieve literariness. Schereschewsky, who had an excellent command of the Chinese language, was known for his skillful use of this kind of phrase in his Mandarin OT and Easy Wenli Bible. Examples of the *chengyu* used by Schereschewsky include "*wanshi wuqiong* 萬世無窮" ("ten thousand generations and without end"), which is the translation of the Hebrew phrase "*min-hāʿôlām wᵉʿaḏ hāʿôlām*" ("from eternity to eternity") in Psalms 106:48, and "*shen bu shoushe* 神不守舍" ("the soul had left the body"), which is the translation of the Hebrew phrase "*napši yāṣʾâ ḇᵉḏabbᵉrô*" ("my soul went out when he spoke") in Song 5:6.[30] The use of *chengyu* also is attested in NT translations by other Protestant missionaries. For example, whereas the translators of the Mandarin Union Version closely followed the syntax of the Greek phrase "*charin anti charitos*" ("grace upon grace") in John 1:16 and translated it as "*en shang jia en* 恩上加恩," the translators of the Wenli Union Version rendered the Greek phrase as "*en zhi you jia wu yi* 恩之有加無已" ("the never ending increase of grace"), in which the idiomatic phrase "*you jia wu yi* 有加無已" was used.[31]

It is noteworthy that the use of *chengyu* by Protestant missionary Bible translators could be under the influence of their Catholic predecessors. The phrase "*wu suo bu neng* 無所不能" ("omnipotent"), the only *chengyu* used in Basset's NT translation (for example, see Mark 10:27 and 14:36), could be found in Marshman's version and the *wenyan* version produced by Morrison with the assistance of William Milne (1823). The phrase also was attested in subsequent Protestant *wenyan* Bible versions, including the NT published in 1837 and translated by Medhurst, Karl F. A. Gützlaff (1803–1851), Elijah C. Bridgman (1801–1861), and John R. Morrison (1814–1843), the Delegates' Version, and the Bible version produced by Bridgman and Michael S. Culbertson (1863).[32]

Chinese Protestant Bible translators transliterated personal names. However, they did not transliterate them entirely in accordance with their Greek or Hebrew pronunciation. For example, Schereschewsky, who was well-versed in Hebrew, sometimes transliterated personal names in the OT according to the English pronunciation, as indicated by the Chinese name of *bāḇel* in Dan 2:12, i.e., *Babilun* 巴比倫 and that of *bilʿām* in Num 24:15, i.e. *Balan* 巴蘭.[33] Also, Protestant missionaries working in non-Mandarin speaking areas might transliterate personal names with reference to the pronunciation of non-Mandarin dialects. John Chalmers (1825–1899) and Rosewell H. Graves (1833–1912), for instance, developed a system of transliteration taking into consideration of the pronunciation of Chinese syllables in Cantonese and Hakka as well as Mandarin. This helps explain why Chinese transliterations of Greek names *Andreas* (Andrew) and *Iōsēph* (Joseph) are *andeliao* 安得寥 and *yuexie* 約燮 in the *wenyan* NT published in 1897 and translated by Chalmers and Martin Schaub (1850–1900), a missionary of the Basel Mission working in Guangdong, instead of traditional Protestant transliterations *andelie* 安得烈 and *yuese* 約瑟.[34]

No matter which pronunciation was adopted as the basis for transliteration, selecting acceptable Chinese characters to transliterate personal names is important, as using characters with improper connotations could attract criticism. *Liubian* 流便, a Chinese name of the biblical character Reuben (see Gen 29:32 and Rev 7:5), is an interesting example. A Chinese transliteration of the Hebrew name *rᵉʾûḇen* and the Greek name *Roubēn*, *Liubian* was used in Bible versions produced by the first generation of Protestant Bible translators, i.e., Marshman, Lassar, Morrison, and Milne, followed by subsequent Protestant Bible versions such as the Bridgman-Culbertson version, the Peking Version, Schereschewsky's Easy Wenli version, and the Mandarin Union Version. The two Chinese characters of transliteration, namely *liu* 流 and *bian* 便, when placed together, could convey the meaning of "flowing faeces" or "flowing urine," since the character *bian* could be used to denote "faeces and urine" collectively, and such a usage is attested in Ming-Qing writings, including Pu Songling's 蒲松齡 (1640–1715) *Liaozhai zhiyi* (*Strange Stories from a Chinese Studio*).[35] While it is uncertain why Chinese Protestant Bible translators in the nineteenth and early twentieth centuries were not alert to this possible improper connotation, the problem has been addressed in Chinese Bible versions published since the 1970s, as indicated by the fact that Reuben became *Liuben* 流本 in the Chinese New Version and *Lübian* 呂便 in the Today's Chinese Version, *Xin biaodian Heheben* (*Chinese Union Version with New Punctuation*, 1988) and the Revised Chinese Union Version.

Changes in the Chinese language over time called for revisions to existing translations. Lexical change is an obvious example. The term "*yichuan* 遺傳" was used as a translation of the Greek word "*paradosin*," which means "tradition," in Matt 15:2 in various Chinese Protestant Bible versions produced in the nineteenth and early twentieth centuries (e.g. the Bridgman-Culbertson version, the Chalmers-Schaub version, and the Easy Wenli, High Wenli, and Mandarin Union Versions). While it was deemed an acceptable Chinese term to render the meaning of "tradition" in the early twentieth century,[36] nowadays it is mainly used as a term with its meaning confined to denote "heredity." Thus, the term "*chuantong* 傳統" was used instead in Protestant Bible versions published in the late twentieth and early twenty-first centuries, including Lü Zhenzhong's (1898–1988) version (1970), the Today's Chinese Version, and the Revised Chinese Union Version.

The role of Chinese assistants or teachers in the enterprise of Protestant missionary Bible translation often has been pinpointed but not studied in depth.[37] The difficulty in identifying those Chinese assistants or teachers, thanks to various unstandardized romanizations of their Chinese names in missionary correspondence and publications, to a large extent accounts for such a lacuna. However, their importance to the translation work and impact on the resultant translations are evident, and one of the few who has received due scholarly attention is Wang Tao (1828–1897), Medhurst's assistant on the translation committee of the Delegates' Version. In his article on the Delegates' Version as Chinese literature, Patrick Hanan argued that it was the first Chinese Bible version with "a claim to literary merit." He explored Wang's contribution to the version's superior Chinese style, of which one of the examples was, according to a quote from Medhurst, as follows: "For many of the happy turns of expression to be met with in the translation of Job, and the Proverbs, as well as the chaste and easy style which prevails throughout we are indebted to him."[38]

Nevertheless, whether the language of a Bible version is idiomatic depends not only on its translators and assistants' linguistic competence; the translation principles adopted for the Bible version are also a determining factor. Published in 1952, Lü Zhenzhong's *Xinyue xinyi xiugao* (*New Testament in Chinese: Revised Draft of New Translation*) is a good example. Aimed at producing a biblical translation for scholars and theology students, Lü preferred a literal translation in terms of syntax. When translating the Bible into Chinese, he paid particular attention to the formal equivalence between Greek and Chinese. This, however, meant that inevitably some sacrifice had to be made in point of style, resulting in unnatural expressions such as "*wo de meng ai de erzi* 我的蒙愛的兒子" ("my beloved son") as the translation of the Greek phrase "*ho huios mou ho agapētos*" in Mark 1:11.[39]

Chinese Protestant Bible Versions and Development of the Modern Chinese Language[40]

From the 1850s and 1910s, Protestant missionaries in China produced a number of Mandarin Bible versions. Their popularity is attested by the huge number of copies printed for distribution: From 1877 to 1936, at least 155,600,833 copies of the Mandarin Bible, including complete Bibles, Testaments, and biblical portions, were published by the American Bible Society and the British and Foreign Bible Society. Moreover, in the late nineteenth century and the first half of the twentieth century, China witnessed the emergence of a national language developed based on Mandarin. Since Protestant Bible translation activities in China overlapped with the development of Mandarin from a lingua franca into a national language for several decades, there have been discussions about whether the former helped pave the way for the latter. Scholars of modern Chinese literature, such as Marián Gálik and Irene Eber, argued that among the Mandarin Bible versions produced by Protestant missionaries, the Mandarin Union Version, published in 1919, was the one that helped codify the Mandarin-based national language, i.e. *guoyu* 國語, and create the new literature in China, owing to the version's success and timing of publication.[41] Nevertheless, influenced by Hu Shi's (1891–1962) view that the success of Mandarin as a national language would require intentional advocacy,[42] some scholars in Chinese Studies were dubious about the contribution of Protestant missionary Bible translators in this regard. Elisabeth Kaske, for instance, argued that "the direct influence of the missionary enterprise on the development of a Chinese national language remained small," because the missionaries were passively driven by Chinese linguistic realities and did not have a "united and active missionary language policy."[43]

In his monograph, *Protestant Bible Translation and Mandarin as the National Language of China* (2017), George Kam Wah Mak explains why Mandarin Bible versions produced by Protestant missionaries were relevant to the development of Mandarin into the national language of China. Mak's monograph shows how these versions, being nationally circulated in the late Qing and Republican era, contributed to the standardization and enrichment of Mandarin.

Mak argued that despite their different degrees of involvement, Protestant Mandarin Bible translators in late Qing and Republican China, notably the translators of the Nanking Version, the Peking Version, and the Mandarin Union Version, engaged in creating favorable conditions for Mandarin's becoming a national language. Determined to produce a Bible version targeting a national audience, these translators, who were helped by their Chinese teachers or assistants as well as their fellow missionaries from different parts of China, endeavored to translate the Bible into a kind of Mandarin that would be "everywhere current" (*tongxing* 通行) in China. In doing so, they set the geographical perimeter of Mandarin as a national language and attempted to create a form of Mandarin that would be acceptable to people of all social classes in China. They adopted either Southern Mandarin or Northern Mandarin, the two contenders for the status of standard Mandarin in late Qing China, as the basis of biblical Mandarin. They employed words and usages having wider currency in their translations, while sometimes including local words such as the interrogative word "*shui* 誰" (who) and the modal particle "*ba* 罷," which were not used in a considerable portion of Mandarin-speaking China at the turn of the twentieth century, but were deemed to be gaining popularity.[44] Through these efforts, the translators were involved in the standardization of Mandarin, as they helped smooth out differences between the varieties of Mandarin and enrich the lexicon of a kind of Mandarin transcending regional boundaries. Moreover, Protestant Mandarin Bible translators attempted to make biblical Mandarin acceptable to not only the uneducated class but also the literati, as they envisioned the potential of Mandarin to be a language for both the common people and the elite. The use of *wenyan* elements such as the connectives "*raner* 然而" (however) and "*huozhe* 或者" (maybe) in the Peking Version and the Mandarin Union Version shows that the translators took account of the literati's taste when translating the Bible into Mandarin.

Besides, using the presence of the neologisms "*shijie* 世界" (world), "*yijian* 意見" (opinion), "*xiaoxi* 消息" (news, information) and "*ziyou* 自由" (freedom) in both the Mandarin Union Version and its predecessors as examples, Mak suggested that being nationally circulating texts, these Bible versions helped enrich the modern Chinese lexicon by facilitating the dissemination of neologisms that are now common words in the Chinese language. Before the massive influx of Japanese loanwords into Chinese started after the first Sino-Japanese War (1894–1895), "*shijie*," "*yijian*," and "*ziyou*," which were missionary neologisms instead of Japanese *kanji* terms derived from *wenyan*, had already been used in Mandarin Protestant Bible versions including the Peking Version, Schereschewsky's 1874 Mandarin OT, and Griffith John's Mandarin NT (1889). The usages of these terms in these Bible versions are not much different from their current usages in modern Chinese. Also, the use of "*xiaoxi*" with the meaning of "news" or "information" in the Nanking Version and subsequent Mandarin Bible versions invalidates Federico Masini's claim that the term's occurrence in *Jiaohui xinbao* (*Church News*) in 1868 was its earliest use as the Chinese word for "information."[45]

An aspect which Mak did not deal with in his monograph is the *chengyu* derived from the Mandarin Bible that eventually became part of the modern Chinese lexicon. Despite being coined by de Poirot, the set phrases "*airen ru ji* 愛人如己" ("love one another as yourself," e.g. Matt 19:19, 22:39, Rom 13:9, Gal 5:14) and "*yi yan huan yan, yi ya huan ya* 以眼還眼，以牙還牙" ("an eye for an eye, a tooth for a tooth," e.g. Exod 21:24, Matt 5:38) were popularized by their use in the Mandarin Union Version.[46]

Concerning their contribution to the development of modern Chinese grammar, Mak pointed out that Mandarin Protestant Bible versions published in the late Qing and Republican era facilitated the spread of the following foreign language-influenced grammatical features that have become part of the grammatical norms of modern Chinese: (1) the transposition of the *yinwei* 因為 subordinate clause; (2) the use of the *bei*

被 passive construction in non-afflictive meanings or situations, without a specified agent of action, and in non-past events or situations; (3) the increasing use of *yi* 以—as a marker of indefiniteness; and (4) the expanded uses of *zai* 在, including the metaphorical use of the locative *zai* phrase, the use of *zai* as the particle heading the locative phrase in sentence-initial position of an existential sentence, and its use as the head of a sentence-initial time phrase.

Nonetheless, according to Mak, among all Mandarin Bible versions produced by Protestant missionaries, the Mandarin Union Version was unique regarding its contribution to the promotion of the nationwide use of Mandarin as *guoyu*. One of the main reasons was its use in promoting Mandarin in place of *wenyan* as the standard written medium, a major function of a national language, outside the church. In addition to serving as a model for literary writing, discussed in detail in John Lai's essay in this handbook, the Mandarin Union Version contributed to the spread and standardization of Mandarin as *guoyu* through the presence of its excerpts in *guoyu* textbooks as usage examples. Its text of the first story of creation in Genesis (1:1–2:3) was used as an exemplar text in *Guowen bai ba ke* (*A Hundred and Eight Chinese Language Lessons*, 1935–1938) edited by Xia Mianzun 夏丏尊 (1886–1946) and Ye Shaojun 葉紹鈞 (also known as Ye Shengtao 葉聖陶, 1894–1988), both of whom were May Fourth writers and language educators. In *Zhongguo yufa lilun* (*Theory of Chinese Grammar*, 1944–1945), which was written as a textbook on Chinese grammar for undergraduates or a reference work for Chinese language teachers in secondary schools, the eminent Chinese linguist Wang Li 王力 (1900–1986) partially quoted Luke 5:13, 5:37, and 14:11 from the Mandarin Union Version to illustrate the usage of the auxiliary verbs "*ken* 肯" and "*bi* 必."

Chinese Protestant Bible Versions as Materials for the Historical Study of the Chinese Language

Recent scholarship on the history of Mandarin has attested to the value of Protestant Bible versions for the historical study of the Chinese language. For example, Mak's monograph showed how the use of these Bible versions as linguistic materials could enrich our understanding of the development of the lexicon and grammar of modern written Chinese. Moreover, some Chinese linguists made use of the Mandarin Bible as empirical evidence in their studies on Mandarin phonology. Ye Baokui, for instance, described the consonants, vowels, and tonal system of late Qing Mandarin with the help of the Romanized Mandarin NT published by the British and Foreign Bible Society in 1888.[47]

Since much of the Protestant Bible translation work in late Qing and Republican China was done in regional dialects, Protestant Bible versions also could be valuable sources for the historical study of Chinese dialects. Major Chinese dialects, except

Northern Mandarin, do not have an established writing tradition. Although some of the Southern dialects do have a literature of sorts, this is mostly confined to writings serving popular cultural functions.[48] Collectively known as *jiaohui luomazi* ("Romanized script by the church") by the Chinese language reformer Ni Haishu (1918–1988), the various romanization systems devised by nineteenth-century Protestant missionaries for not only Mandarin but also almost all the major dialects in China were thus revolutionary, as they demonstrated, for the first time and on a large scale, the possibility and feasibility of writing Chinese with a script other than characters for regular purposes, as well as writing on the basis of one's own dialect instead of Mandarin. Given that these romanization systems were designed mainly as an alternative writing system in Bible translation, as well as for other pedagogical and communicative purposes, it is not surprising that most dialectal Bible versions were printed in romanized scripts, although some of them also were printed in Chinese characters.[49]

Dialectal Bible versions printed in Chinese characters and romanized scripts are among the limited number of writings in the dialects concerned in the nineteenth century, which were not as many as those in Mandarin and *wenyan*. This, along with that romanized scripts also served as a means of phonetic transcription, means that dialectal Bible versions are an invaluable resource for studying the dialects' lexicon, grammar, and phonology at the times when they were produced and published. As indicated by recent scholarship on Chinese historical linguistics, the value of dialectal Bible versions as materials for the diachronic study of Chinese dialects has been recognized by researchers in the field, of which some also utilized Bible versions in dialects such as Cantonese and the Wuhan dialect in their research.[50]

With the help of digital information technology, the accessibility of old Chinese Bible versions has improved greatly. The Bible Society in Taiwan uploaded to its website the scanned images of more than 120 Bible editions in Mandarin, *wenyan*, and simplified *wenyan* (easy *wenli*), as well as more than eighty Bible editions in Chinese dialects and non-Han ethnic groups' languages in Mainland China and Taiwan.[51] Thanks to their digitization projects, the National Library of Australia and the Harvard-Yenching Library allowed online access to old Chinese Bibles in their collections.[52] The United Bible Societies also launched a project of digitizing pre-1960s Chinese Bibles, which was completed in 2019.[53] All these efforts pave the way for wider scholarly use of Chinese biblical texts as a means to study the history of the Chinese language.

Notes

1. Toshikazu S. Foley, *Biblical Translation in Chinese and Greek: Verbal Aspect in Theory and Practice* (Leiden: Brill, 2009), 18, 23. For information on Chinese Protestant Bible versions produced in the late Qing and Republican era, see Hubert W. Spillett, *A Catalogue of Scriptures in the Languages of China and the Republic of China* (London: British and Foreign Bible Society, 1975); Jost Oliver Zetzsche, *The Bible in China: The History of the Union Version or The Culmination of Protestant Missionary Bible Translation in China* (Sankt Augustin: Institut Monumenta Serica, 1999); Daniel Kam-to Choi (Cai Jintu 蔡錦圖), *Shengjing zai Zhongguo: Fu*

Zhongwen Shengjing lishi mulu 聖經在中國: 附中文聖經歷史目錄 (*The Bible in China: With a Historical Catalogue of the Chinese Bible*) (Hong Kong: Logos and Pneuma Press, 2018).

2. John Y. H. Yieh, "The Bible in China: Interpretations and Consequences," in *Handbook of Christianity in China*, Vol. 2: *1800–Present*, ed. R. G. Tiedemann (Leiden; Boston: Brill, 2010), 893.
3. Protestant missionaries in China coined the term *wenli* to denote "the book language as opposed to the colloquial," i.e. *wenyan*. Herbert A. Giles, "The New Testament in Chinese," *The China Review* 10.3 (1881): 151.
4. The OT translation is indeed the one prepared by Walter Henry Medhurst, John Stronach, and William Charles Milne. For the sake of convenience, this essay follows Jost Zetzsche's practice and subsumes the 1852 NT translation and Medhurst, Stronach, and Milne's OT translation under the single term "the Delegates' Version." Zetzsche, *The Bible in China*, 82–107.
5. Letter from W. H. Medhurst, John Stronach, and W. C. Milne to A. Tidman, March 13, 1851, Box 1, Folder 3, Central China Incoming Correspondence, Council for World Mission/London Missionary Society Archives, SOAS Library, University of London.
6. *Records of the General Conference of the Protestant Missionaries of China, Held at Shanghai, May 7–20, 1890* [hereafter cited as *Records 1890*] (Shanghai: American Presbyterian Mission Press, 1890), 37–39.
7. Richard Van Ness Simmons, "Mandarin, Varieties of," in *Encyclopedia of Chinese Language and Linguistics*, ed. Rint Sybesma (Leiden: Brill, 2016). Consulted online on September 30, 2019 <http://dx.doi.org/10.1163/2210-7363_ecll_COM_00000238>.
8. Daniel K. T. Choi and George K. W. Mak, "Catholic Bible Translation in Twentieth-Century China: An Overview," in *Catholicism in China, 1900–Present*, ed. Cindy Yik-yi Chu (New York: Palgrave Macmillan, 2014), 107. For details about the language of de Poirot's translation, see Li Sher-shiueh (Li Shixue 李奭學), "Jindai Baihuawen de jueqi yu Yesuhui chuantong: Shi kui He Qingtai ji qi suo yi *Gu xin Shengjing* de yuyan wenti 近代白話文的崛起與耶穌會傳統—試窺賀清泰及其所譯《古新聖經》的語言問題," in *Chuanbo, shuxie yu xiangxiang: Ming Qing wenhua shiye zhong de Xifang* 傳播、書寫與想像：明清文化視野中的西方, ed. Song Gang 宋剛 (Shanghai: Fudan University Press, 2019), 83–126.
9. William Milne, *A Retrospect of the First Ten Years of the Protestant Mission to China* (Malacca: Anglo-Chinese Press, 1820).
10. "Statement of the Rev J Edkins-Tientsin," enclosed in the letter from J. Hobson to S. B. Bergne, December 9, 1861, the Archives of the British and Foreign Bible Society (hereafter abbreviated as BFBS Archives), BSA/E3/1/4/2, British and Foreign Bible Society's Library (Bible Society's Library), Cambridge University Library.
11. Chauncey Goodrich, "A Translation of the Bible for Three Hundred Millions," *Chinese Recorder and Missionary Journal* 43 (1912): 588.
12. Letter from W. H. Medhurst to G. Browne, October 27, 1853, BFBS Archives BSA/D1/2/113 (BSA/FC/1853/M); Letter from W. H. Medhurst to G. Browne, March 13, 1854, BFBS Archives BSA/D1/2/116 (BSA/FC/1854/M); *Records of the General Conference of the Protestant Missionaries of China, Held at Shanghai, May 10–24, 1877* [hereafter cited as *Records 1877*] (Shanghai: Presbyterian Mission Press, 1878), 223.
13. The Protestant missionaries' conception of "easy *wenli*" is discussed in detail in Liu Yun 劉雲, *Yuyan de shehuishi: Jindai Shengjing Hanyi zhong de yuyan xuanze* 語言的社會史: 近代《聖經》漢譯中的語言選擇 (1822–1919) (Shanghai: Shanghai Renmin Chubanshe, 2015).

14. *Records 1890*, 56–57.
15. *Records 1877*, 221–222.
16. *Records 1877*, 223, 225.
17. *Records 1890*, 42.
18. Ping Chen, *Modern Chinese: History and Sociolinguistics* (Cambridge: Cambridge University Press, 1999), 71.
19. Choi, *Shengjing zai Zhongguo*, 420–422. In his Chinese Bible catalogue, Choi subsumed Nanjing Mandarin under the category "Mandarin dialects." However, this is a problematic classification, since this presupposed Beijing Mandarin has always been the standard form of Mandarin, which was not true. W. South Coblin, "A Brief History of Mandarin," *Journal of the American Oriental Society* 120.4 (2000): 537–552. Also, when the Nanking Version was produced, Medhurst and Stronach did not regard the Nanjing-based form of Mandarin as merely a "dialect," but a standard form. George Kam Wah Mak, *Protestant Bible Translation and Mandarin as the National Language of China* (Leiden; Boston: Brill, 2017), 38–78.
20. Major monographs include Thor Strandenaes, *Principles of Chinese Bible Translation: As Expressed in Five Selected Versions of the New Testament and Exemplified by Mt 5:1–12 and Col 1* (Stockholm: Almqvist and Wiksell International, 1987); Irene Eber, *The Jewish Bishop and the Chinese Bible: S. I. J. Schereschewsky (1831–1906)* (Leiden: Brill, 1999); Foley, *Biblical Translation in Chinese and Greek*.
21. Lihi Yariv-Laor, "Linguistic Aspects of Translating the Bible into Chinese," in *Bible in Modern China: The Literary and Intellectual Impact*, ed. Irene Eber, Sze-kar Wan, and Knut Walf (Sankt Augustin: Institut Monumenta Serica, 1999), 104–106.
22. Yariv-Laor, "Linguistic Aspects of Translating the Bible into Chinese," 107–110; Foley, *Biblical Translation in Chinese and Greek*, 50, 231–232.
23. *Records 1890*, 43.
24. "Meeting of the Board of Revisers," *Chinese Recorder and Missionary Journal* 23 (1892): 26.
25. Yariv-Laor, "Linguistic Aspects of Translating the Bible into Chinese," 111–112; Zetzsche, *The Bible in China*, 327n112.
26. Strandenaes, *Principles of Chinese Bible Translation*, 33, 58, 85; Foley, *Biblical Translation in Chinese and Greek*, 28, 38.
27. Goodrich, "A Translation of the Bible for Three Hundred Millions," 590.
28. Ibid. 590.
29. Patrick Hanan, "The Bible as Chinese Literature: Medhurst, Wang Tao, and the Delegates' Version," *Harvard Journal of Asiatic Studies* 63.1 (2003): 233.
30. Eber, *The Jewish Bishop and the Chinese Bible*, 172.
31. Zetzsche, *The Bible in China*, 254.
32. Toshikazu S. Foley, "Four-Character Set Phrases: A Study of Their Use in the Catholic and Eastern Orthodox Versions of the Chinese New Testament," *Hong Kong Journal of Catholic Studies* 2 (2011): 52–53. Contrary to Foley's claim, the phrase *wu suo bu neng* is not found in Mark 9:22 in Marshman's and Morrison's *wenyan* Bible versions.
33. Eber, *The Jewish Bishop and the Chinese Bible*, 168–169. Eber wrongly cited the number of the biblical verse as Num 14:15 in her work.
34. Zetzsche, *The Bible in China*, 246.
35. Luo Zhufeng 羅竹風 ed., *Hanyu da cidian* 漢語大詞典 (Shanghai: Shanghai Cishu Chubanshe, 2008), 1:1360.
36. See the entry "tradition" in *English and Chinese Standard Dictionary, Small Type Edition*, ed. W. W. Yen et al. (Shanghai: Commercial Press, 1920), 1048; "Yichuan 遺傳," in *Hanyu da cidian*, ed. Luo, 10:1218.

37. Studies that should be mentioned in this regard include Jost Zetzsche, "The Missionary and the Chinese 'Helper': A Re-Appraisal of the Chinese Role in the Case of Bible Translation in China," *Journal of the History of Christianity in Modern China* 3 (2000): 5–20; Thor Strandenaes, "Anonymous Bible Translators: Native Literati and the Translation of the Bible into Chinese, 1807–1907," in *Sowing the Word: The Cultural Impact of the British and Foreign Bible Society 1804–2004*, ed. Stephen Batalden, Kathleen Cann, and John Dean (Sheffield: Sheffield Phoenix Press, 2004), 121–148.
38. Hanan, "The Bible as Chinese Literature," 201, 225.
39. For discussions on Lü's biblical translation, see A. H. Jowett Murray, "Review of Lü Chenchung's Revised Draft of New Translation of the New Testament in Chinese," *The Bible Translator* 4.4 (1953): 167; Robert Kramers, "On Lü Chen-Chung's New Testament Translation," *The Bible Translator* 5.4 (1954); Li Chun (Li Jun 李雋), "*Heheben* xiuding yu *Lü Zhenzhong yiben* 《和合本》修訂與《呂振中譯本》," *CGST Journal* (*Zhongguo Shenxue Yanjiuyuan qi kan* 中國神學研究院期刊) 51 (2011): 87, 90.
40. Unless indicated otherwise, this section draws on Mak, *Protestant Bible Translation and Mandarin as the National Language of China*.
41. Marián Gálik, "A Comment on Three Western Books on the Bible in Modern and Contemporary China," in *Influence, Translation, and Parallels: Selected Studies on the Bible in China* (Sankt Augustin: Institut Monumenta Serica, 2004); Irene Eber, "Introduction," in *Bible in Modern China*, ed. Eber et al.
42. Hu Shi 胡適, "Jianshe de wenxue geming lun 建設的文學革命論," *Xin qingnian* 新青年 4.4 (1918): 296–297.
43. Elisabeth Kaske, *The Politics of Language in Chinese Education, 1895–1919* (Leiden; Boston: Brill, 2008), 65.
44. C. W. Mateer, "The Style of the Mandarin Bible," *Chinese Recorder and Missionary Journal* 31 (1900): 333.
45. Federico Masini, *The Formation of Modern Chinese Lexicon and its Evolution toward a National Language: The Period from 1840 to 1898* (Berkeley, CA: Journal of Chinese Linguistics, Project on Linguistic Analysis, University of California, 1993), 207.
46. Foley, "Four-Character Set Phrases," 85.
47. Ye Baokui 葉寶奎, *Ming Qing Guanhua yinxi* 明清官話音系 (Xiamen: Xiamen Daxue Chubanshe, 2001), 253–265.
48. Chen, *Modern Chinese*, 114.
49. Ni Haishu 倪海曙, *Zhongguo pinyin wenzi yundong shi jianbian* 中國拼音文字運動史簡編 (Shanghai: Shidai Shubao Chubanshe, 1948), 10–23; Chen, *Modern Chinese*, 164–165; Cai, *Shengjing zai Zhongguo*, 420–421.
50. Chi-On Chin, "The Verb GIVE and the Double-Object Construction in Cantonese in Synchronic, Diachronic and Typological Perspectives," PhD dissertation, University of Washington (Seattle), 2009; Zhao Kuixin 趙葵欣, *Wuhan fanyan yufa yanjiu* 武漢方言語法研究 (Wuhan: Wuhan Daxue Chubanshe, 2012).
51. Taiwan Shengjing Gonghui 台灣聖經公會 (The Bible Society in Taiwan), "Zhenben Shengjing 珍本聖經," http://www.bstwn.org, accessed August 31, 2019. The figures do not include bilingual editions.
52. The digitized old Chinese Bibles of the National Library of Australia are part of its London Missionary Society Collection: https://www.nla.gov.au/selected-library-collections/london-missionary-society-collection. The digitized old Chinese Bibles of the Harvard-Yenching Library are results of its Christianity Collection digitization project.

53. Simon Wong, "Digitization of Old Chinese Bibles (pre-1950s)," *The Bible Translator* 68.1 (2017): 11–19; Huang Ximu 黃錫木 (Simon Wong), "Zhonghua Shengjing yiben (1661–1960) shuweihua gongcheng 中華聖經譯本 (1661–1960) 數位化工程," https://www.fhl.net/nbg/reading/reading542630.html, accessed August 31, 2019.

Primary Sources

Bridgman, Elijah C. and Michael S. Culbertson, tr. *Xinyue Shengshu* 新約聖書. Shanghai: Meihua Shuju, 1863.

Bridgman, Elijah C. and Michael S. Culbertson, tr. *Jiuyue quanshu* 舊約全書. Shanghai: Meihua Shuguan, 1863.

Chalmers, John and Michael Schaub, tr. *Xinyue quanshu* 新約全書. Hong Kong, 1897.

De Poirot, Louis Antoine 賀清泰. *Gu xin Shengjing cangao* 古新聖經殘稿. Edited by Li Sher-shiueh 李奭學and Zheng Haijuan 鄭海娟. Beijing: Zhonghua Book Company, 2014.

Jiuyue quanshu 舊約全書. Shanghai: Mohai Shuguan, 1854. [The Old Testament of the Delegates' Version.]

John, Griffith, tr. *Xinyue quanshu Guanhua* 新約全書官話. Hankow: National Bible Society of Scotland, 1889. [Griffith John's Mandarin New Testament.]

John, Griffith, tr. *Xinyue quanshu Wenli* 新約全書文理. Hankow: National Bible Society of Scotland, 1885. [Griffith John's Easy Wenli New Testament.]

Lü Chen-Chung呂振中 (Lü Zhenzhong), tr. *Xinyue xinyi xiugao* 新約新譯修稿 (*New Testament in Chinese: Revised Draft of New Translation*). Hong Kong: The Bible Book and Tract Depot, 1952.

Lü Chen-Chung, tr. *Shengjing* 聖經. Hong Kong: Published for Rev. Lü Chen-Chung by The Bible Society in Hong Kong, 1970.

Marshman, Joshua and Joannes Lassar, tr. *Shengjing* 聖經. Serampore: Mission College, 1822.

Morrison, Robert and William Milne, tr. *Shentian Shengshu* 神天聖書. Malacca: Anglo-Chinese Press, 1823.

Schereschewsky, Samuel Isaac Joseph, tr. *Jiuyue quanshu* 舊約全書. Beijing: Meihua Shuyuan, 1874. [Schereschewsky's 1874 Mandarin Old Testament.]

Schereschewsky, Samuel Isaac Joseph, tr. *Jiuxinyue Shengjing* 舊新約聖經. Shanghai: American Bible Society, 1902. [Schereschewsky's Easy Wenli Bible.]

Shangdezhe 尚德者. *Xin yizhao shu* 新遺詔書. Batavia, 1837. [The New Testament translated by Walter Henry Medhurst, Karl F. A. Gützlaff, Elijah C. Bridgman, and John R. Morrison.]

Shengjing: Xin biaodian Heheben 聖經：新標點和合本 (*Chinese Union Version with New Punctuation*). Hong Kong: United Bible Societies, 1988.

Shengjing xinyiben 聖經新譯本 (*Chinese New Version*). Hong Kong: Tien Dao Publishing House, 1992.

Shengjing: Heheben xiudingban 聖經：和合本修訂版 (*Revised Chinese Union Version*). Hong Kong: Hong Kong Bible Society, 2010.

Shengjing: Xiandai Zhongwen yiben 聖經：現代中文譯本 (*Today's Chinese Version*). Hong Kong: Hong Kong Bible Society, 1979.

Shengjing: Xiandai Zhongwen yiben xiudingban 聖經：現代中文譯本修訂版 (*Today's Chinese Version Revised Edition*). Hong Kong: Hong Kong Bible Society, 1995.

Shengjing Xinyue quanshu: Xin Hanyu yiben 聖經・新約全書：新漢語譯本 (*The New Testament: Contemporary Chinese Version*). Hong Kong: Chinese Bible International Limited, 2010.

Xinjiuyue quanshu: Guanhua hehe yiben 新舊約全書：官話和合譯本 (*Mandarin Bible, Union Version*). Shanghai: British and Foreign Bible Society, 1919. [The Mandarin Union Version.]
Xinjiuyue quanshu: Wenli hehe yiben 新舊約全書：文理和合譯本 (*Wenli Bible, Union Version*). Shanghai: British and Foreign Bible Society, 1919. [The Wenli Union Version.]
Xinyue quanshu 新約全書. Shanghai: Mohai Shuguan, 1852. [The New Testament of the Delegates' Version.]
Xinyue quanshu 新約全書. Shanghai: Mohai Shuguan, 1856. [The Nanking Version.]
Xinyue quanshu 新約全書. Shanghai: Mohai Shuguan, 1857. [The Nanking Version.]
Xinyue quanshu 新約全書 (*The New Testament Translated into Mandarin by a Committee of Peking Missionaries*). 6 volumes. Peking: American Mission Press, 1872. [The Peking Version.]
Xinyue quanshu Guanhua 新約全書官話. Shanghai: American Bible Society, 1872. [The Peking Version.]
Xinyue Shengjing 新約聖經. Shanghai: British and Foreign Bible Society, 1902. [The Easy Wenli Union Version, New Testament.]
Xinyue Shengshu 新約聖書. Shanghai: British and Foreign Bible Society, 1907. [The High Wenli Union Version, New Testament].

CHAPTER 11

ISSUES, CHALLENGES, AND PROMISES IN CHINESE BIBLE TRANSLATION

KUO-WEI PENG

A Brief History of Chinese Protestant Bible Translation from the Publication of the CUV up to the Present Day

In 1919, Two Union Versions (UVs; 和合譯本), the Wenli (文理, i.e., the classical) UV and the Mandarin (官話/國語) UV, were published with the prospect of serving the literati and the wider readership respectively.[1] These two UVs were published during the "New Cultural Movement" (新文化運動; 1915–1923 or 1917–1921) in which Mandarin (normally seen as the oral form of the language at that time) was promoted to replace the classical style used in the Wenli UV (normally the written form for the literati at that time) as the written form for modern Chinese literature. As a result, from the outset, the Wenli UV struggled to gain acceptance and was not published after less than three decades, whereas Mandarin UV was a success from the very beginning and later became the synonym of the Chinese Union Version (CUV) and the standard and most authoritative Chinese Protestant version of the Bible to the present day.[2]

The Mandarin UV (CUV hereafter) was translated during a time when nearly all Chinese people were unfamiliar with Christianity, and the Judeo-Christian culture was very foreign to them. Translators of the CUV, therefore, were concerned more with adaptation for the target audience by translating the sense as well as using a more natural indigenous Mandarin than they were with preservation of formal features of the source texts.[3] According to the distinction made by Christiane Nord, one of the major proponents of *Skopostheorie* (*skopos* theory), a functionalist approach to translation,[4] the CUV can be properly categorized as an "instrumental" translation in that it does not aim at producing in the target language (in our case, Chinese) a kind of "document" of communicative interaction between the source-texts (in our case, the Hebrew, Aramaic, and Greek texts) and the original source-culture audiences (in our case, the first Hebrew and Greco-Roman readers of the Scripture texts), but rather, aims at producing in the target language an "instrument" for a new communicative interaction between the source-texts (the Hebrew, Aramaic, and Greek texts) and the target-culture audience (in our case, Chinese readers), using certain aspects of the source text as a model.[5]

The CUV's instrumental approach to Chinese Bible translation was a sensible one in view of its historical context. It is nevertheless not satisfactory for those who would prefer a documentary approach to Chinese Bible translation that could reveal more formal features of the source-texts. Not long after the launch of the CUV, several attempts were made to produce Chinese translations more formally faithful to the source-texts. A noteworthy one is the NT done by Absalom Sydenstricker and his assistant Zhu Baohui 朱寶惠, which was published in 1929 and, after Sydenstricker's death, it was further revised by Zhu and published in 1936 (Zhu's NT hereafter). Later, Lu Chen-Chung 呂振中 started his very long quest for a more literal, and hence more formally faithful, Chinese Bible translation with the first version of the NT published in 1946, the revised NT in 1952, and the complete Bible in 1970 (LCCV hereafter).

Eugene Nida's groundbreaking works on the theory of "dynamic equivalence in translation" in the 1960s[6] brought a new wave of instrumental Chinese Bible translations by using a more contemporary Chinese style that broke away from CUV's stylistic tradition. In 1979, both the Today's Chinese Version (TCV; 現代中文譯本) and Chinese Contemporary Bible (CCB; 當代聖經) were published. Later, TCV underwent two revisions, one published in 1995 (TCV95) and the other in 2019 (TCV2019); whereas CCB also was revised and published in 2012 with the name of New Living Translation (NLT; 新普及譯本).

The need for TCV and CCB to break away from CUV's style had to do with the dramatic change the Chinese language had undergone since 1919. For this same reason, there had been calls for updating of language for the CUV. The responses to this were the New Chinese Version (NCV; 新譯本) project and the Chinese Union Revision project (和合本修訂計畫). Both projects took a very long time to complete. The NT of NCV was published in 1976 but not until 1992 was the OT completed. As to the Chinese Union Revision project, the NT was published as Revised Chinese Union NT (RCU NT) in 2006, and the complete RCU was finally published in 2010 after almost three decades of work. Later, this version was renamed as the Chinese Union 2010 (CU2010). Between these two publications, in 2003, the "Little Flock" (小群/聚會所) also published its own complete Bible, Recovery Version (CRV; 恢復本), with a Chinese style similar to CUV's.

The second decade of the twenty-first century has seen the burgeoning of Chinese Bible translations. In addition to the aforementioned CU2010, NLT, and TCV2019, the NT of Contemporary Chinese Version (CCV; 新漢語譯本), Chinese Standard Bible (CSB; 中文標準譯本) and Worldwide Chinese Bible (WCB; 環球聖經譯本) were published in 2010, 2011, and 2015 respectively. Moreover, the Deuterocanon (DC) to be used alongside the CU2010 also was published in 2014 to meet the needs of the Chinese Anglican/Episcopal Church; and in 2015, the Four Gospels of the Interconfessional Version (ICV; 共同譯本) was published as a trial.

Apart from the above Chinese Bible versions, which are translations in the traditional sense (i.e., in the form of sentence-by-sentence rendering of the texts), since 2009, the Chinese Union Study Bible (CUSB) series, of which the author is the editor-in-chief and translation consultant, has been producing volumes on individual Scripture books by using *Skopostheorie*'s concept of "translational action."[7] Twelve of them were issued through the end of 2020 (in the sequence of their publications: Galatians, Ruth, Johannine Epistles, Pastoral Epistles, Genesis, Colossians and Philemon, Acts, 2 Peter and Jude, James, the Sermon on the Mount in Matthew, as well as 1 and 2 Thessalonians). The goal of the project is to produce one to three volumes each year until a systematic and comprehensive "translational action" is provided for each and every Scripture book in the Protestant Bible.

The Issue of Authoritative Text: To Break Away from the CUV Tradition or Not?

Since its publication, the CUV has influenced not only the language and vocabulary of Chinese Protestant churches but also the language use of wider Chinese society.[8] Certain terms used in CUV, however, are idiosyncratic and unnatural, such as "*guo-xiao* 果效"[9] (in the sense of "effect" or "outcome") that the natural Chinese term to use today is "*xiao-guo* 效果". Some other terms used convey misleading senses, such as the use of "*xian-zhi* 先知"[10] (with the sense of "someone who foreknows") to render *nāḇiʾ* and *prophētēs*, both of which are nevertheless better understood as a spokesperson or messenger of God other than someone foreknowing, as well as the use of "*yu-yan* 預言"[11] (with the sense of "to foretell") to render the root of *nḇʾ* and *prophēteuō*, both of which are nonetheless better understood as conveying the message from God other than foretelling.

As early as in Zhu's NT, all "*guo-xiao*" are replaced by other terms to avoid the unnaturalness. However, later in LCCV "*guo-xiao*" appears again. In the subsequent TCV and CCB/NLT, "*guo-xiao*" is again avoided whereas both NCV and CRV, which were published roughly in the same period, keep "*guo-xiao*" in the translations. Among the most recent Chinese Bible translations, "*guo-xiao*" is not found in CU2010, a successor of the CUV tradition, but can still be found in CCV and CSB, both of which are actually supposed not to follow the CUV tradition very closely. By using "*guo-xiao*"as a test case, it can be seen that, due to the authoritativeness of the CUV, its idiosyncratic language use will not disappear very soon from later Chinese versions.

As to the terms "*xian-zhi*" and "*yu-yan*," LCCV was the first Chinese Bible to tackle their renderings: "*shen-yan-ren* 神言人" (roughly with the sense of "God's spokesperson") and "*shen-yan-chuan-jiang-shi* 神言傳講師" (roughly with the sense of "preacher of God's message") are used to replace "*xian-zhi*," and the term "*yu-yan*" is used only once. However, among subsequent Chinese Bible translations, including those translated in the last decade, only CRV avoids entirely the uses of "*xian-zhi*"and "*yu-yan*," and TCV tries to minimize the use of "*yu-yan*"; none of the rest has ever tried to deal with the issue of possible misunderstanding caused by these terms. On the one hand, it is understandable for many Chinese versions not to change these key terms out of respect for the authority and popularity of the CUV; on the other hand, seeing that these terms have been misguiding Chinese readers to think the central task of *nāḇiʾ* and *prophētēs* in the Bible to be foreknowing and foretelling the future and, as a result, encouraging certain inappropriate practices in the churches, future translators probably have to rethink seriously whether the renderings for these terms should break away from the CUV tradition.

The authority of the CUV influences not only choices of renderings in subsequent Chinese Bible translations, but also ways they render syntactic structures of the source-texts. Until the end of the twentieth century, an interesting general phenomenon or tendency can be detected among Chinese Bible translations: from time to time, sentence structures and clause orders of the source-texts are preserved in those versions not intended to be formal, such as TCV and CCB/NLT, but not in those versions intended to be formally more faithful to the source-texts than the CUV does, such as Zhu's NT, LCCV, and NCV.[12] The reason is that the latter versions are too closely bound to the CUV's ways of rendering, whereas the CUV is unfortunately more concerned with naturalness of the Chinese and, for this purpose, tends to change syntactic structure freely. As a result, unless it is decided from the outset of a translation project to break away from the CUV tradition, it is unlikely to produce a Chinese version that can reveal formal features of the source-texts in a consistent way.[13]

The influence of the authority of the CUV also can be detected in the choice of base text in subsequent Chinese versions. A good example is the doxological ending in Matt 6:13. Despite the fact that the model text the CUV was supposed to follow did not have the doxology of Matthew's Lord's prayer, CUV Matt 6:13 nevertheless preserves the doxological ending.[14] Many subsequent Chinese Bible translations, such as LCCV, TCV, NCV, CCV-NT, and ICV-Gospels, have removed the doxology from Matt 6:13 and put it in the note based upon contemporary scholarship of NT textual criticism;[15] but the doxology still is preserved at the end of Matt 6:13 in Zhu-NT,[16] CRV, and even some of the most recent Chinese versions, such as CSB-NT, WCB-NT, and CU2010. It is understandable for Zhu-NT and CRV to preserve the doxological ending as both can be seen as Chinese versions in the CUV tradition. As to the CU2010, in the very beginning, some of the internal reviewers advocated to move the doxology from the main text to the footnote, but eventually it was left in the main text due to strong voices from external reviewers.[17] The reason for the inclusion of the doxology in Matt 6:13 in CSB-NT is unclear, but it is a bit strange because this Chinese version seems to plan to break away from the CUV tradition. The footnote in WCB-NT Matt 6:13 indicates that the inclusion is based on the consideration of church tradition. However, this reason is also very interesting because in the same organization's earlier translation, the NCV, which is a version more or less in the CUV tradition, does not have the doxology in the main text, whereas in its second attempt, the WCB-NT, which seems to plan to unbind itself from the CUV tradition, preserves the doxology in the main text.

The purpose of the above examples is not to advocate abolishing the CUV tradition in future Chinese Bible translations, which is entirely unnecessary as the CUV tradition is a precious legacy for Chinese Protestant Christians to cherish. Surely the CUV tradition will continue to serve Chinese Protestant churches for years to come. The above examples do raise questions regarding the way(s) the CUV tradition should or should not be followed at the levels of vocabulary, style, interpretation, and base texts and for what reason(s) the decisions are to be made.

The answers to these questions, as *Skopostheorie* sees it, reside in the "purpose" (*skopos*) of the translation project in question. As the author has discussed,[18] a clearly defined *skopos* (whether it is document-oriented or instrument-oriented; and, if document-oriented, what form of documentary translation to use, while, if instrument-oriented, what form of instrumental translation to use)[19] will help translators of a particular Chinese Bible translation project form principles and guidelines in its relation to the CUV tradition at all levels mentioned so that the CUV tradition can be followed or not followed in a consistent way in the translation process.

The Issue of Syntactic Differences: How Documentary Can It Be? And What's the Purpose of a Documentary Translation?

As mentioned earlier, translators of the CUV adopted an instrumental approach to translation and, since its publication, attempts have been made to produce a Chinese version that is more formally faithful to the source-texts and, hence, more document-oriented than the CUV is. As the author also has pointed out before,[20] there exist huge syntactic differences between Chinese on the one side and the Hebrew, Aramaic, and Greek on the other, and one of the differences is the location of the modifier (adjectives and adverbs) vis-à-vis the modified (nouns and verbs). As a result, this difference makes it extremely challenging, if not impossible, to produce a "literal" or "grammar" translation (i.e., a translation process reproducing the source language form by focusing on "lexical units" of the source-text)[21] of the biblical texts in Chinese. At best, it is possible only to produce a "philological" or "learned" translation (i.e., a translation process reproducing the source-text's form and content by focusing on the "syntactical units" of the source-text)[22] of the biblical texts in Chinese. In most cases, what can be achieved can only be qualified as, in *Skopostheorie*'s terms, an "exoticizing" or "foreignizing" translation, which reproduces the source-text's form, content, and situation by focusing on "textual units" of the source-text.[23]

Ephesians 1:3–14 is a good example to illustrate the challenge. In Greek, this passage is a very long sentence formed by concatenating a series of relative clauses and can be roughly broken down into four main sections (1:3–6, 1:7–10, 1:11–12, and 1:13–14), with the last three sections all beginning with the relative marker, *en hōi* (in whom).[24] As Chinese language does not have any relative marker, it is not possible to formally reproduce these features at the lexical level. It will depend on the creativity of the translators to alert readers certain aspects of the arrangement of the source-text in the translation.

Apparently, translators of the CUV were not aware of this syntactic arrangement because not only did they not explicitly translate the *en hōi* of 1:7 and 1:13, but also they provided no clue about the connections between relative markers and their antecedents. As a result, it is nearly impossible for Chinese readers of CUV Eph 1:3–14 to figure out its internal structure and flow of thought. On this passage, CU2010, being a revision of the CUV tradition, only tries to improve the translation by adding "*zai-ji-du-li* 在基督裏" (in Christ) in the beginning of v. 13 but does not provide any clue about the connection between this "*zai-ji-du-li*" and its antecedent in v. 12. As a result, the improvement is not significant enough.

As far as the reproduction of sentence structure is concerned, so far a better solution can be found in CSB-NT Eph 1:3–14, which uses paragraphing to mark the four main sections and put the antecedents of the relatives, "*zai-ai-zi-li* 在愛子裡" (in the beloved son) or "*zai-ji-du-li* 在基督裡" (in Christ), toward the end of the first three paragraphs and the corresponding relative markers, "*zai-ta-li-mian* 在他裡面" (in him) or "*zai-ji-du-li*" (in Christ), at the beginning of each of the last three paragraphs.

CSB-NT Ephesians 1:3–14 is hardly to be reckoned as a "literal translation" because, without genuine relative markers in Chinese, the subordinate relations in the source-text are not retained in the rendering. It, nevertheless, can be well qualified as a "philological translation" since it reproduces to a degree the arrangement of syntactic units of the source-text. With its success as a philological rendering, it seems unavoidable to ask: is it possible to achieve consistently philological equivalence for all passages of the source-texts in Chinese similar to what has been achieved by CSB-NT Eph 1:3–14?

Theoretically, the answer should be positive, but in practice no Chinese Bible translation of this kind has ever been produced yet. If we compare CSB-NT's rendering of the genealogy of Luke 3:23–38 with some other versions, for example, we find that it is much less formally similar to the source-text than the renderings in Zhu-NT, CCV-NT, WCB-NT are. This example and the discussion on Eph 1:3–14 mentioned above show that even though there may have been some successful philological renderings in Chinese for certain Scripture passages here and there by various Chinese versions since the publication of the CUV, the fruits have not yet been gathered in a particular version to produce a consistent "philological translation." To produce a consistent philological Chinese Bible translation, translators today are encouraged to pay more attention to the issue of consistency in the area of syntactic correspondence and similarity. In addition, more experiments also may be needed for many other source-text syntactic patterns whose philological renderings in Chinese have not been successfully achieved.

A related question also may need to be asked here: what is the purpose to produce a documentary, or more precisely a philological, Chinese Bible translation? Apparently, since the publication of the CUV, the quest for a documentary, or philological, Chinese Bible translation has been related to the instrumental nature of the CUV, which makes the CUV not an adequate tool for serious Bible studies in the church setting, nor for biblical studies in the scholarly arena. For these uses, a documentary Chinese translation has long been desired, but the need has not yet been met to the present day.

In addition to this real need, there also exists a somewhat misleading reason for it. Among Chinese Christians, there has been a popular conviction to equate "formal correspondence in translation" with "faithfulness to the source-text,"[25] and it has been another driving force behind the documentary approach to Chinese Bible translation since the advent of the CUV. To people with this conviction, the closer to the form of the source-text, the better a translation is.

People with such conviction, unfortunately, seldom realize that extremely literal or philological rendering can cause confusion or misunderstanding and can eventually undermine the purpose of the so-called "faithfulness" they pursue. For example, if the phrase "*ʾeṯ-raglāyw baḥᵃḏar hammᵉqerâ*" in Judg 3:24 (a euphemistic idiom for "relieving oneself") is rendered word-for-word as "*ta-zhe-zhu-zi-ji-de-jiao* 他遮住自己的腳" ("he [is] covering his own feet"), most, if not all, Chinese readers will scratch their heads over what the king was really doing by covering his feet and, as a result, the meaning of the resultant Chinese text becomes obscure and unintelligible with such a literal rendering.

On this, *Skopostheorie* has rightly pointed out that the issue of "faithfulness" actually has more to do with the expectation(s) of the readers in the target culture than with the translation's formal correspondence or similarity to the source-text: to one group of target readership, faithfulness can mean faithful reproduction of the form of the source-text; while to another, it can mean the target-text should produce the author's exact opinion.[26] Therefore, in *Skopostheorie*'s view, what are more important in judging the success of a translation are: (1) whether the translation form used is "adequate to" the expectation(s) of the target audience[27] (normally clearly described in the "translation brief")[28] and; (2) whether the translator is "loyal" to the target audience's expectation(s) in producing a translation in line with requirements described in the translation brief.[29] A literal or a philological Chinese Bible transition can be a successful one only if it is produced in a way adequate to the expectation(s) of the intended target audience. As we will see later, nonetheless, the reproduction of the formal features is only one of many possible purposes (*skopoi*) in Chinese Bible translation. To help the Chinese audience understand the message of the Scriptures, there are other needs, hence other purposes (*skopoi*), to cater to.

The Issue of Cultural Differences: What Can "Translational Action" Do to Bridge the Gap?

Skopostheorie sees translating not only as a communicative action[30] but also as an intercultural one.[31] Translation, therefore, is more than a cross-language communication; it is a cross-language as well as a cross-cultural communication. As far as Bible translation is concerned, unfortunately, this cross-language and cross-cultural communication is not always possible to achieve in a satisfactory way by traditional verse-by-verse Bible translation, especially when there exists a great cultural gap between the source and target cultures.

For example, in terms of cross-language communication, the CUV translation of Luke 11:11–12 seems to be fine: it preserves the form of rhetorical questions, and the translation of the questions, though literal, is clear in meaning. There are cross-cultural issues, though. The rhetorical question "*qiu-yu, fan-na-she-dan-yu-gei-ta-ne* 求魚，反拿蛇當魚給他呢?" ("asks for a fish, will give a snake instead of a fish?") in v. 11 may not elicit the expected answer of the source-text if the question is raised to Chinese from the southern provinces in China, such as Canton or Fujian. To them, a snake is not only as edible as a fish, it actually is more expensive, and hence considered better, than a fish. As a result, it is very likely that they would respond "why not?" or "surely!" to this rhetorical question. As to the rhetorical question, "*qiu-ji-dan, fan-gei-ta-xie-zhi-ne* 求雞蛋，反給他蠍子呢？" ("asks for an egg, will give a scorpion?") in v. 12, the response of the Chinese from certain northern provinces in China, such as Hebei, may also differ from the answer the source-text expected because fried scorpions on sticks, along with other fried bugs on sticks, have been consumed as snack there for a very long time. Those fried bugs also are more expensive, and hence considered better, than eggs.

The core of issues of this kind is that, without proper cultural clues provided, readers tend to use their own cultural experiences to make sense of any text in front of them. When the cultural gap is great, this practice will result in unintelligibility or, even worse, misconstruction due to cultural mismatch. This happens very often in the arena of Bible translation in the majority world. While working as a translation consultant in the Asia-Pacific Area, I often heard people of Buddhist background say that they found phenomena of transmigration in the NT. For them, not only did Jesus die and appear again several times (as they read the four Gospels in sequence and were not aware that these Gospels were actually four versions of the same account) but also Herod transmigrated (as they were not aware that Herod was actually a title, not a personal name, and that the Herod in Matt 2:1 was not the Herod in Matt 14:1). This construal, though apparently resulting from a cultural mismatch, makes perfect sense to them according to their Buddhist worldview.

In *Skopostheorie*'s view, there are two ways to tackle the issues caused by cultural differences. The first one is to adapt to the target audience by choosing an appropriate translation form that can serve them well. For target-audience members who are unable *not* to read a text through their own cultural lenses and for those who are likely to get confused over foreign cultural elements in reading the text, the choice of a translation form of an instrument-oriented nature (be it equifunctional, heterofunctional, or homologous)[32] is preferred because these forms have the potential in various degrees to minimize cultural mismatches or hindrances in reading. As to target-audience members who do not have those issues and are keen to experience to a certain degree the cultural "flavor" the source-text uses to communicate with the original source-culture audience, a translation form of document-oriented nature (be it interlinear, literal, philological, or exoticizing)[33] is then preferred.

Skopostheorie holds a very modest and realistic view about translation: each translation commissioning can only achieve certain aspects of cross-language and cross-cultural communication. In *Skopostheorie*'s view, there exists no universal translation that provides a total transfer of information of the source-text so that it can serve all audiences. Therefore, audiences will only be served properly by a translation for which they are the intended audience.

This is why in John 2:4 of CUV, which is instrument-oriented in nature, "*gynai*," the term Jesus addressed his mother, is translated as "*mu-qin* 母親" (mother) and a footnote is added to inform the target audience that the source-text is actually "*fu-ren* 婦人" (woman). In the source culture, addressing one's mother as "*gynai*" was not out of rebuke, nor was it impolite, nor an indication of a lack of affection,[34] whereas in Chinese society where filial piety is paramount, to address one's mother in this way is entirely unacceptable. The change from "*fu-ren*" (woman) to "*mu-qin*" (mother) is, then, to remove a possible cultural obstacle for the target audience so that they are not distracted by this and miss the core message of the account.

Apparently, there are limitations to this approach. First, to gain a fuller appreciation of different facets of the cross-language and cross-cultural communication the source-text generates, audience members would need to resort to more than one translation. Secondly, to avoid possible misunderstandings caused by a cultural mismatch in translation sometimes requires the introduction of the cultural framework of the source-text, but the format of translation per se, i.e., to translate sentence-by-sentence, does not have sufficient, if any, room for this task. As a result, even with the combination of the use of different forms of documentary and instrumental translations, it still is not possible to deal with the cross-cultural aspect of the communication in a satisfying way.

To overcome those limitations, another approach *Skopostheorie* suggests is the use of "translational action." Nord defines "translational action" as "the range of what translators actually do" vis-à-vis "translation" as "what they do when rendering texts"; and in the translation process "translation" in the narrow sense involves the use of some kind of source-text while "translational action" may involve giving advice, issuing warning, and providing any other relevant information so that the source-text can be properly understood by the target audience.[35]

In CUV, there have been sporadic cases of translational action in the form of inline notes, such as the one in John 2:4 mentioned earlier, but its use has been kept to a minimum. The use of translation action increases in some of the later Chinese versions, such as CRV,[36] and especially in some of the most recent ongoing projects, such as CCV-NT and WCB-NT. CCV-NT provides brief introductions for each Scripture book and, at the end of each book, endnotes functioning as translation and textual notes, some of which also repeatedly appear as footnotes in the main text. In addition, maps are inserted in the text wherever necessary. As the notes provided have more to do with translation and textual decisions than cultural information, the translational action of CCV-NT is more concerned with cross-language issues than cross-cultural issues. Moreover, the extensive use of Greek in the notes requires readers to have certain advanced knowledge of *Koine* Greek and, in view of the fact that very few Chinese have gained such knowledge, it raises the question of for whom the notes are designed and whether those notes would intimidate readers who do not have this knowledge. In the introductions, some background information of the book is provided. However, because each one was done by a different writer, it seems that proper coordination among the writers was lacking. As a result, the dates of writing for Matthew and Luke are earlier than that for Mark, and a learned reader would wonder what synoptic hypothesis is followed here.

WCB-NT uses two types of footnotes: one for translation notes (marked with "*yi* 譯") and the other for interpretation notes (marked with "*jie* 解"). Some of the interpretation notes contain cultural information. Nevertheless, the format of footnotes still has the constraint that only piecemeal information of the source culture, not its cultural framework, can be provided.

So far, the most ambitious attempt of translational action can be seen in the ongoing CUSB series. The starting point of this project is what has been discussed above: translation is a cross-language and cross-cultural communication, and in Bible translation the communication between the source-text and its target audience is not always possible to be achieved in a satisfactory way by traditional verse-by-verse Bible translation.[37] Based upon *Skopostheorie*'s concept of "translational action," the project intends to combine parallel versions (CU2010 and TCV95 are placed alongside the running text CUV), introductory materials (both for individual books and for larger collections, such as the Pentateuch, the Prophets, etc.), notes, images, drawings, maps and articles to form a cultural framework by which the target audience is invited to engage in a fuller cross-language and cross-language communicative interaction with the biblical source-texts than what traditional verse-by-verse Bible translation can offer.[38]

On the documentary dimension of communicative interaction, special attention is paid to areas of "textuality" and "background knowledge."[39] For textuality, the focus is on the following: (1) textual variants, which are marked systematically according to the ratings in the Hebrew Old Testament Text Project (HOTTP) final reports[40] for the OT and in the apparatuses of the UBSGNT4[41] and UBSGNT5[42] for the NT; (2) intratextuality of a particular book, which includes syntactic structures (such as the one for Eph 1:3–14 mentioned above), flow of thought, literary design, and rhetorical arrangements, etc. to draw readers' awareness of the structuring of a book; and (3) intertextuality between books, which includes not only quotations but also allusions, echoes, and typologies. As for background knowledge, information about history, geography, culture, fauna, flora, objects, and people are supplied, not only in the form of notes and images but also, in situations in which in-depth and comprehensive discussion of a particular subject is required, by way of articles, which can be as short as a sidebar on a portion of a page but also can be a lengthy one covering several pages.

The scholarship upon which additional materials are based determines the trustworthiness of the end product. From the outset, the guidelines for the CUSB project require additional materials to reflect the consensus of the scholarly world since the 1990s, and when there exists no consensus, to present major opinions in juxtaposition with fair evaluation, if needed.[43] In the volume on Galatians, for example, the topics of "faith in Jesus Christ" versus "faith of Jesus Christ," "legalism" versus "covenantal nomism," as well as "North Galatian hypothesis" versus "South Galatian hypothesis," are all treated in an even-handed manner.[44]

In addition, editors of the project require each and every team member always to think "laterally" when they work on the drafting of the portion they are assigned to. It is very common to see internal disagreements or even conflicts in a publication done by a group of people. For example, in the ESV Study Bible on 1 Corinthians 14:34–35 it comments:

> Since Paul seems to permit wives to pray and prophesy (11:5, 13) as long as they do not dishonor their husbands by the way they dress (11:5), *it is difficult to see this as an absolute prohibition* (cf. Acts 2:17; 21:8–9). Paul is likely forbidding women to speak up and judge prophecies (this is the activity in the immediate context; cf. 1 Cor. 14:29), since such an activity would subvert male headship...[45]

whereas on 1 Timothy 2:12 the author writes in an absolute voice by stating:

> Paul self-consciously writes with the authority of an apostle (e.g., 1 Thess. 4:1; 2 Thess. 3:6), rather than simply offering an opinion. This statement is given in the context of Paul's apostolic instructions to the church for the ordering of church practice when the church is assembled together. In that context, two things are prohibited: (1) Women are not permitted to publicly **teach** Scripture and/or Christian doctrine to men in church (the context implies these topics), and (2) women are not permitted to **exercise authority** over men in church.[46]

Did Paul allow women to speak publicly in church? On this, readers of the ESV Study Bible would be confused by these comments or would be forced to conclude that 1 Corinthians and 1 Timothy might come from the hands of two different authors, which is a scholarly opinion the editorial team of the ESV Study Bible may not want to endorse. This kind of internal tension of the additional materials has to be avoided as it only causes problems and confusion for the audience. The coherency of the cultural frameworks upon which the additional materials are based is paramount.

As to the instrumental dimension of the communicative interaction, the CUSB project is concerned with not only the target audience's proper understanding of the text, which is expected to be achieved when they read the source-texts in their original linguistic and cultural backgrounds, but also the relevance of the message of the source-texts to their contemporary life settings. For the latter, two sets of questions are designed to help readers to find the source-texts' relevancy to their personal lives as well as their communal lives in the wider societies.[47]

It is noteworthy that the CUSB series is intended to provide for the Chinese target audience a fuller cross-language and cross-cultural communicative interaction with the Scriptures without resorting to the generation of a new Chinese Bible translation. It is not because there is no need to revise existing versions or to translate new ones but because the project is more focused on situating the target audience in the cultural framework of the source-texts to minimize possible confusion and misunderstanding caused by cultural differences. Also, it is believed that, with such a framework in place, the target audience can understand any Chinese Bible translation in front of them in a more appropriate way.

Moreover, the additional materials provided in the CUSB series may help the target audience be aware of the translational and exegetical issues of their existing version and, in such a way, pave the way for future revision or new translation work. As for newly issued revisions and translations, information provided by CUSB series can also serve to explain why certain passages are revised or translated in those ways and, thus, to promote their acceptance among the target audience.[48]

Suggestions for New and Ongoing Chinese Bible Translation Projects

The recent burgeoning of Chinese Bible translations and translational actions in the last decade, and the phenomenon that most of those recent Chinese Bible projects tend to unbind themselves from the CUV tradition, indicate that Chinese Bible translation has been stepping into a post-CUV era in which new ways of Chinese Bible translation are to be explored. For this new era, the discussions of the issues of the Chinese Bible identified above may offer some suggestions for new and ongoing Chinese Bible translation projects to consider.

First, on the issue of authoritative text, any new and ongoing Chinese Bible translation project may want to form certain guidelines as well as the reasons behind the guidelines, on the continuity and discontinuity between proper names and terminologies used in the CUV and those in the new project. Similarly, guidelines may also be needed for continuity and discontinuity between style, interpretation, and base texts used in the CUV and those in the new project. To form those guidelines in a consistent way, it is advisable for any Chinese Bible translation to lay out its purpose (*skopos*) in the first place with a translation brief, which normally specifies the intended text function(s), the target-text addressee(s), the prospective time and place of text reception, the medium in which the text will be transmitted, and the motive for production or reception of the text.[49]

Secondly, on the issue of syntactic differences, new and ongoing Chinese Bible translation projects that adopt a documentary approach, such as the CSB project, may want to review all Mandarin versions since the time the CUV project started to collect examples of successful philological renderings. These may contribute to a more consistent Chinese philological translation. As most of Chinese versions produced in the twentieth century are either instrument-oriented or heavily under the influence of the CUV tradition, there may not be enough examples of philological renderings for all kinds of syntactic structures of the source-texts. Chinese translation and biblical scholars are called upon to engage in the discussions and experiments of philological renderings of certain syntactic structures of the biblical source-texts in Chinese for the future of a consistent philological Chinese version.

As far as Bible translation is concerned, consistency is required not only by a document-oriented translation but also by an instrument-oriented one. Even for an instrumental translation, fixed expressions and syntactic patterns of the source-text are expected to be consistently represented by expressions and patterns in the target-text, albeit the target-language expressions may be different in meaning and the patterns may be different in structure from those in the source-text. This is not to say that a "hybrid" translation, i.e., a translation partly documentary and partly instrumental,[50] has to be deemed a bad translation. If the intended audience of a "hybrid" translation is properly informed about the way(s) document-oriented and instrument-oriented parts are distinguished and, in the translation process, the distinctions are executed consistently to meet the expectation(s) of the target audience, then this translation can still be deemed an "adequate" one.

Last but not least, on the issue of cultural differences, new and ongoing Chinese Bible projects employing translational action to deal with cultural differences between the biblical source cultures and the Chinese culture may want to pay attention to the coherency of the constructed or assumed cultural frameworks upon which the additional materials are based. It is undeniable that, in many areas, biblical scholars hold different opinions on the same issue and for many topics there exists no consensus. This does not mean, however, that for the same production in the additional materials provided by the translational action, the scholarship used for one area can be in conflict with that used in another area. As long as there exists coherency in the additional materials that translational action provides, it is not entirely unacceptable for a certain project to adopt a particular scholarly stance with the intention to conform to the views of the intended audience. However, because Bible reading should lead to the audience's transformation, it is preferable for the additional materials provided to be based upon the scholarship acknowledged by a wider spectrum of the scholarly world instead.

An article of mine published several years ago concludes:

> [The suggestions to have multiple Chinese versions of various types] might raise the question whether the plethora of translations would confuse readers. In the functionalist view, the number of translations should not be a cause for confusion if each of them comes with a clearly defined *skopos* [purpose] and is translated in a way adequate to it. The readers will be confused only if the *skopoi* [purposes] of the translations are not clear or if there are translations claiming to achieve certain functions when they are actually unable to do so.[51]

For any translation or translational action, consistency and coherency are two of the key elements to make it adequate to the purpose (*skopos*) defined for it.

Notes

1. The brief survey here is by no means comprehensive. There are also some other personal and sectarian Chinese Bible translations done during this period. However, this essay focuses on the Chinese Bibles aimed at use in the church.
2. See Jost Oliver Zetzsche, *The Bible in China: The History of the Union Version or The Culmination of Protestant Missionary Bible Translation in China* (Sankt Augustin: Monumenta Serica Institute/Nettetal: Steyler Verlag, 1999), 331–332. On the phenomenon of CUV's authority in the Chinese Protestant churches, see Yau-yuk Chong 莊柔玉, *A Study of the Phenomenon of Authoritativeness in the Chinese Translations of the Protestant Bible* [in Chinese] 基督教聖經中文譯本權威現象研究 (Hong Kong: International Bible Society [H.K.], 2000).
3. See the principles discussed in Zetzsche, *The Bible in China*, 324–325.
4. *Skopos* is the Greek word for "purpose." On *Skopostheorie*, see Christiane Nord, *Translating as a Purposeful Activity: Functionalist Approaches Explained* (Manchester: St. Jerome, 1997) and a brief sketch can be found in Kuo-Wei Peng, "Contemplating the Future of Chinese Bible Translation: A Functionalist Approach," *BT* 63, No. 1, (January 2012): 1–16 (1–4).
5. On "documentary" and "instrumental" translation processes, see Nord, *Translating as a Purposeful Activity*, 47.
6. Eugene Nida, *Toward a Science of Translating* (Leiden: E. J. Brill, 1964) and Eugene Nida and Charles R. Taber, *The Theory and Practice of Translation* (Leiden: E. J. Brill, 1969).
7. On "translational action," see Nord, *Translating as a Purposeful Activity*, 16–17. Further discussion of CUSB series' application of the concept of "translational action," see "the issue of cultural differences" below.
8. See, e.g., Wai Boon Chiu 趙維本, *Tracing Bible Translation—A History of the Translation of Five Modern Chinese Versions of the Bible* [in Chinese] 譯經溯源 (Hong Kong: China Graduate School of Theology, 1993), 43–45.
9. Prov 4:23; 11:18; Eccl 4:9; Isa 27:9; 32:17; 1 Cor 14:14; 1 Pet 1:9; Rev 14:13.

10. CUV, passim.
11. Ibid.
12. E.g., the case of 1 John 1:5 discussed in Peng, "Contemplating the Future of Chinese Bible Translation," 12.
13. As already indicated in Peng, "Contemplating the Future of Chinese Bible Translation," 12.
14. On its possible reason, see Kuo-Wei Peng, "The Influence of the KJV in Protestant Chinese Bible Translation Work," in David Burke, John F. Kutsko, and Philip H. Towner, eds., *The King James Version at 400: Assessing Its Genius as Bible Translation and Its Literary Influence* (Atlanta: SBL, 2013), 302–303.
15. See, e.g., Bruce M. Metzger, *A Textual Commentary on the Greek New Testament, Second Edition a Companion Volume to the United Bible Societies' Greek New Testament* (4th rev. ed.) (New York: United Bible Societies, 1994), 13–14.
16. In parentheses, though.
17. See Peng, "The Influence of the KJV in Protestant Chinese Bible Translation Work," 304, 307n61.
18. See Peng, "Contemplating the Future of Chinese Bible Translation," 12–14.
19. On different forms of documentary and instrumental translations, see Nord, *Translating as a Purposeful Activity*, 47–52.
20. Peng, "Contemplating the Future of Chinese Bible Translation," 13.
21. See Nord, *Translating as a Purposeful Activity*, 48–49.
22. Ibid. 48–49.
23. Ibid. 48, 49–50.
24. See Frank Thielman, *Ephesians* (Grand Rapids: Baker Academic, 2010), 43. However, this is not the only possible way to analyze the structure. An alternative analysis can be seen in Andrew T. Lincoln, *Ephesians* (Dallas: Word, 1990), 15–16.
25. See Peng, "Contemplating the Future of Chinese Bible Translation," 11–12.
26. See Nord, *Translating as a Purposeful Activity*, 124–125; Peng, "Contemplating the Future of Chinese Bible Translation," 3–4.
27. On "adequacy," see Nord, *Translating as a Purposeful Activity*, 34–37.
28. On "translation brief," see Nord, *Translating as a Purposeful Activity*, 20–21, 30.
29. On "loyalty," see Nord, *Translating as a Purposeful Activity*, 123–128.
30. Nord, *Translating as a Purposeful Activity*, 22–23.
31. Ibid. 23–25.
32. Ibid. 50–52.
33. Ibid. 47–50.
34. Raymond E. Brown, *The Gospel According to John I–XII* (New Haven: Yale University Press, 1974, 2008), 99; Andrew T. Lincoln, *The Gospel According to Saint John* (London: Continuum, 2005), 127.
35. Nord, *Translating as a Purposeful Activity*, 17.
36. However, many notes in CRV are theological and, therefore, not in line with the aim of "translational action" defined by Nord.
37. See Kuo-Wei Peng, "Reconsider How Bible Translation Is Fulfilled: The Test Case of the Chinese Union Study Bible Series" (paper presented at the International Congress of Ethnic Chinese Biblical Scholars, Hong Kong, August 19, 2014), 2.
38. The translation brief of the project can be seen in Peng, "Reconsider How Bible Translation Is Fulfilled," 5.
39. Peng, "Reconsider How Bible Translation Is Fulfilled," 5–6.

40. Dominique Barthélemy, *Critique textuelle de l'Ancien Testament* (5 vols.; Fribourg/Göttingen: Academic Press/Vandenhoeck Ruprecht, 1982, 1986, 1992, 2005, 2015).
41. Barbara Aland et al., *The Greek New Testament* (4th rev. ed.; Stuttgart: Deutsche Bibelgesellschaft/United Bible Societies, 1994).
42. Barbara Aland et al., *The Greek New Testament* (5th rev. ed.; Stuttgart: Deutsche Bibelgesellschaft/American Bible Society/United Bible Societies, 2014).
43. Peng, "Reconsider How Bible Translation Is Fulfilled," 10.
44. Ibid. 10.
45. Crossway Bibles, *The ESV Study Bible* (Wheaton: Crossway Bibles, 2008), 2213. Italics mine.
46. Ibid. 2328. Boldface original.
47. Cf. Peng, "Reconsider How Bible Translation Is Fulfilled," 6–7.
48. Ibid. 11.
49. See Peng, "Contemplating the Future of Chinese Bible Translation," 3; for detailed discussion, see Nord, *Translating as a Purposeful Activity*, 60.
50. Among English versions, NIV can be categorized as a "hybrid" one.
51. Peng, "Contemplating the Future of Chinese Bible Translation," 14.

Primary Sources

Chinese Contemporary Bible (CCB; 當代聖經). Hong Kong: Tien Dao Publisher, 1979.

Chinese Mandarin Union Version (Mandarin UV/CUV; 官話和合譯本/和合本). Shanghai: British & Foreign Bible Society, 1919.

Chinese Wenli Union Version (Wenli UV; 文理和合譯本). Shanghai: British & Foreign Bible Society, 1919.

Chinese Standard Bible—New Testament (CSB-NT; 中文標準譯本新約). Grandville, MI: Global Bible Initiative, 2008/2011.

Chinese Union Study Bible—1, 2 & 3 John (CUSB-1-3JN; 研讀本系列-約翰一二三書). Taipei: The Bible Society in Taiwan, 2011.

Chinese Union Study Bible—1 & 2 Thessalonians (CUSB-1-2TH; 研讀本系列-帖撒羅尼迦前後書). Taipei: The Bible Society in Taiwan, 2020.

Chinese Union Study Bible—1 & 2 Timothy, Titus (CUSB-1-2TI/TIT; 研讀本系列-提摩太前後書、提多書). Taipei: The Bible Society in Taiwan, 2011.

Chinese Union Study Bible—2 Peter & Jude (CUSB-2PE&JUD; 研讀本系列-彼得後書、猶大書). Taipei: The Bible Society in Taiwan, 2017.

Chinese Union Study Bible—Acts (CUSB-ACT; 研讀本系列-使徒行傳). Taipei: The Bible Society in Taiwan, 2016.

Chinese Union Study Bible—Colossians & Philemon (CUSB-COL&PHM; 研讀本系列-歌羅西書、腓利門書). Taipei: The Bible Society in Taiwan, 2014.

Chinese Union Study Bible—Ephesians (CUSB-EPH; 研讀本系列-以弗所書). Taipei: The Bible Society in Taiwan, 2019.

Chinese Union Study Bible—Galatians (CUSB-GAL; 研讀本系列-加拉太書). Taipei: The Bible Society in Taiwan, 2009.

Chinese Union Study Bible—Genesis (CUSB-GEN; 研讀本系列-創世記). Taipei: The Bible Society in Taiwan, 2013.

Chinese Union Study Bible—James (CUSB-JAS; 研讀本系列-雅各書). Taipei: The Bible Society in Taiwan, 2018.

Chinese Union Study Bible—Ruth (CUSB-RUT; 研讀本系列-路得記). Taipei: The Bible Society in Taiwan, 2011.
Chinese Union Study Bible—Sermon on the Mount in Matthew (CUSB-SotM; 研讀本系列-馬太福音之山上寶訓). Taipei: The Bible Society in Taiwan, 2018.
Contemporary Chinese Version—New Testament (CCV-NT; 新漢語譯本新約). Hong Kong: Chinese Bible International Ltd., 2010.
Four Gospels of the Interconfessional Version (ICV-Gospels; 共同譯本四福音). Taipei: United Bible Societies/the Bible Society in Taiwan, 2015.
Lu Chen-Chung (呂振中) Version (LCCV). Hong Kong: Hong Kong Bible Society, 1970.
New Chinese Version (NCV; 新譯本). Hong Kong: Tien Dao Publishing House Ltd., 1992.
New Living Translation (NLT; 新普及譯本). Hong Kong: Chinese Bible International Ltd., 2012.
Recovery Version (CRV; 恢復本). Taipei: Taiwan Gospel Book Room, 2003.
Revised Chinese Union Version/Chinese Union 2010 (RCUV/CU2010; 和合本修訂版/和合本 2010). Hong Kong: Hong Kong Bible Society, 2010.
Revised Chinese Union Version with Deuterocanon (RCUV with DC; 和合本修訂版[附次經]). Hong Kong: Hong Kong Sheng Kung Hui/Hong Kong Bible Society, 2014.
Today's Chinese Version (TCV; 現代中文譯本). Hong Kong: United Bible Societies, 1979.
Today's Chinese Version 95 (TCV95; 現代中文譯本修訂版). Hong Kong: United Bible Societies, 1995.
Today's Chinese Version 2019 (TCV2019; 現代中文譯本 2019). Taipei: United Bible Societies/the Bible Society in Taiwan, 2019.
Worldwide Chinese Bible-New Testament (WCB-NT; 環球聖經譯本新約). Hong Kong: Worldwide Bible Society, 2015.
Zhu Baohui (朱寶惠) New Testament (Zhu's NT). Hong Kong: Found Treasure Publications (拾珍出版社), 1936/1993.

PART II

EXPRESSION IN LITERARY AND RELIGIOUS CONTEXTS

CHAPTER 12

YIN-YANG (*YIJING*) AND THE BIBLE

CLAUDIA VON COLLANI

Introduction: Chinese Religions

When the first missionaries, i.e., the Jesuits, arrived in China, not only did they bring modern European science and the Christian faith but also they encountered a foreign culture with highly developed religious and philosophical systems. Led by the claim that Christianity as a monotheistic religion was the only true faith, one that would lead mankind to salvation, they observed with curiosity or even suspicion the religions of China. Should they be refuted, or could they be used as a preparation for the gospel of Christ? The attitudes toward this problem changed during the two hundred years of the China mission of early modern times.

The three main religions of China—Confucianism, Daoism, and Buddhism (*san jiao* 三教, three teachings), and with them Neo-Confucianism—were called "sects" by the missionaries. The Jesuits started off in China dressed as Buddhist monks from the West. Soon, however, they were told that the Confucian scholars were the cultural elite. So they adapted to Confucianism, using the Confucian books as a common base for language learning and for discussion and dialogue with the scholars.[1]

Confucianism, Ruism 儒家, constituted the state religion and philosophy of China. The old Confucianism had its base in the "Four Books" (*Sishu* 四書), but especially in the "Five Classical Books" (*Wujing* 五經), among which the *Yijing* 易經, the book of Changes or "*Liber mutationum*," as the missionaries called it, held first place as the most important one.[2] It was followed by the *Shujing* 書經, the "Book of Documents," and the *Shijing* 詩經, the "Book of Poetry" or songs.[3] In the *Shujing* and the *Shijing*, a single high god is mentioned, called *Shangdi* 上帝, Lord-on-High, or Highest Emperor, meaning that he was no worldly ruler. Only the emperor was permitted to offer him sacrifice.[4] In other chapters of the *Shujing*, *Tian* 天, Heaven, as a circumscription of God, comes close to *Shangdi* so that both seem to be identical. *Tian* or *Shangdi* often recalls the God of the Old Testament (OT).[5]

For the missionaries especially, the *Yijing* was a dangerous but fascinating book. It was used for state government, but misused for divination.[6] The sixty-four hexagrams of the *Yijing* consisting of broken and whole lines and were an enigma to be solved. Also, the term "*Taiji*" 太極, mentioned in the third appendix to the *Yijing*, in the *Dazhuan* 大傳 (Great Appendix), played an important role. *Taiji* is represented as a circle, half black and half white, representing *yin* and *yang* moving around each other.[7] The Chinese philosophers considered *Taiji* (supreme ultimate, supreme polarity), which is also identical with the *Dao* (Tao) of the *Daodejing* 道德經, to be the origin of the universe: "Therefore in (the system of) the Yî there is the Grand Terminus [*Taiji*], which produced the two elementary Forms. Those two Forms produced the Four emblematic Symbols, which again produced the eight Trigrams."[8] In this way, the *Yijing* symbolized the cosmogony by the genesis of the sixty-four hexagrams out of the *Taiji*. Not surprisingly, this became the center of conflict because this Chinese philosophical concept about the beginning of the cosmos contradicted the Christian doctrine of the *Creatio ex nihilo*.[9]

Both the Chinese and by the missionaries considered the mythological emperor Fuxi 伏羲 (2952 BCE) to be the author of the *Taiji*.[10] In reality, *Taiji* does not belong to the oldest parts of the *Yijing* but was added and developed much later by philosophers of Neo-Confucianism of the Song dynasty. Zhou Dunyi's 周敦頤 (1017–1073) diagram *Taijitu* and Shao Yong's 邵雍 (1011–1077) philosophy of numbers, for example, have their origins in the *Taiji*.[11] Neo-Confucianism, influenced by Daoism and Buddhism, caused great problems for the missionaries because they mostly misunderstood it. They dismissed Song Confucianism as pure atheism and materialism; most scholars of the Ming and Qing dynasties, therefore, adhering to Neo-Confucianism, were considered to be atheists.[12]

The First Jesuits and Taiji: Critical Voices from Scholasticism

Already during their stay in Japan from 1550 to 1614, the Jesuits had picked up some ideas about Far Eastern religions, especially Zen Buddhism. This encounter, however, was full of misunderstandings on both sides.[13] On the Western side, the reason for misunderstanding was the philosophical-theological education of young theologians in Europe. Especially Neo-Scholasticism and Aristotelianism led to an inflexible worldview in contradiction to modern European science and to other religions and philosophies. Therefore, the attempt to understand other religions and philosophies with the help of Western categories mostly failed, and the debates with Buddhist monks were full of misunderstandings.[14]

Matteo Ricci and *Taiji*

The Jesuits' visitor Alessandro Valignano (1539–1606) became the bridge between the missions in Japan and China. He advocated adaptation to the Japanese culture, but not to its religion. His arguments for debates with Buddhists in Japan were collected as *Catechismus Christianae Fidei, in quo veritas nostrae religionis ostenditur...* (Lisbon 1586).[15] This book also was used in China for debates.[16] The pioneer of the modern China mission, Matteo Ricci (1552–1610), used the arguments from Japan for debates with Buddhist and Neo-Confucian ideas in his famous book *Tianzhu Shiyi* 天主實義 (1603), an introduction to Christianity for non-Christian Chinese scholars.[17] He became the first European to meet and to deal with the concept of *Taiji* and *Yin-Yang*.[18] From the diagram *Taijitu*, Ricci argued that the term "*Taiji*," "Greatest Last One," should and could not be used as a name for God, otherwise called *Shangdi* (supreme emperor) in the Chinese Classical Books: "The theory, from what I have seen of the diagram illustrating the Ultimateless and the Supreme Ultimate, is based on the symbols representing Yin and Yang...."[19] For Ricci, as an adherent of the original old Confucianism, *Taiji* was not authentically Chinese but was only introduced much later by commentaries.[20] Therefore, it could not be identical with the "*summum extremum*," but rather with the "*materia prima*" of the Scholastics and, consequently, it could not be the creator of Heaven and Earth and the source of all things.[21] Later, however, his attitude changed, and he remarked cautiously: "If they finally would understand *Taikieo* (= *Taiji*) to be the first substantial principle, which is intelligent and without end, then we admit that it were God and nothing else."[22]

The Discussion about the Right Terminology: *Taiji* Refused

During their first years in China, the Jesuits had decided to use Chinese names for Christian spiritual concepts. Accordingly, they used the following names: for God, *Tianzhu* 天主 (Lord of Heaven), *Tian* 天 (Heaven), *Shangdi* 上帝 (Emperor-on-High); for angels, *Tianshen* 天神; for the soul, *Linghun* 靈魂; and so forth. After Matteo Ricci's death in 1610, the visitor Francesco Pasio (1554–1612) started a discussion about the name for God in 1612 with a question addressed to the Superior of the China mission, Niccolò Longobardo (1559–1654). This discussion about terms within the Jesuit order continued until 1635. Two positions emerged as a result: supporters of the Chinese names for God on the grounds of theological adaptation and their adversaries, who advocated for Latin terms, because in their opinion the Chinese had no idea about spiritual things. Chinese names could lead to misunderstandings but were preferred by the Chinese. Foreign Latinized names could avoid misunderstanding but sounded barbarian to the Chinese. The discussion became more urgent when the Jesuits, expelled from Japan, arrived in China after 1610: especially João Rodrigues S.J. (1561–1633)—called "the interpreter" in Japan—had his own ideas.[23] In his opinion, following

Valignano's *Catechismus*, there was a hidden doctrine under the outer wrong teachings in the East: "According to the Occidental interpretation, the Great Ultimate [*Taiji*] is something material, is matter without intelligence and without consciousness. Unless there is the infinite, omnipotent, wise, and intelligent factor, how could it ever produce things?"[24] In 1633, Rodrigues was still convinced that the doctrine of the Chinese literati had come to China from the Chaldean diviners via the Persian magician Zoroaster. This doctrine used mathematical figures and two deities called the "Virtue of Heaven" and the "Evil of Earth," symbolized by light and darkness. Rodrigues here evidently spoke about the symbol of *Taiji*, consisting of *Yin* and of *Yang* (light and darkness), as shown in the hexagrams of the *Yijing*, the Book of Changes.[25]

The discussions within the Society of Jesus during the next years brought several treatises pro and contra, which were later destroyed. Niccolò Longobardo became the main opponent of a theological adaptation. Using the *Xingli daquan* 性理大全 (1415), the anthology of Neo-Confucian texts, he wrote the treatise "*Reposta breve sobre las Controversias do Xámti, Tienxin, Limhoên, e outros nomes e termos sinicos...*" (1623).[26] Being a very scrupulous, anxious theologian with many doubts, Longobardo strongly relied on Rodrigues's arguments. He also was convinced that the religions in East Asia had their origin in the Persian magician Zoroaster. Especially the mathematical symbols of the *Yijing*, used by the Chinese literati, played an important role in his argumentation. These symbols coming from Zoroaster contained superstition and were the symbols of the main deities of the Bactrians or Persians.[27] He used *Yijing* and *Daodejing* at the same time when he wrote:

> Even so the Chinese Philosophers, who were the Founders of the Sect of the Learned, have their Symbols consisting of Figures and Numbers, as metaphorical expressions. The principal Symbols have even and odd strokes cross'd in the middle, black and white Points, Figures round and square, the six Position of places in their way of Writing, and other Metaphorical terms and expressions. The Books of the Je King, which contain the Speculative part of the Chinese Doctrine, are full of these Symbols. As to the Mysteries and efficient causes of Numbers, there are two whole Books, which are the 11th and 12th of the Sing Li [*Xingli* 性理], by which it were easy to restore the Science of Pythagorical Numbers, which were lost in the Great West.[28]

These are clear allusions to the *Yijing*, with its hexagrams consisting of six whole and broken lines, and to the figures *Hetu* 河圖 and *Luoshu* 洛書.[29]

In chapter five of his treatise, Longobardo described the Chinese cosmology:

> The form of the Universe is this, Heaven is Spherical, and therefore moves and influences in circulum. The Earth is Square, therefore it lies still in Center, and influences per Quadratum; and four Elements answer to it, one to each of the four Sides, and the fifth to the middle Superficies. Besides Heaven they imagine that infinite Materia Prima, call'd Li [Li, being 理], from which Tai Kie [*Taiji* 太極] flow'd; and they also call it Kung [*Kong* 空], Hiu [*Xu*, vacuum 虛], Tao [*dao* 道], Vu [*Wu* 無], Vu Kie [*Wuji* 無極]; still transparent, rare in the Superlative degree, without knowledge, without

action, nothing Mera Potentia.... This Production of the Universe is assign'd by Fo Hi [Fuxi], and is represented in the figure of the Je King [*Yijing*], call'd Ho Tu [*Hetu*]... Lao Zu [Laozi]: Tao, or the first Chaos produced Unity, which is Tai Kie, or the Materia Secunda. Unity produces Duality, which is Lang I. Duality produced Trinity, which is, Tien Ti [*Tiandi* 天地], Jin [*ren* 人] San Zai [*sancai* 三才], Heaven, Earth, and Man. And Trinity produced all things.[30]

After long discussions within the order, the Jesuits in China decided in the first half of the seventeenth century not to follow the adversaries of Chinese names and ideas. *Shangdi*, *Tian*, *Tianzhu* and other names could be used for the Christian God. Only the attitude towards Song Confucianism remained more or less negative.[31] This changed at least partly when the first translations of some of the Confucian books appeared, namely the *Sapientia Sinica* (1662) and the *Sinarum Scientia politico-moralis* (1667).[32]

Sapientia Sinica (1662): Positive View of *Taiji*

In 1662, the book *Sapientia Sinica* was published as a translation of the *Daxue* (The Great Learning or The Great Doctrine) and of the first five parts of the *Lunyu* (Confucian Analects). It was edited by the Sicilian Jesuit Prospero Intorcetta (1625–1696),[33] but quite probably translated by Inácio da Costa (1603–1666). The two Jesuits, however, had used earlier, unprinted translations of their brethren of the "Four Books" (*Sishu*) since the beginnings of the Jesuit mission in China.[34] The bilingual version in xylographic printing of the *Sapientia Sinica*, however, was not for the European public but only for missionaries learning the Chinese language. The *Sapientia Sinica* shows a graphic illustration of Neo-Confucian cosmology as used by the Neo-Confucian philosopher Shao Yong,[35] demonstrating how all things have their origin in the *Taiji*, being the "*radix prima et summa origo rerum inexhauribilis*" (first root, highest origin, inexhaustible [of all] things): "*Tai kie* produces the two *ŷ* (*yin* and *yang*), the two *ŷ* produce the four pictures (*imagines*), and these (pictures) produce the eight '*sortes*' or '*qua*' (*gua* 卦)." Two lines below, it says: "I do not doubt that the wisest old Chinese wanted to define God, the origin of all things, with the name *Taiji*."[36] In this way, *Taiji* was given a spiritual meaning and could be used or at least discussed as a possible name for the Christian God.

Confucius Sinarum Philosophus (1687)

At the end of the sixteenth century, a Latin translation of three of the Four Books (*Sishu*) was published in Europe, the *Confucius Sinarum Philosophus, sive scientia Sinensis latinè exposita* (Paris 1687), edited by Philippe Couplet (1623–1692).[37] In the lengthy "*Proëmialis Declaratio*" (introduction), dealing with the Chinese books and the accommodation strategy of the Jesuits, the *Yijing* is described as a book about mostly ethical philosophy.[38] According to Chinese tradition, its oldest parts were written by "Fo hi"

(Fuxi), the mythological founder of the Chinese empire. The author(s) of the "*Proëmialis Declaratio*" write(s) that the *Yijing*, being in third place of the Classical Books, constitutes the primary book of Neo-Confucianism.[39] The *Taiji* is the axis or pole of the world, ineffable and spiritual with the power of activity and creativity, moving and resting, so that it nearly seems to be divine. Last but not least, it is the origin of the Neo-Confucianist philosophy.[40] The *Confucius Sinarum Philosophus* writes:

> It is important to know that the Chinese people from ancient time have considered as certitude the existence of a double material element for all things. They call one the *Perfect*, or *Yang*, and the other the *Imperfect*, or *Yin*. These two are produced by *Taiji*, or Great pole, which is understood as a kind of "chaos" or material stuff embracing everything, to the extent that the Chinese pagan and Christian "Doctors" explain it to us as *yuanqi* 元氣 ("*Yven che*"), or "Prime Matter" (*Materia prima*). The riddle of the (original) trigrams of the *Yijing* was solved only a thousand years later by the Chinese ruler Wen Wang, who was in this respect comparable to Oedipus.[41]

This attitude towards the *Yijing* is complemented by the remark that the *Yijing* is being misused by Daoist fortune-tellers and by "atheists" (i.e., Neo-Confucians), and its philosophy as such is pure atheism.[42] Afterwards, a lengthy story of the *Yijing* and a description of the hexagrams is given, together with a map of the hexagrams in the so-called Wen Wang order.[43]

Charles Maigrot: *Taiji* Prohibited

The discussion about the rites and terms then stopped until the end of the seventeenth century because each party was permitted to work at their intention by a papal decree of 1669.[44] This changed with the Apostolic Vicar of Fujian, Charles Maigrot M.E.P. (1652–1730), who became the most important adversary amongst the missionaries against the Chinese rites and against the *Yijing*. His attitude became authoritative for the whole Catholic Church and for the poor reputation of the *Yijing* as a "superstitious book."[45] On March 26, 1693, he issued his famous "mandate" that became the starting point of the new phase of the Rites Controversy (a dispute among missionaries and also between the missionaries and the Chinese government over the validity of the Chinese rituals). Point six of this mandate deals with the *Yijing* and the term "*Taiji*":

> We point out that nothing is to be published in spoken or written form, which could mislead incautious persons to error and could open the way for superstition, such as:
>
> That the wisest old Chinese wanted to call God, the cause of all things, with the name *Tay kie* (*Taiji*); that the book the Chinese call *Ie king* (*Yijing*) is the summa of the best physical and moral teachings.[46]

Maigrot's mandate was sent to Rome and forwarded to the Holy Office in 1698. As a reason, Maigrot stated that all past and contemporary Confucianists were atheists, and that there was no single trace of religion found in China.[47] After long discussions, the mandate was confirmed by the papal decree "*Cum Deus optimus*" (November 20, 1704). Only on point six, no decision was made because the later papal legate to China, Charles-Thomas Maillard de Tournon (1668–1710), was supposed to discuss it with the bishops and missionaries in China. This was never done. Therefore, this point was neither confirmed by the Sacred Congregation nor in the Papal decrees and constitutions.[48]

Joachim Bouvet and His Figurist School

Maigrot's Mandate constituted a great challenge for the French Jesuit Joachim Bouvet (1656–1730), who wanted to defend the accommodation and therefore disprove Maigrot. As the foundation, Bouvet used his European background—Jewish-Christian Cabbala, the allegorical exegetical system, Hermetism, "*Prisca Theologia*," Pythagorean numbers, and Neo-Platonism—for the interpretation of the Daoist, Confucian, and Neo-Confucian literature in China. Bouvet was particularly attracted by the *Yijing* that he considered to be the (then-lost) Book of Henoch.[49] For him, only his Figurist system (see discussion below) offered the right key to understanding the hidden theological meaning in the old books that the Chinese had lost.[50]

The Correspondence with Gottfried Wilhelm Leibniz

Bouvet elaborated his system in the course of his correspondence with the German philosopher and polymath Gottfried Wilhelm Leibniz (1646–1716) between 1697 and 1707. In this exchange, the *Yijing* and Fuxi played an eminent role. Leibniz, at that time working with his binary arithmetic, needed proof of its usefulness. He sent his system to Bouvet, admonishing him to show it to the Kangxi emperor (1654–1722), who was being taught mathematics by Bouvet, to prove the creation of the world out of nothing, namely with only two principles: God, the perfect, one, and nothing, zero, the imperfect.[51] In his answer to Leibniz on November 4, 1701, Bouvet "identified" the binary arithmetic with the so-called *xiantiantu* 先天圖 (Chart of the Former Heaven) arrangement of the sixty-four hexagrams of the *Yijing*, in which the hexagrams start from six broken lines—meaning zero going up to sixty-three with six whole lines.[52] The six grades of the generation represent the six days of the divine creation with the number seven, the last day, on a special place. In the same letter, Bouvet also mentions the *Taiji* as the "premier principle," symbolized by a dot, from where the perfect and the imperfect emanate, represented by the whole and by the broken line.[53] In his answer (May 18, 1703), Leibniz confirmed that in his opinion Fuxi, alias Henoch, had in this way described the creation of the world with the help of zero and one, with the broken and the whole line in the *Yijing*:

> It seems, however, that the eight *gua*, or eight linear figures which are considered fundamental by the Chinese, could perhaps lead to the assumption that Fuxi himself had the Creation in mind in making everything come from the One and the Nothing, and that he extended this to the history of Genesis. For the 0 [zero] can signify the void which preceded the creation of heaven and earth, followed by the seven days .... At the beginning of the first day there existed 1, that is God. At the beginning of the second day, 2, heaven and earth being created during the first. Finally, at the beginning of the seventh everything existed; therefore, the last is the most perfect and the Sabbath... thus 7 is written by 111 without 0.[54]

In the number 111, Leibniz even saw an allusion to the Trinity.[55] Leibniz used the history of Fuxi and the *Yijing* for his article submitted to the Académies des Sciences in Paris, "*Explication de l'arithmétique binaire, qui se sert des seuls caractères 0 & 1; avec des Remarques sur son utilité, & sur ce qu'elle donne le sens des anciennes figures Chinoises de Fohy*," but without any theology.[56]

The *Ain Soph* in Figurism

During the following years, Bouvet even started a private Figurist academy. Together with his approximately ten disciples, he developed his Figurism on the basis of the *Yijing* and the *Daodejing*.[57] In his "*Examen examinis seu responsum ad scriptum censoris anonymi...*" (1713),[58] Bouvet presented his interpretation of the Chinese *Taiji/Dao* with the help of the Christian Cabbala.[59] He was convinced that the Chinese already knew the most important Christian mysteries of faith (i.e. the dogmas).[60] For Bouvet, *Dao* was "beginning and end," identical with eternal law, or the hidden almighty God, the "*Deus absconditus*." He can be represented by the figure of the ten Sephirot of Moses, i.e. the image of *Ain Soph* (*En Sof* = it has no end), partly light, partly dark, meaning the light of the inaccessible Divinity before his emanation through creation. Bouvet confirmed his identification of *Taiji* with the *Ain Soph* with quotations from the Bible proving that God comprehends light and darkness.[61] In Isaiah 45:6–7, one reads: "I am the LORD, and there is no other. I form light and create darkness...." The same idea can be found in Psalm 138:12: "Yea, the darkness hideth not from thee; but the night shineth as the day; the darkness and the light are both alike to thee." In the beginning of his Gospel, John wrote that the symbol of eternal light is illuminating the darkness and that it is stronger than the darkness (1:4–5). Therefore, the *Taiji*/*Ain Soph* is also the symbol for the future Messiah to come, in China the *Shengren* 聖人, the expectation of the whole world.[62]

The Hypostatic Union as Female Theology in Figurism

One of the most difficult dogmas of Christianity, that of the hypostatic union, was explained by the Figurists. This phrase refers to the unity of divinity and humanity in the person of Jesus Christ. Both perfect natures are combined in Christ in one person to a hypostasis (substance).[63] To explain this difficult *mysterium fidei* to the Chinese, Bouvet and his disciple Jean-François Foucquet (1665–1741) used the *Ain Soph* from the Cabbalistic book *Sohar* as a symbol.[64] It resembled the *Taijitu* of Zhou Dunyi. *Dao*, identical with *Taiji*, is ratio, the way and law (the heavenly and eternal one), the uncreated wisdom, with which God created everything. It also stands at the beginning of the *Yijing*, the source of all other classical books of China, with the following definition: "Dao, or (uncreated) wisdom, is like the virtue of both sexes (not in the normal sense, but in the spiritual sense)."[65] In the *Daodejing*, chapter 25, its definition is *youwu huncheng* 有物混成: "The Being with the incomprehensible virtue of both sexes *Yin* and *Yang*."[66] *Yin*, the less perfect, terrestrial spirit and the soul, united since the beginning of the world to *Yang*, the heavenly, perfect spirit and source of light.[67] For the Figurists, only the elements of both sexes together in *Dao/Taiji* can perform creation.[68]

Starting with the circle as a symbol for God, Bouvet introduced a female part into Christology. In the tree of the ten Sephiroth of the *Ain Soph*, the second sephirah is *Hokmah*, God's wisdom, Sophia in Greek. The sephirah Binah is shown as the upper wisdom, "mother of the world," with the seven sephiroth below her as her children. Binah here means female expressing the power of creation, receiving, but also giving birth, a kind of Shakti of the hidden God. The last sephirah, Malkuth, is also called "Shekhinah," who receives from Yesod. In this sephirah, the divine life is like light in a dark mirror and is finally creating, leading the power to the world. This last sephirah is sometimes shown in a very passive way, as night, moon, earth, dry, gate, a transformation of power.[69]

The dark element in *Ain Soph/Taiji* means the female element, the Sophia or Sapientia in the books of Wisdom in the OT, who was present when God created the world: "The Lord created me at the beginning of his work, the first of his acts of long ago. Ages ago I was set up, at first, before the beginning of the earth. . . . When he established the heavens, I was there, when he drew a circle on the face of the depth . . ." (Prov 8:22–27, NRSV). In Jesus Sirach (Ecclesiasticus), she is described in the following way: "I came forth from the mouth of the Most High . . . . I dwelt in the highest heavens, and my throne was in a pillar of cloud. Alone I compassed the vault of heaven and traversed the depth of the abyss" (24:5–7). In the Latin Vulgate translation, she also says: "I am the mother of beautiful love (*mater pulchrae dilectionis*), of fear, of knowledge, and of holy hope; all the delightfulness of the way is in me and the truth, all hope of life and virtue."[70] Bouvet found many other allusions for this creature in Exodus, e.g. in the books of Kings and in Ezekiel. Sophia/Anima lives in the tabernacle, in the oracle of the temple, in the column of fire and of clouds, in the temple of the Lord as his most holy spouse, created from the beginning and hypostatically united to Jesus Christ.[71] This is expressed by the figures of Fuxi and his sister or wife, Nü wa 女媧, representing the anima of Jesus.[72]

Therefore, in Bouvet's opinion, the *Daodejing* was comparable to the books of Wisdom of the OT. Especially chapter 25 describes the *Dao* "without beginning and end." Laozi did not know the real name of this creature before the production of things: "This firstborn creature is standing alone without mutation, before any (other) creature, surrounding the universe without diverging from the way of truth." Hence, she got her name *tianxiamu* 天下母, "mother of all things," i.e. of the universe. For Laozi, this being can only be expressed by the character *Dao*, "Firstborn of all creatures" (before Heaven and Earth) "*xiantian disheng* 先天地生" (chap. 25).[73] She is alone in the world without a companion who resembles her; nobody knows her beginning, way and end. She is the origin of all things.[74]

Negative Theology in Figurism

Other important terms in connection with *Taiji* and *Dao* in Neo-Confucianism are, for example: *Wu*, Non-Being; *You Wu*, Being and Non-Being; *Taixu*, three times greatest void or three times greatest immaterial; *Wuji*, without beginning. For most missionaries, as for Maigrot, these notions from Song Confucianism were the foundations of atheism.[75] In contrast, Bouvet and the other Figurists found in the philosophy of Neo-Confucianists a kind of negative theology. The church father St. Dionysius Areopagites[76] had called God "Nothing," for in "the same way as God is all, He is also Nothing of all." Also, the Hebrews demonstrated this with the symbol of the *Ain Soph*, in China the *Yin-Yang-tu* 陰陽圖. Nothingness in Neo-Platonism corresponds to the Chinese *Wu* and *Taixu*, void, standing for the immaterial, invisible, intelligible, or archetypical world with its eternal ideas of all things in Heaven, from which things have not yet emanated. Laozi wrote: "All things in the universe are produced by Being and Being has been produced by Non-Being." In the *Yijing*, all things are generated by the pre-existent, heavenly and earthly matter. For Laozi and Zhuangzi, Dao is the unexplorable womb of the ideas or examples of all things.[77] It is the archetypical idea of all things, also called the most noble of all things. Heaven and Earth produced all things out of *Taixu*, of Being and Non-Being. *Wanxiang* 萬象, the forms or ideas, are for Laozi identical with *Taixu* or Heaven without matter.

Figurism in Critic and Defence

The system of Figurism, however, was not welcome to most of Bouvet's superiors because of the Rites Controversy. Another reason was that if they identified Fuxi with Enoch and Hermes Trismegistos, considering the *Yijing* as a preparation to Christianity like the OT, then the Chinese perhaps thought they had already everything necessary for salvation and did not need Christianity. Therefore, several Jesuit superiors in China considered Figurism dangerous and forbade Bouvet every discussion with the Kangxi emperor about theology. In the controversy with the Jesuit visitor Giampaolo Gozani (1659–1732), Bouvet gave a short description of his system concerning the *Yijing*.

The *Yijing* has an exterior represented by natural things or symbols, and an interior meaning representing the true hieroglyphic and symbolic philosophy.[78] By means of images and symbols, this philosophy unveils the most important truths of religion.

The natural things or symbols, especially the scientific and mathematical proofs, cover the hidden truths like a veil or enigma. When God created the world, he created everything in "*numero, pondere et mensura*," based on numerical proofs and in a perfect order.[79] The interior meaning represents the "*Invisibilia Dei*" (Rom 1:20),[80] which are God's visible deeds, for they tell about the Creator's glory. In the *Yijing*, they are called "*wanxiang* 萬象" (literally "the ten thousand"] i.e., "all images," or "all symbols."[81] All symbols are related to the three states of the world, i.e., the perfect one, the corrupt one, and the repaired one.[82] Despite the fact that Bouvet was supported by the Kangxi emperor and by the Chinese scholar Li Guangdi 李光地 (1642–1718),[83] the Jesuit superiors accused Bouvet before the Kangxi emperor in 1716. At the end, Bouvet was permitted to work alone until he had finished his work, but he was not allowed to use anybody from outside as a help.[84] Bouvet continued this state until his passing in Peking.

François Noël and *Taiji*: Scholastic Possible

Besides the "great Figurists" (Joseph Henry de Prémare, Jean-François Foucquet, Jean-Alexis de Gollet), the Belgian Jesuit François Noël (1651–1729) also was an adherent of Bouvet's Figurism and therefore dealt with the "Tay Kie" (*Taiji*).[85]

For Noël, the two characters of *Taiji* had the meaning of the highest of all things "*primus rerum Terminus*" (*Terminus* = highest end). It can be used for *natura naturans*, i.e. for God as first author of all things. The Chinese say in this respect: Heaven and Earth are the ones that produced all things. Heaven and Earth, however, are produced by the first terminus, or *Taiji*. *Taiji* is not a name itself because the first principle lacks any name, but *Taiji* gives an idea. For Noël, it seems to have similarity with the expression given by Francisco Suarez S.J. (1548–1617, "*Doctor eximius*") that God cannot be understood (*Dei ineffabilitas*) (I. p. lib. 2 cap. 3) when he wrote: "It is difficult to understand God, but impossible to speak about him." John of Damascus (ca. 650–754) had the same opinion: "Concerning God it is impossible to say what his essence and nature is."[86]

The Chinese express the same idea in a comparable way: the highest Heaven's doings or nature lack voice and smell and sensibility.[87] He is the true effective reason, the *cardo*, the root of all created things. Therefore, he is called "Vu Kie" (*Wuji*), *seu Ens sine termino* (Being without end, or limitation), and also *Taiji*, first last. Beyond, there is nothing because it is the *Ens sine termino*, the same as first end (*primus Terminus*). This includes movement and quietness; it is the way of the law of Heaven or his revolving course without interruption. The meaning of "The nature of High Heaven is without sound and smell" is valid for the Lord or Rector.[88] Therefore, *Taiji* or first terminus, is understood concerning the Lord and Rector of Heaven, and *Shangdi* can also be called *Taiji*, i.e. first or greatest Unity. In old times, *Taiji* was the highest Lord *Shangdi*, the first producer of all things. All scholars explained *Dayi* 大一 the first and greatest Unity, with *Taiji*.[89]

Taiji also can be used for the essence of uncreated and created things. The Chinese say, considering all things, each one has its own singular nature, and in the same way all have one single origin, namely the same. Then, they collectively have the universal essence of all things, which is the one first terminus. The first terminus is the excellence of nature, without form and modus to explain it. It has neither sound nor smell. It is something that is not dependent on the senses.

Taiji or first terminus also can be taken for the whole aggregation of the natural *agentia* (agents). This is proven by the quotation from the Book of Changes: "For in this unique enigmatic symbol and in its six parts or lines the ratio of the first term of the first three principles is contained and can be found (三才 Heaven, Earth, Man, or the whole aggregation of the natural agents). Therefore, these three principles are called three terms (*termini*)."[90]

Taiji, first terminus, is often taken for nature, insofar as nature is taken as the cause of motion and quietness. This is also called *Yin*, quietness, and *Yang*, motion. The origin of the mode *Yin* is *Yang* and the other way around. The terminus consists of these two essences.

Noël argues that also the people of antiquity, such as the Greeks and the Romans, did not venerate nature as such, but they took nature as a circumscription for its author, namely God. So did, for example, the Roman Marcus Tullius Cicero (106–43 BCE) in his book *De natura Deorum*, in which he wrote that many gods were venerated that were in reality but one, the Christian apologist Marcus Minucius Felix (late second century), and Lucius Caecilius Firmianus Lactantius (ca. 250–325) in his *De ira Dei*. Finally, Noël raised the rhetorical question whether the Chinese perhaps knew not only about the unity of God but also about the Trinity. He answered with Suarez that this mystery cannot be seen by only the natural ratio or by the "*lumine naturali*" (*non supernaturali*). Noël does not know the answer and therefore omits it.[91]

The Secularization of *Taiji* and Yin-Yang

The Figurist interpretation of the *Yijing* and its hexagrams found many adversaries that considered this kind of attitude to be ahistorical and contradicting the Chinese way of seeing the *Yijing*. Especially several French Jesuits living in Peking decided to translate the *Yijing* themselves using the historical-critical method. This anti-Figurist group consisted of Fathers Jean-Baptiste Régis (1663–1738), Pierre-Vincent de Tartre (1669–1724), and Joseph Anne Marie de Moyriac de Mailla (1669–1748).[92] They translated single parts of the *Yijing*, but their opus was only published one hundred years later by Orientalist Julius von Mohl (1800–1876) as *Y-King antiquissimus Sinarum liber quem ex latina interpretatione P. Regis aliorumque ex Soc. Jesu P. P. edidit Julius Mohl* (Stuttgartiae et Tubingae 1834–1838) published by J. G. Cotta.[93]

In several dissertations, these authors of the *Yijing* deal with the appendices of the *Yijing* about *Yin* and *Yang*. Régis and Co. refuted the assumption that *Taijitu* was old; in reality, it was not even invented by Zhou Dunyi, Shao Yong (1011–1077), and others, but is of Daoist origin. He described the terms *Wuji* and *Taiji* as "*magnus terminus est sine termino, vel magnus axis sine axe*" (great end without end, or great axis without axis), symbolized by a circle, partly black and partly white.[94] There are many different meanings of *Taiji* that can be found only in the Great Appendix of the *Yijing*. In the Chinese tradition, *xiantian* is said to have be invented by Fuxi, whereas *houtian* was created by Wen Wang. In dissertation five, Régis argues that the diagram *xiantian* (*prioris saeculi mappa* = diagram of the Former Heaven) was not invented by Fuxi—and *houtian* (*posterioris saeculi mappa* = diagram of the Later Heaven) not by Wen Wang. Both are not in the *Yijing*, but originated from the Song Confucians such as Shao Yong, or perhaps the Cheng brothers, Cheng Hao 程顥 (1032–1085) and Cheng Yi 程頤 (1033–1107), and Zhu Xi 朱熹 (1130–1200).[95]

Conclusion

Many missionaries tried to facilitate the way to the new Western religion for the Chinese by interpreting and using the Chinese religions as preparation for Christianity. This was not easy, for especially their European background of Scholastic theology often constituted a great obstacle for them. A special challenge was the question of whether Chinese names and concepts could be used for God and spiritual matters. Figurism, which at first glance seemed to be a strange and outdated method, was an earnest attempt to understand Chinese religion and philosophy and to open the door for a mutual understanding. The Figurists, even more than other missionaries, interpreted the Chinese symbolism of *Taiji* and *Yin/Yang* not in a dualistic way as bad and good, but instead used it in a Christian interpretation as creative male and female forces in a new Christian-Chinese cosmology—as it was no longer permitted to use the term "*Dafumu*大父母," Great-Father-Mother for God. This approach to Christian theology in China was, however, stopped with the prohibition of the Chinese Rites in 1715 and 1742.[96] Only today do we again have the possibility of a new understanding.

Notes

1. Claudia von Collani, "Jesuiten im Gespräch mit chinesischen Gelehrten," *Jahrbuch für Religionswissenschaft und Theologie der Religionen* 2 (1994): 69–87; 3 (1995): 27–49.
2. James Legge, trans., *The I Ching. The Book of Changes*, 2nd ed. (New York: Dover, 1963).
3. Yao Xinzhong, *Routledgecurzon Encyclopedia of Confucianism*, vol. 2 (London, New York: Routledge, 2013), 662.
4. Séraphin Couvreur, *Chou-king: Les Annales de la Chine* (Paris: Cathasia, 1950), 16; s.a. Etienne Ducornet, *Matteo Ricci, le lettré d'Occident* (Paris: Ed. Du Cerf, 1992), 62.
5. Yao, *Confucianism*, 2:535–536.
6. Martino Martini, *Sinicæ Historiæ Decas Prima...* (Monachii: Wagner, 1658), 6.
7. Yao, *Confucianism*, 2:589–590.
8. Legge, *I Ching*, 373.
9. H. Denzinger and A. Schönmetzer, *Enchiridion Symbolorum, Definitionum et Declarationum de rebus fidei et morum* (Freiburg: Herder, 1976), 285, 790, 900. See K. K. Yeo's thesis that the yin-yang lens of interpreting God and humanity (Exod 3:14 and Gen 1:28 respectively)

comes closer to the Hebraic understanding, see Yeo, *What Has Jerusalem to Do with Beijing? Biblical Interpretation from a Chinese Perspective* (Eugene, OR: Pickwick, 2018), 55–69.

10. Philippe Couplet, "Proëmialis Declaratio," *Confucius Sinarum philosophus*...(Paris: Horthemels, 1687), lix, cf. David E. Mungello, *Curious Land: Jesuit Accommodation and the Origins of Sinology* (Studia Leibnitiana Supplementa 25) (Wiesbaden: Franz Steiner, 1985), 266–267.
11. Alfred Forke, *Geschichte der neueren chinesischen Philosophie* (Hamburg: de Gruyter, 1964), 18–40, 45–56; Fung Yu-lan, *A History of Chinese Philosophy*, Vol. 2: *The Period of Classical Learning (from the Second Century BC to the Twentieth Century AD* (Princeton: University Press, 1983), 407–571; Joseph A. Adler, *Reconstructing the Confucian Dao: Zhu Xi's Appropriation of Zhou Dunyi* (Albany: State University, 2014); Yao, *Confucianism*, 2:699–700.
12. Nicolas Standaert, ed., *Handbook of Christianity in China*, Vol. 1: *635–1800* (Leiden: Brill, 2001), 311.
13. Claudia von Collani, "The Opposing Views of Niccolò Longobardo and Joachim Bouvet on Chinese Religions," in Wenchao Li (Hg.), *Leibniz and the European Encounter with China. 300 Years of Discours sur la théologie naturelle des Chinois* (Studia Leibnitiana—Sonderheft Band 52) (Stuttgart: Franz Steiner, 2017), 71.
14. Sangkeun Kim, *Strange Names of God: The Missionary Translation of the Divine Name and the Chinese Responses to Matteo Ricci's Shangti in Late Ming China 1583–1644* (Studies in Biblical Literature 70) (New York: Peter Lang, 2004), 49–55.
15. Urs App, *The Cult of Emptiness; The Western Discovery of Buddhist Thought and the Invention of Oriental Philosophy* (Kyoto: University Media, 2014), 51–60; Collani, "Opposing Views," 71.
16. Matteo Ricci, *Le sens réel de Seigneur du Ciel.* Texte établi, traduit et annoté par Thierry Meynard (Paris: Les belles Lettres 2013), xviii–xxiv.
17. Collani, "Opposing Views," 71.
18. Knud Lundbæk, "The Image of Neo-Confucianism in *Confucius Sinarum Philosophus*," *Journal of the History of Ideas* (1983): 25–26.
19. Matteo Ricci, *The True Meaning of the Lord of Heaven (T'ien-chu Shih-i): A Chinese English Edition*, trans. Douglas Lancashire and Peter Hu Kuo-chen s.j., ed. Edward J. Malatesta (Taipei: Institut Ricci, 1985), 106–107.
20. Lundbaek, "Image," 25.
21. Ricci, *Meaning*, 107–111; Thierry Meynard s.j., ed., *Confucius Sinarum Philosophus (1687).* The First Translation of the Confucian Classics (Rome: Institutum Historicum Societatis Iesu, 2011), 34.
22. Pasquale D'Elia, *Fonti Ricciane*, vol. II (Roma: La Libreria dello Stato, 1949), 297–298.
23. Collani, "Opposing Views," 73–75.
24. Pasquale M. D'Elia, *Galileo in China. Relations through the Roman College between Galileo and the Jesuit Scientist-Missionaries (1610–40)* (Cambridge, MA: Harvard University Press, 1960), 43.
25. Rodrigues, "Letter, 5 February 1633"; see Collani, "Opposing Views," 84.
26. Only parts of Niccolò Longobardo's manuscript of 1623 survived entitled: "Reposta breve sobre las Controversias do Xámti, Tienxin, Limhoên." The manuscript is preserved with its Latin translation in the Archivio della Sacra Congregazione «de Propaganda Fide», SC

Indie Orientale e Cina 1 ff. 145r–168v; 170r–197v (Latin). English translation as Book V "An Account of the Chinese Learned Sect," in *A Collection of Voyages and Travels…, in four volumes*, ed. John Churchill. Vol. 1: D. F. Navarrete: *An Account of the Empire of China, Historical, Political, Moral and Religious* (London: Black Swan, 1704), 183–224.

27. Collani, "Opposing Views," 84–85 and 89. Athanasius Kircher (1602–1680) identified in his *China… illustrata* (Amsterdam: J. à Meurs, 1667), 226, the magician Zoroaster with Noah's bad son Ham. He came from Egypt to Persia and planted colonies in Bactria, then in India and in China.
28. Longobardo, "An Account," 193; cf. Collani, "Opposing Views," 88–89.
29. Fabrizio Pregadio, *The Routledge Encyclopedia of Taoism* (New York: Taylor & Francis, 2011), 1:483–485.
30. Longobardo, "An Account," 198.
31. Kim, *Strange Names*, 183–184.
32. Mungello, *Curious Land*, 250–252.
33. Paolo Beonio-Brocchieri, *Confucio e il Cristianesimo. Traduzione di opere di Propero Prospero Intorcetta S.J.* (Milano: Luni, 2017), vii–viii.
34. David E. Mungello, *The Forgotten Christians of Hangzhou* (Honolulu: University of Hawaii, 1994), 44.
35. See Fung, *History* 2, 454–457.
36. [Ignatio a Costa, Prospero Intorcetta], *Sapientia Sinica* (Kién chām 1662), f. 30v.
37. Mungello, *Curious Land*, 247–286.
38. *Confucius Sinarum philosophus*, xxxviii–liiii.
39. Ibid. xviiijf.
40. Lundbæk, "Image," 23.
41. *Confucius Sinarum philosophus*, xviij.
42. Ibid. xviiijf and xxxviij; Lundbæk, "Image," 25; cf. Meynard, *Confucius Sinarum*, 136.
43. *Confucius Sinarum philosophus*, xviij. Wen Wang was king of Zhou (1112–1050 BCE).
44. Claudia von Collani, "Der Ritenstreit und die Folgen für die Chinamission," *Zeitschrift für Missionswissenschaft und Religionswissenschaft* 90 (2006): 210–225.
45. Claudia von Collani, "Charles Maigrot's Role in the Chinese Rites Controversy," in *The Chinese Rites Controversy: Its History and Meaning*, ed. David E. Mungello (Monumenta Serica Monograph Series 33) (Nettetal: Steyler Verlag, 1994), 154–155.
46. The sentence that the *Yijing* is the "summa of the best physical and moral teachings" was the opinion of the Jesuit Francesco Filipucci (1632–1692), his description containing this sentence seems to have been lost. "Summa" in Scholastic meant the entirety.
47. Collani, "Maigrot's Role," 156.
48. Ibid. 158.
49. Standaert, *Handbook* 1:668–669 and 672–673 (Collani).
50. Collani, "Opposing Views," 90–91.
51. Leibniz, February 15, 1701, in Wilhelm Leibniz, *Der Briefwechsel mit den Jesuiten in China (1689–714).* Französisch/Lateinisch—Deutsch, herausgegeben und mit einer Einleitung versehen von Rita Widmaier, Textherstellung und Übersetzung von Malte-Ludolf Babin (Hamburg: Meiner, 2006), 310–311.
52. Pregadio, *Encyclopedia of Taoism*, 2:1094–1095.
53. Leibniz, *Briefwechsel*, 341–342.
54. Leibniz, 18. Mai 1703, in ibid. 418–421.

55. Cf. Genesis 2:2–3; Leibniz, 18. Mai 1703, in *Briefwechsel*, 421.
56. *Histoire de l'Academie Royale des Sciences*, Année M.DCC.III (Paris 1720), 85–89.
57. Standaert, *Handbook* 1:670–671.
58. Bouvet, "Examen examinis seu responsum ad scriptum consoris anonymi sub hoc titulo examen aliquot propositionum ad R.P. Superiorem P.P. Gallorum," ARSI, Jap. Sin. 177, 240–260.
59. Claudia von Collani, "Cabbala in China," in *Jews in China: From Kaifeng... to Shanghai*, ed. Roman Malek (Monumenta Serica Monograph Series XLVI) (Sankt Augustin: Steyler Verlag, 2000), 527–558.
60. Bouvet, "Examen examinis," f. 246v; cf. Bouvet, Brief and Leibniz, 4. November 1701, in Leibniz, *Briefwechsel*, 354–355.
61. Collani, "Cabbala in China," 529.
62. Joachim Bouvet, "Synopsis sacrae temporum propheticorum doctrinae...," BNF, Ms.n.a.lat. 1173, ff. 19r–20v.
63. Council of Ephesus 431, and other councils.
64. In the Sohar, the Ain Soph is a symbol for God, the creator of the Universe, the "*Deus absconditus*," transcendent, inaccessible, incomprehensible, etc.
65. Joachim Bouvet, "Specimen Sapientiae hieroglyphicae seu Theologiae Symbolicae priscorum Sinarum...," ARSI, Jap. Sin. IV.5.A., 19–20; cf. Legge, *I Ching*, 393.
66. Collani, "Cabbala in China," 542.
67. Bouvet, "Synopsis," 24v–25r.
68. Collani, "Cabbala in China," 542–543.
69. Ibid. 530, 536. The conception of the Sophia is perhaps influenced by Gnosis.
70. Omitted in modern translations. 24:18 (or 24:24). Translation mine.
71. Bouvet, "Synopsis," 23r.
72. Ibid. 25r–v.
73. *Daodejing*, chap. 25; ARSJ, JS IV.5.A, f. 20, Collani, "Cabbala in China," 540.
74. ARSJ, JS IV.5.A, f. 21; *Daodejing*, chap. 25.
75. Collani, "Maigrot's Role," 156.
76. Lived at the end of the fifth and at the beginning of the sixth century.
77. See K. K. Yeo, *Zhuangzi and James* [in Chinese] (莊子與雅各) (Shanghai: Huadong Normal University, 2012), 287–306 on Dao, Hokmah, Sophia, and God.
78. Collani, "Opposing Views," 97–98.
79. Sapientia 11:21 (English: Wisdom of Solomon 11:20).
80. Romans 1:20, cf. Claudia von Collani, "The First Encounter of the West with the *Yijing*: Introduction to and Edition of Letters and Latin Translations by French Jesuits from the 18th Century," *Monumenta Serica* LV (2007): 273 and 285.
81. Wanxiang, literally ten thousand things meaning all things. *Daodejing*, chap. 42.
82. Collani: "First Encounter," 285–286.
83. Ibid. 253–254.
84. Ibid. 251–253.
85. François Noël, *Philosophia Sinica tribus tractatibus, primo Cognitionem Primi Entis, Secundo Ceremonias erga Defunctos, Tertio Ethicam, Juxta Sinarum mentem complectens...* (Prag: Kamenicki, 1711), 137–146; Claudia von Collani, "François Noël and his Treatise on God in China," in *History of the Catholic Church in China: From Its Beginning to the Scheut Fathers and the 20th Century Unveiling Some Less Known Sources, Sounds and Pictures*, ed. Ferdinand Verbiest Institute (Leuven Chinese Studies XXIX) (Leuven: Ferdinand Verbiest Institute, 2015), 61.

86. Collani, "François Noël," 46.
87. Cf. *Shijing*, Ode 235. S. James Legge, *The Chinese Classics IV: The She King* (Taipei: Southern Materials Center, 1985), 431.
88. Collani, "François Noël," 46–47.
89. Noël, *Philosophia Sinica*, 139.
90. Translation mine.
91. Noël, *Philosophia Sinica*, 137–146; cf. Collani, "François Noël," 45–48.
92. Collani, "First Encounter," 258–261.
93. Ibid. 263–266.
94. *Y-king, antiquissimus Sinarum liber quem ex latina interpretatione P. Regis aliorumque ex Soc. Jesu P.P. edidit Julius Mohl.* Vol. 1 (Stuttgartiae et Tubingae: Cotta, 1834–1838), 1:62–78; *Wuji*, a kind of complementation to the *Taiji*, the *coincidentia oppositorum*, as Zhou Dunyi defined: "The Ultimateless (*wuji* 無極)! And yet also the Supreme Ultimate (*taiji*)!" Fung, *History* 2:435.
95. *Y-king, antiquissimus Sinarum liber*..., 62–78; s.a. Collani, "First Encounter," 270. For Song Confucianism, see Forke, *Geschichte*, 45–56; Fung, *History*, 2:435.
96. Collani, "Ritenstreit," 213.

PRIMARY SOURCES

Biblia sacra vulgatae editionis .... Coloniae Agrippinae: Hermann Demen, 1679.

Bouvet, Joachim. "Examen examinis seu responsum ad scriptum consoris anonymi sub hoc titulo examen aliquot propositionum ad R.P. Superiorem P.P. Gallorum," ARSI, Jap. Sin. 177, ff. 240r–260v.

Bouvet, Joachim. "Specimen Sapientiae hieroglyphicae seu Theologiae Symbolicae priscorum Sinarum...." ARSI, Jap. Sin. IV.5.A., 189 pages.

Bouvet, Joachim. "Synopsis sacrae temporum propheticorum doctrinae...." Bibliothèque Nationale, Ms.n.a.lat. 1173, ff. 17r–40v.

Confucius Sinarum philosophus, sive sacientia Sinensis. Adjecta Tabula Chronologica Monarchiae Sinicae juxta cyclos annorum LX. Edited by Philippe Couplet. Paris: Horthemels, 1687.

Confucius Sinarum Philosophus (1687). The First Translation of the Confucian Classics. Translated and edited by Thierry Meynard, S.J. Rome: Institutum Historicum Societatis Iesu, 2011.

Couvreur, Séraphin. *Chou-king: Les Annales de la Chine*. Paris: Les Belles Lettres, 1950.

Kircher, Athanasius. *China monumentis, qua sacris qua profanis, nec non variis naturae & artis spectaculis... illustrata*. Amsterdam: J. à Meurs, 1667.

Legge, James. *The Chinese Classics III: The Shoo King* [in Chinese]. Taipei: Southern Materials Center, 1985.

Legge, James. *The Chinese Classics IV: The She King* [in Chinese]. Taipei: Southern Materials Center, 1985.

Legge, James. *The I Ching. The Book of Changes* [in Chinese]. New York: Dover, 1963[2].

Leibniz, Gottfried Wilhelm. "Explication de l'arithmétique binaire, qui se sert des seuls caractères 0 & 1; avec des Remarques sur son utilité, & sur ce qu'elle donne le sens des anciennes figures Chinoises de Fohy." *Histoire de l'Academie Royale des Sciences*, Année M.DCC.III (Paris 1720[2]): 85–89.

Leibniz, Gottfried Wilhelm. *Der Briefwechsel mit den Jesuiten in China (1689–1714)*. Französisch/Lateinisch—Deutsch, herausgegeben und mit einer Einleitung versehen von

Rita Widmaier, Textherstellung und Übersetzung von Malte-Ludolf Babin. Hamburg: Meiner, 2006.

Longobardo, Niccolò. "Reposta breve sobre las Controversias do Xámti, Tienxin, Limhoên, e outros nomes e termos sinicos: per se determinar quaes delles podem ou nao podem usarse nesta Xpandade. Dirigida aos Padres das Residencias da China, pera a verem, a depois emviare com ou seu parecer sobre ella ao Nosso Padre Visitador em Macao." Archivio della Sacra Congregazione «de Propaganda Fide», SC Indie Orientale e Cina 1, ff. 145r–168v, Latin: "Responssio (sic!) breuis super controuersias de Xám Tí, hoc est de Altissimo Domino, de Tiēn xîn, id est de spiritibus cœlestibus, de Lím-hoên, id est de Anima rationali. De aliisque nominibus ac Terminis sinicis ad determinandum qualia eorum uti possint vel non in hac Xpanitate." Archivio della Sacra Congregazione «de Propaganda Fide», SC Indie Orientale e Cina 1, ff. 170r–197v. English: Longobardo, Niccolò. "An Account of the Chinese Learned Sect." In *A Collection of Voyages and Travels…, in four volumes*. Vol. 1: D. F. Navarrete: *An Account of the Empire of China, Historical, Political, Moral and Religious*. Edited by John Churchill, 183–224. London: Black Swan, 1704.

Martini, Martino. *Sinicæ Historiæ Decas Prima. Res à gentis origine ad Christum natum in extremâ Asiâ, sive Magno Sinarum Imperio gestas complexa*. Monachii: Wagner, 1658.

Noël, François. *Philosophia Sinica tribus tractatibus, primo Cognitionem Primi Entis, Secundo Ceremonias erga Defunctos, Tertio Ethicam, Juxta Sinarum mentem complectens*. Praga: Kamenicki, 1711.

Régis, Jean-Baptiste et al. *Y-king, antiquissimus Sinarum liber quem ex Latina interpretatione P. Régis aliorumque ex Soc. Jesu PP*. Edited by Julius Mohl, 2 vols. Stuttgartiae et Tuebingae: Cotta, 1834, 1839.

Ricci, Matteo. *Fonti Ricciane*, vol. II. Edited by Pasquale M. D'Elia. Rome: La Libreria dello Stato, 1949.

Ricci, Matteo S.J. *The True Meaning of the Lord of Heaven (T'ien-chu Shih-i)*, a Chinese English Edition, translated by Douglas Lancashire and Peter Hu Kuo-chen S.J. Edited by Edward J. Malatesta S.J. (Variétés sinologiques—Nouvelle série 72) Taipei, Paris: Institut Ricci, 1985.

Ricci, Matteo. *Le sens réel de Seigneur du Ciel*. Texte établi, traduit et annoté par Thierry Meynard. Paris: Les Belles Lettres 2013.

Sapientia Sinica, exponente P. Ignatio a Costa Lusitano Soc. Ies. à Prospero Intorcetta Siculo eiusd. Soc. Orbi proposita (Kién Chām 1662).

CHAPTER 13

THE BIBLE AND DAOIST WRITINGS

ARCHIE C. C. LEE

INTRODUCTION

QUITE a few missionaries to China have written on the much-acclaimed Daoist book of *Daodejing* 道德經 and attributed a high regard to it to the extent that even an enunciation of the doctrine of the Trinity can be found in it. J. Edkins argues that the notion of the Trinity is conveyed by the three "foreign" words in the Daoist book of *Daodejing* (chap. 14). He asserts that the name *Jehoveh* is found it.[1] Theos Walter, another Protestant missionary also draws our attention to the rendering of the Christian *Logos* into the Daoist terminology of the *Dao/Tao* 道[2] in the Chinese Bible:

> Our missionaries have used this word *Tao* to represent *logos* in their translation of the New Testament, and the first five verses of St. John's Gospel are nearly as much Taoist as Christian in the Chinese text.[3]

On the academic front, Julia Ching comments on Daoist religious quests, which are better understood in the context of biblical thoughts: "the desire of transcending the limitations of this life" and the "religious striving for the immortality of the whole person"[4] are such examples. The former can be read from the perspective of Adam and Eve wanting to be like God, and the latter expresses a similar concern for the final resurrection of the whole person, both the body and the soul. The aim of this essay explores three aspects on the encounter of the Bible and Daoism. The first is an investigation into the historical encounters of Christianity with Chinese culture as it is witnessed in the documents of Jingjiao, and the second is an attempt to analyze the adoption of Daoist terminology in Chinese Bible translation. Finally, a cross-textual reading of Qoheleth and the Daoist notion of immortality are illustrated in order to bring out the view of humanity in the two traditions concerned. The Daoist writings of *Daodejing*[5] and *Zhuangzi* are selected for focused attention. The objective of this endeavor is to explore the levels of meaning of the biblical texts with the perspectives brought about by the introduction of the Daoist writings to the reading processes. By adopting the method of cross-textual interpretation, this essay intends to go beyond the interest of mere contrast and comparison. Due to the limited scope of this essay, only the Hebrew Bible is covered in this study.[6]

Before proceeding further, the very basic question of what Daoism is has first to be addressed. Chinese sinologist Herrlee Creel, who has written a book with this question as the title, sees it as inappropriate to have a single exclusive definition.[7] Commenting on the same, Julia Ching, a Chinese scholar in Chinese religion, also points out the complexities of the question—in addition to the common use of the word "*dao* 道" by different schools of thought and religion in China, there is also the issue of one English word, "Daoism," designating both philosophical Daoism ("School of the Way," *Daojia* 道家) and religious Daoism ("Religion of the Way," *Daojiao* 道教), not to mention other popular traditions of martial arts, meditation exercises, and breathing techniques (*qigong* 氣功), which are commonly associated with some form of Daoism.[8] "Daoism" is a term first given by the Han dynasty court historiographer, Sima Qian (died 110 BCE), sometimes seen as the "Herodotus of China,"[9] who classifies the then-contemporary schools of thought into "Six Schools," with one of them called "School of the Way" (*Daojia*).

As an organized religion, *Daojia* goes back to the Han dynasty between 200 BCE and 200 CE. Anna Seidel, an outstanding Daoist scholar, attributes its beginning to two popular ingenious politico-religious movements: the Way of Great Peace (太平道) and the Way of the Celestial Masters (天師道), both of which contained messianic elements of "the expectation of an era of peace brought about by a supernatural deliverer from political disorders and social hardship."[10] *Daojia* acknowledges the philosophical thoughts articulated by Laozi in the new religious movement led by Master Zhang Daoling 張道陵 in the second century (approximately in 142 CE).[11] Zhang adopted the teaching of Laozi's *Daodejing* ("Scripture of the Dao and Power/Virtue" 道德經) to instruct its converts.[12] Kaltenmark has a succinct statement to characterize Daoism as:

> a complex and often disconcerting phenomenon: side by side, we find profound insight and puerile suppositions, lofty mysticism and superstitious magic, exhortations to absolute purity and the most primitive obscenity.[13]

Daodejing (*DDJ*) is the fundamental text for both philosophical and religious Daoism. According to tradition, the book is the collection of five thousand words left behind as instructions from Laozi to Yin Xi, the guardian of the Kunlun mountain pass in Western China from where Laozi ascended to the mystical and obscure land of transformation. Daoism regards Laozi's ascent as a return to "Chaos,"[14] a central notion expounded on further below in the context of the translation of the Bible. Despite the span of time between the assumed dates of the birth of Laozi and his legendary pass of Kunlun mountain (tradition has it in 488 BCE), scholars mostly agree that the composition of the book bearing his name was composed in the third century BCE, and it contains materials from ancient oral traditions before they were committed to written form as we know it now.[15]

K. Schipper is doubtful and cautious of the division of Daoism into "two Daoisms," philosophical and religious. He points out the fact that even *DDJ* "was developed in a *religious* context."[16] The phenomenon of rationalizing and philosophizing the book has been influenced, according to Schipper, by the eminent scholar, Wang Bi (224–49 CE), who has incorporated cosmology of the *Book of Change* (*Yijing* 易經) and Buddhist ontology into his commentary on *DDJ*.[17] Wang speculates on the Dao as a concept and adopts dualism to explain away the paradoxes in *DDJ*. The creative power of the Dao as the Mother, the Chaos, and the "Obscure Female" (*DDJ* 6) have therefore no place in his system of School of Mystery ("*Xuanxue*").[18] With the influential exegetical tradition of Wang, Schipper has the following assertion:

> From then on, following Wang Pi's exegesis, the literati made the famous distinction between a "philosophical" Taoism that they claimed was noble and pure, and a "religious" Taoism that was supposedly vulgar and materialistic, that is, the Taoism of the people.[19]

Among missionaries to China, there is sincere appreciation expressed in favor of *DDJ*, but there are also serious biases towards Daoism as a religious institution that has contaminated Laozi, whose "ideas were speedily buried beneath a heap of cabalistic nonsense."[20] One of the most positive assessments of *DDJ* has uplifted it to a level comparable to the biblical teaching of the mystery of God and Jesus' commitment to love one's enemies. The utterance of "requite hatred with goodness" (*baoyuan yi de* 報怨以德, *DDJ* 63) is cited as being identical with "love your enemies, do good to them that hate you" in Jesus' command.[21]

The Christian Message in Daoist Terminology

Historical investigation into the Bible in China in general addresses the three major waves of the coming of Christianity to Chinese territory. Assyrian/Syrian Christianity arrived in China via the Silk Road in the year 635 CE. Since the discovery of the "Nestorian Monument in China" (大秦景教流行中國碑), this first Christian tradition from the Tang dynasty of the seventh century has given us an identifiable name of Jingjiao 景教 which, literarily rendered as "Illuminous Teaching" or "Religion of Light," is the self-designated name of this very first Christian community in China. It has mistakenly been named as "Nestorian Christianity."[22] With the arrival in Guangzhou of Italian Jesuit Matteo Ricci in 1583, a new attempt to renew Christianity in China was initiated in the centuries that followed. Beginning in 1807 until 1949, the Protestant missionary movement exerted its lasting impact in China, with the Chinese translation of the whole Bible by Robert Morrison and William Milne published in 1823.[23] In connection with the Bible and Daoism, Daoist terminology in Jingjiao's Stele of 781 CE and the Protestant translation of the Bible, which have adopted Daoist notions, are the focus of the present investigation.

The unearthing of the Jingjiao Stone in Xian, China in the year 1623 CE is a tremendous breakthrough in understanding the history of Christianity in China in the context of cultural exchange as well as religious interaction of the Christian religion between Western Asia and East Asia via the trade routes in Central Asia. This great Jingjiao stone monument, and subsequent publications of other manuscripts, have surely provided rich historical resources for a glimpse of Syrian Christianity, which came to Chinese soil in the ninth year of the reign of Taizong (627–649 CE) of the Tang dynasty in 635 CE and the establishment of Jingjiao churches in China for the next two hundred years or so. With the imperial endorsement and the court support from the emperor, the first delegates (twenty-one monks) under the leadership of Aluoben 阿羅本 built the Daiqin Temple (大秦寺) and the Scriptural Translation Hall (翻經書殿) to render into Chinese Syriac texts of the Oriental Orthodox brought from Persia to China. It was inscribed in the stele that numerous churches were built over hundreds of Chinese cities (寺滿百城) in the Tang empire. There have been significant studies and research since the seventeenth century, first by the Jesuits and then Protestant missionaries, as well as some eminent scholars.[24]

Besides some unresolved issues, the major consensus among scholars is the influence of Chinese texts of Confucianism, Buddhism, and Daoism on the language of the stele and the other seven Jingjiao writings.[25] The use of Daoist terminology in the expression of Christian theological ideas is particularly evident.[26] The stele even exhibits the incorporation of Daoist tradition into the core of the composition on Christian teachings. The more striking expressions are inscribed as "*changran zhenji, xianxian er wuyuan, yaoran lingxu* 常然真寂, 先先而無元, 窅然靈虛" ("Thus the constant and real tranquility, preceding all and without beginning, all-knowing; everlasting and mysterious").[27] There is also the use of the Daoist idea of "primordial wind," "the two *qi* energies," the "dark void," the "primal conglomeration" and the notion of "emptiness that is not to be filled up" (*yuanfeng, erqi, ankong, hunyuan, xu er buying* 元風, 二氣, 暗空, 渾元, 虛而不盈) in connection with the creation of heaven and earth. The key Daoist notion of the nameless, mysterious, and constant Dao (*zhenchang zhi dao, miao er naming* 真常之道, 妙而難名), whose function does nevertheless brightly manifest, is coopted to support the naming of this Christian religion as Jingjiao, being the Religion of the Luminous Teaching (功用昭彰, 強稱景教). Jingjiao acknowledges the possession of the Old Testament (OT) and the New Testament (NT). In referring to the incarnation and redemption of Jesus the Messiah (分身出代, 救度無邊), the stele sees his coming as "fulfilling the old law as proclaimed by the twenty-four sages" (圓二十四聖有說之舊法).[28] It further designates the NT tradition of twenty-seven books as being handed down to Jingjiao Christians (經留二十七部). Bishop Aluoben, the first of the Jingjiao monks to lead the delegation to China, is attested as demonstrating high virtues. He has detected the will of heaven and he has endured great hardship to bring along the True Scripture

(占青雲而載真經, 望風律以馳艱險) with other religious images from afar to the then-capital of China (遠將經像來獻上京) in 635 CE. Since the royal family has the same surname, Li, as the acclaimed founder and deified Laozi, Daoism was raised to an imperial status in the Tang dynasty. In this respect, the mythical story of the departure of Laozi to the West during the political and moral degeneration of Zhou dynasty and his return is capitalized as the most outstanding and unique ideological persuasion of Jingjiao. The arrival of the teaching of Jingjiao therefore signifies the return of Laozi and his teaching to the East. It claims to be the revival of the light of the Dao at the time of the great Tang era (宗周德喪, 青駕西昇, 巨唐道光, 景風東扇). In fact, Jesus in the conception of Jingjiao is represented as a transformation or manifestation of Laozi. One of the extraordinary physical features of Jesus recorded in the "Sutras of the Mysterious Will on Rest and Joy" (志玄安樂經), a Jingjiao document discovered in Dunhuang, is the mark of the figure ten or the sign of the cross (十), which is also said to be found on Laozi's hand, as described in Daoist sources such as *Shenxian Zhuan* 神仙傳.[29]

Daoist *Hundun* versus "Chaos" in Bible Translation

One of the most interesting features in the area of the encounter of the Bible with Daoist writings is surely the use of Daoist notions in Chinese Bible translation. Reading back from the beginning of the most influential Chinese version used by most Chinese Christian communities, the Mandarin Union Version (1919), one is attracted by the use of "*kongxu hundun* 空虛混沌" for the biblical terms of "*tohu vbohu*" in Gen 1:2.[30] The adoption of an original Daoist term "*hundun*" for the rendering of the Hebrew term "*bohu*" provides a link with the Daoist notion. This translation goes back to Karl Friedrich August Gützlaff 郭實臘, who first used the characters (*fudi hundun* 夫地混沌) in his 1838 Old Testament translation (舊遺詔聖書), which later became the Bible version of Taiping Rebellion of 1853–1864.[31] The terms "*kongxu* 空虛" and "*hundun* 混沌" were later brought together by Bishop Joseph Schereschewsky 施約瑟 in 1874. The phrase has been followed by almost all major Chinese Bibles until today.[32] This standard form has given readers the imagination to understand the biblical and Daoist cosmogony. "Hundun" comes originally from a brief mythological narrative with a deep cosmological explication in Daoism. This amazing piece of myth contains in the last chapter of the supposedly more authentical part of *Zhuangzi* (Inner Chapters, chaps. 1–7).[33] Hundun, the "faceless emperor,"[34] appears as one of the three personified figures, representing the north (*yin*), the south, (*yang*), and the center (the primordial wholeness).[35] The mythical parable runs like this:

> The emperor of the South Sea was called Shu [Brief], the emperor of the North Sea was called Hu [Sudden], and the emperor of the central region was called Hun-tun

> [Chaos]. Shu and Hu from time to time came together for a meeting in the territory of Hun-tun, and Hun-tun treated them very generously. Shu and Hu discussed how they could repay his kindness. "All men (sic.)," they said, "have seven openings so they can see, hear, eat, and breathe. But Hun-tun alone doesn't have any. Let's try boring him some!" Every day they bored another hole, and on the seventh day Hun-tun died.[36]

This Hundun story may have been circulated in ancient times as conveying some form of cosmogony before Zhuangzi adopted it and incorporated it into his work. The names of the two figures, Shu and Hu, may convey some negative message of acting quickly, but being reckless in action. These two rulers are not perceived as being tyrannous and oppressive, but even with benevolent intention, they have done something against the naturalness, simplicity, and spontaneity of Hundun. Their kindness of bringing Hundun into conformity with all humans only brings about the death of the latter when the seventh opening was done on the seventh day. According to the Daoist idea in *Zhuangzi*, which advocates non-action, the two rulers engage in excessive action against the nature of the spontaneity and integrative whole of Hundun.[37] The formless and shapeless Hundun represents the completeness of the primordial nondifferentiated existence. The enforced boring of the holes characterizes the process of cosmogony in which the original wholeness/oneness is being destroyed. Therefore, the term does not imply any idea of disorder and chaos. On the contrary, the Daoist notion of *hundun* conveys a more positive conception. The Dao described in the context of creation mythology is in typically cosmogonic terms. It is characterized as being born before heaven and earth and as the mother of the world.[38] Chapter 25 of *Daodejing* has a profound way of denoting it as in the confused state: "There is a thing confusedly formed (*youwu huncheng* 有物混成)"[39] and it is "without sound and formless" (*jixi liaoxi* 寂兮寥兮).[40]

It is very instructive to trace the meaning of the term "emptiness" (*kongxu*) as the translation of the Hebrew "*bohu*." On the surface, the linguistic feature seems to give an impression of some Buddhist influence. But looking at its adoption and usage in Daoist writings, it seems more likely that it may originate from the Daoist notion of emptiness in a positive manner of advocating a state of being and an attitude toward "emptying" oneself. The term represents a significant understanding in *Zhuangzi* in its exposition of Laozi's typical teaching. The term "*kongxu*" appears three times in *Zhuangzi*:[41] "*xing chong kongxu* 形充空虛" ("Heavenly Revolution," 天運, 3),[42] "*shi wu kongxu* 室無空虛" ("External Things," 外物, 9),[43] and "*yi kongxu buhui wanwu weishi* 以空虛不毀萬物為實" ("All under Heaven" 天下, 5). The character "*xu* 虛," which is used sixteen times, expresses the meaning of the ultimate emptiness of the Great Unity in *Zhuangzi* ("Heaven and Earth" 天地, 8)[44] and implies something to desire and to be pursued. It is in the application of the notion of "emptiness" to the conception of fasting of the heart/mind (*xin zhai* 心齋) in *Zhuangzi* 4 ("Human World" 人間世) that the deepest meaning of Daoism is being fully articulated: "It is only through the Way of emptiness that one can gather emptiness and emptiness is the fasting of the mind" ("唯道集虛。虛者，心齋也").[45]

The Hebrew word "*tohu*" is generally understood to denote the arid wilderness (e.g. drying of wadis, Job 6.18) and the precreation chaotic state (Job 26.7). It is paired with "*bohu*" in two other passages outside Genesis (Isa 34.11; Jer 4.23) to characterize desolation and punishment. By extension, it can also imply emptiness and formlessness, especially when it is applied to the other deities (1 Sam 12.21; Isa 41.29, 44.9) and to defeated nations (Isa 24.10, 34.11, 40.17). The Greek rendering into "chaos" has reinforced the meaning of "void, empty space."[46] Rebecca Watson criticizes Gunkel's book, *Schöpfung und Chaos* (1895), for its connecting the motif of chaos-conflict-creation into Genesis 1 via the Babylonian *Enuma Elish* and turning the formless matter of chaos into a sea-monster that comes to be the opponent of God.[47] After close examination of the relevant texts in the use of the word "*bohu*" in the Hebrew Bible, Watson suggests that any attempt to translate it in terms of "chaos" should first have it further defined. She proposes to best avoid using "chaos" for the Hebrew term in Gen 1:2.[48] This is true to the Daoist notion of returning to the purist and original state of the non-differentiation of the complete *hundun*, which is mistakenly taken as similar to what the Greek word "chaos" meant to convey. It also is in opposition to the meaning of devastation in the biblical perception as conveyed by the prophet Jeremiah, pointing to the destruction of the present creation order, either historically or eschatologically.

Due to the notion of the Dao in its mysterious origin as characterized by emptiness, spontaneity, naturalness, and simplicity, there is the inspiration of Daoism to revert to this desirable state of being and to return to the root:

> I do my utmost to attain emptiness (*xu* 虛);
> I hold firmly of stillness.
> The myriad creatures all rise together
> And I watch their return.
> The teeming creatures
> All return to their separate roots.
> Returning to one's roots is known as still.
> This is what is meant by returning to one's destiny. (*DDJ* 16)[49]

Early Daoism is "politically anarchistic but not ontologically nihilistic."[50] The quest for the "mystical reversal of cosmogony" through meditative, medicinal (alchemical), and ritualistic means of "going back to the undifferentiated beginnings,"[51] is central to Daoism. In societal terms, the call to return to the primal unity of original harmony and natural wholeness of Emperor Hundun of the Center[52] is critical revolt against the hypocritical hierarchy of righteousness and benevolence in civilization governed by Confucian values (*DDJ* 18). It is a return to Dao's "cosmic body."[53] This eschatological quest is not an advocation for anarchy, but a radical criticism of certain negative effects of governmental manipulation and excessive intervention of the ruling power, which sometimes leads to the undesirable institutional oppression, systemic dehumanization, political antagonism, economic exploitation, social segregation, cultural superiority, and racial discrimination. It is not a return to "chaos," but a return to the origin and the source of energies of life. In this regard, Daoism has been treated as a religion of salvation, questing for the return to blissful nature and tranquility. Julia Ching sees in Daoism a conception of the present "fallen state" from the "original state of bliss," and she claims that "it is a salvation religion which seeks to guild its believers beyond this transitory life to a happy eternity."[54] This Daoist dimension of reality may help to enrich the biblical notion of creation and redemption.

Through some form of exercise of spiritual concentration "to retain the One" (*shouyi* 守一), a person is expected to return to the *qi*.[55] The *qi* is one with the "Great One" (*taiyi* 太一) or "Great Ultimate" (*taiji* 太極), an original formless and undifferentiated Oneness underlying all beings and myriad things.[56] The original *qi* of human beings as the primordial breath/vital energy/life principle (*yuan qi* 元氣) is what one inspires to return to as the fundamental roots of life (*ben gen* 本根). In this connection, the notion of the "*ruah Elohim*," translated as the "Spirit of God" that seems to be unrelated to "emptiness," and the darkness in Gen 1:2, can be reviewed in terms of the Daoist notion of "primal *qi*" (元氣) that initiates and sustains the whole creation.

Preservation of Life in Daoism and the Givenness of Life in Qoheleth

As Chinese Bible translations have settled to adopt "*kongxu hundun*" to render the biblical notion of the precreation state of "emptiness and void" in Genesis 1, it is interesting to note that the first term for "emptiness" does appear again, albeit with a reversed order of the two characters, for the notion of "vanity of vanities" in the book of Qoheleth (Ecclesiastes): "虛空的虛空" (*hᵃḇel hᵃḇālim*). The translator may have realized the difference between the use of "*tohu*" in Genesis and Qoheleth's "*habel*" that the transposition of the characters should indicate and signify. As noted above, the two characters come from Daoist writings, though some Buddhist influence on the word "emptiness" (*kong* 空) cannot be ruled out altogether. The fact that Bible translators have conventionally adopted the Chinese title "傳道書" ("Book of the Transmitter of the Dao") for the English name "The Preacher," also opens a way to explore the meaning of the Dao and its implications for understanding Qoheleth and Daoism in the biblical context.

The adoption of the word "Dao" in Daoism is, according to Benjamin Schwartz, drastically different from its former or current usages in other Chinese thought:

> The insistence on the word *tao* represents a striking departure from the centrality of the word Heaven . . . [which] remains the central term even in Analects.[57]

Heaven and earth in the *Analects* may exercise their intention in terms of activity (*you wei* 有為), but the nameless Dao in Daoism is "the beginning of heaven and earth" (*DDJ* 1). Julia Ching notes the triple use of the word "*dao*" in the first sentences of *DDJ*: "The *dao* that can be *dao-ed* is not the constant *dao*."[58] She further underlines an alternative vision of religion in Daoism: "a vision that carries with it a mystical impulse for communication and union with nature, a vision that has been described as 'salvific.'"[59] The very translation of the beginning sentence of St. John's Gospel with the term "*Dao*" for the Greek word "*Logos*" (the Word) is of primal importance in bringing the Bible and Daoism into significant creative interaction. A different Greek word is, however, used to render the way ("*hodos*") claimed by Jesus in the characterization of him being "the Way, the Truth and the Life" (John 14:6). The word "Dao" that has given its name to Daoism has a multiplicity of meanings similar to the Hebrew concept of *derech* which is used in the Hebrew Bible 706 times, one hundred of which are found in the wisdom books of Proverbs and Job (only four times in Ecclesiastes). The primary conception of the term in Daoism refers to a physical road on which people walk and the route people take to reach their destination. It then becomes more abstract to signify the path of life, the style people adopt to conduct their lives, the way of nature as well as the principle that governs the universe. Politically, it refers to how an emperor chooses to rule his empire. In his analysis of the meaning of the Dao (Way), as "the Unhewn, the block out of which things are cut," A. C. Graham further stresses the important concern of Laozi whose concern is not "what is the Way?" but "Where is the Way?" and how the individual and community should conduct themselves in relation to the cosmos.[60] This reminds us of the Hebrew wisdom tradition as expressed in the wisdom poem ending the three cycles of dialogue in the book of Job (4–14, 15–21, 22–27), where the question of "Where is wisdom to be found?" is posted at the end of the wisdom poem (28:28). The leading motif in the Hebrew wisdom tradition is to confirm the pietistic attitude of the sages in their "fear of the Lord" and the corresponding way of life in "staying away from evil."

Daoism acknowledges the mysterious dimension of the Dao, which begets the One and the multitude (*DDJ* 42) and is conceived of as the "mother of all things" (*DDJ* 25). But as commented above in the theme of return to the Dao, there is the quest for an immortal life (*chang sheng* 長生) and an intensive effort to develop a means for the preservation of life (*yang sheng* 養生). The Daoist immortality is basically earthly and bodily, but that does not exclude it from the transcendental dimension of the deepest human aspiration to address the fate of the inescapable physical death of life. In this way, Daoism embarks on a similar search for ways to honestly deal with the human dilemma encountered by Qoheleth. It is more positive in its acceptance of the reality and seeking any means humanly possible to transcend it. This brings us to the Daoist notion of non-action, which has been misunderstood as "doing nothing" and "non-interference." The original wording of non-action (*wuwei* 無為) goes deeper than what it appears to be on the surface. It is a comprehension of reality in its "being so in itself" or its naturalness/spontaneity (*ziran* 自然). The sage knows to follow the principle of "non-action" in order to achieve something, as there is the paradox of "non-action in accomplishing everything" (*wuwei er wubuwei* 無為而無不為, *DDJ* 37). The struggle of Qoheleth is that nothing seems to change despite all natural and human activities that do not have any effect on creation. Qoheleth sees life in the total manipulation of the wholly transcendent God, who sets off the creation order and determines the cosmic cycle as well as the workings of the natural world (1:4–11). There is an appointed time for everything and every human activity (3:1–8), but human beings are conceived as having no knowledge of the divine plan, let alone the ability to change it for the benefit of human welfare, both individual and communal (3:9–12).

Qoheleth can be reconceived as coming close to some aspects of Daoism as advising non-action in the sense of acknowledging the nature (性) of life existence as "being so in itself." It does not advocate counteracting the divine plan, but enjoying the givenness of what life is and accepting it with gratitude. In the face of God being in control in the determination of all things, human effort can only be rendered as "vanity of vanities" and a "pursuit of wind" (1:14, 17; 2:1, 11, 15,17, 19, 21, 23, 26). The final fate of all the ephemeral, the enigmatic, inconsistencies, uncertainties, incomprehensibility, and unpredictability of the world in the hand of God is the inescapable death destined for every mortal (9:2–6). Death is the great equalizer and, therefore, the counsel Qoheleth gives to humanity is to grasp the present and enjoy life in eating, drinking, and celebrating of life with one's family (with a merry heart), taking daily life seriously by having a good appearance (clothes to wear and oil on head), and doing all things at hand with might (9:7–10).[61]

When reading the Garden of Eden story in Genesis 2–3 in a cross-textual framework with Qoheleth and Daoist thought, one comes to the appreciation of these textual traditions in their quest for life in its limitation by death and the quest for immortality. The image of the "tree of life" in Eden may symbolize a life transcending the physical and the corporal existence, which may go beyond the constraints of death. The second tree, the "tree of knowledge," conveys the wisdom and understanding that belongs to God and characterizes both the intellectual cognitive ability to make rational and moral decisions and the power of sexuality to reproduce and procreate. The human reality of the eating of the tree of knowledge and being expelled from the garden signify the definition of human life without immortality, but with the potential for rationality and wisdom. Though the story is traditionally interpreted as inscribing the Christian doctrinal understanding of the Fall and original sin, the words "sin" and "fall" do not occur in Genesis 2–3. What is articulated is the human propensity to rebel against God. The divine curses provide some etiological explanation for the hardship of both male and female experiences, in the field and in pregnancy respectively. The reference to the human condition of being like God underlines the reality of humanity having knowledge to reimagine the world and the sexual ability of procreation to have life continued through the succession of generations. The paradox is that when humans are "being like God," they face the inevitable outcome of the denial of immortality in the divine act of expulsion from the garden to cultivate the earth. One should note at the end of the Eden story that steps and measures were taken by God to ensure any possibility of human approach to the tree of life (Gen 3:22–24).

The story of Adam and Eve in Gen 2:4b–3:24 has been captured by doctrinal reading in the history of reception as one of the most influential narratives of the Hebrew Bible on which the whole teaching of the Christian understanding of original sin is built. It has tremendously shaped both the popular reading of the loss of paradise due to human disobedience against God the creator and the Christian theological understanding of original sin. Its influence on the literary world of the West is especially pronounced. In the long reception of the story, the reality of human existence and the embodied humanistic value have been neglected. Daoism in this respect may help in reconsidering this aspect of the story in the human quest for immortality.[62]

CONCLUSION

The Bible has traveled and taken various journeys all over the world. It has made a great variety of contacts with many Scriptures of other religions in different linguistic and socio-political contexts. Through its translation into vernacular languages and its interpretation by indigenous communities of readers, it has somehow been transformed and taken on new meanings. This is true, if not more so, when the Bible came into the vast geographical scope and complicated religious contexts of China. It encountered the multiplicity of Scriptures on Chinese soil and came to interact with Chinese audiences who have been used to embracing a general open attitude toward other cultures and religions in a more hospitable environment and neighborhood, as witnessed in the experience of Jingjiao in the time of the Tang dynasty.

The striking Daoist expressions in Jingjiao documents (e.g., *changran zhenji, xianxian er wuyuan, yaoran lingxu*) and in Protestant translations of the Bible into Chinese (e.g., "*kongxu hundun*") certainly open up space for reimagining the richness of the creation account in Genesis. The use of the Daoist idea of "primordial wind," "the two *qi* energies," the "dark void," the "primal conglomeration," and the notion of "emptiness that is not to be filled up" (*yuanfeng, erqi, ankong, hunyuan, xu er buying*) in Jingjiao in connection with the creation of heaven and earth further invites Chinese readers of the Bible to reconsider other biblical concepts, e.g. the understanding of "*ruah Elohim*" in Gen 1:2. It is always fascinating to see the interplay of the Bible and Daoist writings and how the latter contributes to explicating the levels of meaning laden in the biblical text.

From the history of Christianity in China,[63] both Catholic and Protestant missionaries were in favor of Confucianism, perceiving Daoism, Buddhism, and Chinese popular religious traditions as idolatrous and superstitious.[64] Such a negative notion has taken hold of the Western conception of China. Though C. Spurgeon Medhurst has designated Laozi as "one of the most thoughtful of Chinese to discover the secret of life" that represents "the search of a blind soul for God," he also affirms that there is in Laozi "no hesitation, no fumbling, no stumbling in his word."[65] He further applies the dynamic analogy of the supplementary roles of the OT and the NT of the Bible to those of Confucianism and Daoism respectively.[66] This statement is valid only if the analogy between the OT and Daoism does not intend to undermine both religious traditions as lower in their contributions to world civilization. In actuality, both the Bible and Daoist writings have achieved a high level of human spirituality that has enriched the religious life of people in both the East and the West.

NOTES

1. J. Edkins, "On the Three Words 'I Hi Wei' 夷希微 in the Tau Te King," *Chinese Recorder* 17 (8, 1886): 306–309.
2. Transliteration of Chinese terminology in this essay normally follows the China Mainland's system of *pingyin* except in quoting works of scholars, in which the original transliteration is kept.
3. Thos Walters, "Lao-Tzu 老子: A Study in Chinese Philosophy, Chapter 1," *Chinese Recorder and Missionary Journal* 1 (June 1868): 32 (31–32).
4. Julia Ching, *Chinese Religions* (Maryknoll, NY: Orbis Books, 1993), 86.
5. Unless otherwise indicated, the English translation of *Daodejing* will be taken from D. C. Lau, *Tao Te Ching* (Hong Kong: The Chinese University Press, 1963). *Daodejing* will be represented by *DDJ* in the rest of the essay.
6. The author has written an essay on the deified Dao in the person of Laozi, who has transformed himself in different historical periods to pass on guidance to rulers and to deliver people from their suffering; see Archie C. C. Lee, "Asians Encountering Jesus Christ: A Chinese Reading of Jesus in the Wisdom Matrix," *Quest: An Interdisciplinary Journal for Asian Christian Scholars* 4 (1, 2005): 41–62.
7. Herrlee G. Creel, *What Is Taoism?: And Other Studies in Chinese Cultural History* (Chicago: Chicago University Press, 1970), 1.
8. Ching, *Chinese Religions*, 85.
9. C. Spurgeon Medhurst, "The Tao The King, An Appreciation," *Chinese Recorder* 30 (11, 1899): 541 (540–551).
10. Anna K. Seidel, "The Image of the Perfect Ruler in Early Taoist Messianism: Lao-Tzu and Li Hung," *History of Religions* 9, No. 2/3 (1969–1970): 216 (216–247).
11. See Michael Strickman, "On the Alchemy of T'ao Hung-ching," *Facets of Taoism, Essays in Chinese Religion*, ed. Holms Welch and Anna Seidel (New Haven and New York: Yale University Press, 1979), 164–168 (123–192), referred to by A. C. Graham, *Disputers of the Tao, Philosophical Argument in Ancient China* (La Salle, IL: Open Court, 1989), 171.
12. See a brief account of the Zhang, his movement and the commentary in Max Kaltenmark, *Lao Tzu and Taoism* (Stanford: Stanford University Press, 1773), 113–117.
13. Kaltenmark, *Lao Tzu and Taoism*, 144.
14. Kristofer Schipper, *The Taoist Body*, trans. Karen C. Duval (Taoiei: SMC Publishing Inc. 1993), 183–184. For the fifth-century tradition of religious Daoist in the belief of immortality and ascension to heaven with Laozi's legend as context, see Livia Kohn, *Taoist Mystical Philosophy: The Scripture of Western Ascension* (New York: State University of New York Press, 1991), 58–64.
15. For the dates and the composition of *DDJ* based on oral tradition, see Schipper, *The Taoist Body*, 184–185.
16. Ibid. 191. The italic is in the original. See the use of "two Taoism" on p. 192.
17. *Commentary on the Lao Tzu by Wang Pi*, trans. Ariane Rump in collaboration with Wing-tsit Chan (Hawaii: University of Hawaii Press, 1979). The commentary has asserted great impact on the interpretative tradition of *Dadejing*; see Schipper, *The Taoist Body*, 192.
18. Schipper, *The Taoist Body*, 193. Huainanzi sums up the role of Dao as the matrix from which the myriad things are proceed: "Dao gave birth to the myriad creatures" (道生萬物, 3/2b). See the list of cosmological texts in Huainnanzi, Charles Le Blanc, *Huai Nan Tzu,*

Philosophical Synthesis in Early Han Thought (Hong Kong: Hong Kong University Press, 1985), 198–199.
19. Schipper, *The Taoist Body*, 194. The tradition of Xianger Commentary, used by the Heavenly Master Sect of Daoism, contains the ancient religious tradition of *Daodejing*.
20. Medhurst, "The Tao The King," 550.
21. Ibid. 543.
22. Jingjiao in China has been inappropriately associated with "Nestorianism" and labeled as being "Nestorian." See the use of the term in Yoshirō Saeki, *The Nestorian Documents and Relics in China* (Tokyo: Maruzen, 1951) and *The Nestorian Monument in China* (London: Society for Promoting Christian Knowledge 1916). Recent studies have corrected the designation concerned and the change is reflected in the titles of recent publications. See Roman Malek in connection with Peter Hofrichter, ed., *Jingjiao: The Church of the East in China and Central Asia* (Sankt Augustin: Institut Monumenta Serica 2006) and Li Tang and Dietmar W. Winkler, eds., *Winds of Jingjiao: Studies on Syriac Christianity in China and Central Asia* (Vienna: Lit Verlag, 2016).
23. For a review of the translation of the Bible into Chinese in the first centenary of Protestant work in China, see Marshall Broomhall, "The Bible in the Chinese Empire," *The Chinse Empire, A General and Missionary Survey*, ed. Marshall Broomhall (London: Morgan & Scott, 1907), 371–418. See also a detailed study of the history of the Mandarin Union Version of 1919 by Jost Oliver Zetzsche, *The Bible in China: The History of the Union Version or the Culmination of Protestant Missionary Bible Translation in China* (Nettetal: Steyler Verlag, 1999).
24. See Matteo Nicolini-Zani, "Past and Current Research on Jingjiao Documents: A Survey," in *Jingjiao: The Church of the East in China and Central Asia*, ed. Malek and Hofrichter, 23–24.
25. For reference to Chinese sources behind the Jingjiao documents relating to Buddhism and Daoism, see Zhu Qianzhi 朱謙之, *Jingjiao in China* [in Chinese] 中國景教 (Beijing: Renmin Publishing Company, 1993), 140–145. It is noted that Zhu has adopted a Marxist material perspective of history in reading the Jingjiao documents with some biases against their religious expressions (14, 148, 165–166). Nestorian Christianity is understood as heresy (90).
26. For a clear and concise popular approach to the Jingjiao texts and the story of their discovery, see Martin Palmer, *The Jesus Sutras: Rediscovering the Lost Religion of Taoist Christianity* (New York: Ballantine, 2001).
27. Besides the title cited above, there is an internet public resource by L. Eccles and Sam Lieu, *Stele on the Diffusion of the Luminous Religion of Da Qin (Rome) in the Middle Kingdom* (https://bit.ly/2wdbNBv [accessed September 15, 2020]).
28. The Hebrew Bible classifies the Bible into twenty-four books.
29. Stephen Eskildsen, *Daoism, Meditation, and the Wonders of Serenity: From the Latter Han Dynasty (25–220) to the Tang Dynasty (618–907)* (Albany: New York University Press, 2015), 326–327. On Jesus Sutra and the text of Discourse on Monotheism, see Jingyi Ji, *Encounters between Chinese Culture and Christianity: A Hermeneutical Perspective* (Berlin: Lit Verlag, 2007), 24–80.
30. The couple of versions at the disposal of the missionaries before 1919 were the King James Version (1611), which uses "without form and void" (so Geneva Bible, 1560) and the Revised Version of 1885 which has "waste and void."

31. There is a rich collection of ancient versions of the various Chinese translation of the Bible online. See http://bible.fhl.net/ob/nob.html?book=18. For the Taiping Bible, see Archie C. C. Lee, "The Bible in China: Religion of God's Chinese Son," *Princeton Seminary Bulletin* 5 (29, 2008): 21–38.
32. http://bible.fhl.net/ob/nob.html?book=210. In Schereschewsky's literary version (文理本) of the Old and New Testament (新舊約全書, 1902 and 1913), a different rendering (地乃空曠混沌) is adopted.
33. For a brief discussion of *Zhuangzi* in comparison with *DDJ* in the context of the theme of *hundun*, see N. J. Girardot, *Myth and Meaning in Early Taoism* (Berkeley: University of California Press, 1983), 77–80.
34. The phrase "faceless Emperor Hun-Dun" is adopted from Girardot, *Myth and Meaning in Early Taoism*, 279.
35. Isabelle Robinet, "Chaos, inchoate state," *The Encyclopedia of Taoism*, ed. Fabrizio Pregadio (New York: Routledge, 2008), vol. 1, 523–525.
36. Burton Watson, tr., *The Complete Works of Chuang Tzu* (New York: Columbia University Press, 1968), 97; David Hawkes, *The Songs of the South: An Anthology of Ancient Chinese Poems by Qu Yuan and Other Poets* (London: Penguin Classics, 1985), 128.
37. See Li Mian, *A Comprehensive Discussion and Chapter by Chapter Commentary of Zhuangzi* [in Chinese] 莊子總論及分篇評注 (Taipei: Taiwan Shangwu Publishing Co., 1990), 188. The term *hundun* is used twenty-five times in the Daoist writings of *DDJ* (four times), *Zhuangzi* (eleven times), and *Huainanzi* (ten times). See the tabulation by Girardot, *Myth and Meaning in Early Taoism*, 121.
38. The motherhood of the Dao is repeated in *DDJ* 1, 20, 52, 59.
39. Lau, *Tao Te Ching*, 37. Girardot, *Myth and Meaning in Early Taoism*, improperly renders as "something chaotic and yet complete," 49.
40. Translation of N. J. Girardot, *Myth and Meaning in Early Taoism*, 49.
41. The character "空" by itself alone appears eight times while that of "虛" sixteen times in *Zhuangzi*.
42. Victor Mair, *Wandering on the Way, Early Taoist Tales and Parables of Chuang Tzu* (New York: Bantam Books, 1994), 134.
43. Ibid. 275.
44. Ibid. 109.
45. Ibid. 32. See also a different translation in Fu Yulan, tr., *Chuang-Tzu, A New Selected Translation with an Exposition of the Philosophy of Kuo Hsiang* (Berlin Heidelberg: Springer-Verlag, 2016), 27.
46. T. H. Gaster, "Chaos," *Interpreters' Dictionary of the Bible*, vol. 1, 552.
47. Rebecca S. Watson, *Chaos Uncreated: A Reassessment of the Theme of Chaos in the Hebrew Bible* (Berlin: De Gruyter, Inc. 2005), 16.
48. Watson, *Chaos Uncreated*, 16, 18. See also T. Fenton, "Chaos in the Bible? *Tohu vavohu*," in *The Earth and the Waters in Genesis 1 and 2*, ed. D. T. Tsumura (Sheffield: Sheffield Academic Press, 1989), 17–43; and T. A. Perry, "A Poetics of Absence: The Structure and Meaning of Genesis 1.2," *JSOT* 58 (1993): 3–11.
49. Lau, *Tao Te Ching*, 23.
50. Girardot, *Myth and Meaning in Early Taoism*, 40.
51. Ibid. 41.
52. On the motif of the Dao and the call to return in *DDJ*, see Girardot, 67–76.
53. Girardot, *Myth and Meaning in Early Taoism*, 294.

54. Ching, *Chinese Religions*, 113.
55. Max Kaltenmark, "The Ideology of the T'ai-p'ing ching," *Facets of Taoism: Essays in Chinese Religion*, ed. Holmes Welch and Anna Seidel (New Haven and London: Yale University Press, 1979), 23.
56. On the cosmic body in Daoist view of the original unity of the *Dao*, see the four texts selected by Livia Kohn, *The Taoist Experience, An Anthology* (New York: SUNY Press, 1993), 191–219.
57. Benjamin I. Schwartz, *The World of Thought in Ancient China* (Cambridge, MA and London: Belknap Press of Harvard University Press, 1985), 195.
58. Ching noted the triple use of the word "*dao*" in the first sentences of *DDJ*, see Ching, *Chinese Religions*, 88. A. C. Graham also notes the nuance and thus has put forth "The Way that can be 'Way'-ed is not the constant Way," *Disputers of the Tao*, 219.
59. Ching, *Chinese Religions*, 88. Ching designates Laozi as a "'divine man' with Messianic qualities" (*Chinese Religions*, 86).
60. Graham, *Disputers of the Tao*, 222.
61. C. L. Seow, *Ecclesiastes, A New Translation with Introduction and Commentary* (The Anchor Bible; New York: Doubleday, 1997), 51–52, 56–57.
62. James Barr, *The Garden of Eden and the Hope of Immortality* (Minneapolis: Fortress Press 1993).
63. For an excellent reference work for the general history of Christianity in China, see *Handbook of Christianity in China*, ed. Nicolas Standaert (Leiden: Brill, 2001).
64. Nettie M. Senger, "Christian Attitudes in Chinese Religions," *Chinese Recorder* 57 (7, 1926): 491 (490–493).
65. C. Spurgeon Medhurst modifies the "blind soul" with an affirmation that Laozi "knows his goal and goes straight towards it," see his "The Tao The King," 540.
66. Ibid. 547.

Primary Sources

Lau, D. C., tr. *Tao Te Ching, A Bilingual Edition*. Hong Kong: The Chinese University Press, 2001.

Mair, Victor. *Wandering on the Way, Early Taoist Tales and Parables of Chuang Tzu*. New York: Bantam Books, 1994.

CHAPTER 14

CHINESE BUDDHIST WRITINGS AND THE BIBLE

LIU BOYUN

Introduction

THE history of the Bible in China can be dated to the seventh century, when a bishop from the Church of the East (Jingjiao)[1] arrived in the capital city of the Tang empire (618–907 CE), bringing with him "Scriptures and images." The translation process of the earliest Christian collection of Scriptures of that period, however, was more complicated and often obscure. We could see that the Church of the East in China in the Tang dynasty was under the influence of the growing Buddhist canon, and came up with many authoritative texts that they called "*jing*," which often is rendered in English as sūtras, Scriptures, or books. Among these sūtras, there are books of the Bible in the modern sense, liturgical books, exegetical works possibly for missionary purposes, and some other books we would not usually call "Scriptures" today. In the Tang dynasty, instead of a Bible, the Church of the East rather had Bibles/sūtras. "Bible" here should be understood in the original sense of the word, *biblia*, a collection of books.

Buddhism had reached in China in the first century during the Eastern Han dynasty (25–220 CE). By the time of the arrival of the Church of the East, Buddhist scholars in China had already translated and composed many important texts. Buddhism was very prominent both culturally and politically in the Tang dynasty. The Church of the East, in over two centuries' time, produced its religious collections. Examining their lexicon, we find that they have borrowed extensively from Buddhist terminology. From the epithets of God, celestial beings, and the clergymen to various religious practices, there is Buddhist vocabulary in all of the Jingjiao texts. However, it does not necessarily mean that the Church of the East made theological compromises in order to make Christian teachings more approachable to the Chinese audience. Although often accused of religious syncretism by modern scholarship, they have kept fundamental Christian doctrines intact.

Catholics who arrived in China in the following centuries were less motivated to translate the Bible into Chinese. In the Yuan dynasty (1279–1368), John of Montecorvino, a papal delegate who later served as the archbishop of Beijing, translated the New Testament (NT) and the book of Psalms into Turkic, the language of the Mongol ruling class. Despite later translation projects such as the Jean Basset translation 白日升譯本 and Louis Antoine de Poirot's annotated translation 賀清泰譯本, it was not until the year 1968 when Catholics published an official complete translation of the Bible in Chinese, the Studium Biblicum version 思高本. Protestants made more efforts in Bible translation and produced numerous versions like the Morrison-Milne Bible 神天聖書, the Delegates' Version 委辦本, the Mandarin Version 北京官話譯本 and the Chinese Union Version 和合本, which is still the most widely used Chinese Bible today. Since then, there have been more translations such as Today's Chinese Version 現代中文譯本 and Chinese New Version 新譯本. These later translations show very little Buddhist influence. However, I would like to argue that there are still some terms that originated in Chinese Buddhism, but they have been so culturally assimilated into Christian vocabulary that readers may not be aware of their sources.

A List of Chinese Bible(s)/Sūtras in the Tang Dynasty

When we are referring to a "Bible" in modern-day China, the meaning is quite clear. It is usually a bound copy of Christian Scriptures, including the Old and the NT, although the number and content of the Old Testament (OT) books may vary depending on whether it is a Catholic or a Protestant Bible,[2] reflecting an age-old controversy introduced to Chinese Christians from the West. However, this was not the case when Christianity first reached China.

The earliest record of Christianity in China is the so-called "Nestorian Stele," set up in the second year of the Jianzhong era of Emperor Dezong of the Tang dynasty (781 CE). According to the inscriptions in Chinese a senior priest, Aluoben 阿羅本,[3] from the Church of the East arrived in Chang'an in the ninth year of the Zhenguan era of Emperor Taizong (635 CE). Aluoben "carried the true Scriptures" with him. What exactly those are, we are not told, although the stele does mention "of Scriptures there were left twenty-seven books,"[4] referring almost certainly to the twenty-seven books of the NT.

What draws our attention here is that the Peshitta NT that the Church of the East regards as authoritative has twenty-two instead of twenty-seven books. Even today, the Assyrian Church of the East still excludes 2 Peter, 2 John, 3 John, and Revelation from their NT canon. Therefore, the Jingjiao Scriptures mentioned here are probably the Harklean Syriac version, completed in 616 CE by Thomas of Harqel, a Miaphysite bishop. This is very significant because Jingjiao had been considered homogenously "Nestorian," although scholars in recent years have challenged this view, claiming that the congregation was more inclusive.[5]

The question now is: were these Scriptures translated into Chinese? The stele does mention translating books and building monasteries,[6] but it does not provide any details. We need to turn to the Dunhuang manuscripts, discovered by Paul Pelliot in 1908, for further information. However, they pose more questions than they can answer. In a text named *Zun jing* (Sūtra of Veneration),[7] it says that 530 Jingjiao "Scriptures" were brought to Chang'an by Aluoben, thirty-five of which have been translated by Jingjing (Adam), the author of the "Nestorian" stele.

From twenty-seven books of the NT to 530 Scriptures, we see a huge discrepancy. Let us now take a look at the thirty-five translated Scriptures for an idea of what the Church of the East regarded as authoritative. These texts are as follows:[8]

1. *Changming huangle jing* 常明皇樂經 (Eternal light royal joy book);
2. *Xuanyuan zhiben jing* 宣元至本經 (Proclaim origin reach root book);
3. *Zhixuan anle jing* 志玄安樂經 (Devoted to hidden peace joy book);
4. *Tianbao cang jing* 天寶藏經 (Heavenly treasure store book);
5. *Duohui shengwang jing* 多惠聖王經 (David sage king book);
6. *A'enqulirong jing* 阿恩瞿利容經 (Evangelium book);[9]
7. *Hunyuan jing* 渾元經 (On the primordial origins book);
8. *Tongzhen jing* 通真經 (Reach truth book);
9. *Baoming jing* 寶明經 (Precious brightness book);
10. *Chuanhua jing* 傳化經 (Preach conversion book);
11. *Qingyi jing* 罄遺經 (Complete bequest book);
12. *Yuanling jing* 原靈經 (Original spiritual power book);
13. *Shulve jing* 述略經 (Transmit summary book);
14. *Sanji jing* 三際經 (Three moments book);
15. *Zhengjie jing* 徵詰經 (Seek ask book);
16. *Ningsi jing* 寧思經 (Peaceful thought book);
17. *Xuanyi jing* 宣義經 (Proclaim righteousness book);
18. *Shilihai jing* 師利海經 (Apostles book);
19. *Baolu fawang jing* 寶路法王經 (Paul dharma king book);
20. *Shanhelv jing* 删河律經 (Zechariah book);
21. *Yiliyuesi jing* 藝利月思經 (Gewargis book);
22. *Ningyeyi iing* 寧耶頤經 (Testament book);
23. *Yizelv jing* 儀則律經 (Ceremonial rules laws book);
24. *Pi'eqi jing* 毘遏啟經 (Benedictions book);
25. *Sanwei zan jing* 三威讚經 (Three majesties praise book);
26. *Moushi fawang jing* 牟世法王經 (Moses dharma king book);
27. *Yiliye jing* 伊利耶經 (Elijah book);

28. *Efulin jing* 遏拂林經 (Ephrem book);
29. *Baoxin fawang jing* 報信法王經 (Messenger dharma king book);
30. *Mishihe zizai tiandi jing* 彌施訶自在天地經 (Messiah self-existent in heaven and earth book);
31. *Simen jing* 四門經 (Tetrabiblos book);
32. *Qizhen jing* 啟真經 (Opening truth book);
33. *Mosajisi jing* 摩薩吉斯經 (Mar Sargis book);
34. *Cilibo jing* 慈利波經 (The Cross book);
35. *Wusana jing* 烏薩那經 (Hosanna book).

Scholars of Jingjiao have been trying to identify what the thirty-five "Scriptures" are. Three can be easily recognized: *Xuanyuan zhiben jing*, *Zhixuan anle jing*, and *Sanwei zan jing* (= *Daqin Jingjiao sanwei mengdu zan* 大秦景教三威蒙度讚), for the original texts have been preserved. The first two are written presumably by Jingjing (Adam), and the third one is part translation and part adaptation of the Syriac *Gloria in excelsis Deo*.[10] Another two well-known texts also can be identified: *Sanji jing*, which may cause some problems in our understanding of the Church of the East, for it bears the same title as a Manichean book; and *Simen jing*, a treatise on astrology by the Egyptian scholar Ptolemy. The others are all shrouded in ambiguity. Many of the titles can be only tentatively translated, and no one knows if they are liturgical or "biblical" in the accepted sense. Our best guesses at the possible "biblical" books are: *Shilihai jing*, which might be the Book of Acts; *A'enqulirong jing*, one of the Gospels, *Moushi fawang jing*, the Pentateuch; *Baolu fawang jing*, one of the Pauline epistles; *Shanhelv jing*, the Book of Zechariah. *Duohui shengwang jing* could be either Psalms or the Psalter for liturgical use.

The Concept of Chinese Bible(s)/Sūtras in the Tang Dynasty

It is perplexing that the same Chinese word, "*jing*," is used to refer to the books of the NT and the 530 Scriptures. All of the thirty-five translated texts bear the word "*jing*" in their titles. Even today, the Christian Bible is called *Shengjing* 聖經 in Chinese. How, then, do we understand the epithet of "*jing*" used by the Church of the East in China?

"*Jing*" was originally used to refer to literary classics that came to be revered by different schools of philosophy during the Warring States period (476–221 BCE), such as the *Daodejing* (also transliterated as *Tao Te Ching*) for the Daoists, and the *liu jing* (six classics) for the Confucians. In the Western Han dynasty (202 BCE–9 CE), the collection of *wu jing* 五經, "Five Confucian Classics" was edited and canonized by decree of the imperial court, namely the *Classic of Poetry*, *Book of Documents*, *Book of Rites*, *Book of Changes*, and the *Spring and Autumn Annals*.

Then Buddhism reached China during the Western Han dynasty. Translation projects of the Buddhist sūtras soon ensued. The Buddhist classics, the *Tripiṭaka* (lit. three baskets), consists of three parts: *Sūtra Piṭaka*, *Vinaya Piṭaka*, and *Abhidharma Piṭaka*. The three terms are respectively translated as "*jing*," "*lv*," and "*lun*" in Chinese. The word "*jing*" is now used to refer to Buddhist sūtras. For example, in the late third century, among the earliest strata of Buddhist translation, the *Sad-dharma Puṇḍárīka Sūtra* (Lotus Sūtra) was translated to *Zhengfahua jing* 正法華經 by Dharma-rakṣa 竺法護 and his team.[11]

Later, "*jing*" became a broader term, loosely referring to all religious classics in the Chinese language. There was a growing Chinese collection of Buddhist sūtras, both in translation, adaptation, and pseudepigraphal composition, covering the three parts of the *Tripiṭaka*. We also see evidence in the Chinese translations of Manichean texts as *jing*.[12] That is why scholars of Jingjiao, such as P. Y. Saeki, Max Deeg, and Martin Palmer, insisted on translating the word "*jing*" used in the Jingjiao text into "sūtra," because of its characteristic appearance in the Chinese literary tradition. In this regard, Jingjiao resembles Buddhism or Manichaeism, two highly Sinicized religions.

When the Church of the East took root in the Tang dynasty, Buddhism was enjoying the peak of its development, forming many different schools of thought and practice.[13] Has then the Chinese Buddhist broad range of sūtras influenced Jingjiao's view of their religious Scriptures? The answer is yes. Throughout their documents, we have hardly, if ever, found any evidence of the idea of the Holy Bible with an OT and a NT. The Peshitta Bible, *textus receptus* of the Church of the East, is never mentioned in the Jingjiao texts discovered in China. Moreover, the Jingjiao canon seems to be a growing collection, with new sūtras created by prominent clergy, including both earlier texts such as *Xuting mishisuo jing* (Jesus Messiah Sūtra) of the "Aluoben's documents"[14] and later texts written by Jingjing, such as *Xuanyuan zhiben jing* and *Zhixuan anle jing*.

Xuanyuan zhiben jing is one of Jingjing's compositions. The title is recorded in the list of sūtras in *Zun jing*. The text was discovered for the first time in Dunhuang in the early twentieth century and is now preserved in Japan. Then in 2006, a *jingchuang* (usually translated as *dhāraṇī* pillar, a traditional term for a Chinese Buddhist funerary pillar) bearing inscriptions of the same sūtra was found in Luoyang with a long colophon. This *dhāraṇī* pillar was set up in the ninth year of the Yuanhe era of the Tang dynasty (814 CE). The Luoyang text encourages the believer to "be empowered by recitation and reading [of the sūtra], have faith in it, understand it, and practice it diligently." In the colophon, it also says, "if anyone can recite and practice [the sūtra], he will definitely receive a radiant[15] blessing, let alone engraving it on a *dhāraṇī*!"[16] This is the language a Buddhist practitioner would use on a powerful sūtra. It also means that *Xuanyuan zhiben jing*, a text written by Jingjing, an eighth-century Jingjiao clergyman, is regarded as the Christian equivalent of the Buddhist *Uṣṇīṣa vijaya dhāraṇī sūtra* 佛頂尊勝陀羅尼經, a very popular text from the early Tang dynasty, and most commonly found on Chinese Buddhist funerary pillars. The Jingjiao pillar discovered in Luoyang follows the typical design of the Buddhist *dhāraṇī*.[17] The wording of the sūtra also indicates that the *Xuanyuan zhiben jing* is regarded as a most preeminent text with great spiritual power.

Similarly, *Zhixuan anle jing*, another text written by Jingjing,[18] also has a structural formula very similar to a typical Buddhist sūtra. It starts with "(I have) heard these Highest Words,"[19] just like a Buddhist sūtra with "Thus I have heard." And it finishes with "When the multitude heard the full speech, they were overjoyed. They paid their respects, and practiced the teaching," which sounds like the common ending of a Buddhist sūtra, "After they heard what the Buddha taught, they were overjoyed, and practiced the teaching."[20] The formulaic resemblance of this Jingjiao text to Buddhist sūtras shows that Jingjing has modeled his writing on Buddhist sūtras and intends for the text to be regarded as authoritative and as a part of Chinese Christian Scriptures.

From the oddly large number of Scriptures brought by Aluoben's and the list of "translated works" in *Zun jing*, we can see that biblical books, biblical paraphrases and interpretations, liturgical books, doctrinal treatises, astrological work, and even a possible Manichean book are clustered together. All of them are called "*jing*" (sūtras), enjoying equal status. Therefore, it is safe to presume that in the Tang dynasty, instead of a closed canon, there was rather a growing canon, in the form of translations, new compositions, and even unusual appropriations of other religions. This is the result of the Church of the East's encounters and dialogues with Buddhism in China, reflecting both imitation and possible competition.

Influence of Buddhist Terms on the Theological Expressions in the Christian Sūtras

There has been a long-time controversy expressing concern over whether the Church of the East in China was orthodox or Nestorian in their doctrine, or if it practiced religious syncretism, and if so, to what extent. First of all, there is no sign of so-called "Nestorianism" in its documents. The accusation of radical Dyophysitism,[21] from the wording of "divided Person of our Three in One" 三一分身 and "The divided Person appeared on earth" 分身出代[22] on the Jingjiao Stele is weak grounds on which to base such a claim. Secondly, we do not have sufficient evidence to say whether the Church of the East in China practiced religious syncretism, though the inclusion of at least one possible Manichean text in its canon does rouse some suspicion.[23] The appropriation of the Buddhist *dhāraṇī* pillar should be viewed as cultural indigenization instead of syncretism, for this kind of funerary pillar itself was a Chinese practice initiated around the time the Church of the East reached China, and should not be seen as traditionally Buddhist. The cross-plus-lotus-flower motif, seen in both the Jingjiao *dhāraṇī* pillar and numerous other stone carvings, including the top part of the Jingjiao Stele, is commonly found across China and India. It, too, should be regarded as a cultural symbol instead of religious syncretism, like variants of the cross around the world.

It is true, however, that the Jingjiao documents do use many terms borrowed from Chinese Buddhism.[24] We will see, from the examples in the following section, that although the Church of the East used Buddhist terms in its texts, it did not compromise its Christian doctrine. On the contrary, these terms could help Chinese-speaking readers to better understand the teachings of the church.

When Buddhist sūtras were first introduced to China, the translators also struggled with rendering the unfamiliar terms into Chinese. One thing they did was to use Daoist vocabulary to convey an essentially Buddhist meaning, such as translating *nirvāṇa* into *wuwei* 無為 (non-action), *bodhi* into *Dao* 道 (the Way),[25] and *Arhat* into *ying zhen*應真 (lit. in accordance with the genuine).[26] The Church of the East used a similar approach when it tried to come up with Christian vocabulary in Chinese. In *Zun jing*, it says, "We reverently worship the mysterious person the royal Father Aloha. The responding person the royal Son Meshiha. The witnessing person Ruha d-qudsha. The above three persons unite together in one body."[27] The phrase "three persons" 三身 is a direct loan of the Chinese Buddhist translation of "*Trikāya*." In Buddhism, "*Trikāya*" means the three bodies of the Buddha, namely, the *Dharmakāya* 法身, the truth-body, unlimited and unfathomable; *Saṃbhogakāya* 報身, the enjoyment body, blissful and bright; and the *Nirmāṇakāya* 應身, the response body, compassionate and visible.[28] In Zunjing, the "responding person" is exactly the same Chinese phrase as "*Nirmāṇakāya*." The concept of "three bodies of the Buddha" can be found in the *Daśabhūmika Sūtra Shastra* (or *Daśabhūmikabhāsya*, lit. Treatise on the Ten Grounds), written by Vasubandhu in the fourth century CE and translated into Chinese as *Shidi jing lun* 十地經論 in the sixth century,[29] and soon greatly popularized as a commentary on part of the *Avataṃsaka Sūtra*, the most important Huayan corpus in the Tang dynasty. Therefore, it can be safely assumed that Jingjiao borrowed the Buddhist term "*Nirmāṇakāya*" to express the person of Christ as the Word Incarnate. It is a very appropriate loan, for it could enable the reader to understand the salvific economy of Christ on earth with the help of the already familiar Buddhist term. Although in Buddhism, there is not one *Nirmāṇakāya* but many, appearing to different people on different occasions, and although *Nirmāṇakāya* can be an apparition instead of a corporeal body, there is no sign of Docetism in the Jingjiao documents. The veneration of the "three persons in one body" has ruled out any unorthodox interpretations.

I have mentioned the "divided Person" on the Jingjiao Stele. It, too, is a loan phrase from Buddhism.[30] For example, in *Kumārajīva* 鳩摩羅什, Jiumoluoshi's early fifth-century translation of the Lotus Sūtra, there are multiple mentions of the Buddha's "reduplication-body" 分身. The *Kṣitigarbha-bodhisattva-pūrva-praṇidhāna Sūtra* 地藏菩薩本願經, translated by Śikṣānanda 實叉難陀 at the end of the seventh century, also mentions Kṣitigarbha emanating a "reduplication-body" to those who are in need. In this sense, a "reduplication-body" is precisely the *Nirmāṇakāya*, although it can be from either a Buddha or a Bodhisattva.[31] Around the same period, the idea of "reduplication-body" was also introduced into Daoism, as we can see in *Benji jing* 本際經 (Sūtra on the Primordial Origin),[32] a very popular Daoist text since the beginning of the Tang dynasty.

Therefore, we can safely say that the Church of the East in China simply adopted some religious terms that were floating around at that time. This translational strategy did not cause corruption to the essential message of Christian texts.

In this vein, Buddhist vocabulary also is incorporated into Jingjiao anthropology. In the Dunhuang Texts, there are three treatises under the collective name of *A Discourse on Monotheism* (一神論, *Yi shen lun*). In the first one, *Yi tian lun diyi* (一天論第一, The Discourse of the Oneness of the Ruler of the Universe, Part I),[33] a catechism on God as the one Creator of the heaven and earth, it says that "the soul and the spirit are made up of 'the five attributes.' "[34] "The five attributes" 五陰 here is apparently a Buddhist term. It also is known as *wuyun* 五蘊 (Sanskrit *pañca-skandha*), or the five aggregates of clinging. It is used here to expound on the constitution of a human being, rather than the original Buddhist approach to account for all sentient beings. So, the Church of the East does not simply implant the Buddhist word in the original sense but modified it according its own doctrines. The following text, *Yu di'er* 喻第二 (The Parable, Part II), further explains its tripartite anthropology, "one human being with both a spirit and a soul will make one complete human being,"[35] markedly different from the Buddhist idea that the body and the spirit/soul are not separate entities. Therefore, we can see that the Church of the East in China uses Buddhist diction extensively, but with caution and adjustments.

Influence of Buddhist Terms on Other Religious Vocabulary in the Christian Sūtras

Apart from the more theological or doctrinal vocabulary, other Buddhist terms also are seen in the Jingjiao documents, such as titles of God, heavenly and demonic entities, and clergymen of the Church of the East in China. In *Xuting mishisuo jing*, the opening verses refers to God as "the Heavenly Revered One" 天尊.[36] In *Shizun bushi lun disan* 世尊布施論第三 (the World Honored One's Discourse on Alms-Giving, part III), the third text of *A Discourse on Monotheism*, Christ is addressed as "the World Honored One" 世尊. Both of the titles are commonly used for a Buddha or a Bodhisattva.[37] In the opening verses of the *Xuting mishisuo jing*, various celestial beings are called by traditionally Buddhist names: Buddhas 佛, *devas* 天, non-humans 非人, and *Arhats* 阿羅漢. Since there is no clear angelology in these texts, we are uncertain what these terms mean exactly. One tentative explanation is that, just as the early Buddhist scholars decided to translate *deva* into *tian* 天, indicating that the Buddha is superior to the god of heaven in traditional Chinese religion, Jingjiao clergy intentionally used Buddhist terminology to refer to the celestial beings, implying that the Christian God is the Lord most high, above the Buddhist pantheon. This was done probably to serve missionary purposes. We have observed a similar case in contemporary Chinese Manichaeism texts, where prominent figures are translated as "Buddhas." Mani himself is rendered the "Buddha of Light" 摩尼光佛.[38] A copy of the *Compendium of the Doctrines and Styles of the Teaching of Mani, the Buddha of Light* 摩尼光佛教法儀略 has been found in the Dunhuang grottos, dated to 731 CE in the Tang dynasty.

As noted in the list of thirty-five Christian sūtras, important biblical figures such as Moses, David, and Paul are entitled "dharma kings" 法王. This is a typical Buddhist designation for a religious leader. Similarly, on the Jingjiao Stele, many of the clergymen are addressed as "monks" (僧 *seng*, from the Sanskrit *saṃgha*).[39] However, as we can see in the Syriac inscriptions, the "monks" are actually "elders" (*qaššīšā*). The Chinese word here does not mean those who have sworn to celibacy and live collectively in a monastery, unlike the Buddhist *bhikkhus* and *samaneras*. Rather, most of those on the list are lay clergy. Only when an additional Syriac word "*yiḥīdāyā*" is attached to *qaššīšā* does it mean a hieromonk or priest-monk. But on the stele, *yiḥīdāyā* is left un-translated. One of the Jingjiao clergyman on the stele is a bishop called Mār Yōḥannān 曜輪, and his title of bishop, *apesqōpā* (from *episkopos* in Greek), is translated as "the Venerable" 大德. This Chinese epithet originally was applied by earliest Buddhist translators on the Buddha (Sanskrit *bhadanta*),[40] but was later used predominantly as the Chinese word for senior monks. In this vein, the *daqin si* 大秦寺 in the Jingjiao documents should not be rendered the "Ta-ch'in monastery,"[41] as most of the modern translations have, but "Daqin Church."[42]

In *Xuting mishisuo jing*, translations of words like the "Devil" and "hell" also are borrowed from Buddhism. They are rendered respectively *yanluo wang* 閻羅王 (Yamarāja) and *di yu* 地獄 (*naraka/niraya*). Similarly, the evildoers are called those who fall into the "evil path" 惡道, which is the Chinese rendering of *akuśala-gatīḥ*, the three lower realms of rebirth (*saṃsāra*). Another name for these people is the "multitude of evil karma" 惡業眾, which is also obviously a loan from Buddhism.

Furthermore, the Chinese translation of certain religious practices, such as almsgiving and prayer rituals, are also loans from Buddhism. In *Shizun bushi lun di san*, almsgiving is rendered *bushi* 布施, as can be seen in the title. The phrase already was used extensively in Chinese classics before the age of Buddhism, such as in "Discourse of the Zhou" in the *Discourses of the States* 國語·周語 and in a lost quotation of the *Book of Odes* in "External Things" in *Zhuang Zi*, a Daoist classic. In the Buddhist translation projects, *bushi* was used to translate the Sanskrit word "*dāna*." By the time Jingjiao worked on its translations and compositions, "*bushi*" already had become a widely known Buddhist term, popularized especially because it is considered the first of the six perfections (波羅蜜, *pāramitā*). Another example is the prayer ritual, or *xiu gongde* 修功德 (merit-making) in the Jingjiao Stele. It is apparently a loan of the Buddhist term "*gongde*," the Chinese translation of "*puṇya*." The service was conducted in an imperial palace, presumably for the well-being of the emperor. A third example is the cloak that Jesus wore as the sick touched him (e.g., Luke 8:44). Believing it to be a religious habit, the author of *Xuting mishisuo jing* rendered it into "*jiasha*" 迦沙 (now commonly written as 袈裟, Sanskrit *kāṣāya*), which originally means a fully ordained Buddhist monk's robe.[43]

One final example is the formulaic ending of *Daqin Jingjiao sanwei mengdu zan*, a reworking of the Syriac *Gloria in excelsis Deo*. The ending words in the original Syriac text are "*l-ʿālmīn āmēn*," usually translated as "forever, amen." The Chinese line reads *qing ning fa'er bu siyi* 清凝法耳不思議. In an English translation of the Chinese version, it has been rendered "Clear and strong is the law; beyond thought or dispute."[44] Now "*qing ning*" means pure and constant, often used in Buddhist texts to describe the essential reality of the Buddha. The following word, instead of "law" in previous English translations, is actually a phonetic loan of *fa'er* 法爾, *dharmatā*, or *tathātā* in Sanskrit, which is often translated as "suchness," indicating the eternal and blissful.[45] It is a perfect equivalent of the word "forever." The examples of Buddhist influence on the Jingjiao sūtras provided are by no means exhaustive. They are simply those that are highly representative, including doctrinal terminology, religious designation, and formulaic diction. A more detailed exploration is definitely in need in the future for a fuller grasp of the earliest Chinese Christian documents.

Incorporation of Buddhist Terms in Later Chinese Bible Translations

As noted above, in the Tang dynasty, there was religious terminology floating around and absorbed into various spiritual traditions, despite their sources in Chinese Buddhism. Even today, when we read the most widely read Chinese Bible versions, we still see religious terms that were originally found in Buddhist texts. However, they have been used so frequently that they have become part of the Christian vocabulary or even everyday words and are no longer questioned for their Buddhist influence. There are a few examples in the next section.

We have seen that in *Xuting mishisuo jing*, "hell" is rendered *di yu* 地獄, a Chinese Buddhist word for "*naraka/niraya*." The same word has been adopted by later translators of the Bible. By the time of the Protestant CUV (Chinese Union Version) and the Catholic SBV (Studium Biblicum version), "*di yu*" had become a received equivalent of "hell" (Greek *gehenna*),[46] though SBV occasionally uses the Islamic term "*huo yu* 火獄" (literally, "fire prison") (Matt 5:22). In the same vein, "*zhi shi* 執事," originally a designation for an official in Chinese classics, later widely used as Buddhist translation for the Buddha's servant[47] or a high-ranking monk in a monastery, was appropriated by the Church of the East to translate the title of "deacon." We see the same rendering in modern Bible translations of CUV and SBV; for example, in 1 Tim 3:12.

Some other cases represent even weaker loans, for they have become everyday parlance, For example, "*ci bei* 慈悲" (compassion) in verses such as Luke 6:36, "*shi jie* 世界" (world) in Matt 13:38, and many other verses in both CUV and SBV. Compassion and wisdom are the most valued qualities of a Bodhisattva, so "*ci bei*" is seen extensively in all Mahayana Buddhist literature. Similarly, "*shi jie*," a coined phrase to translate *lokadhātu*, the combination of time and space, is widely found in Buddhist writings. The two words became so common that the Bible translators did not mind using them at all, and we see numerous examples across CUV and SBV. As of now, people are usually unaware of their Buddhist origins.

NOTES

1. Sometimes translated as the "Brilliant Teaching" or the "Illustrious Religion." I will use Jingjiao and "the Church of the East in China" interchangeably in the following paragraphs.
2. The Orthodox Church in China has not yet published an official complete translation of the Bible, but rather only the Book of Genesis, Psalms, and the New Testament.
3. Also transliterated as Alopen. Max Deeg reconstructs the name as "Ardabān." See Max Deeg, "Ways to Go and Not to Go in the Contextualisation of the Jingjiao Documents of the Tang Period," in *Hidden Treasures and Intercultural Encounters: Studies on East Syriac Christianity in China and Central Asia*, ed. D. W. Winkler and Li Tang (Berlin: LIT 2009), 135–152.
4. I am using A. C. Moule's English translation of the stele. See A. C. Moule, *Christians in China before the Year 1550* (London: Society for Promoting Christian Knowledge, 1930), 34–52.
5. Duan Qing 段晴, "A New Perspective for the *Daqin* Temple and the *Jingjiao* Priests" [in Chinese] 唐代大秦寺與景教僧新釋, in *Religious Beliefs and the Society in the Tang Dynasty* (唐代宗教信仰與社會), ed. Rong Xinjiang 榮新江 (Shanghai: Shanghai Lexicographical Publishing House, 2003), 459–460 (434–472). Max Deeg agrees with her; see "Ways to Go and Not to Go in the Contextualisation of the *Jingjiao* Documents of the Tang Period," 142.
6. Moule, *Christians in China before the Year 1550*, 45.
7. I am using Max Deeg's translation of the Dunhuang text titles. See Max Deeg, "The 'Brilliant Teaching': The Rise and Fall of 'Nestorianism' (Jingjiao) in Tang China," *Japanese Religions* 31.2 (2006): 91–110.
8. For transliterations and translations, see Moule, *Christians in China before the Year 1550*, 55–56; P. Y. Saeki, *The Nestorian Documents and Relics in China* (Tokyo: The Maruzen Company LTD, 1937), 274–275; Hidemi Takahashi, "Transcribed Proper Names in Chinese Syriac Christian Documents," in *Malphono w-Rabo d-Malphone: Studies in Honor of Sebastian P. Brock* (Piscataway, NJ: Gorgias Press), 631–662 (649–53); Matteo Nicolini-Zani, *La Via Radiosa per l'Oriente: I testi e la storia del primo incontro del cristianesimo con il mondo culturale e religioso cinese* (secoli VII–IX) (Magnano, Biella: Comunità di Bose, 2006), 221–224. I have based my translation on all the above with slight modifications.
9. Most scholars read the title as 阿思瞿利容經 Asinqulirong, but it could be a corruption of 阿恩瞿利容經, which corresponds to the Syriac word *ewangeliōn*, a transliteration of the Greek word *euangelion*, "Gospel." For different readings of the title, see Takahashi, "Transcribed Proper Names in Chinese Syriac Christian Documents," 649n89; and Nicolini-Zani, *La Via Radiosa per l'Oriente*, 221.
10. It is written in the seven-syllable genre (七言詩), which could be reflecting both the Chinese literary tradition and the meter of Ephrem.
11. Wang Tiejun 王鐵鈞, *Translation History of Chinese Buddhist Scriptures* [in Chinese] 中國佛典翻譯史稿 (Beijing: Central Compilation and Translation Press, 2006), 65.

12. In the *Compendium of the Doctrines and Styles of the Teaching of Mani, the Buddha of Light* 摩尼光佛教法儀略, each of the seven books is called a "*jing*."
13. See Deeg, "The 'Brilliant Teaching,'" 94–95.
14. *Xuting mishisuo jing* is basically a paraphrase of the Ten Commandments and a condensed version of the life and teachings of Jesus. For an introduction to Aluoben's documents, see Saeki, *The Nestorian Documents and Relics in China*, 113–117. Although the authenticity of the documents has been questioned, no definitive conclusions have been made.
15. It is the same word as in Jingjiao; therefore, it means both "abundant" and "bestowed by God."
16. For the text, see Lin Wushu 林悟殊 and Yin Xiaoping 殷小平, "Textual Analysis and Interpretation of the *dhāraṇī* text of *Daqin jingjiao xuanyuan zhiben jing*" [in Chinese] 經幢版《大秦景教宣元至本經》考釋, in *Journal of Chinese Literature and History* [in Chinese] 中华文史论丛 89 (2008): 331–337 (325–394).
17. Matteo Nicolini-Zani, "The Tang Christian Pillar from Luoyang and Its *Jingjiao* Inscription: A Preliminary Study," *Monumenta Serica: Journal of Oriental Studies* 57 (2009): 104 (99–140).
18. Most scholars believe that this text is composed rather than translated by Jingjing. See Deeg, "The 'Brilliant Teaching,'" 94. A few people, such as Wu Chang Shing, holds that if Jingjing is not the author, at least he took part in the translation process. Wu Chang Shing, 吳昶興, *The True and Eternal Way: Bibliographical Research of Assyrian Church of the East in Tang Dynasty* [in Chinese] 真常之道: 唐朝基督教歷史與文獻研究 (Taipei: Chinese Christian Literature Council Ltd., 2015), 225.
19. I am using Max Deeg's translation. Deeg, "The 'Brilliant Teaching,'" 101.
20. Yan Qiamao 顏洽茂, *An Analysis of the Buddhist Language: A Research on the Buddhist Lexicon in Middle Chinese* [in Chinese] 佛教語言闡釋: 中古佛經詞匯研究 (Hangzhou: Hangzhou University Press, 1997), 39.
21. For the accusation, see Samuel Hugh Moffett, *A History of Christianity in Asia*, Vol. 1: *Beginnings to 1500* (New York: Orbis Books, 2004), 306–307.
22. I am using A. C. Moule's English translation of the stele. See Moule, *Christians in China before the Year 1550*, 36, 45.
23. Kawaguchi Kazuhiko suggests that *Zheng jie jing* 征詰經 might be a corruption of *Cheng gao jing* 澄誥經, which could be a Manichean text. Quoted in Hidemi Takahashi, "Transcribed Proper Names in Chinese Syriac Christian Documents," 651.
24. For a list of Buddhist loan words in Jingjiao documents, see Huang Xianian 黃夏年, "A Preliminary Survey of the Relationship between *Jingjiao* and Buddhism" [in Chinese] 景教與佛教關系之初探, in *Studies in World Religions* [in Chinese] 世界宗教研究 1 (1996): 83–91 (85–86). For Jingjiao's appropriation of Buddhist liturgical formulas, see Wang Chuan 汪娟, "The Adaptation of Buddhist Rituals and Liturgical Texts in the Chinese Christian Manuscripts from Dunhuang" [in Chinese] 敦煌景教文獻對佛教儀文的吸收與轉化, in *Bulletin of the Institute of History and Philology Academia Sinica* [in Chinese] 中央研究院歷史語言研究所集刊 89.4 (2018): 631–661.
25. Max Deeg, "Creating Religious Terminology—A Comparative Approach to Early Chinese Buddhist Translations," *Journal of the International Association of Buddhist Studies* 31 (1–2), 2008 (2010): 111 (83–118).
26. Hubert Durt, "Early Chinese Buddhist Translations: Quotations from the Early Translations in Anthologies of the Sixth Century," *Journal of the International Association of Buddhist Studies* 31.1–2 (2010): 127 (119–140).

27. I am using A. C. Moule's English translation of the text with modifications. See Moule, *Christians in China before the Year 1550*, 55.
28. On the translation history and strategy of the "response body" or "resonant-body" of the Buddha, see Robert H. Sharf, *Coming to Terms with Chinese Buddhism: A Reading of the Treasure Store Treatise* (Honolulu: University of Hawai'i Press, 2002), 100–111. Also see Donghua Zhu, "Ying/ 應/ Nirmāṇa: A Case Study of The Translatability of Buddhism into Jingjiao," in *Winds of Jingjiao: Studies on Syriac Christianity in China and Central Asia*, ed. Li Tang and Diermar W. Winkler (Berlin: LIT 2009), 422–424 (419–433).
29. About the translation project of the Daśabhūmika Sūtra Shastra, see Pan Guiming 潘桂明, *An Encyclopedia of Chinese Buddhism: Sects and Schools* [in Chinese] 中國佛教百科全書·宗派卷 (Shanghai: Shanghai Classics Publishing House, 2000), 51–54.
30. Also see Nicolini-Zani, *La Via Radiosa per l'Oriente*, 194n24.
31. For examples of "reduplication-body" of Avalokiteśvara in the Lotus Sūtra and of Kṣitigarbha in the Kṣitigarbha-bodhisattva-pūrva-praṇidhāna Sūtra, see Sharf, *Coming to Terms with Chinese Buddhism*, 101–102. For "reduplication-body" as an alternative translation of "*Nirmāṇakāya*," see 310n66.
32. On the Daoist understanding of "reduplication-body," see Sharf, *Coming to Terms with Chinese Buddhism*, 69.
33. I am using Saeki's translation. He also notes that the title literally means "shastras on one Deva."
34. Saeki, *The Nestorian Documents and Relics in China*, 177.
35. Ibid. 168.
36. Also translated in English as the more familiar phrase "Lord of Heaven."
37. On evolution of the title "the World Honored One," see Saeki, *The Nestorian Documents and Relics in China*, 231–232. Numerous evidences of the title can be found in Chinese Buddhist texts, for example, the Chinese version of Dīrghāgama Sūtra 長阿含經, translated by Buddhayaśas 佛陀耶舍 and Zhu Fonian 竺佛念 in 413 CE. See Dīrghāgama Sūtra, in *The Taisho Shinshu Daizokyo*, ed. J. Takakusu and K. Watanabe (Tokyo: The Taisho Shinshu Daizokyo Kanko Kai, 1968), 1:1b.
38. Samuel N. C. Lieu, *Manichaeism in the Later Roman Empire and Medieval China: A Historical Survey* (Manchester: Manchester University Press, 1999), 210–219.
39. We have a similar case in the sixteenth century. The Jesuit priest missionary, Matteo Ricci 利瑪竇, did not hesitate to call himself a "Western monk" (西僧) and don a Buddhist monk's robe when he first came to China, following the example of his predecessor and superior, Michele Ruggieri 羅明堅.
40. Deeg, "Creating Religious Terminology," 105.
41. This is Saeki and Moule's rendering. See Saeki, *The Nestorian Documents and Relics in China*, 58; Moule, *Christians in China before the Year 1550*, 39. Nicolini-Zani has the same translation in Italian, "*un monastero di Da Qin*". See Nicolini-Zani, *La Via Radiosa per l'Oriente*, 199.
42. Also see Duan Qing, "A New Perspective for the *Daqin* Temple and the *Jingjiao* Priests," 434–472; and Deeg, "Ways to Go and Not to Go in the Contextualisation of the *Jingjiao* Documents of the Tang Period," 142.
43. See Saeki, *The Nestorian Documents and Relics in China*, 143.
44. This is A. C. Moule's English translation. See Moule, *Christians in China before the Year 1550*, 55. Saeki's translation is similar, "Whose (the Holy Spirit) Purity is absolutely embodiment of Law beyond all thought!" See Saeki, *The Nestorian Documents and Relics in China*,

268. Nicolini-Zani's Italian translation has "*la cui dottrina, limpida e profonda, sorpassa ogni intendimento.*" See Nicolini-Zani, *La Via Radiosa per l'Oriente*, 218.

45. Akira Hirakawa, *A Buddhist Chinese-Sanskrit Dictionary* (Tokyo: The Reiyukai, 1997), 85. For an example of *fa'er* 法爾, see Divākara's 地婆訶羅 Chinese translation of the Lalitavistara Sūtra 方廣大莊嚴經 in 683 CE, collected in J. Takakusu and K. Watanabe, eds., *The Taisho Shinshu Daizokyo*, 3:553b.

46. We need to be reminded that two of the Greek words for "hell," "*hades*," and "*tartaros*," are also of pagan origin. Some modern English translations now transliterate rather than translate them. The Greek word "*Gehenna*" is itself a transliteration of the Hebrew expression (Matt 5:22, 29–30, 10:28, 18:9, 23:15), referring to the valley of Hinnom (in Jerusalem), where children were sacrificed to the pagan gods during the period of Ahaz and Manasseh. This practice is condemned by the prophets (see Jer 7:31–32, 19:2–6, 11–14, 32:35; 2 Kings 23:10). This word is used in the NT (James 3:6; Luke 12:5; Mark 9:43, 47) as a theological metaphor meaning "eternal burning place of curse" and, thus, "hell."

47. See for example in Dīrghāgama Sūtra, in Takakusu and Watanabe, eds., *The Taisho Shinshu Daizokyo*, 1:3a.

Primary Sources

The following is a list of extant original manuscripts and inscriptions of the Jingjiao documents:

Daqin jingjiao liuxing zhongguo bei, Forest of Steles Museum, 781. Henri Havret edited. *La stèle chrétienne de Si-Ngan-fou: Fac-similé de l'inscription syro-chinoise*. Edited by Henri Havret. Variétés sinologiques No. 7. Chang-hai [Shanghai]: Imprimerie de la Mission catholique, 1895.

Daqin Jingjiao sanwei mengdu zan., "Bibliothèque nationale de France, Manuscrit Pelliot chinois 3847, ca. 781 CE." Michel Soymié edited. In *Catalogue des manuscrits chinois de Touen-Houang. Fonds Pelliot chinois de la Bibliothèque nationale*. Edited by Michel Soymié., Volume IV (n° 3501–4000). Paris: Publications hors série de l'École française d'Extrême-Orient, 1991. Pp. 332–33. a. Eloge de la Ste. Trinite, ff. 2 and 3. Pp. 332–333.

Xuanyuan [zhi]ben jing., "Li Shengduo Old Collection, ca. 781 CE." Takeda Kagaku Shinkō Zaidan Kyōu Shooku edited. Pp. 396–97 in In *Tonkō hikyū: Kyōu Shooku zō*. Edited by Takeda Kagaku Shinkō Zaidan Kyōu Shooku. *Eihensatsu* 5. Ōsaka: Takeda Kagaku Shinkō Zaidan, 2011. Haneda Tooru No. 431. [(Not to be confused with Kojima B, a forgery of the same name.] Pp. 396–397.

Xuanyuan zhiben jing dhāraṇī pillar, Luoyang Museum, 814 CE. Ge Chengyong 葛承雍 edited. In *Jingjiao yi zhen: Luoyang xin chu tangdai jingjiao jingchuang yanjiu* [in Chinese] 景教遺珍：洛陽新出唐代景教經幢研究 (*Precious Nestorian Relic: Studies on the Nestorian Stone Pillar of the Tang Dynasty Recently Discovered in Luoyang*). Edited by Ge Chengyong 葛承雍. Beijing: Cultural Relics Press, 2009.

Xuting mishisuo jing., "Takakusu Junjiro Old Collection, ca. 650 CE." Takeda Kagaku Shinkō Zaidan Kyōu Shooku edited. Pp. 83–7 in In *Tonkō hikyū: Kyōu Shooku zō. Eihensatsu* 6. Edited by Takeda Kagaku Shinkō Zaidan Kyōu Shooku. Ōsaka: Takeda Kagaku Shinkō Zaidan, 2012. Haneda Tooru No. 459. Pp. 83–87.

Yi shen lun., "Tomioka Kenzo Old Collection, 642 CE." Takeda Kagaku Shinkō Zaidan Kyōu Shooku edited. Pp. 88–96 in In *Tonkō hikyū: Kyōu Shooku zō. Eihensatsu* 6. Edited by Takeda Kagaku Shinkō Zaidan Kyōu Shooku. Ōsaka: Takeda Kagaku Shinkō Zaidan, 2012. Haneda Tooru No. 460. Pp. 88–96.

Zhixuan anle jing., "Li Shengduo Old Collection, ca. 781 CE." Takeda Kagaku Shinkō Zaidan Kyōu Shooku edited. Pp. 128–32 in In *Tonkō hikyū: Kyōu Shooku zō.* Edited by Takeda Kagaku Shinkō Zaidan Kyōu Shooku. *Eihensatsu* 1. Ōsaka: Takeda Kagaku Shinkō Zaidan, 2009. Haneda Tooru No. 13. Pp. 128–132.

Zun jing, "Bibliothèque nationale de France, Manuscrit Pelliot chinois 3847, ca. 781 CE." Michel Soymié edited. In *Catalogue des manuscrits chinois de Touen-Houang. Fonds Pelliot chinois de la Bibliothèque nationale.* Edited by Michel Soymié., Volume IV (n° 3501–4000). Paris: Publications hors série de l'École française d'Extrême-Orient, 1991. Pp. 332–33. b. Tsouen King, ff. 4 and 5. Pp. 332–333.

Bible versions:

Chinese Union Version (CUV). Nanjing: Amity Printing Co., Ltd, 2000.

Studium Biblicum Version (SBV). Nanjing: Amity Printing Co., Ltd, 2006.

CHAPTER 15

CONFUCIAN CLASSICS AND THE BIBLE

PAULOS HUANG AND K. K. YEO

INTRODUCTION

BOTH the Bible and Confucian classics are texts of *world* civilizations; each not only describes what the world is but also prescribes for followers what the world should be. "Classics," as normative texts that contain eternal principles of cosmic order and transcend historical circumstances of textual traditions, often are claimed by religious communities to be "sacred" and "revelatory" and thus "authoritative." Here lies the crux of the debate in the reading of Confucian classics and the Bible's "Holy Canon" in church history in China. Some Confucian scholars recently have questioned the validity of classifying the Chinese Bible as "Holy" and "canon." The essay gives a brief survey of the encounter between the Confucian and Christian canons, then discusses the issues that arose when the Bible was translated as *Shengjing* (the Holy Canon). The essay ends by reviewing a Christian-Chinese intertextual reading of the Bible and the *Analects* (by K. K. Yeo) and "Sino-Christian academic biblical studies" (by Paulos Huang).

HISTORICAL SURVEY OF VARIOUS ENCOUNTERS BETWEEN THE TWO CANONS

The encounters between the Bible and Confucian classics in China are rather complex and are surveyed selectively here simply to raise the critical issues of the need for such engagements. With the decline of Buddhism in the Northern Song dynasty (960–1125),

Neo-Confucian orthodoxy of the Ming dynasty (1368–1643) redefined sinocentrism, which presented both a challenge and an opportunity for Jesuit missionaries. Matteo Ricci (1552–1610) used the principle of accommodation as he reached out to the Confucian intelligentsia. He aligned with classical Confucianism, preferring Five Classics (*Classic of Poetry*, *Book of Documents*, *Book of Rites*, *Book of Changes*, *Spring and Autumn Annals*) over Four Books (*Great Learning*, *Doctrine of Mean*, *Analects*, *Mencius*), though both are in the Confucian canon. Based on his assumption about the early Confucian theistic belief in *Tian* (Heaven) and *Shangdi* (Lord on High), Ricci interpreted biblical theology and spirituality, although in the moral-religious language of classical Confucianism.[1] Xu Guangqi 徐光啟 and Yang Tingyun 楊廷筠 became Catholic, despite being also Neo-Confucians; they did not assimilate the philosophy and semantic of Confucian scholars such as Zhu Xi 朱熹 (1130–1200) and Wang Yangming 王陽明 (1472–1529). Rather, they regarded biblical anthropology and sanctification as different from Neo-Confucian understandings of self and society, knowledge (*zhi*) and action (*xing*), mind-heart (*xing*), and cosmic principle (*li*).

Besides other non-Christian views that were critical of Christianity, not all Jesuits agreed with Ricci and his followers. Some of his colleagues and his successor, Niccolo Longobardo (1559–1654), opposed him; for example, in the Rites Controversy (1644–1721), they saw the ancestral reverence and worship of *Tian* (heaven) as idolatrous, that is, going against the biblical worship of God.[2]

The Qing dynasty (1644–1911) government was concerned about maneuvering its foreign policy and power equation with foreign imperialism, opium wars, and unequal treaties. For example, much of the confused and split understanding of Chinese personhood as, say, the social against the spiritual, is evident in a bizarre apocalyptic vision of Hong Xiuquan 洪秀全 (1813–1864), the leader of the Taiping Rebellion (1850–1864), in his proclaiming himself as "God's Chinese Son,"[3] the Chinese messiah. Many Chinese Bible versions were rendered in this period, and Bible translators in China used Confucian semantics to translate biblical ethics (*ren-ai* 仁愛, *sheng-jie* 聖潔) and used Buddhist semantic to translate biblical religious concepts (*ti-yu* 地獄, *yin-jian* 陰間). Yet, Hong's "Confucianized doctrine of a Christian God" in the semantic of *Shangdi* (God), *fu* (father), *zi* (son),[4] altered the theological ethics of both Confucian and biblical texts.

From the period of the Republic of China to the recent past, the encounter between Confucian classics and the Bible must be seen in the context of socio-political turmoil and self-determination of national Chinese, as well as the critical issue of "national salvation" (saving China against foreign forces). This encounter is evident in the revolutionary ideology of Sun Yat-sen (1866–1925), who holds to The Three People's Principles (nationalism, democracy, and the people's livelihood) with some biblical values.[5] One also can see hermeneutically the rise of Neo-Confucianism and, in particular, the Cultural Nationalist Confucians from 1920 to 1980 (such as Liang Shuming 梁漱溟, Feng Youlan 馮友蘭, Xiong Shili 熊十力, Tang Junyi 唐君毅, Xu Fuguan 徐復觀, Fang Dongmei 方東美 and Mou Zongsan 牟宗三, Cai Renhou 蔡仁厚), whose reception of European philosophy brings about new issues even to Confucians' understanding of their own classics. But in the nation's polemical context of anti-Confucianism and anti-

Christianity, such as from the May Fourth Movement, some of these Confucians saw Christianity and the Bible as a threat to China and a form of foreign imperialism, though some are sympathetic to biblical values and therefore grant affirmative voices to both Confucianism and Christianity.[6]

On the Chinese church, many Chinese Christians at that time wrestled with the issue of loving socialist China *and* Christianity. The result is the enduring nature of Chinese Christianity dividing into Three-Self Patriotic Churches and the Family Church movement.[7] The consequences of biblical reception of Confucian classics and values in this period are two: (1) on one hand, the works of Wu Leiquan (1870–1944) embraced the national salvation of China, though not so much in identifying with traditional Chinese culture except in Confucian values that have affinity with the "socialist dimensions of Jesus,"[8] while T. C. Chao (Zhao Zizhen, 1888–1979) simply rejected both Confucianist culture and Jesus' teaching as political, eschatological;[9] (2) on the other hand, Watchman Nee (1903–1972) and Wang Mingdao (1900–1988) rejected Confucian values and accepted instead a spiritually focused understanding of the personal regeneration in Christ.[10]

In modern China (after 1980), there have been rigorous engagements between Confucian classics (Four Books and Five Classics) and the Bible, seen in Confucian-Christian research and dialogue by key scholars such as Liu Shuxian 劉述先 (1934–), Yu Yingshi 余英時 (1930–), Julia Ching 秦家懿 (1934–2001), Cheng Zhongying 成中英 (1935–), Tu Weiming 杜維明 (1940–), and Liang Yancheng 梁燕城. Many of these scholars do not abide by the nationalism of previous generations of Confucian scholars; instead they have an academic respect for cultural and religious texts such as Confucian classics, the Bible, philosophies of the East and the West including logic, science, ethics, considering all as valid texts to be examined hermeneutically. For example, these modern Confucians "have enthusiastically adopted the Christian concept of God. This affirmative attitude is not only different from that of the Neo-Confucians, who were against Matteo Ricci in the Ming dynasty, but also different from the attitude of the Cultural Nationalist Confucians."[11]

Confucian classics and the Bible are not the property of China and the West respectively. Thus, a healthy global understanding of shared knowledge and universal ownership of canons has moved the academic studies of Confucianist classics and the Bible to a promising path, contributing toward world civilizations. Here, the scholars of the Chinese Cultural Institute school (*Zhongguo wenhua shyuan pai*), the Boston Confucians,[12] and the cross-disciplinary textual, religious, and philosophical readings of canons in a global context, become significant.

Confucian Classics and Christian Canon

As of 2019, the Chinese Union Version of the Bible (*heheben* 和合本) had existed for one hundred years. However, more and more people in China today dismiss the Bible, emphasizing the importance of reading the Confucian classics. Based on such a background, this section aims to explore how Chinese Christians (missionaries and Chinese) treat Confucian classics and the way they translate and read the Bible in light of the Confucian language/classics and vice versa. In order to do so, it is necessary to explore several issues below.

First, an important issue for Chinese Christians, including missionaries, related to how they treat Confucian classics and related to how Confucians treat the Bible, is that the Bible has been interpreted as the Holy Canon, and Confucian classics have been considered as humanistic canons. In general, there are two criteria for a *jingdian* 經典 (classic) to be treated as a *jing* 經 (canon). The first one is divine authority from God; for example, Christians believe that the Bible is the divine revelation of God in human languages. Thus, the Bible has been believed to be a canon/*jing*. Second, a humanistic authority also can make a classic into a canon; for example, there are two important requirements for Confucian classics to be treated as canons: (1) their royal political influence; and (2) confirmation that these texts written by human beings have reflected, indicated, or represented the Heavenly Way, i.e., the Truth. This is to say, Confucian classics have received their authority and wisdom from human beings, whether they are the reflections of royal rulers or of humanistic scholars.

For Christians (including Chinese and foreign missionaries), Confucian classics do not have the same authority as the Bible, since the divine authority for the Bible as a divine revelation is absolute, eternal, and unchangeable; thus, the Bible has been translated as *Shengjing* 聖經, i.e., the Holy Canon. But to Christians, the humanistic authorities who make Confucian classics as *jing* (canon) are relative, temporal, and changeable. Therefore, although both the Bible and Confucian classics are called *jing*, i.e., canons, they are perceived differently in terms of their authority by different groups of people. Christians consider the Bible to be "the Holy Canon" and Confucian classics to be "canons" only.

For Confucians, the different views of Christians on *jing* is problematic, although in the beginning, when the Bible was translated into Chinese, this was not a significant issue emphasized by Confucians at the end of Ming dynasty and in the Qing dynasty. The Bible has been called *Xinjiueyue quanshu* 新舊約全書 (The Whole Books of New and Old Testaments), *Shengshu* 聖書 (The Holy Books or the Sage Books), *Shengjing* (The Holy Canon), etc. In the recent past, since Chinese nationalism has been revived, some Confucian scholars opposed to Christians calling the Bible *Shengjing* (the Holy Canon). For example, Confucian scholar Lin Anwu 林安梧, from Taiwan and now working in Shandong University, P.R. China, suggests translating the Bible as *Jijing* 基經 (The Canon of Christianity) or *Yejing* 耶經 (The Canon of Jesus or the Canon of Jesus Followers). In his view, "Holy" is too exclusive; only Confucian classics can be called "Holy," and the Christian canon should not be called "Holy"; yet no Confucians have ever called their canons "holy."[13]

This raises the issue of how to interpret the term "*sheng* 聖". Should it be understood as absolutely holy or relatively holy? Many people in the Confucian tradition can be called *shengren* 聖人 (holy men or sages), Confucius is the Top Holy Man, and Mencius is the Secondary Holy Man, etc. In these examples, *sheng* is absolute. But Confucians usually believe that, by self-cultivation of humanistic attempts, human beings can be united with heaven (*tianren heyi* 天人合一)[14] so as to become purely holy. In such a case, *sheng* is potentially achieved by human beings. Such a disputation hints at the difference of authority in the Bible and Confucian classics. It would be helpful for Christians and Confucians to explore this concept more deeply, if a further dialogue is to take place.

Secondly, another important issue for Christians' view of Confucian classics and for Confucians' understanding of the Bible is the question of what kind of authority can raise a *jingdian* (classic) into a *jing* (canon) in the Chinese context. Humanistic texts in China are called "*jingdian*" mostly rather than "*jing*," since not only is there doubt about whether they have divine authority but also there is a challenge as to whether their humanistic authorities are reliable or not. For example, Christians call Confucian classics "*jingdian*" or humanistic relative canon (with relative authority), and Confucians also call the Bible "*jingdian*." When they call each other's canons (the Bible or Confucian classics) "*jing*," they accept them having only relative rather than absolute authority.

Since the end of the Qing dynasty in the beginning of the 1900s, as a result of rationalism, Confucianism has lost its dominant role in China. Thus, Confucian classics have lost their status of being canons and have become humanistic classics. Thus, Confucian classics became *jingdian* (classics) rather than *jing* (canons). Over one hundred years in China, there are few Confucian believers to consider Confucian classics as canons, and *ru* 儒 (Confucians) as a class also have disappeared completely; thus, Confucian classics are considered the object of scientific studies rather than the canons of people's belief. The Bible also has been criticized by those who use the sciences in China to oppose religion, but because Christians have been in China before modern sciences were introduced to China, the Bible has never lost its status of canon, at least for Christians.

Thirdly, because Confucians understand canon in light of humanistic criteria, they treat the Bible also as a humanistic classic rather than as a divinely revealed canon. As far as the tradition of "Western studies" (西學)[15] in China is concerned, theological or religious Scriptures usually also are referred to as "canons," which are primarily the Jewish Bible, the Christian Bible (including the Old and the New Testaments), and the Islamic Qur'an. They are regarded by respective believers as holy and divine and as holding absolute authority.

The Chinese translations of the Bible were most likely started as early as in the seventh century when Nestorianism entered the Tang dynasty of China through Syria, but few manuscripts of biblical translations remain today. In addition to some partial manuscripts of Roman Catholic translations, the earliest Chinese version of the entire Bible was done by British Baptist missionary John Marshman in 1822, and it was called *Xin Jiu yue quanshu* 新舊約全書 (The Whole Book of the Old and New Testaments). In 1919, a *Guanhua hehe yiben* 官話和合譯本 (Chinese Union Version/Mandarin Union Version) was published as the result of an ecumenical cooperation, and this version was becoming so popular in the Chinese church that it took until 1983 and 2010 to have revisions done to this version. Other Chinese translated versions also were done among Roman Catholic, Orthodox, and Protestant churches in China. Almost all of them have translated the Bible with the Chinese term "Shengjing," i.e., the Holy Canon.

Many Confucians, however, have difficulty accepting the Bible as the divinely revealed word of God, but consider it as a humanistic reflection about God. This Confucian view of the biblical canon has an interesting historical reality in that the Confucian classics lost their canonical status between 1905 and 1912. In August 1905, the Queen Cixi and the Emperor Guangxu approved the appeal of ministers represented by Yuan Shikuai and others to abolish the imperial civil examination system from 1906 onwards and to start a new modern education and examination system of mathematics, physics, chemistry, history, geography, zoology, foreign languages, etc. On January 19, 1912, the Education Minister of the Republic of the China at the time, Cai Yuanpei 蔡元培, issued *Putong jiaoyu zanshi banfa* 普通教育暫行辦法 (*The Temporary Methods of General Education*), according to which Confucian canons would not be studied as canons any longer in primary, middle, and high schools.[16] Before Confucian classics lost their status as canons, however, the Bible was accepted to a certain extent *by Confucians* as a canon.[17] Since these Confucians understood the concept of "canon" as a classic that reflects the Way of Heaven, i.e., the Bible was essentially similar to Confucian classics.

Yet, Confucian classics at that time received their authority mainly because of political rulers' power and cultural nationalism. The Bible then also was rejected by many Confucians because of their assumption of the Bible's foreign origin. After 1912, since Confucian classics lost their status as canons, the idea of considering any text a canon was unfamiliar in China, because of the Chinese bias toward science and nationalism. Thus, neither Confucian classics nor the Bible were accepted by many Chinese then as a canon that reflects Truth, and only scientific works could gain such status. The distinction between nationalism and theology in Europe has been largely ignored in Chinese academia.[18] As far as social, political, and cultural authorities are concerned, the Bible is also dismissed by most Chinese for political reasons.

In summary, when Christians translated the Bible into Chinese, they called it "*Shengjing*" (Holy Canon) rather than "*jingdian*" (classic). In the Chinese context, what constitutes a *jing* (canon)? What kind of relationship does it have with the classics, Scriptures and religious canons? If we define the criterion as the question of "whether it holds authority," we may divide works into divine canons/Scriptures (which hold absolute authority) and humanistic classics (which do not hold absolute authority). However, the Confucian tradition has never explained how the Confucian text has fulfilled the aforementioned criteria, especially how its text is classified as divine revelations. Christians think that the Bible is different from Confucian classics in that the Bible contains absolute truth, although both of them have been called "*jing*" (canon).

Jing (Canons) and *Jingxue* (the Studies of the Canons)

The complex relationship between the Bible and *Jing* (Canon) has dominated academic discussion in the contrast between Confucian and the "Western studies." A number of issues can illuminate this relationship.

Firstly, it is important to note the relationship between Western canons (i.e., *jing*) in light of Confucian studies. In Confucian studies, *jing* (canon) has not gained its authority from divine and absolute truth, but from humanistic imperial power, ethical morality, sages' reflection, and so on. Therefore, in light of Confucian studies, the foreign *jing* (canon) can be understood in two senses:

(1) On the one hand, most Confucian scholars do not accept the metaphysical, absolute, and eternal authorities of the Western religious/theological *jing* (canon), i.e., that of the Bible—since traditional Confucians do not recognize the Bible as the divine revelation. Even though there also have been similar "divine revelations" in China—for example, *chenwei* 讖緯,[19] *Hetu Luoshu* (the photos from the Yellow River and the books from the Luo River), the legend of Cang Jie 倉頡 creating Chinese characters, and the worship of Heavenly God in the pre-Qin period—they have not been accepted facts by Confucians.

(2) On the other hand, the relative, temporary, and humanistic authorities of the Western *jingdian* (humanistic classics) are accepted by most Confucian scholars. Thus, most Confucians do not see the Bible as holding absolute, divine, and eternal authority, but consider it as having only relative philosophical, literal, historical, cultural authority. In recent years, some radical nationalist Confucian scholars rejected the Chinese translation of Christmas as *shengdanjie* 聖誕節 (The Holy Birthday) but tried to translate it as *Yedanjie* 耶誕節 (the birthday of Jesus); they rejected a translation of the Bible as *Shengjing* (The Holy Canon) but insisted on translating it as *Jijing* (the canon of Christianity).[20] Professor Lin Anwu called *Lunyu* (*Analects*) "Holy Canon," and he defines it as the classic of a sage.[21]

Secondly, it is important to reflect on the Bible and the Confucian *jing* (canons). There are two sides of the same coin regarding the authors of the Bible. On the one hand, the writers of the Bible were prophets and apostles who were human beings from common people to kings. On the other hand, Christian readers see the above-mentioned people not as the ultimate authors of the Bible, since they were the instruments and servants of God, and God has revealed his message and inspiration to them. Although there are different interpretations about the concept of "inspiration" in China,[22] it is generally believed by the Christian community that the real author of the Bible is God. However, Confucian and Christian scholars alike accept that the authors of Confucian classics were human; even though they were sages and great people, they were human beings. Thus, one can conclude that the authors of Confucian classics were finite human beings rather than the infinite God, Heaven or Truth itself, and Chinese Christians believe the author of the Bible is God, who reveals the Truth to the biblical authors.

According to traditional Christianity, the Bible is the word of God rather than the word of human beings. Yet, in Chinese Christianity, there are also two other broad interpretations. According to liberal theology, the Bible is not the word of God; it is words about God. Since the eighteenth century, historical and form critical schools of biblical studies have held such an opinion. Since Julius Wellhausen (1844–1918) contributed to the composition history of the Pentateuch/Torah, he was credited as one of the originators of the Documentary Hypothesis. Then appeared various schools of biblical studies, such as source criticism, redaction criticism, and form criticism. These kinds of schools were introduced into China and influenced some Chinese theologians. For example, Zhao Zichen 趙紫宸 had written a book, *Yesu zhuan* 耶穌傳 (*A Biography of Jesus*), with a similar liberal theological orientation, and he accepted Jesus only as a great human hero rather than as the divine Son of God, and he accepted the Bible also only as words about God rather than the word of God. Another opinion is that the Bible is a discourse between God and human beings; for example, Archie Lee, a famous Hebrew scholar in Chinese academia, whose opinion lies somewhere between the traditional and liberal interpretations of the Bible.[23]

When Christians and Confucians encounter each other, when the Bible is interpreted in the Chinese context or Confucian classics are interpreted in the Christian context, these questions become important; they are even more important in considering how such readings are done.

An Intertextual Reading of the Analects and the Bible

Despite different cultural contexts and hermeneutical traditions between Christian and Chinese canons, K. K. Yeo and Shi Heng-han nevertheless each have attempted to read the *Analects* [*The Sayings of Confucius*] and the Bible in parallel.[24] First Shi Heng-han's *The Analects of Confucius Meets the Bible* is a dialogue between Christianity and Confucianism, which consists of sixteen topics, including twenty-four sub-topics. It is an interpretation of the *Analects of Confucius* from the perspective of the Bible. Secondly, Shi Heng-han's *The Comparative Reading of Chinese and Western Scriptures* studies the *Analects of Confucius* by comparing those chapters in it with the corresponding ones in the Bible that address similar issues and concepts. In addition, in his study, the author refers to annotations and findings of those missionary and Christian researchers who have studied *the Analects of Confucius* since the Ming and Qing dynasties.

Yeo's intertextual reading is summarized to show his *Christian-Chinese* reading.[25] Once the issue of the Bible as "*Shengjing*" is assumed, Yeo aims to convey the good tidings (gospel) to the Confucian Chinese world and do so in the spirit of friendship and humility, taking a cue from the first two sentences of the *Analects*: "Is it not a delight, having learned something and then practice it? Is it not a joy to welcome friends coming from afar?" (1:1).[26] Learning about "classics," "canons," or "texts" by definition is to *be woven* together to promote a more meaningful life. Both Confucian and Christian traditions are committed to learning and faith (*xin*, *pistis*), because of their shared belief in the messianic mission and betterment of the world. "The Master [Confucius] said: 'What the gentleman seeks is the Way and not food. If he farms, hunger lies therein; if he learns, an official's salary lies therein. [But] what the gentleman worries about is the Way and not poverty.' " (*Analects* 15:32)[27] Similarly, Jesus and the Apostle Paul see themselves as instruments of God for serving *and saving* the world: "through Christ we have received grace and *apostleship* to bring about the *obedience of faith* among all the nations" (Rom 1:5).

Despite the etiological differences between the "naturalistic cosmos" of Confucius and the "created universe" of the Bible,[28] Yeo proposes that both the Bible and the *Analects* texts share the same view of differentiation toward harmony and mutual edification. Both texts accept the existence of the cosmic principle, be they ethical or theological respectively—which together (i.e., theological ethic) give Chinese Christians a holistic analysis of the common issues related to historical process, societal problems, and the brokenness of humanity. Thus, living their belief regarding the mission of God for Chinese Christians means dealing with the embedded issues of life from the bottom up, using both the ethical and theological resources from both canons. This cross-cultural biblical interpretation is consistent with beliefs about God's way of creating the world (Genesis 1) by means of differentiation, so that by differentiating light from darkness, day and night come into harmonious existence. Likewise, the *Analects* say that "the ideal person aims at harmony yet also differences" (13:23; 和而不同). Many Jesuit missionaries to China, such as Matteo Ricci, have testified to this gift of friendship that made them first learn about the Chinese classics and languages before translating the Bible. Many of the Chinese rituals (rites, propriety, 禮), such as ancestral reverence, speak to the cultural expression *of the spiritual quest* of many Confucian Chinese—they in turn, could teach missionaries how to offer priestly and pastoral gifts (considered more important than Western science!) of translating the gospel of Jesus Christ to their Chinese friends.[29]

The Chinese Bible translates the rites of baptism and Eucharist, calling them *holy sacraments* (*sheng li* 聖禮). Biblical sacraments are considered a symbolic yet real way to express a communal life of self-sacrificing love, that Christians are united with Christ, enacting a creation of new community in Christ in which communion (*koinōnia*) and mutual service (*diakonia*). Without losing the biblical narrative of sacraments, the *Analects'* teaching of ritual propriety (*li* 禮), of aesthetic delight (*yue* 樂), and of effortless action (*wuwei* 無為) highlights not the behaviors themselves, such as bowing, but *one's heart* in expressing gratitude, respect, and empathy. The *Analects* mentions that simply taking care of parents out of a sense of duty is similar to animal-keepers "feeding their cattle" (Analects 2:7)! This teaching of the *Analects* echoes the biblical teaching of thanksgiving found in the Bible to honor parents (Exod 20:12; Deut 5:16; Prov 20:20; Matt 15:4; Col 3:20; Eph 6:1–3; 1 Tim 5:8). An intertextual reading of both canons by a Chinese Christian points to the belief that liturgy or religious rite has the power to bring about reconciliation via cruciform love in a broken world. Chinese Christians find the divine power as they live out the experience of grace sacramentally, as they believe the fruit of grace is love in the aesthetic stylized life.

Yeo's intertextual reading of the *Analects* and the Bible seeks to hold in tension the different questions asked by the two canons. One example is the Christian notion of sin as the falling off or falling apart of the relationship between God and humanity that could be seen as the whole of life, while the Confucian understanding of sin as social-moral collapse is only part of the whole. Another example: The Bible may ask, "How is one to be holy?"; the *Analects* ask, "How is one to be human?" The Bible answers: "to be holy/perfect as your heavenly Father is" (Matt 5:48) is to know the acceptance (blessedness) of a forgiving God. Yet, the *Analects*' ethical answers of being benevolent (*ren* 仁), respectful (*jing* 敬), and trustworthy (*xin* 信), also responds to a questing faith, suggesting a Confucian-Christian compound of *being holy and human*. The relationship between Confucian *ren* (love as humanness) and Christian *agapē* (self-sacrificial love) is compounded in the Chinese Bible, which translates the Greek word "*agapē*" as "*ren ai*." *Analects* 4:4 writes, "The Master said, 'If a person were to set his heart on *ren* (benevolence, love, or humanness), he would be free from evil.'" This Confucian understanding of "love" finds its twin or fulfillment in Paul's words: "Bear one another's burdens (concrete expression of love), and so fulfill the law of Christ" (Gal 6:2), and in Rom 13:8, "Leave no debt outstanding, except the debt to love one another."

The classical paradigm of cross-textual readings as inclusivism, exclusivism, pluralism, or relativism can be inflexible and restrictive. Using H. Richard Niebuhr's classical categories of "Christ and culture"[30] as paradigms to view the relationship between the Bible and Confucian classics. While "Christ is against culture" in certain aspects of the encounter, this is not normative. More often than not, it is "Christ above culture," "Christ and culture in paradox," and "Christ the transformer of culture." For example, Yeo's work demonstrates a hybridized Christian-Confucian hermeneutic in the matter of God and *tian* (Heaven). It also shows that in the matter of an ethic based on the Spirit and an ethic based on self-cultivation, the two need to co-exist in tension. Yeo also shows how Confucian ethics on ritual (*li*) and music (*yue*) can clarify a Christian theology that does not spell out their significance in the highest order, and he demonstrates how the Christian understanding of cruciform love can fulfill the Confucian ideal of benevolence (*ren*) while also learning from it, especially its social dimension. The relationship between human nature and grace (for Christians) and the relationship between human nature and goodness (Confucius) are different, yet, both command the love of neighbor/others. Though the *Analects* and the Bible have different understandings of human nature, Yeo illustrates that both speak of freedom—though the former speaks of moral freedom and the later, spiritual one—and a combined voice of both will move followers of both traditions to serving the world. Finally, Yeo points out that it is their commitments to the receptivity of God's faithfulness and *tian*'s endowment that encourage Christian Chinese to live a life of righteousness, order, and beauty (Matt 5:20; Rom 2:5–13).[31]

Sino-Christian Academic Biblical Studies

The ways to read both Confucian classics and the Bible beg the methodical question about Chinese biblical study. Paulos Huang has worked diligently in major universities in China, and he provides a roadmap in his cutting-edge scholarship on "Sino-Christian academic biblical studies."[32] Huang wants to avoid both Confucian-centrism or Han-centrism and the biased Enlightenment presuppositions. Instead, he proposes "the *globalized* great *national* studies" as the context to read any canonical texts in China, especially the Chinese Bible. That is, Sino-Christian *academic* biblical studies could be done in a *global* dialogue and effort.[33]

Huang's book proposes a rather complex yet systematic approach to Sino-Christian academic biblical studies. He affirms the sacredness of the Bible canon; thus, the absolute authority of this *shengjing* (sacred text). For him, the Age of Reason has erroneously constructed a binary system of sacredness and secular; thus, it has risked doubting or even replacing holiness with secularism. The "globalized great national studies" of China will treat the Bible as a historical text, a literature, and "a holy canon" acknowledged by its believers in its multi-disciplinary studies. Later, in the same work, Huang combines the best of Chinese *jingxue* (studies of canon) and proposes *shengjing kaoshixue* 聖經考釋學 to read the Bible, thus focusing on textual exegesis (*kaoshi* 考釋) and commentary (*shiyi* 釋義). Finally, Huang pays attention to using literary methods to read *jing*/canon, thus doing a biblical hermeneutic in reading both Confucian and the Bible canons in dialogue (or intertextually). In Huang's book, he states that the contemporary context of reviving Confucian classics in mainland China has been taken as an especially important background for biblical studies.[34]

Conclusion

The key to understanding these two traditions and their studies of canons lies in the authority of the texts that elevates a classic into a canon. In other words, where does the authority come from? The answer determines whether the authority of a canon is metaphysically absolute, eternal, and unchangeable. If not, is it physically relative, temporal, and changeable instead? This is an essential issue for emphasizing the importance of reading Confucian canons today and for promoting Confucianism outside China, as significant as reading the Bible in China is meaningful for both people in China and also in other parts of the world.

Notes

1. Matteo Ricci, *The True Meaning of the Lord of Heaven (T'ien-chu Shih-i)* [A Chinese English Edition], tr. Douglas Lancashire and Peter Hu Kuo-chen, ed. Edward J. Malatesta (Taipei, Paris: Institut Ricci, 1985). For more scholars, sources, and literature that belong to the similar assimilation approach as Ricci, see Paulos Huang, *Confronting Confucian Understandings of the Christian Doctrine of Salvation: A Systemic Theological Analysis of the Basic Problems in the Confucian-Christian Dialogue* (Leiden: Brill, 2009), 9–10; John D. Young, *Confucianism and Christianity: The First Encounter* (Hong Kong: Hong Kong University Press, 1983), 27–38; K. K. Yeo, "Paul's Ethic of Holiness and Chinese

Morality of *Renren*," in Charles Cosgrove et al., *Cross-Cultural Paul: Journeys to Others, Journeys to Ourselves* (Grand Rapids: Eerdmans, 2005), 104–140.

2. See sources and scholars that are critical or even anti-Christian in their approach, see Huang, *Confronting Confucian Understandings*, 9–11.
3. Jonathan D. Spence, *God's Chinese Son: The Taiping Heavenly Kingdom of Hong Xiuquan* (New York: W. W. Norton & Company, 1996).
4. See Carl S. Kilcourse, *Taiping Theology: The Localization of Christianity in China, 1843–64* (New York: Palgrave Macmillan, 2016), 107–131.
5. For Sun Yat-sen the idea of a righteous nation and the democratic politics and socialism could work together, thus his effort to harmonize his Three Principles with Marxism. See W. Bauer, *China and the Search for Happiness* (New York: Seabury Press, 1976), 348; K. K. Yeo, *Chairman Mao Meets the Apostle Paul* (Grand Rapids: Brazos, 2002), 58–84 on Confucian views of history.
6. On Neo-Confucian sources and scholars and the Cultural Nationalist Confucians, see Huang, *Confronting Confucian Understandings*, 11–13, 55–58.
7. K. K. Yeo, *What Has Jerusalem to Do with Beijing? Biblical Interpretation from a Chinese Perspective* (Eugene, OR: Pickwick, 2018), 221–241.
8. Wu Laiquan, *Christianity and Chinese Culture* [in Chinese] (Shanghai: Youth Association, 1936), 71–72, 90–92.
9. Zhao Zichen, *Yesu zhuan* [in Chinese] *Biography of Jesus* (Shanghai: Qingnian shuju, 1935), 6–8, 674–675. Zhao rejected Confucian teaching about self-perfection as well as the liberal theology that sees Christ as the moral example in atonement theory.
10. Watchman Nee, *The Spiritual Man* (Anaheim: Living Stream Ministry, 1998).
11. Huang, *Confronting Confucian Understandings*, 62.
12. See Robert Cummings Nevill, *Boston Confucianism: Portable Tradition in the Late-Modern World* (New York: SUNY, 2000). Concerning the primary sources and literatures on the encounter between Christian Bible and Confucian classics, Paulos Huang has made a detailed study in his *Confronting Confucian*, "1.4 Previous research," 19–29; "2.3 The Confucians who have mostly commented in the Christian doctrine of salvation," 51–68.
13. Paulos Huang, "Canons and the Studies of Canons in Chinese Context" [in Chinese] 漢語語境裡的 "經" 與 "經學", *Guandong Journal* 2 (2019), 5–21.
14. Paulos Huang, "Does Tianrenheyi Belong to Only China—An Analysis in the Light of Western Studies" [in Chinese] '天人合一'乃國學所獨有的嗎? —西學視野中的分析, in *China Forum Jilin University* 3 (2018): 313–325; Paulos Huang "Rediscussion on the Question Whether Tianrenheyi Belongs to only China: And a Dialogue with Professor Lin Anwu" [in Chinese] 再論天人合一是否為儒家所獨有:兼與林安梧教授對話, *Journal of Hunan University* 33 (January 2019): 24–31.
15. This essay uses the word "Western" generically (as East and West) and not ideologically (democracy and colonizing powers).
16. Although some of Confucian texts are still studied in schools, they are considered only as common classics rather than canons with authority. See Li Tiangang 李天綱, "Year 1905—The Vanishing of the Imperial Civil Education System" [in Chinese] 1905年—科舉制的幻滅, http://www.aisixiang.com, http://www.aisixiang.com/data/7177.html [accessed May 1, 2020]; Huang Yusheng 黃裕生, "Please Do Not Let the Return after One Hundred Years as Reviving the Ancient: A Reflection on Return of Confucian Canons into Civil Education" [in Chinese] 莫使百年回歸成復古—關於儒家經典重歸國民教育的思考, *Journal of Qi and Lu* 6 (March 8, 2018): 35–40.

17. For example, the Neo-Confucians (sixteenth–seventeenth centuries) had understood Confucian classics as authoritative canons, and when they encountered the Bible, it was possible for them to accept it as a foreign canon. For example, Xu Guangqi, Yang Tingyun, and Li Zhizao had not only accepted such an interpretation but also had converted to Christianity. Even those Neo-Confucians who did not accept Christianity, for example, Yang Guangxian 楊光先, Lin Qilu 林啟陸, and Shi Feiyin Tongrong 釋費音通容 (1593–1661), considered the Bible as a canon, even though they did not accept it as having the same authority as Confucian classics have; cf. Huang, *Confronting Confucian Understandings*, 51–54.
18. Paulos Huang, "The Western Studies Should Not Be Castrated Anymore in the Cultural Construction" [in Chinese] 文化建設中不能再閹割西學, *International Journal of Sino-Western Studies* 2 (2012): 1–4.
19. *Chenwei* is a divination combined with mystical Confucian beliefs (prevalent during the eastern Han dynasty, 25–220). *Chen* is the text of prophecy, foreboding, and augury by shaman, and sometimes it is combined with certain divine photos and mystic Confucian beliefs. And *Wei* is a kind of text of interpreting Confucian canons from the viewpoint of theology. They are collections from ancient times rather than one sole author's speech or text. Such texts had very close relationships with the official ideology of the East Han dynasty, the authority of East Han Guangwu emperor Liu Xiu (光武帝劉秀) and their ceremony system.
20. Wang Dasan 王达三, "On the Reflection and Suggestion to Change the Holy Birthday, i.e. Christmas into the Name as the Birthday of Jesus" [in Chinese, 2018] 關於把 '聖誕節' 正名為 '耶誕節' 的思考和建議; Lin Anwu 林安梧, "Christmas Should Be Called 'the Birthday of Jesus,' Confucian Religion is a Religion of Enlightenment" [in Chinese] '聖誕節' 應該叫 '耶誕節', 儒教是覺性的宗教, https://www.rujiazg.com/article/15532; Lin Anwu, Yan Binggang 颜炳罡, Xie Wenyu 謝文郁, "Holy Birthday? Jesus' Birthday?—A Brilliant Dialogue between Confucian and Christian Scholars" [in Chinese] '聖誕'? '耶誕'? 一儒家學者與基督教學者的精彩對話, https://mp.weixin.qq.com/s? [all accessed June 3, 2019].
21. For example, professor Lin Anwu, a student of Mou Zongsan, has given around twenty lectures with the title "A Translation and Interpretation of the Analects as the Holy Canon" [in Chinese] 論語聖經譯解, in the Center for Yi and Chinese Ancient Philosophies, Shandong University. Lin says: "*Ti wei Lunyu shengjing yijie, tebie biaoju qi wei Shengjing, ci shengren zhi jingdian ye*" 題為論語聖經譯解，特別標其題為 '聖經', 此聖人之經典也, translated into English as "I use the title A translation and interpretation of the Analects as the Holy Canon, and it is especially called as the Holy Canon, since it is the classic of a sage").
22. Paulos Huang, "Martin Luther's Position of Inspiration in the Light of the Study of Finnish School" [in Chinese] 從芬蘭學派來看馬丁. 路德研究的默示觀, *Religious Study* 3 (2015): 223–230.
23. Cf. Paulos Huang, "A Literature Work, a Humanistic Classic, God's Words, or a Record on the Discourse between God and Human Beings? A Dialogue between Paulos Huang and Archie Lee on the Studies of Hebrew Bible" [in Chinese] 文學作品、人文經典、神的話語、還是神人交碰的記錄? 黃保羅與李熾昌關於希伯來《聖經》研究的對話 (August 2, 2018). For example, Meng Zhenhua in Nanjing University (Jiangsu Province), Jiang Zongqiang in North Western Normal University (Lanzhou, Gansu Province) and Lin Yan in Shenzhen University (Shenzhen) use this approach.
24. K. K. Yeo, *Confucius and Paul* [in Chinese] 孔子與保羅 (Shanghai: East China Normal University Press, 2009), 21–32 on the succinct summary of his intertextual readings of the

two texts, the English edition of the work is *Musing with Confucius and Paul*, 33–44; Shi Heng-tan, *The Analects Meets the Bible: The Frontal Encounter between Chinese Culture and Christianity* [in Chinese] 論語遇上聖經： 中國文化與基督教的正面交鋒 (Beijing: World Publishing, 2014); Shi Heng-tan, *The Comparative Reading of Chinese and Western Scriptures* (2018, China Social Sciences Publishing House). See also Yeo, *What Has Jerusalem to Do with Beijing?*, 132–166 on two essays regarding Confucian classics and Amos and Romans, and Yeo, "A Confucian-Christian Vision of the Transformative Mission of God," in Edmund Chia, ed., *Confucianism and Christianity* (Routledge, forthcoming).

25. See K. K. Yeo, "Beyond Chalcedon? Towards a Fully-Christian and Fully-Cultural Theology," in *Jesus Without Borders*, ed. Gene Green et al. (Grand Rapids: Eerdmans, 2014), 162–179.
26. Unless otherwise noted, translations of the Bible texts and the *Analects* in this section are Yeo's.
27. Chi-chung Huang, *The Analects of Confucius (Lunyu): A Literal Translation with an Introduction and Notes* (New York: Oxford University Press, 1997), 157.
28. Though it is also true as Huang as argued that, "During the development of Chinese thinking, there has been degeneration from theism to humanism, and the concept of *Shangdi* (Sovereign on High) has changed from that of a personal deity into an impersonal Heaven..." (Huang, *Confronting Confucian Understandings*, 82).
29. K. K. Yeo, *Ancestor Worship* [in Chinese] 祭祖迷思 (Hong Kong: Chinese Christian Literature Council, 1996).
30. H. Richard Niebuhr, *Christ and Culture* (New York: Harper & Brothers, 1956).
31. K. K. Yeo, "Introduction: So Great a Salvation: Soteriology in the Majority World," in *So Great a Salvation*, ed. Gene Green et al. (Grand Rapids: Eerdmans, 2017), 1–13 (8, 11).
32. Paulos Huang, *Sino-Christian Academic Biblical Studies in the Light of the Globalized Great National Studies* [in Chinese] 大國學視野中的漢語學術聖經學 (Beijing: Minzu Press, 2012).
33. As he draws from the insight of Jin Huimin 金慧敏, see Jin Huimin, "Redefining Global Knowledge," *Theory, Culture and Society* 24 (2007): 276–280.
34. Concerning the Bible and Confucian classics and Chinese translation and interpretation of the Bible, please refer to the latest publication of Paulos Huang, "A Report on the Workshop of Spiritual Humanism: Martin Luther and Confucians," *International Journal of Sino-Western Studies* (online version: www.SinoWesternStudies.com accessed May 1, 2020) 16 (2019): 173–234.

Primary Sources

Bible: Chinese Union Version [in Chinese] 聖經 (和合本). Shanghai: China Christian Council, 2006.

Confucius Sinarum Philosophus (1687). The First Translation of the Confucian Classics. Translated and edited by Thierry Meynard, S.J. Rome: Institutum Historicum Societatis Iesu, 2011.

Huang, Chi-chung. *The Analects of Confucius (Lunyu): A Literal Translation with an Introduction and Notes*. New York and Oxford: Oxford University Press, 1997.

Huang, Paulos. *Sino-Christian Academic Biblical Studies in the Light of the Globalized Great National Studies* [in Chinese] 大國學視野中的漢語學術聖經學. Beijing: Minzu Press, 2012.

Matteo Ricci, Mateo, S.J. *The True Meaning of the Lord of Heaven (T'ien-chu Shih-i)* [A Chinese English Edition]. Translated by Douglas Lancashire and Peter Hu Kuo-chen S.J., edited by Edward J. Malatesta S.J. (Variétés sinologiques—Nouvelle série 72). Taipei, Paris: Institut Ricci, 1985.

Shi Heng-tan. *The Analects Meets the Bible: The Frontal Encounter between Chinese Culture and Christianity* [in Chinese] 論語遇上聖經: 中國文化與基督教的正面交鋒. Beijing: World Publishing, 2014.

Wu Laiquan, *Christianity and Chinese Culture* [in Chinese]. Shanghai: Youth Association, 1936.

Yeo, K. K. *Confucius and Paul* [in Chinese] 孔子與保羅. Shanghai: East China Normal University Press, 2009.

Zhao Zichen, *Biography of Jesus* [in Chinese] 耶穌傳. Shanghai: Qingnian shuju, 1935.

CHAPTER 16

THE BIBLE IN MODERN CHINESE FICTION

CHLOË STARR

Introduction

The appearance of the Bible in Chinese fiction takes many forms, from fleeting echo or allusion to direct quotation and extended exegesis. When drawn together, the range and number of references to the Bible, and the degree of biblical literacy apparent in modern fiction, might surprise even specialists in Chinese literature. The marginalization of the topic as a subject for study in mainland China has obvious historical causes—from the perceived link between the Bible and imperialist predation of Chinese culture, to the anti-religious ideology of the PRC—and it is only in the last few years that there has been a surge of interest in Chinese Christian fiction.

Many early studies focused on the reception of Christianity or Jesus by authors, and considered the Bible only tangentially. Pioneering volumes in the broader field of Chinese Christian literature from Yang Jianlong 楊劍龍 or Ma Jia 馬佳 in the 1990s have been followed in this century by studies from Qi Hongwei 齊宏偉, Liu Lixia 劉麗霞, and a raft of outstanding younger scholars.[1] Recent scholarship among Chinese academics has included studies of individual authors and works of fiction, as well as analyses of faith narratives, or categories such as "spiritual literature."[2] Despite an exciting proliferation of academic studies of the Bible as literature, and new journals devoted to the topic, there have been few studies of the Bible *in* literature.[3] Exceptions include Lewis S. Robinson's 1999 essay, which considered Republican-era fiction; Marián Gálik's survey of the Bible in twentieth-century literature, which examines the Bible both as a source for creative literature and as the subject of biblical studies; and a recent monograph by Cao Jian 曹堅, which considers in detail fictional works based on Hebrew Bible characters and subjects.[4]

Secondary scholarship on Chinese Christian literature has adopted a variety of approaches to its history, development, and literary expression, including chronological, biographical, and thematic.[5] Lewis Robinson's 1986 monograph, which offered a seminal contribution to the study of Christianity and Chinese literature, presented chronological case studies of texts from the mainland and Taiwan, delineating periods of greater attraction or aversion to Christianity.[6] Robinson has divided Republican and Nationalist Christian literature into three phases, determined by its relationship to Scripture: the May Fourth era through until 1927, when a "largely humanistic" approach governed both romantic and realist writers' approach to Scripture; 1928 to 1937, when suspicion and skepticism reigned and irony and satire were the dominant modes of approaching the Scriptures; and the period from 1937 to 1949, when a more politicized use of the Bible prevailed, whether by more patriotic-leaning authors or those using biblical themes to allegorize the current political situation, in an era of more positive embrace of Christian presence in China.[7] Other scholars have foregrounded the use made of the Bible by writers. Liu Zhifang 劉志芳, for example, categorizes the influence of the Bible on modern fiction in three modes, which might be described as autobiographical, intellectual, and social: where authors combine their own feelings with biblical material; use biblical material to express philosophical ideas on humanity; or use the Bible to address national and social crises.[8] Bible reading is analysed by Liu (and others) as a secular pastime, conditioned by the political situation and attitudes toward the church, with the underlying assumption that Western imperialism would militate against intellectuals having any faith-based involvement with Scripture.

The 1920s and '30s have attracted the lion's share of scholarship to date, with much of this focused on the impact of "Christian culture" on writers (too often seen as monolithic and static, omitting the possibility that Christianity can become part of Chinese culture). As the field has developed, a canon of Christian writers emerged. Yang Jianlong offered an early iteration of this, devoting chapters to fifteen well-known and lesser-known names, from Lu Xun 魯迅 or Bing Xin 冰心 to Xu Yu 徐訏, including a few modern writers like Bei Cun 北村 or Taiwanese author Zhang Xiaofeng 張曉風. Others followed this lead: an almost identical set of writers is used by Qi Hongwei in his study of literary suffering. Qi and Yang both divide writers into the categories of (baptized) Christians and those merely interested in Christian culture, with reasons including the utility value of Christian culture for society (as "medicine" to save the country) and the Bible's value as a treasury of world literature and as study-guide for writing in the vernacular. The trend to distinguish between Christian and non-Christian authors has persisted in scholarship, often without good grounds (literary or theological) regarding the use of biblical material. Given that various names in the canon changed their views or attitudes (and even their faith) over the course of their writing lives, an absolute distinction as a basis for literary analysis may be difficult to sustain. (In the shifting sands of the Republic, for example, Bing Xin was baptized, as was Lao She, while Guo Moruo and Lu Yin 廬隱 (Huang Shuyi) affiliated themselves with Christianity early in their writing careers).

Concrete narrative studies have proved a fruitful mode of analysis. In his 2012 study of narration in the Bible and modern fiction, Yang Jianlong utilizes both author-based and literary analyses to explore the influence that the Bible had on modes of narration during the New Culture Movement. As Yang shows, writers were "consciously or unconsciously" influenced by the literary forms and structure of the biblical narrative, seen in characterization, development of spirit (*jingshen* 精神), and use of allusions and language.[9] Yang describes themes taken from biblical stories or narrative structure that reappear in modern Chinese literature: sin and repentance (in Lu Yin, Guo Moruo 郭沫若 and Zhang Ziping 張資平); the fall and salvation (in Bing Xin, Xu Yu, and others); testing, suffering, and character development (in Xu Dishan 許地山 and Su Xuelin 蘇雪林 in particular). He notes how the Bible narratives enabled writers to cast off some of the shackles of traditional literature, such as heavy-handed moralistic teaching, or an exclusive concentration on characters' outer worlds, by introducing more interior reflection, and ordinary, non-heroic, characters. Thematic studies can threaten to reduce a work of literature to a single topic, but Yang's research shows convincingly how the narrative forms of the Bible (including U-shaped trajectories, etc.) affected Chinese writers, and how a variety of Bible editions played into modern literature.

The current essay approaches the Bible in fiction through the type, and degree, of engagement. This ranges from direct, sustained dialogue with the Bible, as in the many semi-fictional Lives of Christ produced in the first half of the twentieth century, or stories based on a particular biblical scene or pericope, through to much more diffuse or passing references to biblical themes or allusions present in a variety of short stories and novels. The essay begins with two particular types of depiction: representation of the physical Bible in literature, whether as talisman, moral guide, or synecdoche for its Western imperialist purveyors, and direct citation of Bible passages in stories or novels. The second half of the essay considers literary or thematic engagement. The aim is extensive, to show something of the range of fiction connected to the Bible in China, and also particular, to examine individual works and analyse the engagement in question. There is no attempt to distinguish between "Christian" or faith-based use or appropriation and non-Christian or secular use—or even to separate evangelical motivation from satirical deployment of biblical passages, a point especially germane in periods when religious affiliations might rapidly mutate or be obscured for political reasons. The focus here is on how authors draw on, converse with, and utilize the Bible in their writing, and only secondarily on potential reasons for their homage.

The essay spans the Bible in Chinese vernacular fiction by mainland authors from around the time of the May Fourth Movement, or New Culture Movement, to the present.[10] The imaginative, creative fiction by Chinese writers from this period onward is arguably quite different in category to the "Christian literature" of the late Qing, although there are continuities with some of the earlier, church-based didactic literature in its fictionalizing of the Bible.[11] The publication of the vernacular Union Bible translation in 1919 marks a convenient starting point for a century of engagement, especially as it coincides with the national vernacular movement, the upsurge of periodical and print press increasing the circulation of all forms of literature, and the coming of age of a generation educated in missionary schools and colleges in China with background knowledge of the Bible. This is the first time in Chinese history when secular authors routinely make passing references to biblical characters or themes, and when a sizeable number of Christian authors are writing literature for a national stage. It is also the time when a flourishing indigenous church is debating the need (in meetings such as the 1923 National Council of Churches) to create and promote a Chinese Christian fiction, and when a growing number of theological educators are penning fiction in their spare time to explore the Christian faith. As the works cited display, the Bible flourished in literary representation in the 1920s and 1930s and has re-appeared most notably in the record in the post-Mao era, especially the 1990s onward.

One aspect that this survey can only touch upon is the relationship between the promotion of the study of biblical literature by literary critics and its popularization among writers and readers. In the May Fourth era, an influential writer and critic like Zhou Zuoren 周作人, despite claiming little knowledge of religion and no interest in doctrine, set out to write about how "the spirit and form" of the Bible could impact "the research and creation of Chinese new literature."[12] Zhou proposed that the Bible be read in its own stead as a work of literature, that Western biblical study provided a model for studying the Chinese classics as literature, and that (à la Trotsky or Kropotkin), the quality of art lay in the strength of the transmission of feelings experienced—and that the highest form of art was religious art, since the highest feelings of humanity are religious ones. The circulation of such ideas was an important element in the reception of the Bible in the period, and, as Zhou's more famous brother Lu Xun proved, writers and intellectuals might come to the Bible as much through literary criticism as through reading Scripture directly. In contemporary China, the engagement with Christianity and the Bible by cultural critics and academics such as Liu Xiaofeng 劉小楓 once again has had a significant effect on the reception and appreciation of Christianity and its sacred writings among the wider populace.

The Bible as Book and Inscription

The physical Bible can take on a raft of different connotations. It can be a symbol of freedom or capitulation, a draw to a spiritual life or a sign of its casting off, as when "even the church schools threw their Bibles to the ground and joined the ranks" of striking students and workers in Lao She's 老舍 novel set in the 1920s.[13] The Bible can function as a marker of identity or denote a particular type of person, giving the reader a window into an author's perception of Christianity and the religious. When "the devout Mr Johnson," a missionary headmaster is observed reading "a thick red book" by his pupil (and cleaner) in Xiao Qian's 蕭乾 1936 short story "Cactus Flower" (Tan 曇), we are in no doubt as to the connotations of "the Bible, translated into Chinese with notes in the Latin alphabet. From the day he first set foot in this dark continent more than ten years ago, that book had been his faithful companion."[14] The Bible here is guidebook for the authoritarian, the paternalistic, and patronizing, those "savage" and "barbaric" foreigners who cannot forget "the dirt the yellow race carried from birth" but who outwardly claim to be one family with them in God.[15] For certain school children in missionary schools or colleges, the Bible represents institutional regulation of a particularly limiting type. In Yu Dafu's 郁達夫 renowned 1921 short story, "Sinking" (*Chenlun* 沉淪), the melancholic, nature-loving protagonist recalls the "superstitious restrictions" of his Presbyterian college, a place "notorious for its despotic administration" and "minimal freedom," where students were not allowed to go outside or read secular books on a Sunday, but "could only pray, sing psalms, or read the Old and New Testaments."[16]

Yet if the Bible is the companion of the hypocritical missionary, or instrument to chafe juvenile minds, it is also a tool of liberation and education. In Xu Dishan's novella, "Yuguan" (玉官, published posthumously in 1941), Xingguan's Bible has "dog-eared corners" and "slips of paper sticking out as markers," showing how many times a day its owner consults it. By it she has learned to read, and by it she teaches her fellow villager Yuguan "this foreign language," as the future Bible Woman grasps within a week how to sound out the phonetic transliteration and read Scripture for herself.[17] On first acquaintance with her neighbor's Bible and its worn gilt and dulled leather, Yuguan finds its stories ridiculous and chuckles to herself at the notion that everyone was a sinner in need of salvation or that all creatures were created by God. Despite her misgivings, she furtively steals glances at her neighbor's book, but cannot make head nor tail of its "foreign" language. As the story unfolds, the Bible emerges as the means of Yuguan's intellectual, physical, and economic liberation. The Bible is an effective bribe to bring Yuguan to church, while Yuguan's literary emancipation goes hand in hand with her physical liberation, since unbinding her feet is a condition of employment by the mission agency. The promise of a salary for becoming a "handmaid of the Bible" offers economic independence as well as the chance to educate the next generation (her son obtains a fee-waiver at the mission school). One of the central storylines elucidates how Yuguan, whose work is to distribute Bibles and catechize women, is transformed from someone who preaches the Bible without believing all that she proclaims to an eventual believer who embodies its tenets and values. Along her pilgrimage way, Yuguan, whose theology of inculturation has much to teach professional theologians, discovers that the *Yijing* 易經 is at least as effective as the Bible at repelling Chinese ghosts, but that Bible reading and biblical guidance (alongside the wisdom of the Confucian classics and the pragmatic teachings of modern science) gives her the strength and courage to repel even marauding communist soldiers. As she saves a band of women from certain rape, she discovers that "the Old and New Testaments were capable of checking the living devils."[18]

Inscriptions outnumber references to the Bible as a physical book. Offering a brief biblical verse or quotation as an epigraph at the front of a novel is a relatively frequent phenomenon, but in some fiction much lengthier biblical passages are transcribed into the story. While the insertion of external texts—poems, songs, documents, or even drama scripts—was a fairly common novelistic technique in late imperial fiction, for characterization or plot purposes, it is less common in modern (print) fiction and bears particular scrutiny. In some stories, Bible excerpts comprise the majority of the work. The most extreme example of this in a work still categorized as fiction is Mao Dun's 茅盾 (Shen Yanbing 沈雁冰) short story "The Death of Jesus" (耶穌之死, 1942), almost the entirety of which is a compilation of Bible verses. As an end note alerts readers: "If you want to know the sources for material in this piece, please see the four gospels in the New Testament."[19] There are minimal intrusions from the narrator linking Bible passages together in Mao Dun's remarkable story, with occasional chapter-end comments. Divided into nine parts, the first is the only section without biblical citation and reads in its entirety: "How did the Pharisees and Jesus forge their enmity? It is a long story." Mao Dun's tale is precisely this story: a weaving together of all of the gospel passages in which Jesus dialogues with his "enemies," first the Pharisees and scribes, then the chief priests and elders, and finally the worldly powers of Pilate and Herod. Jesus' teaching, the narrator notes, caused many to put their faith in him, but led to the hatred of those who usurp authority to bless or who pretend to do good.[20] Every parable has but one purpose, to lambast hypocrites and establish true order, as when Jesus reproves his hearers: "The Kingdom of God will be taken from you and given to the commoners (proletariat, 百姓) who will produce fruit."[21]

The effects of Mao Dun's creative retelling are striking: an extended litany of challenge emerges, as Jesus questions, vilifies, and antagonizes those in positions of power and authority. As commentators have noted, to anyone used to the Gospel depiction of Jesus as healer, teacher, and prophet, this concentrated compilation seems skewed or distorted. Liang Gong writes that Mao Dun bids farewell "to the Son of God, Messiah or Christ, Savior, magician doing miraculous deeds, doctor, religious activist, thinker, poet, and orator" in his redaction.[22] It is true that Mao Dun's stitching together of Scriptures, in translation and paraphrase, produces a quite different effect from an individual Gospel: a record of confrontation, argument, word play, and pointed parables as Jesus parries his questioners—but like the Gospel writers, Mao Dun's narrative is governed by his particular interests. In genre, it resembles the "collected sayings" tracts that Qing missionaries produced, compiling lists of scriptural references to gambling or other vices, but because it is framed by a fiery John the Baptist and by Jesus' death, the story also reads as a chronological tale. Mao Dun's aim is simple: to show how Jesus courted death in exposing the powers that be. An ulterior aim, as commentators have suggested, is to instill courage in readers, and a radical defiance or contumacy in the face of Japanese occupation.

Like the Synoptic Gospel writers, Mao Dun employs the prophet Isaiah to set the scene. The verses from Isaiah 1, 2 and 40 highlight how citation-as-political-allegory might work: rulers who love bribes and chase gifts (1:23) find that "your cities are burned with fire; in your very presence aliens devour your land" (1:7, NRSV). The text serves both to condemn war and to offer a pacifist revision of reality. Mao Dun carried his Bible with him to the unoccupied west of China, and it was the only book he carried back from occupied Hong Kong; a radically subversive text passed by guards who took it as a sign of innocent piety. As Lewis Robinson shows, Mao Dun's target in this story was not just foreign invaders, but the Nationalist Guomindang government and its "Christian" leaders, making his political allegory a "stroke of genius" in avoiding censorship and appealing to Christians in the southwest. The oppressive activities of the Guomindang during the United Front; the hypocrisy of leaders; extrajudicial trials; and the eventual transfer of the kingdom to "the people" are all signaled through Jesus' rebukes of Pharisees and rulers.[23]

If the Bible makes a cameo appearance in many works of fiction and is frequently present in direct quotation, in some stories it has its own role, more akin to that of a character. In the first chapter of Zhang Ziping's long novel *God's Sons and Daughters* (*Shangdi de ernümen* 上帝的兒女們, 1931), the Bible is muse and companion for the young protagonist, Ruiying, but becomes a more disturbing dialogue-partner as the pivot around which her budding sexual feelings and ethical questioning are explored. The short Bible extracts in Zhang Ziping's novel are interwoven into the text and reified in the lives of characters. In the first chapter, Ruiying has spent the morning reading and returns to the Bible after lunch on a hot, sultry day. There is something both furtive and bold about her deliberate choice of 2 Samuel 13 to read, and the story causes Ruiying to flush, but, curiosity piqued, she cannot put the book down. Through her response to the story of Tamar, we sense a young woman on the cusp of adulthood, just beginning to fathom the ways of the world. As the focus shifts between the biblical texts and Ruiying's responses, the interaction between Bible and girl composes a character portrait. We see the intellectual scope of Ruiying's faith shifting as her reading provokes a new questioning. When Ruiying reads that because Tamar was a virgin, it was difficult for Amnon to get close to her, she wonders: how could the author describe these things in such an explicit way, so boldly?[24] After reading of Amnon's plan, she skips ahead verses, eager to discover the outcome. Excited at Tamar's resistance, Ruiying's feelings turn to hatred for Amnon at his assault, and she muses on the worthlessness of a virgin "once she had lost the final boast."[25] Sleepy in the heat, the Bible passage is recast as a fantasy in Ruiying's mind, and she becomes Tamar to her brother.

The guise of young children allows Zhang Ziping to disclose some of the Bible's perceived character-flaws, as Scripture returns to center-stage at the end of the first chapter of *God's Sons and Daughters* as the unmasker of innocence. As Ruiying is plagued by her younger brother who wants tickling, we discover that she missed her father preaching about "our ancestors" that morning: not Adam and Eve, but the apes from which all humans are descended. Her brother's innocent defense of Scripture in the family discussion—those scientists are mad, wanting to be descendants of apes not God—turns poignant when his questioning brings Ruiying back to the question of incest. "Sis, Cain and Seth were both born of Adam and Eve, but then who were their wives?" "Yes, who?" she asks in return, unwilling to expose her own accumulated questions on the passage. "Cain and Seth must have taken their sisters as wives, mustn't they, sis? But the person who wrote Genesis didn't explain this clearly."[26] As she flicks through to Genesis 4 in her Bible, Ruiying confirms that the text indeed "does say just that he had a wife, not who she was." Thinking back to Tamar and her suggestion that a marriage with her brother might have been permitted had he but asked, "Ruiying, who had reached marriageable age, and A-Bing, who had developed early, glanced at each other briefly" before walking away, a cold breath of air enveloping both. The narrator has the final word: the siblings had read Genesis but had not read as far as Leviticus, where they would have seen the punishments mandated for incest.

A modern novel in which extended scriptural quotation appears is Bei Cun's 1992 *The Baptising River* (or *The River of Baptism*, 施洗的河 *Shixi de he*). Bei Cun is one of a number of authors, including Shi Tiesheng 史鐵生 (1951–2010) and recent émigré Shi Wei 施瑋, whose writings have been described and studied as "spiritual literature" or spiritual reportage (神性寫作). Bei Cun's *The Baptising River* has been praised for responding to the "spiritual void" of the post-Mao era and exposing a character's soul to readers.[27] Bei Cun is a relatively well-known intellectual convert, and *The Baptising River*, his first post-conversion novel set in the wartime 1940s, follows the life course of its protagonist, Liu Lang, from his abused childhood to his abusive, dissipated adult life. Liu makes three key boat trips, as he journeys downstream to college, succeeds his father as a triad boss, and is eventually baptized in the muddy effluvium of the river. The novel is bookended by an epigraph from Matt 4:17, "Repent, for the kingdom of heaven has come near" (NRSV) and concludes with a long quotation from Ezekiel 33, spanning verses 1–12. There are other snatches of Scripture in the novel, in the speech of a university girlfriend who is forever quoting the psalms at Liu, to little effect, and in the Job-like cries of the opium-addicts Tang and Liu Lang himself ("Why wasn't I allowed to die when I came out of the womb? Why didn't my birthday become a dark night? . . ."[28])—but it is the final long passage from Ezekiel that is the most visible and challenging scriptural intrusion. Like the hymn texts and extempore conversion prayer of Liu in the penultimate chapter of the novel, the biblical quotation is indented and italicized, marking a significant change of voice and style of narration.

The Bible passage includes the charge to Ezekiel to act as a watchman for the people of Israel, with the injunction that if he did not speak out "to dissuade them from their ways" then the wicked would die but he would be held accountable for their blood; and a fervent call to the people to turn from their ways and live ("turn back, turn back from your evil ways; for why will you die, O house of Israel?").[29] The passage, addressed in the novel to Liu Lang's old rival and friend Ma Da, whom he is trying to convert, complements the Matthean epigraph and operates at the levels of protagonist, author, and reader. The sin and death that pervade the novel are recast in the quotation, as the universalizing effect of the specific biblical charge to the Israelites apostrophizes the reader. While the call to repent presages the eventual *metanoia* and baptism of the protagonist Liu Lang, it is also clear from the appendices to the book that, as author, Bei Cun began writing anew as a Christian novelist, and he took his role in warning through fiction seriously.[30] The quotation shows some of the pitfalls of introducing long biblical extracts into fiction, however. If the speed of Liu Lang's conversion and baptism seems improbable, the shift of voice to "Christian" character remains unconvincing, the disjunction pointing to Bei Cun's early search for an authentic Christian expression. The loan of a scriptural voice offers an alternative authority and allows Liu Lang to express his new vision without resorting to the hackneyed language of his conversion prayer. In Bei Cun's later novels, the Christian voice is more subtle, and better integrated; Scripture need no longer be inserted wholesale to create a voice for a modern Chinese Christian.

Literary Engagement with the Biblical Text

Literary engagement with the Bible runs the gamut from direct quotation of Scripture through to a more diffuse Christian imaginary, where elements of biblical morality can be inferred or glimpses seen of biblical motifs or characters. The Bible may be present in a story as the absent archetype, as when Lu Xun refers to the "Creator" (*zaowuzhu* 造物主) as weak or faint-hearted in his Wild Grass (*Yecao* 野草) collection,[31] or when Shi Tiesheng sketches an omnipotent "Almighty God" attempting to do something of which "He" is ontologically incapable, namely, to dream.[32] In this category of allusion and evocation, we might also place Christ-like figures such as Mr Huang in Lao She's short story, "Temple of Great Compassion," a gentle, much-mocked figure who sacrifices himself for the sake of his student charges, who is described as an "angel" and who offers pre-emptive forgiveness to his murderer, but is never directly associated with Christianity, or the hypocritical religious figures who populate Lao She's stories and are notable for their distance from biblical tenets. Rev. Yi (variously translated as Rev. Eden, Ely, or Evans) in Lao She's novel *The Two Mas* (二馬, 1929) is one such figure with an inverted or estranged relationship to the Bible, whose selfish attitude and sense of racial superiority contradicts any Christian ideal; the closest he comes to a Bible is when it evaporates before him, aware that his speech "was somewhat contrary to biblical style so he inhaled on his pipe, swallowing in one gulp both the smoke and his words."[33]

The array of scattered references to the Bible in early twentieth-century literature testifies to the impact of mission colleges and of new curricula, as well as to the influx of foreign and translated literatures and their reproduction in the new print media. Their sum is noteworthy, but the incidental nature of many of these references—as with later equivalents in Nationalist or People's Republic of China literature—makes them difficult to systematize.[34] The remainder of this essay considers fiction with more extensive biblical reference and grappling: works that draw directly on biblical scenes or characters and fictional or semi-fictional Lives of Christ.

Although uplifting motifs like creation, hope, and salvation have furnished literary reflection, Chinese authors frequently have found recourse in darker themes: in suffering, theodicy, and revenge; in Job, Sampson, and Christ. Three very different twentieth-century interpretations of the crucifixion exemplify this. Lu Xun's dense prose-poem, "Revenge II" (復仇其二, 1925), opens with Christ already nailed to the cross, "Because he thinks he is the Son of God."[35] If the poem begins with the question of faith or delusion, in its reworking of the gospel narratives and alternation between third-person depiction and the inner voice of Christ,[36] it foregrounds the relationship between source text and imagination, between the reading of Scripture and the writing of fiction, exegesis and eisegesis. In five hundred characters, "Revenge II" offers a reflection on the impotence of religion; a meditation on pain, torture, and the madness it induces; and an allegory of the fate of the nation, channeled through the cruel apathy of bystanders. If salvation was a rallying cry for May Fourth writers, there is no resurrection here. Lu Xun turns to the psychic cost of self-sacrifice, as he transforms the archetype of salvation into a meditation on "revenge," Christ's revenge on his crucifiers. As the protagonist's body convulses with pain, the thought that "these curse-worthy people are themselves crucifying their own son of God soothes his pain," and he refuses the wine offered to him, to "be able for as long as possible to pity their future and hate their present."[37] As the skies turn dark and the dying figure cries out, "*Eloi, eloi, lama sabachthani*," he apprehends that "God had abandoned him—he was, after all, just a 'son of man.'"[38]

If watching the depiction of a compatriot's execution by the Japanese appalled Lu Xun and provoked him to activism, his Bible reading centered around human suffering. The passion, the book of Lamentations, Job, and fictional accounts of early Christian martyrdom raised for him profound philosophical, theological, and social questions, which "Revenge II" leaves open, polyvalent.[39] The late twentieth-century writer Wang Meng was similarly drawn to the shocking power of the most "wretched" of gods through the many crucifixes he saw in churches and galleries around Europe. Wang Meng's 王蒙 "On the Cross" (十字架上, 1988), written when he was Minister of Culture at the tail-end of a period of relative artistic freedom, evinces an erudition to his reading of the Bible, notwithstanding its fantastic embellishments. Written in nine short parts, "On the Cross" incorporates poetry, drama, and parody, offering travelogue, spiritual reflection, and satire. While Lu Xun's terse prose focuses on Christ, Wang Meng's relaxed narrative switches between auto-biographical reflection and depiction of Christ, the voices merging in places, as the meaning of Christ's life in a contemporary society of "nakedly bestial self-interest" is scrutinized.[40] The story culminates in a pastiche of the book of Revelation with speeches from four oxen.

A riotous medley of pop-culture and high-culture references, Wang begins in what the reader takes to be his own voice, describing the uplifting effects of church architecture and organ music, whose reverberations overwhelm him with "feelings of universal love."[41] The cross is approached slowly, obliquely. In section II, the child Christ is shocked into realizing his identity as savior after a fight over a mango; in section III, his ability to heal is set against an inner tension between the weight of his mission and distress at human sin. In section V, Wang asks "How did Jesus end up on the Cross?" before turning the question to himself: "are you willing to ascend the cross?" The winnowing and "clean-up campaign" that Wang imagines will accompany the Messiah raises existential questions, since no one is perfect or able to judge reliably; no one can be certain they themselves are not "depraved chaff."[42] For all its bright irony ("It was a magnificent ceremony," begins the depiction of Christ's execution), Wang Meng's story offers as biting a social critique as Lu Xun's condemnation of bystanders. Jesus himself bears little relation to the Gospel versions—alarmed before Pilate as he realizes he might be freed and his life's mission imperiled, he cries out not to be released, and is aghast at members of the public approaching him for judgment and healing when he can do nothing for them from the cross—but the portrait is of a credible savior. Wang Meng's Christ faints repeatedly, and his unclear state of consciousness mirrors the lack of clarity of the rabble of bystanders debating if he is a fraud, and the ambivalence of the author and his Christ as to the resurrection, as the latter wonders whether, even resurrected, he will ever be able to fulfill the contradictory prayers of humanity.

If Lu Xun's focus is Christ, and through Christ the world, and Wang Meng sets up an interchange between the two, Gu Cheng's chapters "The Cross," "The New Testament," and "The Wound" in his long novel *Ying'er* 英兒 (1993) are insertions into an ongoing meditation on death and lost loves; the "wound" is the protagonist's own gaping loss at his lover's desertion, not that of Christ. The novel was one of his last compositions before poet Gu Cheng killed his wife, Xie Ye, and committed suicide, and its setting and themes—the bucolic life on a Pacific island of the protagonist Li Cheng and his two wives, including the eponymous *Ying'er*—bear more than a passing semblance to Gu Cheng's own life. Critics have read the novel as biography, as a modern-day, destructive journey to the West, and as a study in masculinity and the male imaginary, but only rarely considered its religious timbre. Jesus, hanging on the cross, appears from below in apt metaphor, "a big tree before a great storm, or half a rack of lamb on a wooden frame,"[43] but there is no pain or terror in this crucifixion, just a thirsty, bored Christ, musing on the nature of water, gravity, and God. This may be "the most important moment in history," but in the quotidian scene a dispassionate Christ watches Mary haggle with other women over the price of linen for a shroud and eventually morphs into a man from Beijing whose wives are laughing at him. In the light of Gu Cheng's suicide, the questioning of Christ ("Are you dying of your own volition?" . . . "No-one is helping me to kill myself, apart from God"[44]) takes on a poignant, personal hue.

In contrast to such highly fictionalized interpretations, a number of twentieth-century Chinese theologians and writers penned biographies of Jesus with varying degrees of imaginative interpolation and addition, but more closely based on the Gospel accounts. Often indebted to Ernest Renan's 1863 *Vie de Jésus* (and later imitators), with its close exploration of Galilean life, portrayal of Jesus as a revolutionary, and eschewal of the more miraculous aspects of Jesus' gospel ministry, these include Zhao Zichen's 趙紫宸 *Life of Jesus* (耶穌傳, 1935), Zhang Shizhang's 張仕章 *The Revolutionary Carpenter* (革命的木匠, 1939), and Zhu Weizhi's 朱維之 *Jesus the Proletarian* (無產者耶穌, 1950)—the latter two heavily invested in the project of Christian socialism.[45] Both Zhu and Zhao appraise the literary aspects of the Gospel as well as drawing on biblical studies and Marxist scholarship in their writing.[46] But while Zhao and Zhang Shizhang's biographies bring Jesus' story alive with vernacular dialogue and vivid scenery (Mary, chiding the child Jesus in the temple in the first scene of Zhang's account, scolds him with the colloquial immediacy of any fraught Chinese mother[47]), Zhu Weizhi's treatise on the property-less Jesus, and the task he has set himself of disrobing Jesus of "the strange attire and trappings that two thousand years of feudalism and capitalism have given him,"[48] is an intellectual rather than literary project.

Zhao Zichen's *Life of Jesus* is the most innovative of the three biographies. One of the earliest of the semi-fictional memoirs of Jesus in Chinese, Zhao's biography was reprinted at least five times before 1949—although Zhao himself turned sharply away from this "unbridled" application of imagination to Scripture, as his theology veered from a liberal, contextualized cast toward a more evangelical orthodoxy.[49] Zhao engages with the Bible in ways both theological and literary. His poetic license with the biblical text is measured, balancing the "living spirit" of imagination with historical reality, and claiming to use the twin tools of reason and empathy to flesh out the spare biblical narrative. Zhao humanizes characters, adding greater depth to a figure like Mary Magdalene or giving Joseph a fuller role in Jesus' upbringing, while re-imagining whole incidents in light of his theological preoccupations (recreating Judas as a thwarted revolutionary in a two-thousand-character interlude in Chapter 15, for example, strategizing a different path for the same liberationary ends as Jesus, but falling prey to the tactics of the high priest). Zhao re-arranges the units of Scripture to make a more coherent narrative, and in so doing, changes the tenor of passages, so the parable of the laborers in the vineyard becomes directed at the disciples, who have just been arguing about their place in the kingdom. Zhao shares with many of his contemporaries an aversion to the non-scientific and the miraculous and often uses the formula "people said . . ." to explain the supernatural: "people said" that Jesus fasted for a whole forty days, and "people said" a herd of pigs leapt off a cliff when the "legion" entered them. It is the angle and the light that make witnesses think Jesus has walked on water rather than waded along the shoreline.

In terms of narrative, Zhao's *Life of Jesus* is highly Sinicized and inculturated. The story teems with poetic figures of speech and four-character phrases. John the Baptist is described as an "unmovable Mount Tai," while Herodias' daughter sings like "dew weeping on a lotus flower" or "the wind soughing through bamboo."[50] Zhao wrote his 250-page biography in less than a month, and we can assume that the references and literary associations came naturally to him from his memory bank as he reworked the Bible text. Each chapter is headed by a couplet drawn from the classics, offering a commentary on the biblical texts from within the Chinese tradition. Chapter 5, for example, begins with a line from a Tang poem by Liu Yuxi describing a "thousand league iron chain" in a historical sea battle, and alludes to Jesus as liberator, who breaks through the mental and physical chains that bind his people. While Zhao draws on biblical scholarship and prior Lives of Jesus in his descriptions of the land, he also writes within a tradition of Chinese travelogue and landscape depiction, where place is a source of historical and national memory, revisited through centuries of literary descriptions and carved inscriptions. As Jesus climbs the hills and gazes out over the land of Israel, he reflects on the historical memories filtered through the biblical texts set out in the landscape before him in the manner of a Chinese scholar—at Deborah's feats at Mount Tabor, on Saul on Mount Gilboa—and is prompted to his own theological reflection on his mission as Messiah.

While the literary imaginations of the fiction authors discussed above find rich source material in the scriptural narratives to a variety of ends, the intent of the biography writers is frequently more deliberately theological and academic: to enable a deeper knowledge and understanding of Christ's life among readers (albeit in line with their own political or social views etched into the re-telling of Jesus' life) and as part of their own quest to better comprehend the Scriptures.

Notes

1. See Yang Jianlong, *Crying Out in the Wildernes* [in Chinese] 曠野的呼聲：中國現代作家與基督教文化 (Shanghai: Shanghai Jiaoyu, 1998); Ma Jia, *Wandering under the Cross* [in Chinese] 十字架下的徘徊：基督宗教文化和中國現代文學 (Shanghai: Xuelin, 1995); Qi Hongwei, *Literary Suffering* [in Chinese] 文學苦難：精神資源 (Jiangxi: Jiangxi Renmin, 2008); Liu Lixia, *The Historical Actuality of Chinese Christian Literature* [in Chinese] 中國基督教文學的歷史存在 (Beijing: Social Sciences Academic Press, 2006).
2. See e.g. Jing Yaping 荊亞平, *The Narration of Faith in Contemporary Chinese Novels* [in Chinese] 當代中國小說的信仰敘事 (Shanghai: Xuelin, 2009).
3. See, for example, the *Journal for the Study of Biblical Literature* [in Chinese] 聖經文學研究 published jointly by Henan University and Cheng Chi College, Chinese University of Hong Kong.
4. See Marián Gálik, "The Bible in the Literature of the Chinese Mainland in the Twentieth Century," *Asian and African Studies* 16 (2007): 1, 68–80. Gálik's important study *Influence, Translation and Parallels: Selected Studies on the Bible in China* is divided into two parts, separating academic study of the Bible and biblical literature from case studies of literary works, from Mao Dun 茅盾 to Gu Cheng 顧城. Lewis S. Robinson, "The Bible in Twentieth-Century Chinese Fiction," in *Bible in Modern China: The Literary and Intellectual Impact*, ed. Irene Eber et al. (Sankt Augustin: Institut Monumenta Serica, 1999), 237–277. Cao Jian, *Chinese Biblical Anthropology: Persons and Ideas in the Old Testament and in Modern Chinese Literature* (Eugene, OR: Pickwick, 2019).
5. Material in these introductory paragraphs draws on Chloë Starr, "Reflecting the Bible" [in Chinese] 折射聖經：晚清和民國的 "基督教文學", *Journal for the Study of Biblical Literature* 聖經文學研究 19 (2019): 62–108.
6. Lewis S. Robinson, *Double-Edged Sword: Christianity & 20th Century Chinese Fiction* (Hong Kong: Tao Fong Shan, 1986), chapters 1–3.
7. See Robinson, "The Bible in Twentieth-Century Chinese Fiction," 237, and *Double-Edged Sword*, where the chapters in part I correspond to this division.
8. See Liu Zhifang, "The Influence of the Bible on the Modern Chinese Novel" [in Chinese] 聖經對中國現代小說的影響, *Journal for the Study of Biblical Literature* 18 (Spring 2019): 113–138.
9. Yang Jianlong, *The "May Fourth" New Literature Movement and Christian Culture* [in Chinese] "五四"新文化運動與基督教文化潮 (Shanghai: Shanghai Shiji, 2012), 287.
10. Taiwanese, Hong Kong, and diasporic writers are not considered in this survey, given their different histories and concerns.
11. See Starr, "Reflecting the Bible," 65–75.

12. Zhou Zuoren 周作人, *The Bible and Chinese Literature* [in Chinese] 聖書與中國文學 (Shanghai: Shangwu, 1925), 6.
13. Lao She, *The Two Mas* [in Chinese] 二馬, tr. Kenny K. Huang and David Finkelstein (Hong Kong: Joint Publishing Co., 1984), 45.
14. Xiao Qian, "Cactus Flower," in Xiao Qian, *Chestnuts and Other Stories* (Beijing: Panda Books, 1984), 106.
15. Ibid. 106, 107.
16. Yu Dafu, "Sinking," tr. Joseph S. M. Lau, in *Columbia Anthology of Modern Chinese Literature*, ed. Joseph S. M. Lau, C. T. Hsia, and Howard Goldblatt (New York: Columbia University Press, 1995), 50.
17. Xu Dishan, "Yü-kuan," tr. Cecile Chu-chin Sun, in *Modern Chinese Short Stories and Novellas 1910–49*, ed. Joseph S. M. Lau, C. T. Hsia, and Leo Ou-fan Lee. (New York: Columbia University Press, 1981), 57.
18. Ibid. 75.
19. Mao Dun, *The Death of Jesus* [in Chinese] 耶穌之死 (Shanghai: Zuojia Shushi, 1945), 28.
20. Ibid. 7.
21. Ibid. 12, 13.
22. Liang Gong, "The Image of Jesus in *The Death of Jesus* by Mao Dun," in Roman Malek S.V.D., ed., *The Chinese Face of Jesus Christ*, vol. 3a (Sankt Augustin: Institut Monumenta Serica, 2005), 935–942 (938).
23. Robinson, *Double-Edged Sword*, 171–178.
24. Zhang Ziping, *God's Children* [in Chinese] 上帝的兒女們 (Shanghai: Guangming Shuju, 1931), 2.
25. Ibid. 4.
26. Ibid. 11.
27. See, e.g., Xie Youshun 謝有順, "Can Writing Come Home? Bei Cun and His *Baptizing River*" [in Chinese] 寫作能回家嗎?—北村和他的《施洗的河》, in Bei Cun, *The Baptizing River* [in Chinese] 施洗的河 (Guangzhou: Huacheng, 2016), 314–329, or Xie's longer essay "The Retreat of the Avant-Garde and Its Deeper Reconstruction—With a Discussion of Bei Cun's *Baptizing River*" [in Chinese] 先鋒性的萎縮與深度重建：兼談北村的《施洗的河》, *Dangdai zuojia pinglun* 5 (1993), 36–41.
28. Bei Cun, *The Baptizing River*, 273.
29. Ibid. 299; translation from NRSV.
30. The novel was first published in serialized form in Huacheng 花城 magazine in 1993 and republished in book form by several different presses.
31. In the 1926 short story "Among Pale Blood-stains" [in Chinese] 淡淡的血痕中. Lu Xun, *Wild Grass* [in Chinese] 野草 (Beijing: Renmin Wenxue, 2003), 77.
32. As the narrator notes in Shi Tiesheng's humorous sketch, which riffs on Laozi as well as the biblical God, "we are only able to dream when we are unable to fulfil our aspirations." Shi Tiesheng, "Dream Scenario," tr. Michael S. Duke, in *Worlds of Modern Chinese Fiction*, ed. Michael S. Duke (Armonk, NY: M.E. Sharpe, 1991), 120.
33. Lao She, *The Two Mas*, 14.
34. For examples and an overview of stories with biblical references, see Gálik, "The Bible in the Literature," or Cao Jian, *Chinese Biblical Anthropology*.
35. Lu Xun, *Wild Grass*, 14.
36. The figure referred to as "he" throughout is not explicitly identified as Christ.
37. Lu Xun, *Wild Grass*, 14, 16.
38. Ibid. 16.

39. See Qi Hongwei 齊宏偉, *Lu Xun: Dim Conscious and Bright Transcendence* [in Chinese] 魯迅：幽暗意識與光明追求 (Jiangxi: Jiangxi Renmin, 2010), 79–86.
40. Wang Meng, "On the Cross," tr. Janice Wickeri, *Renditions* 37 (Spring 1992): 43–68 (54).
41. Ibid. 46.
42. Ibid. 54.
43. Gu Cheng 顧城 and Lei Mi 雷米, *Ying'er* [in Chinese] 英兒 (Taipei: Tushen, 1993), 207.
44. Ibid. 209.
45. For a discussion of these three centered on Zhu Weizhi's work, see Chin Ken-pa, "W. T. Chu's Jesus the Proletarian," *Stasis* 3.2 (2015): 132–144.
46. Such as Kautsky's *Foundations of Christianity* (1908), translated into Chinese in 1932 by Tang Zhi and Ye Qifang (Shanghai: Shenzhou Guoguang, 1932).
47. Zhang Shizhang, *The Revolutionary Carpenter* [in Chinese] 革命的木匠 (Shanghai: Jidujiao Xinwen She, repr. 1949), 4–5.
48. Zhu Weizhi, *Jesus the Proletarian* [in Chinese] 無產者耶穌 (Shanghai: Guangxue hui, 1950), preface, 2.
49. See Chloë Starr, *Chinese Theology: Text and Content* (New Haven: Yale University Press, 2016), 75–76. Zhao's later biography of St Paul is quite different in style. For a more detailed study of Zhao's *Life of Jesus*, see, e.g., Starr, *Chinese Theology*, chap. 3.
50. Zhao Zichen, *Life of Jesus* [in Chinese] 耶穌傳, reprinted in *Complete Works of Zhao Zichen* 趙紫宸文集, vol. 1 (Beijing: Shangwu, 1935), 486, 546.

Primary Sources

Bei Cun 北村. *The Baptizing River* [in Chinese] 施洗的河. Guangzhou: Huacheng, 2016.

Duke, Michael S. D., ed. *Worlds of Modern Chinese Fiction*. Armonk, NY: M.E. Sharpe, 1991.

Gu Cheng 顧城 and Lei Mi 雷米. *Ying'er* [in Chinese] 英兒. Taipei: Tushen, 1993.

Lao She 老舍. *The Two Mas* (二馬). Translated by Kenny K. Huang and David Finkelstein. Hong Kong: Joint Publishing Co., 1984.

Lau, Joseph S. M., C. T. Hsia, and Howard Goldblatt, eds. *Columbia Anthology of Modern Chinese Literature*. New York: Columbia University Press, 1995.

Lau, Joseph S. M., C. T. Hsia, and Leo Ou-fan Lee, eds. *Modern Chinese Short Stories and Novellas 1910–49*. New York: Columbia University Press, 1981.

Lu Xun 魯迅. *Wild Grass* [in Chinese] 野草. Beijing: Renmin Wenxue, 2003.

Mao Dun 茅盾. *The Death of Jesus* [in Chinese] 耶穌之死. Shanghai: Zuojia Shushi, 1945.

Shi Tiesheng 史鐵生. *Think on Soul* [in Chinese] 靈魂的事. Tianjin: Tianjin Jiaoyu, 2010.

Shi Wei 施瑋. *Letting Go of Eden* [in Chinese] 放逐伊甸. Beijing: Zhongguo Dianying, 2007.

Xiao Qian 蕭乾. *Chestnuts and Other Stories*. Beijing: Panda Books, 1984.

Wang Meng 王蒙. "On the Cross." Translated by Janice Wickeri. *Renditions* 37 (Spring 1992): 43–68.

Zhang Ziping 張資平. *God's Children* [in Chinese] 上帝的兒女們. Shanghai: Guangming Shuju, 1931.

Zhang Shizhang 張仕章. *The Revolutionary Carpenter* [in Chinese] 革命的木匠. Shanghai: Jidujiao Xinwen She, repr. 1949.

Zhao Zichen 趙紫宸 (T. C. Chao). *Life of Jesus* [in Chinese] 耶穌傳. Reprinted in *Complete Works of Zhao Zichen* [in Chinese] 趙紫宸文集, vol. 1. Beijing: Shangwu, 2003. Pages 449–636.

Zhu Weizhi 朱維之. *Jesus The Proletarian* [in Chinese] 無產者耶穌. Shanghai: Guangxue hui, 1950.

CHAPTER 17

THE BIBLE AND MISSIONARY NOVELS IN CHINESE

JOHN T. P. LAI

INTRODUCTION

MATTEO RICCI (1552–1610) and Michele Ruggieri (1543–1607), together with other Jesuit missionaries, inaugurated Catholic missions to China in the late sixteenth century. Protestant Christianity in China began with Robert Morrison (1782–1834), of the London Missionary Society, who first set foot in Canton (Guangzhou) in 1807. On the basis of Jean Basset's (1662–1707) partial translation of the Chinese Catholic Bible, Morrison completed and published the first Chinese translation of the New Testament in 1813 and the entire Bible ten years later.[1] Against the backdrop of the global missionary movement in the nineteenth century, China became a major missionary field for translation, publication, and circulation of the Bible and Christian tracts.[2] Biblical stories and Christian messages were disseminated among the Chinese audiences in a wide array of modes, including hearing biblical stories paraphrased or recapitulated in sermons, singing of hymns and making use of liturgical texts, reciting catechisms and trimetrical primers, consulting Bible dictionaries and commentaries, among others.[3] Meanwhile, missionaries were aware of the popularity of Chinese vernacular novels because of the long tradition of public storytelling and novel reading known as *shuoshu* 說書, in cities and villages alike. Some missionaries embarked on the production of a sizable number of Christian novels in the Chinese language. Since the Chinese form of public storytelling was widely followed for reading of Christian novels, fictional representation of the Bible—tailored to the aesthetic interests and cultural habits of the Chinese audience—was generally better received than mere translations of the Bible.

Patrick Hanan (1927–2014) made important contributions with his pioneering study on the "missionary novels" produced by Protestant missionary writers in nineteenth-century

China, against the literary context of the rise of modern Chinese fiction.[4] Missionary novels, as defined by Hanan, are "narratives (in the form of novels) that were written in Chinese by Christian missionaries and their assistants".[5] These novels in Chinese, regardless of their length, convey profound religious messages as they are influenced or shaped by Christian values and images. Invariably interconnected with the Chinese Bible, these novels make creative use of traditional Chinese literary forms to express Christian thoughts, rewrite biblical stories, and attune the gospel message in the Chinese cultural milieu.[6] Missionary novels in Chinese can be categorized according to a combination of three main aspects, namely denominational traditions (i.e., Protestant and Catholic), the nature of the texts (i.e., original or translated works), and the chronology of publication (from early Qing to Republican periods). While the earliest missionary novels extant in Chinese flowed from the pens of Jesuits in the seventeenth century, the literary activities and output of Protestant missionaries were more vibrant and voluminous during the nineteenth century. Our discussion will commence with, and place greater emphasis on, Protestant fictional productions in the late Qing period, followed by Catholic endeavors in the early Qing and Republican eras.

Protestant Novels: Original Works

Prior to the First Anglo-Chinese War (1839–1842), scores of Protestant missionaries were stationed in South East Asia to prepare for the opening up of China by undertaking the composition of biblical texts in local languages. The majority of their Chinese works were published by missionary presses in Malacca, Singapore, and Batavia (Jakarta).

Interreligious Dialogues between Friends

The first Protestant missionary novel in Chinese, *Zhang Yuan liang you xianglun* 張遠兩友相論 (*Two Friends*, 1819; hereafter *Two Friends*) was produced by William Milne (1785–1822), of the London Missionary Society, and based in the Anglo-Chinese College, Malacca. In the form of a dialogue novel in which stories are largely conveyed through dialogue, the twelve-chapter *Two Friends* encapsulates twelve lively conversations between Zhang, a Christian, with his non-Christian friend, Yuan, concerning such religious topics as sin, repentance, everlasting life, resurrection, and reincarnation. Adopting a familiar Chinese setting and non-confrontational tone, the novel undertakes extensive interreligious dialogues between Christian doctrine and Chinese thoughts in Confucianism, Buddhism, Daoism, and Chinese folk religions.[7] Repeatedly revised in different dialects and reprinted until the late 1930s, *Two Friends* emerged as the most widely distributed and well-received Chinese missionary novel promoting Christianity in China.[8]

Inspired by Milne's successful fictional attempt, Prussia-born Karl Friedrich August Gützlaff (1803–1851), initially sent by the Netherlands Missionary Society, became the most prolific missionary novelist in Chinese among all nineteenth-century Protestant missionaries to China. Gützlaff preached in Siam and Batavia before embarking on his Chinese missions in the early 1830s.[9] He translated the Bible into Thai and Japanese and also revised Robert Morrison's Chinese Bible, which was subsequently adopted and modified by Hong Xiuquan (洪秀全, 1814–1864) in his Taiping Heavenly Kingdom. Author of over sixty Chinese Christian works ranging from catechisms and evangelical tracts to biographies of biblical figures,[10] Gützlaff was dedicated to the composition of more than ten Christian novels, such as *Shuzui zhi dao zhuan* 贖罪之道傳 (*The Doctrine of Redemption*, 1834; hereafter *Doctrine of Redemption*), *Changhuo zhi dao zhuan* 常活之道傳 (*The Doctrine of Eternal Life*, 1834), *Zheng xie bijiao* 正邪比較 (*Orthodoxy and Heresy Compared*, 1838), and *Huizui zhi dalüe* 悔罪之大略 (*The Treatise on Repentance*, 1839; hereafter *Treatise on Repentance*), which manifest vivid features of traditional Chinese fiction characterized by nascent narrative.[11] He remarked that narrative writings, as the most effective means of conveying the divine truths and capturing readers' interests, should make up the majority of missionary publications.[12] Gützlaff's earliest novel, *Doctrine of Redemption*, often incorporates lengthy scriptural quotations, to the extent of an entire biblical chapter, followed by theological elucidation through conversations and interreligious dialogues between Christian and non-Christian characters. A companion to his Bible translation, *Shengshu zhushu* 聖書註疏 (*Explanation of the Scriptures*, 1839), employs a fictional framework to provide succinct summaries of each biblical book and to situate Scripture history in the Chinese dynastic timeline. Gützlaff's fictional works also frequently quote from, or paraphrase, vernacular Chinese novels such as *Romance of the Three Kingdoms* and Confucian classics such as *The Works of Mencius*, as an aesthetic and hermeneutical strategy for better understanding and reception of the biblical messages.[13] The fictional experiments of early missionaries, especially Milne and Gützlaff, prepared the ground for further flourishing of Protestant literary cultivation in the second half of the nineteenth century. Fictionalized biography of biblical figures constitutes another major type of missionary novel in Chinese.

Fictionalized Biography of Biblical Figures

While James Legge (1815–1897), of the London Missionary Society and based in Hong Kong, has been remembered for his monumental legacy in translating Chinese Confucian classics such as the *Four Books* and *Five Classics* into the English language,[14] which established his prestige in sinology and earned him the first professorship of Chinese in Oxford University in 1876. Much less academic attention has been paid to his composition of a couple of fictionalized biographies of biblical figures in Chinese, particularly *Yuese jilüe* 約瑟紀畧 (*Brief Biography of Joseph*, 1852; hereafter *Brief Biography of Joseph*)[15] and *Yabolahan jilüe* 亞伯拉罕紀畧 (*Brief Biography of Abraham*, 1857). By dramatizing the plot and revealing the characters' disposition to enhance the aesthetic beauty of the narrative, *Brief Biography of Joseph* constitutes one of the most intriguing adaptations reworking the life of Joseph chiefly according to the book of Genesis into the form of a classical Chinese novel.

Brief Biography of Joseph purposefully imitates the literary style of a Chinese historical biography, which contains features of both historical narrative and biography. It exhibits the literary form and narrative features of *zhanghui xiaoshuo* 章回小說 (chaptered novel), a major type of Chinese novel during the Ming and Qing periods, with each chapter headed by a couplet giving the gist of its contents. Around the mid-Ming era, the chaptered novels witnessed a period of great prosperity, with many works mainly basing themselves on subject matters of existent historical narratives. Prominent works of these historical novels or "fictionalized history" (*yanyi* 演義) include *Sanguo yanyi* 三國演義 (*Romance of the Three Kingdoms*) and *Shuihu zhuan* 水滸傳 (*Water Margin*). *Brief Biography of Joseph* places great emphasis on the authenticity and historicity of the biography of Joseph by situating the story in the Chinese historical framework. The beginning of the novel puts the Hebrew/Christian tale into the context of Chinese dynastic history, "During the time of the Shang Dynasty, in the Far West dwelled a man named Joseph" (*Taixi Shangchao shi, ren you Yuese zhe* 泰西商朝時, 人有約瑟者). Joseph has thus gained authenticity as a historical figure whose biography attained heightened credibility.

A salient feature of the *Brief Biography of Joseph* lies in Legge's attempt to offer a Confucian interpretation of the biblical story. *Brief Biography of Joseph* attaches great importance to the paternal role in building an ordered and harmonious family that is highly valued by Confucian ethics. The poem in chapter one attributes the brothers' betrayal of Joseph to Jacob, who failed to properly handle the father-son relationship due to his deliberate indulgence towards Joseph. The chapter-end commentary responds to this view by reiterating the importance of proper family management, "though Joseph's dream sparked off his brothers' vicious plot, the underlying cause for their jealousy was Jacob's partiality towards his children. The ones who manage a family must be vigilant!" (*Zhu xiong yu sha Yuese, sui you Yuese zhi shuo meng, jiujing shi you qi fu zhi pian'ai ye. Zhijia zhe ke bushen yu* 諸兄欲殺約瑟，雖由約瑟之說夢，究竟實由其父之偏愛也。治家者可不慎歟). The commentary further illustrates the principle of filial piety by condemning the betrayal of Joseph as not only a demerit on the part of the brothers, but, more significantly, an unfilial act toward their father who was deceived and made to grieve, hence violating the prevalent obligation in Confucian teaching of a child to a parent.

Most strikingly, Joseph was portrayed as a "Confucian sage" (*shengxian* 聖賢) who possesses the ideal personality and moral paradigm of Confucianism, with both talents and virtues. Joseph's rejection of the attempted seduction by his master Potiphar's wife consolidates his image as a sage with high moral standards. The poem in chapter two alludes to the famous saying from *The Works of Mencius* that "To enjoy food and delight in the appetite of sex is nature" (*shi se, xing ye* 食色, 性也),[16] and stresses that "Master Joseph" (*Gong Yuese* 公約瑟) can stand even firmer than many ancient sages and heroes by resisting the lust for food and sex; therefore, Joseph could enjoy "a good reputation for a thousand generations" (*jujian qianzai zhu fangming* 拒奸千載著芳名). Joseph is acclaimed as a sage on the grounds of his steadfast resistance to carnal temptation by "having righteousness in both nature and emotion, together with profound self-cultivation" (*xingqing zhi zheng, daoxue zhi shen* 性情之正，道學之深), as stated explicitly in the commentary in chapter two.

Taking advantage of the Confucian discourse resources, *Brief Biography of Joseph* often adapts or quotes directly from Confucian classics to interpret the story of Joseph. In the commentary of chapter six, "since our ancestors committed sins and their sons followed suit, the mind of man was becoming restless, prone to err and its affinity to what is right was becoming small" (*Di zi shizu fanzui, zisun xiaoyou. Yuan shi renxin ri wei, daoxin ri wei* 第自始祖犯罪，子孫效尤。爰是人心日危，道心日微), the last sentence is a quotation from "The Counsel of the Great Yu" of *The Book of Documents* (*Shangshu* 尚書), which says "The mind of man is restless, prone to err; its affinity for the right way is small" (*renxin wei wei, daoxin wei wei* 人心惟危，道心惟微)[17] As a matter of fact, Legge argued in his paper "Confucianism in Relation to Christianity" that passages from Confucian classics like this one from *The Book of Documents* could be appealed to "in support of the Christian doctrine however we may phrase it, that there is not, and has not been on earth, a just man, doing good and not sinning."[18] By so doing, Legge borrowed the Confucian understanding of humanity and worldview to illustrate the history of human beings as described in the Bible, stating that after our ancestors committed sins, all men have gone astray from the right path of God. The same commentary further employs Confucian notions and expressions to elaborate on God's plan for human salvation.

Summarizing the relation between Confucianism and Christianity, Legge stipulated that the *Di* (帝 Lord) and *Shangdi* (上帝 Lord on High) of "the Chinese classics is God—our God—the true God"[19] and came to the conclusion that many important points of Confucianism were "defective rather than antagonistic…that missionaries should endeavor not to exhibit themselves as antagonistic to Confucius and Confucianism."[20] Legge's sympathetic attitude toward Confucianism explains his approach of placing the Joseph story into a fictionalized biography with vivid Confucian characteristics. By incorporating a large number of direct quotations and indirect references from Chinese classics, *Brief Biography of Joseph* deliberately represented this biblical story in such a manner so that educated Chinese readers would find the language of the novel more familiar, thus facilitating their reception of the biblical contents and values of the work. Manifesting the Confucian poetics and moral function of Chinese novels, *Brief Biography of Joseph* is a classic example of the inter-textual relationship between the Bible and Chinese vernacular novels.

Literary Advocacy for Social Reform

While Legge's fictionalized biographies are rooted in biblical contexts, some missionary novels strive to integrate the biblical narrative art with the specific socio-cultural milieu of late imperial China. Griffith John (1831–1912), of the London Missionary Society and based in Hankow (Hankou), composed the sixteen-chapter *Yin jia dang dao* 引家當道 (*Leading the Family in the Right Way*, 1882), narrating the conversion story of an ordinary Chinese. "Family" constituting the main thread, the novel portrays the life experiences of different family members, particularly the father figure, Mr. Li. Unable to resist all manner of temptations, Mr. Li forsook his happy and harmonious family and indulged in sex, gambling, and opium-smoking. With its narrative structure and themes resembling the biblical parable of the Prodigal Son, the novel highlights the positive impact of the Christian gospel in leading not only Mr. Li back home but ultimately his entire family in the right way. The entire Bible, according to Northrop Frye (1912–1991), is a "divine comedy," with the biblical narratives largely based on a grand U-shaped structure, following the "paradise–sin–disaster–repentance–redemption" pattern.[21] Mr. Li's story epitomizes such a "divine comedy" in which his initial trials and tribulations plunge his early life to a threateningly low point, after which his encounter with the gospel engenders a fortunate twist in the plot that sends the conclusion up to a happy ending. From a broader perspective, the novel advocates social reform through tackling such major Chinese issues as polygamy, gender inequality, foot-binding, and opium-smoking by means of biblical values and teachings.

Along the same line of expressing social concern through the composition of Christian novels, some 150 "New Age Novels" were submitted for the 1895 fiction contest organized by former Anglican missionary John Fryer (1839–1928) in the aftermath of the First Sino-Japanese War (1894–1895), seeking effective ways to purge Qing China of the social concerns of opium-smoking, foot-binding, and the eight-legged essay (a standardized essay style for the civil service examination in imperial China, which was often blamed for the country's cultural and socio-political stagnation).[22] Heavily influenced by literary productions of Western missionaries, some Chinese Christian authors conducted their own experiments in terms of literary creation and religious poetics, and these novels preserved their religious voices and social concerns. A typically intriguing example is *Qu mo zhuan* 驅魔傳 (*Story of Demon Banishing*) by Guo Zifu 郭子符, a Chinese literatus from the Shandong Province. Readers are struck by the multifarious and multi-religious celestial world, an ingenious adaptation of the biblical account of the eternal battle between the creator God and the fallen angel-turned-Satan—who heads a large throng of demons with vivid Chinese characteristics such as the demons of opium and of foot-binding—which personifies and denounces the social malaise of late Qing China.[23]

Protestant Novels: Translated Works

Throughout the nineteenth century, the English works of quite a few renowned Christian authors were translated into Chinese by Protestant missionaries.

Allegory of Spiritual Pilgrimage and Warfare

The Pilgrim's Progress by John Bunyan (1628–1688) usually remained the number-one priority. Profoundly inspired by and copiously alluding to the Bible, *The Pilgrim's Progress* portrays the spiritual pilgrimage of Christian, the protagonist, in the genre of a religious allegory. This Christian classic was first introduced to the Chinese world by William Muirhead (1822–1900) of the London Missionary Society, based in Shanghai as early as 1851, and indeed was the first English allegorical novel to be rendered into Chinese. During the last decades of imperial China, this classic was translated, predominantly by Western missionaries, into more than ten Chinese linguistic forms, ranging from classical Chinese, Mandarin vernacular, local dialects, and romanization, to braille. It is worth noting that some earlier translations not only adopted the literary form and narrative features of traditional Chinese fiction but also were substantially annotated to elucidate its copious Christian metaphors and biblical references.

The earliest extant Chinese translation of *The Pilgrim's Progress* constitutes *Tianlu licheng* 天路歷程 (*Progress on the Path to Heaven*, 1853) in classical Chinese by William Chalmers Burns (1815–1868), an English Presbyterian missionary.[24] Targeted at an intended readership of educated Chinese, Burns from time to time resorted to Confucian terminology and concepts to convey Christian messages. The allegory commences by a graphic depiction of Christian, the protagonist, who, being weighed down by a "great burden upon his back," spares no effort to shed this burden. An unmistakable allusion to the Bible, this central image symbolizes the burden of "iniquities" and "original sin" for humankind, as expressed in Ps 38:4, "For mine iniquities are gone over mine head: as a heavy burden they are too heavy for me" (KJV). Burns rendered the "great burden" as "*daren* 大任" (great office or mission), which puts on a vivid Confucian color with its direct reference to *The Works of Mencius*, "Thus, when Heaven is about to confer a great office (*daren*) on any man, it first exercises his mind with suffering, and his sinews and bones with toil."[25] Burns's translation of "*daren*" drastically transformed the derogatory Christian concept of the personal burden of sin to a commendatory term loaded with the Confucian connotation of moral and social obligation.[26] In the China Centenary Missionary Conference held in Shanghai in 1907, Burns's translation of *The Pilgrim's Progress* was acclaimed as the third most effective and well-received works of proselytization in the Protestant missions in China since the time of Robert Morrison. Arthur Henderson Smith (1845–1932) even declared that *The Pilgrim's Progress* was the best translation ever made by a foreigner into Chinese, and that it was "evidently as much a classic with the Chinese as with the Western church".[27]

While Burns's translations of *The Pilgrim's Progress* are substantially annotated to stipulate biblical references and elucidate religious metaphors, *Shenglü jingcheng* 勝旅景程 (*Bright Journey of the Victorious Traveler*, 1870; hereafter *Bright Journey of the Victorious Traveler*)[28] by Thomas H. Hudson (1800–1876), of the General Baptist Missionary Society, stands out from the rest to interpret biblical messages in the framework of Confucian teachings. Demonstrating a remarkably domesticating approach to translation, *Bright Journey of the Victorious Traveler* inherits the literary tradition of fiction annotation to interpret Christian thoughts of the text by making profuse references to traditional Chinese religious and philosophical concepts, especially from Confucian classics. Alluding to Eccl 1:2 "vanity of vanities; all is vanity," the Vanity Fair, symbolizing worldly frivolity and ostentation, constitutes a prominent scene in *The Pilgrim's Progress*, where Christian and Faithful were slandered and persecuted. "Vanity Fair" was translated by Hudson as "*Fuyun Shi* 浮雲市" (Floating Cloud Fair), where multitudes of "floating cloud commodities" were on display and sale. Most intriguingly, Hudson followed the Chinese literary tradition of fiction annotation to supplement notes and commentary at the top of a page, "Confucius said, 'Riches and honours acquired by unrighteousness are to me as a floating cloud.' Both Christian and Faithful are righteous people who believe in the Lord. How would they desire to purchase commodities of unrighteousness?"[29] The words of Confucius were taken from the *Analects*, "With coarse rice to eat, with water to drink, and my bended arm for a pillow;—I have still joy in the midst of these things. Riches and honours acquired by unrighteousness are to me as a floating cloud."[30] Hudson's employment of the figurative term "floating cloud" captured the unsubstantial and ungraspable nature of the Fair and its commodities. With a direct quote from the *Analects*, Hudson's annotation goes a step further to interpret all commodities of the "Floating Cloud Fair" as "unrighteous." This foregrounds the antagonism between the "righteousness" of the Christian pilgrims originating from their faith in Jesus Christ, and the "unrighteousness" of all worldly possessions that might lead the pilgrims astray from their path to heaven. In this connection, Hudson reinterprets some biblical notions, for instance "vanity," by making extensive references to traditional Chinese religious and literary sources, especially from Confucian classics. On the other hand, Hudson might have modified subtly the philosophical connotation of some Confucian concepts like *yi* 義 (proper and just) by juxtaposing it with the Christian term "righteousness," which conveys the theological implication of the doctrine of "justification by faith."[31]

Apart from being the first Chinese translator of *The Pilgrim's Progress*, William Muirhead also accomplished the first Chinese rendition of Bunyan's allegory *The Holy War*, entitled *Renling zhanji* 人靈戰紀 (*Man Soul Warfare*, 1884; hereafter *Man Soul Warfare*), telling the story of the town Mansoul (Man's soul), which is besieged by the hosts of the devil and ultimately rescued by the troops of Emmanuel, the son of Shaddai (Almighty). On the basis of Muirhead's rendition in classical Chinese, a Cantonese version of *The Holy War* was brought out in 1887 by Emma Young, an American woman missionary of the Southern Baptist Convention. The popularity of the Chinese *The Holy War*, however, failed to be on a par with that of the Chinese *The Pilgrim's Progress*, largely corresponding to the reception of their originals in the English-speaking world. Donald MacGillivray (1862–1931) observed the undesirable reception of Muirhead's *Man Soul Warfare*: "Chinese do not take to it, as we might expect. Perhaps if *illustrations* [italics original] were added they would."[32] In this light, the insertion of attractive illustrations is thought to play a significant role in the story of missionary novels in Chinese.

Contextualization of Gospel Accounts

In the process of rewriting the Bible into literary works, a major challenge faced by the writers is harmonization of the different perspectives of biblical accounts, especially the four Gospels, as demonstrated in *Zhengdao qimeng* 正道啟蒙 (*Enlightening the Right Way*, 1864; hereafter *Enlightening the Right Way*) by William Chalmers Burns. *Enlightening the Right Way* was largely based on the structure of a Sunday-school textbook of biblical stories, *The Peep of Day* by Favell L. Mortimer (1802–1878). Although the overall framework of the original was retained, some chapters were combined, some omitted and added in *Enlightening the Right Way*, resulting in a fifty-chapter work that centers on the life and work of Jesus Christ.[33] Burns adopted a most liberal strategy for translating *The Peep of Day* to an extent that *Enlightening the Right Way* could be considered a drastic rewriting of the original text by harmonizing different Gospel accounts. Burns freely supplemented additional narratives and comments to every chapter, which is also concluded by a Chinese poem to give a summary and commentary of the central teachings. *Enlightening the Right Way* displays vivid narrative features of a traditional Chinese novel, particularly incorporating Chinese story-telling traditions for dissemination of the biblical messages.

Typically, the rewriting of the first miracle performed by Jesus in turning water into wine at the wedding feast in Cana involves substantial contextualization of biblical narratives in chapter 18 of *Enlightening the Right Way*. By assuming the role of an omniscient narrator, Burns consciously controlled the point of view of interpreting the biblical narrative and commanded a panoramic view of the world of the story. Burns supplemented a narrator's commentary about the running out of wine in the middle of the wedding feast by stating, "I guess the host might not be wealthy and the guests might be so multitudinous that wine ran out after a short while." Narration interspersed with comments was the dominant mode of narration in traditional Chinese novels, especially during the Ming and Qing periods. The contextualized rewriting of biblical accounts facilitate the flow of scriptural reading for Chinese readers.

The depiction of the image of Jesus is also a prominent point of interest in this chapter. According to chapter two of the Gospel of John, Mary probably just laid out the need for wine in mundane terms, while Jesus's answer "Woman, what have I to do with thee? Mine hour is not yet come" (KJV) conveys profound symbolism and theological implication that the hour of his death/glorification has not yet come. In *Enlightening the Right Way*, Jesus immediately instructed the servants to take action after Mary mentioned the shortage of wine, omitting Jesus's response to his mother. With careful comparison of the two texts, Jesus in the Gospel of John, in the eyes of Chinese readers, might appear to be disrespectful, if not rude, at the reasonable request of his mother to take some remedy for the shortage of wine; whereas Jesus in *Enlightening the Right Way*, who took immediate action responding to his mother's plea, presented an image of a filial son. The portrayal of such a culturally acceptable image of Jesus seems intended to facilitate reception of the biblical messages among the Chinese audience.

It is highly remarkable that Burns provided a long explanation on the supposedly Christian attitude toward drinking near the end of the chapter. Burns added this passage to explain why Jesus allowed the people to have more wine, while agreeing that drunkenness was deplorable. First, wine made of grapes, different from liquor commonly found in China, is supposed not to make people drunk so easily. Besides, moderate drinking would be perfectly acceptable. Everything made by God is originally good for our use. If things are not properly used or are abused, adverse consequences would result. In other words, Burns was concerned about the problem of the misreading of this Gospel account on the part of Chinese readers that God encourages drinking by turning water into wine. By engaging the biblical accounts with Chinese social and cultural contexts, *Enlightening the Right Way* drastically shifts the focus of discussion from showing the divinity of Jesus as presented in this miraculous narrative to the issue of drinking, thus rendering the text vivid with moral and social significance.[34]

Imagination of Heavenly Paradise

During the early years of China missions, most attention was paid to converting adult men. In the course of time, missionaries realized the importance of targeting Chinese women and children, who were generally more open to the gospel message. The younger generation, if converted, would lay a firm foundation for the future Chinese Church. Founded in 1878, the Chinese Religious Tract Society placed great emphasis on furnishing illustrated works for Sunday Schools and providing suitable literature for young people.[35] A number of Chinese translations of Christian children's novels were issued in the early 1880s, such as *Guina zhuan* 閨娜傳 (1882; translation of *Cottage on the Shore, or Little Gwen's Story*) and *Haitong gushi* 孩童故事 (1883; translation of *The Swiss Boy*).[36]

Among many Christian children's novels being translated, *Anle jia* 安樂家 (*Sweet Home*, 1882; hereafter *Sweet Home*) by Mary Harriet Porter (1846–1929) of the American Board of Commissioners for Foreign Missions, emerged as a highly popular Chinese translation of *Christie's Old Organ; or, "Home Sweet Home"* (1874) by Mrs. O. F. Walton.[37] The favorite tune of old Treffy, a forlorn barrel-organist, is "Home, Sweet Home," which rekindles the sweet memory of a ragged orphan, Christie. When Treffy's health is deteriorating, Christie takes over playing the old organ. Treffy, ignorant of religion, becomes terrified of his imminent death, and Christie makes every effort to convince his dying friend of salvation in Christianity. Treffy finally passes away with heavenly hope, and Christie gets married and finds his sweet earthly home while looking forward to the eternal home above.[38] This novel demonstrates vivid artistic creation, as shown in the visual, auditory, and psychological representation through image, music, and dream. The protagonists, Treffy and Christie, are homeless wanderers in the world, suffering from poverty, loneliness, fear, and disease. Amid all these vexations shines through the biblical motif of hope and thirst for the heavenly paradise, as envisioned in the book of Revelation; this guiding light is to become a strong motivation throughout their ardent religious pursuit.[39]

Conversion of a Jewish Girl

While the majority of Protestant translated novels have their original texts in English, the first German-Chinese translated Christian novel *Jinwu xingyi* 金屋型儀 (*Exemplar in the Golden House*, 1852; hereafter *Exemplar in the Golden House*) is a typical example of acculturation and appropriation, with its literary and religious components blended into the Chinese cultural framework. Rendered by Ferdinand Genähr (1823–1864)—a Rhenish missionary to China, from Hermann Ball's *Thirza; oder die Anziehungskraft des Kreuzes* (English translation by Elizabeth Maria Lloyd: *Thirza; or, the Attractive Power of the Cross*)—the work tells the story of Thirza, a Jewish girl, who converts to Christianity against the staunch opposition of her father, an orthodox Jew.[40] While the source text depicts the entrenched religious conflict between Judaism and Christianity, the narrative focus of the target text has been subtly shifted to Christian thoughts and Chinese (chiefly Confucian) traditions, by the conscious representation of the image of the female protagonist as an ideal Chinese Christian who could integrate the virtues of Confucian ethics with her Christian faith.[41] Genähr's attempt to rewrite and indigenize the Jewish conversion story was undoubtedly a timely measure if the novel is put back to its Qing contexts of xenophobia, anti-Christian sentiments, and the widespread confrontation between Christianity and local religious culture of China.

It is noteworthy that some missionary novels, like *Sweet Home* and *Exemplar in the Golden House*, share a common feature in showing the pursuit of salvation by the protagonist (usually a child or teenager) against a background of poverty, suffering, and death. Meanwhile, it is often the converted children who lead adults to embrace the eternal hope in Christ. As Gillian Avery rightly put it, "children are not only shown as better than their parents, but are frequently the instruments of their parents' salvation."[42] The tales of children's conversion in these missionary novels was intended to prove to be morally and spiritually uplifting to the adults.

Catholic Novels

While this essay focuses on Protestant missionaries' production of novels in the nineteenth century, the origin of missionary novels could be traced back to the early Qing period, particularly two Catholic works.

Early Qing Works

The two works are by Joseph Henri Marie de Prémare (1666–1736), a French Jesuit missionary to China and renowned for his French translation of *Zhaoshi gu'er* 趙氏孤兒 (*The Orphan of Zhao*; French: *Tchao Chi Cou Ell*, 1735).[43] Prémare's first fictional work is

Meng meitu ji 夢美土記 (*Dreaming about the Paradise*; hereafter *Dreaming about the Paradise*), a short story of some three thousand Chinese characters composed in 1709, with *Lüren* 旅人 (*Traveler*) pointing the way of ascending to the heavenly paradise.[44] *Dreaming about the Paradise*, according to Li Sher-shiueh, is the very first story in Chinese that structures itself on Western fiction, on the grounds that its plot is modeled on Marcus Tullius Cicero's (106–43 BCE) "*Somnium Scipionis*" (Dream of Scipio). Li also argued that *Dreaming about the Paradise* is an allegory of Jesuit Figurism because the story makes profuse allusion to Chinese classical sources, with a provocative claim that ancient Chinese sages had some knowledge of Christianity through the revelation from the true God. In this light, it has repeatedly been contended in the story that Christian truth and the way to Paradise can be discovered in such pre-Qin Chinese classics as the *Yijing* 易經 (*Book of Changes*), the *Shijing* 詩經 (*Book of Poetry*), and the *Shangshu* 尚書 (*Book of Documents*).[45]

In addition to *Dreaming about the Paradise* in classical Chinese, Prémare composed a novel in vernacular Chinese, *Ru jiao xin* 儒交信 (*A Confucianist Befriends a Believer*, ca. 1718–1721; hereafter *Confucianist Befriends a Believer*).[46] The six-chapter novel adopts an accommodative approach to engender a series of Confucian-Christian dialogues between a Confucian scholar Li Guang 李光 and Sima Shen 司馬慎, a literatus who acknowledged a belief in Catholicism. Sima, arguably the incarnation of Prémare himself, succeeds in convincing Li to embrace Catholicism by underscoring the compatibility between Catholic doctrines and the teachings of Confucius embodied in classical Confucian texts, especially the *Yijing*. With the assertion that "Yi being the invisible Sage; The Sage being the visible Yi" (*Yi zhe, wuxing zhi shengren; shengren zhe, youxing zhi Yi* 易者, 無形之聖人; 聖人者, 有形之易) and that "Hexagrams Qian and Kun being the Sage" (*Qian Kun jiu shi shengren* 乾坤就是聖人), Sima affirms that the incarnated Jesus Christ is precisely the Sage of Yi. Li Sher-shiueh has rightly maintained that the central theme of the novel is that "Jesus did not destroy Confucius; rather, Confucius was thus named all because of Jesus' help" (*Yesu bu mie Kongzi, Kongzi dao chengquan yu Yesu* 耶穌不滅孔子，孔子倒成全於耶穌), as stipulated by Sima in chapter two.[47]

It is worthy of attention that a network of intertextual influences could be identified between the early Qing Catholic and late Qing Protestant missionary novels, despite any denominational differences and debates. Notably, Gützlaff's *Doctrine of Redemption* apparently alludes to the dream narrative and heavenly scenery of Prémare's *Dreaming about the Paradise*.[48] Similarly, Milne's *Two Friends* is reminiscent of the non-confrontational interreligious dialogues between scholarly friends as portrayed in Prémare's *Confucianist Befriends a Believer*.

Republican Works

After the prohibition of Catholicism by the Kangxi (1654–1722) and Yongzheng (1678–1735) emperors, a new wave of Catholic missionaries returned to China in the wake of the First Anglo-Chinese War.[49] While many Protestant missionaries opted for the composition of novels for their proselytizing purposes in the late Qing period, the

Catholic presses in China published a large corpus of fictional literature during the Republican era (1912–1949). With the collapse of imperial regime in 1911, the Republic of China saw an urgent need to establish new moral, social, and political orders. Several series of fictional literature, including biblically inspired novels, were issued by these Jesuit presses during the early Republican period. This corpus of literature comprises three major types of texts: first, Chinese translations of French Catholic novels; second, original novels composed by Chinese Jesuits; and third, Catholic plays, which are chiefly dramatic adaptations of biblical narratives and hagiographies.[50]

With a vividly moralistic and religious emphasis, some Catholic novels were intended to contribute to the construction of the new moral and social orders of the Republic of China by means of Catholic ethics and values. These novels, for example, *Xiaonü jiufu* 孝女救父 (*The Filial Girl Saves Her Father*, 1917) and *Nü junzi* 女君子 (*A Noble Woman*, 1923), attempted to infiltrate Catholic thoughts and virtues, in conjunction with traditional Chinese ones, such as chastity, filial piety, forgiveness and reconciliation, for the edification and moral transformation of Chinese readers. The preface of *Daozhen Lai Hua* 道眞來華 (*Daozhen Comes to China*, 1916), from the series of original novels, further elaborated the far-reaching impacts of fiction: "A work of moral fiction serves as an effective tool for social reform. Its enchanting narrative and elegant wording will not only enlighten the mind, but also touch the heart of the readers. Encountering the virtues of loyalty, filial piety, chastity and righteousness, the readers would imitate; perusing the stories of the wicked and malicious, they would detest. The gradual transformation of people's mind and moral constitutes the key to national strengthening."[51] The social relevance and significance of these Jesuit works becomes more prominent when they are examined against the cultural, social, and political landscape of the early Republican era, notably the May Fourth new literary and cultural movements, the advocacy of *renge jiuguo* (人格救國 national salvation by character), and the anti-imperial/anti-Christian movements in the 1920s.

Conclusion

While Western missionaries to China, Protestant and Catholic alike, spared no effort in the translation and circulation of the Bible, they recognized the fact that the Bible per se, with all its cultural and theological peculiarities, was too alien and difficult for most Chinese readers to comprehend. Missionary novelists were well aware of the fact that literary representations of the biblical narratives might provide greater leeway and ample possibilities to indigenize the Christian messages by offering their intended Chinese audiences culture-specific commentaries and nuanced interpretations. In the process of literary representation of the Bible, missionary novelists had to resolve some major challenges, principally the degrees of fictionalization and contextualization of the Bible that would be desirable in the Chinese contexts. The reverence for the canonical status of the Bible remained a high priority in the literary experiments of missionary writers. The necessary objective of presenting a full and accurate account largely restricted the degree to which the scriptural narrative could be modified. Moreover, in the literary system of traditional Chinese literature, fiction had long occupied a peripheral position compared with poetry and classical prose until the late nineteenth century. There was no comparison between the canonical status of the Bible as a religious Scripture and the inferior literary status of vernacular novels. Missionary novelists had to execute a fine balancing act between the conveyance of biblical messages and the creation of fictional works. This dilemma was succinctly expressed by James Legge, who ardently defended his "bold" attempt to rewrite the Holy Scriptures into the form of a Chinese novel. He reiterated in the preface of *Brief Biography of Joseph* that "This work, albeit in the form of a novel, neither fabricates information nor supplies 'branches and leaves' as one pleases. In conformity with the historical accounts of the Bible, the novel refrains from making any addition or deletion."[52] Strict adherence to the biblical narrative was claimed to be Legge's guiding principle in the composition of the novel. While most novels produced by missionaries endeavored to fulfill the predominant function of proselytization, the introduction of literary elements and commentary to the biblical narratives was supposed to be a means to the end of leading the interested audience to reading of the Bible itself.

The representative missionary novels discussed above have manifested the multiple representations and reappropriations of Christianity, where biblical imageries and symbolism were transformed by linguistic manipulation into new contextualized forms that nurtured distinctive new fruits of literature and expanded the religious imagination of Chinese readers and writers. By way of illustration, a number of the "New Age Novels" in 1895 are heavily inspired by William Burns's translation of *The Pilgrim's Progress* as manifested by their imitation of its allegorical genre and rhetorical devices. Typically, *Wuming xiaoshuo* 無名小說 (*Unnamed Novel*, 1895) by Zhang Tianshu 張佃書 manifests rich intertextual relations with Burns's *Tianlu licheng* by transforming the entire allegory into a piece of traditional Chinese *shidiao* 時調 (popular tune) in twelve stanzas, being sung by a character in the novel. The *shidiao* exhibits the hybridity of multiple religious expressions, with the Confucian, Buddhist, and Daoist elements intricately intermingled to accommodate and communicate Christian thoughts and biblical imageries in *The Pilgrim's Progress*.[53] In this regard, our understanding of Chinese Christian literature may hence be enriched by highlighting the intertextual connections between missionary literature and fictional works produced by Chinese Christian authors. Furthermore, the late Qing Chinese translations of *The Pilgrim's Progress* facilitated the introduction of Western narrative elements and Christian poetics for the experimentation of modern Chinese fiction. The literary and religious motifs of the spiritual journey and pilgrimage in *The Pilgrim's Progress* left evident traces in the novels of some modern Chinese writers, particularly Xu Dishan 許地山 (1894–1941). His novels—*Shangren fu* 商人婦 (*The Merchant's Wife*) and *Yu Guan* 玉官 (*Lady Jade*), with their explicit references to the title *Tianlu licheng*—narrate the solitary journeys of adventure of the female protagonists, bearing a striking resonance to, and refashioning of, the spiritual odyssey undertaken by Christian in *The Pilgrim's Progress*. And ultimately, the literary fruits of the missionaries not only had facilitated reception of the Bible and spread of the associated religious message but also had reshaped and modernized the literary and social landscapes of the late Qing period and the May Fourth new literary movement.

Notes

1. See John T. P. Lai, "Robert Morrison's Chinese Literature and Translated Modernity," in *A New Literary History of Modern China*, ed. David Der-wei Wang (Cambridge, MA: Harvard University Press, 2017), 56–62.
2. John T. P. Lai, *Negotiating Religious Gaps: The Enterprise of Translating Christian Tracts by Protestant Missionaries in Nineteenth-Century China* (Sankt Augustin: Institut Monumenta Serica, 2012), 44–47.
3. Chloë Starr, ed., *Reading Christian Scriptures in China* (London and New York: T&T Clark, 2008), 32–48; Lai, *Negotiating Religious Gaps*, 119–144.
4. Patrick Hanan, "The Missionary Novels of Nineteenth-Century China," *Harvard Journal of Asiatic Studies* 60.2 (2000): 413–443.
5. Ibid. 413.
6. See John T. P. Lai 黎子鵬, *Attuning the Gospel: Chinese Christian Novels of the Late Qing Period* [in Chinese] 福音演義：晚清漢語基督教小說的書寫 (Taipei: National Taiwan University Press, 2017).
7. See William Milne, *Zhang Yuan liangyou xianglun* [in Chinese] 張遠兩友相論 (Malacca: Anglo-Chinese College, 1831). For an annotated edition of *Zhang Yuan liangyou xianglun*, see John T. P. Lai, ed., *Selected Christian Narrative Literature of Late-Qing China* [in Chinese] 晚清基督教敘事文學選粹 (New Taipei: CCLM Publishing, 2012), 1–46.
8. See Daniel H. Bays, "Christian Tracts: The Two Friends," in *Christianity in China: Early Protestant Missionary Writings*, ed. Suzanne Wilson Barnett and John King Fairbank (Cambridge, MA: Harvard University Press, 1985), 19–34.
9. For the life and work of Gützlaff, see Jessie Gregory Lutz, *Opening China: Karl F. A. Gützlaff and Sino-Western Relations, 1827–1852* (Grand Rapids: William B. Eerdmans Publishing, 2008).
10. For the list of Gützlaff's works in Chinese, see Alexander Wylie, *Memorials of Protestant Missionaries to the Chinese* (Shanghai: American Presbyterian Mission Press, 1867), 56–63.
11. For an annotated collection of Gützlaff's novels, see John T. P. Lai, ed., *The Doctrine of Redemption: The Collected Christian Novels of Karl Friedrich August Gützlaff* [in Chinese] 贖罪之道傳：郭實獵基督教小說集 (New Taipei: CCLM Publishing, 2013); Oh Soon-bang, Li Sher-shiueh, and John T. P. Lai, eds., *Christian Fiction in Qing China, 1709–1907: An Anthology with Commentary and Annotations* [in Chinese] 清代基督宗教小說選注, vol. 1 (Taipei: Institute of Chinese Literature and Philosophy, 2018), 227–291.
12. *The Thirteenth Annual Report of the American Tract Society* (New York: American Tract Society, 1838), 133–134.
13. See John T. P. Lai, "Gützlaff, Karl F. A.," in *Encyclopedia of the Bible and Its Reception*, eds. Eric J. Ziolkowski et al. (Berlin and New York: De Gruyter, 2015), 10:1024–1025; Lai, *Literary Representations of Christianity in Late Qing and Republican China* (Leiden: Brill, 2019), 17–37; Lai, ed., *The Doctrine of Redemption*, xiii–xci.
14. See James Legge, tr., *The Chinese Classics: With a Translation, Critical and Exegetical Notes, Prolegomena, and Copious Indexes*, 5 vols. (Hong Kong: Hong Kong University Press, 1960).

15. See James Legge, *Brief Biography of Joseph* [in Chinese] 約瑟紀畧 (Hong Kong: London Mission Press, 1870). For an annotated edition of *Brief Biography of Joseph*, see Oh, Li, and Lai, eds., *Christian Fiction in Qing China*, 1:293–328.
16. Legge, *The Chinese Classics*, 2:397.
17. Ibid. 3:61.
18. James Legge, *Confucianism in Relation to Christianity: A Paper Read before the Missionary Conference in Shanghai on May 11th 1877* (Shanghai: Kelly & Walsh, 1877), 7–8.
19. Ibid. 3. See also Lauren Pfister, "Nineteenth-Century Ruist Metaphysical Terminology and the Sino-Scottish Connection in James Legge's *Chinese Classics*," in *Mapping Meanings: The Field of New Learning in Late Qing China*, ed. Michael Lackner and Natascha Vittinghoff [*sic*] (Leiden; Boston: Brill, 2004), 615–638.
20. Legge, *Confucianism in Relation to Christianity*, 10.
21. Northrop Frye, *The Great Code: The Bible and Literature* (San Diego, New York, and London: Harcourt Brace Jovanovich, 1983), 169.
22. These manuscripts were deposited in the C. V. Starr East Asian Library, University of California, Berkeley, and reprinted in Zhou Xinping 周欣平, ed., *The Collected New Age Novels of the Late Qing Period* [in Chinese] 清末時新小說集, 14 vols. (Shanghai: Shanghai guji chubanshe, 2011).
23. See John T. P. Lai, "Fictional Representation of the Bible: Chinese Christian Novels of the Late 19th Century," *Literature and Theology* 28.2 (June 2014): 213–217.
24. William Chalmers Burns, tr., *Progress on the Path to Heaven* [in Chinese] 天路歷程 (s. l.: s. n., 1853).
25. Legge, trans., *The Chinese Classics*, 2:447.
26. See John T. P. Lai 黎子鵬, *The Afterlife of a Classic: A Critical Study of the Late-Qing Chinese Translations of* The Pilgrim's Progress [in Chinese] 經典的轉生—晚清《天路歷程》漢譯研究 (Hong Kong: Christian Study Centre on Chinese Religion and Culture, 2012), 108–115.
27. *China Centenary Missionary Conference Record: Report of the Great Conference Held in Shanghai, April 5th to May 8th, 1907* (New York: American Tract Society, 1907), 196–197.
28. Thomas Hall Hudson, tr., *Bright Journey of the Victorious Traveler* [in Chinese] 勝旅景程 (Ningpo: Ningjun Kaimingshan fuyindian, 1870). For an annotated edition of *Bright Journey of the Victorious Traveler*, see Lai, *Selected Christian Narrative Literature of Late-Qing China*, 227–399.
29. Hudson, tr., *Bright Journey of the Victorious Traveler*, 56.
30. Legge, tr., *The Chinese Classics*, 1:200.
31. See Lai, *Attuning the Gospel*, 53–78.
32. D. MacGillivray, *New Classified and Descriptive Catalogue of Current Christian Literature, 1901 (Wen-li and Mandarin)* (Shanghai: Society for the Diffusion of Christian and General Knowledge among the Chinese, 1902), 87.
33. William Chalmers Burns, tr., *Enlightening the Right Way* [in Chinese] 正道啟蒙 (Peking: Fuyintang, 1864). For an annotated edition of *Enlightening the Right Way*, see Lai, *Selected Christian Narrative Literature of Late-Qing China*, 80–180.
34. See Lai, "Fictional Representation of the Bible," 209–213.
35. Donald MacGillivray, ed., *A Century of Protestant Missions in China (1807–1907)* (Shanghai: American Presbyterian Mission Press, 1907), 621.
36. See Lai, *Negotiating Religious Gaps*, 135–136.
37. Mary Harriet Porter, tr., *Sweet Home* [in Chinese] 安樂家 (Shanghai: Chinese Religious Tract Society, 1882). For an annotated edition of *Sweet Home*, see Oh, Li, and Lai, eds., *Christian Fiction in Qing China*, 2:159–221.

38. Humphrey Carpenter and Mari Prichard, *The Oxford Companion to Children's Literature* (Oxford: Oxford University Press, 1985), 116.
39. See Lai, *Attuning the Gospel*, 79–98.
40. Ferdinand Genähr, tr., *Exemplar in the Golden House* [in Chinese] 金屋型儀 (s. l.: s. n., 1852). For an annotated edition of *Exemplar in the Golden House*, see Oh, Li, and Lai, eds., *Christian Fiction in Qing China*, 2:3–36.
41. Lai, *Attuning the Gospel*, 19–51.
42. Gillian Avery, *Nineteenth-Century Children: Heroes and Heroines in English Children's Stories 1780–1900* (London: Hodder and Stoughton, [1965]), 81.
43. See Knud Lundbæk. *Joseph De Prémare, 1666–1736, S.J.: Chinese Philology and Figurism* (Aarhus: Aarhus University Press, Acta Jutlandica, 1991).
44. For an annotated edition of *Meng meitu ji*, see Oh, Li, and Lai, eds., *Christian Fiction in Qing China*, 1:11–28.
45. Li Sher-shiueh 李奭學, "Dreaming about the Paradise: The First Chinese Mimesis of a Western Story: A Preliminary Study of 'Meng Meitu ji'" [in Chinese] 中西合璧的小說新體—清初耶穌會士馬若瑟著〈夢美土記〉初探, *Hanxue Yanjiu* (*Chinese Studies*) 29.2 (2011): 81–116.
46. For an annotated edition of *A Confucianist Befriends a Believer*, see Oh, Li, and Lai, eds., *Christian Fiction in Qing China*, 1:37–91.
47. Li Sher-shiueh李奭學, "'Jesus Did Not Destroy Confucius; Rather, Confucius Was Thus Named All Because of Jesus' Help': A Close Look at Joseph Prémare's *Rujiaoxin*" [in Chinese] 「耶穌不滅孔子，孔子倒成全於耶穌」—試論馬若瑟著《儒交信》, *Logos & Pneuma: Chinese Journal of Theology* 46 (Spring 2017): 27–73.
48. Li Sher-shiueh, *Transwriting: Translated Literature and Late-Ming Jesuits* [in Chinese] 譯述: 明末耶穌會翻譯文學論 (Hong Kong: The Chinese University Press, 2012), 438–439.
49. D. E. Mungello, "The Return of the Jesuits to China in 1841 and the Chinese Christian Backlash," *Sino-Western Cultural Relations Journal* 27 (2005): 9–46.
50. John T. P. Lai, "Performing Religion: Chinese Catholic Biblical Drama in the Republican Era," *Journal of Chinese Religions* 45.1 (May 2017): 39–62; *Catalogus Generalis Librorum Catholicorum qui in Sinis Eduntur* (*General Catalogue of Chinese Catholic Books* 中華公教圖書總目) (Hong Kong: Catholic Truth Society, 1941), 193–201.
51. Han Tianmin 韓天民, *Daozhen Comes to China* [in Chinese] 道眞來華 (Sienhsien: Imprimerie de Tchely S.-E., 1916), preface, 5.
52. Legge, *Brief Biography of Joseph*, preface, 1.
53. Lai, *Attuning the Gospel*, 159–188.

Primary Sources

Catalogus Generalis Librorum Catholicorum qui in Sinis Eduntur (General Catalogue of Chinese Catholic Books 中華公教圖書總目). Hong Kong: Catholic Truth Society, 1941.

Lai, John T. P. 黎子鵬, ed. Selected Christian Narrative Literature of Late Qing China [in Chinese] 晚清基督教敘事文學選粹. New Taipei, CCLM Publishing, 2012.

Lai, John T. P., ed. *The Doctrine of Redemption: The Collected Christian Novels of Karl Friedrich August Gützlaff* [in Chinese] 贖罪之道傳：郭實獵基督教小說集. New Taipei: CCLM Publishing, 2013.

Lai, John T. P., ed. *Daode chuhai zhuan: Selected New Age Novels by Late Qing Chinese Christians* [in Chinese] 道德除害傳—清末基督徒時新小說選. New Taipei: CCLM Publishing, 2015.

Lai, John T. P., ed. *Gusheng Ruose juben: An Annotated Anthology of Chinese Catholic Biblical Plays of the Republican Period* [in Chinese] 古聖若瑟劇本—民國天主教聖經戲劇選輯. New Taipei: CCLM Publishing, 2019.

Li, Sher-shiueh 李奭學 and Lin Hsi-chiang 林熙強, eds. *Christian Literature in Chinese Translation, 1595–1647: An Anthology with Commentary and Annotations* [in Chinese] 晚明天主教翻譯文學箋注. Taipei: Institute of Chinese Literature and Philosophy, Academia Sinica, 2014.

Oh, Soon-bang 吳淳邦, Li Sher-shiueh, and John T. P. Lai, eds. *Christian Fiction in Qing China, 1709–1907: An Anthology with Commentary and Annotations* [in Chinese] 清代基督宗教小說選注. Taipei: Institute of Chinese Literature and Philosophy, 2018.

Wylie, Alexander. *Memorials of Protestant Missionaries to the Chinese: Giving a List of Their Publications and Obituary Notices of the Deceased*. Shanghai: American Presbyterian Mission Press, 1867.

Zhou, Xinping 周欣平, ed. *The Collected New Age Novels of the Late Qing Period* [in Chinese] 清末時新小說集. 14 vols. Shanghai: Shanghai guji chubanshe, 2011.

CHAPTER 18

CATHOLIC TRACTS AND PARABOLIC STORIES IN MING-QING CHINA

SHER-SHIUEH LI

Introduction: Problems of "*Shengjing*"

In the Chinese-speaking world today, the Bible is generally translated as the *Shengjing* 聖經. This term, when it made its first appearance in the Christian circle of the Ming dynasty, addressed different contents notwithstanding. In 1605, Matteo Ricci 利瑪竇 (Li Madou, 1552–1610) published a book titled *Shengjing yuelu* 聖經約錄. For this book, however, the "*sheng*" of "*shengjing*" is an adjective describing "*jing*," which means classics or any Chinese texts that are honorable, sacred, or holy. So, in the context of *Shengjing yuelu*, the term "*shengjing*" signifies nothing more than honorable or divine texts. As expected, it includes some creeds that are taken as prestigious and essential for Christianity. These creeds, prayers, and other texts include *Tianzhu jing* 天主經 (The Lord's Prayer), *Shenmu jing* 聖母經 (The Hail Mary), the *Tianzhu shijie* 天主十誡 (Ten Commandments), *Shenhaojing* 聖號經 (The Sign of the Cross), *Aijin shishiduan* 哀矜十四端 (The Fourteen Works of Mercy), the *Zuizhong qiduan* 罪宗七端 (The Seven Deadly Sins), *Kezui qiduan* 克罪七端 (The Seven Virtues), *Tianzhu shande* 天主三德 (Faith, Hope, and Love), *Renshen wushi* 人身五司 (Five Senses of the Body), *Shenyou sansi* 神有三司 (The Three Faculties of the Soul), 阨格勒西亞撒格辣孟多 (Seven Sacraments), *Shi'er yapoluo shinbolu* 十二亞玻斯多羅性薄錄 (*apostolicos simbolos*), etc.[1] Though the *Shengjing yuelu* is not the translation of the full Vulgate Bible, the creeds and prayers therein are indispensable and thus essential to Catholic and therefore Christian belief. Obviously, Christianity did not monopolize "*shengjing*"; it also could be applied to any other sacred texts of traditional Chinese religions or even eminent philosophy at that time.

So far as all biblical stories are concerned, the *Shengjing yulu* does not tell us anything except the Eight Beatitudes of Jesus at the Sermon on the Mount (*zhenfu baduan* 真福八端; Matt 5:3–12) and the Ten Commandments. Compared with the Nestorian translation of the partial imports of the Bible, Ricci did not offer a lot, even if the Nestorian Stele, and thus Nestorian Christianity, were found by members of the Society of Jesus, the Catholic order to which Ricci belonged. One thousand years ago, when the Nestorians came to China, they had translated at least thirty short books of the Bible, although they have been consigned to oblivion. The "*Xutin* 序聽" in *Xutin Mishisuo jing* 序聽迷詩所經 is generally supposed to mean Jesus,[2] and the text in its totality is a much shortened story of Jesus' life, starting from his trinitarian ontology as shapeless and intangible and continuing through His (God) bestowing possibly the Ten Commandments and, finally, to Jesus' Nativity and Resurrection. This text looks more like a simple *harmonia evangelica* version of the life of Jesus, although its Chinese style, in sharp contrast to the magnificently poetic translation of the Marian hymn "Sanwei mengdu zhang 三威蒙度讚," or the Magnificat (Luke 1:46–55),[3] is not as strong and its names therein difficult to identify.

Jesuit Tracts and the Bible

The Ten Commandments were the first biblical text to have been translated into Chinese by the Ming Jesuits. In 1584, Michele Ruggieri 羅明堅 (Luo Mingjian, 1543–1607), virtually the earliest Jesuit who went to China, published his *Tianzhu shilu* 天主實錄. In this book, which one hitherto has to anoint as the first catechism in Chinese, Ruggieri retold something about the Bible. Whereas he has put down several stories from the holy book—the creations of the heavens, the waters, the earth, and Adam and Eve, for instance—he translated directly from the Bible only the Ten Commandments, whose title in its highlighted version is *Zhuchuan Tianzhu shijie* 祖傳天主十誡. Just like the Sermon on the Mount, Ruggieri had the Ten Commandments rendered in Chinese idioms. In a sense, these translations were so done all because, linguistically or culturally, they are highly Sinicized. To meet Chinese ethical requirements, for example, Ruggieri had to replace the Christian understanding of "honoring" one's parents with the Confucian sense of "filial piety" to them.[4]

Ricci made almost no contribution to the rendition of the Bible. He was nevertheless a good translator of other genres: maxims on friendship, proverbial teachings by Stoic scholars, and medieval as well as humanistic dialogues in the transmission of Christian faith. *Jiaoyou lun* 交友論, *Tianzhu shiyi* 天主實義, *Jiren shipian* 畸人十篇, and *Ershiwu yan* 二十五言 were all unprecedented works in the history of China,[5] not to mention in the development of Christianity in that land. These tracts are replete with illuminative, moral stories used to teach and to defend Christian tenets. He did not translate the Bible though; instead, he taught the messages thereon through Christian and pagan stories. Paganism and Christianity are mingled in his tracts to form a kind of

Augustinian *eloquentia et sapientia* so as to convince the Chinese of the superiority of the Christian religion.

The almost complete life of Jesus based on the Gospels had not appeared in the Ming until Giulio Aleni 艾儒略 (Ai Rulu, 1582–1649) published its formidable *Tianzhu jianshen yanxing jilue* 天主降生言行紀略 or *A Synoptic History of God's Descending to the World* (1635). Aleni humbly says in his preface to the book that he "dares not say" that he "was translating the Gospels" (*bugan yan yijing* 不敢言譯經).[6] *Tianzhu jianshen yanxing jilue* is commonly believed to have been translated from Ludolph of Saxony's (ca. 1295–1378) *summa evangelica*, the *Vita Jesu Christi* (1374), which was not only the first Life of Jesus in history but also an influential biography at the turn of the Middle Ages. This notwithstanding, I opine that Aleni translated a large part of the Gospels by consulting the *Via Jesu Christi*, and this, together with the Vatican ban on Bible rendition, is most likely the reason he disavowed identifying himself as a translator.[7] Without doubt, Aleni's synoptic history of Jesus was the first fuller history of Jesus, spanning from nativity to ascension and including numerous episodes of Jesus' miracles done in a short life in this world. In *Tianzhu jianshen yanxing jilue*, Aleni formally depicted the Gospels with the term "*shengjing*,"[8] a label that, in history, was to be followed by his Jesuit brothers to designate the Bible. It is certainly the Vulgate version, since Aleni has overtly suggested this in his "*wanrilue jingshuo* 萬日略經說,"[9] which can be deemed an introduction to his book.

Since Aleni's *Tianzhu jianshen yanxing jilue* is comparatively a fuller rendition of Jesus' life, most major parables of Jesus are well kept in Chinese. We can see here and there the "Parable of the Prodigal Son," the "Parable of the Good Samaritan," the "Parable of the Budding Fig Tree," etc. What is intriguing is that the first parable that the Jesuits rendered is the renowned "Parable of Sowing Seeds," which, however, does not appear in any biblical story or text ever translated into Chinese, but in a hagiography entitled *Shen Ruosafa shimo* 聖若撒法始末:

> 吾主有云：「有農播種，或下於路傍者，鳥啄食之。或下於磽确之地，隨生隨稿 [sic]，為其土薄而根不深也。或下於荊棘之中，荊棘擁蔽之，亦不長發。惟下於肥饒之土，自秀而實矣。」[10]
>
> . . . [My Lord] said, "A sower went out to sow. And as he sowed, some seed fell on the path, and birds came and ate it up. Some fell on rocky ground, where it had little soil. It sprang up at once because the soil was not deep, and when the sun rose it was scorched, and it withered for lack of roots. Some seed fell among thorns, and the thorns grew up and choked it. But some seed fell on rich soil, and produced fruit. . . ." (Matt 13:1–8)[11]

Before the middle of the nineteenth century, *Shen Ruosafa shimo* had been taken as part of the *Vitae Patrum*, or one of the lives in the *Desert Fathers*. Scholars since the second half of the nineteenth century, however, have been inclined to hold that it is a Christianized life of the Buddha, though titled *Barlaam and Ioasaph*, and the most popular version of which was written in Greek by St. John Damascene (ca. 676–794). It is when Barlaam would like to illuminate his disciple Ioasaph, an Indian prince who obviously is the young Buddha, that the above parable is told. The Chinese version of this romance of the Christian Buddha was translated in 1602, making the "Parable of Sowing Seeds" the first parable of Jesus to ever appear. Niccolò Longobardo 龍華民 (Long Huamin, 1559–1654), a Jesuit who succeeded Ricci to preside over the see in China, is perceived to be the translator of the hagiographical romance.[12]

Politics of Translation

The Chinese Jesuits were permitted to render the Bible in 1615. But formally, no genuine attempts to translate the Bible were made before 1636; an interesting topic of debate is thus formed.[13] With the exception of a Vatican interdict, one of the discourses to defend the Jesuits refraining from translating the complete Bible is the controversial idea of "biblical insufficiency from divine perfection,"[14] so much so that the first generation of Jesuits thought it more important to render church creeds, liturgical prayers, and sacraments as found in the *Shengjing yuelu*. Chances are that the idea was correct, and so Aleni, being a proliferate translator, resisted the claim of "translating" even the selected Gospels in the preface to his *Tianzhu jiangshen yenxing jilue*.[15]

Aleni finished "his" version of Jesus' life in 1635, immediately followed by an album of fifty-three pictures of a graphic, translated biography of Jesus from Jerónimo Nadal's (1507–1580) *Evanglicae Historiae Imagines* (1593). This was popular in the Renaissance since it was often included in Nidal's *Adnotationes et Meditationes in Evangeliae* (1595), a meditative commentary inspired by the *Spiritual Exercises*, on the Sunday readings by one of the closest followers of St. Ignatius of Loyola (1491–1556).[16] In addition to *Tianzhu jianshen jixiang* 天主降生言行紀像 (1635?), Aleni also gave his graphic life of Jesus a very Confucian title: *Tianzhu jiangshen chuxiang jingjie* 天主降生出像經解 (hereafter abbreviated as *Chuxiang jingjie*).[17] "*Jingjie*" is a special genre commonly referring to texts interpreting Confucian canons. Aleni, actually, had moved one more step forward than Ricci had done by calling his Chinese life of Christ a "*jing*," having the narrative of Jesus' life equal especially the sacred texts of Confucianism. Thus, he named the Old Testament (hereafter OT) "*Gujing* 古經" and the New Testament (hereafter NT), the "*Xinjing* 新經".[18] These two terms were to be employed by his Qing brothers in the same order.

What is curious is that, in his *Chuxiang jingjie*, Aleni, with the exception of headings, did not completely render the captions of Nadal's original into Chinese. On the contrary, he transplanted words in the *Vita Jesu Christi* into his *Chuxiang jingjie*, making them the explanation of the pictures therein.[19] The Chinese *Vita Christi*, therefore, looks more like a "*shengjing*" than the *Shengjing* (Chinese Bible) can be. In terms of translation, Aleni even had the pictures of his *Chuxiang jingjie* transcribed from copper-plate etchings into engravings since, up to this point, the Chinese remained ignorant and unable to produce etchings. The engravers from Fujian, part of which was Aleni's diocese or parish in the mid-seventeenth century, must have contributed greatly to the formation of this "Chinese, graphic Bible." It takes little imagination to see that the first European work in *harmonia evangelica* has transformed itself into a Chinese classic, regardless of the contents of its text or its sub-text.

Given the publication of *Chuxiang jinjie*, the Jesuits were moving closer toward the modern, translated title of the Bible that Ricci had intimated with his collection of creeds, prayers, etc. As expected, the next holy book the Jesuits published in China bore the title "*Shengjing*" without hesitation, and that is Manuel Dias Jr.'s 陽瑪諾 (Yang Manuo, 1574–1659) *Shengjing zhijie* 聖經直解. "*Shengjing*" refers not only to the four Gospels, or *evangelia* (*Erwanrilue* 阨萬日略) in Dias's words, but also other books in the OT and NT.[20] Unlike Aleni, Dias designated the OT or Judaism *Gujiao* 古教, while the NT or Christianity was called *Xinjiao* 新教. He also penned the Four Gospels (*Sishi Shengjing* 四史聖經),[21] a term adopted by other Jesuits in the Qing dynasty. The *Shengjing zhijie* appeared only one year after Aleni published his *Chuxiang jingjie* as illustrations of the *Tianzhu jiangshen yanxing jilue*. Obviously, Dias did not mean to translate the Bible as a whole, not even the whole NT. The title *Shengjing zhijie* comprises two parts: One is *Shengjing* and the other, *zhijie*. By *Shengjing*, Dias did mean part of the Bible, but he did not have the ambition to which Aleni aspired. He translated a mere fifty-five verses or parts from the Gospels for Sunday and feast-day reading. Dias, as he was to work on the Bible, was superbly careful about the Chinese style that equals *jing*. The result is an antique, though not obsolete, style, one that has been employed in Chinese classics, which was difficult not only for non-native speakers but also for native speakers of Chinese to understand completely. Dias, like several other Jesuits, began his studies of Chinese with the *Shujing* 書經,[22] and for him, therefore, this Confucian text was certainly representative of what a genuine *jing* is. The style of his "*Shengjing*," of course, was created by imitating as closely as possible that of the *Shujing*. Let us, for example, take Dias's translation of Luke 21:25–33, which serves as the first passage of his *Shengjing zhijie*:

> 維時, 耶穌語門弟子曰: 「日月諸星, 時將有兆: 地人危迫, 海浪猛鬨, 是故厥容憔悴, 為懼且傒所將加於普世。諸天之德悉動。乃見人子乘雲來降, 威嚴至極。始顯是事, 爾皆舉目翹首: 蓋爾等真福已近。」又指喻曰: 「視無花果等樹始結實時, 即知夏日非遙。爾輩亦然, 見行玆兆, 則知天國已近。肆予確說, 於人類未滅前, 必僉驗之地。天可毀, 予言不能不行。」[23]
>
> [Then] . . . [Jesus] said to . . . [his disciples], "There will be signs in the sun, the moon, and the stars, and on earth nations will be in dismay, perplexed by the roaring of the sea and the waves. People will die of fright in anticipation of what is coming upon the world, for the powers of the heavens will be shaken. And then they will see the Son of Man coming in a cloud with power and great glory. But when these signs begin to happen, stand erect and raise your heads because your redemption is at hand." He taught them a lesson. "Consider the fig tree and all the other trees. When their buds burst open, you see for yourselves and know that summer is now near; in

> the same way, when you see these things happening, know that the kingdom of God is near. Amen, I say to you, this generation will not pass away until all these things have taken place. Heaven and earth will pass away, but my words will not pass away...." [Translation mine.]

Partly due to Dias's difficult style of Chinese, and partly due to his practical need, he annotated his translation by borrowing traditional Chinese ways of annotation, i.e., by using the *zhen* 箴 and the *zhu* 注. On the part of the *zhen*, he gave commentaries on the passages he translated, while on the part of *zhu*, he explained what is meant by the translated characters. The second part of the title *Shengjing zhijie*, like *jingjie* has showcased earlier, is also a particular Confucian genre that commenced in the Song dynasty (960–1279) with *Xiaojing zhijie* 孝經直解 or the *Interpretation of the Classic on Filial Piety*. The most renowned *zhijie* in the Ming dynasty surely was Zhang Juzheng's (張居正, 1525–1582) *Sishu zhiji* 四書直解, which in the Jesuit pedagogical history in China, had turned out to be one of the most important textbooks for them to study not only Chinese but also Confucianism. Generally, the part of *zhijie* for a particular book is given in vernacular Chinese. But interestingly, Dias did not do so: his *zhijie* was written in literary Chinese, albeit much easier to understand than the style of his text.

Paganism and Christianity

Whereas most scholars hold that the *zhijie* part of *Shengjing zhijie* is based on Sebastian Barradas's (1542–1615) *Commentaria in Concordiam et Historiam Evangelicam* (1617),[24] I doubt that this is correct, on account of the wide coverage of classical *exempla* in this part, which can be scarcely found in Barradas. An *exemplum* has been defined as a short narration given as truthful and intended to be inserted into a speech, usually a sermon, to convince an audience by means of a salutary lesson.[25] The classical type of *exemplum*, as those also enlisted to teach in Ricci's *Jiren shipian* and *Jiaoyou lun*, is commonly pagan in nature. I quote one to demonstrate its paganism: "Occasio is a bald man chasing on a ball and with a lock on his forehead." One should catch Occasio's lock to "correct one's mistakes, or he escapes."[26] This is an interesting representation of the Occasio myth in classical antiquity, as it also goes superbly well with the old Chinese idiom, *ji buke shi* 機不可失 (not to lose an opportunity). Dias puts Occasio as *ji*. I would argue that Dias, as he says in the epilogue of this large book, annotated his arduous work with fourteen *juan* "by imitating" his "precursors" and by what he "has learned" (*zhushu jiuwen* 祖述舊聞).[27] Again, it is all because Dias followed what he had heard that he confused the Sisyphus story with the Prometheus one on the part of *jian*:

> 古賢欲警嗇人，設寓言曰：「有吝人心腸不憐，既亡，下地獄。罰應其吝，鷹立胸上，剖裂心腸，抓啄無已。異矣，鷹僅叫盡，心腸又萌，鷹始再吃，如是于無窮也。」[28]

> By giving a fable, an ancient sage was to warn people not to be stingy: "A miser, who was stingy, went to hell after he had died, and his punishment was correspondent to his stinginess: An eagle standing on his chest fed on his liver, which, as the eagle stopped crying, would grow back only to be fed again. It would so happen endlessly." [Translation mine.]

One knows that it is Prometheus—because of his theft of fire for man and other heroic deeds good for the development of human culture—whom Zeus punished by having his liver fed to an eagle. For mankind, Prometheus is, hence, a hero rather than a miser as Sisyphus is. Should Dias have "translated" his *zhijie* from Barradas, Prometheus would not have been mistaken for Sisyphus. Classical *exempla* or their Christian counterparts can be found in such tracts as *Jiren shipian*, *Jiaoyou lun*, or even Diego de Pantoja's 龐迪我 (Pan Diwuo, 1571–1618) *Qike* 七克 (1604; *Seven Conquests*), which teaches how to "conquer" the seven deadly sins with seven virtues. Later works such as Nicholas Trigault's 金尼閣 (Jin Nige, 1577–1628) *Kuangyi* 況義 (1625) and Alfonso Vagnone's 高一志 (Gao Yizhi, 1566–1640) *Lixue guyan* 勵學古言 (1632) are also full of *exempla*,[29] pagan or Christian. If spoken by Jesus, these works would be nothing short of parabolic texts for readers.

In the Zikawei Library of Shanghai, a pamphlet-like (seven folios only) translation of the Bible, whose title is *Sishi hebian* 四史合編 or the *Four Gospels Harmonized*, is found.[30] The date and the translator of this book remain unknown, while it goes quite well with the *zhijie* tradition. That is to say, the biblical texts have been translated into literary Chinese, whereas the *jie* 解, or "annotation," are given in good Mandarin Chinese. Titled *hebian* or "harmony" nevertheless, this book deals with only a minor part of Luke. The *jie* part, however, tells a good number of related events or stories in the other books of the Gospels, and so the true "harmony" can be found only in this part. Since, in the translated Luke, there are two illustrations (Annunciation and Visitation) re-worked from *Chuxiang jinjie*, the partially translated Luke would not have been done before 1635; in all likelihood, it was rendered as late as the mid-Qing.

In addition to the short parts of the Gospels, Dias also translated a tract entitled *Shen Ruoshe xingshi* 聖若瑟行實 (1644), or a biography of St. Joseph, Mary's husband.[31] He might have translated the book in response to Vagnone's *Shenmu xingshi* 聖母行實 (1629), which in three fascicles deals with Mary's life, Mariology, and the Marian miracles.[32] Just as the first fascicle of Mary's biography addresses Mary's life, spanning from her maidenhood to her Assumption, so Dias's *Shen ruoshe xingshi* also is derived from such apocryphal Gospels like the *Protoevangelium of James*.[33] Accordingly, *Shen Ruoshe xingshi* begins with Mary's life, which ushers in the early life of Joseph as an artisan, followed by his marriage to Mary. But this marriage is one without sex, and Joseph has to understand that his wife becomes pregnant because of the care of the Holy Ghost. Joseph humbly accepts God's arrangement, and, as has been told in the Gospels, he happily receives Jesus as his son. He realizes that he is to look after Jesus, even when Jesus challenges other teachers at a young age. St. Joseph is anointed the patron of the Church.

Early Catholic Chinese *Shengjing* and Chinese Cultures

In 1634, the Vatican placed a veto on the translation of the Bible into any "dialects," including Chinese. Dias's *Shengjing zhijie*, probably because it was translated from readings for Sunday school and also for priests only, survived from the veto. Not until the early Qing could one see again a translation of the Vulgate. What was next to Dias's work was Jean Basset's 白日昇 (Bai Risheng, ca. 1662–1715) influential translation of the Gospels into a text in *harmonia evangalica*. The *Sishi youbian Yeshu Jilishidu fuyin zhi hebian* 四史攸編耶穌基利斯督福音之合編 (ca. 1702–1707; hereafter abbreviated as *Sishi youbian*) was "influential" because it had great impact on future translations of the Bible, Catholic or Protestant. Robert Morrison (1782–1834), before he started to work on *Shentian shenshu* 神天聖書 (1823), the first Protestant Bible translated into Chinese, had read a copy of Basset's translation and consulted it intensively.[34] Louis de Poirot 賀清泰 (1735–1813), while translating his renowned *Guxin shengjing* 古新聖經, the first Catholic attempt to render the complete Vulgate Bible, also might have consulted Basset's work.[35] Even Gabriele Allegra 雷永明 (Lei Yongmin, 1907–1976), when he began to render what we know today as the John Duns Scotus Bible in Chinese, also had a copy made of Basset's work by Ying Chianli 英千里 (1900–1969) in London.[36] Basset was a member of the Mission Étangere, Paris. Despite the fact that his translation is commonly abbreviated as the *Sishi youbian*, which means a gospel harmony of a Diatessaron, it also covers the Acts, the book of Hebrews, and some other parts of Paul's letters. In spite of its great impact on later translations, the *Sishi youbian* was not translated into literary Chinese; it is much worse than the strenuous style of Dias's *Shengjing zhijie*, and this may account for the reason, although it is well known, why it has not been published even today.

The interdictions of Bible translation were evoked once again and reinforced in 1728, when *Sacra congregatio christiano nomini propagando* issued its verdict that no translations could be done: All Catholics had to rely on the *Vulgatam Clementinam* for understanding God.[37] What made matters worse is that Emperor Yonzheng (1723–1735) of the Qing dynasty at that time also gave a verdict on missionary works: No books by missionaries could be published under his reign.[38] This verdict notwithstanding, translation of the Bible into Chinese never ceased. Some twenty-five years after the *Sishi youbian* was completed, François Xavier d'Entrecolles 殷弘緒 (1664–1741) "published" his *Xunwei shenbian* 訓慰神編 (1730?),[39] which brought stylistic and formalistic variety to the Catholic rendition of the Bible as of that time. I highlight the word "published" because it was truly published around 1730. D'Entrecolles was a French Jesuit whose parish was in Jianxi, but he visited Beijing several times and served for a long time as the head of the French missionaries. He was unafraid of political repression, to the extent that he gathered together his followers and preached secretly during the Yonzheng reign. His Chinese was so excellent that he was one of the few early translators of famous Chinese short stories into French. Scholars know less about d'Entrecolles because his translation of the *Xunwei shenbian* was done during the period when translation of the Bible was apparently prohibited, and publication of missionary books was even more strictly prohibited. To the best of my knowledge, the *Xunwei shenbian* was the third attempt of early Catholic missionaries at translating the Vulgate Bible, only after Dias and Basset.

Xunwei shenbian is actually the translated book of Tobias (Tobit) in the OT, but accompanying the translation are d'Entrecolles's personal annotations and commentary on the text. The text of *Xunwei shenbian* begins with a poetic patchwork collected from the lines in the Guofeng 國風, the Ya 雅, and the Zhousong 周頌 sections of the *Shijing* 詩經, supposedly the earliest collection of poetry in China, to echo the different parts of Tobias. To underpin his points, d'Entrecolles also cited Zhu Xi's commentaries on the *Shijing*. This act of citation was not so commonly seen in the Jesuits in that they did not admire the Neo-Confucianists, and Zhu was one of them. Following such novel critics as Jing Shengtan 金聖嘆 (1608–1661) and Mao Zhonggang 毛宗崗 (1632–1709), d'Entrecolles supplied many comments in colloquial Chinese over the course of Tobias' story, although he translated the story in excellent literary Chinese. And he closed the book with a description and discussion of nine virtues that he located in the story of Tobias. In a word, the design of the translated "Tobias" shows eminently good knowledge, and great command, of Chinese literature.

D'Entrecolles arrived in China when the translation of the Bible had been forbidden, but he continued editing and publishing the book of Tobias to make it into a single book, i.e., *Xunwei shenbian*. He braved double jeopardy actually: one challenge came from the Vatican and the other from Beijing. Missionaries and converts suffered greatly at the hands of the Qing government for their faith. In this circumstance, d'Entrecolles knew more that he had to teach (*xun*) and to give comfort (*wei*) to his followers because they were in great danger due to persecution of Christians at the hands of Emperor Yonzheng. There are four copies of Tobias in the Dead Sea Scrolls, and the story was therefore written in Aramaic.[40] Nevertheless, d'Entrecolles's Tobias was without doubt translated from the Vulgate Bible, as no Protestant Bibles at that time would have included this particular book.

Before Louis de Poirot attempted to translate the complete Vulgate Bible, Joseph de Prémare's 馬若瑟 (Ma Ruoshe, 1666–1736) had echoed Dias's biography of St. Joseph with his own biography of the same saint: *Shenmu jingpei Shen Ruoshe zhuan* 聖母淨配聖若瑟傳 (ca. 1725), or *St. Joseph: The Pure Spouse of St. Mary*. But instead of translating the character "*zhuan* 傳" as biography, I prefer to interpret it as "commentary," in the sense that it is a strong explanation and defense for Dias's biography of St. Joseph. The saint, again, is interpreted as a devoted husband with no desire for sex with his wife Mary, and he has from the beginning known well God's plan to have Mary conceive and give birth to Jesus, who is God Himself. St. Joseph was therefore Jesus' "foster father" (*juifu* 鞠父), and hence Mary's "pure spouse" (*jingpei* 淨配). There is no conflict of any form in this structure of the "*Sancta Familia*" (*shenjia* 聖家).[41]

Not only did Prémare respond to Dias; in 1740, Joseph Anne Marie de Moyriac de Mailla 馮秉正 (Feng Bingzheng, 1669–1748) also published a book which, by imitating the partial title of Dias, was called *Shengjing guanlu* 聖經廣益 (1740). It reprinted Dias's translation of the sentences in the Gospels for other purposes: Mailla appropriated Dias's text in order to help his readers promote their spiritual life by meditating on the life of Jesus as Dias had rendered it.[42] Mailla might have been motivated by St. Ignatius of Loyola's (1491–1556) famous *Spiritual Exercises* in compiling his own tract. The echo of Dias's *Shengjing zhijie* is strongly heard.

The first attempt made by Catholic missionaries to translate the Vulgate Bible in full happened in the last decade of the seventeenth century, most likely after Poirot had completed his rendition of the same Bible in Manchurian. Poirot worked in the Qing court as a painter for his emperor in the daytime, and, as he returned to his church at night, he served as a translator. He was probably the last Jesuit in the transitional period between the Ming and the Qing. Pursuant to a letter from his Jesuit fellow Giuseppe Panzi 潘廷章 (1773–1812?), Poirot may have begun to work on the Bible in 1790,[43] though we have no sure evidence of this starting date. He died in the reign of the next emperor, Jiaqing. It is not certain when he stopped his translation. All we know is that he sent back to the Vatican a request to publish his translation.

As a painter, Poirot was not quite outstanding; he was, however, very much famed for his partial translation of the Bible, not only because this was the first Jesuit attempt to translate the Vulgate in its entirety but also because this was, in the history of Catholicism in China until today, possibly the last attempt to translate the same version of the Bible. Poirot had been strongly influenced by St. Jerome in the style of his translated Bible. In the second preface to his translation, he highlighted the so-called "Dream of St. Jerome" and came to the conclusion that the Bible is for people to understand, and because of this, one should translate it in the middle style that St. Augustine has designated in his *On Christian Doctrine*. As a result, Poirot decided that he should render the Bible in vernacular Chinese rather than the "high style" Dias and d'Entrecolles selected for their translations.[44] In actuality, Poirot mixed the middle and the low styles in creating his own translation. As his Bible was a translation from Latin, the style he came up with is almost the first long sample of the "Europeanized style" (*Ouhua ti* 歐化體) that is widely used or spoken in the Chinese-speaking world today. When Poirot put his translation down in stylized Chinese form, his style met quite well the one employed in Jerome's Vulgate Bible in that his was in typical colloquialism. Let us take an example from Poirot's translated Gen 1:2–5:

> 陡斯的聖神在水上行著，陡斯降旨命明光生，明光就生。陡斯看著這明光好，把明光從暗影分開。明光叫「白日」，暗影叫「黑夜」。有了早晚，就成了第一日。[45]
>
> [While] the [...Spirit of Deus] swept over the waters... [Deus] said, "Let there be light," and there was light .... [Deus] saw how good the light was... [Deus] then separated the light from the darkness .... [Deus] called the light "day," and the darkness he called "night." Thus evening came, and morning followed—the first day. [Translation mine.]

The *Guxing Shengjing* was the first Bible translated into vernacular Chinese, especially in the dialect of Beijing, the capital of Ming and Qing China.

Conclusion: More on Poirot

Poirot's Vulgate includes more than 1,400,000 Chinese characters, mostly due to his inclusion of a large body of annotations. It seems to be the Catholic tradition in China for a translated Bible to include annotations. With the exception of Basset, Dias, and d'Entrecolles so translated their *Shengjing zhijie* and *Xunwei shenbian*, and Poirot was not an exception. His annotations ranged from astrology to astronomy, from anthropology to theology, and from the human sciences to the social sciences. He even went so far as to cover such details as "currency exchange" and an explanation of capacity measure. Nothing in the history of translating the Vulgate Bible into Chinese had been so "scholastic" as Poirot's.

With the exceptions of Solomon's *Song of Songs* and most of *Prophets*, Poirot almost completed the entire Vulgate. He was the first person to translate the full NT. In 1803, Poirot wrote the *Propaganda Fide* for permission to publish his Vulgate, but he received a response that praised his enthusiasm but turned down his request.[46] It is not clear whether this letter or his death in 1813 prevented Poirot from completing the Vulgate Bible. It should be remembered that very likely Morrison had read Poirot's Gospels before he started to work on his rendition, and it is for sure that Allegra completed his Scotus Bible by consulting Poirot's *Guxin shengjing*,[47] which, as mentioned earlier, means the OT and the NT. When history marked its way into the turn of the Qing dynasty, Poirot's Bible circulated in manuscript or its copies in Beijing, Shanghai, and St. Petersburg.[48] It was not until 2016 that Poirot's effort was brought to modern readership in printed form.[49] Again, nothing in the history of translating the Vulgate Bible into Chinese has been as "dramatic" as Poirot's version, and "*Shengjing*" has since become the ingrained title of the Bible in Chinese. In the Chinese-speaking world today, when it comes to the "*Shengjing*," one would think of the Bible without hesitation: Christianity monopolized this Chinese term.

Notes

1. Li Madou 利瑪竇, *Shengjing yuelu* [in Chinese] 聖經約錄 ("A Synoptic Handbook of the Holy Texts"), in *Yeshuhui Luoma dan'anguan Ming Qing Tianzhujiao wenxian* 耶穌會羅馬檔案館明清天主教文獻 (*Chinese Christian Texts from the Roman Archives of the Society of Jesus*; hereafter *YMQW*), ed. Nicolas Standaert, Ad Dudink, and Nathalie Monnet (Taipei: Ricci Institute, 2002), 4:87–116.
2. Weng Saozhun 翁紹君, an., *Hanyu Jingjiao wendian chuanshi* [in Chinese] 漢語景教文典詮釋 (*Annotations of Chinese Nestorian Documents*) (Hong Kong: Hanyu Jidujiao wenhua yanjiu shuo, 1995), 83n1.
3. Weng, *Hanyu Jingjiao wendian chuanshi*, 189–198.
4. Luo Mingjian 羅明堅 (Michele Ruggieri), *Tianzhu shilu* [in Chinese] 天主實錄 (*True Accounts of God*), in *YMQW* 4:82–83.
5. Li Madou, *Jiaoyou lun* [in Chinese] 交友論 ("Treatise on Friendship"), in *Tianxue chuhan* 天學初函 *The First Box of Western Learning*, ed. Li Zhizhao (1629; Taipei: Xuesheng, 1965),

1:291–330; Li Madou, *Tianzhu shiyi* [in Chinese] 天主實義 ("The True Meaning of the Lord of Heaven"), in *Tianxue chuhan*, ed. Li Zhizhao (1629; Taipei: Xuesheng, 1965), 1:351–636; *Jiren shipian* [in Chinese] 畸人十篇 ("Ten Chapters from a Strange Man"), in *Tianxue chuhan*, ed. Li Zhizhao (1629; Taipei: Xuesheng, 1965), 1:93–282; Li Madou, *Ershiwu yan* [in Chinese] 二十五言 ("Twenty-Five Passages"), in *Tianxue chuhan*, ed. Li Zhizhao (1629; Taipei: Xuesheng, 1965), 1:325–350.

6. Ai Zhulue 艾儒略 (Juius Aleni), *Tianzhu jianshen yanxing jilue* [in Chinese] 天主降生言行紀略 (*A Synoptic History of God's Descending to the World*), in *YMQW* 4:29.
7. Pan Feng-chuan has a different idea; see her "Shu er bu yi? Ai Rulue *Tianzhu jiangshen yanxing jilue* de kuayuyan xushu chutan [in Chinese] 述而不譯？艾儒略天主降生言行紀略的誇語言敘事初探 ("Translation as Narration: Giulio Alen's Cross-Language Narratives of *A Brief Record of the Words and Deeds of the Incarnation*"), *Zhongguo wenzhe yanjiu jikan*中國文哲研究集刊 34 (March 2009): 111–167.
8. Ai, *Tianzhu jianshen yanxing jilue*, in *YMQW* 4:23.
9. Ibid. 4:26.
10. Long Jinhua 龍精華 (Long Huamin 龍華民), tr., *Shen Ruoshafa shimo* [in Chinese] 聖若撒法始末 ("Life of St. Ioasaph") (Minzhong Tianzhutang 閩中天主堂 edition, 1645), in *Faguo guojia tushuguan Ming Qing Tian zhujiao wenxian* [in Chinese, hereafter *FMQTW*] 法國國家圖書館明清天主教文獻 (*Chinese Christian Texts from the National Library of France*), ed. Standaert, Dudink, and Monnet (Taipei: Ricci Institute, 2012), 15:238–239. Long Huamin's 1602 original has been lost; nowadays, only this modified 1645 version by Zhong Geng 張賡 is available.
11. For this essay, I use the New American Bible (New York: Catholic Press, 1970).
12. For discussions about *Shen Ruoshafa shimo*, see Li Sher-shiueh李奭學, *Yishu: Mingmo Yeshuhui fanyi wenxue lun* [in Chinese] 譯述：明末耶穌會翻譯文學論 (*Transwriting: Translated Literature and Late Ming Jesuit*) (Hong Kong: Chinese University of Hong Kong Press, 2012), 61–106.
13. Pan, "Shu er bu yi? Ai Rulue *Tianzhu jiangshen yanxing jilue* de kuayuyan xushu chutan," *Zhongguo wenzhe yanjiu jikan*, 112–113.
14. Zhuan Xintian 莊心恬, *Yeshuhui de zhai shiyin—Zhonghua diguo zhi zhong de Ruxue xingxian* [in Chinese] 耶穌會的再適應—中華帝國志中的儒學形像 (*The Re-accommodation of the Society of Jesus*) (Xinbei: Daoxian, 2014), 40–41.
15. Ai, "Preface" to his *Tianzhu jianshen yanxing jilue*, in *YMQW* 4:29.
16. John O'Malley, *The First Jesuits* (Cambridge, MA: Harvard University Press, 1993), 7–14.
17. This title appears in Aleni's preface to his *Tianzhu jianshen yanxing jixiang* (Jinjian: Jinjian Ginjiaotang, 1637), 1a.
18. Ai, *Tianzhu jianshen yanxing jilue*, in *YMQW* 4:23–24.
19. Cf. Pan, "Shu er bu yi? Ai Rulue *Tianzhu jianshen yanxing jilue* de kuayuyan xushi chutan," 139–140.
20. Yang Manuo 陽瑪諾 (Manuel Dias Jr.), *Shengjing zhijie* [in Chinese] 聖經直解 (*Vernacular Interpretation of the Shengjing*), in *Tianzhujiao dongchuan wenxian sanbian* [in Chinese; hereafter *TDW*] 天主教東傳文獻三編 (*The Third Collection of Catholic Writings in China*), ed. Wu Xiangxiang (Taipei: Xuesheng, 1965), 4:1558–1568.
21. Yang Manuo, *Shengjing zhijie*, in *TDW* 4:1569.
22. Liam Matthew Brockey, *Journey to the East: The Jesuit Mission to China, 1579–1724* (Princeton: Princeton University Press, 2007), 265.
23. Yang Manuo, *Shengjing zhijie*, in *TDW* 4:1571–1573.

24. Nicolas Standaert, "The Bible in Early Seventeenth-Century China," in *Bible in Modern China: The Literary and Intellectual Impact*, ed. Irene Eber et al. (Jerusalem: The Hebrew University of Jerusalem, 1999), 44–45n42.
25. Cf. Joan Young Gregg, *Devils, Women, and Jews: Reflections of the Other in Medieval Sermon Stories* (Albany: State University of New York Press, 1997), 11–16.
26. Yang Manuo, *Shengjing zhijie*, in *TDW* 4:1798–1799.
27. Ibid. 6:2954.
28. Ibid. 6:2947. For the story of Prometheus, see Hesiod, *Theogony* (Cambridge, MA: Harvard University Press, 1982), 507–616; and his *Works and Days*, in Apostolos N. Athanassakis, tr., *Hesiod: Theogony, Works and Days, Shield* (Baltimore: Johns Hopkins University Press, 1983), lines 47–105.
29. Pan Diwuo 龐迪我 (Diego de Pontoja), *Qike* [in Chinese] 七克 ("Seven Conquests"), in *Tianxue chuhan*, ed. Li Zhizhao (1629; Taipei: Xuesheng, 1965), 2:689–1126; Jin Nige 金尼閣 (Nicholas Trigault), *Kuangyi* [in Chinese] 況義 (*Morals Drawing from Comparison*), in *FMQTW* 4:305–343; Gao Yizhi 高一志 (Alfonso Vagnone), in *Lixue guyan* [in Chinese] 勵學古言 (*Classical Chreiai on Learning*), in *FMQTW* 4:1–66.
30. Anonymous, *Sishi hebian* [in Chinese] 四史合編, *Harmony of the Four Gospels*, kept in the Zikawei Library of Shanghai, Dudink number: SH 252B/ZKW–x; see Adrian Dudink, "The Chinese Christian Texts in the Zikawei 徐家匯 Collection in Shanghai: A Preliminary and Partial List," *Sino-Western Cultural Relations Journal* 32 (2011): 18.
31. Yang Manuo, *Shen Ruoshe xingsh* [in Chinese] 聖若瑟行實 ("Biography of St. Joseph"), in *FMQTW* 15:125–158.
32. Gao Yizhi, *Shenmu xingshi* [in Chinese] 聖母行實 ("A Biography of St. Mary"), in *Tianzhujiao donchuan wenxian sanbian*, ed. Wu Xianxian (Taipei: Xuesheng, 1965), 2:1273–1552.
33. Anonymous, *Protoevangelium of James*, in *The Lost Books of the Bible*, ed. William Hone (repr. New York: Bell, 1979), 17–91.
34. See the detailed discussion in Jost Oliver Zetzsche, *The Bible in China: The History of the Union Version or the Culmination of Protestant Missionary Bible Translation in China* (Sankt Augustin: Monumenta Serica Institute, 1999), 25–58.
35. Haijuan 鄭海娟, "Wenben zhi wan: *Guxin shengjing* yu qianhoudai Shenjian hanyiben zhi guanxi 文本之網: 古新聖經與前後代聖經漢譯本之關係," *Tsing Hua Zhongwen xuebao* 11 (June 2014): 279.
36. This copy by Yin Qianli (Ignatius Yin) is now kept in the library of Studium Biblicum Franciscum, Hong Kong.
37. Peter Guilday, "The Sacred Congregation *de Propaganda Fide* (1622–1922)," *The Catholic Historical Review* 6.4 (January 1921): 478–494.
38. Xiao Jingshan 蕭靜山, *Tianzhujiao chuanxing Zhongguo kao* [in Chinese] 天主教傳行中國考 ("History of Catholicism in China"), in *Zhongguo Tianzhujiao shiji huibian* [in Chinese] 中國天主教史籍彙編 (*Collection of Books on Catholicism in China*) (Xingbei: Fu Jen Catholic University Press, 2004), 195–205.
39. For a modern, annotated edition, see Yin Hongxu 殷弘緒 (François Xavier d'Entrecolles), *Xunwei shenbian* [in Chinese] 訓慰神編 ("A Holy Story for Teaching and Comfort"), in *Qingdai Jiduzhongjiao xiaoshuo xuenzhu* [in Chinese] 清代基督宗教小說選注 (*Christian Fiction in Qing China, 1708–1907: An Anthology with Commentary and Annotations*), ed. and an., Wu Chunbang, Li Sher-shueh, and Lai Tze Pan (Taipei: Zhongyan yanjiuyuan Zhongguo wenzhe yanjiushuo, 2018), 1:121–179.

40. Bruce M. Metzger and Michael D. Coogan, *Oxford Companion to the Bible* (Oxford: Oxford University Press, 1993), 746–747.
41. Ma Ruoshe, *Shenmu jingpei Shen Ruoshe zhuang* [in Chinese] 聖母淨配聖若瑟傳 ("St. Joseph: The Pure Spouse of St. Mary"), in *Qingdai Jiduzhongjiao xiaoshuo xuanzhu*, ed. Wu, Li, and Lai, 93–128.
42. Feng Bingzheng 馮秉正, *Shengjing guangyi* [in Chinese] 聖經廣益 ("*The Benefits of the Shengjing*"), in *FMQTW* 14:147–560.
43. Erling von Mende, "Problems in Translating the Bible into Manchu: Observations on Louis Poirot's Old Testament," in *Sowing the Word: The Cultural Impact of the British and Foreign Bible Society, 1804–2004*, ed. Stephen Batalden, Kathleen Cann, and John Dean (Sheffield: Sheffield Phoenix Press, 2006), 151; Louis Pfister, *Notices biographiques et bibliographiques sur les Jesuites de L'ancienne mission de China, 1552–1773* (Shanghai: Imprimerie de la Mission Catholique, 1932–1934), 2:969.
44. He Qingtai 賀清泰 (Louis de Poirot), "Second Preface" to his trans. and an., *Guxin shengjing cangao* [in Chinese] 古新聖經殘稿 (*Remnants of the Chinese Vulgate Bible*), ed. Li Sher-shiueh and Zheng Haijuan (Beijing: Zhonghua, 2014), 1:3–4.
45. Li and Zheng, *Guxin shengjing cangao*, 1:3.
46. N. Kowalsky, "Die Sacra Congregatio 'de Propaganda Fida' und die Übersetzung der Hl. Schrift," in *Die Heilige schrift in den katholischen Missionen*, ed. J. Becknann (Schöneck-Beckenried: Neue Zeitschrift für Missiionswissenschaft, 1966), 30.
47. Gabriele M. Allegra, *"Memorie" Autobiografiche del P. Gabriele M. Allegra O.F.M.: Missionario in Cina*, ed. Serafino M. Gozzo (Rome: np., 1986), 92–93, and 108.
48. Cf. *Guxinshengjing cangao waierzhon: Beitang ben and ManHan hebi ben* 古新聖經殘稿外二種：北堂本與滿漢合璧本 [in Chinese] (*The Other Two Remnants of Guxin shengjing: The Beitang Version and the United Version of the Man and the Han Language*), ed. Li Sher-shiueh and Ukida Keiichi (Osaka: Kansai University Press, 2018). Also see He Qingtai, *Guxin shengjing* [in Chinese] 古新聖經 ("The Old and the New Testaments"), in *Xujiahui Changshulou Ming Qing Tianzhujiao wenxian Xubian* [in Chinese] 徐家匯藏書樓明清天主教文獻續編 (*Sequel to Chinese Christian Texts from the Zikawei Library*), ed. Nicolas Standaert, Ad Dudink, and Wang Renfang (Taipei: Ricci Institute, 2013), vols. 28–34.
49. See n. 45 about the version edited by Li and Zheng.

Primary Sources

Ai Zhulue 艾儒略 (Juius Aleni). *Tianzhu jianshen yanxing jilue* 天主降生言行紀略 ("A Synoptic History of God's Descending to the World"). In *YMQW* 4:29.

Allegra, Gabriele M. *"Memorie" Autobiografiche del P. Gabriele M. Allegra* O.F.M.: *Missionario in Cina*. Edited by Serafino M. Gozzo. Rome: np., 1986.

Anonymous. *Protoevangelium of James*. In *The Lost Books of the Bible*. Edited by William Hone (New York: Bell, 1979), 17–91.

Anonymous. *Sishi hebian* 四史合編 (*Harmony of the Four Gospels*). [Kept in the Zikawei Library of Shanghai, Dudink number: SH 252B/ZKW–x.]

FMQTW = *Faguo guojia tushuguan Ming Qing Tian zhujiao wenxian* 法國國家圖書館明清天主教文獻 (*Chinese Christian Texts from the National Library of France*). Edited by Nicolas Standaert, Ad Dudink, and Nathalie Monnet.

Feng Bingzheng 馮秉正. *Shengjing guanyi* 聖經廣益 ("The Benefits of the *Shengjing*"). In *FMQTW* 14:147–560.

Gao Yizhi 高一志 (Alfonso Vagnone). *Lixue guyan* 勵學古言 ("Classical Chreiai on Learning"). In *FMQTW* 4:1–66.

Gao Yizhi. *Shenmu xingshi* 聖母行實 ("A Biography of St. Mary"). In *Tianzhujiao donchuan wenxian sanbian*. Edited by Wu Xianxian (Taipei: Xuesheng, 1965), 2:1273–1552.

Guxinshengjing cangao waierzhon: Beitang ben and ManHan hebi ben 古新聖經殘稿外二種：北堂本與滿漢合璧本 (*The Other Two Remnants of Guxin shengjing: The Beitang Version and the United Version of the Man and the Han Language*). Edited by Li Sher-shiueh 李奭學 and Ukida Keiichi 內田慶市. Osaka: Kansai University Press, 2018.

He Qingtai 賀清泰 (Louis de Poirot). "Second Preface" to his translated and annotated *Guxin shengjing cangao* 古新聖經殘稿 (*Remnants of the Chinese Vulgate Bible*). 9 vols. Edited by Li Sher-shiueh 李奭學 and Zheng Haijuan 鄭海娟. Beijing: Zhonghua, 2014.

He Qingtai. *Guxin shengjing* 古新聖經 ("The Old and the New Testaments"). In *Xujiahui Changshulou Ming Qing Tianzhujiao wenxian Xubian.* 徐家匯藏書樓明清天主教文獻續編 (*Sequel to Chinese Christian Texts from the Zikawei Library*). Edited by Nicolas Standaert, Ad Dudink, and Wang Renfang 王仁芳 (Taipei: Ricci Institute, 2013), vols. 28–34.

Hesiod. *Theogony.* Cambridge, MA: Harvard University Press, 1982.

Hesiod, *Works and Days*. Translated by Apostolos N. Athanassakis (Baltimore: Johns Hopkins University Press, 1983), lines 47–105.

Jin Nige 金尼閣 (Nicholas Trigault). *Kuangyi* 況義 (*Morals Drawing from Comparison*). In *FMQTW* 4:305–334.

Li Madou 利瑪竇 (Matteo Ricci). *Jiaoyou lun* 交友論 ("Treatise on Friendship"). In *Tianxue chuhan* 天學初函 (*The First Box of Western Learning*). Edited by Li Zhizhao 李之藻 (1629; Taipei: Xuesheng, 1965), 1:291–330.

Li Madou. *Jiren shipian* 畸人十篇 ("Ten Chapters from a Strange Man"). In *Tianxue chuhan* (*The First Box of Western Learning*). Edited by Li Zhizhao (Taipei: Xuesheng, 1965), 11:325–350.

Li Madou. *Tianzhu shiyi* 天主實義 ("The True Meaning of the Lord of Heaven"). In *Tian xue chuhan* (*The First Box of Western Learning*). Edited by Li Zhizhao (Taipei: Xuesheng, 1965), 1:351–636.

Li Madou. *Ershiwu yan* 二十五言 ("Twenty-five Passages"). In *Tianxue chuhan* (*The First Box of Western Learning*). Edited by Li Zhizhao (Taipei: Xuesheng, 1965), 1:93–282.

Li, Madou. *Shengjing yuelu* 聖經約錄 (*A Synoptic Handbook of the Holy Texts*). In *YMQW* 4:87–116.

Long Jinhua 龍精華 (Long Huamin 龍華民), tr. *Shen Ruoshafa shimo* 聖若撒法始末 (*Life of St. Ioasaph*). In *FMQTW* 15:238–239.

Luo Mingjian 羅明堅 (Michele Ruggieri). *Tianzhu shilu* 天主實錄 (*True Accounts of God*). In *YMQW* 4:82–83.

Ma Ruoshe 馬若瑟 (Joseph de Prémare). *Shenmu jingpei Shen Ruoshe zhuang* 聖母淨配聖若瑟傳 (*St. Joseph: The Pure Spouse of St. Mary*). In *Qingdai Jiduzhongjiao xiaoshuo xuenzhu.* 2 vols. Edited and annotated by Wu Chunbang 吳淳邦, Li Sher-shueh 李奭學, and Lai Tze Pan 黎子鵬 (Taipei: Zhongyan yanjiuyuan Zhongguo wenzhe yanjiushuo, 2018), 1:93–128.

Pan Diwuo 龐迪我 (Diego de Pontoja). *Qike* 七克 ("Seven Conquests"). In *Tianxue Chuhan* (*The First Box of Western Learning*). Edited by Li Zhizhao (Taipei: Xuesheng, 1965), 2:689–1126.

QJX 清代基督宗教小說選注 (*Christian Fiction in Qing China, 1708–1907: An Anthology with Commentary and Annotations*). 2 vols. Edited and annotated by Wu Chunbang 吳淳邦, Li

Sher-shueh 李奭學, and Lai Tze Pan 黎子鵬. Taipei: Zhongyan yanjiuyuan Zhongguo wenzhe yanjiushuo, 2018.

The Lost Books of the Bible. Edited by William Hone. New York: Bell, 1979.

The New American Bible. New York: Catholic Press, 1970.

TDW = *Tianzhujiao dongchuan wenxian sanbian* 天主教東傳文獻三編 (*The Third Series of the Collection of Catholic Writings in Chinese*). 6 vols. Edited by Wu Xiangxiang 吳相湘. Taipei: Xuesheng, 1965.

Weng Saozhun 翁紹君, an. *Hanyu Jingjiao wendian chuanshi* 漢語景教文典詮釋 (*Annotations of Chinese Nestorian Documents*). Hong Kong: Hanyu Jidujiao wenhua yanjiu shuo, 1995.

Yang Manuo 陽瑪諾 (Manuel Dias Jr.). *Shen Ruoshe xingshi* 聖若瑟行實 (*Biography of St. Joseph*). In *FMQTW* 15:125–158.

Yang Manuo. *Shengjing zhijie* 聖經直解 (*Vernacular Interpretation of the Shengjing*). In *TDW* 4:1558–1568.

YMQW = *Yeshuhui Luoma dan'anguan Ming Qing Tianzhujiao wenxian* 耶穌會羅馬檔案館明清天主教文獻 (*Chinese Christian Texts from the Roman Archives of the Society of Jesus*). Edited by Nicolas Standaert, Ad Dudink, and Nathalie Monnet. Taipei: Ricci Institute, 2002.

Yin Hongxu 殷弘緒 (François Xavier d'Entrecolles). *Xunwei shenbian* 訓慰神編 (*A Holy Story for Teaching and Comfort*). In *QJX* 1:121–179.

CHAPTER 19

ADOPTION OF CHRISTIAN ANTHROPOLOGY BY CHINESE INTELLECTUALS

CAO JIAN

INTRODUCTION

MODERN China from the mid-1910s until the 1940s experienced a period of intellectual ferment. The worship of science was prevalent, and the interest in European and American philosophy was strong. It also was a period of new moral standards, such as freedom, equality, and universal love of human beings. Some intellectuals turned to Chinese traditional culture, some attempted to reconcile Chinese and foreign ideas, and others argued for a value system that originated not in science but in religion, ethics, and aesthetics.[1] In their search for justification in a scriptural text, both Christian and non-Christian intellectuals found the Old Testament (henceforth OT) a rich and promising source, arguing for the value of Hebrew culture, especially the monotheistic idea of God, at times of cultural and national crises.

Monotheism is not only the central idea of the OT and the greatest contribution the Hebrew culture made to European culture but also the most stimulating biblical idea for modern Chinese intellectuals. In this paper, three major topics will be taken up. First, it will explore the ways in which the Chinese OT and its idea of God were anthropologically interpreted by Chinese intellectuals in light of modern scientism, Western philosophy, and Chinese traditional culture. Second, it will analyze how the idea of one God was utilized by Chinese intellectuals in their efforts to explain human nature and to promote individual morality. Finally, it will discuss how universal love, which was of special importance in the context of monotheism, was interpreted by Chinese intellectuals. These three topics lead to a common interest or agenda of the time: building up a society of human perfection. This essay is based primarily on the actual writings of Chinese authors, and two major groups of intellectuals will be considered: Christian converts, primarily Protestant, and non-Christians.

Idea of God in Light of Scientism, Western Philosophy, and Chinese Tradition

Scientism challenged the traditional authority of the OT and led to a controversy among Chinese intellectuals. To those with absolute faith in rationalism, like Cai Yuanpei, faith in God does not help one find the truth of the world, for God is not the final reason for everything. In other words, the OT demonstrates an early stage of human civilization when science and philosophy were intertwined with myth and religion. Thus, the idea of God is inevitably an incomplete system. Cai argued that when philosophy develops independently as a result of the growth of science, there is no longer a need for religion.[2] And faith in God does not help a person develop his morality. It is not religious doctrines like the Ten Commandments, but "human conscience" or the will to be moral, that is the only true criterion of human values. Cai believed that human conscience, as a psychological phenomenon, is powerful because everyone recognizes an idea emerging from conscience and follows it voluntarily.[3]

Wider distribution and reading of the Chinese OT—including the Delegates' Version, the Chinese Mandarin Version, and the Union Version, to name just a few dominant ones—showed its lasting power even within a hostile context. What on earth is the Bible's authority? asked some Chinese intellectuals. To them, that authority seemed to consist first and foremost in the higher criticism of OT studies. It was believed that the application of scientific methods helped expose the true meaning of the OT to the people. The understanding was that textual research by means of historical criticism helps reveal the historical evolution of an OT idea like that of God.[4] For some, this historical evolution is even the process of revelation facilitated by God's will. Yuan Ding'an believed that the OT authors had views that were identical with Darwin. After the fall of Adam and Eve, for example, God intended to show the effect of sin and evil through the cruelty of competition for survival and evolution. God did that for humanity's sake. Spencer's social evolution theory is wrong in denying God's role.[5]

In addition, the authority of the OT is indicated by the fact that it communicates eternal values in its attention to religious experiences, problems of the human mind, and the needs of spiritual life, all of which remain the same throughout history.[6] Many Chinese Christian intellectuals believed that science alone is not enough because it does not provide moral education, as demonstrated by World War I. In contrast, OT teachings are full of life and excel in communicating moral messages. In a translated article, Xu Baoqian highlighted the OT's emphasis on benevolence as the highest moral value. That emphasis is demonstrated in the establishment of the moral idea of God, namely the development from the God of revenge of antiquity to the God of justice and benevolence of the prophetic period.[7] Li Rongfang related this moral value to human survival and evolution. The family of Noah, for example, survived not because of their superior intelligence or physical prowess, but because of their superior morality.[8]

To non-Christian intellectuals with a keen interest in cultural problems and a sympathy for religion, the authority of the OT was first in its importance to Hebrew culture. However, while Christian intellectuals always believed that in medieval times, Hebrew culture was as important as Greek culture and the two combined to form a merged culture,[9] non-Christian intellectuals differed among themselves. In Cai Yuanpei's view, religion—Hebrew culture especially—should be blamed for the scholasticism of the medieval period. The weak point of scholasticism was its focus on deduction, because it blindly used simplistic OT ideas to explain the origin of the world without serious investigation.[10] Zhang Dongsun had a more favorable view of Hebrew culture; he spoke highly of Hebrew culture as one of the two sources for Western culture and wrote that Westerners fortunately absorbed Hebrew culture and, as a result, had Christianity for moral cultivation. Zhang made this point as an addition to Liang Shuming, who proclaimed that Western culture is focused on external material profits.[11]

During the New Culture Movement, European philosophy was widely translated and introduced to China as a leading branch of scientific learning that could reveal the truth of the world. Some Christian intellectuals found inspiration in atheistic philosophers. Zhu Weizhi, for example, tried to reconcile two views of Song of Songs—the modern understanding of it as a lyric of sexual love and the traditional interpretation of it as a religious book about God's love for human beings, because religious psychology relates to the love between man and woman. In that regard, Zhu turned to Sigmund Freud and Kuruyagawa Hakuson for theoretical support.[12]

Other Christian intellectuals considered philosophy and faith in God as one and the same. Yuan Ding'an argued for a "philosophy of theism" and proposed verifying God through the philosophical method. Actually, many great philosophers since antiquity—from Socrates to Darwin—have believed in a monotheistic God. Since it is human intuition to probe the question of the deity, as did Moses (Exod 33:8–13) and Gideon (Judg 6:36–40), faith in God is meaningful to human life. Therefore, the existence of God can be verified through the "pragmatist method" advocated by such philosophers as William James and Hu Shi. Unlike Laozi's "inconceivable" *dao* 道 (the Way), a "dominant, sympathetic, and anthropomorphic" God whose ultimate purpose is people can be ascertained in religious life through conscious communication with him.[13]

Wang Guowei argued that all world religions have dualistic elements. It is significant that he analyzed these elements from a philosophical viewpoint. The opposition between good and evil is a universal phenomenon in human experience, which leads to endless disputes in the world as well as to such differences as between politics and morality, religion and philosophy. In the biblical tradition, the diametrically opposed characters of Jehovah and Satan reflect the impact of Zoroastrianism. The motif of Adam and Eve's fall shows the struggle between good and evil. Similarly, in the Chinese tradition, *shen* 神 (god) and *mogui* 魔鬼 (devil) can be contrasted. Evidence of dualism also can be noted between *xing* 性 (nature) and *qi* 氣 (matter), *liangzhi* 良知 (innate knowledge) and *wuyu* 物慾 (material desires), as advocated by Lu Xiangshan and Wang Yangming. Therefore, Lu and Wang were dualists, despite their faith in humanity's *xingshan* 性善 (natural goodness), whereas Mencius was self-contradictory.[14]

Feng Youlan also believed that religion is inherently philosophical. However, the philosophy of Christianity attested to in the OT is different from the philosophy of Confucianism. First, in the philosophy of Christianity, God the Creator and humanity the created are opposites (Gen 2:7 and Isa 45:6–7). There is no internal link between the two except the covenantal relationship. In Confucianism, the "thing-itself" of the human spirit has cosmic implications. Secondly, in the philosophy of Christianity, the ideal world, in which human beings once lived and should return to, was concrete (Genesis 2–3). In Confucianism, it is abstract. Thirdly, in the philosophy of Christianity, the lost paradise cannot be restored without absolution of men's sin. Who will be redeemed and who will not depends not on men's achievements and virtues but totally on the will of God. In Confucianism, human beings can restore the ideal world they had lost with their own will power. Those unique OT ideas in Christian philosophy explain why modern science and progressivism developed nowhere else except in Europe. The cardinal ideas of progressivism are that human and nature are opposed to one another, and human can control nature with human intelligence. As Feng understood it, that reflects the relationship of human and God in the OT. The confidence in human knowledge about nature and power over nature is inspired by the idea of an anthropomorphic God as the world's creator and governor with unlimited wisdom and power. As to the concrete vision of paradise, it explains why modern Europeans hoped and worked so hard for a better world. Finally, under an autocratic God, people obviously can protest and hope to establish a human kingdom with their own power.[15]

With the revived interest and confidence in traditional Chinese culture among many Chinese intellectuals after World War I, discussions of OT ideas were frequently undertaken in parallel with ideas from Chinese traditions. Wu Zhenchun emphasized that in an age of evolutionary religion and changing academic thought, it is even more meaningful to mediate between the classics of Christianity and Confucianism. On the subject of humanity's origin, for example, Wu believed that Gen 2:7, the opening sentence of *Zhongyong* 中庸 (the Book of the Mean)—"What Heaven has ordained is called nature"—and Zhu Xi's commentary to it all expressed the same idea.[16] In fact, in Zhu's commentary, "nature" is not limited to human; it embraces that of animals also, a difference that Wu neglected.

Yuan Ding'an explored the subject of God as the Creator in greater detail. According to Chinese etymology, he wrote, the authoritative dictionary *Shuowen jiezi* 說文解字 (Origin of Chinese Characters) by Xu Shen states that "the heavenly god draws forth all things on the earth," whereas the *Shuowen jiezi xizhuan* 說文解字系傳 (Notes on the *Shuowen jiezi*) by Xu Kai 徐鍇 states that "the heavenly lord lowers energy of life to inspire all things on the earth." According to the OT, God created the embryonic world at the very beginning and then simply commanded the production of things from the land. "Command" means that God spoke, and speech has the energy of life. Therefore, that all things were produced by God's command is the same as Xu Kai's idea. God's work at the second stage, stating and drawing forth things, confirmed God as the Creator at the first stage. Scientists describe the second stage of God's work, while religious leaders reveal the first. The use of *tianshen* 天神 (the heavenly god) does not exclude the existence of other gods. Although Xu Kai stated *zhu* 主 (lord) instead, *tianzhu* 天主 (the heavenly lord) in his day did not have monotheist implications either. Nonetheless, Yuan equated *shen* and *zhu* to God, as did, of course, many missionaries. He believed that genuine Confucianism had a monotheist faith. But later, Confucianism became a polytheistic religion due to the lack of a clear monotheistic theory, and as a result of the impact of Buddhism, Daoism, and superstitions.[17]

Idea of God and Perfect Personality: Discussions on Human Conscience, Desire, Free Will, and Suffering

Chinese intellectuals did not limit themselves to attacking or defending the OT idea of God. They also applied it in their search for both individual and social redemption. Among them, Christian intellectuals in particular had an interest in the relevance of the idea of God to human personality and suffering. They generally held that individual redemption lies in moral perfection. To show that faith in God is important to the moral integrity of an individual, many Christian intellectuals emphasized the perfection of God or God the highest good.[18]

This understanding of God reveals a possible influence of Immanuel Kant. According to ideas Kant introduced at the time, the highest good meant being transcendental and being perfect. Being transcendental meant transcending everything and being free from limitations of the environment. Although this was nearly impossible in the mundane world, human beings can get increasingly closer to that goal through endless effort. Being perfect means a perfect combination of morality and pleasure. Since the motive of morality goes beyond the bounds of nature, the combination of morality and pleasure is impossible unless there is a reason both inherent and transcendental, namely God, which not only provides grounds for nature but also has morality.[19]

The human world is wicked. In Chinese culture, Xunzi advocated that human beings are bad by nature and must be reformed by education and cultivation. However, many Christian intellectuals believed that, since human was created in the image of God, he is naturally good. Some suggested that even Adam and Eve's fall implies that human beings are good by nature. Natural goodness is "human conscience" and is put by God in the heart of every human, including Cain.[20] Natural goodness is the deity in the heart as expressed by the Chan Buddhist saying, "The heart is Buddha and Buddha is the heart." That is why conscience can be called "heavenly conscience" (天良). For the same reason, conscience is natural principle, and no one can deny it or cast it aside. Yuan quoted from

Shiji 史記 (Records of the Grand Historian), saying "the great Supreme God has conferred natural goodness even on inferior people."[21] Others explained that natural goodness referred to "the heart of right and wrong" (*shifei zhixin* 是非之心) as advocated by Mencius. Plato had said that the heart of right and wrong equips a person with innate knowledge and ability.[22] Yuan Ding'an noticed that Cheng Yi 程頤 highlighted the origin of innate knowledge and ability in *tian*. Although human beings are naturally good, they are inclined to be spoiled and bad because God granted them desires and free will to choose good or evil. Inherited from Adam and Eve, desire can lead to immorality. A person is good when, following his conscience, he overcomes desire.[23] Desires are of three kinds: sensuality, selfishness, and willfulness. Each kind can be beneficial or harmful. Religion aims to develop their helpfulness and check their harmfulness.[24]

The interpretation of free will reveals once more the possible impact of Kant. Kant had stated that God allows for the existence of evil and gives human beings the freedom to choose good or evil so that they can exercise their moral responsibility.[25] Christian intellectuals regarded men's free will as evidence of human freedom. Adam and Eve had the freedom to decide what to accept and reject. Similarly, the covenant between human and God meant freedom of faith as was preserved by the Israelites. Therefore, the OT emphasizes self-determination according to one's conscience, using neither coercion nor cajolery.[26] Moreover, without free will, there would be no evolution to perfection of human beings, and they would not renew themselves ever newer from day to day. The function of the Bible and Holy Spirit is not to compel but to help human beings to evolve until they become as perfect as God. Human beings should follow their conscience to understand this will of God so that they can obey it out of their own free will. Therefore, men's free will and God's will are not mutually exclusive.[27]

The ideas of desire and free will led to discussions about the secondary good as well. The highest good, when applied to humankind, means absolute faithfulness and obedience to God, whereas the secondary good means following desire. Human beings are sinful when they choose the secondary good rather than the highest. Li Rongfang resorted to Chinese tradition for support. According to *Daxue* 大學 (the Great Learning), the ultimate goal is to "rest in the highest good" (*zhiyu zhishan* 止于至善), which means dutifulness or righteousness (*yi* 義). Mencius said, "Life is what I want; dutifulness is also what I want. If I cannot have both, I would choose dutifulness rather than life" (6A:10). The gist of Li's argument is that when a person must choose, the choice is related to morality.[28] More than that, the morality of a sage like Moses must be attributed to God, and "sageliness" is identical to holiness. Yuan Ding'an believed that the Chinese tradition confirmed his view, arguing that the perfect moral integrity of a Confucian sage is a result of modeling after *tian* or God. Zhou Dunyi, for example, advocated that a sage is one who learns from *tian* (*sheng xi tian* 聖希天).[29] Obviously, God is equated by Yuan Ding'an to Zhou Dunyi's *tian*. However, Zhou defines sagehood in terms of *cheng* 誠 (sincerity). To be sincere is to be true to the innate goodness of one's nature bestowed by heaven and to actualize one's moral potential. With the modeling of a sage from *tian*, *tianren heyi* 天人合一 (the unity of heaven and human) comes true.[30]

Unlike their Christian contemporaries, non-Christian intellectuals did not necessarily concur that God endowed humans with free will and that this free will is related to morality. Like Feng Youlan, Xu Zhimo portrayed God as one who tried to restrain men's free will. God regretted having created humans in God's image and planned to recreate humans without breathing spirit/life into his nostrils. In another poem, Xu admired the knowledge and light as represented by the serpent. Adam was a "fool" who obeyed God blindly and lived without free will to open his eyes to see "heaven and earth," "the light," and "the marvelous world."[31]

Turning now to the topic of suffering—which may be viewed by atheists as a fact rather than a problem and by polytheists as a commonplace phenomenon due to conflicts between gods—the Israelites who believed in a monotheist and merciful God required an explanation for the problem of suffering. To Christian intellectuals, the Bible explains human suffering most comprehensively because it was written by a people who had undergone centuries of suffering and oppression. God let the Israelites live in the Egypt because only then would the Israelites be prepared to risk leaving the house of slavery and reap the benefits for their future.[32] So Christian intellectuals explained suffering as God's will that human evolve a perfect personality. Li Rongfang held that suffering as God's punishment for sins is compulsory in the process of human evolution because only through punishment can human beings recognize their sins as did Jacob and Joseph.[33] The idea of suffering is certainly not alien to the Chinese tradition. According to Mencius, to confer a great office on a person, heaven also exercises the person's mind and body with suffering, which is similar to the biblical sense of suffering.[34] According to authentic Jewish exegesis, for example, eating the forbidden fruit is punished, but rewarded too, as knowing good and evil is the essential human ability for moral judgment, which is gained through the same event. Punishment in the human world is thus established as a necessary motivation for action and progress.[35]

Zhao Zichen introduced the evolution of the idea of suffering. In the early stages when a tribe or a clan was considered the unit of moral responsibility and a disaster was seen as God's punishment for the offense, the suffering of an individual, whether innocent or not, was considered part of God's punishment for the wrongdoing of a king like Saul (2 Sam 21:1–14) or an ancestor like Achan (Josh 7). But with the development of civilization, the individual became a unit of moral responsibility. Prophets like Jeremiah and Ezekiel introduced a new ethical idea of individual retribution, while the book of Job rejected the idea that suffering was God's punishment. In some later books of the OT such as Prov 3:11–13, suffering was interpreted as God's means of training and educating human for moral improvement. Because of the Babylonian exile, suffering of a righteous person or nation also began to be interpreted as a universal and cardinal principle of the human world. This was understood as God's plan, that righteous men sacrificed their lives for a better society.[36]

Although non-Christian intellectuals resorted to the OT in their search for a possible solution to the problem of suffering, they were more interested in the end of suffering than taking it for granted, and they related suffering less to human perfection. Wang Guowei, for example, traced the reason for human suffering to the mistake made by the first ancestors of humankind, described in both the book of Genesis and the first chapter of the *Dream of the Red Chamber*. However, he denied the possibility of happiness for the majority, as expressed in the biblical idea of redemption. One must rely on free will for release from suffering, and a natural release can be achieved only temporarily in art.[37] Obviously, Wang's ideas of free will and release are not concerned with religious issues.

Idea of God and a Perfect World

To Chinese intellectuals, it was not enough to search for the perfect personality. It was more important to educate or integrate moral doctrines into the heart of humankind to achieve a perfect society. Do the OT and faith in God contribute to the rebuilding of the nation and the making of a perfect world? How was that question approached by both Christian and non-Christian intellectuals? And how was the OT with its idea of God relevant to their views about education and universalism?

With a common belief in the aesthetic function of empathy as the key to uniting people, some leading intellectuals resorted to aesthetic education. Aesthetics refers to more than mere art; it is a more general appreciation of beauty, of harmony, and idealization, to which monotheistic sentiment was believed to be particularly helpful.[38] Early in 1917, Cai Yuanpei wrote an article calling for replacing religion with aesthetic education. Cai's article led to controversies among his contemporaries in subsequent years. Many non-Christian intellectuals supported Cai's idea, but some also disagreed with him. The writer Shen Congwen admitted that Cai made a great contribution to national rebuilding with his call for aesthetic education, but Shen did not believe that replacing religion with aesthetic education was useful. To make his point, he distinguished *shen* from *shangdi*. *Shangdi* refers to the OT Creator God, whereas *shen* is an abstract and pantheistic idea of deity. Nonetheless, both *shen* and *shangdi* are relevant to his admiration of "beauty."

On the one hand, everything in nature is created by God and has its own life. On the other hand, "beauty" is omnipresent in everything that has life. The pantheistic idea of *shen* is a symbol for and is synonymous with "beauty." Although one cannot reach God, one can reach that which God has created, namely beauty or *shen*. In other words, if a person approaches a creature from a pantheistic perspective, he will find beauty in it. Therefore, the highest meaning of life is to know that *shen* is in life. Shen Congwen's view implied that the pantheistic idea of *shen* is superior to but dependent on the monotheistic idea of *shangdi*.

Shen Congwen's interpretation of beauty also suggested the impact of the Chinese tradition, especially Daoism. He wrote that beauty found in a creature represents the highest "virtue," which leads to human wisdom. This implies the Daoist idea that "virtue" is the reflection of *dao* in the phenomenal world. Therefore, the "disintegration of *shen*" leads to all kinds of disorder, evil, and immorality. If people were to "recreate," that is follow, *shen* and establish a new religion of beauty and love, it could stimulate the desire to be an upright person. Like the Daoist *dao*, the abstract *shen*, or "beauty," or "love," will stop human degeneration, promote spiritual life, and arouse the sincere desire for a better future. National restoration would then become possible.[39]

Therefore, though both Shen Congwen and Cai Yuanpei advocated for the dominant role of beauty or art in national rebuilding, Shen tried to reconcile his ideas with religion, whereas Cai emphasized the opposition between aesthetic education and religion. However, the OT's influence on aesthetics was generally recognized by these Chinese intellectuals. Indeed, even Cai admitted that in medieval Europe, many works of art were inspired by the OT.[40] The reason for combining art and OT motifs, especially God, is that with the help of art, religion diverts a believer's attention and leads him to the noumenal world so that he can forget for a moment the phenomenal world of suffering.[41] Like Kant, Cai stressed the universal nature of the appreciation of beauty and its capacity to provide a feeling of emotional detachment.[42]

Christian intellectuals disliked Cai's idea of replacing religion with aesthetic education. On the one hand, they highlighted the importance of religion and the Bible to aesthetics. There is a kind of uncultivated and unsophisticated beauty in the occupations and trifles of the OT prophets, which may inspire masters of fine arts.[43] Art is part of human life, and the Bible is a document about human life; therefore, art must also be a part of the Bible.[44] The OT stories, moreover, reveal eternal truths as do fine arts because both OT myths—like those in Genesis—and works of fine art portray the nature of human life with simple and practical symbols.[45] On the other hand, Christian intellectuals denied the universal value of art, declaring that improper and excessive use of art endangers religious faith. To Liu Tingfang, the second of the Ten Commandments (Exod 20:4) forbids art to negate theology so that human beings will not sully their outlook of God with material expressions. He explained that, although most people have to resort to art when they hope to express a spiritual idea like that of God, there is a decline in the worship of God when fine arts become popular. Fine arts are likely to become coarse and crude forms of humanization (*renhua zhuyi* 人化主義) and make people forget the original intention of religion.[46]

Since the basic setting of the current anti-Christianity movement was anti-imperialist nationalism, many Chinese Christian intellectuals claimed that nationalism in a broad sense agrees with the principles of monotheism, and monotheism helps accomplish nationalism. Christian intellectuals did not find a conflict between serving people or country and serving God. Indeed, the OT was sometimes considered a literature of nationalism. All the OT historical books hold the same national as well as philosophical idea that Israel had the heavenly mandate to represent God before the nations.[47] This kind of "religious nationalism" was considered the focus of all the OT books; whereas the historical literature describes the rise and fall of the Israelites, the prophetic literature is concerned with national restoration. Even the psalms, which seem to be works of religious philosophy, do not lack a nationalistic flavor, as is evident in Psalm 122.[48]

Christian intellectuals called for a heavenly kingdom on earth, namely a perfect society with universal love and world peace and, in that respect, the OT with its idea of God was particularly valuable and inspiring. Since human must love God and other people to complete the law, the prophet Amos introduced to the Jews a God of universal love for all nations (9:7).[49] Universalism was the destiny of human evolution. Universal love was the prerequisite for many other virtues necessary for a perfect society, such as equality and mutual aid.[50] Darwin was wrong to ignore the role of universal love in the spiritual realm. "Survival of the fittest" meant not physical fitness like that of "the heroes of old, men of renown" (Gen 6:4)[51] but moral fitness like that of Noah and his family.[52] The defeat of Germany and the survival of Poland in World War I revealed the same.[53]

Of course, Christian intellectuals did not believe that universal love could be disseminated by Judaism. Instead, it was Christianity that makes universal love possible. Even those who believed that Judaism was originally universal resolved the contradiction by stating that Judaism was later spoiled. According to Yuan Ding'an at a later time, by stressing the way of holiness, Judaism lacked learning and no longer practiced the way of love. Although Judaism spared no effort in attacking evil, it denounced aliens without respecting their value as human beings. The ancient Hebrews and the ancient Chinese had almost identical notions about deity and had the same limit: prejudice or discrimination against the aliens.[54] Still, not all Christian intellectuals believed in the universal love of Christianity. Xu Baoqian thought that Judaism excludes outsiders as does Christianity. In contrast, Chinese culture incorporates things of a diverse nature.[55]

Universalism was considered by some as closely related to humanism. The Bible is sacred because it upholds all humanity. If one takes a monistic and practical outlook on life, he will regard human relations as the supreme and genuine principle. Zhao Zichen argued that the primary essence of modern culture is humanism or the high regard for character. The main concern of the Bible is the human being (Gen 9:5–6). Man is the center because God, living in man, is the center of the whole world. Faith in God and universal love in the world are the main ideas of the Bible, and these created the foundation for culture and made genuine democracy possible.[56] For the sake of universalism, therefore, there is the need to emphasize human relations based on peace, equality, mutual love, and aid among human beings and nations, which only faith in God can help achieve. Li Rongfang simply emphasized the love between husband and wife as the foundation of family life and of society. Therefore, the motif of God creating women (Gen 2:18–24) is valuable because God considered it impossible for man to achieve happiness without a partner's cooperation, especially love from a woman.[57] It also was claimed that both Mozi's theory of universal love and Peter Kropotkin's theory of mutual help were testimonies of God's revelation.[58]

Non-Christian intellectuals generally traced the origin of universalism to the Chinese tradition, as did Kang Youwei. But the OT attracted their attention as another source during the New Culture Movement. Even the Communist leader Chen Duxiu wrote that the problem of Christianity in modern Chinese society is a major issue worthy of study. The Chinese have not yet benefited from the religious spirit of Christianity; that spirit is the spirit of universal love and can be traced back to the OT. Chen declared that the basic teachings of Christianity are faith and love and human dignity in God's image, as stated in Gen 9:5–6.[59]

To those who wanted to reconcile, nationalism is the only path one must follow to realize universalism, the ultimate goal advocated by the OT prophets. But how to justify nationalism and the diversity among nations within the context of the universalist ideal? The answer is that diversity was planned for the purpose of human evolution toward a perfect world. God stopped human beings from building the Tower of Babel and scattered them over the face of the earth. As a consequence, people began to speak different languages. God did that not as judgment on man's ungrateful and sinful attempts to make for himself a name, but rather for humanity's sake because a people can develop only when independent and separated from others. Because of their differences, the nations make different contributions to a perfect world. The same is true of individuals and families. Independent individuals are the prerequisite of happy families, and independent families are the prerequisite of flourishing countries, whereas independent countries are the prerequisite of the Confucian belief in a common human nature and universal moral values.[60] Therefore, neither individualism nor nationalism hinder but promote the realization of universalism. Chinese nationalists who fought for national self-determination actually aim for universalism in the long run. Before the Chinese reach the goal of a harmonious world, they must strive for liberation and freedom of China.[61]

The OT ideal of universalism is not foreign to Chinese traditions. The genealogy of Genesis 10 reveals that all human beings can be traced to one ancestor; that one should be respectful toward others in society because "all within the Four Seas are brothers."[62] The traditional Chinese ideal of *datong* 大同 (Great Harmony) is also that of a perfect society. Confucius presumably declared that when the great *dao* prevails, the whole world will be harmonious. The prerequisite of realizing the ideal of Great Harmony is that human beings should consider each other brothers.[63] In short, both the follower of Confucian *dao* and the follower of God aim for a morally ideal world. In this way, a moral foundation was laid for nationalism and universalism. Inevitably, for those who believed in national salvation as basically a religious problem of morality, one that precedes political and social concerns, it must start from individual reform, which surely leads to social reforms.

Conclusion

The attempt made here is to show how the OT idea of God relates to current diverse anthropological concerns of May Fourth intellectuals. For most of them, faith in God was a concern secondary to their interpretation of the problems of their times. The monotheistic idea was, moreover, transposed into a new cultural context with different assumptions and readers. In the process, Chinese intellectuals resorted to different resources to legitimize their contextualized reading of the OT. Western ideas of science and philosophy, especially the evolutionary theory, were considered, whereas the use of Chinese conventions was not limited to Confucianism and attention also was paid to

Daoist ideas. Chinese argumentation tends to be inclusive rather than exclusive on nearly every topic. The introduction of the OT took the same course.

However, the gap between biblical monotheism and the Confucian non-theistic view is obvious. But what equally matters is the fact that despite that obvious gap between the OT and Confucian views, Chinese intellectuals still were attracted by OT motifs. Even more significantly, they were able to transform them in the new context and made use of them for their own purpose. Therefore, we need to keep in mind that when observing the uses of OT ideas in Chinese intellectual history, it is important to understand the changed meanings. In the transforming process, accommodation was the most fruitful way of action, not only as a strategic method but also as a cultural imperative.

To orthodox Confucian gentry and anti-Christian intellectuals, the principle differences between the OT and Confucian teachings supported their opposition to the OT. But other intellectuals took these differences for granted. They tended to highlight the incompleteness of both Confucian and OT texts while asserting that both were canonical and complementary. These two traditions together encourage a complete obedience of faith. A balanced worldview that is both theo-centric and anthropo-cosmic could be most beneficial; otherwise, religion would become divorced from ethics, alienating divine grace from human endeavor. Christian intellectuals in particular believed that no cultural system is beyond God's power, and the OT is meaningless if not reconciled with Chinese culture—though by doing so, they may have endangered the uniqueness and authority of the OT.

The idea of God that can help reform Chinese society through moral teachings is not opposed to the Confucian belief in the basic goodness of human nature that can be transformed through effective moral education. Individual moral character ultimately can save a country by removing corruption, greed, and injustice from human hearts. Only by reconciling both views could Chinese Christian intellectuals identify themselves as Chinese as well as Christian. Some common emphases can be identified among the Chinese interpreters: a keen awareness of the OT's authority; a clear aim to cultivate morality; and the final purpose to benefit the whole nation. Underlying these emphases is a Chinese pragmatic concern for life at the present time. It is in response to evil, suffering, and injustice that Chinese interpreters attempted to find meaning in the OT for their own day. Such an approach to the OT indeed may have made them oblivious to historical and cultural gaps and led them to misinterpretations of the OT at times. Yet this closer contact with the OT text enabled many Chinese intellectuals to find an inner logic in the OT and the book's existential claims on a reader's life.

NOTES

1. D. W. Kwok, *Scientism in Modern Chinese Thought from 1900 to 1950* [in Chinese] 中國現代思想中的唯科學主義 1900–1950, trans. Lei Yi (Nanjing: Jiangsu Renmin Chubanshe, 1989), 112.
2. Cai Yuanpei, "Philosophy and Science" [in Chinese] 哲學與科學 (First published in 1919), in *Complete Collection of the Works by Cai Yuanpei* [in Chinese] 蔡元培全集, ed. Gao Pingshu (Beijing: Zhonghua Shuju, 1984), 249.

3. Cai Yuanpei, "Outline of Philosophy" [in Chinese] 哲學大綱 (First published in 1915), in *Complete Collection of the Works by Cai Yuanpei*, 133–134.
4. Shi Qide, "The Conflict of Science and Religion" [in Chinese] 科學與宗教的衝突, trans. Zhao Zichen, *Zhenli yu shengming* 真理與生命 4.12 (April 1930): 17.
5. Yuan Dingan, *Philosophy of Theism* [in Chinese] 神的哲學 (Shanghai: Christian Literature Society, 1924), 46–49, 54, 57–61, and 101–104.
6. Cheng Zhiyi, "The Method of Studying the Bible" [in Chinese] 研究聖經的方法, *Zhenli yu shengming* 6.1 (October 1931): 58–59.
7. W. P. Montague, "Liberation of Faith" [in Chinese] 信仰的解放, trans. Xu Baoqian, *Zhenli yu shengming* 7.3 (December 1932): 28.
8. Li Rongfang, "Social Ethics in Some Early Hebrew Stories" [in Chinese] 希伯來早年故事中的社會倫理, *Zhenli yu shengming* 5.1 (November 1930): 38–39.
9. Peng Bide, "A Review of Li Shicen's *Life Philosophy*" [in Chinese] 評李石岑人生哲學之一端, *Zhenli yu shengming* 2.11 (June 15, 1927): 303.
10. Cai Yuanpei, "Chinese Renaissance" [in Chinese] 中國的文藝中興 (first published in 1923), in *Complete Collection of the Works by Cai Yuanpei*, 809.
11. Zhang Dongsun, *Thought and Society* [in Chinese] 思想與社會 (first published in 1946) (Hong Kong: Longmeng Shudian, 1968), 188.
12. Zhu Weizhi, "The Song of Songs and The Nine Songs" [in Chinese] 雅歌與九歌 (first published in 1947), in Zhu Weizhi, *Essays on Literature and Religion* [in Chinese] 文藝宗教論集 (Shanghai: Qingnian Xiehui Shuju, 1951), 107–108.
13. Yuan, *Philosophy of Theism*, 10, 54, 62–65, 77–79, 103, 125, 134, 136, 139–140, 143, 148–149, 159, and 163–164.
14. Wang Guowei, "The Philosophical and Educational Thoughts of Schopenhauer" [in Chinese] 叔本華哲學及其教育學說, in *Collected Works by Wang Jing'an* [in Chinese] 王靜庵文集 (Tainan: Shengmian Chubanshe, 1978), 190–191.
15. Feng Youlan, "Progressivists" [in Chinese] 進步派, in Feng, *The Philosophy of Life* [in Chinese] 人生哲學 (Shanghai: Commercial, 1926).
16. Wu Zhenchun, "Christian and Confucian Scriptures" [in Chinese] 基督教經與儒教經, *Shengming* (Life) 3.6 (March 1923): 1–2 and 5. For the English translation of the sentence and Zhu's commentary, see W. T. de Bary and I. Bloom, *Sources of Chinese Tradition*, 2nd ed. (New York: Columbia University Press, 1999), 735.
17. Yuan, *Philosophy of Theism*, 4–5, 10, 54n6, 71, 121, 154–155 and 160–162.
18. Liu Qiang, "A Look at Christianity" [in Chinese] 從社會科學上觀察, *Zhenli yu shengming* 4.15 (July 1930): 14–22.
19. Guo Bendao, "Kant's Ideas about the Reality of God, Conservation of Human Soul and Free Will" [in Chinese] 康德之上帝存在靈魂不滅及意志自由論, *Zhenlii yu shengming* 7.1 (October 1932): 26–32.
20. Li Rongfang, "The Murderer Cain" [in Chinese] 凶犯該隱, *Zhenli yu shengming* 10.2 (April 1936): 80.
21. Yuan, *Philosophy of Theism*, 31–34 and 80–87. See the Chinese in Ruan Yuan, ed., *Notes and Commentaries to the Thirteen Classics* [in Chinese] 十三經注疏 (Yangzhou: Jiangsu guangling guji keyinshe, 1995), 162.
22. Zhao Zichen, "The Place of the Bible in Modern Civilization" [in Chinese] 聖經在近世文化中的地位, *Shengming* 6 (January 1921): 11 and 18. See Mencius' words in *Mencius* 2A:6 and the English translation in Mencius, *Mencius*, trans. D. C. Lau (Hong Kong: Chinese University of Hong Kong Press, 2003), 73.

23. Yuan, *Philosophy of Theism*, 80–87.
24. Xu Dishan, "What Kind of Religion Do We Want?" [in Chinese] 我们要甚麼樣的宗教, *Shengming* 3.9 (May 1923): 1.
25. Guo, "Kant's Ideas," 28.
26. Yuan Dingan, *Introduction to Judaism* [in Chinese] 猶太教概論 (Shanghai: Commercial, 1935), 25–26.
27. Wang Shanzhi, "What I Have Learned in Bible Reading" [in Chinese] 考察聖經的心得, *Shengming* 3.6 (March 1923): 9. See the Chinese quotation in chap. 42, *Liji* 禮記 (*The Book of Rites*) and its English translation in Confucius, *Ta Hsüeh and Chung Yung* 大學与中庸 (*The Highest Order of Cultivation and On the Practice of the Mean*), trans. A. Plaks (London: Penguin, 2003), 7.
28. Li, "The Origin and Effect of Sin" [in Chinese] 罪的来源與效果, *Zhenli yu shengming* 10.1 (March 1936): 11–14. See the Chinese of the quotation in *Mencius* 6A:10 and its translation in Mencius, *Mencius*, 253.
29. Yuan, *Philosophy of Theism*, 8–9 and 138–139. See the quotation in Zhou Dunyi, "The Almanac" [in Chinese] 通書, in *Complete Works of Zhou Dunyi* [in Chinese] *Zhouzi quanshu* 周子全書 (Taipei: Commercial, 1978).
30. J. Adler, "Zhou Dunyi," in de Bary and Bloom, *Sources of Chinese Tradition*, 1:676.
31. Xu Zhimo, "Another Experiment" [in Chinese] 又一次實驗, and "The Origin of Humankind" [in Chinese] 人種的由來, in *Complete Works of Xu Zhimo* [in Chinese] 徐志摩全集, ed. Zhao Xiaqiu et al. (Nanning: Guangxi Minzhu Chubanshe, 1991), 1:162–163 and 351–354.
32. Yuan, *Philosophy of Theism*, 91–94 and 98.
33. Li, "Social Ethics in Some Early Hebrew Stories," 37–38 and 41–42.
34. Yuan, *Philosophy of Theism*, 91–94 and 98. See Mencius' argument in *Mencius* 6B:15.
35. G. Patt-Shamir, "Confucianism and Judaism: A Dialogue in Spite of Differences," in *The Jewish-Chinese Nexus: A Meeting of Civilizations*, ed. M. A. Ehrlich (London: Routledge, 2008), 61–64.
36. Li Rongfang, "The Social Ethics of the Flood" [in Chinese] 洪水的社訓, *Zhenli yu shengming* 10.5 (October 1936): 282–283.
37. Wang Guowei, "A Study of the *Dream of the Red Chamber*" [in Chinese] 红樓夢評論, in *Collected Works by Wang Jing'an*, 92–93, 102–103, and 106.
38. Lee Mei-Yen, "An 'Aesthetic Education': The Role of 'Sentiments' in the Transition from Traditional Confucianism to Modern Aesthetics," *IIAS Newsletter* 47 (Spring 2008): 19.
39. Shen Congwen, "Beauty and Love" [in Chinese] 美與愛, in *Collected Works by Shen Congwen* 沈從文文集, ed. Shen Congwen (Guangzhou: Huacheng Chubanshe, 1984), 11:376–379.
40. Cai Yuanpei, "About Replacing Religion with Aesthetic Education" [in Chinese] 以美育代宗教說 (First published in 1917), in *Collected Works by Cai Yuanpei on Aesthetic Education* [in Chinese] 蔡元培美育論集, ed. Gao Pingshu (Changsha: Hunan Education, 1987), 45.
41. Cai Yuanpei, "Aesthetic Education to Replace Religion" [in Chinese] 美育代宗教 (first published in 1932), in *Collected Works by Cai Yuanpei*, 276.
42. W. J. Duiker, *Ts'ai Yüan-p'ei: Educator of Modern China* (University Park: Pennsylvania State University Press, 1977), 28.

43. Lu Zhiwei, "Christianity and Fine Arts" [in Chinese] 基督教與美術, *Zhenli yu shengming* 2.7 (April 15, 1927): 177–178.
44. Zhao, "The Place of the Bible in Modern Civilization," 14.
45. Li Rongfang, "The Origin of Man and his Wife" [in Chinese] 人的來源與他的配偶, *Zhenli yu shengming* 9.1 (March 1935): 474–478.
46. Liu Tingfang, "The Image of God" [in Chinese] 神的形象, *Zijing* 4.2 (April 1933): 176–181 and 187.
47. Li Rongfang, "Introduction to the OT" [in Chinese] 舊約導言, *Shengming* 6 (January 1921): 2.
48. Yuan, *Introduction to Judaism*, 94–96.
49. Li, "Social Ethics in Some Early Hebrew Stories," 34; and Li Rongfang, "The Table of Nations" [in Chinese] 民族統系表, *Zhenli yu shengming* 10.7 (December 1936): 434.
50. Liang Junmo, "The Meaning of Human Life and the Bible of Christianity" 人生意義與耶教聖經, *Daguang bao* 2 (December 25, 1922): 6–7.
51. All Bible verses quoted in English are from the New International Version (NIV).
52. Li, "Hongshui de shexun," 287.
53. Wang, "What I Have Learned in Bible Reading," 3–6.
54. Yuan, *Introduction to Judaism*, 3–10, 13–22, and 32–33.
55. See Xu Baoqian, "The Future of Christianity in China" [in Chinese] "Jidujiao zai zhongguo de qiantu" 基督教在中國的前途, *Zhenli yu shengming* 1.13 (December 15, 1926): 336.
56. Zhao, "The Place of the Bible," 15 and 17.
57. Li, "Social Ethics in Some Early Hebrew Stories," 35–37.
58. Yuan, *Philosophy of Theism*, 80–87 and 115–120.
59. Chen Duxiu, "Christianity and the Chinese" [in Chinese] 基督教與中國人, *Xin qingnian* 7.3 (February 1, 1920): 5.
60. Li Rongfang, "God Confused the Languages" [in Chinese] 口音變亂, *Zhenli yu shengming* 10.8 (January 1937): 491–495.
61. Li, "The Table of Nations," 433–435.
62. Li, "Social Ethics in Some Early Hebrew Stories," 39–40. See the quotation in *Lunyu* 12:5 and its English translation in Confucius, *The Analects*, trans. D. C. Lau. 2nd ed. (Hong Kong: The Chinese University Press, 1992), 111.
63. Li, "The Table of Nations," 433–435. See the Chinese quotation from *Liji* in Ruan, *Notes and Commentaries to the Thirteen Classics*, 1414.

Primary Sources

Li Rongfang 李榮芳. *OT Selections for Present-day Youth* [in Chinese] 現代青年舊約必讀. Shanghai: Zhonghua Jidujiao Nüqingnianhui Quanguo Xiehui, 1933.

Wu Leichuan 吳雷川. *Christianity and Chinese Culture* [in Chinese] 基督教與中國文化. Shanghai: Guji chubanshe, 2008.

Yuan Dingan 袁定安. *Philosophy of Theism* [in Chinese] 神的哲學. Shanghai: Christian Literature Society, 1924.

Zhao Zichen. 趙紫宸 *Selected Works by Zhao Zichen* [in Chinese] 趙紫宸文集, Vol. 1. Edited by Yanjing yanjiuyuan. Beijing: Commercial Press, 2003.

Zhu Weizhi 朱維之. *Essays on Literature and Religion* [in Chinese] 文藝宗教論集. Shanghai: Qingnian Xiehui Shuju, 1951.

[This paper is a phrasal achievement of the following research projects: (1) "Historical consciousness of Jews in modern era" (18YJA730001) supported by Research and Planning Fund for Humanities and Social Sciences of the Ministry of Education; (2) "Construction of a new notion of history for the State of Israel" (19VJX057) supported by National Social Science Fund.]

CHAPTER 20

CHRISTIAN POETRY FROM TANG TO REPUBLICAN ERA

ZHAOHUI BAO

INTRODUCTION

UNLIKE biblical poetry, whose literary cultures and theological formulations are well developed, Christian poetry in China is still a new development.[1] It is difficult to define what constitutes Chinese Christian poetry, but there are two criteria one may use. First, does the work itself fulfill the requirements of poetry? Second, does it contain enough Christian elements to be considered Christian? And what is the minimum ratio of the two criteria needed for the work to be classified as "Christian poetry?" This essay wrestles with these questions, focusing on works written in the Chinese language using the poetic elements of Christian motifs or biblical genres as Chinese Christian poetry, even though the writers may be foreign missionaries or non-Christians who nevertheless have favorable impressions of Christian or biblical literature.

TANG, SONG, YUAN DYNASTIES

Chinese Christian poetry first appeared in the eighth century during the Tang dynasty. A Nestorian (at that time called Jingjiao [Luminous Religion] in China) monk, Jingjin 景淨, who was born and lived in China, might be the one who compiled the earliest Chinese hymn, "In Adoration of the Majesty of Trinity for Obtaining Salvation" (三威蒙度讚),[2] which was mainly adapted and translated from the Western Roman Catholic hymn, "Gloria in Excelsis" of the Syrian text. This hymn includes such sentences as: "Glory to God in the highest, a peace to the earth again" (無上諸天深敬嘆,大地重念普安和)[3]—parts of it came from "*Te Deum Laudamus*."[4] It used several Buddhist terms to praise the Majestic Trinity, such as *Shi Zun* 世尊 (Revered One of the world), *ku jie* 苦界 (the bitter and suffering realm), and *jiu du* 救度 (salvation). It adopted a seven-character poem form with rhythm, which was a popular literary form in the Tang dynasty. The main idea of the hymn was to praise the Trinity, the loving Father and the bright Son and the sanctified Holy Spirit. Because of them, the world would return to peace and kindness. It praises the Father as the resource of all goodness and eternity (James 1:17): "eulogizing your grace and kindness, to bring the light of the gospel to shine China" (我今一切念慈恩, 嘆彼妙樂照此國). It praises the Son as the Messiah and the Lamb of God (John 1:29; Rev 5:6), "to bear the burden the sin of the world and work hard, to forgive the peoples accumulated with sins" (大普耽苦不辭勞, 原赦群生積重罪). The earliest scroll of "In Adoration of the Majesty of Trinity for Obtaining Salvation," which was made between the tenth and the eleventh centuries, was found in 1908 in Dunhuang by French Sinologist Paul Pelliot.

Jingjiao, or Nestorianism, did not have any impact on the culture of the Tang dynasty. Therefore, it is rather difficult to find Tang poetry to explain Jingjiao's doctrine except "In Adoration of the Majesty of Trinity for Obtaining Salvation." In 845 CE, Emperor Wu Zong of Tang ordered the destruction of statues of Buddha throughout the country and, since Jingjiao is similar to Buddhism in the external form, Jingjiao declined from the end of the Tang dynasty but started to revive only in the Yuan dynasty. Although the Yuan dynasty had a lot of Nestorian Christians, most of them were Mongolian and Semu people. They might write Christian poetry in their own languages.[5]

Ming Dynasty

The Jesuit missionaries had vigorous preaching and effective works in China; many Chinese elites, including government officials and literati such as Xu Guangqi (1562–1633), Li Zhizao (1565–1630), Wang Zheng (1571–1644), and Wu Li (1632–1718), were baptized and wrote Catholic poetry in the Ming dynasty. Xu Guangqi was born in Shanghai; he was the famous scientist and once served as the head of government of the ritual administrative department. He cooperated with Matteo Ricci in translating *The Elements of Euclid* into Chinese. He was baptized by a missionary, Joannes de Rocha (1566–1623), in Nanjing in 1603. Xu wrote more than ten Catholic poems, including "In Adoration of Jesus Icon" (耶穌像讚), "Praise to Madonna Icon" (聖母像讚), "Praise to the Catholic Regulations and Commandments" (聖教規誡箴讚). "In Adoration of Jesus Icon" described the relationship between Jesus Christ as the Creator and the human being and described his nature as the original source of all beings, as well as his supreme status and mysterious truth: "his status over all things, his truth wonderful and endless" (位至尊而無上, 理微妙而莫窮). In "Praise to Madonna Icon," he considered Madonna as Jesus' mother and described her noble and holy character: "her blessing was unsurpassable, her beauty was unmatched" (福既極而難並, 美非常而莫倫). Both of these poems adopted the style of parallel prose (駢體文) and used six-character sentences (六字句) in their composition. The poems also used antithesis and "semantic confrontation" (語義對仗) in adjacent sentences: "her blessing was unsurpassable, her beauty was unmatched." The match of sound (the last word of the former sentence features an oblique tone 並 and the last word of the latter sentence features a level tone 論) parallels the match of wording used in the same sentence, such as "unsurpassable" (難並) and "unmatched" (莫倫).

The title of this hymn, 聖教規誡箴讚 (meaning "Praise to the Catholic Regulations and Commandments"), is mixed with the two ancient styles of proverb and praise in verse. The first two sentences of the text give praise to God and the rest use the style of proverb. In a literary critic work titled *Dragon-Carving and Literary Mind* (文心雕龍), Liu Xie 劉勰 (465?–520?) defined proverb (箴) as: "Proverb, the same of pronunciation needle in Chinese, as the pass-through word, it means preventing and curing disease with acupuncture, the metaphor of an instrument called stone needle and capable of curing disease" (箴, 針也, 所以攻疾防患, 喻針石也). In "Praise to the Catholic Regulations and Commandments," because of human fallibility, Xu Guangqi suggested that human beings should forsake heresy and return to the truth swiftly, for "if one once had a real repentance, God must forgive you forever" (鑒爾一息, 貰爾百年).

Another Chinese Catholic, Wang Zheng, was born at Ting Yang, a small city in the northwest of China, during the Ming dynasty. He was an inventor and a local officer. In 1616, he met Missionary Diego de Pantoja (1571–1618), the assistant of Matteo Ricci in Beijing, and Wang studied Catholic doctrine with him. Deeply influenced by Diego de Pantoja, Wang was soon baptized. In 1644, the last emperor of the Ming dynasty, Chongzhen, committed suicide. Li Zicheng, the leader of the Rebellion, wanted Wang Zheng to be his official. In order to be loyal to the previous Ming dynasty, he chose to go on a hunger strike and died. Wang's publications include poetic texts such as: "On Fearing God and Loving People" (畏天愛人極論), "the Contract of the Benevolence Agency" (仁會約), "Chanting about Living in the Mountains" (山居咏), and "Matching the Rhyme to Tao Yuanming's Verse of Homeward Bound I Go" (和陶靖節先生歸去來辭). "Matching the Rhyme to Tao Yuanming's Verse of Homeward Bound I Go" imitated the rhyme of "Homeward Bound I Go" by Tao Yuanming (352–427) in the Eastern Jin dynasty. This verse used "step rhyme" (步韻), which is a later author replying (附和) to an original poem by writing a poem using the original poem's rhyming words, thus using the same rhyme sequence as the original poem. In this case, the original poem, "Homeward Bound I Go" (歸去來兮辭) expresses Tao Yuanming's idea that he wanted to be a reclusive person and live in the countryside, avoiding secular disturbance and people. His free and unfettered thought and chosen life was influenced seriously by the Daoist Zhuangzi. But in Wang Zheng's later poem, he stressed Catholic theology: "in adoration of one Savior, only majestic God" (欽崇一主, 惟上帝尊). In other words, Wang Zheng saw himself as a prodigal son previously, though he always quested for faith, such as from Buddhism and Daoism. Now he found the true faith in Christ. In this verse, "to wash his heart by the holy water, to exorcise unclean clothes" (願洗心兮聖水, 更祓除其裳衣), he desired to be transformed and to "cleanse ourselves from every defilement of body and spirit" (2 Cor 7:1). He hoped that he would march forward courageously in faith, "not flowing in secular wave" (毋隨波而逐流), and did his best for God, because "only those things saved by true God would be kept" (惟有真神萬世留).

The representative Catholic poet in the Ming dynasty was Wu Li. He was a famous poet and painter, born in Changshu in southern China. As an adherent of a former dynasty, he did not want to receive an official post from the Qing government, so he made his living by selling his paintings. In 1680, he made a great decision to follow Jesuit missionary Philippe Couplet (1623–1693) to visit the Pope in Rome, to prepare himself to be a priest. When the six priests passed through Macao, Philippe Couplet was informed that he would only be allowed to take only the two youngest priests to Rome. As an older man, Wu Li stayed in Macao and studied theology at San Ba Catholic College there for years. In 1688, he was ordained as a priest and was responsible for a Shanghai pastoral parish at the age of 56. He wrote more than one hundred Catholic poems called "Heavenly Poems" (天學詩), most of which were included in the *San Ba Collection of Poems* (三巴集). He had a collection of sacred songs entitled *Heaven Music's Sound Spectrum* (天樂正音譜), which were filled with lyrics according to Chinese traditional *qu* 曲 tunes.

Wu Li's "Shepherd Ci" (牧羊詞) described vividly his pastoral life in his later years, and reflected his high spiritual quality of diligence, as he took care of his sheep. At that time, he lived in the Adoration of One Church in an urban area of Shanghai. He traveled to and fro between the west of Huangpu river, the east of Huangpu river, and Jiading, the northwest of Shanghai. He knew his flock's various situations well and tried his best to shepherd them. Below is the text of the entire poem translated into English:[6]

> Crossing Huangpu River to suburban shepherding, successively ask about how are the sheep.
> Fat sheep, can have more groups? Lean sheep, a lot!
> Grass declining, long distance causing shepherding late, my sheep sick only I know.
> Go and guide to sing without sleepiness, protect and drive out wolves without lying.
> Hope to shepherd strongly for long years, morning set off for southeast, twilight of northwest.

A Catholic poet, Zhang Xingyao (1633–1715?), in the Ming dynasty is also worth mentioning. He had a collection of poems called *Praising to a Warning from the Holy Roman Catholic* (聖教讚銘), which included thirty-eight poems and was divided into eight modules. These poems were created from 1678 to 1692, upon the request of Jesuit missionary Prospero Intorcetta (1625–1696). Each of these poems was composed near a painting hanging at the Savior Church in Hangzhou, placed there to help people read the pictures through the interpretation of the poems intertextually, and that frequently attracted the literati.

This style of poem is called "Zan 讚," which is a style used to praise someone's action or merit. According to the eulogy, Zan here is divided into six parts, including praising apostles, martyr, teaching saints, and so on. This poem also is called "Ming 銘." Ming as a style is used to warn oneself or others. In this collection of poetry, there are only four poems that are considered Ming, such as "warning for death's coming" (死候銘) and "warning for trial" (審判銘), which mentioned that a human being's death was befalling and there will be judgment after death (Heb 9:27). Whether it is the style of Zan or Ming, both of them adopted the writing form of pre-Tang poetry (古體詩), with sixteen lines and four characters in each line, and a strict requirement for the same rhyme in the last word of each sentence or paragraph.

In addition to national Chinese Catholic poets, some Jesuit missionaries translated and compiled religious poems in Chinese, such as *Songs of Holy Dream* (聖夢歌) by Giulio Aleni (1582–1649) and *Harpsichord and the Meaning of Song* (西琴曲意) by Matteo Ricci (1552–1610). *Harpsichord and the Meaning of Song* was the earliest Chinese poetry collection, sung in Chinese royal court, composed by Ricci. *Harpsichord and the Meaning of Song* had eight chapters, dedicated to the Emperor Shenzong of the Ming dynasty. These songs adopted the rhythm of Chinese poetry and combined the style of Italian lyric poetry. The lyrics of the first chapter's title was "our hope in the heaven" (吾願在上). The song described the difference between human beings and grass and trees. The former's foundation was forward to heaven, and the latter's foundation was under the earth. It also praised God in creating everything and showing mercy to all creation. So the poem appealed to the well-educated and guided them to turn to God: "what the well-educated want to know, [is] to know God; whom the well-educated want to learn from, [is] to learn from God; the well-educated give people the teaching to let them know God" (君子之知, 知上帝者, 君子之學, 學上帝者, 因以擇誨下眾也).[7]

Jesuit Michele Ruggieri (1543–1607) was the first missionary to write Chinese poetry in the Ming dynasty. His thirty-four poems are collected in the Roman Jesuit Archives (Archivum Romanum Societatis Iesu–ARSI) today in Vatican City. He wrote some of his poems purely for friendship, and some involved Christian teaching and contents, such as in "Travel to Hangzhou": "Why carrying thousands of books? To proclaim the name of God" (攜經萬卷因何事? 隻為傳揚天主名).

Qing Dynasty

In 1724, Emperor Yongzheng issued a ban on Catholic missionary works in all provinces of China. From that time on, the Qing government banned missionaries from preaching until the Opium Wars. The common Chinese folks had a negative impression of the Chinese who believed in Christianity, because of Western imperialism. This negatively influenced Chinese people toward believing in Jesus and further affected the creation of poetry. Throughout this period, there were no outstanding Chinese Christian poets. Hong Xiuquan (1814–1864), founder of Taiping Heavenly Kingdom, had a collection of poems, *The Poetry of Heavenly Father*, but most of them were religious ethics poems that Hong Xiuquan wrote for the purpose of governing and admonishing his imperial harem. The genre of his poetry was popular poetry (俗體詩), and some even were doggerel. The doctrine expounded in his poems is considered heretical and a misinterpretation of the

Bible. He had another collection of poems called *Juvenile Learning Poetry* (幼學詩), with thirty-four five-character-quatrain poetry. Its contents involved honoring God and Jesus, and the relationship among humans themselves. British Missionary W. H. Medhurst considered the poems enjoyable reading, and most were in line with the teachings of the Bible.[8]

In this period, some non-Christians who had a favorable impression of Christianity also wrote Christian poetry. To commemorate the crucifixion of Jesus Christ, Emperor Kangxi (1654–1722) of the Qing dynasty wrote popular seven-character regulated verses (七言律詩) titled *The Death of Christ* (基督死), which described the passion of Christ. You Tong (1618–1704), a famous poet and dramatist, had two well-known "Bamboo Branch Ci" (竹枝詞), which were poems imitating ancient folk songs, *Europa Zhuzhi Ci* 歐羅巴竹枝詞. The first poem's last sentence mentioned the missionaries "tried to write a song about Jesus' cross" (試作耶穌十字歌). The second poem mentioned bells and pianos ringing through the church and the people pouring wine in front of the tomb to commemorate Matteo Ricci (杯酒還澆利泰西).

As non-Christians, You Tong tried to understand Catholicism and Chen Weisong (1625–1682), a leader of Yangxian School of Ci (陽羨詞派), followed the Ci tune of "The River All Red" (滿江紅) to write "To the Gentleman Surnamed Lu Who Came from the West with Still Using the Former Rhyme" (贈大西洋人魯君仍用前韻) in dedication to the Jesuit missionary Francois de Rougemont (1624–1676). Furthermore, Wu Youru (1840–1893), a painter of the Shanghai School, followed the Ci tune of Bodhisattva Barbarian 菩薩蠻 to write Ci on his scroll of painting called "Red Chapel" (紅禮拜堂); Huang Zhenxian (1848–1905), an outstanding poet and diplomat, wrote "Lament on Removal of Chinese Overseas Students in American Fu" (罷美國留學生感賦), which referred to the participation of Chinese overseas students in holy communion and reading of the Scripture. These students were sent by the Qing government to America to pursue religious studies. Although these non-Christian authors did not scorn Christianity and tried to describe the biblical faith as objectively as possible, they took often confused Christian faith with Western culture.

Missionaries in the Qing dynasty translated Hebrew poetry, such as the book of Psalms, into Chinese verse. The Delegates' Version (1854) was translated by Walter Henry Medhurst, a missionary of the British London Missionary Society, and his work was embellished by Wang Tao (1828–1897). Among High Wen Li Version, it was the most widely circulated version. Walter Henry Medhurst used classical Chinese to translate faithfully from the Greek and Hebrew Bible in order to attract Chinese intellectuals. He translated the Psalms using the style of Ci 辭.

John Chalmers (1825–1899), a missionary of the British London Missionary Society, published *A Specimen of Chinese Metrical Psalms* (中文韻律詩篇選輯) with poetic translations in Hong Kong in 1890. In his preface to this book in English, he stated that the style of the translated version was inspired by the *Nine Songs of Chuci* 楚辭 and a portion of the "Fu on Pheasant Shooting" (射雉賦). The missionary of the China Inland Mission, Frederick William Baller (1852–1922), one of the translators of the Chinese Union

Version of Bible, published a translated version of the rhyme style of Mandarin poetry called *the Essence of Psalms* (詩篇精意) in Shanghai in 1908.

Republican Era

In the era of the Republic of China (1919–1949), freedom of religion was allowed, and church-affiliated universities as well as Christian primary and secondary schools were prominent—all these nurtured the flourishing of Christian poetry. Zhao Zichen (1888–1979, or T. C. Chao), born in Huzhou city of the Zhejiang province, was a famous Protestant theologian and writer. He was baptized as a Methodist and once served as the dean of the faculty of liberal arts of Soochow University, as well as the dean of the school of religion of Yanjing University (1928–1950). He published several collections of poetry, including two hymnals titled *Christian Fellowship Hymns* (團契聖歌集) and *Hymns for the People* (民眾聖歌集), then *The Sound of Glass* (*The Collection of Poetry and Ci*) (玻璃聲 [詩詞集]). He was brought up in an exquisite traditional culture and therefore able to compose poems written in Ci with five-character-quatrain (五言絕句). He followed the Ci tune of "The River All Red" to write "Postscript to the Biography of Jesus" (耶穌傳跋). The upper part of this Ci is as follows: "In three-two-year reach at the top, leave messages two thousand year later, ask which emperor since ancient times, use thorns as crown?" (三兩年中凌絕頂, 二千載后留消息, 問從來那個帝王頭, 纏荊棘?) The Ci tune of "The River All Red" is very suitable for expressing grief, so it was suitable for him to write this Ci to describe Jesus' tragic life.

A famous writer named Bing Xin (originally known as Xie Wan-ying, 1900–1999), was baptized in a pastor's house when she studied at Yanjing University from 1920 to 1923. She wrote sixteen Christian poems in 1921, which are mostly based on the Bible. In the preface to a publication of five Christian poems for the first time, she mentioned: "I felt when I read the Holy Bible—whether early in the morning or late at night—the words and sentences of this book always showed the beauty of transcendence. Among them, there had especial one or two verses which were like a picture because it was full of sacred, solemn, bright and mysterious image. I excerpted my favorite several verses and demonstrated them."[9] Based on Psalms 57:7–8, Bing Xin composed "At Dawn," using the rhetorical question to ask, "Who urged me to wake up at dawn?" (誰感我醒了, 阿們). Her answer is her adorable Lord of all creation. Then the poem turns to God in praise, for "in your majestic quietness and brightness" (在你的嚴靜光明裡), the author's "heart is steadfast" (我心安定).

Timothy Liu Tingfang (1891–1947), who earned his bachelor of theology degree at Yale Divinity School in 1918, was an ordained priest of the Congregational Church and served as the dean of the school of religion of Yanjing University (1925–1926) and chairman of the Board of National Christian Universities of China (1930). He wrote several modern Christian poems, such as "Resurrection," "Faith," "Not to Mourn the Dead," which were published in the Christian literary Chinese journal called *Amethyst*. Based on John 20:27 and Hebrews 13:8, Liu wrote a poem entitled "Faith": "I don't need extend my right hand. / to touch his side punctured by a gun, / I absolutely believe, / Jesus Christ lives, living to today."[10]

Lu Zhiwei (1894–1970), baptized in 1911 when he studied at Soochow University, earned his PhD in philosophy at the University of Chicago and served as acting president of Yanjing University (1934–1941). He published a collection of poetry, *Crossing a River* (渡河) and became a pioneer in modern colloquial language poetry-writing. In the preface to the collection of poetry, he professed that he was a Christian and had a deep experience with the passion of Christ, his resurrection, love and forgiveness. His poem, "This is what I heard" (如是我聞), in the collection of poetry shows his faith profession: "Those idolatrous Christians, will never be considerate of Jesus' love."[11]

Chen Mengjia (1911–1966), a famous modern poet and paleographer, is recognized as one of the Four Great Poets of the Crescent School in the 1930s. He was born into a family of Protestant pastors and baptized at birth. He wrote several Christian poems, such as "One Wild Flower" and "Ancient Jesus Told People," both of which are included in *Mengjia's Poetry Collection*. In "Ancient Jesus Told People," he portrays the passion of Jesus: "suffering in the world, don't have to be sad, the heaven has built beautiful tower and terrace for you."[12]

Liu Tingwei (1903–1994), whose brother was Timothy Liu Tingfang, served as an acting dean of the biology department of the University of Shanghai. He published a collection of Christian poetry, "My Cup." Jesus once drank that bitter cup at the garden of Gethsemane (Matt 26:39). The author used "my cup" as the title of collection of poems to express that he was willing to join Jesus in drinking the bitter cup as part of following him. "Morning Prayer" was one of his masterpieces, which compared favorably with "Evening Prayer" of Bing Xin and Liang Zongdai (1903–1983), a poet and a translator who could have been baptized during Christian middle school and later served as the dean of the faculty of law of Peking University. Below is part of "Morning Prayer," which reflects the biblical psalm but in modern colloquial Mandarin: "You teach me to sing" (你教我歌唱) in place of the commonly used phrase in Psalms "Praise the Lord" (Psalms 103, 104, 146, 150, etc.), then "Like pine branch dripping" (像滴雨的松枝) and "Like spring water gurgling" (像奔流的泉水) imitating creation psalms' (Psalms 47, 93, 96–99) praising God with and in creation.[13]

In the challenging area of translating biblical poetry into Chinese, one writer, Xu Dishan (1894–1941), translated Song of Solomon in *The Modern Reader's Bible: The Books of the Bible with Three Books of the Apocrypha Presented in Modern Literary Form*, edited by Richard G. Moulton, into modern vernacular Chinese with strong literary features and expressions in accordance with Chinese habits in 1921. For example, he translates "Thy two breasts are like two fawns that are twins of a roe, which feed among the lilies"[14] into Chinese: "你的雙乳，好像麐鹿孪生的一對小鹿，在百合花間游牧".[15] It was the first time for the Chinese people to translate a biblical book independently.

Chen Mengjia published Song of Songs in the form of modern poetry in Shanghai in 1932, translating "Thine eyes are as doves behind thy veil, Thy hair is as a flock of goats"[16] into Chinese: "你面纱里的眼好像鸽子眼，你的秀发像一群山羊."

Biblical literature scholar Zhu Weizhi (1905–1999) translated the fifth chapter of Lamentations in the style of Nine Songs (九歌體) among Chu-Ci in 1939, according to Charles Foster Kent's edited volume, *The Songs, Hymns, and Prayers of the Old Testament* (1914). Section 1 of chapter five of the English version is "Remember, O Jehovah, what hath befallen us, look and see our disgrace."[17] Zhu Weizhi's translation is: "耶和華眷念兮，我所遭遇! 同胞受辱兮, 乞予目注!"[18]

A Catholic scholar John C. H. Wu (1899–1986) published "The First Draft of the Translation of Psalms" in a form of pre-Tang poetry and Chu-Ci style in Shanghai in 1946. His Chinese translation of section 3 of chapter one of Psalms is: "譬如溪畔樹，及时結嘉實。歲寒葉不枯，條鬯永無極。"[19]

The above translations are all rendered by Chinese Christian writers and theologians who were formed in exquisite Chinese culture and excellent foreign language. They took the literariness of the biblical poetry as the fundamental point for the translation of Psalms and Songs of Solomon and therefore preserved the unique literary form and taste. The Chinese Union Version of the Bible (1919), however, adopted a colloquial and prose approach to translate biblical poetry, similar to that of other biblical literary genres, resulting in the decline of the aesthetic quality of the poetic genre.

Conclusion: Critical Assessment

From the perspective of composing Chinese Christian poetry in the past dynasties, the narration of biblical themes and biblical historical scenes occupied a prominent place in poems. Writers also used biblical and theological words to express the relationship between individuals and God and the world in Chinese Christian poetry. The insight of Russian formalist literary critic Roman Jakobson (1896–1982), regarding two main functions of language as poetics and referential, may be applied to Chinese Christian poems. As far as literary language is concerned, the poetic and aesthetic functions of language are first presented before the referential function and other functions.[20] When Chinese poets relied too much on biblical themes, scenes, and biblical words, they paid more attention to the referential rather than the poetic function of language. The result is that homogenization in their writing became inevitable, which is a limitation of their writing. A brief history of Chinese Christian poetry indicates its variety of styles, expressions, and levels of linguistic and cultural embodiment.

As for translating Hebrew poetry into Chinese poetry, missionaries and Chinese Christian writers as well as translators have been successful in their works of translations. There also are some unsatisfactory attempts. In his translation, Zhu Weizhi did his best to respect the style of "Kinah" in the Hebrew "Lamentation" poem. He translated "Lamentation" in the style of "Nine Songs" among Chu-Ci and achieved good results. Hebrew poetry is different from Chinese or Anglo-Saxon poetry. The biggest characteristic of Hebrew poetry is parallelism, including synonymous, antithetical, and synthetic parallelism; traditional Chinese poetry also requires parallelism, but not to the same extent. Frederick William Baller used seven-character quatrains, and John C. H. Wu used the pre-Tang poetry with five characters to co-translate *Psalms*, such as 1:1:

> 福氣千般享不窮，休隨惡類計謀行。
> 路中不作横人伴，褻慢邪流切莫從。(Frederick William Baller's)
> 長樂唯君子，為善百祥集。莫偕無道行，恥與群小立。
> 避彼輕慢徒，不屑與同席。(John C. H. Wu's)

These translations paid attention to phonetic rhythm, and they stressed the rhyme at the end of a sentence, but they lacked the logical rhythm and parallelism of Hebrew poetry.

The contribution of Chinese Christian poetry to Chinese writing lies first in the breakthrough of writing style, offering an "I and Thou" dialogical writing style. Especially in the light and revelation of the divine subject "Thou," the poet's writing has become a respectful listening and writing process. In the process of respectfully listening, the intonation, posture, and vocabulary of the poet's writing changes unwittingly; as such, Chinese poetry acquires an introverted, soothing, moderate, and pure character.

Another contribution of Chinese Christian poetry to Chinese writing is the breakthrough of writing object and content, which provides a divine dimension for literary writing. The writing content of Chinese literature is mainly concerned with the country, society, history—lacking a transcendental dimension—while Chinese Christian poetry writing fulfills this lack. Chinese Christian poetry writing also has activated theological thinking in Chinese, which restates the themes that have long existed in traditional Christian theology, such as Christ, revelation, redemption, and so on, with a stronger sense and clearer perception. Christian religion also has been vividly "displayed" through artistic activity in poetry.

However, there also is a need for improvement in the writing of Chinese Christian poetry. Chinese Christian poets could benefit from paying *more* attention to how the tradition influences their poetry writing and the ways it can enrich their writing; that is, they should not assume that writing a poem at the level of Christian confession or biblical motifs naturally makes for an excellent poem. In fact, some poets who may be far from the Christian traditions could have a more profound perception regarding the reality than many priests and Christian theologians. This may be because poetry is the expanding horizon of universal human existence rather than the final judgment of existence. Poetry often begins with the experience of existence, engenders a sense of awakening that bridges time and eternity, materiality and spirituality, and human beings with all of creation. Poetry contains the dimension of religion but is not limited to the dimension of religion.

For Chinese Christian poets, first and foremost, they can pay attention to spiritual independence, and spiritual independence is neither simply inherited from sacred tradition of the Bible nor achievable through self-expression of biblical faith. It may be easy for Christian poets to present a large number of theological images and lexicon in their works because they are immersed in or disciplined in the traditions of the faith and the Bible, and even church teaching. Yet, if Chinese Christian poetry emerges from a "clan" culture or mentality, then it will hinder readers in appreciating the Bible or Christianity. Christian poets need to use more creative biblical and theological metaphors to produce more personal and creative writing.

Notes

1. See K. K. Yeo, *Classical Rhetoric: Greco-Roman Culture and Biblical Hermeneutic* [in Chinese] (Hong Kong: Logos and Pneuma, 2002), and K. K. Yeo, *Zhuangzi and James* [in Chinese] (Shanghai: Huadong, 2012), 3–20, 97–125.
2. A. E. Moule translated this title "A Hymn of the Brilliant Teaching to the Three Majesties for obtaining salvation" (*Christians in China before the Year 1550* [London: S.P.C.K., 1930], 53). The manuscript of Jingjiao is now collected in the National Library of France, Paris.
3. The English translation of Chinese poetry in this paper is that of the author.
4. This is modern Catholic scholar Fang Hao's view (*The History of Chinese and Western Traffic* [in Chinese], vol. 2 [Taipei: Huagang Publishers Ltd, 1953], 217). The text adopts his opinion.
5. "In the Yuan Dynasty, both Nestorianism and Catholicism, the main devotees were not Han, but Mongolians who ruled the Han, Shemuans, and other foreign minorities during the period." Leung Ka-lun, *Blessing to China: Ten Lectures on the History of the Church in Modern China* [in Chinese] (Hong Kong: Tien Dao Christian Media Association, 1988), 24.
6. Wu li, *The Collection of Wu Yushan with Annotation* [in Chinese], ed. with annotation by Zhang Wenqin (Beijing: Zhong Hua Book Company, 2007), 264–265: 渡浦去郊牧, 紛紛羊若何? 肥者能幾群? 瘠者何其多! 草衰地遠似牧遲, 我羊病處惟我知。前引唱歌無倦惰, 守棧驅狼常不臥。但願長年能健牧, 朝往東南暮西北.
7. Matteo Ricci, "Harpsichord and the Meaning of Song," in *The Collection of Ricci's Chinese Translation* [in Chinese], ed. Zhu Weizheng (Shanghai: Fudan University Press, 2001), 241.
8. In response to the concerns of European and American countries about the Taiping Heavenly Kingdom incident, Walter Henry Medhurst submitted a report "Papers Respecting the Civil War in China" to the British Government in 1853, and edited and translated official books of the Taiping Heavenly Kingdom, such as *Juvenile Learning Poetry*. Walter Henry Medhurst sympathized with the Taiping Heavenly Kingdom, so according to errors in biblical teachings involved in publications, he took a more tolerant attitude.
9. This passage of Bing Xin originally appeared as the first Christian poem "At Night" [in Chinese], see Timothy Liu Tingfang and other (editors-in-chief), *Life* 1.8 (March 1921), here taken from *Bing Xin Collection* [in Chinese], ed. Zhuo Ru, vol. 1 (Fuzhou: Hai xia wen yi chu ban she, 1994), 182.
10. Timothy Liu Tingfang, "Faith" [in Chinese], *Amethyst* 8.1 (1935): 150–151: 我也無須伸我右手, 撫摸槍刺的脅旁。我卻絕對地深信, 基督是活著, 活到如今.
11. Lu Zhiwei, "This Is What I Heard" [in Chinese], in *Crossing a River* (Shanghai: Yadong Library, 1923), 95: 那些拜偶像的基督徒, 總不會體貼耶穌的愛了.
12. Chen Mengjia, "Ancient Jesus Told People" [in Chinese], in *Mengjia's Poetry Collection* (Shanghai: Shanghai Crescent Bookstore, 1933), 40: 在人間受些苦難, 都不必悲傷, /天上為你們造了美煥的樓台.

13. Liu Tingwei, "Morning Prayer" [in Chinese], in *My Cup* (Shanghai: National Association of Young Women's Christian Association, 1932), 34–37.
14. Richard G. Moulton, ed., *The Modern Reader's Bible: The Books of the Bible with Three Books of the Apocrypha Presented in Modern Literary Form* (New York: The Macmillan Company, 1907), 891.
15. Comparing the translation of the Chinese Union Version (1919): "你的兩乳好像百合花中吃草的一對小鹿，就是母鹿雙生的."
16. Moulton, *The Modern Reader's Bible*, 891.
17. Charles Foster Kents, *The Students' Old Testament: The Songs, Hymns, and Prayers of the Old Testament* (New York: Charles Scribner's Sons, 1914), 79.
18. Comparing the translation of the Chinese Union Version of the Bible (1919): "耶和華啊，求你纪念我们所遭遇的事，觀看我们所受的凌辱."
19. Comparing the translation of the Chinese Union Version of the Bible (1919): "他要像一棵樹栽在溪水旁，按時候結果子，/葉子也不枯乾。凡他所作的盡都順利."
20. "Poetic function is not the sole function of verbal art but only its dominant, determining function, whereas in all other verbal activities it acts as a subsidiary, accessory constituent. This function, by promoting the palpability of signs, deepens the fundamental dichotomy of signs and objects." Roman Jakobson, "Closing Statement: Linguistics and Poetics," *Style in Language*, ed. Thomas A. Sebeok (Cambridge, MA: MIT Press, 1960), 356.

Primary Sources

Aleni, Giulio 艾儒略. "Songs of Holy Dream" 聖夢歌. In *Roman Jesuit Archives Catholic Documents of Ming and Qing Dynasties*. Edited by Nicolas Standaert and Adrian Dudin, vol. 6 (Taipei: Ricci Institute, 2002), 435–464.

Baller, Frederick William 鮑康寧. *The Essence of Psalms* [In Chinese] 詩篇精意. Shanghai: The American Presbyterian Mission Press, 1908.

Bing Xin 冰心. "At Dawn" [In Chinese] 黎明. Originally in *Life* 1.8 (March 1921), ed. Timothy Liu Tingfang et al., here taken from *Bing Xin Collection* 冰心全集, vol. 1, ed. Zhuo Ru 卓如 (Fuzhou: Hai xia wen yi chu ban she, 1994), 166.

Chalmers, John 湛約翰. *A Specimen of Chinese Metrical Psalms* [In Chinese] 中文韻律詩篇選輯. Hong Kong: Manüt'ong Printers, 1890.

Chen Mengjia 陳夢家. *Song of Songs* [In Chinese] 歌中之歌. Shanghai: Liang You Book Printing Co., 1932.

Chen Mengjia. "Ancient Jesus Told People" [In Chinese] 先古耶穌告訴人. In *Mengjia's Poetry Collection* 夢家詩集 (Shanghai: Shanghai Crescent Bookstore, 1933), 40.

Chen Mengjia. "One Wild Flower" [In Chinese] 一朵野花. In *Mengjia's Poetry Collection* (Shanghai: Shanghai Crescent Bookstore, 1933), 3.

Hong Xiuquan 洪秀全. *The Poetry of Heavenly Father, Juvenile Learning Poetry. Hong Xiuquan and Hong Rengan Volume of Modern Chinese Thinker Series* [In Chinese] 中國近代思想家文庫·洪秀全 洪仁玕卷. Edited by Xia Chuntao 夏春濤. Beijing: Renmin University of China Press, 2015.

Jingjin 景淨. "In Adoration of the Majesty of Trinity for Obtaining Salvation" [In Chinese] 三威蒙度讚. The National Library of Paris, Pelliot Chinois 3847.

Liu, Timothy Tingfang 劉廷芳. "Faith" [In Chinese] 信. *Amethyst* (紫晶) 1.8 (1935): 150–151.

Lu Zhiwei 陸志韋. "This Is What I Heard" [In Chinese] 如是我聞. In *Crossing a River* 渡河 (Shanghai: Yadong Library, 1923), 93–95.

Liang Zongdai 梁宗岱. "Evening Prayer" [In Chinese] 晚禱. In *Liang Zongdai's Anthology* 梁宗岱文集, Vol. 1: *Volume of Poetry & Articles* (Beijing: Central Compilation & Translati on Press, 2003), 31–32.

Liu Tingwei 劉廷蔚. "Morning Prayer" [In Chinese] 早禱. In *My Cup* 我的杯 (Shanghai: National Association of Young Women's Christian Association, 1932), 34–37.

Ricci, Matteo. "Harpsichord and the Meaning of Song" [In Chinese] 西琴曲意. In *The Collection of Ricci's Chinese Translation* 利瑪竇中文著譯集. Edited by Zhu Weizheng 朱維錚 (Shanghai: Fudan University Press, 2001), 239–244.

Ruggieri, Michele 羅明堅. *Chinese Poems*. The Roman Jesuit Archives (Archivum Romanum Societatis Iesu–ARSI), Jap. Sin. II 159.

Wang Zheng 王徵. *The Collection of Wang Zheng* [In Chinese] 王徵集. Edited by Lin Lechang 林樂昌. Xian: Northwest University Press, 2015.

Wu Li 吳歷. *The Collection of Wu Yushan with Annotation* [In Chinese] 吳漁山集箋注. Edited with annotation by Zhang Wenqin 章文欽. Beijing: Zhong Hua Book Company, 2007.

Wu, John C. H. 吳經熊. *The First Draft of the Translation of Psalms* [In Chinese] 聖咏譯義初稿. Shanghai: Commercial Press, 1946.

Xu Dishan 許地山. "New Translation of Song of Songs" [In Chinese] 雅歌新譯. *Life* (生命) 2.5 (1921): 1–18.

Xu Guangqi 徐光啟. *The Collection of Xu Guangqi's Poems and Articles* [In Chinese] 徐光啟詩文集. Edited by Li Tiangang 李天綱. Shanghai: Shanghai Classics Publishing House, 2011.

You Tong 尤侗 and Chen Lunjiong 陳倫烱. *Foreign Bamboo Branch Ci Records on Maritime Areas and States* [In Chinese] 外國竹枝詞 海國聞見錄. Beijing: Zhong Hua Book Company, 1991.

Zhu Weizhi 朱維之. "A Mournful Song after the Disaster—The Fifth Lamentation of Jeremiah" [In Chinese] 劫難之后的哀歌—耶利米哀歌之五. *Truth and Life* (真理与生命) 12.1 (March 1939): 36–38.

Zhang Xingyao 張星曜. *Praising to a Warning from the Holy Roman Catholic* [In Chinese] 聖教讚銘. The National Library of Paris, Pelliot Chinois 7067.

Zhao Zichen 趙紫宸, *The Sound of Glass* (The Collection of Poetry and Ci) [In Chinese] 玻璃聲 [詩詞集]. Edited by Yanjing Research Institute, *Zhao Zichen's Antholog*, Vol. 6. Beijing: Commercial Press, 2004.

CHAPTER 21

THE BIBLE AND CHRISTIAN POETRY IN MODERN CHINA

GUANGQI RONG AND ZHAOHUI BAO

Introduction

THE pursuit of Chinese intellectuals for a modern cultural, economic, and political system since the late Qing dynasty parallels the transition movement of Chinese literature during that same period. The intense interest in science and technology, the publishing industry and education, and medical treatment in China at that time was influenced by Catholicism introduced to China in late Ming and early Qing dynasties and by Protestantism introduced in 1807 when Robert Morrison (1782–1834) arrived in Guangzhou. At the beginning of 1919, the Chinese Union Version (CUV) of the Bible was published, marking an unprecedented biblical-cultural mutual transformation. This essay looks at another religious-cultural phenomenon, specifically Chinese Christian poetry, in the contemporary People's Republic of China era. This essay surveys Chinese poems in the twentieth century that are in dialogue with biblical faith and poetry, examining how the Bible was expressed in Chinese poems and how Chinese poets have been influenced by the Bible in their life experience and imagination for the world.

The Emergence of China's Christian Poetry

Contemporary Chinese literature is influenced by the Bible, enabling Chinese poets, namely Bing Xin 冰心 (1900–1999) and Mudan 穆旦 (1918–1977), to employ biblical images or stories such as Eden, Adam, Eve, the serpent, God, Jesus, the cross, thistle, sinners, prayer, or the prodigal son. The relationship between Mudan's poems and Christianity has been sufficiently studied.[1] The preface of his long poem, "Indistinct Appearance" (隱現 *yin xian*), has "Let's see distinctly, my Lord," can be interpreted to echoing the long biblical tradition regarding the elusive presence of God (Genesis 28; Exodus 3, 33; Jeremiah 11; Ezekiel 5; Job 1–2, 38–40; Psalms 13, 16; Matthew 18; Revelation 21) and yet also the concrete incarnation of Christ (John 1), as well as the intruding presence of "the Coming One" (1 Thessalonians 4–5) in biblical eschatology.[2] Mudan's "indistinct appearance" is about the elusive presence of God in the context of absurdity and vanity (Eccl 1–2), but acknowledging the "witty ignorance" of humanity in its brokenness: (1) "too many wars" within and without, with ourselves and with others; (2) "too many complaints" consisting of "living deaths" and "dying lives"; (3) "too many . . . divisions, conspiracies, or revenges."[3] Despite all these universal human predicaments in being "pushed into the extremes," the poet is encouraged to write the message of hope in the phrase "turning around and meeting you."[4] His intention for the final words is to lead the readers into believing the time has come, that their "distorted lives" will find "soothing," and their "drained hearts" will find "kneading" from the Lord of life.[5] He uses the language of "Lord of the spring of life" to bid his Christian readers to "hear [the] gushing sounds [of the Lord]."[6] Those who are familiar with the Bible may realize that the poem borrows in form and structure from Ecclesiastes, narrating the complex social reality of the modern world, including China, in its structure and embodying the indistinct characteristics of truth and the poet's incessant pursuit for truth.

From 1949 to 1978, there appeared a few Christian poems attributed to the political oppression of Christians. In the 1980s, when Christian culture was popular globally, many Chinese poets would mention biblical images even though they were not Christians. Haizi's 海子 (1964–1989) "Jesus (Lamb of the Holy)" is an example, where he seems to write of Jesus' "bronze lips fly away," in the first-century context of the persecution of the Roman empire.[7] Haizi writes of the grief of Jesus and how the author himself identifies with that grief in the world in which he ultimately finds utter despair.[8] In this poem, as well as other poems, Haizi employs the images of Jesus or the lamb (John 1:29; Rev 5–7), expressing his own despair toward the world and his loneliness in the world while sensing beauty and consolation through the image of the lamb.

Since the 1990s, Christian poems have been emerging widely with the increasing number of Christians in China. In contemporary Christian literature, Shi Wei 施瑋 (1963–), a poet, novelist, and theorist, is a trailblazer in this genre. She proposes that Christian literature is to be "spiritual literature" (靈性文學 *ling xing wen xue*). The traditional "temperamental literature" (性靈文學 *xing ling wen xue*) she states, "emphasizes the writers' subjectivity and sentiment, corresponding to aspirational literature (言志文學 *yan zhi wen xue*)," while spiritual literature underlines "divinity within humanity" (性中之靈 *xing zhong zhi ling*), which "comprehends beauty, virtue, and the existence of the Spirit (Spirit within sentiment, not by human's effort, but by the aroma and radiance tinged with inner spirit and its expression and action (sentiment's spirit [靈之性 *ling zhi xing*])."[9] The "spirit" in "spiritual literature" means that divinity does exist in humanity, expecting writers, especially poets, to respond to the call of the Divine and write the words in accordance with biblical revelation. For a human is "a living soul (有靈的活人 *you ling de huo ren*)" (Gen 2:7), whose inner spirit is created by God according to God's own image and form—of meaning, glory, purpose, and dignity.

The works by Shi Wei and Lu Xixi 鲁西西 (1966–) are more outstanding compared with those of other female Christian writers in contemporary China. Shi Wei has written many novels, the latest one (in 2014) being a long poem named *Brilliant Christ* (輝煌的基督 *hui huang de ji du*); later, its name was changed to *Emmanuel* (以馬內利 *yi ma nei li*).[10] It is a finely constructed long poem, threaded with events in Jesus' life according to the Gospels, integrated with the author's sentiments, thoughts, and beliefs, thus allowing readers to perceive more profoundly the biblical narratives. Following its preface is the first chapter named "Christmas Snow" (聖誕雪 *sheng dan xue*), of which the first few lines read:[11]

> On Christmas, a pure snow
> beyond the high sky, falls
> thickly and softly covering this mortal world
> the surging dust and voice
> the stir of body and soul
> The merchants clamor desperately
> ending in mutely shivering phantasms
> The holy bends down
> like snow, fragrant and magnanimous
> towards the feeble and fruitless soul murmuring.

The author moves readers by blending her understanding about the redeemer with her imagination of snow: "The holy bends down / like snow...." The stainless Son of God is originally divine but chooses to be born in the mortal world as a human being. This is the humble descent ("bending down" 俯下身來 *fu xia shen lai*) of the Divine toward humanity, embodying God's magnanimity. The divine attributes and the salvation significance are fused with the imagination of the snow narrative, thus an example of eloquent Christian poetry inspiring readers to find the Divine in biblical faith and poetic imagination.

Lu Xixi distinguished herself in the 1990s and professed herself as a Christian. Compared with other female poets, her works are refreshing and filled with brilliant sentiment, and "Joy" (喜悦 *xi yue*) is such an example. She writes of joy that overflows her whole being, so that her "shoulders shimmer," her "neck and waist [as the] two sisters turning opposite directions into dance," her "arms wave delicately," her "tiptoe, instep and heel...."[12] Her inner joy bursts around her and "turns around, from [her] head to tiptoe, enlightening [her] into blue, purple and vermilion as a neon lamp."[13] Reading her poems, one would think of Paul's writing of joy despite the affliction he and his congregations experienced (Phil 1:12–30, 4:4; 1 Thess 2:19).

What distinguishes Lu Xixi from her peers is that her poems feature mystery and religious connotation. In the field of literature, expression of experience is expected to be literary rather than religious, yet literary words can be implicated in religion. It is particularly difficult for Christian poets to excel in their poems because there are gorgeous Psalms in the

Bible set as a precedence, as well as the poetical texts of the Israelite prophets and the book of Wisdom. Nevertheless, Lu Xixi excels in that she does not interpret the Psalms literally or paraphrase hymns, and she is able to retain her own sophisticated existential experience *and* her Christian comprehension of life experience. Another of her poems, "Wind interface" (風的界面 *Feng te jie mian*), has similar embodiment of this poetic quality:[14]

> What I admire most in the world is the wind,
> It's the most talkative I've ever seen.
> I envied it when it opened its mouth and the tree understood it,
> The leaves above, shaking their heads, nodding their heads.

Some poets have internalized the spiritual character of Christ and used spirituality to look at daily life, thus creating new words to rename old things. Lu Xixi is a good example in this regard, an approach illustrated by her "Five Forms of Willow" (柳樹的五種形式 *Liu shu de wu zhong xing shi*)[15] and "Joy" (喜悅 *xi yue*). In the poem, "Five Forms of Willow," willows regard their leaves as "a younger sister or a limb of the tree" (一個妹妹或樹的一個肢體, *yi ge mei mei huo shu de yi ge zhi ti*). The willows also appear as loved ones: "Willow trees, / the wind loves you when you make the branches droop, / spring comes when you dry up, and the young leaves within you are revealed by it."[16] The willow also maintains its own quietness. Its sleep is not affected by the external environment, even if the leaves leave it, it is still "with three or two dead branches, sleep in earnest" (用三兩根枯枝，認真地睡 *Yong san liang gen ku zhi, ren zhen de shui*). The willow is also generous, "a rich man, a creditor" (一個富戶，一個債主 *yi ge fu hu, yi ge zhai zhu*), "loaned out large large leaves" (大片大片地借出葉子 *da pian da pian di jie chu ye zi*) in summer, and "gives green in large quantities" (大把大把地給出綠色 *da ba da ba di gei chu lü se*) in autumn, and "free from all debts" (免了一切的債 *mian le yi qie de zhai*) in the winter.[17] In classical Chinese poetry, the willow is associated often with connotations of separation and fraternity. But in Lu Xixi's poem, the willow no longer has a sentimental meaning of sadness and separation; instead, it is infused with new content of joy, generosity, and love—which are deeply rooted in the poet's faith of love. In observing the willow, the poet is full of tenderness and thoughtfulness because of her faith and her understanding of love; thus, she meticulously senses the growth and surging of willows and, at the same time, gives the willow lifelike joy and love of life.

Song Xiaoxian's 宋曉賢 (1966–) long poem, "Daily Repenting" (日悔錄 *ri hui lu*),[18] may be less arresting than his masterpiece, "Lifetime" (一生 *yi sheng*),[19] but is qualified to be a simple yet dynamic work that is deeply introspective of individual life. It is not a penitential poem but a poetic penitential work. One of his other poems, "God" (上帝 *Shangdi*), strikes a similar chord with the poem, "Ernste Stunde" (嚴重的時刻 *yan zhong de shi ke*), by Rainer Maria Rilke. The poem, "God," responds to the miraculous grace of God's salvation:[20]

> Where it is beyond my hearing
> a voice tenderly calls me
> Where it is beyond my seeing

a pair of eyes look at me
Where it is beyond my touch
a hand gently strokes me
Where it is beyond my imagination
Somebody quietly keeps me in mind.

A few lines below by Song Xiaoxian convey to readers an image of a poet who thinks that his pen is happier than himself even when he is writing about prayers, as in, "When writing down the word 'resurrection' / my slow pen / is instantly liquid / gushing like spring." His poem, "Happiness" (幸福 *xing fu*) reads:[21]

Depressed by the afternoon anguish
I'm drenched in sweat
writing a paragraph of prayer
I'm alone bending over the desk
regardless of sweaty lappet
Realizing the moment is approaching
I write even more modestly
Hardly when writing down the word "angel"
I feel the pen is smooth
For the word "God"
it turns out slow.

When talking about the reason for writing *Daily Repenting*, the poet explains:

> ...Due to the East Asians' face culture, my repenting may make the others feel uncomfortable, sentimental, superficial or even ridiculous. My paltry soul, however, needs refreshing so as to be healthy, thus necessitating somebody's beginning. Each interrogation in the poem is against me alone. Repeated daily interrogating gives rise to repeated repenting, leading, however, to the ultimate peace.[22]

The significance of the writing style of "*Daily Repenting*" is the daily jotting down of the Christian prayer and sanctification.

A poet and an economist, Su Xiaohe 蘇小和 (1968–), published *Little Song of Songs* (小雅歌 *xiao ya ge*). As a Christian poet, he regards this anthology of poems as his first worship act of sacrifice to God. In the poem, "Little Song of Songs" (小雅歌 *xiao ya ge*), he is aware of his own smallness and God's greatness:[23]

Heaven and earth is one of your words
My boundless dream is your sigh.
You always live in all directions
I can only climb along the path on the earth.

As a famous Christian writer, Bei Cun 北村 (originally known as Kang Hong, 1965–) has published more than ten Christian poems, such as "Something Fragrant" (芳香的事

fang xiang de shi) and "Paradise" (天堂 *tian tang*).[24] His poems exhibit shining hope and a lively imagination, such as in the poem "Remembrance" (思念 *Si nian*), in which he expresses the reversal of life after meeting God:[25]

when I saw you at the first time, I was blind
From now on, you'll be the only one to lead my way
When I heard you at the first time, I was deaf
From now on, I can only touch you
The first hug with you, I get sick
Only trembling in your arms
The first time I love you, I'm dead
It can only be buried by you.

The description of Jesus' image in Bei Cun's series not only enriches the shaping of Christological image but also deepens and broadens the theological content of Jesus' person and works. In Bei Cun's poetry, for example, he uses "you" and "he" to refer to Jesus: (1) "your voice in all the cold" (in his poem "Lover" 爱人 *ai ren*); (2) "He is thinner than he was in heaven, yet closer to the likeness of my heart" (in his poem "He and Me" 他和我 *ta he wo*); (3) "He is herding sheep in heaven (in "Imagination" 想象 *xiang xiang*).[26]

He also used "us" to express the presence of Jesus with humanity: (1) "Tonight we can at least get hurt together" (in "Lover"), and (2) "Life of humiliation is our food" (in "Lover").[27]

Furthermore, he used the image of "younger brother" to describe Jesus giving up everything for the love of mankind: (1) "A little brother in rags, wearing a happy grain of wheat" (in "Younger Brother" 弟弟 *di di*); (2) he mentions the loneliness of the younger brother: "Who listens to my brother's love, a lonely tent" (in "Younger Brother").[28]

In the poem, "Deep Valley" (深谷 *shen ku*), he portrays Jesus as becoming the "pale child" in the quietest place, "making the deepest sound ever."[29]

In short, by describing the events in the life of Jesus Christ, Bei Cun himself becomes the viewer of the times and the communicator of God's mission. Bei Cun's poems rewrite his understanding of the image of Jesus Christ with his own experience and language.

Consciousness in Contemporary Chinese Christian Poetry

We realize from Bei Cun's writings that his contemporary Chinese Christian poets choose not to employ common materials and words from the Bible but instead choose to feel and view the larger emerging world as they imagine it by means of the biblical aesthetic and divine Spirit. Their poems provide new sensibilities and appeal to God's revelation as mediated in the Bible.

Of the poems written by Jiang Qingyi 姜慶乙 (1969–), a poet blind from the age of 12 and writing in the braille alphabet, one example is "The Titleless Poem" (無題, *wu ti*):[30]

As a blind person
I'm a boundary tablet erecting
between the light and the lightless
As a miserable man
I hear the call
"yes, I'm here"
Misery keeps me waiting here
...
When removing the sunglasses
and more surplus in the world
breeze feeling His curable fingers
as image extricated from language
"presenting" before my eyes intimately
I'm silent, afraid that beauty might
miss my kinsfolk once again.

The poems express the author's dependence on God's sustaining and creative grace for his works. His poems, however, are neither confessional nor contain any apparent religious wording. He simply has immersed himself in feeling and "presenting" this world by means of his fingers and eyes and allowing the Spirit to flow into the words. Encountering such poems, many readers are moved by his sensual and experiential word-pictures.

This sort of writing reflects contemporary Christian writers' artistic consciousness. Contemporary Chinese Christian poetry has developed since the 1990s. Every literary genre shares certain generalities in conveying experience and constructing aesthetics. And Christian poetry aims to make sense for both Christians and non-Christians. In terms of experience, Christian literature is the same as general literature in using symbols of common situations. In terms of aesthetics, Christian poetry uses artistic language to embody truth and salvation without any preaching or propaganda expressions. Art and poetry offer representational understanding to people with representational words that appeal to sense, experience, and imagination.

An artist and poet, Daozi 島子 (originally known as Wang Min, 1956–), has written several Christian poems with the skills of Western modernist poetry and wild imagination, such as "Annunciation" (天使報喜 *tian shi bao xi*) and "Elegy of the Tianjin Explosion" (津門大爆炸挽歌 *Jin men da bao zha wan ge*).[31] Around 11:30 p.m. on August 12, 2015, a fire and explosion occurred in the dangerous goods warehouse of Ruihai Company in Tianjin Port, killing 165 people. This poem was the author's elegy to the victims. In the same year, the government engaged in the cross-removal campaign in Zhejiang province. So, the author wrote the following sentence: "Amen and the balance of justice was locked in a dark prison; Jealousy and hatred ferment in the syringe of the system" (阿們和天平一起被鎖進黑牢; 嫉恨在制度的藥囊裡發酵 *a men he tian ping yi qi bei suo jin hei lao; ji hen zai zhi du de yao nang li fa jiao*).

Daozi also writes "The Song of Consolation" (安慰之歌 *an wei zhi ge*):[32]

> Console the big rock, console
> the brothers who rolled the big rock up the hill, console for
> he with the rock cultivated the breeze
> console spring wind, console
> my mother whose crystal womb blood drained
> ...
> console disease, console
> the sword broken in the sands
> when burning strawmen and feathers
> waking the harp music of the angel, console
> angel, and please console
> the bronze mirror polished by blood, console mirror
> console the clear spring and the sisters, console in their midst
> the most beautiful of whom handing over Bible and oil lamp.
> console night, console oil lamp,
> ...
> console the hay, console morning stars, console their illuminating
> for they are eyes in the manger.

In this poem, Daozi writes by combining poetic and religious experiences. The former traces images in the past ages, such as "womb blood" (宫血 *gong xue*), "feathers" (羽毛 *yu mao*), "bronze mirror" (銅鏡 *tong jing*), "Bible and oil lamp" (經書和油燈 *jing shu he you deng*), the latter presenting us with peace and serenity after being genuinely comforted. What is most interesting are the last lines: "console the hay, console the morning stars, console their illuminating / they are eyes in the manger" (安慰乾草，安慰晨星，安慰它們照見/ 馬槽裏的眼睛 *an wei gan cao, an wei chen xing, an wei ta men zhao jian/ ma cao li de yan jing*). The author means in the lines before "the morning stars," that whatever is contained in the images needs consolation, consolation from God, for only God can endow us with genuine consolation. And "the morning stars" (晨星 *chen xing*), a biblical allusion to Job 38:4, can be used in the last lines both as an object and a subject, with the former conveying the morning stars being consoled while the latter conveying the morning stars worthy of being consoled for "they are eyes in the manger." The significance here is that whatever is created can be redeemed and comforted from the void, and whatever promised before "the morning stars" can be fulfilled because of the baby in the manger. Common readers can appreciate the lines' beauty but may fail to feel the significance of salvation connoted between the lines as deep as those who know the biblical theology/faith. That is to say, as a Christian, Daozi expresses his ideas of grace and salvation not directly but resorting to artistic sensibilities that link all human common experience. Catering to such a universal reception of aesthetics, his poems provide many readers with a shareable general human experience.

Li Jianchun 李建春 (1970–) is one of the poets born in the 1970s adhering to an exceedingly mature style, whose poems were published in the series of the *Chinese*

Poetry Review.[33] He could have belonged to a group of poets who possesses intellectual rigor in his Christian writing, but he gradually bid explicit Christian writing farewell, devoting himself instead to writing courageously artistic long poems of biblical depth regarding the human predicament:[34]

> How can I bear, in a state of seemingly ascending,
> descending once more? Or departing?
> You say it is an order. "You should learn from me."
> ...
> Love can melt cement, steel and glass. I love.
> The midday clouds are burning. In the turn-plate near the trade plaza,
> stays instant serenity. Scarce open ground for the sky
> ...
> The midday cloud disperses. Please pity my wild heart.
> To learn from you is nearly impossible.
> I love the world, ceaselessly,
> as you ordered, and I put on the beautiful crown of thorns.

Not impacted by the spirit of the time, Li Jianchun's writing is rather developed in themes such as the ego's sin, the world's depravity, and God's holy grace. What he writes about is not the subject of traditional religious poems. He learns from God's revelation on how to treat the self and the world, by which he offers spiritual explanation and historical contemplation. Expressed amid beauty and the crown of thorns, new life and the corresponding price, new poetic aesthetics and the corresponding arts, Li's poems present a kind of "enduring" aesthetic, that is, his surging sentiment and experience are expressed very sternly and abstinently, contained in the vast and remote realm and peculiar images and words.

Rong Guangqi 榮光啟 (1974–) is a poetry critic, but his poems have gained much attention recently for their artistic connotation. Despite his widely known Christian identity, he chooses not to avoid depicting lust or sin, but to realize warm and brilliant sentiment concerning self, life, the world, and existence. He refuses to present sex ambiguously in a nihilistic or decadent attitude as many contemporary poets do. Below is his piece on "Creation" (創造 *chuang zao*):[35]

> This is not average repetition
> but inner joy surged from mutual affection
> indicated by fresh fluid and slight fatigue
> Discarding books, project, writing and vigil
> we can still excel
> What else source of confidence can we acquire but this?
> When I feel guilty of indulgence
> you hug me, saying like the original wife:
> you see, we are in creation, creation praising God
> What else source of happiness can we acquire but this?

Sex in this poem is endowed with significance for it is in accord with God's creation, accompanied not by "guilt of indulgence" but by "source of happiness" despite its repetition style. In his poems, "lust" usually can be distilled, transcending sinful lust permeated in modern literary works. This capability for rewriting "lust" originated from his familiarity with the biblical celebration of life in accordance with God's good creation.

Liheng 黎衡 (1985–) is a poet who pays much attention to poetic art when dealing with Christian materials. He tries to link biblical words with the present existential situation so that readers can figure out the words they are familiar with when reading his poems:[36]

> Nobody else in the wilderness
> rainstorms for forty days and gravels for forty days
> The universe wriggling its hungry stomach
> ...
> the future surging blood
> Patience makes the closed door
> broke open by the fountain from the dead bottom of the sea
> Your dream is covered with dust, wherein you are walking incessantly
> towards yourself, and you yourself are the nation,
> the mountain, the white clothes
> And you become a wandering harp in your decay.

Jesus' temptation in the wilderness is a classical theme in Christian poetry. However, Liheng turns it into a new theme, not interpreting the words of the Bible in poetic words, but within short and simple lines, he conveys Jesus' sacrifice, suffering, death, and the future Jesus opens up for readers:[37]

> The wind blows wherever it will, and you hear the sound it makes
> but do not know where it comes from and where it's going
> ...
> We walked the opposite way, amid the unknown guide-boards
> dangling around, ...
> ... Being lost we feel hungrier
> and more ignorant. I suddenly remembered a church nearby,
> then took you to look for it, "the wind spinning ceaselessly."
> Over the slope, through the grove, led by the song of choir,
> we found it, in the infinite serenity of the wind.

The poem is inspired by John 3:8. When dealing with the biblical theme, Liheng carries with it his own personal life, everyday experience, to the swirl of faith and the incessantly spinning wind. Readers find the church "in the infinite serenity of the wind (在風的無限安靜中 *zai feng de wu xian an jing zhong*)." The last sentence is exceedingly meaningful, as "serenity" is like peacefulness in the center of the storm. The storm and serenity are in the journey of going astray and mending the way.

Li Hao 李浩 (1984–), a Catholic poet, has accomplished long poems such as "Dispelling Ladders" (消解之梯 *xiao jie zhi ti*), "Poems of Still Life" (靜物詩 *jin wu shi*), "White Canyon" (白色峽谷 *cai se xia gu*), and "My Horse Is My Hometown" (我的馬是我的故鄉 *wo de ma shi wo de gu xiang*):[38]

> From the height over me drops a brilliant red flower. Speedy
> agony confounds me. The light fails to flash before the thunder.
> . . .
> For once I tell, the other being will be on the way
> losing his feet, shadow, idea and soul. Alas,
> please forgive me, I'm not a physician, but I can surely cure
> common illness. Its prescription is with my blood
> made into medicine curing the others' blood.

Jesus' incarnation is the subject matter of this poem. Li Hao marvels at Jesus' condescension and the healing effect of Jesus' blood. When reading Li's poems, Christian readers are drawn to admire the metaphorical language, which is achieved indirectly by employing universalized language and individualized sense and avoiding theological words such as "Jesus," "incarnation," and "salvation." It portrays modernist alienation and the redemption for suffering. This is indeed remarkable for contemporary Christian poets, who present understandable poems for Christians as well as admirable works for readers in the universal literary field.

Conclusion: Assessment

Because the written language in verses, odes, or songs of ancient China is basically poetic, Chinese poetry demands antithesis and rhymes. Therefore, pioneers in the vernacular language movement in the May Fourth period (1919), such as Hu Shi and Chen Duxiu 陳獨秀 (1879–1942), proposed that literature revolution start with poems. Hu Shi published Talk on New Poetry (談新詩 *tan xin shi*) in 1919, maintaining that the appearance of new poetry is an event since the Xinhai Revolution in 1911 (辛亥革命 *xin hai ge ming*), signifying that Chinese people have figured out a new way of expression. The Chinese Union Version Bible was translated in 1919 as well and set an example for the vernacular language, for poems in vernacular language, in particular Christian poems, which have had a profound influence in form and content on the modern Chinese language.

Psalms, Song of Songs, and Ecclesiastes are all poetic models for Chinese modern writers such as Bing Xin, Cao Yu 曹禺 (1910–1996), and Mu Dan, who either express their emotions in Christian style or organize their narrations inspired by the Bible. Apocalyptic literature, such as Daniel and Revelation, endows them with imaginative inspirations. Jesus' image is usually a trope employed by them to lament their plight, embodied in, say, *Wild Grass* (野草 *ye cao*) by Luxun and *A Nazarite's Death* (一個拿撒勒人的死 *yi ge na sa le ren de si*) by Ai Qing 艾青 (1910–1996). The words, images, themes, stories, narratives, and portraits of Jesus are generally in dialogue with modern writers' imagination and ethos, constituting their writing's context. Even non-Christian writers feel like talking about their situations in terms of the mythos of the Bible. Lü Yuan 綠原 (1922–2009), for instance, chose to admonish his generation by writing the poem, "Rereading Bible," when he was aware that he could not gain freedom of speech. Thus, the Bible has become an important literary resource and referential context for Chinese writers to express themselves since the May Fourth movement.

Many contemporary Chinese poets still draw materials from the Bible and regard Jesus' life and teaching as the narrative core of their poetic works. *Emmanuel*, by Shi Wei, was originally named *Brilliant Jesus*. Li Jianchun has written a long poem named "Christmas Journey" and many dramas of saints. Many Christian poets, however, would prefer not to adopt Christian or biblical elements in their writing explicitly, for their purpose is to allow readers to fathom the concepts of life, world, and values of the Bible through these modern Chinese poetic works. The biblical faith renews their lives, and Christian writers would present different connotations, and thus richness, of the thriving of life amidst all challenges.

Despite the church growth movement in China, there still exists religious prejudice driven by consumerism, atheism, and domination. Chinese Christian writers and their works are trying to highlight human flourishing and divine grace and hope, human dignity and freedom. Many poets are able to internalize biblical symbols and inspiration, so that the materiality of everyday life would thrive in the face of whatever social-political challenges confront them. And they are inspired by Christian elements to present the concepts of life, world, and values from the Bible. Realizing that cresative and impactful works are nurtured through grace and love from the depth of the soul, Chinese Christian poems breathe heavily of the contextual life situation of the peoples and the indispensable artistry of Chinese poetic forms and language. I see the following three areas in which these Christian writers aspire to improve themselves: (1) incessantly renewing their individual lives in biblical spirituality; (2) delving into the concreteness of individual and social contexts of China, thus making their poems the means of the immediate life of, as they believe, serving God, demonstrating the power of the gospel to care and transform people's lives; (3) exploring in the aesthetic poetic field new form and language and expressions so as not to fall behind the times with respect to expression, imagination, and creativity—ultimately constituting what it means to be in the *imago Dei* and Christians.

Notes

1. Wang Benchcao 王本朝, *Christian Culture and Chinese Literature in the Twentieth Century* [in Chinese] 20 世紀中國文學與基督教文化 (Hefei: Anhui Education Publisher, 2000); Duan Congxue 段從學, *Mudan's Spiritual Structure and the Issue of Modernity* [in Chinese] 穆旦的精神結構與現代性問題 (Beijing: People Publisher, 2014).

2. On biblical theology of God's presence, see K. K. Yeo, *Eschatology and Hope: First and Second Epistles to the Thessalonians* [in Chinese] 末世與盼望: 帖前與帖後現代詮釋 (Beijing: Religious Culture, 2007), 381–409; K. K. Yeo, *Chairman Mao Meets the Apostle Paul* (Grand Rapids: Brazos, 2002), 27–56.
3. Mudan, "Indistinct Appearance" [in Chinese] 隱現, in *Complete Version of Mudan's Poems* [in Chinese] 穆旦詩全集, ed. Li Fang (Beijing: Chinese Literature Press, 1996), 214.
4. Ibid. 214.
5. Ibid.
6. Ibid.
7. Haizi, "Jesus (Lamb of the Holy)" [in Chinese] 耶穌 (聖之羔羊), in *Complete Version of Hazi's Poems* [in Chinese] 海子詩全編, ed. Xichuan 西川 (Shanghai: Joint Bookstore,1997), 307.
8. Ibid. 307. Despite his successful teaching and research career and prolific writing of poems, Haizi committed suicide at the age of 25. On scholarly studies of Haizi, see Marián Gálik, *Influence, Translation and Parallels: Selected Essays on the Bible in China* (Sankt Augustin, 2004); *Undying Haizi*, ed. Cui Weiping 崔衛平 (Beijing: The Publisher of China Literary Federation, 1999); Li Si, *The Poetic Development of the Chinese Poet Haizi (1964–1989): A Case Study of Changing Aesthetic Sensibilities in Modern China* (New York: Edwin Mellen, 2016); Xiaoli Yang, *A Dialogue between Haizi's Poetry and the Gospel of Luke: Chinese Homecoming and the Relationship with Jesus Christ* (Leiden: Brill, 2018).
9. Shi Wei, *No. 100 of the Xincheng Road*, vol. 1 of the Novels of the Series of the Spiritual Literature 靈性文學叢書小說卷第一輯·新城路 100 號 (Beijing: China Radio and Television University Press, 2008), 2.
10. (Hongkong Chinese Bible Association, 2014).
11. Shi Wei, "Christmas Snow," in *Emmanuel* (Hong Kong: Chinese Bible International Limited, 2014), 8.
12. Lu Xixi, "Joy," in *Selections of Lu Xixi's Poetry* (Beijing: Guangming Daily Press, 2004), 31.
13. Ibid. 31.
14. Lu Xixi, "Wind Interface," in *Selections of Lu Xixi's Poetry* (Beijing: Guangming Daily Press, 2004), 215 (English translation is Bao's).
15. Lu Xixi, "Five Forms of Willow," in *Selections of Lu Xixi's Poetry* (Beijing: Guangming Daily Press, 2004), 27–29.
16. Ibid. 28. The corresponding Chinese characters of the sentence is: "柳樹啊, / 你使枝下垂的時候風愛你, / 你枯干的時候春天降臨, / 親自將你內裡的嫩葉顯露" (English translation is Bao's).
17. Ibid. 29.
18. Song Xiaoxian, *Daily Repentance* 日悔錄 (Shanghai: Joint Publishing Co., 2014).
19. Song Xiaoxian, "Lifetime" 一生, in *China New Poem Almanac in 1998*, ed. Yangke (Guangzhou: Huacheng Press, 1999), 1–2.
20. Song Xiaoxian, "God" [in Chinese] (上帝 *Shangdi*), in *Daily Repentance* 日悔錄, prepublication draft (personal collection): 在我的耳力達不到的地方,/有一個聲音輕喚著我/在我的目力達不到的地方/有一雙眼睛注視著我/在我的肌膚觸不到的地方/有一隻手輕輕撫摸着我/在我想象不到的地方/有一個人悄悄想念着我. Noteworthy is the fact that censorship often deleted a lot of quality material nevertheless deemed politically incorrect; thus, these verses were deleted when published. I was privileged to read it as I was asked to write a foreword.

21. Song Xiaoxian, "Happiness" [in Chinese] 幸福, in his *Daily Repentance* 日悔錄, prepublication draft (personal collection): 午後的苦悶中/我大汗淋漓/寫着一段禱告詞/我一個人趴在桌上/顧不上汗濕的衣襟//我知道那一刻臨近/筆觸就更加虛心/剛寫下"天使"一詞/頓感筆頭變輕/剛剛提到"上帝"/在一刻比我幸福/筆杆又變得死沉//剛觸到"復活"二字/我那枯澀的筆尖/頓時墨水汩汩/如泉水湧出//這是企盼已久的時刻/我覺得我的鋼筆/在一刻比我幸福. [It was censored when published.]
22. The postscript on *Daily Repentance* was censored when published.
23. Su Xiaohe, "Little Song of Songs" [in Chinese], in *Little Song of Songs* 小雅歌 (Beijing: New World Publishing House, 2013), 24.
24. Bei Cun, "Something Fragrant" 芳香的事 and "Paradise" 天堂, in *Violin and Stove* 琴與爐, ed. Shi Wei (Beijing: China Radio and Television Publishing House, 2008), 40–41, 35–36 respectively.
25. Bei Cun, "Remembrance" [in Chinese] 思念, in "Bei Cun's Poetic Works—special column for Bei Cun the poet-Blog China" (北村詩歌作品—詩人北村的專欄—博客中國), http://shirenbeicun.blogchina.com/2988213.html.
26. The corresponding Chinese characters of the three sentences are: "所有的寒冷中有你的聲音" (愛人), "他比在上面時更清瘦, 更接近我心的模樣" (他和我), "他已在天上放羊" (想象). Bei Cun, "Lover" 愛人, "He and Me" 他和我and "Imagination" 想象, in *Violin and Stove* [in Chinese] 琴與爐, ed. Shi Wei (Beijing: China Radio and Television Publishing House, 2008), 27–28, 37, 46 respectively (English translation is Bao's).
27. The corresponding Chinese characters of the two sentences are: "今夜我們至少可以一同受傷," "終生屈辱是我們的糧食." Bei Cun, "Lover," 27 (English translation is Bao's).
28. The corresponding Chinese characters of the two sentences are: "衣裳襤褸的弟弟, 披戴幸福的麥粒," "誰聆聽弟弟的愛情, 孤獨的帳篷." Bei Cun, "Younger Brother" (弟弟 *di di*), in *Violin and Stove*, 33 (English translation is Bao's).
29. The corresponding Chinese characters of the sentence is: "發出了有史以來最低沉的聲音". Bei Cun, "Deep Valley" (深谷 *shen ku*), in *Violin and Stove*, 44.
30. Jiang Qingyi, "The Titleless Poem" (無題 *wu ti*), in *The Way of the Blind* (盲道 *mangdao*) (Wuhan: Changjiang Literature and Art Press, 2014), 78.
31. Daozi, "Annunciation" [in Chinese] 天使報喜 and "Elegy of the Tianjin Explosion" (津門大爆炸挽歌), in *Selective Poems by Daozi* 島子詩選 (Hong Kong: China International Culture Press, 2015), 79, 80–81.
32. Daozi, *Selective Poems by Daozi*, 37.
33. The series of poetry named *Department Store's Grammar* 百貨大樓的語法 were published in *Language: Formal Nomenclature* [in Chinese] 語言: 形式的命名, ed. Sun Wenbo 孫文波, Zangdi 臧棣, and Xiao Kaiyu 肖開愚 (Beijing: People's Literature Publishing House, 1999), 129–137.
34. Li Jianchun, "Praying in the Street Garden" [in Chinese] 街心花園祈禱, in *Encountering Rain on the Road: Selections within Twenty Years* 出發遇雨: 二十年詩选 (Guangzhou: Huacheng Publishing House, 2012), 3.
35. Rong Guangqi, "Creation" [in Chinese] 創造, *Monthly Poetry* 10 (2016): 39.
36. Li Heng, "Glory" [in Chinese] 光榮, *Today* 5 (2010): 65.
37. Li Heng, "From the Breeze" [in Chinese] 來自風, *Poetry Forest* 5 (2014): 6.
38. Li Hao, "Dispelling Ladders" [in Chinese] 消解之梯, in *Storm* (Shanghai: Joint Publishing Co., 2014), 149–161.

Primary Sources

Daozi 島子. *Selective Poems by Daozi* [in Chinese] 島子詩選. Hong Kong: China International Culture Press, 2015.

Ephphatha: Selections of the Contemporary Catholic Chinese Poems [in Chinese] 厄法達: 當代天主教漢語詩選. Edited by Ren Andao 任安道. Taipei: Showwe Publishing House, 2018.

Haizi 海子. *Complete Version of Hazi's Poems* [in Chinese] 海子詩全編. Edited by Xichuan 西川. Shanghai: Joint Bookstore, 1997.

Li Jianchun 李建春. *Encountering Rain on the Road: Selections within Twenty Years* [in Chinese] 出發遇雨: 二十年詩選. Guangzhou: Huacheng Publishing House, 2012.

Li Hao 李浩. *Storm* [in Chinese] 風暴. Shanghai: Joint Publishing Co., 2014.

Li Heng 黎衡. *Circular Morning* [in Chinese] 圓環清晨. Beijing: Sunlight Press, 2015.

Lu Xixi 鲁西西. *Selections of Lu Xixi' s Poetry* [in Chinese] 鲁西西詩歌選. Beijing: Guangming Daily Press, 2004.

Mudan 穆旦. *Complete Version of Mudan's Poems* [in Chinese] 穆旦詩全集. Edited by Li Fang 李方. Beijing: Chinese Literature Press, 1996.

Rong Guangqi 榮光啟. *Orchard Downs* [in Chinese] 噢恰當. Shanghai: Joint Publishing Co., 2014.

Shi Wei 施瑋, ed. *Violin and Stove* [in Chinese] 琴與爐. Beijing: China Radio and Television Publishing House, 2008.

Shi Wei. *Emmanuel* [in Chinese] 以馬内利. Hong Kong: Chinese Bible International Limited, 2014.

Song Xiaoxian 宋曉賢. *Daily Repentance* [in Chinese] 日悔錄. Shanghai: Joint Publishing Co., 2014.

Su Xiaohe 蘇小和. *Little Song of Songs* [in Chinese] 小雅歌. Beijing: New World Publishing House, 2013.

CHAPTER 22

LOCALIZATION OF BIBLE PRINTING IN CHINA

WANG ZI

Introduction

By the end of 2018, China had become the largest Bible printing country in the world. The Nanjing Amity Printing Company has printed 186 million copies of the Bible for more than 110 countries around the world, a record set in less than two hundred years from the first Chinese translation of the Bible (the Marshman version) printed in 1822 outside China—in Salampur, India. This essay gives a historical survey of Bible printing in China to show: (1) the development of Chinese Christianity in the works of printing and publishing; and (2) that printing and publishing are windows of dialogue between Chinese and foreign cultures.

The Catholic Missionaries: Printing of the Bible Graphic/Illustrative Book

Christianity has come to China four times, namely, Nestorianism in the Tang dynasty, Arkagun 也裏可溫[1] in the Yuan dynasty, Catholicism in the Ming and Qing dynasties, and Protestantism in the late Qing dynasty and early Republic of China. During the Tang and Yuan periods, missionaries did not fully introduce the Bible to China; they made few attempts to translate the Bible in fragments, to say nothing of printing the Bible. This situation remained until the sixteenth century, when in 1541, the Pope sent Jesuit missionary-scholar Francis Xavier to preach in East Asia, and their missionary strategy changed. Catholic missionaries used to focus on oral sermons as they in their mission work in India and Japan, but they shifted their strategy to printing and publishing instead when doing mission works in China. The change of strategy related deeply to their understandings of China as a country that valued books, and their interest was to missionize the Chinese upper class, especially scholar-officials. Catholicism then did not emphasize lay reading of the Bible; rather, the Catholic intention for catechism called for published materials, though their publications relating to the Bible are mostly illustrative books.[2]

In the early days, the religious copperplate etchings the Jesuits brought to China were to attract the royal family and the bureaucrats who marveled at "the heavenly mother (the Virgin Mary)... with appearance as if she is alive, her body and arms seem to reach out of the frame, and her face is so vivid that there is no difference from the living person."[3] The rare and lifelike copperplate etchings aroused great interest in the Chinese, rapidly becoming an effective means of Catholic mission. The earliest known Chinese illustrative book with biblical images is the *Apology of True Religion* (*Bian Zheng Jiao Zhen Chuan Shi Lu* 辯正教真傳實錄), written and printed by Spanish Dominican Fr. Juan Cobo (1546–1592) in Manila, Philippines in 1593.[4]

The famous Jesuit missionary, Matteo Ricci (1552–1610), quickly found an opportunity to cooperate with Chinese commercial publishers to spread the copperplate etchings with Catholic and biblical themes. At that time, the well-known Chinese ink-maker, Cheng Dayue 程大約 (1541–1616), was trying to compile an ink-painted illustration. The illustration titled *Cheng's Selection of Ink Works* (*Chengshi Moyuan*, 程氏墨苑) was published in Anhui in 1594, which collected a lot of poetry, calligraphy work, and paintings, among them three biblical story paintings and one icon painting. These four engravings were made using the Huizhou woodcut technique, meanwhile trying to recreate the three-dimensional effect of the original copperplate etching. They are simply exquisite to see. The three biblical story paintings in *Cheng's Selection of Ink Works* are based on the story of Sodom in Genesis 19, the passages of Jesus' walking on the sea of Galilee in Matthew 14, and the two disciples meeting the risen Christ in Luke 24. Each of them is accompanied by a paragraph of interpretation phoneticized in the Roman alphabet and written by Matteo Ricci to explain its religious meaning. Interestingly, in Matteo Ricci's retelling of the Catholic stories, he used many common Confucian terms, such as "gentlemen" (*junzi* 君子), "the mandate of Heaven" (*tianming* 天命) and "true son of God" (*zhen tian zhu zi* 真天主子). Similarly, the four engraved works were made in distinct Chinese Hui style, while the images of the figures and articles, such as their hairstyle, costumes, and sea-craft, preserved the foreign features.

In the era of Matteo Ricci, although the copperplate etchings brought by European missionaries attracted much attention of the Chinese, the equipment of copperplate painting and engraving was not brought to China due to the difficulty of shipping. The one who first brought the European copper-engraving techniques to China was missionary Matteo Ripa (1692–1745) one hundred years later.[5] He arrived in Beijing in 1711 to serve as a court painter and spread the copperplate painting technique to China. He also was keen to promote the combination of Western methods of representation and the Chinese painting style. During the Emperor Qianlong period, copper-engraving techniques had fully developed, but for court use only. It was not until 1888 that copper-engraving technology was finally applied by the Chinese, for some of them had studied in Japan.[6]

After the Opium Wars, with the signing of a series of Chinese and foreign treaties, missionaries in China gained some freedom, and subsequently the printing of Catholic Bible illustrative books became popular. There were no fewer than twenty modern printing institutions in the whole country established by Catholic missionaries. Among them, T-Usey Press (上海土山灣印書館), Hong Kong Nazareth Press (香港拿撒勒出版社), and Henri Vetch Peking (北京遣使會印字館) distinguished themselves. Especially after the opening of Shanghai as a seaport, church publishing institutions, government offices, and private publishing houses emerged one after another. Over time, Shanghai has gradually replaced Hong Kong as the center of modern Chinese publishing industry. In 1847, the Jesuits set up their Chinese headquarters in Tushanwan (Xujiahui, Shanghai) and later established the Tushanwan Painting Studio and T-Usey Press (1867) whose printing had much to do with biblical cultures and theologies.[7]

T-Usey Press originally used Chinese traditional engraving and ancient book binding technology and engraved a large number of Chinese-language books written by foreign missionaries in the late Ming and early Qing dynasties, including Matteo's *The True Meaning of the Lord of Heaven* (*Tianzhu shiyi* 天主實義). Later, T-Usey Press introduced a litho printing machine, thus expanding its business to lithographic printing, typographic printing, and color printing.[8] A major feature of its publications is the modern Catholic catechism written in Shanghai dialect, in addition to the Bible (dialect version), the dialectical explanatory, and interpretation of the catechism. By 1900, there were as many as 292 Chinese publications printed by T-Usey Press.[9]

The most exquisite Bible albums printed by T-Usey Press are *Illustration to the Life of Jesus Christ* (*Dao Yuan Jing Cui* 道原精萃, 1887); *Colorful Illustration to Old Testament* (*Wucai Gushi Xiangjie* 五彩古史像解, 1892) and *Colorful Illustration to New Testament* (*Wucai Xinshi Xiangjie* 五彩新史像解, 1892). Prior to these three works, Nanjing Catholic Church had printed *Illustration to the Typology of Savior* (*Jiushizhu Yuxiang Quantu* 救世主預像全圖) and *Illustration to Savior's Deeds* (*Jiushizhu Shixing Quantu* 救世主實行全圖) in 1869, which presented the whole Bible to Chinese Christians in images, thus overcoming the problem that there was no complete Chinese Bible in the late Ming and early Qing dynasties, but only biographies adapted from the Bible. This set of two illustrative books features printmaking at the top and a headline layout at the bottom; it also inserts some images of Buddhist and fairy beings (mythology), showing the fusion of the biblical story and Chinese culture at the early stage of enculturation. After the takeover of the Nanjing Catholic Church, the Jesuits published *Colorful Illustration to Old Testament* and *Colorful Illustration to New Testament*, marking the completion of Bible picture books in China. This set of two books corresponds to the two testaments of the Bible and includes 118 and 106 illustrations respectively. The illustrations are on the right-side, odd-numbered pages, drawn by Liu Bizhen 劉必振 (a famous Chinese artist, 1843–1912) and his students. The interpretations are on the left-side, even-numbered pages, with writings in the vernacular Chinese and in question-and-answer style. The atlases are large format 32 (size of the page), and 228 pages in all, published by T-Usey Press. At least six editions were printed before 1936. *Colorful Illustration to Old Testament* presents some Bible maps, and it is the first book in the Chinese collection of Bible stories to include Bible maps, which gives readers a geographical understanding of Middle Eastern history.

The graphic Bible books published by Catholic missionaries have been widely distributed and have promoted greatly the development of copper-plate printing technology and Chinese art in modern times.

Protestantism in Qing Dynasty China: Printing of the Bible

Protestant missionaries continued the strategy of Catholic missionaries of focusing on printing and publishing, given the fact that the Qing government had strictly restricted activities by foreigners in China.[10] Protestant missionaries found printing and publishing to be the only missionary option in this predicament, as attested to in a letter written by Protestant missionary Robert Morrison (1782–1834) to the London Missionary Society.[11] The Printing technology was developed fully in Europe in the late eighteenth and early nineteenth centuries. Before coming to China, the London Missionary Society had inquired about the situation of printing in that country. In 1800, Pastor William Moseley published a booklet titled *A Memoir on the Importance and Practicability of Translating and Publishing the Holy Scriptures in the Chinese Language*, which traces the experience of Jesuits in China; as a result, the booklet became a source of reference for Protestant missionaries. Despite restrictions on missionary activities in China, the maturity of printing technology in Western Europe and the experience of printing and publishing by Jesuits in China were a great help in boosting Protestant missionary works in printing the Bible.

The Foreign Bible Societies: Financial Source

In 1807, Morrison arrived in China and began to prepare for three tasks assigned to him by the London Missionary Society: learning Chinese, compiling a Chinese-English dictionary, and translating the Bible into Chinese. Morrison translated and published a Chinese translation of the New Testament (henceforth NT) in 1814. However, the circulation of the Bible was not successful in China then because of the ban on mission and evangelism by the Chinese emperor. So, Morrison decided to go to Malacca to establish a missionary station to preach the biblical message to the Chinese in Java and Malacca in the Malay kingdoms. In 1815 he, along with his co-worker William Milne (1785–1822) and a Chinese Christian printer Liang Fa 梁發, took some Chinese books and printing papers as they departed Guangzhou and arrived in Malacca by sea. They founded a free school there called Liyi Hall 立義館, which later grew into a prestigious school renamed as Ying Wa College 英華書院. And the affiliated printing house also was established simultaneously to print Bible and religious books. In 1819, Morrison completed the translation of the Old Testament, which was published in Malacca in 1823. Even though Joshua Marshman had published his translation one year earlier than Morrison's translation, the latter is the more influential translation, for subsequent Protestant translators consulted Morrison's translation—and Morrison has consulted the NT translated by Jean Basset M.E.P. (1662–1707) and a Confucian convert Johan Su (?–1734).[12]

The translation and printing of the Morrison's Chinese Bible was funded primarily by the British and Foreign Bible Society—£3,500 in the years of 1812 and beyond.[13] This Bible society, founded in 1804, is a trans-denominational Christian organization that promotes and sells the Bible. Later, this Bible Society also supported the translation work of Walter Medhurst (1796–1857) and Karl Friedrich August Gützlaff (1803–1851), and it authorized Liang Fa to print some Scriptures in Guangzhou for distribution. In 1836, the British and Foreign Bible Society sent George Tradescunt Lay (ca. 1800–1845) to China as the representative of the society in China. He carried 10,000 copies of the Gospel booklets to places such as Borneo and Medan, and also shipped some copies of the Bible to China via the opium trade ship. Two years later, he hired six Chinese Christians who had been trained by the London Missionary Society in Malacca to promote distribution of the Bible in the inland China. Thus, the British and Foreign Bible Society had branches in China.

The signing of the Treaty of Nanking in 1842 ceded Hong Kong to Britain and opened up five trading ports to foreign nations, giving missionaries an opportunity to enter inland China for mission work. The British and Foreign Bible Society took this opportunity to print 20,000 to 30,000 copies of the single-volume Bible for distribution. In 1852, the Bible Society paid 1,300 pounds for the publication of the Delegates' Version of the Bible (DV, 委辦本),[14] and it established its committees in Shanghai, Guangzhou, Hong Kong, Tianjin, and Beijing.[15] When it learned that the Taiping Rebellion (1850–1864) adopted the teachings of Christianity, the British and Foreign Bible Society, believing that they had a responsibility to interfere and lead this indigenous Christian movement, or so-called Semi-Christianity in China, to the right path, i.e., to become the true Christianity,[16] launched the "Million copies of Bibles" plan. They raised a significant amount of money while hiring a group of Chinese Christians as salesmen in Shanghai, Hong Kong, Ningbo, Fuzhou, Xiamen, and Guangzhou to vigorously distribute the Bible. However, this plan was not very successful; as although 250,000 copies of the Bible were printed, only 30,000 copies sold according to statistics from 1860.

In addition to the British and Foreign Bible Society, the National Bible Society of Scotland and the American Bible Society also participated in the printing and publishing ministry to China. The National Bible Society of Scotland established its China headquarters in Hankou in 1863. It founded a printing factory there in 1885 and printed copies of the Griffith John version and Beijing dialect version. Since 1890, it began to hire salesmen, up to three hundred at one time, to promote distribution of the Bible.[17] The American Bible Society started to participate in the Chinese ministry in 1833. It took part in printing the Delegates' Version of Bible and supported the publication of the NT, which was translated by Josiah Goddard, and the whole Bible translated by Medhurst and Gützlaff. In 1875, the American Bible Society collaborated with the American Presbyterian Church to print the Bible at the American Presbyterian Mission Press in Shanghai. Its Chinese headquarters was located in Shanghai, and its branch offices were located in Guangzhou, Chongqing, Chengdu, Jiujiang, and Beijing. Between 1875 and 1905, the American Bible Society had invested more than $900,000 in the Bible printing in China.[18] Later on, it teamed up with the British and Foreign Bible Society and the National Bible Society of Scotland to print different Chinese versions of the Bible.

American Presbyterian Mission Press: Technical Innovation

The printing house founded by Morrison and Milne in Malacca used mainly block printing technique. When Medhurst came to Shanghai in 1843, he transported some printing equipment to Shanghai and established the London Mission Press. Later, in support of the "Million copies of Bibles" plan, the British and Foreign Bible Society assisted in the import of several large yak-powered printing presses from Great Britain. However, due to the poor performance of this kind of machine and the illegibility of printed works, they eventually were returned to Britain, and the press had to use manual printing. Before 1860, the London Mission Press had published 171 books, and there were some texts on science in addition to missionary books. In the 1870s, with the rise of the American Presbyterian Mission Press (美華印書館), the London Mission Press gradually withdrew their works.

In 1844, the American Presbyterian Mission Press was founded in Macau and was originally called Macao Presbyterian Mission Press (華英校書房). In the next year, it was moved from Macau to Ningbo, and its name was changed to the Chinese and American Holy Classic Book Establishment (華花聖經書房). In 1860, it was moved again from Ningbo to Shanghai and was hosted by William Gamble (1830–1886) from the United States, who changed its name to American Presbyterian Mission Press. American Presbyterian Mission Press used and subsequently developed the Chinese metal type, which was praised as the one that "opened the door to early modern Chinese publishing."[19]

Metal Type

Before American Presbyterian Mission Press was founded, Bible printing in China commonly used wood-type printing. Wood type has many shortcomings, mainly its illegible presswork. But because it is easy to make and light to carry, the wood type remained the first choice of missionaries, particularly during the persecution when the portability of wood types meant escaping or avoiding the Chinese official search.

After 1845, the five trading ports were re-opened, and missionaries in China gained increasing freedom to do mission work. In this new situation, American Presbyterian Mission Press began to print in batches with metal type. Medhurst, in 1843, did a comparative study on Xylography, lithography, and movable metal-type printing, analyzing their different manpower, materials and equipment, cost and time consumption. He concluded that metal type was more economical and could effectively shorten the production cycle.[20] Metal type also could be melted to recreate new types in the case of heavy consumption. Therefore, movable metal-type printing technology gradually became the first choice for Euro-American missionaries in printing the Bible and religious materials.

Divisible Type

The technical difficulty in Chinese metal-type printing is in the integration of the Chinese metal type into the Western mechanized printing production process. In order to solve this problem, French missionary Marcellin Legrand invented the "divisible type" in printing Chinese characters. The divisible type not only could reduce the cost of metal type making but also made it the right size, which is only equivalent to half of the great primer (36 pounds). The design principle of divisible type is to use the fewest possible elements to present Chinese characters without changing the composition of Chinese words.[21] The genius here is to disassemble the structure of Chinese characters, by extracting key strokes or core constituent elements, so as to effectively organize and improve the typographic effect and speed of Chinese metal movable type. This is a modular and overall design concept.

In the design of Chinese metal type, Legrand used "the radical" and "the root" corresponding to Chinese characters. In order to facilitate the uniform font size, the proportion of radicals is specified to account for one-third of the entire word-block, and the roots account for the other two-thirds. For example, if three of the radicals (口, 月, 木) are placed alongside four of the roots (土, 巴, 幾, 内) respectively, we will have twelve different Chinese characters (吐, 吧, 嘰, 呐, 肚, 肥, 肌, 肭, 杜, 杷, 機, 枘). This kind of radical-root combinations can create 22,741 Chinese characters, which is extremely efficient and convenient, without the trouble of creating the actual 22,741 word-blocks.

Hong Kong Typeface and Font Size

Even though divisible-type print has many advantages, its disadvantages are also obvious, such as: (1) the mechanical combination cannot highlight the beauty of the Chinese characters; and (2) the combination of two parts to form a complete Chinese character also brings challenges for typographical printing. Therefore, after repeated research, British missionary Samuel Dyer (1804–1843) decided to return to the traditional European method, which was based on the stipulated characters to make the final type by stamping. Dyer has researched and produced Chinese metal type in Penang, Malacca, and Singapore. After his death, his successor Alexander Stronach (1800–?) continued the work and completed 3,891 stipulated characters in Hong Kong, which was called "Hong Kong Typeface."[22] This method of making a single metal type by the process of "stipulated character-type matrix-type" had been used in the Chinese and American Holy Classic Book Establishment, until William Gamble later succeeded in making Song typeface with the electroplating method.

William Gamble came to China to host American Presbyterian Mission Press in 1858 and began to use the electroplating method to make Chinese metal type. Based on the unique 40,919 Chinese characters included in *Kangxi Dictionary* (a forty-two-volume Chinese dictionary compiled during the reign of Emperor Kangxi in the Qing dynasty), Gamble studied 130,000 Chinese characters in all different versions of the Bible and twenty-seven other books published by American Holy Classic Book Establishment and American Presbyterian Mission Press. Gamble then succeeded in developing a Song typeface (also known as Meihua typeface or Shanghai typeface).[23] The electroplating stipulated character could not only save cost and time but also produce a smaller metal type with elegant definition of Chinese strokes.

One of its main values is to establish the concept of "font size" in Chinese characters. This is a systematic font design concept and allowed for the possibility of later printing of bilingual works, such as a dictionary with 11-point movable type, which proved to be not only clear and intuitive but also greatly readable. The 1–7 type sizes often mentioned in the history of Chinese printing and publishing are directly related to the design of William Gamble.[24] His design accurately sets the object and context for text reading, grasps the different functions of different font sizes in different people and communication contexts, and helps people quickly and effectively understand the text they read.

Another important achievement of Gamble is that, in the past small fonts were not easy to stamp and form. For example, Morrison's *A Dictionary of the Chinese Language* used 5.3 mm^2 hand-engraved metal type. Then the electroplating method of William Gamble, the small metal type that is literally flat and beautiful in appearance, was developed. This font size is able to make the Bible verses and lines printed as close as possible, and the whole Bible could be printed in one volume, even when printed in the Chinese-English interlinear format. Furthermore, the small print makes it possible to mix Chinese characters with Arabic numerals, notes, and other symbols, making the Scripture verses able to be read with ease on the eyes.

Another contribution of Gamble is his carefully selected 6,000 Chinese characters, which could satisfy almost all the needs of the actual printing work at that time; they therefore were used widely in missionary and East Asian cultural circles. Gamble's work has an impact more far reaching than simply Bible printing, for it has revolutionized conceptually in layout design to solve the problem of presenting different sizes of Chinese characters since Morrison.[25] From then on, many printing organizations purchased the series of Song typeface, and Chinese characters in publications presented a diversified appearance that decreased or ascended incrementally by font size.

Scales and Types of Printing

American Presbyterian Mission Press was one of the largest publishers in Shanghai at the time and printed whatever amount the Bible societies ordered, including the Bible, the hymnals, the doctrinal handbooks, the church school textbooks, and two journals, *Chinese and Foreign Gazette* (*Zhong Wai Xin Bao* 中外新報) and *The Chinese Christian Intelligencer* (*Tong Wen Bao* 通問報), as well as dozens of books on the natural sciences.[26]

After the outbreak of the Anti-Japanese War in 1937, American Presbyterian Mission Press was relocated to Wuhan; unfortunately its printing machines later were stolen by the Japanese army, and the press ceased to exist.

Bible Printing in the Republic of China: The Beginning of Localization

Entering the early twentieth century, especially after the revolution of 1911, the Chinese modern commercial printing house developed rapidly, and the printing industry in China was more cost saving and efficient. At the beginning of the twentieth century, most of the Bibles issued in China once were printed in a Japanese printing house, which is the Fukuin printing company in Yokohama. Soon after, two Chinese Christians who once worked at American Presbyterian Mission Press started their own press, the Commercial Press. Gradually the Commercial Press developed and accepted most of the Bible printing works from the British and Foreign Bible Society and the American Bible Society. The location of the Commercial Press was in Shanghai, and it became one of the world's major Bible printing centers.[27]

The Shanghai Commercial Press was bombed by the Japanese army in 1931, and a large number of Bible print templates and product inventories were turned into ashes. When the Japanese invaded inland China, the foreign Bible societies tried their best to print and publish the Bible in Hankou, Chengdu, and Chongqing. In the 1930s and 1940s, there was often a set of Bible fonts that were delivered by plane to the printers in these inland cities. The printing of the Bible was extremely difficult during the war. From 1941–1945, the printing output of the Bible was not recorded. But, by 1947, the victory of the Communist regime was confirmed, and the Bible societies had to rush to work overtime to print the Bible again. They hoped that by overproducing Bibles, they would be available to China for the next three years in response to the unpredictable future.

There are two major features in Protestant printing and publishing of the Bible in China. One is the large number of copies produced; the American Bible Society alone published more than 84 million Chinese Bibles during the Republic of China (1912–1949). It is estimated that the Chinese Bible output of the British and Foreign Bible Society was about twice that of the American Bible Society. The output of the National Bible Society of Scotland was about half the amount produced by the American Bible Society. Thus, the total output of the three Bible societies in Republic China was more than 200 million. The British and Foreign Bible Society declared that, in China a country called the "home of books," no book was more accessible, or cheaper, than the Bible.[28]

Another feature was the variety of versions. In particular, the high illiteracy rate in China hindered the spread of the gospel through printing. To overcome this obstacle, Bible societies tried to use the Roman alphabet to phoneticize Chinese dialects to make it easier for Christians everywhere to read the Bible in their mother tongues. The Bibles that were circulated at that time were mainly the Union Mandarin version (the official language 和合官話本), which later on became the most influential version in China until today. There were also a considerable number of local dialect versions of the Bible in China. The Shanghai dialect Pinyin Bible was published in 1850, followed by the Roman alphabet phonetic version of Minnan and Ningbo dialects Bible. In 1877, almost eleven dialect versions of the Chinese Bible were published. In the twentieth century, dialect versions of Bible have not met the needs of missionary activities satisfactorily, since ethnic minorities or tribes in China have not yet had written languages or scripts/texts. The languages of these peoples have no similarities with Chinese characters, so the missionaries translated the Bible into their local languages. In 1940, there were as many as thirty-nine Bibles in different dialects and national languages in the local language of ethnic minorities. In addition, it is worth mentioning that the Chinese Braille version of the Bible, the first Chinese book ever published for the blind, was published in the 1930s. After this, the Chinese Braille Bible appeared in the vernacular version, such as the Cantonese version and the Fuzhou dialect version. By 1949, the number of Braille Bibles produced by Bible societies reached 1,192 copies. This illustrates the efforts of foreign missionaries who want to convey biblical messages and cultures to languages and people (Rev 5:9, 7:9, 14, 13:7, 14:6) from all walks of life in China.[29]

Bible Printing in New China: Facing the World

Prior to the founding of New China in 1949, Christian publishing organizations had been seen as a trend toward collaboration in joint publishing.

Joint Publishing

In 1942, the Youth Association Press (青年協會書局) (Shanghai) and Canadian Mission Press (Chengdu), the Christian Literature Society for China (Shanghai), and *the Christian Farmer* (Peking) established United Christian Publishers in Chengdu. Although they were different in theological position and also in ideological and social perspectives, they established working guidelines for cooperation in Christian missions.[30]

From March 16 to March 22, 1951, The Central Publishing Office held a Christian publishing conference in Beijing and adopted the document, "Direction of Christian Publishing in the Future." The purpose of this document was to immediately stop accepting foreign subsidies by any means, to thoroughly eliminate all influences of imperialism, and to actively promote the Three-Self Movement. The document claimed that the Christian publishing industry should gradually move toward unified management.[31] As a result, the China Christian Publishers' Association was established finally in December 1956. Meanwhile, in order to implement the spirit of this publishing conference, twenty Christian publishers across the country conducted self-reviews of their publications; among them, only 49 percent were allowed to continue to be sold after the review. After this situation, publication of the Bible was basically at a standstill after 1955, with a circulation of only about one hundred copies per year.[32] When the Cultural Revolution broke out in 1966, the China Christian Publishers' Association was swept away, and all the printing and publishing of the Bible were stopped at that time.

The Reform and Opening Up: Amity Printing Co., Ltd.

Though the turmoil of the Cultural Revolution came to an end in 1976, the Christian printing and publishing industry did not regain its vitality until its national reform. In 1986, with the strong support of the Chinese government and all walks of life, the Amity Foundation and the United Bible Societies (of the church universal) jointly established Nanjing Amity Printing Co., Ltd., and it became the only company in China with the exclusive right to print the Bible.[33] After more than thirty years of growth, Amity Printing Company has developed into a modern thin-paper printing company. To date, 186 million copies of the Bible—for all kinds of organizations around the world—have been printed, including Chinese and minority languages for Chinese Christianity and Catholicism, as well as more than one hundred foreign-language Bibles, including those in English, German, French, and Spanish. *The Guardian* once commented that China, the largest atheist country in the world, has turned into the largest Bible printer in the world.[34]

At present, the printing and publishing of the Bible in China is authorized by the National TSPM (Three-Self Patriotic Movement Committee) and CCC (China Christian Council). Thus, Bibles in China are not considered a public publication, for they do not have an International Standard Book Number (ISBN). This is the reason given by the government, which recently prohibited selling of Bibles publicly, either online or in bookstores. Therefore, people can purchase Bibles only in churches. Since the Bibles supplied to the Chinese market still partially use paper donated by the United Bible Societies, the price of Bibles in China remains low, ranging from 7 yuan to 10 yuan for ordinary paperbacks. Thus, Bibles are relatively easy to buy in China.

In response to the question of whether the Bible is a public publication in China, Wang Zuo'an, then director of the State Administration of Religious Affairs, answered in an exclusive interview with Phoenix Satellite TV's "Question and Answer China" in 2011:

> The religious policies and regulations of China do not restrict the publication of the Bible. The current situation of publication of Bible in China is due to the fact that the Bible printing is authorized by the National TSPM & CCC. The National TSPM & CCC enjoy the benefits as publishers. This is actually the privilege we give to the Chinese churches. The Chinese churches need that support.... The printing,

> publishing and distribution of the Bible as a capital chain can solve the problem of funding and help many churches. Therefore, the Bible is not a public publication in China. This is fundamentally a matter of "self-support."[35]

Bible Reading in the Twenty-First Century: Online Resources

With the advent of the Internet, people have more diverse channels and ways to read the Bible. Established in 2015, Hong Kong for Harvest Technology and Culture Development Co. Ltd. developed the "WD Bible" application.[36] The app provides more than twenty Bible translations, including: Chinese Union Versions ("*Shangdi*" version and "*Shen*" version); Contemporary Bible Revised (simplified characters); Modern Chinese Translation (simplified characters); Chinese Union Version Revised (traditional characters); New International Version; American Standard Version; New English Version; Holman Christian Standard Bible. These translations are officially authorized by the copyright owners. The interface of "WD Bible" is simple and exquisite, using paper colors to try to recreate the paper-reading experience, including the passages, the underlining of the name of the person and place, the layout of poetry, the addition of dots, the use of subtitles, and so on. Users also can choose the list version or the Chinese-English version, according to their reading preferences. It supports different font and size choices, night mode, background color adjustment, brightness settings, page swiping from left to right or up and down, note-taking and highlighting. It is very convenient to use. Meanwhile, it also has a voice function, with which users can listen to the Mandarin, Cantonese, English, Hebrew, and Greek Bible, as well as some spiritual reading materials. In "WD Bible," users also can set up their own "Reading Plans," providing a variety of solutions to help users adhere to daily readings.

In addition to these applications designed for the general public, with the rise of Euro-American classical studies in Chinese academic circles in recent years, more and more online databases have emerged. For example, the "I Love Classics Database," a classical open-source digital resource website, contains Bibles in different languages, such as Hebrew, Greek, and Latin, for free use by Chinese scholars.

Conclusion: China and the World

Beginning with the printing and publication of the first Chinese Bible and continuing to become the largest Bible printing base in the world, China has been developing its Bible printing for nearly two hundred years. Early missionaries brought advanced printing technology and design concepts from Europe to China, which promoted the emergence and spread of the Chinese Bible. As Christianity continued to be integrated into Chinese society, the Chinese took over the task of Bible printing from foreign missionaries. And after the reform and opening up in China, with the leading printing technology, Chinese

Bible printing serves the global requirements of reading the Bible. It can be said that the two hundred years of development of Bible printing in China have witnessed the entry of Christianity into China, its integration into Chinese society, and its emergence as a bridge between China and the world. To many Chinese Christians, the development of Chinese Christianity in the works of printing and publishing is thought to echo the prophetic declaration that "the earth will be full of the knowledge of the Lord as the waters cover the sea" (Isa 11:9; Hab 2:14). To them the printing and publishing of the Bible in China is a testimony to the Word incarnate in contexts, cultures, and languages serving as a catalyst of transformation and reconciliation (cf. John 1, 17, 20–21; Rom 5:11; 2 Cor 5:18) to a world looking for meaning, friendship, and creativity.

NOTES

1. In Yuan dynasty, there were Nestorianists, Catholics, and some other Christian sects, yet the Chinese then couldn't tell the differences among them and called them all as "*Arkagun*" (or "*arka'un*").
2. For more, see Leorenzo Ditommaso and Lucian Turcescu, eds., *The Reception and Interpretation of the Bible in Late Antiquity* (Leiden: Brill, 2008); Christopher Rowland et al., *The Oxford Handbook of the Reception History of the Bible* (Oxford: Oxford University Press, 2011); M. B. Laufer, *Christian Art in China* (Beijing, 1910); John E. McCall, "Early Jesuit Art in the Far East IV: In China and Macao Before 1635," *Artibus Asiae* XI (1948), 45–69; Nicolas Standaert, *An Illustrated Life of Christ Presented to the Chinese Emperor: The History of the Jincheng Shuxiang* (Sankt Augustin: Institut Monumenta Serica, 2007).
3. Gu Qiyuan 顧起元, *Tales from Guests* [in Chinese] 客座贅語, vol. 6 (Beijing: Zhonghua Book Company, 1987), 193–194.
4. Henri Bernard-Maitre, tr. Xiao Junhua, *The Missionary History of Catholics in China in Sixteenth Century* (Shanghai: The Commercial Press, 1936), 179.
5. Feng Xiaojuan, "Missionaries and Copperplate Etchings in the Court of Qing Dynasty," *Art Education Research* (December 2018), 10–11.
6. Xiaojuan, "Missionaries and Copperplate Etchings," 12.
7. De Lixian 德禮賢, *The Missionary History of Catholics in China* [in Chinese] 中國天主教傳教史 (Shanghai: The Commercial Press, 1933), 103.
8. Zou Zhenhua, "T-Usey Press and the Development of Printing and Publishing in Shanghai" [in Chinese], *Journal of Anhui University (Humanities and Social Sciences)* 3 (2010): 8.
9. Wu Hongliang, "From *Dao Yuan Jing Cui* to *Xin shi Xiang jie*" [in Chinese], *Literature and Art Studies* 2 (1997): 148.
10. For more, see Alexander Wylie, *Memorials of Protestant Missionaries to the Chinese: Giving a List of Their Publications, and Obituary Notices of the Deceased, With Copious Indexes* (Shanghai: American Presbyterian Mission Press, 1867); Macintosh Gilbert, *The Mission Press in China* (Shanghai, The American Presbyterian Mission Press, 1894); K. S. Latourette, *A History of Christian Missions in China* (London, Society for Promoting Christian Knowledge, 1929); J. M. Braga, *The Beginning of Printing at Macau* (Lisboa: Separate de Studia, 1963); Herbert Hoi-Lop Ho, *Protestant Missionary Publications in Modern China*

(1912–1949): A Study of Their Programs Operations and Trends (Hong Kong, Chinese Church Research Center, 1988); Chen Jianming 陳建明, *The Literature Ministry of Protestantism in Modern China* [in Chinese] 激揚文字, 廣傳福音: 近代基督教在華文字事工 (Taipei: Cosmic Care, 2006); Su Jing 蘇精, *Missionaries and the Changing of Chinese Printing* [in Chinese] 鑄代以刻: 傳教士與中文印刷變局 (Taipei: Taiwan University, 2014).

11. Su Jing 蘇精, *Robert Morrison and Chinese Printing and Publishing* [in Chinese] 馬禮遜與中文印刷出版 (Taipei: Taiwan Student's Publishing House, 2000), 50.
12. See Song Gang's essay in this Handbook.
13. Luo Weihong 羅偉虹, *The History of Chinese Christianity (Protestantism)* [in Chinese] 中國基督教(新教)史 (Shanghai: Shanghai People's Publishing House, 2018), 186.
14. The Delegates' Version was translated by the committee, which comprised twelve people from different missions. During the translation, there was a major disagreement on how to translate the divine name. Some insisted that "God" should be translated as "*Shangdi*" (上帝), while others believed that it should be translated as "*Shen*" (神). Out of this disagreement, the translation committee spilt into two groups. The British and Foreign Bible Society published the Delegates' Version with "*Shangdi*" and the American Bible Society later published it with "*Shen*," which was called the Bridgeman version. The disagreement on the translation of the divine name also divided developers of the Union version. Thus, there was a Union Version with "*Shangdi*" and a Union Version with "*Shen*." Interestingly, to keep them in the same format, a blank space was left before "*Shen*" when they printed the Union Version with "*Shen*."
15. Luo, *History of Chinese Christianity*, 186.
16. Cf. Prescott Clarke and J. S. Gregory, *Western Reports on the Taiping* (Canberra: Australian National University Press. 1982), 145, 153.
17. Luo, *History of Chinese Christianity*, 187.
18. Ibid. 188–190.
19. Hu Xueyan, "One of the Earliest Modern Publisher in China: American Holy Classic Book Establishment," *Publication and Historical Data* 1 (2010): 78.
20. Walter Henry Medhurst, "Estimate of the Proportionate Expense of Xylography, Lithography and Typography, as Applied to Chinese Printing," *Chinese Repository* 3 (1834): 246–252.
21. Samuel Wells Williams, "Movable Types for Printing Chinese," *Chinese Recorder* 6 (1875): 29.
22. Su Jing, *Robert Morrison and Chinese Printing and Publishing*, 202.
23. K. T. Wu, "The Development of Typography in China during the Nineteenth Century," *The Library Quarterly* 22.3 (1952): 288–301.
24. Cao Ruping, "Choice and Enlightenment: the Chinese and American Holy Classic Book Establishment and Chinese Metal Type Printing," *Modern Publishing* (May, 2017): 76.
25. Feng Jinrong, "William Gamble and the American Presbyterian Mission Press," Department of History in Fudan University, ed., *Chinese Publishing and East Asian Cultural Exchanges in History* (Shanghai: Baijia Publisher, 2009), 307–308.
26. Luo, *History of Chinese Christianity*, 193–194.
27. For more, see Herbert Hoi-Lop Ho, *Protestant Missionary Publications in Modern China (1912–1949): A Study of Their Programs Operations and Trends* (Hong Kong: Chinese Church Research Center, 1988); Zhao Xiaoyang, "The Youth Association Press and

Chinese Christian Literature Ministry," *Studies on Eastern and Western Cultures, Institute of Modern China History in CASS* (Beijing, The Social Science Documentation Publishing House, 2005), 415–439; Zhao Xiaoyang, "The Final Destiny of Protestants' Literature Ministry in China," *Religious Studies* 3 (2009): 129–133.

28. Herbert Hoi-Lop Ho, trans. Chen Jianming and Wang Zaixing, *Protestant Missionary Publications in Modern China (1912–1949): A Study of Their Programs Operations and Trends* (Chengdu: Sichuan University Press, 2004), 126.
29. On the way the biblical warrant of the gospel informs and inspires scholars to translate the Bible into various vernaculars, see K. K. Yeo, "Beyond Chalcedon? Towards a Fully-Christian and Fully-Cultural Theology," in *Jesus Without Borders*, ed. Gene Green et al. (Grand Rapids: Eerdmans, 2014), 162–179; K. K. Yeo, "Introduction: So Great a Salvation: Soteriology in the Majority World," in *So Great a Salvation*, ed. Gene Green et al. (Grand Rapids: Eerdmans, 2017), 1–13.
30. For more, see Zhu Jinping 朱晋平, *Chinese Communism's Transform of Private Publishing Companies (1949–1956)* [in Chinese] 中國共產黨對私營出版業的改造 (Beijing: Party School's Publisher, 2008); Xing Fuzeng 邢福增, *The Failure of Christianity in China?: Chinese Communist and History of Christianity* [in Chinese] 基督教在中國的失敗?: 中國共產運動與基督教史論 (Hong Kong: Logos & Pneuma Press, 2013); Chen Ling, "Reasons and Results of Christian Publishing's Joint in New China," *Dong Yue Tribune* 5 (May 2018), 78–90.
31. Chi Nai 赤耐, ed., *Religion Work in Contemporary China* [in Chinese] 當代中國的宗教工作, vol. 2 (Beijing: Contemporary China Publisher, 1998), 261.
32. Luo, *History of Chinese Christianity*, 688.
33. For more information, visit the website: http://www.amityprinting.com.
34. *The Guardian*, May 2, 2016.
35. "Why the Bible Cannot Be Sold Publicly in China?," *Gospel Times*, April 5, 2018.
36. For more information, visit the website: https://wdbible.com/app.

Primary Sources

The Bible, Bridgmans Version (*Shen*) [in Chinese]. Shanghai: American Presbyterian Mission Press, 1863.

The Bible, Delegates' Version (*Shangdi*) [in Chinese]. Shanghai: London Mission Press, 1852 (New Testament), 1854 (Old Testament).

The Bible, Joshua Marshman's Version [in Chinese]. Salampur: Np., 1822.

The Bible, Robert Morrison's Version [in Chinese]. Malacca: Np., 1823.

The Bible, Shanghai dialect Pinyin Version [in Chinese]. Shanghai: T-Usey Press, 1850.

The Bible, Union Mandarin Version [in Chinese]. New York: American Bible Society, 1919.

Cobo, Fr. Juan. *The Apology of True Religion* [in Chinese] 辯正教真傳實錄. Manila: Np., 1593.

Cheng Dayue 程大约. *Cheng's Selection of Ink Works* [in Chinese] 程氏墨苑. Anhui: Zi Lan Tang, 1594.

Colorful Illustration to Old Testament [in Chinese] 五彩古史像解. Shanghai: T-Usey Press, 1892.

Colorful Illustration to New Testament [in Chinese] 五彩新史像解. Shanghai: T-Usey Press, 1892.

Illustration to the Life of Jesus Christ [in Chinese] 道原精萃. Shanghai: T-Usey Press, 1887.
Illustration to the Typology of Savior [in Chinese] 救世主預像全圖. Nanjing: Nanjing Catholic Church, 1869.
Illustration to Savior's Deeds [in Chinese] 救世主實行全圖. Nanjing: Nanjing Catholic Church, 1869. Amity website: http://www.amityprinting.com. WD Bible website: https://wdbible.com/app.

PART III

INTERPRETATION AND METHODS OF READING

CHAPTER 23

A HISTORY OF BIBLICAL INTERPRETATION IN CHINA

JOHN Y. H. YIEH

INTRODUCTION

WHEN Nestorian Christians first arrived in Chang-an (Xian) in 635 CE, Emperor Tang Taizong (598–649) asked them to translate their Scriptures "in the imperial library" for his private reading and, impressed with "the rectitude and truth of the religion," the emperor ordered its dissemination.[1] Unfortunately, none of their translated Scriptures survived. In 1583, Matteo Ricci (1552–1610) came to Beijing to preach Catholicism with remarkable success, yet during the one-hundred and fifty years of Catholic mission in China, only parts of the Bible were translated into Chinese for catechetical and liturgical uses. It was not until 1807, when the first Protestant missionary from England to China, Robert Morrison, made his primary task to translate the Bible into Chinese as a tool to propagate Christianity. He printed the first complete Bible in Chinese (*Shentian shengshu*) in Malacca in 1823. In the year 1919, the Union Version (*heheben*), a joint project by missionary translators from several missions, became the most popular version broadly circulated and profoundly influential in the Chinese church and society.[2] In 2019, the Amity Printing Company in Nanjing, which began to print the Chinese Bible in 1988, celebrated the printing of 200 million copies. In the last two hundred years, the Bible has been used for devotion at homes, for worship in churches, and for research in universities. As Ding Guangxun stated in a plenary address to the AAR & SBL annual meeting in 1990, "Most Chinese Protestants are Bible-loving, Bible-possessing, and Bible-reading Christians."[3] A significant number of sermons, commentaries, and research studies on the Bible also have been published.[4] This essay seeks to construct a history of biblical interpretation in China to see how the Bible has been received, interpreted, and appropriated by the Chinese people.

Why a History of Biblical Interpretation in China?

The purposes of constructing a history of biblical interpretation are: (1) to preserve a record of the circulation and reception of the Bible in China; and (2) to assess its major interpretations and effects on Chinese people. It is only in the context of history that can we recognize the creative insights of a special interpreter, and only in light of history can we assess the impact of a particular interpretation. Besides historical purpose, a history of biblical interpretation in China may provide fascinating examples and thought-provoking cases for cross-cultural comparison and hermeneutical reflection on the theories and practices of biblical interpretation. While tracing the Bible's encounters with the Chinese people and reviewing its various interpretations, we also may learn how the Bible was translated into a new language, how it was received by a new people, how it was interpreted in a new culture, how it was used to address new situations, and how it helped form and shape a new nation. In order to answer these historical and hermeneutical questions, a good history of biblical interpretation in China should combine three related approaches: history of reception (*Rezeptionsgeschichte*), history of interpretation (*Auslegungsgeschichte*), and history of effects (*Wirkungsgeschichte*).

A history of biblical interpretation in China also may reveal the distinctive features and common patterns of "Chinese" biblical interpretation by showing how Chinese readers interact with the Bible. First of all, China has a long and rich history of scriptural interpretation in its philosophical and religious traditions. Elite scholars and common folks alike are familiar with the basic teachings and major interpretations of the Four Books and Five Scriptures of Confucianism, the Dao De Jing of Daoism, and the Jing (Sūtras) and Lü (Vinaya) of Buddhism. Nurtured in a multi-religious culture reverencing traditional classics and Scripture, it is natural for Chinese readers to hold some similar perspectives on the Bible. By observing how they interact with the Bible as a "foreign" Scripture and comparing their reading of the Bible to other Chinese texts, we may detect some patterns of culturally distinctive "Chinese" interpretation.

Secondly, most Chinese Protestant Christians subscribe to Reformed theology and revere the Bible as the most authoritative text for their faith and life (*sola scriptura*).[5] Christians are encouraged to read the Bible for daily devotion and participate in Bible studies in church groups. The Bible is internalized to inform their belief system and shape their way of life. By observing how the Bible is interpreted, preached, and taught, we may gain an insight into indigenized doctrines and contextualized theologies of the Chinese church.

Thirdly, the history of the Bible in China coincides with a tumultuous history when China went through radical changes. The imperial system was overturned to become a new republic and is now ruled by the Communist Party, the feudal society broke down into chaos and developed through industrialization into a Chinese style of socialism, and the traditional culture metamorphosized through critical exchanges with foreign influences to become modern and global. To address the crisis caused by those changes, Christian scholars and church leaders have sought answers in the Bible, claiming that the Bible holds the key to transforming the society and changing lives. By analyzing the presumptions, approaches, and outcomes of major interpreters and their approaches, we will be able to learn something about the art and practice of biblical "interpretation."

How Best to Conceive a History of Biblical Interpretation?

How can a history of biblical interpretation in China be properly conceived? In the West, a history of biblical interpretation often is conceived as a history of intellectual evolution marked by paradigm shifts in interpretive methodologies.[6] The history of biblical interpretation in China is best conceived, however, as a history of social revolution rather than intellectual evolution, in which the Bible is received, interpreted, appropriated, and consequential. Brought to China as a "foreign'" Scripture, the Bible has to prove its truth and merit to earn the welcome of Chinese readers, and its interpreters have to engage the political, social, and cultural settings of China in a compelling way. For both reasons, a history of biblical interpretation in China needs to intersect closely with the national history and the church history of China.

In an essay, "Chinese Biblical Interpretation: History and Issues,"[7] I have proposed to divide the history of Chinese biblical interpretation into four stages, using the metaphor of human growth from infancy, childhood, adolescence, to growing pains. I follow the same division to highlight the most significant socio-political events and church challenges that constitute the historical contexts of biblical interpretation in each period.

Anti-Foreignism and "Difficult Infancy" (1807–1860)

When Protestant missionaries landed in China, they began to produce Gospel tracts for dissemination, not realizing that only a few literati could read, and those Gospel tracts often were discarded with disdain because missionaries were regarded as invaders who forced their way into China "on the gunboat of the British Navy."[8] Even though the imperial ban against foreign contact had been in place since 1721, Western powers continued to knock at China's door in pursuit of trading opportunities, such as smuggling opium grown in India into China, using drug money to purchase Chinese silk, porcelain, and spices, and selling those goods to Europe to make a fortune. The Opium Wars and various unequal treaties made it possible for missionaries to move into China to preach the gospel, but these humiliating events also created a deep anti-foreign resentment among the people. Though missionaries produced several impressive Chinese translations, the Bible was met with suspicion from literati who were otherwise accustomed to a multi-religious culture and would have been interested in reading it as a new Scripture.[9]

To adapt to the low literacy rate and anti-foreign sentiment, missionaries began to tell Bible stories in the familiar Chinese genre of *Sanji Jing* 三字經 (three character or trimetric classic), traditionally used to teach basic moral principles to young children. Storytelling turned out to be a simple and useful form of biblical interpretation. Reading the Bible is a political act, and socio-political condition dictates how it is received.

Popularists' Uprising and "Traumatic Childhood" (1860–1911)

In this era, Western countries gathered incredible wealth from the industrial revolution and colonial exploitations, and the revival movements of the foreign church sent a great number of missionaries to China.[10] With more resources, missionaries replaced their initial strategy of "direct evangelism" (preaching on the streets and distributing Gospel sheets) with "indirect evangelism" (opening schools, orphanages, and hospitals).[11] As a result, they made many converts and built many churches.[12] Missionaries' decision to add philanthropy to evangelism was motivated by their new vision "not just to save the heathen soul, but to remake his world"; nevertheless, the radical expansion of Christianity in China could be conceived, in William Hutchison's view, as a "moral equivalent for imperialism."[13] The anti-foreign and anti-Christian hostility became violent, and local riots attacking missionaries and Christians (*jiao-an* 教案) dramatically increased,[14] evident ultimately in the horrific Boxers' Uprising in 1900 endorsed by the Empress Dowager Cixi.[15]

In response to such harassment, missionaries strengthened their mission of education, raising students to explain the gospel to their compatriots. The Bible was preached in churches and taught in schools by missionaries and foreign teachers who imported a variety of biblical interpretations developed and debated in the West. Chinese Christians were being trained and were still searching for their own voices in biblical interpretation.

Student Protests and "Challenging Adolescence" (1911–1949)

In this period, China faced many crises: new political system, foreign aggressions, moral corruptions, civil wars, and Japanese invasion. The nation recognized that it was weak and in danger of being colonized, but the government proved to be incompetent and corrupt. Intellectual leaders were keen on finding a way to save China from foreign aggression and self-destruction. As a result, the New Cultural Movement and the May Fourth Movement drew a huge following among impassioned college students who believed China needed modernization, science, and democracy. Traditional culture, religions, and Christianity, on the other hand, were the roadblocks to progress that should be removed.

In such anti-Christian climate, the church faced three major challenges, all of which affected biblical interpretation. The first concerned missionaries' institutional leadership.

In 1922, the "Anti-Christian Alliance" demanded that higher education be independent of missionary control. In reaction, missionaries began to transfer their leadership in the church and in the school to Chinese Christians. Chinese leaders were now given the pulpits and lecterns. The second was the big question: Can Christianity save China?[16] Many Christian scholars joined the Indigenization Movement to write and show how the Bible and Chinese culture share common visions in ethics and can be integrated to build a moral society and a strong nation.[17] Some (e.g., Wu Leichuan, Zhao Zichen) went further to argue that Jesus' example and teaching as presented in the Gospels are the best remedies that can transform society as well as save souls. The third was a practical question: Can the Bible help people deal with the challenges of life, such as temptations and suffering? Several theologians and preachers (e.g. Jia Yuming, Wang Mingdao, Ni Tuosheng) rose to national acclaim as they unraveled the spiritual teaching of the Bible to advise Christians on how to live a faithful life in an age of depravity and despair.

Communist Rule and "Growing Pains" (1949–2019)

The hallmark of this era is the tension between the state and the church, which has induced conflicting approaches to biblical interpretation. At the founding of the PRC, the Communists tried to build a socialist nation while fighting US imperialism in the Korean War, so they demanded support from all religious groups. Among Protestants, Wu Yaozong tried to rally support for the new government, asking church leaders to pledge allegiance by signing the "Christian Manifesto" (1950). Others, like Wang Mingdao and Ni Tuosheng, were skeptical of the Communist Party because of its espousal of atheism. The dissension over this document divided the Chinese church into two camps: The Three-Self Patriotic Movement (TSPM) churches and the unregistered churches.

In the past seventy years, the People's Republic of China has survived and thrived through several political transformations—the Cultural Revolution, Reform and Opening, Chinese Style of Socialism, and One Belt One Road—to become an economic superpower in the world. The Chinese church also has gone through challenges and ordeals, but its membership grows rapidly in the TSPM churches and especially the unregistered churches. Sadly, the division and distrust between the two camps remain strong today, and both sides use biblical interpretation as a theological weapon to attack each other. Biblical interpretation in the TSPM churches tends to focus on God's love, social service, and good citizenship, while that in the unregistered churches tends to insist on the purity of the gospel, spiritual growth, and separation from the world. It should be noted that, since 2000, a third group of biblical interpreters has appeared, namely, a growing number of academics in universities carrying out interesting projects to research the Bible as a literary, cultural, or religious text. In terms of contexts, the religious policy of 2017 on the implementation of the "Sinicization of religions" (宗教中国化), which is regarded as part and parcel of Xi Jinping's vision for a New Era,[18] needs to be closely watched for its potential impact on Chinese biblical interpretation.

What Should Be Included in a History of Biblical Interpretation?

Having considered socio-political and church contexts, we may ask: what subject matters should be included in a history of biblical interpretation in China? To show how the Bible has been interpreted in China, a proper history should of course include a critical assessment of major interpreters and influential approaches, and we should look for them in four areas (Bible translation, teaching for the church, interpretation for the society, and research in the universities) where the Bible has been earnestly read and critically studied. To facilitate hermeneutical reflection on the traits and contributions of Chinese biblical interpretation, a good history also should include an investigation into the reception, appropriation, and consequences of the Bible. In this essay, I mention only a few interpreters and approaches as examples and register a few issues deserving further reflection.

Noteworthy Examples: Major Interpreters and Influential Approaches

Who are the shakers and movers of biblical interpretation in China, and what notable contributions have they made?

Bible Translation

Every translation is interpretation. So, a comparison of different versions of the Chinese Bible, e.g. Robert Morrison (1823), Karl Gützlaff (1838), The Delegates' Version (1856), and The Union Version in Mandarin (1919), may shed light on translators' interpretation of the Bible as well as their understanding of Chinese culture, as evident in the so-called "interminable term question."[19] It also would be interesting to find out how Bible translation can influence recent constructions of Sino-Christian theology because of its emphasis on the Chinese linguistic context.

Teaching for the Church

In the second stage of the history, missionary teachers used the Bible to teach doctrine and train preachers. Their denominational affiliations and theological positions obviously affected the way they taught the Bible. Those from mainline churches, such as Anglicans and Presbyterians, would teach students to read the biblical text in historical contexts. Missionaries in the China Inland Mission tended to focus on the gospel message in the Bible. As a result, the theological fight between liberals and conservatives in the West was transplanted into China.

What is remarkable in the third stage of the history was the rise of prominent Chinese theologians and preachers, whose writings and sermons exhibit a wide range of interpretive approaches to the Bible. The following are notable examples.

Jia Yuming (1880–1964) was a Presbyterian pastor and professor of North China and Nanjing Seminaries. He headed a Chinese Christian Bible institute and edited a bulletin entitled *Ling Guang* (*Spiritual Light*) Magazine. He was nominated as vice-chairman at the World Gospel Conference in Holland (1948) and chosen as vice-chairman of the Committee of the Chinese Church Three-Self Patriotic Movement (1954).[20] A prolific author, Jia published several Bible commentaries and popular textbooks on Christian doctrines such as *Study of Theology*, *Basic Bible Truth*, and *Total Salvation*. His Calvinist teaching on soteriology and sanctification have been influential in conservative churches. His view on Christian spirituality has caught much attention recently. Tse Lungyi argues that Jia Yuming interprets Paul's idea in Philippians 1:21—"For to me, living is Christ"—to mean "*theosis*" as understood in the Eastern Orthodox tradition, which is the final goal on the Christian path to sanctification.[21] Kwok Wei-luen further argues that Jia's view of *theosis* as the final destination of the Christian journey to the "abundant life" that Christ has promised can be compared to Mencius' idea of *jing xin zhi xing* 盡心知性, which suggests a life-long journey of moral cultivation to recover the goodness or conscience in human nature that has been drowned out—though, for Jia obviously, that goodness or conscience is God.[22] I would add that Jia's interpretation of "*theosis*" reflects his education in Chinese classics and may have been shaped by his life experience with the devastation of wars and violence. Like many people in his generation seeing the frailty and uncertainty of life, he longed to be in union with God, the source of abundant life. His interpretation of the Bible was always grounded on careful exegesis of the text in the historical context and his explanation of theological messages was highly imaginative and memorable. He wrote beautifully and his argument was compelling; he was good at using the Reformed principle of *scriptura scripturam* (以經解經) to interpret obscure Scripture with explicit Scripture. In his long career as a theological educator, he trained many Bible-based pastors and preachers for the Chinese church.

Wang Mingdao (1900–1991) was founder of Christian Tabernacle, a large independent church in Beijing, publisher of a religious newspaper, *Spiritual Food Quarterly* (靈食季刊), and a famous itinerant preacher nationwide.[23] He did not receive formal theological training, but his biblical preaching was forthright and inspirational with a clear focus on pure doctrine and holy life. This focus attracted many pious followers who desired to live an ethical life in a society characterized by moral decay aggravated by wars and poverty. He was greatly admired by conservative Christians because of his courageous refusal to sign the "Christian Manifesto," his passionate debate with the leaders of the TSPM, and his suffering in jail for the sake of faith from 1955 to 1980. He was charged as an "anti-revolutionary" by the authorities, but he was really anti-TSPM for theological reasons. He refused to sign the Manifesto because he believed only the gospel can save people from sin and corruption and the church must separate itself from the state. He saw his debate with the leaders of the TSPM as a battle between gospel truth and Modernist heresy. In a famous article, "We are for the Faith," he called Wu Yaozong and Ding Guangxun "wolves in disguise among the sheep" and declared that he would never be in cohort with that "party of unbelievers."[24] Against the "social gospel" embraced by the TSPM, he once wrote: "the social gospel is a counterfeit medicine conjured up by the devil...I oppose the social gospel and warn those who preach it: lest the curse that Paul pronounced upon preachers of 'another gospel' fall upon them."[25] Wang became a model of disobedience for faith. His article, "We are for the Faith," has been evoked repeatedly by the unregistered churches in their protests against the authorities; for instance, the Shouwang Church in Beijing that lost their place of worship in 2011 and the churches in Jejiang Providence whose crosses were taken down in 2015.

Ni Tuosheng (1903–1972) was founder of an indigenous Chinese church nicknamed "Little Flock," which has grown to be a broad network of several hundred churches in China and southeast Asia and now including the United States. He called himself "Watchman Nee," because he believed he was a seer of divine revelation and his commission from God was to teach people to know and experience God in Christ.[26] He was and remains influential among fundamentalist Christians because of his volumes of biblical expositions and his martyrdom (1952–1972). His widely circulated books include *The Spiritual Man* (3 vols., 1928), *The Normal Christian Life* (1957), and *Love Not the World* (1968). These titles are indicative of Ni's overall concern for Christian spirituality. To "live by the Spirit, not to gratify the desires of the flesh" (Gal 5:16) is a central theme in his biblical teaching on Christian life. He advocated for so-called "spiritual interpretation" (靈意解經). The purpose of biblical interpretation, for him, is to discern God's revelation in the words of the Bible through the help of the Holy Spirit. The words of the Bible could be used to communicate divine revelation to the first readers, because the authors of those biblical words have been inspired, i.e., sanctified, by the Holy Spirit. Likewise, readers today need to be sanctified and belong to the Holy Spirit (1 Cor 2:9–13).[27] The key to Ni's "spiritual interpretation" is the sanctified reader more than any clever method. Like Jia, Ni's spiritual interpretation follows the Reformed principle of *scriptura scripturam* (using explicit Scripture to interpret obscure Scripture) and requires a cogent process of inference-making (cross-referencing other texts in the Bible).[28] In practice, however, his choice of the text for cross reference and the process of his inference-making are not always cogent or convincing. Sometimes his interpretation looks like an allegorical interpretation in the fashion of the ancient Alexandria School, and other times it seems to be an arbitrary construal from his own theological world.

During the Cultural Revolution, we don't know how Christians held on to faith or how they might have read the Bible under the dire circumstances. But an oral history project interviewing Christians released from labor camps records personal testimonies and anecdotal stories to show many of them kept their faith by reciting biblical verses from memory and singing hymns that contain biblical words, which gave them comfort, hope, and joy in those difficult times.[29] More research needs to be done.

In the fourth stage, one of the most powerful voices in Chinese biblical interpretation was Bishop Ding Guangxun (K. H. Ting; 1915–2012), chairman of the Chinese Council of Churches and the TSPM and President of Union Theological Seminary in Nanjing.

The God of love and the Cosmic Christ are two pillars of his theological system and the keys to biblical interpretation. He recognized that Communist China is the social reality in which the Chinese church is called to testify and to serve. For him, therefore, the main concern of the church is to connect the two C's, Christianity and Communism.[30] In contrast to fundamentalist church leaders who believed Christians are in the world but not of the world and their life should be kept holy by separation from the way of the world, Ding urged Christians to be faithful disciples of Christ and loyal citizens to the nation at the same time. In his sermons and speeches, he often encouraged Christians to serve the needs of society with open heart and charitable actions as they have received grace from God. In order to connect the two C's, Ding Guangxun also launched a controversial movement called "theological reconstruction,"[31] urging the church to preach more of God's inclusive love and to de-emphasize (*danhua*) the doctrine of "justification by faith" which assumes everyone is a sinner and which can be off-putting to the Chinese people.

Interpretation for the Society

Toward the end of the first stage, there was a little-known but fascinating Chinese interpreter of the Bible, Hong Xiuquan (1814–1864), the rebel king of the Taiping Heavenly Kingdom. He may be the only person who actually was converted by the Gospel tract and turned into the legendary leader of a peasant uprising that took over one third of the nation and established a kingdom in Nanjing (1850–1864).[32] The story in the Gospel tract helped him recognize God and Jesus in his vision on the sick-bed, and he believed he was the younger brother of Jesus sent back to earth for a mission. He began to read the Chinese Bible intently and decided to become a Christian. When rejected by American Baptist missionary Issachar Roberts, he baptized himself in the river and founded the Society of God-Worshippers in his hometown. As he roamed through villages and towns, many poor peasants who were angry with corrupted officials accepted his message of divine love and human equality and followed him in large groups, eventually turning into an army of tens of thousands, and in three years he took over Nanjing and assumed it as his capital city. Hong followed biblical teachings to treat all his followers kindly and equally as brothers and sisters and encouraged them to share everything in common, as did the first church in Jerusalem. His land redistribution policy shows his care for poor peasants and might have been inspired by the God in the Bible who promised his people a land of milk and honey where all can work hard to raise their families. Based on the vision of Gal 3:28, he prohibited ethnic, class, and gender discrimination. In his army, women served as officers, and in his royal court as ministers. He also printed a Chinese Bible with his own annotations for circulation in the kingdom. He ordered his citizens to follow the teaching of the Bible and banned alcohol, tobacco, opium, gambling, slavery, and prostitution.[33] Some annotations in his Taiping Bible illustrated his esoteric reading of the Scripture, similar to the *Pesherim* in the Dead Sea Scrolls, to prove his identity as the second son of God and support the legitimacy of his kingdom.

In the third stage of the history, in response to college students who were anti-tradition and anti-Christian, several Christian scholars rose to contend that Christianity actually could save China from moral degeneration and foreign aggressions, if the ethical and social messages of the Bible were followed. Wu Leichuan (1870–1944), the first Chinese Chancellor of Yenching University, argued that the essence of Christianity was neither the church nor its doctrines, but Jesus Christ who could reform society and save China.[34] The Gospels in the New Testament, Wu maintained, portray Jesus as a moral teacher whose compassion for the poor and willing sacrifice for the kingdom of God set up a good example of moral virtue, love, and courage. Jesus' teaching, especially the Lord's Prayer, is a useful blueprint to establish an ideal society inhabited by virtuous people in China.[35] Modernization and science were indeed necessary to build a strong China, but moral character was the foundation of a healthy nation in which progress can be made and prosperity achieved, Wu argued.[36] Jesus Christ was precisely what Chinese people needed to know and imitate so that their moral character could be transformed and, if a significant number of people would do so, the corrupted society could be reformed.[37] A scholar of Chinese Classics, Wu Leichuan believed in the deeply held Confucian theory of moral primacy and its educational process called "*neishen waiwang*" (become a sage inside and govern the society outside): *xiushen, qijia, zhiguo, pingtianxia* (cultivate one's moral self, keep the family in order, rule the nation effectively, and make the world peaceful). In his view, the contribution of the Bible is to present Jesus Christ as the perfect model of moral virtue. Imitating Jesus is the right remedy to cure the ailment of the nation.

To defend Christianity against Modernists' and Nationalists' accusation that Chinese Christians were unscientific and unpatriotic, Zhao Zichen (T. C. Chao, 1888–1979), well respected theologian and professor of religious studies at Soochow and Yenjing universities, made a similar argument to uphold Jesus Christ as the best model to transform moral character and thereby reform the society.[38] In his *Life of Jesus*, Zhao describes his threefold approach to the materials in the Gospels in writing a biography of Jesus as historical, imaginative, and existential, and he has a younger generation of Christians as his targeted readers.[39] Chloë Starr characterizes this biography of Jesus as "a literary testament that combines a 'scientific' world-view with a passionately Chinese flair in its narrative form and social commitment."[40] In his writings on Christology published in this period of time, Zhao described Jesus as an ethical person who appreciated family relationship, honoring God as Father, and loving all people as siblings. Jesus exhibited a perfect character that he was not born with but was built up through his human experiences so that his followers might imitate him to become moral. Jesus also was concerned about the Jewish society of his time. That is why, unlike John the Baptist who retreated to the Jordan River, Jesus traveled to many cities and towns to meet people in various conditions, eager to change their lives and improve their society. It is interesting to note that, like Wu Lei-chuan, Zhao defended Christianity by arguing Jesus Christ could save China by inspiring his followers to imitate him and undergo moral transformation via the Confucian route of virtue ethics. Both scholars are Chinese and Christian.

K. K. Yeo, an overseas Chinese biblical scholar teaching in Chicago, Beijing, and Jerusalem, has brilliantly maintained the same scholarly effort to wed Chinese culture with the Christian Bible. In *Rhetorical Interactions in 1 Corinthians 8 and 10: A Formal Analysis with Preliminary Suggestions for a Chinese, Cross-Cultural Hermeneutic*,[41] he used a rhetorical-critical approach to analyze Paul's interaction with new converts. More importantly, he developed a cross-cultural hermeneutic to engage the centuries-old controversy of ancestor worship in the Chinese church. In *What Has Jerusalem to Do with Beijing: Biblical Interpretation from a Chinese Perspective*, his cross-cultural hermeneutic is further developed and tested by more case studies on other Chinese and biblical themes (e.g. *yin* and *yang*, *li* and *ren* [Torah and Spirit]).[42] Through critical comparisons, he demonstrates there are many concerns and perspectives shared in common by the Christian Bible and Chinese culture, and both can be mutually illuminative and complementary. Yeo reads the Bible culturally and reads cultures biblically. He is also keen on showing how reading Chinese culture and the Christian Bible cross-culturally can have important and practical implications for contemporary society and culture in China. Thus, in *Musing with Confucius and Paul: Toward a Chinese Christian Theology*, he advances from biblical interpretation to construct a Chinese Christian theology that can address political, social, and cultural issues in China today.[43]

Research in the Universities

Since 2000, several Centers for Christian Studies have been established in major universities, so Christianity and biblical studies are accepted as legitimate subjects of academic research in China.

Several scholars teaching in universities have made their marks in three strands. The first strand is to study the Bible as a literary classic in world literature. Most notable is Zhu Weizhi of Nankai University, a trailblazer specializing in literary analysis of the Bible, who translated John Milton's *Paradise Lost* and *Paradise Regained* into Chinese and published the first major book on the Bible as literature.[44] Liang Gong of Henan University follows Zhu's work to study the Bible as a discipline in comparative literature. He also introduced many critical methods of literary analysis from the West to China.[45] The second strand is to study the Bible as a cultural text in the Western tradition. Yang Huilin, professor of Renming University, considers himself an intercultural interpreter. He has brought Western theological methodologies to Chinese academia and explained Chinese Christianity to the English world.[46] Liu Xiaofeng of Renming University has been called a "Cultural Christian."[47] He reads the Bible not to find traditional Christian theology but as a textual source to construct a Sino-Christian theology (*hanyu shenxue*) in the context of Chinese language and culture. The third strand is to read the Bible as a religious text that creates a Christian religious tradition. You Bin of Central Minzu University has published in the field of Hebrew Scripture and established the Institute of Comparative Scripture and Religious Dialogue to study the Bible as a religious text of Christianity. The most important method he adopts is the so-called "scriptural reasoning" in contemporary religious dialogue that encourages deep listening to the scriptural reasons under each religious doctrine and practice so that we can reach a better understanding of each religion or a better quality of disagreement.

Hermeneutical Questions: Reception, Interpretation, Appropriation, Consequences

To facilitate hermeneutical reflection on issues concerning biblical interpretation in China, questions in the following four areas also should be considered, if evidence allows.

Reception

How was the Bible welcomed or rejected in each period, and why? Throughout its history in China, the Bible has been rejected by literati, popularists, college students, and red guards because missionaries were considered accomplices of Western imperialism. But it also has been cherished by Christians and studied by academics. Chinese Christians love the Bible because they believe it contains revelation of God's love and Christ's salvation, spiritual guidance on living a Christian life, and uplifting teachings that may cultivate moral character, transform society, and save China from self-destruction in a time of ethical crisis. Academics like it because it is a literary, cultural, and religious text in *world* heritage.

Interpretation

How has the Bible been interpreted in China? It has been cited to tell the gospel story and translated for readers at different levels of learning. In the process of translation, some theological views and cultural understandings have surfaced. It has been taught at seminaries and schools to explain Christian doctrine and prepare sermons for the church. Missionaries have brought in competing approaches to biblical interpretation, both conservative and liberal. Among Chinese interpreters, we have seen a wide range of interpretive approaches: Hong Xiuquan's esoteric reading, Jia Yuming's methodical exegesis, Wang Mingdao's moral discernment, and Ni Tuosheng's spiritual interpretation.

Appropriation

How has the Bible been used in China? First and foremost, it has been used in the church to teach Christian doctrine and nurture Christian life. Remarkably, it has also been used to implement the laws in Taiping Heavenly Kingdom, to engage theological debates between conservatives and liberals, to compare with Chinese classics on cultural themes, and to show how it can cultivate moral character to reform society. It also has been studied as an important text in world civilization.

Consequences

What impact has the Bible exerted on China? In the enterprise of Bible translation, the exchange of cultural tradition and printing technology between China and the West took place.[48] Bible translation also gave birth to the academic discipline of Sinology in Europe. The Union Version has supported the spread of the Vernacular Chinese Movement (*baihuawen yundong*) and inspired imagination and creativity in modern

Chinese writers such as Lu Xun, Bing Xin, Xu Dishan, and Lao She.[49] To college students who thought modernism and science were the only answers to national crises, the Bible presents Jesus Christ as a social reformer and a role model of compassion and sacrifice for an ideal society. Inside the church, the Bible has been interpreted to develop a social gospel and social service for the TSPM and spiritual truth and conservative pietism for unregistered churches. Biblical interpretation has built up the church in China. It also has divided the church in China. The wide-ranging impact of the Bible should be further explored.[50]

Conclusion: What Is Next?

These prolegomena provide a rationale, a method, and a few samples of basic contents to be further investigated for a thorough and comprehensive history of biblical interpretation in China. This sketch of the history in four stages shows how the Bible is dearly beloved and earnestly interpreted in China in the last two centuries, though at times it has been banned and burned. As a religious text, it has nurtured the faith and life of Chinese Christians and strengthened the identity and mission of the Chinese church. As a cultural text, it has introduced Christian religion and Western literature to the Chinese imagination and has trained many Sinologists, who in turn introduced Chinese culture to the West. As a social text, it has offered spiritual ideas and social ideals to the Chinese people with a potential to help them build moral character, ethical society, and a strong nation. The many ingenious ways it has been interpreted and appropriated by Chinese scholars and Christian preachers can serve as interesting cases to prompt fresh approaches to the search for biblical meaning and biblical relevance. The most noticeable among them are the "cross-cultural hermeneutic" that perceives the Christian Bible and Chinese culture as mutually illuminative and functionally complementary in their common goal to transform the reader and renew society (Wu, Zhao, Ding, Yeo, You), and the so-called "spiritual interpretation" that combines the Reformed principle of "*scriptura scripturam*" with a Chinese cultural emphasis on being a reader whose mind and heart must be sanctified by the Holy Spirit (Jia, Wang, Ni). Much remains to be gained and more research needs to be done!

Notes

1. A. Wylie, "On the Nestorian Tablet of Se-gan Foo," *Journal of American Oriental Society* 5 (1855–1856), 275–336 (282).
2. Jost Zetzsche, *The Bible in China: The History of the Union Version of The Culmination of Protestant Missionary Bible Translation in China* (Sankt Augustin: Monumenta Serica; Steyler Verlag, 1999). Philip Chia 謝品然, Ken-pa Chin 曾慶豹, eds., *Ever Since God Speaks Chinese: The 90th Anniversary of the Chinese Union Version Bible* [in Chinese] 自上帝說漢語以來:《和合本》聖經九十年 (Hong Kong: CABSA, 2010).

3. Ding Guanxun, "A Christian's Approach to the Bible," in *God Is Love: Collected Writings of Bishop K.H. Ting* (Colorado Springs: Cook Communications Ministries International, 2004), 79–91.
4. This is amply evidenced by the erudite essays and rich bibliographies in this Handbook.
5. Aiming Wang, *Church in China: Faith, Ethics, Structure: The Heritage of the Reformation for the Future of the Church in China* (Bern: Peter Lang, 2009), 473–570.
6. In *A Short History of the Interpretation of the Bible* (Robert Grant with David Tracy, *A Short History of the Interpretation of the Bible*, rev. Eng. ed. [Philadelphia: Augsburg Fortress, 1984]), Grant and Tracy survey major interpretive approaches to the Bible chronologically. See also the four-volume *History of Biblical Interpretation* by Henning Reventlow (trans. Leo Perdue and James Duke [Atlanta: Society of Biblical Literature, 2009–2010]), who follows chronological order across geographical regions to discuss different methods used in biblical interpretation.
7. John Yieh, "Chinese Biblical Interpretation: History and Issues," in *Ways of Being, Ways of Reading: Constructing Asian-American Biblical Interpretation*, ed. Mary Foskett and Jeffrey Kuan (St. Louis: Chalice, 2006), 17–30.
8. G. Thompson Brown, *Christianity in the People's Republic of China* (Atlanta: Knox, 1983), 36. Georg Evers, "Christianity in China—A Case of Missed Opportunities?" in *China and Christianity*, ed. Felix Wilfred, Edmond Tang, and George Evers (London: SCM, 2008), 32.
9. Paul Cohen, *China and Christianity: The Missionary Movement and the Growth of Chinese Anti-Foreignism, 1860–1870* (Cambridge, MA: Harvard University Press, 1963).
10. There were eighty-one missionaries in 1858, but the number jumped to 1,324 representing more than 130 denominations by 1893. Leung Ka-lun 梁家麟, *Blessing Upon China: Ten Talks on the Contemporary Church History of China* [in Chinese] 福臨中華: 中國近代教會史十講 (Hong Kong: Tian Dao, 1988), 68; Wang Chih-hsin 王治心, *History of Christianity in China* [in Chinese] 中國基督教史綱, 3rd ed. (Hong Kong: Chinese Christian Literature Council, 1979), 199.
11. Wei Waiyang 魏外揚, *Missionary Enterprises and Modern China* [in Chinese] 宣教事業與近代中國 (Taipei: Cosmic Light, 1978).
12. Leung, *Blessing Upon China*, 90.
13. Daniel Bays, *A New History of Christianity in China* (Malden, MA: Wiley-Blackwell, 2012), 71.
14. S. C. Lu, *The Origin and Cause of Anti-Christian Movement Officials and Gentry, 1860–1874* (Taipei: Institute of Modern History, Academica Sinica, 1966).
15. According to one statistic, five bishops, forty-eight priests, 18,000 Catholics, 188 ministers, and 5,000 Protestant Christians were murdered by the Boxers. By the time the soldiers from the Alliance of Eight Nations burned down Beijing in revenge, additional 100,000 people were killed, and the Chinese capital city totally ruined. Wang Chih-hsin 王治心, *History of Christianity in China* [in Chinese] 中國基督教史綱, 3rd ed. (Hong Kong: Chinese Christian Literature Council, 1979), 231.
16. For the historical context of this issue, see Ying Fuk-Tsang邢福增, "'Christianity Saving the Nation' in the Beginning of the 20th Century: An Example of Chinese Church's Response to the Context of the Tim [in Chinese] 二十世紀初年的「基督教救國論」(1900–1922)—中國教會回應時代處境一例, in *Conflict and Congruence: Essays on Modern History of Chinese Christianity*衝突與融合: 近代中國基督教史研究論集 (Taipei: Cosmic Light, 2006), 71–102.
17. N. Z. Zia謝扶雅, *Christianity and Chinese Thought* [in Chinese] 基督教與中國思想 (Hong Kong: Chinese Christian Literature Council, 1971). Ng Lee Ming 吳利明,

Christianity and Social Change in China [in Chinese] 基督教與中國社會變遷 (Hong Kong: Chinese Christian Literature Council, 1981). Zhang Xiping, Zuo Xinping 張西平、卓新平, eds., *Exploration on Indigenization: Scholarly Essays on Chinese Christian Culture in the 20th Century* [in Chinese] 本色之探: 20世紀中國基督教文化學術論集 (Beijing: China Broadcasting and Television Press, 1998). Duan Qi段琦, *Historical Documents on Indigenization of Chinese Christianity: A Historical Record of Confusion and Struggle of Chinese Christianity on Its Journey to Indigenization* [in Chinese] 中國基督教本色化史稿: 中國基督教在本色化道路上徬徨、苦鬥的歷史紀錄 (Taipei: Cosmic Light, 2005).

18. Benoît Vermander, "Sinicizing Religions, Sinicizing Religious Studies," *Religions* 10.137 (2019): 1.
19. Irene Eber, "The Interminable Term Question," in *Bible in Modern China: The Literary and Intellectual Impact*, ed. Irene Eber (Institut Monumenta Serica: Steyler, 1999), 135–168.
20. Kwok Wei-Luen 郭偉聯, *Objection to Unification: The Entanglement of Jia Yuming, Fundamentalism, and Unification Movement* [in Chinese] 反對合一: 賈玉銘、基要主義與合一運動的糾結 (Hong Kong: Tiandao, 2002).
21. Tse Lung Yi 謝龍邑, *Christ Person: The Spiritual Theology of Jia Yuming* [in Chinese] 基督人: 賈玉銘的靈命神學 (Taipei: China Evangelical Seminary, 2008).
22. Kwok Wei-Luen, "Jia Yuming's View of Sanctification and the Confucian View of Human Nature" [in Chinese] 賈玉銘的成聖觀與儒家心性學, in *Christianity and Chinese Culture*基督教與中國文化, ed. State Administration of Religious Affairs Center of Religious Studies (Beijing: Religion and Culture, 2013), 69–83.
23. For his biography and impact on Chinese Church, see Lam Wing-hung Lam, 林榮洪, *Wang Mingdao and the Chinese Church* [in Chinese] 王明道與中國教會 (Hong Kong: China Graduate School of Theology, 1982).
24. Wang Mingdao 王明道, *We are For the Faith* [in Chinese] 我們是為了信仰 (Hong Kong: Spiritual Stone, 1994), 288–330.
25. Wang Mingdao, *Spiritual Food* (Southampton: Mayflower Christian Books, 1983), 127.
26. For a biography written by his successor, see Witness Lee, *Watchman Nee: A Seer of the Divine Revelation in the Present Age* (Anaheim: Living Stream Ministry, 1991).
27. Lam Wing-hung, *The Spiritual Theology of Watchman Nee* [in Chinese] 屬靈神學: 倪柝聲思想的研究 (Hong Kong: China Alliance Press, 2003), 132–158.
28. Leung Ka-Lun, "A Defense for Spiritual Interpretation of the Chinese Church," in *The Role and Interpretation of the Bible in the Life of the Church in China*, ed. Choong Chee-Pang (Geneva: The Lutheran World Federation, 1997), 45–46.
29. An oral history project on DVD, see Yuan Zhiming 遠志明, *The Cross–Jesus in China* [in Chinese] 十字架—耶穌在中國 (Rohnert Park, CA: China Soul for Christ Foundation, 2003), Vol. 3: *Kubei* 苦杯 (Cup of Suffering).
30. Ding Guangxun, "To Testify for Christ in China," *Union Theological Journal* n.s. 1 (1984): 11–17. Ding Guangxun, "On theological education in my country—a prepared paper for a conference," *Union Theological Journal* n.s. 1 (1984): 46–49.
31. Philip Wickeri, *Reconstructing Christianity in China: K. H. Ting and the Chinese Church* (Maryknoll: Orbis, 2007), 333–369.
32. Jonathan Spence, *God's Chinese Son: The Taiping Heavenly Kingdom of Hong Xiuquan* (New York: W. W. Norton, 1996).
33. J. C. Cheng, "Chapter V: The Taiping Bible," in *Chinese Sources for the Taiping Rebellion: 1850–1864* (Hong Kong: Hong Kong University Press, 1963), 81–91.

34. Wu Leichuan 吳雷川, *The Hope of Christians* [in Chinese] 基督徒的希望 (Shanghai: Youth Association, 1940), 12–15. Tsai Yen-zen 蔡彥仁, "Scriptural Interpretation and Cultural Exchange: Wu Leichuan as An Example" [in Chinese] 經典詮釋與文化匯通: 以吳雷川為例, *Taiwan Journal of East Asian Studies* 1 (2004) 2: 305–330.
35. Wu Leichuan 吳雷川, *Christianity and Chinese Culture* [in Chinese] 基督教與中國文化 (Shanghai: Youth Association, 1936), 61–65. Grace Hui Liang, "Interpreting the Lord's Prayer from a Confucian-Christian Perspective: Wu Leichuan's Practice and Contribution to Chinese Biblical Hermeneutics," in *Reading Christian Scriptures in China*, ed. Chloë Starr ed. (London: T&T Clark, 2008), 118–133. John Yieh, "Reading the Sermon on the Mount in China: A Hermeneutical Enquiry into Its History of Reception," in *Reading Christian Scriptures in China*, ed. Chloë Starr (London: T&T Clark, 2008), 143–162.
36. Chin Ken-pa 曾慶豹, "Introduction" 導論 [in Chinese], in *Christianity and Chinese Culture: The Collected Works of Wu Leichuan (I)* 基督教與中國文化: 吳雷川著作集 (一) 附錄耶穌的社會理想 (Taipei: Olives, 2013), xii–cix (xix).
37. Wu Leichuan, *Jesus' Social Ideals* [in Chinese] 耶穌的社會理想 (Shanghai: Youth Association, 1934). Wu Leichuan, *Christianity and Chinese Culture* 基督教與中國文化 (Shanghai: Youth Association, 1936), 82–98.
38. Winfried Glüer 古愛華, *Zao Zichen's Theological Thought* [in Chinese] 趙紫宸的神學思想, trans. Joe Dunn 鄧肇明 (Hong Kong: Chinese Christian Literature Council, 1998). [German original: Winfried Glüer, *Die Theologische Arbeit T. C. Chao's in der Zeit von 1918 bis 1956* (1979)].
39. Zhao Zichen 趙紫宸, *Life of Jesus* [in Chinese] 耶穌傳 (Shanghai: Youth Association, 1935). Collected in Zhao Zichen 趙紫宸, *Collected Works of Zhao Zichen*, vol. 1 趙紫宸文集第一卷, ed. Yengjing Institute (Beijing: Shangwu, 2003), 449–631. Richard X. Y. Zhang, "Representing the Gospels to the Chinese Mind: T. C. Chao's Approaches to Biblical Texts in The Life of Jesus," in *Reading Christian Scriptures in China*, ed. Chloë Starr (London: T&T Clark, 2008), 134–142.
40. Chloë Starr, "Zhao Zichen and a Creative Theology: *The Life of Jesus* (1935)," in *Chinese Theology: Text and Context* (New Haven: Yale University Press, 2016), 73–99.
41. Leiden: Brill, 1995.
42. Harrisburg, PA: Trinity Press International, 1998; 2nd ed. Eugene, OR: Pickwick, 2018.
43. K. K. Yeo, *Musing with Confucius and Paul: Toward a Chinese Christian Theology* (Eugene, OR: Wipf & Stock, 2008).
44. Zhu Weizi 朱維之, *Twelve Lectures on Biblical Literature* [in Chinese] 聖經文學十二講 (Beijing: Renming Literature, 1989). Lo Lung Kwong盧龍光 and Wang Lixin王立新, eds., *Biblical Literature and Culture: A Festschrift in Memory of Professor Zhu Weizi on His Hundredth Birthday* [in Chinese] 《聖經》文學與文化: 紀念朱維之教授百年誕辰論集 (Tianjin: Nankai University Press, 2007).
45. Liang Gong 梁工, *Contemporary Literary Theories and Biblical Criticisms* [in Chinese] 當代文學理論與聖經批评 (Beijing: Renming, 2014).
46. Chloë Starr, "Yang Hulin: An Academic Search for Meaning," in *Chinese Theology: Text and Context* (New Haven: Yale University Press, 2016), 240–262.
47. Fredrik Fällman, *Salvation and Modernity: Intellectuals and Faith in Contemporary China* (Lanham, MD: University Press of America, 2008), 21–39.
48. Su Ching 蘇精, *Morrison and Chinese Printing Publication* [in Chinese] 馬禮遜與中文印刷出版 (Taipei: Student Books, 2000).

49. Liang Gong, "Twenty Years of Studies of Biblical Literature in the People's Republic of China (1976–1996)," in *Bible in Modern China: The Literary and Intellectual Impact*, ed. Irene Eber (Institut Monumenta Serica: Steyler, 1999), 383–408.
50. For more examples of interpretation and consequences, see John Yieh, "The Bible in China: Interpretations and Consequences," in *Handbook of Christianity in China*. Vol. 2: *1800 to the Present*, ed. R. G. Tiedemann (Leiden: Brill, 2010), 891–913.

Primary Sources

Wang Mingdao 王明道. *Spiritual Food*. Southampton: Mayflower Christian Books, 1983.
Wang Mingdao. *We Are for the Faith* [in Chinese] 我們是為了信仰. Hong Kong: Spiritual Stone, 1994.
Wu Leichuan 吳雷川. *Christianity and Chinese Culture* [in Chinese] 基督教與中國文化. Shanghai: Youth Association, 1936.
Wu Leichuan. *The Hope of Christians* [in Chinese] 基督徒的希望. Shanghai: Youth Association, 1940.
Zhao Zichen 趙紫宸. *Life of Jesus* [in Chinese] 耶穌傳. Shanghai: Youth Association, 1935.
Zhu Weizi 朱維之. *Twelve Lectures on Biblical Literature* [in Chinese] 聖經文學十二講. Beijing: Renming Literature, 1989.

CHAPTER 24

STUDY OF THE BIBLE IN CHINESE ACADEMIA

YANG HUILIN

Introduction

THE research and study of the Bible in Chinese academia can be traced back generally to the period of the Republic of China (1912–1949), but the history of academic teaching of the Bible in Chinese universities—not counting teaching in seminaries and Bible colleges—is recent. Although one can find related studies and teaching of the Bible in the fields of philosophy, ethics, history, and arts in universities, they are limited to certain aspects and hardly exist as an independent discipline as we find in Euro-American biblical studies. Furthermore, religious studies as an academic discipline, with students ranging from undergraduate to doctoral level, can be found only in a number of Chinese universities.

The few examples of universities that offer biblical studies given below are not meant to be exhaustive,[1] but they suggest a marginalization of Bible courses being offered in Chinese universities in the past, not to mention that the status of these course offerings today is difficult to gauge. One may explain this phenomenon citing factors of China's temperament, tradition, and sociological reality, and observe that biblical studies in China often have emerged from other disciples. For example, Wang Xiaochao 王曉朝 has taught and mentored his students in the use of the Bible but only in the areas of early Christianity, Christian ethics, or ancient Mediterranean cross-cultural studies (at both Zhejiang University and Tsinghua University). Though Zhu Donghua 朱東華 has taught the Gospel of John and Nestorian textual history at Tsinghua, his colleague Tian Wei 田薇 leans more toward Christian aesthetic and comparative religions.

Peking University has had at least three research centers that could have promoted biblical studies: Centre for Christian Studies, Hebrew-Jewish Culture Research Institute, Ancient Near Eastern Research Centre. Yet, biblical and biblically cognate languages, including ancient Near Eastern languages, Hebrew, Greek, and Latin, are taught without textual exegesis in these centers. In the Department of Religious Studies, Wu Yipeng 吳玉萍 for her tenure at Peking University has taught the Gospels to undergraduate students. Her colleague, Xu Longfei 徐龍飛, has taught biblical languages and historical-critical biblical interpretations, but often under the umbrella of historical or philosophical theology.[2] His colleague, Sun Shangyang 孫尚揚, focuses his research on the sociology of religion and Catholic missionaries to China, though one of his students, Wang Zi 王梓, was able to write a dissertation on "On Being Human: The Encounter between Ancient Roman Culture and Early Christianity in 1 Corinthians" in Pauline studies (under co-supervision with K. K. Yeo 楊克勤). Among his prolific works in foreign philosophy, Zhao Dunhua 趙敦華, former departmental chair of Philosophy and Religious Studies at Peking University, published a two-volume on biblical theology titled *Philosophy of Biblical History*.[3] Two doctoral students of Zhao, Hua Wei 花威 and Yu Liang 余亮, have worked on Romans and Ecclesiastes respectively, but since their teaching-research field (*jiao yan shi* 教研室) is foreign philosophy, Hua Wei's dissertation is "*Voluntas et Gratia*: Augustine's Philosophy of Will" (2012) and Yu Liang's is "A Study of the View of Time in the Book of Ecclesiastes" (2013).[4] Doctoral dissertations in Bible-related topics often are produced in China academia outside the Department of Philosophy and Religious Studies, and Peking University is no exception. Che Jinshan 車槿山 is a professor in the Department of Chinese Language and Literature at Peking University, yet his research foci are French critical theory and Sino-French comparative literature. And one of his students, Zhang Xin 張欣, wrote her PhD dissertation on "The Transformation of the Image of Jesus" (2008).[5] Zhang is now directing the Center for Studies of Christian Literature & Arts at Beijing Normal University and teaching biblical literature courses. With the help of Li Sher-shiueh 李奭學 from Academia Sinica Taiwan, Che's other student, Zheng Haijuan 鄭海娟, was able to complete her dissertation on Poirot's *Guxinshengjing* 賀清泰《古新聖經》研究 (2012).[6]

In Shanghai at Fudan University, the two professors in the religious studies department who are more likely able to offer Bible courses are Liu Ping 劉平 and Zhu Xiaohong 朱曉紅. Yet, it is possible to find a quality doctoral dissertation from outside the religious studies department; for example, Xing Mei 邢梅 wrote "A Study on the Syntax of Mandarin Chinese Union Version of the Bible" 《聖經》官話和合本句法研究 (2012) under Shen Xiaolong 申小龍 in the Department of Chinese language and Literature of Fudan University.

Liang Hui 梁慧 at Zhejiang University, Hangzhou, has long taught Bible courses and mentored Master's-student theses and PhD dissertations in biblical hermeneutics (sometimes under co-supervision with K. K. Yeo),[7] but often under the field of (comparative) literature, as she also is appointed to the Centre for Christianity and Cross-Cultural Research. The Department of Religious Studies at Wuhan University, Wuchang, has offered courses in biblical exegesis and Introduction to the Old Testament and New Testament, but still historical and comparative theology courses dominate.

On Jewish studies, especially Jewish biblical studies, Xu Xin 徐新, founder and director of the Research Institute of Jewish Culture at Nanjing University, focuses on Jewish civilization, while his colleague, Meng Zhenhua 孟振華, concentrates on the Hebrew

Bible and Jewish culture. Cao Jian 曹堅 at Sun Yet-sen University, Guangzhou, is probably the most qualified to teach the Hebrew Scriptures there, being the first mainland Chinese to earn a PhD in Hebrew studies from Hebrew University, Jerusalem.[8] His senior colleague, Gan Yang 甘陽, and former colleague Liu Xiaofeng 劉小楓, though they know biblical studies, invest most of their academic lives in Christian thought and Greco-Roman classical studies.[9] Shandong University, Jinan, has the Centre for Judaic and Inter-Religious Studies, and the Hebrew Bible is taught there. Fu Youde 傅有德 is the director of the Centre and the chief editor of the Centre's journal, *The Journal of Jewish Studies* 猶太研究. His colleague, Xie Wenyu 謝文郁, conducts research on the Gospel of John but in the context of Christian philosophy, Greek language, and culture. Mu Tao 沐濤, in the history department of East China Normal University, Shanghai, studies Jewish culture, while his colleague Zhang Ying's 張纓 research interest is in Old Testament (OT).

Another research center worth mentioning is the Centre for Christian Studies at Sichuan University, Chengdu. Major research interests of the Centre include biblical studies, but under Christian history, culture, and ethics. Chen Jianming 陳建明 is the director of the Centre, and his colleagues are Lin Qinghua 林慶華, who focuses on Thomistic theology, and Tian Haihua 田海華 and Zha Changping 查常平, who concentrate on New Testament (NT) studies.

Zhang Xiping 張西平, director for Overseas Chinese Studies at Beijing Foreign Languages University, focuses on historical theology of Catholics in China. One of his students, Zhu Jing 朱菁, wrote on Jean Basset's New Testament but from the historical perspective on issues of Bible translation.[10] Last but not least, You Bin 游斌, a prolific biblical scholar who studied NT at Peking University (1999) under Yang Shi 楊適 in Greek philosophy, is now a "Yangtze River Scholar" at Minzu University of China. Youbin has published in OT studies and, in 2017, established an academy of religious studies to promote Christian studies and equip church theologians in China (in collaboration with Fujian Seminary and Northeast Seminary).

For reasons stated above, to study and teach the "Bible as literature" is the most obvious feature of academia in the PR China's; we will look at Renmin University later on as one of the strong examples. It will be shown that the Chinese academic tradition places special emphasis on classics. This tradition pays attention to both religious and non-religious classics, thus providing a unique opportunity and natural method for the study and teaching of the Bible in higher education.

Bible as Literature and Chinese Academic Tradition

It is well-known that learning and mastering "Six Arts" represents the Chinese academic and cultural spirit. The so-called "Six Arts," as recorded in *Zhou Li*, originally included studying and learning the knowledge of rites, music, archery, horsemanship, calligraphy, and mathematics. Confucian scholars in the Han dynasty referred to the "Six Classics" as the "Six Arts." The Six Classics—*Book of Poetry*, *Book of Documents*, *Book of Rites*, *Book of Music*, *Book of Changes*, and *Spring and Autumn Annals*—were redacted by Confucius. According to Zhang Taiyan 章太炎 (1869–1936):

> In ancient times, when children were eight years old, they moved out to live in outer courtyard and start learning the "minor/primary learnings" [rites, music, archery, horsemanship, calligraphy, and mathematics]... and at the age of 15, they turned to "great learnings," which is also called "Six Classics." The wording of these two learnings seems to be different, but the principles are the same. The ancient Chinese first became literate, and then were taught to pursue and explore the ultimate *Dao*.[11]

After the 1919 "New Culture Movement," China established many modern higher institutions and the learning of "Six Arts" and "Six Classics" was gradually replaced by Western disciplines. This traditional learning spirit is immanent and has left clear marks, and in the studies of literature, history, and philosophy, the influence remains the deepest. This tradition offers resources for the study and teaching of the Bible in at least two areas.

First, according to the descriptions in *Book of Rituals* and *Chuang Tzu* (*Zhuangzi*), the essence of "Six Arts" lies in the cultivation of one's character, propriety, and metaphysical thinking so that the way to "search for truth" (*wei dao*), "to teach/learn" (*wei jiao*), and "to behave oneself" (*wei ren*) are strongly connected to each other and mutually reflects each other. In this sense, "Six Arts" or "Six Classics" not only are literary but also serve as the foundational education of literature, history, and philosophy. Even the so-called "minor/primary learning" (*xiao xue*), a critical interpretation of ancient texts offering specialized training of philology and exegesis, is classified in the category of "*Jing* 經" (similar to Scripture) in *The Si Ku Quan Shu* 四庫全書 (*Complete Library in the Four Branches of Literature*), because although the "primary learning" originated from the "children's literacy education,"[12] it is a necessary preparation for students to study the "great learning" (*da xue*), or Scripture-like classical texts. This tradition is similar to the medieval tradition of learning "liberal arts"; to learn grammar, rhetoric, and logic is to train in the basic yet comprehensive capability so that one can then interpret and understand the sacred text.[13]

Second, there is no clear distinction between religious and non-religious classics in the Chinese tradition. Confucius in the *Analects* highlighted the principle of education: "Set your heart upon the Way; rely upon moral power; follow goodness; enjoy the arts."[14] And in another verse, he stressed that one should "Draw inspiration from the Poems; steady your course with the ritual; find your fulfillment in music."[15] One can see clearly that literature plays a crucial role in cultivating perfect character of a person. And when Zeng Xi 曾晳, one of Confucius' disciples, mentioned that his educational ideal was to get along with students to "enjoy the breeze on the Rain Dance Terrace, and go home singing," Confucius "heaved a deep sigh and said 'I am with Dian [Zeng Xi].' "[16] Zhang Taiyan provided a further lesson to the story:

> Teachers should stay with the students every day, climbing, swimming, drinking and composing poems,... waiting for the students' self-enlightenment, instead of

> pushing or imposing on them.... The students could not be attracted by your teachings unless they understand why Confucius agreed with Zeng Xi.[17]

In the Chinese context of scriptural reading, "analyzing poetry metaphorically with Buddhist *Zen* idea" became a unique hermeneutical landscape of Chinese Buddhism, and in *The Complete Collection of Poems in Tang Dynasty*, there are 115 "monk poets" and more than 2,800 "monk poems." In the Song dynasty, Yan Yu 嚴羽 even advocated that "poetry is like *Zen*," because "epiphany with insights and enlightenment is manifested both in *Zen* and in poetry."[18] In a similar pattern, when the Assyrian Church of the East (commonly yet wrongly labeled as "the Nestorians") brought Christianity to China in the Tang dynasty, the Bible was widely interpreted and explained through Buddhist terms and ideas. The conceptual system of Buddhism was the first interpretative structure Christian thought relied upon in China. In other words, the Nestorian church frequently used Buddhist terms to translate important Christian concepts in their written Scriptures. For example, God was translated as "*Fo* 佛" (Buddha); Christ as "*Shi Zun* 世尊" (Bhagavat); "baptism" as "*Shou Jie* 受戒" (initiation into monkhood or nunhood); "faith," "hope," and "love" as "*San Chang* 三常" (the Three Virtues); Simon Peter as "*Cen Yin Seng Jia* 岑隱僧伽" (a hermit and monk), etc. Besides, the *Shi Zun Bu Shi Lun* 世尊布施論 (*Tales of Bhagavat Distributing Alms*) consisted of stories from the Gospels, and the meaning of *Xu Ting Mi Shi Suo Jing* 序聽迷詩所經 was rendered as the "Bible of Jesus Christ." And after Emperor Wudi of the Tang dynasty suppressed the Buddhist religion in the year of Huichang 會昌滅法, a number of Nestorian classics that had become scattered were mistakenly regarded as Buddhist classics and were thus mixed within the Buddhist treasures preserved at Dunhuang, which have become a precious cultural heritage today.[19] In the Ming dynasty, Matteo Ricci composed his *Catechismus Sinicus* 天主實義 in the form of a dialogue between a Chinese literatus and a European scholar.[20] In the late Qing dynasty and early Republic of China, there appeared many narrative literatures based on the Bible.[21] When Young John Allen 林樂知 published *The Church News* 中國教會新報 and *The Global Magazine and A Review of the Times* 萬國公報, "Bible stories" were still some of their prime content.[22] Accordingly, the Bible as literature and comparative studies on the relationship between Christianity and literature occupied a noticeable position in academic research and teaching.

For instance, as early as the 1930s, the YMCA Press published a series of books written by Christian writers, including two separate books with the same title *Christianity and Chinese Culture* 基督教與中國文化, by Wu Leichuan 吳雷川 and Xu Baoqian 徐寶謙. A more influential book by Zhu Weizhi 朱維之, *Christianity and Literature* 基督教與文學, also was published in this series. Zhu Weizhi's further research can be seen in his two monographs, *Twelve Lectures on Biblical Literature* 聖經文學十二講 (People's Literature Press, 1989) and *History of Ancient Hebrew Literature* 古希伯來文學史 (Higher Education Press, 2001). Some of Zhu's students, such as Liang Gong 梁工 and Wang Lixin 王立新, have become the new generation of scholars engaging in the study of the Bible as literature.

Bible as Literature and the Related Studies in the Past Four Decades

Wu Leichuan, Xu Baoqian, and Zhu Weizhi opened two new paths in the study of the Bible as literature. One is to study Christianity and Chinese culture, especially modern Chinese literature. The main outcomes of this track can be seen in the following works: *Wandering under the Cross* 十字架下的徘徊 (Xuelin Press, 1995) by Ma Jia 馬佳, *The Voice of the Wilderness* 曠野的呼聲 (Shanghai Educational Press, 1998) by Yang Jianlong 楊劍龍, *Chinese Literature and Christian Culture in the 20th Century* 20 世紀中國文學與基督教文化 (Anhui Educational Press, 2000) by Wang Benchao 王本朝, *Christian Culture and Tragic Consciousness of Modern Chinese Drama* 基督教文化與中國現代戲劇的悲劇意識 (Shanghai SDX Joint Publishing Company, 2002) by Wang Lieyao 王列耀, *Chinese Modern Literature and Christianity* 中國現代文學與基督教 (Shanghai University Press, 2003) by Xu Zhenglin 許正林, *Chinese and Western Literature and Religious Philosophy* 中西文學與宗教哲學 (Peking University Press, 2003) by Gao Xudong 高旭東, and another one specifically on the relationship of Christianity and contemporary Chinese popular culture, *The Cross Crowded with Onlookers* 被圍觀的十字架 (People's Publishing House, 2010) by Chen Qijia 陳奇佳.

Another path is comparative studies of Christianity and Western literature out of the contexts of Chinese scholars, such as seen in Table 24.1.

If the above-mentioned research has revealed a pattern, it can be roughly summarized as: Christian theological and hermeneutical studies (Liu Xiaofeng, Yang Huilin); Hebrew culture and literary text studies (Archie Lee, Liu Hongyi, Wang Lixin, You Bin) or Greco-Roman cultures and NT studies (K. K. Yeo); and biblical criticism and the history of Bible as literature (Liang Gong, Liu Yiqing, Liu Jianjun, Liang Kun, Chu Xiaobai). These studies also have directly influenced the curriculum of Chinese language and literature or foreign languages and literatures in higher educational institutions.

Studying and Teaching Bible in China's Academia Today

The undergraduate curriculum in Chinese universities contains several levels: general education courses, specialized compulsory courses, specialized optional courses, and elective courses. Courses related to the Bible or biblical cultures are found normally in elective courses. In other words, students can decide to take a course or not according to their own interests. Such courses generally account for two credits, which means about thirty-six teaching hours. Furthermore, courses related to the Bible are offered primarily in the Department of Foreign Languages and Literature. Some key universities also

Table 24.1 Comparative Studies of Christianity and Western Literature

Author	Title	Publisher & Year
Liu Xiaofeng 劉小楓	*Delivering and Dallying* 拯救與逍遙	Shanghai People's Publishing House, 1988
	Ad veritatem crucifixam 走向十字架的真	Hong Kong SDX Joint Publishing Company, 1990
	Narratio instincta descenti Spiritu Sancto 聖靈降臨的敘事	Beijing SDX Joint Publishing Company, 2003
Yang Huilin 楊慧林	*Sin and Redemption: The Spirit of Christian Culture* 罪惡與救贖	Oriental Press, 1995
	The Background and Cultural Extension of Christianity 基督教的底色與文化延伸	Heilongjiang People's Publishing House, 2001
	The History of European Medieval Literature 歐洲中世紀文學史	Yilin Press, 2001
	Theological Hermeneutics 神學詮釋學	Shanghai Translation Publishing House, 2002; Fujian Educational Press, 2018 revised edition
	On the Boundary between Literature and Theology 在文學與神學的邊界	Fudan University Press, 2012
Liu Hongyi 劉洪一	*Cultural Studies of American Jewish Literature* 美國猶太文學的文化研究	Jiangsu Literature and Art Press, 1995
	Essentials of Jewish Culture 猶太文化要義	The Commercial Press, 2004
	Biblical Narrative Studies 聖經敘事研究	The Commercial Press, 2011
Wang Lixin 王立新	*Historical Documents, Historical Framework, Historical Concepts of Ancient Israel* 古代以色列歷史文獻、歷史框架、歷史觀念研究	Peking University Press, 2004
	Literary Studies of Hebrew Bible in the Context of Ancient Jewish History and Culture 古猶太歷史文化語境下的希伯來聖經文學研究	The Commercial Press, 2014
	Exploring the Secret: Hebrew Literature and Western Literature 探賾索幽	Central Compilation and Translation Press, 2014
Liang Gong 梁工	*Bible and Literature* 聖經與文學	Times Literature and Art Press, 2006
	Oriental and Western Literature in the Horizon of the Bible 聖經視閾中的東西方文學	Zhonghua Book Company, 2007
	Introduction to Western Biblical Criticism 西方聖經批評引論	The Commercial Press, 2006
Archie Lee 李熾昌 and You Bin 游斌	*Life Speech and Community Identity: Five Volumes of Hebrew Bible Research* 生命言說與社群認同	China Social Sciences Press, 2003

(Continued)

Table 24.1 Continued

Author	Title	Publisher & Year
Archie Lee 李熾昌	*Cross-Textual Reading of the Hebrew Bible* 希伯來聖經的跨文本閱讀	Shanghai SDX Joint Publishing Company, 2015
You Bin 游斌	*The Literary, Historical and Thought World of the Hebrew Bible* 希伯來聖經的文本、歷史與思想世界	China Religious Culture Publisher, 2007
	Holy Book and Holy People: Historical Memory and Ethnic Construction in Ancient Israel 聖書與聖民	China Religious Culture Publisher, 2011
Liu Yiqing 劉意青	*Literary Interpretation of the Bible* 聖經的文學闡釋	Peking University Press, 2004
K. K. Yeo 楊克勤	*Biblical Rhetoric* 聖經修辭學	China Religious Culture Publisher, 2007
Liu Jianjun 劉建軍	*Christian Culture and Western Literary Tradition* 基督教文化與西方文學傳統	Peking University Press, 2005
Liang Kun 梁坤	*Eschatology and Redemption: Religious Cultural Interpretation of the Theme of Russian Literature in the 20th Century* 末世與救贖	Renmin University of China Press, 2007
Chu Xiaobai 褚瀟白	*Space Narration and Eschatological Consciousness: Research on Christian Literature in Late Classical Age* 空間敘事與終末意識	China Social Sciences Press, 2016

offer such courses in the Department of Chinese Language and Literature or the Department of Philosophy (see examples given in the first section of this essay). Accordingly, textbooks for these courses are compiled by faculty members who have majored in foreign languages and literatures. In any public bookstore, one can easily find a textbook like *An Introductory Course of Biblical Culture* 聖經文化導論 (student and teacher's books, Shanghai Foreign Language Educational Press, 2012) by Ren Dongsheng 任東升, Zhang Delu 張德祿, and Ma Yuelan 馬月蘭, which is listed in the series of "New Century Textbooks for English Major Undergraduates." The major drive to set up courses or compose textbooks related to the Bible is to help students understand the cultural history and the context of English language and literature.

Many universities do not offer courses related to the Bible for undergraduates but do offer elective courses related to the Bible in graduate programs, such as Western Classics Study or Selective Lectures on Western Literature (or Culture). The quality and content of such courses may vary according to different faculty resources. In a survey appearing in the Institute of Sino-Christian Studies (Hong Kong) *News Letter* (Autumn 2018) on courses related to the Bible for undergraduates in major Chinese universities in the academic year 2018, there is a course entitled Biblical Interpretation offered by professors in the English Department of Sichuan University, while some courses like Selected Readings of Greek Texts (including Texts from the NT), Basic Classical Hebrew (including Texts from the OT), and Selected Readings of Latin Texts (including Biblical and

Patristic Texts) are listed in the curriculum of the School of Liberal Arts (Chinese Linguistics and Literature) at Renmin University of China (in Beijing).

Regarding the research and teaching of the Bible as literature, many famous academic works pertinent to biblical studies have been translated into Chinese, some of which contain a preface written by non-Christian professors. For instance, Northrop Frye's *The Great Code: The Bible and Literature* (Peking University Press, 1998) was included in the Series of Frye Studies, with a preface by Wang Ning 王寧; *People of the Book: Christian Identity and Literary Culture* by David Jeffrey (Renmin University of China Press, 2005) was included in the Series of Christian and Western Literature, with a preface by Yang Huilin under the title, "For the Forgotten Poetic Wisdom." In addition, *Dictionary of Biblical Tradition in English Literature*, edited by David Jeffrey, was translated by Liu Guangyao 劉光耀 and his team (Shanghai SDX Joint Publishing Company, 2014), and it has become an important reference book for related research and teaching.

The more church-based series, the "Daily Study Bible" 每日研經 series, is slightly different from the above-mentioned translations. It focuses more on the interpretation of the biblical text itself, but it is also widely consulted and studied by Chinese researchers and scholars both inside and outside church circles. The Chinese version of this series was originally published by Hong Kong Christian Literature and Art Publishing House, and the mainland edition was republished as *Annotations to the Old Testament* by John Gibson (China Christian Association, 1990) and *Annotations to the New Testament* by William Barclay (China Christian Association, 1988).

In recent years, the most important publication project is "The Biblical Library" series 聖經圖書館, published by East China Normal University Press, edited by K. K. Yeo and Liang Hui. This series includes twenty-one volumes so far, published as textbooks for Christian studies, focusing on biblical studies, such as in Table 24.2.[23]

Apart from co-directing with Zhao Dunhua the MA program in Christian Studies and mentoring PhD students majoring in biblical studies at Peking University (in the Department of Philosophy and Religious Studies) from 2005 to 2017, Yeo also has edited (as executive editor with Zhao Dunhua as the series editor) the Peking University Christian Cultures Series, and fifteen volumes have been published thus far. This series not only included translation works to promote dialogue between Chinese scholars and international biblical scholars[24] but also encourages Chinese biblical scholars to produce works for the Chinese readers out of the Chinese context.[25]

In a similar vein, the exchange and cooperation between secular universities and church-based seminaries are gradually growing. University scholars are invited to lecture at seminaries or speak at academic conferences representing different voices from different circles, and seminary students can audit university courses. The MA in Christian Studies program at Peking University, since 2002, has offered intensive courses in summer (July) and winter (January) breaks to students with accredited college or university degrees, who then need to complete thirty-two credit hours of courses plus a thesis project to earn the MA degree conferred by the university. The MA program provides the background for preparation for the doctorate in religious studies or to provide the foundation for a career in religious leadership. Of the twelve courses in

Table 24.2 "The Biblical Library" Edited by K. K. Yeo and Liang Hui

Author	Title	Translator
Everett Ferguson	*Backgrounds of Early Christianity*	Li Lishu 李麗書
James S. Jeffers	*The Greco-Roman World of the New Testament Era*	Xie Fenfen 謝芬芬
R. E. V. Voorst	*Reading the New Testament Today*	Leng Xin 冷欣 and Yang Yuanzheng 楊遠征
Barry L. Bandstra	*Reading the Old Testament: Introduction to the Hebrew Bible*	Lin Yan 林豔 and Liu Hongyi 劉洪一
John H. Walton	*Ancient Near Eastern Thought and the Old Testament: Introducing the Conceptual World of the Hebrew Bible*	Li Lishu 李麗書
James C. VanderKam	*The Dead Sea Scrolls Today*	Liu Boyun 柳博贇
Shimon Bar-Efrat	*Narrative Art in the Bible*	Li Feng 李鋒
Walter Kasper	*The God of Jesus Christ*	Lou Xuanmin 羅選民
Alister E. McGrath	*A Fine-Tuned Universe: The Quest for God in Science and Theology*	Cai Qin 蔡蓁
Vernon K. Robbins	*Exploring the Texture of Texts: A Guide to Socio-Rhetorical Interpretation*	Huo Chengju 霍成舉
E. Rosenstock-Huessy	*The Christian Future: or the Modern Mind Outrun*	Xu Weixiang 徐衛翔
Leon Morris	*The Atonement, Its Meaning and Significance*	Yu Xiaofei 喻小菲 and Cui Ciaoxiong 崔曉雄
K. K. Yeo	*Confucius and Paul* (2010); *Eve, Earth and God* (2011); and *Chuang Tzu and James* (2012)	K. K. Yeo 楊克勤

this MA program, half of the them are in Bible and theology (historical and systematic) areas, mostly taught by world-renowned international faculty; and the other half pertaining to Christianity and society, ethics, Chinese cultures, and topics in Christian studies, which are taught by Peking University professors. Other than the number of Bible courses offered in the Yenching University (1921–1951) curriculum, it is rare to have such a concentration of academic studies of Bible and theology courses offered in any universities in China—to have the Bible studied and taught in the perspective of historical and literary criticism, and theological as well as philosophical perspectives.

Renmin University of China (RUC) has always been a leading institution in study of the Bible as literature and interreligious perspectives. Since 2006, RUC has recruited sixty representatives from the five religions—Protestantism, Catholicism, Buddhism, Taoism, and Islam (each religion can send twelve candidates) to have a four-month intensive study. Since 2012, the Chinese education ministry issued special permission to RUC to recruit five students from each religion to study in the MA program of religious studies every other year. The program takes three years to complete. Christian priests and pastors study in the same classroom and stay in the same dormitory as secular students, Buddhist monks and nuns, Muslim imams. and Daoist priests, so as to provide a practice of natural inter-religious dialogue in their daily lives.[26] Although only RUC can offer a degree program for religious workers, it signifies also a possibility of bridging the gap between secular higher-education institutions and Christian seminaries, Buddhist colleges, and Islamic *pesantrens*. The Bible component in the curriculum is found only in the interreligious course(s), and much more can be done, for example, in teaching the Bible as literature to this group.

With more and more international exchanges in Chinese academia, many foreign scholars have participated directly in the research and teaching of the Bible in China. For example, the Center for the Study of Theology and Literature, established by David Jasper at Glasgow University, co-sponsored the "Beijing-Scottish Seminar" with Chinese scholars and co-compiled a special issue for the journal *Literary and Theology* published by Oxford University. David Jasper also served as a distinguished professor of "Yangtze River Scholars" at Renmin University of China, and his Theological Trilogy has been translated and will be published in China soon. Several books by Roland Boer, like *Criticism of the Marxist Bible*, *Bible and Popular Culture*, *Critiques of the Heaven: Marxism and Theology*, and *Critiques of Religion: Marxism and Theology*, have been translated into Chinese and have received engaging responses in Chinese academic circles.

On the other hand, American and British theologians who have initiated the Scriptural Reasoning movement have interacted with Chinese scholars in the past years, extending comparative studies of the Bible, Qur'an, and Tanakh to the study of the Bible translated into Chinese and Chinese classics translated into foreign languages. For this reason, David Ford of Cambridge University wrote special articles to reflect on his interactions with Chinese scholars: "Deep Reading, No Map" and "Flamingo, Taiji and Scriptural Reasoning with Six Text: A Report on China's Trip."[27] Peter Ochs, from the University of Virginia, wrote an article for the *Journal of Renmin University of China*, "Scriptural Reasoning: From Practice to Theory," in which he commented on the different academic interests of Chinese scholars in "Scriptural Reasoning."[28] Since 2011, the International Comparative Literature Association (ICLA) has established the "Research Committee on Scriptural Reasoning and Comparative Literature" and has organized roundtables related to this theme in Paris (2013), Yanbian (2014), Beijing (2016), and Kaifeng (2017). Recently, several young Chinese scholars have published new works, such as *Self and Other: A Study in the Perspective of Scriptural Reasoning on The Analects Translated and Interpreted by James Legge* by Qiu Yexiang 邱業祥; *In the Tent of Lao Tzu: Scriptural Reasoning Based on Different Translations of Tao Te Jing Translated by James Legge and Lin Yutang* by Guan Ensen 管恩森; and *Collected Interpretations of the Selected English Versions of the Chapter "Xue Er" in the Analects* by Jiang Zhe 姜哲. Among them, a "non-religious interpretation" of the Bible and Chinese classics is the dominant tone, as Chloë Starr observed: "If Abrahamic Scripture Reasoning began with theists and theologians, Chinese Scripture Reasoning has been developed by textual theorists and comparatists," and so, "any Scripture Reasoning using the Chinese classics will necessarily be interdisciplinary," because "one of the things that Chinese thinking can bring to

Scripture Reasoning is a fluidity of interpretation," the model of which "is a textual web of association around a keyword."[29]

In terms of academic journals, the biannual *Journal for the Study of Christian Culture* 基督教文化學刊, founded by the Institute for the Study of Christian Culture (edited by Yang Huilin), Renmin University of China in 1998, has already published forty issues consecutively, through which the unique characteristics of interdisciplinary studies by China's academia could be clearly recognized. Subsequently, more than ten issues of *Theological Aesthetics* 神學美學 (edited by Liu Guangyao) and *Journal for the Study of Biblical Literature* 聖經文學研究 (edited by Liang Gong) have been published in the past years. The academic journals are all initiated by the scholars engaged in comparative literature, but their authors have expanded to the fields of religion, philosophy, history, anthropology, sociology, and other disciplines. The journals have become a typical interdisciplinary research platform.

In addition to monographs, translations, and journals, Chinese scholars, in cooperation with universities or research institutes at home and abroad, have successively organized quite a few international forums or conferences, such as the "International Conference on Bible and Classics Interpretation" (Henan University), "Symposium on Christianity and Literature" (Nankai University), "Christianity in China: Perspectives and Methods of Comparative Research" (Peking University), "Humanities and Theology" (Renmin University of China), "International Forum on the Study of Bible" (Chinese Academy of Social Sciences). In recent years, the topic of "Literature and Religion" has been listed as a panel or roundtable at the annual conferences of the Chinese Comparative Literature Association (CCLA).

Conclusion

Understanding is an interpretation. In the Chinese context and framework of understanding, "comparison" must be presupposed as the premise for the understanding of anything coming from other cultures. The research of Wang Guowei 王國維, a great scholar in modern China, was once summarized by another master, Chen Yinke 陳寅恪, as the effort to "prove by interpreting" (釋證 *shi zheng*), "to correct by providing supplements" (補正 *bu zheng*), and "to prove by comparing" (參證 *can zheng*). The "interpretation" (釋證 *shi zheng*) refers to the collation of "ancient documents" coincident with "unearthed literature," and the "supplementary" and "comparison" refer to the use of the learnings from abroad, i.e. the "old books of different nationalities" and "foreign concepts." Chen Yinke even believes that "for the future studies of humanities in our country, there is no way out of such three methods."[30]

In this regard, in order to understand the Bible appropriately as the absolute Other in the Chinese context, it is specifically necessary to reinterpret and even reshape Western and foreign learnings to stimulate and revitalize the unique problems raised from

Chinese perspectives. In this case, talking about studying and teaching Bible in China's academia, the following words of Martin Heidegger are well worth pondering: "Poets, when they are in their being, are prophetic, but they are not 'prophets' in the Judeo-Christian sense of the word. . . . His dream [the poet's] is divine, but it does not dream a god."[31] This, to me, also explains the internal causes of the "Bible as literature" in China.

NOTES

1. Other universities or research institutes in China that touch on Bible related studies are: The China Academy of Social Sciences, Beijing (Zuo Xinping 卓新平); The Xu Ricci Dialogue Institute at Fudan University (Li Tiangang 李天綱); Institute for Jewish Research at Henan University (Liang Gong 梁工); Research Institute for Middle East Studies at Shanghai Foreign Languages University; Shanghai Centre for Jewish Researches at Shanghai Academy of Social Sciences (focuses on Jews in Shanghai); Research Institute for Christian Culture at Shanxi Normal University, Xian (You Xilin 尤西林); Research Centre for Chinese Christianity at Fujian Normal University (Lin Jinshui 林金水); Shanghai University (Tao Feiya 陶飛亞, Zhou Ping 周平), Beijing Normal University (biblical literature taught by Zhang Xin 張欣), and Nanjing Theological Seminary.
2. Xu Longfei, *Metaphysical Way: Study of Methodology on Christian Philosophy* [in Chinese] 形上之路 (Beijing: Peking University Press, 2013); Xu Longfei, *Aesthetic Way* [in Chinese] 循美之路 (Beijing: The Commercial Press, 2018); *Eternal Way* [in Chinese] 永恒之路 (Beijing: The Commercial Press, 2018).
3. Zhao Dunhua, *Philosophy of Biblical History* [in Chinese] 聖經歷史哲學 (Nanjing: Jiangsu People's Publishing House, 2011).
4. Yu Liang's dissertation was revised and published as: *A Study of the View of Time in the Book of Ecclesiastes* [in Chinese] 《傳道書》的時間觀研究 (Taipei: Huamulan Culture Publishing House, 2015).
5. Published as: *Jesus as Mirror* [in Chinese] 耶穌作為明鏡—20 世紀歐美耶穌小說 (Beijing: China Religious Culture Publisher, 2010).
6. Zheng and Li were able to get it revised further and published: Louis Antoine De Poirot 賀清泰, *Guxin Shengjing Cangao* [in Chinese] 古新聖經殘稿, ed. Li Sher-shiueh 李奭學 and Zheng Haijuan 鄭海娟 (Beijing: Zhonghua Book Company, 2014).
7. For example, Zhang Zhaoyang 張詔陽, "On Paul Ricoeur's Narrative and Biblical Hermeneutics" [in Chinese] 論保羅·利科的敘事詮釋學及聖經詮釋 (2017); Zhang Chun 張春, "On Sugi's Postcolonial Biblical Critical Hermeneutic" [in Chinese] 蘇吉薩拉迦的後殖民主義聖經批評理論 (2018).
8. His revised dissertation is published as: Cao Jian, *Chinese Biblical Anthropology: Persons and Ideas in the Old Testament and in Modern Chinese Literature* (Eugene, OR: Pickwick, 2019).
9. Liu Xiaofeng 劉小楓 and Gang Yang 甘陽 have edited a 500-volume series titled "Classici et commentarii: Hermes" 西方傳統 經典與解釋 on Greek and Latin texts, published by Huaxia Publishing House and East China Normal University Press since 1986.
10. Zhu Jing 朱菁, "The Chinese Translation of the New Testament of the Basset and Xu Version" [in Chinese] 漢譯新約《聖經》"白徐譯本"研究 (PhD dissertation, 2014, Beijing Foreign Studies University: Comparative Literature and Cross-Culture Studies).

11. Zhang Taiyan, "*Brief Introduction of Minor Learnings*" [in Chinese] 小學略說, in *Collected Speeches of Zhang Taiyan* 章太炎國學講演錄, ed. Zhu Zugeng, Wang Qian, Wang Chengliu, et al. (Beijing: Zhonghua Bookstore, 2013), 110.
12. Zhang Taiyan, "Preface to *Shuo Wen Jie Zi*" [in Chinese] 說文解字序, in *Collected Speeches of Zhang Taiyan*, 51.
13. O. B. Hardison, ed., *Medieval Literary Criticism: Translations & Interpretations* (New York: Frederick Ungar Publishing Co., 1974), 9.
14. Simon Leys, tr., *The Analects of Confucius*, 7.7 (New York; London: W. W. Norton & Company, Ltd., 1997), 29. "志於道、據於德、依於仁、游於藝" (論語·述而).
15. Leys, tr., *The Analects of Confucius*, 8.8, 36. "興於詩、立於禮、成於樂" (論語·泰伯).
16. Leys, tr., *The Analects of Confucius*, 11.26, 53.
17. Zhang Taiyan, "Confucian School of Idealist Philosophy Appropriate for Today" [in Chinese] 適宜今日之理學, in *Collected Speeches of Zhang Taiyan*, 30–31.
18. Yan Yu, Collation and Annotation of Canglang Poetry [in Chinese] 滄浪詩話校釋, coll. & annot. Guo Shaoyu (Beijing: People's Literature Press, 1983), 11–12.
19. Yang Huilin, "The Chinese Union Version of the Bible and Its Hermeneutical Analysis," in *China, Christianity and the Question of Culture* (Waco, TX: Baylor University Press, 2013), 199–211.
20. Matteo Ricci, *Catechismus Sinicus, with Commentaries and Notes* [in Chinese] 天主實義今注, by Thierry Meynard (Beijing: The Commercial Press, 2014).
21. William Milne 米憐, et al. tr., *Selected Christian Narrative Literature in Late Qing Dynasty* [in Chinese] 晚清基督教敘事文學選粹, ed. Lai Tsz Pang (New Taipei: CCLM Publishing Group Ltd., 2012).
22. John Chalmera 湛約翰, et al. tr., *The Lost Pearls: Selected Chinese Protestant Bible in Late Qing Dynasty and Early Republic Period* [in Chinese] 遺珠拾穗: 清末民初基督新教聖經選輯, ed. Cai Jintu (New Taipei: CCLM Publishing Group Ltd., 2014), iv.
23. The sixteen-volume Cambridge New Testament Theology manuscripts were submitted to the publisher in 2013 as part of The Biblical Library series which, when published [in Chinese], will further enhance the work of biblical study for the Chinese world.
24. For examples [in Chinese], the translations of Stanley Romaine Hopper, *The Crisis of Faith*, trans. Qu Xutong 瞿旭彤 (2006); Roland Murphy, *The Tree of Life: An Exploration of the Wisdom Literature*, trans. Duan Suge 段素革譯 (2010); Tremper Longman III, *How to Read Exodus?*, trans. Duan Suge (2010); Gene Green, Steve Pardue, K. K. Yeo, eds., *Jesus beyond Borders*, trans. Duan Suge (2017).
25. For examples [in Chinese], the writings of Wang Zi 王梓 in *Reading Scripture and World Civilizations* [in Chinese] 經典解讀與世界文明, ed. K. K. Yeo and Wang Zi (2017); Justin Tan, *Suffering and Wisdom—Job* [in Chinese] 苦痛與智慧 (2010); K. K. Yeo, *Eschatology and Hope* [in Chinese] 末世與盼望 (2007), K. K. Yeo, *Biblical Rhetoric* [in Chinese] 聖經修辭學 (2007), K. K. Yeo, *Biblical Civilization: Introduction to Early Judeo-Christian Cultures* [in Chinese] 聖經文明導論 (2011).
26. So far three classes have graduated, and fourteen are sent by Protestant churches, and eight are sent by Catholic churches.
27. Chloë Starr, *Chinese Theology: Text and Context* (New Haven: Yale University Press, 2016), 347.
28. Peter Ochs, "Scriptural Reasoning: From Practice to Theory," trans. Wang Hai, *Journal of Renmin University of China* 5 (2012): 2–7.

29. Chloë Starr, "Yang Huilin: Searching for Meaning," in *Chinese Theology: Text and Context*, 252, 261–262.
30. Chen Yinke, "*Preface to the Posthumous Writings of Master Wang Jing'an*" [in Chinese] 王靜安先生遺書序, in *Collection of Wang Guowei on Learnings* 王國維論學集, ed. Fu Jie (Kunming: Yunnan People's Publishing House, 2008), 508–509.
31. Taken from Jacques Derrida, *Acts of Religion*, ed. Gil Anidjar (New York: Routledge, 2002), 54n9. Originally M. Heidegger, *Andenken* (1943), 4:114.

Primary Sources

Academic Journals:

Fu Youde, ed. *The Journal of Jewish Studies* [in Chinese] 猶太研究. Jinan: Shandong University (2002–).

Liang Gong, ed. *Journal for the Study of Biblical Literature* [in Chinese-English] 聖經文學研究. Kaifeng: School of Literature, Henan University (2006–).

Liu Guangyao and Yang Huilin, eds. *Theological Aesthetics* [in Chinese] 神學美學. Xiangyang: Hubei University of Arts and Science (2008–).

Xu Zhiwei, ed. *Regent Review of Christian Thoughts* [in Chinese] 基督教思想評論. Vancouver: Regent College (2008–).

Yang Huilin, ed. *Journal for the Study of Christian Culture* [in Chinese] 基督教文化學刊. Beijing: The Institute for the Study of Christian Culture, Renmin University of China (1999–).

You Bin, ed. *Journal of Comparative Scripture* [in Chinese-English] 比較經學. Beijing: Minzu University of China (2014–) [in print and on web: http://pppan777.wixsite.com/icsird/publicaiton].

Zhang Qingxiong, *Christian Scholarship* [in Chinese] 基督教學術. Shanghai: School of Philosophy, Fudan University (2002–).

Scholarly Series:

Fu Youde, ed. "Chinese Translation of the Masterpieces of Jewish Culture" Series [in Chinese] 漢譯猶太文化名著譯叢. Jinan: Shandong University Press, 1999–, 14 vols.

Liu Xiaofeng and Gang Yang, eds. "Classici et commentarii: Hermes" [in Chinese] 西方傳統經典與解釋. Huaxia Publishing House and East China Normal University Press, since 1986–, over 500 volumes.

Yeo, K. K. and Liang Hui, eds. "The Biblical Library" [in Chinese] 聖經圖書館. Shanghai: East China Normal University Press, 2000–), 21 vols.

Yeo, K. K. and Hua Wei, eds. "Classics and Civilization" [in Chinese] 經典與文明. Shanghai: Shanghai People's Publishing House, 2017–, 2 vols.

You Guanhui and Sun Yi, eds. "Christian Cultures Translation Series" [in Chinese] 基督教文化譯叢. Shanghai: Shanghai People's Publishing House, 2003–, 24 vols.

Zhao Dunhua, ed. "Peking University Christian Cultures Series" [in Chinese] 北京大學基督教文化研究系列. Beijing: China Religious Culture Publisher, 2006–, 15 vols.

CHAPTER 25

PATRISTIC BIBLICAL INTERPRETATION IN CHINA

JUSTIN T. T. TAN

INTRODUCTION

PATRISTIC biblical interpretation in China has not attracted much attention until the second half of the twentieth century. The flourishing of the particular area of study began when universities in China saw the impact of Christianity in general and Christian Scripture in particular, with the flowering of Christian intellectual investigations, as more and more intellectuals began to see the enduring value of Christianity toward the reconstruction of social and religious mores.

Patristic biblical interpretation in China often is taken as part of patrology and appear in conjunction with patristic theology and spirituality. Only in recent times has the study in this particular area taken off, due to increasing interest in investigation of the theological and spiritual roots of Christianity, as this religious outlook becomes more acceptable in China. The works of the early fathers are sourced for their rich variety of theological outlook, and their seemingly endless ways of expressing the message of the Bible that are devoid of too much historical criticism. For example, the ancient dichotomy of the so-called "Alexandrian" school and the "Antiochene" school of biblical interpretations are taken as examples of hermeneutical variety, not as a choice about which is more orthodox. So in effect, the investigation of patristic biblical interpretation takes on a slightly different approach from what is more conventional in the West: the fact that two approaches to the Bible existed that can be traced back to the ancient fathers of the church would mean that no one way should dominate the other in the exposition of the Bible. But the most notable difference is the approach from the cultural milieu of the patristic era, seeing their biblical interpretation as a way of adapting and transforming the prevalent cultural mindset. This suits the situation of Christianity in China well, as scholars are concerned about presenting the Christian and biblical message through cultural eyes.

This essay chronicles this process, first by tracing the developments of patristic biblical studies in China from the early days of the Tang and Ming dynasty (albeit briefly), then introducing notable translations of patristic texts that have enshrined in them some biblical interpretations and, finally, investigating modern Chinese scholars' work, which sets the tone for further studies in this particular area.

Early Works on Patristic Biblical Interpretation

Biblical Interpretation in China can be traced to the earliest known missionary movement during the Tang dynasty (618–907). The first Christian communities in China were founded around monasteries, established with the blessing of the emperor, the most famous of which were the Da Qin monasteries. Besides the literature pertaining to monastic practices, i.e. fasting, meditation and daily offices, other materials of edification and studies like patristic literature also could be found. Together with these were surely the study of the Bible through patristic eyes.[1] But it is difficult to pinpoint exactly how and where the patristic texts are being utilized. The monks were interested only in whatever texts pertained to the purpose of establishing the monastic order; thus, texts like *Apophthegmata Patrum* and other writing of the desert fathers were favorites, insofar as the monastic life of prayer and struggle against the world was a top priority.[2] Biblical interpretation was thus subsumed in some theological formulation as missionary texts.

The Jesuits of late Ming and early Qing China (ca. 1600–1700) attempted not only to present the Christian message but also to introduce the Chinese to the classics of the Western Christian Church. The lives of the saints were partly translated into Chinese as part of edification and devotional material for the spiritual life, of which the desert fathers have some particular interest, notably the work by Jesuit missionary Johan Adam Schall and Chinese convert Wang Zheng 王徵: *chong yi tang ri ji sui bi* 崇一堂日記隨筆 (*Chongyitang Daily Anecdotes*),[3] published in 1638, consulting Athanasius' *Vita Santi Antonii* and other related Latin works. Indeed, the desert fathers' anecdotes served the teaching of the Jesuits well, in that they served as a corrective for the overt emphasis on extreme asceticism, which was likely rejected by the intellectual converts of the time. *Chongyitang Daily Anecdotes* indeed has much value of its own in introducing the early Christian fathers to the Chinese people, and a comparison could then be made with the Confucius ethos of the sage and the Catholic way of "saintliness."

Another Jesuit, Alfonso Vagnore (ca. 1568–1640), attempted to paraphrase the lives of the ancient Christian saints in his work, *tian zhu shengjiao sheng ren xing shi* 天主聖教聖人行實 (*Lives of Catholic Saints*), including parts of Augustine's *Confessions*, St Anthony's life based on Athanasius's biography, and some of the female saints, the purpose of which was to make a model of perfect Christian life as practiced by the saints and their so-called miraculous encounters with God as a means to introduce the Christian gospel to the Chinese.[4]

John T. P. Lai 黎子鵬 has compiled and edited a magnum opus on Christian publications from 1860–1911 in China. A breathtaking view of Christian literature with annotations to all entries makes this an indispensable resource in the study of Chinese Christianity. Of interest in the entries is one dated 1860, on the Orthodox liturgy, by a Russian monk, Gury Karpov. He based his liturgical order on the Nicene Creed[5] and expounded on each order of service using patristic interpretation of the Bible, much the same as the way his mother Orthodox Church in Russia. This could be seen as the first endeavor to introduce the product of Russian patristic studies into China. But the period in question was inundated with gospel tracts, basic expositions of the biblical stories, commentaries on short passages like the Lord's Prayer and the Ten Commandments, and materials for liturgy and worship. Although some attempts were made to systematize the Christian belief, these were done mainly as a primer and introduction to theological ideas. The obvious lack of translated patristic materials in this period can be traced to the flurry of excitement in propagating the Gospel and the attempt to make the Christian message clear to the populace. Serious study of Christian philosophy was rare, and there was little interest in classic Christian writers. Even the Protestant greats were ignored, and there are only a few that introduced the Catholic saints.

In all, this period's usage and quotations from the patristic era was characterized by edification of the converts to the Christian faith and introduction of the Christian worldview and theological tenets. Attempts to introduce patristic biblical interpretation were rare and included those only viewed as the orthodox view of the Bible; thus, there was no incentive to be involved in serious interpretation of the biblical texts, let alone to engage with the fathers on biblical interpretation.

Contemporary interest in the Bible and patristics in China began towards the end of the twentieth century. Intellectuals agreed that, in order to understand and learn from the progress of Christianity in the "West," they would have to rediscover the rich and deep well from which the nourishment was drawn. And patristic studies was a much-neglected sphere of study, often ignored by modern interpreters of Christianity. There was a rush to learn from modern Western hermeneutics, which had in the main treated patristic studies as theologically fanciful and biblically unsound in interpretation. However, it is still safe to say that the interest in patristic studies is still in its heyday.

Most of the study of patristic biblical interpretation is confined to a section in textbooks on the history of biblical hermeneutics. It has not been representative of serious studies of the fathers, often sidelined as glib in the vast hermeneutical history, and mostly through allegorical eyes.[6] And here lies the dilemma in the history of Chinese interpretation of the Bible. On one hand, with the influence of conservative missionaries and a distinct lack of biblical investigative tools like lexicons and biblical archaeological resources, "spiritual" interpretations of the biblical texts became the norm; on the other hand, there was also a strong rejection of the ways of so-called patristic allegorical interpretation, which was not viewed with positive eyes. As a result, Chinese Christian scholars would rather study the theological treatises of the fathers, as they were seen as historical theological foundation of the Christian tenets.

Recent Studies and Publications of the Patristic Corpus

It is well known that the patristic corpus that was being translated into the Chinese language is scanty. Almost every scholar working in this field laments over the frustration of assessable material.[7] The situation is remedied somewhat by rapidly increasing number of translations by several centers in China on the works of the fathers; also, there are increasing numbers of scholars who are doing research overseas on their doctoral studies, learning the ancient original languages, so that they can in fact gain access to the original texts without translation into Chinese. This has indeed gained momentum recently and helped enhanced patristic research in China.

From 1912–1949, with the rapid increase of the number of Christians in China, the need for more substantial literature in Christian philosophy and theology became more acute. The establishment of the Christian Literature Society for China (廣學會)[8] had been instrumental in introducing more scholarly translated works to China, among the publications are Bible study tools and lexicons and biblical commentaries. Although patristic materials also were published, they were confined to mainly theological treatises.[9] Most of the patristic biblical interpretation works are an aside to them, but some of the patristic preaching corpus has been translated to illustrate how the fathers understood Scripture, and how this could be used in the exposition of the Bible in Sunday preaching in China.

Meanwhile, an ambitious project was started in the 1940s on, making available ancient Christian classics in the Chinese language. Named the "Christian Classics Library" 基督教歷代名著集成, it quickly became a classic series in itself. In all, there are thirty-two volumes published, covering the fathers and medieval classics, and up to the Enlightenment period. Of interest are the first ten or so volumes on the fathers, but this mainly covers theological treatises. On biblical interpretations and commentaries, they are sadly lacking, and only snippets of the sermons by some fathers are included. Perhaps they are viewed as the most important contribution of the fathers, but in terms of patristic studies, the series was a defining movement towards rectifying the neglect in this area of research. By all counts, it has influenced historical theological studies across China, Hong Kong, and Taiwan. Theological seminaries in these three regions would have tried to remedy the lack of patristic materials by stocking foreign language translations, especially English, and some even stocked Migne's *Patrologia graeca* and *Patrologia latina*,[10] but the evidence of usage is rare.

Other series from the Catholic tradition also have contributed much toward this, especially from the output of Fujen University Press in Taiwan (輔仁大學神學論集). A variety of patristic studies is made available: on monasticism are John Cassian's *Conferences and Institutions*;[11] *The Sayings of the Desert Fathers*;[12] and *The Lives of the Desert Fathers*;[13] and resources on John Chrysostom.[14] A Translation of Pope Benedict XCI's *I Padri Della Chiesa*[15] also is made available to Chinese readers. And a multi-volume translation of F. Cayre's *Compendium de Patrologie* is one of the most valuable resources for teaching on the early fathers.[16]

In Hong Kong, the baton for publishing translating Christian classics goes to the Institute of Sino-Christian Studies (漢語基督教文化研究所). The institute has provided for young scholars from all over China in their research into Christianity and its impact, especially in academic research. Every year students are invited to study with financial and academic support through Tao Fong Scholarship. Among some of the notable studies are patristic theology and biblical interpretation. Some of these students have gone on to become scholars in their own right. Among them are Zhang Xuefu 章雪富 of Zhejiang University, whose work on Christian Platonism helps to trigger interest in the studies of the fathers in the heart of Chinese academia. There is now diverse interest in patristic contribution to Christian thought, rejuvenated by modern translations of some of the fathers, notably Augustine, Athanasius, Basil of Caesarea, John Chrysostom, Cyprian, Justin Martyr, and Ambrose.[17]

An attempt at translating these texts into the Chinese language has met with mixed results. Other modern translations of the patristic texts come from selected series edited by He Guang Hu 何光滬;[18] to date, some ten volume have been published, of which are patristic works of Augustine (*Moral Treatises* 道德論集, *Enchiridion* 論信望愛, *The Harmony of the Gospels* 論四福音的和諧);[19] Gregory of Nazianzus (*Theological Orations* 神學講演錄); Athanasius (*On the Incarnation* 論道成肉身); Eusebius (*Church History* 教會史); Ambrose (*Exposition of the Christian Faith* 論基督教信仰); The Desert Fathers (*The Sayings of the Desert Fathers* 沙漠教父言行錄); Origen (*Contra Celsius* 駁塞爾修斯); Gregory of Nyssa (*The Life of Moses* 摩西的生平); Basil of Caesarea (*Hexaemeron* 創世六日). Most of the translations are based on English translated works, and because most of the translators lack knowledge of the original language, these so called "secondary" translations inevitably contain some errors,[20] but overall, they are invaluable in ongoing patristic studies.

Interest in the works of the fathers has been enhanced by the translation of patristic biblical interpretations from the English series, edited by Thomas C. Oden, *Ancient Christian Commentary on Scripture*, now being translated into Chinese and published in Taiwan. The Chinese editor, Simon Wong 黃錫木, recognizes the importance of the patristic contribution to the richness of the biblical text but also laments the lack of material in Chinese and is hopeful that the series can work toward remedying the neglect in the Chinese-speaking world. Beginning in 2005, the series translation is now nearing completion. This no doubt will be appreciated greatly by Chinese academia and churches alike.

Recent Interest and Themes

The interest in patristics as a discipline of philosophy and theology is a recent phenomenon. Although materials on this research area have yet to become abundant, nevertheless there are good signs that this is happening. Certainly, scholarship in China's main focus is still the philosophical and theological treatises of the ancient fathers, but there are already some scholars who are very much engaged in the patristic interpretation of Scripture.

Recent Patristic Research

Wang Xiaochao 王曉朝 begins with an introduction to the study of the Bible in his 2003 book,[21] which is included in the Tsinghua Philosophy Research series (清華哲學研究系列). He basically categorizes patristic studies under philosophical investigation. This has indeed become a norm that other patristic scholars are pursuing, nonetheless, Wang's work has triggered much interest in this period of investigation. Contemporaneous to Wang is Chen Cun Fu 陳村富, who is also a patristic scholar in his own right. Since 1991, he has helped established the Centre for the Study of Christianity (基督教研究中心) under the auspices of Hangzhou University (now Zhejiang University). The Centre focuses on three areas of research: early Christianity and patristic studies, contemporary theology and religious philosophy, and history of Christianity in China and its modern situation. Together with some of the younger scholars, he edits an anthology on religion and culture.[22] The anthology looks at patristic studies from the perspective of mutual influence of the pervading Greek culture and the so-called Hebrew biblical culture, and how these affect the formulation of Christian theology and biblical interpretation. Another interesting study, also from Zhejiang University, is Hu Long Biao 胡龍彪 on Boethius,[23] which introduces the Chinese audience to Boethius' philosophy and theology.[24]

Typology as a Legitimate Interpretation

Some scholars who studied overseas and are returning to China, Hong Kong, and Taiwan, have contributed new insights into this field, especially from their own cultural perspective.

Chan Man Ki 陳文紀, a Hong Kong scholar, concentrates his efforts in biblical interpretation in his doctoral thesis on the book of Ruth.[25] He takes his cue from the historical and cultural context in which the book is being interpreted, first from rabbinic literature and then attempts to view it from the patristic context. Noting that there is indeed a very strong influence of context over biblical hermeneutic, as is evident in rabbinic literature, where Ruth's foreign ethnic background was never mentioned, instead she was praised as a pious Jewish woman par excellence. Chan sees this rabbinic reading as a typical interpretation of the *midrash*. Chan then sees a similar paradigmatic reading in the commentaries on the book of Ruth in the patristic context. Although they come from two different religious traditions, they are of a similar cultural and historical backgrounds. And this has made it distinctly unique in the history of biblical interpretation, in that each selected as its cultural target in expounding the biblical text. The Christian fathers' approach to the book of Ruth is thus very different from their contemporaneous Jewish counterpart (and by implication, to the biblical texts as a whole). The point of contention is the place of the Old Testament in the new Christian faith, but in order not to adopt the extreme views of a Marcionite or that of Tertullian, Christological interpretation of the text gradually became the norm through the use of typology. The early fathers, according to Chan, use the hermeneutics of the *midrash* to formulate this: The promise in the old is fulfilled in the new, the old events, characters and systems are but prefigurations of the new.[26] The eschatological view of history and the advent of the messiah become the formative influence in interpreting Scripture.

Chan uses the interpretation of the book of Ruth to test his case.[27] Based on the eighth-century exegete Rabanus Maurus, the "*Gloss of Ruth*" comments on the Vulgate text, and the so-called "Gloss Additions," which include snippets of comments by John Chrysostom, Theodoret, and Ambrose. Commenting on Ruth 2:8 and 22, the "Gloss" warns the Christian against "gleaning in another field," meaning not being lured away from the true faith into heresy. On the relationship between the law and the gospel, the "Gloss" proposes embracing both, but working towards the gospel of grace, commenting on Ruth 3:18, "For the man [Boaz] will not rest, but will settle the matter today." This means that the church will be faithful to its promise, and it will be fulfilled, what is promised in the old will be fulfilled in the new; therefore, Christians should diligently study and meditate on the law, knowing that there lies the promise. Ruth is praised because she was able to discard her pagan belief to come to the true faith.

Chan's work put Chinese reading of the fathers in the category of the Gospel's commentary of culture. The fathers are viewed as innovative thinkers, attempting to transcend culture to present the true faith. Typology is the obvious hermeneutical tool to cross the barrier of the Old and New Testament on the one hand, and the separation of Christians from the non-Christian culture on the other. This has great implications in the Chinese context, in that like Ruth, Christians are living in the midst of a hostile culture. Chan's interest is thus not about the debate over the legitimacy of typology, but its legitimate application.

Patristic Allegorical Interpretation and Its Implications

The debate on the allegorical interpretation of Scripture has been a contentious one in the Chinese church. Some would insist that allegory is the high fruit of the understanding of the biblical text. The patristic allegorical interpretation then became the "grandfather" of most hermeneutical endeavors. Some modern Chinese exegetes have rejected this wholesale as too fanciful. But the fact is that without acknowledging it, the Chinese church in the twentieth century has relied on allegorical biblical interpretation for close to one hundred years, in understanding the spiritual meaning of the biblical text and edification of Christians.

Of all the models of allegorical interpretation, Origen's works on the Bible have become the focus point. A recent report on Origen studies in China has really put him on the intellectual map.[28] Origen is viewed as a Christian intellectual *par excellence*. The controversy during Origen's lifetime and subsequent years aside, Chinese academics are more interested in the way Origen presented the Christian message in the Greek world, which was thus more objective and, on the whole, shed a more positive light.

Interestingly, some fruits of patristic biblical interpretation come from Jewish studies in China. There have been increasing studies of this kind, mainly because of the admiration of the customs and religion of the Jewish people, but also because biblical studies under the guise of ancient Judaism is more palatable to the current climate of the intelligentsia. One of the interesting studies is included in the Doctoral Jewish Studies series, edited by Fu Youde 傅有德. The author, Li Yong 李勇, focuses his study on the allegorical interpretation of Scripture, entitled "Allegory: From Philo to Origen."[29]

Li Yong's investigation explores the dichotomy between "Athens and Jerusalem,"[30] or the dialogue between the Hebrew and Greek mindset. He proposes that the way to reconcile the two theological and cultural mindsets is through allegorical interpretations of religious texts as demonstrated by the early fathers. He uses Origen's Commentary on the Gospel of John as his working text to articulate how Origen manages to transfuse the Hebrew/Greek mindset into a distinctly Christian mindset, all through the common denominator of allegory. Li Yong has then taken a positive outlook toward the use of allegory, contrary to most modern patristic interpreters, seeing it as a somewhat successful attempt to interpret biblical texts into the Greek philosophical milieu. Li is adamant that Origen subscribed to Trinitarian theology and therefore was thoroughly Christian (although he ignores the extent to which a mature Trinitarian theology had yet to be formulated in Origen's time). But according to Li, Origen had to address the "inevitable" dichotomy of the interface between Greek and so-called Hebrew culture, thus finding allegory as the most probable pathway. Using St Paul's catchphrase, "Not of the letter but of the Spirit; for the letter kills, but the Spirit gives life" (2 Cor. 3:6), Origen saw a fourfold premise for interpreting Christian Scripture: (1) the traditional allegorical interpretation of sacred texts in the Greek tradition, notably the Stoics; (2) the translation of this method in Judaism as authoritative license, notably Philo; (3) the contemporary Greek use of allegory as norm, making allegorical interpretation of the Christian Scripture more palatable to the wider world; and (4) the frequent usage of hidden meanings (e.g. the parables and imageries) in the New Testament itself.

Origen then utilized the tripartite approach to interpretation: the Body = literal meaning; the Soul = extrapolation of the literal meaning according to reason; and the Spirit = the spiritual/allegorical meaning behind the text. Li finds ample illustrations of this approach in Origen's commentary on the Gospel of John.[31] Although Origen's later works point toward a binary interpretation of literal and spiritual meaning, it works much the same as the tripartite one. Origen then classified the idea of wisdom, again in a tripartite way: the wisdom of the "world," the wisdom of the wise, and the wisdom of God. This, according to Li, enabled Origen to transcend the Greek wisdom tradition into a very Christian one; in that the ultimate wisdom lies hierarchically with God. Thus, allegory works in such a way as to highlight the superiority of the Christian message.

In the environment of mainly Greek and anti-Christian mindset, Li perceives that allegorical interpretation of Christian Scripture became the "inevitable" pathway of contextualizing the Christian message. Therefore, Li generally looks at Origen's allegorical interpretation in a more positive light. He refutes Martin Luther's criticism of Origen's ways, and noted that Origen could not be accused of taking the literal scriptural texts lightly in order to project the higher spiritual/allegorical meaning.[32] Compared to later usage, Origen's interpretation is much more restrained and was always bounded by his tripartite/binary system.

From what we can perceive above, Li indeed approaches patristic biblical interpretation from a much more rounded standpoint, showing the modern Chinese reader how to appreciate an often belittled way of viewing allegory, and presents a corrective to the pervading condemnation by modern Chinese scholars.

In a similar vein, Justin Tan 陳廷忠 attempts to reintroduce Augustine's biblical interpretation to the Chinese world as well. In his 1999 article,[33] Tan states that, "For Augustine, the task of interpretation should always be governed by the principle of dual Charity: interpretation must be carried out with the aim of seeking God and loving him, and through loving God, to love others as well."[34] Augustine follows Tyconius's seven rules of scriptural interpretation but points out that it should always be under the authority of the church; he also sees the validity of variant interpretations of the same biblical texts, but, "as the texts may [also]... be exposed to heretical interpretation, Augustine introduced the Dogma of the Church as a guide against heretical abuses of Scripture."[35] This he does through four-fold hermeneutics of the neo-Platonic tradition, *historia*, *aetiologia*, *analogia*, and *allegoria*. His understanding of the law and grace is typical of his interpretation of the biblical text. First, he adamantly insists on the unity of the two testaments. But just as the ancient Israelites were accused of legalism by strict observation of the law, so exegesis also could be accused of literalism. Reason is important in human progress, but if one cannot come to God by reason, then at least he/she could obey Him through the law; according to Augustine, this in itself is grace, "but for the believers, the Law was our pedagogue in Christ, and this also is grace. What was discarded is not the Law, but the veil (2 Cor. 3:14), which is virtually the literal meaning of the Old Testament text. In Christ, the veil has been removed and the *allegoria* revealed."[36]

Again, the move to objectively appreciate patristic allegorical interpretation becomes more viable. Indeed, Justin Tan, in his primer to the translation of Gregory of Nyssa's Life of Moses, pushes for more positive evaluation of the use of allegory as an important pathway to understanding the formulation of Christian theology in the age of the early fathers.[37]

For earlier pastors and biblical scholars in China, cultural distance between the Chinese and biblical background became acute when these two clashed in the early 1900s. Missionaries who came in the heyday of Chinese evangelism could be distinctly differentiated between conservatism and liberalism. Hudson Taylor is a case in point.[38] His conservative stance on the unique authority of the Bible saw him rejecting the so-called historical-critical method that was pervasive in his Victorian age. He subscribed to what one scholar called "the oldest form of interpretation," implying patristic hermeneutics, namely Christological typology and allegory.[39] For Taylor and most of the contemporary missionaries, allegorical and typological interpretation are time-tested fool-proof ways of teaching and understanding the Bible. In time, this was adopted by Chinese pastors and teachers and has influenced Chinese Christians for generations.

Evangelists like John Sung 宋尚節 were at one extreme of the spectrum of biblical interpretation, seeing the biblical text as codes to the deep things of God and, therefore, interpretation as a requirement to decode them. Thus, the Exodus that is recorded in the Old Testament is pregnant with codes: "Egypt represents the World. The Israelites in Egypt represent the nominal Christian, those who are not born again . . . . The Pharaoh represents the Devil. The meaning of the Exodus is then release from sin. Moses represents Jesus rescuing his children from sin."[40] This was encouraged by the missionaries, holding to a distinctly patristic allegorical interpretation as a viable interpretive tool. One scholar viewed this as indigenization of the "Western Allegorical interpretation."[41]

Some would view the allegorical interpretation as toxic to the truthful understanding of Scripture, believing that the Chinese church has been negatively influenced by it for too long, and that it therefore should be discarded in favor of the modern hermeneutical technique that is closer to the original meaning. But from the recent revival of the interest in patristics, allegorical interpretation has enjoyed a renewed perspective.

Liang Ka-lun 梁家麟 also takes a more sympathetic view of allegorical interpretation as practiced by Chinese pastors and teachers in the early 1900s.[42] Taking his cue from the ancient fathers, he sees the main motive of allegorical interpretation as apologetic; from Origen on, the defense of the faith requires it to confirm that all Scripture interpretation must conform or be made to conform to orthodox teaching of the Church, as against the likes of Gnostic teachings and heretics. Liang finds the Chinese correspondence in one school of interpretation of the Chinese sacred texts, called *gongyang xue* 公羊學, akin to patristic allegorical interpretation; both attempt to find the hidden spiritual meaning of the sacred texts. And Liang goes so far as to propose that the reason allegorical interpretation became a popular hermeneutical tool came from this in-grained respect and common usage in interpreting texts. The subsequent expositors of the Bible, like Wang Mingdao 王明道 and Jia Yuming 賈玉銘, adopted Christological interpretation of the texts.[43] But according to Liang, there is no need for panic over whether they will lead Christians astray or into heresy, because they are very careful to conform their exposition to orthodox beliefs and do not understand the Bible according to their whims. Therefore, Liang proposes that allegorical, especially typological, biblical interpretation, should have its place in expounding the Bible. There is much to gain from it, especially in edification of Christians and encouraging meditation on the spiritual meaning of the biblical texts.[44]

Conclusion

The study of patristic biblical interpretation amongst Chinese scholars indicates a distinct sense of wanting to let the early fathers speak again to their philosophical and theological context, with the aim of presenting Christianity to a challenging world. The investigators in China are able to examine patristic texts objectively, having deliberately discarded the traditional bias in the West, which primarily rejects the most popular interpretation of the Bible: typology and allegory. Prior to the influence of the historical-critical method, these two methods were used widely in the Christian churches, mainly for their usefulness in edification and also for making the message of Christianity come through the texts in a non-Christian world. From the second half of the twentieth century, more and more scholars who might or might not come from a traditional Christian background have entered into this area of patristic biblical interpretation, having little or no burden of history, and are able to see and appreciate it on its own terms. And this in itself is an objective contribution to the study of Christian Scripture in China.

Notes

1. M. Nicolini-Zani, "Christian Monastic Literature in China," in *Light a Candle: Encounters and Friendship with China*, ed. R. Malek and G. Criveller (Sankt Augustin: Institut Monumenta Serica, 2010), 296–298.
2. M. Nicolini-Zani, "Christian Monastic Literature in China," 302–303.
3. See Sher-shiueh Li 李奭學, *Transwriting: Translated Literature and Late-Ming Jesuits* [in Chinese] 譯述：明末耶穌會翻譯文學論 (Hong Kong: Chinese University, 2012), 107–149.
4. Li, *Transwriting*, 205–253.
5. John T. P. Lai 黎子鵬, ed., *The Chronicles of Christian Publishing Enterprise in China (1860–1911)* [in Chinese] 中國基督教文字事業編年史 (1860–1911) (Hong Kong: Christian Literature), 8–9 on Eastern Orthodox.
6. One textbook, Liang Gong 梁工, ed., *Xifang shengjing piping yinlun* [in Chinese] 西方聖經批評引論 *Introduction to Western Biblical Interpretation* (Beijing: Commercial, 2006), uses five pages to describe the patristic contribution of the first five centuries of the Christian era, almost all on introducing their allegorical interpretation.
7. Cf. Wang Xiaochao 王曉朝, "On Patristic Methodological Issues" [in Chinese] 教父學的若干方法論問題, *Zongjiao yu wenhua* 4 (2001): 145–147; Richard X. Y. Zhang 張賢勇, "Two Notes on Some Volumes Devoted to Patristic Studies" [in Chinese] 教父學述介二題, *Logos & Pneuma: Chinese Journal of Theology* 道風：基督教文化評論 14 (2001): 295.
8. Formerly called "The Society for the Diffusion of Christian and General Knowledge among the Chinese."

9. See Herbert H. L. He 何凱立, *Protestant Missionary Publications in Modern China 1912–1949: A Study of Their Programs Operations and Trends* [in Chinese] 基督教在華出版事業 (Sichuan: Sichuan University, 2004), 72–82.
10. Matteo Nicolini-Zani spotted these in the Holy Spirit Seminary College, Hong Kong, and the Hong Kong Franciscan Studium Biblicum; and the Shanghai Catholic Theological Seminary (not complete). See his article, "Patristic Studies in Contemporary China: A Survey with Appended Bibliography," *Theology Annual* 29 (2008): 80. (The author owes a great debt to Nicolini-Zani's article in chronicling recent patristic studies in China, and would like to express deep gratitude.)
11. Paul Jen 任佩澤, tr., *Jean Cassien: Conferences Institutions* [in Chinese] 若望伽仙: 會談錄, 隱院規章 (Hong King: Caritas Printing Training Centre, 1982).
12. Fu Wen-huei 傅文煇, tr., *The Sayings of the Desert Fathers* [in Chinese] 曠野之聲 (Taipei: Kuangchi, 1982).
13. Ren Da Yi 任達義, tr., *The Lives of the Desert Fathers* [in Chinese] 曠野聖祖的生活 (Hong Kong: Yong Ling Press, n.d.).
14. Joseph Au 區華勝, tr., *St. John Chrysostom* [in Chinese] 金口若望 (Taipei: Wisdom Press, 2007).
15. Grace Liu Chia-ling 劉嘉玲, tr., *I Padri della Chiesa—Da Clemente Romano a Sant' Agostino* [in Chinese] 教父—從聖克勉到聖奧斯定 (Taipei: Kuangchi, 2012).
16. F. Cayre, *Compendium de Patrologie* [in Chinese] 教父學大綱, 4 vols., tr. Wu Ying Feng 吳應楓 (Taipei: Kuangchi, 1975).
17. Some other examples are listed below: Tertullian, *De anima*, *De resurrectione carnis*, *Apologeticus*; Origen, *Περὶ Ἀρχῶν*. To date there are about fifteen volumes on "Christian literature from the Hellenistic period to the fifteenth century."
18. Published in Mainland China by SCX Joint Publishing, Beijing.
19. Interestingly, Augustine's *Confessions* and the *City of God* have gone through several translations in the past fifty years. So, the influence of these two works should not be underestimated.
20. A translation of Origen's *De principiis* has created a heated dialogue, mainly on the fact of this so-called secondary translation; see Nicolini-Zani, "Patristic Studies in Contemporary China," 82–83.
21. Wang Xiaochao, *Patrology: Early Christian Philosophy under the Perspective of Culture* [in Chinese] 教父學研究: 文化視野下的教父哲學 (Hebei: Hebei University Press, 2003).
22. Chen Cun Fu 陳村富, *Religion and Culture: Early Christianity and Patristic Studies* [in Chinese] 宗教與文化: 早期基督教與教父學研究 (Beijing: The Oriental Press, 2001).
23. Hu Long Biao 胡龍彪, *The Latin Patristic: Boethius* [in Chinese] 拉丁教父波愛修斯 (Beijing: Commercial, 2006).
24. Other publications include Zhang Xuefu 章雪富, *Christian Platonism* [in Chinese] 基督教柏拉圖主義 (Shanghai: Shanghai People Publishing House, 2001) on the Alexandrian Fathers.
25. Chan Man Ki 陳文紀, *A Comparative Study of Jewish Commentaries and Patristic Literature on the Book of Jonah* [in Chinese] 燃亮傳統: 路得記的猶太釋經與教父釋經比較 (Hong Kong: Chinese Bible International Limited, 2013).
26. Ibid. 11–330.
27. Ibid. 333–377.
28. Matteo Nicolai-Zani, "Alijah, Origen in China: A Report on Origenism and Patristic Studies in Contemporary China," in *Adamantis: Journal of the Italian Research Group on*

"*Origen and the Alexandrian Tradition*" 13 (2007): 341–378; subsequently published in a revised and updated version as "Patristic Studies in Contemporary China: A Survey with Appended Bibliography," *Theology Annual* 29 (2008), 63–146.

29. Li Yong 李勇, *Allegory: From Philo to Origen* [in Chinese] 寓意解經: 從斐洛到奧利金 (Shanghai: Shanghai Joint Publishing Company, 2014).
30. This is allegedly coined by Tertullian, see ibid. 1–3.
31. Frustrated by the non-existence of this work, he attempts his own translation (albeit from an English translation) and included it in his book; see Li, *Allegory*, 200–377.
32. Ibid. 176–184.
33. Justin Tan 陳廷忠, "Augustine the Ancient Exegete [in Chinese] 古典詮釋者奧古斯丁," *CGST Journal* 中國神學研究院期刊 27 (1999): 59–79.
34. Ibid. 77, the following is the gist of content of his article.
35. Ibid. 78.
36. Ibid. 79.
37. Shi Min Min 石敏敏, tr., *Gregory of Nyssa's The Life of Moses* [in Chinese] 摩西的生平 (Beijing: SCX Joint Publishing, 2010), 1–12.
38. Cf. C. E. M. Wigram, *The Bible and Mission in Faith Perspective: J. Hudson Taylor and the Early China Inland Mission* (Zoetermeer: Utigeverij Boekencentrum, 2007), 127–141.
39. Alec Motyer, foreword to J. Hudson Taylor, *Union and Communion* (Ross-shire: Christian Focus, 1996), 8–9.
40. This is quoted by Ka-lun Leung 梁家麟, *Far Ahead and Lagging Behind: Studies in Contextual Hermeneutics and Theology* [in Chinese] 超前與墮後: 本土釋經與神學研究 (Hong Kong: Alliance Bible Seminary, 2003), 25–26.
41. Che Ming Tan 陳濟民, *Understanding Principles of Biblical Interpretation* [in Chinese] 認識解經原理 (Taipei: Campus Evangelical Fellowship, 1988), 68.
42. Leung, *Far Ahead and Lagging Behind*, 1–58.
43. Jia Yuming, a well-respected theologian and biblical scholar, adamantly says that, "All Scripture's main thrust is redemption; that is the full salvation plan that is prepared by God for humanity. It has Jesus as its core, and the Cross as its theme. All of the Old Testament has no other main message than the Cross, and all of the New Testament has no other starting point than the Cross. From all Scripture, every book, every chapter, every page, are the figure of Jesus revealed. And both the Old and New Testament's message is none other than the life, death, resurrection, ascension and the coming again of Jesus, and their consequences," quoted by Leung, *Far Ahead and Lagging Behind*, 25.
44. Leung, *Far Ahead and Lagging Behind*, 43–49.

Primary Sources

Jones, Francis P. 章文新, ed. *Christian Classics Library* [in Chinese] 基督教早期文獻選集. Hong Kong: Chinese Christian Literature, 1959 onwards.

Oden, Thomas C. (Simon Wong 黃錫木 series editor of the Chinese Version), ed. *Ancient Christian Commentary on Scripture* [in Chinese] 古代基督信仰聖經注釋叢書. Taipei: Campus Evangelical Fellowship, 2005 onwards.

Pang, Chen Ying 逄塵瑩, tr. *Soyons l'âme du monde—Textes choisis des chrétiens des premieres siècles* [in Chinese] 當為世界之魂: 初世紀基督信徒文選. Taipei: Kuangchi, 2006.

CHAPTER 26

NEW TESTAMENT MONOGRAPH AND COMMENTARY IN CONTEMPORARY CHINA

ZHA CHANGPING

Introduction

Biblical studies in the Chinese academic world is a small part of Christian studies. Until 1996, apart from two volumes by Zhu Weizhi 朱維之 on literary themes in the Bible,[1] other works published all have been popular works.[2]

At the beginning of this century, several biblical studies works used an integrated perspective, such as *Biblical Language and Thought*[3] written in Chinese by the Austrian author Leopold Leeb 雷立柏, and Sun Yi's 孫毅 *Introduction to the Bible*.[4] Sun Yi's text organized his sections as historical background, main themes, and key scriptural texts.[5] Liang Gong's 梁工 *Study of Biblical Narrative Art* uses narrative criticism of biblical studies from the 1970s in light of the historical methods of biblical studies.[6] His method comes from studies of secular literature, especially fictitious novels. It neglects historical backgrounds, material sources, form features, and redaction process of the biblical text. Liang Gong suggests that narrative criticism of the biblical texts needs other methodological supplements such as those of hermeneutics, sociology, reader-response criticism, and feminist criticism.[7] Subsequently, Liang edits *Introduction to Western Biblical Criticism*[8] and started publishing the journal, *Biblical Literature Studies* in 2007.[9] His main focus is on the relationship between the Bible and literature. But compared with other fields of Christian studies, it remains true that such works on the "study of the Bible are few,"[10] as Wen Yong 文庸 goes on to say, that Chinese biblical studies is "just taking its first steps."[11]

Biblical studies in China more than twenty years ago was characterized by two aspects: (1) more studies of the constituent parts than of whole books of the New Testament (hereafter NT); and (2) more research in religious studies than in the theology of NT texts. There is also a further overarching tendency toward historical studies (characters, events, or themes) rather than exegesis, interpretation, and hermeneutic of the NT.[12]

Because of efforts made by scholars such as Choong Chee Pang 鐘志邦 (Zhong Zhibang), Xie Wenyu 謝文郁, Yang Yan 楊硯, K. K. Yeo 楊克勤 (Yang Keqin), Zha Changping 查常平, and Zhao Dunhua 趙敦華, NT scholarship during the recent past (1976–2018), especially the last ten years, has transformed drastically the ways the New Testament is studied in China.

The Rhetorical Literary Perspective

Various Chinese scholars have developed their frameworks from foreign, especially Euro-American, academic (hereafter "Western" or "West") disciplines and applied them to Sino-theological studies. One example can be seen in the field of rhetorical study. Traditional biblical studies highlighted the structure of the text and its relationship to smaller textual units and suggested that the biblical language would lose its significance if the biblical text were separated from its production situation, process, and its textual reception. The Bible has a message only as the scriptural text is connected with the concrete life situations of readers, and these connections exist in the interactive dialogue between the text and the rhetorical functions of textual utterance, speaker, and reader. Such is the conclusion of K. K. Yeo, a prolific writer and Christian studies program co-director at Peking University (2005–2017), in his introduction to classical Greco-Roman and modern rhetorical criticism. Rhetorical studies concern the relationship between speaking and thinking, as Yeo writes:

> Rhetorical study aims, through its analysis of the structure of language and the concrete situations in which the functions of such rhetorical study are brought into play, to study and to observe the responses of the listeners.[13]
>
> The situation of a rhetorical unit is not only "a viewpoint on life," but also an "ideological" guidance and cultural exhortation given by both the speaker (author) and addressee (reader) on life, their experiences and traditions.[14]
>
> Therefore, to understand the word in rhetoric is to do theology, namely, to observe and name how God works in the process of human communication. The purpose of rhetorical criticism of the NT is not merely human activity but is more fundamentally connected with the work of God (Word) in the historical progress.[15]

K. K. Yeo has written on rhetoric in his *Classical Rhetoric: Greco-Roman Culture and Biblical Interpretation*, and elsewhere on the way in which Augustine "Christianized" the rhetoric of Marcus Tullius Cicero.[16] In the volume on rhetoric, Yeo discusses the history and theory of classical rhetoric as a backdrop to the NT and the interactions between the text of the NT and classical Greek, Roman, and Hebrew cultures, from which he gradually builds up a theory of classical biblical interpretation. Yeo suggests that there are particular characteristics of rhetoric in the NT that emerge in comparison with the style of argumentation in Greco-Roman culture. He argues that the NT rhetoric:

> ... is not a presentation of truth, but a persuasive narrative proclamation. For biblical narrative proclaims and evokes faith, hope and love. The particularity of the NT rhetoric lies in its affinity with the gospel of Christ, and therefore the NT rhetorical purpose is to build up and transform individuals, groups, and society.[17]

And he writes, "The NT rhetoric includes a proclamation in the statement of truth."[18]

Yeo also applies this "rhetorical interaction" to study Paul's letters, including 1 Corinthians, and 1 and 2 Thessalonians, researching how Paul used rhetorical skills to interpret and preach the Bible to different peoples in different cultural situations.[19] Yeo believes that the uniqueness of Paul's theology lies in "the interpretation of the present by the eschatological future, of suffering by hope, and of sin and evil by the Lord's *parousia*."[20] Paul's concept of history is Christ-centered. It means that, in Paul's view, history would develop under God's sovereignty and grace and be given value as well as meaning in Jesus Christ:

> ... who will come again as Lord and grants present struggling a purpose and goal by which Christians believe and preach that all history is in God's salvation and control. Therefore, they may live a dynamic faith in love, and be confident in the real hope of the Lord's Coming.[21]

Paul's rhetoric, as Yeo notes, is based on persuasiveness and adherence to the teaching of Jesus, and not on the foundations of logical argumentation of analysis. "Because Paul's rhetoric is crucifixion-centered, it has a function of self-criticizing. The rhetoric of crucifixion is not to maintain or boast its own authority, but to sacrifice 'small self' (*xiao wo*—individuals) in order to fulfill 'great self' (*da wo* 大我—greater humanity)."[22]

Paul's thought originates from the rabbinic Jewish tradition that rearranges Hebrew religious beliefs into Greco-Roman argumentative discourses. Therefore, the multicultural study of Pauline rhetoric, such as Yeo's analysis of Paul's use of different cultural perspectives between Jewish and Gentile Christians in 1 Corinthians 10:1–22, serves to show the principles of Yeo's "Cross-Cultural Rhetorical Hermeneutics." In drawing on recent theories of rhetoric by Kenneth Burke and Chaïm Perelman, Yeo emphasizes the importance of exegetes' acceptance of each other in the process of interpreting the Bible.[23] Yeo investigates how Paul responded to proto-Gnostic teachings of wisdom, human, and gender in the Corinthian situations.[24]

In summary, "Paul's letters are rhetorical, interactive, and besides, theological (that is to say, have essential content),"[25] according to Yeo's cross-cultural rhetorical interpretation. He uses abundant academic achievements in Western rhetoric, both traditional and modern, and introduces them to Chinese biblical studies. He also practices dynamic cross-cultural interpretation as he reads biblical verses and Chinese literature, such as his theology of ecological feminism, as he offers his readers in China a new perspective regarding the interrelationship of humans and ecology.[26]

Socio-Rhetorical Study of the Synoptic Gospels

As for study of the Synoptic Gospels in Chinese scholarship, there is only one work written by Yang Yan, *The Camel through the Eye of a Needle: Luke's Warning and Persuasion of the Rich*.[27] By choosing some passages about the rich in the third Gospel, such as Jesus' warning, "Woe to you who are the rich" (Luke 6:24; NRSV throughout this essay), "How hard it is for those who have wealth to enter the kingdom of God" (Luke 18:24), Yang Yan uses socio-rhetorical criticism to interpret all nine passages on the rich in the Gospel of Luke. Her research proposes that Luke's particular redaction and intention in these passages is disclosed in the comparative interpretation of the Synoptic Gospels and in the immediate context so as to weaken human hostility against the rich and to warn them regarding wealth.

On the intertextual understanding between the Gospel of Luke and Greco-Roman literature, rhetoric, and socio-cultural setting, she suggests that Luke hopes to have a direct dialogue with Greco-Roman ethics on wealth in light of political ideology, including topics such as wealth hoarding, wealth management, almsgiving, and benefaction. In doing so, Luke's purpose is to exhort the rich to live a social life of discipleship and to show that the Christian community then is not anti-social, because it cares for the needs of the poor and it promotes *Pax Romana* for the welfare of the empire. The aim of all these redactions of Luke enables Yang: (1) to search for the survival of the Christian community in the context of the control and suppression of associations or *collegia* by the Roman empire; and (2) to differentiate the Christian community from others who do not jeopardize regional social security in contrast to the misunderstanding of the Roman rulers.[28]

Taking nine passages in the Gospel of Luke as an example, Yang's work tries to make the point that, "the teachings of the earlier Christian community are affected by Roman social politics, and the community responds to Roman social cultures"[29] through admonishing the rich to the work of benefaction.

More than twenty years ago, socio-rhetorical criticism came into being.[30] It was applied to the study of the letters and the Gospels in the NT. Yang applies socio-rhetorical criticism to the topic of wealth in the third Gospel, thus marking a significant beginning in the Chinese academy of biblical studies in mainland China.

In Taiwan, however, Wu Zhuhui 吳主惠 hoped to search for the "equality of the historical Jesus and the Christ of faith" in his *Jesus' Life* (*Explanation of the Gospel of Mark*).[31]

Dong Junlan 董俊蘭 thought the best way to study the Gospels is not to distinguish the issue of authorship, the borrowed traditions, and the identity of Jesus, but to consider all the Lukan writing as a "witness" to the Gospel writers, and then to seek after their *kerygma* (proclamation), which they would have preached to their readers.[32] In Hong Kong, Vincent Cheung 張永信 (Zhang Yongxin) published two volumes of the Gospel of Mark in 2010,[33] and Sun Po-ling 孫寶玲 published *Mark: The Beginning of the Gospel* 馬可福音—福音之始 in 2011.[34] The former leads readers to understand the specificity of Jesus Christ in the Gospel of Mark, while the latter combines current biblical studies with the practice of faith to build up Christians. Besides, in the past ten years, a few professional essays about the Gospels were published in China, such as Zha Changping's "The Three Dimensions of Christian Classical Text in History: A Case Study of the Gospels (基督教歷史經典文本的三個層面—以福音書為例)"[35] and his series of papers on the social logic of the Gospel of Mark.[36]

Two Studies on the Gospel of John

In the study of the Gospel of John, Xie Wenyu, a professor at Shandong University, in his writing, *The Way and Truth: The Gospel of John in the History of Western Thought*,[37] interprets the Gospel in the context of classical Western thought and sees the text not only as a religious one but also as a philosophical one. Xie demonstrates his Chinese existential concern and perspective in presenting the Gospel of John to Chinese readership. The book contains strong Chinese elements.

In tracing the understandings of the Gospel of John by Christian theologians in history, Xie delineates a unique concept of truth he believes is nurtured by the Gospel, namely the redemptive truth given by the Trinitarian God in contrast to the rational concept of truth proposed by Greek philosophers. Further, Xie makes distinctions between two epistemologies in approaching truth: In Greek philosophy, truth is assumed to be the target of knowing, but without the knowledge of the locality of truth—and philosophers take pains to find ways to approach it. In this epistemology, human beings find ways to pursue truth. Xie's understanding is that the Gospel of John advocates a different way; that is, truth itself came to readers as a human being, claiming that he is the truth giver. Thus, when people come to him/truth and believe in him, they will then become truth receivers.

Since the Gospel of John was written in Greek and contains several similar crucial concepts as those employed by Greek philosophers, Xie argues, the Gospel writer and readers share the same existential concerns and thinking with other Greek language users.[38] Consequently, they respond to issues or perplexities encountered by Greek thinkers; otherwise, the teaching of Christ would not attract many readers. In Xie's argument, the Gospel has offered convincing answers to those issues the Greek philosophers could not overcome and, therefore, there is an existential connection between the Gospel of John and Greek philosophy. Xie then moves on to provide a new interpretation of the Gospel in the history of thought, as well as a new Chinese translation of the text.

To defend the above thesis, Xie discusses in the introduction to his book key issues originating from the Gospel, such as *Logos*, reason and faith, the sonship of Jesus Christ, truth, life, and authorship of the Gospel. Under the title of "Christ and Messiah," Xie addresses the issue of Jesus' sonship. Xie argues that the contemporary Pharisaic Jews had their own conception of "messiah," in which they thought the true messiah must be a savior who was an anointed political leader—thus, someone who would lead them to destroy Roman rule and establish an independent kingdom. Xie analyzes the Pharisees' epistemology this way:

> Pharisees conceived the notion of Messiah according to the Hebrew scriptures, ... They believed that, as long as they read and discuss the holy scriptures hard enough, they would be able to achieve the correct understanding of Messiah, ... In this epistemology, ... the Pharisees were trapped by their own notion of messiah in judgment and rejection of God's revelation. When Jesus declares that the revealed letters must be understood through God's revelation, he insists on a consistent epistemology in the tradition of the Hebrew scriptures. That is, people cannot see the true Christ (or Messiah) if they employ their own judgment; rather, they can see the true Christ only through God's self manifesting, which is Jesus himself.[39]

Xie categorizes the former as the rational epistemology of truth, which is associated with Plato's theory of truth, and the latter using the name of the epistemology of redemptive truth, which was rejected by Plato as a *doxa* (opinion), such as people accepting other's opinions without rational discernment. He further analyzes Plato's criticism of *doxa*. When Plato rejected *doxa* as it is accepted in emotion, he proposed that all true knowledge comes from rational judgment. However, Xie writes: "It is impossible for us as human beings to have any knowledge if we do not trust in others. Trust is indeed a window to receive knowledge from others. And more importantly, trust is the starting point for us to gain knowledge of the world."[40]

As Xie points out, Plato failed to realize the essential function of trust as an emotion or feeling in epistemology. In the Gospel of John, the epistemology of *doxa* is revived, but it is called the epistemology of redemptive truth, and the term "*doxa*" is no longer a negative word. In English translation, the word is rendered as "glory," followed by the Latin's *gloria*, which refers to God's knowledge in the Gospel.[41]

Following this new epistemology, Xie believes that the Gospel of John stresses that human beings are unable to recognize the true God; in other words, unless God or the Truth comes and reveals himself to human beings, the pursuit of truth will be in vain. Now, Xie writes, God reveals himself through Jesus:

> who cannot be seen by reason in judgment, but can only be seen in faith. Faith is the starting point in understanding Jesus Christ. In this way, people must accept Jesus' claim that he is Christ in faith, and then they can witness Jesus' words as the truth itself, and in due course they come to understand Jesus as the true Christ.... As the receivers, we may understand Jesus' claim after we have received the truth in faith. Consequently, our trust in Jesus' self-claim is the only way to the truth. This is what we call the theory of the redemptive truth.[42]

According to Xie, this also is called the "sonship of Jesus." Xie delineates Jesus as the only Son of God from these two sides: (1) from the Father's side, he sent Jesus to the world and let him speak and do things on his behalf, and he will not send any others; (2) from Jesus' side, he only speaks and does what the Father wants him to say and do. It follows that Father and Son speak and do the same things.

According to Xie, the Gospel distinguishes two concepts of life. He writes:

> The authority of life is in God. In receiving Jesus' giving in faith, people receive life. This is the eternal life. People are reborn in believing in Jesus Christ and so have the new starting point (born again) in their existence, which is new life. Meanwhile, a life without Jesus' giving is moving towards death, such as a human being is fully controlled by his or her desires, emotions.[43]

In Plato's thought, a true life is a life starting with the truth, and a life without the truth is a destructive course toward death. Now, the Gospel provides a life in Jesus' giving, which is also a life with the truth. Such a life is what the Greek philosophers had been pursuing all along but could not find. This good news was very much attractive to Greek thinkers indeed.[44]

Xie's delineation of the Gospel's epistemology of redemptive truth, in my consideration, is an important and unique contribution to contemporary Chinese biblical scholarship. Introducing the historical context in thought to biblical studies may offer a new tool for intercultural studies of the Scriptures, especially for those who engage in comparative studies between the Bible and other cultural classics, including Greek texts and Chinese texts.

Xie Wenyu's *The Way and Truth* was published in The Biblical Library series, edited by K. K. Yeo and Hui Liang in China. Yeo, in the series "Prospectus," writes that:

> The Biblical Library seeks to promote the wholistic approach to Scripture through methodological and exegetical studies, historical research and reflection, and finally through philosophical and conceptual inquiry. Being grounded on the Chinese horizon but committed to benefit global biblical interpretations, the objective of the Series is consistent with classical Confucianist, Daoist, rabbinic, and Greco-Roman studies. . . . The Series encourages the intertextual and cross-cultural reading of the Bible with the varied cultures of China.[45]

The Way and Truth represents this kind of reading of the Bible as it engages with Hebraic, Greek, and Chinese cultures.

Besides this series, the "Tiandao Biblical Commentary" series—completed by Chinese scholars overseas, first published in Hong Kong then republished by Shanghai Joint Publishing Company in mainland China—also has promoted biblical studies in the Chinese academy. *A Commentary of John's Gospel*,[46] written by a Singaporean Chinese who lectured actively in China, Choong Chee Pang, is representative of this series. Lacking Chinese resources in Chinese academia in diaspora even, Choong mainly consulted European and North American biblical scholarship, focusing on studies of original words and then going through exposition and application of the message in the context of traditional Chinese texts or semantics. He considers "Word of life" as the core thesis of John's Gospel and recognizes that most scholars establish the essence of John's Gospel as a Hebraic one that "is rooted in the life and the lives of Jesus' disciples... [and] is the confession of Jesus by the author John and his contemporary believers."[47] Choong claims that he would understand "symbolic speech" of the Gospel if it were couched in historical facts and history, since the NT connects most clearly and closely with Judaism.[48]

As for the relationship between John's Gospel and the Dead Sea Scrolls, Choong adopts directly the point of the Oxford scholar John Ashton as follows:

> The symbolism of light and truth is used to greater effect than at that in the Qumran,... for Jesus is identified not only as the light of the world (8:12) but also as the truth (14:6). For John the main task of the "spirit of truth" will be to recall to his disciples' minds the words of Jesus and lead them into all truth (14:26; 16:13).[49]

Choong agrees with the views of most scholars after the Second World War, that the shaping of the Gospel of John was independent of the Synoptics. Choong sees the main purpose of John's Gospel as a mission to Greek-speaking Jews, strengthening in them faith in Jesus as the Christ, the Son of God—and helping them find eternal life in his name.[50]

For Chinese readers, Choong's comparative study between *Laozi*'s Dao and the Greek understanding of *Logos* in the Bible is important, because it deepens their understanding of the eternal spiritual *Logos* of becoming material flesh (*sarx*), Jesus of Nazareth, who embodied both of them in history.[51]

Cross-Cultural Readings of the Bible

It should be relatively easy for scholars trained in Chinese academic traditions to do comparative research on the Bible and Chinese classical texts. However, this sort of comparative research has been limited to date to theological discussions of such major systematic categories as the doctrine of God, Christology, and pneumatology, and often limited to the literature and traditions of Hebrew, Greek, Christian, and Chinese thought. In addition to many essays,[52] a few books about them in Chinese academic circles were published. K. K. Yeo's *Confucius and Paul: Encountering of Tiandao with Word*[53] and *Zhuangzi and James: Metaphor of Life, Wandering in the Heavenly Grace*[54] are examined here.

Based on "the literary and commentary readings"[55] and on cross-cultural hermeneutics of *The Analects of Confucius* and *The Epistle to the Galatians*, Yeo points out that the question proposed by Confucius is about how to form community of human-human relationships by force or by virtue, while the question proposed by Paul is about how to become God's people by obeying religious rites or receiving the freedom of God's grace. Both of them shared the essence of theological ethics—"the common goodness in different communities."[56] However, as Yeo notes, it is necessary to know the essential differences between the world views of Confucius and Paul, which include differences: (1) between the natural and the created cosmos; (2) between the concept of recycled history and the eschatological concept of Christ-centered history; (3) between human nature as good and that which is under the power of sin; (4) between the virtue ethics of self-cultivation and the grace-filled life of faith in God; (5) between the cultivation of becoming a gentleman (*junzi*; exemplary person) and restoration of becoming God's people; and (6) between the social concept of harmonious morality, which is based on hierarchy, and the faith community of inclusion of individuals based on God's redemptive grace.[57] Since Paul's theological ethics begins with a divine-human relationship, therefore, Yeo argues that Paul envisions the world to be saved by the transcendent One. Confucius' virtue ethics begins with a human-human relationship; therefore, Yeo argues Confucius advocates for socio-spiritual harmony as the saving of the world. The author's aim of cross-cultural intertextual interpretation lies in the construction of Sino-theology, whose foundation based on Christ's teachings and works enable his followers to participate and "live out faith, hope, and love."[58] To Yeo, the content of Chinese Christian life is about God's unconditional love and transcendental love to ground "human freedom and rights"[59] in God's mercy, as well as infusing the truth of "benevolent human" (*renren* 仁人)[60] in mutual love based on God's love (*agapē*).

Prior to the intertextual reading, Yeo sees the ethics of Paul as belonging to the theological sphere, the ethics of virtue pertaining to the anthropological realm. This is the reason the intelligentsia in China commonly laud the Greek tradition and ignore the Jewish tradition or the Hebraic nature of the Pauline letters. Since there is no transcendental authentic dimension of the relationship between the human and the divine in Confucian ethics, a cross-cultural reading is helpful for transcending and critiquing the human-centered subject of Chinese culture.

Yeo's other representative work by means of rhetorical interactive interpretation, as well as cross-cultural, is *Zhuangzi and James*. As for the reason Yeo works on intertextual interpretation between *Zhuangzi and James*, he writes that:

> culture and theology is deeply relevant for each other, because Chinese text of wisdom (*Zhuangzi*) belongs to a category of culture, while the foreign text of wisdom (*James*) belongs to a category of theology. Yet, theology without culture will be like a ghost which has a soul without a body, and the culture without theology will be like a corpse without a soul. Theology needs culture to be nourished, but culture needs theology to break through and correct itself.[61]

Finally, he hopes to shape a new Sino-theology by cross-culturally interpreting the classics of *Zhuangzi* and *James*, moving toward "a unity with Dao, and making friends with God."[62] In Sino-theology, he writes:

> maybe wisdom of life does not lie in simply deleting suffering, but more so in treasuring life and knowing oneself through interpreting suffering from God's perspective/Word. So heaven and earth will live in peace/harmony with me, . . . that it is Dao and

> God to move my heart, to delight my emotion, and to nourish my psyche so that we may live in peace/*shalom*, as well as to return continuously to Dao and God.[63]

However, there would be a significant difference between the personal God of *James* and the impersonal Dao in *Zhuangzi*—at least when these texts are read independently. When researchers highlight comparisons among texts during cross-cultural reading, they will hesitate to wonder about this particular judgment of the difference in meaning. As a Christian scholar, K. K. Yeo has emphasized a "life approach of heavenly grace," because he believes that in life "all that is good, all that is perfect, is given us from above" (James 1:17a).[64] But as a Chinese scholar, when he cites the verse, it gives the impression to readers that he has omitted its latter part, which is connected with the sovereignty of the God of the Bible, "it comes down from the Father of all light; with him, there is no such thing as alteration, no shadow caused by change" (James 1:17b). This ambiguous reading seems to indicate a potential limitation of cross-textual interpretations in present Chinese scholarship. Yeo's cross-textual interpretation is more sophisticated, one that he has demonstrated elsewhere to practice this biblical mandate of translating biblical truth in vernaculars and by doing so could "save" vernaculars or cultures.[65] He sees this work as a "sacred task" of a Chinese Christian scholar.[66] Without cross-cultural biblical interpretation, both biblical messages and cultures will "die."[67] Yeo demonstrates this double-saving effect of cross-cultural biblical interpretation in the use of *dao* and *ren* in the Gospel of John and Pauline epistles respectively in the Chinese Bible.[68]

The History-logic Perspective of the New Testament

In 2011, Zha Changping, a multi-discipline-gifted Christian professor in NT studies at Sichuan University, published *Introduction to the Logic of the World-Picture of the New Testament*, Volume 1: *The History-Logic of the New Testament*.[69] He assumes that any tradition of cultural thought is formed by its historical canons, whose thinkers inherit and then interpret. The historical canon in the revealed religion of Judeo-Christianity is the Bible. Zha's methodology of history-logic abstracts the logical principles of any historical text by interpreting the four concepts of language, time, justice, and faith in the text. Recently, he expanded the concepts of the four into seven dimensions of the logic of world-picture, to include the concepts of ego/self, the natural world, and history.[70]

The key words in the study of the NT by means of "history-logic" are "history" and "logic." In the genetic, philological, and historical senses, the term "history" means event, human's speaking, and facts. The meanings of "logic" include the Bible, which he regards as "God's Word" (as in God's *Logos*), and also human words, and methods in the Hebraic and Greek traditions. When applying history-logic to the theological research of the NT as a hermeneutical frame, then Zha regards the NT as "God's Word that has been revealed in Jesus Christ and his historical event." He considers the narratives and references in all the Gospels as related to this historical event. The human words as proclaimed by the apostles ultimately speak of Jesus Christ but, for the authors of the NT, Zha argues that the most important meaning of both the Bible and human words is the NT, which promises the way of salvation for human beings.

In Zha's understanding, there is a parallel relationship between the three meanings of history or logic: the event of Jesus Christ revealed in the Bible is also a historically written one; the human words spoken by the authors of the NT are also those speaking of this historical event; the approach to the salvation of human beings shown in the Gospels is an eternal *Logos*, whereby human beings will obtain liberation and new life through what God has done in Christ Jesus (from the bondage of laws and sins).

In the study of history-logic, Zha argues that, first, it is important to pay attention to the concept of language in a historical text. Additionally, any particular historical text will be written down for a specific time in history and also will include the concept of time and the conceptual reflection of time. Second, in considering the concept of time in a historical text, the scholar using a history-logic perspective lives among interpersonal relationships, an expression of the concept of justice, that is, an ideal correlation held by people. Thus, Zha concludes that, in the history-logic study of biblical texts, it is necessary to pay attention to the concept of justice in a historical text, and ultimately, in order to live a just life, it is impossible for a person to live in this world without faith.

According to Zha, the ultimate question is: what kind of objective goal will a person choose to be his faith, and will this choice give him the ultimate meaning of life? The scholar using the history-logic method always states any historical text, such as the NT, in his own faith. On the contrary, any historical text in itself registers and bears witness to the Bible regarding the faith of the biblical writers. Thus, the four dimensions of language, time, justice, and faith in the NT become the objects of history-logic study.

On the language of the NT, Zha suggests that all the following references point to Jesus as the Christ: the many parables used in the Synoptic Gospels, the historical narrative in Acts, the invitation of Jesus to his hearers in the Johannine dialogues, the theology of Paul on the cross of Christ, and the rhetorical-theological responses in Paul's letters, the imperative mood in the Catholic Epistles, and the apocalyptic symbolic language in Revelation.

Zha views the concept of time in the NT as eschatological. This time begins with God's creation in the past, the First Advent of Christ marks the beginning of the end of time, and his Second Advent in the future will consummate God's creation. When viewed through this lens, history is revealed from creation in the beginning to the end of time, in which God finally fulfills his salvation of human beings through Jesus Christ.

Zha explains that salvation history of the NT is understood primarily by many Christians in the factual historical sense. From this perspective, the relationship between humans and humans is based on the central value of the relationship between God and humanity. Zha thinks that the relationship between God and humans belongs to the quest for human faith. The relationship between humans and humans also is maintained as the question of justice. Zha interprets that this just relationship between humans and humans, according to the NT, is based on the relationship between humans and the God of Jesus Christ. Zha argues that because Jesus Christ serves as a mediator between humans and God, it is impossible to establish a just relationship between humans and humans with any ethical, political, economic, and juristic aspirations. He further explains that both the concepts of justice and faith form the inherent properties of the NT as a historical text.

Zha reads the concept of justice in the NT as the righteousness of God/Christ shown through love, though a social theory of justice (human-centric) in the relationship between humans and humans that is nevertheless based on the relationship between humans and God (theodicy). He explains that the cross on which Jesus Christ was crucified symbolizes this concept of justice. Because of Jesus' vicarious death, Zha sees God's love as shown to the people; by virtue of Christ's resurrection, the righteous/just relationship will maintain God as God in heaven and humans as humans on earth. However, all the efforts to examine the history-logic of the NT will point toward faith in Christ, whose life is that of a Trinitarian God. For Zha, methodologically, the concept of the Trinitarian God implies the need to grasp a thing in terms of both absolute correlative perspective (the unity of Tri-unity = *agapē* = love) and absolute differential perspective (tri- of Tri-unity = *dikaiosynē* = righteousness/justice). That is, the God of the NT is one who has an absolute correlation in his absolute differences (three Persons of Father, Son, and Holy Spirit), as well as one who has absolute differences in God's absolute correlation (unity).

In the philological sense, Zha sees the unique feature of the NT as its *signifié* of words, which in turn is the Jesus Christ of history. According to this view, the NT recorded the historical events, which include the Logos/Word of God becoming the flesh of the historical Jesus and, simultaneously, the historical Jesus in the flesh becoming God's *Logos*. Both of these may be named as the "Christ-event." The former signifies the birth of Jesus by the Holy Spirit, Jesus' preaching of human love for his God and for his neighbor as himself, Jesus' vicarious death for God's salvation and for human redemption from sins on the cross. The latter means Jesus' resurrection from the dead, his ascension, return, and rendition of judgment. The central proposition of the history-logic of the NT is, therefore, faith in Christ, vis-à-vis, making a decision to believe in the event of God's Word becoming flesh, the historical Jesus, and the proclaimed (*kerygma*) Christ.

Compared to Sino-theology, the content of Zha's concept of faith in the study of the history-logic of the NT has an affinity with biblical theology, but he seeks to explain the concepts of language, time, justice, and faith in the NT as a historical text. Thus, this study of the NT belongs to a discipline of human social sciences. The study of the history-logic of the NT will enlarge the horizons of biblical studies in Chinese academia (from the concept of faith to that of justice in the text of the NT, from its concept of time to that of language), and advance its vertical depths (from the historical facts of Jesus Christ to the historical words of the NT writers speaking of Christ, again to the historical event of Christ).

The Perspective of the Philosophy of Biblical History

In the same year, 2011, Zhao Dunhua, a distinguished professor in the philosophy department of Peking University, also published his *Philosophy of Biblical History* (two volumes). The purpose of his book was to interpret philosophically the history of the Bible. In accordance with the Protestant catalogue of the Bible, he tries "to grasp the development of salvation history"[71] and to explain the formation and development of the philosophical contents of biblical revelation. He highlights the historical value of the witness of the Holy Spirit and works hard to understand biblical history based on the relatedness and differences between world history and salvation history. His discussions of ten philosophical premises for interpreting biblical history have made a creative contribution to Chinese biblical studies.[72] In the early historical background from the first two centuries of the common era, Zhao researches the formation of the NT. Because he values the historical elements in the NT, he somehow ignores the Catholic Epistles in which the Christian ethic of living seems to be the major content.

Conclusion

This survey on the major commentaries and monographs of NT studies is rather selective. Paulos Huang, an overseas Chinese Christian scholar, once provided his own succinct reflection: "In the present context of the Chinese academic world, biblical studies should be done not only from the perspective of history but also from the perspectives of literature and theology."[73] A final analysis of New Testament studies shows that the deep integration of Christian faith with the concrete situation in China in the past forty years has yet to come to fruition. NT studies in the Chinese academic world will progress in three ways: (1) interpreting Scripture as linguistic text; (2) the theological understanding of the Chinese tradition; and (3) the practice of engaging NT texts in the contemporary situation at its depth.

Chinese academics, especially those in NT studies, have a great interest in modern Euro-American cultures. Many biblical scholars assume that NT documents originated mainly from the two traditions: classical Hellenism (especially Greek thought) and Judeo-Christianity, and that both have been interactive throughout history. Scholars in the Chinese academic world in the twentieth century, however, have based their NT studies mainly on the rational philosophy of the classical Greek source, and therefore have understood and interpreted "Western culture" while neglecting the classical perspective of Judeo-Christian traditions originating in the Middle Eastern world. The works made by some Chinese scholars in biblical studies have begun to change this one-sided bias. But much more could be done for this young discipline in China.

Some potential topics of NT studies for NT scholars in China to pursue include the following queries: (1) what kind of world-picture logic, such as rhetorical argumentation, literary elements, and cross-cultural meanings, are found in the individual books of the NT? (2) What are the concepts of language, time, ego/self/personhood, nature, society, history, and the divine in the NT—especially in the Gospel of Matthew, Gospel of Mark, Acts, the Catholic Epistles, and Revelation—that often are neglected in Chinese NT scholarship? (3) What is the relationship between the logic of the world-picture of the NT and Chinese Christian lives as well as Chinese society today?

Notes

1. Zhu Weizi, *Twelve Lectures on Biblical Literature* [in Chinese] 聖經文學十二講 (Beijing: People's Literature Publishing House, 1989); and his *Christianity and Literature* [in Chinese] 基督教與文學 (Shanghai: Shanghai Shudian, 1992). *Twelve Lectures on Biblical Literature* systematically introduces the history of the Hebrew people, the influence of biblical literatures of the East and West, the origin and content of the Bible, the apocrypha, pseudepigrapha, and the Dead Sea Scrolls to its readership, while *Christianity and Literature* discusses the relationship between Christianity and Jesus, the Bible, hymns, prayer, and teaching, treating in detail the effects of Christianity on later poems, prose, novels, and drama.
2. E.g. Wen Yong's *Shengjing Lice: A General Understanding of the Bible* [in Chinese] 聖經蠡測 (Beijing: Today's China, 1992); Zhuo Xinping's *An Appreciation of the Bible* [in Chinese] 聖經鑒賞 (Beijing: Zongjiao Wenhua, 1992); or Cai Yongchun's *Introduction to the New Testament* [in Chinese] 新約導讀 (Beijing: Today's China, 1992).
3. Leeb Leopold, *Biblical Language and Thought* [in Chinese] 聖經的語言和思想 (Beijing: Zongjiao Wenhua, 2000).
4. Sun Yi, *Introduction to the Bible* [in Chinese] 聖經導讀 (Beijing: Renmin Daxue, 2005).
5. See Zha Changping, "Studying the New Testament in the Chinese Academic World: A Survey, 1976–2006," in *Reading Christian Scriptures in China*, ed. Chloë Starr (New York: T&T Clark, 2008), 81–82.
6. Liang Gong, *Study of Biblical Narrative Art* [in Chinese] 聖經敘事藝術研究 (Beijing: Commercial Press, 2006).
7. Ibid. 378–388.
8. Liang Gong, ed., *Introduction to Western Biblical Criticism* [in Chinese] 西方聖經批評引論 (Beijing: Commercial Press, 2006), 378–388.
9. Liang Gong, ed., *Biblical Literature Studies* [in Chinese] 聖經文學研究 (Beijing: People's Literature Publishing House, 2007).
10. Wen Yong, "A Missing Area in Biblical Studies" [in Chinese] 《聖經》研究的一個誤區, *World Religion Data* 4 (1990): 53.
11. Ibid. 54.
12. See Zha Changping, "Studying the New Testament in the Chinese Academic World: A Survey, 1976–2006," in *Reading Christian Scriptures in China*, ed. Chloë Starr (New York: T&T Clark, 2008), 82–83.
13. K. K. Yeo, *Eschatology and Hope: First and Second Epistles to the Thessalonians* [in Chinese] 末世與盼望：帖前與帖後現代詮釋 (Beijing: Zongjiao wenhua chubanshe, 2007), 54. See also his English work on the reception of Thessalonian correspondence in Maoist China:

Chairman Mao Meets the Apostle Paul: Christianity, Communism, and the Hope of China (Grand Rapids: Brazos, 2002).

14. Yeo, *Eschatology and Hope*, 59.
15. Ibid. 60.
16. K. K. Yeo, "Cicero and Augustine's Rhetorics" [in Chinese] (西塞羅與奧古斯丁的修辭學), in *Christian Cultural Review*, ed. Liu Xiaofeng (Guiyang: Guizhou Renmin, 1999), 140; K. K. Yeo, *Classical Rhetoric: Greco-Roman Culture and Biblical Interpretation* [in Chinese] 古修辭學: 希羅文化與聖經詮釋 (Hong Kong: Hanyu Jidujiao wenhua yanjiusuo, 2003). This book is republished in simplified characters and retitled as *Biblical Rhetoric: Greco-Roman Cultures and New Testament Interpretation* [in Chinese] 聖經修辭學: 希羅文化與新約詮釋 (Beijing: Zongjiao wenhua chubanshe, 2007). See his earliest interest in classical Greco-Roman rhetoric in his English work: *Rhetorical Interaction in 1 Corinthians 8 and 10: A Formal Analysis with Implications for a Cross-Cultural, Chinese Hermeneutic* (Leiden: E. J. Brill, 1995).
17. Yeo, *Biblical Rhetoric*, 241.
18. Yeo, *Eschatology and Hope*, 45.
19. Yeo, *Eschatology and Hope*, 45; Yeo, *Rhetorical Interaction in 1 Corinthians 8 and 10.*
20. Yeo, *Eschatology and Hope*, 10–11.
21. Ibid. 409.
22. Ibid. 66.
23. See Zha Changping, "Studying the New Testament," 88–89.
24. K. K. Yeo, *Biblical Civilization: Introduction to Early Judeo-Christian Cultures* [in Chinese] 聖經文明導論: 古希伯來及早期基督教文化 (Beijing: Zongjiao wenhua chubanshe, 2011), 162–195.
25. Yeo, *Eschatology and Hope*, 62.
26. K. K. Yeo, *Eve, Gaia and God* [in Chinese] 夏娃、大地與上帝 (Shanghai: East China Normal University Publishing House, 2008), 6.
27. Yang Yan, *The Camel through the Eye of a Needle Luke's Warning and Persuasion of the Rich* [in Chinese] 穿過針眼的駱駝《路加福音》對富人的警告與勸導 (Shanghai: Shanghai Joint Publishing Co., 2017).
28. Ibid. 291–296.
29. Ibid. 297.
30. See Vernon Robbins, *Exploring the Texture of Text* (Harrisburg: Trinity Press International, 1996), translated into Chinese 探索文本的紋理: 社會-修辭解釋法導論 by Huo Chengju (Shanghai: East China Normal University Publishing House, 2012).
31. Wu Zhuhui 吳主惠, *Jesus' Life* (*Explanation of the Gospel of Mark*) [in Chinese] 耶穌的生平（《馬可福音》講解）(Tainan: Taiwan Church Publishing House, 1973), 7.
32. Dong Junlan 董俊蘭, *Witness of the Gospel of Mark for the Misunderstood Messiah* [in Chinese]馬可福音的見證—被誤解的彌賽亞 (Tainan: Taiwan Church Publishing House, 1977), 10.
33. (Hong Kong: Tiandao Publishing House, 2010).
34. (Hong Kong: Mingdao Press Ltd., 2011).
35. *Religious Studies* 4 (2011): 167–172.
36. Zha Changping, "The Background for the Social Logic of the Gospel of Mark" [in Chinese] 《馬可福音》的社會邏輯所發生的背景, *Journal of Southwest Minzu University* 9 (2012): 77–81; Zha Changping, "The Relationship Between Jesus and the Members of Jewish Institution in the Gospel of Mark" [in Chinese] 《馬可福音》中耶穌與猶太宗教制度成員

的關係, *Religious Studies* 3 (2012): 171–176; Zha Changping, "Two Groups in the Gospel of Mark Based on the Relationship Between Jesus and Jewish People" [in Chinese] 《馬可福音》中的兩個群體—從耶穌與猶太會眾的關係看, *Journal of Southwest Minzu University* 8 (2013), 67–70; Zha Changping, "Two Groups in the Gospel of Mark Based on the Relationship between Jesus and Gentiles, Disciples and John the Baptist" [in Chinese] 從耶穌與外邦人、門徒、約翰的關係看《馬可福音》中的兩個群體, *Religious Studies* 3 (2013): 221–225.

37. Xie Wenyu, *The Way and Truth: The Gospel of John in the History of Western Thought* [in Chinese] 道路與真理—解讀《約翰福音》的思想史密碼 (Shanghai: East China Normal University Publishing House, 2012).
38. Ibid. 2, 9.
39. Ibid. 2, 18–19.
40. Ibid. 25.
41. Ibid. 26.
42. Ibid. 39–40.
43. Ibid. 39, 47–48.
44. In addition, the theory of truth by grace was discussed in the Tian Wei's 田薇 earlier paper, "The Doctrine of Word's Becoming the Flesh in *John's Gospel* [in Chinese] 從《約翰福音》'道成肉身'對希臘哲學困境的回應談起 responding to the Plight of Greek Philosophy" (in *Regent Review of Christian Thoughts* 2 [2005]: 127–137), which understands the salvation message of modern culture by means of the biblical tradition.
45. Yeo, "Prospectus," in Xie, *The Way and Truth* [front matter page].
46. Choong Chee Pang, *A Commentary of John's Gospel* [in Chinese] 約翰福音注釋, 2 vols. (Shanghai: Shanghai Joint Publishing Co., 2010).
47. Choong, *A Commentary of John's Gospel*, 1:4.
48. Ibid. 1:8.
49. John Ashton, *Understanding the Gospel of John* (Oxford: Oxford University Press, 1993), 214.
50. Choong, *A Commentary of John's Gospel*, 1:14.
51. Ibid. 1:62–81.
52. See Zha, "Studying the New Testament," 86–88.
53. K. K. Yeo, *Confucius and Paul: Encountering of Tiandao with Word* [in Chinese] 孔子與保羅: 天道與聖言的相遇 (Shanghai: East China Normal University Publishing House, 2010). See also his English version: *Musing with Confucius and Paul: Toward a Chinese Christian Theology* (Eugene, OR: Cascade Books, Wipf & Stock, 2008); and K. K. Yeo, ed., *Navigating Romans through Cultures: Challenging Readings by Charting a New Course* (Edinburgh: T&T Clark International, 2004), translated into Chinese (《羅馬書》文化巡航: 新航程下的閱讀) by Li Xi (Beijing: Religious Culture Press, 2018).
54. K. K. Yeo, *Zhuangzi and James: Metaphor of Life, Wandering in the Heavenly Grace* [in Chinese] 莊子與雅各：隱喻生命、遨遊天恩 (Shanghai: East China Normal University Publishing House, 2012). See also his numerous authored and edited works in English: *What Has Jerusalem to Do with Beijing? Biblical Interpretation from a Chinese Perspective* (Eugene, OR: Pickwick, 2018); co-authored (with Charles Cosgrove and Harold Weiss), *Cross-Cultural Paul: Journeys to Others, Journeys to Ourselves* (Grand Rapids: Eerdmans, 2005); and co-edited (with Gene Green and Steve Pardue), Majority World Theology Series of 6 vols. (Eerdmans and Langham, 2014–2019; omnibus by IVP, 2020).
55. Yeo, *Confucius and Paul*, 10.

56. Ibid. 10.
57. Ibid. 23–32.
58. Ibid. 405.
59. Ibid. 409.
60. Ibid. 414.
61. Yeo, *Zhuangzi and James*, 4–5.
62. Ibid. 381.
63. Ibid. 420.
64. Ibid.
65. Yeo, "Introduction: So Great a Salvation: Soteriology in the Majority World," in *So Great a Salvation: Soteriology in the Majority World*, ed. Gene L. Green et al. (Grand Rapids: Eerdmans, 2017), 1–13. See his sophisticated diverse methods of cross-cultural hermeneutics in *What Has Jerusalem to Do with Beijing?*, 45–47.
66. Yeo, "The Sacred Task of the Bible Interpreter: The Method of a Chinese Christian," *Word & World: Reading the Bible in Context* 2 (December 2016): 16–19.
67. Yeo, "Chapter 18: Asian and Asian-American Biblical Interpretations," in *Scripture and Its Interpretation: A Global, Ecumenical Introduction to the Bible*, ed. Michael Gorman (Grand Rapids: Baker Academic, 2017), 324–335.
68. Yeo, "Beyond Chalcedon? Towards a Fully-Christian and Fully-Cultural Theology," in *Jesus Without Borders: Christology in the Majority World*, ed. Gene L. Green et al. (Grand Rapids: Eerdmans, 2014), 171–178.
69. Zha, *Introduction to the Logic of the World-Picture of the New Testament*, Vol. 1: *The History-Logic of the New Testament* [in Chinese] 新約的世界圖景邏輯（第一卷）引論 新約的歷史邏輯 (Shanghai: Shanghai Joint Publishing Co., 2011).
70. See his forthcoming work in the second volume of *The Logic of the World-Picture of the New Testament*.
71. Zhao Dunhua, *Philosophy of Biblical History* [in Chinese] 聖經歷史哲學 (Nanjing: Jiangsu People's Publishing House, 2011), 1:35.
72. Ibid. 1:13–36.
73. Paulos Huang, *Sino-Christian Academic Biblical Studies in the Light of the Globalized Great National Studies* [in Chinese] 大國學視野中的漢語學術聖經學 (Beijing: Ethnic Publishing House, 2012), 82.

Primary Sources

NT works in Chinese only.

Choong, Chee Pang 鐘志邦. *A Commentary of John's Gospel* 約翰福音注釋. 2 vols. Shanghai: Shanghai Joint Publishing Co., 2010.

Dong, Junlan. *Witness of the Gospel of Mark for the Misunderstood Messiah* 馬可福音的見證—被誤解的彌賽亞. Tainan: Taiwan Church Publishing House, 1977.

Liang, Gong 梁工. *Study of Biblical Narrative Art* 聖經敘事藝術研究. Beijing: Commercial Press, 2006.

Sun, Yi 孫毅. *Introduction to the Bible* 聖經導讀. Beijing: Renmin Daxue, 2005.

Xie, Wenyu 謝文郁. *The Way and Truth: The Gospel of John in the History of Western Thought* 道路與真理—解讀《約翰福音》的思想史密碼. Shanghai: East China Normal University Publishing House, 2012.

Yang, Yan 楊硯. *The Camel through the Eye of a Needle: Luke's Warning and Persuasion of the Rich* 穿過針眼的駱駝 《路加福音》對富人的警告與勸導. Shanghai: Shanghai Joint Publishing Co., 2017.

Yeo, K. K. *Biblical Civilization: Introduction to Early Judeo-Christian Cultures* 聖經文明導論: 古希伯來及早期基督教文化. Beijing: Zongjiao wenhua chubanshe, 2011.

Yeo, K. K. 楊克勤. *Biblical Rhetoric: Greco-Roman Cultures and New Testament Interpretation* 聖經修辭學: 希羅文化與新約詮釋. Beijing: Zongjiao wenhua chubanshe, 2007.

Yeo, K. K. *Confucius and Paul: Encountering of Tiandao with Word* 孔子與保羅: 天道與聖言的相遇. Shanghai: East China Normal University Publishing House, 2010.

Yeo, K. K. *Eschatology and Hope: First and Second Epistles to the Thessalonians* 末世與盼望: 帖前與帖後現代詮釋. Beijing: Zongjiao wenhua chubanshe, 2007.

Yeo, K. K. *Eve, Gaia and God* 夏娃、大地與上帝. Shanghai: East China Normal University Publishing House, 2008.

Yeo, K. K. *Zhuangzi and James: Metaphor of Life, Wandering in the Heavenly Grace* 莊子與雅各: 隱喻生命、遨遊天恩. Shanghai: East China Normal University Publishing House, 2012.

Zha, Changping 查常平. *Introduction to the Logic of the World-Picture of the New Testament*, Vol. 1: *The History-Logic of the New Testament* 新約的世界圖景邏輯(第一卷)引論 新約的歷史邏輯. Shanghai: Shanghai Joint Publishing Co., 2011.

Zhao, Dunhua 趙敦華. *Philosophy of Biblical History* 聖經歷史哲學. 2 vols. Nanjing: Jiangsu People's Publishing House, 2011.

Zhu, Weizi 朱維之. *Twelve Lectures on Biblical Literature* 聖經文學十二講. Beijing: Renmin Wenxue chubanshe, 1989.

CHAPTER 27

THE CHINESE FACE OF JESUS CHRIST

ROMAN MALEK

FORM

JESUS Christ has been the subject of manifold and intensive reflection in the Chinese context and has shown various faces. It is said that in no other centuries have as many books been written on Jesus as in the last two.[1] Furthermore, there are numerous publications on the understanding of Jesus in non-Western contexts, especially in individual Asian countries.[2] The fascination of Jesus seems unbroken so that one may say with the Chinese theologian Choan-seng Song: "Jesus' light has burned on and has ignited countless new lights in the world, becoming the source of courage and hope to millions and millions of people during the past two millennia."[3]

Literature outside China, which puts forth the question of the Chinese face of Jesus Christ, however, is neither very extensive nor manifold. *Christus kam bis nach China* (Christ came to China) is the (inadequate) German title of the famous work by Jacques Gernet.[4] "Did Jesus Christ really come to China?" asks Claudia von Collani in one of her works.[5] *Preaching Christ in Late Ming China* is the title of the dissertation by Gianni Criveller.[6] The same author published a series of articles in the Hong Kong journal, *Tripod*, under the title "Dialogues on Jesus in China," which, however, concentrate on texts written mostly by Jesuit missionary Giulio Aleni (1582–1649).[7] *Le Christ chinois* is the title of a book published by Benoît Vermander with Chinese and Western contributions on Jesus.[8] The numerous Western christological works often speak about the Asian—including Chinese—understanding of Jesus. *Der andere Christus*, e.g., is the title of a book published by Hermann Dembowski and Wolfgang Greive, which also contains contributions on the Chinese understanding of Jesus.[9] Most of the materials so far published on Jesus in China are of mission-historical, literary, art-historical, and—as one might expect—theological nature.[10]

In the Chinese world, there are innumerable larger and smaller works of biblical, apologetical, catechetical, liturgical, general theological, literary, and art-historical nature on Jesus Christ, which within the Sinological and mission-historical research have been noted, but have not yet been appropriately investigated. A comprehensive interdisciplinary work on the manifold faces and images of Jesus in China, which unites the Sinological, mission-historical, theological, art-historical, and other aspects, so far has been a desideratum.

Who is Jesus of Nazareth or Jesus the Christ for the Chinese? "What is Jesus?" *Yesu shi shenme dongxi* 耶穌是什麼東西?—was asked in China.[11] How did the foreign missionaries who came from diverse Occidental contexts and epochs present Jesus Christ to the Chinese in their specific contexts? What did the Chinese think about this Savior Jesus? How did they themselves understand and portray him? Which face did they give to Jesus Christ, whether as the "believed-in Savior" or as the rejected "stranger" or "barbarian"?

Who then is Jesus of Nazareth for China and the Chinese? How was he proclaimed and perceived in China? As Jesus of Nazareth, as Jesus the Christ, as the Son of God and Redeemer of humankind, as "stranger" and "barbarian," as the "prisoner" or the opponent of Confucius, of Laozi or Buddha, as rebel or revolutionary, as exemplary person, the gentleman (*junzi*)? How is his face portrayed in Chinese history, beginning with Nestorianism (the "Religion of Light" or "Luminous Religion," jingjiao 景教) in the seventh to ninth centuries, via the Franciscan mission of the thirteenth and fourteenth centuries, the old China mission of the Jesuits and other congregations in the seventeenth and eighteenth centuries, the complicated "colonial" mission history of the nineteenth and twentieth centuries up to the present time, i.e., after the so-called "Liberation" (*jiefang* 解放) of 1949? What did the face and image of Jesus look like in the theology proclaimed in China as well as in pastoral and liturgical practice? Which face did he have for Chinese converts or within Chinese criticism of Christianity for non-Christian scholars? What does his face look like today, within oppressed Christian churches and among intellectuals or even in the many Christian sects now existing everywhere in China? In which way has Jesus Christ influenced China at all? Could it be that the "Chinese Revolution" is unthinkable without him and his message? Choan-Seng Song, for example, says: "In Asian works of art it seems that God comes to the people in more and more recognizable forms.... the Word became flesh, not just in Bethlehem two thousand years ago, but *now* in *Asia*.... The incarnation has become transposed in Asian Christian art."[12]

Emmanuel Lévinas calls it "visage,"[13] and the idea of the "icon," "face," and "image," also the German word "*Antlitz*," is included. In the Chinese language, there are various equivalents of these terms: "*mianrong* 面容," "*miankong* 面孔," "*mianmao* 面貌," "*mianmu* 面目," "*mianpang* 面龐," or "*lian* 臉" ("physical face"), "*mian* 面" ("honorific face"), and "*xingxiang* 形象" (manifestation, "enfacement")—terms that evoke many associations.[14] Similarly, according to the Chinese understanding, face is "what presents a person, it is the presentation by means of which a person stages his social existence and communicates its meaningfulness... it presents the identity as well as the individuality of a person."[15] In such a way, face is "the unmistakable clue to one's personal uniqueness and provides the basis of the identity of a person." Face is "a mark of identification."[16] Lévinas says that the face "speaks," manifests itself, is expression and a vivid presence, and that all this is already the "speech."[17]

Neither foreign nor Chinese Christianity construed a uniform face of Jesus Christ. The "appearance of his countenance" (Luke 9:29) has always been associated with a variety of views about his person, his life, his message. Each generation, each country, and every Christian (and non-Christian) brings in an individual perspective to this mosaic.

The "coming of Jesus to China," the forming of the "appearance of his countenance" within the Chinese context, was accompanied and limited by various factors. Choan-seng Song speaks about a difficult "theological leap from Israel to Asia"—or China.[18] Sinologist Jacques Gernet states an incompatibility between Christian and Chinese thought. Catholic theologian Paul Welte talks about a conflict between China and Christianity with its adhesion to Israel and Jesus Christ. Christians, says Welte, confess that Jesus Christ is the only mediator of salvation.[19]

There is a gap especially clearly visible in Chinese anti-Christian literature. Missionaries, too, had difficulties explaining the uniqueness of Jesus. Chinese converts on their part tried to adapt the Jesus Christ in their own ("syncretistic") way.[20]

Proclaiming Jesus in China, the missionaries as well as the Chinese touched on very fundamental questions concerning the Occidental and the Chinese context. These were questions on the understanding of religion, the problem of incarnation and redemption, the problem of the cross (the redeeming death of Jesus), the question of godhood and humanity (transcendence, man, person, soul). Thus, the questions connected with the Chinese faces and images of Jesus, as Jacques Gernet writes, raise:

> ...indeed important problems of historical psychology, including Chinese and European corporal as well as mental attitudes towards religious representations, history of religious feelings and history of religion in China...as well as—not less important subject—the history of Christianity itself.[21]

For Chinese Christianity up to the present time, these questions have remained crucial and are not to be given up; they are connected with a continuing, not-yet-finished process of searching, which has to be faced with all risks and limits.[22] That the Chinese and Christian identity in principle is being challenged by the perplexity of the experience of the Other and the "stranger," of Jesus Christ, is clearly referred to.

Before Jesus was proclaimed as the incarnation of God and redeemer of the world, a Chinese equivalent for the Christian term "God" had to be found. It is known that in China, due to the peculiarity of the Chinese language, for a long time there was no agreement about this question, that it culminated in the Catholic "Rites Controversy" and the Protestant "Term question," and even until today has not been solved,[23] which does not surprise as no other people in the world esteemed the name as much as the Chinese.

For most non-Christian Chinese, the conviction that Jesus was God's Son, God's incarnation in history, that God, therefore, took on bodily shape and walked on earth in human form, was simply irrational. Given that Jesus the Heavenly Lord (*Tianzhu* 天主)

was born in the Han dynasty, the question arose where God had been in the many dynasties before. Many authors of anti-Christian writings, which have emerged since the seventeenth century and have hardly been investigated so far, stress this point.[24]

As the Chinese pay great attention to the family background of a person, they were very interested to learn more about Jesus' parents. Jesus' miraculous birth by a virgin seemed strange to the Chinese.[25] The fact that Jesus had contacts with people of low social status and doubtful origin the Chinese connected with his "illegitimate" birth. Jesus had tax collectors and fishermen as disciples. Furthermore, many Chinese were astonished that one of his disciples, who had followed Jesus for many years, in the end betrayed him.[26]

In addition, from the Confucian perspective Jesus was anything but a praiseworthy son who showed proper filial piety (*xiao* 孝) toward his parents. In reference to the passage in Mark 3:35, some Chinese authors criticized the fact that Jesus did not even accept and respect his own mother. His disciples as well were accused of offending, in their human relationships, the Confucian teaching of loyalty and respect for parents. In anti-Christian literature, the authors emphasize that Jesus' teaching (like the teaching of the Chinese "arch-heretic" Mozi from the sixth/fifth century BCE) would destroy the five human relationships in Chinese society. Jesus in the seventeenth century, as Mozi before, was stylized as a type of heterodox and foreign teacher, thus the heretic par excellence.

The fact that Jesus performed miracles to heal the sick was regarded by Chinese literati as evidence that Christianity was a heresy (*xiejiao* 邪教). Within Christian apologetics, Jesus' ability to heal the sick was interpreted as a sign of his being the Son of God.[27]

The most controversial issue of the christological discussion in China was the claim that Jesus, by sacrificing his own life on the cross, had saved mankind from the destruction resulting from original sin. Confucius and Mengzi emphasized good human nature more than its inclination towards evil.[28]

Thus, the Christian teaching of salvation through Jesus from a Chinese perspective was not understandable. As the Lord of Heaven (*Tianzhu* 天主) was unparalleled in majesty and of infinite compassion, Chinese scholars argued, why did he not simply grant amnesty for the crimes of humanity, and why did he have to atone for human wickedness with the self-sacrifice of his only son? Why was he unable to arrange for people not to commit any further crimes?[29] Yang Guangxian 楊光先, an orthodox Confucian of the seventeenth century and adversary of Jesuit Johann Adam Schall von Bell (1592–1666), was surprised that Jesus could save mankind as a whole, but himself was condemned to the most dishonorable death of all. How, Yang asked, could he possibly be the Lord (*Tianzhu* 天主) who had created Heaven?[30]

In order to make the Christian teaching of salvation through Jesus understandable to the people, missionaries discovered that they (like the earlier "Nestorians") could borrow religious terms and thoughts from Chinese Buddho-Daoist folk religion, in which the merits of the ancestors, the immortals, and the bodhisattvas may be accumulated and transferred to later generations.[31]

Theologian Aloysius Pieris distinguishes between three "Christs," who claim Asia's—and China's—following: the Euro-Church Christ of the official Roman Church; the non-Western Christ of scholars and intellectuals; and the truly Asian (Chinese) Christ.[32] All these "Christs" can be met in China. In the history of Christianity in China, however, one also can find the "inclusive" and "aggressive" Jesus of the Christians; Jesus as the "unreasonable," "incomprehensible" (strange) person, Jesus Christ on the cross ("scandal"), and Jesus as friend, brother, bodhisattva, as the incarnated Dao. The "Chinese Jesus Christ," thus, has many faces, which manifest themselves in manifold images.[33]

The entire history of Christianity in China was a conflict between two mission strategies, which are reflected by the different faces and images of Jesus. One strategy defined the proclamation of Christianity as the task to, in one way or other, obtain a place for Jesus Christ in China. The other one tried to articulate the consequences of Jesus being recognized and proclaimed as the one who actually does not have a place in China, as he, for instance, was not born in China, thus being a "stranger" or "barbarian."[34]

Studying these competing strategies against the background of Chinese history or the individual epochs of the history of Christianity in China, one finds that this conflict is repeated in all epochs. There are the following time periods: (1) the Tang- and Yuan dynasties, seventh–ninth centuries and twelfth–fourteenth centuries, with "Nestorianism" and Manichaeism as well as the so-called "Franciscan" mission under the Mongols; (2) the Ming and mid-Qing dynasties, end of the sixteenth century up to the eighteenth century, what was called "old China mission" of the Jesuits and other congregations, with the so-called "Rites Controversy" and the banning of Christianity followed by its persecution; (3) the modern era, which usually is connected with the Taiping Rebellion, the "Unequal Treaties," and modern Protestant and Catholic Missions of the nineteenth and twentieth centuries; and, finally, (4) the present time, i.e., especially the time after the founding of the PR China in 1949 ("Liberation"), within which we can distinguish between the time before and after the so-called "Cultural Revolution" (1966–1976).

Contents

The message of Jesus, the Messiah and Savior, was brought to China when the largest part of Europe and the rest of the world still did not know it, namely, in the Tang dynasty (618–907) around the year 635. It is said that there were 530 "Nestorian" texts, of which only a few have been preserved. The still existing ones, however, give evidence of a high degree of inculturation of theology of the East Syrian Church in China, which also may be traced back to the spiritual atmosphere at the beginning of the Tang dynasty: China was in her heyday, its culture at a high level, so all teachings were welcome. Most of the preserved "Nestorian" texts talk about Jesus, the Messiah.

The Buddha, the *buddhas*, *devas*, demons, *arhats*, and angels are not only often mentioned and named with terms that stem from Buddhism but also are brought into relationship with Christian teaching. That in the Tang time, with its cultural and religious pluralism, people had no problems proclaiming Christian salvation with terms derived from Buddhism or Daoism has to be especially emphasized here.

In the "Nestorian" texts, Jesus as well as Christ is transcribed as *Yishu* 遺書 and *Mishihe* 彌師訶 (Messiah); once in a while the term "Lord of the Universe" is used. Trinity is translated as *sanyi* 三一 ("three-one"). The cross in the Jesus-Sūtra, according to Acts 5:30, is translated with "tree" (*mu* 木), but also generally with the "ten-character" (*shizi* 十字). Around 1300 CE, Christian monasteries in China were called "ten-character-monasteries."[35] An inscription of the year 1281 says that the Nestorians erected the cross in their homes, drew it in their churches, wore it on their heads, and hung it on their chests. In sharp contrast to the role of the cross in the Tang dynasty is the question of the cross in the Jesuit mission of the Ming (1368–1644) and Qing (1644–1911) dynasties.

It might be said about the writings of the East Syrian Church and its Christology that the Christian message was described in a very "mystical" way and that those who proclaimed it exerted all efforts to preserve the substance of the gospel but, at the same time, attempted to represent it in Buddhist and Daoist terms, so that Jesus, the Redeemer, became a folk religious Buddha-Messiah. This early synthesis is symbolically portrayed in the so-called "Nestorian Cross" (without the corpus), whose base is the lotus flower: "Christ and the Buddha embracing each other."[36]

To summarize Sino-Christian synthesis during the Tang dynasty, one can state an old Buddhist saying: "There is a jewel in the heart of the lotus." The East Syrian Christians, with regard to the iconographical presentation of their faith, limited themselves to the cipher of the cross and the lotus or referred to the metaphor of Jesus Christ as Messiah and light. Interesting and reciprocally supplementing faces and images of Jesus from the Tang, however, also can be found in Chinese Manichaeism.

The first known face of Jesus in China from Tang to Yuan thus was the "Buddho-Daoist Messiah" of the East Syrian Church community which, in China, experienced a heyday from the seventh to the ninth century. Aloysius Pieris calls this attempt "inreligionization" (in contrast to inculturation). With regard to the "Nestorian" experiment we see, as Pieris writes, how a meta-cosmic religion (namely, Christianity) develops a new Asian identity within the idiom and the ethos of another meta-cosmic religion (namely, Buddhism). Thus, Christian soteriology was formulated within the terminological framework of the Buddhist or Daoist *Weltanschauung* by using the Dao- or Buddha/Avalokiteśvara/Guanyin-model to develop "a Buddho-Daoist Christology." The time of the "Buddho-Daoist Christ" was not due to any church interventions, but to the banning of all so-called "foreign religions," imposed by the Chinese emperor in the year 845. To these "foreign religions" belonged Buddhism as well as Christianity, Manichaeism, and Zoroastrianism (the "Religion of the fire"). Therefore, we do not have any possibility of discovering to what extent the "Buddho-Daoist Christ" of the East Syrian monks/scholars attracted the masses of Chinese.

Numerous excavations—also in recent times—give witness to the typical "Nestorian Crosses" everywhere in China, in Mongolia, in Xinjiang down to the Southern Chinese coast in Quanzhou. These "Nestorian Crosses" are the only "images" of Jesus in China of the Mongolian Yuan dynasty (thirteenth–fourteenth century).

The East Syrian and Manichaean approach, however, even though it showed the enormous power and ability of inculturation of the Christian message into the Chinese context, after the imperial ban of "Nestorianism" fell into oblivion and was unknown even to the Jesuits when they arrived in China at the end of the sixteenth century. Only gradually did they draw, as their writings on "Nestorianism" show, new ideas from the "Nestorian Stele," which then became known and was made available by them to the world. The same was true for their encounter with the Jews of Kaifeng.

The second "christological breakthrough" in China opened up with the arrival of Jesuits Michele Ruggieri (1543–1607) and Matteo Ricci (1552–1610). Ruggieri was an advocate of the dialogical approach toward the Chinese Buddho-Daoist folk religion. In this spirit, he wrote the twelve Jesus-poems "On the Birthday of God." Matteo Ricci, on the other hand, rejected Daoism and Buddhism as incompatible with Christianity and relied on the "cosmic religiosity" of Confucianism. His work, *Tianzhu shiyi* 天主實義 (The True Meaning of the Lord of Heaven), was instrumental in this respect. In this catechism, the name of Jesus is mentioned only once. The title "Christ" Ricci does not mention at all. Ricci speaks about *Tianzhu* 天主, the "Lord of Heaven," whom he understands as God and the Son of God, the Lord. In Ricci's writings, the aspect of the passion is missing and everything sounds very "Chinese": A wise man has been born; a holy one who proclaimed to the people the Dao 道 in order to put the disturbed harmony of the world in order again. Ricci focused on the Chinese inclination toward ethics, so that the incarnated God was presented only as a sage and his salvation deed explained as an example of virtue. Ricci thus seems to have been very careful with a direct proclamation of Jesus, his salvation deed, and his death on the cross. At the end of his catechism, however, Ricci encourages the Chinese to go to the "Fathers" to look for the "True Teaching" as presented in a more complete way in other books. In view of the lack of understanding of the Chinese of the crucifixion of Jesus, Ricci—as the early church—adopted the "arcane discipline" when explaining the Passion. The mendicants in their letters and reports said that, in the interest of his mission strategy, he did not fully proclaim the Christian teaching of salvation.

George Dunne (1905–1998) states that the most serious charge against the Jesuits, without any doubt, was the claim that the Jesuits had concealed the teaching of Christ's crucifixion. This charge was believed by so many that in the end it became an historical commonplace (the problem with the "preaching of the cross").[37] Thus, French philosopher Blaise Pascal (1623–1662) also made an influential statement about the "concealment of the cross" in the China Mission of the Jesuits.

Earlier research, however, has proved that the Jesuits wrote extensively about the life of Jesus (including Jesus' passion and death on the cross), mostly in translations of the Gospels, accounts of the passion, Jesus-Litanies, etc. They also made efforts to portray Jesus Christ in pictures. Was it then de facto only the influential Ricci who "concealed" the passion and the cross?[38]

The Franciscans, for instance, report about their own mission that in 1691 they brought to China "*una imagen de un crucifijo de bronce, otra de un Salvador…*"; they often talked about "*la s. imagen de N. Señor crucificado*." Letters written by the Franciscans several times mention churches dedicated to the name of Jesus.[39] The Dominicans, too, used to proclaim the cross in a direct way.[40]

A look at the newer Chinese literature and art shows clearly that the question of the cross for today's Chinese writers and artists remains of greater relevance than ever,[41] that they are struggling with possible interpretations of Jesus and the cross,[42] the self-manifestation (*doxa*) of God as self-ef(-)*face*-ment.

In the context of the Jesuit mission in China, the attempts of the so-called "Figurists" to find Jesus Christ the Savior in the figures of Chinese mythology and ancient history have to be mentioned.[43] In Macao, we furthermore find images of Jesus from the rich Sino-Lusitanian tradition, which also are re-presented by the poems of the Chinese Jesuit Wu Li or Wu Yushan (1632–1718).[44]

The Jesuits' attempts to proclaim Jesus Christ and to present the "countenance of his appearance" provoked different reactions among the Chinese. Since the seventeenth century in China, large numbers of anti-Christian treatises, pamphlets, and compilations from Confucian and Buddhist apologists and critics were published. These writings not only illustrate the conflict between Christianity and Chinese culture but also provide source material for the Chinese, non-Christian, and non-church understanding of Jesus.

According to *Poxieji* (1640), a collection of memorials, proclamations, and reports opposing Christianity, the Jesuits planned to impose the idea of Jesus on the Chinese. One of the authors, Shen Que 沈㴶 (d. 1624), from the Ministry of Rites, like other literati scholars found the story of Jesus' life incredible. One scholar not only found the miraculous birth of Jesus beyond reason but also thought a religion glorifying the immoral act of an unmarried woman was nothing less than fabulous. If God, or Jesus, were so powerful, it was furthermore argued, surely he must have foreknown Judas' betrayal. If Jesus were really such a perfect person, why did he choose to die like a criminal? And above all, why did God descend only to one particular country, but not China?

On the other hand, Chinese criticism has elicited apologetical writings by missionaries and converts and has given rise to more theological precision but also to a dialogue with Chinese thought. This may be seen, for instance, from the writings of the Jesuit missionary Ludovico Buglio (1606–1682), especially his *Budeyi bian* 不得已辨 (1665) against Yang Guangxian 楊光先. The writings by converts are particularly important as they represent attempts at a "Sino-Christian Christology."[45] Xu Guangqi 徐光啓 (1562–1633), for instance, wrote "Eulogy on the Portrait of Jesus" (*Yesu xiang zan* 耶穌像讚),[46] and thought that the Lord Jesus (*Tianzhu*) was simply synonymous with God (*Tianzhu*). It was God himself descending to earth with the name of Jesus to show his divinity with universal fraternity. It seems that Xu had an ambiguous concept of the incarnation—an ambiguity, reminiscent of the ancient apologists who wrote before the full elaboration of the Trinity doctrine in the fourth century.

It is an interesting fact that in the midst of Confucian and Buddhist criticism of Jesus and Christianity, around the year 1701, a "story of Jesus" with his picture was published in a folk-religious, Buddho-Daoist work entitled *Shenxian gangjian* 神仙綱鑑 (*Mirror of Divine Immortals*) or *Lidai shenxian tongjian* 歷代神仙通鑑 (*General Record of Divine Immortals over Successive Generations*).[47]

During the period after the Opium Wars (1840–1842) and in the context of the Taiping Rebellion (1851–1864), "modern" faces and images of Jesus have emerged.[48] Around the year 1850, in China a totally new image of Jesus developed—this time not a critical one, and also not a church one. It was the syncretistic Chinese face of Jesus as the "Elder Brother" of Hong Xiuquan 洪秀全 (1814–1864), the leader of the Taiping, the "Younger Brother of Jesus," and the new Messiah of China and the world. Under the "Heavenly Father, the only God," a new trinity of the Sons of God came into being: Hong Xiuquan and Yang Xiuqing 楊秀清 (1821–1856) with Jesus Christ (who was understood as fire and light). Among the vast literature on *Taiping tianguo* 太平天國, however, one hardly finds any monographs on the understanding of Jesus or the Christology of Hong Xiuquan.

The Chinese criticism of Christianity, as well as of the person and teaching of Jesus, was continued in the nineteenth century; the topics also were similar to those of the time of the Jesuit mission. Many Chinese entertained doubts regarding reports of the Gospels on Jesus' death and resurrection.[49] Other authors believed that Jesus really died on the cross and regarded this as evidence that he had been a criminal punished by Roman authorities. Similar to the people who had mocked Jesus on the cross, the Chinese could not believe that the man nailed on the cross was the savior of humankind.[50]

Even though non-Christian Chinese in general were not much impressed by the historical Jesus, they often had a totally different opinion about his teaching. There are numerous portrayals of Jesus as a teacher of the people in the West, comparable with Confucius and Mencius. Some scholars even admitted that some elements of Jesus' teaching were to be adapted by the Chinese; they had the impression that the "Teaching of the Lord of Heaven" (*Tianzhujiao* 天主教) was not so radically different from many of the Chinese schools of thought. The converts, on the other hand, preached a kind of synthesis of Confucianism and Christianity or (more seldom) of Buddhism and Christianity. In this spirit, the proclaiming of Jesus' teaching in China started changing. The statement of the centenary conference of the Protestant Missions in China in 1907 indicates the missionaries' stress on the "person and work of Jesus Christ" as represented in the Bible. In affirmative theology, especially of American missionaries, the central point was God's incarnation in man through Jesus Christ; on that foundation liberal missionaries built a theology that, in varying degrees, asserted the (Confucian) innate goodness of man and bright prospects for human society.

At the end of the nineteenth and the beginning of the twentieth centuries, from the confrontation of (especially Protestant) Christianity with Islam, further interesting faces and images of Jesus unfolded.[51]

Long before "Liberation" in the year 1949, in China there were new christological attempts leading up to a radical Confucian adaptation of Jesus. In the Confucian view, he is regarded as the perfect, holy man (*shengren* 聖人), the gentleman (*junzi*) who practices virtue in a most outstanding way. Common to all these attempts is the emphasis on the ethical dimension in Jesus' teaching (similar to Matteo Ricci).

During the first decades of the twentieth century, probably most non-church publications on Jesus and China written by Chinese were produced, with many positive (among others, Chen Duxiu), but also very negative (e.g., Zhu Zhixin 朱執信, 1885–1920) voices. Representative of this non-church understanding of Jesus of that time is a statement by Chen Duxiu 陳獨秀 (1879–1949), the personification of the "New Culture" and the later co-founder of the Chinese Communist Party, who in 1920 in his article "Jidujiao yu Zhongguoren 基督教於中國人" (Christianity and the Chinese People), asked the readers of *Xin qingnian* 新青年 (*La Jeunesse*) to earnestly study Christianity: "Knock at Jesus' door and ask that his lofty and magnificent character and his warm sympathetic spirit be united with us."[52] But as Chen Duxiu, the intellectuals of that time ignored some aspects of the Christian faith, like Jesus' virgin birth, his miracles, his saving death, and his resurrection. They emphasized the brotherly love, humanity, and his sincere personality (*renge* 人格) instead. This attitude also influenced some converts. Jesus' resurrection was regarded by rational Confucians as totally inconceivable; they believed that the body of Jesus was stolen by his disciples. After the disciples had done this, they spread the rumor that Jesus had been resurrected on the third day.

In the Protestant church in the 1930s, signs of a genuine Chinese theology with many interesting and new facets of the understanding of Jesus developed. Some of these voices were compiled as the series of articles, *Jesus As I Know Him* (published also by the Associated Press, Shanghai, in book form in Chinese [1929] and English [1930]). Zhao Zichen designed in the Confucian spirit a Christology in which Jesus' humanity and his perfect personality (*renge*) were emphasized.[53] Much stronger than with the Jesuits in the seventeenth and eighteenth centuries, Jesus became the "prisoner of Confucius." Another picture was sketched by Wu Yaozong, who understood Jesus within the context of the *Social Gospel*, which at that time was popular also in China.

In the early decades of the twentieth century, several Catholic missionary painting schools came into being: in Beijing the *Ars Sacra Pekinensis*; in Shanghai the paintings from Tou-se-we (Tu-shan-wan); then the paintings by Leo van Dijk (1878–1951) and Edmond van Genechten (1903–1974); both Scheut missionaries (C.I.C.M.), with numerous (not undisputed) paintings of Jesus in "Chinese style."[54]

With the "victory" of the Communists and the so-called "Liberation" of 1949, new faces and images of Jesus emerged. "The realization of Communism is the fulfillment of the hopes of Jesus," a circular of the CCP said.[55] The famous writer, Guo Moruo郭沫若 (1892–1978), at that time Vice-Prime Minister, in a hymn on the seventieth birthday of Stalin (December 16, 1949), wrote that the redeemer of ancient times, Jesus, died once and is said to have been resurrected. "Jesus' death was real, but his resurrection was invented."[56] Jesus, the illegitimate son of a carpenter, and his bride made a revolution against the Jewish religion; he was a proletarian revolutionary.

During the time of the Cultural Revolution (1966–1976), in Europe and America, there followed the infamous comparisons between Marx, Mao, and Jesus, as well as the reinterpretation of Christology in the spirit of the Maoist "New Man."[57] Under Chinese influence at that time, there arose in the West new images of Jesus, which might be summarized under the slogans "Jesus-Revolution" or "Words of the Chairman Jesus," modeled on the so-called "Mao-Bible" (*Mao yulu* 毛語錄, "Mao's Sayings") or the "red precious book" (*hong baoshu* 紅寶書).[58] The topic "Jesus Christ in China" has, of course, above all a deep theological dimension.[59]

The so-called "Cultural Christians" in the People's Republic of China also contribute new elements to the mosaic of the non-church Chinese images of Jesus.[60] One of the more recent publications of the Institute of Sino-Christian Studies in Hong Kong carries the symptomatic title "Christ's Mundane Face" (*Jidu de chenshi mianrong* 基督的塵世面容).[61]

The Chinese faces and images could be further enriched by glimpses of the faces of Jesus in Korea—with interesting borrowings from China[62]—and interpretations of Jesus Christ in light of *yin-yang* 陰陽, *Yijing* 易經, and Neo-Confucian philosophy,[63] in Japan, Vietnam, or Asia in general.

Conclusion

The various forms of Christian and non-Christian Chinese faces and images of Jesus have changed over the course of time. What is important, however, is the fact that christological discussions, as structured in the history of Occidental Christianity, were continued in another cultural context and against a complex religious background. Was China then a field for philosophical-theological—or more concrete christological—new approaches? What did the theological transfer of ideas and interpretations look like, i.e., which "equivalents" to or "deviations" from "Occidental Christology" are visible in China and what was actually transferred in the practical proclamation of the faith? The result might be that the Chinese context limited the possibilities for the unfolding of a specific face and image of Jesus much more than other contexts. Xenophobia and strong nationalism, for example, in the past prevented many Chinese from developing a Christian understanding of Jesus.[64]

Lévinas is right in pointing out regarding "face" that the "*absolute experience is not disclosure but revelation*: a coinciding of the expressed with him who expresses, which is the privileged manifestation of the Other, the manifestation of a face over and beyond form. Form—incessantly betraying its own manifestation, congealing into a plastic form... alienates the exteriority of the other."[65] The face of an individual, especially that of Jesus Christ, ultimately is unknowable, indefinable, and irreducible to images or ideas. Which faces and images of Jesus Christ will the Chinese context still generate? Which position will such a Jesus gain in this vast part of Asia? Will he remain a *vox clamantis in deserto*?

Notes

1. Among the famous works on Jesus in the twentieth century is the one by Jaroslav Pelikan, *Jesus through the Centuries: His Place in the History of Culture* (New Haven: Yale University Press, 1985), which has been translated into many languages, *inter alia* into Chinese: *Lidai Yesu xingxiang jiqi zai wenhua shishang de diwei* [in Chinese] 歷代耶穌形象及其在文化史上的地位 (Xianggang: Daofeng, 1995).

2. See, among others, Hans Waldenfels, "Modelle christlicher Soteriologie in außereuropäischem Kontext," *Zeitschrift für Missions- und Religionswissenschaft* 71 (1987) 4: 257–278; R. S. Sugirtharajah edited, *Asian Faces of Jesus* (Maryknoll: Orbis, 1993); Volker Küster, *The Many Faces of Jesus Christ: Intercultural Christology* (Maryknoll: Orbis, 2001); Georg Evers, "Heutige Christologien in Asien," *Neue Zeitschrift für Missioswissenschaft* 55 (1999), 297–311; Georg Evers, "Jesus Christ and the Gentile Mission," in *Studia Missionalia* 51 (2002), *passim*.
3. *Jesus, the Crucified People* (Minneapolis: Fortress, 1996), ix.
4. *Chine et Christianisme. Action et réaction*. Bibliothèque des histoires (Paris: Gallimard, 1982).
5. See, for instance, "Did Jesus Christ Really Come to China," *Sino-Western Cultural Relations Journal* XX (1998): 34–48. Cf. Roman Malek, *The Chinese Face of Jesus Christ* [hereafter *CFJC*], vol. 4a, *Annotated Bibliography* (Sankt Augustin: Steyler, 2015), 197–198.
6. *Preaching Christ in Late Ming China: The Jesuits' Presentation of Christ from Matteo Ricci to Giulio Aleni* (Taipei: Taipei Ricci Institute, 1997).
7. See Malek, *Chinese Face of Jesus*, vol. 4a (entry on Gianni Criveller, 201–203).
8. *Le Christ chinois: Héritages et espérance*. Préface de Claude Larre. Collections Christus No. 87. Essais (Paris: Desclée de Brouwer, 1998).
9. *Der andere Christus: Christologie in Zeugnissen aus aller Welt* (Erlangen: Ev.luth. Missionsverlag, 1991).
10. All ascertainable Chinese works on Jesus as well as Western editions and references regarding the Chinese faces and images of Jesus have been compiled in Malek, *CFJC*.
11. See "What Is Jesus?" by Zhu Zhixin (1885–1920) in *CFJC* 3a: 1197–1207.
12. Choan-Seng Song, *The Compassionate God: An Exercise in the Theology of Transposition* (London: SCM Press, 1982), 4.
13. See his *Totalité infini: Essai sur l'exteriorité* (Den Haag: Le Livre de Poche, 1961). German: *Totalität und Unendlichkeit: Versuch über die Exteriorität*. Übers. von W.N. Krewani (Freiburg: Verlag Karl Alber), 63.
14. See Hu Hsien Chin, "The Chinese Concepts of 'Face,'" *American Anthropologist* 46 (1944): esp. p. 45; Cheng Chung-ying, "The Concept of Face and Its Confucian Roots," *Journal of Chinese Philosophy* 13 (1986): 334–345.
15. Cheng, "The Concept of Face and Its Confucian Roots," 329.
16. Ibid. 329.
17. Cf. E. Lévinas, *Totalité infini: Essai sur l'exteriorité*, 63 and 87.
18. German version "Von Israel nach Asien—ein theologischer Sprung," *Europäische Theologie herausgefordert durch die Weltökumene* (Genf: Studienheft, 1976), 10–29.
19. Paul Welte, "Basic Problems of a Chinese Contextual Theology," *Tripod* 17 (1983): 55.
20. This is verified especially in the contributions of Paul Rule, Whalen Lai, Dominic Sachsenmaier, Jessie G. Lutz, Roman Malek, Gotelind Müller, Winfried Glüer, Matthias Christian, and Poling J. Sun in the respective volumes of *CFJC*.
21. Letter to the author, December 14, 1998.
22. As discernable from the contributions by Liu Xiaofeng and Wolfgang Kubin in vol. 3b of *CFJC*.
23. It will surely take a long time before Catholics and Protestants will call on the one God by the same name, e.g., like in liturgical texts with *Shangzhu* 上主, and not like in the Lord's Prayer today, differently, with *Shangdi* 上帝 or *Tianzhu* 天主.
24. The texts by Wen Xiangfeng (1577–1642) and Yang Guangxian (1597–1669) in *CFJC*, vol. 2, are some samples.

25. See P. K. Kwok, "Chinese Non-Christian Perceptions of Christ," *Concilium* (1993/2): 115.
26. Cf. Kwok, "Chinese Non-Christian Perceptions of Christ," 115. In the 1940s Wu Leichuan also refers to these differences in comparison with the disciples of Mozi. See the contribution by R. Malek, *CFJC*, vol. 3a.
27. Compare the views on Jesus' miracles held by, e.g., Wu Leichuan, Zhu Zhixin, and many other intellectuals in the first decades of the Republic in the *Anthology* of *CFJC*, vol. 3a.
28. See among others Wolfram Eberhard, *Guilt and Sin in Traditional China* (Los Angeles: University of California Press, 1967); and Wu Pei-yi, "Self-Examination and Confession of Sins in Traditional China," *HJAS* 39 (1979): 5–38. See Liu Xiaofeng, *Zhengjiu yu xiaoyao* [in Chinese] 拯救與逍遙 (Shanghai: Fengyun shidai, 1988; new edition 2001); Zhuo Xinping, "The Concept of Original Sin in the Cultural Encounter Between East and West," in *Christianity and Modernization. A Chinese Debate*, ed. Ph. L. Wickeri and L. Cole (Hong Kong: DAGA Press, 1995), 91–100.
29. See Kwok, "Chinese Non-Christian Perceptions of Christ," 118.
30. Regarding Yang Guangxian's views which are representative of the Chinese anti-Christian criticism, see the text of Ludovico Buglio, *CFJC*, vol. 2.
31. Exemplary for this question is J. D. M. Derrett, Hans-Joachim Klimkeit (1939–1999), Gunner B. Mikkelsen, Steve Eskildsen, and Yves Raguin (1912–1998) in *CFJC*, vol. 1, with the relationship between Buddhism and Christianity in the context of "Nestorianism" and Manichaeism.
32. A. Pieris, *An Asian Theology of Liberation* (Edinburgh: T. & T. Clark International, 1988), 127–129. Mark Fang Chih-jung, "Confucius et Jésus face à leurs disciples," in B. Vermander s.j., ed., *Le Christ chinois: Héritages et espérance.* Collections Christus No 87. Essais (Paris: Desclée de Brouwer, 1998), 123–139.
33. K. K. Yeo, "Chinese Christologies: Images of Christ and Chinese Cultures," in *The Oxford Handbook on Christology*, ed. Francesca Murphy (Oxford: Oxford University Press, 2015), 393–407; K. K. Yeo, "Beyond Chalcedon? Towards a Fully-Christian and Fully-Cultural Theology," in *Jesus Without Borders: Christology in the Majority World*, ed. Gene L. Green et al. (Grand Rapids: Eerdmans, 2014), 162–179.
34. C. S. Song (*Jesus, the Crucified People*, ix), e.g., posed the following question: "Did Jesus, born in Palestine two thousand years ago, expect his influence to go beyond the land of his birth and his impact to long outlive him? The answer is probably no."
35. With regard to the "ten-character-monasteries," see Georg Schurhammer s.j., "Der 'Tempel des Kreuzes' 十字寺," *Asia Major* 5 (1928–1930): 247–255.
36. Cf. Michael von Brück, "What Do I Expect Buddhists to Discover in Jesus? 'Christ and the Buddha Embracing Each Other,'" in *Buddhist Perceptions of Jesus. Papers of the Third Conference of the European Network of Buddhist-Christian-Studies*, ed. Perry Schmidt-Leukel, Josef Thomas Götz, Gerhard Köberlin (St. Ottilien: EOS, 2001), 158–175.
37. Cf. G. H. Dunne, *Generation of Giants: The Story of the Jesuits in the Last Decades of the Ming Dynasty* (Notre Dame: Kessinger, 1962).
38. In Athanasius Kircher's (1602–1680) *China illustrata*... (Amsterdam: a Jacobum à Meurs, 1667; repr. Kathmandu 1979), between pp. 112–113 (illustr. Cc), Ricci is being portrayed together with Xu Guangqi and the cross between both. In J. B. du Halde's *Description géographique, historique, chronologique... de l'empire de la Chine...*, t. 3 (La Haye: Scheulees, 1736), between pp. 86–87, Ricci is portrayed in a pose pointing to the cross.
39. *Sinica Franciscana. Relationes et Epistolas Fratrum Minorum Hispanorum in Sinis qui a. 1684–92 missionem ingressi sunt.* Collegit, ad fidem codicum redegit et adnotavit P. Fortunatus Margiotti O.F.M., pars prior et pars altera (Rome, 1975), VIII/1, 237, 325, 378, 715, 900, 925.

40. As Miguel Ángel San Román and Benno Biermann demonstrate (in *CFJC*, vol. 2).
41. See Wang Xuefu 王学富, "Zhongguo wenxuezhong de Yesu xingxiang" [in Chinese] 中國文學中的耶穌形象, in *Jinling shenxue zhi* 金陵神學誌 22–23 (1995/1–2): 59–65. Cf. also Marián Gálik, "Zwischen dem Garten von Gethsemane und Golgatha: Die letzte Nacht und der letzte Tag Jesu in der modernen chinesischen Literatur (1921–1942)," in *China heute* XX (2001/1–2): 39–44.
42. As the sample texts of Wang Meng (*On the Cross*), Han Bide, Wang Weifan, and Choan-seng Song show (see *CFJC*, vol. 3b).
43. Claudia von Collani gives a detailed report on these attempts (*CFJC*, vol. 2).
44. On the Sino-Lusitanian Christian art in Macau, see Roman Malek (Hrsg.), *Macau. Herkunft ist Zukunft* (Sankt Augustin: Steyler, 2000), esp. 361–402, 469–484.
45. As the Dominic Sachsenmaier, Whalen Lai, and Paul Rule verify (in *CFJC*, vol. 2).
46. For the English translation, see Wang Xiaochao, *CFJC*, 2:755.
47. Karl L. Reichelt and E. T. C. Werner (in *CFJC*, vol. 2) have translated this story in order to accomplish the mosaic of the faces and images of Jesus in the Qing dynasty.
48. Ralph R. Covell and Jessie G. Lutz in *CFJC*, vol. 2. Margo S. Gewurtz gives concrete and specific examples of the proclamation of Jesus in China of this time (in *CFJC*, vol. 2).
49. Cf. Paul A. Cohen, *China and Christianity: The Missionary Movement and the Growth of Chinese Antiforeignism 1860–1870* (Cambridge, MA: Harvard University Press, 1963).
50. See P. A. Cohen, *China and Christianity*, 42.
51. Regarding this question in general, see the contribution of Françoise Aubin, "L'Apostolat protestant en milieu musulman chinois," in *Actes du IVe Colloque International de Sinologie de Chantilly, 1983* (Taipei: Institut Ricci, 1991), 12–74.
52. "Jidujiao yu Zhongguoren" [in Chinese] 基督教於中國人, *Xin qingnian* 7 (February 1, 1920): 18.
53. See W. Glüer, *Christliche Theologie in China: T.C. Chao, 1918–1956* (Gütersloh: Mohn, 1979), with a complete bibliography of Zhao Zichen's writings (pp. 278–293).
54. For a critical interpretation of these pictures, see among others Xaver Bürkler, "Katechismus-Illustrationen in China: Christliche Stimmen zur chinesisch-christlichen Kunst," in *Neue Zeitschrift für Missioswissenschaft* 8 (1952): 294–301; Ekman P. C. Tam discusses the understanding of Jesus of Karl L. Reichelt (in *CFJC*, vol. 3a). Poling J. Sun introduces "Jesus in the Writings of Wang Mingdao," and Anthony S. K. Lam, "The Images of Jesus in *Kung Kao Po* 1928–1930," the Catholic diocesan paper of Hong Kong (in *CFJC*, vol. 3a).
55. Quotation from Johannes Schütte, *Die katholische Chinamission im Spiegel der rotchinesischen Presse: Versuch einer missionarischen Deutung* (Münster: Aschendorfer, 1957), 76.
56. Cf. J. Schütte, *Die katholische Chinamission*, 78.
57. See Michael Chu, ed., *The New China: A Catholic Response* (New York: Paulist Press, 1977), here esp. Gerald O'Collins S.J., "Christ and China," 124–145.
58. See, e.g., Johannes Lehmann, *Mao, Marx und Jesus* (Wuppertal: Jugenddienst Vlg., 1969); Gustav Weth, *Zwischen Mao und Jesus: Die große chinesische Revolution fordert die Christenheit* (Wuppertal: Brockhaus, 1968); Gustav Weth, *Chinas rote Sonne: Unsere Welt zwischen Mao und Jesus* (Wuppertal: Brockhaus, 1972); Paul E. Kaufmann, *Confucius, Mao and Christ* (Hong Kong: Asian Outreach, 1975).
59. That these faces and images may enrich our mosaic with the faces and images of Jesus, is shown in *CFJC*, vol. 3b, by Marián Gálik and Wang Xiaochao; the latter gives a short introduction into the "Marxist Interpretations of Jesus in China (1949–1999)."

60. These are persons who do not belong to a church, but work intensively, especially on an academic level, on Christianity and theology.
61. In *Daofeng—Logos & Pneuma* 17 (2002), see also K. K. Yeo, *Confucius and Paul* (Shanghai: East China Normal University Press, 2010).
62. See Hector Diaz, M.G., *A Korean Theology. Chu-Gyo Yo-ji: Essentials of the Lord's Teaching by Chóng Yak-jong Augustine (1760–1801)* (Immensee: Neue Zeitschrift für Missionswisenschaft, 1986).
63. See, e.g., the writings of Jung Young Lee also relevant for China: *The Theology of Change: A Christian Concept of God from an Eastern Perspective* (Maryknoll: Orbis, 1979); Jung Young Lee, *The Trinity in Asian Perspective* (Nashville: Abingdon Press, 1996).
64. Cf. Kwok, "Chinese Non-Christian Perceptions of Christ," 119.
65. Emmanuel Lévinas, *Totality and Infinity: An Essay on Exteriority*, trans. Alphonso Lingis (The Hague/Boston/London: Martinus Nijhoff Publishers, 1979), 65–66. Italic his.

Primary Sources

Gernet, Jacques.*Chine et christianisme. La première confrontation* (Édition revue et corrigée; Paris: Gallimard 1991; new ed. 2009). Italian trans.: *Cina e cristianesimo* (Casale Monferrato 1984); English trans.: *China and the Christian Impact: A Conflict of Cultures*, trans. Janet Lloyd (Cambridge—Paris, 1985); German trans.: *Die Begegnung Chinas mit dem Christentum* (revised edition; Sankt Augustin 2012). Chinese trans.: Xie Henai 謝和耐, *Zhongguo wenhua yu jidujiao de chongzhuang* 中國與基督教的衝撞, trans. Geng Sheng 耿昇 (Shanghai: Guji 1989, 2003); *Zhongguo yu Jidujiao: Zhong Xi wenhua de shouci zhuangji* 中國與基督教: 中西文化的首次撞擊 (Beijing: Shangwu yinshuguan, 2013).

Roman Malek, ed. *The Chinese Face of Jesus Christ*. Volume 1 (Sankt Augustin—Nettetal, 2002); Volume 2 (Sankt Augustin—Nettetal, 2003); Volume 3a (Sankt Augustin—Nettetal, 2005); Volume 3b (Sankt Augustin—Nettetal, 2007); Volume 4a, *Annotated Bibliography* (Sankt Augustin—Nettetal, 2015). *CFJC* 1–4.

CHAPTER 28

JESUITS' *CONVENEVOLEZZA* IN PRINTED ILLUSTRATIONS OF THE GOSPEL

QU YI

Introduction

In the year 1582, the first Jesuits reached the territory of Ming dynasty (1368–1644), China. The arrival of the Jesuits was of great importance not only for the mission but also for the transmission of European science and culture to China. It marks the beginning of a new period of Sino-European artistic exchange as well. The Chinese reaction to European architecture, sculptures, and paintings is well documented. However, most of the European-style buildings, sculptures, and paintings were unfortunately damaged or altered. On the contrary, the printings that could be reproduced in larger quantities were more widespread, well accepted, and more easily handed down. Some earliest printing series are still well preserved in European libraries and archives.

The Evangelicae historiae Imagines (EHI)

Archbishop Celso Costantini (1876–1958) identified, in the 1930s, the illustrations in the *EHI* compiled by Jesuit Jerónimo Nadal (1507–1580) in 1595, which served as templates for *Guicheng* and *Jingjie*.[1]

In 1548, the founder of the Jesuit Society, Ignatius of Loyola (1491–1556), published the *Exercitia spiritualia*, which laid the foundation of the spiritual exercises of Catholicism.[2] *Exercitia spiritualia* is a guide for those who follow the spiritual exercises; it teaches them how to pray, meditate, and make decisions in their lives. One of Loyola's most important followers, Jerónimo Nadal, inherited and developed Loyola's spirituality. Because Nadal understood Loyola's *Exercitia spiritualia* so well, he was asked to compile an illustrated guide for meditation based on Loyola's *Exercitia spiritualia*. Thirteen years after the death of Nadal, in 1593, the *EHI* was finally published in Rome.[3]

The *EHI*, with 153 folios, describes the entire narrative of the life of Jesus, as well as scenes selected from the life of the Virgin Mary in the four Gospels: from the annunciation to the childhood of Jesus, his ministry, passion, resurrection, and ascension to the assumption of Mary. Important pericopes were portrayed in great detail with several illustrations, such as the Passion of Jesus in thirty-three illustrations.

The plate layout of the *EHI* consists of three parts. In the top table on the page is the days of the liturgical calendar, a quotation from the Bible, two numerical orders in Arabic and Roman, and sometimes the title of the illustration and the age of Jesus. In the middle part, illustration takes up most of the space. In the illustration, there are scattered capital letters to be seen. The arranged alphabetic order gives the reading sequence of the illustration. The table under the illustration contains explanatory comments. These are guided by capital letters corresponding to the alphabetic sequence noted above in the illustration. Each engraving, without caption and explanations, is 169 mm high and 140 mm wide.

The *EHI* has a visualized representation. On the top row, the theme of the illustration is marked out explicitly for the reader. The illustration can be read furthermore by the means of explanatory comments in the lower table. Capital letters denote the order of the illustration sequence. When one reads the *EHI*, it is possible to catch the theme of the story according to the words in the top table and then observe the illustration in the middle according to the notes below in order to experience and participate in the narrative of the Gospel from one scene to another. In this way, the reader conducts a meditation in the light of the Jesuit's spiritual exercises.

The *EHI* arrived in China at the latest in 1605. Matteo Ricci (1552–1610) wrote on May 12th of that year to Pater John Alvarez in Portugal and asked for a second exemplar of the *EHI*, because he had traded the first one for the Bible from Pater Manuel Dias (1574–1659). Ricci regretted his decision and assessed the *EHI* to be "more useful than the Bible" even.[4]

Song nianzhu guicheng (Rules for Reciting the Rosary)

It is estimated that, today,[5] the existing *Guicheng* 誦念珠規程 has seven copies in two versions total.[6] The first edition was accomplished around 1620 in Nanjing, and it has six copies, while the second edition, preserved in the Biblioteca nazionale Centrale di Roma, came from the woodblock printed in Beijing in 1638.

The first five pages of the first edition begin with a dialogue between a teacher and a student, and these are missing from the second edition. This dialogue concerns the meaning and practice of the rosary. Otherwise, the contents of the two editions are identical, and the illustrations of the later edition are rougher than those of the first one. After the dialogue comes the first illustration. The illustration is followed by a corresponding text consisting of a title, introductions for the recitation, sacrifice (*xian* 獻), and prayer (*qi* 祈). The other fourteen illustrations are constructed in the same way.

The fifteen illustrations are reproduced after the foreign templates in the *EHI*. They present the fifteen Mysteries of the Rosary, which are meditations on episodes in the lives of Jesus and Mary, from the Annunciation to the Coronation of the Virgin. The accompanying texts explain the fifteen Mysteries and give examples for sacrifice and prayer.

Each Mystery of the Rosary is accompanied by an illustration on the right side and an explanatory text on the left side. Because the traditional Chinese reading order is from right to left, Chinese readers of *Guicheng* see illustrations first and then texts. In contrast to the *EHI*, no explanation is listed on the illustration of *Guicheng*. One finds the title and the content of the illustration first in the text. The *EHI* depicts the Gospel narrative and is made for the purpose of meditation, while *Guicheng* introduces the rosary to the Chinese and teaches them how to pray and meditate.

Tianzhu jiangsheng chuxiang jingjie (Explanation of the Canonical Book about the Lord of Heaven's Incarnation with Selected Images)

Jingjie 天主降生出像經解,[7] the second Chinese Christian book, was published by Giulio Aleni (1582–1649) in Jinjiang in 1637.[8] This book introduces for the first time to the Chinese the life of Jesus with printed illustrations. With a total of fifty-seven woodcuts, *Jingjie* was the largest woodcut-project in Chinese missionary history.[9]

Like *Guicheng*, *Jingjie* also is reproduced in woodcuts after the *EHI*. Even though the 153 scenes in the *EHI* are reduced to fifty-seven in *Jingjie*, the original iconography is mostly preserved. And except for the first two illustrations with the presentation of the map of Jerusalem and the "Salvator Mundi" (Savior of the World), *Jingjie* adopts the layout of the *EHI*. Those illustrations are divided into three parts. In the top table, the title gives the theme of each woodcut. Titles, however, are not a direct translation from the Latin in the *EHI*. Illustration occupies a large part of the woodcut in the middle. In the lower table, one could grasp the explanation of the illustration through the description of scenes lead by Heavenly Stems (*Tiangan* 天干). The Heavenly Stems also are scattered throughout the illustration and indicate the order of the description.

Illustrations

Many authors assume that the woodcuts in *Jingjie* are less Sinicized than those in *Guicheng*.[10] Although in terms of style, the illustrations in *Guicheng* indeed follow more Chinese pictorial conventions, those illustrations in *Jingjie*, however, featuring a selection of Chinese elements and themes, also show an adaptation of Confucianism clearly, as the following four points explain.

Sinicized Interior

The sixth page of *Guicheng*, the first picture, depicts the "Annunciation" in the Gospel of Luke (1:26–38) (Fig. 28.1). The lower part of the image features five steps leading to an open interior. Directly above the stairs in the room, a woman with a halo kneels before a small square table with curved legs, on which lies an open book. Her right hand rests on her chest, and her head bends slightly to her right side, facing the viewer. From the left top corner radiates a beam of light that focuses on her. In the clouds, a bird flies toward her, symbolizing the Holy Spirit. At the left of the illustration, a young man is stepping on the clouds and moving toward the kneeling woman. He is presented as having two wings on his back. The forefinger of his right hand stretches upwards, while his left hand holds a bouquet of lilies. This illustration shows a very common theme of Christian art, which is interpreted as the annunciation. However, this is different from the illustration in the *EHI*, which presents the annunciation scene in an Italian town; as we read in the comments in the *EHI*,[11] the scene in *Guicheng* takes place in a Chinese environment (Fig. 28.2).

Though the composition of the Chinese annunciation is faithfully imitating the original one in *EHI*, it is assembled with Chinese components. Instead of a humble room with a wood roof and cracked walls in the *EHI*, the scene of the annunciation in *Guicheng* is presented in an elegant building with a typical Ming dynasty interior and a traditional garden. Instead of a lectern, Mary kneels before a square table with curved legs, typical of Ming period furniture. Behind Mary stands a relatively low and wide bed with a mat on it. On the bed, there is a basket with needlework, including scissors, wool, and cloth, which indicate women's work and could be seen also in other Ming dynasty prints. In contrast to the illustration of the *EHI*, the curtain behind the bed on the annunciation of *Guicheng* disappears. A screen behind the bed replaces it, covering the rear part of the room. The screen shows a landscape scene with mountains, stones, and trees. In the upper left, the house is surrounded with woodwork, roof, and walls, which are partly hidden by the clouds and rays of light. At the left edge of the image a palm, a railing, and some stones can be seen. Their presence obviously indicates an elegant property with the garden of a Ming dynasty family. The interior also displays much traditional Chinese furniture and other Chinese elements. But at the same time, all the essential elements of the Christian annunciation are visible as well in order to make the reader recognize the theme of the image at first glance.

A screen also can be seen on the illustration, "Foot Washing" (literally: Lessons of humility by Foot washing, *Zhuo zu chui xun* 濯足垂訓; Fig. 28.3) in *Jingjie*. It illustrates the Gospel of John (13:1–10) and shows how Jesus washed his disciples' feet and dried them with a cloth during the last supper on the eve of the crucifixion. In the illustration, Jesus and his disciples are presented in three scenes. On the top left, we see the scene of communion through an open door in the back room. The scene of foot washing takes place on the stage in another room in front of the door. The left corner shows the moment in which Jesus stands up at the supper and holds the clothes in his right hand. His disciples follow him. In the middle of the illustration, the twelve disciples sit in a semicircle waiting for Jesus to wash their feet. Jesus kneels before a foot basin and asks to wash the feet of his first disciple, Simon Peter.

Particularly noticeable in this illustration is the triad folding screen behind the foot-washing scene, on which a landscape with clouds, birds, sky, mountains, rivers, and so on can be seen. These elements give the picture a typical Chinese pastoral atmosphere.

As Wu Hung 巫鴻, in his book *The Double Screen*, defines the function of the folding screen, it not only divides the space as a three-dimensional object in the room but also its surface serves as one of the most popular media of artistic presentation.[12] Ledderose deems that the landscape painting on the screen symbolizes a high social status of the secular figures in front of the screen.[13]

Landscape has become one of the most important subjects on the folding screen in the Tang dynasty. The short handscroll, "Collation of books" (*Kanshu tu* 勘書圖) by Wang Qihan 王齊翰 from the Southern Tang dynasty, is probably one of the earliest handscrolls; on it there is a screen with a landscape representation shown behind a scholar (Fig. 28.4). The presentation of the landscape on the screen reflects the innermost soul of the scholar in front of it, which orients him toward an ideal atmosphere, away from the real world.

In the Song dynasty, a description of landscapes on screens has been continued and further developed in literati paintings. At this time, there is no longer a single literatus, but often a group of literati are depicted before the screen. The integration of the landscape-screen with the literati-depiction has evolved into a general paradigm of the sophisticated literati tradition. The painting, "The eighteen scholars" (*Shiba xueshi tu* 十八學士圖; Fig. 28.5), which is attributed to Liu Songnian 劉松年 (ca. 1155–1218) from the Southern Song dynasty, places a folding screen before a group of scholars at the court of Taizong, the second emperor of the Tang dynasty. They gather at a garden terrace and play the Four Accomplishments 四藝, namely lyre-playing, chess, calligraphy, and painting.

In the Southern Song dynasty, illustrations of didactic Confucian classics also present screens with landscape depiction, such as the painting of "Dissemination of perfect virtue" (*guang zhi de* 廣至德), the thirteenth chapter of the classic "Book of Filial Piety" 孝經, attributed to Ma Hezhi 馬和之 (1131–1162) (Fig. 28.6). The folding screen takes up a large part of the upper half of the painting, which depicts the landscape with mountains, trees, a river, and cottages on a flat terrain. The idyllic landscape implies a harmonious society under the guidance of Confucian ethics.

As Matteo Ricci perceptively realized, antique art works as well as their reproductions played a central role for the Chinese in the seventeenth century.[14] A lot of handscrolls with landscape depiction of early times were reproduced in the Ming period, such as "Han Xizai evening banquet" (*Han xizai* 韓熙載夜宴圖; Fig. 28.7) attributed to Tang Yin 唐寅 after Gu Hongzhong from the tenth century; "High officials play chess" (*Gaoshi ti tu* 高仕棋圖; Fig. 28.8) copied by Qiu Ying 仇英 (1482–1559), whose original is attributed to Wang Wei 王維 (699–761); and "Whiling away the summer" (*Xiaoxia tu* 消夏圖; Fig. 28.9) by an unknown artist painted after Liu Guandao 劉貫道 from the thirteenth century.

All these paintings have landscape depictions on a screen, which connects the spiritual world of the literati. However, painters in the Ming period changed the motives from their predecessors. Wu Hong observes that Ming dynasty painters pursued the strategy of retaining the original figure depiction, while at the same time updating the internal display on the painting.[15] By imitating the ancient masters with some variations, the painters of the Ming dynasty placed the original paintings in their actual situations, which also reflected aesthetic interests of the Ming dynasty. The Jesuits were surely familiar with this artistic practice. By adding a typical Chinese screen on the woodcut, "Lessons of humility by foot washing," they updated the biblical story of foot washing in the seventeenth century and translocated it to the residence of Confucian literati and officials in the Ming dynasty.

The landscape-screen on the woodcut, "Lessons of humility by foot washing" inherited the literati tradition from the Southern Song dynasty. However, the Confucian literati in front of the screen are replaced by Jesus and his disciples. The screen here is representative of an aristocratic dwelling, while the idyllic landscape on the screen indicates a harmonious Confucian society. Here, however, these Confucian elements are placed in the Christian context. In the process of their missionary work in China, the Jesuits gradually became more and more familiar with many different Chinese religious traditions. They also are aware of the extent to which Confucianism as an ancient philosophical tradition and political thought has shaped and influenced Chinese culture and society for hundreds of years.

After the "Annunciation," follows the second illustration of *Guicheng*, the "Visitation" (Fig. 28.4), which also is embedded in a Chinese environment. This time, the visitation does not only take place in a Chinese courtyard but also is depicted in the Chinese painting style. In the lower part of the illustration, we can see an enclosed courtyard in Ming style with an open door. Outside the enclosure, in the lower right corner, a horse is tied to the tree. Inside the fence, there are two men wearing hats. They greet each other. The man on the right carries a stick with a parcel hanging on his shoulder. From this detail, he could be identified as Joseph, who traveled with his wife Mary from Nazareth. He is being received by Zachariah, husband of Elizabeth on the left. On the first level, two men stand, and up three steps, we see the two women embracing each other. The woman on the right, with a halo, is Mary. She is being welcomed by her relative, Elizabeth. Like the "Annunciation," the "Visitation" also is staged in a Chinese environment. The screen wall facing the gate of the house on the top right indicates a Chinese forecourt in the interior. The large garden with a screen wall, railing, and palm tree suggests that it is a gorgeous and elegant mansion.

Except for the objects, Chinese characteristics emerge from the composition and the perspective of this illustration. In the *EHI*, the main theme is illustrated at the bottom right of the image (Fig. 28.5). Right in front of the door is a donkey tied to the tree. The two women stand in the center, while a group of men are presented in the background beside the door. The viewer's standpoint is from the interior. Elizabeth and Zachariah are greeting Mary and Joseph coming into the room through the door. The most significant group in the illustration is the two women, presented largest and arranged in the foreground in the center. Here the central perspective is taking place. In contrast, the viewer's standpoint of the Chinese illustration is located outside the fence. This composition is very common of woodcut illustrations in the Ming period. In the Chinese version, the groups of women and groups of men are arranged from top left to the bottom right in a diagonal axis. Although Mary and Elizabeth are the most important group, they are not reduced in terms of perspective. On the contrary, they are displayed in the middle on the largest panel, while the horse, which stands in the foreground, is the smallest figure in the illustration; the illustration is produced using a hierarchical perspective, which means that the size and position of a figure are arranged depending on its property in the image, not its spatial arrangement.

Added Elements in Chinese Convention

It is noteworthy that illustrations are often produced with added elements in Chinese convention or with Chinese style. Below are two examples of added elements.

Added a Dog

According to the Bible, Jesus, with his twelve disciples, had the Last Supper before he went to the Mount of Olives and was going to suffer (Matt 26:20–29, Mark 14:17–25, Luke 22:14–38). Interestingly, on the illustration of "The Last Supper" (literally: Holy Communion Ceremony, *Li sheng ti da li* 立聖體大禮; Fig. 28.6), a dog is added under the table of the meal, which does not appear in the *EHI* and is not mentioned in the Gospels. The reason a dog is added could be found in the Chinese painting tradition. "Amusement in the Palace" (*Gong yue tu* 宮樂圖; Fig. 28.13), by an anonymous artist of the Tang dynasty (618–907), is possibly the first scroll painting that contains a dog under the table (Fig. 28.13). On the table, there are some cups and a pot. Women seated around the table are either drinking or playing musical instruments. A servant girl is keeping time to the music. The facial expressions of the women convey a harmonious and artistic atmosphere, in which even the dog under the table is resting quietly. The description of the dog supports a peaceful and carefree mood of the illustration.

In "Appraising ancient works in the grove" (*Zhu lin pin gu tu* 竹林品古圖; Fig. 28.14), from an album by Qiu Ying, a dog description also could be seen. This time, there are two dogs playing in the upper right corner of the painting. Two folding screens split the painting into two areas. Two officers are sitting inside the screens, recognizable by their official caps laid on the table. On the other three tables behind them and in the foreground on the ground, there is some antique bronzeware. Maids and servants are presenting the scholars with more ancient items, such as porcelain or scrolls. Outside of the screen, on the right edge of the painting, a houseboy is preparing tea on a stove. In the upper part and behind the railing, there is a bamboo grove in which a servant is preparing a chessboard on the stone table near where the two dogs are playing. The appraising of ancient artworks, tea-tasting and chess-playing are considered typical elegant activities of Chinese scholars. The screens, artificial rocks, and bamboo grove correspond to the surroundings of the scholars, while the presentation of the dogs playing reflects a playful mood of the painting.

In contrast to the two paintings, which render a pleasurable scene, "The Last Supper" presents a serious occasion, in which Jesus has had the last meal with his disciples before proceeding to the passion. The dog under the table reduces the sadness of this evening and evokes a peaceful ambience, which in the Christian context emerges only after the subsequent passion takes place.

Added Floral Decoration

Apparently, the Chinese print-makers had made efforts to decorate all kinds of surfaces in the illustrations with Chinese patterns, such as the floral decoration on the tablecloth of "The encounter of Jesus with the sinner" (literally: Absolution of the guilty woman—*She hui zui fu* 赦悔罪婦; Fig. 28.7), on the blanket of "The parable of the rich man and the poor Lazarus" (literally: Different retribution of the poor and the rich—*Pinfu si hou shu bao* 貧富死後殊報; Fig. 28.8), on the water bottle and footbath of "The foot washing" (*Zhuo zu chui xun*; Fig. 28.3), and on the curtain of "The Last Supper" (*Li sheng ti da li*; Fig. 28.6).

Two decorative motifs can be seen: the pine-needle pattern and the lotus-flower decoration. The pine-needle pattern was depicted commonly on Chinese textiles such as curtains, tablecloths, and blankets. Instead of an apricot-blossom motif, with its clearly sketched contour lines, which are often seen in Ming prints, the pine-needle patterns in *Jingjie* are drawn with simple crossed lines without petals or leaves. The lotus-flower decoration appears on the porcelain, such as the water bottle and the footbath. In the late Ming period, porcelains pieces often were decorated with the lotus-flower pattern.

This tradition has been maintained in *Jingjie*. In contrast to the pine-needle motif on the textiles, the lotus flower on the porcelain is depicted with stems and tendrils in soft and saturated lines.

Not all surfaces on the porcelain in *Jingjie* are decorated with floral motifs. In the illustration, "The Wedding at Cana" (literally: Showing miracle on the wedding—*Hun yan shi yi* 婚筵示異) and "Jesus and the Samaritan woman" (literally: Fetching water and teaching the public in Sychar—*Xi jia ji shui hua zhong* 西加汲水化衆), the surfaces of the water bottle are like those in *EHI*, unpainted. According to Jonathan Hay, the decorative objects in the Ming period have great social importance because they show at first glance the social status of their owner, in order to distinguish them from the poor and the uneducated.[16] The social status of Cana and Samaritan families are not emphasized in the Bible. In contrast, the decorative motifs on other illustrations conveyed the treasure of the vessels; for instance, in the "Encounter of Jesus with the sinner," in which the sinner woman washes Jesus' feet using her hair and precious ointments; and in "The parable of the rich man and the poor Lazarus" (Fig. 28.8), where the rich man lies on a bed covered by splendid decorated floral motifs.

The flower motifs on the curtain and tablecloth in the "The foot washing" and "The Last Supper" allow the Ming people to associate with an interior environment of the Confucian upper class, where, in fact, Jesus gathered with his disciples before his passion. Thereby, a higher status of Jesus could be suggested to late Ming readers. The Jesuits must be aware that, in the late Ming period, decorations on the items could reflect the social status of their owners and probably required Chinese print makers to take this into account. The added floral decorations are also the early signs of European interest in Chinese decorative motifs on textiles and porcelains, which were gradually attached with more attention, more and more appreciated and copied later by the Europeans.

Landscape in Chinese Painting Style

The sixth illustration in *Guicheng* is the "Agony in the garden of Gethsemane" (Fig. 28.9). In this narrative, Jesus went with his disciples to the garden of Gethsemane. He then led the disciples back and went alone to pray. The Chinese illustration is composed similarly to its European model. On the right side, Jesus kneels and prays, while the angel descends from the left corner of the illustration. On the left, his disciples and the town of Jerusalem can be seen.

The arrangement of Chinese illustrations is very similar to the European style. However, the Chinese artists have not placed Jesus and his disciples in the garden of Gethsemane, but in the garden of a typical Chinese pictorial style. In the *EHI*, Jesus kneels on the hill with dense covered trees, grasses, and plants (Fig. 28.10). In the Chinese illustration, a bare rock divides the illustration into two halves from the left bottom to the top right. In the middle, a rock stretches to the left, on which Jesus kneels.

His head is depicted in profile. His view is directed towards the angel, who flies down from the clouds. In his left hand, the angel holds a chalice, while his right hand points upwards. In the background, there are jagged projecting rocks. The mode of composition, in which the illustration is diagonally divided by rocks and mountains, is very common in Ming prints. On the left side at the bottom, which is separated by the rocks, the disciples are waiting for the praying Jesus. They sit in a landscape surrounded by trees and rocks. Their heads are supported on their hands as if they are asleep. Above them, behind the fence of the garden, a river flows above a bridge. Behind the bridge, on the left side of the illustration, the city of Jerusalem is depicted. All of these, from the city gate, the wall of the garden, to the trees and rocks, and even the pines growing out of the rocks, are drawn in the Chinese style.

Let us now look at "The Crucifixion" (Fig. 28.11) and "The Assumption" (Fig. 28.12), where not only the trees and mountains are illustrated in Chinese style but also the composition is modified from the European model. In "Crucifixion," the Chinese simplified the complicated background from the European style (Fig. 28.13). The entire architecture-complex of the city of Jerusalem in the background is replaced by mountains, which are sunk from both sides into the middle. In this way, the cross in the middle could be upraised.

To express the meaning of Christianity to the Chinese audience, Chinese artists emphasize the important elements in the illustrations, which requires a rudimentary knowledge of biblical texts. For example, in the lower part of the image in illustration 20, "The Assumption," the disciples are looking up at Jesus Christ floating into heaven. In the middle stand two angels. One of them lifts his hands to the sky. Behind them there is a slope, which stresses the central axis. Above that, in the middle, Jesus Christ flutters in the air. Compared with Western illustrations (Fig. 28.13, Fig. 28.14), we recognize clearly in these two Chinese woodcuts that they are divided into three levels; namely, the lower part occupied by the disciples; the middle part for the two angels; and the upper part with Jesus in the cloud accompanied by angels playing trombones on both sides.

Illustrations done in the Chinese traditional literary painting style make it clear that the Jesuits were familiar with the challenge of being accepted by the Chinese at the beginning of their missions. Therefore, they adapted pictorial representations to the traditional Chinese painting style. They also tried to approach the world outlook of the literati and officials in the Ming dynasty. This approach, using landscape depiction in the woodcuts, reflects the Jesuit's "top down" strategy, which means attempting to take root first in the class of officials and literati, in order to win the entire population from the upper class. The landscape depiction makes clear the Jesuits' efforts to connect with the Chinese literati and officials.

Changed Theme

"The Announcement of the Birth of John the Baptist" (literally: Saint John was bred before the Lord of Heaven—*Sheng ruo han xian tian zhu er yun* 聖若翰先天主而孕) (Fig. 28.15) is the first engraving in the *EHI*, in contrast to the narrative cycle of the life of

Jesus in *Jingjie* that does not begin with the "Announcement." It seems that for Aleni, there is no readily completed model to copy. In order to represent this narrative, he took the ninetieth illustration in the *EHI*, namely "The parable of the Pharisee and customs" (Fig. 28.16). The temple in which the Pharisees and customs prayed is transformed into the temple where Zachariah received God's proclamation from the angel Gabriel. In comparison to the European model in the *EHI*, the Chinese illustration has two added figures in the middle courtyard of the temple, namely the priest Zachariah, who burns incense in the temple, and the angel who speaks to him, telling him that God has answered his prayer and his barren wife Elizabeth was going to give birth to a son, John the Baptist, the precursor of Jesus.

The reason Aleni selected "The Announcement of the Birth of John the Baptist" as the first illustration for the illustrated life of Jesus can go back to the life of Confucius.[17] According to the legend of "The Prayer and Ritual on Mountain Ni" (*Daosi nishan* 禱嗣尼山), the parents of Confucius still had no child in their old age. The mother from the family Yan 顏 went therefore to the Mountain Ni to pray for the birth of a son. After ten months of pregnancy, she finally gave birth to Confucius.[18] This story often appears in the illustrated *Legend of Confucius* (*Shengji tu* 聖跡圖). For the Chinese in the late Ming period, it is hard to understand that Jesus Christ, who lived after Confucius, nevertheless should be the only god in the world. How should one understand the great Saint of Confucianism in a Christian context? One explanation is that, like John the Baptist, Confucius is a precursor of Jesus. The first illustration in *Jingjie*, "The Announcement of the Birth of John the Baptist," can remind the Chinese reader of the association with the legend of "The Prayer and Ritual on Mountain Ni" in the illustrated legend of Confucius. The Jesuits represented Confucius for the Chinese in the Christian context, just as John the Baptist was represented as a precursor of Jesus, so that the later coming (of Jesus) could be better understood and accepted for the Chinese.

Conclusion

The Jesuits' steep training in biblical and theological studies make them familiar with the Gospel stories yet able strategize in how to proclaim the gospel in and to contextual recipients. Fundamentally, their missionary work in China intensified the artistic exchange between China and Europe. Nowadays, some available print series in European libraries and archives enable us to gain an insight into the earliest cultural exchange under Catholic auspices, especially their understanding of text and images.

Guicheng and *Jingjie* are the first two illustrated Christian books printed in China. Interior settings on some illustrations are different from their European templates and they are replaced by constructing a Ming period ambience, so that the cultural distance between biblical history and the Chinese reader could be bridged and the Chinese could receive and understand biblical themes easily.

Landscape is an important subject in traditional Chinese literati painting. Landscapes in *Guicheng* are depicted in Chinese literati style and show stylistic similarity with the woodblock prints in Huizhou. Because in China, landscape painting was cultivated by the politically or economically powerful literary elite, it occupied the highest rank in the hierarchy of painting genres. Because of the higher status of landscape painting, it is less influenced by foreign painting.[19] Therefore, the Jesuits used the traditional Chinese style in landscape painting, in order to approach Chinese literati and officials.

Since the fourteenth century, the terminology of *convenevolezza*, i.e. the application of contemporary costume and theater designs in the artistic representation of historical narratives, was much discussed in Italian art circles.[20] Jesuit missionaries also were familiar with this concept. In the seventeenth century, soon after the beginning of their missionary activities in China, the Jesuits chose this artistic method for conveying Christian ideas to the Chinese more effectively. This can be seen in their biblical illustrations for the Chinese public.

Not only through the Chinese contemporary costumes, furniture, decorations, but also through the added *Bildsujet* (depicted subject) and the landscape depiction in traditional Chinese style, the historic and cultural distances were bridged. The life of Jesus was translocated and took place in a Chinese milieu in the seventeenth century. The *convenevolezza*, which is fixed in Confucian soil in *Guicheng* and *Jingjie*, reflects the Jesuits' attempt to be close to the ethics and aesthetics of Confucianism, which was dominant and influential in the society of the late Ming period. Through this approach, the Jesuits wanted to gain the acceptance of Christianity first by the educated and then to promote their missionary work further through the upper class. From an artistic aspect, these two books revealed Jesuits' accommodation policy at the beginning of their Chinese missionary activities.

The robust understanding of the biblical text by the Jesuits translated to the use of images and word-pictures as a vehicle of communion with Christ and the gospel event. This suggests the Jesuit's confidence and aspiration to translate the European biblical interpretation into the Chinese context and artistic style for the sake of the new audience of the literati in China. For the Jesuits, this is how the Word/*Logos* is incarnated pictorially—taking on the Chinese body of artistic expression—full of grace and truth to the elite class.

APPENDIX

FIGURE 28.1 "The Annunciation," in *Song nianzhu guicheng*, ca. 1620, Nanjing, Archivum Romanum Societatis Iesu (Jap. Sin. I, 43b).

FIGURE 28.2 "The Annunciation," in *Evangelicae Historiae Imagines* (Rome, 1593), plate 1.

FIGURE 28.3 "Foot washing" (literally: Lessons of humility by foot washing 濯足垂訓), in *Jingjie*, 1637, Fuzhou, Bibliothek National de France, Chinois 6750.

FIGURE 28.4 "The Visitation," in *Song nianzhu guicheng*, Archivum Romanum Societatis Iesu (Jap. Sin. I, 43b).

FIGURE 28.5 "The Visitation," in *Evangelicae Historiae Imagines* (Rome, 1593), plate 2.

FIGURE 28.6 "Last Supper" (literally: Holy Communion ceremony 立聖體大禮), in *Jingjie*, 1637, Fuzhou, Bibliothek National de France, Chinois 6750.

FIGURE 28.7 "The encounter of Jesus with the sinner" (literally: Absolution of the guilty woman 赦悔罪婦), in *Jingjie*, 1637, Fuzhou, Bibliothek National de France, Chinois 6750.

FIGURE 28.8 "The parable of the rich man and the poor Lazarus" (literally: Different retribution of the poor and the rich 貧富死後殊報), in *Jingjie*, 1637, Fuzhou, Bibliothek National de France, Chinois 6750.

FIGURE 28.9 "Agony in the garden of Gethsemane," in *Song nianzhu guicheng*, Archivum Romanum Societatis Iesu (Jap. Sin. I, 43b).

FIGURE 28.10 "Agony in the garden of Gethsemane," in *Evangelicae Historiae Imagines* (Rome, 1593), plate 107.

FIGURE 28.11 "The Crucifixion," in *Song nianzhu guicheng*, Archivum Romanum Societatis Iesu (Jap. Sin. I, 43b).

FIGURE 28.12 "The Assumption," in *Song nianzhu guicheng*, Archivum Romanum Societatis Iesu (Jap. Sin. I, 43b).

FIGURE 28.13 "The Crucifixion," in *Evangelicae Historiae Imagines* (Rome, 1593), plate 130.

FIGURE 28.14 "The Assumption," in *Evangelicae Historiae Imagines* (Rome, 1593), plate 148.

FIGURE 28.15 "The Announcement of the Birth of John the Baptist" (literally: Saint John was bred before the Lord of Heaven 聖若翰先天主而孕), in *Jingjie*, 1637, Fuzhou, Bibliothek National de France, Chinois 6750.

FIGURE 28.16 "The parable of the Pharisee and customs," in *Evangelicae Historiae Imagines* (Rome, 1593), plate 90.

Notes

1. Pasquale M. D'Elia, *Le origini dell'arte cristiana cinese (1583–1640)* (Rome: Accademia d'Italia, 1939), 57–66; Richard Hadl, Rezension zu D'Elia "Le origini dell'arte cristiana cinese (1583–1640)," [Roma 1939], *Artibus Asiae* 9 (1946): 237–238.
2. Ignatius von Loyola, *Exercitia spiritualia* (Rome: Antonio Blado, 1548).
3. Jerónimo Nadal, *Evangelicae historiae imagines. Ex ordine Evangeliorum, quae toto anno in Missae sacrificio recitantur; in ordinem temporis vitae Christi digestae* (Antwerpen: Martinus Nutius, 1593).
4. Cf. Rong Zhenghua 榮振華, *Zai Hua Yesuhuishi liezhuan ji shumu bubian* [in Chinese] 在華耶穌會士列傳及書目補編, trans. Geng Sheng 耿昇 (Beijing: Zhonghua shuju, 1995), 186–187.
5. See Pasquale M. D'Elia, *Le origini dell'arte Cristiana cinese (1583–1640)* (Rome: Accademia d'Italia, 1939), 67–121; Monique Cohen, Nathalie Monnet, *Impressions de Chine. Catalogue rédigé par Monique Cohen et Nathalie Monnet. Exposition présentée dans la Galerie Colbert de la Bibliothèque nationale du 8 septembre au 6 décembre 1992* (Paris: Bibliothèque nationale, 1992); Gauvin Alexander Bailey, *Art in the Jesuit Missions in Asia and Latin-America, 1542–1773* (Toronto: University of Toronto Press, 1999), Lin Xiaoping, "Seeing the Place: The Virgin Mary in a Chinese Lady's Inner Chamber," in *Early Modern Catholicism: Essays in Honour of John W. O'Malley*, ed. Kathleen M. Comerford-Hilmer M. Pabel (Toronto: University of Toronto Press, 2001), 182–210; Chen Hui-Hung, "A European Distinction of Chinese Characteristics. A Style Question in Seventeenth-Century Jesuit China Missions," *Taiwan Journal of East Asian Studies* 5.1 (June 2008): 1–32; Qu Yi, "Song nianzhuguicheng (Die Anweisung zur Rezitation des Rosenkranzes) Ein illustriertes christliches Buch aus China vom 17. Jahrhunderts," *Monumenta serica* 60 (2012): 195–290; Jeremy Clarke, *The Virgin Mary and Catholic Identities in Chinese History* (Hong Kong: Hong Kong University Press, 2013), 13–14; Rui Oliveira Lopes, "L'art dans les missions jésuites en Chine. Une édition illustrée du xviie siècle de la Méthode de prière du Rosaire," *Histoire De L'Art* (Asie-Occident) 82 (2018): 141–154; Xiao Qinghe 肖清和, "Hermeneutic and Change" Quan shi yu qi bian [in Chinese] 詮釋與歧變：耶穌形象在明清社會裡的傳播及其反應), in *Guangdong shehui kexue* (廣東社會科學) 4 (2011): 137–147; Chu Xiaobai 褚瀟白, *Rhetoric of Icons* [in Chinese] Shengxiang de xiuci 聖像的修辭: 耶穌基督形象在明清民間社會的變遷 (Beijing: China Academy of Social Science, 2011).
6. Archivum Romanum Societatis Iesu, Rome (Jap. Sin. I, 43b); Biblioteca nazionale central di Roma, Rome (Fondo Gesuitico 72.B.298); Biblioteca Apostalica Vaticana, Vatican City (Borgia Cinese 336.5); Bibliotheque Nationale de France, Paris (Chinois 7382, 6861); Österreichische Nationalbibliothek, Wien (Sin. 1607); Getty Research Institute Los Angeles (Research Library 1374–1445).
7. Secondary literature before 2007, see Nicolas Standaert, *An Illustrated Life of Christ Presented to the Chinese Emperor. The History of Jincheng shuxiang (1640)* (Sankt Augustin, Nettetal: Steyler Verlag, 2007), 14n10. Secondary literature from 2008 onward, see: Chen Hui-Hung, *Preaching Christ in Late Ming China. The Jesuits' Presentation of Christ from Matteo Ricci to Giulio Aleni* (Taipei: Ricci Institute, in collaboration with Fondazione Civiltà Bresciana, 1997); Chen Hui-Hung, "A European Distinction of Chinese Characteristics," 1–32; Junhyoung Michael Shin, "The Reception of the '*Evangelicae historiae imagines*' in Late Ming China: Visualizing Holy Topography in Jesuit Spirituality and Pure Land Buddhism," *Sixteenth Century Journal* 40.2 (2009): 303–333; Junhyoung Michael Shin, "The Supernatural

in the Jesuit Adaptation to Confucianism: Giulio Aleni's Tianzhu jiangsheng chuxiang jingjie [in Chinese] 天主降生出像經解 (Fuzhou, 1637)," *History of Religions* 50.4 (2011): 329–361; Junhyoung Michael Shin, "Jesuit Mnemonics and Topographic Narrative: '*Evangelicae Historiae Imagines*' in Late Ming China (Fuzhou, 1637)," *Archiv für Reformationsgeschichte* 103 (2012): 237–271; Junhyoung Michael Shin, "The Jesuits and the Portrait of God in Late Ming China," *Harvard Theological Review* 107.2 (April 2014): 194–221; Mateo Borao/Eugenio José, "La version china de la obra ilustrada de Jerónimo Nadal 'Evangelicae historiae imagines,'" *Revista Goya* 330 (2010): 16–33; Qu Yi, "Konfuzianische Convenevolezza in chinesischen christlichen Illustrationen. Das Tianzhu jiangsheng chuxiang jingjie von 1637," *Asiatische Studien* 66.4 (2012): 1001–1030.

8. Following exemplares of *Jingjie* are preserved in European libraries: Archivum Romanum Societatis Iesu (Jap. Sin. I, 187, 188); Bibliothèque nationale de France, Paris (Chinois 6750; OE 166); Bodleian Library, Oxford (Sinica 60); Franciscan Archive, Madrid (26/2); Biblioteca Apostolica Vaticana (Raccolta Prima III 339; Rossiani Stampati 3476; Borgia Cinese 410; Borgia Cinese 443 [1]; Barberini Oriente III, 134 [1]; Raccolta Generale Oriente III 226 [3], III 247 [6] and [7]).
9. The space of this print was surpassed until 1887 by a printed work with the same title, which contains 146 illustrations after Abbe Pierre Florentin Lambert Brispot's reproduction of Nadal and is a part of the collection of six Catholic works titled *Daoyuan jingcui* [in Chinese] 道原精萃 (*The Essence of the Writings about the Fundamental Teaching*).
10. Cf. Gianni Criveller, *Preaching Christ in Late Ming China. The Jesuits' Presentation of Christ from Matteo Ricci to Giulio Aleni* (Taipei: Ricci Institute Variétés Sinologiques, Fondazione Civiltá Bresciana-Annali, 1997): 239; Standaert, *An Illustrated Life of Christ Presented to the Chinese Emperor*, 14–15.
11. In the comments, under the letter D is to read: "*cubiculum, quod visitur laureti agro piceno, ubi est mary*," which means: "room, also can be seen in the region Laureti, where Mary lives." The small village Laureti (Italy) in the vicinity of Recinata in the region Piceno is still a pilgrimage site for many Christians.
12. Wu Hung, *The Double Screen: Medium and Representation in Chinese Painting* (Chicago: University of Chicago Press, 1996), 9.
13. Lothar Ledderose, *Ten Thousand Things: Module and Mass Production in Chinese Art* (Princeton: Princeton University Press, 2000), 164–185.
14. "In this kingdom they make much of antique things; and yet they have no statues nor medals.... But more than all these things are valued paintings by famous persons, without color, but in ink alone; or letters by ancient writers on paper or on cloth, with their seals to confirm that they are genuine" (Translation after Craig Clunas, *Art in China. Oxford History of Art* [Oxford: Oxford University Press, 1997], 151–156). Cf. Pasquale M. D'Elia, *Fonti Ricciane. Documenti originali concernenti Matteo Ricci e la storia delle prime relazioni tra l'Europa e la Cina (1582–1597)* (Rome: Libreria dello Stato, 1942), 1:91.
15. Wu Hung, *The Double Screen: Medium and Representation in Chinese Painting* (Chicago: University of Chicago Press, 1996), 187.
16. Jonathan Hay, *Sensuous Surfaces: The Decorative Object in Early Modern China* (Honolulu: University of Hawai'i Press, 2010), 21.
17. With regard to the depiction of the life of Confucius see: Julia K. Murray, "The Temple of Confucius and Pictorial Biographies of the Sage," *Journal of Asian Studies* 55.2 (1996): 269–300; Julia K. Murray, "Illustrations of the Life of Confucius: Their Evolution, Functions, and Significance in Late Ming China," *Artribus Asiae* 57.1–2 (1997): 73–134; Julia K. Murray,

Mirror of Morality: Chinese Narrative Illustration and Confucian Ideology (Honolulu: University of Hawai'i Press, 2007).

18. Cf. Sima Qian 司馬遷, *Shiji* 史記 (*Records of the Grand Historian*), Cap. 47: "Kongzi shijia" 孔子世家 (Confucius family).
19. Lothar Ledderose, "Chinese Influence on European Art, Sixteenth to Eighteenth Centuries," in *China and Europe: Images and Influences in Sixteenth to Eighteenth Centuries*, ed. Thomas H. C. Lee, Institute of Chinese Studies Monograph Series (Hong Kong: The Chinese University Press, 1991), 221.
20. Reiner Haussherr, *Convenevolezza. Historische Angemessenheit in der Darstellung von Kostüm und Schauplatz seit der Spätantike bis ins 16. Jahrhundert* (Wiesbaden: Steiner, 1984), 11.

Primary Sources

Anonymous. "Whiling away the summer" (*Xiaoxia tu* 消夏圖). The Palace Museum, Beijing. Ink and color on silk. [Early Ming dynasty.]

Anonymous artist at the Tang dynasty (608–907). "Amusement in the Palace" (*Gongle tu* 宮樂圖). National Palace Museum Taipei, Taiwan. Color on silk. [Tang dynasty.]

(Attributed to) Liu Songnian 劉松年 (ca. 1155–1218). "The eighteen scholars" (*Shiba xueshi tu* 十八學士圖). National Palace Museum, Taipei, Taiwan. A copy of Ming dynasty, section of a handscroll, ink and color of silk. [Ming dynasty.]

Ma Hezhi 馬和之 (1131–1162). "Dissemination of perfect virtue" (*Guang zhi de* 廣至德). National Palace Museum, Taipei, Taiwan. 13th chapter of the Classic "Book of Finial Piety" (*Xiao jing* 孝經), a section of a handscroll, ink and color on silk.

Qiu Ying 仇英 (ca. 1482–1559). "High officials play chess" (*Gaoshi ti tu* 高仕棋圖). Shanghai Museum. Album, ink and color on paper. [Ming dynasty.]

Rong Zhenghua 榮振華. *Zai Hua Yesuhuishi liezhuan ji shumu bubian* 在華耶穌會士列傳及書目補編. Translated by Geng Sheng 耿昇. Beijing: Zhonghua shuju, 1995. [A Chinese translation of: Joseph Dehergne, *Répertoire des jésuites de Chine de 1552 à 1800*].

Song nianzhu guicheng 誦念珠規程 (*Rules for Reciting the Rosary*, henceforth: *Guicheng*). Nanjing: João da Rocha, ca. 1620. [Archivum Romanum Societatis Iesu.]

Tang Yin 唐寅 (1470–1524). "Han Xizai evening banquet" (*Han xizai yeyan tu* 韓熙載夜宴圖). Chongqing Municipal Museum. Ink and color on silk. [Ming dynasty.]

Tianzhu jiangsheng chuxiang jingjie 天主降生出像經解 (*Explanation of the Canonical Book about the Lord of Heaven's Incarnation with Selected Images*). Fuzhou: Giulio Aleni, 1637. [Bibliothek National de France.]

Von Loyola, Ignatius. *Exercitia spiritualia.* Rome: Antonio Blado, 1548.

Wang Qihan 王齊翰. "Collation of books" (*Kanshu tu* 勘書圖), handscroll, ink and color on silk. Nanjing University Library. [Tenth Century.]

CHAPTER 29

CHRISTIAN BIBLICAL TRADITION IN THE *JING* CHINESE CULTURE

YANRONG CHEN

INTRODUCTION

EUROPEAN missionaries in the early modern period arrived in China in the second half of the sixteenth century. However, when European vernacular-language Bibles emerged apart from the Latin Vulgate Bible, the China mission still lacked a Chinese Bible. The practice of translating the Bible began in the early stage but only led to incomplete or unpublished translations in the end. The simple fact can be surveyed by examining a series of individual efforts, including translations of sections of the Old Testament by Antonio Laghi F.M. and Francesco Jovino F.M. (1677–1737), the only published book of Tobit by François Xavier d'Entrecolles S.J. (1664–1741), a partial set of the New Testament books by Jean Basset M.E.P. (1662–1707), and the most complete version of the Bible except for some prophetic books done by Louis de Poirot S.J. (1735–1813).[1] These manuscripts were denied publication and not even used at that time.

Nevertheless, the expression of the Bible in Chinese was not limited to a translation of the book. Biblical contents were vastly and effectively integrated into Chinese culture, and biblical interpretations were intertwined with the realms of literature, images, ritual, and everyday life.[2] As far as biblical words are concerned, pieces and bits of the Bible can be found in numerous Chinese Christian texts that were composed in different language styles and literary forms. Selected gospel readings and epistles for use in liturgy had appeared already in numerous Chinese texts. Our understanding of those Christian texts within the conventional frame of Chinese translations of the Bible is thus disrupted because there is not an existing category or protocol to describe them.

This alternative perspective presents seemingly contradictory facts that raise a question about "text" and "translation." "Text" is a cultural device, especially given the weight of written culture in Chinese history. On the other hand, "translation" in its modern sense is a practice or process of a masterpiece being translated into a book for Chinese appreciation of the European Catholic biblical literature; yet, it cannot immediately fit into the history of Christianity being introduced into the Chinese language. The "translation" of the Bible was, in fact, a process of producing, circulating, printing, distributing, reprinting, and reproducing a mass of texts, the Chinese Christian texts that continuously conveyed biblical words and messages to Chinese audiences. Following this inquiry is the discovery of transformations of the Bible into a wide range of texts, from recording sermons and prayer books to handbooks for performing and attending rituals to manuals for guiding spiritual exercises. These were important to the literary interests and everyday devotional life of Chinese Christians.

These Chinese Christian texts delivered biblical words and messages from the late sixteenth through the eighteenth centuries. Overall, they collectively comprised a textual foundation of Chinese reception of the Bible. One primary mechanism of the emergence of these texts was the integration of the biblical tradition into a Chinese culture of *jing* 經. The Chinese character, although having more vibrant and more complex connotations, often is referred in English as "classics" and "Scriptures." I use "sacred texts" as an equivalent phrase because it allows more space for preserving the inclusion of the character's meanings and more possibilities for comparing different traditions—in which the current dual-focused emphasis on the Christian Bible in China is involved.[3] The next section of this essay will elaborate on the birth of a Christian biblical tradition in the Chinese culture of sacred texts.

In order to give these Chinese Christian sacred texts the place they deserve, this essay showcases some examples. A methodological challenge emerges due to the diverse genres of Chinese Christian texts that expressed the Bible. It is difficult, if not impossible, to account for each sacred text in either the convention of the European Catholic or Chinese literary history, certainly not promising to detail Chinese Christian sacred texts that innately had textual features representing both sides. Moreover, the majority of the Chinese Christian sacred texts cannot fit precisely into existing modern categories of either European genres (e.g., commentaries, liturgical books, manuals of spiritual exercises, an illustrated life of Christ) or Chinese genres (e.g., primers, poetry, scholarly treatises), at least not without a process for understanding their textuality. My presentation of individual texts endeavors to check its genre against Christian literature in the European Catholic tradition as well as to explain textual features that corresponded to the inherent plasticity of the Chinese culture of sacred texts. Sometimes, a text's contents, forms, and styles resonate in both traditions.

This essay first outlines the formation of Christian discourse in the Chinese *jing* culture; afterward, it outlines a series of types and demonstrates them with examples. Each section of this essay presents a type of Christian sacred texts. Like all literature, the particular form of any text is shaped by the needs and issues of its own world and thus is resistant to any ahistorical classification of genres. I identify the types of Chinese Christian sacred texts by recognizing their biblical contents and forms of composition, with an emphasis on their purposes to Chinese audiences and their Christian religiosity. Organizing these types in clusters provides a possible way to understand their composition, but the organization itself does not claim to be a typological categorization of Chinese

Christian sacred texts, and delineating each section remains flexible and negotiable. The goal is to outline a broad but clear spectrum constituted by these texts case by case, in order to provide an insight into the diversity and inclusion of Chinese Christian sacred texts.

Chinese Christian Sacred Texts Born in Chinese Culture of *Jing*

Sacred texts exist and develop in different traditions and cultures with every tradition's own cultural underpinnings. The role of the Bible in the church tradition in early modern Europe, in fact, did not exactly match the status of scriptures, canons, and classics across other traditions in China or, more generally, in East Asia.[4] For instance, the notion of the Bible as Holy Scripture in Christianity means that the Bible is a complete set of the doctrine that is central to the faithful and their religious life and that it has the authority to regulate the belief system as the ultimate source of truth through revelation. In China, the authority of a sacred text can be claimed in different ways, and the process of recognizing its authority intertwines with historical conditions, and reaching a consensus on which text is a sacred text is flexible but can take a long time. Canonization of a sacred text always comes with critical examination and doubts to a certain degree. The forms of sacred texts vary as well. There is not a single work in the Confucian, Buddhist, or Daoist tradition that has an exclusive place and can be directly compared with the status of the Bible in Christianity.[5]

Sacred texts in China speak for a cultural phenomenon, and the idea of sacred texts has developed in history.[6] Understanding the role of sacred texts in the Chinese context has to start with its language. The Chinese word for "sacred texts" is *jing* 經, a character having its etymological origin in textiles. The first meaning of this character denotes the fixed lead thread or warp of cloth, insofar as the weft threads are woven into warp threads to make a fabric. Its extended meaning refers to authority, orthodoxy, and the essential way toward truth and principle. Confucianism became the official ideology in China before Christ was born, and clusters of Confucian classics changed from five titles to thirteen titles as more and more commentaries upon classical texts emerged and were respectfully endorsed as canons too in later periods.[7] Other schools, such as the Legalists, the Mohists, and medical schools, also had their own *jing* texts. Religious traditions—including both native Daoism and alien Buddhism that was introduced to China from India—had been producing various types of *jing* all along. The term for Sanskrit sutra in Chinese is *jing*, and the Daoist canons starting from *Daodejing* (transliterated also as *Tao Te Ching*) adopts the very same word. One difference from dominant Confucianism is that a large body of Buddhist and Daoist *jing* is transmitted both orally and in writing, in both literary and vernacular Chinese, carrying out not only religious teachings but also rituals and exercises. Popular or folk religions in China have a similar scenario.[8]

To Chinese literati, uneducated commoners, ritual experts, and laity, *jing* had different meanings across different traditions in different contexts. Confucian *jing* constituted the curriculum for Chinese students to study, to recite, and to write exegesis. Widely spreading Buddhist and Daoist *jing* for religious practitioners vastly enriched the scholarly denotations of this term *jing*. As a whole, activities associated with *jing* involved copying, transcribing, disseminating, citing, reciting, printing, writing commentaries, and more. Vocabularies derived from the culture of *jing* thus have proliferated in everyday Chinese language. The Chinese character *jing* is variously translated into English at the expense of losing its cultural connotations. Given its complexity, as seen in all the traditions in China, I adopt a compound collocation of "sacred texts" to take into account the role of *jing* in Chinese literary culture as a whole.

Therefore, what the Catholic missionaries encountered was a contemporaneous Chinese culture of sacred texts that encompassed different domains. When the pioneer Jesuits Michele Ruggieri S.J. (1543–1607) and Matteo Ricci S.J. (1552–1610) arrived in late Ming China by the end of the sixteenth century, the entire Chinese society in general was immersed in the culture of sacred texts. They confronted the prevailing sacred texts across different traditions. Having come from the biblical discourse in the church tradition, the missionaries soon became acquainted with the significance of sacred texts to Chinese literati who studied them. Already at the very beginning of his arrival in 1595, Ricci started learning the six Confucian classics.[9] It was not long before they learned of other religions' sacred texts, such as the Buddhist sūtra and Daoist prayers.

European missionaries, in collaboration with their Chinese contacts, found a way to express biblical messages and words by imitating Confucian literary works, sometimes by mirroring Buddhist and Daoist texts used in religious practice. Although they had to bridge the gap in intercultural hermeneutics between the Christian biblical tradition and the imperative Chinese culture, it was possible for them to use creativity and flexibility at a certain level to produce Chinese Christian discourse in the hybrid culture of Chinese sacred texts while retaining the church's authority. They came up with a Christian discourse of *jing* in order to claim Chinese Christian sacred texts, in an attempt to empower Christian literature and give it due credit and to assume their position in the mainstream Chinese traditions.

The impact of bringing a new minor tradition of Christianity into the non-Christian context as part of the Chinese *jing* culture is significant. It is evident that the Christian conversion of Chinese often was referred to as accepting Christian sacred texts, expressed as "*lingjing* 領經," "*chengjing* 承經," or "*shoujing* 受經" in Chinese.[10] With these words, Chinese convert Fan Zhong 范中 claimed his Christian identity.[11] Chinese Christians through the nineteenth century were exposed to such a tradition, having access to biblical contents, although without an authorized Chinese Bible.[12] Non-Christian and anti-Christian groups even recognized the presence of Christian discourse in generic Chinese sacred texts.

Echoing the diverse genres of sacred texts in other religious traditions in China—as in Daoism, *jing* included written prayers, dispatches, certificates, commands, and talismans, and Buddhist *jing* ranged from sutra to commentaries, from mantra to precepts—various types of Christian sacred texts were produced and circulated during the two hundred years.[13] It is difficult to describe their features collectively, for some originated from the European Catholic tradition, while others were inspired by specific forms of Chinese writing. All of them were indebted to European missionaries and Chinese workers, including collaborative writers, revisers, correctors, carvers, publishers, and religious leaders. Examples of these works will be introduced in the following sections.

Commentaries Accompanying Bible Verses

Writing a commentary on existing classics and scriptures is a universal practice in all traditions of sacred texts, the same as it is in Christian literature and other traditions in China. A significant creation of Chinese Christian work in this regard is a large-volume book titled *Shengjing zhijie* 聖經直解 (*Straight Explanation of Sacred Scriptures*). The book of *Shengjing zhijie* was composed by Portuguese missionary Manuel Dias S.J. (Jr) (1574–1659) and published between 1636 and 1642. Since then, it has received broad readership and has proved to be versatile for readers.

The book of *Shengjing zhijie* increasingly has become known in recent years in the history of the Chinese Bible.[14] Its nature as the most comprehensive and exemplary work of Christian sacred texts calls for more scholarly attention. The content of this book covers biblical narratives, verses, and references. The variety of biblical content is shaped primarily in two forms: Scripture and commentaries. The section of Scripture includes precisely translated Bible verses selectively arranged according to the regulation of gospel readings on Sundays and major feast days over a liturgical year. Accompanying the Bible verses are commentaries formed with two specific formats of Chinese commentary writing: numerous interlinear annotations to explain words and biblical references and long commentaries to govern potential interpretations of the gospel readings.

This book was valued highly among interllectuals as it took into account Chinese scholarly conventions for Christian Bible verses. For rendering the gospel verses, it adopted literary written Chinese, a high style of literature and classics. In writing, for both interlinear annotations and long commentaries, it prepared rich and persuasive expositions. The sophisticated language use and writing form in the book of *Shengjing zhijie* provided literary readers access to the vast Christian biblical and exegetical tradition.

Moreover, this book was designed carefully with respect to its paratextual elements, editorial apparatus, and printed presentation, having great potential to meet the various needs of different audiences. The section of Bible verses could be used for multiple purposes, as of gospel readings in liturgical contexts or studying practices. The commentaries also could be used by ritual experts for exegesis references while preparing sermons. In the absence of a Chinese-language Bible, the book of *Shengjing zhijie* stood out for conveying comprehensive biblical contents to Chinese audiences.

Possessing all of these textual features, *Shengjing zhijie* became a Christian sacred text useful to readers of diverse backgrounds. It had a wide circulation and long-term impact upon later Chinese Christians, leading them to research into theology or other matters concerning Christianity. The entire book was studied and cited by later Christian scholars. It was often recommended in other books as one of the essential elements of Christian literature. Some suggested it for learning Christian teachings, and some prescribed where and when to read it. Non-Christian scholars too referred to the book of *Shengjing zhijie* as a vital source for them to learn of biblical chronology and Christian worldviews. Missionaries—not only Jesuits—critically reviewed the book of *Shengjing zhijie* and agreed that it was an outstanding work. From a reception perspective, being recognized among missionaries demonstrated its status as a classic of Christian sacred texts.

Beyond the Christian community, the book of *Shengjing zhijie* represented a Christian book that could ascend to the level of Chinese sacred text, substantiating a Christian discourse comparable to other traditions in China. One textual feature, among other factors that leveraged its role, is the commentary writing developed therein. Another book *Guxin Shengjing* 古新聖經 (*Old and New Holy Scriptures*) compiled by the end of the eighteenth century also continued this writing form.

The book of *Guxin shengjing*, authored by Louis de Poirot S.J. (1735–1813), is considered famous for its comprehensiveness in translating the Old and New Testaments into Chinese.[15] What has been missing in previous studies is a proper understanding of various commentaries included in this book. The book of *Guxin shengjing* actually followed along the line of Christian sacred texts; the commentaries accompanying Bible verses take up more than half of the book. The down-to-earth commentary methods adopted in the book of *Guxin shengjing* were very simple, basically written for pastoral needs and ordinary audiences without scholarly training. It was based on the reason Louis Poirot used to justify his choice of everyday language on the street, considered effective for spreading the gospel to commoners.

Although Louis Poirot used the colloquial Chinese of his time to translate Bible verses, a style distinct from the erudite language of *Shengjing zhijie*, the preferences in language style did not undermine their shared editorial principle. In terms of literary composition, the book of *Guxin shengjing* followed the commentary convention initiated by *Shengjing zhijie*, despite their differences in adopting either a high-culture or low-culture approach. By accompanying Bible verses with commentaries, both works stood for Chinese Christian sacred texts. Their shared purpose was to add commentaries to assure the authority of the Bible verses, to guide readers' interpretations of the words, and to claim Christian sacred texts in the indigenous Chinese culture.

Manuals Regarding Rituals and Exercises

While gospel verses could be useful in different contexts of religious practice, there is another cluster of Christian sacred texts particularly made for use in liturgy and spiritual exercises. These works echoed the indigenous traditions in China as well. Buddhist rituals had sacred texts for performing rites (e.g., *zhaiwen* 齋文 and *zhuanjing wen* 轉經文) and for making confession (e.g., *chanwen* 懺文). Texts of similar use were dispersed in Daoist rituals too (e.g., *daowen* 導文 and *sanhua ci* 散花詞). In this regard, a handful of Christian works for one to conduct and to attend liturgy were prepared, such as the Chinese Breviary titled *Rike gaiyao* 日課概要 (1674) and a Chinese manual of the ministry of sacraments titled *Shengshi lidian* 聖事禮典 (1675). More texts for praying and meditation practice also came along. Although they were not authorized by Rome at that time, these works formed a concrete collection of canons for Chinese liturgy, representing Christian rituals and practices in the Chinese context.

Among other liturgical works, the Missal called *Misa jingdian* 彌撒經典 (*Classic and Canon on Mass*) in the Chinese language was completed in 1670. Following *Missale Romanum* (1570), this book was published as a ritual manual to prepare Chinese native clergies for performing the liturgy.[16] As *Missale Romanum* prescribed the mass in the European Catholic, the book of *Misa jingdian* showed what kind of a mass Chinese Christians could possibly celebrate, from a textual perspective. Generally speaking, the European and Chinese editions of the missal had the same principle for visualizing and regulating the stages and process of the mass, but with distinct formats to present the ritual as featured in its own cultures. For example, the Roman missal had headings printed in red (*rubrica*) to guide its users, in contrast to engravings of the rest of the text in black. The Chinese missal was carved all in black woodblock printing, but it used different sizes of Chinese characters. It created "rubric marks" with a purposeful arrangement of differently sized characters to signify their textual functions during the mass.

Mirroring the Roman missal in every aspect, the Chinese book *Misa jingdian* also rendered readings from the Bible in the Chinese language, which included passages from the epistles called "*jingshu* 經書" in Chinese, verses from the Gospels called "*wanrilüe jing* 萬日略經," offertory prayers that are generally referred to as "*zhuwen* 祝文", and hymns from the book of Psalms translated as "*shengyong* 聖詠" in Chinese. These texts presented the main difficulty in making the Chinese missal, as its author Lodovico Buglio S.J. (1660–1682) expressed in his own words.[17]

The gospel readings in this book were, in fact, copied with revisions from the Bible verse commentaries in the book *Shengjing zhijie*, as mentioned above. Buglio's use of *Shengjing zhijie* was not an isolated instance; Joseph A. M. de Moyriac de Mailla S.J. (1669–1748) also took the available Chinese translation of the Bible verses directly from *Shengjing zhijie* in creating his meditation book for daily life *Shengjing guangyi* 聖經廣益 (*Wider Benefit from the Sacred Scriptures*).[18] *Shengjing guangyi* was published in 1740, and it provided guidelines for spiritual exercises and meditations upon Bible verses. If gospel readings throughout a liturgical year were needed, later missionaries already knew that the earlier sacred text, *Shengjing zhijie*, was their source to rely upon.

In the European tradition of Christian literature, the texts of litany, rosary, and other texts for spiritual exercises belong to devotional works. To Chinese clergies and other kinds of religious leaders in local communities, the books of liturgy, like *Misa jingdian*, prescribed what ritual experts should do and say, and how to do it and to say it, and thus these were sacred texts. The faithful also were taught to follow strictly the instructions about what to meditate on, how to meditate, why to meditate and how to do daily exercises. These works, as another integral part of Christian sacred texts, were valued very highly by practicing Christians because the words contained therein, such as prayers and hymns, were repetitively framed in the forms of indigenous Chinese sacred texts, and Christians were familiar with them. The Christian books containing various prayers were catechetical, a concept that will be introduced in the next section.

Handbooks to Foster Routine Religiosity

From the beginning of the China mission, missionaries had to respond to the Chinese demand for Western sacred texts.[19] Also in order to meet pastoral needs when there was not a Chinese Bible, a large number of educational books—including fundamental doctrines and prayers—emerged to guide new conversion and to help converted Christians maintain their Christian religiosity. These works had catechetical compositions in nature but were not limited to the catechism in a modern sense, at least not the catechism characterized by the modern church.[20] They included a wide range of Christian books, borrowing forms from Buddhist and Daoist sacred texts and providing guidance for learning Christian doctrines and explanations of religious practice.

The earliest catechetical text in this cluster was derived from *Doctrina Christiana*. Matteo Ricci composed *Tianzhu jiaoyao* 天主教要 (*Essential Teachings of the Lord of Heaven*) in 1605 to present a full account of Christian truth to converts and Christians-to-be.[21] Contained in this book were basic prayers such as the Our Father, Hail Mary, and Ten Commandments, common prayers and doctrines, which were considered as primary Christian counterparts to Buddhist prayers and disciplines. In the following years, this book was revised and published under the title *Shengjing yüelu* 聖經約錄 (*Concise Records of Holy Texts*). The new title was widely distributed all over the country, and books following this trend were increasingly produced. Some focused on single prayers—like the book on the rosary, *Song wuzhu yesu nianzhu moxiang guitiao* 誦吾主耶穌念珠默想規條 (*Rules for Reciting the Rosary and Meditating*) composed by Nicolo Longobardo S.J. (1559–1654)—whereas some collected prayers and instructions comprised one anthology, like a book of euchologion, *Shengjiao rike* 聖教日課 (*Daily Exercises of Holy Teaching*). Some were composed in the form of questions and answers, such as *Jingdian jilüe wenda* 經典紀略問答 (*Questions and Answers on the Records of Classics*), composed by Jean Basset M.E.P. (1662–1707).

These Christian sacred texts containing prayers and doctrines were popular.[22] On the one hand, they were in accordance with *Doctrina Christiana* of the church tradition; meanwhile, they mirrored non-Christian traditions of sacred texts in China. For example, a book focusing on the Lord's Prayer, *Tianzhu jingjie* 天主經解 (*Explanations to the Heavenly Lord's Prayer*), combined prayers and commentaries. The widely circulating *Tianzhu jingjie* was prepared by Giacomo Rho S.J. (1592–1638) around 1630 to 1635. The only sixty-seven-character Lord's Prayer was printed in the first chapter, and the rest of this book expounded on the prayer with commentaries from multiple perspectives in more than a hundred pages. Overall, the exposition in the book of *Tianzhu jingjie* made it an essential reference for anyone wanting to learn the Lord's Prayer.

Christian books of this type are usually of less interest to modern researchers, in comparison to the ones involving philosophical arguments. However, they were essential for converts and their Christian religiosity. Corresponding to the constituents of the indigenous Chinese culture of sacred texts, each piece of Christian doctrine and prayer was referred to as a sacred text. Individual items that were already rendered into Chinese by the late seventeenth century included, but not limited to, *Tianzhu jing* 天主經 (Our Father or the Lord's Prayer), *Tianshen chao tianzhu shengmu jing* 天神朝天主聖母經 (the Hail Mary, or *salutatio angelica*), *Tianzhu shijie* 天主十誡 (the Ten Commandments or the Decalogue), *Shi er yabosiduoluo xing bo lu* 十二亞玻斯多羅性薄錄 (the Apostole's Creed of the Twelve Apostles, or *Symbolum [duodecim] Apostolorum*), *Shenghao jing* 聖號經 (the Prayer of the Sign of the Cross), *Xingshen aijin zhixing shisiduan* 形神哀矜之行十四端 (the fourteen works of charity, in material/bodily and spiritual sphere), *Zhenfu baduan* 真福八端 (the Eight Beatitudes from the Sermon on the Mount), *Zuizong qiduan* 罪宗七端 (the Seven Capital Sins), *Kezui qiduan you qide* 克罪七端有七德 (the Seven Remedies or Opposing Virtues), *Xiang tianzhu you sande* 向天主有三德 (the Three Theological Virtues), *Shen you wusi* 身有五司 (the Five Senses of the Body), *Shen you sansi* 神有三司 (the Three Faculties of the Soul), *Egelexiya sagelamengduo you qi* 阨格勒西亞撒格辣孟多有七 (the Seven Sacraments, or *Ecclesiae Sacramenta*).[23]

The missionary Giulio Aleni s.j. (1582–1649) once highlighted five fundamental Christian doctrines as necessary items for examining one's soul. He selected *Xinjing* 信經 (the Credo), *Shijie* 十誡 (the Ten Commandments), *Aijin shisi duan* 哀矜十四端 (the Fourteen Works of Mercy), *Qike* 七克 (the Seven Victories), and finally, to complete [the account of] the Lord's grace, *Sagelamengduo zhi qi* 撒格辣孟多之七 (the Seven Sacraments).[24] These five were put in parallel with the Confucian "Five Classics," the compulsory materials for Confucian students to learn by heart in order to survive the civil examination.

To Chinese audiences, receiving Christian prayers and reciting those words by heart manifested one's conversion to Christianity. The recitation of repetitive Christian prayers was well adapted to Chinese forms of prayers, especially from the Buddhist tradition. Except for sūtra, the canonized scriptural texts that we are acquainted with, there are many other Buddhist genres for just saying prayers, such as *yuanwen* 願文 or *fayuan wen* 發願文 and *qingqi wen* 請啟文. These Buddhist texts used repetition of stereotyped forms and refrains; Christian prayers were composed in a similar pattern, repetitively and concisely. The beginning and end of every sentence often was structured with the same fixed phrases. They were written in colloquial Chinese, giving easy access to everyone, including the illiterate who could be taught to memorize and recite the prayers. A likely scenario is that Christian priests, clergies, catechumens, and practicing converts recited Christian prayers in a manner similar to what Buddhist ritual experts did with their prayers. This practice can be described as "*nianjing* 念經" or "*songjing* 誦經" in

Chinese. The reception of these Christian sacred texts that can be described as "*chengjing* 承經" or "*shoujing* 受經" signals one's Christian identity.

Catchy Primers of Biblical Narratives

Another group of catechetical Christian sacred texts was composed entirely by following regular forms of Chinese verses, totally beyond the scope of genres common to the European church tradition. In most cases, they were written in reoccurring rhymed verses to facilitate the learning process of pupils and adults with limited literacy. The composition of these books was an imitation of Confucian primers but were used for Christian education. While conveying Christian teachings, they made catechetical instruction of Christianity memorable so that biblical narratives could be effectively promoted and popularized among large audiences.

The most famous book of this type is *Sizi jingwen* 四字經文 (*Four-Character Classic Text*), authored by Guilio Aleni, as mentioned earlier.[25] The writing form of this book followed the pattern of a particular Chinese schoolbook, *Sanzi jing* 三字經 (*Three-Character Classic*). While *Sanzi jing* had three characters in a line, and every other line rhymed at the last character, *Sizi jingwen* was composed in the same format but with only four characters. Also, in parallel to *Sanzi jing* that imparted the elementary Confucian moral education and state ideology, the Christian *Sizi jingwen* succinctly recorded the life and deeds of Jesus, his teachings, the biblical chronology, and the historiography of creation and salvation.

A Chinese Christian, Yan Zanhua 嚴贊化, whose Christian name was Ambrose, composed a similar work titled *Shengjiao jianyu* 聖教簡語 (*Plain Words of Holy Teaching*) by following the same verse form with four characters in each line. The composition in rhymed doggerel was independent of and different from the book of *Sizi jingwen*.

Another book of this type incorporated other textual features, and it was again commentary. *Tianxue mengyin* 天學蒙引 (*Instruction of the Heavenly Learning*), probably by a Chinese Christian Zhou Zhi 周志, is an interesting work in this regard, although the existing scholarship has neglected this book's compilation. It was composed in rhymed verses with seven characters in a line, in combination with commentaries written in prose form accompanying the rhymed verses. The writing of commentaries bore a resemblance to abridged commentaries of Confucian classics for students preparing for the civil service examination.

Whether being written by European missionaries or Chinese Christians, with four or seven characters in a line, these three examples matched a typical writing model of Confucian classics for primary education in the traditional society. Such a composition may not escape the influences of the sacred texts of other religious traditions either; after all, Buddhism had created new writings and shaped the Chinese literary history from the second century. Buddhist chant and hymn called "*jisong* 偈頌" had become a form of Chinese poetry a thousand years ahead of European missionaries' arrival in China.

As far as this type of Christian sacred texts is concerned, it was prevalent among children, young pupils, illiterate or semi-illiterate adults, women, and the majority of the population who could not receive adequate education. The rhymes accelerated memorization, so readers could easily recite at least part of the book. Simple expressions and straightforward narration also made it easier for readers to comprehend biblical messages, helping to improve common folks' Christian literacy.

Images and Biography Writings Combined

Iconography is indispensable in Christianity. Images are part of the Chinese culture of sacred texts too, as Confucian and other religious traditions never fall short of drawing, carving, and painting practices as an expression of devotion. Buddhists are especially passionate in this faculty. At the time of the arrival of European missionaries, images often were inserted to make illustrated books, a fashion in the printing industry and the current Chinese book market. Some Chinese Christian sacred texts were produced in line with this fashion too. A perfect example of a creative continuation of the European church tradition in the Chinese book culture involves two interconnecting books prepared by the same aforementioned author Giulio Aleni, *Chuxiang jingjie* 出像經解 (*Explanation of Illustrated Classic*) and *Yanxing jilüe* 言行紀略 (*Abbreviated Records of Words and Deeds*).

The book of *Chuxiang jingjie* was famous to art historians in China and Europe, as it was based on the great *Evangelicae Historiae Imagines ex Ordine Evangeliorum, Quae Toto Anno in Missae Sacrificio Recitantur* of Jerónimo Nadal S.J. (1507–1580).[26] However, the editing of texts and images in this book diverged from those of European origin so they could better serve Chinese audiences' background and reading habits. In addition, the Chinese crafesmen employed the distinct techniques of woodblock carving. While choosing and rearranging illustrated pages from *Evangelicae Historiae Imagines*, the book of *Chuxiang jingjie* built up a general narration to coherently present the life circle of Jesus, along with select motifs in which Chinese audiences at the time were most interested. It contained a series of major events in a person's life in a chronological sequence (birth, circumcision, death), stories of miracles (the ministry of Jesus), the Catholic teachings of worldly matters and afterlife imagery (heaven, hell, resurrection). These subjects were illustrated with images particularly appealing to Chinese audiences of the time, providing a visualization of the life of Jesus Christ.

The book of *Yanxing jilüe* is the one with literary and explanatory compositions to serve as a biographical writing on the life of Jesus. It often is regarded as one of the most important sources that introduced Jesus and Christianity to Chinese audiences in modern studies.[27] At the time of its production, the composite nature of *Yanxing jilüe* resonated the genre of European gospel harmony and the form of writing Chinese biography; integrating both methods almost promised its popularity among broad audiences of the time. The book of *Yanxing jilüe* did enjoy huge success in terms of reaching out to readerships beyond the literati and the Christian community. Due to wide distribution in the circle of literary readers, the popularity of *Yanxing jilüe* earned this book a classic status. In the eyes of Chinese Christians, the book of *Yanxing jilüe* was a major work of Christian sacred texts. This recognition often resulted in *Yanxing jilüe* and *Shengjing zhijie* being regarded together as Chinese substitutes of the Bible.[28]

It was noted on almost every page throughout the illustrated book of *Chuxiang jingjie* that one can refer to the book of *Yanxing jilüe* for further reading. The two books formed a pair and were meant to be read side by side. One who followed the notes in *Chuxiang jingjie* would be directed to the location of the same theme developed in *Yanxing jilüe*. Therefore, *Chuxiang jingjie* visualized part of what was narrated in *Yanxing jilüe*, and vice versa; *Yanxing jilüe* elaborated on what was portrayed in *Chuxiang jingjie*. By way of integrating the biographical nature and powerful visualization, the two books together could provide audiences a unique experience of "reading" and "seeing" the life of Jesus Christ. Visualizing biographies was a popular manner used to present the life of heroic or saintly individuals in Chinese history—in particular during the Ming and Qing era. Pictorial biographies of Confucius, as well as those of Buddha and Daoist deities, continued the current trend of illustrated Chinese books in late imperial China.[29] In this context of prevailing illustrated biographies and sacred texts, *Chuxiang jingjie* and *Yanxing jilüe* introduced elements of the Christian tradition.

Other Genres for the Reading Public

The above types and examples of Christian sacred texts laid the textual foundation to prepare conversion and to sustain Christian religiosity in late imperial China. In addition to practicing Christians, the Chinese outside of the Christian circle, such as friendly scholars and opponents, also were exposed to Christianity because of the large number of Chinese Christian texts that were written mainly for non-Christian readers. These works included theological writings, apologetic writings, argumentative treatises, spiritual writings, devotional writings, sermons, individual notes, digests, and commentary layers. Not all of these genres echoed the Christian literature of the church; for instance, biographies of saints did not necessarily confirm the genre of hagiography in the European tradition but remained in line with the Chinese fashions of biography and historiography writing. These diversified Chinese Christian compositions did not speak for sacred texts but had a meaningful impact in terms of introducing Christianity to large audiences. Sometimes, biblical elements were contained as well. In the end, the circulation of these texts disseminated knowledge of biblical and Christian ideas to non-Christian Chinese too.

The most famous work in this regard is *Tianzhu shiyi* 天主實義 (*True Meaning of the Heavenly Lord*) by Matteo Ricci published in 1607. Ricci drafted the book of *Tianzhu shiyi* as a *catechismus* (not in the modern sense of catechism) to present Christian ideas based on natural theology to people who were hardly acquainted with Christian teachings. This book was welcomed among Chinese scholars as a Christian work to engage the literati, Buddhists, and Daoists in dialogue. In this book, Ricci introduced to his Chinese interlocutors the concept of Christian sacred texts (*jing*).

Already at the very beginning upon his arrival, Ricci soon was aware of the Confucian *jing* and, meanwhile, he took action accordingly. In the book of *Tianzhu shiyi*, Ricci inserted Christian connotations for the indigenous Chinese notion of *jing*, with which the collocations alluding to Christian sacred texts can be spotted throughout the book.[30] The occurrences of the character "*jing* 經" in Christianity appearing in the book of *Tianzhu shiyi* testified to Ricci's considerations and his execution of creating Christian sacred texts, although they were merely a vague concept that awaited more development and texts to substantiate. Given the wide circulation of the book *Tianzhu shiyi*, the concept of Christian sacred texts was made known even to outsiders.

For years after the time of Ricci, for instance during the ban on Christianity in the eighteenth century, official documents often reported on confiscated books of Christian sacred texts to the state authority. Activities of Christian communities were found to include "manufacturing Western *jing* volumes in Chinese" 用漢字編造西洋經卷. Also, local governors recognized churches and the places producing Christian books as "*Tianzhu jingtang* 天主經堂," literally meaning a hall of the Heavenly Lord's *jing*.[31]

Conclusion

While a handful of incomplete Chinese translations of the Bible presented continuous efforts with limited echoing results, the Bible was eventually "translated" or received into a wide variety of Chinese genres within the context of the *jing* culture. "Translating" the Bible in China meant looking for the Chinese to embrace the Bible, and the contextualization would involve adaptation, rewriting, circulation, and interpretation beyond biblical translation in its modern sense. In the end, the "Chinese Bible" was, in many ways, a textual phenomenon consisting of numerous Christian sacred texts, more prosperous and more dynamic than a Chinese book of the translated Bible.

The Christian sacred texts showcased in this essay were delivering biblical narratives, words, and messages to Chinese audiences at different levels from the late sixteenth through the eighteenth centuries. Overall, these Chinese Christian sacred texts included Bible verses, prayers, commentaries, catechetical instructions, liturgical books, Christian primers, images, prose, and rhymed lines, reading guides, and so forth, all useful for establishing Chinese Christianity without an authorized publication of the Bible in China. Through these works, Chinese people of different backgrounds and purposes had access to the Christian Bible and recognized a Christian tradition within the Chinese context of sacred texts. What occupied the life of Chinese Christians was the Bible being assimilated into the Chinese culture of sacred texts—with both written and oral channels laying the textual foundation for Chinese Christian religiosity. These Chinese Christian sacred texts testified to and represented the mechanism of continuous reception of the Bible in China. Viewing this history in a bigger picture, one can find that Chinese Bible reception was a case of creatively inserting and integrating the biblical stream into local cultures, a case of a meeting between the Christian tradition of sacred texts and that in China, a case of transmitting the Bible worldwide in world Christianity.

NOTES

1. Nicolas Standaert, "The Bible in Early Seventeenth-Century China," in *Bible in Modern China: The Literary and Intellectual Impact*, ed. Irene Eber et al. (Sankt Augustin: Steyler Verlag, 1999), 31–54.
2. Joseph Dehergne, "Travaux des Jésuites sur la Bible en Chine," in *Le siècle des lumières et la Bible*, ed. Yvon Belaval and Dominique Bourel (Paris: Beauchesne, 1986), 211–228.
3. Thomas Jansen, "Sacred Text," in *The Wiley-Blackwell Companion to Chinese Religions* (Chichester: John Wiley & Sons, Ltd, 2012), 283–308; K. K. Yeo, *Musing with Confucius and Paul: Toward a Chinese Christian Theology* (Eugene, OR: Wipf and Stock Publishers, 2008).
4. Jiang Wu and Lucille Chia, eds., *Spreading Buddha's Word in East Asia: The Formation and Transformation of the Chinese Buddhist Canon* (New York: Columbia University Press, 2016).
5. Alvin C. Kibel, "The Canonical Text," *Daedalus* 112.1 (1983): 239–254.
6. John B. Henderson, *Scripture, Canon and Commentary: A Comparison of Confucian and Western Exegesis* (Princeton: Princeton University Press, 2014).
7. Ibid. 50.
8. Jansen, "Sacred Text," 288.
9. Matteo Ricci, *Lettere: 1580–1609*, ed. Piero Corradini and Francesco D'Arelli (Macerata: Quodlibet, 2001), 247.
10. Standaert, "The Bible in Early Seventeenth-Century China," 46.
11. Yanrong Chen, "The Reception of the Bible: Building a Christian Textual Community in Late Imperial China" (Doctoral Dissertation, KU Leuven, 2017), 122.
12. Chloë Starr, "Reading Scripture in Nineteenth-Century China," in *Reading Christian Scriptures in China* (Edinburgh: T&T Clark, 2008), 32–48.
13. Jansen, "Sacred Text," 285.
14. Yanrong Chen, "The *Shengjing Zhijie*: A Chinese Text of Commented Gospel Readings in the Encounter between Europe and China in the Seventeenth Century," *Journal of Early Modern Christianity* 1.1 (2014): 165–193.
15. Li Shixue 李奭學, "Louis de Poirot and His "Guxin Shengjing" at the Linguistic Crossroads of China" [in Chinese] 近代白話文、宗教啟蒙、耶穌會傳統—試窺賀清泰及其所譯《古新聖經》的語言問題, *Zhongguo wenzhe yanjiu jikan* 42 (2013): 51–108; Zheng Haijuan 鄭海娟, "Annotating the Bible in Mid-Qing China: Poirot's Efforts" [in Chinese] 薪傳與新詮:《古新聖經》的解經之道, *Wenbei: Bijiao jingxue yu bijiao wenhua* 1 (2014): 55–84; Song Gang 宋剛, "The Translation of the Bible and Exegesis of the Jesuit Louis Antoine de Poirot during the Qing Period" [in Chinese] '本意' 與 '土語'之間: 清代耶穌會士賀清泰的《聖經》漢譯及詮釋, *Guoji hanxue* 5 (2015): 23–49.
16. François Bontinck, *La lutte autour de la liturgie chinoise aux XVIIe et XVIIIe siècles* (Louvain: Nauwelaerts, 1962), 181–182; Audrey Seah, "The 1670 Chinese Missal: A Struggle for Indigenization amidst the Chinese Rites Controversy," in *China's Christianity: From*

Missionary to Indigenous Church, ed. Anthony E. Clark, Studies in Christian Mission 50 (Leiden: Brill, 2017), 86–120.

17. Bontinck, *La lutte autour de la liturgie chinoise aux XVIIe et XVIIIe siècles*, 156–157.
18. Nicolas Standaert, "The Spiritual Exercises of Ignatius of Loyola in the China Mission of the 17th and 18th Centuries," *Archivum Historicum Societatis Iesu* 161 (2012): 73–124.
19. Ricci, *Lettere*, 406.
20. Nicolas Standaert, ed., *Handbook of Christianity in China*, Vol. 1: *635–1800* (Leiden: Brill, 2001), 608–616.
21. Gianni Criveller, *Preaching Christ in Late Ming China: The Jesuits' Presentation of Christ from Matteo Ricci to Giulio Aleni* (Taipei: Ricci Institute, 1997), 40; Matteo Ricci, *Fonti Ricciane: Documenti Originali Concernenti Matteo Ricci e La Storia Delle Prime Relazioni Tra l'Europa e La Cina (1579–1615)*, ed. Pasquale M d'Elia (Rome: La libreria dello stato, 1942), 289–293.
22. Standaert, *Handbook of Christianity in China*, 1:629.
23. Erik Zürcher, *Kouduo Richao: Li Jiubiao's Diary of Oral Admonitions: A Late Ming Christian Journal* (Sankt Augustin: Institut Monumenta Serica, 2007), 109–110.
24. Ibid. 516–517.
25. Eugenio Menegon, *Un Solo Cielo: Giulio Aleni SJ (1582–1649): Geografia, Arte, Scienza, Religione Dall'Europa Alla Cina* (Brescia: Grafo, 1994), 160–162; Criveller, *Preaching Christ in Late Ming China*, 254–259; Gail King, "The Gospel for the Ordinary Reader: Aspects of Six Christian Texts in Chinese from the Late Ming Dynasty," *Monumenta Serica* 57.1 (2009): 167–194; Gu Weiying (Ku Wei-ying) 古偉瀛, "*Sizi jingwen:* benwei hua yu Taiwan tianzhujiao" [in Chinese] 四字經文: 本位化與台灣天主教, in *History of Catechesis in China*, ed. by Rachel Lu Yan et al. (Leuven: Ferdinand Verbiest Institute, 2008), 319–337.
26. Hieronymus Natalis, *Imagenes de La Historia Evangelica* (Barcelona: El Albir, 1975).
27. Standaert, "The Bible in Early Seventeenth-Century China," 31–54.
28. Chen, "The Reception of the Bible," 170.
29. Julia K. Murray, *Mirror of Morality: Chinese Narrative Illustration and Confucian Ideology* (Honolulu: University of Hawaii Press, 2007); Julia K. Murray, "Illustrations of the Life of Confucius: Their Evolution, Functions, and Significance in Late Ming China," *Artibus Asiae* 57.1/2 (1997): 73–134.
30. Chen, "The Reception of the Bible," 119–121.
31. *Documents on Catholic Missionaries' Activities in China During the Early Qing and Mid Qing* [in Chinese] 清中前期西洋天主教在華活動檔案史料 (Beijing: Zhonghua shuju, 2003), 2:839.

Primary Sources

Dudink, Ad and Nicolas Standaert. "Chinese Christian Texts Database," n.d. https://www.arts.kuleuven.be/sinologie/english/cct.

Natalis, Hieronymus. *Imagenes de La Historia Evangelica*. Barcelona: El Albir, 1975.

Qing zhongqianqi xiyang tianzhujiao zaihua huodong dang'an shiliao [in Chinese] 清中前期西洋天主教在華活動檔案史料. 北京: 中華書局, 2003.

Ricci, Matteo. *Fonti Ricciane: Documenti originali concernenti Matteo Ricci e la storia delle prime relazioni tra l'Europa e la Cina (1579–1615)*. Edited by Pasquale M d'Elia. Rome: La libreria dello stato, 1942.

Ricci, Matteo. *Lettere: 1580–1609*. Edited by Piero Corradini and Francesco D'Arelli. Macerata: Quodlibet, 2001.

Standaert, Nicolas, ed. *Handbook of Christianity in China*, Vol. 1: *635–1800*. Leiden: Brill, 2001.

Zürcher, Erik. *Kouduo Richao: Li Jiubiao's Diary of Oral Admonitions: A Late Ming Christian Journal*. Sankt Augustin: Institut Monumenta Serica, 2007.

CHAPTER 30

SINO-CHRISTIAN THEOLOGY AND THE BIBLE

PAN-CHIU LAI

INTRODUCTION

DURING the 1980s, a small group of intellectuals in mainland China began their academic studies of Christianity, especially Christian theology. As most of them were not formally committed to any Christian church, they were conventionally called "cultural Christians" (*wenhua jidutu* 文化基督徒). They tended to use the term "Sino-Christian theology" (or simply "Sino-theology"; *hanyu shenxue* 漢語神學) to identify their theological endeavor. However, as there is no particular theological position commonly shared by this group of intellectuals, the term "Sino-theology" refers to a loosely connected cultural qua theological movement rather than a strictly defined school of theology.[1] The main aim of this essay is to survey and analyze the relationship of Sino-Christian theology with the Bible, especially academic study of the Bible. A similar survey was published in 2006.[2] Nonetheless, due to the rather dramatic developments of the movement since then, it is necessary to provide a more updated study by supplementing information about the most recent developments.[3]

Regarding the term "Sino-theology," there are two preliminary remarks to be made. First, in the relevant literature, one may find roughly two types of definition of Sino-theology. Broadly speaking, "Sino-theology" could refer to any theology written in the Chinese language (*han yu* 漢語), rendering it possible to trace the history of Sino-theology back several hundred years. However, more often, scholars may prefer to use "Chinese theology" to denote this broader sense of Sino-theology.[4] In the narrow sense of the term, Sino-theology may designate specifically the theological thinking of "cultural Christians" or scholars from mainland China pursuing academic studies of Christianity. In this sense, Sino-theology often is associated with sort of philosophical or rational expressions of individual religious beliefs in academic settings of mainland China and is an alternative that is radically different from "indigenous theology" advocated by the Chinese churches and seminary-based dogmatic theology.[5] The following discussion is confined to Sino-theology in its narrow sense.

Second, Sino-theology underwent a certain "paradigm shift" in the last ten to twenty years.[6] In terms of religious background, unlike the "cultural Christians" of the first generation, many of the younger Chinese scholars engaging in academic studies of Christianity have their respective church affiliations. Some of them even prefer to identify themselves as "Christian scholars" in order to highlight their religious identity and to differentiate themselves from "cultural Christians."[7] In terms of academic approach, the more recent studies of Christianity in Chinese academia became increasingly multi-disciplinary, involving not only the more traditional historical, philosophical, and systematic theological methods but also the more contemporary social-scientific methods. Together with this multi-disciplinary approach to the study of Christianity is a change of vision from a more restricted vision of "Sino-Christian theology" to a broader vision of "Sino-Christian studies."[8] Furthermore, "Sino-theology" is no longer considered to be mere philosophical expressions of individual religious beliefs in the academic setting. Instead, there are many recent studies concerning Chinese "public theology"[9] or Christian theological participation in inter-disciplinary studies of public issues.[10]

This essay focuses on articles published in *Dao Feng* 道風 (*Logos & Pneuma*, 1994–), a journal published by the Institute of Sino-Christian Studies (ISCS), which is a Hong Kong-based organization aiming at the promotion of Sino-theology. It changed its Chinese sub-title from *han yu shen xue xue kan* 漢語神學學刊 (*Chinese Journal of Theology*) to *ji du jiao wen hua lun ping* 基督教文化論評 (*Christian Cultural Review*) since 2000 without changing the sub-title in English. The journal published Chinese articles only, but it published both original articles written in Chinese as well as Chinese translations of articles originally written in other languages until 2005. Since 2006, it has published original Chinese articles only.

Based on reasons discussed later, this essay takes 2006 as the dividing line for the development of the relationship between Sino-theology and the Bible embodied in the publications of *Logos & Pneuma*.[11]

Early Development of Sino-Christian Studies of the Bible

When Sino-theology emerged as a cultural qua theological movement in the 1980s, the principal force in biblical scholarship in the Chinese-speaking world consisted of researchers from theological seminaries, especially those outside mainland China. In comparison to biblical studies in, say, Hong Kong, the research strength of mainland China scholars was relatively weak in this area. Articles on biblical studies by mainland

China scholars were meager, and very few scholars from mainland China could master the methodology generally adopted by contemporary biblical scholarship. Admittedly, the under-development of biblical studies in mainland China was mainly due to its unfavorable external environment,[12] but this seemed to be exacerbated by the failure of advocates of Sino-theology to take seriously the importance of the Bible to Christianity and to recognize properly the academic character of biblical studies.

Leung Ka-lun 梁家麟 (also known as Liang Jialin), a church historian who taught at the Alliance Bible Seminary in Hong Kong, once criticized the theology of "cultural Christians," especially the methodological separation of their theological thinking from biblical studies:

> Most of them are interested merely in Christian thought and its philosophical implications and the main subjects of their studies are those theologians in history who were original in theological and philosophical thinking (especially modern theologians), so that they do not follow the conventional approach (or tradition) of theological studies: exegesis → Biblical theology → historical theology → systematic theology → applied theology → practical theology; they rather deal with the thinking of those theologians separately without taking Biblical studies into account. For them, it is less important whether these thoughts are orthodox or heterodox, and even whether they are conformable to the teaching of the Bible is not a matter of their concern. Therefore, the so-called Christian theological thought is actually the thought of some historical figures who proclaimed themselves Christians. Normally it is impossible to do such kind of theological research in theological seminaries.[13]

Though Liang's own understanding of the relationship between biblical studies and theology is rather naive, his observation of the separation between theological thinking and biblical studies among the cultural Christians is rather perceptive. Generally speaking, cultural Christians seldom quote the Bible in their theological writings, and even fewer devote themselves to in-depth research into biblical studies. Their research and writings bear no close relation to the Bible or biblical studies. Moreover, cultural Christians are not supposed to be church members, and Sino-theology presupposes no particular confessional stance with regard to the inspiration and the authority of the Bible. All of these factors create the impression that Sino-theology is not very "biblical," or at least less "biblical" than the non-church (*Mukyōkai*) movement in Japan.[14] One may then have to question whether Sino-theology should be an integral part of Christian theological studies.

Against this query, Sino-theology can justify its approach to the Bible with certain theological reasons. In view of the curriculum of theological studies as a whole, biblical studies is merely a branch of the theological encyclopedia. Moreover, Christian theology is not necessarily confined to, or identical with biblical theology, being capable also of presenting itself in the form of philosophical theology or apologetic theology. Accordingly, Sino-theology as apologetic theology can organize itself around the critiques raised by the non-Christians against the Christian faith instead of proceeding directly from the inherent doctrines of Christianity. Apologetics may make reference to the Bible indirectly, implicitly, and occasionally, rather than persuade its opponents by quoting the

Bible directly as an authoritative text or proof text.[15] In the rather complicated academic environment of mainland China, with its millions of non-Christians, it is quite understandable and even reasonable that Sino-theology makes very scarce reference to the Bible. The question of whether Sino-theology is Christian is thus not to be determined by the frequency of direct biblical quotation.

It also is important to note that, from its very beginning, Sino-theology professed to assume an ecumenical or non-denominational stance, permitting it to make use of theological resources from any denomination of Christianity. In fact, ISCS publishes books from various branches of Christianity, including Catholic, Orthodox, and Protestant. Therefore, Sino-theology is under no obligation to take the Protestant stance of *Sola Scriptura* and to adopt the linear and irreversible approach suggested by Liang Jialin. In other words, the question as to whether Sino-theology is Christian cannot be reduced to the question of whether it is biblical.

Certainly, in terms of theological position and methodology, one can confidently argue that even though Sino-theology is seemingly not very biblical at the present stage, it cannot be proved that it is not Christian. However, the way Sino-theology conceives of the relationship between theology and biblical studies remains an inevitable question. The reason is that even Roman Catholicism and Orthodox Christianity, despite their recognition of the importance of tradition and of upholding no principle of *Sola Scriptura*, also affirm the importance of the Bible and its close relationship with tradition.

Admittedly, biblical studies constituted only a tiny proportion of the publications of ISCS. This assessment can be confirmed by a very simple review of the articles published in *Logos & Pneuma* in the first half of its history, namely from 1994 to 2006. In terms of quantity, the proportion of the articles on biblical studies is slight: on average less than one article per issue, which usually consists of more than ten articles. As for the background of the authors of articles related to biblical studies, the majority are scholars from theological seminaries in Hong Kong and Taiwan, rather than scholars from the universities of mainland China. With regard to the main themes of the publications, only "*Genesis* and Modern Political Philosophy"[16] seems closely related to the Bible; even then, the articles published under this main theme focus more on political philosophy than on the interpretation of *Genesis*. Furthermore, among the three articles included, only one of them is authored by a Chinese scholar,[17] whereas the other two are translated from publications of Georg Jellinek (1851–1911) and Leo Strauss (1899–1973) respectively.

Among the articles more directly related to biblical studies, other than some occasional and short book reviews and reading notes,[18] one can find only one article giving a detailed linguistic study of the Bible[19] and a survey of the development of Old Testament studies.[20] However, the major concern of all these articles remained the theological-philosophical ideas in the Bible, e.g., on suffering,[21] the idea of human being,[22] social ethics,[23] doctrine of God,[24] Christology[25] and so on. Without paying enough attention to the fine analysis of Scriptural texts, most of these discussions focus on some rather general theological ideas. The only article embracing an attentive interpretation of a biblical text is nevertheless a translated article, which also focuses its attention on theological thinking—on the question of "poverty and affluence."[26] So to sum up, in its first twelve years of publication, *Logos & Pneuma* provided very few articles offering in-depth exploration of Scriptural texts or biblical criticism, and the standard of its research has been far from in line with the international norm in biblical scholarship. With regard to other theological journals published in mainland China, such as *Jidu jiao wenhua xuekan* 基督教文化學刊 (*Journal for the Studies of Christian Culture*, 1999–) and *Jidu zhongjiao yanjiu* 基督宗教研究 (*Study of Christianity*, 1999–), the situation is quite similar.

The current underdevelopment of biblical studies in mainland China may result from several factors discussed below.

The Political Atmosphere

In mainland China, the Bible is usually regarded merely as a sacred object for Christians' worship and devotion, so it is only supplied in churches and not available in bookstores. In other words, it is an object of religious piety rather than a subject of academic study. The political factor is well exemplified by a conference held in Kaifeng, Henan province, in September 2002, which was co-sponsored by Henan University and the Association of Chinese Comparative Literature. While most of the papers presented at the conference pertained to biblical studies, the conference was held under the title "Hermeneutics of Classics and Communication of Culture." According to the editors of the conference volume, the word "Bible" was dropped in the official title of the conference because it was too politically sensitive. Conference organizers had even once planned to publish a collection of the papers in a very remote province in order to avoid attention from the government. Although the collection was finally published by a renowned publisher in Beijing,[27] the incident showed that biblical studies remains, in the minds of scholars at least, a rather sensitive discipline in mainland China.

The Rigidity of the Requirements of the Discipline

For most current scholars in mainland China, Christian studies or theological studies is still a brand-new field to which they switch their studies from other academic disciplines such as history, literature, and philosophy. It is straightforward for those scholars to shift their studies from history to church history, or from sociology or anthropology to empirical or field studies of Chinese Christianity, for it requires no essential change in methodology. The change from philosophy to philosophical theology or systematic theology, though different in their methodology and required background training, remains not so difficult. However, in pursuing biblical studies, those scholars from other disciplines almost need to start afresh as beginners due to the rigidity of requirements for training. With regard to New Testament studies, one's previous knowledge, if any, of the Greek language, as well as the history and culture of the ancient Greco-Roman world, could be of little help. For Old Testament studies, the case is more complicated in that it requires proficiency in several ancient languages (including Hebrew), knowledge of ancient myths, history, culture and society, etc., as well as an understanding of the methodologies of modern biblical studies. It is not easy for scholars in mainland China to overcome these hurdles by themselves and to reach the international standard in biblical scholarship.

The Ignorance of the Academic Character of Biblical Studies

In its "Notes for Contributors," *Logos & Pneuma* shows a rather interesting attitude worthy of rumination:

> [The journal] treasures the intellectual, cultural, and academic character of the contributions, and no articles of sermon, spirituality, and pure exegesis will be accepted. All the results of academic studies of Christian theology from the perspective of different disciplines (systematic-fundamental theology, Biblical Scholarship, Church history, the history of dogma, the history of Jewish thought), Christian human sciences (philosophy, ethics, history, philology and aesthetics), Christian social sciences (politics, sociology, psychology and anthropology), and religious dialogue are warmly welcomed.[28]

One may perhaps be puzzled by the question concerning why, on the one hand, the research products of biblical scholarship are welcomed, while on the other, "pure exegesis" is rejected. Though no clear definition of "pure exegesis" is given in the "Notes for Contributors," one can infer from the context that "pure exegesis," comparable to sermons or literature of spirituality, is supposed to be lacking in "intellectual, academic, and cultural character."

Queries Concerning Sino-Theology and Biblical Studies

The exclusion of "pure exegesis" is queried by Lai Pan-chiu 賴品超 (also known as Lai Pinchao) in a paper presented at the third roundtable symposium of Sino-theology held by ISCS in September 2005. Due to the political censorship in mainland China, Lai's paper, together with the other papers presented at the symposium, were eventually published in Shanghai in 2009,[29] with Lai's paper further reprinted in Hong Kong in 2010,[30] long after the publication of its English version in 2006.[31] Lai's queries can be summarized below.

The prevalent exegetical practice of some Chinese churches might have given people such an impression or prejudice that "pure exegesis" is something without "intellectual, academic, and cultural character." However, anyone familiar with the development of biblical scholarship outside Asia might notice that many social-scientific studies of the Bible were published long before the emergence of Sino-theology. In Asian contexts, many Asian theologians tend to express their theological thinking by means of biblical interpretation. In spite of their emphasis on the Asian contexts, their interpretations are not without "intellectual, academic and cultural character," which can be seen from the considerable references to the results of the contemporary Western academia, the analyses of the historical context of biblical documents, the training in original languages involved, and the background knowledge in history, archaeology, and even sociology. Sometimes, this kind of contextual exegesis also encompasses social and cultural analysis of contemporary contexts.[32]

In a sense, one could say that exegesis is fairly intellectual in that even the most basic exegesis indeed requires knowledge of the Scriptural texts, as well as the history and culture involved. Moreover, probably no classical text in this world other than the Bible has been studied by so many methods, and one should not forget that hermeneutics, a prominent discipline of contemporary humanities, has been conducted for a rather long time in the context of biblical exegesis. Furthermore, the methodology of contemporary biblical scholarship is quite similar to the methodology adopted by contemporary international academia as the methodology of studying and interpreting texts in general. Therefore, biblical exegesis also may be seen to be quite academic. Finally, without confining their studies to the Scriptures as ancient classics having a far-reaching influence on human history, exegetes may study the Scriptures with contemporary social or cultural problems in mind. For example, the "cross-textual reading" of the Scriptures advocated by Archie C. C. Lee 李熾昌 (also known as Li Chichang) illustrates clearly how one's cultural context might affect one's reading of the Scriptures, and how biblical exegesis may play a vital role in cross-cultural dialogues.[33] All these speak well for the cultural character of exegesis.

The line of demarcation between "pure exegesis" and "biblical scholarship" is blurred, and it is too simplistic to make a sharp division between "biblical scholarship" and "pure exegesis" in the measure of the so-called "intellectual, academic, and cultural character," because even the most "pure exegesis" more or less measures up to the criterion. There is no reason for Sino-theology to preclude biblical exegesis from its horizon. If one of the aims of ISCS is to improve the academic status and level of Christian studies in mainland China, it has to pay adequate attention to or even work energetically to promote biblical studies, including biblical exegesis. Therefore, in order to show how to interpret Scripture with the tools of the contemporary methodology in humanities and social sciences, and also to show that exegesis can be highly "intellectual, academic, and cultural," it is advisable for ISCS to be more open to academic exegesis of the Bible and to translate more books on exegetical methodology and/or books on biblical interpretations and hermeneutics. If biblical studies were to attain its due academic status in China, the academic status and the legitimacy of Sino-theology would be consolidated and strengthened.

Late Development of Sino-Christian Studies of the Bible

Lai's query made in 2005 seemed to make a certain immediate impact on ISCS, especially *Logos & Pneuma*. It is interesting to note that starting from issue no. 24, the phrase "pure exegesis" in the "Notes for Contributors" was deleted.[34] In an editorial note added to the aforementioned conference-paper-turned-book-chapter authored by Lai, the editor acknowledged that this modification was made in response to Lai's criticism or suggestion made at the conference held in 2005.[35]

This modification of "Notes for Contributors" means that academic papers of "pure exegesis" are now welcome by *Logos & Pneuma*. It is noticeable that, since then, the journal published several special issues related to biblical studies, and ISCS also published an edited volume on Sino-Christian scriptural hermeneutics edited by Jason Lam.[36] The three special issues are: "Biblical Studies and Chinese Academia,"[37] "Comparative Scripture as Sino-Christian Theology,"[38] and "New Testament Studies and Sino-Christian Theology."[39] Apart from the articles included in these three special issues, there are some other noteworthy articles on biblical studies.[40] Some of these articles might belong to the category of "pure exegesis,"[41] and their approaches are also similar to the academic studies of the Bible in international academia, including the use of postcolonial theory[42] and speech act theory.[43] Based on this rather brief survey, one may find that biblical studies plays a rather important role in *Logos & Pneuma*, and this is in sharp contrast with the underdevelopment of biblical studies in the first twelve years of publication of the journal. It is noteworthy that in 2019, *Logos & Pneuma* makes "The Future of Sino-Christian Studies" the main theme of its fiftieth volume, which serves as a milestone for its publication. Excluding the short introduction of the main theme, the first among the six articles included is about the methodology of Chinese biblical studies.[44] This signifies that in the years to come, biblical studies may continue to play an important role in Sino-Christian studies.

Regarding the rather dramatic contrast of the role of biblical studies in the early (before 2006) and recent (after 2006) developments, there are two further observations to be made. One concerns the background of contributors, and the other the methodology, especially its relationship with Sino-theology or Sino-Christian studies. Regarding the background of contributors, it is noticeable that some of them are professed Christians from Hong Kong and even overseas, e.g., Choong Chee Pong 鍾志邦 from Singapore and Wan Sze-kar 温司卡 from the United States. Among the scholars from mainland China, some of them were trained in Hong Kong, including some PhD graduates of the Chinese University of Hong Kong.[45] Furthermore, there are many co-authored or co-edited publications concerning biblical studies resulting from the collaboration between scholars from Hong Kong and mainland China. For example, one may notice the book on the Hebrew Scriptures or Old Testament co-authored between Archie C. C. Lee from Hong Kong and You Bin 游斌 from mainland China.[46]

For co-edited publications, one may recall the series of biblical studies co-edited by Lo Lung-kwong 盧龍光 (also known as Lu Longguang) from Hong Kong and Liang Gong from mainland China.[47] All these indicate not only the importance of academic collaboration between Hong Kong and mainland China but also the impossibility of restricting participants of Sino-theology or Sino-Christian studies as a movement to scholars from mainland China, especially those without church affiliation.

Regarding methodological issues, it is noticeable that in addition to the publications calling for the development of biblical studies as an academic discipline in China,[48] there are some innovative explorations and experiments aiming at the development of some sorts of biblical studies with Chinese characteristics. Taking the volume on "Sino-Christian Scriptural Hermeneutics" edited by Jason Lam as a focus of discussion,[49] one may find that there are many methodological issues raised, ranging from the basic concept and "Problematik" of Sino-Christian Scriptural Hermeneutics[50] to the relationship among the Bible, Sino-theology, and the Christian tradition[51] and the development of a "Critical Sino-Public Biblical Theology."[52] In addition to these relatively more theoretical studies, there are also studies of concrete and historical cases of biblical hermeneutics in the Chinese context. Notable examples include Chinese translations of the Bible,[53] modern Chinese Christians' interpretation of the Bible[54] using the cross-textual hermeneutics as a strategy to study of Chinese Christian writings of the Ming and Qing dynasties,[55] and the cross-cultural encounter of the Chinese and Christian exegetical traditions during the Ming and Qing dynasties.[56] A slightly different study is a constructive experiment in addressing the issue of theological diversity within the Bible by casting light from Chinese Buddhist approaches on doctrinal classification.[57]

These studies indicate that there are three possible areas of development for Sino-Christian scriptural hermeneutics: (1) case study of the Chinese Christian interpretations of the Bible;[58] (2) methodological explorations, especially the "comparative," "dialogical," "cross-cultural," or "cross-textual" approach to the Christian and Chinese scriptures;[59] and, (3) constructive attempt to compare Christian and Chinese Scriptures or their hermeneutical traditions.[60] All these areas take seriously the importance of Chinese Scriptures or classical texts for the interpretation of the Christian Bible. In fact, this sort of comparative/dialogical/cross-textual approach can be adopted by those from a more church-based background.[61] Furthermore, it also is possible to conduct some sorts of comparative or dialogical studies between Christianity and Chinese religions that are based on but not restricted to the study of Chinese and Christian Scriptures.[62]

It is noticeable that these areas highlight characteristics of the Chinese context and assume that some Chinese Christians would interpret various passages of the Bible in ways that are radically different from interpretations prevalent in the Western world, partially due to the existence of other Scriptures or classical texts. It is thus quite understandable that this sort of comparative/dialogical/cross-textual approach is welcome by Chinese scholars. For example, You Bin launched a journal called *Comparative Scripture* (2013–) in order to promote comparative studies of the Scriptures. Different from the practice of "scriptural reasoning" advocated by some Euro-American scholars aiming at the parallel readings of the Scriptures from Judaism, Christianity, and Islam, "comparative Scripture" covers also Scriptures beyond the Abrahamic religions. Given the very rich Chinese scriptural traditions, it is quite reasonable to expect that through making references to Chinese scriptural traditions, including its hermeneutical traditions, Sino-Christian studies of the Bible will make significant contributions to international academia. However, one has to be reminded that comparative Scripture does not necessarily involve the Bible. It is interesting to note that Liang Hui gave an example that compares a rabbinic text with a Confucian classic, instead of a particular text from the Bible, in order to illustrate her "dialogical hermeneutics" or "comparative scriptural studies."[63] This reminds us once again that the relationship between Sino-Christian theology and the Bible is not restricted to Sino-Christian studies on the Bible. In fact, Sino-Christian theology may raise even more fundamental questions concerning the relationship between Christian theology and the Bible.

Theology and the Bible from a Chinese Perspective

One of the characteristics of Sino-theology is its use of materials from traditional Chinese culture, especially Chinese classical texts or Scriptures. But if one investigates the way in which Chinese culture conceives of the transmission of tradition, one may find that Confucianism (especially the tradition of "*xin-xue* 心學," literally speaking, "heart-mind learning") and Buddhism (especially the Ch'an school) emphasize the transmission of "heart-mind" over that of "Scripture," which is only the testimony to the former.[64] Similarly, the Bible reads, "Do all you can to preserve the unity of the spirit.... There is one body and one Spirit... one and the same hope... one Lord, one faith, one baptism, and one God..." (Eph 4:3–6; Jerusalem Bible). It is noteworthy that there is no mention of "one Scripture." In fact, the canon adopted by Roman Catholicism is slightly different from that of Protestantism. Therefore, instead of adhering to "one Scripture," Sino-theology could inherit the ecumenical Christian tradition in terms of "one Spirit" or "one heart-mind," which may include not only the faith, love, and hope belonging to the domain of Spirit or heart-mind but also the object or content of faith (one Lord, one God), the one heart-mind attested to, and the liturgy (one baptism) testifying the transmission of the one heart-mind.

With this understanding, we may revisit to the question concerning Christian identity of Sino-theology, especially whether Sino-theology is a continuation of and belongs to the Christian tradition. According to the analysis given by Christoph Schwöbel concerning how to understand the continuity of the tradition in the history of Christianity, there are three different models. The first model, introduced by Irenaeus of Lyon, is to understand tradition as a "continuous chain" of the original message that is preserved in the unbroken apostolic succession from apostles to the present Pope. The second understanding of tradition is the "consensus model," which suggests that the Christian tradition is preserved in one consensus of faith, e.g., the *consensus fidelium* suggested by Vincent of Lérins, which means the faith held by all Christians of all times. The third model adopts the strategy of "return to the origin" of the tradition, called by Reformers *ad fontes*, namely, returning to the Bible as the yardstick for tradition.[65]

As many cultural Christians do not have strong connections with Christian churches and sometimes even consider themselves outside the ecclesiastical polity, it is not easy for Sino-theology to adopt the first model, which comes rather close to the stance of Roman Catholicism. In fact, it also is difficult to demonstrate the concrete ecclesiastical (not to say "apostolic") succession of Sino-theology in historical terms. The adoption of the third model may not be helpful either because Sino-theology as a whole remains not very "biblical" in its appearance. Therefore, the second model is perhaps a more feasible approach to understand how even the theological activities of cultural Christians can continue the Christian tradition. This is because despite having no formal affiliation to a Christian church, they do share to a certain extent the faith of Christians. As Schwöbel points out, the problem of the second model lies in its need for the third model as a supplement, for what the consensus of Christians of all generations and all places signifies remains rather unclear.[66] Certainly, the stress on consensus in the second model and the emphasis on Scripture in the third model do not conflict with each other.[67] For Sino-theology, the virtue of the second model, nevertheless, might precisely lie in its seeming limitation pointed out by Schwöbel. The distinctiveness of Sino-theology lies in its emphasis on the language it employs. Owing to the close linkage between language and its living context, the consensus of Christians in the Chinese context is not necessarily expressed in an unambiguous universal language (comparable to Esperanto) and thus cannot be identical with the language of the Scriptures or ecumenical creeds. It, nevertheless, shall and can be reinterpreted or translated in the Chinese context. If the mission of theology is to construct the future of the tradition by using inherited faith and resources,[68] compared with the other two models, the second model of understanding the continuation of tradition can furnish Sino-theology with greater hermeneutic space, and more possibilities for participating in and therefore enriching the Christian tradition.[69]

Conclusion

Other than its contributions to the understanding of Scripture and the transmission of the Christian tradition, Chinese cultural resources also may inspire some alternative paths for approaching the relationship between theology and biblical studies. For instance, the Chinese Buddhist method of doctrinal criticism, which attempts to criticize, rank, and organize the Scriptures according to their different theological contents, may provide for biblical theology a possible method for handling the question of theological diversity within the canon.[70] The method is similar to "content criticism" in biblical studies, also called "theological criticism," for the "content" refers to theological content. Underlying this kind of theological criticism is the presupposition that the ultimate authority does not lie in Scriptural texts but with the Holy Spirit, who inspired the Scriptures. The theological criticism is not to use a non-theological or non-Christian authority to reject the Bible; but, as Luther also had said, to "urge Christ against Scripture." It presupposes that the Bible was written by human beings susceptible to mistakes and thus bears the theological opinions and orientations of the authors or the editors.[71] Therefore, with regard to the relationship between theology and the Bible, it is not necessary for theology to be unilaterally determined by the Bible or biblical studies, whereas theology also can conduct a critique of the theological formulations in different parts of the Bible; by doing so, a hermeneutic circle may be formed. It is possible that this approach to biblical studies has been carried out secretly throughout the entire history of Christianity, but has been seldom adopted publicly and systematically, with the exception of obvious examples such as Martin Luther and Origen. However, almost every school of Chinese Buddhism regards this kind of doctrinal criticism as an indispensable component; in fact, Zhang Chunyi (1871–1955), a Chinese promoter of Mahayana Christianity, already has tried to apply the method to the criticism of different Scriptural texts.[72] In short, Sino-theology is capable of making its unique contribution to the Christian tradition as a whole by making use of its cultural resources.

Notes

1. Yang Huilin and Daniel H. N. Yeung, eds., *Sino-Christian Studies in China* (Newcastle: Cambridge Scholars Press, 2006); Lai Pan-chiu and Jason Tsz-shun Lam, eds., *Sino-Christian Theology: A Theological qua Cultural Movement in Contemporary China* (Frankfurt am Main: Peter Lang, 2010); Lai Pan-chiu, "Sino-Theology as a Non-Church Movement: Historical and Comparative Perspectives," ed. Jan A. B. Jongeneel et al. (Frankfurt am Main: Peter Lang, 2011), 87–103.
2. Lai Pan-chiu, "Sino-Theology, Bible and the Christian Tradition," *Studies in World Christianity* 12.3 (2006): 266–281.
3. Some parts of this chapter are derived from: Lai, "Sino-Theology, Bible and the Christian Tradition," 266–281; reprinted with corrections in Lai and Lam, eds., *Sino-Christian Theology*, 161–177.
4. For example, Chloë Starr, *Chinese Theology: Text and Context* (New Haven, CT; London: Yale University Press, 2016).
5. Lai Pan-chiu, "Typology and Prospect of Sino-Christian Theology," *Ching Feng (New Series)* 6.2 (2005): 211–230.
6. Sun Shangyang, "The Possible Contribution of Christianity and Sino-Christian Theology to Chinese Social and Cultural Construction" [in Chinese] 基督宗教和漢語神學對中國社會文化建設的可能功能, *Logos & Pneuma* 46 (2017): 291–295. All articles published in *Logos & Pneuma* are in Chinese, but for reasons stated in n. 11, hereafter no Chinese title will be provided for articles published in *Logos & Pneuma*.
7. Gao Xin, "Preliminary Survey on the New Generation of Scholars of Christian Studies in Mainland China," in *Sino-Christian Theology: A Theological qua Cultural Movement in*

Contemporary China, ed. Lai Pan-chiu and Jason Tsz-shun Lam (Frankfurt am Main: Peter Lang, 2010), 225–237; Naomi Thurston, *Studying Christianity in China: Constructions of an Emerging Discourse* (Leiden: Brill, 2018).

8. Lai Pan-chiu, *Sino-Christian Theology in the Public Square: From Theology to Christian Studies* [in Chinese] 廣場上的漢語神學: 從神學到基督宗教研究 (Hong Kong: Logos & Pneuma Press, 2014); Xie Zhibin, "From 'Multidisciplinary Studies' to 'Interdisciplinary Studies': An Overview and Prospect for 'Across Disciplines' Character of Sino-Christian Studies," *Logos & Pneuma* 41 (Autumn 2014): 103–126.
9. Yang Huilin and Xie Zhibin, eds., "Sino-Theology and Public Space," *Logos & Pneuma* 32 (Spring 2010): 19–145; Lai Pan-chiu and Xie Zhibin, eds., "Public Theology in the Chinese Context," special issue, *International Journal of Public Theology* 11.4 (2017): 375–500; Alexander Chow, *Chinese Public Theology: Generational Shifts and Confucian Imagination in Chinese Christianity* (Oxford: Oxford University Press, 2018).
10. Xie Zhibin, ed., "Dignity, Morality and Rights: Inter-Disciplinary Studies," special issue, *Logos & Pneuma* 49A (Winter 2018): 21–142.
11. The articles published in *Logos & Pneuma* are accessible free of charge (with time lag of a few months) at the website of the Chinese University of Hong Kong Library, http://repository.lib.cuhk.edu.hk/en/item/cuhk-475760 (accessed April 23, 2019). Starting from no. 7 (1997), both the English title and an abstract are provided for each of the original Chinese articles. The articles published in *Logos & Pneuma* are indexed by both Web of Science (starting from 2007) and Scopus (starting from 2008) according to English titles provided by the journal, including the journal title *Logos & Pneuma*, as well as the titles of the articles. These made the Chinese title as well as the transliteration of the title not so necessary for reference checking. So, when referring to articles published in *Logos & Pnuema*, no Chinese title or transliteration will be provided in order to keep the endnotes succinct.
12. Choong Chee Pong and You Bin, "Introduction to the Main Theme," *Logos & Pneuma* 31 (Autumn 2009): 19–24.
13. Leung Ka-lun, "Another Debt That We Owe?" [in Chinese] 又是我们欠的債嗎?, in *Cultural Christian: Phenomenon and Argument* 文化基督徒: 現象與論爭, ed. Institute of Sino-Christian Studies (Hong Kong: Institute of Sino-Christian Studies, 1997), 108.
14. Lai, "Sino-Theology as a Non-Church Movement," 103.
15. Lai, "Typology and Prospect," 218–221.
16. Liu Xiaofeng, "Genesis and Modern Political Philosophy," *Logos & Pneuma* 15 (Autumn 2001): 9–82.
17. Lin Guoji, "*Creatio ex nihilo* and the Social Contract Theory," *Logos & Pneuma* 15 (Autumn 2001): 13–41.
18. For examples, Liu Yihuan, "Conjectures on Few Possible Errors in the Union Version Chinese Translation of the New Testament," *Logos & Pneuma* 6 (Spring 1997): 222–231; Eric K. C. Wong, "Book Review: *He Who Has Ears Let Him Hear: Revelation and Exegesis*," *Logos & Pneuma* 18 (Spring 2003): 291–295; You Bin, "Whose Bible? Which Theology?—A Review of James Barr's *The Concept of Biblical Theology: From the Perspective of Old Testament*," *Logos & Pneuma* 19 (Autumn 2003): 281–286.
19. Liu Xiaofeng, "A Semantic Exploration of σῶμα in the Pauline Letters," *Logos & Pneuma* 20 (Spring 2004): 149–167.
20. Mark Fang, "Old Testament Theology in Present and Past," *Logos & Pneuma* 3 (Autumn 1995): 73–86.

21. Liu Xiaofeng, "Job and the Crisis of the Ancient Concept of Wisdom," *Logos & Pneuma* 5 (Autumn 1996): 79–115.
22. Tan Lizhu, "Human Beings' Worldly Understanding of the Narrative of Temptation in the Bible," *Logos & Pneuma* 8 (Spring 2004): 173–195.
23. Mark Fang, "The Concept of State and Community in the Old Testament," *Logos & Pneuma* 1 (Summer 1994): 263–269.
24. Mark Fang, "The Mystery of Holy Trinity," *Logos & Pneuma* 17 (Autumn 2002): 139–152.
25. Liu Xiaofeng, "Christ in 'Romantic Gospel,'" *Logos & Pneuma* 12 (Spring 2000): 59–88.
26. R. Brändle, "Money and Grace—On 2 Corinthians 8 & 9," trans. Chengjun Diao, *Logos & Pneuma* 8 (Spring 1998): 137–143.
27. Lo Lung-kwong and Liang Gong, eds., *The Bible and Literary Interpretation* [in Chinese] 聖經與文學闡釋 (Beijing: People's Literature Publishing House, 2003).
28. "Notes to Contributors," *Logos & Pneuma* 1 (Summer 1994): 4.
29. Li Qiuling and Yang Xinan (Daniel H. N. Yeung), eds., *Modernity, Transformation of Tradition and Sino-Christian Theology* [in Chinese] 現代性、傳統變遷與漢語神學(Shanghai: East China Normal University Press, 2009).
30. Lai Pan-chiu, "Sino-Christian Theology, the Bible, and the Christian Tradition" [in Chinese] 漢語神學、聖經與普世基督宗教傳統, in *An Initiative Proposal on Sino-Christian Scriptural Hermeneutics* [in Chinese] 漢語基督教經學芻議, ed. Lin Zichun (Jason Tsz-shun Lam) (Hong Kong: Logos & Pneuma Press, 2010), 95–113.
31. Ibid. 266–281.
32. For example, Li Chichang (Archie C. C. Lee), ed., *The Asian Context and Biblical Interpretation* [in Chinese] 亞洲處境與聖經詮釋 (Hong Kong: Christian Literature Council, 1996).
33. Li Chichang (Archie C. C. Lee), "Engaging *Lamentations* and the *Lament for the South*: A Cross-Textual Reading" [in Chinese] 哀江南賦與哀歌之相融: 跨文本閱讀之例証, *Religion Studies* 宗教研究 1 (2003): 196–207.
34. "Notes to Contributors," *Logos & Pneuma* 24 (Spring 2006): 4.
35. Lai, "Sino-Christian Theology, the Bible," 104.
36. Lin Zichun, ed., *An Initiative Proposal on Sino-Christian Scriptural Hermeneutics.* Hereafter cited as *An Initiative Proposal.*
37. Choong Chee Pong and You Bin, eds., "Biblical Studies and Chinese Academia," *Logos & Pneuma* 31 (2009): 19–175.
38. You Bin and Gao Zhe, eds., "Comparative Scripture as Sino-Christian Theology," *Logos & Pneuma* 42 (Spring 2015): 17–145.
39. You Bin, "New Testament Studies and Sino-Christian Theology," *Logos & Pneuma* 48 (Spring 2018): 17–178.
40. For examples, Jiang Zongqiang, "On the Monotheism of Isaiah 40–55," special issue, *Logos & Pneuma* 45A (Winter 2016): 297–316; Tian Haihua, "The Feminist Biblical Interpretation and Theology of Phyllis Trible," special issue, *Logos & Pneuma* 45A (Winter 2016): 529–550; Jiang Zhenshuai, "The Social Space in the Hebrew Bible: The Case of the Priestly Texts in the Torah," *Logos & Pneuma* 49 (Autumn 2018): 291–320.
41. For example, Yang Junjie, "*Kai perisson echōsin*: A New Reading of John 10:10b," *Logos & Pneuma* 42 (Spring 2015): 47–67.
42. Wan Sze-kar, "'Peace and Security': A Postcolonial Rereading of 1 Thessalonians," *Logos & Pneuma* 31 (Autumn 2009): 109–127.
43. Hong Xiaochun, "An Analysis on the Value of Speech Act Theory for Biblical Studies: With an Interpretation of 1 John as Example," *Logos & Pneuma* 48 (Spring 2018): 122–145.

44. Liang Hui, "Dialogic Hermeneutics: The Methodological Exploration of Chinese Biblical Studies from the Perspective of Comparative Scriptural Studies," *Logos & Pneuma* 50 (Spring 2019): 33–68.
45. For examples, Meng Zhenhua, "The Gatekeepers and the Ideas of Identity in the Bible in the Post-Exilic Period," *Logos & Pneuma* 31 (Autumn 2009): 83–108; Jiang, "On the Monotheism"; Tian, "Feminist Biblical Interpretation"; Hong, "Analysis on the Value of Speech Act Theory."
46. Archie C. C. Lee and You Bin, *Discourse of Life and the Communitarian Identity: Studies of the Megilloth of the Hebrew Bible* 生命言說與社群認同: 希伯來聖經五小卷研究 (Beijing: China Social Sciences Press, 2003).
47. Lo Lung-kwong and Liang Gong, eds., *An Interpretation of the Bible* [in Chinese] 聖經解讀 (Beijing: Religion Culture Publishing House, 2003); Lo and Liang, eds., *An Interpretation of the Torah & Narrative Books* [in Chinese] 律法書、敘事著作解讀 (Beijing: Religion Culture Publishing House, 2003); Lo and Liang, eds., *An Interpretation of Biblical Poetry & Wisdom Literature* [in Chinese] 詩歌書、智慧文學解讀 (Beijing: Religion Culture Publishing House, 2003); Lo and Liang, eds., *An Interpretation of the Prophets & Apocalyptic Literature* [in Chinese] 先知書、啟示文學解讀 (Beijing: Religion Culture Publishing House, 2004); Lo and Liang, eds., *An Interpretation of Four Gospels* [in Chinese] 四福音書解讀 (Beijing: Religion Culture Publishing House, 2004).
48. You Bin, "Towards a Sino-Christian Scriptural Hermeneutics: On the Nature and Approaches of Biblical Studies in the Chinese Academic Context," *Logos & Pneuma* 31 (2009): 43–64, repr. in *An Initiative Proposal*, 73–93; Paulos Huang, *Sino-Christian Academic Biblical Studies in the Light of the Globalized Great National Studies* [in Chinese] 大國學視野中的漢語學術聖經學 (Beijing: The Ethnic Publishing House, 2012).
49. Lam, *An Initiative Proposal*.
50. Jason Tsz-shun Lam, "The Concept and Problematic of Sino-Christian Scriptural Hermeneutics" [in Chinese] 漢語基督教經學的概念與問題意識, in *An Initiative Proposal*, 27–72.
51. Lai, "Sino-Christian Theology, the Bible."
52. Philip Chia, "Chinese Language, Bible and Theology: Towards a Construction of a Critical Sino-Public Biblical Theology" [in Chinese] 漢語、聖經、神學: 邁向一個批判的漢語公共聖經神學之建構, in *An Initiative Proposal*, 127–163.
53. You Bin, "Translation of the Bible, Invention of Written Words and Social Transformation: An Example of a Minority Group in Southwest China in Adopting the Bible" [in Chinese] 聖經翻譯、文字創制與社會轉型—以中國西南少數民族的聖經接受為例, in *An Initiative Proposal*, 389–406.
54. Liang Hui, "How Do Modern Christians Read the Bible? The Examples of Wu Leichun and Chao Tsu-Chen" [in Chinese] 中國現代基督徒是如何讀聖經的?—以吳雷川與趙紫宸處理聖經的原則與方法為例, in *An Initiative Proposal*, 341–355.
55. Archie C. C. Lee, "The Strategy of Cross-Cultural Hermeneutics: A Study on the Writings of Christians during Late Ming and Early Qing Dynasties" [in Chinese] 跨文本閱讀策略: 明末清初中國基督徒著作研究, in *An Initiative Proposal*, 319–340.
56. Li Tiangang, "Cross-Textual Hermeneutics: The Encounter between Theology and Chinese Classical Studies" [in Chinese] 跨文本詮釋: 神學與經學相遇, in *An Initiative Proposal*, 277–318.
57. Lai Pan-chiu, "On the Theological Diversity of the Bible from the Perspective of Chinese Buddhism: A Thought Experiment of Sino-Christian Theology" [in Chinese] 從中國佛教看聖經的神學分歧: 漢語神學的一個思想實驗 in *An Initiative Proposal*, 357–388.

58. For example, Liang Hui, "Mencius' Classical Interpretive Method of 'Tracing the Original Intention from the Understood Meaning' and Biblical Hermeneutics: Exploration of Wu Leichuan's Biblical Reading Strategies," *Logos & Pneuma* 31 (Autumn 2009): 153–715; and Chloë Starr, ed., *Reading Christian Scriptures in China* (London: T&T Clark, 2008).
59. For example, Liang, "Dialogic Hermeneutics."
60. For example, Shi Heng-tan, *Lunyu yushang Shengjing: Zhongguo wenhua yu Jidujiao di zhengmian jiaohui* [in Chinese] *The Analects Meets the Bible: The Frontal Encounter between Chinese Culture and Christianity* 論語遇上聖經: 中國文化與基督教的正面交鋒 (Beijing: World Publishing, 2014); K. K. Yeo, *What Has Jerusalem to Do with Beijing? Biblical Interpretation from a Chinese Perspective* (Eugene, OR: Pickwick, 2018).
61. For example, Samuel Hio-kee Ooi, *A Double Vision Hermeneutic: Interpreting a Chinese Pastor's Intersubjective Experience of Shi Engaging Yìzhuàn and Pauline Texts* (Eugene, OR: Pickwick Publications, 2014).
62. For examples, Yang Keqin (K. K. Yeo), *Confucius and Paul* [in Chinese] 孔子與保羅 (Shanghai: East China Normal University Press, 2009) and his *Zhuangzi and James* [in Chinese] 莊子與雅各 (Shanghai: East China Normal University Press, 2012); Lai Pinchao (Pan-chiu Lai), *Mahayana Christian Theology: Thought-Experiments of Sino-Christian Theology* [in Chinese] 大乘基督教神學: 漢語神學的思想實驗 (Hong Kong: Logos & Pneuma Press, 2011).
63. Liang, "Dialogic Hermeneutics."
64. Lai Pan-chiu, "Inheriting the Chinese and Christian Traditions in Global Context: A Confucian-Protestant Perspective," *Religion & Theology* 10.1 (2003): 7–11.
65. Christoph Schwöbel, "Rationality, Tradition and Theology: Six Theses," in *Identity and Change in the Christian Tradition*, ed. Marcel Sarot and Gijsbert van den Brink (Frankfurt am Main: Peter Lang, 1999), 179–180.
66. Schwöbel, "Rationality, Tradition and Theology," 181.
67. Lai, "Inheriting the Chinese and Christian Traditions," 11–16.
68. Delwin Brown, *Boundaries of Our Habitations: Tradition and Theological Construction* (Albany, NY: State University of New York Press, 1994), 148.
69. Lai, "Inheriting the Chinese and Christian Traditions," 19–21.
70. Lai, *Mahayana Christian Theology*, 69–102.
71. *A Dictionary of Biblical Interpretation*, ed. R. J. Coggins and J. L. Houlden (London: SCM Press, 1990), s.v. "Sachkritik," by Robert Morgan.
72. Lai, *Mahayana Christian Theology*, 39–68.

Primary Sources

He Guanghu & Yang Xinan (Daniel H. N. Yeung), eds. *Sino-Christian Theology Reader* [in Chinese] 漢語神學讀本, 2 Volumes. Hong Kong: Institute of Sino-Christian Studies, 2009.

Lai, Pan-chiu, and Jason Tsz-shun Lam, eds. *Sino-Christian Theology: A Theological qua Cultural Movement in Contemporary China*. Frankfurt am Main: Peter Lang, 2010.

Lin, Zichun (=Lam, Jason Tsz-shun), ed. An Initiative Proposal on Sino-Christian Scriptural Hermeneutics [in Chinese] 漢語基督教經學芻議. Hong Kong: The Logos & Pneuma Press, 2010.

Shi, Heng-tan. *The Analects Meets the Bible: The Frontal Encounter between Chinese Culture and Christianity* [in Chinese] 論語遇上聖經: 中國文化與基督教的正面交鋒. Beijing: World Publishing, 2014.

CHAPTER 31

SCRIPTURAL REASONING IN CHINA

YOU BIN

Background

China has been a multi-ethnic and multireligious nation since its origin. Located in the southeastern part of Eurasia, the geographic and ecological diversity presented a diversity of cultures and religions within China. It is usually described as a "starry" origin of Chinese civilizations. As a matter of fact, Confucianism and Daoism could be represented as repositories of these diversified cultures while being united by their founding figures and authoritative Scriptures. The lovely story of Confucius, the founder of Confucianism, consulting about the rituals with Laozi, the founding figure of Daoism, is a reflection of the strong interactive, even complementary, relationship between these two traditions.

With the openings of more trade roads, a closer relationship was developed between China and the world. Chinese civilization has carried out more in-depth and diverse interactions in all four directions with other nations and cultures. Through the Silk Road, the Porcelain Road, and the Spice Road on land and at sea, the religions that have originated and grown in other parts of the world also entered China, further enriching the diversity of Chinese civilization. Buddhism that originated in India came to China through the "Silk Road," and Chinese monks also went to India to seek "the True Scriptures" through the same road. Buddhism gradually became an integral part of Chinese culture. Before the rise of the Islamic empires, the Christian church was widely distributed throughout West Asia and the Middle East. It also entered China through the Silk Road. Jingjiao 景教 (commonly called "Nestorianism") in the seventh century CE represents the earliest attempt to spread the gospel in China, and its achievements are still inspiring for theological construction of today's Chinese Christianity. With the rise of Islam, various ethnic groups in the Middle East and Central Asia also brought Islam into China, and through the numerous works of "*Hui* Confucians" (*Hui* is the name of a Chinese Islamic ethnic group), the Islamic religion also has become an integral part of Chinese civilization. Catholic missionaries entered China in the sixteenth century through the Age of Discovery. They brought Christian faith to Chinese people while making a great exchange between China and Europe. They produced Christian theological works in Chinese terms, on the one hand, and introduced Chinese religions and cultures to Europeans, on the other. The first versions of the Confucian *Analects* and the Daoist *Daodejing* in European languages were translated during this period.

Respect for Scripture (or sacred books) had been a prominent phenomenon for Confucianism. Daoism followed a similar pattern in making and respecting Scriptures in its process of transformation into a religion of revelation. Buddhism adopted the term *Jing* in its translation of Indian *Sutra* into the Chinese language. In the process of strong interactions between the three religions, the immersion with the sacred texts and their interpretation of other religions was so outstanding among Chinese Confucian intellectuals or religious professionals that even "multiple religious identities" was not a criticism, but a pride, for them.

Furthermore, Confucian scholars, Daoist priests, and Buddhist monks began to develop a kind of interreligious commentary on their Scriptures. It is commonly believed that interreligious learning in crossing the border into Daoism and Buddhism had caused Confucian thinkers in the Song Dynasty (960–1279) to transform it into Neo-Confucianism, while Daoism and Buddhism more or less adopted into their beliefs and practices Confucian moral codes as being rooted in Confucian Scriptures. To appreciate Confucian Scriptures also had been a cultural strategy for those late Islamic and Christian scholars. To find the right Chinese term for the Abrahamic highest God, *Shangdi*, *Shen*, or *Tian*, Christian missionaries had to undertake a huge research project into ancient Confucian Scriptures. For Matteo Ricci, his first doctrinal work, *Tian Zhu Shi Yi* (*The True Meaning of the Heavenly Lord*), quoted dozens of passages from Confucian and Daoist Scriptures to elaborate his understanding of the Christian God. Chinese Muslims accepted the ethical framework of human life from Confucian Scripture, though insisting on the Islamic ontological belief in the human relationship with God. It is safe to say that the theological systems of Chinese Christian and Islamic thinkers were constructed in the interreligious reading and interpretation of the Abrahamic and Confucian Scriptures.

This brief introduction about the interreligious learning and comparative theological construction among Chinese religions might be helpful for us to understand why and how Scriptural Reasoning, originating out of the Anglo-Saxon context, would be received, practiced, and extended in China.

A Short Introduction of Scriptural Reasoning

To describe it simply, Scriptural Reasoning is an interreligious practice that Jews, Christians, and Muslims participate in regularly, reading passages from their respective Scriptures together.[1] It improves participants' awareness of their own religious identity and their understanding of others' religious convictions, both represented by the scriptural texts of the different faith traditions. On the one hand, SR participants respect the authority of their own Scriptures; on the other hand, they maintain openness to the sacredness of those of others. The goal of Scriptural Reasoning is not an agreement between various religious traditions but rather growth in understanding of these traditions and deeper exploration of the meaning of the texts. While participants are reading these texts together, the content of those texts would be interpreted and shared among them. In this process, the various traditions that worked and continue to work with the texts, and the possible engagement of these religious texts with a range of contemporary issues, would be involved, in an effort to make both the texts and traditions to be relevant to the contemporary world.

According to Miikka Ruokanen, a Finnish theologian and analyst of SR, SR has the potential to move interfaith dialogue away from some abstractions of religions to concrete, life-relevant texts commonly shared by religious communities. It offers a more flexible tool for developing richer, more complex, and sensitive interfaith dialogue. SR is a democratic movement as it is based on equal participation of all discussants, lay people or professionals, and is open to its results. SR insists on the value of reciprocity in recognizing oneself in relation to the other, discovering one's own identity by negotiating it through dialogue with others. Its intent is to foster a life attitude of living with deep differences with other faiths while struggling for the sake of the public good by reaching mutual appreciation through a cross reading of Scriptures together. In its full sense, SR is a comprehensive method of dialogue, encompassing and parsing the intellectual, emotional, artistic, and moral aspects of religion.[2]

As a method of reading Scriptures among different religions, Scriptural Reasoning had gained much attention and discussion around the world. It exerted much influence upon biblical studies, a general study about religious Scriptures, and interreligious engagement. In the early 1990s, Scriptural Reasoning began to be practiced among the Abrahamic religions, mainly organized by the University of Cambridge in the UK, and the University of Virginia in the United States. In recent years, Scriptural Reasoning began to attract the attention of Chinese scholars of religious studies. They adapted SR into Chinese cultural contexts and made some great changes to it. Since there is much overlap with the Bible as Christian Scripture in the Chinese religious context, biblical scholars in China also tend to have a strong interest in this practice of SR between the Bible and Scriptures of other Chinese religions.

This essay explores the way SR is being practiced in China and discusses further how it could impact biblical studies in China. It addresses this topic in four sections: perception, extension, and application of SR in China, and then some prospects for SR in China.

Perception of Scriptural Reasoning in China

Soon after the Virginia and Cambridge scholars began to practice SR in the Western context, Chinese scholars, such as Yang Huilin of Renmin University and You Bin of Minzu University of China, noticed this approach to Scriptures and interreligious dialogue at the beginning of the twenty-first century. Yang Huilin first introduced SR to the Chinese audience in an article.[3] You Bin further applied SR as a part of his methodology of biblical or Christian theological studies in the Chinese context. He extended SR into a general method of interreligious dialogue and even established a center of Comparative Scripture and Interreligious dialogue.[4] Through a one-year experimental SR project, with representatives from six religious or cultural traditions in Beijing sponsored by Minzu University and Helsinki University, SR as a way of cross reading religious or classic texts and interreligious dialogue became widely known in China. At the academic level, SR even caused a methodological reflection on studies about the translation of the Chinese Bible and missionary translation of the Chinese classics into Western languages, along with the history of cultural exchange between China and the West.[5] SR and its theoretical ideals about cultural and religious dialogue even became the research methodology for analyzing missionary achievements in the Bible and Chinese classics translators such as James Legge.[6]

Some advantages of SR were much appreciated by Chinese scholars. First, the role of Scriptures or classics is very much respected in this practice. China has a long-standing tradition of respecting authoritative texts in its cultural and philosophical formation. Confucian authoritative texts were named *Jing*, translated as "the principle of the cosmos." When the Bible was translated, it took after the Confucian name of *Jing*, a name being widely adopted by various Chinese religious traditions. Scriptures playa paramount role in almost all Chinese religions and cultures. For Abrahamic religions in China, Scripture is regarded as "the Word of God," while Scripture is regarded as the breath of the Creator God in Daoism, and similarly the works of Sage Confucius or the preaching of Buddha. All Scriptures enjoy the highest authority in religions. Chinese scholars appreciated that SR takes the texts of Scripture, rather than abstract philosophical principle or ideas, as the starting point or foundation for interreligious dialogue. In this way of reading and interpreting the texts of Scripture, the result of interreligious dialogue could be both foundational and fundamental. By "foundational" I mean that the Scriptures are all foundational to Christian life; the result of interreligious dialogue could be inspiring to the normal lives of the people. By "fundamental," I mean that Scriptures are the authoritative texts for religions, the new understanding or interpretation of the text could be normative and authoritative to the relevant religions.

Second, the particularity of every religion is always respected in SR. This is very much welcomed by Chinese biblical and religious scholars, as religious pluralism is always the dominating cultural background in China's history. Unlike the previous "global ethic" or "ultimate reality" models for interreligious dialogue that presupposed some universal and abstract principle or ideas of all religions, SR takes the particularity of every religion through its beginning to the end. SR does not believe that interreligious dialogue ought to proceed from the common points of dialogical partners. On the contrary, it encourages religions involved in the dialogue to uphold their particularity. It tries to reveal the particular meaning of each religion even if there are seemingly identical ideas, themes, or figures between them because significance or meaning could vary in the different religious systems. Chinese scholars appreciate the fact that SR does not want to produce some mega-religion that could unite all religions into a family, but to enrich and develop the particularity of each religion in the dialogue. This is what "improve the quality of differences" means in SR interreligious practice. That is to say, though religious differences would be still there even after the dialogue, people nevertheless would understand and appreciate each other more deeply. Upholding the particularity of each religion in the process of dialogue would make participants learn from each other in border crossing. Through mutual learning between participants, the particularity of each religion would develop further, and in this sense, the SR interreligious dialogue would help the religions involved "become a better self."

Third, the value of "openness" in SR is very much appreciated by religious scholars in China. Though the texts in SR would be taken from the Scriptures of particular religions, their meaning is open to all participants in the process of reasoning. The first step in SR is to interpret the texts by the representatives of that religion or tradition in accordance with its own meaning system. The representative of a religious tradition in SR can use his academic background to provide sufficient explanation for a certain paragraph of text, a certain person or symbol; nonetheless, he or she does not have the sole, exclusive right of interpreting the text. On the contrary, in the SR process of interreligious conversation, the text would be "de-familiarized." This would result in new, and creative, interpretations of those once-familiar texts. In the process of SR, participants begin to reflect upon the theological understanding of the sacred texts as a mirror to other religions, some neglected tradition would be re-discovered or enriched, and some new horizon of interpretation would emerge. In an ultimate sense, the "de-familiarization" would give birth to an experience of encountering the ever-renewing God or ultimate reality of any religion.

In short, the nature and method of SR have special appeal to Chinese religious persons and scholars in the university as it combines respect for authoritative texts with openness to unknown dialogical partners, religious affiliation with intellectual argumentation, and loyalty to a home faith with a sympathy to other religious traditions. SR could be practiced as a way of interreligious dialogue, and also be of methodological inspiration to studies of the multireligious situation in Chinese culture and history. In their adaptation of SR to religions in China, some interesting extensions they made would be of special interest for both religious and biblical studies.

Extension of Scriptural Reasoning in China

Scriptural Reasoning could be described as a new effort of contemporary European and American religious scholars in response to their multireligious situation. However, similar practices and theoretical reflections have constituted a continuing tradition in the history of Chinese religion. Due to the "starry" multicultural coexistence since the origin of Chinese civilization, and the interaction between religious traditions of the northern pastoral nomads and those of the southern agricultural settlers, and the entry of Abrahamic and Indian religions from the West into China along the Silk Road, the diversity of religions and their deep interreligious learning have always been a basic cultural reality for Chinese religion. There is congenital adaptability between SR and theological or religious studies in China. Therefore, we can see that Chinese religious and biblical scholars extended SR in its scope and theoretical presuppositions. Three extensions could be easily identified in the SR movement in China.

First, SR in China is extended to a discipline of so-called "comparative scripture," a combination of scripture reasoning and comparative theology in the academic and cultural context of China. In the process of practicing SR among religious representatives, scholars of SR in China are not satisfied with the nature of social or religious friendship building among different religions, and they wish to, on the one hand, produce something more systematic and coherent and, on the other, investigate the history of religious dialogue or interreligious learning in Chinese civilization. Their acquaintance with comparative theology, represented by Francis Clooney, and the series, *Christian Commentaries on Non-Christian Sacred Texts,* edited by Catherine Corneille, had pushed the Chinese SR scholars to see how they can absorb the advantages of those two academic approaches into SR practices, and to improve its visibility and influence in their university settings. According to You Bin of Minzu University of China, the discipline of comparative Scripture is, on the one hand, an academic branch in which sacred texts could be read interreligiously and their history of interpretation could be compared; on the other hand, comparative Scripture could be an interreligious learning in border crossing with the purpose of strengthening the ability of the home tradition in facing the challenges of the modern world through the deep learning from scriptural inspiration or interpretation of the guest religion(s). In the sense of the latter, the comparative Scripture could be viewed as a theological enterprise in a multireligious or cross-cultural context.[7]

Second, SR in China begins to see what values or principles the ancient Chinese wisdom could provide to enrich its theory and practice. SR had proposed some values, for example, to celebrate the particularity, to improve the quality of differences, etc. Nevertheless, according to SR scholars in China, there is a resource in the ancient wisdom of Chinese civilization that could signify, enrich, and expand the horizon of SR, because interreligious learning and dialogue have been a fundamental logic or structure for the formation of Chinese civilization. From its beginning, Chinese ancient civilization has not been singular but has multiple origins. To describe it in a metaphorical way, Chinese civilization is of "starry" multiple origins. Therefore, to celebrate the value of plurality, border-crossing learning is inherent in Chinese culture. Some philosophical values or wisdom had been discovered and embraced by SR in China. For example, "A variety of thing is fostered and the Dao(s) would be parallel without contradiction" (萬物並育而不相害、道並行而不相悖), a saying from *The Book of Means*, is interpreted as a Chinese value for an ontological celebration of the plurality of religions. Another saying of Confucius in the *Analects*, "cultivating oneself while putting others at ease" (修己安人), is Chinese wisdom about mutual enrichment between self and others in a single activity. It could uphold the value of "double renaissance" of both the home and guest tradition in interreligious dialogue in China, as corresponding to the value of "improving the differences" of SR, so that all participants in SR could be enriched through the border-crossing reading of the scriptural texts.

Third, SR began to extend to Eastern religious traditions in its practice in China. Usually, SR in the United Kingdom and the United States would have participants from Judaism, Islam, and Christianity. In this sense, SR is a friendship-building activity of inner Abrahamic religions. Nonetheless, SR in China will have to include sacred texts from so-called Asian religions or traditions: Confucianism, Daoism, and Buddhism. The practice of SR in Minzu, in reality, invited participants from the three Chinese religions to share their perspectives on various themes based on their sacred texts. With the inclusion of these three Chinese religions, not only is there a greater difference in their understanding about different themes, but also more fundamental challenges would rise up against the presuppositions of SR. For example, the idea of Scripture itself was challenged by Chinese religions, that there is no such idea of divine inspiration or revelation in these religions as there is in the Abrahamic traditions. Scripture is more like a repository of life wisdom or philosophical argumentation. And the flexibility of Chinese religions would challenge the identity of religions with Scriptures. For example, in the Confucian tradition, its Scripture is mainly the "five scriptures" (五經, Five Classics), but after the Song dynasty (960–1279), Neo-Confucianism had formed the Four Books (四書), though two of them came from a single *The Book of Rites* in the "five scriptures," to supersede the role of Scripture. The massive collection of Scriptures or sacred texts in Chinese religions would challenge the impression of a single volume, a closed book as Scripture in theology, and make it difficult to select passages for different sessions of SR in practice. Nevertheless, the inclusion of the Eastern religious texts into SR had very much extended the horizon of participants from both Abrahamic and Chinese traditions, and the theological brainstorming between the West and East would make a deeper intellectual exchange for those participants.

Fourth, scholars began to adapt the theoretical and methodological implications of SR into biblical studies in China. For Chinese biblical scholars, the question of how to do comparative studies between the Bible and Chinese Scriptures, or how to develop a cross-textual reading of biblical texts in China, is always a prior research presupposition.[8] SR brought a new vision and practice to biblical studies in China. It argues that the purpose of comparative reading of Scriptures, Christian and Chinese, is not to find commonality or some universal ground, but to enrich each other and to improve the quality of difference through the border-crossing deep learning, which could help biblical studies in its interaction with Chinese Scripture to build up its Christian identity. In the SR session about the formation of Scripture in Chinese religions, the Confucian scholar's argument that the five scriptures laid the scriptural foundation for the "five-thousand-year-old Chinese civilization," can inspire biblical scholars to explore the cultural identity of the Bible in China. Likewise, the Jewish, even ancient Near Eastern, origin of the Bible, can shed light on the cultural continuity of the Jewish Tanakh into the Christian New Testament, therefore also into Chinese Bible.[9]

In conclusion, religious scholars creatively adapted SR to a Chinese context. This expanded the meaning of SR, theoretically and methodologically, in the cross reading of Abrahamic and Eastern religious texts. With its combination with Chinese pluralist values and its inclusion of Chinese religious texts, its impact on Chinese religious studies, especially upon the biblical studies, would appear in the future, while the original meaning of SR would be enriched with Chinese significance.

Practice of Scriptural Reasoning in China

Chinese scholars not only introduced SR involving the Scriptures of the Abrahamic traditions into Chinese academia but also began to practice SR after the inclusion of Chinese religions. The first experiment of SR in China was carried out in Beijing as a cooperative project between Minzu University of China and the University of Helsinki from 2014 to 2015. For the first time, SR included the sacred texts of Daoism, Confucianism, and Buddhism (sometimes even the Theravada tradition was represented too) alongside the canonical texts of Christianity, both Catholic and Protestant as they are listed as two separate religions in China, and of Islam. The Scriptures of all the faith traditions of China were represented in this dialogue. Professors You Bin and Miikka Ruokanen were the moderators of the experiment, and Dr. Li Huawei followed the whole experimental process as a participatory researcher.[10] Two SR groups, one consisting of members of scholars and professionals of the Chinese religions, and the other made up of young students, met simultaneously at Minzu University once a month, for a total of ten sessions, each of which lasted about three hours.

The topics of each session, proposed by the project moderator but also discussed and agreed to by participants of the SR groups themselves, were the following: the creation of the universe, the problem of poverty, the problem of suffering and evil, the role of women in religion and society, the definition of a good society, the definition of saintliness, our responsibility for the environment, the circumstances of and after death, etc. Before each meeting, every member of the SR groups chose a passage from the sacred texts of her/his tradition and prepared a short, written commentary on that extract for group discussion. As a matter of fact, the texts chosen were sometimes very different in the two groups. During the meeting itself, each member gave an oral presentation and explanation upon the texts, followed by a Q & A and an open discussion.

For the dialogue and discussion of the different religious texts, SR sessions operated according to the following principles: (1) All participating members are required to abide by the facilitation of the moderators. For each session, a scholar representing a particular faith tradition will serve as the moderator, deliberating on the schedule and the order of and allotted time for each speaker. (2) Each text is to be read carefully. Special attention is paid to the rhetorical use of words, syntax, intonation, and context. (3) Discussion first focuses on the text at hand. If other sources are quoted, its relation to the text at hand will be explicated. Those who belong to the tradition of the given text may be more familiar with it, but those who are from other traditions may offer new revelations through their intuition, speculation, doubts, and even misunderstandings. (4) Discussions in and of the original languages of the texts is be expanded on for richer understanding, while philological details is to be relevant to the discussion at hand. Nevertheless, discussions in and of the original languages may not hinder creative exegeses. (5) Participants are welcome and even encouraged to offer bold new interpretations of texts and to question others. Unfamiliarity, after all, is what instigates interpretation and dialogue. Showing respect for the texts of other traditions and for the traditions themselves is a necessary precondition. (6) SR does not advocate suspending one's own belief but rather welcoming the integration of one's own faith tradition to one's interpretation with the following caveats: (a) a personal religious stance does not enhance the authority of any given interpretation; it is rather thorough analysis of texts, inclusive of the existing, laboriously developed exegetical tradition within a religion, and prudent and moderate reasoning that contribute to the depth and breadth of dialogues; and (b) interpretations is not to remain fixed, since the meaning of a particular text never remains unchanged, as much for insiders of as for outsiders to a faith tradition. (7) Comments from others are to be heard attentively and affably. One can then ask where they obtained the interpretation, so as to know the reasons and assumptions behind their comments. They are invited to elucidate any point that is unclear.

SR, as practiced in the experimental sessions, follows these procedures. The responsibility of a moderator is to ensure an ordered, effective, and beneficial discussion following the above principles. The first step of SR is reading the text. Time allotted to reading each text will not exceed three minutes. The second step of SR is the interpretation of the text by one who comes from that religion or tradition. This will not exceed five minutes. The third step of SR is dialogue. Participants may raise questions, ask for clarification, offer their own interpretations, make comparisons, or delve deeper into the texts. A moderator will keep time, facilitate the questioning process, and offer brief summaries of the discussion at hand. At the end of each session, the moderator, or a participant appointed by the moderator, will give a summary for the whole session. In different traditions, the interpretation of texts cannot be separated from their specific rituals. In such cases, ritual recitations or hymns would be utilized to allow a deeper understanding of the text.

Li Huawei did sociological research about the impact of SR on participants from all Chinese faith traditions. Among the nineteen questionnaires that were filled out by representatives of various faith traditions, fourteen showed a positive attitude toward other religions and an interest in knowing more about other religions after SR. Sixteen have sympathy toward other religions. As for the effects of SR, eighteen out of nineteen participants agreed that SR is conducive to develop a deeper understanding of other religions. The same percentage of participants showed that the conversations in SR would be helpful, though not obvious, to understand their own faiths too. The research shows that SR is effective in promoting mutual understanding between the religions.

As "particularity" is the first value of SR, it encourages participants to bring religious identity and theological reflection into the conversation. Seventeen out of nineteen people felt no restriction in showing their religious identity for most of the time. The value of "reciprocity" also has been proven in SR practices, as fourteen participants felt that those of other faith traditions showed genuine interest in knowing more about their faith, and sixteen believed that those of other faiths had reached an understanding about their religions.

For participants, to join SR to discuss different themes gives them an opportunity to reflect on their strength and potential to respond to modern issues. They believed that Chinese religions could contribute greatly to Chinese education, individual and social morality, environmental protection, social development, and charity work. Joining hands together, Chinese religions, understanding each other better, can help the shaping of a good society. In the civil area, like promoting women's social status, providing a spirituality to face the challenges of modern life, and forming an organizational basis for social development and solidarity, they believed that religions could play their special roles. Furthermore, the positive influence of religions upon morality can contribute to the rule of law, social justice, and equality of all citizens.

Participants also felt happy and that the SR process had been effective in showing a clear purpose of offering a democratic occasion and equal opportunity for each member to participate actively in the discussion. The procedure of SR ensured a free and coherent argument about the important issues all religions are facing. With the experience of SR, participants began to think more about concrete means of fostering moral education in their faith communities in order to strengthen their ability to deal with all important civil and moral issues. In the spirit of friendship fostered in SR, religious professionals showed a willingness to cooperate through religious charities for social-justice issues, and for the welfare of the people, for the equality of women and men, and for environmental protection, etc.

Prospects for Scriptural Reasoning in China

It seems that the principle of particularity, celebrating differences, and jointly building a civil society learned through the spiritual traditions of SR could find their echo in ancient Chinese wisdom, which somehow is commonly shared by Chinese religions. SR provided religions in China an opportunity to meet regularly and to speak to the issues of civil society in responding to common themes in the SR sessions. The significance of the biblical texts could shed much light on comparative reading with Chinese religious texts. As a matter of fact, all participants claimed that they benefited from their participation in the SR groups. The majority of participants showed their favor over the procedure and methods of SR, agreeing that it will be continued with regular and irregular publications on its latest achievements, as the publication would urge participants to reason with the texts more fully and deeply; in addition, circulation of the SR sessions could exert more influence on the general society. There are at least three directions along which SR could contribute more to Chinese religions, society, and culture.

The first is to promote the practice of SR among religious communities. The experimental sessions of SR were mainly conducted in an academic context. The social and cultural power of SR could be released if SR could be done within religious communities at various levels. If the SR procedures, and the different civil or cultural themes of previous SR, could be worked out as a handbook, it would give an impetus for living religious communities to practice SR on their own. Civil topics, for example, the social status of women, environmental protection, etc., would help religious communities in China to develop closer cooperation with other faith communities in various projects. If SR could be more fully practiced by living religious communities, it would not be confined in the textual sphere; rather, it would extend to different forms of artwork, for example, concert or painting exhibitions, etc., that surely reflect more lively and deeply the spiritual traditions of the Scriptures.

The second is to develop a deep, sophisticated, and systematic interpretation of some texts of particular religions after receiving inspiration from SR. One of the purposes of SR is to develop a friendship between different religions through the cross reading of texts together. Another goal is to uphold the particularity of every religion. Nevertheless, the particularity of every religion depends on the growth and transformation of these religions themselves. Therefore, one important goal of SR would be a theological interpretation of some particular texts, passages, or chapters of Scriptures along with the particular tradition. A deep, sophisticated, and systematic interpretation of scriptural texts needs to be done with inspiration from the SR sessions. Ideally, it would be a theological achievement if there could be a stronger interaction between the scriptural interpretation and theological argument. To help religions to be creatively transformed in the process of reasoning about all these modern issues with the scriptural interpretation would be a final goal for SR in China. This would be extremely important for biblical studies in China, as a systematic theology rooted in the biblical texts while being nourished by Chinese cultures would be the foundation upon which Chinese Christian identity could be built.

The third is to have a strong integration of SR with the study of Chinese religions. China has a long history of interreligious dialogue. Interreligious commentary, or even interfaith borrowing, could take place between the native Chinese religions, Confucianism and Daoism, and also between the so-called foreign religions, such as Buddhism, Islam, and Christianity and the two native religions above. SR could, on the one hand, provide a methodological inspiration for understanding the nature and practice of interreligious learning in China, and then further about the nature of Chinese religiosity of "multiple religious belongings" and, on the other hand, become more fruitful in rooting in the rich soil of Chinese culture of interreligious dialogue.

Notes

1. For a general introduction to SR, see https://www.interfaith.cam.ac.uk/.
2. Miikka Ruokanen and Li Huawei, "Scriptural Reasoning as a Method of Interreligious Dialogue in China," *Journal of Comparative Scripture* 8 (2016): 15–17.
3. See Yang Huilin's 楊慧林 argument for the aspects and significance of Scriptural Reasoning for the construction of public theology, see "The Significance of Scriptural Reasoning and Theological Studies in Public Life" [in Chinese] "經典辯讀"的價值命意與"公共領域"的神學研究, in *Journal of Yangtze River Academy* 長江學術 1 (2009): 51–52.
4. See You Bin, "Comparative Scriptural Studies as an Approach of Doing Biblical Studies in China: Taking Zhu Xi's Scripture Reading Strategy as a Case Study," *Gregorianum* 92.4 (2011): 665–686.
5. Yang Huilin, *Scriptural Reasoning: A Dialogue Between West and East* [in Chinese] 經文辯讀: 中西之間的思想對話, and a series of articles on the implication of the theory and practice of SR for Chinese culture and religious studies, *Journal of Renmin University of China* 人民大學學報 5 (2012): 1–36.
6. Qiu Yexiang 邱業祥, *Self and Other: A Study of James Legge's Translation and Interpretation of Analects from the Perspective of Scriptural Reasoning* [in Chinese] 自我與他者: 經文辯讀視域中的理雅各《論語》譯解研究 (Beijing: China Social Science Press, 2017).
7. You Bin, "Comparative Scriptural Studies as an Approach of Doing Biblical Studies in China," 665–686.
8. See Archie C. C. Lee, "Scriptural Translations and Cross-Textual Hermeneutics," *The Oxford Handbook of Christianity in Asia*, ed. Felix Wilfred (Oxford: Oxford University Press, 2014), 121–133; and K. K. Yeo, *Musing with Confucius and Paul: Toward a Chinese Christian Theology* (Eugene, OR: Wipf and Stock, 2008).
9. You Bin, "The Sinicization of Christianity Calls for an Awareness of 'Greater Theology'" [in Chinese] 基督教中國化呼喚大神學意識, *Preface of Apostles' Creed: A Chinese Catechism* 《使徒信經》要理問答 (Beijing: Religious Culture Press, 2018), 1–13.
10. For a more detailed analysis, see Li Huawei, "Practice of Scriptural Reasoning in China: Analysis of the Experiment of Interreligious Dialogue between the Six Religions of China, 2014–15," *International Journal of Sino-Western Studies* 9 (December 2015): 149–164. And Miikka Ruokanen and Li Huawei, "Scriptural Reasoning as a Method of Interreligious Dialogue in China," 9–35.

Primary Sources

Clooney, Francis. *Comparative Theology: Deep Learning across Religious Borders*. London: Wiley-Blackwell, 2010.

Ford, David F., and Chad Pecknold. *The Promise of Scriptural Reasoning*. Oxford: Blackwell, 2006.

Ochs, Peter. *Come, Study! Teaching and Learning Scriptural Reasoning*. Stanford: Stanford University Press, 2012.

You, Bin, ed. *Journal of Comparative Scripture*, vols. 1–8. Beijing: Religious Culture Press, 2013–2018.

CHAPTER 32

THE BIBLE AND CHINESE MINORITY CULTURES

SHI HENGTAN

Introduction

THERE are officially fifty-six ethnic groups that constitute a large family of the Chinese nation, but the actual number of ethnic groups far exceeds that count. Ethnic minorities mainly live in border areas, especially in the southwest of China. Missionaries who came to China preached the gospel not only to the Han people but also to minority nationalities—especially Protestant missionaries since the nineteenth century. However, generally the Han people have a sense of cultural superiority, and thus a feeling of hostility, as well as fear, toward anything that is "foreign." When they accept Christianity, they also take a pragmatic attitude of hoping Christianity will meet their practical need. Ethnic minorities are very different from the Han people. They have long lived in isolation and suffered cultural discrimination from the Han nationality. When they encounter Christianity, they regard it as an opportunity to achieve their national rebirth and liberation. Their ancient myths and legends are quickly replaced and renewed by the Christian faith.

The Bible and Minority Culture in Southwest China

Since the signing of the Yantai Treaty 煙台條約 in 1876, missionaries have gradually entered Guizhou and Yunnan provinces in the southwest China.

The Spread of Christianity in Minority Areas in Southwest China

In 1877, missionaries of the China Inland Mission, Charles Henry Judd and James F. Broughton, entered Guizhou from Hunan province to missionize. In 1881, Mr. and Mrs. Clarke, a missionary couple from the China Inland Mission, came to Dali City in Yunnan and planted the first church there. In 1904, Samuel Pollard, pastor of the Methodist Church, missionized in Shimenkan Village, Weining County, Guizhou province, at the junction of Yunnan and Guizhou.

In 1902, William Young, a missionary of the American Baptist Foreign Mission Society, preached among the Lahu people and Wa people communities in the southern part of the Sino-Burmese border in southwestern Yunnan. In 1921, he established a church in Lancang Nuo Fu. In the twenty years following, over two hundred churches were built, and more than sixty thousand followers became Christians.

In 1913, Bathow preached in the northern part of the Sino-Burmese border. Following him, James O. Fraser and some missionaries of the China Inland Mission, such as Allyn B. Cooke and a couple, John and Isobel Kuhn, also went to Lushui, Bijiang, Fugong and other counties to build churches, and a large number of Lisu people and Nu tribal group became Christians.

Around 1913, American Presbyterian missionaries Gao Meixin, Cliffton Dodd, and others came to preach in Jinghong City from Thailand. On October 15, 1917, they began to establish missionary sites in Jinghong to carry out permanent missionary work. Missionaries frequently visited and preached in Xishuangbanna. They learned that if some people there were believed to be "*pipa* ghosts,"[1] the whole family would be expelled from the village. As more and more "*pipa* ghosts" families were isolated from traditional Dai society, they lived together to form new "*pipa* ghost villages." Moreover, families of leprosy patients also were expelled from their original villages and formed their own communities. Three such villages have converted to Christianity thus far. Dai priests and Christians often performed rituals to cast out ghosts in the name of God according to their understanding of the Bible's teachings, and rejected their own traditional Buddhist beliefs. They believed that "witches" among them needed to admit that the God of the Bible has more power than their own gods and ghosts.

At the beginning of the seventeenth century, Jesuits came to Tibet to preach. In 1856, the Moravian Mission came to Tibet. In the nineteenth century, Biet Felix, a French missionary, established a church in Upper Yanjing Village, Naxi Nationality Township, Mangkang County, Changdu District in Tibet. In 1865, Father Deng Deliang, a missionary of Paris Foreign Missions Society, established a church there, the only existing Catholic Church in Tibet Autonomous Region. The Catholics in Upper Yangjing Village still live a different life from those around them, and the story of the movie *Ticket* 車票 revolves around the Catholic Church there.

The common feature of the transmission of Christianity to minority groups is the publication of literature, especially the Bible, as a tool intended to assist Christians in learning the written form of Christian doctrine and etiquette, as well as the oral form of singing hymns. In most cases, the two approaches are parallel and cooperative, but sometimes one is dominant and the other is secondary. Most missionaries adopt the first way as they preach to the Han nationality and the second way as they work among minority nationalities. There are some differences between minorities and the Han people. Since singing is common among minority peoples, it is easy for them to learn Christian poetry. In fact, minority peoples learn most Christian teachings from Christian hymns.

Creating Words, Translating Bibles, and Composing Hymns

Bible translation is the incarnation in language as the Bible becomes vernacular, thus fulfilling the culture, and as the vernacular "re-presence" of the Bible and its teachings.[2] Many missionaries have edited dictionaries before translating the Bible. Samuel Pollard, an Englishman, created a script for the old Miao language in 1905, with the help of his Miao followers John Chang, Jacob Yang, and Li Stephen, a teacher of the Han nationality. Later generations named this writing system, "Pollard Miao alphabet" or "Pollard script." He also took charge of the translation work of some Miao textbooks, such as the *Miao Primitive Reading Book*, which contains Miao's historical legends, poems, stories, etc., as well as scientific knowledge and common sense of daily life. These publications were sold in churches and schools. In 1917, the New Testament (henceforth NT) in Huamiao script was printed and published in Yokohama, Japan. By 1929, it was produced in three editions, and 10,000 copies were printed. In 1923, with the help of local Black Miao Christians, M. H. Hutton 胡致中 and other missionaries created a new Miao writing system, borrowing letters from Chinese phonetic signs. In 1935, they translated and published the NT.

Wendaocheng 文道成, a Canadian missionary, led Yi followers Ann Wenliang 安文良, Wang Xingju 王興舉, and Jacob Yang 楊約瑟, to create a set of Yi scripts with phonetic characters and translated *Song of Odes to the Lord* 頌主聖歌 (a total of sixty hymns) in this new Yi language, which was printed and published in Kunming in 1935. From 1912 to 1919, two missionaries, James O. Fraser and Rev. Bathow, created Lisu script. In 1937, Allyn B. Cooke, a missionary, translated and published the *Lisu Eulogy of the Lord* 頌主歌曲 (now known as the Lisu Hymn 傈僳文讚美詩), collecting 319 hymns in all.

Hu Guding 胡古丁, a missionary, trained eight Dai missionaries and fifty-six doctors in Xishuangbanna, and sent some of his followers to Thailand to study the Bible in English and Thai. The missionaries set up a primary school to teach the languages of Chinese, English, Dai, and to teach the Bible. American missionaries took charge of the English courses. With the help of Dai Christians and Thai missionaries, American missionaries translated the Old Testament and some hymns into the Dai language. In the marketplace, they used pictures to tell biblical stories to multi-ethnic people who came to the streets, and that facilitated the preaching of Christianity and helped Christians in understanding Christian doctrines.[3]

In 1890, Ola Hanson, an American Baptist missionary, collected 25,000 Kachin words and created the Kachin script based on the Roman alphabet. Later, he wrote many books, including *Doctrine Questions and Answers*, *Pinyin Manual*, *Scriptures for Day Class*, and *Kachins: Their Customs and Traditions* 克欽人的傳統習俗, and completed the translation of the Kachin Bible. He also translated more than four hundred hymns and composed more than two hundred hymns himself.

Church schools also offered music courses to teach Western music theory. The church introduced trumpets, organs, and other Western musical instruments, popularized the musical staffs, and taught hymns, scientific vocalization, and four-part choruses. From 1905 to 1908, Shimenkan church of the Christian Methodist Church and Gerb Church of the China Inland Mission co-edited the compilation of *Psalms* 詩篇歌, a total of fifty hymns. In 1932, the Shimenkan church mimeographed the *Odes to the Lord* 協合頌主聖詩調, a music piece composed for four voices.

In 1939, Gerb Chuch's missionary Liu Gusen 劉谷森 and his wife, together with their Miao coworker Yang Zhicheng 楊志成, selected 213 poems, and edited and published them in one book, named *Hymns* 讚美詩. In 1939, the translation of the *Odes to the Lord* 頌主聖歌 was supplemented by eighty re-editions, and in 1948, 275 hymns were re-edited. The melody of "Ancient Song," sung by Dahua Miao in the past, has a sad and sorrowful tone, for it reflects the despair of life. Now the hymn is full of excitement, expressing the praise of God and the hope of life.

In Tibet, Rev. H. A. Jaeschke of the Moravian Mission in Germany wrote several preaching pamphlets and school textbooks in Tibetan and began to translate the Bible. He translated the entire NT with the assistance of a Tibetan Lama and his colleague F. S. Redslop, and the first standard Tibetan NT book (lacking only Hebrews and Revelation) was translated in 1875.

Spiritual Songs of the Miao People

The hymn is often called a "spiritual song," because it is thought that, when Christians are filled with the Holy Spirit, they sing a hymn spontaneously. These kinds of spiritual songs are often sung in the native language, and the folk music familiar to that nationality. Once the people reach a state of religious trance, they compose these songs. Most of these songs disappeared rather quickly, but some good lyrics were preserved and circulated, such as Yang Marco's 楊馬可 "Come to worship the Lord" 齊來敬拜主, "Praise My Heavenly Father" 讚美我天父, Yang Yongfang's 楊永芳 "Ode to Peace" 和平頌, "Wonderful Power" 奇妙的大能, "Christmas Carol" 聖誕佳音歌, and so on. Yang Yongfang said in an interview, "It seems that from the heaven down into my heart, in my heart it seems that the heaven sends out such a song."[4]

In 2008, Guizhou Christian Church published *Guizhou Spiritual Songs* 貴州靈歌 compiled by Wu Wanhua 吳萬華, in which 1,248 pieces were collected. Some of the contents of spiritual songs are directly from the Bible, some are the visions and dreams of Christians, and some convey their emotions after the experience of being saved. The spiritual songs seemed to imbue the Miao people with a sense of vigor and happiness.

The Hymns of the Lisu People

The hymns of the Lisu People consist of the translation of Western hymns and the creation of Lisu Christians. For example, in the *Lisu Spiritual Songs* 靈歌, the 140th "Lord Jesus, My Road" 主耶穌，我的路 is said to have been written by Moses from Luxi County, Dehong Prefecture. The seventeenth, fifty-seventh, and eightieth hymns are also the works of Lisu Christians. These songs were taught and sung only after the revision of missionary Allyn B. Cooke.

In the past thirty years, there have been a large number of self-compiled hymns. Initially, this was the spontaneous creation of ordinary Christians with the inspiration of the Holy Spirit, and the quality was not high. Later, some music-savvy professionals greatly improved their level of creation and injected personal style into the hymns. Li Weicai 李衛才 is well-regarded among them.[5]

Miao and Lisu Christians sing in solo, duets, and chorus. They especially love to sing at multi-voice, unaccompanied chorus. Usually, there are dozens of people in the choir. At important gatherings, there will be thousands of people. In singing, the harmony between the voices shows their strong musical talent and skills.

These hymns also have a great attraction for young urban people in contemporary society, and some have come to church as a result. Zhang Yu narrates a young musician in Lizhong City who smoked, drank, and smoked marijuana. After going to the Lisu Church, he believed in Christianity and began to quit smoking and drinking. He sang hymns all day and learned Lisu.[6]

Opening Schools and Developing Education

Samuel Pollard planted churches, ran a hospital, and built a school in Shimen Kankan, which made this remote Miao village the cultural center of Wumeng Mountains in the following decades, famous both at home and abroad. Samuel Pollard had a famous slogan, "Where there is a church, there is a school."

At the Miao Church Primary School in Sappushan, A. G. Nicholls 郭秀峰, a missionary of the China Inland Mission, compiled a set of Miao literacy textbooks for Bible lessons. Some of the contents of the first lesson in Chinese are expressed in the form of *Three-Character Scriptures* 三字經, such as: "Since the beginning, there has been God, creating all things, creating heaven and earth, the great foundation, and he is the human father, is present everywhere" (自太初, 有上帝, 造萬物, 造天地, 大根本, 乃人父, 處處在). The second lesson also is related to the Bible: "God is all-knowing, all-powerful and all-present, without beginning or end, without change" (神是自有永有, 無始無終, 無變無異, 全知、全能、全在).[7] In the curriculum of church schools in Jingpo ethnic minority areas in western Yunnan, English and Jingpo are the main subjects in the first grade, and Bible learning is promoted as the main course in the third and fourth grade.

Miao followers also compile textbooks. In the summer vacation of 1932, Zhu Huanzhang 朱煥章 and Zhang Chaolun 張超倫, Wang Jianming 王建明 and Yang

Hanxian 楊漢先, who used to be Christian classmates in Shimenkan and were studying in Chengdu at that time, compiled a set of *Night Textbooks for Miao People in Yunnan, Guizhou and Guizhou* 滇黔苗民夜課讀本 in their spare time. Any Christians and non-Christians who went to the thirty-five churches set up by Shimenkan parish in the border areas of Yunnan, Guizhou, and Sichuan provinces were required to read these textbooks.

The education initiated by missionaries such as Samuel Pollard 柏格理 has been widely used in the Yunnan and Guizhou minorities areas. The second delegation of the Central Visiting Mission found in 1951 that 90 percent of the Miao people in the counties could understand the Latin alphabet of the Miao language spelled by Western missionaries. All the Black Yi and Lisu Christians living in the valley could understand the Latin alphabet of the Black Yi and Lisu language.[8]

The Baptist Church founded twenty-one church schools in Lancang County, Yunnan province. Among them, there were more than two hundred male and female students in Nuofu Church School in 1923. In 1936, American Pastor Bei Wenhua 貝文華 founded a church school named Mengjiaming Dao Yuan in Mengjia Village in western Yunnan province. In addition to Chinese textbooks, the school also taught the Old Testament and the NT, *Odes to the Lord* 頌主聖歌, and some books complied by their own teachers, such as oral English textbooks, abacus and written arithmetic textbooks.

In 1916, the Bible School was founded in Dading County, Guizhou province. The students are mainly Christians, Yi and Miao children, and orphans adopted by the church. The main courses are the Bible and the hymn. The church covers living expenses and books of the students.

As for the relationship between reading and religion, Wang Mingji 王明基, a Shimenkan preacher, said, "We believe in religion [Christianity] mainly to get books to read. We believe not because of wanting to go to heaven, but to get foreigners to run schools for free, so we actively participate in religious activities."[9] Chen Xuhui explains, "Christianity makes us learn cultural knowledge. We are very happy and proud.... With culture, you will not be bullied."[10] Others believe that Jesus sent them books, creating a desire for God.[11] In the 1930s and 1940s, there was a reading "fever" among Miao people in northeast Yunnan and northwest Guizhou. Poor families also want to send their children to school; families with children in school feel honored and people with knowledge are respected.

Word Ministries Including Newspapers, Magazines, Brochures

The Miao people in Shimenkan have sorted out the Miao people's *Ancient History and Legends* 古史傳說 and circulated a newspaper in the Miao language called *Semimonthly* 半月刊 to publicize Christian doctrine and scientific-cultural knowledge.

In the 1920s, Lisu Christians Lawada and Lemaida adopted the Lisu brochure "Mayimi" 馬益米, with comprehensive biblical contents, when they preached in Weixi

County, Yunnan province. Afjia, a Naxi Christian, also uses color pictures to tell biblical stories in Fugong County. Li, a Dai Christian, also sells biblical books and wall-charts in various languages to the Dai people in Mengjia. Guiyang Mainland Association has *Spiritual Newsletter* 靈通讯 and Christian Evidence Mission has *Wilderner Language* 曠野人語 (founded on September 1, 1946).

The main works of Vial Paul, a French Catholic missionary, include the Yi classics, *The Origin of the Universe* 宇宙流源, *Yi Nationality: History, Religion, Customs, Language and Letters* 倮倮, 歷史, 宗教, 習俗, 語言和文字, *Research on Yi Language in Yunnan* 雲南彝族文字研究, *Yi Language Grammar* 彝語語法, *French-Yi Dictionary* 法倮字典.

From 1919 to 1920, the Tibetan Sacred Teaching Bureau of Dajianlu published 115,000 religious short stories and pamphlets, which were distributed to Tibetans. The bookstore also gave free books to all missionaries working on the Tibetan border and hired many people to travel there to promote the sales of religious books and single volume editions of the Bible, amounting to more than 1,000,000 copies.[12]

The Bible and the Lifestyle of Minority Nationalities

As we have seen already in this essay and will see in the examples to follow, the relationship between the Bible and the cultures of minority nationalities is neither a simple nor a linear issue. While Christian mission works came to the minority nationalities with good intentions of bringing and/or strengthening resources of literacy, education, social welfare, and the arts, two critical questions surface in our description: (1) Whether cultural imperialism is implicit both in the Christian mission activities and in the biblical messages they bring that are meant to benefit recipients. In other words, do the Bible and culture exist as two separate entities? If not, what is the relationship between them? (2) What do the cultures of the minority nationalities have to contribute to the Bible, especially in terms of translation, expression, interpretation, or even content?[13]

These two questions are especially important when we discuss the Bible and the lifestyle of minority cultures, such as traditional customs and cultural practices. For example, the remnants of the original group marriage system—public marriage housing system (公房制度),[14] transfer marriage system (轉房制度),[15] aunt and cousin marriage (姑舅表婚)—were changed as the biblical message of marriage was taught by missionaries in the minorities areas. Monogamy was implemented strictly, and consanguineous marriage within three generations (in some places, five generations) was prohibited. Some traditional customs such as accepting betrothal gifts were eliminated, and the mutual respect and love between husband and wife of the biblical teaching was encouraged. Zhang Jucheng writes:

> The missionaries set a rule that Christians are not allowed to marry in traditional arranged marriage and should get married according to church's marriage discipline, that is, men over 20 years old and women over 18 are free to find a marriage partner by themselves. Men are not allowed to pay women's dowry asked by the women's

> parents. Anyone who cannot afford a small feast can get married on Sundays or during festivals. Some people became Christians because they like the rules of marriage in the church that men do not need to give money to their partners' parents, which made it easier for them to start a family.[16]

As Christians, they were not allowed to take part in folk entertainment activities and sing Miao folk songs at ordinary times and during festivals. Love songs and step-by-step folk dance were forbidden.[17] In traditional Miao custom, a young man had to marry his uncle's daughters, which led to serious inbreeding. It was eliminated completely among Christians since the church opposed it severely.

In daily life, missionaries, emphasizing the moral aspect of their Christian tradition, were opposed to smoking, drinking, and waste, advocating for a frugal and healthy lifestyle and cultivated civilized living habits. For example, in Fugong County, Ma Daomin 馬導民 and other missionaries once set ten commandments for new Lisu Christians: (1) Do not smoke; (2) Do not drink; (3) Do not steal; (4) Do not gamble; (5) Do not tease women; (6) Do not believe in ghosts and gods; (7) Folk songs and dancing are prohibited; (8) Marriage is prohibited between Christians and non-Christians; (9) Betrothal gifts are not allowed; (10) Christians and non-Christians shall not work together.[18]

The survey of missionary activities in minority cultures raises the question whether missionaries are able to teach the Bible without cultural prejudice. In leisure time, for example, the church requires Christians not to play billiards, mahjong, not to gamble, and, if watching TV, to pay more attention to news and less to entertainment. Christians are encouraged to listen to the Gospel Broadcast in Lisu on a Thai radio station every evening from 9:00 to 9:30 p.m.[19] Christians often read *The Winds of Heaven* magazines 天風, while Catholics read more *Faith* newspapers 信德 and *Ark* magazines 方舟.

At that time, ethnic minority people kept what missionaries perceived as "outdated" habits due to poor natural conditions and an underdeveloped economy. Hygiene was not a top priority in their culture, so the missionaries required them to pay attention to hygiene when they became Christians. To help Christians develop healthy living habits, the church even regarded hygiene as one of its ten commandments. Historically, Lahu people had no toilets. It was customary for non-Christians of Lahu and Wa nationalities to live together with animals, people living upstairs and animals living downstairs. But after becoming Christians, they were taught to live differently. After coming to church, the Jingpo people's living habits were also transformed, and they shook hands and said "hello" to each other in greetings. They paid more attention to hygiene and cleanliness. Weddings were held in the church, which helped people save money. When people died, cows were no longer killed and sacrificed to ancestral ghosts, and no more "*Bugongo*" (sacrificial dance) took place.[20]

The biblical message of sharing and equality had contributed enormously to establishing mutual and harmonious relationships among people in different social classes and ethnic groups. They were taught the biblical message of loving one's neighbor, believing that it will reduce the gap between the rich and the poor. In the past, the Yi people had a strict social hierarchy, and there was a huge gap between chiefs and slaves. After the introduction of Christianity, some Yi nationality Nuosu chiefs were able to sit together on an equal footing with their former Miao slaves, listening attentively to the preaching of the Bible and the singing of hymns.

In the past, armed struggles between different ethnic groups often occurred because of various contradictions. The Nu people came to the Nujiang areas first. Then came the Lisu people. So, the Lisu people fought against and looted the territory of the Nu people. They often fought with weapons and sometimes killed people. After the introduction of Christianity, this situation changed.[21]

Christian belief is thought to achieve unity among all ethnic Christians in the church by giving them an undivided heart in spite of their different nationalities. In traditional ethnic villages, Christians coexisted with other non-Christians. In the process of integration into minority society, Christians also rooted their beliefs in this land. At present, relations among different nationalities are relatively more harmonious than they have been in the past.

Bible and Minority Festivals

The Bible also has brought about changes in the content and form of minority festivals. Christian festivals gradually have replaced traditional festivals of minorities. For example, the broad season 闊時節 of the Lisu New Year is usually the cherry blooming season, from the beginning of December to the first ten days of the first month of the following year. In 1990, the Lisu Autonomous Prefecture of Nujiang designated December 20 of the Gregorian calendar as the statutory festival of the broad season of the state, with a period of about twelve days. The festival has been replaced by Christmas among Christians. The ceremony of burning incense to daffodils and mountain gods was replaced by celebrating the birth of Jesus.

The Miao Church also competes with the Miao traditional festival "Flower Ground Festival" 花場節 on the fifth day of May in the Lunar calendar, while the Yi Church competes with the traditional Torch Festival by holding a graduation ceremony for volunteer refresher classes.

In the Lisu area, no matter what kind of festivals are celebrated, they are held as group activities and centered on worshiping and experiencing of the Holy Spirit, with few secular activities. During festivals, Christians often sing hymns in succession for several days and nights. There are various competitions as well, such as the Bible speech contest for priests, hymn-singing competitions for old people, children, and women, and Bible-Scripture recitation competitions for all Christians, and so on.

On Christmas Eve, Christians in the upper Yanjing Village of Mangkang County in Tibet usually drink wine made by churches wearing national costumes. They often dance the "*guozhuang* dance" (鍋莊舞) and "string dance" (弦子舞) until dawn.

The Bible and Minority Culture in Other Regions

In 1882, (R. P. Jean-Baptiste) Steenman (Shi Tianji 石天基), a Catholic missionary of the Congregation of the Immaculate Heart of Mary, went to preach in Yili, Xinjiang. In January 1877, Easton and Parker entered Eastern Xinjiang, distributing Bibles and preaching biblical messages passionately. In 1892, Swedish Protestant Missionary of the Swedish Mission Society N. F. Howie Jill took Kashgar as the center to preach the gospel.

The Swedish Mission Society established three primary schools in Kashgar, Shache, and Yingjisha. It was reported that, "There are 56 boys and 18 girls in the primary schools. There was also a vocational school and there are 8 boys and 7 girls, all of whom were taught knowledge of practical occupations."[22] The missionaries adapted the Bible into scriptural songs, translated them into Uygur, taught students to sing, and translated many Swedish folk songs into Uygur.

The Swedish Mission Society successively translated, printed, and published parts of the Bible, such as Genesis, Job, and Psalms, into Uygur. In 1935, missionaries Albert and Osler Hermanson translated the NT into Uygur, which was later published in Cairo by the British Foreign Bible Society. It also has published anthologies of hymns, promotion materials, and brochures, etc. The books translated and published by missionaries include *Uygur Grammar* 維吾爾語語法 and *History of Central Asia* 中亞史.

George W. Hunter, a missionary of the China Inland Mission of England, knows many languages, such as Han, Uygur, Kazakh, and Mongolian. Since 1906, he has gone to Yili, Kashgar, Brake, and other places to preach and distribute various texts of Christian books. Since 1914, Percy Mather, another missionary of the China Inland Mission, has become an important co-worker.

In 1880, the Missionaries of Congregation of the Immaculate Heart of Mary founded the Boys' School in Sanshenggong District, Inner Mongolia. In addition to studying the Bible, students also read Chinese traditional classics. By the time the last member left China in 1955, the Congregation of the Immaculate Heart of Mary had set up 960 primary and secondary schools.

Father Antoine Mostaert, an authority on Mongolian linguistics, Mongolian history, and folklore archaeology, has published the *Mongol Language Collection* 蒙語集 and the *Mongol-Chinese Dictionary* 蒙漢大詞典. Father Jozef Van Oost collected, recorded, compiled, and printed a variety of Mongolian and Han folk songs. He also combined the melody and color of Ordos folk songs with Catholic music and created many hymns. Father Leo Van Dijk imitates Chinese painting, paints Catholic images, integrates Chinese and Western art, preaches Christian doctrine and culture through art, while Father Edmond Van Genechten is skilled at Chinese art and woodcut art. They have a far-reaching impact on Chinese Christian art.[23]

In 1882, some missionaries of the Swedish Alliance Mission in China came to Inner Mongolia to preach the gospel. Then Otto Oberg and his wife established a church in Shaerqin, Salazi Town (now Tumoteyou Banner in Baotou City). In 1886, British missionary of The China Inland Mission G. George came to Hohhot city to preach and established the Church of Jesus. The Swedish Alliance Mission in China (Associate Mission of the China Inland Mission) was the main body of the China Inland Mission in Inner Mongolia.

In 1926, the Swedish Mongol Missionary Church published about seven thousand Christian books at Harun Usu Printing House, including *New Testament Essentials*, *Biblical Questions and Answers*, *Praise Poetry*, and *The Legend of Blessed General*. Later, in Hadan Sumo, it published the *Story of Believing in Jesus' Salvation*. In 1952, the NT in Mongolian was published in Hong Kong.[24]

In 2009, the church in Inner Mongolia staged the first large-scale singing and dancing sacred opera, *Esther*. Their tour has continued since 2010. They have been to Israel and many provinces, cities, and autonomous regions of China. The film was produced by Beijing Film Studio at the end of the same year. Yu Guojun, the composer, created all the music of the holy drama. He fused ancient Jewish folk songs and church tunes with changes from traditional local opera patterns, displayed the psychological activities of the characters, and promoted the development of the plot, all of which embodied the extensive and deep integration of the Christian holy drama genre and traditional music in the Yinshan cultural area.

Yu Lifang 余麗芳, a follower of Hohhot, wrote a hymn, "I Want to Follow the Lord" (我要跟隨主), on the basis of Ordos folk songs. It has been widely sung among Mongolian followers. Some other hymns are inspired by and created with a passage of traditional Mongolian folk songs; for example, "The Greatest Commandment" (最大誡命) comes from the Chahar folk song, "The Yellow Horse" (黃驃馬); "God Loves the World" (神愛世人) from the Ordos folk song "On the Road" (在路旁); and "My Beloved" (我心所愛) is based on the melody of the well-known "Senjidema" 森吉德瑪.

At present, there is an active Mongolian Christian singer called Yu Wenhai 宇文海. His representative works include "Grassland Children Singing for the Lord," "Heavenly Father Calling," "Happy Grassland," "Live for the Lord," "Your Love Is Better than Wine," and so on. He also has published an album titled *Paradise Hymn* 天堂讚歌.

In 1867, Alexander Williamson, a Scottish missionary, disseminated the Bible and preached the gospel along the Ashe River in Heilongjiang province on the northeast Sino-Korean border. He baptized the Korean people in Manchuria in 1873 and established the first church in Ji'an County in 1884. In 1887, Xu Xianglun 徐相侖, Bai Hongjun 白鴻俊, and others translated and published the first Korean Bible in Shenyang. In 1906, Li Xiang 李相 came to Yanbian and opened the first modern Korean educational institution, Ruidian Private School in Longjing. He combined education with missionary work to propagate anti-Japanese ideology and national independence consciousness to Korean people. In 1911, when Li Donghui 李東輝 came to Yanbian, he set up a Christian Missionary Mission with Korean, Chinese, and Russian Christians and launched the "Million Salvation Movement." They advocated the activity of "one village, one villa, and one school" in Yanbian. By December 1911, forty schools had been established, and by 1916, seventy-one Christian schools had been established.[25]

Some Korean people live in the cold northeastern region of China and they have a cultural practice of drinking alcohol to keep warm. The church admonishes Christians to abstain from drinking, following church tradition (rather than Bible teachings). Most Christians strictly abide by the teaching, go to church two or three times a week, and pray constantly. They are keen to study the Bible and eager to preach the gospel to relatives and friends. Compared to Chinese Christians, many Korean Christians incorporate singing and dancing into their worship, and many of their worship styles are warm and passionate. Among them, there have been famous singers like Fang Chushan 方初善.[26]

Conclusion

In contemporary Chinese society, the Han nationality remains the largest people group, concentrated in urban areas and with a long history and profound culture. The influence of Christianity and the Bible on them has been slow but gradual. In short, renewed Han cultures may contribute to Chinese Christian theology, while ethnic minorities have more vitality and space for embodying the biblical faith, especially in music and dance and other art forms. From the above description, we can see that, compared with the Han nationality, some ethnic minorities accept Christian faith more readily, and their cultures also have contributed to the diverse and robust expressions of the gospel while, at the same time, they have been changed by the biblical messages. The Miao and Lisu and Lahu nationalities living in southwest China are rather religious people. The Bible translation work there was the earliest among minority groups in China, and it is in biblical translation that one sees biblical influence on their cultures and ways of life. This shows that, in the missionizing work, there will be collision, convergence, and mutual transformation of faith and cultures.

Notes

1. "*Pipa*" ghost is a Chinese transliteration of the Dai language; "*pipa*" is regarded as the most vicious ghost in Dai society. Dai people think that these ghosts are ominous and unclean and bring diseases and disasters to people.
2. K. K. Yeo, "Beyond Chalcedon? Towards a Fully Christian and Fully Cultural Theology," in *Jesus without Borders: Christology in the Majority World*, ed. Gene L. Green et al. (Grand Rapids: Eerdmans, 2014), 162–179, also K. K. Yeo, *What Has Jerusalem to Do with Beijing? Biblical Interpretation from a Chinese Perspective*, 2nd ed. (Eugene, OR: Pickwick, 2018), 3–52.
3. Li Shoulei 李守雷, "The Regional Adaptation and Change of Christianity in Xishuangbanna" [in Chinese] 西雙版納地區基督教的地域適應與變遷, *International Journal of Sino-Western Studies* [國學與西學國際學刊] 12 (2016): 5–6.
4. Chen Bei 張蓓, *The Place Is Far Away and the Singings are Beautiful—Dahua Miao's Christian Music* [in Chinese] 地遠歌長—大花苗的基督教音乐 (Beijing: Religious Culture Press, 2018), 140.

5. Yang Minkang 楊民康, *Nationalization and Modernity: A Study of Ethnic Minority Christian Ritual Music in Yunnan* [in Chinese] 本土化與現代性: 雲南少數民族基督教儀式音樂研究 (Beijing: Religious Culture Press, 2008), 94.
6. See Zhang Yu 張羽, "Re-Walking the Missionary Way: A Lecture on the Holy Testament of West China (Part I)" [in Chinese] 重走傳教士之路—華西聖約講座(上) (Zhang Yu's Magic Book Public Wechat on September 4, 2018).
7. See Chen Jianming 陳建明, "Modern Christianity in Southwest Ethnic Minority Areas and Its Impact" [in Chinese] "近代基督教在西南少數民族地區的文字布道及其影響," *Studies in World Religions* [世界宗教研究] 6 (2011): 113.
8. Wang Cong 王聰, "Church Schools in Southwest Minority Areas during the Republic of China and Their Contemporary Enlightenment" [in Chinese] 民國時期西南少數民族地區的教會學校及其當代啟示, *Journal of the Legion College of Education* [兵團教育學院學報] 3 (2015): 31.
9. Shen Hong 沈紅, *Structures and Subjects: Shimenkan, a Rising Cultural Community* [in Chinese] 結構與主體: 激蕩的文化社區石門坎 (Social Sciences Literature Publishing House, 2006), 355.
10. Chen Xuhui 陳徐慧, *Interaction between Christianity and Religious Beliefs of Ethnic Minorities: Investigation and Reflection on Rural Christianity of Lisu Nationality in Central Yunnan* [in Chinese] 基督教與少數民族宗教信仰的互動—滇中北傈傈族鄉村基督教的調查與思考 (Master's Degree Thesis, Department of Philosophy and Religion, Central University for Nationalities, 2007), 5.
11. See Wang Shude 王樹德, trans. Dongrenda (東人達) "Shimenkan and HuaMiao Minority" [in Chinese], in *In Unknown China* 在未知的中國 (Yunnan People's Publishing House, 2002), 434.
12. See Chen Jianming, "Modern Christianity in Southwest Ethnic Minority Areas and Its Impact," 112.
13. See Yeo, *What Has Jerusalem to Do with Beijing?*, 3–52.
14. Public housing system means that young men and women can get together in public housing before they are married. When night falls, young men and women make appointments at the public house, burn a fire in the fire pond, play the pipa, blow the oral chords, talk about love, and sing love songs, and then stay in the public house. After 1949, this situation ceased to exist.
15. The transfer marriage system refers to a son marrying his father's concubine and a brother marrying his sisters-in-law after the death of their parent and brother respectively. It is a disguised form of polygamy. This marriage system is still prevalent among nomadic minorities.
16. Zhang Jucheng 張巨成, "On the Christian Culture of the Minority Nationalities in Yunnan in Modern Times" [in Chinese] "論近代雲南少數民族基督教文化," *Exploration of Yunnan Students* [雲南學生探索] 6 (1996): 51.
17. Step-by-step folk dance is a dance performed by Lisu people on important festivals and wedding days. It is played with a piccolo and not sung. Usually after a full meal, men, women, old and young join hands and dance in a circle with the rhythm of the piccolo. Young people usually dance until dawn.
18. *A Brief History of Christian Communication in Fukung* [in Chinese] 福貢基督教傳播史略, trans. Fu Abe 傅阿伯 and Hu Zhengsheng 胡正生 (Dehong: Selected Literature and History of Nujiang, Selected from the First to the Twentieth Episodes, Dehong National Publishing House, 1994), 1092–1103.

19. Du Zhongfeng 杜忠鋒, *The Spread of Christianity and the Construction of Ethnic Minorities' Daily Life World: Based on the Ethnographic Survey in Village Bingzhongluo* [in Chinese] 基督宗教傳播與少數民族日常生活世界的建構—基於雲南丙中洛鄉的民族志調查, *Yunnan Province* (PhD Dissertation, College of Media and International Culture, Zhejiang University, 2012), 129.
20. See *A Survey of Ethnic Folklore and Religion in Yunnan* [in Chinese] 雲南民族民俗和宗教調查, by Revised Editorial Committee of the Series of Surveys on Social History of Ethnic Minorities in China [in Chinese] 中國少數民族社會歷史調查資料叢刊 (Beijing: Nationalities Publisher, 2009), 296.
21. See Zhang Yu, "*Re-Walking the Missionary Way (Part I)*" [in Chinese] 重走傳教士之路—華西聖約講座(上), in "Zhang Yu's Magic Book, Public Wechat" [張羽魔法書公共微信], September 4, 2018.
22. *The Christian Occupation of China (1901–1920)* (Part I) [in Chinese] 中華歸主：中國基督教事業統計 (1901–1920) (上), ed. the Special Committee on survey and occupation China continuation Committee 1918–1921, trans. the World Religious Research Institute of the Chinese Academy of Social Sciences (Beijing: China Social Sciences Press, 1987), 560.
23. See Li Changxian's 李昌憲 research on Christian Missionary Activities in Inner Mongolia during the late Qing dynasty and the Republic of China (1900–1949) [in Chinese] "清末民國時期 (1900–1949) 內蒙古地區基督教傳教活動研究" (Master's Degree Thesis, School of History and Culture, Central University for Nationalities, 2011), 71.
24. See Liu Chunzi 劉春子, "Preliminary Study on the History of Protestant Christianity in Western Inner Mongolia" [in Chinese] 內蒙古西部地區基督教新教歷史初探 (Master's Thesis, Mongolian Research Center, Inner Mongolia University, 2000), 32–33.
25. Wu Qianshi 吳千石 and Guo Meiying 郭美英, "On the Characteristics of Korean Anti-Japanese National Education in Yanbian Area in Modern Times" [in Chinese] 淺談延邊地區朝鮮族近代反日民族教育的特點, *Journal of Yanbian Institute of Education* 6 (2013): 66.
26. See Xuan Qianze's 玄千澤, "Research on Korean Christian Belief in Yanbian Area" [in Chinese] 延邊地區朝鮮族基督教信仰調查研究 (Master's Thesis of Yanbian University, 2018), 21–37.

Primary Sources

Black Yi Bible 黑彝文聖經. Nanjing: Chinese Christian Association, 2016.

Dai Hymn, KiulungKiang 傣文讚美詩. Kunming: Presbyterian Church of America, 1935 edition; printed by XiShuangbanna Christian Association in 1994.

Dai New Testament 傣文新約全書. Nanjing: China Christian Association, 1993.

Dai Old Testament 傣文舊約全書. Jinghong: Translated and printed by the Dai ministry team of Manyun Church in Jinghong, 2018.

The Holy Bible in Blue Hmong 藍苗文聖經. Seoul: Korean Bible Society, n.d.

Lahu New Testament 拉祜文新約全書. Kunming: Yunnan Christian Association, 1985.

Lisu Bible 傈僳文聖經. Nanjing: China Christian Association, 2008.

Lisu Hymn Book 傈僳族讚美詩, anonymous editor. Nanjing: China Christian Association, 1992.

Miao Bible 苗文聖經. Nanjing: Chinese Christian Association, 1988.

New Compilation of Yiwen Praise Poems 彝文讚美詩新編, Shan Yulin edition. Kunming: A Yingte Church, Peace Village Committee, Jiulong Town, Luquan County, 2013.

Sacred Hymn with Notes to Kachin 景頗文讚美詩, anonymous editor. Nanjing: China Christian Association, 1992.
Ta Hwa Miao Hymnbook 苗文頌主聖歌, anonymous editor. Kunming: Yunnan Christian Association, 1983. *Ta Hwa Miao Hymnbook*, editor of Revision Group of Ta Hwa Miao Hymnbook. Kunming: Yunnan Christian Association, 2010 edition.
Wa Bible [Phuk Lai Sigang Khri Paraog] 佤文聖經. Nanjing: Chinese Christian Association, 2016.
White Yi Bible 白彝文聖經. Nanjing: Chinese Christian Association, 2014.

CHAPTER 33

SACREDNESS IN THE BIBLE AND CHINESE CULTURES

CHAN TAK-KWONG

Introduction

HISTORICALLY, sacredness has its root grounded in the Latin term "*sacrum*," whereas holiness has been rooted in the Germanic word, "*Heilig*." Today, what is sacred or holy has become an important issue for modern religious studies and theology.

Max Müller, a famous scholar of religion studies, asks for an open mind or equanimity in the study of different world religions. Another scholar, Nathan Söderblom, said at the beginning of the twentieth century that "holiness" is the great word in religion, and it is even more essential than the notion of God. Real religion may exist without a definite concept of divinity, but there is no real religion without a distinction between holiness and profanity.[1]

Correspondingly, we find the transition from discussing God to discoursing on sacredness in theology, which has brought forth without precedence an attitude of openness and dialogue with other religions.

In this regard, this essay is an introduction to the meaning of sacredness or holiness in the Bible and Chinese culture, ending with a synthesis of this vital concept. The methodology of this essay consists of doing pertinent research on biblical theology, Chinese philosophy, and religious studies.

Sacredness in the Bible

Sacredness in the Bible can be studied from the perspectives of theology and exegesis. On the one hand, biblical theology considers sacredness as the specific or unique nature of God, whether it is the essence of God himself or the way of manifestation, sanctification, or consecration attributed to human beings. On the other hand, biblical exegesis is studying and exploring the vocabularies used for sacredness in the Bible. For example, in the different forms of translation according to their contexts, the root or basic form of *qdš* (Hebrew adjective *qādôš*) in the Old Testament (henceforth OT) and *hagi-* (Greek adjective *hagios*) in the New Testament (henceforth NT) mean "sacredness, holiness, consecration, sanctification, and purification." Correspondently, the NT interpretation of sacredness takes its departure from the OT, and finds its accomplishment in the incarnation of Jesus and the gifts of the Holy Spirit mentioned in the NT texts. Both biblical theology and biblical exegesis are important methods for arriving at a full understanding of sacredness in the Bible.[2]

Hence, for the purpose of the present essay, this section provides only a succinct systematic study of the three stages related to the development of sacredness in the Bible. The first stage corresponds to the sacredness of the numinous God introduced by the theologian Rudolf Otto. According to Otto, the sacredness or *numen* of God, which is characterized by the "wholly other," is a mystery beyond the sphere of the usual, the intelligible, filling the mind with blank wonder and astonishment.[3] This stage, though it is difficult to illustrate empirically, is necessary and serves as the foundation for further development in the next two stages.

The second stage corresponds to sacredness in the OT, and is explained in terms of the binary model of integrity and alterity, a thesis proposed by William Paden, a scholar of religious studies.[4] This stage is a sort of *exitus* (depart from God), characterized by a dual, if not dualistic, order of development originating from the first stage. The proposal of a binary model is not totally new, since sacredness as "alterity" or "otherness" is a topic of traditional theology, yet "sacredness as integrity" is a favorite issue for scholars of religious studies, though not totally unknown in theology.

According to anthropologist Mary Douglas, granted that the root of holiness means separateness, the next idea that emerges from holiness is "wholeness and completeness." As it is, holiness is exemplified by completeness, in view of a systematic ordering of things. Therefore, holiness requires that individuals shall conform to the class to which they belong, where different elements of things shall not be confused.[5]

Thus, the third and final stage corresponds to the eschatology of the NT or Christian theology, which is a theme about the last things or the end of the world, characterized by the coming of the kingdom of God or the second coming of Christ (*parousia*). This stage is important as the coming together or wholeness of the two models of the previous second stage. At the same time, it is a process of *reditus* (return to God) corresponding to the first stage at the end of human history.

Sacredness of the Numinous God

To describe this numinous or ineffable nature of God, sometimes called the "wholly other," is a difficult if not an impossible task. According to the Exodus narrative, Moses once tried to ask the name of God, yet God answered with a mysterious name: "I am who I am" (Exod 3:14), one in which the character of the divine name is concealed rather than revealed.

In Hebrew grammar, speaking three times is a way to express something of the highest degree or uniqueness in nature. We can cite the example of the prophet Isaiah (Isa 6:3) of the Seraphim angels proclaiming three times the "holy" (*qdš*) in the celestial court. Notably, Yahweh is praised three times also in Ps 99: 3, 5, 9, "Holy is he (Yahweh)."[6] It is a way to confess that Yahweh of Israel is the only God or God of the highest majesty.

The NT maintains that only God is "the holy one" (Rev 15:4), the only source of sanctification for humanity. Further, this God is immensely elevated, dwelling in inaccessible light (1 Tim 6:16).

In sum, at this stage, sacredness is a word symbol that seems to hide itself behind the greatness of the things being described or of engaged action. This is perhaps the place where the language of sacredness finds its perfection.

Sacredness of Integrity and Alterity

To avoid sheer nihilism, sacredness of the "wholly other" has become understandable to humanity with the binary model of integrity and alterity. This is the level of God-human relationship, with the rise of human consciousness characterized by an opposition between what is sacred and what is profane.

Although in principle, any single experience or example could entail both elements of integrity and alterity, e.g., when "clean" is opposed to "unclean," "clean" conveys the idea of separateness or "alterity," yet "clean" itself presupposes a systematic ordering of the idea of things for human beings to correspond, hence a kind of integrity that one may not infringe upon. For the sake of clarity, this essay explores each model below—i.e., integrity and alterity—with its own examples from the OT.

Sacredness of Integrity

Sacredness of integrity implies togetherness or partnership. Here, sacredness presents itself as a kind of order, an authentic and harmonious one in which God and human beings may enter into mutual relationship. Theology of creation and covenant implies such a kind of order. Hence, to be God's chosen people as his own among nations urges the people to lead a life of sacredness of integrity. The people can come close to one accord with the Holy God through sanctification, where Moses is the mediator. Here is a series of examples bearing the word *qdš*.

THE THORN BUSH THEOPHANY (EXOD 3)

The background of the theophany in the Exodus narrative is the God-given vocation of Moses at the burning bush. It reveals that God has seen the sufferings of his people and will lead them from the bondage of the Egyptians to a land flowing with milk and honey.

The reaction of Moses in saying, "I must go across and see this strange sight, and why the bush is not being burnt up" (Exod 3:3), gives the impression that sacredness attracts more than it frightens. The admonition of Yahweh to Moses to come no closer but to take off his sandals shows that the place upon which Moses is standing is "holy ground" (Exod 3:5). Indeed, such an experience does not mean punishment nor death, but rather it is a sign of respect, with a liturgical flavor.

PREPARATION FOR THE COVENANT AT SINAI (EXOD 19)

Before the Sinai theophany, the Israelites were ordered to take three days of purification or sanctification. Accordingly, washing clothes (Exod 19:11), standing in probably for sexual abstinence and avoiding defilement, has to do with the idea of integrity, an important element of the prescription of God.

THE PURIFICATION OF BATHSHEBA (2 SAM11)

David laid with Bathsheba just after she had purified or sanctified herself (*qdš*, *Hithpael*) from her period (2 Sam 11:4). It was assumed that menstruation makes a woman "dirty," and that purification may be obtained after washing. In fact, the law of the Levites makes it clear that the unclean period lasts for seven days, during which it is impure for a man to touch a woman (Lev 15:19). Thus, the sacredness attested to here signifies a kind of integrity, in which menstruation and the loss of blood are symbols of order destruction, causing a danger to purity and integrity.

INVOCATION OF THE HOLY NAME

Yahweh God, the holy one of Israel, is a favorite name for invocation, and it is read in a number of biblical passages of the Psalms and prophetic writings (Ps 71:22; Isa 5:24; Hab 3:3). Also mentioned in the Bible is the idea that the people of Israel are expected to trust in the holy name (Ps 33:21), because the mutual relationship between God and human, therefore integrity, is implied.

RULES CONCERNING CLEAN AND UNCLEAN ANIMALS (LEV 11–16)

Written after the Babylonian exile, this passage of the Levirate Law talks about the rules on clean and unclean animals. Those animals lacking one of the three elements are unclean, i.e., cloven hoof, a parted foot, a ruminant; although pigs have a cloven hoof and parted foot, they are without a ruminant. Again, "clean" and "unclean" presupposes a systematic ordering of things, a kind of integrity not to be infringed upon. Thus, the reason for the rule being given in the conclusion of the passage, "For it is I, Yahweh, who am your God. You have become holy because I am holy: do not defile yourselves with all these creatures that swarm on the ground" (Lev 11:44).

THE SACREDNESS OF THE PRIEST (LEV 21–22)

Besides some verses of Leviticus insists on the integrity of an offering without blemish (Lev 22:17–25), the priests themselves are required to be without physical defect, e.g., infirmity such as being blind or lame, disfigured or deformed, having an injured foot or arm, a hunchback, rickets, ophthalmia, or a scab, or running sores, or someone who is a eunuch (Lev 21: 19–20).

THE LEVIRATE DECALOGUE (LEV 19)

The priestly document of the Levirate Decalogue underlines sacredness, characterized by Yahweh demanding that his people be holy based on the ground that Yahweh himself, the God of the Israelites, is holy (Lev 19:1–2). This is remarkably different from the other two Decalogues of the Elohist document (Exod 20) and of the Deuteronomic document (Deut 5).

Sacredness of Alterity

Alterity is another model of sacredness, in which sacredness presents itself not as the "wholly other," yet as "the other" or alter opposed to integrity, imbued with its transcendent and supernatural character. The Israelites are prescribed to keep their status of otherness, not to be mixed up with the profane or with the way of other nations. The biblical passages after the Babylonian exile emphasized the ritual and external aspect of the sacredness, intensifying the antagonism between the sacred and the profane, which are characteristics of alterity. This can be seen in the following examples.

AWFULNESS BEFORE THE HOLY GOD (1 SAM 6–7)

This is an ancient text where God is called "the Holy One," and the people at Beth-Shemesh have an awful experience of God, saying, "Who can stand his ground before Yahweh, this holy God" (1 Sam 6:20). The background of the passage is the ark of God, which brought disaster to the Philistines and even killed seventy local people at Beth-Shemesh.

CITIES DECLARED SACRED OR INVIOLABLE (JOSH 20)

Cites of refugee or cities declared sacred or inviolable (*qdš, Piel*) is an idea initiated by Yahweh, who ordered the Israelites to designate some of their cities to provide refuge for those who commit homicide inadvertently without intent, e.g., the city of Kedesh, Shechem (Josh 20:7). These cities are not to be under jurisdiction of the secular power. Some other passages of the OT, e.g., Deuteronomy (Deut 19:2–7) conveyed a similar idea of refuge city in which "homicides" may take refuge, with the verb "to set apart" (*bdl, Hiphil*). Hence, sacredness also has the meaning of "to set apart."

IMMENSURABLE FORGIVENESS OF THE HOLY ONE (HOS 11)

The prophet Hosea described the contrast of forgiveness between God and human beings saying, "I will not execute my fierce anger; I will not again destroy Ephraim; for I am God and no mortal, the Holy One in your midst, and I will not come in wrath" (Hos 11:9). Hence, the Holy One of Israel brought immensurable forgiveness and salvation to God's people, which is opposed to the revenge-seeking finitude of humanity.

THE HOLY ONE'S IMPLACABLE OPPOSITION TO SIN (ISA 1:5)

The Holy One of Israel is irreconcilable with sin (Isa 1:4; 5:18–19, etc.). Isaiah conveyed the idea that the Holy One of Israel is implacably opposed to sin: "Disaster, sinful nation, people weighed down with guilt, race of wrong-doers, perverted children! They have abandoned Yahweh, despised the Holy One of Israel, they have turned away from him" (Isa 1:4). Therefore, sacredness is irreconcilable with sin, generally including moral and religious sin.

THE LAW OF HOLINESS (LEV 17–26)

The law of holiness, with its origin dated back to the pre-exilic period during the reign of King Josiah, was one of the oldest laws for the priests of Jerusalem. The law began with the ritual for the sacrifice (Lev 17) and ended with benediction and malediction (Lev 26). Sacredness in this passage has both liturgical and moral aspects; examples are given below. Lev 20:26: "Be consecrated to me, for I, Yahweh, am holy, and I shall set you apart from all these peoples, for you to be mine." Being the conclusion of Lev 20, this passage condemned idolatry and sexual crimes; because Israelites were chosen and sanctified, their behaviors had to be different from those of the pagans.

Priests also are segregated from other lay Israelites. Hence, their marriages are restricted only with virgins of his clan, i.e., they will not marry a woman profaned by prostitution or one divorced by her husband, "for the priest is consecrated to his God" (Lev 21:7).

INSTRUCTIONS ON THE SANCTUARY BUILDING AND ON ITS MINISTERS (EXOD 25–31)

Levirate instructions on the building of the sanctuary and on the minsters of sacrifice were priestly documents. They emphasized the rite of purification or consecration from the profane as the prerequisites for coming close to Yahweh. To avoid danger of penalty of death, Aaron the high priest is to put on a liturgical vestment with rings of gold in the fringes and a golden rosette with a plaque, on which is written, "consecrated to Yahweh" (Exod 28:33–37).

THE TORAH OF EZEKIEL (EZEK 40–48)

What is sacred and profane in the Torah of Ezekiel is the law for the Jewish people after the Babylonian exile. It is characterized by external and liturgical characters of sacredness, which implies also an idea of opposition between the sacred and the profane. The Torah narrated the teaching of the priests to make people understand the difference between the sacred and the profane, the clean and the unclean (Ezek 44:23). Since the liturgical vestments of the priests are sacred, they are reserved to be used only during worship in the holy places and be taken off when the priests go out of the holy places (Ezek 42:14). Finally, there will be construction of an enclosing wall of the temple separating the sacred from the profane (Ezek 42:20).

Sacredness at the Eschaton

Sacredness at the *eschaton* or *parousia*, a perspective of Christian theology regarding the second coming of Christ at the end of human history, is a stage where all oppositions or divisions through the mediation of Jesus are to be transformed by God the Father into a harmonious whole at the end of human history, e.g., the sacred and the profane, the awfulness and the fascination, etc. The binary of the models of integrity and alterity of the second stage is one of the exemplary cases.

This stage is also the *reditus* to the archaic beginning of sacredness of the numinous God. For the Christian tradition, the *eschaton* began with the incarnation of the God-human Jesus, with whom the barrier or veil between the sacred and profane was removed or torn into two. In Pauline theology, Jesus is the one sent by God to become for us justice, sanctity, and salvation (1 Cor 1:30), a work accomplished in the Holy Spirit (Rom 15:16; 1 Cor 6:11).

Pre-figuration in the Old Testament

Christian interpretation takes its departure in the OT, where the sacredness at the *eschaton* also is attested in some passages of the OT, revealing the new relationship between the sacred and the profane.

We shall give illustration by an example narrated by the book of the prophet Zechariah. Written after 300 BCE, third Zechariah narrates the vision at the *eschaton* or the day of the Lord, which is the coming of the kingdom of God at the end time. The sacredness of God being "all in all" (1 Cor 15:28) is read in the scene of the removal of the dividing line between the sacred and the profane. According to the description, when all people go up to Jerusalem to celebrate the feast of tabernacle, every profane object such as kitchen pots and even dirty things such as horses of war will be changed into objects and instruments of the temple, absorbed and transformed by the holiness of God (Zech 14:20–21).

Incarnation and life of Jesus

According to the Gospel of Luke, the sacredness or holiness of Jesus goes back to the beginning of His birth or incarnation, when the angel said: "the Holy Spirit will come down upon you . . . . And so, the child will be holy and will be called Son of God" (Luke 1:35). The holiness of Jesus was the work of the Holy Spirit.

Correspondingly, the Bible mentioned the presentation of Jesus at the temple, according to what was written in the law of Moses: "Every first-born male must be consecrated to the Lord" (Luke 2:23; Exod 13: 2–3). The meaning of the consecration in the life of Jesus is part of the integral plan of God.

In the NT, the life and activities of Jesus are described by the Gospel writers as the manifestation of God, where the whole person of Jesus was in perfect cooperation with the divine plan for salvation, e.g., the baptism, the walking on the sea, the transfiguration, the miracles, and finally the resurrection.

For Johannine theology, the "I am" of Jesus (John 8:58) intends to remind readers of the "I am who I am" of the self-presentation of Yahweh at the burning bush. John portrays the incarnated body of Jesus as the new holy place or canopy of God, the only mediator between God and humankind. With the cleansing of the Jerusalem temple, Jesus announced the coming of the *eschaton* (John 2:13–22), and proclaimed a kind of worship not binding to any holy places, a worship "in spirit and truth" (John 4:21–24). This new worship shall be realized at the end time according to the book of Revelation: "I could not see any temple in the city since the Lord God Almighty and the Lamb were themselves the temple" (Rev 21:22).

Unclean spirit cast out by the Holy One of God

The synoptic Gospels reported an opposition between the Holy and the unclean in the curing of a demoniac at Capernaum (Mark 1:24; Luke 4:34). When Jesus taught at Capernaum, there was a man with an unclean spirit, shouting: "What have you to do with us, Jesus of Nazareth? Have you come to destroy us? I know who you are, the Holy One of God." The demoniac presented here is someone with an unclean spirit, which is cast out by the Holy One of God.

Hallowed be thy name

The first of the three invocations in the Lord's prayer, i.e., "hallowed be thy name" (Matt 6:9; Luke 11:2), conveys the idea that the name of God will be hallowed at the messianic time or the end time at the *eschaton*, initiated by the coming of Jesus. The context of the meaning is that God's most intimate message of fatherhood is revealed by his Son Jesus, who conveys the will of the Father to be also the will of the disciples when they proclaim his name of holiness in the imitation of Jesus. Hence, to the Gospel writers, Jesus is the mediator between the essential sanctity of God and the sanctification entrusted by grace to humankind. To the Gospel writers, the vocation to follow the holiness of Jesus is the will of God.

New relation of the sacred and the profane

As high priest, Jesus is the minister of the sanctuary of the real tabernacle according to the book of Hebrews (8:2). The book believes that Jesus is the mediator of a new and higher covenant (Heb 8:6; 12:24), he establishes a new relationship between the sacred and the profane, the outside and the inside. Hebrews (13:11–14) illustrates the idea that, like the sacrifice of the animals whose blood is taken into the sanctuary by the high priest for the rite of expiation and is burnt outside the camp, Jesus too suffered outside the gate to sanctify the people, old and new, with his own blood. This prefigured how Jesus was to be killed outside the walls of Jerusalem, thus according to Matthew, when Jesus died, "the veil of the Sanctuary was torn in two from top to bottom" (27:51). It was the symbol of the end of the exclusive privilege of the Jewish period of the OT. Hereafter, sacredness, in biblical theology, will be handed down by Jesus, by the spiritual temple of the church, among those who worship the Father "in spirit and truth" (John 4:23).

Persecution and consecration by the Holy Father

Before returning to his Father, Jesus the high priest prayed to his father for protection of his disciples, according to the Gospel of John. It is where the theme of persecution and consecration is found. Among the six times of appellation to God the Father (John 17:1, 5, 11, 21, 24, 25), "Holy Father" was employed only once (John 17:11b). The context of the passage is twofold. On the one hand, the disciples were called to be holy and consecrated by the truth of the Word of the Father. On the other hand, the disciples had to remain in the world, facing hatred, evil, and persecution.

The Holy Spirit and sanctification

According to the Gospels, forgiveness of sin is the sign of sanctification by the Holy Spirit. The disciples of Jesus believed they were baptized in the Holy Spirit (Matt 28:19), in which the grace of the Holy Spirit is a gift of purification or sanctification. Jesus, after having risen from the dead, appeared to His disciples and said: "Receive the Holy Spirit. If you forgive anyone's sins, they are forgiven; if you retain anyone's sins, they are retained" (John 20:22–23). The first Christians recognized the accomplishment of the promise of the OT in the forgiveness of sin, which is a sign of eschatology.

Sacredness of the Christian community

According to Pauline theology, the Christian community is the temple of the Holy Spirit: "Do you not realize that your body is the temple of the Holy Spirit, who is in you and whom you received from God?" (1 Cor 6:19). The sacredness of the Christian community is seen also in its role as mediation of grace and blessing, the real meaning of priesthood and sacrifice, i.e., being a chosen race, a kingdom of priests, a holy nation, a people to be a personal possession to sing the praises of God (1 Pet 2:9; Exod 19:5–6).

Sacredness at the end time of life

According to the book of Revelation, the Christian community has also the image of a bride, as the author proclaimed: "And I saw the holy city, the new Jerusalem, coming down out of heaven from God, prepared as a bride adorned for her husband" (Rev 21:2). During her life of tribulations on earth, the church, in faith and hope, eagerly exclaimed to Jesus her bridegroom to come, as we read: "The Spirit and the Bride say, 'Come!'" (Rev 22:17).

Summary of Sacredness in the Bible

Sacredness in the Bible is characterized by the three stages of development and the process of *exitus* and *reditus*. The sacredness of the numinous God is the ultimate source or ground of the process. *Exitus* is explained by the binary model of integrity and alterity, seemingly a kind of dialectical relationship of human experience of the sacredness in the OT. The history of the Jewish people since the Babylonian exile until the time of Jesus was characterized by turmoil and oppression. Therefore, the experience of sacredness was more in the favor of alterity than integrity, marked by the transcendence and otherness of God. The Israelites are called to keep their sacred status or identity to behave differently from the world.

Reditus in biblical theology began with the first coming of the God-human Jesus, or the primary phase of the *eschaton* or *parousia*, which is characterized by the removal or tearing of the barrier between the sacred and the profane. At the final phase of the *eschaton*, everything will be absorbed and transformed by the sacredness of God, whose glory fills up the whole universe, as Paul said in his letter to the church in Corinth: "God may be all in all" (1 Cor 15:28).

Finally, alterity and integrity together form a unitary whole. Alterity represents some sort of exterior but dynamic aspect of the "God-human" relationship, where God appears as the other or alter in a supernatural way, breaking the ordinariness of daily life with the marvelous and with surprise, the so-called "shock of sacredness." Integrity, on the contrary, represents some sort of interior or static aspect of the "God-human" relationship, where God is found in intimate relation with the inner part of human, a kind of familiarity without distance or words being necessary. Within this binary model, a tension or a balance in-between, the life of Christians goes back to the source of the sacredness, the deep mystery of the numinous God.

Sacredness (*Sheng*) in the Chinese Culture

The biblical translation and equivalence of sacredness in Chinese vocabulary is *sheng* 聖. Generally, the word "*sheng*" in Chinese culture is used for a sacred or ideal person, including the honorific title addressed to persons like emperors the *shengshang* 聖上 and the proficient of cultural achievement, e.g., Confucius (551–479 BCE) is called the *shengren* 聖人.

When sacredness or *sheng* is applied to Chinese religions, e.g., the Taoist religion and the Buddhist religion, the usage of the word is similar to that of the Bible, designating religious objects (*shengwu* 聖物), birthdays (*shengdan* 聖誕), doctrines (*shengdao* 聖道), and sites and events (*shengji* 聖跡). The difference between the Christian religion and the Chinese religions is mainly the perspective or interpretation of theology or religion studies, which we shall discuss at the end of the essay.

To limit or to choose the scope of this essay to parallel the study on sacredness in the Bible, we focus on some ideas typical of the Chinese culture. The relationship between sacredness and God is similar to the relation between *nature* (*benxing* 本性) and Heaven (*tian* 天) or *nature* (*ziran* 自然) and *Dao* 道.[7] The sacred person (a sage in Confucianism or true person in Daoism) is the ideal person who transforms himself according to the human *nature* ordained by Heaven (Confucianism) or models himself after the cosmic *nature* of Dao (Daoism), where Heaven or Dao is the ultimate source of the *nature*.

Confucianism

We limit our studies to the passages with the terminology of *sheng* in the Confucian classics. According to that tradition, the *sheng* or sacredness is represented by the ideal person, the sacred human being, or the sage, the one who transforms himself according to the *nature* ordained by Heaven.

Sacred Person/Sage and Human Nature

The ideal or the wording: "Sacredly (sagely) within, and kingly without" (*nei sheng wai wang* 內聖外王), despite its origin enunciated at chapter 23 ("The World") in the book of *Zhuangzi*, is typical of the spirit of Confucianism. Accordingly, a person is said to be the exemplar of the pattern of comprehensive unity, aspiring to the interfused value of the inwardly sacred and outwardly kingly achievement.

"Sacredly/sagely within" signifies the cultivation of the inwardness of a person that is of primary importance, and the cultivation has to do with modeling after the *nature* of a human, which is ordained by Heaven (Supreme Lord for Confucius). Such illustration is found in the opening sentences of the Confucian classic, *Doctrine of the Mean*:

> What is ordained of Heaven is called the essential *nature* of a human,
> To follow our *nature* is called the Way,
> Cultivating the Way is called education.

Basically, the *nature* of a human, with its focus on the natural order or law of reason and morality, is a far-reaching topic. Many scholars have found correspondences between the Confucian *nature* of a human and the natural law theory of Western philosophy.

Additional remarks on the idea of kingly achievement or the movement from inward to outward, from the *nature* of a human to the *nature* of things, ending with a Trinitarian life of harmony with Heaven and Earth, is illustrated by the quotation from chapter 22 of The *Doctrine of the Mean*:

> Only those who are absolutely sincere can fully develop their *nature*.
> If they can fully develop their *nature*, they can then fully develop the *nature* of others.
> If they can fully develop the *nature* of others, they can fully develop the *nature* of things.
> If they can fully develop the *nature* of things, they can fully participate in the transforming and nourishing process of Heaven and Earth.
> They can thus form a trinity with Heaven and Earth.

In sum, the inwardly sacred person, after having achieved the perfection of his *nature*, modeled after the infinitely and continually creative power of Heaven, need to go further to establish a well-disposed order in which all people and all creatures will be able to lead a life of similar perfection.

Sacredness and Transformation According to the Nature of Goodness

Mencius (371–289 BCE?) mentioned *sheng* (sacredness) and transformation into the *nature* of goodness. Sacredness is to be transformed in order to be divine, and such transformation is mystically realized beyond our knowledge.

Such idea has its origin in the six steps of cultivation proposed by *The Works of Mencius*, book 7, chapter 25. The six steps are: good, true, beautiful, great, sacred, and divine:

> Good person: one who commands our liking (because of his virtue).
>
> True person: one who is sincere with himself.
>
> Beautiful person: one who (whose goodness) is extensive and solid.
>
> Great person: one who (whose goodness) is abundant and is brilliantly displayed.
>
> Sacred person/sage: one who is great and is completely transformed (to be goodness itself).
>
> Divine person: a sage who is beyond our knowledge.

The first three preliminary steps of good, true, and beautiful are explained in the following. Mencius, going for the innermost motive of kind and just action, has found the foundation of moral character in good conscience (goodness). This conscience has found within itself all the potency of exalted life waiting for fulfillment (truth). When fulfillment is complete, it will give rise to the perfect beauty of personality (beauty).

Further explanation of the next three advanced steps of great, sacred, and divine is given in the following. Going outward means that greatness will be achieved when the beautiful personality is brilliantly manifested (greatness). This greatness, inasmuch as it comes to the completely transformed to be goodness itself, will issue in what is called sacredness (sacredness). And sacredness, becoming so rich in nature as to be far above the human power of comprehension, will be called the divine.[8]

Daoism

Daoism could be differentiated between Daoist philosophy and Daoist religion. Though with different accents, Daoist philosophy is metaphysical whereas Daoist religion is theistic. The idea of modeling after *nature* is their common characteristic.

Sacredness and Modeling after Self-Nature

According to Daoist philosophy, though the ultimate source of *nature* is Dao, Dao is said to model itself after *self-nature*. Hence, we read in the book of *Laozi*, "Dao imitates her natural self" (*Dao fa ji ren* 道法自然), which means what the Chinese word "自然" (*ziran*, literally, *self-nature*) implies, a kind of spontaneity or freedom from attachment (*wuwei* 無為) or a deep mystery of no-thingness (*wu* 無) in the philosophy of the Laozi (born 570 BCE?) and Zhuangzi (399–286 BCE). Let us quote the whole passage for illustration: "Human models himself after earth, earth models itself after heaven, heaven models itself after Dao, and Dao models itself after Nature" (*Laozi*, chap. 25).

Hence, modeling or imitating as employed here has a different meaning from the usual understanding. Far from winning and acquiring something exterior, it is the attitude of inwardness that nothing is by design to be won or acquired.

Sacredness and Modeling after Cosmic Nature

Daoist religion consists of many elements from folk religion, where modeling after cosmic *nature* is characterized by correspondence of one's life or behavior with the naturalness and normality of things or happenings.

Since life and death are of primary concern of religions, it is pertinent to give here an example. According to the Daoist religion, what is natural (*ziran* 自然) for human beings is to lead long life and to die a natural death, with male descendants performing ancestral worship. In this case, a normal procedure (*zhengchang* 正常) of funeral and interment would be enough, since the deceased has led a blissful life on earth and become an ancestor in order to enjoy the offerings of his offspring. Hence, worship and prayers are executed in conformity to this idea of *nature* and normality.

On the other hand, in the case of unnaturalness (*fei ziran* 非自然), e.g., a premature death or death by accident or sickness, with no male offspring or descendant to perform ancestral worship, there is no blessing for the life on earth of the deceased nor a peaceful afterlife for them to have their offspring perform the sacrifice, according to Daoist religion. The deceased would become ferocious ghosts (*ligui* 厲鬼), and an un-natural procedure (*fei zhenchang* 非正常) or grand ceremony of funeral and interment would be required to appease the resentment of the diseased and to console the grief of those alive. Worship and prayers to the gods are increased and multiplied in this context.[9]

Synthesis

Generally, the idea of *nature* in Chinese culture is similar to sacredness of integrity, a kind of systematic ordering of things in our context of biblical studies. To go one step further, in the Bible, sacredness at the final completion of sanctification is to be united with God. For the Chinese culture, it is to be one with Heaven or Dao, which is a more ultimate principle than the personal God (except for Confucius). The Chinese believe that human *nature* or cosmic *nature* is the magnificent realm of the confluence of life, even as a sacred system of value and beauty.

For Christian theology, sacred value or the ultimate principle is not God himself. The first principle does not create, nor is it found by itself. Only a personal God, not nature, is able to provide the answer to the first cause of creation that guarantees the meaning of human life. The cosmic order in the Bible is not self-created, self-rooted, or designed, and the principle of nature cannot become itself the fountain of morality. Biblical theology claims that one needs a God as the creator who possesses intellect and will, personal love, and who is to be the fountain of all value and the good.

However, Chinese thought conceives of creation as a natural process of the world emerging or evolving out of primordial reality, rather than as a willful act of an omnipotent God. From the Chinese perspective, the dualistic character of Christian theology poses a serious intellectual stumbling block, as well as an ontological rupture between God and the world and the alienation of man from God, as the fundamental religious truth.

Conclusion

Although this essay has pointed out many similarities of sacredness between the Bible and Chinese culture, they are very different in origin and in presentation. As it is, this does not provide an answer to the confrontation between these two different traditions. It is concerned only with the question of whether or not the numinous God of sacredness and the mysterious Heaven or Dao of *nature* have anything in common.

Further, in accordance with its very theme on sacredness, this essay also has investigated the common ground of the opposition between the OT and the NT, integrity and alterity, divine revelation and humanism, the sacred and the profane, as well as the mystical character and the harmonious whole of everything.

Finally, it is the finding of this essay that, despite different interpretations, both the biblical and the Chinese traditions would agree that each human being is destined to be a sacred or divine person.

Notes

1. Nathan Söderblom, "Holiness" in *Encyclopedia of Religion and Ethics*, vol. 6, ed. James Hastings (Edinburgh: T&T Clark, 1981), 731–741 (731).
2. Gilbert Maurice, "Le sacré dans l'ancien Testament," dans *L'éxpression du sacré dans les Grandes religions*, Vol. 1: *Proche-Orient ancien et traditions Bibliques, coll. Homo Religiosus*, ed. Julien Ries et al. (Louvain-la-Neuve: Centre d'histoire et de religion, 1978), 205–289; Ponthot Joseph, "Sacré et saintété dans le Nouveau Testament," in *L'éxpression du sacré dans les grandes religions*, ed. Julien Ries et al. (Louvain-la-Neuve: Centre d'histoire et de religions, 1986), 289–330.
3. Rudolf Otto, *The Idea of the Holy: An Inquiry into the Non-rational Factor in the Idea of the Divine and Its Relation to the Rational* (London: Oxford University Press, 1958), 26.
4. William Paden, "Sacred as Integrity: "Sacred Order" as a Model for Describing Religious Worlds," in *The Sacred and Its Scholars: Comparative Methodologies for the Study of Primary Religious Data*, ed. Thomas A. Idinopulos and Edward A. Yonan (Leiden: E. J. Brill, 1996), 3–18.
5. Mary Douglas, *Purity and Danger: An Analysis of the Concepts of Pollution and Taboo* (New York: Routledge, 1996), 42–58.
6. Unless otherwise noted, all biblical quotations are taken from the New Jerusalem Bible.

7. "Nature" as a term is italicized as a special meaning in the Chinese nature mentioned in this paper.
8. Thomé H. Fang, *Creativity in Man and Nature: A Collection of Philosophical Essays* (Taipei: Linking Publishing Company, 1983), 22.
9. *Zhongguo yiji chongbai yu shengzhe chongbei* [in Chinese] 中國遺跡崇拜與聖者崇拜 (Culte des sites et culte des saints en Chine), ed. Francisus Verellen and Lin Fu-shih (Taipei: Yunchen, 2000), 11–56.

Primary Sources

Chan, Wing-Tsit. *A Source Book in Chinese Philosophy*. Princeton: Princeton University Press, 1973.

The Doctrine of the Mean. Translated by James Legge, in his *The Chinese Classics*, vol. 1. Oxford: Clarendon Press, 1895.

Laozi, Laozi. Daodejing. Translated and notes by Edmund Ryden. Oxford: Oxford University Press, 2008.

Mencius, *The Works of Mencius*. Translated by James Legge, in his *The Chinese Classics*, vol. 2. Oxford: Clarendon Press, 1895.

The New Jerusalem Bible. Edited by Henry Wansbrough. Garden City: Doubleday, 1985.

Zhuangzi. *The Complete Works of Chuang Tzu*. Translated by Burton Watson. New York: Columbia University Press, 1968.

PART IV

RECEPTION IN INSTITUTIONS AND THE ARTS

CHAPTER 34

THE BIBLE AND POPULAR CHRISTIANITY IN MODERN CHINA

JOSEPH TSE-HEI LEE AND
CHRISTIE CHUI-SHAN CHOW

Introduction

The one hundredth anniversary of the publication of the Mandarin language Chinese Union Version (CUV, 和合本) in 2019, which remains the most widely used translation in the Chinese world, has prompted a spate of conferences and publications on the history of the Bible in China. The historiography of the indigenization of Christianity worldwide is full of stories of vernacularizing the Bible to empower ethno-cultural communities. Much emphasis was placed on literary, philosophical, and theological impacts of Bible work, but little attention has been given to the Bible in Chinese popular religious life.[1]

This essay draws on the latest scholarly research and fieldwork to explore how ordinary Chinese Protestants used the Bible to cope with a multitude of challenges in different temporal and spatial settings. It particularly looks at the influential role the Bible played in the sphere of popular Christianity. Xi Lian defines the phenomenon of popular Christianity as a form of "lively, indigenous Protestantism," which emerged outside the Western denominational missions throughout the late nineteenth and early twentieth centuries and which "retained its antiestablishment predilection" against the state-controlled Three-Self patriotic churches after 1949. This study builds on Lian's conceptualization to examine the widespread use of the Bible among the lay populace who were affiliated with, but outside the denominational churches, and who did not necessarily adopt an anti-state posture. It seeks to capture the religious fervor and creativity of ordinary believers who were traditionally excluded from the concerns and pursuits of Chinese Christian elites in cosmopolitan cities.[2] Greatly influenced by a climate of rising nationalism, Chinese Catholics and Protestants, as well as some Christian-inspired sectarians, skillfully adopted and adapted foreign theological currents into local cultural temperament and developed their own unique doctrinal markers and faith practices. A closer look at the Chinese reception of the Bible reveals various strategies for reading, practice, and deployment of scriptural teachings for spiritual and political purposes at the grassroots level.

Studying the localization of Christianity in Papua New Guinea, Harvey Whitehouse highlights the doctrinal and imagistic modes of biblical understanding.[3] The doctrinal mode refers to "the power of the Word," namely the "argument-based verbal and textual codification" of the Bible, and the imagistic mode captures the use of "climactic and revelatory ritual episodes" and ceremonies for transmitting scriptural teachings.[4] These two modes of biblical engagement coexisted with and complemented each other from the beginning of the Protestant expansion into China. Beginning with an overview of the cultural influence of the Bible in the mid-nineteenth century, this essay argues that the Bible was leveraged by peasant converts looking for new cosmologies, values, and norms to advance revolutionary changes in society. The rise of the Taiping Movement provides one example of how that happened. The twentieth century witnessed multiple levels of direct engagement with biblical texts, unmediated by foreign missionaries, among Chinese evangelists and congregants. Some drew on new biblical inspirations to found independent churches and sectarian groups, and some relied on the practice of bibliomancy to seek guidance in times of chaos. These examples offer complex view regarding the symbiosis between Bible reading and conversion in China.

The Bible as a Cosmological and Revolutionary Text

For many nineteenth-century Protestant missionaries, their first primary task of proselytization was to create new linguistic devices for translating the Bible, because the ability to comprehend the Bible would point Chinese faith seekers to belief in salvation by faith in Jesus Christ. In rural China, where literacy was taken as a sign of status, the ability to write and read publicly was important because it transformed Christians into a group of reading congregants and knowledgeable evangelists in their social circles. Translating the Bible was the missionaries' conscientious effort to enable believers to discern the text in their native tongues. The decision to standardize the doctrines through Bible study often coexisted with the urge to integrate the Gospel with preexisting worldviews. This missionary project to deepen the popular understanding of the Bible contributed to the transition of Chinese conversionary experience from *chuan* 傳 (preaching) to *bai* 拜 (worshipping) and *xin* 信 (believing).[5] The evangelistic, ritualistic, and fideistic elements suggest that the correlation between the Bible and popular Christianity was never a clear-cut, one-way process. The complexity could be known only through Chinese everyday encounters with the sacred.

Advocating a rupture between Christianity and Chinese culture over the interpretation of the sacred, most of the missionaries strove to displace longstanding philosophical and religious traditions to make room for Christianity. A theological vacuum about the role of ancestors arose in Chinese churches, and this was reinforced by the missionaries' demand for ritual purity among native converts, who were instructed to adhere to the iconoclastic practices of the missionaries. Shaped by the Second Great Awakening and a literal reading of the Bible, most Anglo-American and European missionaries of the evangelical tradition perceived conversion as "a specific and datable experience" of dramatic transformation, and they were believed to have undergone a single experience of conversion because they went abroad to turn "sinners" and "heathens" to God.[6] In the late nineteenth-century Chaozhou-speaking region of Guangdong province, American Baptists and Scottish Presbyterians expected Chinese converts to confess their belief in Christ as Savior publicly, to reject non-Christian rituals such as ancestral worship, geomancy (*fengshui* 風水), and temple ceremonies and to join a Christian community. Burning ancestral tablets, smashing household deities, and boycotting temple affairs were the sorts of attitudinal and behavioral changes the missionaries expected from Chinese Christians.[7] However, first-generation Chinese Christians were not in a supportive environment to nurture their faith. They faced the threat of harassment when they refused to take part in community rituals. Thus, missionary correspondence tells tales of humble Christians being forcefully expelled from their lineages due to their refusal to participate in ancestral worship and temple festivals.

The transformative power of the Word, they believed, came in the form of translated biblical passages. During the seventeenth and eighteenth centuries, the Spanish Dominicans came to rural Fujian province and permitted the laity to blend the biblical teachings and liturgical sacraments with preexisting social and religious customs. In this process of localization, the Dominicans acted as ritual specialists, exorcists, and faith healers among Catholics and non-Christians alike. Of all the sacraments, the Christianization of ancestral veneration and death management was the most illustrative. The Fujianese Catholics were instructed to pray to God and the saints for the salvation of their ancestors rather than looking up to the ancestors as divine figures and asking for material benefits. When displaying the hope of salvation for themselves and their ancestors, the Catholics rejected the conventional idea that their fate was to be decided by the ancestors. The Catholic doctrine of universal salvation subverted the verticality of the Chinese kinship system and transformed the cosmological relationship with ancestors. In Catholic families, ancestors now depended on the living to pray for their salvation.[8] This example corrects the misconception that everyday beliefs and practices of Catholic laity, often labeled as superstition or magic, were thought to be oriented towards utilitarian ends. Popular invocations to God and biblical saints were made to save one's ancestors, cure illnesses, and gain protection against misfortune. These innovative liturgies enabled local Catholics to make sense of the world and express their ethical and spiritual concerns. The commoners had a fresh understanding of biblical virtue in that being a good Catholic was bound with the fulfillment of one's duties to respect ancestors and living family members. A century later, Chaozhou-speaking Protestants in neighboring Guangdong province found in the Bible new insights that surprised the missionaries. Reading the Bible directly, some Chaozhou Baptists found it morally feasible to respect their dead ancestors. Viewing the Old Testament through a Confucian lens, they expressed profound sympathy for Abraham, who at first had no male descendant, but they were pleased to learn that God promised Abraham a son to continue the family line and to bless all the nations of the earth. Furthermore, the offering of Isaac by Abraham as a sacrifice to God in Genesis 22 was in line with the Confucian principle that family patriarchs had absolute power over the life and death of their children. The Chinese derived from this story the message that no one could interfere with Christian patriarchs except God. They found much comfort in biblical references to worshipping God as the God of Abraham, Isaac, and Jacob. Even though the Chinese were instructed to reject ancestral worship, they argued that God was the God of one's ancestors, families, and lineages.[9] They placed biblical accounts of Abraham, Isaac, and Jacob alongside their own family histories and drew out relevant moral lessons for themselves. Embracing these biblical narratives, these Baptists displayed a deep commitment to "perform the scriptural teachings" (*xingdao* 行道) in their Christian households.[10] American Baptist missionary Jacob Speicher, who was based in the district city of Jieyang, framed these accounts as the victory of Christian monotheism, and he never confronted local congregants over their literal understanding of the Bible, lest he lose control over his flock.

While Protestant missionary movements, which were born out of the European Reformation, had disenchanted the world through a rationalistic approach towards human destiny, fast-growing churches in rural China reenchanted the world by recognizing the interdependence between material and cosmological universes. Nineteenth-century Hakka-speaking members of the Basel, Rhenish, and Berlin missions in eastern Guangdong province derived from the Bible a new conception of the human relationship with the sacred.[11] Traditional beliefs in a powerful world of gods, ghosts, and ancestors who were able to affect the human domain, shaped Chinese perception of the Bible. Prior to their conversion, they treated local deities, ancestral spirits, and wandering ghosts with fear and awe. They prayed to these gods with sacrifices and offerings in exchange for protection. But when they read the biblical accounts of exorcism, they were fascinated by the absolute authority of Jesus Christ. Upon conversion, they were convinced that being given the biblical power by Christ to mediate between the supernatural and material domains, Christians ought to exercise their spiritual agency and to influence the state of affairs in both worlds. They challenged the basic assumptions of popular religious practices and rejected the subordinate transactional relations with other deities.[12] Their dissatisfaction with the inadequacy of popular religions and their desire for protection were powerful reasons for joining the church.

The cosmological interface between Christianity and popular religions was a consistent theme in local Chinese church memory, and the Bible emerged as a sacred object in the imagination of ordinary Christians. In a remote Hakka-speaking village, some Baptist women tore down the old paper deities and "put up the Holy Spirit instead" by worshipping the Bible and religious tracts at an altar and using them to ward off harmful spirits.[13] They regarded the Word as an important medium of transmitting God's authority from the chapel to the home. A similar practice continued in a Hong Kong Cantonese Lutheran church during the 1980s, when an educated seminarian was shocked to see an elderly female congregant offering incense to the Bible at home.[14] These stories resonated with the ritual of worshipping temple deities printed on colorful papers. Unless these believers had something visual and tangible to worship, they found it hard to understand the Christian God as transcendent and immanent.

The cultural influence of the Bible clearly depended on the educational standard of recipients. As with other rural societies, a cultural barrier separated the literati from numerous semi-literate or illiterate peasants in China. The educated class had an extensive knowledge of Chinese characters and the ability to write them. Below them were those semi-literate or illiterate commoners who recognized some characters but could not write them.[15] Therefore, providing Christians with a means of reading the Bible in their native tongues was of top priority.[16] During the 1860s, a linguistic revolution was set in motion in Xiamen, Fujian province and Taiwan, where English Presbyterian missionary wives used the Xiamen [Amoy] romanized script to teach women so that they could "read just as fluently and intelligently as most people at home [Scotland] would do." "The romanized Colloquial opened up the Scriptures to them" and "enabled them to consult the Bible freely for themselves."[17] In 1874, English Presbyterian missionary William Duffus vernacularized the Chaozhou dialect in Guangdong, using alphabets with eight accents to transcribe every sound and tone.[18] He and John Campbell Gibson translated the Bible, pamphlets, and hymnals into the phonetic script because classical Chinese was "a dead language" to dialect speakers as Latin and Greek were to ordinary Europeans.[19] This decision was of great historical significance because it not only made the Bible easily accessible but also provided Christians with "an easy channel for intelligent self-education." Instead of memorizing thousands of characters as Confucian scholars would do, local Christians only needed "to learn about twenty simple letters, and to practice their phonetic use in representing the sounds of their own mother-tongue as used in daily speech." As Christians began "to read the Word of God for themselves,"[20] they formed a self-instructing church on Chinese soil.[21] Qiu Jiaxiu 丘加修, an ordained Presbyterian minister, recalled that at age 12 he studied Chinese characters, the hymns, the Gospel of Luke, mathematics, and the romanized Chaozhou script in a village church school. After spending a week mastering the phonetic script, he could read aloud the Bible in public.[22]

One far-reaching impact of the vernacular Bible was the empowerment of female converts through the Biblewomen (i.e., Chinese Christian evangelists) training program. American Baptist missionary Adele M. Fielde was the first to organize the systematic training of Biblewomen in Chaozhou. Upon training, the Biblewomen traveled to places where access was denied to foreigners and anti-missionary sentiment was rife and preached to fellow women in the private domain. Even though biblical literalism advocated the scriptural treatment of women's subordination to men over ecclesiastical and spiritual matters, this program ensured a certain extent of authority for women to be involved in ministerial work under the formal church hierarchy.[23] In areas distant from Protestant mission headquarters in the treaty ports of Shantou and Xiamen, the vernacular Bible enabled Chinese recipients to join an extensive network of Bible-reading communities and to tap into a global religious awareness made possible by modern print culture that transcended linguistic, spatial, and class divisions.[24]

An idea of the complexity involved in Sino-Christian interactions can be gained from the Christian-inspired Taiping Movement in southern China, where Hong Xiuquan (1814–1864), a disillusioned Confucian scholar, inspired by a Protestant tract and some biblical materials, proclaimed himself the Chinese son of God and the younger brother of Jesus. Hong led the Society of God Worshippers (Bai Shangdi Hui), a movement that developed into a popular uprising against the Qing dynasty (1644–1911), defeating the imperial armies, and founding the Heavenly Kingdom of Great Peace (Taiping Tianguo) in Nanjing, which governed China's economic heartlands from 1853 to 1864.

By compiling their own Taiping Bible, the Taiping rebels perceived themselves as the new elect of God. Hong Xiuquan drew on his reading of the first books of the Hebrew scripture, especially the first three of the Ten Commandments, to advocate monotheistic ideals that flew in the face of Confucianism, Buddhism, and Daoism. Prohibiting the worship of idols as blasphemy, Hong rebuked the Chinese imperial cult and the authority of the Manchu emperor. He also modified biblical passages to ban alcohol sale and consumption, opium-smoking, and gambling.[25] Inspired by the book of Revelation, Taiping rebels believed themselves to be launching a political revolution that facilitated the advent of the Christian God's kingdom on earth. They propagated a doctrine of universal brotherhood and sisterhood under God. Women were to be treated as equals of men, permitted to hold office, able to join the army, and allowed to take government examinations. Civil service examinations were based on biblical rather than Confucian principles. More remarkable was the Taiping land reform, which divided all land among families of the Taiping soldiers and their supporters according to family size, with men and women receiving equal shares.[26] After the Heavenly Kingdom fell in 1864, the Qing imperial government effaced all evidence of the Taiping. The Taiping Movement, far from giving rise to a native tradition of Christianity, caused Protestant influence to wane and led to greater suspicion and hostility among the Chinese literati towards any form of Christianity in the late nineteenth century.

Despite the failure of Taiping Christians, the early twentieth century witnessed the proliferation of several independent, popular Christian movements such as Watchman Nee's 倪柝聲 (Ni Tuosheng, 1903–1972) Local Church (*Difang Jiaohui* 地方教會) or Assembly (*Zhaohui* 召會), also called "the Little Flock" (*Xiaoqun* 小群), the True Jesus Church, and the Jesus Family. As with Uchimura Kanzō's (1861–1930) Non-church movement in Japan, Watchman Nee's Local Assembly rejected ordained priesthood as an intermediary between believers and God and asserted the biblical principle of the priesthood of all believers. By casting off ecclesiastical leadership and Western denominationalism, Nee strove to conform to a timeless, biblical model of churches as the local manifestation of the body of Christ in the Apostolic Age.[27] Similarly, in 1917, Wei Enbo 魏恩波 (or Paul Wei) had a vision of encountering Jesus in the river outside Beijing. Since then, Wei called for a restoration of the direct charismatic scripts of the New Testament, and the scriptural teachings of Jesus. When he referred to his movement as the "True Jesus Church" (*Zhen Yesu Jiaohui* 真耶穌教會), the Chinese word "*Zhen*" (True) signified an immediate return to the purest mode of biblical Christianity.[28]

The Bible as a Spiritual Guide

Coinciding with the spread of the doctrine of bible inerrancy, the compilation of the CUV in 1919 reinforced the widespread idea that God could speak directly to his Chinese followers through a faithfully translated sacred text and provide answers in all of life's situations. But when the Bible was banned from circulation during the Maoist era (1949–1976), reading the Scripture in public was deemed subversive. Christian leaders of all stripes were compelled to show submission to the socialist order, and both denominational and independent churches found themselves embroiled in a process in which personal faith and biblical adherence were made subservient to politics. Yet, the Bible-centered, Christ-focused discourse empowered Christian religious prisoners to resist the ideological control of the Maoist state. When a young Seventh-Day Adventist evangelist, Robert Huang 黃兆堅 (Huang Zhaojian), was jailed from 1964 to 1972, he turned to his biblical knowledge and pastoral skills to network with Christian cellmates. He recalled writing down some biblical verses on tissue paper for fellow Christians and hiding them in Mao's Little Red Book, the only reading material permitted in prison. In the summer of 1967, after reading the front-page story of the Arab-Israeli War of June 5–10, 1967, in the *Liberation Daily*, he allegedly invoked biblical end-time prophecies to interpret the Six-Day War as a temporal marker in the Christian eschatological calendar in order to encourage other believers.[29]

Despite the state's seemingly totalitarian rule, clandestine evangelistic activities existed beneath the surface of the Maoist regime. Some Seventh-Day Adventist Christians in East China's Wenzhou enmeshed the Bible with the practice of divination, known as *qiuwen* 求問 (spiritual inquiring), to seek divine guidance and to assert their personal piety in opposition to the Communist state's atheistic propaganda. The art of bibliomancy, in which a biblical verse is randomly selected for divination, embedded itself in the broad spectrum of Chinese Christianity. While prominent preachers like Wang Mingdao and Watchman Nee drew on the Bible to oppose the Communist's interference in the spiritual affairs of the church, pro-government thinkers like Wu Yaozhong (Y. T. Wu) and Bishop Ding Guangxun (K. H. Ting) appropriated biblical passages to accommodate Christianity with socialism. Yet, the practice of bibliomancy led ordinary Christians to adhere to a biblical message they believed to be true and relevant to themselves. As clergymen were incarcerated and ordered to abandon their ministries, bibliomancy helped several women in rural Wenzhou to imbue their faith with Chinese cultural flavor.

Although Adventist women, like their female Catholic and Protestant contemporaries, saw the family as their primary sphere of action, their convictions led them to take an active role in ecclesiastical affairs. As Bible literalists, they believed that the Scripture directly addressed their problems and revealed deeper truths about China. Wu Guiying 吳桂英 and Huang Meide 黃美德, the matriarchs of the Chen family, an influential Adventist family in rural Wenzhou, practiced bibliomancy during troublesome times. They usually prayed in a quiet room and opened the Bible randomly with their eyes closed. They pointed to specific passages and wrote down the verses. Repeating this step twelve times, they collected twelve sets of verses, because they perceived "twelve" as the "perfect" biblical number.[30] Most of the verses they gathered during the 1950s warned about the immanent return of Jesus Christ and the demise of the Communist state. In 1955, the matriarchs referred to Josh 3:1–17, when the Israelites are called upon to cross the River Jordan after three days at camp, a pivotal moment for God's chosen people to reach the Promised Land. Interpreting these verses, they predicted that in three years' time, in 1958, Jesus would return and rescue faithful Christians.[31] After this prophecy failed to materialize, some congregants became disillusioned. In 1956, Huang Meide and her husband, Pastor Chen Dengyong 陳登庸, identified a verse in 1 Sam 11:9: "Thus shall you say to the inhabitants of Jabesh-gilead: 'Tomorrow, by the time the sun is hot, you shall have deliverance.'" (*Mingri taiyang jinwu de shihou, nimen bi de jiejiu*; cf. Chinese Union Version: 明天太陽近午的時候，你們必得解救). Reading it through a Chinese lens, they rendered "*Mingri taiyang jinwu*" as the peak of the summer of 1957 with "*wu*" as the Dragon Boat Festival and "*nimen bi de jiejiu*" as a symbol of regime change. Such an interpretation was deeply subversive, as the Chens placed God's authority above the socialist state and subjected the latter to the spiritual judgment of the Divine.[32]

Bibliomancy served as a valuable Bible-reading tool for women to stay vigilant in their ministries in times of chaos. On November 11, 1964, Huang was inspired by Job 5:24: "You shall know that your tent is safe, you shall inspect your flock and miss nothing" (NRSV). That verse assured her of divine protection. On November 16, she held clandestine worship at home. The police raided her home and captured her and another woman, only releasing them after beating them up. Returning home wounded, Huang found Jeremiah 44 through bibliomancy, which describes the desolation of Jerusalem. The Bible seemed to have foretold her suffering.[33]

Like her mother-in-law, Huang practiced bibliomancy and carefully copied down selected biblical verses without giving commentaries. These records were written in red, blue, and black colors, and one can imagine that the red verses might be those that inspired her the most. After the arrest of her husband, Pastor Chen, in 1961, Huang took on the daunting task of preserving the Seventh-Day Adventist ministry for a few years. Although she did not theorize which hermeneutical principle guided her reading of the selected verses, nor how those texts informed her action, she always rejoiced that on each occasion, the Lord gave her "invaluable" biblical signs, "comfort and peace," and inner strength.[34] In 1981, Huang retrieved her mother-in-law's two notebooks. "How faithful our mother was! She has drunk the cup of bitterness. We should keep on fighting for our ministry," Huang writes in her diary.[35] Throughout the 1980s, Huang turned to bibliomancy to seek out ideas to reclaim former mission properties from the district authorities,[36] pastor ordinary believers, and advise her husband on how to respond to hostile officials.[37]

The conventional scholarship on bibliomancy resonates with these Adventist stories.[38] Performing what Theodore Ziolkowski calls the "epiphany of the book," the inquirer gains "moments of insight" from the Bible for particular answers.[39] Bibliomancy appears to be similar to the Chinese ritual of divination, in which worshippers reach out to deities using devices like wooden or bamboo divination sticks and consulting *The Book of Changes* for guidance.[40] As with popular religious specialists who circulated the precious volumes (*baojuan*) and conducted spirit-writing in the sand to transmit heavenly messages, both Wu and Huang treated the Bible as a divine object for spiritual consultation.[41] Convincing as it seems, this scholarly understanding fails to comprehend the appeal of bibliomancy among the Christian masses. Believing in the Bible, Wu and Huang regarded it as a master script for practical consultations and saw bibliomancy as key to cultivating an intimate relationship with God.[42] In contrast to seeking guidance through spirit mediums, bibliomancy was designed to turn people's attention to God in times of crisis. Therefore, practicing Christians should embrace bibliomancy as a spiritual pedagogy to ask "the Holy Spirit to teach you everything, and remind you of" what Jesus had "said to you" (John 14:26).[43] By isolating the randomly chosen biblical verses from the entire Scripture, they created *a* bible within *the* Bible, placing specific texts under intense scrutiny.

The practice of bibliomancy exhibited innovative modes of survival among Chinese Christians during the darkest moments of modern Chinese history. When organized churches and religious activities were banned in public, humble Adventists acquired a special way to approach the sacred text for unique situations. They were determined to extract spiritual insights from the chosen verses, to lead their clandestine churches, and above all, to motivate themselves to be faithful to God. Historical urgency and contingency had much to do with the appeal of bibliomancy. In Maoist China, reading any religious literature was itself a political act, and the Adventists embraced this practice because of their belief in the efficacy of the Bible. The art of bibliomancy appears to be of little significance in Chinese history, but as shown by lesser known evangelistic agents such as Wu and Huang, this mode of Bible reading inspired a handful of house-church followers to resist the anti-religious policies of the Maoist regime and pointed to their deep faith in the "malleability" of Christianity.[44]

The Bible as a Revelatory Text

The 1980s and 1990s saw the proliferation of numerous Christian autonomous house churches that refused to join the Three-Self Patriotic Movement based on their biblical convictions. Despite their conservative theological orientation, these autonomous churches took the Bible seriously, treating it as "a revelatory text inspired by the Holy

Spirit and accordingly an authoritative scripture."[45] Some urban house churches, such as the Ark Church (Fangzhou jiaohui 方舟教會) and Watchers Church (Shouwang jiaohui 守望教會) in Beijing, attracted disillusioned intellectuals after the Communist crackdown on the prodemocracy student movement in Tiananmen Square in June 1989 and provided them with a biblical worldview towards personal struggle and social engagement. In 1998, several urban house churches from across the country issued a faith statement to reassert their belief in the Bible and the universal principle of religious liberty. It was the interpretation of biblical social ethics that put them at odds with the Communist state.

At the other end of the theologian spectrum, a number of Christian apocalyptic groups organized themselves around charismatic leaders of different house churches. As with mid-nineteenth-century Taiping leader Hong Xiuquan, Wu Yangming (1945–1995), in western Anhui province, came across a reference to himself in Luke 2:34: "This child is destined for the falling and rising of many in Israel, and to be a sign that will be opposed" (NRSV). Styling himself as the Established King (*Beiliwang*), the reincarnated Christ, he built a theocratic movement that hailed himself as the father-king (*fuwang*) and gave biblical names to his followers. Setting two dates for the end-time, he proclaimed that his movement would overthrow Satan (i.e., the Chinese Communist state) and bring in "a new heaven and a new earth." He was arrested and executed in 1995.[46] One of Wu's subordinates, Liu Jiaguo (1964–2003), built a splinter group called the "Lord God Sect" (*Zhushenjiao*) and borrowed the Old Testament to create his own Ten Commandments, blending biblical teachings with demands for submission and self-sacrifice. Influenced by the dispensationalist ideas of Watchman Nee's Local Assembly, Liu advocated for the divine punishment of the corrupt Communist regime during the end time and urged his devotees to surrender their belongings to him. He was arrested in 1998 and put to death in 2003.[47]

Reinterpretation of the Bible plays a decisive role in contemporary Chinese debate about challenges posed by these Christian sectarian movements, which are persecuted by the Chinese government as "evil cults" (*xiejiao* 邪教), a political stigma imposed by the state and a religious brand subject to criticisms by officially registered patriotic churches and unofficially recognized house churches.[48] Indigenous Christian sectarians are widely thought to be influenced by Chinese folk religions,[49] but this analytical paradigm overlooks a sociocultural process of utilizing the Bible to construct a new Chinese Christian orthodoxy. This process is particularly crucial in China, where neither the Three-Self Patriotic Movement nor the Communist state has the authority to institutionalize and monopolize core Christian beliefs and practices in the public domain.

The most famous Christian sectarian group is probably the Lightning of the East (also known as "Eastern Lightning"), in reference to Matt 24:27: "For as the lightning comes from the east and flashes as far as the west, so will be the coming of the Son of Man" (NRSV). This biblical reference is thought to denote China as the exact location where the Almighty God is born. Widely called "The Church of Almighty God" today, it is believed to have been founded by Zhao Weishan (1956?–) in northern China. When the movement was denounced by the government as the second "evil cult," following the suppression of the Falun Gong in 1999, Zhao Weishan left China and now resides in the United States. Since spreading from its homeland of Heilongjiang province in northeastern China, to Hong Kong, South Korea, the United States, and Europe, however, Zhao's group has become an organized, proactive, and widespread transnational movement with a sophisticated body of teachings.[50]

The Church of Almighty God might be best described as "Sinocentric," placing China at the heart of Christian salvation in the end time. Criticizing China as the land of the "great red dragon," an apocalyptic symbol of Satan in the book of Revelation,[51] it is for the purpose of saving Chinese that the Almighty God has become an incarnate Chinese woman named "Deng," who strives to recruit Chinese believers to save all nations. Thus, the ministry of The Church of Almighty God is reminiscent of the biblical understanding of the chosen people. This group has produced countless religious texts, including *The Scroll That the Lamb Opened* (*The Scroll*) and *The Word Has Appeared in the Flesh* (*The Flesh*), both of which introduce the most fundamental elements of the group's teachings derived from the Bible.[52]

The Church of Almighty God's revelations constitute the single source of authority beyond the Bible. Proclaiming that it would be misleading for the Christian God to reincarnate in a male body, the feminization of the Almighty God places women on equal footing with men, revealing a strict gender compartmentalization of salvation in its theology.[53] Modelling itself on the Four Gospels, the group's portrayal of the Almighty God resonates with the Jesus story. Born into a humble family in northern China, Deng dropped out of school in 1989. Inspired by the Holy Spirit in a house church, she started her ministry in 1991, setting out to purify the world against Satan, a biblical metaphor for Chinese Communists.[54]

The Church of Almighty God's appropriation of the Bible is an essential way of sustaining its identity as distinct from other Christian communities. Drawing on the Union Bible to create its own Bible, The Church of Almighty God quotes extensively from biblical narratives and vocabulary to construct theological worldviews and revelatory messages and to critique the secular world. In presenting herself as the chosen one to save China, the Almighty God argues for a direct relationship with the Divine. Her repudiation of Scripture is comparable to the doctrinal position held by the Friday Apostolics in Zimbabwe, who reject the authority of the Bible and seek for an immediate divine presence through the prophet's speech acts, spiritual healings, and singings.[55] Just as the Friday Apostolics are suspicious of the religious adequacy of the Bible in bringing people to God, The Church of Almighty God seeks to overcome this God-man distance through the revelations of a female savior. The movement is probably the most innovative and ambitious indigenous Christian-inspired group in today's China. Any Chinese Christian who attempts to monopolize the interpretation of Christian faith is confronted by the group's redefinition of the right way to approach God. Its remarkable expansion worldwide challenges mainland and overseas Chinese Christians to re-read and reinterpret the Bible. One single lesson to be learnt from these interactions is that the landscape of Chinese Christianity is highly fragmentary and characterized by various modes of reading and acting on the Bible.

Conclusion

The CUV has been central in the making of Chinese Christianity from the nineteenth century to the present. The Chinese church history abounds with examples of genuine, bottom-up efforts to engage with the Christian God through an independent reading of the Bible unmediated by Western theology and practice. The teachings of some prominent Chinese preachers and Christian-inspired sectarian leaders are treated as of equal or similar authority to the Bible. The most notable historical precedents include the Taiping Uprising and The Church of Almighty God today. Even though these followers have distinguished the Bible from their founders' writings, frequent references to the latter in public worship and private mediation have prompted followers to re-read the Bible and appreciate the salvific significance of Christ through their founders' revelatory words. These Christian sectarians have purposefully appropriated new biblical insights to seek specific guidance, often following the pattern of theological fulfillment or that of restoration. For example, Taiping leader Hong Xiuquan treated the Bible as a revolutionary text that inspired him to imagine and fight for an alternative political system. Inspired by the Old Testament, and especially Revelation, Hong's biblical commentaries and spiritual teachings were taken as additional revelations from God, and this new understanding superseded the common knowledge of Protestant Christianity in existing mission-churches. In the early twentieth century, Watchman Nee's Local Assembly and the True Jesus Church criticized many existing denominations as decadent, and they proclaimed to have rediscovered, restored, and reformatted biblical wisdom once held by the early Apostolic church. During the Maoist era, some humble Adventist women practiced the art of bibliomancy to sustain their clandestine ministry when the state prohibited public circulation of the Bible. Today, The Church of Almighty God has gone further to argue that God's revelation never ends with the canonization of the Bible, and that God continues to reveal deeper truths to those people who are open to the ongoing work of the Divine.

In short, the Bible, once translated into Chinese, has had immense consequences at the popular religious level. It has inspired certain elements of creative dissent for people who struggle on the fringes of society. The innovative Bible-reading methods have "prophesied an impending fiery end to the corrupt and unjust world and promised a complete deliverance in the coming millennial kingdom."[56] Offering comfort in this world and a promise of salvation in the afterlife, the Bible provided transcendent meanings for the destitute in the past and will remain relevant to people trapped in crisis situations in contemporary China.

Notes

1. John Y. H. Yieh, "The Bible in China: Interpretations and Consequences," in *Handbook of Christianity in China*, Vol. 2: *1800–Present*, ed. R. G. Tiedemann (Leiden: E. J. Brill, 2010), 891–913; George Kam Wah Mak, *Protestant Bible Translation and Mandarin as the National*

Language of China (Leiden: E. J. Brill, 2017); George Kam Wah Mak, "Building a National Bible Society: The China Bible House and the Indigenization of Bible Work," in *The Church as Safe Haven: Christian Governance in China*, ed. Lars Peter Laamann and Joseph Tse-Hei Lee (Leiden: E. J. Brill, 2019), 205–237; Chloë Starr, *Reading Christian Scriptures in China* (New York: T&T Clark, 2008).

2. Xi Lian, *Redeemed by Fire: The Rise of Popular Christianity in Modern China* (New Haven: Yale University Press, 2010), 12.
3. Harvey Whitehouse, *Arguments and Icons: Divergent Modes of Religiosity* (Oxford: Oxford University Press, 2000), 34.
4. Whitehouse, *Arguments and Icons*, 52.
5. Joseph Tse-Hei Lee, "Preaching (*chuan*), Worshipping (*bai*), and Believing (*xin*): Recasting the Conversionary Process in South China," in *Asia in the Making of Christianity: Agency, Conversion, Indigeneity, 1600s to the Present*, ed. Jonathan Seitz and Richard Fox Young (Leiden: E. J. Brill, 2013), 81–108.
6. Jessie Gregory Lutz, *Opening China: Karl F. A. Gützlaff and Sino-Western Relations, 1827–1852* (Grand Rapids: William B. Eerdmans, 2008), 7.
7. Joseph Tse-Hei Lee, *The Bible and the Gun: Christianity in South China, 1860–1900* (New York: Routledge, 2003), xxviii.
8. Eugenio Menegon, *Ancestors, Virgins, and Friars: Christianity as a Local Religion in Late Imperial China* (Cambridge, MA: Harvard University Asia Center, 2009), 299.
9. Jacob Speicher, *The Conquest of the Cross in China* (New York: Fleming H. Revell, 1907), 252–254.
10. Sarah Allan, *The Way of Water and Sprouts of Virtue* (Albany: State University of New York Press, 1997), 100–101.
11. Jessie Gregory Lutz and Rolland Ray Lutz, *Hakka Chinese Confront Protestant Christianity, 1850–1900, with the Autobiographies of Eight Hakka Christians, and Commentary* (Armonk, NY: M. E. Sharpe, 1998), 152–159.
12. Robert P. Weller, *Unities and Diversities in Chinese Religion* (Seattle: University of Washington Press, 1987), 88–89.
13. Louise Campbell, "Kaying," in *Oriental Gardens and the Lord God Planted a Garden Eastward* (Chicago: Women's American Baptist Foreign Missionary Society, 1915), 131–132; Meir Shahar and Robert P. Weller, "Introduction: Gods and Society in China," in *Unruly Gods: Divinity and Society in China*, ed. Meir Shahar and Robert P. Weller (Honolulu: University of Hawai'i Press, 1996), 28–29.
14. Joseph Tse-Hei Lee recalled this story told by a Lutheran seminarian in 1988.
15. Herbert A. Giles, *From Swatow to Canton [Overland]* (Shanghai: Kelly and Walsh, 1877), 11.
16. "Mission Notes," no date, Library of the School of Oriental and African Studies, University of London, The Presbyterian Church of England Archives, Foreign Mission Committee (hereafter cited as SOAS), series 1, box 31, folder 8.
17. John Campbell Gibson, Shantou to H. M. Matheson, London, August 31, 1875, SOAS, series 1, box 41b, folder 6.
18. Adele Fielde, *A Pronouncing and Defining Dictionary of the Swatow Dialect* (Shanghai: American Presbyterian Mission Press, 1883), ii and iv; John Campbell Gibson, *Manual of Swatow Vernacular* (Swatow: English Presbyterian Mission Press, 1923), 3.
19. George A. Hood, *Mission Accomplished? The English Presbyterian Mission in Lingtung, South China: A Study of the Interplay between Mission Methods and their Historical Contexts* (Frankfurt, Germany: Peter Lang, 1986), 119.

20. John Campbell Gibson, *Mission Problems and Mission Methods in South China: Lectures on Evangelistic Theology* (Edinburgh and London: Oliphant, Anderson & Ferrier, 1902), 212–213.
21. Hur L. Mackenzie, Shantou to H. M. Matheson, London, January 14, 1876, SOAS, series 1, box 42a, folder 2. For a similar Cantonese linguistic experiment, see Yin-Ping Lee and Shin Kataoka, "Malixun dui zhongwen de renshi (Robert Morrison's knowledge of Chinese Language)," *Zhongguo yuwen yanjiu* (Studies in Chinese Language) 2 (2006), 21–36.
22. "*The Lingdong Convention of the Church of Christ in China: Biographical Sketches of Ninety-Six Protestant Ministers*" [in Chinese] 偽中華基督教會嶺東大會: 有關九十六名牧師傳略" (1948), Shantou Municipal Archives 汕頭市檔案館, *The Archives of the Republican Regime* 舊政權檔案, call no. 12/11/16.
23. Ellen Xiang-Yu Cai, "The First Group of Chaoshan Biblewomen," in *Christianizing South China: Mission, Development, and Identity in Modern Chaoshan*, ed. Joseph Tse-Hei Lee (New York: Palgrave Macmillan, 2018), 15–36; Oi-Ki Ling, "Bible Women," in *Pioneer Chinese Christian Women*, ed. Jessie Gregory Lutz (Bethlehem, PA: Lehigh University Press, 2010), 246–265.
24. Melissa Wei-Tsing, *China and the True Jesus: Charisma and Organization in a Chinese Christian Church* (Oxford: Oxford University Press, 2019), 71.
25. P. Richard Bohr, "Taiping Religion and Its Legacy," in *Handbook of Christianity in China*, Vol. 2: *1800–Present*, ed. R. G. Tiedemann (Leiden: E. J. Brill, 2010), 371–395; Jonathan D. Spence, *God's Chinese Son: The Taiping Heavenly Kingdom of Hong Xiuquan* (New York: W. W. Norton, 1996).
26. Weichi Zhou, "Correspondence between the *Taiping Heavenly Chronicle* (*Taiping tianri*) and the 'Revelation,'" in *Yearbook of Chinese Theology: 2015* (Leiden: E. J. Brill, 2015), 71–107.
27. David Woodbridge, *Missionary Primitivism and Chinese Modernity: The Brethren in Twentieth-Century China* (Leiden: E. J. Brill, 2018), 69; Joseph Tse-Hei Lee, "Watchman Nee and the Little Flock Movement in Maoist China," *Church History* 74.1 (2015): 68–96.
28. Melissa Wei-Tsing Inouye, *China and the True Jesus: Charisma and Organization in a Chinese Christian Church* (Oxford: Oxford University Press, 2019), 110.
29. Joseph Tse-Hei Lee, "Faith and Defiance: Christian Prisoners in Maoist China," *Review of Religion and Chinese Society* 4.2 (2017): 167–192.
30. Interview with Chen Yajun by Christie Chui-Shan Chow, August 18, 2012; interview with Chen Dengyong by Christie Chui-Shan Chow, August 6 and 26, 2012.
31. Chengqian Shu, *Wushinian jiaohui shenghuo huiyi* [in Chinese] (*Memoirs of Church Life in the Last Fifty Years*), 156–157.
32. Chengqian Shu, *Wushinian jiaohui shenghuo huiyi*, 156–158.
33. Entry for November 20, 1964. Huang Meide's diary.
34. Entries for November 1, 1985, November 2, 1986, and November 2, 1986. Huang Meide's diary.
35. Entries for April 28 and July 1, 1981. Huang Meide's diary.
36. Entries for November 25, 1980; April 29 and July 22, 1981; September 18, 1982; September 1 and December 7, 1983; January 15 and April 8, 1985; August 14 and 29, 1986; February 9, 1987; November 15 and December 9, 1990. Huang Meide's diary.
37. Entry for May 20, 1987. Huang Meide's diary.
38. Robert Wiśniewski, "Pagans, Jews, Christians, and a Type of Book Divination in Late Antiquity," *Journal of Early Christian Studies* 24.4 (2016): 553–568; Pieter W. van der

Horst, "Ancient Jewish Bibliomancy," *Journal of Greco-Roman Christianity and Judaism* 1 (2000): 9–17.

39. Theodore Ziolkowski, "'*Tolle Lege*': Epiphanies of the Book," *Modern Language Review* 109.1 (January 2014): 1.
40. Adam Yuet Chau, *Miraculous Response: Doing Popular Religion in Contemporary China* (Stanford: Stanford University Press, 2006); Stephen L. Field, *Ancient Chinese Divination: Dimensions of Asian Spirituality* (Honolulu: University of Hawai'i Press, 2008).
41. Daniel L. Overmyer, *Precious Volumes: An Introduction to Chinese Sectarian Scriptures from the Sixteenth and Seventeenth Centuries* (Cambridge, MA: Harvard University Asia Center, 1999); David K. Jordan and Daniel L. Overmyer, *The Flying Phoenix: Aspects of Chinese Sectarianism in Taiwan* (Princeton: Princeton University Press, 1986); Jean DeBernardi, *The Way That Lives in the Heart: Chinese Popular Religion and Spirit Mediums in Penang, Malaysia* (Stanford: Stanford University Press, 2006).
42. "Sermon theme #260," in Chen Dengyong, *Five Hundred Sermon Outlines.*
43. "Sermon theme #341," in Chen, *Five Hundred Sermon Outlines.*
44. Albert Wu, "Forever a Patriot: Chinese Christians and the Repudiation of American Liberal Protestantism," *Journal of the American Academy of Religion* 85.1 (2017): 112–135.
45. Yieh, "The Bible in China," 905.
46. Xi, *Redeemed by Fire*, 221.
47. Ibid. 222.
48. Emily Dunn, *Lightning from the East: Heterodoxy and Christianity in Contemporary China* (Leiden: E. J. Brill, 2015); Kristin Kupfer Kupper, "Images of Jesus Christ in Christian Inspired Spiritual and Religious Movements in China Since 1978," in *The Chinese Face of Jesus Christ*, Vol. 3b (Sankt Augustin: Institut Monumenta Serica and China-Zentrum, 2007), 1365–1375.
49. Daniel H. Bays, "The Growth of Independent Christianity in China, 1900–1937," in *Christianity in China: From the Eighteenth Century to the Present* (Stanford: Stanford University Press, 1996), 307–316; Daniel H. Bays, "Chinese Protestant Christianity Today," *China Quarterly* 174 (2003), 488–504; Richard Madsen, "Chinese Christianity: Indigenization and Conflict," in *Chinese Society, Change, Conflict and Resistance* (London: Routledge Curzon, 2003), 271–288; Kupper, "Images of Jesus Christ"; Emily Dunn, "'Cult,' Church and the CCP: the Case of Eastern Lightning," *Modern China* 35.1 (2009): 96–119; Emily Dunn, "Netizens of Heaven: Contesting Orthodoxies on the Chinese Protestant Web," *Asian Studies Review* 31.4 (2007): 447–458.
50. Dongsheng Wu, *The Secrecy of Evil Cult: A Study on the Regime of Evil Cult Assembly in Today's China* [in Chinese] (Beijing: Social Sciences Academic Press, 2004), 41n1.
51. Anonymous, "China as Red Dragon," https://en.godfootsteps.org/about-us-02.html.
52. Dunn, *Lightning from the East*, 20.
53. Anonymous, "The Word Becoming Flesh Twice Completes the Significance of the Incarnation," *The Scroll That the Lamb Opened*, 116. http://english.hidden-advent.org/book/0034.php.
54. Anonymous, "A Brief Introduction about the Background of the Appearance and Work of Christ of the Last Days in China," https://www.holyspiritspeaks.org/about-us-02/.
55. Matthew Engelke, *A Problem of Presence: Beyond Scriptures in an African Church* (Berkeley: University of California Press, 2007).
56. Xi, *Redeemed by Fire*, 232.

Primary Sources

Anonymous. "A Brief Introduction about the Background of the Appearance and Work of Christ of the Last Days in China." https://www.holyspiritspeaks.org/about-us-02/.

Anonymous. "China as Red Dragon." https://en.godfootsteps.org/about-us-02.html.

Anonymous. "The Word Becoming Flesh Twice Completes the Significance of the Incarnation." *The Scroll That the Lamb Opened*, 116. http://english.hidden-advent.org/book/0034.php.

The Archives of the Republican Regime [in Chinese] 舊政權檔案. Shantou Municipal Archives 汕頭市檔案館. Shantou, Guangdong province, China.

Campbell, Louise. "Kaying." In *Oriental Gardens and the Lord God Planted a Garden Eastward*. Edited by Nellie G. Prescott. (Chicago: Women's American Baptist Foreign Missionary Society, 1915), 131–132.

Chen, Dengyong. *Five Hundred Sermon Outlines*. Wenzhou, Zhejiang province, 2013. Personal acquisition by Christie Chui-Shan Chow.

Fielde, Adele. *A Pronouncing and Defining Dictionary of the Swatow Dialect*. Shanghai: American Presbyterian Mission Press, 1883.

Giles, Herbert A. *From Swatow to Canton [Overland]*. Shanghai: Kelly and Walsh, 1877.

Gibson, John Campbell. *Manual of Swatow Vernacular*. Swatow: English Presbyterian Mission Press, 1923.

Gibson, John Campbell. *Mission Problems and Mission Methods in South China: Lectures on Evangelistic Theology*. Edinburgh and London: Oliphant, Anderson & Ferrier, 1902.

Huang, Meide. Diary. Wenzhou, Zhejiang province. Personal acquisition by Christie Chui-Shan Chow.

The Presbyterian Church of England Archives, Foreign Mission Committee. Library of the School of Oriental and African Studies, University of London. London, UK.

Shu, Chengqian. *Memoirs of Church Life in the Last Fifty Years* [in Chinese] 五十年教會生活回憶. Internal publication, Wenzhou, Zhejiang province, 2002.

Speicher, Jacob. *The Conquest of the Cross in China*. New York: Fleming H. Revell, 1907.

CHAPTER 35

BIBLICAL ECCLESIOLOGY AND THE CHINESE CHURCH

EVAN LIU

Christianity in China: From Survival to Revival

When the Communist Party of China (CPC) came to power in 1949 and shut the door to outsiders for almost three decades from 1951 to 1978, churches in Eastern Europe and North America wondered whether churches in China would survive. Before 1949, the Roman Catholic Church had claimed many dioceses and ordained Chinese bishops. The Russian Orthodox Church assigned their priests to lead the different orthodoxy parishes in northeastern China. And, since the first foreign Protestant missionary Robert Morrison (1782–1834) arrived in the Guangdong province in 1807, Protestant denominations had a long history of outreach and establishment of denominational churches among the Chinese people.

The withdrawal of foreign missionaries in China began when the Chinese full-scale civil war resumed in 1946, and the number of missionaries was further reduced when the CPC expelled more than three thousand foreign missionaries in 1951. By the end of 1952, without freedom to approach the Chinese people, very few missionaries remained.[1]

In 1954, the Chinese government formed the National Committee of the Three-Self Patriotic Movement to manage all the visible churches and forced them to become the State Three-Self Churches (self-governing, self-propagating, and self-supporting). The Three-Self Patriotic Movement in 1951 aimed to cut off all religious connection between Chinese churches and the outside world. Protestant Chinese churches seemed able to give up the connection because they had gone through indigenization before 1949. However, the Chinese Catholic and Orthodox churches encountered challenges without communion with the Roman pope or the Russian archbishop.

During the Great Cultural Revolution (GCR, 1966–1976), Three-Self churches were shut down. Some public churches refused to cooperate with the shutdown and became the first group of underground churches after 1949. And, despite an immense national crisis with the GCR, many underground churches experienced rapid growth.[2]

Also, during the GCR, communications with the Vatican and Moscow were cut off. As a result, the Chinese Catholic and Orthodox churches lacked bishops ordained by outside authorities. And, Chinese bishops who had been previously ordained by outside authorities were detained by the government during this time. Thus, liturgical services and religious activities of those churches were discontinued, and the details of those church situations remain unclear.

When the GCR ended right after Chairman Mao's death in 1976, China reopened the door to the world by 1979. One phenomenon that was astounding to the outside world was that, rather than decreasing, the number of Chinese Protestant Christians increased to around 3 million by 1982. This was more than three-fold the 700,000 Protestant Christians in China before 1949.[3] In fact, the number of Chinese Protestant Christians continues to rise rapidly today, so much so that the Amity Foundation in Nanjing has printed 88.9 million copies of Chinese Bibles during the time of its establishment from 1988 through 2011.[4]

By 1981, China began to allow religious communications with the outside world, but the CPC—in an effort to guard political stability—has not permitted Chinese Catholic and Orthodox churches to build a formal relationship with outside religious authorities.

Chinese Three-Self Patriotic Churches

The Chinese Three-Self Patriotic Protestant (TSP) churches were generated from the Three-Self Patriotic Movement (TSPM) in 1951. The movement was initiated by the CPC through the national religious bureau to promote indigenization of all Chinese churches to uphold self-governance, self-support, and self-propagation. Later, it formed the Three-Self Patriotic Movement Committee (TSPMC) of the Protestant Churches of China and the China Christian Council (CCC).[5]

Indigenization contained three dimensions. The first was to mobilize all Protestant churches in China to join TSPM and become Three-Self Patriotic churches. The second was to remove any denominational connections from the churches and move them into a post-denominational stage. And, the third was to Sinicize (中國化) Christian religion and make Chinese Christianity fit the development of socialistic China.[6] To reach such a goal, Three-Self theologians like Zhao Zichen 趙紫宸 (1888–1979) and Wu Leichuan 吳雷川 (1870–1944) attempted to interpret Christian theology through Confucianism and the modern scientific worldview.[7] According to these theologians, Christianity is a kind of ideology to explain the world and its purpose based on the visions cast by Jesus. Zhao Zichen contended that Jesus was no more than a suffering hero and a moral example and, through following Christ, one continued to develop his moral character until he could become a benefactor to his own country and contributor to the peace of the world. Wu Leichuan, agreeing with Zhao, embraced the idea that individual righteousness could never be granted by belief and must be gained through self-effort.[8]

The first chairman of the TSPM, Wu Yaozong 吳耀宗 (1893–1979), argued to place national salvation as the priority. For him, salvation has nothing to do with the individual; instead, it is about the liberation and improvement of social justice.[9] Later, another leader of the Three-Self movement, K. H. Ting 丁光訓 (1915–2012), contended that the Christian doctrine of justification by faith devalued ethics and should not be uplifted. Ting blames the tendency to see "faith" as an automatic trigger for "righteousness," as if it were an impersonal price paid in exchange for a personal virtue. He proposed that the nature of being Christian was one of love and love could be best demonstrated by loving one's own country, namely by demonstrating patriotism. Patriotic love could help Chinese churches become Sinicized and liberated from denominational bondage.[10] This socio-moralistic interpretation of Christianity became the guiding principle held by the majority of Three-Self churches in China.

Most TSP churches are composed of Mandarin-speaking Han people and the rest are minorities who speak different languages and dialects. Since TSP churches are government-approved churches, they enjoy the privilege of holding religious activities and services in their public church buildings. However, they cannot freely evangelize outside their sanctioned regions and sanctioned buildings, and all religious ceremonies or events must be conducted by legitimated clergies recognized by CCC and TSPMC. This policy, called the "Three Designation Principles," was included in Document 19 issued by CPC in 1982 and prescribed the government's legitimated religious activities from then on.[11]

While most TSP churches reject any denominational background, operate their ministries with absolute obedience to the government, and propagandize religion from the perspective of socio-morality and science, there are some TSP churches that play the role of mediator between the local authority and local underground churches.

Among TSP churches, 2.5 percent are affiliated denominational churches, such as True Jesus Church, Little Flock, and Seventh-Day Adventist, which had existed in pre-CPC China. They all are publicly designated as TSP churches rather than being called by their denominational names, although they always prefer to restore their tradition by any means possible.[12] The denominational churches' public label as TSP churches is informed by K. H. Ting, the former chairman of CCC, who insisted that denomination is the major hindrance for churches in reaching ecumenical unity, which to him is equivalent to a type of religious colonialism. Ting urged that all TSP churches in China shall reach unity by entering the post-denominational stage and upholding the universalism of Jesus Christ. TSP churches can participate in China's socialistic construction proactively and demonstrate Christian belief to the whole society.[13]

Furthermore, there are some TSP churches that have underground ministries, such as church planting and cross-provincial evangelism implemented by True Jesus Church, Little Flock, or other churches who want their Christian traditions to survive and revive.

Their strategy is to sponsor many underground church missions and assist the newly planted family churches to grow. On many occasions, TSP churches could serve as an umbrella for underground churches and encourage them to promote the gospel mission in China. Thus, it too naive to conclude that TSP churches are always opposed to underground family churches without consideration of the overlapping areas of outreach.[14]

The official data in 2005 claims that there are more than 50,000 TSP churches with 25 million attendants in China.[15] There are around twenty-five official seminaries and Bible schools in China, and TSP churches recruit graduates from the official seminaries or Bible schools. They primarily train students to use religious knowledge to serve the development of socialism in China and to create harmony with other religions rather than evangelizing for more people to become Christians.[16] The local TSP pastoral ordination requires permission from the corresponding religious bureau and CCC because an ordained TSP pastor is equivalent to an official clergy and receives payment from the local government. Nevertheless, though church leadership is under the auspices of the government to serve the CPC's ideology, many members in TSP churches are Christians.

Chinese TSP and Catholic Underground Churches

The concern of "biblical ecclesiology" is predominantly a Protestant agenda. Catholic and Orthodox understandings of "ecclesiology" do not have to stress "biblical" for they have their long traditions in creeds, polity, and liturgy—though these traditions have gone through various renewal and modernization such as the Vatican II. The history of the Chinese Catholic church can be traced back to Matteo Ricci 利瑪竇 (1552–1610), a Jesuit missionary who successfully built the first Catholic Church in Beijing in 1605 at the time of the Ming dynasty.[17] After the construction of the first Catholic church, the Catholic mission entered a golden time of outreach to Chinese officials and intellectuals until 1715, when Pope Clement XI issued a decree claiming that the controversy of Chinese traditional ritual ceremonies went against Catholic belief. In 1721, Emperor Kangxi (1654–1722) stated his defiance against the pope's decree and began to forbid foreign missionary work in China from then on. In 1742, Pope Benedict XIV issued a Papal Bull to forbid all Chinese Catholic adherents from being involved with Chinese ancestral honorary rites, Confucius' honorary rites, and other traditional rites. This decree destroyed the relationship between the Roman Catholic Church and the Qing government and caused an escalated expulsion of Catholic missionaries by the Qing government. The Chinese Rites Controversy finally was resolved in 1939, when Pope Pius XII issued a decree to permit Chinese Catholic members to attend traditional rites without contradicting Catholic belief.[18]

During the years following 1949 because of political situation in China, Chinese Catholic churches had a difficult situation because of their submission to the Vatican. It eventually led to a split into Catholic Three-Self open churches and Catholic underground churches in China. The TSPM in 1951 later resulted in the establishment of the Chinese Patriotic Catholic Association (CPCA), the Chinese Catholic Bishops' Conference (CCBC), and the Chinese Catholic Affairs Committee (CCAC). Those organizations aimed to make Chinese Catholic churches more indigenous and pay homage to the CPC.[19] The pope would no longer have any supervisory power over Chinese Catholic churches, and insistence for Chinese churches' independence was affirmed in Document 19.[20] As a result, the issue of whether Chinese churches belonged to the governmental body of the CPC or to the body of the Roman Catholic Church split Chinese Catholics into two groups: patriotic adherents to the TSPM and those faithful to the papacy.

The patriotic adherents formed Chinese TSP Catholic churches (Open Church) under the supervision of the government, and Chinese faithful to the papacy refused to follow the TSPM, naturally forming Catholic underground churches. All Chinese Catholics faithful to the papacy secretly followed Chinese bishops and priests appointed by the Holy See.

Navigating the relationship between the Vatican and Beijing became a difficult issue for various successors in the papacy. In 1995, Pope John Paul II made his exhortation to Catholic churches in China and called them to forgive, forebear, and reconcile with one another within the whole community without distinguishing whether their brothers and sisters belonged to the open church or the underground church.[21] This exhortation eased the bilaterally hostile relationship. However, since the CPC never withdrew its control over the appointment of sacra offices, the schism and intensity between the Vatican and Beijing continued into 2009.

On November 10, 2009, Tarcisio Cardinal Bertone, Secretary of State for the Holy See, presented his letter to all Catholic clergies in China and exhorted adherents of TSP churches and underground churches to reconcile and procure unity by holding the Eucharist as the center of the whole communal body. The letter urged all Chinese bishops and priests to not hesitate to reconcile and unite if any opportunities for reconciliation occurred; it also emphasized that the first priority of the Chinese faithful was to give up the hostile attitude toward the other side. The letter also hinted that the pope would not forbid underground bishops from seeking government approval to resolve the conflict to reduce pressure against the underground church body.[22]

From then on, the tension between Beijing and the Vatican was eased, even as the papacy continued to insist on his sovereignty over sacra offices and the authority to reject the inauguration of some bishops appointed by the CPC.

Despite historical challenges of Chinese Catholic churches, the data speaks loudly again regarding the survival and resilience of the church in China. According to official data, the number of Chinese Catholic members was around 3.5 million in 2000.[23] Another report estimated that there were about 12 million Catholics in China by the end of 2014,[24] among which were, "74 bishops and more than 2,000 priests in the Open

Church and 46 bishops and at least 1,000 priests in the Underground Church."[25] The TSP Catholic churches have about nineteen seminaries and claim 1,000 seminary students. It is likely that underground churches have their own seminaries and students too and, according to some estimations, underground Catholic members could total another 10 million.[26]

Chinese Recovering Russian Orthodox Churches

During and following the GCR, Chinese Orthodox Churches (COC) were not many in number and they existed only as separate individual communities in northeastern China because foreign bishops were expelled from China and the CPC forced Chinese bishops to stop their ministries. In 1951, the TSPM did not establish any official Chinese Orthodox organizations and assigned COC to the supervision of local religious bureaucratic authorities.

The Eastern Orthodox Church in China holds a significantly longer history than that of the Roman Catholic Church and that of the Protestant Church. According to the Nestorian His-An monument, the Eastern Orthodox Church sent Aluoben 阿羅本, a Nestorian missionary, to China in 635 and set the historical stage for the introduction of Christianity into China. Another Eastern Orthodox missionary, Mateus Escandel, a former hermit at Mt. Sinai, entered China during in the fourteenth century and, during the Ming dynasty, lived and taught in a place called Cohilouza, not far from Beijing. Later, he was martyred, and his death in 1399 caused an earthquake that shook Beijing according to *Peregrinaçam*—a travel log written by Portuguese adventurer Ferñao Mendes Pinto (1509–1583).[27]

The first known Orthodox Church in Beijing could be traced back to 1685. When Qing troops captured fifty young Russian soldiers during a war against Russia and pardoned them to serve Emperor Kangxi, an Orthodox priest, Fr. Maxim Leontiev was among the captives. He later ministered to those Russians by accepting an empty Buddhist temple from the emperor to use as a church.[28]

In 1715, Tsar Peter the Great supported the emergence of the Chinese Russian Mission and thus more and more Orthodox churches were built in China. The first Orthodox Church in Wuhan was established in 1876, the first in Harbin in 1898, and the first in Shanghai in 1902.[29] By 1949, China had five bishops, 300,000 adherents, 310 parishes, and an Orthodox university in Harbin, the northeastern city. Among them were 10,000 Chinese adherents, which included some ordained deacons, priests, and bishops.[30]

Following the political pressures in 1949, most Russian Christians left China, and the Russian Orthodox Church had to allow Chinese churches to be independent in order to survive the religious crisis. However, the autonomous Chinese Orthodox Church did not last long after the only two native Chinese bishops died, and other Chinese clergies were forced by the CPC to stop their services.[31]

In Beijing, the last Chinese native priest was Fr. Alexander Du, whose service was never reactivated by the CPC after 1949; he died in 2003 without being able to see any Orthodox churches reopen.[32] From 1949 on, all Orthodox churches in China showed no obvious signs of restoration until 1984, when the parish in Harbin was officially reopened under the presiding of Fr. Gregory Chiu, whose office was permitted by the CPC. However, when he died in 2000, all liturgical services were discontinued until 2014, when a newly ordained Chinese priest was able to succeed in Chiu's position and restart everything.[33]

Meanwhile, in 1996, the Russian Ecumenical Patriarchate inaugurated a metropolitanate in Hong Kong to claim jurisdiction over China and some other East Asian countries.[34] In 1997, the Moscow Orthodox Patriarchate claimed its ecclesiastical support for the Autonomous Chinese Orthodox Church in electing bishops and other clergies. However, this posed a dilemma because the CPC did not permit any foreign clergies or Chinese clergies ordained by foreign churches to serve in China until 2014. In that year, the priest Fr. Alexander Yushi, ordained in St. Petersburg and recognized by the CPC, was able to serve in a church in Harbin after the restoration of Russian Orthodox jurisdiction over Chinese orthodox churches.[35]

In 2003, Moscow patriarchal priest Fr. Dionisy Pozdnyaev, from the Russian Orthodox Church, moved to Hong Kong to found and minister to the Church of Sts. Peter and Paul. He was very concerned and sought to address the lack of religious support for new Orthodox Christians in China. At the time, many Christians had broken ties with their existing social networks after conversion to the Orthodox religion, and this resulted in individual communities having only two to three people, making it difficult for Christians to form a sustainable network of spiritual support.[36] Thus, many new secret believers would have no regular way to approach the sacraments.[37] The priest, Fr. Dionisy Pozdnyaev, insisted on the indigenization of the Chinese Orthodox Church by training Chinese seminarians, ordaining them as native priests, and ensuring their recognition by the authority to teach and serve publicly someday.[38]

Pozdnyaev also worked toward having an increase of Chinese Orthodox members by emphasizing an open invitation to all who had family heritage or birth into the Chinese Orthodoxy, as well as to any others who wanted to join. In 2004, Pozdnyaev estimated that there were 10,000 Chinese Orthodox members on the northern border of China, 250 in Beijing, and around fifty in Shanghai.[39] And, the Moscow Orthodox Church announced to the Religious Affairs Bureau in Beijing that, by 2004, eighteen Chinese students had studied at Orthodox seminaries in Moscow and St. Petersburg.[40]

Then, in 2013, the Orthodox Parish of Sts. Peter and Paul was formerly inaugurated in Hong Kong by using an apartment to conduct services in Slavonic, English, and Chinese. The parish also commenced translating and publishing works in order to support churches in mainland China for recovery and revival.[41] Later, the Hong Kong parish opened another small house-church parish in Shenzhen of mainland China, which provided services for foreign Orthodox members in the Russian language as well as cultural seminars for Chinese visitors. However, since the government did not grant permission for Orthodox missionary work in China, the parish in Shenzhen promised the local government that they would not proselytize anyone beyond sharing knowledge of Orthodoxy when inquired by Chinese visitors.[42]

Today, some Russian Orthodox missionaries predict that the Orthodox Church in China will experience radical growth since they surmise that Chinese people have empty hearts after the Great Cultural Revolution and want to find meaningful faith to fill a vacancy inside.[43] They continue to find lost ecclesiastic estates in China in order to either buy them back or appeal to the local government for return. And, the Hong Kong Orthodox Parish has become the best connection and support for the mainland Orthodox Church to advance and expand.

Throughout these efforts, all the anticipated progress requires great patience for the reorganization of the CPC's regard toward the Eastern Orthodox as a world religion rather than a Russian ethnic minority belief, which was largely dependent on the diplomatic relationship between Russia and China.[44] However, the issue of jurisdictional conflict may arise if the Chinese government allows all foreign Orthodoxy churches—such as Greeks, Antiochians, and Serbs—in addition to Russia, to have their own missions in China.[45]

So far, there is not even an Orthodox theological school in China because of the CPC's restriction.[46] And, regarding the role of women in ministry, the Chinese Orthodox Church allows women to become catechists but not to hold any higher office.[47]

In sum, the Chinese Orthodox Church has not been restored to its pre-1949 thriving state yet. Nevertheless, many underground works are being fostered to a gradually expanding scale with those foreign missionaries' passion and persistence.

Chinese Protestant Underground Family Churches

The fourth group of churches in China are Protestant Family Churches, also called "underground churches." The origin of underground churches in China could be retrieved to TSPM in 1951, which divided Chinese Protestant churches into two wings. The left-wing churches were very willing to affiliate TSPM and become TSP churches, but the right-wing churches refused to let politics mix with religion and refused to let atheistic authority interfere with church issues.

Because some of them refused to accept the TSPM policy, right-wing church leaders were jailed until the late 1970s and the early 1980s. Some famous among them were Wang Mingdao 王明道 (1900–1991), Samuel Lamb 林獻羔 (1924–2013), and Allen Yuan 袁相忱 (1914–2005). However, once they were released from prison and settled in an urban neighborhood, they quickly formed family churches by opening their houses and continuing to evangelize without any connection to TSP churches. Majority of the family churches under those leaders' influence also rejected any connection with TSP churches and with anyone who cooperated with TSP churches.[48]

Most family churches are typically small in size and are usually characterized by close relationships and familiarity among congregants. One distinguishing feature of family churches that demonstrates strong intimacy within the church network is the very common use of sibling language and the title of "brothers and sisters," which they attribute to the Bible. Members treat going to a family church fellowship as returning to a spiritual home. This home-return ecclesiology is quite popular in a Chinese Christian's mindset. Sometimes, if a Chinese family has converted to Christianity, it can influence a large social network.

An illustration of this is the revival of rural churches from the mid-1980s to the mid-1990s, which were led by traveling evangelists. For example, once the head of a village became Christian, not only did his whole immediate family convert to Christianity but also the whole village would shift from worshiping other gods to Christian worship. Sometimes, several neighborhood villages also joined the gathering when they heard the gospel spreading from the converted village. This phenomenon is called a "gospel revival" or "furnace gathering"[49] and is very similar to the story of the Samaritan woman, who shares her testimony about Jesus to the whole village after she encountered Jesus at the well (John 4:28–29).

There are many claims about miraculous healings and deliverances in rural Chinese churches. Rural Christians seem to believe in Jesus quickly once they believe that the power of Jesus is superior to Chinese gods by experiencing relief from physical sickness, psychological torture, or what is believed to be demonic bondage.[50]

During the urbanization in the 1990s, the second revival from urban areas launched and generated numerous city family churches. In urban areas, many Chinese intellectuals have been attracted by Bible-study groups led by well-educated evangelists or missionaries, either on university campuses or in the marketplace. By studying the Bible, they feel they find hope for a meaningful life full of God's love and truth.[51] From 1990 on, a large number of Chinese students went overseas to study, and a significant percentage of them became Christians in the Euro-American world. Upon return to China, many either formed urban house churches or joined local existing house churches.[52]

Since the gospel spreads rapidly in China through family churches established in both rural and urban areas, these members have encountered increasing hostility and opposition socio-politically. In the 1990s, free evangelists would be arrested easily and put into prison by the local authorities. Financial forfeiture is also a common penalty for a family church gathering once it is detected by the local authorities, who would condemn the family church for not being legally registered as an authorized religious gathering group under the Religious Affairs Bureau. However, registration is solely dependent on the local government's appraisal, one that is based on unclear rules that may vary from place to place. Thus, a large percentage of family churches are unable to obtain legal permission for gathering even if they attempt to apply for registration.[53]

Without and unaware of their ecumenical and universal church traditions, Chinese churches often construct their ecclesiology based on their study of the Bible. For example, they believe that suffering with Christ and denying oneself is the mark of obedience and glorification to God. For many decades, this posture has not changed among family churches, in fact they see "*ding shi zi jia* 釘十字架" (crucifixion with Christ) as their motto to demonstrate their decision to be Christians at any cost.[54] Many family church leaders are proud of being persecuted for their faith, and even consider persecution of a candidate as one of the criteria to install the person to be head of a large family church network or not.[55]

According to the family church tradition, they see church planting as significant way of assembling a small group of Christians in one's house for close fellowship, Bible study, and evangelism in the neighborhood. In contrast to foreign church planters, whose first priority is to look for a church building in a new area to hold services, Chinese church planters prefer to build a close fellowship among Christians.

Along with the rapid growth of family churches in China, many underground seminaries and Bible schools are secretly formed. Most Bible schools recruit Christian students with any background and teach them how to practice Christian discipleship and evangelism. The study can last for three months, six months, or a year, and then the students are quickly dispatched to evangelize and plant churches.[56]

Almost every underground school focuses on training students for missions and evangelism. Before 2000, underground churches focused their missions primarily on domestic China and, after 2000, the mission focus began to shift from China to other countries. Two international mission movements originated from family churches and are well known around the world as, "Back to Jerusalem" (BTJ)[57] and "2030."[58] Most recently, many Chinese urban family churches are focusing more on having small organic churches with a good knowledge of the Bible and a powerful social impact without falling into the program- and number-driven institutional church model that exists outside China.

Biblical Ecclesiastic Image in Chinese Church: Family, Suffering, and Mission

The above study surveys different types of the existential Chinese churches, and this section discusses the similarities and differences between Chinese churches and the biblical ecclesiastic image. How does the biblical vision of ecclesiology play out among them?

In the New Testament (henceforth NT), *ecclēsia* is described with phrases such as, "the church of God" (1 Cor 10:32; 11:22; Gal 1:13; 1 Tim 3:5), "the churches of God" (1 Cor 11:16; 2 Thess 1:4), "the churches of Christ" (Rom 16:16), and "the churches in Christ" (Gal 1:22). *Ecclēsia* is described with attributes such as: "the property of God" (Eph 1:14), "the body of Christ" (Col 1:24), "God's household" (1 Tim 3:15), "God's temple" (1 Cor 3:16–17), "God's people" (1 Peter 2:9), "God's priests" (1 Peter 2:9), "Christ's body" (Eph 1:23), "Christ's bride" (Eph 5:25; Rev 22:17), "God's lampstand" (Rev 1:20), "ministerial society" (1 Tim 5:17), and "holy nation" (1 Peter 2:9).[59] And, the Greek term *ecclēsia* denotes "assembly," "solidarity of a community," and the "consolidating act of a group."[60]

Chinese underground family churches often see themselves in this meaning of *ecclēsia*—Christ-followers who form a distinctive community with a unified identity. Chinese underground family churches also see themselves as a unique social unit that is qualified by their belongingness to God, which, in their understanding, is the *ecclēsia* that appears in the NT text with the genitive *tou theou, tou Christou* or the dative *en Christo* on some occasions (cf. Rom 16:16; 1 Thess 1:1, 2:14; 2 Thess 1:1). In addition to this understanding, other types of Chinese churches may regard themselves as the part of the governmental, Russian Orthodoxy or Vatican Catholic body as well.

Plainly, *ecclēsia* in the NT is not to be simply understood as a church building but rather as the spiritual gathering or meeting of Christians, and Chinese Christians believe in their gathering God's presence is there with them. Some Chinese Christians consider the paradigm of *ecclēsia* shift from the image of a religious space to the image of an organic together-entity characterized by mutual love of Christians to one another, and corporate mission to the world.[61] Since Chinese underground family churches cannot legally use any religious building for gatherings, they interpret *ecclēsia* not as a space but about life togetherness and fellowship.

The Chinese church is aware of Paul's teaching when he uses a familial metaphor in reference to the church's conduct codes (1 Tim 3:15) and discusses the selection of good stewards among the early *ecclēsia* depending on whether they could manage their private households well (1 Tim 3:5).[62] The Chinese underground family churches advocate this particular aspect of Paul's instruction for choosing church leadership. Furthermore, a pastoral house in the underground family churches easily become a church house that is often visited by church members for counseling, prayer, accommodation, or a meal. Majority of underground family churches understand the biblical concept means the church and household become two sides of the same coin—"the household as the basic unit in the church" and "the church as a social structure modeled on the household."[63]

Evidently, the meeting places among Christian groups in the first century were commonly private houses, with the head of the household in the core leadership team (Rom 16:5; 1 Cor 16:19; Col 4:15; Philemon 1:2). Based on the discovery of the capacity of a Roman house, a Pauline church was usually limited to thirty to forty people.[64] Since Chinese Catholic underground churches and Protestant family churches have no official approval to conduct public services, they have to meet at houses and have encountered a similar situation as that of the first-century churches. Underground Christians are accustomed to meeting at member's house, holding the Eucharist, and participating in worship and fellowship there.

The metaphor of the relationship among congregants as familial in God prevails in the NT letters, and the reference to believers as brothers and sisters occurs around 180 times.[65] This familial relationship resonates with the Chinese church because of the cultural value of family. Even still, Paul's teaching of the family *of God* is counter-cultural to the Chinese understanding of family because Paul refers to fellow believers as "brother" (*adelphos*) or identifies the church groups or workers as "brothers" (*adelphoi*) about 127 times,[66] especially in addressing greetings at the beginning of his letters to different churches (Col 1:1–2; 2 Cor 1:1–2). Because those in the Chinese church understood the concept of family literally, in terms of a biological or genealogical relationship, it became necessary for them to embrace a new definition of this relational bond, as they perceived what they believe the Bible is saying: fellow believers as brothers and sisters in the family of God.

It is important to stress that *all types* of Chinese churches have commonly used familial language, and the usage of "brothers" and "sisters" in the Chinese church shows an endearing and trusting relationship among a community of believers, with no connotation of disrespect because Christians consider all to be God's children with equality in the biblical sense.

Roman families were not based solely on kinship but "by the relationship of dependence and subordination."[67] Thus, a whole family house (*oikos*) conversion to Christianity or believing in God in the first century could mean a broader relational network change (Acts 10:2, 16:31, 18:8). This situation of the whole family conversion because of one leading role is not common in the urban area but is in the rural area of China, of which an example was previously discussed. The difference with urban Christians is that they tend to be very independent and individualistic. Even though they would like other family members to be Christian, they cannot exert enough influence upon their families quickly and take time to patiently proselytize others. In the rural area, a village Christian head can quickly attract many others to Christianity due to his or her strong influence over the whole community, which is similar to the social dynamics of the NT era.

Christian family churches in the first century faced heavy persecution, and they were insulted by the surrounding society (1 Pet 4:14–16).[68] In the first three centuries, many were arrested and even martyred. Early Christian churches regarded those sacrifices as a worthwhile imitation of Christ suffering on the cross and believed there would be a reward from heaven in the end.[69] The Chinese underground Catholic churches and Protestant family churches also carry a cross similar to first-century churches through the tribulations from surrounding society. According to Tertullian, "the blood of Christian is seed" (*Apol.* 50.14), and many Chinese underground church leaders would interpret his saying with the conviction that the blood of Christian martyrs is the seed for gospel revival in China.

An underground church could be shut down, dismissed, fined, and its leaders interrogated and detained by the local authority.[70] Furthermore, since a new regulation on religious affairs was enacted on February 1, 2018, with more details than the previous one, the stressful situation and hardship for underground churches has increased even more. Larger church gatherings are now wrestling to find an efficient way to function well as they split into multiple smaller cell groups and experience intense intervention from local authorities.

The early church's astounding growth phenomenon is inevitably associated with the apostolic mission and planting of churches (Matt 28:19–20). Most NT writers also were, traditionally, profound missionaries, such as Paul, Peter, Mark, Luke, John, etc. They had a fearless heart for mission work as they faced political trials and tribulations (Acts 4:19).

Most underground Protestant churches are horizontal in nature and they love to proclaim the gospel and outreach to as many Chinese people as they can.[71] They also seek to involve in the cross-cultural and cross-national mission field without much concerned about government policy, and as they are taught in their church, to realize the great commission of Matthean teaching (28:18–20).

Conclusion

In summary, first-century Christians regarded *ecclēsia* as the house of God and defined Christians' relationship with one another based on Christ as the head of the family, *pater familias*. They regarded and called one another as "brother" or "sister," met in private homes, suffered for the sake of Jesus, and preached the gospel to the world.

In the modern era, a great challenge was posed for Chinese churches when Christianity was confronted by Chinese cultural, political, and nationalistic systems. They have to grapple with religious Sinicization, patriotic opposition, social restriction, and political persecution. Their unique status presumes that Chinese churches cannot copy foreign or neighboring Korean church models, nor can those models be easily adapted.

In their alignment with church traditions, Chinese Catholic and Orthodox churches adapt their ecclesiology in the complex Chinese situation. Because of their young history, Chinese Protestant family churches seek the Bible for guidance. According to the previous discussion: (1) most of them are indigenous, autonomous, and meet in private houses; (2) they are horizontal in terms of church administration and count each other as brother or sister in their Father's house; (3) they are not much bound by denominational traditions and are active in evangelism to expand Christianity from China to other countries; (4) they regard suffering for Christ's sake as the token of being a family member in God's house; and (5) their concept of church is not about a church building with large gathering but a group of Christ's faithful followers, they perceived, to be indwelled by the Spirit of God as the *ecclēsia*.

The central challenge and task of the Chinese church today is to find an effective expression of the Christian faith within the context of its special social and political context and without deviating from the biblical *ecclēsia* model.[72] The challenge of the Chinese church is also to explore an innovative and effective operational model of its own.

Notes

1. Tian'en Zhao 趙天恩, *Contemporary Chinese Christianity Development History 1949–1997* [in Chinese] 當代中國基督教發展史 1949–1997 (Taipei: Zhongfu Publisher, 2010), 67.
2. Xi Lian, *Redeemed by Fire: The Rise of Popular Christianity in Modern China* (New Haven: Yale University Press, 2010), 197–203.
3. Kim-Kwong Chan, "Religion in China in the Twenty-First Century: Some Scenarios," *Religion, State & Society* 33.2 (2005), 96.

4. Michael Nai-Chiu Poon, *The Rise of Asian Pacific Christianity and Challenges for the Church Universal in Asian Handbook for Theological Education and Ecumenism* (Eugene, OR: Wipf & Stock, 2013): 54 (38–58).
5. Chan, "Religion," 92; Mark Galli, "The Chinese Church's Delicate Dance: A Conversation with the Head of the Protestant Three-Self Patriotic Movement," *Christianity Today* 48.11 (2004), 68; on the political theology of TSPM see also K. K. Yeo, *What Has Jerusalem to Do With Beijing* (Eugene, OR: Pickwick, 2018), 221–241.
6. Wen Ge, "In Search of the Ecclesial Identity of the Post-denominational Churches: A Case Study of the Contemporary Chinese Ecumenical Theology in the Making," *Asian Journal of Theology* 29.2 (2015): 179–180; see also Britt Towery, "The Contribution of Lao She to the Three-Self Principle and the Protestant Churches of China," *Missiology* 22.1 (1994): 96–97.
7. Jingyi Ji, *Encounters between Chinese Culture and Christianity: A Hermeneutical Perspective* (London: Global, 2007), 212.
8. Veli-Matti Kärkkäinen, "Chinese Theology," in *Global Dictionary of Theology* (Downers Grove: Intervarsity, 1989): 163.
9. Kärkkäinen, "Chinese Theology," 164; K. K. Yeo, "Chinese Theology," in *Evangelical Dictionary of Theology*, ed. Daniel Treier and Walter Elwell, 3rd edition (Grand Rapids: Baker Academic, 2017), 171–172.
10. K. H. Ting, "Retrospect and Prospect," *International Review of Mission* 70 (1981): 32; see also Ge, "Ecclesial Identity," 186.
11. Jiexia Zhai, "Pentecostal Christianity and Church-State Relations in China: The Case of the True Jesus Church Movement," *The Review of Faith & International Affairs* 11.3 (2013): 44.
12. Zhai, "Pentecostal," 91.
13. Ge, "Ecclesial Identity," 175, 186.
14. Zhai, "Pentecostal," 50; see also Xie, "Religion and Modernity in China," 92.
15. Chan, "Religion," 96.
16. Evan J. Liu, "The Exodus of Underground Christian Seminary Education in China," *Asian Journal of Religion and Society* 5.2 (2017): 44.
17. William T. Liu and Beatrice Leung, "Organizational Revivalism: Explaining Metamorphosis of China's Catholic Church," *Journal for the Scientific Study of Religion* 41.1 (2002): 122.
18. Tiangang Li 李天鋼, *Chinese Rites Controversy* [in Chinese] 中國禮儀之爭 (Shanghai: Shanghai Classic Publisher, 1998), 80–100.
19. Chan, "Religion," 92.
20. Beatrice Leung, "The Impact of Modernization on the Catholic Church in China," *Missiology* 13.3 (1985): 327.
21. Jean-Paul Wiest, "The Current Status of the Catholic Church in the People's Republic of China," *Missiology* 23.3 (1995): 290.
22. John L. Allen Jr., "Playing 'Spin the Pope' in China," *National Catholic Reporter*, January 29, 2010; Moody, "Limitations," 420–421.
23. Liu and Leung, "Organizational Revivalism," 133.
24. Paul P. Mariani, "The Four Catholic Bishops of Shanghai: 'Underground' and 'Patriotic' Church Competition and Sino-Vatican Relations in Reform-Era China," *Journal of Church and State* 58.1 (2016): 38.
25. Chan, "Religion," 97.
26. Wiest, "Status," 287.

27. Kevin Baker, "Wise Men from the East: The Influence of Eastern Christianity in China, 635–1986," *Phronema* 8 (1993): 50, 52.
28. Baker, "Wise Men," 51; Dionisy Pozdnyaev, "Orthodoxy in Greater China Laying the Foundation for an International Orthodox Presence," *Road to Emmaus* 19.1 (2016): 6.
29. Baker, "Wise Men," 54.
30. Pozdnyaev, "Orthodoxy in Greater China," 6; see also Baker, "Wise Men," 52, 55.
31. Pozdnyaev, "Orthodoxy in Greater China," 6.
32. Dionisy Pozdnyaev, "The Pearl of Great Price: Resurrecting Orthodoxy in China," *Road to Emmaus* 6.4 (2005): 35.
33. Ibid.
34. Pozdnyaev, "Orthodoxy in Greater China," 9.
35. Ibid. 11.
36. Ibid. 24; see also Papiy Fu, "I Was Born in an Orthodox World': Early Memories of a Chinese Christian," *Road to Emmaus* 6.4 (2005): 58.
37. Pozdnyaev, "Orthodoxy in Greater China," 27.
38. Dionisy Pozdnyaev, "Beyond the Great Wall: Orthodoxy in China," *Road to Emmaus* 4.2 (2003): 32.
39. Pozdnyaev, "The Pearl of Great Price," 37.
40. Ibid. 38.
41. Pozdnyaev, "Orthodoxy in Greater China," 21; see also Christy Ma, "Opportunities and Challenges for Liturgical Inculturation in the Mission Church of Hong Kong," *The Greek Orthodox Theological Review* 61.1–2 (2016): 191.
42. Pozdnyaev, "The Pearl of Great Price," 31.
43. Pozdnyaev, "Beyond the Great Wall," 44.
44. Pozdnyaev, "The Pearl of Great Price," 29–30.
45. Pozdnyaev, "Beyond the Great Wall," 33; see also Fu, "Early Memories," 59.
46. Pozdnyaev, "The Pearl of Great Price," 37.
47. Ibid. 38.
48. Mark Galli, "Delicate Dance," 70.
49. Yalin Xin, "Inner Dynamics of the Chinese House Church Movement: The Case of the Word of Life Community," *Journal of the International Association for Mission Studies* 25.2 (2008): 165–167.
50. Xie, "Religion and Modernity in China," 83.
51. Donald E. MacInnis, "Religious Revival in China," *The Christian Century* 98.11 (1981): 347.
52. Xie, "Religion and Modernity in China," 77–78.
53. Siu Chau Lee, "Towards a Theology of Church-State Relations in Contemporary Chinese Context," *Studies in World Christianity* 11.2 (2005): 263.
54. Teresa Zimmerman-Liu, "The Divine and Mystical Realm," *Social Sciences & Missions* 27.2 (2014): 260–263; cf. Lian, *Redeemed*, 215.
55. Xin, "Dynamics," 162–163, 181.
56. Ibid. 157–158.
57. BTJ emphasizes that Chinese Christians should receive the evangelistic token from foreign missionaries and send out 100,000 missionaries to those Islamic countries west of China and out to Israel. See Paul Hattaway, "A Captivating Vision: Why Chinese House Churches May Just End Up Fulfilling the Great Commission," *Christianity Today* 48.4 (2004): 84.

58. The focus of the 2030 movement is that the Chinese Family church feel their obligation to pay off the "gospel debt" to foreign Protestant missionaries who came to China from 1807 and were expelled from China in 1952. The founders of this vision were primarily from underground churches of Beijing, and they are all highly educated and represent the elite Christian class in urban underground churches.
59. P. T. O'Brien, "Church," in *Dictionary of Paul and His Letters: A Compendium of Contemporary Biblical Scholarship*, ed. Ralph P. Martin, Gerald F. Hawthorne, and Daniel G. Reid (Downers Grove: InterVarsity, 2009), 123–131.
60. Everett Ferguson, *The Church of Christ: A Biblical Ecclesiology for Today* (Grand Rapids: Eerdmans, 1996), 130.
61. Mary L. Coloe, *Dwelling in the Household of God: Johannine Ecclesiology and Spirituality* (Collegeville: Liturgical Press, 2007), 199; see also Yulin Liu, *Temple Purity in 1–2 Corinthians* (Tübingen: Mohr Siebeck, 2013), 1.
62. Fredrik Ivarsson, "Christian Identity as True Masculinity," in *Exploring Early Christian Identity*, ed. Bengt Holmberg (Tübingen: Mohr Siebeck, 2008), 167.
63. David C. Verner, *The Household of God: The Social World of the Pastoral Epistles* (Chicago: Scholars Press, 1983), 1.
64. Balch David, "Rich Pompeiian Houses, Shops for Rent, and the Huge Apartment Building in Herculaneum as Typical Spaces for Pauline House Churches," *Journal for the Study of the New Testament* 27.1 (2004): 28; K. K. Yeo, *Musing with Confucius and Paul: Toward a Chinese Christian Theology* (Eugene, OR: Cascade Books, 2008), passim.
65. David J. Feddes, "Caring for God's Household: A Leadership Paradigm among New Testament Christians and Its Relevance for Church and Mission Today," *Calvin Theological Journal* 43.2 (2008): 284.
66. Reidar Aasgaard, "Brothers and Sisters in the Faith: Christian Siblingship as an Ecclesiological Mirror in the First Two Centuries," in *The Formation of the Early Church*, ed. Jostein Ådna (Tübingen: Mohr Siebeck, 2005): 314.
67. Wayne A. Meeks, *The First Urban Christians: The Social World of the Apostle Paul* (New Haven: Yale University Press, 2003), 30.
68. G. K. Beale, *The Book of Revelation: A Commentary on the Greek Text* (Grand Rapids: Eerdmans, 1999), 233; Robert H. Mounce, *The Book of Revelation* (Grand Rapids: Eerdmans, 1998), 80.
69. Rodney Stark, *The Rise of Christianity: A Sociologist Reconsiders History* (Princeton: Princeton University Press, 1996), 188–189.
70. Jeff M. Sellers, "Crushing House Churches: Chinese Intelligence and Security Forces Attack Anew," *Christianity Today* 48.1 (2004): 63.
71. Xiaheng Xie, "Religion and Modernity in China: Who Is Joining the Three-Self Church and Why," *Journal of Church and State* 52.1 (2010): 76.
72. Yeo, *Musing with Confucius and Paul*, 402–432.

Primary Sources

Author's personal interviews with three-self underground churches in China, for security reason not listed here.

Catholic Letter about reconciliation of Chinese underground catholic and Three-Self Catholic members: http://www.vatican.va/holy_father/benedict_xvi/letters/2007/documents/hf_ben-xvi_let_20070527_china_en.html.

Fu, Papiy. "'I Was Born in an Orthodox World': Early Memories of a Chinese Christian." *Road to Emmaus* 6.4 (2005): 57–59.

Ma, Christy. "Opportunities and Challenges for Liturgical Inculturation in the Mission Church of Hong Kong." *The Greek Orthodox Theological Review* 61.1–2 (2016): 191–207.

Pozdnyaev, Dionisy. "Beyond the Great Wall: Orthodoxy in China." *Road to Emmaus* 4.2 (2003): 32–44.

Pozdnyaev, Dionisy. "Orthodoxy in Greater China Laying the Foundation for an International Orthodox Presence." *Road to Emmaus* 19.1 (2016): 6–27.

Pozdnyaev, Dionisy. "The Pearl of Great Price: Resurrecting Orthodoxy in China." *Road to Emmaus* 6.4 (2005): 31–38.

CHAPTER 36

THE SOCIO-POLITICAL IMPACT OF THE BIBLE IN CHINA

BENOÎT VERMANDER

Introduction

In 1929, ten years after its release, the Mandarin Union Version (*heheben* 和合本) had already sold one million copies of its New Testament translation; additionally, half a million complete Mandarin Union Bibles had been issued.[1] Sales sharply increased at the time of the Sino-Japanese war.[2] The recent period has known similar exuberance in the printing and distribution of various Bible translations. The Catholic Studium Biblicum version sold 4.5 million copies in mainland China from 1993 to 2018; the corresponding figure would be around 183 million copies for Protestant Bibles,[3] though these figures warrant scrutiny.[4]

The 1919 publication of the *heheben* constitutes a milestone when assessing the impact that the biblical text was and is still having upon Chinese society and culture. Among other leading intellectuals, Zhou Zuoren 周作人 (1885–1967) praised the literary qualities of the Mandarin Union Version's vernacular and predicted that it would greatly help in the reform of Chinese language and literature.[5]

The impact of the biblical text on China's society and culture extended far beyond the inspiration it provided for language reform and literary storytelling. And such impact has not been strictly religious either. The China of today has been shaped partly by two centuries of Bible translations and by an even longer period of Christian propagation rooted in biblical narratives and teachings. At the same time, the Bible's impact on China has been circuitous, ambiguous, and controversial. This essay seeks to offer insights discussing to what extent and through which channels the Bible has become part and parcel of Chinas' socio-political references and controversies.[6]

Before the Mandarin Union Version

The history of Protestant translations of the Bible into Chinese was already over one hundred years long when the Mandarin Union Version was published. These translations, as well as the debates surrounding them, had been impacting the collective psyche for a long time before 1919. Let us mention here the most notorious example: the pamphlet "Good Words to Exhort the Age" (*Quanshi liangyan* 勸世良言) by Liang Fa 梁發 (1832). This pamphlet narrates the conversion of the author: "Every Sunday, when I did not need to work, I loved to read the Holy Bible. When there were things I did not understand, I would ask Mr. Mi [William Milne, of the London Missionary Society] for explanations."[7] This particular pamphlet, which included large excerpts of the Morrison-Milne Bible translation, had a formative influence on Hong Xiuquan 洪秀全 (1814–1864), the future leader of the Taiping Rebellion. The biblical readings of the rebels' leader inspired his vision of the coming of the heavenly kingdom. They decisively helped him to make sense of his visions, they validated his mission, and they provided him with a moral and legal code.

When looking back to the seventeenth and eighteenth centuries, any direct impact of the biblical text on Chinese society and culture would be much more difficult to discern. One of the reasons the Jesuits had translated only excerpts aimed at liturgical and catechetical use was their concern as to the effect and reception of a text replete with stories of regicide and other disturbing political events. They were keenly aware of the subversive nature of the biblical text as well as of the way it might be received and interpreted by a power not inclined to see its legitimacy being questioned. Gospel narratives by Giulio Aleni and exegetical commentaries by Manuel Diaz Jr., among others, did play an important role in shaping Christian communities but had no discernible effect on society at large.

The comparison between the early missionary period and the one that followed suggests a preliminary lesson: the story of the translation and diffusion of the Bible in China during the nineteenth century and the first half of the twentieth century is not independent of the story of China's political demise. Largely due to the context in which these events occurred, they had unintended social, cultural, and political consequences. We will need to keep this in mind when assessing the socio-cultural impact of the Bible during the latter half of the last century as well as its present effects.

The Bible and the Attempts at a New Social Order

Hong Xiuquan was not alone in dreaming of a Warrior God imposing a new social order on a China torn by unrest and divisions, nor did the demise of his movement signal the end of such a dream. The warlord Feng Yuxiang 馮玉祥 (1882–1948) converted to Methodism in 1914 and built up a "Christian army," the routine of which mixed physical drills with gospel singing: "Just as a father gathers his family about him for Bible reading and prayers, so the captains and corporals of the army conduct the service for those committed to their care."[8] Among the military elite, Zhang Zhijiang 張之江 (1882–1966) provides us with another example of a leader firmly engaged in spreading the Bible among soldiers and society. And the support of Chiang Kai-shek 蔣介石 (Jiang Jieshi) for translation of the Psalms untaken by Catholic scholar Wu Jingxiong 吳經熊 is well documented.[9]

Even more significantly, the story that most influenced the historical narrative proper to Sun Yat-sen seems to have been the one of Moses: From early on, the departure from Egypt and the crossing of the Red Sea constituted the paradigm of national revolution. Later on, Sun Yat-sen compared the challenging period following the Xinhai revolution to the forty years in the desert.[10] Following a different line of interpretation, Protestant theologian Chen Chonggui 陳崇桂 (1883–1963) was trying to unearth meaning in the post-revolutionary historical trials by meditating on the consequences of Samson's reprehensible behavior.[11]

Both Sun and Mao were influenced in one way or another by the figure of Hong Xiuquan, a fact that indicates "how the Bible was read as a political text with apocalyptic promises for the oppressed and how its grand vision of the kingdom of God unleashed a force so powerful that not only Hong Xiuquan and his generation, but also the entire course of history of the twentieth-century China was dramatically changed."[12] Biblical readings were indeed inspiring attempts at "saving the nation," and this beyond the circle of political and military leaders.[13] As an example, theologian Wu Leichuan 吳雷川 makes the kingdom of God a blueprint of socioeconomic reform, starting with one of property system.[14] Sometimes, it was the figure of Jesus himself who was said to possess inspiring, or even redeeming, effect. In an article called "Christianity and the Chinese People," the founder of both the *Xinqingnian* 新青年 (*New Youth*) journal and the Chinese Communist Party (expelled from it in 1929), Chen Duxiu 陳獨秀 (1879–1942), famously wrote: "Crossing through the door of Jesus himself, we should internalize, make our own, the great characteristics of Jesus and his profound concern for humanity."[15] The portrait of Jesus he drew stressed features-relevant for the building-up of a new Chinese civilization: the spirit of sacrifice; the spirit of forgiveness; equality; and universality in love. Jesus, he concluded, was, first and foremost, the friend of the poor.

However, for most theologians and Christian teachers, the social inspiration drawn from the Bible was inseparable from the lessons it also was conveying on self-cultivation: the common point of the varying biblical hermeneutics that followed the May Fourth movement was that "regeneration of self, society and ultimately nation must begin with moral cultivation."[16] Moral regeneration was the seed from which national salvation was supposed to emerge. In this respect, the Bible was conveying lessons akin to the ones stressed by Chinese classics (*jing* 經) and thus was asserting its place as the classic par excellence.

National rejuvenation was not only a man's task but also a woman's duty as well. Bible models of the woman, notably the one offered in Proverbs 31, influenced the way Christian Chinese women understood their status and mission within the family, the church, and society at large, both in Catholic and Protestant environments. There is no doubt that biblical reading and church teaching played mainly in favor of female empowerment, even if social and religious constraints made such processes fall short of full-fledged emancipation.

The Bible and Institutional Building

Besides such lofty dreams of Bible-inspired national rejuvenation (and often ignoring or belittling such dreams), Christian organizations were busily engaged in down-to-earth institutional endeavors. For instance, Jesuits in Shanghai were conceiving of their enclave of Xujiahui 徐家匯 (Zikawei) as a kind of "counter-society" that was progressively providing the faithful with schools and a university, an observatory, a museum of natural history, orphanages offering professional training, and institutions of clerical education. Still in Shanghai, the YWCA soon specialized in social work, especially child-labor campaigns and programs of popular education in various factories; nearby the Bund, the *Missions Building* was home to the National Christian Council, the American Bible Society, the National Bible Society of Scotland, the London Missionary Society, and the China Council of the Presbyterian Church. Among other missionary institutions, St John's College, founded in 1879 by American Anglicans, became a full-fledged university accredited in the United States in 1905, with an associated middle school, attracting the children of Shanghai's Chinese elite. Shanghai also was home to the Seventh-Day Adventists' headquarters in China; based in the city, *Shizhao Yuebao* 時兆月報 (*The Signs of the Times*) was the most widely circulated Christian periodical in the mid-twentieth century, with around 130,000 copies per issue sold in 1937.[17] The large Moore Memorial Church (*Mu'en Tang* 沐恩堂), founded in 1887 as the Central Methodist Church, nurtured strong connections with the Soong family and other elite circles, becoming known as Shanghai's "social club."[18] In Moore Memorial Church, as was also the case for the YMCA and many other places of worship, the "Social Gospel," rather than Evangelism, was the dominant doctrine.[19]

However, the biblical interpretation promoted by the (American-led) "Social Gospel" movement was soon to be challenged by other exegetical trends, which opposed both its theological modernism and its foreign missions' flavor. The prominent evangelist Wang Mingdao 王明道 (1900–1991) used to call the Social Gospel "fake medicine."[20] Reflecting shifting trends within Chinese Christianity, Shanghai thus became the hotbed of an indigenous Church infused with both Christian nationalism and evangelical undertones. The aftermath of the Boxer Rebellion played a crucial role in the process of indigenization. The Centenary Missionary Conference was held in Shanghai in 1907, one hundred years after the arrival of Robert Morrison, and called for the formation of a

Chinese church that should pass beyond missionary control and guidance. Yu Cidu 余慈度 (1873–1931), a woman preacher who played a major role in evangelical revivalism, organized preaching sessions in a suburb northeast of the city center. On the Protestant side at least (though similar trends could be discerned in some Chinese Catholic quarters), a "literal interpretation of the Bible and emphasis on divine inspiration by the Holy Spirit gave new power to ordinary believers."[21] If institutional building had anchored biblical reading in Chinese communities, the appropriation of the Bible that followed deeply challenged the hierarchical order and the ways of proceeding on which the religious establishment was relying.

The Literary Imagination and Its Social Impact

Other contributions in this volume focus on the influence of the Bible upon the culture, arts, and literature of modern and contemporary China. Suffice it here to say that Ai Qing 艾青, Mao Dun 茅盾, Lu Xun 魯迅, Lao She 老舍, Ba Jin 巴金, Guo Moruo 郭沫若, and Shen Congwen 沈從文 figure among the many Chinese writers, intellectuals, and artists who read and quoted the Bible or took their inspiration from its figures and stories, though for different purposes and to varying extent.

Bible reading was not confined to the search for new and inspiring narratives. It was part of a debate on what could be labeled "literary ethics." In a manifesto for an emerging literary movement ("Humanist literature" [*Ren de wenxue* 人的文學]), Zhou Zuoren promoted a humanistic thinking that stressed healthy self-appreciation. Quoting the commandment, "Thou shalt love thy neighbor as thyself" (which he attributes directly to Jesus, apparently ignoring its roots in Lev 19:18), Zhou notes that loving others without first loving oneself represents an impossible task.[22] The "modern humanism" he aspires to build does not borrow from Confucianism (which he rejects as radically as Chen Duxiu does); rather, besides explicit references to Christianity, Zhou finds inspiration in the works and life of Leon Tolstoi, for instance. Rival conceptions of what "humanism" was meant to be would soon see the light of the day. Through the prism of this new concept, they would reinterpret the Confucian tradition in various ways and criticize Zhou and Chen's borrowing from Christianity and "universal values" as vehicles for Western expansionism in China. The fact that well-known Christians such as Zhao Zichen 趙紫宸 (C. T. Chao, 1888–1979) were among the promoters of a "Chinese Humanism" (contrasted to the blueprint that the early articles of *New Youth* had sketched) shows that the intellectual and political debate of Republican China was shrouded in innumerable contrasts and nuances.[23] Individual parameters made the matter even more intricate. The convoluted travels of Lin Yutang 林語堂 between Chinese culture and Christianity, as well as the influence that such travail entailed on Lin's ever-evolving political views, is a case in point.[24]

In a short and famous text called "Revenge (II)" 復仇 (其二), Lu Xun dealt with the meaning (or lack thereof) to be found in Jesus' crucifixion:

> Because he thinks himself the Son of God, the king of the Jews, he is to be crucified. . . . All around is hate, pitiable, execrable. . . . He has not drunk the wine mixed with myrrh. He wants to remain sober to savior the Israelites' treatment of their Son of God, and to have longer to pity their future but hate their present. . . . God has forsaken him, and so he is the son of man after all. But the Israelites are crucifying even the son of man. Those who seek most of blood and filth are not those who crucify the Son of God, but those who crucify the son of man.[25]

One may be entitled to think that Lu Xun here "depicts the death of Jesus as the ultimate expression of futility";[26] it also has been suggested that Lu represents Christ "as a sadistic and whimsical deity who enjoys suffering on the cross, because he knows that his own anguish will cause the Israelites much greater anguish in the future."[27] However, the crux of the text probably lies elsewhere, namely in the transition from the term "Son of God" to "son of man": it may well be the frequent depiction of Christ as "Son of God" independently from Jesus' humanity that lies at the center of Lu Xun's criticism. And the (re)discovery of Jesus' disgraced humanity goes along the recapturing of China's history as one of blood, tears, and hunger, further darkened by religious, social, and political hypocrisy. In that respect, the text of Lu Xun was indeed premonitory of the way the figure of Jesus was going to further inscribe itself into the political narrative of China.

The Bible and Martyrdom

And indeed, the theme of "*kenosis*"—of a God divested from his own divinity—was to become a dominant feature of Christian historical experience and spiritual interpretation, this at least from the 1950s until the end of the Cultural Revolution. For many believers in China and beyond, Ni Tuosheng 倪柝聲 (Watchman Nee) (1903–1972), leader of the Christian Assembly (*Jidutu Juhuichu* 基督徒聚會處), has become a symbol of the kenotic trials experienced by Chinese Christianity. Denounced as a counterrevolutionary in the 1950s, he died in prison in 1972. "Explaining the Scriptures" was the first task that Watchman Nee had been assigning to himself, and the way he confronted and understood his trials could not be separated from his understanding of the Bible as the "living Word" that is unceasingly challenging earthly powers: "The Bible is the Supreme Court," Nee used to declare.[28] Such unwavering reliance on the Bible as being "spoken for today" may explain "the spiritual depth of indigenous church leaders," which David Mungello contrasts, probably with some injustice, with "the foreign-mission Christianity of Zhao Zichen" and other leaders and theologians.[29]

However, many Christians who entered into dialogue or collaboration with the new regime were also to experience and meditate upon a truly kenotic experience. Jesuit

Alyosius Jin Luxian 金魯賢 (1916–2013), who was to be official bishop of Shanghai from 1985 onwards, mentions in his memoirs the difficulties he had encountered during his training with a number of foreign missionaries.[30] In a different way, his years in prison would deepen his experience of lowering and humiliation. And this experience would not stop at the time of his liberation, around 1982: "During my 27 years in jail everyday I sang to myself the song 'The Society of Jesus is my mother,' believing [mistakenly] that all the Jesuits in the world were praying for me, from which thought I derived both peace of mind and inner strength."[31] The insistence on *humiliation*—be it brought by foreigners or one's own people—captures much of the kenotic experience lived and expressed by Chinese Christians. The biblical narrative is encapsulated in the story of the passion.[32]

Among other testimonies that have been gathered sometimes decades after the events, Henrietta Harrison, while investigating the memory of a Catholic village in Shanxi Province, mentions the following: Zheng Fentao, a Catholic woman, was executed in the spring of 1970, "though, as a poor village woman, she was shot in prison rather than receiving the full panoply of public execution. . . . Her terrified daughter-in-law could not even find out which grave was hers and never managed to retrieve her body."[33] Harrison aptly shows how such story is now remembered and associated with both ancient local tales and the biblical narrative itself, composing a communal and spiritual identity.

The aftermath of the persecution has sometimes witnessed a revival of the opposition between the "institutional Church" (now led by Chinese clergy) and believers who claim to rely first and foremost on the Word of God. Harrison mentions a Catholic lay preacher, confessor of the faith during the Cultural Revolution, who has this to say (or rather to sing in a rhyme) about priests of a new generation: "They've set up a church of reinforced concrete, / But they've broken the church of the heart and soul."[34] That the covenant between God and his people can only be "written on the heart" (Jer 31:33), and is always betrayed when translated into compromises, institutions, and stone buildings, remains an underlying *leitmotif* for many Chinese Christians, whatever their denominations may be.

The Bible, Marxism, and Political Accommodation

If Bible narratives were associated with experiences of *kenosis* and martyrdom, they also could be used in order to nurture and justify the new course taken by national rejuvenation. The aforementioned figure of Watchman Nee is thus often contrasted with the one of Bishop Ding Guangxun 丁光訓 (K. H. Ting). For Ding, the radical nature of the political change having intervened required an equally radical change in structures and ways of thinking;[35] hence the frontal conflict with Wang Mingdao, the firmest opponent of a theology of *aggiornamento*, that inevitably intervened.[36] The numerous publications of Ding make ample use of biblical quotations, be it for asserting that loving one's nation is a cardinal virtue or for stating that both Chinese classics and the Bible consider that goodness is inscribed into a person's nature. As to the theme of the "Cosmic Christ," developed by Ding in his post-1978 writings, it is marked by references to the latter Pauline letters. Ding presents the focus on Christ's cosmic dimension as a path through which collaboration between believers and non-believers may receive its full theological meaning. One can find here both contrasts and analogies with the theology of another Protestant thinker of the time, Wang Weifan 汪維藩 (1927–2015). Analogies have to do with a common desire to reconcile the Bible and Chinese Classics into a hermeneutic centered on life, healing, and reconciliation. However, Wang Weifan exhibits more reverence towards classical biblical hermeneutics and pre-1949 Chinese theologians, as well as a sensitivity more spiritual, or even mystical, than the one of the politically minded Ding Guangxun. Especially worthy of attention is Wang's commentary on the Song of Songs that stresses that the trials undergone during the first decades of the new regime have *dispossessed* the Chinese Church of Christ—but only so that the church may rather become the *possession* of Christ himself.[37]

Ding's hermeneutical endeavor was not opposed to, but was going further than the one propounded by the biblical scholar Li Rongfang 李榮芳 (1887–1965), who was seeing in Jeremiah and Jesus embodiments of the precept of "loving the Church and loving the nation" (*ai jiao ai guo* 愛教愛國), a precept that should, according to Li, characterize Chinese Christians.[38] Progressively, the first imperative (*ai guo* 愛國) was taking precedence over the second, and could not be practically separated any more from the one of "loving the party" (*ai dang* 愛黨). As the relationship between state and religions progressively stabilized, leaders of both the Catholic Patriotic Association and the Three-Self Church were (and are still) striving to find biblical ground for presenting the guidance of the Party as a form of obedience to God's commandments.[39]

Around 1990, criticisms as to the nature of such arrangements became stronger. Christian churches (argued researcher Tang Yi 唐逸 and other observers) were losing prophetic relevance while remaining unable to accommodate actual Chinese cultural patterns.[40] It is noteworthy that arguments exchanged during the period considered remained generally oblivious to the (rather intense) Marxist-Christian dialogue that had been taking place in other parts of the globe. The encounter between biblical hermeneutics and Communist/Maoist thought as it happened in China after 1950, and in a new format after 1980, was less a "dialogue" than a one-way accommodation, which eventually brought few intellectual fruits. However, the time may have come for conducting a new and more sober assessment of the texts that Ding and others produced, so as to better analyze the deadlocks and the openings repeatedly met by Chinese biblical hermeneutics in the political context in which it took and takes place.[41]

The current context makes such assessment more complicated and urgent at the same time. From 2017 onwards, the question of adjusting biblical hermeneutics to the Party's directives has regained an importance that it had lost in the decades of the policy of Reform and Opening. Academics promoting the Party line stress and praise anew the compliance exhibited in the past by Ding and other church leaders.[42] Xi Jinping's report at the start of the Nineteenth Congress of the Chinese Communist Party in October

2017, reads as follows: "We will fully implement the Party's basic policy on religious affairs, uphold the principle that religions in China must be Chinese in orientation [must "Sinicize," *Zhongguohua* 中國化, in the original Chinese] and provide active guidance to religions so that they can adapt themselves to socialist society."[43] *Zhongguohua* means first that the faithful must follow the Party's leadership and adhere to socialist values; on this basis they must work toward more Chinese "religious values," more Chinese religious symbols, and a more Chinese practice of the faith.[44] This goes along with two emerging trends: restrictions as to the circulation of the Bible, especially on the Internet;[45] and efforts deployed so as to further "Sinicize" its tradition and exegesis,[46] though such efforts, at the time of the writing of this contribution, remain inchoative.

The document entitled "Principle for Promoting Chinese Christianity in China for the Next Five Years (2018–2022)," compiled by the China Christian Council and Three-Self Patriotic Movement, explicitly states:

> Contents of the Bible that are compatible with the core values of socialism should be deeply researched in order to write books that are popular and easy-to-understand. . . . Bible study needs to be strengthened to establish a correct view of the Bible and the biblical hermeneutics in conformity with the situation in China as a foundation for deepening the development of theological thought.[47]

In other words, the biblical text remains a disputed asset, and the control of its interpretation a locus of political influence.

The Bible and Intellectual Reconstruction

After the Cultural Revolution, a "culture fever" (*wenhua re* 文化熱) generated massive enthusiasm for classics of "world literature," seen as a source of beauty and meaning after a period defined by folly and ugliness. It is against such background that the "cultural Christians" (*wenhua jidutu* 文化基督徒) movement is to be assessed: the Bible was seen as a "classic" through which to tackle and understand phenomena such as "radical evil"—or even the basic opposition between "good" and "bad," which Chinese traditional cultural resources were deemed unable or reluctant to confront.[48] The "Sino-theology" (*hanyu shenxue* 漢語神學) that developed out of such readings was meant to make Chinese people develop a theological voice anchored in their own language and experience.[49] The literary style proper to the Bible narrative, as well as the variety of formats to be found in Chinese literature, inspired such attempts at developing a theological "discourse" that would challenge Western/professional biblical scholars and theologians.

However, already in the middle of the 1990s, the movement—if it can be qualified as such—diverged in several directions.[50] Some of its members integrated church organizations, mostly underground. Others have continued to undertake comparative research on the basis of philological and philosophical concerns. Such is the case of Yang Huilin 楊慧林 (b. 1954), who highlights the fluidity of interpretations that characterizes the Chinese hermeneutical tradition for crisscrossing it with methods and concerns inspired by the "Scriptural Reasoning" movements and others aiming at developing a form of "textual hospitality."[51] Similar concerns can be seen in the attempts at cross-reading Confucian and Christian classics in light of the current ecological crisis.[52] In any case, the intellectual impact achieved by the Cultural Christians movement decisively contributed in the introduction of courses on the Bible and Christian thought in many universities.

An intellectual sub-current that issued from the movement has recognized its flag bearer in the person of Liu Xiaofeng 劉小楓 (b. 1956), whose initial exegetical endeavor was soon recast by the reading of political philosophers such as Leo Strauss and Carl Schmitt. Liu's shift from theology to politics led him to advocate for a reappraisal of Chinese classics.[53] In the positioning he progressively adopted, the literary scholar (including the Bible scholar) is meant to be the advisor of the prince. Bible studies are integrated into a reinterpretation of world classics that is itself determined by a preexisting political philosophy.

Reading the Bible in the "Reform and Opening Era"

Conversions to Christianity multiplied after 1980s, and that happened in all sectors of society. However, in contrast to a period where Christian belonging was equated with "backward mentality," observers were struck, from the middle of the 1990s onwards, by the spread of the phenomena in urban, well-educated strata. Business owners, executives, doctors, professors, and teachers were all part of the cohorts of new converts. This did not happen without consequences for the way of interpreting the Bible and applying it to social and political issues.

Though the diversity of situations and standpoints hampers generalizations, it can be argued that the shift in China's Christian population triggered a style of biblical readings influenced by one form or another of American conservatism, be it the prosperity gospel or firm adherence to liberal democracy and free markets as fruits of Christian values and worldview. The reasons for this are many: once the ideological illusions of the 1960s and 1970s dissipated, the West's perceived prosperity could not be separated, in the eyes of many middle-class Chinese, from its religious traditions;[54] the failure of the Tiananmen movement redirected many of its leaders and participants toward house churches activism;[55] Christian bosses and executives were finding in the gospel not only religious justifications to their emerging prosperity but also a code of conduct to which they could anchor their professional practices and strategies—and the building-up of social networks with like-minded entrepreneurs soon solidified their newfound beliefs.[56] New translations of *The Protestant Ethic* testify to the continuing impact of Weber's theses on today's China.[57] It can thus be argued that "Christianity's gains among the upper strata of Chinese society, particularly the intellectuals, means that elements of Western Protestant ideals, values, and idioms are finding their way, in however small measure, into the cultural synthesis of a future China."[58]

Such trends sometimes remained in the domain of the private: Pentecostal forms of piety and fundamentalist understanding of the biblical text can nurture a community outlook without impacting its relationship to the external world (or lack thereof). Other times, they evolved into nascent public theologies. This has notably been the case with Wang Yi 王怡 (b. 1973), a former law professor who has become the leader of the Early Rain Church (*Qiuyu jiaohui* 秋雨教會) in Chengdu. For Wang, Puritan Calvinism provides for both a constitutional polity and a transcendent power, thus grounding absolute moral principles as well as the separation of church and state.[59] The summary of Wang Yi's thought provided by Fällman well captures its political dimension:

> Wang Yi has promoted liberalism as his preferred political ideology, while linking both liberalism and constitutionalism to Christian faith and the relation between human beings and God. From previously merely promoting constitutionalism and the rule of law, with his Christian interpretation, Wang . . . likens the constitution to a contract, just like God's covenant with humanity, and argues for a God-given freedom depending on voluntary submission to God.[60]

Even before he had articulated his religious stance, Wang Yi was counted among prominent "public intellectuals (*gonggong zhishifenzi* 公共知識分子)" (such a label has been less and less in use as the Xi Jinping era has asserted renewed ideological objectives).[61] The (failed) attempts by the Beijing-based *Shouwang* 守望 (Watchers) Church, around the years 2010–2011, to enter into public dialogue with the government on the churches' registration system represented another effort at anchoring public theology into the Chinese context.

Still in Beijing, the Ark (*Fangzhou* 方舟) Church has been home to writers Bei Cun 北村 (b. 1965) and Yu Jie 余杰 (b. 1973, exiled to the United States since 2012), the name of the latter often being associated with his friend, dissident and Nobel Peace Prize winner Liu Xiaobo 劉曉波 (1955–2017). For Bei and Yu, as well as for like-minded intellectuals, cultural reconstruction and Christianity's social impact could not be separated. Yu's biographies of present-day Chinese Christians aim at nothing less than rebuilding Chinese culture by placing "God" at its root; the same ideal permeates the testimonies of any of Yu's interviewees.[62] The style and content of such writings strongly contrast with those produced by academics and leaders of the official church.

This does not mean that the various interpretations of the Bible and of its social and political teaching propounded in China have remained fully entrenched. In August 2013, at a forum held at Oxford University, Chinese scholars representing a wide range of backgrounds (including a number of avowed Christians as well as liberals, Confucians, and representatives of the New Left) worked out a text entitled (in probably too optimistic a fashion) the "Oxford Consensus" (*niujing gongshi* 牛津共識). It holds to the principles of people's consent, fairness and justice, pluralism, and fair world order.[63] References to particular canons are not to be found in this text. However, the underlying message is that the Bible can be interpreted in a way that concurs with social and political insights offered by other traditions, at least in the sense that, while a nation shares the same origins and destiny, its people may diverge as to the path to be followed.

As already noted, the (economically) liberal and (socially) conservative lines of biblical interpretations flourished during the "Reform and Opening" era and have somehow accompanied its development. Xi's "New Era" seems to restrict the array of biblical interpretations being publicly discussed and clearly attempts at restraining the Bible's impact on Chinese society and polity. However, as the biblical text has become part of commonly accepted and oft-quoted references, its interpretation has spread much beyond the realm of confessional readings and thus may be extremely difficult to contain. This was actually the objective that the first generation of Cultural Christians was aiming at, without finding ground at that time for furthering its endeavor. In November 2018, participating in a workshop, a sociologist working at Shanghai Academy of Social Sciences was mobilizing biblical references[64] as he was assessing current relationships between residents and non-residents of Shanghai across various neighborhoods of the metropolis.

A last point deserves mention: mainland Chinese society and theology have been little impacted by the political interpretations of the Bible developed in other Chinese society, especially Taiwan. It means that Asian styles of liberation theologies, such as the one developed by Choan-Seng Song 宋泉盛 (b. 1929), marked by the specific Taiwanese political experience, have not been discussed much within mainland China. As a consequence, the influence of Bible readings developed within the Asian continent as a whole remains marginal in China—and Bible readings proper to mainland China are similarly marginal in the rest of Asia.[65] The "Asian" and "Chinese" impacts of the Bible remain very distinct. Their respective narratives and assessments would certainly need be crisscrossed, so as to allow for a richer interpretative framework in China proper.

Conclusion: A *Jing* for All Seasons

From its introduction through the first Protestant translations onwards, the Bible in China has been the object of a "conflict of interpretations." For sure, this was and still remains the case for other periods and cultures. However, the relatively short time, as well of the intensity through which these varying interpretations developed, may constitute a distinctive feature. Three factors at least played a crucial role in the way the Bible's various understandings impacted the Chinese nation as a whole: (1) translations were accompanied by the import of foreign exegetical methods and results, which historical circumstances made politically loaded; (2) at the same time, the new "classic" was automatically read and interpreted through the rich Chinese hermeneutical tradition; and (3) the rhythm, intensity, and scope of the social and political upheavals that China underwent during the last one hundred and fifty or two hundred years could not but deeply affect reading strategies, since the Christian canon was entering China at the same time the country was confronting Western "modernity."

At least seven reading strategies emerge from our narrative:

1. The Bible sometimes was read line with other apocalyptic writings characteristic of Chinese political and religious traditions. If such reading is nowadays subject to severe and convergent prohibitions (by both the State and the Churches), it certainly remains virtually present.
2. In the aftermath of the Taiping rebellion, the good news of the coming of the kingdom was read through a more Confucian prism: the Bible was seen as an agent of political and social change, and thus of national renewal, provided that its message of personal cultivation first was anchored solidly in the mind and deeds of its readers.
3. Such reading was revamped and reinterpreted later on according to changing political circumstances. Interpreting the historical situation that was proper to China became key in deciding which interpretation to give to the biblical text. This still governs the way the "Sinicization" of biblical reading is presented today as an objective to be progressively achieved.
4. Against the above-mentioned models, a more fundamentalist reading of the Bible evolved and developed from the 1920s until the present. Its rejection of any political stance became a political stance in and of itself. While it renounced a "nationalistic" understanding of the Bible, at least as determined by any Party line, it was strongly anchored into a popular and very immediate experience of Bible reading.
5. From the 1980s onwards, a new model of biblical reading emerged, which was emphasizing the counter-cultural elements proper to biblical narratives and teachings set against traditional Chinese culture and recent political upheavals. Such reading has continuously oscillated between hermeneutical attempts inserted into a Christian theological framework, on the one hand, and enterprises that make biblical readings dependent on an interpretative strategy extending to world classics as a whole, on the other hand.
6. Western-style, evangelical readings have penetrated a number of family churches. They stress the biblical roots of constitutionalism, democratic values, economic liberalism, and social ethics. They contrast it with China's contemporary ethos, which could be reformed only through exposure to an authentic Christian and biblical culture.

7. Independent of both confessional affiliations and intellectual/political factions, "inchoative" readings are developing, which integrate biblical material into discussions of issues such as ecology, migration, justice, or even with personal ethics.

Needless to say, these modes of reading were selected according to the social and political impact that they entail. However, we should not forget that most believers read the Bible primarily for inner nourishment and reformation, without their rumination of the text directly impacting their stance in society—though any kind of reading eventually influences one's understanding of the social environment. Bible reading nurtures emotions, strengthens knowledge, and through sharing and study sessions, inserts the faithful into a reading and worshipping community. The way Bible reading shapes believing communities directly impacts the social fabric.

This analysis could be furthered by taking into account exegetical styles and methods. The variety of settings, interpretations, and social impact has characterized biblical readings from the time the Bible was introduced into China, and particularly since it became part of the general debate on modernity and national essence. Though the future of biblical reading in China will be determined partly by political factors and partly by the congregations' inner evolutions, the text, most probably, will prove able to generate new, surprising, and impactful interpretations. Its future lies in its readers.

Notes

1. Jost Oliver Zetzsche, *The Bible in China: The History of the Union Version or the Culmination of Protestant Missionary Bible Translation in China* (Sankt Augustin: Monumenta Serica Institute, 1999), 331.
2. Archie C. C. Lee, "The Bible in Chinese Christianity: Its Reception and Appropriation in China," *The Ecumenical Review* 67 (2015): 102.
3. Lin Lin, "Sigao shengjing chuban faxing wushi zhounian zuotanhui zai beijing juxing (Seminar held in Beijing for the fifty years anniversary of the printing and distribution of the Studium Biblicum Bible)" [in Chinese] *Xinde* (*Faith Weekly*) (October 19, 2018): http://chinacatholic.org/News/show/id/43836.html (accessed November 21, 2018).
4. For instance, they are not fully congruent with the ones released in: Information Office of the State Council 2018.
5. Zuoren Zhou, "Shengshu yu Zhongguo wenxue [in Chinese] (The Bible and Chinese Literature)," *Xiaoshuo Yuebao* (*The Short Stories Monthly*) 12.1 (1921): 7–13; Zetzsche, *The Bible in China*, 333–334.
6. We will limit our inquiry to mainland China. For a synthesis on theologies developed in the whole of the Chinese world, including "homeland theologies," see Matteo Nicolini-Zani, "The Development of Chinese Christian Theology in the Last Decades: Between Indigenization and Contextualization," *Tripod* 155 (Winter 2009): 31–54. For a hermeneutical reading of the biblical text anchored in the Chinese tradition as developed in the context of overseas Chinese communities, see K.K. Yeo, *What Has Jerusalem to Do with Beijing? Biblical Interpretation from a Chinese Perspective* (Eugene, OR: Pickwick Publications, 2018; 1st ed.: 1998). See also, from the same author, *Musing with Confucius*

and Paul: Toward a Chinese Christian Theology (Eugene, OR: Cascade Books, 2008). The Chinese version of this last work, published by East China Normal University Press in 2010, has been well read in academic circles.

7. Janet Chen, Pei-Kai Cheng, and Michael Lestz, with James Spence, *The Search for Modern China: A Documentary Collection* (New York and London: W.W. Norton & Company, 2014), 117.
8. Georges T. B. Davis, ca. 1919, quoted in Chen, *The Search for Modern China*, 208.
9. John Ching Hsiung Wu, *Beyond East and West* (New York: Sheed and Ward, 1951), 285–324, esp. 314.
10. Yat-sen Sun, *Sun Zhongshan quanji, 11 (1924.9–1925)* [in Chinese] (*Complete Works of Sun Yat-Sen*, vol. 11) (Beijing: Zhonghua shuju, 1986 [1924]), 537–538; Chen, "Modern Chinese Attitudes," 23.
11. Sze-kar Wan, "Competing Tensions: A Search for May Fourth Biblical Hermeneutics." In *Reading Christian Scriptures in China*, ed. Chloë Starr (London: Bloomsbury Publishing, 2008), 97.
12. John Y. H. Yieh, "The Bible in China: Interpretations and Consequences," in *Handbook of Christianity in China*, Vol. 2: *1800–Present*, ed. Robert Tiedemann (Leiden: E. J. Brill, 2010), 895.
13. Some Christian posters dated 1907 to 1951, collected by the Center for Global Christianity and Mission at Boston University, are indicative of the popular impact of Christianity, especially when it comes to visions of family and of national salvation. See http://ccposters.com (accessed September 15, 2020).
14. Chloë Starr, *Chinese Theology: Text and Context* (New Haven: Yale University Press, 2016), 139–142.
15. Duxiu Chen, "Jidujiao yu Zhongguoren (Christianity and the Chinese People)" [in Chinese], in *Xinqingnian* (*New Youth*) 7.3 (February 1920), 19.
16. Wan, "Competing Tensions," 214.
17. Benoît Vermander, Liz Hingley, and Liang Zhang, *Shanghai Sacred: The Religious Landscape of a Global City* (Seattle: University of Washington Press, 2018), 21–25.
18. John Craig William Keating, *A Protestant Church in Communist China: Moore Memorial Church Shanghai, 1949–1989* (Bethlehem, PA: Lehigh University Press, 2012).
19. This illustrates the paradoxical positioning of Christianity from the end of the nineteenth century till the dawn of the new regime: it was at the same time a "foreign religion" and a crucial agent in the process of national modernization. See Peter van der Veer, *The Modern Spirit of Asia: The Spiritual and the Secular in China and India* (Princeton: Princeton University Press, 2014), 105.
20. Xi Lian, *Redeemed by Fire: The Rise of Popular Christianity in Modern China* (New Haven: Yale University Press, 2010), 118–122.
21. Henrietta Harrison, *The Missionary's Curse, and Other Tales from a Chinese Catholic Village* (Berkeley: University of California Press, 2013), 205.
22. Zuoren Zhou, "Literature of Humanity" (1918), In *Modern Chinese Literary Thought: Writings on Literature, 1893–1945*, ed. and trans. Kirk A. Denton (Palo Alto: Stanford University Press, 1996 [1918]); Zuoren Zhou, "Ren de wenxue (Literature of Humanity)" (1918), in *Zhou Zuoren sanwen quanji*, vol. 2 (Nanning: Guangxi Normal University Press, 2009), 85–93.
23. Ke Zhang, "La formation du concept d'humanisme confucéen," in *Chine France—Europe Asie: Itinéraire de concepts*, ed. Michel Espagne and Li Hongtu (Paris: Editions Rue d'Ulm, 2018).

24. See esp. Yutang Lin, *From Pagan to Christian* (Cleveland: World Publishing Company, 1959).
25. Xun Lu, *Silent China: Selected Writings of Lu Xun*, trans. Gladys Yang (Oxford: Oxford University Press, 1973), 120–121.
26. Lewis S. Robinson, *Double-Edged Sword: Christianity and 20th-Century Chinese Fiction* (Hong Kong: Tao Fong Shan, 1986), 78.
27. C. J. Alber, "Wild Grass; Symmetry and Parallelism in Lu Hsün's Prose Poems," in *Critical Essays on Chinese Literature*, ed. W. H. Nienhauser Jr. (Hong Kong: The Chinese University of Hong Kong, 1976), 10.
28. Wan, "Competing Tensions," 100.
29. David E. Mungello, "Reinterpreting the History of Christianity in China," *Historical Journal* 55 (2012): 547.
30. Luxian Jin, *The Memoirs of Jin Luxian*, Vol. 1: *Learning and Relearning, 1916–1982*, trans. William Hanbury-Tenison (Hong Kong: Hong Kong University Press, 2012); see also Paul Mariani, *Church Militant: Bishop Kung and Catholic Resistance in Communist Shanghai* (Cambridge, MA: Harvard University Press, 2011).
31. Jin, *The Memoirs*, 288.
32. See Benoît Vermander, "Humility and Humiliation; Kenotic Experience in Modern Chinese Painting, and in the Historical Experience of Chinese Christians," in *Chinese Spirituality and Christian Communities: A Kenotic Perspective*, ed. Vincent Shen (Washington, DC: The Council for Research in Values and Philosophy, 2015): 85–101.
33. Ibid.
34. Harrison, *The Missionary's Curse*, 192.
35. Philip L. Wickeri, *Reconstructing Christianity in China: K. H. Ting and the Chinese Church* (Maryknoll, NY: Orbis Books, 2015).
36. Starr, *Chinese Theology*.
37. Alexander Chow, "Wang Weifan's Cosmic Christ," *Modern Theology* 32.3 (July 2016): 388.
38. Archie C. C. Lee, "The Bible in Chinese Christianity: Its Reception and Appropriation in China," *The Ecumenical Review* (2015): 105.
39. "Obeying the law is a basic Christian concept as the Bible clearly teaches. 'Remind them to be submissive to rulers and authorities, to be obedient, to be ready for every good work' (Titus 3:1). Chinese Christianity, through study and implementation of the new regulations, will strengthen the establishment of China's national law and religious regulations; . . . continue to strengthen the establishment theological thinking; strive to promote and implement sinicized Christianity; will work towards realizing the struggle towards the goal of 'two one hundred years' and contribute to realizing the Chinese people's great rejuvenated Chinese dream to enable Chinese Christianity to promote 'Love of country, love of religion; glorify God, benefit people.'" Qinghua Yue, "Yi fa ban jiao, gu ben qiang shen [in Chinese] (Teach According to the Law, Strengthen the Body)," *Tianfeng* 13 (September 2017): https://mp.weixin.qq.com/s/-hbMGlUSy8UIx_6ocdwe5A (accessed November 21, 2018). *Tianfeng*, in which this contribution was published, is the official magazine of the China Christian Council and Three-Self Patriotic Movement.
40. Yi Tang, "Chinese Christianity in Development," *China Study Journal* 6.2 (August, 1991): 4–8; Anonymous, "Christianity and Chinese Culture," *China News Analysis* 1452 (January 15, 1992): 1–9.
41. See Starr, *Chinese Theology*, 211–212.
42. Zhigang Zhang, *Zongjiao zhongguohua yili yanjiu* [in Chinese] (*Sinicization of Religions: A Theoretical Study*) (Beijing: Religious Cultures Publishing House, 2017): 95–114.

43. Xi Jinping, *Report Delivered at the 19th National Congress of the Chinese Communist Party*. http://www.xinhuanet.com/english/special/2017-11/03/c_136725942.htm (in English); http://finance.sina.com.cn/china/gncj/2017-10-18/doc-ifymvuyt4098830.shtml (in Chinese), October 18, 2017 (accessed December 5, 2018).
44. See notably Zhang Zhigang, *Zongjiao zhongguohua*.
45. Ian Johnson, "China Bans Online Bible Sales as It Tightens Religious Controls," *New York Times*, April 5, 2018, https://www.nytimes.com/2018/04/05/world/asia/china-bans-bible-sales.html?module=inline (accessed December 14, 2018).
46. Uncanews, "Bible rewrite helps stoke censorship fears in China" (April 5, 2018): https://www.ucanews.com/news/bible-rewrite-helps-stoke-censorship-fears-in-china/81983 (accessed November 23, 2018).
47. Ucanews, "Protestant five-year plan for Chinese Christianity" (April 20, 20180: https://www.ucanews.com/news/protestant-five-year-plan-for-chinese-christianity/82107 (accessed November 23, 2018).
48. Huilin Yang, *China, Christianity, and the Question of Culture* (Waco: Baylor University Press, 2014), esp. 61–75; Alexander Chow, "The East Asian Rediscovery of 'Sin,'" *Studies in World Christianity* 19.2 (2013): 129–131; Frederik Fällman, *Salvation and Modernity: Intellectuals and Faith in Contemporary China* (Lanham: University Press of America, 2008).
49. See Xiaofeng Liu ed., *"Dao" yu "Yan". Hua wenhua yu jidu wenhua xiangyu* [in Chinese] (*The "Way" and the "Word": The Meeting between Chinese Culture and Christianity*) (Shanghai: Sanlian, 1995), esp. the editor's preface.
50. See notably Qiuling Li, "Historical Reflections on 'Sino-Christian Theology,'" *China Study Journal* (Spring-Summer 2007): 54–67; Xiangchen Sun, "The Possibility of Sino-Christian Theology: From 'Cultural Christianity' to 'Christian Scholars,'" *China Study Journal* (Autumn-Winter 2009): 35–44.
51. Starr, *Chinese Theology*, 240–262.
52. Pinchao Lai [Lai Pan Chiu] and Lin Hongxing, *Ru Ye duihua yu shengtai guanhuai* [in Chinese] (*Confucian-Christian Dialogue and Ecological Concerns*) (Beijing: Religious Cultures Press, 2006).
53. Xiaofeng Liu, *Sino-Theology and the Philosophy of History: A Collection of Essays*, trans. Leopold Leeb (Leiden: E. J. Brill, 2015); Frederik Fällman, "Public Faith? Five Voices of Chinese Christian Thought," *Contemporary Chinese Thought* 47.4 (2016): 223–234.
54. Nanlai Cao, *Constructing China's Jerusalem: Christians, Power and Place in the City of Wenzhou* (Palo Alto: Stanford University Press, 2010). Recent shifts would need further assessment. For instance, new converts show a propensity to stress the link between the adhesion to Christianity and an attitude of cultural openness. See Pierre Vendassi, *Chrétiens de Chine. Affiliations et conversions au XXIe siècle* (Rennes: Presses Universitaires de Rennes, 2016), 74–80.
55. Alexander Chow, "Calvinist Public Theology in Urban China Today," *International Journal of Public Theology* 8.2 (2014): 158–175.
56. Cao, *Constructing China's Jerusalem*.
57. Zhejun Yu, "Xin yiben daodu (Reading Guide of the New Translation)" [in Chinese], in *Xinjiao lunli yu zibenzhuyi jingshen* (*Die Protestantische Ethik un der Geist der Kapitalimsus*), ed. Max Weber. Translated by Yu Zheyun (Hangzhou: Zhejiang University Press, 2018): 1–25.
58. Xi Lian, *Redeemed by Fire: The Rise of Popular Christianity in Modern China* (New Haven: Yale University Press, 2010), 244.

59. Chow, "Calvinist Public Theology".
60. Fällman, "Public Faith," 228.
61. Wang Yi and around one hundred members of his church were arrested on December 9, 2018. His friends made public a letter he wrote before his arrest. It notably states: "I firmly believe that the Bible has not given any branch of any government the authority to run the church or to interfere with the faith of Christians. Therefore, the Bible demands that I, through peaceable means, in meek resistance and active forbearance, filled with joy, resist all administrative policies and legal measures that oppress the church and interfere with the faith of Christians." Yi Wang, "My Declaration of Faithful Disobedience," trans. Brent Pinkall and Amy Cheung, in *China Partnership*, http://www.chinapartnership.org/blog/2018/12/my-declaration-of-faithful-disobedience?fbclid=IwAR1oE33gadaCnBt3wEaonvR5rZfzJrXv31CHqMbU388WH9a_yuqK40NveDs (accessed December 13, 2018).
62. Starr, *Chinese Theology*, 272–277.
63. Ming Chen et al. "The Oxford Consensus," *The New York Times* (October 23, 2013), http://www.nytchina.com/china/20131023/c23consensus/en-us/ (accessed November 26, 2018).
64. These references had to do both with the welcome to be extended to "the Stranger" and with the relativity of such concept.
65. Benoît Vermander, "Speaking of Harmony in Many Tongues: The Crafting of a Pan-Asian Theology," *Revue des sciences religieuses* 91.2 (2017): 269–286.

Primary Sources

See resources listed in notes.

Chen, Janet, Pei-Kai Cheng, and Michael Lestz, with James Spence. *The Search for Modern China. A Documentary Collection*. New York and London: W.W. Norton & Company, 2014.

Liu, Xiaofeng, ed. *"Dao" yu "Yan". Hua wenhua yu jidu wenhua xiangyu (The "Way" and the "Word". The Meeting between Chinese Culture and Christianity)* [in Chinese]. Shanghai: Sanlian, 1995.

Wang, Weifan. *Zhongguo shenxue ji qi wenhua yuanyuan (Chinese Theology and Its Cultural Sources)* [in Chinese]. Nanjing: Nanjing Jinling Xiehe Shenxueyuan, 1997.

CHAPTER 37

THE BIBLE AND THE PUBLIC SQUARE IN CHINA

PHILIP P. CHIA

INTRODUCTION

IT is not the intention of this essay to provide a history of Christianity and the Bible in China by combing through the massive historical materials, nor to describe the historical development of the translation of the Bible into Chinese since the entry of Christianity into China. The focus of this essay, however, is to extract materials, historical and contemporary, that have implications for understanding the significance of the Bible as it has manifested itself outside the Christian church or Christian community into the public arena since its entry into China. This also could provide insights into historical lessons about how the Bible and the public square in China could better relate to each other. A healthy relationship between the Bible and the public square could or would have impacted on the nation as a whole, as China progresses into prosperity, with Christianity and the Bible as a potentially positive and constructive force in its peaceful rise to global status within the world community.

Although Christianity came into China as early as the seventh century (635 CE) during the Tang dynasty (618–907), it was not until the sixteenth century, with "the Protestant Reformation and the creation of the Portuguese and Spanish seaborne empires,"[1] that an influx of missionaries launched themselves into this land of the Middle Kingdom. Although much missionary work in the land had been done, albeit some with limited access and constraints due to political policy, it was not until 1822 that the first Protestant translation of the Old and New Testament Bible into Chinese was completed. This was credited to Joshua Marshman (1768–1837) in India and, subsequently, in 1823, the Robert Morrison (1782–1834) version was published by the British and Foreign Bible Society. In 1968, the first Catholic Chinese Bible came into existence, credited to

Gabriele Maria Allegra O.F.M. (1907–1976). With the existence of a completed Chinese Bible, along with various portions of the Bible being translated at various periods and localities into various dialects,[2] the availability of these Bible translations to the common people signified the presence and potential use of biblical texts and teachings, which often were used alongside various Chinese classical teachings in public life. The message and teaching of the Bible were granted access by the common people often via the Christian intellectual community and also through publication and education; it was in this way that the Bible presented itself as it entered the public arena with a powerful influence in the lives of the Chinese people.[3]

There were major concerns and conflicts during the sixteenth century as Catholic and Protestant missionaries made their way into Chinese culture. The religious power and Christian belief of the global church were in tension and conflict with the everyday practice of the Chinese people, whose worldview and anthropological understanding were very different from the Christian West and ruled by the imperial court of the absolute authority of the emperor. One of the most discussed events in Chinese Christian history is the Rites Controversy (1704 prohibition–1939 approval).[4] Since that time, for almost 150 years (1800–1950), the tension between the Chinese church, foreign mission, and the State has been the testing ground for engagement between Western-oriented Christianity and Eastern cultural China.[5] The presence and potential of the Bible for resolving any of these tensions have often been overshadowed by the polity and authority of the missions or church governance. Orders of the church or Protestant theology often overwrote grievous cultural issues.

Several events contributed to years of anti-imperialist, anti-foreign, and anti-Christian social upheaval: the Opium War (*Yapian Zhanzheng*) (1840) between the British and China, which brought about the "unequal treaties" (*bupingdengtiaoyue*) era—British (1842), Americans (1843), and the French (1844); and the Treaty of Nanjing (1842), whereby Hong Kong was ceded to Great Britain; the Taiping Heavenly Kingdom (*Taipingtianguo* 太平天國) Civil War (1850–1864), which resulted in an estimated death of between 20 to 70 million; the Boxer Rebellion (*Yihetuan* Movement 義和團運動, 1899–1901), which began with the murder of five Catholic bishops and the death of nearly 30,000 Catholic faithful. Years of social unrest resulted at the local and national level, with Christianity and politics, both internal and international, fully at play as the people of the land were struggling to survive a transition from an imperial dynasty system of government to a new system of national autonomy. Following the Wuchang Revolt led by Sun Yat-sen, who proclaimed the Republic of China in 1911, a post-Imperial dynasty China came into existence. The years between 1920–1950, though traumatic, were full of excited Protestant missionaries who led evangelization missions in China. Christian churches in China during this period, however, were characterized by split and division, as Daniel Bays noted, "The missionary community in China remained split between liberals or modernists on one side, and conservatives or fundamentalists on the other."[6] From the May Fourth Movement (1919), due to the Treaty of Versailles, to the anti-religious and anti-superstition movement especially among Chinese intellectuals, reactions toward "capitalism, imperialism, colonialism" and religious superstition, which led to the anti-Christian Movement (1922–1927), the rise of Chinese nationalism, coupled with a strong sense of anti-Christian sentiment, granted a force of resistance to Christian occupation of the nation. The Chinese translation of the Bible came into existence during this period of national difficulties. What effect could have linked the century of national unrest with decades of intense Protestant missions and Bible teachings? It is no wonder that, at the end of the 1949 era, when missionaries and mission organizations had all been driven out once again from this Middle Kingdom, the twofold question most deeply asked, as a way of deep reflection and re-evaluation, was "Did Christianity fail in China?" and "Did Christianity fail China?"

The Context and Controversy of the Bible in the Public Square

With the very brief introduction above, the following shall highlight four specific contexts in the recent history of Christianity in China, serving as the background for investigating the relations between the Bible and the public square. First, the Rites Controversy (1704–1939); second, the Taiping Rebellion (1850–1864); third, the Boxer Rebellion (1899–1901); and fourth, the powerful Protestant publication mission of the "literature" amid "The Multiple crises of Chinese Christianity 1927–1950."[7]

Although the Rites Controversy was the most discussed and studied historical event of Christianity in China, its outcome clearly has been a struggle for control between religious and political powers.[8] The cultural insensitivity of Western Christian missions on the one hand, and condescension, domination, and hegemony of the powerful West on the other, all led to a disastrous dissolution in global relations at that historical juncture. The Bible, however, was never caught in the crossfire between the Pope and the emperor. It would appear to be a pure power struggle between the "two empires." But the fallout from the Rites Controversy did have serious implications for Protestant missions later on, even lasting to this very day, whereby paying respect to ancestors by bowing with incense is considered by some as equal to idol worship, which is prohibited by the Bible. The Bible in the public square, especially in the daily cultural life of the common Chinese family and society, came squarely into tension with the Confucius rites that have been accepted as the norm of governance for a normal structured human societal relationship. The Bible, which came with its religious regulations, was found to be intolerably in opposition to the Chinese culture of Confucian rites. The tension also necessarily caused a reevaluation of mission strategy for the Chinese. The approach went from targeting the top Chinese elite in the intellectual community as an entry point for mission strategy to reaching the majority of people at the grassroots level, who were mostly illiterate at the marketplace and common people. Both approaches gained their own effective ground in the race into the public square. From the time of the Italian Jesuit Matteo Ricci (1552–1610) and Kangxi's 1692 edict of toleration for mission and Christianity, down to the prohibition of the "rites" by the Pope in 1704, the Bible has had very little role in the expansion of Christianity in China. It was those hundreds of educated Jesuits, coming with modern science and astronomy into China between 1580–1780, who gained public access to the people of China.

Toward the downfall of the Qing dynasty in late nineteenth-century China, there was an unpleasant historical context filled with Western imperialism and colonialism intruding on this Middle Kingdom. The ever-weakening Qing dynasty with its ineffective governing, and the Western predators who came with great dominating firepower that could easily subdue the imperial power of the dynastic rulership, added up to a growing strong sentiment of nationalism with elements of anti-imperialism, anti-foreigners, and anti-Christianity. Desperately in search of a national solution to counter the impotence of the Qing imperial power, the stage was set for the Taiping Rebellion (1850–1864). The leader, Hong Xiuquan, who started the most devastating civil war in the history of Christianity and China, the Taiping Rebellion, found confirmation of his dream vision, "to chase the demons," in a booklet published by Liang Afa, a Chinese Christian convert who summarized the Protestant teaching of the Bible as a form of evangelism and heavenly teaching. The use of the Bible in the free-form of contextual interpretation, applying his understanding of the teaching of Jesus to the immediate context of national crisis, Hong Xiuquan initiated the biggest civil war in modern Chinese history, the Taiping Heavenly Kingdom, which conservatively estimated resulted in the deaths of 20 to 70 million. The Bible in the public square of China under Hong Xiuquan became a weapon of political rebellion against the late Qing dynasty, with a mission to liberate the nation. This is clearly an unchecked use of the Bible teachings applied to public and national life. This same historical event also instilled a deep national distrust that kept coming back to haunt the immediate and future ruling authorities about the power of religion, especially that of Christianity, even unto this day.

Following this Taiping crisis, thirty-five years later in 1899, the murder of five Catholic bishops brought about another crisis known as the Boxer Rebellion (*quan luan* 拳亂), or Boxer Uprising, whereby the anti-imperial, anti-foreigner, and anti-Christian sentiment again fueled social unrest at a national level due to the corrupted and extremely fragile and impotent rule of the imperial court, which eventually brought an end to the Qing dynasty later on.

The Rites Controversy, the Taiping Rebellion (1850–1864), Boxer Rebellion (1899–1901), the Anti-Christianity Movement (1922–1927), all happened following the entry of the Protestant missionary Robert Morrison, who landed in Macau in 1807. With the first Chinese Bible published in 1823, there was a sharp increase during this period in Protestant converts compared with the Catholics who had already been in China for centuries. The Bible has never gained a proper entry into the public square, except as a powerful cultural and political tool for proselytization and domination. Worst of all, it even appeared to be the cause of several movements of social unrest, local and national, individual, family, and society, as the nation transitioning in its State system from thousands of years of absolute monarchy rule to a republic as the Qing dynasty came to an end. Devoting an entire chapter to discussing the problems and issues of Chinese Christianity prior to 1949, Daniel Bays elaborated under the title, "The Multiple Crises of Chinese Christianity, 1927–1950,"[9] highlighting various contexts that had given rise to those crisis moments. There can be no separation between state-politics and the church-religion.

The Concentration and Conservation of the Bible in Public Square

During the 150 years of missionary endeavor (1800–1950), the growth of the Christian community in China demonstrated the great effort of missionaries' communicative skill and strategy. With the Protestants coming in the era after the Reformation, the importance of the Bible became a focus of missionary effort. Concentration on making available the sacred Word of God, through translation of the Bible into various vernaculars, was a key strategy of Protestant missionaries. Due to a large portion of the population remaining illiterate, and in order for the Bible to be accessible to all people rather than just the educated elites, the translation of the Bible into a common Chinese language had gone through various phases of development in order to achieve the status of a common-language version. At the same time in the early twentieth century, there was also the transformation process taking place in the Chinese language, taking a "language" turn from "classical" to "common" Chinese language, attempting to unify both the written and spoken Chinese language. From the Morrison Chinese Bible Version of 1823 to the common Union Version of 1919, the transformation of Chinese language from classical *wenyuanwen* 文言文 to modern vernacular Mandarin Chinese *baihuawen* 白話文 represented almost a century of translation effort on the part of the missionaries and their Chinese helpers. For the Bible to relate itself to the general wider public, a *public* language was unavoidably needed for the Bible and its audience. The Protestant Bible translators contributed tremendous language and cultural efforts to the birth of the modern vernacular Mandarin Chinese language.

With the Bible as the major focus of the teaching of Protestant Christianity, the emphasis on Jesus as the Son of God and his ethical teaching carried extremely significant weight in the faith of the Christian community. This also was a time of cultural reflection among the Chinese intellectual community, whereby the traditional Chinese Confucius-based cultural values had been called into question, considered to be the source of a weak nation in the face of powerful foreign nations, thus seeking changes to transform the traditional culture. Christian faith from abroad served the purpose of a nation under foreign siege and desperately wanting to learn from the powerful West so as to be strong. The ethical and spiritual emphasis of the Protestant missionary teaching of the Bible also raised the authority of the Bible to a higher level, deeming it the Word of God. By emphasizing the ethical and spiritual concerns of the Bible, a sense of conservatism among Protestant Christian teaching of the Bible drew acceptance among Chinese Christians, who traditionally already had a strong sense of revering the transcendent, spiritual, and religious world. The ethical teaching of Jesus was especially attractive at a time when the nation was at a crossroad in terms of establishing Chinese national, social, and human value, given the fact that it had been a nation under imperial rule for ages. As surveyed by one historian, "In 1853 there were 350 Chinese Protestants, whereas Catholics were then estimated at 330,000. Protestants grew to 37,289 in 1889 and at which time Catholics approached 500,000."[10] It is clear that there were differences between Catholics and Protestants in their mission strategy and concentration, drawing religious authority from different sources. Catholics came to China much earlier than Protestants, and the number of converts showed a sizable gap between the two; yet the Bible was never the focus of the missions, until Protestant missionary Robert Morrison came to China and had the Bible translated into Chinese. To Protestant missions, the authority of the Bible and its teaching was a major concern and thus they made translation of the Bible a major task of the mission.

As the focus of Protestant missionaries was to translate the Bible into various dialects, they established local churches as they were evangelizing at the grassroots level. Illiteracy was common and thus, they had to rely on preaching and verbal communication, drawing lessons from the Bible. Since the majority of the population was in the rural area, reaching the masses of people required a separate mission strategy. This brought about the China Inland Mission, founded in 1865 by James Hudson Taylor (1832–1905). By adopting a new strategy, unlike those with institutional organization and regulation-based mission organization, Taylor demonstrated a very successful mission model that was different from those of the city-based mission organization.[11] Daniel Bays writes:

> In 1895 the China Inland Mission (CIM) had 641 missionaries, 462 Chinese helpers, and 260 stations and outstations with 5,211 communicants. By the time of Taylor's death, at Changsha in 1905, the number of missionaries had increased to 828. By that time, it [CIM] was almost three times larger than the next largest group, the British Church Missionary Society CMS.[12]

The mission strategy of the CIM may be understood as a mission model that reached out to the massive public population and, in doing so, required a well thought out strategy.

On the other horizon, there were those institutionalized mission organizations that took their mission strategy to the general public through education, schools, colleges, hospitals, and relief activities. It was in good faith that "Christian civilization" as shown by the colonial West is exactly what China needed and thus served as much of the foreign mission strategy. This awareness of the cultural hegemony of the West was seriously reflected in the post-1949 evaluation of foreign mission strategy. The Bible has yet to chart its course into the public arena in China.

The intense activities of the Protestant missionary works of the conservative evangelicals and fundamentalists, plus an emphasis on the Bible being the Word of God with unique authority over humanity and individual life, together put great effort in Christian publications as a form of spreading the gospel, especially with gospel tracts. *The Bible Magazine* (1913–1951, first phase), founded by the Canadian missionary Robert Alexander Jaffray (1873–1945), was the first of its kind, with the Bible as its core focus informing readers with a variety of Bible messages that provided important orthodoxy to evangelical faith. A proven successful mission model included a devotional emphasis and a focus on developing good Christian personal ethics in Christian life as a witness and testimony to the public community. The life-changing gospel message attracted many converts, and the Bible, besides being instrumental for Christians in getting to know God, remained a challenge in engaging the broader public in society and at the national level with national and societal concerns.

The Culture and Control of the Bible in the Public Square

With the Chinese-language Bible readily available to the Chinese audience, though not yet available in quantities for members of the public still working hard to become literate, its existence created a new public arena for the Bible to reach out to the general Chinese public outside of the church and Christian community, especially to the Chinese intellectual community. The Bible in the public square, venerated through literature and education, has proven to be one of the most effective means of spreading Christian religious ideas and the concept of human dignity.

Prior to 1949, with the backdrop of the May Fourth movement, the ethical teaching of the Bible became much sought-after for creative writing and composing among intellectuals, including one of the founders of the Chinese Communist Party, who was the first party general secretary in 1921, Chen Duxiu 陳獨秀; he wrote "Christianity and Chinese" (基督教與中國人 *ji du jiao yu zhong guo ren*) in a positive light. Other writers who utilized the Bible as a source for their creative fictional writings were Yü Dafu 郁達夫, Kuo Mo-jo 郭沫若, Pa Chin 巴金, Lu Hsün 魯迅, Hsü Ti-shan 許地山, and Mao Tun 茅盾.[13] The so-called "public intellectuals" of the early days of the Republic together constituted the progressive Chinese spirit of the era. The positive and potential influence of these intellectuals, whose fictions incorporated very positive views of the Bible, greatly helped the acceptance of the Bible among the general public, thus gaining access among the intellectual elites as well as in the public life of the common people, especially during this period of social turmoil and corruptive authority as the nation was transitioning from imperial rule to a republic. The teaching of Jesus on the Mount was among the most favorite Bible texts that appealed to the public, who had been traditionally concerned about personal ethics in the Confucian mode.

Prior to 1949, there had not been a lack of Christian theologians, pastors, and intellectuals who strived hard to represent the teaching of the Bible to the public. As in the collected series of essays presenting Christian views of the "society," "Images of Jesus," and "Christian Student Movement," Chin Kenpa presented a handful of examples from the "public theologians" of the times.[14]

Protestant press missions have proven to be a very successful strategy for reaching out to the general public. As noted by Charbonnier:

> In 1845, there were twenty American Protestant missionaries in China, as against ten English and one German. By 1855, there were forty-six Americans and twenty-four English. These emissaries from the New World brought, together with the Christian faith, a message of democracy, science, and progress, ideals that were to be diffused among Chinese students and intellectuals by means of abundant Christian literature.[15]

With the influx of Christian literature, however, there also was a hidden danger in the minimum regulations on the quality and orthodoxy of those publications, and the effect of their reception could be disastrous.

A case in point was the Taiping Rebellion. There were among those literatures published with good intention an influential booklet by Liang Afa, the *Quan shi liang yan* (Exhortations for our time), which "was made up of biblical texts, which formed a summary of Protestant teaching," and a copy landed in the hands of Hong Xiuquan, having "an unsettling effect on the mind of a Hakka . . . who later became the leader of the Taiping rebellion."[16] Charbonnier vividly described the case:

> He [Hong Xiuquan] thought he had found in the Bible a striking explanation of his dreams and a confirmation of his mission; God the Father and Jesus, big brother, were urging him to destroy the idols. . . . He had had a vision of an old man urging him to destroy demons. . . . He later baptized himself and preached his version of the Bible to his parents and friends, whom he also baptized.[17]

Naturally, the authorities reacted sharply and forbade the distribution of Christian literature; that was not entirely unreasonable, given the effect of the reception of one single booklet, and there occurred the most serious civil war in the recent history of Christianity in China. Charbonnier well concluded, "The Taiping were not recognized as Christians by Protestants, and even less by the Catholics."[18]

On the effects of Christian publication, Charbonnier provided a stock check for the late nineteenth century and the direction of the literature crusade as the Bible message was being imparted and introduced to the public square. He writes:[19]

> The 1877 General Conference of Protestant Missionaries also received statistics about Protestant publications in China: forty-three books of pamphlets of biblical commentaries, 521 books on theology, twenty-nine lives of saints, eighty-two catechism, fifty-four prayer books and rituals, sixty-three collections of hymns, seven periodicals, and 101 tracts. This rich crop of publications was not only due to the diversity of denominations and nationalities. Protestants were above all Christians of the Book. They preached the Word, but they did so with the Bible in hand. The Bible was at the heart of their publications, as they produced apologetic and devotional literature . . . they also tried to reach intellectuals and followed more or less the same path as the Jesuits in trying to reach the scholar-gentry. Aiming at reaching greater numbers, they imitated the Confucian tracts, which has popularized the moral norms of self-perfection. The German pioneer of missionary work in China, Karl Gutzlaff, had produced a booklet of thirty pages called, *The Model of the Perfect Man*. He took up the Confucian ideal of *junzi*, "the gentleman," completing it in a Christian direction; Jesus in his relation to the Father and the eight Beatitudes indicates the way to perfection.

Evidently, the invention of the printing press not only helped the Reformation with a wider distribution of the Bible but also the technology had well served Christian missions in China during the twentieth century. Unchecked religious power, however, as seen in the case of the Taiping Rebellion, although rare, but nevertheless raised a legitimate question concerning a modern-day Western idea of "freedom of speech" and the legitimacy for a public policy to control and regulate religious community.

The first fifty years of the twentieth century, 1900–1950, presented China as a land that was marked with chaos and relentless struggle, both internally and externally, for nationality and identity, as the ancient culture came into contact with and encountered challenge from a foreign culture that demonstrated its national strength and power with modern science and technology. This also was a time when the Western Christian mission was most active and seemingly had achieved its height in religious and cultural expansion into China. The role and value of the Bible in the public square, however, remains a blur and unsettled in China. Perhaps this was largely due to the fact that the Bible was often only a tool for the expansion of Christianity, in that the Bible was used mostly to support and strengthen preachers teaching of religious spirituality for personal nourishment in faith. This might have had some traditional influence from the Taoist or even Confucianist concept of the being. The Bible, as the Word of God, naturally carried with it some sort of "heavenly authority." Thus, it was a convenient tool for religious powers to exert authority by its leaders over its followers in the name of the Bible and also often under the power of Christian institutions and administrations.

Although the centrality of the Bible for Protestants was unquestionably crucial and subtle, as the Bible was being introduced into China and implemented into Chinese culture, unavoidably the text of the Christian Bible would be met with the rich text-based religious traditional culture of the Chinese intellectual tradition. As Chinese intellectuals approached the biblical text, it was natural for them to deal with it as they would with Confucian classics. Perhaps this is what Alexander Chow would understand as the

"Confucian imagination," developing the idea further to argue that "the Confucian imagination has a strong influence in certain aspects of Chinese Christianity and one of its key intellectual products: Chinese public theology."[20] According to Chow, "both Christianity and Confucianism offered resources for engaging the Chinese civil society."[21] Given the nature of the Bible as Protestantism deemed it, and with the Reformation as the backdrop, perhaps there was an ongoing cry for some form of "public theology" that would address the issues and situations of not just Chinese civil society, but also of humanity in the public life of the created world, whereby humanity was at risk, threatened day by day by their own invention of reality..

The Current Construction of the Bible in the Public Square

There was a period of "closed door" policy in China after 1949, when the Communist Party ruled China with its atheistic oriental Marxism. Seeds that had been sowed prior to its closing seemed to have sprouted behind the "bamboo curtain." The Christian community's growth in quantity after the door was re-opened had speedily reached an alarming level in the view of the ruling party, who were concerned about the threat of religious power that could endanger its regime. Christian concerns about public issues or civil society was almost a taboo subject in most Christian discussions within the Christian community in China. Christianity still is considered by the Chinese Communist regime today as a foreign power from non-Communists with the ill-intention of influencing and toppling Communist Party-ruled China.

It was within such a threatening and controlled atmosphere that the Bible, however, miraculously continued to survive and even prosper in China. In fact, it just celebrated in 2019 the hundredth anniversary of the Chinese Union Version (CUV) of the Bible with 100 million printed copies of the CUV in 2012 and 200 million printed copies in 2019. Although minimum space is given in the public square for any concerns and construction of the Bible in China, the biblical faith community is growing with a peaceful and loving concern for the well-being of the nation. Although the Bible is a controlled item in China, as it is not available in bookstores except in some of the official churches with internal bookstores for their members, and although manuscripts on the biblical text are legally required to go through stringent government censoring and approval before publication, nevertheless, the biblical faith community in China continues to press on for a positive contribution of their biblical faith toward the development and building of a healthy nation. The anticipated transformational power of the Bible in personal and individual life will drive the biblical faith community towards contributing perceived positive outcomes in the public arena with a "public-turn" in their understanding of the Bible mandate for contemporary humanity.

The Challenge and Contribution of the Bible in the Public Square

Having made a constructive analysis by means of two concepts, namely "generational shifts" and the "Confucian imagination," Alexander Chow concluded that "In mainland China, Chinese public theology still remains in its nascent stages. To move forward, it needs a critical and constructive engagement with its Christian and Chinese foundations."[22] If public theology is in such a "nascent stage," perhaps the challenge can be addressed by promoting education on the need and value of the Bible in the public square to Christians and non-Christians alike.

For ages, the Bible has been the source of inspiration and innovation for humanity, and the Bible can contribute its great wisdom potential in public discourse and address issues in Chinese civil society, if the "public" nature of the Bible can be released into the public square. With the growing interest in the theological arena for public theology,[23] there is a great need for a public theology that draws from the Bible as the foundational source of its development. A recent new endeavor is the establishment of The Centre for Advanced Biblical Studies and Applications (CABSA), as an attempt to tackle the issue of the Bible, the church, and the public. Founded in Hong Kong as a non-profit organization in 2004, the Centre has published a series of publications under the main series of "Bible and Public Theology." Prior to 2004, discussion of the term "public theology," much less the public-ness of the Bible, was seldom heard or mentioned within the global Sino-Christian community.[24] Centuries of modern critical studies of the Bible carried a strong tradition of biblical scholarship that was not sensitive to the need for a critical public biblical scholarship. Recent investigations by biblical scholars[25] of public theology have demonstrated the impact of the Bible in the public square as it contributed toward a potentially enriched nation-state and pluralistic cultural society.[26]

Hermeneutical and theological challenges are equally important; if the effect of conscious reading with a public sense is to be effective, cultural considerations cannot be underestimated or taken for granted.

The recent rise of right-defending professional lawyers (維權律師 *wei quan lü shi*) in China since 2004, with a large proportion of the community being Christian, and the witnessing of their Christian commitment against injustice and the defense of their constitutional rights, may be grounded in their biblical faith. Though there may be some initial concern by the church, or even attempts to keep a distance from Christians taking action in public or taking part under the public glare in defense of their constitutional rights, the scenario is changing as the pressure from authority grows. With the award of the 2016 Nobel Peace Prize given to public intellectual Liu Xiaobo, who is a Christian, the presence of a Christian public intellectual in the public square no longer can be kept in the dark, as the death of Liu was noticed by the global human conscience.

The relationship of the Bible and the public arena in China or Chinese communities in the diaspora intensely challenges their confessional theological beliefs, as well as their understanding and undertaking of their social responsibility in the public square. Given the major content of theological beliefs, which are mostly doctrinal and dogmatic in nature, perhaps the most urgent challenge to the Chinese Christian community worldwide is the construction of a practical and positive set of biblical and theological ideas for a biblical-based Chinese public theology.

Conclusion

This brief exploration of the Bible in the public square, has traced the movement in its historical development and reviewed the challenge of the Bible's presence in the public square to a complex Chinese society, whether it is over mainland China, Hong Kong, Macau, Taiwan, or the Chinese diaspora. As long as the Bible-believing community continues to exist in various walks of life and professions, given a glocal way of life, the Bible as the Christian and spiritual resource for humanity in the public square will continue to be a challenge both to that Bible-believing faith community and to Chinese civil society, as well as to the state authority that accommodates and resists it.

Notes

1. Daniel H. Bays, *A New History of Christianity in China* (Oxford and New York: Wiley-Blackwell, 2012), 19.
2. Kam-to Daniel Choi, *The Bible in China: With a Historical Catalogue of the Chinese Bible* [in Chinese] (Hong Kong: Institute of Sino-Christian Studies, 2018), 420–553.
3. Lewis S. Robinson, "The Bible in Twentieth-Century Fiction," in *Bible in Modern China: The Literary and Intellectual Impact*, ed. Irene Eber et al. (Sankt Augustin: Institut Monumenta Serica, 1999), 237–278. Also, Robinson's PhD dissertation at the University of California, Berkeley, 1982, entitled *Double-Edged Sword: Christianity and Twentieth-Century Chinese Fiction.*
4. Jean-Pierre Charbonnier, *Christians in China: AD 600 to 2000*, trans. M. N. L. Couve de Murville (San Francisco: Ignatius, 2002), chap. 15 "Catholic Faith and Confucian Rites: The Chinese Rites Controversy. Political Context and Religious Motivation," 246–270; Bays, *A New History of Christianity in China*, 28–32.
5. Ibid. 2.
6. Ibid. 121.
7. Ibid. 121–157. Contexts for post-1949 will be discussed in the last two sections before the conclusion.
8. As Daniel Bays puts it vividly, "Christianity was proscribed, categorized as a heterodox ideology, and officially forbidden to be practiced for about 120 years, from 1724 to the 1840s. This was almost the same number of years as from Matteo Ricci's establishing residence in Beijing in 1600 until Yongzheng's decree, during most of which time Christianity was legally or by practice sanctioned" (*A New History of Christianity in China*, 32).

9. Ibid. 121–157.
10. Charbonnier, *Christians in China*, 351.
11. Bays, *A New History of Christianity in China*, 68–69.
12. Ibid. 69; Charbonnier, *Christians in China*, 357.
13. Robinson, "The Bible in Twentieth-Century Fiction," 237–278; Robinson, *Double-Edged Sword*. Cf. Choi, *The Bible in China*, 569–595; *Gleaning in the Undiscovered Talent: Selections of the Protestant Bible in the Late Qing and Early Republic China* [in Chinese], ed. Chin Kenpa and Johnson Wu (Taipei: Olive Press, 2012); *Wan qing jidujian shushi wenxue xuan cui* [in Chinese] 晚清基督教叙事文學選粹 (Taipei: Olive Press, 2012).
14. Chin Kenpa, ed. *Collected Essays on the Public Theology of Chinese Christianity*, Vol. 1: *Social Thought* [in Chinese] (Hong Kong: CABSA, 2012); Chin Kenpa, ed. *Collected Essays on the Public Theology of Chinese Christianity*, Vol. 2: *Image of Jesus* [in Chinese] (Hong Kong: CABSA, 2012); Chin Kenpa, ed. *Collected Essays on the Public Theology of Chinese Christianity*, Vol. 3: *Christian Student Movement* [in Chinese] (Hong Kong: CABSA, 2015).
15. Charbonnier, *Christians in China*, 352.
16. Ibid. 353.
17. Ibid.
18. Ibid. 354.
19. Ibid. 359–360.
20. Alexander Chow, *Chinese Public Theology: Generational Shifts and Confucian Imagination in Chinese Christianity* (Oxford: Oxford University Press, 2018), 165. He argued further "that this Confucian imagination has offered a particular shape to certain forms of Chinese Christianity and, by extension, Chinese public theology," 130.
21. Ibid. 128.
22. Ibid. 165.
23. Sebastian Kim and Katie Day, *A Companion to Public Theology* (Netherlands: E. J. Brill, 2017).
24. See K. K. Yeo, "Theology and the Future of Global Christianity: Glocal and Public Theologies," in *Theology and the Future: Evangelical Assertions and Explorations*, ed. Trevor Cairney and David Starling (Edinburgh: T&T Clark, 2014), 45–61; Xie Zhibin, *How Public? Why Theological?: A Review and Prospect of Sino-Christian Public Theology* [in Chinese] (Occasional Paper Series No. 25; 8/2016; Hong Kong: Centre for the Study of Religion and Chinese Society, Chung Chi College, The Chinese University of Hong Kong, 2016).
25. Philip P. Chia, "Biblical Studies and Public Relevance: Hermeneutical and Pedagogical Consideration in Light of the Ethos of the Greater China Region (GCR)," in *Transforming Graduate Biblical Education: Ethos and Discipline*, ed. Elisabeth Schüssler Fiorenza and Kent Harold Richards (Atlanta: SBL, 2010), 93–107; Philip P. Chia, "Sino-Biblical Theology: Toward a Critical Sino-public Biblical Theology," in *Toward a Sino-Christian Biblical Studies*, ed. Jason Lam (Hong Kong: DaoFeng, 2010), 127–64; Philip P. Chia, "After Crossing: The Relevance of Public Culture to Biblical Interpretation," collected in *Essays in Honour of Professor Archie Lee*, ed. L. K. Lo (Hong Kong: Chung Chi Divinity School, 2010), 212–224; Philip P. Chia, "Biblical Studies in the Rising Asia: An Asian Perspective on the Future of the Biblical Past," in *The Future of the Biblical Past*, ed. Roland Boer and Fernando Segovia (Atlanta: SBL, 2012), 81–96; Philip P. Chia, "Occupy Central: Scribal Resistance in Daniel, the Long Road to Universal Suffrage," in *Interested Readers: Essays on the Hebrew Bible in Honor of David J. A. Clines*, ed. James K. Aitken, Jeremy M. S. Clines, and Christl M. Maier (Atlanta: SBL, 2013), 247–264.

26. See the attempt of K. K. Yeo in reading Isaiah, Amos, and Revelation in relation to the socio-political issues in China, *What Has Jerusalem to Do with Beijing? Biblical Interpretation from a Chinese Perspective*, 20th anniversary edition (Eugene, OR: Pickwick, 2018), chaps. 5, 8, 9. Also, Alexander Chow, *Chinese Public Theology*; Lai Pan Chiu, *guang chang shang de han yu shen xue* [in Chinese] *Sino-Christian Theology's Public Square* (Hong Kong: Logos & Pneuma Press, Institute of Sino-Christian Studies Ltd, 2014).

Primary Sources

Chin, Ken Pa 曾慶豹, ed. *Collected Essays on the Public Theology of Chinese Christianity*, Vol. 1: *Social Thought* [in Chinese] 中國基督教公共神學文選 (一): 社會思想. Hong Kong: CABSA, 2012.

Chin, Ken Pa, ed. *Collected Essays on the Public Theology of Chinese Christianity*, Vol. 2: *Image of Jesus* [in Chinese] 中國基督教公共神學文選 (二): 耶穌形象篇. Hong Kong: CABSA, 2012.

Chin, Ken Pa, ed. *Collected Essays on the Public Theology of Chinese Christianity*, Vol. III: *Christian Student Movement* [in Chinese] 中國基督教公共神學文選 (三): 學生運動篇. Hong Kong: CABSA, 2015.

Kim, Sebastian and Katie Day. *A Companion to Public Theology*. Netherlands: E. J. Brill, 2017.

CHAPTER 38

THE BIBLE AND ETHICS IN CHINESE SOCIETY

BERNARD K. WONG AND SONG JUN

INTRODUCTION

THE question this chapter attempts to answer is: How do Chinese Christians read the Bible for ethics? Several assumptions and clarifications must be explicated. First, the interest is in how Chinese Christians read the Bible in the ecclesial setting. Thus, the comparison of the Bible with Chinese classics, or juxtaposing biblical ethics with indigenous Chinese ethics, is not the focus. Second, the assumption is that there is a certain "Chinese" way of reading the Bible. It is widely accepted that there is no universal, objective way to interpret a text. All readers bring with them, in Gadamer's words, a "fore-structure" in their interpretation. Understanding of the text is a "fusion of horizons" between the interpreter's fore-structure and the world of the text.[1] The "Chinese" way of reading involves a "fore-structure" that is common to Chinese Christians. Analysis shows that they demonstrate a pattern of interpretation that corresponds to Confucian ideologies. The task is thus to explicate how Confucianism influences Chinese Christians in their appropriation of the Bible for ethics. Third, it must be asserted, on the other hand, that there is not a single Chinese way to read the Bible. Every interpreter is located in a particular context with specific concerns and is influenced by different theological traditions. Therefore, no single interpreter can represent the whole tradition, nor should we reduce all Chinese interpreters to a few types. Hence, the essay adopts Jeffrey Siker's method in his *Scripture and Ethics: Twentieth-Century Portraits* by selecting several representative figures and analyzing "each author's writings and then see how the Bible is used within the context of each author's larger constructive theology and ethics."[2] Then, it attempts to locate a common way of interpretation among them and to see whether a trend can be discerned. Fourth, this essay only serves as an introduction to the subject; performing an exhaustive analysis that includes all significant voices is not the purpose. Texts from earlier Christian entrances into China—during the Tang dynasty (seventh century) and Yuan dynasty (thirteenth century)—are excluded, for they have little impact on Christianity in China today. Only Christians in the Protestant tradition are included as they represent the majority of the Christian population in China. Analysis starts from the first Protestant Chinese pastor, Liang Fa 梁發, in the early nineteenth century. Articles published in *The News of Churches* 教會新報 in the late nineteenth century are then examined. Moving into the early twentieth century, the writings of Jia Yuming 賈玉銘, Zhao Zichen 趙紫宸, and Wu Yaozong 吳耀宗 are discussed. The analysis ends at Ding Guangxun 丁光訓 and Wang Weifan 汪維藩, who were still writing in the early twenty-first century. The essay first outlines the theological tradition and social context of each, followed by a discussion, by looking at some examples, about how each writer interprets the Bible for ethics. Although the figures covered represent different theological traditions, all of them served in mainland China, where the majority of Chinese Christians are located. It is important to acknowledge that no women interpreter has been included. The reason is that influential leaders in the Chinese church have been primarily made up to the time of writing, and we hope the situation will change in the future. Finally, the essay concludes by describing several factors that influence how Chinese Christians appropriate the Bible for ethics.

Confucian Ethics

Confucianism was the dominant ideology in China when Christianity entered in the late Qing dynasty. It is appropriate to begin by offering a brief outline of Confucian ethics. The source of knowledge and human morality, for Confucianism, is "heaven" (*tian* 天). The aim of a human person is to know and attain union with this heaven (*tian-ren heyi* 天人合一). Mencius 孟子 says:

> He who has exhausted all his mental constitution knows his nature. Knowing his nature, he knows Heaven. To preserve one's mental constitution, and nourish one's nature, is the way to Heaven.... the cultivation of his personal character... is the way in which he establishes his Heaven-ordained being.[3]

It is through knowing and nourishing one's nature and "cultivating one's personal character" (*xiushen* 修身) that a person knows and finds union with heaven.[4] Ethics is thus not the acceptance of a set of external rules but the cultivation of what lies within one's own nature. But this "nature" that one finds within also must be expressed outward, and the "extension of oneself toward others" (*tuiji jiren* 推己及人) is the basis of Confucian interpersonal ethics.[5] Confucius' saying, "Do not do to others what you would not want others to do to you"[6] exemplifies such a notion. Norms for different spheres of relationships—between king and subjects, father and children, husband and wife, and among siblings and friends—are developed, enabling people to live together in harmony. Although Confucian ethics begins from the personal, an individual is considered subservient under the common good. As such, the largest sphere—one's country—has precedence over the smaller spheres.[7]

To summarize: "knowing one's nature" is the source of Confucian ethics, and the "cultivating of one's personal character" is the practice of ethics. "Cultivating one's personal character" entails the "extension of oneself" toward the larger spheres in concrete ways. The collective and communal is emphasized over the individual in a hierarchical relational structure. A person should begin from the self then extend outward, aiming at the largest sphere of the world:

> The ancients who wished to illustrate illustrious virtue throughout the [world], first ordered well their own States. Wishing to order well their States, they first regulated their families. Wishing to regulate their families, they first cultivated their persons. Wishing to cultivate their persons, they first rectify their hearts. Wishing to rectify their hearts, they first sought to be sincere in their thoughts. Wishing to be sincere in their thoughts, they first extended to the utmost their knowledge. Such extension of knowledge lay in the investigation of things.[8]

In the individual dimension, a person should begin from "investigation of things" and walk step by step toward "cultivating one's person." When expressed outwardly, this ethics finally brings about the right government of states and peaceful society.[9] A staged process of "investigating things [*gewu* 格物], extending knowledge [*zhizhi* 致知], being sincere in thoughts [*zhengxin* 正心], rectifying their hearts [*chengyi* 誠意], cultivating their persons [*xiushen* 修身], regulating their families [*qijia* 齊家], ordering their States [*zhiguo* 治國], and making the world peaceful [*pingtianxia* 平天下]" is the path to a virtuous life. In short, the phrase, "inner sageliness and outer kingliness" (*neisheng waiwang* 内聖外王) captures this ideal.

However, a person needs an optimal environment in order to achieve the ultimate aim of making the world peaceful. When conditions are favorable, the cultivation of one's person can be congruent with one's actions in the public. But under unfavorable situations, a person may only be able to strive for personal virtue:

> If poor, [the men of antiquity] attended to their own virtue in solitude; if advanced to dignity, they made the whole [world] virtuous as well.[10]

Therefore, Confucian ethics is pragmatic; inner sageliness must be expressed outwardly as kingliness for the benefit of society. Yet pragmatism also means that when circumstances do not allow, a person is justified to withdraw from the public into the private pursuit of sageliness.

With this outline of Confucian ethics, it is now possible to analyze how representative Chinese church leaders and theologians appropriate the Bible for ethics.

Liang Fa (1789–1855)

Liang Fa was the second Protestant Chinese convert and the first Chinese pastor. Ethics is significant in his understanding of Christianity and the Bible. The sign of being a Christian, for Liang, is to do good whole-heartedly. The Bible is "a good book that exhorts people away from evil for doing good work."[11] He suffered persecution and believed that moral improvement was the best way for Christians to defend themselves against attacks from nonbelievers.[12] Besides, Christianity and Confucianism are compatible in terms of ethics: "The principles of Confucianism—benevolence, justice, courtesy, wisdom—are good and exemplary. They are... compatible with the Truth that saves the world."[13] This same strategy of using morality to bring Christianity into China had been adopted during the first Christian entry in the Tang dynasty, as well as subsequent entries during the Ming and Qing dynasties.[14]

Hence, Liang uses the Bible mainly for moral exhortation, which also supports his apologetic strategy. For instance, in his sermon on 1 Thess 5:21–22, he interprets Paul's admonition "to test everything" to mean "to discern good and evil," so that a person should become prudent or "moderate" (*zhongyong* 中庸),[15] an important Confucian virtue. The ability to "discern good and evil" is the virtue of wisdom (*zhi* 智), one of the five principles of Confucian ethics.[16] Then Liang exercises this wisdom and says that the highest "true good" is the love of God and neighbors, and the second highest one is respecting your parents—filial piety—and loving your family, followed by truthfulness and propriety.[17] These goods align with the first Confucian principle of ethics—benevolence (*ren* 仁), which teaches that a benevolent person should love others, beginning with the family.[18]

Liang's sermon on 1 Cor 4:20 is based on the Chinese Bible translated by Morrison. The last word of the verse, "For the Kingdom of God depends not on talk but on *power*" (NRSV), was mistranslated into "*morality* [*de* 德]" so he thought Paul was saying: "the kingdom of God depends not on talk but on *morality*." Then he interprets the verse to mean that as "heaven"—kingdom of God—is holy and without sin, only blameless people can enter. He further says that, while it is true that a believer is cleansed by Christ's blood, it is by obeying God's decrees and doing good works throughout her life that she will be granted "joy in heaven."[19] Although Morrison's mistranslation contributes to Liang's interpretation, Liang also disregards the context of the verse, for the "kingdom of God" could not have meant the "heaven" that one enters after death. Besides, Paul is not teaching morality in that pericope. This example demonstrates Liang's neglect of context in his biblical interpretation, as well as his tendency to read morality into the Bible. Perhaps it is importunate to expect our first Chinese pastor to follow today's hermeneutical principles. Yet it is notable that Liang's biblical interpretation aligns with the Confucian hermeneutical tradition. Sze-Kar Wan points out that in Confucianism, hermeneutics of classical text has morality as its purpose: "The hermeneutical task... was not how one could understand the thought of the original author.... The question, instead, was how one could become moral.... Exegesis was designed to induce, to provoke, to stimulate readers to moral action."[20] Though a Christian pastor, Liang's biblical interpretation is deeply shaped by the Confucian tradition.

The News of Churches

Liang ministered in China in the early nineteenth century, when Christianity was officially banned by the Qing government. When the ban was lifted after the Opium Wars in the 1840s, Western missionaries were able to evangelize in China more freely. But the same war prompted many Chinese nationals to consider Christianity a part of Western aggression. Thus, Chinese Christians had to defend their faith, and the main strategy was to demonstrate the compatibility of Christianity and Confucianism in terms of ethics.[21] Examples are found in the publication *The News of Churches*, launched by the American Missionary Young John Allen 林樂知 in 1868. For instance, one writer explains that the Confucian teaching, "Do not do to others what you would not want others to do to you," though different in wording, is identical in meaning to "Do to others as you would have them do to you" in Matt 7:12.[22] Another writer argues that the Confucian five principles of morality (*wulun* 五倫)—applicable to five different kinds of relationship—all can be found in the Bible.[23] In the same vein, the Confucian "three prohibitions of a noble person" (*junzi sanjie* 君子三戒)—against lust, violence, and greed—all find correspondence in the Ten Commandments.[24] Besides, poems expounding on the Ten Commandments were composed[25] and Jesus' Two Greatest Commandments of love were discussed for moral teaching.[26] In these poems and discussions, Confucian terminology and concepts often were employed.

Jia Yuming (1880–1964)

The Chinese church grew rapidly in the late nineteenth and early twentieth centuries. Western missionaries established schools as a means to evangelize. Jia Yuming was educated at such schools and was formed theologically in the fundamentalist tradition while he pursued a life of prayer and spirituality. He became a pastor and later taught at several seminaries and founded a school of Christian spirituality.[27] In his *Systematic Theology* (*Shendaoxue* 神道學), he avers that Christians should aim at experiencing the abundant life of God through a three-stage process: from "life," through "abundant life," to "perfect salvation" (*wanquan dejiu* 完全得救). Christians who have arrived at the final goal are "Christ-people whose persons are infused with the Logos."[28] Similarly, Jia argues that there are three stages of sanctification, from sanctification in status, through sanctification in living, to total sanctification.[29] This approach to ethics shares many characteristics with the Confucian tradition. It is the cultivation of the person, not the discernment of right and wrong or the conforming to rules, that is the gist of ethics. Jia's staged process bears similarity with the Confucian step-by-step pursuit toward "cultivating one's personal character." The Christian notion of turning from the old self to become Christ-people is, again, not unlike the Confucian notion of "union with heaven."

Within this ethical framework, Jia interprets the Pauline epistles not for their theological contents but to promote a path of spiritual progress. In *Perfect Salvation*, Jia uses Romans to construct a spiritual journey of the author. The epistle, he suggests, begins with the "old Paul" who obeyed the law and lived in sin (chaps. 2 and 3). This "old Paul" journeyed on to become the "new Paul" who was justified by faith (3:20 to chap. 5), through "Saint Paul" who struggled with sins, died, and was resurrected with Christ (chaps. 6 to 8), and finally became the "great Paul" who loved his compatriots and preached to the Gentiles to the extent that he was willing to give up his life (chaps. 9 to 16).[30] Underlying Paul's spiritual journey was a transformation of the self. First, the "egoist self" (*ziwo* 自我) must be given up. Next, with Christ living within and the old self gone, the person becomes a "true self" (*zhenwo* 真我). The next stage is "lamb-self" (*yangwo* 羊我), meaning the sanctification of the self. Finally, the person becomes the "great self" (*dawo* 大我), to live and die together with Christ, offering oneself as a sacrifice for others. Practically, it means serving "the least of these brothers."[31] Note that the final destination of Paul's journey—to become the "great Paul" and the "great self"—advocates an ethical ideal of benefiting others through self-giving. The Confucian notions of "extending oneself toward others" and "inner sageliness and outer kingliness" are evident.

Trained in the fundamentalist tradition and influenced by dispensationalism, Jia sees little reason for active Christian participation in the political sphere so his "outer kingliness" falls short of the Confucian ideal of "peaceful world."[32] When interpreting Phil 4:8–9, Jia says that the relationship between the "inner man" and the "outer man" is that of consistency: we should practice what we think and believe.[33] This practice does not necessarily have any political purpose. When commenting on Rom 13, Jia affirms that although Christians are citizens of their earthly nations, their core identity is always citizens of God's kingdom. Only personal morality—honesty, trustworthiness, charity, diligence—are mentioned. As the world is dark, Christians should stay alert, avoid evil, and pursue things spiritual.[34] Pietism and an otherworldly tendency is apparent in Jia's biblical interpretation.

Zhao Zichen (T. C. Chao) (1888–1979)

The early twentieth century was a time of turmoil for China, and the general sentiment among intellectuals was to seek a way to save the nation and rebuild the Chinese culture. While Jia's passion for spirituality and his fundamentalist theology steered him away from speaking much on social and political issues, his contemporary, Zhao Zichen, was much more concerned about them. Although his theology shifted from the liberal tradition to a more conservative outlook after being captured and imprisoned during the Sino-Japanese War, the theme of "national salvation by character" (*renge jiuguo* 人格救國)

remains dominant throughout. In 1948, when China was facing the crises of social chaos and civil war, Zhao avers that "the totality of all problems in China is a moral problem," and the only solution is Christian ethics.[35] Although Confucianism also emphasizes morality, its reliance on the goodness of human nature and the lack of a transcendent dimension renders its ethics ineffective in changing human behavior. The Christian doctrine of sin and external salvation can remedy this shortfall. The aim of ethics, for Zhao, is to attain the "supreme good" (*zhishan* 至善):

> What is the supreme good?...Towards God: to do God's will...towards the self: to build up one's human character[36] [*renge* 人格] to the full statute of Christ, to become a human being that God wills...towards the whole world: to make peace, to build God's kingdom, to demonstrate God's love and justice.[37]

This expression reveals a resemblance with the Confucian notion of "cultivating one's personal character" then "extending oneself toward others" to arrive at the goal of "making the world peaceful."

How does a person build up her "human character" and obtain this "supreme good" of building "God's kingdom"? Zhao quotes the first Beatitude ("Blessed are the poor in spirit, for theirs is the kingdom of heaven") and argues that the feeling of "poor in spirit" prompts a person to embark on a journey toward "God's kingdom." The journey is full of hardship and persecution; thus, the last Beatitude is "Blessed are those who are persecuted for righteousness' sake."[38] This interpretation is an abridged version of his earlier exposition of the eight Beatitudes, where they are treated as steps toward building up "human character." The first half is about cultivating the individual person, and the second half is on living with others in society. The inner qualities that the first four Beatitudes encourage include the feeling of dissatisfaction, a mournful heart for social evil, humility, and a thirst for righteousness. The fifth to seventh Beatitudes concern how one should live in society: forgiving others to foster justice, living in right human relationships, and making peace. The last Beatitude warns of hardship along the journey, but also promises a great reward: hope and future for the nation and the world.[39] Therefore, Zhao adapts the Bible into his aim of "national salvation through character," and his ethics fall within the Confucian framework of "inner sageliness and outer kingliness." As social transformation is his concern, the "human character" that he encourages is not Jia's charity, honesty, and trustworthiness, but justice and right relationships in society, or "making the world peaceful" in Confucian terms.

Wu Yaozong (Y. T. Wu) (1893–1979)

While Zhao championed the contribution of Christianity to save the Chinese nation, his contemporary, Wu Yaozong, went further by selecting elements in Christianity that fitted his overall agenda of national salvation. In his autobiography, he recounts two major shifts in his thinking.[40] Before accepting Christ, he was burdened by the suffering of the world, but at the same time discouraged by the sheer scale of the problem and his own frailty. The first major shift happened in 1917, when he first read the Sermon on the Mount. It was Jesus as a human person—not as God—that attracted him. Jesus' examples and teachings motivated him to holy living, giving him hope that the ideal world could be realized.[41] Being Jesus' disciple, for Wu, meant having one's "human character" (*renge* 人格) "Christianized."[42] The second shift happened during the Anti-Christian Movement in the 1920s, where he struggled with the accusation that religions were the "opium of the people." He came to embrace dialectical materialism, an ideology that was gaining popularity at the time. Although materialism was against religion, he developed a synthesis of the two by gleaning useful elements from each.[43] The resulting synthesis rejects the supernatural dimension of Christianity. Jesus' teaching about God providing for the birds of the air and lilies of the field, Wu argues, means that humans should believe that through mutual trust and effort, everyone will have enough to eat. "Men do not live by bread alone" means that human beings essentially are social and dependent on society. In the hostile world, the powerless may be robbed of their basic needs. That is why Jesus stands in solidarity with the poor, to incite the vision of mutual help and sharing whereby everyone's needs can be satisfied.[44]

In the 1940s, Wu embraced socialism even more, claiming that Jesus was a "social revolutionary," transforming how people assign human worth.[45] He interprets Jesus' "feeding of the five thousand" not as a supernatural miracle but a "great moral teaching and a way to social reform."[46] Among those who followed Jesus into the wilderness, Wu explains, many had brought food but were too selfish to share with others. What Jesus did was to ask his disciples to share what they had, thereby setting a good example for others to follow, so everyone ended up having enough to eat. Wu interprets the parable of the laborers in the vineyard (Matt 20:1–16) also in a socialist way. The "landowner" in the parable is not an "employer" in the capitalist system but "the whole society," for "people are their own masters." Therefore, the parable teaches that "everyone should contribute whatever she could and take whatever she needed." How much a person contributes and how much she takes do not need to be equal, so the capitalist notion of equal exchange is rejected.[47] As capitalism was alleged to have colluded with Western imperialism at the time, this interpretation divorces the Bible from this ideology. Wu ends his exposition with: "The world is changing, and the power to change is in the people's hand."[48] The Bible is interpreted to support the Marxist proletariat revolution. But he is still in the tradition of "national salvation by character," for it is not merely political change but also the people's willingness to contribute and share that makes social transformation possible.

Ding Guangxun (K. H. Ting) (1915–2012)

Wu became the first chairperson of the National Committee of the Three-Self Patriotic Movement, an organization that regulates the official Chinese church after the

Communists took government in 1949. His successor, Ding Guangxun, carried out in 1996 a theological reconstruction following President Jiang Zemin's appeal that all religious groups should "reform any religious system or doctrine that is incompatible with socialism."[49] Ding claimed that as the church and even the biblical authors themselves reconstructed their theologies continually, such exercise in his time was justified and would even benefit both the nation and the church. Except for "basic doctrines," such as the Trinity, Christ's incarnation, death, and resurrection, all other doctrines can and should be reviewed in the changing context.[50] The context, for Ding, was that the Communist Party was much more effective than Christians in eradicating moral evil: "While Christians have been proclaiming against opium and prostitution for a century without success, these ills were wiped clean within months after the New China was established." Therefore, Christians must rethink "the division between believers and nonbelievers," and the doctrine of salvation should be reconstructed.[51] Specifically, the doctrine of justification by faith should be "played down."[52] Ding uses Jesus' teaching in Matt 25:31–46 (the sheep and the goat) to argue that God will judge a person based solely on how she treats her neighbors and not because of her faith. Therefore, Christians should not claim that morally good nonbelievers, such as atheist Communists, will be condemned to hell.[53] In this regard, Ding's view in fact goes further than "national salvation by character": a person's salvation also depends on her moral behavior.

This theological reconstruction governs how Ding interprets the Bible. He accentuates Scriptures that portray God as love to counter the understanding of God as an authoritative and condemning sovereign that is popular among Chinese Christians.[54] Biblical passages that describe a loving God, such as the prodigal son, the lost sheep (Luke 15), and Jesus' weeping for his friend (John 11:33–35) and for Jerusalem (Luke 19:41) are considered normative to define God's essence as love. God and Abraham's discussions on Sodom (Gen 18:20–35) are interpreted as affirming God's love and mercy for all people while the narrative about the subsequent retribution on the city is ignored. For passages that narrate God's anger and judgment, Ding opines that they were recorded due to the biblical authors' misunderstanding about God. God's revelation is progressive, he avers, and human understanding of God finally arrives at "God is love" (1 John 4:16) as the apex. If God is love, then God is always benevolent. Christians should not suggest that natural disasters and human evil are the "signs of end time" so as to undermine the efforts to building up the church and the nation.[55]

Ding's biblical interpretation serves to support his theological reconstruction, while reading an ethic out of the Bible is not his main concern. Yet an ethic of love, defined as not condemning others, serving one's neighbors, and active construction of church and the socialist nation, results. For instance, Ding's sermon on "feeding of the five thousand" exhorts Christians to care for all people, including nonbelievers, to work for social structures that can produce and distribute food to all, and to live in harmony with one another.[56] This ethic, nonetheless, would render Christianity "compatible with socialism."

WANG WEIFAN (1927–2015)

While Ding was educated in the more liberal Anglican tradition, his colleague at the Nanjing Union Theological Seminary, Wang Weifan, was nurtured in the evangelical faith. He held onto this tradition all through his active engagement with the Three-Self Patriotic Movement and Ding's theological reconstruction.[57] Wang is well-versed in Chinese classics, and his theology and biblical interpretation are infused with concepts and maxims familiar to the Chinese. Yet he asserts that it is the Bible, not any Chinese tradition, that is the "source, foundation, and basis" of Christian theology. While people of all cultures can know God through the Bible, the Chinese culture, for Wang, is blessed with a holistic and integrated way of thinking that helps the Chinese understand Christianity in ways unlike that of the West. The Chinese culture avoids Western dualisms and is better able to handle the issues of "love of God and love of neighbors," "spirituality and service," and "faith and work." Besides, the Chinese way of thinking integrates knowledge with practice, resulting not in mere pragmatism, but a holistic practice that originates from a person's inner being. Chinese Christians also emphasize one's own spirituality, affection toward one's family and country, and reliance upon one's church community while not rejecting rationality and logical thinking.[58] Wang formulates a biblical interpretation method of "in between East and West," that is, using the Chinese way of thinking while not abandoning valuable traditions from the West to come up with results that are different from those of the West.[59]

In an essay that discusses the meaning of the phrase, "the one who is righteous will live by faith," which appears in four different places of the Bible, Wang refers to Gal 5:6—"faith working through love"—to argue that "faith" is not merely cognitive but must be integrated with practice. While this interpretation is not unique, Wang adds that this holistic view of "faith" is consistent with the Chinese mode of thinking that unites knowledge and practice, nature and action, and inner and outer. He then argues that those obtaining God's "righteousness" should walk a life-journey "from faith to faith" (Rom 1:17), that is, to grow spiritually. Quoting the Confucian text, "righteousness is the accordance of actions with what is right" (*yizhe, yiye* 義者，宜也),[60] and Mozi's 墨子 saying, "righteousness is benevolence" (*yi, liye* 義，利也), Wang says that in the Chinese context, "the one who is righteous will live by faith" should be interpreted to mean: "A person saved and justified by God, reconciled with God into proper relationship, must by faith maintain this relationship and lead a life of righteousness through actions, benefitting others, and emulating Christ."[61] Here, Wang merges Confucian concepts with Western hermeneutical methods to come up with interpretations that the Chinese can appreciate easily. Finally, he exhorts his readers to live like Christ, sacrificing oneself for others, for the church, and for the nation.[62] The Confucian ethical approach of "cultivating one's character," "extension of oneself toward others," and "inner sageliness and outer kingliness" is again apparent. Wang's interpretation of this biblical phrase pregnant with theology does not rest on the clarification of doctrine; the formation of

Christians from inner being to outward actions is his ultimate goal. It is the Chinese way of integrating knowledge with practice that informs this hermeneutic.

The above example shows that Wang uses traditional Chinese sayings and concepts to help Chinese Christians understand the Bible. Another example involves his interpretation of Paul's saying in Acts 26:19—"I was not disobedient to the heavenly vision." "Disobedient," he points out, can mean "disloyal" and "rebellious," the opposite of filial piety (*xiao* 孝) extolled in Chinese culture. After quoting Confucius, "filial piety is the foundation of morality" (*fuxiao, de zhibenye* 夫孝, 德之本也), Wang argues that if showing filial piety toward one's parents was deemed essential, how much more must Christians obey God.[63] Although "filial piety" may not be identical with "obedient," Wang's interpretation can easily resonate with Chinese readers. Yet Wang sometimes goes too far in using Confucian concepts. The word translated into "act like men" (NASB) in 1 Cor 16:13 should mean "be courageous." But Wang imports much more meaning into the word by quoting a famous Confucian text that expounds on "being a man" (*dazhangfu* 大丈夫), causing over-interpretation of the Bible.[64]

Conclusions

The above analysis reveals three main factors that influence how Chinese Christians read the Bible for ethics, described as follows.

Confucianism

All interpreters examined in this essay are influenced by Confucianism, though in different ways and to varying degrees. Two main areas of influence are identified. First, interpreters of classical Confucian text have morality as their hermeneutical purpose, and right behavior is important in this tradition. These biblical interpreters also demonstrate such hermeneutical purpose: from Liang of the nascent Chinese church underscoring the ethical function of Christianity, through Jia embracing a spirituality of "cultivating the person," to the twentieth-century theologians advocating "national salvation by character." Second, the interpreters adopt the Confucian motto, "inner sageliness and outer kingliness," as the framework for ethics. They believe that good behavior flows from a person's inner being, and the cultivation of personal character is the common theme of their ethics. Persons of excellent moral character, such as Jesus or Paul, often are revered as models for Christians to emulate. With the exception of Wu, who interprets the Bible to support a social-political ideal, others tend to assume that national crises can be solved by improving personal morality. Nevertheless, Wu also thinks that moral behaviors are essential for the social system he advocates.

Social and Historical Context

Although all the interpreters are influenced by Confucianism, which Confucian elements they use and how they use them vary according to their social and historical contexts. When Christianity was considered part of Western aggression, the Bible often was compared with Confucian classics to demonstrate that it agrees with Confucian ideals, frequently by means of ethics. In the early twentieth century, concerns over the crumbling nation prompted Christian intellectuals to pursue the path of "national salvation by character." All the interpreters follow the Confucian framework of "inner sageliness and outer kingliness" in their approach to ethics, and the differences lie in how they understand "outer kingliness." While Jia exhorts an "outer kingliness" of upright behavior when treating one's neighbors, Zhao and Wu believe that salvation of the Chinese nation depends on it.

Besides, the interpreters' social locations also influence their use of the Bible for ethics. As a socialist and a Christian, Wu attempted to harmonize the two. He also severed Christianity from Western ideologies to ensure that the official church would survive under Communist rule. Ding's task as the leader of the official church was to resolve the tension between the ruling party and Christianity; thus, he reconstructed the doctrine of justification by faith to render Christianity "compatible with socialism." Finally, Wang represents how Chinese Christians appropriate the Bible for ethics when national salvation is no longer a burning issue nor Christianity considered an alien religion. The Bible, not Confucian values, becomes the source of ethics while Confucian concepts and languages are used to help the Chinese understand the Christian faith and the ethics that ensue. Yet one can argue that his theology was influenced by his social location as a faculty member of an official seminary: by claiming that Christianity is compatible with the Chinese culture and that the Bible can promote public morality, his theology also aligns with the agenda of the government.[65]

Theological and Intellectual Tradition

A person's theological and intellectual tradition strongly influences how she reads the Bible. We can distinguish our interpreters along the line of liberal versus fundamentalist/evangelical traditions. On the liberal side are Wu and Ding, who tend to apply biblical teachings in the social and political spheres. Socialism exerts strong influences on Wu's theology, while Ding follows his Anglican tradition to bridge Christianity and the socio-political sphere.[66] They also place less emphasis on traditional doctrines and the authority of the Bible. On the other hand, Jia and Wang represent the fundamentalist/evangelical tradition. Jia is passionate about spirituality and describes moral pursuit as a journey that aims at becoming "Christ-people" while saying little about the political sphere. Wang's evangelical background caused him to hold high esteem for the Bible and traditional doctrines when developing his "in between East and West" method of interpretation. Zhao's theological tradition is more difficult to classify, for he shifted from the liberal tradition toward the more conservative side. Yet as an intellectual, he always advocates the Christian contribution to society.

A related factor is the educational background of these interpreters. Zhao, Wu, and Ding received higher education in theology in the West.[67] This may have contributed to the more liberal outlook of their theology. Jia did not study abroad but received a Western education at schools run by missionaries of the fundamentalist tradition. Liang and Wang never received a Western education, nor did they obtain any higher degree within China. Yet their deep knowledge about Chinese classics shapes how they interpret the Bible.

To conclude, social and historical contexts, as well as theological and intellectual traditions, affect how these interpreters read the Bible. What is common among them is the influence of Confucianism in their appropriation of the Bible for ethics. The Bible is God's revelation for the world, a revelation that can be received into all cultures. Confucianism, with its classical texts, thinking pattern, and ethical framework, will continue to shape how Chinese Christians read the Bible for ethics. Perhaps this Chinese way of reading will even inspire Christians of other cultures in their own hermeneutics of the sacred text.

Notes

1. Hans-Georg Gadamer, *Truth and Method*, trans. Joel Weinsheimer and Donald G. Marshall, 2nd ed. (New York: Continuum, 1989), 268–306.
2. Jeffrey S. Siker, *Scripture and Ethics: Twentieth-Century Portraits* (Oxford: Oxford University Press, 1997), 6.
3. Mencius, "Tsin Sin" part 1 [in Chinese] 盡心一, trans. James Legge, *The Chinese Classics, with a Translation, Critical and Exegetical Notes, Prolegomena, and Copious Indexes*, Vol. 2: *The Works of Mencius*, 3rd ed. (Hong Kong: Hong Kong University Press, 1960), 448–449.
4. Tang Kailin 唐凱麟 and Zhang Huaicheng 張懷承, *Becoming Human and Becoming Sage: The Essence of Confucian Ethics* [in Chinese] 成人與成聖—儒家倫理道德精粹 (Changsha: Hunan University Publishing, 1999), 49–51.
5. Tang and Zhang, *Becoming Human and Becoming Sage*, 62–63.
6. Confucius, "Yan Yuan" [in Chinese] 顏淵, trans. Lao An, *Translations of Confucian Classics: The Analects of Confucius* (Shandong: Shandong Friendship Press, 1992), 169.
7. Tang and Zhang, *Becoming Human and Becoming Sage*, 74.
8. Confucius, "The Great Learning" [in Chinese] 大學, trans. James Legge, *The Chinese Classics, with a Translation, Critical and Exegetical Notes, Prolegomena, and Copious Indexes* (Hong Kong: Hong Kong University Press, 1960), 1:357–358.
9. Tang and Zhang, *Becoming Human and Becoming Sage*, 87.
10. Mencius, "Tsin Sin," part 1, 453.
11. Liang Fa, *Good Words to Exhort the World* [in Chinese], from the Harvard University Collection 《勸世良言》美國哈佛大學藏本 (Taipei: Taiwan Student Publishing, 1965), 302–305.
12. Ibid. 311–312.
13. Ibid. 136.

14. Yang Huilin, *China, Christianity, and the Question of Culture* (Waco: Baylor University Press, 2014), 47–49.
15. Liang, *Good Words to Exhort the World*, 399.
16. Tang and Zhang, *Becoming Human and Becoming Sage*, 192.
17. Liang, *Good Words to Exhort the World*, 400–401.
18. Tang and Zhang, *Becoming Human and Becoming Sage*, 168–170.
19. Liang, *Good Words to Exhort the World*, 247–249.
20. Wan Sze-Kar, "Competing Tensions: A Search for May Fourth Biblical Hermeneutics," in *Reading Scriptures in China*, ed. Chloë Starr (London: T&T Clark, 2008), 114.
21. Yang, *China, Christianity, and the Question of Culture*, 50–52.
22. Author unknown, "Asking about the Jesus Religion: Zhongyong of Confucianism is Compatible with the Jesus Religion" [in Chinese] 耶穌教或問：儒教中庸與耶穌教同, in *The News of Churches*, ed. Young John Allen (Taipei: Taiwan Huawen Publishing, 1968), 2:839–840.
23. Author unknown, "Clarification of Christian Doctrines" [in Chinese] 消變明教論, in *The News of Churches*, 2:613–614.
24. "Clarification of Christian Doctrines," 641–647.
25. *The News of Churches*, 1:386, 406–407; 2:633.
26. Ibid. 2:573, 593–594.
27. Xie Longyi 謝龍邑, *Man of Christ: Spiritual Theology of Jia Yuming* [in Chinese] 基督人—賈玉銘的靈修神學 (Taipei: China Evangelical Seminary Press, 2008), 44–56.
28. Jia Yuming, *Systematic Theology* [in Chinese] 神道學 (Taipei: Youth for Christ Publishing, 1971), 423–425.
29. Jia, *Systematic Theology*, 501–504.
30. Jia Yuming, *Perfect Salvation* [in Chinese] 完全救法 (Hong Kong: Bellman House Publishers, 1987), 261–265.
31. Ibid. 276–280.
32. Wan, "Competing Tensions," 103.
33. Jia Yuming, *Commentary on Philippians* [in Chinese] 腓立比講義 (Zhongli: Christian Tian Ren Publishing, 1968), 81–83.
34. Jia Yuming, *Commentary on Romans* [in Chinese] 羅馬新講義 (Hong Kong: The Bellman House, 1970), 203–210.
35. Zhao Zichen, "Christian Ethics" [in Chinese] 基督教倫理, in *Works of T. C. Chao* (Beijing: The Commercial Press, 2003), 2:495–496.
36. Depending on context, "人格" can be translated as "human character" or "human personhood."
37. Zhao, "Christian Ethics," 504.
38. Ibid. 505.
39. Zhao Zichen, "Jesus' Philosophy on Being Human, 1: Doctrine of Human Personhood" [in Chinese] 耶穌的人生哲學之第一講—人格主義, in *Works of T. C. Chao*, 1:205–216.
40. Wu Yaozong, "Christianity and Materialism: A Christian's Confession" [in Chinese] 基督教與唯物論—一個基督徒的自白, *University Monthly* (July 1947). Quoted in *The Collected Works of Y. T. Wu* [in Chinese] 吳耀宗全集, vol. 3, book 2, ed. Ying Fuk-tsang (Hong Kong: Chinese University of Hong Kong, 2018), 184.
41. Wu Yaozong, "My Own Religious Experience" [in Chinese] 我個人的宗教經驗, *Life* 3.7–8 (April 1923). Quoted in *The Collected Works of Y. T. Wu*, 1:92–95.

42. Wu Yaozong, "Who Are Jesus' Disciples" [in Chinese] 誰是耶穌的門徒, *Truth Weekly* 1.9 (May 1923). Quoted in *The Collected Works of Y. T. Wu*, 1:104–105.
43. Wu, "Christianity and Materialism," 185–191.
44. Wu Yaozong, "The Jesus I Know" [in Chinese] 我所認識的耶穌, *Truth and Life* 3.11 (October 1928). Quoted in *The Collected Works of Y. T. Wu*, vol. 2, book 1, ed. Ying Fuk-tsang (Hong Kong: Chinese University of Hong Kong, 2017), 308–309.
45. Wu Yaozong, "The Jesus I Know" [in Chinese] 我所認識的耶穌, *Herald* 2.4 (1940). Quoted in *The Collected Works of Y. T. Wu*, vol. 2, book 1, 633.
46. Wu Yaozong, "Five Loaves and Two Fish: Christianity Speaks, part 5" [in Chinese] 五餅二魚—基督教講話之五, *Tian Feng* 17 (September 1945). Quoted in *The Collected Works of Y. T. Wu*, vol. 3, book 1, ed. Ying Fuk-tsang (Hong Kong: Chinese University of Hong Kong, 2018), 96.
47. Wu, "Five Loaves and Two Fish," 97–98.
48. Ibid. 101.
49. Ren Jie, *Religious Policy of the Chinese Communist Party* [in Chinese] 中國共產黨的宗教政策(Beijing: People Publishing House, 2007), 197–203.
50. Ding Guangxun, "The Inevitability and Imperative of Adjusting Theological Thinking" [in Chinese] 調整神學思想的難免和必然, *Tian Feng* (Mar 2000). Quoted in *On the Construction of Theological Thinking* [in Chinese] 論神學思想建設 (Shanghai: Three-Self Patriotic Movement, 2000), 37–38.
51. Ding Guangxun, "The Cosmic Christ" [in Chinese] 宇宙的基督, speech given at "Friends of the Chinese Church" 中國教會之友 gathering in England, July 1991. Quoted in *Collection of Bishop K. H. Ting's Essays* [in Chinese] 丁光訓文集, ed. Frances Fang (Hong Kong: Chinese Christian Literature Council, 1999), 92.
52. Fredik Fällman, "Hermeneutical Conflict? Reading the Bible in Contemporary China," in *Reading Scriptures in China*, ed. Chloë Starr (London: T&T Clark, 2008), 52.
53. Ding Guangxun, "On the Question that Christians Should Think Deeply: Ethics and Morality" [in Chinese] 談基督徒一個思想深處的問題, speech given at the Northeast Conference for Five Religions, 1996. Quoted in *Collection of Bishop K. H. Ting's Essays* [in Chinese], 293–295.
54. Ding Guangxun, "How Chinese Christians Read the Bible" [in Chinese] 中國基督徒怎樣看待聖經, speech given at the American Academy of Religion and Society of Biblical Literature in 1990. Quoted in *Collection of Bishop K. H. Ting's Essays*, 85.
55. Ding Guangxun, "What Kind of God to Believe In" [in Chinese] 信一位怎樣的上帝, *Nanjing Theological Review* (Aug 1999): 14–16.
56. Ding Guangxun, "Give Ye Them to Eat" [in Chinese] 你們給他們吃吧, sermon delivered in Toronto, November 1979. Quoted in *Nanjing Theological Review* (December 1995): 85–88.
57. Kevin Xiyi Yao 姚西伊, "Wang Weifan's Evangelical Thinking and His Influence on Theology of the Chinese Church" [in Chinese] 汪維藩的福音主義思想兼論其對當代中國教會神學之意義, in *A Watchman Vigilant in Spirit and Pure in Heart: The Study on the Thought and Ministry of Wang Weifan*, ed. Kevin Xiyi Yao and Song Jun (Hong Kong: Christian Study Centre on Chinese Religion and Culture, 2015), 6–7.
58. Wang Weifan, "Introduction," in *Walking Alone for Ten Years: Selected Works of Wang Wei-fan (1997–2007)* [in Chinese] 十年踽踽: 汪維藩文集 (1997–2007) (Hong Kong: Christian Study Centre on Chinese Religion and Culture, 2009), xiii–xiv.
59. Wang Weifan, "An Attempt to Construct a Chinese New Testament Hermeneutics" [in Chinese] 創建中國新約詮釋學之芻議, in *Walking Alone for Ten Years*, 162.

60. "Doctrine of the Mean" (中庸), trans. Legge, *The Chinese Classics*, 1:405.
61. Wang Weifan, "Interpretation of 'The One Who is Righteous Will Live by Faith' Using Semantic Analysis" [in Chinese] 按語義釋經學方法理解「惟義人因信得生」, in *Walking Alone for Ten Years*, 93–95.
62. Wang, "Interpretation of 'The One Who is Righteous Will Live by Faith,'" 96.
63. Wang Weifan, *Life and Vision of Paul* [in Chinese] 保羅的異象人生 (Nanling: Guangxi Three-Self Patriotic Movement, 2007), 5. See also Song Jun 宋軍, "An Analysis of Wang Weifan's Traditional Chinese Cultural Approach to Biblical Interpretation" [in Chinese] 試論汪維藩聖經注釋中的中國傳統文化進路, in *A Watchman Vigilant in Spirit and Pure in Heart: The Study on the Thought and Ministry of Wang Weifan*, 162.
64. Wang, *Life and Vision of Paul*, 75. See also Song, "An Analysis of Wang Weifan's Traditional Chinese Cultural Approach to Biblical Interpretation," 171.
65. Alexander Chow 曹榮錦, "Christian Intellectual Who Responds to the Spiritual Crisis of China" [in Chinese] 竭力應對中國精神危機的基督徒知識分子, in *A Watchman Vigilant in Spirit and Pure in Heart: The Study on the Thought and Ministry of Wang Weifan*, ed. Kevin Xiyi Yao and Song Jun (Hong Kong: Christian Study Centre on Chinese Religion and Culture, 2015), 203.
66. Chow, "Christian Intellectual Who Responds to the Spiritual Crisis of China," 189.
67. Zhao studied at Vanderbilt University in the United States, and both Wu and Ding studied at Union Theological Seminary in New York and Columbia University.

Primary Sources

All in Chinese:

Ding Guangxun 丁光訓. *Collection of Bishop K. H. Ting's Essays* 丁光訓文集. Edited by Frances Fang. Hong Kong: Chinese Christian Literature Council, 1999.

Jia Yuming 賈玉銘. *Commentary on Philippians* 腓立比講義. Zhongli: Christian Tian Ren Publishing, 1968.

Jia Yuming, *Commentary on Romans* 羅馬新講義. Hong Kong: The Bellman House, 1970.

Jia Yuming. *Systematic Theology* 神道學. Taipei: Youth for Christ Publishing, 1971.

Jia Yuming. *Perfect Salvation* 完全救法. Hong Kong: Bellman House Publishers, 1987.

Liang Fa 梁發. *Good Words to Exhort the World* 勸世良言, from the Harvard University Collection. Taipei: Taiwan Student Publishing, 1965.

The News of Churches 教會新報, in 6 vols. Edited by Young John Allen. Taipei: Taiwan Huawen Publishing, 1968.

Wang Weifan 汪維藩. *Walking Alone for Ten Years: Selected Works of Wang Wei-fan (1997–2007).* 十年踽踽: 汪維藩文集 (1997–2007). Hong Kong: Christian Study Centre on Chinese Religion and Culture, 2009.

Wu Yaozong 吳耀宗. *The Collected Works of Y. T. Wu* 吳耀宗全集. Edited by Ying Fuk-tsang. Hong Kong: Chinese University of Hong Kong, 2015.

Zhao Zichen 趙紫宸. *Works of T. C. Chao* 趙紫宸文集. Beijing: The Commercial Press, 2003.

CHAPTER 39

THE BIBLE IN CONTEMPORANEOUS STRUGGLES FOR BASIC LEGAL FREEDOMS

TERENCE C. HALLIDAY

INTRODUCTION

A disproportionate number of leading rights lawyers in China are Protestant Christians.[1] These *weiquan*[2] 維權 or notable activist lawyers[3] present a sociological puzzle. Why are Christians over-represented in the vanguard of rights lawyers?[4] What beliefs motivate these lawyers to practice what is a risky and often dangerous way to earn a living? More precisely, what are the biblical foundations on which Protestant Christian activist lawyers build not only their practices but also their vision of a renewed China?

This set of questions must be contextualized within an interdisciplinary scholarship on the conditions under which legal professions mobilize across time and place[5] for a liberal legal vision of political society that establishes and protects basic legal freedoms.[6] The discovery of an explicitly Christian leading edge for legal rights advocacy in China echoes findings from elsewhere.[7] Drawing on a substantial body of original research,[8] this chapter examines the biblical premises and understandings that motivate and sustain Protestant activist lawyers[9] in the pursuit of their legal and religious ideals in an increasingly repressive political context.

Why do these Christian lawyers matter? If they are so few, if their practices and clients are very often marginal, why should scholars take note either of them or their biblical foundations? They matter because lawyers like these have had transformative roles in other times and places, including northeast Asia. They are consequential for the maintenance of power as signified by the Party-state in its extensive and costly efforts to control them. Several have had high profiles in the international media and have helped shape international public opinion and foreign relations with China beyond the capacity of China's local churches. Some have met with foreign leaders, testified before the US Congress and met with European parliamentarians and foreign offices. They matter also because several have had strong relationships with international NGOs which support and defend them, thus expanding the networks and resources of the global church. The Christian lawyers matter in particular because they stand potentially as a fulcrum between China's largest aggregation of civil society groups, the unofficial Protestant churches,[10] and international religious and rights organizations. Their views and their social ties domestically and internationally may come to shape China's public theology and China's future, an aspiration for the lawyers, and a present and future danger for the Party-state.[11]

Callings and Consciousness

China's Christian activist lawyers in this study ranged in age from their early 30s to early 50s. Most originated from outside Beijing but were drawn to the capital for work and solidarity with likeminded practitioners. While a few had academic qualifications from elite universities in Beijing and elsewhere, most had qualifications from provincial institutions. While some had begun their legal careers practicing commercial or civil law, almost all were predominantly committed to criminal defense law with particular emphasis on vulnerable populations or the "weak parties."[12] These include criminal cases that arise out of land takings, environmental protests, forced abortions, to name a few prominent examples, and many cases that result from restrictions on worship and evangelism, destruction of church property, persecution of church leaders, and allegations of financial improprieties, principally of Protestant Christians but also other religions, and, most fiercely, Falun Gong practitioners. In these respects, like other *weiquan* and notable activist lawyers, the Christian lawyers are engaged nationwide with the deepest and most widespread grievances that permeate Chinese society, grievances that make these lawyers and their cases and publicity particularly sensitive to public and state security.

It is useful to distinguish among three groupings who are within or proximate to the Christian circles of activist lawyers. First, the great majority are those who are self-declared and practicing Christians. Second, there are several who declared themselves as "seekers," sometimes adding that they were attending a Bible-study group or reading the Bible or that they had not yet been baptized. Two of these seekers later reported they had been baptized as Christians. Alongside the seekers were two notable leaders of China's activists who were not themselves Christians but had a strong empathy for the Christian lawyers. One had been mentored by a well-known Christian lawyer; another could be found from time to time in meetings on cases with the Christians. And, third, there were a small number of informed Christians, trained as lawyers or lawyer-intellectuals and lawyer-academics, who were not all connected socially with the lawyer practitioners but had valuable perspectives on the Christian activists and on Christianity more generally in the current configuration of power in China.

Discovering and discerning the levels, forms and substance of biblical underpinnings proved challenging.[13] Christian rights lawyers fell into three discernible classes of biblical awareness. The first group of four lawyers, repeatedly interviewed over the six years, had a relatively sophisticated biblical knowledge. They could point to sections of Micah and Amos in the Old Testament or to the Gospels, e.g., the Lord's prayer, or Romans, and the most literate, Li Baiguang 李柏光,[14] who had an extraordinary almost photographic memory, could quote chapter and verse and recite the text itself with ease. They drew from these doctrines and ethics and guides to practice as well as wisdom on how to deal with the Party, authorities, and the future. A second and much larger group had a sporadic knowledge of the Bible, at most able to refer to a passage or two. The most frequently cited text, sometimes in association with the inspiration of Martin Luther King, was Amos 5, "let justice roll down like waters, and righteousness like an ever-flowing stream." This functioned rather like a slogan or banner or perhaps more saliently as a kind of theological-legal liturgy. The third group exuded a diffuse biblical sensibility. That is, they made no reference to particular biblical passages and seemed not to know any they could name in the moment when prompted to do so. Rather they spoke of Christian doctrines, used biblical metaphors or images, exuded a biblical ethos, and bore Christian witness in ways they could not articulate biblically, as I shall show below. Two conclusions can be drawn from this overview. Taken as a whole the Protestant lawyers did not have an explicit, textually grounded, knowledge of the Bible. Rather they seemed to be anchored by a tiny number of lawyer-leaders in whose circles they moved and who concomitantly were inspirational and prophetic in their attraction to rights practice and were better-grounded theologically.

For several of the lawyers the reading of the Bible was decisive in their spiritual biographies. One of the most biblically literate of the lawyers described how he became a Christian during the SARS epidemic. "I accidentally bumped into a friend was a reading a Bible in the classroom" where they were confined in his elite university "so I told him I am interested in reading the Bible too." He'd read Buddhist books and had even been a member of Falun Gong. His Bible reading and his friend led him to their house church "and very soon I became a believer." Li Baiguang recounts how he experienced what he viewed as a sequence of miracles before he became a Christian. Subsequently, during a case, he himself was arrested and spent thirty-seven days in prison. In jail "I started to read the Bible, e.g., Psalm 23" and a year after he was released he became a Christian. One of the lawyer-intellectuals recalled how he first "knew about Christianity through Christians." He discovered "another kind of life, another way to live." This started him reading the Bible, indeed, researching it to discover why house church leaders he was defending on charges of proselytizing and indoctrination were instead "mellow and peaceful." Both lawyers were sentenced to death, yet they faced it with "courage and peace," confident there would be "a second judgment in heaven." Four years after he first encountered Christians, he himself was baptized, converting from "a believer in law to a believer in Christ." Another defense lawyer started his career in the police. A friend gave him a Bible and brought him to a house church with many lawyers in the congregation. He became a Christian shortly afterwards after watching a DVD of a survivor of the June 4 massacre who himself had become a Christian. Each of these lawyers are first-generation Christians. Two built upon the transformative power of the Bible in their lives to lead wider circles of Christian lawyer believers, not only in matters of faith, but in the practices they developed.[15]

Invariably the encounters of Christian lawyers with the Bible are embedded in social contexts. They arise out of social settings, as in several instances of conversion. Repeatedly Christian lawyers stress the role of Bible-study groups in their past and present lives. These groups drew lawyers out of individualistic understandings of faith to its wider significance for law, society, and politics. The Bible-study groups have taken several forms.

Several of the more prominent lawyers point to a Christian legal intelligentsia that conducted Bible studies for other lawyers. The most notable was the Bible-study group or salon led by Dr. Fan Yafeng 范亞峰.[16] This circle, and the Ark Church, also led by Dr. Fan, attracted at various times several of the most prominent Christian rights lawyers, some of whom saw, for the first time, how a line of biblical interpretation might shape a coherent understanding of China's legal system, politics, and Christian concept of a good society and what role lawyers might play in bringing it about (see below). The detention and long house arrest of Dr. Fan signified the dangers that the Party saw in lawyer-leaders committed to shaping China with Christian values.

He was not alone as a lawyer-intellectual exercising leadership within the legal community and not only with rights lawyers. An influential house church quietly drew law students, law faculty, and practitioners into a thoughtful community of faith where biblical understanding was a building block of Christian vocation, even if it exercised great caution in its direct engagement with what might be labeled "political." A bold and vocal younger lawyer describes how his path to Christian faith was influenced and inspired by a Bible-study group led by a professor whose conviction was that "studying the Bible could change China, a belief in Christ that is not only good for myself but for the society and the state." Yet another Bible-study group was led by a scholar who had recently received his doctorate in law from a distinguished university.[17]

Bible studies appear in other guises. The now banned and disbanded (in 2011) Shouwang church in Beijing had Bible studies in which young professionals, including a younger generation of activist lawyers, found fellowship as well as vocational grounding. Bible studies feature not only in the round of church life but also as a safer alternative to attendance at a house church for the more politically toxic lawyers. "The police are always at my house" so "I usually go to a Bible study" rather than bring trouble to a house church. Bible study groups might be accommodated in a law firm, as Li Baiguang initiated in his firm, or bring together lawyers and journalists, as another rights lawyer indicated.[18]

In sum, while the Bible study was an essential element in the devotional life described by some, for most it transcends the solitary spiritual life. The Bible provides the commons in which Christian lawyers congregate as a place of mutual support, solidarity, learning, and most importantly for our purposes, an incubator for discussions over the proper calling of Christian lawyers in an unjust society ruled by a hostile Party.

Guiding Biblical Principles

Several core doctrines or principles recur in lawyers' biblical understandings of callings, practice and wider visions of law in society.[19]

Human Nature

Some juxtapose Christian understandings of human nature with Confucian, Communist, and popular beliefs. "For Confucianism, man can be perfect; Communism requires a person to be morally perfect" and "Chinese people believe in the goodness of all humans." Christians, by contrast, it was said, have a "more correct view of human nature. . . . Everyone is a sinner before God." "We are all sinners, none is righteous." If this is so, it has radical significance for concepts of dignity and equality.[20]

Dignity

Frequently affirmed, sometimes explicitly, more often implicitly, is the belief that "God created man according to his image. I understand that our dignity and rights come from God's image." As a result, the imprint of God endows "dignity and freedom" on all human beings. If the dignity of any person is infringed it is an affront to that person's Creator, whether or not they are Christian believers. "All sinners are created by God and in the image of God and all sinners have dignities and rights that should be protected." To uphold the dignity of all persons therefore leads from the beliefs that we are all God's creatures and all of us bear the stamp of God, or in classic theology, the *imago Dei* (the image of God).[21]

Equality

If everyone is a sinner, "everyone is equal." Repeatedly, lawyers reiterate this radical equality of all persons with such statements as "because we are all sinners, Chairman Mao is the same sinner as I am." Or, "because every person is a sinner . . . no one can think he is superior to another." And, if "everyone according to this belief is a sinner, then all sinners are equal whether you are an ordinary citizen or the president."[22]

Equity, in a lawyer's view, can also to be substantive:

> I believe on the basis of Christian belief that real equity can be realized. No matter who he is, a rich man or beggar, everybody is equal in the eyes of God. For example, last year I was working on a case where a peasant worker, he was taking a train and the head of the train bound him with plastic tape and he died. According to Chinese law, the compensation for a peasant is much lower than compensation for a city person. We required the court to give the same compensation to the peasant because he and his co-worker believed that each life is equal so there should be the same compensation. I used the media to put the court under very heavy pressure and it gave up and gave the same level of compensation. In another case I helped a lot of house churches to get the same rights as Three-Self churches because I believe that they have the same rights—the equality to worship their Lord.[23]

Freedom

This motif is ubiquitous in lawyers' understandings of their faith and work. "Jesus came," said a leading Christian lawyer, "to set us free." This means our freedoms and rights are not grants from the government. Rather, "freedoms and rights are given by God." These endowments on humans mean that "God lives in every Christian's heart" and thus reinforces the "freedom of conscience to think and believe," the autonomy of the self, and the independence of the person. Any limitation or restriction on rights or freedoms, therefore, "is against the law of God." Moreover, these freedoms should lead to "freedom from the terror of power," including "bad things from China's traditional culture and Communist control." The freedom of conscience, the ability to think and believe, an independent personality, and a recognition that a believer ultimately is accountable only to God are preconditions for civil society and are "quintessential" for "democracy and freedom" in China.[24]

Justice

Because justice and righteousness derive from the very character of God, who is "righteous and just," one said, they are foundational to Christian rights aspirations. For Christians, justice should reach far beyond "sacrifice" or religious ritual. And that justice should be focused disproportionately on the weakest in society—the "widows and orphans" repeatedly privileged in the Bible (Isa 1:17; Ps 68:5; Jas 1:27). To strive for justice requires that Christian rights lawyers should defend believers in other religions and other ethnic groups. "Just as I am Han, I defend Tibetans. I want to show the world that justice means not doing justice just with your own group." Thus it is imperative, said several lawyers, for Christians to defend the brutally persecuted Falun Gong believers for whom both the Christian and other rights advocates share a particular empathy. In fact, said a lawyer, the principle of defending the weak should extend to all "people who are violated by the public power, whether rich or poor."[25]

Another lawyer stated:

> I could even say that under this ultimate governing power [in contemporary China] everybody can be weak, even government officials themselves. I have taken a case in which a high-ranking official was interrogated in a prison and charged with criminal charges and he was beaten up even though he was a high-ranking official.[26]

Love

For Christians, stated lawyers, the most important of the Biblical ideals is love—"that God loves us and we need to love others and to help and defend others." "Justice can only be built on love," said another, "and at the same time justice guarantees that love can continue." If the Old Testament places a greater emphasis on justice, a lawyer observed, the New Testament emphasizes the "love of Jesus Christ." The secular law of China itself, the theological arguments suggest, should be infused by care for all others, no matter what their attributes, and justice should be held in balance with love.[27]

Fairness

The issue of unfairness experienced by lawyers personally, in Chinese society and its legal system, repeatedly motivates them to drive toward a legal system and society that is fair. For one Christian lawyer it arises from his childhood: "I grew up in a rural area. Since I was a child I had a strong sense of fairness in my heart, not necessarily fighting for equality or justice. But I cannot take unfairness." For another fairness should be inscribed in the Criminal Procedure Law "to guarantee the justice of the procedure." Unfairness extends to the lawyers themselves: "we are facing a lot of risks. Although we are not doing illegal things, we are suffering a lot of persecution from the government and mafia."[28]

Forgiveness

Given the severity of repression many of these lawyers have experienced, and continue to experience, forgiveness could be infused by love. "The Bible teaches 'love your enemies.' This has a huge impact on me." It opens up the prospect of an inner peace in the face of outer persecution.[29]

> In Romans 12 it says to "bless those who curse you." Forgiving those who persecute us will help us have a peaceful heart, to really live out God's life because the core of forgiveness is love and the core of God is love (1 John 1).[30]

Forgiveness should extend, said a few, to those who persecute them. "I think that basically we have to forgive police and government officials for the harms they do us and their misconduct."[31]

> When we forgive our enemies, as Martin Luther King said, you attract your enemies into your league and they become your brothers. When we could bring our enemies into our league through our forgiveness we can eventually realize our dream of peace and rule of law.[32]

The practice of forgiveness might also extend into lawyers' practice:

> Forgiveness is important, not to hold a grudge against the government. If you are negotiating with the government and take a more mellow way than an antagonistic way, a more cooperative and peaceful way, it might help move things forward.[33]

Underlying all these particularities are general convictions that ensure both that these lawyers will hold the regime accountable and that their ultimate loyalty lies not to the Party-State but to their faith.

The incipient subversiveness of these beliefs can be observed in statements about ultimate loyalty. Repeatedly it is stated and implied that loyalty to the Kingdom of God, to God's law, will prevail over China's law. "Divine rights are the magna carta for Christians" and "if the teaching of God . . . conflicts with the government's law," then the Christian lawyer "has to obey God's word." In fact, whether in business or the military or any type of work, only if "we act according to God's law and principles" will there be "freedom and justice and righteousness." This means that any reforms of the law or legal system must "be as close as possible" to "God's law."[34]

Building the rule of law in China, and doing rule of law work, therefore, is not merely a lawyerly or philosophical ideal. It is doing "work for Christ."[35] Indeed, the foundation of rule of law in China for these lawyers is the work and Word of God itself.

Practice

Biblically infused guidance is brought to bear by the Christian lawyers on the nature of legal practice itself. This has manifested itself in several ways.

First, they feel called and have chosen to adopt a type of legal practice which springs from their commitment to the ideals of justice, freedom, equality, and fairness, among others. Common to all *weiquan* lawyers, they seldom represent white-collar offenders or Party cadres who have fallen afoul of the criminal law on corruption or fraud or related charges. Most often they represent the weak, poor, and helpless, especially those most vulnerable to the arbitrary and predatory power of the state. And since many, if not most, instances of deep-seated grievance in China can turn into offenses that fall under the criminal law, the Christian criminal defense lawyers span the spectrum of troubles experienced by laborers, migrant workers, women, victims of pollution, aggrieved citizens whose homes or livelihoods have been lost in land takings, among others.

Overwhelmingly, the Christian lawyers find themselves called to defend fellow Christians and other religious believers on an array of eclectic charges: corruption, larceny, stealing church moneys, public disturbance, proselytizing, illegal church property construction and location, illegal meetings, property takings, splittism, leaking state secrets and inciting violence. While unofficial churches, their leaders and members, are by far the most common clients, other cases may involve "evil cults" (e.g., Eastern Lightning), Three-Self Churches, and Falun Gong.

Second, the Bible as a source of guidance not infrequently is mentioned by lawyers who seek to discern how they should comport themselves as advocates for clients in particular cases. In courts loaded against a fair trial a reflective lawyer in a younger cohort of theologically informed practitioners called upon higher Christian ideals as a justification for advocacy that widely used social media to rouse local publics. Outraged citizens on the steps of a courthouse or in front of a police station could pressure court and Party officials and at the same time lift public legal consciousness about rights. A small number of Christian lawyers well connected with international organizations might publicize cases outside China in ways that brought unwanted publicity to local courts, judges, police, and Party cadres. Christian diehard lawyers likewise felt justified in their combination of hyper-proceduralism inside the court with rousing of publics outside the court.

In his later years of practice, Li Baiguang took a different view:

> After reading the Bible I rarely use the media to publicize my case. . . . I realized that as a Christian I should be low key and do the work secretly, quietly, just like the Bible says: what you have done in your right hand, you shouldn't let your left hand know. The Lord teaches us to be peaceful and kind and not create conflicts.[36]

In fact, this shift to a quieter form of advocacy was also accompanied by his preference to solve problems for his church clients less through the criminal law and more through administrative law and its procedural intricacies. The path of quietude was a course also chosen by a lawyer whose cases had attracted unwarranted pressure from the Justice Bureau and public security:

> Right now when I go back to read Bible verses on meekness and obedience, then quietly doing the work it seems more important. Right now I am trying to figure out the best approach for myself.[37]

A leading Christian rights lawyer pointed to another conundrum he had confronted. His notability as a fearless advocate for "the public interest" had brought "praise and glory on his head" inside China and from world leaders and international rights groups. But was this self-glorifying? And did it actually make a difference for solving problems in society?

> I was confused. . . . A scripture solved the problem for me. In the Bible the Lord's Prayer says all glory, power, authority belongs to the Father. For the human rights lawyer the glory doesn't belong to me but to God. If you have a sober mind your glory belongs to God. When you think about that you relax totally. You will not be over self-confident. . . . [I]f you see this glory as God's glory, it is not under your control.[38]

Not least, all the Christian rights lawyers wrestled with the relationship between the choice and outcomes of a particular case and its wider significance. A notable lawyer-intellectual close to the Christian circle, but not a Christian himself, had divided all *wei-quan* lawyers into two classes: "those that take human rights cases with the intention of bringing about fundamental change in the law, and they use the cases and the media to achieve this," in contrast to "those that defend human rights cases in each case, not because they are trying to bring a change in the system." A leader of the Christian circle preferred a more differentiated categorization of practice where he accorded the highest value of eight types of lawyers to "constitutional lawyers, who pay utmost attention to public interest. They not only have a constitutional perspective. They carry out constitutional actions. In each individual case they try to change the constitutional system." Eighty percent of this first type of lawyer, he estimated, were Christians. For them, every case is part of a transformative struggle. "Just by doing cases only we are quietly changing the social structure without people seeing it obviously."[39]

Transformative Struggle

The motif of transformation infuses the self-reflections and orientations of the Christian lawyers: transformation on the road to personal faith, transformation in the instance of a case, and ultimately transformation in the society itself.

Basic Legal Freedoms

The Christian rights lawyers speak most authoritatively about the institution of law where they have established their professional credentials. All envision a future China where rule of law is fully institutionalized. In their everyday practice, and in their reactions to successive reforms of the Criminal Procedure Law in 1996 and 2012, they emphasize the fundamental civil rights of procedural justice not only in the law but actualized in practice: freedom from arbitrary arrest, detention, torture in custody, and execution; fair trials; procedural protections for defendants; access to lawyers and legal representation when under investigation or on trial; access to evidence and fair rules for testing evidence; *habeas corpus*, or the right not to be detained indefinitely without representation or trial; and proportional sentences.

Alongside procedural legal rights Christian lawyers join other activist lawyers to insist upon the core political rights of freedom of speech, religion, and association. "If we could have freedom of speech," declared a well-known Christian lawyer, "it would be a great and splendid thing." Religious freedom repeatedly is stressed by lawyer-leaders because it speaks to the inner qualities of a person, to "the freedoms of your soul, your mind, your heart." To fight for this freedom addresses a spiritual vacuum, a collapse of belief, in China's society.[40]

Freedom of speech and the necessity of a freedom of association to construct civil society are frequently linked by activist lawyers. Once you permit religious freedom, and human beings can "live autonomously and independently," then an accompanying freedom of association allows "people to solve problems by themselves. You wouldn't need the government to solve everything." These foundations for a vibrant civil society "would balance the relationship of the state to society."[41]

Property rights are similarly seen as integral to the Christian faith:

> In the Ten Commandments it says clearly you are not allowed to steal other people's property. . . . Very clearly our faith has told us that we have the right to property. [But] the reality is that some church properties have been violated . . . . [A]lso, many people's houses have been torn down. Farmers' and peasants' land has been taken. All these have contributed to the instability of China's society.[42]

It becomes the responsibility of lawyers not only to represent clients, but to speak out to the public as rights advocates and spokespersons:

> I seek to protect rights and to improve the sense of protection of rights. For example, the rights of speech, religious freedom, rights of protest have always been trampled by the government. When lawyers intervene, they criticize and speak out on behalf of the public, and hopefully that will reduce the government attacks on individual rights.[43]

Civil Society

The lawyers insist that a defense of basic legal freedoms requires a robust civil society where citizens can organize themselves free of control by the state or Party. Most salient to Christian lawyers is the defense of religious groups, most especially, but not only, unregulated Protestant "house" churches. Said one activist lawyer:

> I believe that the Chinese house church right now is a very important component of Chinese civil society. The house churches represent the exercise of religious freedom according to international standards and the Chinese constitution.[44]

A staple of practice, therefore, has been defending unofficial churches from administrative and criminal charges ranging from persecution of believers for worshipping or evangelizing or printing and circulating Christian literature to the particularly dangerous charge that they are "evil cults." Several prominent churches in Beijing and other cities were shut down and some leaders, notably Wang Yi (王怡)[45] in Chengdu, Sichuan Province, have been detained, disappeared, and charged with the serious crime of "inciting subversion of state power" (*shandong dianfu guojia zhengquan zui*). Defense of property rights have become more frequent as churches are ordered to remove crosses in some provinces to the extreme of being forcibly destroyed. A Christian lawyer-leader spoke approvingly of the Old Testament story where the king Ahab (and Queen Jezebel) was held accountable for seizing property of Naboth the Jezreelite by force (1 Kgs 21:14 "stoned him to death"). Beyond particular cases some lawyers believe they have a prophetic responsibility to "speak for the church" in the public sphere to the extent they can.[46] Indeed, before the crackdown on lawyers in mid-2015, several Christian lawyers leveraged social and other media to voice their defense of voluntary association, freedoms of speech and religion, in China.

Alongside churches they have envisaged a society dense with social groups not beholden to the state, not least independent bar associations and more informal networks of Christian lawyers. Buttressing associations they imagine a rich public square where open expression of ideas, peaceful debate, and varieties of opinion can be expressed with limited constraint by state authorities.

Restraints on Power

Christian lawyers insist that basic legal freedoms cannot be protected without checks and balances that hold the Party-state security apparatus at bay and keep the Party away from the administration of justice. Frequently expressed in terms of independence of courts and judges, this systemic demand goes to the heart of rule of law as classically understood. Li Baiguang anchors his advocacy for rule of law in Scripture:

> Actually, the Bible mentions rule of law, e.g., in Esther, rule of law means act according to the law. So when the king acted he acted according to the law. I don't see the principle of democracy in the Bible but I do see the rule of law in the Bible, i.e., it is the law that rules, the ruler should act under law and to protect citizens safety, freedom, life and property. Rule of law restrains the power of the ruler to protect the rights of citizens.[47]

He expresses the view, widely shared, it is said, among house churches and their leaders, that Scriptures such as Romans 13, 1 Peter 2, and Titus 3 assure us "that these rulers are permitted by the Lord. They are God's servants. And God teaches us to be obedient to them because their powers are granted by God."[48] At the same time, his dictum on restraint expresses a conditional obedience to rulers and a systemic limit to their powers. Like all other Christian lawyers, for instance, he opposed the active intervention into trials of the Political Legal Committee, usually chaired by the jurisdiction's police chief, and mobilized on so-called sensitive cases, insofar as it represents a direct incursion of the Party into the workings of justice.

From Law to Politics

For some, however, their biblical understandings impel them to go beyond a lawyers' political liberalism. A notable Christian lawyer who has suffered severely for his beliefs stated that when "I became a Christian after I came to Beijing . . . later I found out in the Bible there are lots of ideas that are consistent with what I am pursuing—democracy, constitutionalism, rule of law."[49] Another lawyer recounted of Dr. Fan Yafeng's teaching:

> . . . the best way to glorify God . . . , to care for the weak in China and to defend civil rights is to focus on rule of law and democratic reform in China. Lawyers should stand at the frontier of the rule of law and democratic reform. My practical experience is consistent with Dr Fan's analysis. . . . All these lawyers who go to his group are lawyers who embrace a bright future for China as a democracy and they are all trying to do positive work to help with that.[50]

Here in close juxtaposition are master ideals of a social and political order—constitutionalism, democracy, and rule of law brought into engagement, indeed authorized, by the preeminent Christian ideal of glorifying God. Similar resonances of the biblical and political arise repeatedly in comments of the Christian rights lawyers even if there are variations in views about how Christian lawyers should properly relate to the rulers of a Party-state hostile to them and their co-religionists.

Conclusion

Lawyers, in virtue of their education and their practice, have a unique social location in any society. The very essence of law in a modern society concerns the language of the state, expressed through constitutions, statutes, regulations, and rules which govern society in various degrees through the institutions of law itself. Lawyers are integral to systems of justice, whether for public or private law, criminal or civil law. They are invariably implicated in the state's governing institutions and its efforts to shape legal consciousness and legally acceptable behavior.

This essay reveals that a biblical current flows strongly through the callings and beliefs of Christian rights lawyers. For lawyer-leaders especially this driving force reaches from their macroscopic conceptions of the legal and political institutional order of the society itself to the microscopics of its vast and most vulnerable, weak and marginal populations.

Christian lawyers bring the authority of a document they consider divinely endowed to appraise China's society, law, and politics as they are now and to imagine China's society, law, and politics as they might be. In contexts where pressure from Party-state authorities readily shifts towards persecution to loss of livelihood, detention, disappearance, imprisonment, and torture,[51] all within an ambience of apprehension, fear, and even terror, the everyday recourse of the Christians is to their Bibles and the Bible-study groups, house churches and fellowship groups that center their activities upon it.

Key questions remain. First, both in mainland PRC and in Hong Kong there are lawyer-intellectuals such as Wang Yi, former law professor, now imprisoned house church pastor in Chengdu, Fan Yafeng in Beijing, and Benny Tai,[52] currently a law professor at the University of Hong Kong, whose writings and leadership have galvanized local groups, and in some cases their writings are available more widely. If the biblical knowledge and theological understandings of most Protestant Christian rights lawyers is fairly shallow, it remains a critical question of how a strong intellectual and pastoral link might be forged between lawyer-intellectuals and practitioners who can weld sophisticated theological awareness with realities of everyday legal practice in an unfree state.

Second, the quickening outbreaks of protest in Hong Kong over the last two decades are marked by the leadership of Roman Catholic and Protestant Christians, several of whom are lawyer-leaders with an acute commitment to rule of law and a vibrant civil society. How essential will the authority, biblical and ecclesiastical, of these leaders prove in the defense of basic legal freedoms in Hong Kong as it negotiates the interpretation and even survival of a "one-country two-systems" constitutional arrangement? And since it appears both the Roman Catholic and Protestant churches are divided theologically on who they should support and how, will deepening crisis stimulate a deepening recourse to theological understandings and biblical reinterpretation?

Third, the protests in Hong Kong around rule of law and freedoms of speech and assembly have posed an acute question for many Hong Kong Christians and, by implication, for the PRC on the mainland. Are there biblical and theological grounds to justify violence against an unjust state? The Roman Catholic catechism speaks directly to this issue.[53] How does Protestant biblical interpretation, and how do lawyers themselves who are generically committed to a legal and orderly path to transformation, reach to this most vexing of issues? It is plain that until the present Christian lawyers on the mainland abhor the prospect of violence. May hardening repression inside China, and the example of Hong Kong, impel China's current advocates of peaceful change to consider its limits?

Notes

1. For the period, 2010–2015, on which this chapter focuses, an estimate of approximately 40 percent, or 100–150 of 400 activist lawyers nationwide, comes from rights lawyers themselves and specialist academic observers. That proportion may have changed since the crackdown against rights lawyers that began on July 9, 2015 (see Pils, below, note 4). In an authoritarian state there is no rigorous way of testing its accuracy.

2. Fu Hualing and Richard Cullen, "*Weiquan* (Rights Protection) Lawyering in an Authoritarian State: Building a Culture of Public-Interest Lawyering," *The China Journal* (2008): 59.
3. Sida Liu and Terence C. Halliday, "Political Liberalism and Political Embeddedness: Understanding Politics in the Work of Chinese Criminal Defense Lawyers," *Law and Society Review* 45 (2011): 1540–5893.
4. On human rights and rights lawyers more generally in China see Eva Pils, *China's Human Rights Lawyers: Advocacy and Resistance* (London and New York: Routledge, 2015); Eva Pils, *Human Rights in China* (Cambridge: Polity Press, 2018); Eva Pils, "The Party's Turn to Public Repression: An Analysis of the '709' Crackdown on Human Rights Lawyers in China," *Asian Journal of Law and Society* 3 (2018): 1–48.
5. See Terence C. Halliday and Lucien Karpik, eds., *Lawyers and the Rise of Western Political Liberalism: Europe and North American from the Eighteenth to Twentieth Centuries* (Oxford: Clarendon Press, 1997); Terence C. Halliday, Lucien Karpik, and Malcolm M. Feeley, eds., *Fighting for Political Freedom: Comparative Studies of the Legal Complex for Political Change* (Oxford: Hart Publishing, 2007); Terence C. Halliday, Lucien Karpik, and Malcolm M. Feeley, eds., *Fates of Political Liberalism in the British Post-Colony: The Politics of the Legal Complex* (New York: Cambridge University Press, 2012).
6. Historically and comparatively, lawyers of diverse political viewpoints have most often found common ground for collective action in their commitment to (1) a moderate state where executive power is balanced, checked, and restrained; (2) a vibrant civil society of voluntary associations independent of state control and a lively public square; and (3) a legal system where basic legal freedoms and core political rights are established and protected. Halliday et al, *Fighting for Political Freedom*. This bundle of elements comprises a lawyers' concept of political liberalism.
7. Cf. note 5 for national case studies on eighteenth-century France, twentieth-century Brazil, Kenya, South Korea, and Singapore, and twentieth-first-century Zambia, where Roman Catholic and Protestant Christians press for protection of basic legal freedoms within the wider institutional framework of political liberalism.
8. See Sida Liu and Terence C. Halliday, *Criminal Defense in China: The Politics of Lawyers at Work* (New York: Cambridge University Press, 2016). This essay draws on extensive and repeated interviews of approximately twenty Christian rights lawyers in Beijing from 2010 to 2015. The study, part of a larger research project conducted jointly by the author and Professor Sida Liu, Department of Sociology, University of Toronto, was financially supported by the National Science Foundation in the United States and by the American Bar Foundation, an independent institute of advanced interdisciplinary empirical research on law, lawyers, and legal institutions worldwide. The content and interpretation of findings are entirely independent of any sponsoring institution and are those of the author alone. I am particularly grateful for the continued collaboration and insight of Professor Liu. Not least we express great appreciation to those repressed rights lawyers, for their courage and forthrightness, over years of meetings, often in difficult circumstances.
9. Hereafter I abbreviate China's Protestant rights activist lawyers to "Christian lawyers."
10. Valuable social scientific studies of China's Christian churches include: Nanlai Cao, *Constructing China's Jerusalem: Christians, Power, and Place in Contemporary Wenzhou* (Stanford: Stanford University Press, 2011); Li Ma and Jin Li, *Surviving the State, Remaking the Church* (Eugene, OR: Pickwick Publications, 2018); Carsten Vala, "Protestant Christianity and Civil Society in Authoritarian China," *China Perspectives* 3 (2012): 43–52;

Carsten T. Vala, *The Politics of Protestant Churches and the Party-State in China: God above Party?* (Abingdon, Oxon: Routledge, 2018); Geida Wielander, *Christian Values in Communist China* (London: Routledge, 2013).

11. For a discussion of China in the contexts of party-states more generally, see Stein Ringen, *The Perfect Dictatorship: China in the 21st Century* (Hong Kong: Hong Kong University Press, 2016).
12. B1127. To protect the informants and to maintain their confidentiality, each lawyer-informant is given a distinctive alpha-numeric code. Information that might allow lawyers to be identified has been excluded, a standard practice for protection of research subjects. The primary sources are in the confidential research archive of the principal investigators.
13. Sets of questions and modules to reach biblical foundations were developed by asking (a) what are principal biblical doctrines of concepts that inform their views and behavior, (b) what are particular biblical texts that have been especially meaningful, and (c) what comments did they have on a sequence of statements about doctrine and defense practice that had been offered in earlier interviews by others. This social science methodological technique creates a triangulation of methods to discover an underlying set of beliefs or practices from different data sources, each of which may reveal a different but complementary facet of the phenomena being studied.
14. I name this one leading rights lawyer because he is now deceased (1968–2018). He rose to prominence in the early 2000s, was harshly treated by China's security apparatus, then continued a different kind of practice until his untimely death, under circumstances some consider suspicious. For an excellent journalistic account of his life and work, see https://chinachange.org/2018/03/20/the-might-of-an-ant-the-story-of-lawyer-li-baiguang/.
15. B1116, B1103, B1105, B1107.
16. On Fan Yafeng and his circle of eminent rights lawyers, see Lian Xi, "'Cultural Christians' and the Search for Civil Society in Contemporary China," *The Chinese Historical Review* 20 (2013): 70–87.
17. B1402.
18. B1323, B1104, B1116.
19. This section is an elaboration of Liu and Halliday, *Criminal Defense in China*, 105–106.
20. B1004, B1114, B1001, B1121, B1111.
21. B1006, B1121, B1125. Cf. K. L. Dearborn, "Image of God," in *Evangelical Dictionary of Theology*, ed. Daniel J. Treier and Walter A. Elwell (Grand Rapids: Baker Academic, 2017), 415–417.
22. B1001, B1111, B1114, B1125, B1104.
23. B1001.
24. B1116, B1001, B1125.
25. B1108, B1111, B1108.
26. B1001.
27. B1001.
28. B1129, B1108.
29. B1138.
30. B1138.
31. B1104.
32. B1108.
33. B1129.
34. B1101, B1108, B1311.

35. B1106.
36. B1103, B1113.
37. B1117.
38. B1104, B1125.
39. B1311.
40. B1101, B1108.
41. B1123, B1005, B1005.
42. B1001.
43. B1101.
44. B1108.
45. On Wang Yi's theology, see Chloë Starr, "Wang Yi and the 95 Theses of the Chinese Reformed Church," *Religions* 7 (2016): 142–157. On Wang Yi's church, through the seasons of the Christian year, see Ian Johnson, *The Return of Religion after Mao* (New York: Pantheon, 2017).
46. B1001.
47. B1103.
48. B1103.
49. B1108.
50. B1111.
51. An exemplar of extremes of suffering and resilience of faith is renowned China rights lawyer, Gao Zhisheng: Zhisheng Gao, *Unwavering Convictions: Gao Zhisheng's Ten-Year Torture and Faith in China's Future* (Chicago and Durham: American Bar Association Section on International Law and Carolina Academic Press, 2017); Eva Pils, "Rights Activism in China: The Case of Lawyer Gao Zhisheng," in *Building Constitutionalism in China*, edited by Stephanie Balme and Michael Dowdle (New York: Palgrave Macmillan, 2009), 243–260.
52. Benny Tai, "Public Theology, Justice and Law: A Preliminary Note," *Interface* 15 (2012): 3–25.
53. See *Compendium of the Social Doctrine of the Church*, by Pontifical Council for Justice and Peace (Washington, DC: United States Conference of Catholic Bishops, 2005), 172.

Primary Sources

See note 12.

CHAPTER 40

THE BIBLE AND ICONOGRAPHY IN CHINA

NICOLAS STANDAERT

INTRODUCTION

THE general image of the Jesuit mission in China in the seventeenth and eighteenth centuries is one of a rationalistic approach to the proclamation of faith. In the initial phase of evangelization, missionaries did not proclaim the narrative of the Gospels, but tried to convince the Chinese counterpart of subjects such as the existence of God, the (immortality of the) soul, heaven and hell with reward and punishment, with arguments based on Aristotelean philosophy and Thomistic theology. This image is further supported by the fact that Jesuits were involved in scientific activities such as astronomy and calendar reform and that, in a certain sense, they preferred translating mathematical handbooks to the Bible. Yet, this overall impression is only one part of the story and neglects other aspects of the Jesuit mission: the narrative approach of mission by preaching the life of Christ with the support of images. Jesuit missionaries imported religious prints and illustrated books directly from Europe, used them as illustrations during their preaching, and distributed them to converts. Moreover, they commissioned local artists to produce woodblock prints of biblical images on the basis of European models.

This chapter discusses the link between the Bible and iconography in three steps: first, it sketches the background of the use of images in the Jesuit tradition in Europe; next, it gives an overview of the major publications or productions in China by dividing them into sources from the late Ming (1582–1644) and early Qing (1644–1722) dynasties; finally, it sketches how Chinese and European traditions were interwoven in these images.[1]

Use of Images in the Jesuit Tradition in Europe

The Jesuit order originated at the time when the print culture in Europe was in full development. Not only was there a sharp increase in printed books in the late sixteenth century but also illustrated books and separate prints became more popular, enhanced by the advancement in copper-etching techniques. Though there were some internal debates about the role of images in liturgy and meditation, the Jesuits very quickly took advantage of the modern media of their time and extensively used visual artefacts in their apostolic activities. They had close contacts with engravers and printers, especially in the major printing centers such as Augsburg, Munich, and Antwerp, which further facilitated the publication of prints with biblical scenes or saints. In addition, they actively promoted the spread of *emblemata*, which are pictorial images that represent allegories or concepts, such as moral virtues. They introduced a new type of these allegorical images by bringing them together in a narrative sequence based on the Gospel, or on classical and Christian symbols.

In general, early seventeenth-century Jesuits attributed four functions to the use of images. First was the didactic function, since they were of the opinion that the transmission of knowledge was helped not only by the written word but also by visual images. This was particularly but not exclusively the case for less educated and illiterate people. Secondly, they valued the fact that images helped the process of remembering, since memory is activated by the sight of images. Thirdly, they attributed an empathic function to images, since visual materials arouse not only intellectual but also emotional responses. Finally, in line with the Catholic tradition, Jesuits supported the cultic function of images, encouraging people to venerate Christ and the saints through images.[2]

One of the major and early emblem texts is Jerónimo (Hieronymus) Nadal's (1507–1580) *Evangelicae historiae imagines* (*Images of the Gospel Story*), a collection of 153 large folio copperplate engravings of gospel scenes, posthumously published in Antwerp (s.n. [M. Nutius]) in 1593. A companion volume of Nadal's contains the contemplative texts referring to each picture, *Adnotationes et meditationes in Evangelia* (*Annotations and Meditations on the Gospels*), Antwerp: M. Nutius, 1594.[3] The illustrations had been made by famous Flemish and Dutch engravers of that time: the Wierix brothers of Antwerp, Jan (1549–ca. 1618), Hieronymus (ca. 1553–1619) and Antoon II (ca. 1555–1604), Karel van Mallery (1571–1635), Jan Collaert (1566–1628) and Adrian Collaert (1560–1618), mostly after the designs of Giovanni Battista Fiammeri S.J. (1530–1609) and Bernardino Passeri (1540–1596). In Nadal's eyes, the pictorial images of the life of Christ were not merely artistic images of a text, but they formed an essential part of the meditative prayer (*meditatio*).[4] His work can be considered a complement to the *Spiritual Exercises* of Ignatius Loyola (1491–1556), the founder of the Society of Jesus. This booklet introduces the retreatant to a series of "exercises," i.e., meditations and contemplations on the life of Christ, and it insists on the use of images and senses in this way of prayer. In the first stage of a prayer exercise, Ignatius suggests a "composition of the place," which consists in "seeing with the sight of the imagination the physical place where the thing is found which I want to contemplate. By physical place I mean, for example, a temple or mountain where Jesus Christ or Our Lady is found, according to what I want to contemplate."[5] Moreover, the person who is praying is encouraged to apply all the senses, and not only sight, during the meditation, by trying to see, hear, feel, touch, and smell what is going on in the scene depicted. In other words, readers/viewers first "compose" the Gospel scenes, and then position themselves within the sites, finally moving themselves around in the scene in order to convert them into a private interiorized meditative prayer. As a result, an encounter can take place.[6] Nadal's *Adnotationes et meditationes* is entirely built on these principles. In fact, his treatise initiated a new genre of devotional literature keyed to the imagining potential of prints. Each image is marked with a series of capital letters that are related to a list of annotations below. In contrast with other earlier meditative texts, in Nadal's case, the entire book is built around the images, rather than having the engravings merely function as illustrations.[7] Nadal's work inspired other illustrated books on the life of Christ. For instance, Bartolomeo Ricci S.J. (1542–1613): *Vita D.N. Jesu Christi et verbis Evangeliorum in ipsismet concinnata* (*The Life of Jesus Christ Arranged According to the Words of the Gospels*), Rome: B. Zanettum, 1607, contains a chronological life of Christ with 160 illustrations (and two maps), eighty of which are based on the illustrations in Nadal. Bartolomeo Ricci's work follows the example of Nadal but is less sophisticated and focuses on the principal scene of the illustrations in Nadal. The images in Nadal's work became also a source of inspiration for local adaptations in various cultures in Latin America and also in China.

Major Publications in China

Late Ming

The communication between Europe and China happened partly through books. When they arrived in China in the late sixteenth century, the Jesuits were surprised to find a print culture in China that was in many regards more efficient, more developed, and cheaper than in Europe. This context shaped their apostolate in two ways: on the one hand, it encouraged them to ask for books and prints in Europe they could use in their preaching; on the other hand, these European models gave rise to the production of Chinese prints that were locally produced. The early transfer of books can be illustrated with Nadal's work.[8] As early as 1599, the Jesuits in China had asked for a copy of Nadal's book, and it is certain that by 1605 they had one in their residence in the south of the country. In one of his letters, Ricci wrote that Nadal's book "is of even greater use than the Bible, in the sense that while we are in the middle of talking we can also place right in front of their eyes things that with words alone we would not been able to make clear."[9]

In the 1630s, at least two other sets (one in Nanjing and one in Fuzhou) were available in China, where they were the source of Chinese versions.

Regarding the production of new illustrations in the late Ming dynasty, one can distinguish four different series of prints that are closely related to biblical iconography and that are still existent.[10]

The first series in chronological order is a set of four engravings:[11] they were reproduced, at the suggestion of well-known Jesuit missionary Matteo Ricci S.J. 利瑪竇 (1552–1610), in an "album of ink cakes" *Chengshi moyuan* 程氏墨苑 (*The Ink Garden of Mr. Cheng*). The compiler was a famous master in woodcut printing, Cheng Dayue 程大約 (1541–1616?), who published his album shortly after 1605 with reprints in 1610.[12] The engravings, with a short explanation by Ricci (entitled *Xizi qiji* 西字奇蹟 *Remarkable Examples of Western Writing*), comprise two scenes from the life of Christ: *Christ Appearing to Simon Peter and the Miraculous Draught of Fishes* and *The Journey to Emmaus*; these separate prints were originally designed by Maarten de Vos (1532–1603) and engraved by Antoon Wierix II. There is one image related to the Old Testament: *Lot at the Destruction of Sodom and Gomorrah* from the Dutch engraver Crispijn de Passe de Oude (ca. 1564–1637). The fourth woodblock print is an image of the Virgin with child that is probably a reproduction of a print made in Japan, representing the *Nuestra Señora de L'Antigua* from the cathedral in Sevilla, Spain. The reproduction of these European prints is very precise, and the images are arranged in the album under the section of "Buddhist and Taoist subjects" (*zihuang* 緇黃). It is noteworthy that the first Chinese reprints of biblical iconography appeared in a context that was not directly related to mission propagation but to the commercial selling of inkstones.

The second series of engravings appeared in an illustrated version of the rosary entitled *Song nianzhu guicheng* 誦念珠規程 (*Rules for Reciting the Rosary*), translated by the Portuguese Jesuit João da Rocha S.J. 羅儒望 (1583–1623) and published in Nanjing ca. 1619.[13] Its fifteen woodcut illustrations are derived from the above-mentioned copperplate engravings in Nadal's *Evangelicae historiae imagines*. They represent fifteen mainly biblical scenes (the Annunciation, Visitation, Nativity, etc.) that accompany the mysteries that are reflected upon during the recitation of the rosary. Thus, only these scenes have been selected and the annotations were left out, since the explanation is given in the text of the treatise on the rosary. The illustrations of *Song nianzhu guicheng* are well known because, more than others, they have been transformed according to Chinese pictorial conventions. The scenes have been reduced to straightforward rendering of the main scene that is meditated on. The objects (e.g., furniture, windows, clouds) have been adapted to Chinese style, the disposition of the actors has sometimes been rearranged, secondary elements have been deleted, while in some scenes the environment has been reorganized (adding a door and a wall; opening the back scene of the room). Chinese prints usually contain little shadowing, since volume or perspective is rarely represented with the *chiaroscuro* method. In these prints, the shadowing of objects and on faces has been left out. Moreover, the European geometric perspective has been replaced by the Chinese isometric perspective. European prints of that time use geometric perspective with a single vanishing point, while Chinese prints used isometric perspective with parallel vanishing points. These adaptations are clear examples of cultural interaction that benefited from the artisanship of the local engravers.

The third series consists of approximately fifty-six engravings of the illustrated life of Christ entitled *Tianzhu jiangsheng chuxiang jingjie* 天主降生出像經解 (*Explanation of the Images of the Lord of Heaven's Incarnation*), first published by Giulio Aleni s.j. 艾儒略 (1582–1649) in Jinjiang (Quanzhou) in 1637.[14] Most of these Chinese woodcuts also were reproduced after Nadal's work. Moreover, the illustration of *The Four Evangelists* from Bartolomeo Ricci's *Vita D.N. Jesu Christi* was partly used for the frame of the image of Christ as *Salvator Mundi* at the beginning of Aleni's work. The illustrations follow the life of Jesus in chronological order, and the annotations marked by references in the illustrations have been included at the bottom of the image. The woodcuts adopt fewer Chinese pictorial conventions than *Song nianzhu guicheng*. For instance, the primary and secondary scenes have been maintained, there is some shadowing, and the images follow the geometric perspective of the European original. Yet, there are some adaptations, such as the combination of two original prints in one new print, the transformation into more Chinese expressions of vegetation and rocks, and the addition of a group of Chinese devotees in one of the final prints. As regards the general structure of *Tianzhu jiangsheng chuxiang jingjie*, the arrangement of the pictures belongs to the genre of the "harmony of the Gospel" (*harmonia evangelica*), which is an attempt to organize the material of the four distinct Gospels into a chronological sequence and a consistent narrative text. This was a popular genre in the sixteenth and seventeenth centuries in Europe. The instructions on the meditations of the "Life of Christ" in the *Spiritual Exercises* also follow the same structure.

Tianzhu jiangsheng chuxiang jingjie often has been treated together with *Tianzhu jiangsheng yanxing jilüe* 天主降生言行紀略 (*Short Record of the Words and Deeds of the Lord of Heaven's Incarnation*), published for the first time in 1635. However, this is not a translation of Nadal's commentary, but a similar harmony of the Gospel based on *Vita Jesu Christi e quatuor Evangeliis et scriptoribus orthodoxis concinnata* (*The Life of Christ Arranged from the Four Gospels and Orthodox Authors*) of Ludolphus de Saxonia (1300–1378). First published in 1474, this *Vita Jesu Christi* was a very popular text in the sixteenth and seventeenth centuries and was published and translated in the main European cities. The work had also a special influence on the Society of Jesus, since Ignatius of Loyola was converted to a new lifestyle by reading *Vita Jesu Christi*, and his *Spiritual Exercises* bear its influence, especially with regard to the use of active imagination. That Aleni took Ludolphus de Saxonia's *Vita Jesu Christi* as the first work to be translated instead of the Gospels themselves shows how the didactic and spiritual dimension of the life of Christ was preferred to the exegetical or liturgical dimension. *Tianzhu jiangsheng yanxing jilüe* and *Tianzhu jiangsheng chuxiang jingjie* thus complement each other.

The fourth series belongs to the woodcut book entitled *Jincheng shuxiang* 進呈書像 (*Images in a Booklet Presented to His Majesty*), composed by Johann Adam Schall von Bell s.j. 湯若望 (1591–1666), and probably produced in Beijing in 1640.[15] It contains forty-eight illustrations, one of which is the reproduction of the original front cover representing the four evangelists and another one being a double-page illustration of the three Magi adoring the child Jesus. The remaining forty-six illustrations represent scenes from the life of Christ, from the Annunciation to the Ascension. Each illustration is accompanied by a short explanatory text. The original work on which the Chinese book is based is not a printed work, but a manuscript containing miniature paintings, which was especially prepared as a gift to the Chinese emperor by Maximilian I, Duke of Bavaria (1573–1651). It was acquired in 1617 by Nicolas Trigault S.J. 金尼閣 (1577–1628), a missionary who had returned from China to recruit new missionaries and gain support for the China mission in Europe. Trigault carried the manuscript book to Macao in 1620, where it remained for a long time because it could not be delivered due to conflicts at the Chinese court. Ultimately, it was presented to the Chinese emperor by Schall von Bell twenty years later, but before doing so, Schall had a Chinese version made and printed. Unfortunately, the original work seems to be lost, but thanks to a large number of other original sources, we are fairly well informed about its production process. It appears that the miniature paintings were based on a wide variety of prints, mainly from Dutch and Flemish engravers. They belong to different categories. First, the most frequently represented source work is Nadal's *Evangelicae historiae imagines* with at least ten illustrations, and together with a few illustrations from Bartolomeo Ricci's *Vita D.N. Iesu Christi*. Second, some illustrations that have their origin in biblical "series" of prints. There are three series, all related to the *Passion of Christ*: by Joannes Stradanus (Jan van der Straat) (1523–1605), Hendrick Goltzius (1558–1617), and Jacques de Gheyn II (1565–1629) with Zacharias Dolendo (b. between 1561 and 1573, d. before 1604). The third category consists of some nine illustrations that do not belong to such a "series" but are copies from separate prints by engravers who were active in Munich and neighboring Augsburg in the 1610s. They can be divided into two groups: those by Johann Matthias Kager (1575–1634) and those by the Sadeler family, consisting of Raphaël Sadeler (1560 or 1561–1632) I, Raphaël II (1584–?), Aegidius II (ca. 1570–1629), and Jan I (1550–1600).

A comparison of the original European prints with the Chinese prints reveals a wide variety of similarities and differences: some Chinese prints are copies in the same direction as the original; others are mirror images of the original. In some cases, the picture-within-the-picture, a characteristic of Nadal's illustrations leading to temporal displacement from the principal scene,[16] has been preserved, and in others these have been deleted. Some Chinese illustrations are clearly the combination of two original prints, in some cases possibly even prints from two different sources (combining the works by Nadal and B. Ricci). The question is whether these changes were introduced by the Chinese woodcutters or were already present in the original miniatures. Most possibly they occurred in the different stages of reproduction. There are good reasons to assume that the illuminators in Munich did not follow the prints slavishly but that they introduced the omission or replacement of figures or altered the background. This does not exclude the possibility that other changes are due to the Chinese woodcutters or to the Jesuits in Beijing. Certain Chinese pictorial conventions have been adopted, such as the absence of shadowing. Another major difference is the representation of perspective. The shape of the tiles in different prints of *Jincheng shuxiang* shows that the woodcutter adopted isometric perspective. Chinese characteristics also are present in the shape of waves, clouds, rocks, and trees. Some adaptations are more subtle. The eyes of the figures, for instance, usually have a shape that is closer to those in Chinese prints than in European prints of that time. As in the case of the previous changes, they show artistic intercultural processes in the production of new images.

Early Qing (1644–1722)

The above-mentioned four series belong to the Ming dynasty, which came to an end in 1644. In the early Qing, especially during the sixty-year reign of the Kangxi emperor, there were no longer such important publications. Still there are a few important sources that can be linked to biblical iconography and can inform us about other means of transmission and reception.

The first source is the reproduction of some of these prints in books. An example is a work related to the "Calendar-case," an anti-Christian campaign that was initiated by Yang Guangxian 楊光先 (1597–1669) and took place in 1665. In his *Budeyi* 不得已 (*I Can No Longer Stand It*), Yang attacked both Christian doctrine and Western astronomy and geography.[17] Hereto he reproduced three of Schall's "offensive" pictures from *Jincheng shuxiang*, to demonstrate the heterodox nature of foreign doctrine. His core idea is that *Jincheng shuxiang* shows that Jesus was a rebel condemned to crucifixion, a fact about which, according to him, others remained silent. The three pictures that are reproduced are *Christ's Entry into Jerusalem*, *The Crucifixion*, and *Christ on the Cross*. They show the circulation of early prints outside the Christian community and the further adaptation of these prints to a Chinese context.

The second case is the reproduction of these illustrations in paintings. A first example is a set of six polychrome album paintings on silk, bearing the false signature of the famous painter, Dong Qichang 董其昌 (1555–1636).[18] The signature is false because several scenes of the album are adaptations of allegorical elements selected from a secular commemorative print published in Leuven in 1652, which makes the album of a later date.[19] One of the paintings—*Jesus amidst a Crowd of Publicans and Pharisees*—is derived from a biblical print by the Flemish master Antoon Wierx, which also appears in Nadal's treatise. Though the orginal function and purpose is unknown, it shows that these biblical models continued to circulate, that they were also reproduced as paintings and that they could be combined with other non-biblical models. Another example of a print becoming a painting is the biblical scenes on a Coromandel screen, unfortunately undated, but possibly from the seventeenth or eighteenth century.[20] These screens, mainly made for export, were made of Chinese lacquer from Fujian, Zhejiang, Jiangsi, and Anhui. They were called "Coromandel" because they were shipped to European markets via the Coromandel coast in east India. One of these screens reproduces eight biblical scenes, among which are *Christ Appearing to Simon Peter and the Miraculous Draught of Fishes* and *The Journey to Emmaus*, which were present in the above-mentioned *Chengshi moyuan*. Though there are no positive proofs for a direct link between both, this case not only proves the continued reproduction of biblical images, but also affirms that there was a wide variety of means in doing so.

The third case is of different nature: it concerns two Chinese manuscripts with descriptions of European prints that were presented to the Kangxi emperor in 1708 and in 1720. The illustrations corresponding to these descriptions, however, are missing. The details of the descriptions, however, help to identify the original European texts that were given to the emperor.

The first manuscript has no title in Chinese, only one in Latin: *Exemplar explicationis figurarum sive imaginum tam Veteris quam Novi Testamenti, oblatae Imperatori (Linguâ Tartaricâ) anno 1708 (Explanation of the Figures and Images of Both the Old and New Testament, Offered (in Manchu) to the Kangxi Emperor in the Year 1708)*.[21] The text consists of the description of, in total, 468 images (*tu* 圖): the Old Testament (starting with creation, ending with the Maccabees); the New Testament, the life of Jesus from Annunciation to Ascension, with chronological but also thematic series (e.g., parables, beatitudes, Our Father, etc.); the Acts of the Apostles with at the end the martyrdom of the apostles; twelve articles of the creed. The text is an explanation in Chinese of the illustrations in *Theatrum Biblicum* (first edition 1639) by Claes Jansz. Visscher (ca. 1587–1652).[22] Visscher was a Dutch draughtsman, engraver, and publisher, who became prominent for the publication of biblical picture books. These are not illustrated Bibles (i.e., the Bible text with illustrations), but books with pictures that narrate biblical stories, with only some brief scriptural references or a short explanation. Visscher specialized in the reprint of the work of earlier engravers. He managed to acquire the original woodblocks or copperplates, which he used to compose new books. This was also the case of *Theatrum Biblicum*, a work that included reproductions of prints from the sixteenth and seventeenth centuries. One copy of this work (probably the edition of 1643 or 1650) seems to have been presented to the Kangxi emperor, and an anonymous person, possibly a missionary, composed the Chinese explanation of the illustrations. How the work came to China and who made the translations is uncertain. Some sources, however, indicate that "the Moscovites," which refers to a delegation of Russian diplomats, may well have presented it, and subsequently some Jesuit missionaries explained the illustrations of the work to the emperor in 1706. This transmission via Russia is a possibility since *Theatrum Biblicum* was known in Russia as "The Bible of Piscator." It became one of the most influential works for biblical representations and served as a model for prints as well as for paintings by Russian artists, who decorated the walls of churches across central Russia based on this work.

The second manuscript is entitled *Shen xianxian tuxiang jielüe* 神顯現圖象解略 (*Brief Explanation of Illustrations of Manifestations of Angels*), which can be dated to 1720.[23] There also is an Italian title written on the cover: *Storia del Nuovo Testamento e apparizione degli Angeli* (*Story of the New Testament and Apparition of the Angels*). It consists of the depiction of three series of illustrations: (1) angels; (2) the parables of Jesus; and (3) three secular illustrations about courage. The sources of the second and third series could not yet be identified, while the section on the angels can be identified as having *Biblisches Engel- u. Kunst Werck* (1694; repr. 1700, 1705, 1715) as its primary source. The work was compiled by the German Baroque engraver, illustrator, and publisher Johann

Ulrich Kraus (also Krauss, Krauß, 1655–1719), who belonged to a well-known circle of artists in Augsburg in the late seventeenth and early eighteenth centuries. The work consists of thirty illustrations in which thematically angels appear, usually two scenes on each page from both the Old and New Testament. For instance, for the theme "the angels nursing the sick," there is the healing of a sick man at the pool of Bethesda (John 5:1–9) and Tobias healing his father with fish gall following the instructions of the angel Raphael (Tobit 11:7). The flamboyant and at times exuberant cartouches, with arabesques, flowers, *putti*, and swags make up the decoration. There are some indications that the emperor indeed had seen European images of "humans with wings."

It appears that after the Ming, European books with prints continued to travel to China until the mid-Qing. Moreover, these not only came from different origins (the Low Countries, or Augsburg in Germany) but also they arrived through different channels, not only via Catholic missionaries but also via Russian delegations. Finally, these illustrated books were considered valuable means for transmitting the biblical stories to the Kangxi emperor. These efforts are similar to the life of Christ presented by Adam Schall von Bell to the Chinese emperor at the end of the Ming. They reveal some of the less known encounters between the emperor and missionaries.

Interwoven Images

These sources show in various ways how the images were culturally interwoven. From an historical point of view, it appears that despite the fact that a full Bible translation into Chinese was not published in the seventeenth and eighteenth centuries, that there were a variety of visual "translations." Biblical images and illustrated Bibles were not only sent to China but also were printed in China. The presence of print culture in both China and Europe facilitated this process. The audience to which the images were destined consisted of ordinary, often illiterate, Christians as well as higher officials or even the emperor. It is difficult, though, to assert how widely the prints circulated. The number of reprints and the reception history give some indication, but this provides only limited insight in the iconic circuit. Still one can point to the role of the Christian community in this process, such as in Fujian. In one of the final images of the *Tianzhu jiangsheng chuxiang jingjie*, a Chinese community replaces the Western community. It is remarkable that the community in which the images were received is itself represented in the print. To a certain extent, such converted images could become a power of conversion: because images became Chinese, Chinese could become Christians.

From the point of view of the artistic value in intercultural contacts, the images represented the interweaving of European and Chinese visual traditions. The description of the prints has shown that there is a broad variety in degrees of adoption of local Chinese pictorial conventions. The degree of adoption can be made visual as a grading scale. On one end is the total adoption and on the other end no adoption at all (a simple reproduction of the original). In certain cases, such as in *Song nianzhu guicheng*, the adoption was rather extensive. In other cases, it was not the accommodation to local conventions but the maintenance of the culture of origin that was stressed, such as the prints in *Chengshi moyuan*. In most cases, the prints can be situated in between: between adoption and non-adoption, familiarity and strangeness. As in other parts of the world, these images had to be both recognizable and different to be attractive.

These images also are revealing from the point of view of print culture and, more specifically, the relationship between the text and the images. The Christian illustrated biblical works often refer to the illustrations as "*xiang* 像" and not as "*tu* 圖." Recent research has pointed at the differences between these concepts. Various features are known as *tu*: pictures, maps, diagrams, charts, and tables, and therefore *tu* seemingly covers any form of representation in visual form at all. Yet, function rather than form makes a *tu*. Thus, the body text and *tu* differ not because the first consists of text and the second images, but because the latter serves largely to illustrate the former.[24] The word "*xiang*" or image, by contrast, is consistently used for any sort of portraiture and has dense connections to ideas about representation. *Xiang* not only means "image," connoting resemblance and implying an act of perception, but also "figure," which refers to activities that are involved in "figuring" the situation revealed by the act of divination. *Xiang* can also be connected with the "personator" of the dead, a young descendant of the deceased who temporarily adopted the identity of the recently departed and participated as guest of honor in a commemorative funerary meal. Personators were considered literally to image (*xiang*) the dead, and in fact many scholars believed the custom of personation was the forerunner to the custom of using painted and sculpted images of the deceased at sacrificial offerings. In this context, the body of the personator represented another human body not by correlation but by incarnation.[25] An image thus manifests the subject. The choice of *xiang* in the titles these works therefore seems to clarify further the meaning of the Christian biblical books. The images are not simply illustrations of a text, as would be the case with *tu*, but are themselves the most important aspect of the work, the text being an explanation of the images. Moreover, the woodprints are "images," i.e. portraits of Jesus, which represent him as an incarnated subject, figuring acts by himself. The images therefore function not only as sacred objects of worship or meditation but also as sacred subjects that can cause an effect.

These images are, from the point of view of spiritual cultivation, also significant for visually oriented contemplation, which is another way in which the interweaving was expressed. Many of them, especially the Nadal images, originated from a context of biblical meditation as exemplified by the Ignatian methodology. Moreover, it can be pointed out that these images entered a Chinese context in which such meditation practices were not strange. Michael Shin Junhyoung, for instance, explored the receptive potential of these works in the context of the indigenous Buddhist tradition in China. He argues that *Tianzhu jiangsheng chuxiang jingjie* could be eagerly received and fully functional among the Chinese audience since it was already familiar with a similar tradition drawn from the *Guan wuliangshou jing* 觀無量壽經 (*Sūtra of the Contemplation of the Infinite-Age Buddha*) of so-called Pure Land Buddhism. According to the sūtra, the practice of visualizing the Pure Land through different scenes will absolve one of accumulated sins and enable one to achieve salvation, that is, rebirth in the Pure Land. This meditative methodology is very similar to that of *Tianzhu jiangsheng chuxiang jingjie*. Just like its European counterpart, the sūtra's detailed descriptions of colorful lakes and streams, jewel trees, beautiful pavilions, with grandiose deities inhabiting them lead the Buddhist practitioner to create in mind a holy space. As with Nadal's images, the practitioner not only visualizes the holy topography but also enters the visualized Pure Land to be reborn, travel, meet with and hear from the Buddhas. Shin concludes that the Pure Land meditative methodology predisposed the Chinese audience to be susceptible to a Chinese version of the Ignatian visual meditation.[26] There are several indications that these visual contemplation exercises of the latter actually were put into practice. One can get a glimpse from some practices in the Fujian community of the 1630s. The most important source for information about the Fujian community is the *Kouduo richao* 口鐸日抄, an extensive record of missionaries' conversations with converts and interested literati in Fujian selected from the ten-year period of March 13, 1630, to July 4, 1640. More than twenty-five Christians participated in the recording and editing of this work.[27] Besides theological or moral questions, it also contains the explanation of series of images or exchanges about practical matters such as meditation.[28] In fact, there is a close link between biblical texts, biblical iconography, and meditation. In *Kouduo richao*, one can observe that missionaries not only explain the life of Jesus or other themes on the basis of images but also explain how to meditate with these biblical scenes. They encourage the application of the three faculties of the soul, which are memory, intellect, and will. The idea of the three faculties of the soul was in the Christian spiritual literature first exposed by Augustin. Ignatius of Loyola got to know it as a method for meditation through the work of Lodolphus de Saxonia. Especially the "application of the senses" (to see, hear, smell, taste, and touch) in meditation or contemplation is helpful for stimulating the faculties. The method of contemplation is explained in *Kouduo richao* in three steps: (1) to memorize the facts; (2) to deduce the meaning; (3) to disclose the inner feeling. One can notice the influence of meditation methods as outlined in Ignatius' *Spiritual Exercises*, with concrete images or with the use of imagination. Memory enables a person to bring to awareness the theme of the prayer that is proposed and the images and impressions that one has about the theme. One can memorize them and recall them in order to activate the intellect and understanding. Understanding can activate the analysis of the scriptural passage that makes it possible to set the will into motion, which can lead to remorse, self-improvement, or firm decisions to mend one's ways. This method of prayer is a discursive mental prayer especially suited for "beginners" (*incipientes*). The explicit reference to the method in the Fujian community shows how it was applied to beginners in China as well.

Conclusion

This essay underscores the fact that biblical iconography had a didactic function in China in the seventeenth and eighteenth centuries. Biblical stories, often treated as historical events, and biblical themes not only were explained by words but also were illustrated visually with images produced either in Europe or in China. Yet, these images also functioned as a means for spiritual cultivation, inspired by the *Spiritual Exercises* of Ignatius of Loyola, and welcomed in a culture with a tradition of visual meditation. One of the purposes of the visual meditation according to the *Spiritual Exercises* is to create a space in which an encounter can take place. Experience suggests that the encounter according to this specific method leads to "inner transformations" or "displacements." The whole setting of the images encourages such displacements. Since the religious pictures, as for instance included in *Song nianzhu guicheng* and *Tianzhu jiangsheng chuxiang jingjie*, were expected to fix the details of dramatic scenes from the Gospels in Chinese minds, they can be considered another type of visual translation of the methods of the *Spiritual Exercises*. Moreover, a detailed analysis of the Chinese versions of the prints, in comparison with contemporary Chinese prints, shows that in the new composition similar "displacements" as in the European prints take place. The theme expressed by the biblical scenes was often an encounter between biblical figures and the person watching or meditating on the prints so they could encounter mentally the persons represented in the images. Such an encounter also may lead on to a "re-location" or "repositioning" that becomes flesh in the real life of the one who, through the composition, allows him- or herself to be set in motion. This may well have been the significance of biblical iconography in a Chinese context.

Notes

1. This essay is partly based on earlier publications by the author: Nicolas Standaert, "The Bible in Early Seventeenth-Century China," in *Bible in Modern China: The Literary and Intellectual Impact*, ed. I. Eber et al. (Nettetal: Steyler Verlag, 1999), 31–54; "Chinese Prints and Their European Prototypes: Schall's *Jincheng shuxiang*," *Print Quarterly* 23.3 (2006), 231–253; "The Composition of Place: Creating Space for an Encounter," *The Way: A Review of Christian Spirituality* 47.1 (2007), 7–20; *An Illustrated Life of Christ Presented to the Chinese Emperor: The History of Jincheng shuxiang (1640)*, (*Monumenta Serica Monograph Series* LIX) (Sankt Augustin Nettetal: Steyler Verlag, 2007); "Ignatian Visual Meditation in Seventeenth-Century China," in Halvor Eifring, ed., *Meditation and Culture: The Interplay of Practice and Context* (London: Bloomsbury, 2015), 24–35, 218–219; "Dutch, Flemish and German Engravings Presented to the Kangxi Emperor," *Sino-Western Cultural Relations Journal* 38 (2016), 1–27. Extensive references to primary and secondary sources can be consulted at: Ad Dudink & Nicolas Standaert, Chinese Christian Texts Database (CCT-Database) (http://www.arts.kuleuven.be/sinology/cct). This includes updates of secondary sources and information about the location or reprints of primary sources.
2. Peter Van Dael, "'De Christelijcke leeringhe met vermaeck gevat': De functie van illustraties in boeken van jezuïeten in de Nederlanden tijdens de zeventiende eeuw," *De zeventiende eeuw* 14.1 (1998): 122.
3. Nadal's writing has been studied extensively; see Maj-Brit Wadell, *Evangelicae Historiae Imagines: Entstehungs-geschichte und Vorlagen* (Göteburg: Lindgrens, 1985); Pierre-Antoine Fabre, *Ignace de Loyola: Le lieu de l'image* (Paris: Vrin, 1992), esp. 163–296; Paul Rheinbay,

"Nadal's Religious Iconography Reinterpreted by Aleni for China," in *"Scholar from the West": Giulio Aleni S.J. (1582–1649) and the Dialogue between Christianity and China* (*Monumenta Serica Monograph Series* XLII), ed. Tiziana Lippiello and Roman Malek (Nettetal: Steyler Verlag, 1997), 323–334; Walter S. Melion, "The Art of Vision in Jerome Nadal's *Adnotationes et meditationes in Evangelia*," in *Annotations and Meditations on the Gospels*, vol. 1, ed. Jerome Nadal (Philadelphia: Saint Joseph's University Press, 2003), 1–96; Ralph Dekoninck, *Ad imaginem: Statuts, fonctions et usages de l'image dans la littérature spirituelle jésuite du XVIIe siècle* (Genève: Droz, 2005). The illustrations have also been republished, and for a reprint and a translation: see Jerome Nadal, *Annotations and Meditations on the Gospels*: Vol. 1: *The Infancy Narratives*, trans. F. A. Homann (Philadelphia: St. Joseph's Univ. Press, 2003), Vol. 3: *The Resurrection Narratives*, trans. F. A. Homann (Philadelphia: St. Joseph's Univ. Press, 2005), and Vol. 2: *The Passion Narratives*, trans. F. A. Homann (Philadelphia: St. Joseph's University Press, 2007).

4. On these characteristics, see Fabre, *Ignace de Loyola*; Melion, "The Art of Vision"; Jeffrey Chipps Smith, *Sensuous Worship: Jesuits and the Art of the Early Catholic Reformation in Germany* (Princeton: Princeton University Press, 2002), chap. 2; Dekoninck, *Ad imaginem*, chap. 3.
5. *The Spiritual Exercises of Saint Ignatius*, trans. George E. Ganss (St. Louis: The Institute of Jesuit Sources, 1992), n. 47.
6. Melion, "The Art of Vision," 3.
7. Smith, *Sensuous Worship*, 43.
8. On European books on the Bible, including illustrated Bibles and biblical exegesis, that were sent to China in the late seventeenth and early eighteenth centuries, see Noël Golvers, *Libraries of Western Learning for China: Circulation of Western Books between Europe and China in the Jesuit Mission (ca. 1650–ca. 1750)*, Vol. 3: *Of Books and Readers* (Leuven: Ferdinand Verbiest Institute, 2015), 48.
9. Cf. Joseph Dehergne, "Une vie illustrée de Notre-Seigneur au temps des Ming," *Neue Zeitschrift für Missionswissenschaft* 14 (1958): 104; Jonathan D. Spence, *The Memory Palace of Matteo Ricci* (London and Boston: Faber and Faber, 1990), 62–63.
10. For an overview and bibliography of Chinese reproductions of European prints, see Erik Zürcher, "Prints and Painting in the Seventeenth Century," in *Handbook of Christianity in China*, Vol. 1: *(635–1800)*, ed. Nicolas Standaert (Leiden: Brill, 2001), 809–822. For the reproduction of these prints together with the originals, see *Chūgoku no yōfū gaten: Minmatsu kara Shinjidai no kaiga, hanga, sashiebon* 中国の洋風畫展：明末から清時代の繪畫。版畫。插繪本 (Machida: Machida shiritsu kokusai hanga bijutsukan, 1995). For discussions of the place and "influence" of these prints, see esp. Craig Clunas, *Pictures and Visuality in Early Modern China* (London: Reaktion Books, 1997), 172–183; Gauvin Alexander Bailey, *Art on the Jesuit Missions in Asia and Latin America, 1542–1773* (Toronto: University of Toronto Press, 1999), chap. 4.
11. There is extensive literature on these prints: e.g. Berthold Laufer, "Christian Art in China," *Mitteilungen des Seminars für Orientalische Sprachen an der Königlichen Friedrich-Wilhelm-Universität zu Berlin* 13 (1910): 106–111; Paul Pelliot, "La peinture et la gravure européennes en Chine au temps de Mathieu Ricci," *T'oung Pao* 20 (1921): 8–9; Pasquale M. d'Elia, *Le origini dell'arte cristiana cinese (1583–1640)* (Rome: Reale Accademia d'Italia, 1939), 57–66; Jozef Jennes, *Invloed der Vlaamsche prentkunst in Indië, China en Japan tijdens de XVIe en XVIIe eeuw* (Leuven: Davidsfonds, 1943), 93–100; Spence, *The Memory Palace*, 59–64, 128–132, 201–204, 262–265; Bailey, *Art on the Jesuit Missions*, 98; Carmen

Guarino, "Images of Jesus in Matteo Ricci's Pictures for *Chengshi moyuan*," in *The Chinese Face of Jesus Christ*, vol. 2, ed. Roman Malek (Nettetal: Steyler Verlag, 1997), 417–436; *Chūgoku no yōfū gaten*, 66–69; see other references in CCT database.

12. On Cheng Dayue and his *Chengshi moyuan*, see Lin Li-chiang, "The Proliferation of Images: The Ink-Stick Designs and the Printing of the *Fang-shih mo-p'u* and the *Ch'eng-shih mo-yüan*" (PhD diss. Princeton Univ., 1998). According to Lin Li-chiang, the fourth image, was not included in the earlier versions of *Chengshi moyuan* (published in 1605) but was added to the version published around 1610.
13. On these prints, see d'Elia, *Le origini dell'arte cristiana cinese*, 67–121; Jennes, *Invloed der Vlaamsche prentkunst*, 109–112; Bailey, *Art on the Jesuit Missions*, 102–104; *Chūgoku no yōfū gaten*, 475–480; Lin Xiaoping, "Seeing the Place: The Virgin Mary in a Chinese Lady's Inner Chamber," in *Early Modern Catholicism: Essays in Honour of John W. O'Malley*, ed. K. M. Comerford and H. M. Pabel (Toronto: Toronto University Press, 2001), 183–210; see other references in CCT database.
14. For an analysis of different editions of this text, see Dehergne, "Une vie illustrée"; according to Sun Yuming, "Cultural Translatability and the Presentation of Christ as Portrayed in Visual Images from Ricci to Aleni," in *The Chinese Face of Jesus Christ*, ed. Roman Malek (Nettetal: Steyler Verlag, 2003), 2: 477n20, thirty-seven copies have survived. She distinguishes two groups: (1) *Tianzhu jiangsheng chuxiang jingjie* (Jinjiang, 1637), with a foldout map of Jerusalem and fifty-six illustrations; (2) *Tianzhu jiangsheng yanxing jixiang* [in Chinese] 天主降生言行紀像 (not long after 1637) without map and with only fifty-one illustrations. There is extensive literature on these prints: d'Elia, *Le origini dell'arte cristiana cinese*, 121–124; Jennes, *Invloed der Vlaamsche prentkunst*, 113–116; Rheinbay, "Nadal's Religious Iconography"; Bailey, *Art on the Jesuit Missions*, 102–104; *Chūgoku no yōfū gaten*, 73–106; Junhyoung Michael Shin, "The Reception of the *Evangelicae historiae imagines* in Late Ming China: Visualizing Holy Topography in Jesuit Spirituality and Pure Land Buddhism," *The Sixteenth Century Journal* 40.2 (Summer 2009), 303–333; and Junhyoung Michael Shin, *The Jesuits, Images, and Devotional Practices in China and Japan, 1549–1644* (Seoul: Seoul National University Press, 2017); see other references in CCT database.
15. See Standaert, "Chinese Prints and their European Prototypes"; Standaert, *An Illustrated Life of Christ*. For copies and reprint of this work, see also CCT database.
16. See John F. Moffitt, "Francisco Pacheo and Jerome Nadal: New Light on the Flemish Sources of the Spanish 'Picture-within-the-Picture,'" *The Art Bulletin* 72.2 (1990): 631–638; see also Fabre, *Ignace de Loyola*, 285; Standaert, "The Composition of Place."
17. See Xiang Da 向達, "Ming-Qing zhi ji Zhongguo meishu suo shou Xiyang zhi yingxiang" [in Chinese] 明清之際中國美術所受西洋之影響, *Dongfang zazhi* 東方雜誌 27.1 (1930): 35; Hsiang Ta, "European Influences on Chinese Art in the Late Ming and Early Ch'ing Period," in *Renditions* 6 (1976), 160–161; Huang Yilong 黃一農, "Xin faxian de Yang Guangxian 'Budeyi' yishu Kangxi jian keben" [in Chinese] 新發現的楊光先《不得已》一書康熙間刻本, *Shumu jikan* 書目季刊 27.2 (1993): 3–13. For copies and reprint of this work, see CCT database.
18. Cf. Jozef Jennes, "L'art chrétien en Chine au début du XVIIe siècle (Une parure d'Antoine Wierx identifiée comme modèle d'une peinture de Tong K'i-tch'ang)," *T'oung Pao* 33 (1937): 129–133; Laufer, "Christian Art in China," 100–104. It is now kept in the Laufer Collection of the Museum of Natural History, New York.

19. Cf. Noël Golvers, "A Chinese Imitation of a Flemish Allegorical Picture Representing the Muses of European Science," *T'oung Pao* 81 (1995): 303–314.
20. *Le Musée de l'Orient, Lisbonne*, ed. Alexandra Curvelo et al. (Paris: Musées et monuments de France, 2008), 70–72.
21. BAV (Biblioteca Apostolica Vaticana, Rome), Borgia Cinese, 318.2; see CCT database.
22. This summary is based on the following publications about Visscher and his print Bibles: Wilco C. Poortman, *Bijbel en Prent: Deel IIa Boekzaal van de Nederlandse Prentbijbels* (Gravenhage: Boekencentrum, 1986), 26–33; Peter van der Coelen, "Claes Jansz. Visschers bijbelse prentenboeken," *De boekenwereld* 11 (1994–1995): 106–119.
23. BAV (Biblioteca Apostolica Vaticana, Rome), Shelf: Borgia Cinese, 316.17; see CCT database.
24. Lucille Chia, "Text and *Tu* in Context: Reading the Illustrated Page in Chinese Blockprinted Books," *Bulletin de l'École Française d'Extrême-Orient* 89 (2002): 242.
25. Deborah Sommer, "Destroying Confucius: Iconoclasm in the Confucian Temple," in *On Sacred Grounds: Culture, Society, Politics, and the Formation of the Cult of Confucius*, ed. Thomas A. Wilson (Cambridge, MA: Harvard University Asia Center, 2002), 101–103; Standaert, *An Illustrated Life of Christ*, 77–78.
26. Shin, "The Reception of the *Evangelicae historiae imagines*."
27. For the Chinese text and an annotated English translation, see *Kouduo richao: Li Jiubiao's Diary of Oral Admonitions: A Late Ming Christian Journal*, 2 vols., trans. Erik Zürcher, ed. Roman Malek (Sankt Augustin and Brescia: Institut Monumenta Serica & Fondazione Civiltà Bresciana, 2007).
28. See for this and the following topics, e.g., *Kouduo richao*, I.30, I.40, II.11, III. 42; VI.9, VI.22, VII.37, VIII.21, VIII.35.

Primary Sources

See note 1 and also of those primary texts discussed in the main text.

CHAPTER 41

INCULTURATION OF CHRISTIAN PICTURES IN THE REPUBLIC OF CHINA

XIAOBAI CHU

THIS essay investigates Christian pictures in the inculturation movement of Chinese churches in the Republic of China, which includes: (1) the paintings 聖像 by Fu Jen Catholic University 輔仁大學; (2) the comic-strip book 連環畫 published by the Chinese Christian Painting Press of the Gospel 中華基督福音畫社; (3) the pictures 圖像 on *Kung Kao Po* 公教報 (a Catholic newspaper in Hong Kong); and (4) several pictures 繪畫 in the books published by Tou-se-we Painting House 土山灣畫館. The primary Chinese artists of these works and the foreign missionaries who promoted them all aimed to implement the spirit of inculturation of Christianity in China. This means that they hoped to make the Christian church eliminate the images of the foreign religion and have their own Christian art become an integral part of Chinese culture. As artists, their effort was to localize Christian art. These attempts were limited to the field of visual arts, though; the essential issue it identified was based on the inculturation of Christianity in China in the first half of the twentieth century.

PAINTINGS FROM FU JEN CATHOLIC UNIVERSITY

In September 1935, in order to cooperate with the National Congress Catholic Action in Shanghai, teachers and students of the art department at Fu Jen Catholic University (Peking)[1] held a painting art exhibition in Shanghai. More than one hundred works were exhibited in this exhibition, and all of them made an attempt to promote the localization of Christian art in China.[2] Since this exhibition, the artists of Fu Jen Catholic

University have held more exhibitions, and more Christian works of art were exhibited in Shanghai, Tianjin, Peking, and even in Paris and Vatican City.[3]

The leading painter in Fu Jen Catholic University was Chen Yuandu 陳緣督.[4] In 1929, Chen Yuandu met Celso Constantini (1876–1958), a senior representative from the Roman Catholic to China, in a Chinese painting exhibition. Celso Constantini praised Chen's paintings and encouraged him to try Christian painting in the Chinese style. The purpose of Celso Constantini was very clear: he was sent to China by the Pope to implement the policy of localization. When he was in his hometown in Italy, Celso Constantini loved art very much. He not only created his own sculptures but also, he wrote books on religious art. In 1912, he convened the artists to set up the "Society of Holy Art" 聖教藝術友誼社 to study how to integrate art and religion.[5] When he came to China and started to become familiar with Chinese ancient art, he immediately realized that "in a country with ancient art and real artistic value, Catholic art should also cooperate with the trend of missionary innovation."[6] He also carefully studied the creation of Christian art in China from the Yuan dynasty to the Ming and Qing dynasties through historical materials. After his study, he came to the conclusion that "in Chinese missionary areas, from the sixteenth century to the previous years, except for a few exceptions . . . works of Catholic arts have been totally foreign."[7] During his stay in Beijing, he visited almost all the local exhibitions of Chinese paintings and eventually met Chen Yuandu at a small solo exhibition in 1929. Celso Constantini greatly appreciated the aesthetic value in Chen Yuandu's traditional Chinese paintings. At the same time, he introduced Chen to Christian gospel and European religious paintings. Later, this Chinese painter was baptized and given the Catholic name Luke. Since then and before 1949, he had created a large number of paintings on Christian subjects as a professor of art at Fu Jen Catholic University. The exhibitions of Christian art in the 1930s were all promoted by him, and his own paintings also accounted for a large proportion of them.

As we know, since the Renaissance, European religious paintings have used the principle of perspective to enable paintings to approach "reality" to the greatest extent. In contrast to this, scattered-point perspective is used in the Chinese painting tradition, and the understanding of fixed-point perspective was not introduced to China until the end of the Ming dynasty. In short, European painting pursues the effect of visual expressiveness and visual impact while, in the Chinese tradition, the way of expression of painting, together with the habit of appreciation of painting, is very different. Chinese hand scrolls and long-scrolls require a calm, melodious, and soothing attitude of appreciation. The so-called "seeking meaning beyond words" is the pursuit of endless aftertaste in the whole process of appreciation.

In the 1930s, Western paintings had long been familiar to the Chinese people, and there were many Chinese artists who adhered to the practice of Western paintings. More attempts were made to combine Chinese and Western fine arts.[8] When Luke Chen and other painters of Fu Jen Catholic University tried to localize Christian art, they also hoped that through the combination of Chinese and Western styles, Christian paintings would have a strong power of expression and conform to the aesthetic way of traditional

Chinese paintings as well. They chose *kiginu* instead of paper as the vehicle for their paintings since *kiginu* has the ideal quality of being absorbent. It is different from the raw and the ripe *Xuan* paper 宣紙. The raw *Xuan* paper is suitable for freehand brushwork and the ripe *Xuan* paper for fine brushwork. The water-absorbing capability of *kiginu* is just between these two materials, which allows it to show the dual functions of narration and expression of the painting in a relatively comprehensive way. This silk painting tradition often appeared in the mainstream of Chinese painting before paper technology was improved, especially before the freehand literati painting took its own unique style. Thus, it enables the painters to control the contrast in the form on one hand, to somehow present the basic principles of European painting; on the other hand, it also can realize the strengths of traditional Chinese painting in terms of composition and tone.

With regard to the subjects, the Holy Family and the Virgin Mary with the child Jesus accounted for a high proportion of artworks. When Celso Constantini met Luke Chen the first time, he told Chen the story of the Virgin Mary and asked him to paint a Chinese-style Virgin Mary with the child Jesus. Several days later, the painting, "Madonna Venerated Baby Jesus" (see Fig. 41.1), was born and received Celso Constantini's great appreciation; it was later reproduced in various church magazines and the Vatican even published a set of commemorative stamps with the image. In the following almost two decades, a large number of paintings with the theme of Virgin Mary and child Jesus emerged. The image of the Virgin Mary in these paintings is similar to the image of Guanyin (bodhisattva of great mercy) in the Chinese folk Buddhist religion. For instance, the poised and dignified Virgin Mary is like the Sun-Moon Guanyin, the elegant and quiet one is like the Water-Moon Guanyin, the simple and plain one is like the Fish-Basket Guanyin, and the most are those who hold babies like the Sender of Sons Guanyin (see Fig. 41.2 and Fig. 41.3). The Holy Family also is a subject often chosen by painters. Luke Chen's "The Child in the Crib," Lu Hongnian's 陸鴻年[9] "Flight to Egypt" (see Fig. 41.4), Wang Suda's 王肅達[10] "He Was Subject to Them" (see Fig. 41.5), and "The Newborn Shepherd" (see Fig. 41.6) are all excellent examples of this type of painting.[11]

Whether depicted in "Virgin Mary and Baby Jesus" or the "Holy Family," these themes themselves are full of strong emotional implications, especially focusing on the happy family atmosphere. The emphasis on family ethics is one of the essentials of Chinese traditional culture. With strong emotional character, the family theme can show a happy and harmonious family atmosphere. Therefore, even though not intentionally depicting this theme, the painters at Fu Jen Catholic University also tended to add children to their paintings. For instance, Luke Chen's "Jesus and Children" depicted Jesus with many children. In fact, in the history of European religious painting, both the theme of Virgin Mary and child and the theme of the Holy Family also have been extensively expressed. Depicted by famous painters such as Titian, Da Vinci, and Fra Angelico, paintings with the Holy Family theme have become almost the classic visual expression of European Christian paintings. It also is not deniable that there have been different styles of paintings on other subjects in the European tradition, such as the Last Supper, the Crucifixion, the Pietà, Jesus and his disciples, etc. However, in Christian paintings by the Fu Jen faculty, these popular European themes have not been equally developed. A large number of works focus on family themes, while the use of other themes still is relatively rare. As Celso Constantini rightly put it: "The theme of family is so rich in a human touch with the sweetest feeling, even the non-Christians can easily understand."[12] It is obvious that Celso Constantini had already realized that Chinese religion and culture tend to emphasize human relations, kinship, and ethical spirit. Expressing the core of Christian thoughts through paintings from the perspective of family ethics can highlight a loving God within family-like relations, by which to show the relevance between the Christian God and the traditional Chinese way of Heaven.

Another striking feature of these paintings is the use of visual symbols commonly found in traditional Chinese paintings, such as pine and bamboo, clouds and water, and moon-shaped courtyard doors. On Luke Chen's first Christian painting, "Madonna Venerated Baby Jesus," in the medium shot behind the main characters, there appear pines and cypresses symbolizing fortitude and moral integrity, and the noble peony symbolizing auspiciousness and wealth with traditional brushwork. If you look into the distance, you can see green mountains and rivers, which are no different from the conventional expression of visual symbols in silk paintings of the Song dynasty. In Luke Chen's other painting, "Jesus and Children," not only did Jesus' clothes become completely Chinese but also the children are typical of folk children of the Qing dynasty. In addition, the background also uses bamboo, which has rich symbolic meanings. The image of children is full of the folk information found in traditional Chinese New Year paintings and engravings. Bamboo is an indispensable spiritual symbol in traditional Chinese literati paintings. They are integrated in a painting expressing Christian religion, showing the pioneering artistic power of the painter. In contrast, Lu Hongnian is more inclined to express the pure Chinese traditional folk images. The most typical works are "Our Lady's Lantern Festival" (see Fig. 41.7). Many of the children in these two paintings carry colorful lanterns around the Holy Mother and child Jesus. This is a typical festive and peaceful image of the Lantern Festival. Lu Hongnian is also very good at expressing daily life scenes of the Holy Family with the distinct sense of the four seasons, which is also a common visual symbolic technique in Chinese landscape painting.

Comic Strip of the *Scriptural Pictures*

In 1937, the Chinese Christian Painting Press of the Gospel in Jia Xing published a book of comic strips, *Scriptural Pictures* 救主聖跡, which contains 226 pictures by Chinese artist Tang Xiaofeng 唐曉峰. Judging from the pictures in the book, the artist was not only familiar with the biblical stories but also had a good understanding of the European Christian tradition of visual arts.[13] For example, in the No. 13 picture in the book, "Simian and Anah the Prophetess Visit Child Jesus" 西面與女先知亞拿見耶穌,[14] the seven lampstands behind the main characters are a sign that conforms to the traditional symbol system of the Old Testament. We learn that Tang Xiaofeng was a painter specializing in the Shanghai style of calendar paintings. Shanghai Style art in the 1930s to 1940s was a typical product of the integration of foreign and native artistic characteristics. We also know that he was a painter who was good at religious paintings. The monthly calendar paintings and the picture sheets of the gospel published by Shanghai Evangelical Book Bureau all came from him. After his main work as a calendar painter, he carefully read the four Gospels of the Bible and "painted more than 200 pieces pictures of the holy acts of Jesus. Imitating the style of popular comic strips at that time, he put all the pictures into two thick volumes."[15] That is to say, the painter himself was an insider with external vision.

In the preface to the *Scriptural Pictures*, Tang Xiaofeng told readers of his purpose for making the book:

> In order to teach the gospel to the village women, children, and ordinary people, we have compiled all the biblical stories and all kinds of historical legends about the Holy Way. With moving pictures and simple explanations, we hope that the general illiterate and literate people can see the Holy Way clearly, and thus can increase their interest in the Holy Way. . . .[16]

Since this comic-strip book was intended for "fulfilling the mission of popularizing the gospel" and the potential readers were the "village women, children, and ordinary people," the various images it presented needed to be related to the living context of the normal people in China at that particular period of time. In terms of techniques of expression, the comic strips by Tang Xiaofeng combined the traditional Chinese line drawing, European realistic painting style, and the popular comic painting of the time. The figures in the paintings are mainly plain drawings, while the animals, houses, and some distant scenes are drawn in European style. But this is not a rigid rule. The artist also flexibly uses the forms of cartoon when it comes to problems that are difficult to deal with. For instance, in order to express the Christian idea that the price of sin is death, the artist puts a large black Chinese character "sin" in front of the black background full of white skeletons. At the same time, as a painter familiar with the Western Christian tradition of art, he also refers to the composition of famous Christian paintings. For example, the Virgin Mary in the history of European Christian paintings often appears as a pious reader of the Bible, and the Virgin Mary in Tang's comic strip is consistent with this tradition.

Like all calendar painters, Tang Xiaofeng was particularly good at character painting. The image of Jesus presented by him is a Confucian scholar in ancient China, while contemporaries of Jesus are all dressed in ancient costumes, and the background scenes are replaced by Chinese classical style as well. But there also are some exceptions. Sometimes the images show their strong characteristics of the time by dressing the costumes of Republican time. For example, in the No. 154 picture,[17] there is a typical capitalist character lying on a coin with the words "third year of the Republic of China." His fat body is supported by this huge coin, which echoes the words in the Gospels about "how hard it is for those who have wealth to enter the Kingdom of God." By depicting Jesus and his contemporaries as ancient Chinese, Tang tries to integrate Jesus into Chinese ancient history. At the same time, he expresses Jesus' prediction of the future by using the specific scenes of Republican China. As we know, the time of Republican China was no longer the period of self-seclusion; on the contrary, it was experiencing a rapid transformation of modernization. This state was illustrated in one particular picture (No. 111):[18] Jesus stands on the globe with the words, "Africa, Australia, Asia, America, and Europe," and says to a group of people dressing in ancient Chinese costume that Jesus is the light of the world. In this picture, the Shanghai calendar painting style with mixed features of Chinese and Western paintings creates a strong sense of time and space, by which Jesus Christ seems to be fixed in eternality. However, the image of Jesus in a typical ancient Chinese scholar style still affirms the special emphasis on nationalism in the period of the Republic of China.

It is worth noting that, like Luke Chen and his colleagues in Fu Jen Catholic University, the author of the *Scriptural Pictures* also naturally emphasizes traditional Chinese virtues, such as filial piety and diligence, from his local experience. The text in the No. 25 picture describes the growing experience of Jesus from childhood to adulthood: "Jesus lived with his parents. He had never disobeyed his parents, always liked to be happy and obedient, and carefully learned carpenter's craftsmanship under his father's leadership. He also did everything he could for his parents and never had been lazy. As soon as he got some spare time, he engaged himself in studying. Every day, he worked very hard."[19] Such imaginative exertion is completely consistent with the Chinese people's criteria for judging "good children" or a "good person."

Thus, the gospel story in the comic book is no longer about an ancient history in remote Israel, but a story in Chinese historical memory. Even if some details are fictional, if we can understand that "nationalism" itself is also a form of "imaginary community," then this fiction is not deceptive. Of course, it is still not simple to determine to what extent this fiction can really fit the "imaginary community" by producing certain effects on specific groups of people.

Pictures on the *Kung Kao Po*

Founded in 1928 and still published in Hong Kong today, the *Kung Kao Po* was the oldest newspaper in Hong Kong. Before 1949, this Catholic Church publication also had a certain readership in Shanghai and other cities. At the start of publication, the circulation of this newspaper had already reached 10,000.[20] In regard to the missionary work, Catholicism paid much more attention to personal network instead of publication in the twentieth century in China. Therefore, at the end of the Qing dynasty and the beginning of the Republic of China, the newspapers and periodicals for missionary work were not as prosperous as those in Protestantism. However, the *Kung Kao Po* inherited the Catholic tradition of image-oriented missionary work and published some portraits in the first two years of its publication.

Among these portraits, in terms of the subject matter, there are three portraits of the Virgin Mary and baby Jesus, five portraits related to Christmas, seven portraits related to Jesus' mission, and one portrait of a missionary saint in ancient China. In terms of the painting style, there are four classical Western paintings, eleven Chinese paintings and one modern painting. These paintings demonstrate almost all the important themes of the traditional Western Christian paintings except the Crucifixion. Although the cross as a symbol of the Crucifixion is depicted in a sketch style picture: Holding a cross, Jesus Christ is above the clouds in the picture, while at the bottom of the picture, a priest also holds a cross to respond.[21] Below this picture, the author gives a long interpretation of the significance of the redemption and the victory of the cross. As to the style, the combination of Chinese and Western features presents a universal image of Jesus. Obviously, the editors of this journal consciously presented the universality of Jesus and, at the same time, tried to integrate his Person into Chinese history.

From the text published by the editors of the journal, we can see the pertinence of this adaptive effort according to the characteristics of the times. Every issue of the column, "Principles of Catholicism" in the *Kung Kao Po*, published "A Brief History of Jesus." In the second issue publishing "A Brief History of Jesus," the visit of the three wise men from the East at the birth of Jesus is described as follows:

> In the horse stacks, the worshippers are not the poor and ignorant shepherds, but the most noble and wise ones. However, today's Catholic church does not make a difference between the poor and the rich, the native and the foreign. What only matters is the faith in God and His Words. As for those who have true knowledge and profound learning, their learning must be especially tally with the religion. Since the religion and the learning are not against each other, they form an integral part instead. Examining the ancient history in China, the moral principles and their statements of the sages and philosophers were totally consistent with Catholic religion. It is thus a big mistake that today's people regard Catholic religion as a foreign religion and criticize it.[22]

The unity of learning and religion which is, to a large extent, a tit-for-tat comparison with the non-scientific or even anti-scientific denunciation of religion at that time, is emphasized in an obvious way here. At the same time, the author tries to wash away the name of Christianity as a foreign religion, which is also a special response to the feeling of the times that Christianity was always to be condemned as a weapon of Western imperialism. Sometimes, this adaptation seems to be too arbitrary. For example, in order to show the consistency of filial piety with the Chinese tradition in Christianity, the author intends to add his own explanation of the miracle of "turning water into wine" in the section of "Jesus shows his transcendental omnipotence" in "A Brief History of Jesus":

> At the wedding banquet in Cana, Jesus expresses his love and respect for the Virgin Mary and made it clear that the Virgin Mary has great power to ask the Son to have miracles. Although sometimes the time has not been yet arrived to have the miracle, Jesus would not like to break his mother's will since he has enough filial piety to her. How can people bear that if the mother has asked for help from her son and son refuses to do that for her? Now Virgin Mary is the Queen of Heaven, and her influence over the Son of God has not been slightly less than the time in Gana. . . .[23]

It seems that the painter wants to use the miracle of Jesus "turning water into wine" to respond to the famous twenty-four filial piety stories in China. This also shows that since Christianity entered China, its symbol system has been one of the most difficult problems to resolve in terms of the collision and entanglement with Chinese tradition in ethical level, especially in respect of filial piety.[24] During the whole period of Republican China, Catholics had continued to work tirelessly to align Christian ethics and Chinese filial piety. The effort in the field of visual arts is one of the examples.

Pictures in Books Published by Tou-se-we Painting House

From the mid-nineteenth century to the 1940s, the Zi-ka-wei area of Shanghai had become headquarters for the Chinese Jesuits. Around the headquarters were the observatory, the Bibliotheca, Jesuit Theologate, St. Ignatius College, St. Ignatius Cathedral, Major and Minor Seminary, the Society of Carmel, Good Shepherd Convent, and other more than twenty-one institutions of education, culture, science and technology, and social charity. This area was thus known as "the Vatican of the far East." Among these church institutions, one orphanage won a reputation for its "Tou-se-we Orphanage Craft Workshop" 土山灣孤兒院工藝場, which made the Catholic community there become "the most large-scale and influential source of Western culture transmission in modern China" in the late nineteenth and early twentieth centuries.[25] The Painting House of this Orphanage Craft Workshop was established in the 1860s. Its birth was a symbol that the earliest school of teaching Western painting appeared in Shanghai in the middle of the nineteenth century. The students of Tou-se-we Painting House were to be the first group of artists who mastered the oil painting and sculpture of Western technique. The famous Chinese painter Xu Beihong 徐悲鴻, made these comments about the Painting House: "This place offered its great contribution to the cultural communication between China and the West. It was the cradle of the Western painting in China."[26]

The establishment of Tou-se-we Painting House was mainly for training artists in the technique of Christian painting and sculpture. The fund for the orphans in Tou-se-we orphanage were donated by both Chinese and Western Catholic churches.[27] Those orphans then received four years of basic cultural education, including Chinese, arithmetic, character learning, Catholicism, and other subjects. The task of learning basic culture in Tou-se-we was arduous. According to the memories of those who experienced it, students were expected to read the Bible from 7 to 12 a.m. and study culture courses from 1 to 6 p.m.[28] On average, at the age of 13, they were given some technical skills according to the qualifications of each student, and then they graduated at the age of 19. Tou-se-we Painting House mainly trained orphans with artistic ability. It adopted the apprenticeship system and classified teaching according to the time order of their admission. The education system was generally four years; if one studied oil painting, it would be extended for one year. In addition to a small amount of painting supplies imported from Europe, color and canvas coating materials should be made locally, so the pupils learned how to grind and modulate color at the beginning of their study. Foreign and Chinese missionaries taught them different painting skills, such as pencil painting, pen painting, color painting, and oil painting. The most works done in the classroom were copying the models.[29] After two exams a year, the top three students were rewarded and encouraged. A little allowance was available during the apprenticeship period, and a piece-by-piece remuneration also was available after the completion of the teacher's degree.[30] After graduation, since these pupils had already mastered the skills of making a living and could support themselves in society, "it was up to them whether they would like to work in the Painting House or move out to make a living."[31] Thus, the formal Western art education system and methods finally appeared in modern China.[32]

The works of Tou-se-we Painting House are primarily Catholic icons.[33] According to records, members also sometimes copied famous European Renaissance paintings. While the Catholic missionaries at the end of the Ming dynasty and at the beginning of the Qing dynasty used Western religious paintings as a supplement to their missionary work, and the iconography was at that time used only as a "lead" to draw attention, the paintings in Tou-se-we Painting House in Shanghai were not only a "lead," but a large-scale and systematic way to integrate missionary work with teaching and market operation. This combination of scale, systematization, and marketization shows that the situation of Christianity had greatly improved in some cities of China at this time, and the Christian communities had become increasingly large as well, which provided a considerable market for the icons. At the same time, consumers of the paintings also had undergone important changes. Previous missionary paintings were mainly used as a supplementary tool to preach the gospel. As regard to Tou-se-we paintings, even though they still played the role of preaching the gospel, their main purchasers should undoubtedly be Catholics. The supply of icons produced by Tou-se-we Painting House was to meet the needs of Catholic churches' decoration and the spiritual practice of Catholics all over the country. They were very often in short supply:

> Most of the icons favored by Chinese Catholics were painted and printed in Tou-se-we, and the decorations and tools used in the cathedrals can be seen in almost every church in the vast and boundless empire of China.[34]

What was the reason Tou-se-we paintings were so widely appreciated in that period? "The paintings are so exquisite that one could not help showing extreme admiration for them."[35] In fact, this statement points out the reason. The works by Tou-se-we Painting House were indeed very rich. However, it is a pity that very few of them were preserved during the last century. Nevertheless, it is still fortunate that three books with pictures published by Tou-se-we survived, which can give us precious materials to study the works of the Painting House. Actually, from the perspective of the development history of modern Chinese art, "the achievement of books with pictures is the sign of the mature time of Tou-se-we Painting House."[36] The three books preserved well today are the *Essence of Tao* 道原精萃 (1887), *Picture Interpretation of Ancient History* 古史像解 (1892), and *Picture Interpretation of New History* 新史像解 (1892). The first book, which contains more than three hundred pictures, is about the dogma of Christianity, and the second and third books are about the Old and New Testament, which contain almost three hundred pictures in all. Although these books were first published in the late nineteenth century, they also were published again and again in the Republic of China. And especially in the 1920s and 1930s, they became quite popular in Christian circles. This is the reason these pictures also belong to the Republican time.

From these three books, we can see that, after mastering the techniques of foreign paintings, the Chinese painters in Tou-se-wei Painting House were allowed to create freely. Sometimes they also could combine Chinese painting elements into European-style paintings. The works from the *Essence of Tao* are models of their achievement. For instance, there is one picture called "Jesus Christ Wearing the Crown of Thorns."[37] The painter depicted the shape of the face by using lines instead of the wide range of contrast between light and shade typical of European painting. This is different from the European style of painting, but also different from the traditional Chinese painting with regard to the use of lines. The use of lines in Chinese painting emphasizes the beauty of the lines themselves; that is, a kind of smooth rhythm, while the lines in this picture serve the shape and structure completely. It follows the structure-first principle in European painting instead of considering the actual meaning of lines in traditional Chinese painting. This method of using lines enables the works completed by Westerners on bronze plates to be reproduced in another painting medium—traditional Chinese wood plates. There is one image of Jesus Christ with the crown of thorns on his head and his eyes lowered, yet there is no bitterness or anger in his eyes; he seems to look lovingly down upon all living beings.

The other two books painted and published in Tou-se-we also display this artistic feature. The *Book of Picture Interpretation of Ancient History* was first published in 1892. It is a color set printing and lithographic printing according to the analysis of the particles produced on the paper. In this picture book, the images are vivid in form and color. There are seven colors: green, brown, red, light red, blue, yellow, and flesh color, plus black lines, which need to be printed eight times. In many places, new colors are produced by repeated the printing of two other colors. The first colorful picture in the *Book of Picture Interpretation of Ancient History* depicts the scene of a group of Chinese children learning the Old Testament under the guidance of their elder. The basic sense of perspective and the mastery of the proportions of the figures in this painting show the painter's proficiency in European painting techniques, and the overall representation of Jesus Christ is based entirely on the style of Catholic iconography, while in details, the way of depicting the cloud below Jesus, the other figures, and furnishings are all of the authentic Chinese style. It is so well executed that the foreign and Chinese features co-exist in one picture in a harmonious way.

Conclusion

Inculturation is a complex concept, and the process of inculturation must be long and complex, because the "local" itself is not immutable, especially for Chinese society in a rapid transitional period.

During the one hundred years from the late Qing dynasty to the Republic of China, on one side, Chinese society experienced social changes that had not been seen in the past thousand years. On the other side, the national crisis in this period of time covered up all kinds of complexity to some extent, and thus made all the cultural forms conform as the most rapid response to the mission of national salvation and rejuvenation. When this kind of nationalism becomes the mainstream of the time, recognition of the local culture will inevitably lose the complex dimension it should have and become over-simplified.

Whether the mixed Chinese and Western style pictures published in the *Kung Kao Po* and the Catholic books, or the semi-Chinese and thorough Chinese portraits created by Fu Jen Catholic University and the Chinese Christian Painting Press of the Gospel, all of them were pioneers in exploring the possibility of the inculturation of Christian art in China. Although some of these efforts were made too rashly and were over-simplified, they were still worthwhile attempts to seek the connection between Christianity and Chinese culture. It seems that they all tried to make an issue of the form of the pictures, but in essence, they were paying more attention at a deeper level, that is, to associate images in the Bible with Chinese history and culture, especially to implant the image of Jesus into the Chinese interpretation of history of redemption.

APPENDIX

FIGURE 41.1 "Madonna Venerated Baby Jesus," by Chen Yuandu, 1928 (from Sepp Schüller, *Neue Christliche Malerei in China* [Düsseldolf: Mosella-Verlag, 1940], 66).

FIGURE 41.2 "Maris Stella," by Luke Chen, unknown time (from Sepp Schüller, *Neue Christliche Malerei in China* [Düsseldolf: Mosella-Verlag, 1940], 56).

FIGURE 41.3 "Madonna with Virgin Musicians," by Chen Yuandu, 1938 (from Fritz Bornemann, *Ars Sacra Pekinensis: Die Chinesisch-Christliche Malerei An Des Katholischen Universität in Peking* [Mödling bei Wien: Druck Und Verlag Missionsdruckerei St. Gabriel, 1950], 59).

FIGURE 41.4 "Our Lady's Lantern Festival," by Lu Hongnian, 1936 (from Fritz Bornemann, *Ars Sacra Pekinensis: Die Chinesisch-Christliche Malerei An Des Katholischen Universität in Peking* [Mödling bei Wien: Druck Und Verlag Missionsdruckerei St. Gabriel, 1950], 171).

FIGURE 41.5 "He Was Subject to Them," by Wang Suda, 1940 (from Fritz Bornemann, *Ars Sacra Pekinensis: Die Chinesisch-Christliche Malerei An Des Katholischen Universität in Peking* [Mödling bei Wien: Druck Und Verlag Missionsdruckerei St. Gabriel, 1950], 127).

FIGURE 41.6 "The Newborn Shepherd," by Luke Chen, unknown time (from Sepp Schüller, *Neue Christliche Malerei in China* [Düsseldolf: Mosella-Verlag, 1940], 106).

FIGURE 41.7 "Our Lady's Lantern Festival," by Lu Hongnian, 1936 (from Fritz Bornemann, *Ars Sacra Pekinensis: Die Chinesisch-Christliche Malerei An Des Katholischen Universität in Peking* [Mödling bei Wien: Druck Und Verlag Missionsdruckerei St. Gabriel, 1950], 171).

NOTES

1. Fu Jen Catholic University in Peking was founded in 1925. Its predecessor was Fu Jen Society affiliated to Peking Catholic University. In 1927, it was renamed Private Fu Jen University. In 1931, it was formally filed at the Ministry of Education of the Central Government of Nanjing. It was taken over by the Central People's Government in October 1950. By 1952, the faculty was reorganized and merged with Beijing Normal University. Fu Jen Catholic University in Peking thus has a history of twenty-seven years.

2. Luke Chen 陳路加, "An Appreciation of the Catholic Art Exhibition in Shanghai," *Fu Jen Magazine*, vol. II (1936) (Fu Jen Catholic University in Peking, published in Techny, Illinois, USA), 82–83.
3. Fritz Bornemann, *Ars Sacra Pekinensis: Die Chinesisch-Christliche Malerei an der Katholischen Uniersität (Fu Jen) in Peking* (Mödling bei Wien: Verlag Missions druckerei St. Gabriel, 1950), 12.
4. Chen Yuandu (1902–1967), original name was Chen Yu. In 1917, he started to study Chinese painting, and joined the Chinese Painting Institute in 1923. In 1926, he participated in the founding of Hushe Painting Association. He taught at the National Peking Academy of Art and Jing Hua Academy of Fine Arts. In 1932, he was baptized, named Luke, and appointed professor of art at Fu Jen Catholic University in Peking. Since then, a group of Christian painters formed around him. He organized several Christian art exhibitions in Shanghai and Beijing. Since the 1950s, he taught in Beijing Normal University of Art and the Central Academy of Arts and Crafts.
5. Celso Constantin, *Cultivate in China: Recollections of Celso Constantin* [in Chinese] 在中國耕耘—剛恆毅樞機回憶錄 (Taipei: Congregatio Discipulorum Domini Press, 1980), 30–42.
6. Celso Constantin, *Chinese Catholic Fine Arts* [in Chinese] 中國天主教美術 (Taipei: Guangqi Publishing House, 1968), 12.
7. Gu Weimin, *A History of Christian Arts in Modern China* [in Chinese] 近代中國基督宗教藝術發展史 (Hongkong: Tao Fong Shan Christian Center, 2006), 136.
8. During that period of time, Chen Baoyi, Feng Gangbai, Ni Yide, Pan Yuliang, and other painters adhered to the Western painting, while Wang Yuezhi, Liu Haisu, Lin Fengmian, Guan Liang, Xu Beihong, and Wang Yacheng were excellent in the combination of Chinese and Western painting. See Ruan Rongchun and Hu Guanghua, *History of Modern and Contemporary Chinese Art* [in Chinese] 中國近現代美術史 (Tianjin: Tianjin People's Art Publishing House, 2005), 132–144.
9. Lu Hongnian (1914–1989) was a student of the Department of Fine Arts of Fu Jen Catholic University in 1930s. After his graduation in 1936, he was appointed as a lecturer there. In 1950, he was baptized and named John Lu. Since 1953, he taught at the Central Academy of Fine Arts.
10. Wang Suda (1911–1963) was a student of the Department of Fine Arts of Fu Jen Catholic University in 1930s. He was appointed as a teacher in Fu Jen Catholic high school after his graduation in 1936. In 1937, he was baptized and named George Wang.
11. See pictures in Sepp Schüller, *Neue Christliche Malerei in China* (Düsseldolf: Mosella-Verlag, 1940), 85; Fritz Bornemann S.V.D., *Ars Sacra Pekinensis: Die Chinesisch-Christliche Malerei An Des Katholischen Universität in Peking* (Vienna: Druck Und Verlag Missionsdruckerei St. Gabriel, Mödling bei Wien, 1950), 59, 127, 121.
12. Celso Constantin, *Cultivate in China: Recollections of Celso Constantin* (Taipei: Congregatio Discipulorum Domini Press, 1980), 385.
13. Tang Xiaofeng, *The Scriptural Pictures* [in Chinese] 救主聖跡 (Jiaxing: the Chinese Christian Painting Press of the Gospel, 1937), the preface.
14. See the thirteenth picture in *The Scriptural Pictures* by Tang Xiaofeng, 13.
15. Ibid. preface.
16. Ibid. preface.
17. See the 154th picture in ibid. 154.
18. See the 111st picture in ibid. 111.
19. Ibid. the preface.

20. Lin Ruiqi, *The Research on Kung Kao Po (1928–1931)* (Hongkong: Catholic Holy Spirit Research Center of Hongkong Parish, 2003), 9–37.
21. See "I am the Light of the World," a modern painting by Alvares in Fr. A. Granelli, ed., *Kun Kao Po* (Hong Kong: Vicariate Apostolic of Hong Kong, August 1, 1929), 1.
22. Ibid. (September 9, 1928).
23. Ibid. (March 1, 1929).
24. In China, "filial piety" is the basic content of family system in the patriarchal society. In a society where "the filial piety is the most important value," the worship of ancestors is the basic ethical norm that every Chinese people need to abide by. The question whether Chinese Christians could worship their ancestors aroused great controversy among the missionaries since the late Ming dynasty, and eventually led to the Rites Controversy in the Qing dynasty. The Vatican believed that worship of ancestors was not in conformity with religious rules, and the Qing government banned Christian missionary work in China. During the last decades of the Qing dynasty, the local squires called on the people to expel the foreign religion and initiated numerous religious cases.
25. Su Zhiliang, "Origin and Evolution of Tou-se-we," in *Shanghai Xinming Evening News* (June 16, 2008), B-5.
26. Ibid.
27. Zhang Wei, "The Tou-se-we in Old Shanghai: The Cradle of Chinese Modern Arts and Handicraft," *Shanghai Arts and Handicraft* 2 (1998): 18.
28. Meng Qing, "The Disappearing Tou-se-we," *Chinese Religions* 6 (2003): 41.
29. Zhou Xiufen, ed., *Zikawei in History* (Shanghai: Sanhua Advertising Co., 2005), 114.
30. Zhang Hongxing, "In Memory of the Earliest Cradle of Western Art: The Artistic Career of Shanghai Tou-se-we Orphanage," *Southeast Culture* 5 (1991): 126.
31. Zhang Wei, "The Tou-se-we in Old Shanghai," 18.
32. Li Chao, "The Disappearing Cradle," 44.
33. Zhu Boxiong and Chen Ruilin, *Fifty Years of Chinese Western Painting (1898–1949)* (Beijing: People's Fine Arts Publishing House, 1989), 29.
34. J. de. ca. Serviere, *Missionary History in Jiangnan*, trans. by the translation group of historical materials in Shanghai Diocese (Shanghai: Shanghai Translation Publishing House, 1983), 2:294.
35. Zhang Wei, "The Tou-se-we in Old Shanghai," 18.
36. Luan Rongchun and Hu Guanghua, *The History of Modern Art in China* (Tianjin: Tianjin People's Art Publishing House, 2005), 29.
37. See "Jesus Christ Wearing the Crown of Thorns," by Liu Bizhen in Liu Bizhen, *The Pictures of Essence of Tao* (Shanghai: Tou-se-we Cimutang, 1904), 28.

Primary Sources

Bornemann, Fritz. *Ars Sacra Pekinensis-Die Chinesisch-Christliche Malerei an der Katholischen Uniersität (Fu Jen) in Peking*. Mödling bei Wien: Druck Und Verlag Missionsdruckerei St. Gabriel, 1950.

Chinese Artist: The Life of Christ by Chinese Artists. London: Roffey & Clark Ltd., 1954.

Fleming, Daniel Johnson. *Each with His Own Brush: Contemporary Christian Art in Asia and Africa*. New York: Union Theological Seminary, 1938.

Kung Kao Po (The Catholic Newspapers in Hong Kong), 1928–1931.

Liu Bizhen. *The Pictures of Essence of Tao*. Shanghai: Tou-se-we Cimutang, 1904.
Picture Interpretation of Ancient History. Shanghai: Tou-se-we Publishing House, 1926.
Schüller, Sepp. *Neue Christliche Malerei in China*. Düsseldorf: Mosella-Verlag, 1940.
Tang Xiaofeng. *The Scriptural Pictures*. Jiaxing: Chinese Christian Painting Press of the Gospel, 1937.

CHAPTER 42

THE BIBLE AND CHINESE CHURCH MUSIC

SUN CHENHUI

Introduction

In many ways, Chinese and biblical cultures share a commonality in their poetic languages, passion of the people for music, and their yearning for the aesthetic. At the time of the OT, rich and diverse musical forms were used widely in various ritual and non-ritual activities, and this has been true since ancient China. During the NT period, these musical forms then were seen rarely in Greco-Roman cultures. But musical instruments are mentioned in the NT, and the apostle Paul encouraged believers to praise God with psalms, hymns, and spiritual songs.[1]

Traditions and Functions of Instrumental Music

There is no doubt that, in Mesopotamian and ancient Egyptian cultures, Hebrew instruments and their music and worship styles were not the traditions of today's Chinese or foreign world. In the Chinese Union Version of the Bible published over one hundred years ago, Chinese translators used frequently the terms of Chinese-specific musical instruments, such as *di* 笛, *sheng* 笙, *gu* 鼓, *bo* 鈸, *luo* 鑼, *pipa* 琵琶, *se* 瑟, *guqin* 古琴 and other silk 絲弦 instruments, hoping that Chinese readers would praise God in their own languages and music.

Musical instruments in the Bible may be divided into three categories: stringed instruments, wind instruments, and percussion instruments. People used them to practice psychotherapy, exorcism, and worship activities. Among these functions, the most important one was to praise God in a liturgical setting, and music was performed either by a single instrument or a band or orchestra. During the reign of King David and his son, King Solomon, large-scale comprehensive orchestras, combining vocal music, instrumental music, and dancing, were arranged for the purpose of worship (see the psalms). As early Christianity developed, instrumental music did not become mainstream church music,[2] and the situation improved slightly only until the Baroque period, where instrumental music in Western Europe flourished as a whole.

Christianity was introduced to China along with Middle Eastern and Euro-American church music. Missionary history, taking place over 1,384 years, came in four waves, namely: (1) during the Tang dynasty; (2) during the Yuan dynasty; (3) at the end of the Ming dynasty; and (4) at the beginning of the Qing dynasty and during the Opium War. The descriptions of church liturgies and worship life and the use of musical instruments during the Ming and Qing period were found in the letters of many foreign missionaries to China.[3]

In modern China, one of the major features of Chinese Mass ceremonies was the performance of Chinese music (*zhongyue* 中樂), Chinese folk music (*mingyue* 民樂), or wind and percussion music of folk traditions (*bayin hui* 八音會 or *yinyue hui* 音樂會)—not for entertainment purposes but as an integral part of worship in church life. Bands would play music to replace recitation of the Scriptures, which was called locally "blowing the Scripture" (*chui jing* 吹經). For example, recitation of the Lord's Prayer and the Hail Mary in the holy rosary was replaced by the music of a band. This form of Catholic church music presentation is gradually disappearing but can be seen still in some northern Chinese provinces, mainly in Shanxi and Shaanxi, and especially was observed widely in some cities such as Taiyuan, Xinzhou, Jinzhong, Yuci, and Qixian. The musical band, called *yinyue hui*, in the Catholic archdiocese of Taiyuan, comprises civil (*wen jia ju* 文家具) instruments and martial (*wu jia ju* 武家具) instruments[4] and may be divided into four categories: (1) wind music; (2) plucked string music; (3) bowed string music; and (4) percussion music—thus including *dizi* 笛子, *guanzi* 管子, *sheng* 笙, *banhu* 板胡, *gehu* 革胡, *dihu* 低胡, *erhu* 二胡, *zhongruan* 中阮, *sanxian* 三弦, *pipa* 琵琶, *yunluo* 雲鑼, *chazi* 鑔子, *dagu* 大鼓, *paiban* 拍板. Nowadays, the band generally uses numerical notation, while musicians over 50 years of age also can play with *Gongche* notation 工尺譜. The "band" (locally called *Tianyue hui*, Heavenly Musical Band 天樂會) in the Catholic diocese of Guanzhong in Shaanxi also consists of civil and martial musical groups. Musical instruments include not only traditional Chinese percussions, such as *yunluo* 雲鑼, *nao* 鐃, *biangu* 邊鼓, *bangu* 板鼓, and *dagu* 大鼓, but also brass instruments, woodwind instruments, and the accordion introduced by the young musicians.

Traditional Chinese culture, especially dimensions of the aesthetic, including music, song, and poetry, are highly stylized and diversified. Yet, because it probably has been influenced by Confucian ethics, the culture of music is not simply about musical performance but about enhancing the aesthetic way of life and social ethics. Yeo writes, "Through the improvisation of music, ethics and politics will not be artificial activities but *artful living* of goodness. Once beauty is predicated upon goodness (virtue) and truth (*dao*), rituals and poetry will not be pursued self-consciously, selfishly, or for certain ulterior motives. Confucius taught that a person ought to be lifted by poetry, formed by rituals (*li*), and perfected by music (Analects 8:8)."[5] Thus, folk wind and percussion music is used widely in weddings and funerals in local traditions, to shape community, lifting their spirit of celebration and mourning respectively. But for a long time, wind and percussion musicians occupied a lowly position in traditional Chinese culture.[6] The folk culture that they represented has been passed down deeply and widely in China for the past one thousand years. And due to intermingling with local cultures, often the visions of life reflected in their music are fundamentally different from that in foreign value systems, especially Western musical principles. That is, traditional Chinese musical cultures may have had little to do with the notion of sacredness of church music since biblical times. Therefore, the application of folk music in modern Chinese mass ceremonies is more of a transition or a combination of traditional Chinese emotions and expressions of biblical or Christian religious culture, especially that which was transmitted to China through foreign missionaries or the force of globalization. Over the course of time, this special feature of mixing Chinese musical instruments with Christian liturgical texts died out gradually and is seen rarely in contemporary Chinese Catholic masses. Many Christian believers find it noisy and vulgar; thus, they are against such performance in the church. That being said, in Catholic ceremonies outside the church, such as pilgrimage, holy icon parades, and shrove ceremonies, where sacred ceremonies often are combined with folk culture, the *yinyue hui* 音樂會 ("band" music) has not totally lost its popularity, though almost attracting only senior citizens. Such animated activities that involve folk culture provide space for the band. Christian folk band music has never been really integrated with local Chinese culture. Though not completely eliminated, this band is fading away gradually and will eventually vanish along with the deconstruction and reorganization of traditional Chinese culture, as is the case with today's Chinese rural culture.

This brief review points to the crux of the matter, raising the question regarding challenges of church music in Chinese culture: (1) Are Chinese musical instruments in and of themselves inferior for use in Christian worship as compared to instruments in the Middle East and Europe? (2) What is "musicality" and, if there is such criterion used in Christian worship, would the *yinyue hui* feature less musicality? Is it possible that the "noisy and vulgar" reception of the audience of this music has to do with the musical performance itself, rather than the use of Chinese music? Could it be that the integration of so-called Christian music expressed in Chinese musical instrument was not done properly or beautifully? (3) Could it be that the Chinese church is still in the young age of forming its Christian identity? Thus, in order to differentiate from their own culture, why is it that many Chinese Christians "are adamant that singing traditional hymns . . . [in the United States] country music is acceptable, while singing hymns with traditional Chinese music . . . is prohibited"?[7] The challenging task of constructing a robust identity of "fully Chinese and fully Christian" music remains a significant one for the Chinese church.

Setting aside the challenges but still guiding us to consider the big picture of Chinese Christian music, the historical survey below may help. Ever since the first arrival of modern Western-style bands one hundred years ago, they have been relatively well received in China.[8] Due to the lack of professional musicians and relevant teaching staff, there are not many Western bands in churches, even in the big cities. However, in rural churches, Western-style military bands, military percussion bands, drum and trumpet bands, brass bands, and orchestras have mushroomed all over China. In visiting rural churches in China, one may be very impressed with the popularity, the huge number of such musicians involved, the entry-level performance, and the indigenization of the sound effects. In contrast to Western bands in modern China, when Western music was deemed as upper-class entertainment and the teachers were either foreigners or Chinese musicians with diplomas in Western music as well as experience teaching and playing mostly European classical music, contemporary rural Western bands has evolved by catering to people in the countryside and without the benefit of professional teachers and musicians. The characteristics of rural Western bands include a raw but joyful timber, a simple and loud performance, full visibility of percussion instruments, as well as delightful solos and ensembles, much like a Western version of the folk wind and percussion music. Such quasi-Western military bands focusing on brass music or percussion music have gained a great deal of popularity in churches across the country, replacing the old folk-music bands.

Pipe organs, one of the most representative musical instruments in Western churches, can barely be seen in contemporary China, however. In extremely rare cases, the churches keep the old pipe organs installed during the Republic of China period, such as the pipe organ (unserviceable) near the lectern on the second floor of the Catholic Church in Daming, Hebei Province. Nowadays, for the purpose of accompaniment, Catholic churches usually use stage pianos or electronic organs, while Protestant churches tend to use pianos or digital pianos. With the development of international exchanges and the improvement of economic conditions, many churches have started to purchase pipe organs. Nevertheless, due to the expense of purchase and maintenance, and the lack of professional organists, only a few churches have purchased traditional, large-size, mechanic church organs. With a reasonable price and acceptable acoustic quality, new electronic organs become the first choice for many churches. As a compromise, some churches have installed metal pipes on their electronic organs to create the solemn impression of traditional mechanic pipe organs.

The shortage of instruments and organists, as well as people's lack of knowledge in pipe-organ music, makes it difficult for pipe-organ music to develop in Chinese society. Meanwhile, Chinese churches rarely have the budget, the human workforce, or the vision to duplicate the complete musical setting of Western churches. As a result, most Chinese Christians are relatively unfamiliar with pipe-organ music, though in some cities where Western classical music has more popularity, such as Beijing, Shanghai, Xiamen, and Guangzhou, especially through the understanding of Bach and his music, the situation is better. The impressive sound effect and the solemnity brought by pipe organs are almost absent in Chinese musical traditions. The musical experience and related imagination with organ music in Western worship are very different from those of Chinese music. Putting cultural differentiation aside, this limited experience and imagination in China continue to be obstacles in pipe-organ music being introduced and integrated with the best Chinese soil; in addition, most churches simply cannot afford to buy and maintain an organ. There is more organ music used in churches in Hong Kong and Taiwan, compared with those churches in China.

Traditions of Vocal Music—Choirs

Ever since the choir of King David and professional temple musicians (1 Chr 15, 25:7), traditions of vocal music have developed steadily in Christian music, bringing to Christianity the reputation of a "singing religion."[9]

Historically, Chinese Catholic choirs used to sing Western traditional chants in Latin with Chinese characters as phonetic annotation in modern times. After the 1980s, they sing mainly Chinese chants. Chinese Protestant choirs tend to sing European and American quadraphonic hymns, some original hymns, and Western classical music, all of which are translated or written in Chinese, though some choirs sing in English depending on their educational level, and this tradition has remained unchanged. Chinese Orthodox choirs sing Russian chants in Russian or the old Slavic language. The small number of believers who are either of Russian ethnic identity or Russian descendants in North China have little influence on Chinese culture or Chinese music.

The development of Chinese church music is still in its initial phase, so it is the common goal of all the churches to build up choirs of professional quality. At present, the choirs sing mostly monophonic or polyphonic chants or hymns in Chinese, focusing on traditional Western church music and newly created chants in the style of Western church chants they are accustomed to. Usually, churches have several choirs for different occasions, such as choirs to sing in Chinese, English, or Latin, as well as children's choirs or youth choirs. Every choir may have different music styles and different types of members. For example, youth choirs comprise basically young singers, often singing popular chants with electro bands; choirs in Chinese sing at the major musical and worship services of their dioceses, and the music styles are relatively traditional. Musical activities organized by the churches include music-sharing concerts, international exchange concerts, music training, and music production.[10]

In the twenty-first century, tourism has drawn people's attention to the remote areas in China, and local governments are promoting the local cultural brands, hence the Protestant music of minority ethnic groups that was unrevealed for over one hundred years is gradually known to the world. In the past one hundred years, thanks to the efforts of China Inland Mission and other international missions, Protestantism has developed steadily in ethnic groups (nationalities) in remote mountainous areas of China. The minority ethnic groups have made full use of their excellent singing and dancing talents in the Western church music, interpreting it in their unique ways. In this regard, the Lisu ethnic group and the Huamiao ethnic group in Yunnan and Guizhou provinces in southwest China have outstanding musical performances. They are very skilled in presenting the quadraphonic Western hymns and Western classical music in local singing methods and local languages. Some other ethnic groups have Bible Scriptures and hymn notes created by foreign missionaries around one hundred years ago, written in local languages, and some still are in use today. This cultural-biblical encounter and cross-pollination is probably exhibiting its best marriage. The Christian culture of these ethnic groups is becoming the hot spot for researchers on anthropology, ethnology, and religious studies, as well as the tourism industry.[11]

Psalms, Hymns, and Spiritual Songs in China

The early church did not make music for its own sake, for the sake of expressing its faith in Christ and in the proclamation of the word of God, as Yeo writes, "Early Christian music gave expression to the new faith of the early believers, a worshipful response to God's salvation in Christ, and a liturgical call for the faithful to glorify God and serve one another."[12] The apostle Paul mentioned three forms of music in Ephesians and Colossians: psalms, hymns, and spiritual songs (Col 3:16; Eph 5:8–19), all for worshipping purpose, as the work of Geoffrey Wainwright has shown, that the singing and confession of faith are formative activities of the early church.[13] Most scholars think that psalms might be some kind of poem in the Old Testament, and hymns may be newly created poems of the early church; the interpretation of spiritual songs is controversial, however, and perhaps they are songs written by believers.[14] The Christian worship music has a long and rich history, but the core stays within these three forms, which almost always are sung with music accompaniment.

Hymns in China

When Protestantism came to China in the nineteenth century, the translation of hymns was taken more as text rather than music. The quadraphonic hymns though were adopted in churches and religious educational institutions as basic curricula on Western classical music and choral music. Chinese churches today are recovering their rich liturgical and worship resources, even though a lot of these are from outside China.

Protestant hymns have experienced the following phases of development in China: (1) the compilation and translation of Western hymns (1818–1860); (2) the compilation of hymns in Chinese dialects (1850–1870); (3) the emergence of hymn composition in the vernacular (1900–1936), such as the publishing of *Putian song zan* 普天頌讚 (*Hymn of Universal Praise*, 1936);[15] (4) the development of hymns in overseas Chinese communities after 1949; and (5) the development of hymns in mainland China since 1983. Because Chinese dialects and Mandarin are tonal, thus musical, as such the hymn singing in Chinese churches gives worship added layer of musicality. J. Gelineau, in his article

"Music and Singing in the Liturgy," has insightfully spoken of "the relative importance given to the verbal and the musical elements varies in inverse proportion," from reading Scripture to cantillation, to psalmody, to chant, to hymn, to jubilus, and finally to instrumental music.[16] In terms of musical style, these hymns may be divided into European traditional hymns and Chinese original hymns.

European traditional hymns were the dominant type of hymns in China, and it is still the case today. The first hymnal in China, *Yangxin shen shi* 養心神詩 (*Cultivating Heart Hymns*), collects mostly British church hymns with only thirty hymns originally in Chinese. This hymnal was edited and translated in 1818 by British missionary Robert Morrison (1782–1834). Then, another hymnal, *Putian song zan* (*Hymns of Universal Praise*), a comprehensive collection of hymns in China for over one hundred years, was published by the Society for the Diffusion of Christian and General Knowledge Among the Chinese in Shanghai (上海廣學會) in 1936. Another hymnal, *Zanmeishi xinbian* 讚美詩新編 (*The New Hymnal*),[17] is a standard Chinese Protestant hymn book with four hundred hymns, first published in 1983, and the main contents of all these books are a collection of various European and American hymns from the past two hundred years.

Chinese original hymns are not produced frequently in China; those that are may be divided into the following categories: (1) original lyrics with an existing folk melody or with a revision of an existing folk melody; (2) original hymns in Western style; and (3) original hymns in Chinese style.

Regarding hymns with original lyrics and an existing folk melody, it is a common creation technique in Chinese traditional music to write new lyrics for existing melodies, thus presenting the cultural preference for *qiu wen* 求穩 (stability) and *jian bian* 漸變 (gradual change). The famous *Lao baban* 老八板 (old eight beats) is the traditional Chinese tune with the most versions of lyrics for hymns in modern China.

The use of a revised folk melody is an adaptation or reconstruction of folk music. For example, the hymns "*Women zheci juhui you ge yuangu* 我們這次聚會有個緣故" (*There Is a Reason for Our Gathering Today*; 1883) and "*Zhu ci pingan* 主賜平安" (*Jesus Gives Me Peace*), written by Xi Shengmo 席勝魔, a pastor in Shangxi Inland Mission, were the earliest known hymns with folk-music features. All poems in the hymnal, *Minzhong shengge ji* 民眾聖歌集 (*Hymns for the People*) (1931),[18] were composed by Tzu-Chen Chao 趙紫宸 (1888–1979), dean of the school of theology and leader of Christian Fellowship in Yenching University, and the tunes are composed by Bliss Wiant 范天祥 (1895–1975), American missionary and dean of the department of music at Yenching University. This hymnal adopted Chinese folk melody for the harmony and was a good attempt at Chinese-style hymns. Another hymnal, *Yesu jiating shige* 耶穌家庭詩歌 (*Jesus Family Songs*), published in Mazhuang, Shandong, in the 1950s, also adopted folk music. The lyrics came from the easily understood doctrine written by Jing Dianying 敬奠瀛 (1890–1957), founder of the Jesus Family 耶穌家庭; hence, the songs were suitable for rural believers who were mostly illiterate at the time.

Original hymns in Western style often were created by Christian musicians and pastors with Western music educational training, such as: "*Shougao zhe* 受膏者" (*The Anointed*), a major choral work written by Ma Geshun 馬革顺 (1914–2015) and published by Chinese Baptist Press in 1954; "*Shengdan qu* 聖誕曲" (*Christmas Song*), a major choral work written by composer Zhang Xiaohu 張肖虎 (1914–1997); the hymns created by Pastor Su Zuoyang 蘇佐揚 (1916–2007), Pastor Shi Qigui 史奇珪 (1929–), and musician Yang Lufu 楊旅復 (1916–2014). These pastors and musicians were pioneers and developers of Chinese choral music and church music.

Examples of original hymns composed in Chinese style are among the 512 hymns in *Putian song zan* (Hymn of Universal Praise) published in 1936; seventy-two hymns were in Chinese tunes, either created by Chinese musicians or imitated by Western missionaries. Similarly, in the four hundred hymns in *Zanmeishi xinbian* 讚美詩新編 (*The New Hymnal*) published in 1983, 102 hymns were written and/or composed in Chinese tune by Chinese believers, among which fifty-six hymns were newly created texts.

The majority of hymns in China have been translated from Western hymns. However, despite a relatively small number, these hymns with vernacular lyrics and indigenous folk melody, with revision of existing folk tunes, and with originally composed hymns in the Chinese style are actually closer to the mind and heart of Chinese believers. Due to stylistic differences and the cultural barrier between Chinese music and Euro-American music, the general public tends to prefer their own familiar cultural style, especially in matters of faith and spirituality. This is significant because if the Bible itself suggests there is no revealed language or music and instrument, then the argument must follow that God's self-revelation and the content of Scriptures can be expressed in diverse languages. In the matter of church music and hymn-texts, Chinese Christians can better understand the content of the hymns to sing gospels or be immersed in biblical Scriptures if only they use the language of their heart and elements of their ecology of life.

Contemporary Chants

In the 1990s, Lü Xiaomin 吕小敏, a Christian woman convert with a middle-school educational background who was raised in a peasant family, wrote and composed a collection of oral folk hymns called *Jianan shi xuan* 迦南詩選 (*Canaan Hymns*) with lyrics and tunes. Her songs spread like wildfire from rural churches in Henan Province to big cities and finally became popular in overseas Chinese churches. As of 2011, she had written over one thousand hymns. The songs are of pentatonic scale with cordial and smooth melodies, as well as catchy lyrics. All these songs have similar styles that described the joys and sorrows in personal religious experience and thus found kindred spirits in the hearts of believers. Meanwhile, some musicologists critiqued her songs in such areas as simplified folk music style, colloquial lyrics, and occasional reference to sensitive topics. Yet, Chinese Canadian composer Huang Anlun 黃安倫 adapted some of these songs into choral compositions and made a recording. The promotion of these musicians further broadened reception of the songs by urban and overseas Chinese church choirs. In his movie titled "1942," Feng Xiaogang 馮小剛 used her song, "*Shengming de he* 生命的河" (*The River of Life*), as the closing theme song but with a new melody.

Nevertheless, these hymns—technically "songs"—do not completely meet the emotional expectations of urban youth. With urbanization further progressing in China at a swift pace, rural culture has less and less influence on rural youth. Youth today yearn for a new cultural language to express their spiritual need. Religious groups such as small-size gatherings and fellowships of urban cultures have come to rural China and supplied the musical needs of this generation of believers in terms of diversification and rejuvenation of musical styles and lyrics. Thus, lively and terse songs in pop style, such as that of Xiaomin, are steadily gaining favor.

At the beginning of the twenty-first century, starting from first-tier Chinese cities such as Beijing, Guangzhou, and Shanghai, some song sheets printed on single pieces of paper gained rapid popularity in a number of churches. These songs were modern popular style hymns from Taiwanese or American Chinese churches, with beautiful melodies and catchy lyrics, providing an entirely new musical experience for believers. Inland churches gradually learned about some famous overseas Chinese Christian musical groups, such as Stream of Praise 讚美之泉, Clay Music 泥土音樂, and Melody of My Heart 我心旋律. The songs that they created used basically pop music or the style of worship and praise music in the United States as reference. These styles have become a globalized trend. People in contemporary society tend to prefer more convenient, simple, and direct musical language in order to express their strong emotions, and Chinese Christians are no exception.

In such a context, the modern music style and modern Chinese lyrics from songs created by overseas Christian musical groups continue to inspire urban youth. As this music circulates gradually to mainland China, it appeals to young Christians. Although the mainstream inland churches persist in singing traditional European and American hymns and Western classical music that have been sung for the last two hundred years, the young and popular trend is irresistible. Meanwhile, with the development of media and communications, the worship and praise style has spread from first-tier urban churches in China to rural areas, including areas where minority ethnic groups live. Protestant gatherings of various sizes, such as evangelical music concerts, vocal concerts, praise and worship celebrations, and youth fellowships, all are flourishing over China, thus providing young people who have contact with Christianity, believers or not, with an entirely new way to know foreign Christian traditions.

Amidst the clash of global forces influencing Christian worship in China, modernization and contextualization of church music expressions also is encouraging the creativity of inland young Christian musicians. More and more original local Christian musical works can be seen on the Internet and, despite uneven quality, many believers still have a strong desire to create original church music and songs. In the whole Chinese-speaking world, it is not rare to see the popularity of some famous Christian musicians as well as theirs works, but unfortunately churches often do not encourage the work of music (except for some areas such as Wenzhou). Church music is now divided into two trends: traditional quadraphonic hymns and young pop-style music. In mainland China, the new musical development of Catholicism is much slower and more traditional, but the situation concerning Protestants, especially the emerging churches, is undergoing drastic change.

Music Style and Aesthetics

In the biblical period, "early Christian music was influenced by Jewish and Greco-Roman cultures, both of which has rich musical heritages. Temple worship and early Christian worship center on word or text with melody rather than on performance of instrumental music alone, although there is no evidence of prohibition to instrumental music."[19] The Bible shows the contextualized music model of the Jewish people, with the artistic style of their own ethnic group, as well as the cultural influence of other ethnic groups, though some of the cultural elements have been re-interpreted by the Yahwist faith. With the passing of time, styles and aesthetics of worship music continue to change. The history of Christian music in China has witnessed such cultural factors as contextualization, Westernization, popularization, and diversification.

Chinese-Style Music Works

Christianity originated in the Middle East and developed in North Africa, in the East (Orthodox Christianity) and West. The origin of worship music in the Bible is stamped with diverse cultural distinctiveness from the East and the West, but for Chinese believers, the history of Christian music means, for the most part, traditional European and American church music. Even today, Christian music in China is still mostly the translation of traditional chants, European and American hymns and Western classical music works, with very few Chinese-style Christian music works and very limited participation or contribution from professional composers. In the course of its development during the last few hundred years in China, Christian music has not yet formed its own musical system.

Except for some original Western-style church music works of high quality, most local music works in China are the result of borrowing of material from outside China, a quick fix for practical need (e.g., use in church service), and sometimes a misuse of music theory and biblical interpretation. Churches, mission-groups, missionaries, and believers hold different opinions regarding the use of Chinese traditional music in the worship life of the church, and few of them support such a position of appropriating Chinese traditional music in Christian worship. In the past four hundred years since the Ming and Qing dynasties, a small number of foreign missionaries attempted to use Chinese *Gongche* notation and folk music, and some Chinese intellectuals also made special efforts to mix Chinese with foreign music styles. The fact that some of them were able to create some high-quality, Chinese-style, Christian music works indicate that such enterprise can and must be done.

The following are the best representatives of indigenous Catholic music with Chinese traditional music style in the last four hundred years: (1) *Shengyue jing pu* 聖樂經譜 (*Scores of Sacred Music*), a collection of Chinese Catholic music compiled by French

Jesuit missionary Jean Joseph Marie Amiot; (2) *Tianyue zhengyin pu* 天樂正音譜 (*Compendium of Correct Sounds of Heavenly Music*), a Catholic hymn collection written by calligrapher and painter Wu Yushan 吳漁山 in the Qing dynasty with existing Chinese tunes of *Nanbei qu* 南北曲 (southern and northern songs); (3) the four Catholic chants created by modern composer Jiang Wenye 江文也; (4) the Chinese-style piano suites composed by Portuguese priest Aureo Castro 區師達 in Macau; and (5) *Zhonghua heyi misa* 中華合一彌撒 (Chinese Mass Unity), mass music created by contemporary musician Geng Hui 耿輝 in Taiyuan with northwestern folk-music style.

During its circulation in China in the last two hundred years, Protestant hymns mostly have translated Western hymns with Western music, but there are still some good indigenous music works, such as: (1) the aforementioned *Minzhong shengge ji* (*Hymns for the People*) in the Republic of China period, written by T. C. Chao and composed by Bliss Wiant in Chinese tunes for the harmony; (2) Chinese-style hymns in the contemporary *Zanmeishi xinbian* (*The New Hymnal*); (3) *Jianan shi xuan* (*Canaan Hymns*) written by Henan Christian Lü Xiaomin; and (4) sacred music works created by contemporary Chinese Canadian composer Huang Anlun.

These music works are the voice of Chinese Christians and are representative of their aspiration to use Chinese musical language. Unlike music works created by professional musicians, the aforementioned *Jianan shixuan* (*Canaan Hymns*) is unique in that it is the religious confessions of general rural believers in China. Therefore, in spite of the popularity of worship and praise music all over the world, including China, these indigenous songs still have a powerful emotional connection and influence in the Chinese-speaking world.

Trends of Music Aesthetics

In contemporary Chinese churches, there are two trends of music aesthetic: high-quality, traditional foreign classical music and modernized pop music. The former is the orthodox representation of church music in the Christian West, and the latter is the preference of the young generation of Christians in China.

To do traditional church music, good choirs are the common priority of development for Chinese church music, so it is still the mainstream music aesthetic choice for Chinese churches to construct a Western church music culture. Nevertheless, it is usually more contextual/indigenous in rural churches. For example, rural believers tend to add glides in the songs, which makes Western hymns sound utterly different, and the Chinese singers are not aware at all of their mistake although, of course, the choirmaster can point out this mistake to them. Such cultural difference is less obvious in urban churches. In rural churches, folk-percussion music and the seedling songs called *yangko* 秧歌 dance are very effective tools for sharing the gospel. In some places, this form of performance even has become the cultural and artistic feature strongly promoted by local governments; this is ironic as the Chinese government does not encourage religious belief.

Despite rural churches in China having their unique music features, like urban churches, they all regard pop electro bands as the most popular and most fashionable music expression, even in worship. The main reason is that, based on the rapid development of Christianity in today's China, the composition of believers tends to be younger and better educated than ever before. This huge internal change of Christianity in China, together with the increasing use of the internet and media in Chinese society, make pop music not only the cultural and aesthetic preference of the younger generation but also the cultural connection among social classes and different age groups. This is unprecedented in the history of music development in China.[20]

Chinese Christian Music and Biblical Vision

Music as a system of harmony and aesthetic always has had its positive effects on the worship and missional lives of Chinese Christian communities. Following the OT and NT communities, the Chinese church always has been adaptive and creative in using both instrumental music in their liturgical, social, and ethical life. Perhaps this expansive use of Christian music has to do with the Chinese language (which is tonal and pictographic) and the cultures in China, which are aesthetic. Thus, Chinese Christian music can be incorporated easily into cantillation (proclamation), verbo-melodism (chant), hymn-singing, or simple instrumental music for meditation.[21]

The Chinese church loves to sing, and singing together creates harmony musically, but also desired to form the "one body in Christ." Christian music in worship or mission contexts is thought to demonstrate the power of the gospel of salvation via aesthetic means, thus "'sing psalms, hymns, and spiritual songs to God' (Col 3:16; Eph 5:18–19) [is] tying love of God to music—the unifying (unison) and harmonizing (harmony) effect on a community."[22] The Chinese church has demonstrated that even though music itself may not save the world, music in the context of biblical proclamation and worship is believed to move believers and listeners into God's glory and salvation—especially in its mending the brokenness, healing the hurt, as well as drawing people to one another and ultimately to God. Indeed, the music and lyrics of the book of Revelation remains one of the rich sources from which the Chinese church can draw.

Conclusion

Christian music has a history of thousands of years, and nowadays various branches of churches all over the world seem to share a similar opinion about sacred music: as long as it is appreciated, any music genre may enter the churches, though with different priorities and purposes. In some highly diverse cultures, such changes greatly enrich sacred music and people's understanding of worship, but it also can cause confusion and conflict in China, which is relatively unified in terms of politics, society, and culture; Chinese churches do need to wrestle with more and more diversity of music coming to them without stifling creativity.

Due to historical reasons—suspicion of anything that is foreign and the current social-political climate of restriction—the challenge is that musical development of Chinese churches tends to be homogenous and conservative because people are unwilling to be stimulated by something from outside. As a result, Chinese Christians do not understand or are not willing to understand their own musical traditions, and they can only learn about the Christian music culture of the outside world through fragmented and sometime distorted information—without any access to the international community of people from different cultures and different religions.[23] The music development of Chinese churches, like local theology, needs to address the diverse, problematic, and powerful external cultural system on a fragmented, narrow, and biased basis. Therefore, the primary mission of music development in Chinese churches is to broaden the horizon and improve itself in a fast and comprehensive manner.

At present, as Christian music education in China cannot be integrated into social music education, this can be done only through the individual efforts of music professionals, musicians, music teachers, and music scholars. The nurturing of the Chinese Christian music culture requires the efforts of several generations.

Notes

1. See Geoffrey Wainwright and Karen B. Westerfield Tucker, eds., *Oxford History of Christian Worship* (Oxford: Oxford University Press, 2006), 24–35; see also K. K. Yeo, *Musing with Confucius and Paul* (Eugene, OR: Cascade Books, 2008), 231–240 on "music and its lyrical quality in the NT."
2. Thus the difficulty of researching this area; see Wendy J. Porter, "Misguided Missals: Is Early Christian Music Jewish or Is It Graeco-Roman?" in *Christian-Jewish Reactions through the Centuries*, ed. Stanley S. Porter and Brook W. S. Pearson (Sheffield: Sheffield Academic, 2000), 202–227. Taken from Yeo, *Musing with Confucius and Paul*, 231n149.
3. The earliest mention of Chinese musical instruments could be traced to the description written by French missionary P. Pierre Jartoux (1668–1721). See my former Chinese works, Sun Chenhui, *Catholic Music in North China* [in Chinese] 天音北韻—華北地區天主教音樂研究 (Beijing: Religious Cultures Press, 2012); Tao Ya-bing 陶亞兵, *Musical Exchanges in Ming-Qing* [in Chinese] 明清間的中西音樂交流 (Beijing: Eastern Publisher, 2001).
4. "Civil" or *wen* refers to those musical instruments used by civil officials or scholars (called *wen* in Chinese). "Martial" or *wu* refers to those musical instruments used in battle or by martial artists.
5. Yeo, *Musing with Confucius with Paul*, 229.
6. Musician register (*hu ji zhi du yue ji* 戶籍制度樂籍), a residential permit system that existed for thousands of years in China: musicians were in special register as a lower caste and served as slaves generation after generation. The musician slavery system began in the

Northern Wei dynasty and ended in the first year in the Yongzheng emperor's reign in Qing dynasty. Though some obtained citizenship, most musicians occupied servant status. These bearers of traditional Chinese music had a very low social position, especially the female musicians, who often were forced into prostitution.

7. Yeo, *Musing with Confucius with Paul*, 251.
8. During the large-scale circulation of modern Western music in China in the last one hundred years, most Chinese people find that Chinese traditional music is "inferior" to Western music which is perceived to be more elegant. The music preference of urban families tends to be Western classical and pop music, piano, and violin, instead of Chinese traditional music. The music education in contemporary China has illustrated the same problem. In the meantime, people have very limited knowledge of traditional Chinese music and other types of music. To a certain extent, the mainstream attitude of Chinese people regarding music appreciation is that Western music represents a superior, finer, and more elegant music culture.
9. Porter, "Misguided Missals," 204. See Luke 7:32; Matt 13:17, 26:30.
10. See Sun Chenhui, *Gregorian Chant in Tibet* (Centre for Catholic Studies. Shatin, Hong Kong: The Chinese University of Hong Kong, 2010).
11. See Sun Chenhui, *Hymns in Lisu and Huamiao in China* [in Chinese] (Taipei: Huamulan Publisher, 2015).
12. Yeo, *Musing with Confucius and Paul*, 235.
13. Jeffrey Wainwright, *Doxology: The Praise of God in Worship, Doctrine and Life* (New York: Oxford University Press, 1980), 156–163, 194–217.
14. Donald P. Hustad, *Jubilate II: Church Music in Worship and Renewal* (Carol Stream: Hope Publishing Company, 1993), 472–476.
15. Edited by six hymnal united committees (Shanghai: Shanghai Guang xue hui, 1936).
16. J. Gelineau, "Music and Singing in the Liturgy," in *The Study of Liturgy*, ed. Cheslyn Jones et al., rev. ed. (Oxford: Oxford University Press, 1992), 504.
17. Nanjing: China Christian Council, 1991.
18. Another hymnal edited by Tzu-chen Chao is *Fellowship Hymns* [in Chinese] (團契聖歌集, 1931), but this hymnal is mainly a translation of foreign hymns.
19. Yeo, *Musing with Confucius and Paul*, 233.
20. Due to the broad geographic range and the long history, as well as the highly diversified customs in different areas, Chinese music always has had very strong local features. Besides, the music aesthetics of the upper class and that of the lower class are not the same. As an emotional expression, music appreciation has never been unified in Chinese history. However, contemporary pop music from the outside world is changing the landscape of church music. It seems that pop music is becoming the common music language of all the Chinese people.
21. Yeo, *Musing with Confucius and Paul*, 233, 244–249.
22. Ibid. 236.
23. The traditional music culture in China has suffered serious destruction in the past one hundred years. At present, people are passionate with the revival of the traditional culture as a way to regain cultural confidence for political reasons. Nevertheless, Christians in China, especially urban believers, are reluctant to do so. In comparison, Christians in Hong Kong, Macau, Taiwan, and overseas Chinese communities are more naturally attached to their traditional music. Meanwhile, as denominational traditions of foreign churches were eradicated in China, Chinese churches have very limited choice and resources in sacred

music. Protestant music basically follows the choice of North American evangelists, which means European and American hymns and worship and praise music style, while Catholic music focuses on traditional chants. Compared with urban churches, rural churches have relatively more flexibility in making connection with local cultures.

Primary Sources

Aureo de Castro Nunes e Castro. *Aurei Carmina Pianoforte et Organo*. Macau: Macau Catholic Dioecesis Macaonensis, 2001.

Clay Music 泥土音樂: http://www.claymusic.org.

Jean Joseph-Marie Amiot. *Musique sacrée. Recueil des principals priéres mises en musique chinoise*. Manuscript. BNF collection Bréquigny 14.

Jiang Wenye 江文也. 聖詠作曲集第一卷 1947; 聖詠作曲集第二卷 1948; 第一彌撒曲 1948; 兒童聖詠歌集第一卷 1948 [all in Chinese]. Beijing Franciscan Biblical Institute 北平方濟各聖經學會.

Lü, Xiaomin. *Canaan Hymns* [in Chinese] *Jianan shi xuan* 迦南詩選. [Internal publication with no publisher and year.]

Melody of My Heart [in Chinese] 我心旋律: http://www.momh.org/.

Minzhong shengge ji 民眾聖歌集 [in Chinese] *Hymns for the People*, by Zhao Zi-chen. In Zhao Zi-chen, *Tzu-chen Chao Sacred Music Collection* 趙紫宸聖樂專輯. Edited by Yenjing Research Institute 燕京研究院编. Beijing: Commercial Press, 2013.

The New Hymnal [in Chinese] *Zanmeishi xinbian* 讚美詩 (新編) (線譜本). Nanjing: China Christian Council, 1991.

Putian song zan 普天頌讚 [in Chinese] *Hymn of Universal Praise*. Edited by six hymnal united committees. Shanghai: Shanghai Guang xue hui, 1936.

Stream of Praise [in Chinese] 讚美之泉: https://sop.org/.

Wu Li 吳歷. *Tian yue zheng yin pu* 天樂正音譜 [in Chinese] *wu yu shan ji jian zhu* 吳漁山集箋注. Beijing: Zhonghua Books, 2007.

Yangxinshenshi 養心神詩 [in Chinese]. http://hb.fhl.net/gbdoc/ob/ro.php?book=29&procb=0 [Paper version now collected by Taiwanese church elder Mr. Lai Yong-xiang 賴永祥.]

Zhao Zi-chen. Zhao Zi-chen shengyue zhuanji [in Chinese] 趙紫宸聖樂專輯*Tzu-chen Chao Sacred Music Collection*. Edited by Yenjing Research Institute 燕京研究院編. Beijing: Commercial Press, 2013.

Zhonghua heyi isa 中華合一彌撒 [in Chinese] *Chinese Mass Unity*. Geng Hui 耿輝. In《中文彌撒作品集》*Collection of Chinese Missals*. [Internal document of Taiyuan Catholic Diocese 天主教太原教區, 2014].

CHAPTER 43

CONTEXTUALIZING HYMNS AND SONGS FOR THE CHINESE CONTEXT

FANG-LAN HSIEH

Introduction

Chinese Christians were introduced to singing psalms, hymns, and spiritual songs in the early nineteenth century, when Protestant missionaries arrived in China to bring the gospel to the Chinese. Some missionaries, after they had learned the language and with the assistance of their Chinese tutors, began to write Christian tracts and translate foreign, mostly Euro-American hymns into Chinese.[1]

Understanding that hymns were a powerful means to evangelize the Chinese and to teach new Christian biblical truths, other early Chinese missionaries learned the Chinese language and translated hymns into Chinese. The first Chinese hymnal was translated and printed by Robert Morrison (1782–1834) in 1818, titled *Yangxin shenshi* 養心神詩 (*Sacred Odes to Nourish the Mind*). It was a text-only hymn book of twenty-seven leaves, including a translation of psalms and hymns commonly used in England and probably well-known by Morrison, the first Protestant missionary to China.

Early Chinese Christian Poems

There are two sources of early Chinese Christian poems, and we will look at the Nestorian hymns and the early Catholic hymn-text briefly before we focus on Protestant hymns and songs.

Nestorian Hymns

Prior to the Protestant missionaries, the Nestorians arrived in China in the seventh century. The so-called "Jingjiao" (Luminous Religion) was well received and flourished during the Tang dynasty (618–907); however, the Nestorian religion along with Buddhism was banned in 845 and mostly has disappeared in China since then. Few documents have been preserved regarding the liturgy and music of Nestorian Christians in China; nevertheless, two Nestorian Chinese hymns, along with some documents and numerous relics were uncovered in 1908 at a cave in Dunhuang by a French sinologist Paul Pelliot (1878–1945). Unfortunately, one of the hymns, *Daqin jingjiao dasheng tongzhen guifa zan* 大秦景教大勝通真規法讚 ("The Nestorian Hymn in Adoration of the Transfiguration of our Lord"), was lost during World War II. The other, *Daqin jingjiao sanwei mengdu zan* 大秦景教三威蒙度讚 ("The Highest Heavens with Deep Reverence Adore"), survived. It is the earliest existing Christian hymn: a hymn text traced back to the eighth century.

The text of "The Highest Heavens with Deep Reverence Adore" was translated by a Nestorian missionary Jing Cheng 景淨 in 760 CE from a liturgical text by Assyrian Bishop Alopen Abraham. The hymn contains eleven stanzas with four lines each and seven characters in each phrase. It was probably adapted from *Gloria in Excelsis Deo* and could be sung by the Nestorian Christians during the worship service.

The text is a hymn praising the Holy Trinity, as shown in the Chinese title. The fifth and sixth characters in the title, "*Sanwei* 三威" (see Fig. 43.1), literally mean "the Three Majesties," i.e., the Holy Trinity. Other characters in the title, such as the seventh and eighth characters, "*mengdu* 蒙度" ("obtaining salvation," see Fig. 43.1), and the ninth character, "*zan* 讚" ("hymn," see Fig. 43.1), were also Buddhist terms. "*Zan*" was a term that often appeared in the metrical eulogies and hymns of praise to Buddha. Furthermore, Jing Cheng borrowed several other Buddhist terms in the text. For instance, the terms he used to describe God—a Merciful Father, a Holy Lord, a Just King who "saved those who fall" in stanza 9—reflect his knowledge of Buddhism, and he used terms that the Chinese already knew to convey the Christian message. The hymn concludes with the words "*busiyi* 不思議" (see Fig. 43.1), meaning "Amen" in Buddhist expression. The hymn tune CHENG CHING TSAN 誠敬讚 was composed by Ji-fang Liang 梁季芳 (1906–1988) in 1934. The hymn was first collected in the 1936 *Putian songzan* 普天頌讚 (*Hymns of Universal Praise*) and again in the 2006 new revised edition of the hymn book.[2]

Catholic Church Music

The Roman Catholic Church began to send missionary priests to China in the late thirteenth century. The Franciscan priest John of Montecorvino (1247–1328) arrived in Beijing in 1294. The Jesuits came to China: Michele Ruggieri (1543–1607) in 1579 and Matteo Ricci (1552–1610) in 1582. Not much information regarding the liturgical music

FIGURE 43.1 *Hymns of Universal Praise* (1936), "The Highest Heavens with Deep Reverence Adore" (no. 2). Used by the permission of Chinese Christian Literature Council Ltd. (H.K.), extracted from the *Hymns of Universal Praise.*

of early Chinese Catholics has been preserved, except one collection called *Tianyue zhengyin pu* 天樂正音譜 by Yushan Wu 吳漁山 (1632–1718).[3] The collection, published around 1700, contained Wu's compositions of nine sets of masses. The masses were written in the style of ancient Chinese *yayue* 雅樂,[4] with strong influences of Western chants which Wu learned at the seminary in Macao.

Wu also was the author of the hymn text, "Lord, Before All Time Thou Wast" (*Yangzhi ge* 仰止歌). The hymn text came from his collection of poems *Mojing shichao* 墨井詩抄. He used the Chinese classical poetic style, a seven-character *lüshi* 七言律詩 to write this hymn of two stanzas, with four lines of seven characters each.

The text in stanza 1, as translated by Ivy Balchin (1914–2002) and Heyward Wong 黃永熙 (1917–2003), poetically depicts the way the Lord, being the "Judge of all," formed the world and gave himself to it; therefore, nations will fall "at Thy cross."[5] The second stanza contrasts the turning aside of "Satan's power" and the backdrop of "heaven's ladder," with the consequence that believers can lay their "burdens... on Christ."[6]

Emperor Kangxi (1654–1722) of the Qing dynasty also wrote Christian poems. He was a well-educated scholar. He sponsored the compilation of a multi-volume dictionary called the *Dictionary of Kangxi* and also wrote several poems, including a few hymn texts.

The emperor had the chance to hear the gospel through the Jesuits. He studied the Bible and Christian literature. Once, he was so moved by the crucifixion of Jesus on the cross that he wrote a poem, "From the Cross the Crimson Flow" (*Kangxi shijia ge* 康熙十架歌). The poem, which probably was not used at a liturgical setting, consists of two stanzas; four lines each vividly describe the scene in which Jesus was crucified on the cross. The text was translated into English by Ivy Balchin in 1975 with a tune *KANG HSI* composed by Heyward Wong, as the first stanza uses word pictures of "crimson flow" to describe the cross event that shares blessings universally. Yet, the hymn paints the suffering of the cross with vivid words such as "tried... bruised and torn... denied... to the whip his flesh is bare."[7]

Early Chinese Christian Hymns

From the mid-nineteenth century, a number of missionaries who had mastered the Chinese language began to compile new hymnals for their congregations. They not only revised existing hymn texts translated by earlier missionaries but also translated new ones into various dialects. Using hymns in Fuzhou, Xiamen, Guangzhou, Ningbo, Mandarin, and other local dialects, the missionaries were able to use the hymns to bring the gospel and to teach the biblical truths.

The hymnals compiled by missionaries rarely contained hymns written by Chinese; whereas, some missionaries had encouraged Chinese Christians to write hymns. The 1912 edition of *Songzhu shige* 頌主詩歌 (*Blodget and Goodrich Hymnal*),[8] a hymn book which was esteemed as "the best hymn-book in China"[9] at that time, contains hymns by Chinese. "God of Heaven Whose Boundless Love" (*Shangdi lianai zui shenhong* 上帝憐愛最深宏) with the tune PEKING was a Christmas hymn written by Chaohai Ren 任朝海, a pastor in Beijing. Another hymn, a mission hymn, with the tune name O SAVE MY COUNTRY LORD (*Zhonghua guizhu* 中華歸主) was composed by En Pu 恩普.

Hsi Sheng-mo

The *Shansi China Inland Mission Hymnal* included twenty-eight hymns written by Hsi Sheng-mo 席勝魔 (1835–1896). This text-only hymnal was issued by China Inland Mission (CIM) in Shanxi in 1901. Hsi was a Confucian scholar and a pastor in Shanxi. He was an opium smoker, who converted to Christianity after missionaries shared the gospel with him, and he believed he was healed by the Holy Spirit after ten years of addiction to opium. Later, he changed his first name from Zi-zhi 子直 to Sheng-mo, meaning "the Overcomer of Demons."

Hsi recognized the power of congregational singing and wrote several hymns and tunes. He loved to sing and liked to lead singing during meetings. As regarded by the British missionary C. S. Champness, Hsi's hymns and tunes are "Chinese of the Chinese" in their style.[10] One of his hymns, "There Is a Reason for Our Gathering Today" (*Women zheyici de juhui you ge yuangu* 我們這一次的聚會有個緣故), was often sung during revival meetings in China. The text has a strong gospel message, full of provocative questions regarding drinking, smoking, or gambling preventing one from receiving salvation. In the beginning and ending of the first stanza:

> There is a reason for our gathering today,
> It is the Holy Spirit that leading the church moving forward, . . .
> Is it drinking? Is it smoking? Is it gambling?
> Please tell me [Jesus] what else you can't give up to follow me and enjoy the everlasting life?[11] [English translation mine.]

In 1906, the CIM published a collection of twenty-five hymns of Hsi, titled *The Songs of Pastor Hsi* (*Xishengmo shige* 席勝魔詩歌).[12] The majority of the tunes were Chinese songs, or new tunes composed by Hsi. The hymn texts were translated into English by Francesca French (1871–1960), a missionary in Shanxi. The gospel song book was printed in London in 1920.

One of Hsi's hymn, "A Song of Compensation," was well-liked by Shanxi Christians. The hymn brought a strong message of comfort to those Christians who suffered from famine, hunger, disease, financial difficulties, and even persecution. The text has four stanzas with a refrain. Each stanza states a phase of difficulty in life (such as poverty, shame, trials, sorrows) and concludes with a refrain that gives a message of hope and peace "in the Lord."[13]

Dora Yu

Dora Yu or Ci-du Yu 余慈度 (1873–1931) was a prominent female evangelist and Bible teacher in the first part of the twentieth century. She inspired and trained many young men and women to become full-time ministers and evangelists, including brothers Wang Zai 王載 and Wang Zhi 王峙, and Watchman Nee 倪柝聲.

Yu published a gospel song book, *A Hymn Book for Revival and Evangelistic Meetings* (*Fengxing budao shige xuanji* 奮興佈道詩歌選集). The song book, considered one of the earliest hymnals by Chinese Christians for Chinese churches, was printed by the Presbyterian Mission Press in Shanghai in 1909 and contained one hundred and ten gospel songs with music.[14]

Jia Yuming

Jia Yuming 賈玉銘 (1880–1964) was a prolific author who wrote several theology books and Bible commentaries. He also wrote hymns and gospel songs, which were published in four books—*Hymns for Spiritual Fellowship* (*Lingjiao shige* 靈交詩歌, 1930), *Triumphal Hymns* (*Desheng shige* 得勝詩歌, 1938), *Hymns for Spiritual Fellowship and Triumph* (*Lingjiao desheng shige* 靈交得勝詩歌), and *Voices from the Hearts of Saints* (*Shengtu sinsheng* 聖徒心聲, 1943).

The New Hymnal (*Zanmeishi xinbian* 讚美詩新編) selected five of Jia's hymns from his *Shengtu singsheng*, including "The Lord's Grace Is New Each Day" (*Zhuen rixin ge* 主恩日新歌). In the hymn, the writer repeatedly uses the word "new" as in "new grace" (stanza 1), "new life" (stanza 2), "new thinking" and "new power" (stanza 3), and "new experience" (stanza 4) to remind Christians that God's grace is new each day.

His "Christians Love One Another" (*Xintu xiangai ge* 信徒相愛歌), a hymn often sung by Chinese Christians, was written for a Christian student group in the early twentieth century. Jia's elegant and yet colloquial text portrays the sweet fellowship among Christians through the love of Christ.

Wang Zai

Wang Zai or Leland Wang 王載 (1898–1975) was a significant twentieth-century Chinese evangelist. He gave up his promising naval career and became a full-time evangelist in 1921. He conducted many evangelist and revival meetings in China, North America, Europe, Austria, and New Zealand.

Wang compiled a volume of gospel songs titled *Evangelistic Hymns: for Church Worship, Gospel Services and Revival Meetings* (*Fuxing budao shi* 復興佈道詩), published by Alliance Press in 1923. The words-only gospel song book contained one hundred and twenty hymns. The song book was well-received and was reprinted in twelve additional printings.

His "I Praise My Lord Whose Boundless Grace" ("The Song of Holding the Plow" or "*Fuli ge* 扶犁歌") was written in 1929. The hymn text reminds Christians, as Jesus said in Luke 9:62, "No one who puts a hand to the plow and looks back is fit for service in the kingdom of God" (NIV). The text of four stanzas begins by reminding Christians to praise God for His boundless grace and His care for our bodies, minds and health. Wang concluded the hymn by encouraging Christians to bring "God's glorious name" to the end of the world.

Wang Ming-dao

Wang Ming-dao 王明道 (1900–1991) was a well-respected evangelist and pastor. He was wrongly imprisoned by the Chinese government for his faith from 1955 until 1980. Wang was a writer who wrote many articles which were published in *Liangshi jikan* 糧食季刊 (*Spiritual Food Quarterly*), a periodical Wang established in 1927 that ran for twenty-eight years. The autobiographical information of the first half of his life and writings were included in *My Fifty Years* (*Wushi nianlai* 五十年來) and published in 1950. *The Last Forty Years* (*You sishi nian* 又四十年) was compiled by Chinese Pastor Chang-xin Wang 王長新 and published posthumously in 1997.

One of Wang's hymn texts, "This House, O God, We Dedicate" (*Jinri wozhong huanji songen* 今日我眾歡集頌恩),[15] is a hymn celebrating church dedication. The text has four stanzas. Stanza 4 states that the dedication of God's house should remind us to rededicate ourselves because our bodies are God's temple.

John Sung

John Sung 宋尚節 (1901–1944) was a renowned evangelist who played a significant role in the revival movement in China, Southeast Asia, and Taiwan. He traveled tirelessly and preached fearlessly to the multitudes. Tens of thousands of Chinese had come to know Jesus Christ through his preaching and teaching ministry. Some of Sung's preaching, sermons, Bible-study notes, and testimonies have been collected and published as a set of six volumes.

Sung also wrote several hymns, eleven of which are collected in *Revival Hymns and Choruses*.[16] The *Chinese Praise*[17] included one of his hymn texts, "Spiritual Life" ("*Shu Ling Sheng Huo* 屬靈生活"). Sung reminds us that we must die with Jesus on the cross, and be buried and resurrected with him. We must let "the Lord lives in us" (*zhu zhu limian* 主住裡面), so "He can occupy all" (*zhanling yiqie* 佔領一切, stanza 1), "He can change all" (*bianhua yiqie* 變化一切, stanza 2), "He can fulfill all" (*shixian yiqie* 實現一切, stanza 3), and "He can connect all" (*lianluo yiqie* 聯絡一切, stanza 4), perhaps echoing the message from the epistle of Ephesians.

Watchman Nee

Watchman Nee 倪柝聲 (1903–1972) was an influential preacher and evangelist. In 1920, when he was only 17 years old, Nee became a Christian at Dora Yu's evangelistic meeting and committed to serve the Lord. Later, he was under the mentorship of the British missionary Margaret Emma Barber 和受恩 (1866–1930). Barber was a poet who wrote hymn texts.[18] Nee's love of writing gospel songs was probably inspired by her.

Nee wrote several Christian books that have been translated into English, such as *The Spiritual Man* (1928) and *The Normal Christian Life* (1957), just to name a few. He also wrote several hymns and gospel songs; some were collected in *The Hymnary* (*Shengtu shige* 聖徒詩歌).[19] One of them is often sung by Chinese Christians, "Olives That Have Known No Pressure" (*Ni ruo buya ganlan chengzha* 你若不壓橄欖成渣). The hymn has five stanzas, which are paired with the beautiful melody, "O Ye Thirsty Ones that Languish," by American songwriter Stephen Collins Foster (1826–1864). The fifth stanza describes the Christian life in light of John the Baptist's confession that Jesus "must increase, but I must decrease" (John 3:30, NRSV), using the metaphor of olives being pressed, out of which issued the sweetness and preciousness of life with Jesus:

> Oh, I'll praise Thee, e'en if weeping mingles with my song.
> Thine increasing sweetness calls forth grateful praises all day long.
> Thou hast made Thyself more precious than all else to me,
> Thou increase and I decrease, Lord—This is now my only plea.[20]

Each stanza concluded with the refrain:

> Each blow I suffer, is true gain to me;
> meici de daji, doushi zhenliyi 每次的打擊，都是真利益；
>
> In the place of what Thou takest,
> ruguo ni shouqu de dongxi 如果你收去的東西，
>
> Thou dost give Thyself to me.
> ni yi ziji lai daiti 你以自己來代替.[21]

The refrain has an echo in pairing two themes from the biblical texts: (1) Paul's understanding that suffering strengthens believers, such as in 2 Cor 1:3–9, 11:16–33, 12:7–8; and (2) the providential perspective of Job that "the Lord gave, and the Lord has taken away" (1:21; NRSV), but the refrain stresses that Jesus gives himself "in the place of" the taking away. The hymn most likely reflects Nee's own experience. Nee had a difficult life. He experienced the Second Sino-Japanese War (1937–1945) and faced many tests and trials, including persecution and imprisonment for his faith, from 1952 until his death in 1972. The refrain of the hymn text may sound sentimental or even romantic, but it actually reflects his strong faith in Christ, even to his death in jail.

John E. Su

John E. Su 蘇佐楊 (1916–2007) was a pastor, evangelist, and writer. Beginning in 1935, when he was still studying at the North China Theological Seminary in Shandong,

Su composed hymns as well as the so-called "scriptural choruses" (*jingwen duange* 經文短歌), short songs quoting or paraphrasing Bible passages that were simple and accessible. By 2007, he had written over three hundred hymns and six hundred scriptural choruses.

Su published a collection of his hymns in 1935 titled *Heavenly People Hymnal* (*Tianren shengge* 天人聖歌), for which he composed the majority of the hymn tunes or harmonized Chinese folk songs. He also wrote some texts for the hymns.[22] Su's hymns, as well as his scriptural choruses, were centered on melody, often drawing on Chinese folk or folk-like tunes, with accompaniments arranged in Western harmonic style. The combination of Chinese and Western styles made his hymns and choruses appealing to Chinese Christians, some becoming quite popular. A notable one is his "The Lord Is My Shepherd" (*Shipian ershisan pian* 詩篇二十三篇), a Chinese folk song with the text of three stanzas paraphrased from Psalm 23. The hymn was popular among Chinese Christians for decades, for Shen-yin Wang 王神蔭 (1915–1997) mentioned that, when he visited several churches after the Cultural Revolution (1966–1976), many Christians still could sing the hymn by memory."[23]

Su published his scriptural choruses, titled *Heavenly People Choruses* (*Tianren duange* 天人短歌), in Shanghai in 1937. He composed scriptural choruses to assist Chinese Christians in memorizing Bible verses. He composed melody with closely matched biblical text to make the song unforgettable.

Several choruses have been popular among Chinese Christians and some were included in other Chinese hymnals, such as "The Mountain Shall Depart" (*Dashan keyi nuokai* 大山可以挪開; text Isa 54:10), "Although the Fig Tree" (*Suiran wuhua guoshu* 雖然無花果樹; text Hab 3:17–18), and "A Bruised Reed" (*Yashang de luwei* 壓傷的蘆葦; text Matt 12:20 and Heb 4:15).

Contextualization of Chinese Hymns

T. C. Chao 趙紫宸 (1888–1979) was a significant Chinese theologian, Christian writer, and educator. He penned over thirty books on various subjects, including theology and philosophy, as well as several collections of sermons and poems. One of his most significant contributions to Chinese Christianity was his endeavor to contextualize the Chinese faith to meet the needs of Chinese society and its culture. He believed that the Chinese church must establish its own creeds and liturgy, "severing relationships with the ancient traditions of the Western churches on the one hand and combining the best elements of their own culture with the essence of Christianity on the other hand, both in order to produce a Christian religion acceptable to the Chinese mind and heart."[24]

He worked diligently also to contextualize the Chinese hymns. He is regarded as the father of Chinese Christian hymnody. His first hymn book, *Christian Fellowship Hymns* (*Tuanqi shengge ji* 團契聖歌集), was the result of his attempt to contextualize the Chinese hymns. The hymn book was published in 1931 by Yenching University in

Beijing. Chao translated 124 hymns and eighteen responsive readings into the *wen-li* or classical style of Chinese. His colleague at the university, the music missionary Bliss Wiant 范天祥 (1895–1975), was the music editor of the hymn book. Some of the hymn texts he translated displayed the influence of Chinese society dominated by Buddhism, nationalism, and Chinese culture. For instance, the opening lines of stanzas 1 and 2 of Martin Rinkart's "Now Thank We All" are translated into Chinese by T. C. Chao as follows:

Stanza 1
Now thank we all our God
With heart and hands and voices,

Stanza 2
O may this bounteous God
Thro' all our life be near us.[25]

Chao translated the phrase in stanza 1, "Now thank all our God," into Chinese as "*wu zhong zai zhu tangjie* 吾眾在主堂階." In the phrase, "with heart and hands and voices," Chao chose the Chinese words "*wutitoudi* 五體投地," which literally mean with "the entire body lying down on the floor," to express the most humble and sincere attitude of worshipping God. Again, the words he used for God, *shenming* 神明, and the description of God in stanza 2 as a merciful one, *dacibeishen* 大慈悲神, were terms from Buddhism.

Shortly after the publication of *Christian Fellowship Hymns*, Chao and Wiant compiled yet another new hymnal, *Hymns for the People* (*Minzhong shengge ji* 民眾聖歌集), which also was published by Yenching University in 1931. While *Christian Fellowship Hymns* was compiled for the faculty and students at the university, the new hymnal was intended for congregational use, those not as learned as university professors and students. The former hymn book consisted of foreign hymns and tunes, whereas the latter included fifty-four newly written hymns with Chinese tunes.

Chao wrote all the texts for the hymnal, using Chinese in the colloquial style, in contrast with the *wen-li* style of the previous hymn book. Wiant collected and arranged Chinese melodies, including ancient Chinese tunes, folk melodies, Buddhist tunes, and new Chinese tunes, all in four-part harmony.

This pivotal collection of hymns was a pioneering work of Chinese hymnody, with hymn texts solely written by Chinese. In the preface, Chao mentioned the principles he applied for writing hymn texts:

1. being realistic, not abstract;
2. sounding as simple as a folk song;
3. challenging enough for the congregation;
4. contemplating some aspects of Chinese heritage;
5. conveying personal spiritual experiences;
6. praising God;

7. reflecting a Christian's daily life;
8. encouraging Christians to care for social concern and their country;
9. containing rich biblical imagery and spiritual insight as an efficient tool for teaching doctrines.

One text of Chao probably is the most well-known Chinese hymn to Christians outside China, "Song of Early Morning" (*Qingchen ge* 清晨歌). The hymn was an indigenous hymn in every aspect. Based on Ps 19:1–6, Chao's text described the heart and soul of a rice farmer, who appreciated the simple life and was able to labor diligently on the beautiful land that God created. Since China was an agricultural society, in which many households lived on farming, the hymn resonated well with the people. The original hymn tune was arranged and harmonized by Wiant, though later a new tune by Te-ai Hu 胡德愛 was paired with Chao's text in *Hymns of Universal Praise.* Hu's tune, which was edited by her teacher Wiant, became popular among both Chinese and foreign Christians.

Hymns of Universal Praise (*Putian songzan*)

In the fall of 1931, the Church of Christ in China[26] initiated a hymnal project. Six denominations[27] whose combined membership equaled three-quarters of the entire Protestant church membership of China responded to the invitation and participated in the compilation of a new union hymnal.

Consisting of Chinese pastors, missionaries, and musicians, the union hymnal committee of twenty-three members was formed to undertake the epoch-making hymnal project. The committee's first chairman was Robert Ferris Fitch 費佩德 (1873–1954), a missionary who returned to America in 1932. Fitch was followed by Timothy Tin-fang Lew 劉廷芳, who was also the chairman of the literary sub-committee of the project. Ernest Y. L. Yang 楊蔭瀏 of the Chinese Anglican Church served as the associate editor of the hymn texts and translated and wrote over two hundred hymns. In order to fulfill his task as an editor, Yang "reread the entire Bible three times during the three years, that he might better be imbued with its language, its message, and its elevated mood."[28]

Timothy Tin-fang Lew

Timothy Tin-fang Lew 劉廷芳 (1891–1947) was a well-known educator, author, and hymnal editor. He was regarded as one of the most important Chinese Christian leaders in the early twentieth century. *Hymns of Universal Praise* collected several hymn texts he translated or wrote, including the communion hymn, "The Bread of Life for All Men Broken" (*Jinsheng ge* 覲聖歌). The hymn he wrote in 1934 has been translated into English by Walter Reginald Oxenham Taylor (1889–1973), a Church of England missionary to China, in the bi-lingual edition of the hymnal.

The text depicted the suffering and death of Jesus Christ in the first and second stanzas, whereas the third stanza expressed the expectation for eternal hope and blessing. The hymn was intended to strengthen Chinese Christians' faith during difficult times, especially when many of them suffered and died during the Second Sino-Japanese War.

Ernest Y. L. Yang

Ernest Y. L. Yang 楊蔭瀏 (1899–1984) was a scholar, educator, and musician who played Chinese instruments *pipa* 琵琶 and *sanxian* 三弦 and took piano lessons and music theory classes from American missionary Louise Strong Hammond 郝路義. As a scholar, Yang was a Chinese music historian. His monumental two-volume set of *Ancient Chinese Music History* (*Zhongguo gudai yinyue shigao* 中國古代音樂史稿) was published in 1981.

Yang translated and wrote hymn texts for the first Chinese ecumenical hymnal. He wrote a text for a famous ancient lute tune called "Three Ceremonies at Yangguan" (*Yangguan sandie* 陽關三疊).[29] A famous painter and poet in the Tang dynasty, Wei Wang 王維 (699–761), composed the tune to bid farewell to a friend who was called to the army. Yang's hymn text of "Our Parting Blest by Christian Bonds" (*Sandie lige* 三疊離歌) has three stanzas. He changed from the sadness of sending off friends to praying for fellowship in the future, alluding to the Old Testament theme of a "loving God" guiding his people through the wilderness, rough terrain ("over hill"), and chaos ("deep sea") in the refrain of the hymn. The refrain also looks forward to the New Testament themes of fellowship in Christ and unity in the body: "one Lord, one faith, one baptism" (Eph 4:5, NRSV).[30]

The New Hymnal (*Zanmeishi xinbian*)

The Three-Self Patriotic Movement (TSPM) and China Christian Council (CCC) established a music work group in 1981 to pursue the compilation of a new hymnal for the churches. The group immediately made an announcement in the Christian journal *Tian Feng* 天風, a publication of the CCC, to solicit new texts and tunes for the hymnal. In 1982, the Chinese Christian Hymnal Committee was organized to promote church music in China, with eleven members selected for the New Hymnal Editorial Committee to undertake such a project. In a rather short time, *The New Hymnal* (*Zanmeishi xinbian* 讚美詩新編) was printed by the Council in 1983. The hymnal was widely adopted by Three-Self churches in China, with a total distribution of about nine million copies through 1998, as stated in the preface of the bilingual edition of the hymnal (1999).

The hymnal greatly relied on Chinese hymns published before 1949 and on newer ones published overseas. It consisted of four hundred hymns, with two hundred and ninety-two from the missionary era. Following the recommendation of Bishop Zi-gao Shen 沈子高 (1895–1982), one of the three advisors of the Chinese Christian Hymnal

Committee, the hymn book continued to carry on the concept of the contextualization of Chinese hymns that was initiated by T. C. Chao, Timothy Tin-fang Lew, and Ernest Y. L. Yang. Yang also was involved as an advisor for the new hymnal project.

"Three-Self" Hymns

Several patriotic hymn texts that promoted the TSPM were selected for the hymn book, some newly written for the hymnal. Texts of numbers 124–128 and numbers 175–178 were filled with patriotic and "Three-Self" sentiment, as exemplified in "May God Bless China" (*Qiu zhu fuyou zhonghua ge* 求主福佑中華歌). The text was penned by Yan-li Sun 孫彥理 (1914–1995), a pastor in Shanghai. Written in 1981, the text of five stanzas depicted how blessed was China and her people, and the third stanza proclaimed that "God is pleased with Three-Self spirit," and therefore urged the faithful to demonstrate their love to both their "homeland and . . . faith." Each stanza was followed by the refrain of admonishing the children of "beauteous" and "glorious China" to love her and to pray to their "Savior . . . to bless China."[31]

The text "I Love Christ's Church" (*Jiaohui wo suoai ge* 教會我所愛歌) was also in line with the "Three-Self" concept. The text of five stanzas written by Wen-hao Cai 蔡文浩 (1913–1993) described Christ's church as God's own house (stanza 1), God's own folk (stanza 2), God's own flesh (stanza 3), God's own bride (stanza 4), and God's own lamp (stanza 5). The refrain repeatedly stressed the importance for Chinese Christians to "Promote 'Three-Self' by God's grace," and the unity they maintain "in God's spirit."[32]

Hymns of Chinese Heritage

A few hymns written for Chinese Christians to celebrate important days and festivals were selected for the hymn book. Honoring parents and respecting the elderly had been a noble Chinese tradition. Following the similar biblical teachings, Chinese Christians had written a few hymns along this line. In addition to "Who's Been Born without Two Parents?" (*Xiaoqin ge* 孝親歌) came from *Hymns of Universal Praise*, the hymnal also included hymns to celebrate the Chinese New Year, weddings, birthdays, funeral services, farewell parties, and the dedication of a new house.

The New Hymnal Supplement (*Zanmeishi xinbian buchongben*)

More than two decades later, a supplement to the hymnal was published in 2009. The supplement, titled *The New Hymnal Supplement* (*Zanmeishi xinbian buchongben* 讚美詩新編補充本), was edited by De-hua Lin 林德樺, a retired church music professor in

China. The hymn book contains two hundred gospel songs and hymns, including "Amazing Grace" and hymns written by contemporary hymn writers, such as Brian A. Wren (1936–). In addition, it includes new hymn texts and tunes written by Chinese Christians. Da-wei Wang 王大衛 (1951–), who wrote one hymn for the 1983 edition, also wrote texts and tunes for this hymn book. Wang's "The Lord is the Way, the Truth, and the Life" (*Zhu shi daolu zhenli shengming* 主是道路真理生命) was based on John 14:6. The text proclaims Jesus is "the bread of life" (stanza 1), "the light of the world" (stanza 2), "the gate of the sheep" (stanza 3), "the good shepherd" (stanza 4), "the source of life" (stanza 5), and "the true vine" (stanza 6), with the refrain accentuating Jesus' message from the gospel of John.

A unique hymn, "Praise God, Boarder People" (*Bainjang xintu zanmei shen* 邊疆信徒讚美神), was written by Yao-jun Qian 錢耀君. The hymn speaks for Christians who live on the frontier of China. The text has three stanzas, with the third stanza stating that "We live in the love of Jesus, even though we are poor, we still want to praise the Lord. . . ." The refrain repeatedly intends to remind Christians that praising the Lord will bring them blessings, hope, and peace. Qian also composed the hymn tune, which uses a pentatonic scale and a simple melodic line similar to the music of the ethnic groups in that region.

Contemporary Hymn Writers and Christian Music Groups

The Chinese church in the twenty-first century has been continuously influenced by the foreign, mostly European and American church in worship and music. Several contemporary Chinese hymn text writers and composers, as well as Christian music groups, are actively involved in writing and composing hymns as well as praise and worship songs.

David P. L. Yeung

David P. L. Yeung 楊伯倫 (1931–) is a church musician and composer in Hong Kong who wrote more than seventy hymns and anthems. Some of his compositions are written in four-part harmony that could be sung by congregations, such as "May the Spirit Revive Me" (*Yuan na linghuo fuxing wo* 願那靈火復興我). The hymn was written in 1956 and first appeared in *Hymns of Praise* (*Zanmei shi* 讚美詩, 1978). Since then, the piece has been included in other hymnals.

The text has four stanzas, with each one advising Christians not to leave their first faith (*qichu de xinxin* 起初的信心, stanza 1), first hope (*qichu de xiwang* 起初的希望, stanza 2), first love (*qichu de aixin* 起初的愛心, stanza 3), and first faith-hope-love (*qichu de xinwangai* 起初的信望愛, stanza 4), but instead to repent and pray for the spirit to revive them.

I-To Loh

I-To Loh 駱維道 (1936–) is a pastor, ethnomusicologist, hymnologist, and a composer in Taiwan. He has worked arduously to indigenize Taiwanese hymns and promote Asian hymnody. When he was a teenager, he went on mission trips with his father Hsien-chun Loh 駱先春 (1905–1984) to remote mountains and villages. While there, he was fascinated by the aboriginal songs and later arranged some of them as hymn tunes for the 1964 edition of *Seng-Si* 聖詩 (*Hymns*), a hymnal for the Presbyterian Church in Taiwan. "God Created Heaven and Earth" (*Chinchu siongte cho thintoe* 真主上帝造天地 in Taiwanese) was based on an aboriginal tune, TOA-SIA 大社. The hymn has been collected in several Chinese and American hymnals.

Loh's publications include *New Songs of Asian Cities, Hymns from the Four Winds*, and *Sound the Bamboo: CCA Hymnal 2000*. He is the editor of the 2009 edition of *Seng-Si* and has translated and written hymn texts in Taiwanese for the hymnal; for instance, Loh wrote a beautiful Taiwanese hymn "*Tiohng chu siongte chhiun sinkoa*" 著向主上帝唱新歌 with text based on Psalm 98 for a Brazilian tune "*Cantai ao Senhor*." This joyful song shows Loh's interest in global hymnody as well.

Lü Xiaomin

The song book *Canaan Hymns* (*Jianan shige* 迦南詩歌) contains gospel songs written by Lü Xiaomin 吕小敏. Born in a little village in Henan, she had little education or musical training; however, she is a prolific writer who has written more than sixteen hundred gospel songs. Xiaomin often sings her songs and brings the gospel to many house-churches in China.

Most of her songs are brief, similar to choruses or refrains of traditional hymns or gospel songs. Her texts are simple and colloquial, not in any Chinese classical poetic forms, and they resonate well with Chinese Christians who have similar life experiences as hers. Her melodies are tuneful, similar to Chinese folk melodies. Her gospel songs have become popular among Chinese Christians outside China, partially due to the work of Huang Anlun 黄安倫 (1949–), a Chinese Canadian composer who has beautifully arranged some of her songs for mixed chorus with orchestral accompaniment.

A popular song of Xiaomin is "At Five O'clock in the Morning in China" (*Zhongguo de zaochen wu dianzhong* 中國的早晨五點鐘). The song is written in a free style of three short stanzas; each stanza begins with "Five o'clock in the morning of China, you heard the sound of prayer." It portrays the spiritual life of many house-church Christians in China who gather and pray at the church at five o'clock in the morning. Because the Chinese language is pictorial in its script and expression, the third stanza describes the prayers of Chinese Christians "soaring over the highest mountains" and "melting the ice off the coldest hearts," and these Chinese Christians are being delivered from bondage and wars as they look for peace and well-being. The song concludes with praying for a good harvest year. It speaks for Xiaomin and many Christians who have difficult lives as farmers in villages in Henan and other parts of China.

Heavenly Melody

Heavenly Melody 天韻合唱團 is Taiwan's pioneering Christian vocal ensemble group. The mixed chorus of eight to twelve singers started in 1963 under the leadership of Doris Brougham 彭蒙惠 (1926–), the missionary who established the Overseas Radio & Television Inc. 救世傳播協會 in Taipei. The primary goal of this group is to share "God's love" around the world through music compositions and live concerts. Over the years, the group has performed in thirty countries on five continents, as stated in its website.[33]

The group sings in diverse musical styles ranging from classic hymns to contemporary praise and worship songs. In the beginning, Heavenly Melody sang songs translated from Western hymns and choral music. In the 1970s, they began to write and sing their own compositions. One of the most popular pieces among Chinese churches is "Flowers of the Field" (*Yedi de hua* 野地的花), with text by Linda Yeh 葉薇心 (1951–) and music by Wen-dong Wu 吳文棟. The song was included in the first recording issued by the group in 1979. Since then, it has been sung by many Christians in Taiwan and China, as well as by Mandarin-speaking Christians worldwide. The melody sounds like a folkish student's song, in a style that was popular on college campuses in Taiwan in the 1970s. The text of the first stanza is based on Matt 6:26–32, though it does not render the multiple rhetorical questions of the gospel text into Chinese. The first stanza paints the teaching of Jesus (1) in contemporary Chinese vernacular that is easy to understand and (2) in colorful expressions of "flowers of the field" and "birds in the heavens":

> Flowers of the field are dressed in bright array,
> *yedi de hua chuanzhuo meili de yishang,*
> 野地的花，穿著美麗的衣裳，
>
> Birds in the heavens, never worry for a day,
> *tiankong de nia-or, conglai bu wei shenghuo mang,*
> 天空的鳥兒，從來不為生活忙，
>
> Our gracious Father watches over all, He cares so much for us.
> *ta geng ai shishang ren, wei tamen yubei yongsheng de lu.*
> 祂更愛世上人，為他們預備永生的路.[34]

The repertoire of the group has changed over the years. Their current musical style lies between classical and popular music. The melodies are usually tuneful, and the texts are biblical and evangelical, as in their latest recording (CD #24) "Eternal Covenant" (*Yongheng youyue* 永恆•有約) issued in 2016. Seven out of ten pieces of the CD have texts based on Bible passages. The text of "The Greatest Love" (*Zuida de shi ai* 最大的是愛), for instance, is written by Linda Yeh and based on 1 Corinthians 13 and 1 John 4:7, 16. The music is composed by one of the singers, Esther Liao 廖雅惠, a seminary-trained musician.

Stream of Praise

Based in California, the Chinese music ministry team, Stream of Praise Music Ministries 讚美之泉, was formed to evangelize Chinese through contemporary Christian songs at concerts and worship seminars. Since 1995, the team has released several CDs and has traveled worldwide, including the United States, Canada, Panama, Taiwan, Hong Kong, Australia, New Zealand, Singapore, and Malaysia, as mentioned on its website.[35]

Their praise and worship song "Let Praise Arise" (*Rang zanmei feiyang* 讓讚美飛揚) is quite popular among Chinese youth, who often learned such songs at the concerts presented by Stream of Praise Music Ministries, or through the CDs and DVDs the ministry team produced. This tune contains frequent syncopations, unusual melodic progressions, and a low tessitura that makes the song less singable and memorable than a traditional hymn.

River of Life Christian Church Music Ministry

River of Life Christian Church 矽谷生命河靈糧堂 was founded in 1995 by Liu Tong 劉彤 in California and, since then, it has more than two hundred branches in Mongolia, Africa, Europe, and North America. The church ministry has four focuses, with the first one being Worship and Praise. The music team of the church has produced CDs containing more than one hundred songs. One of them, "Here in Your Presence" (*Yujian ni* 遇見祢), is written by Tiffany Wang 施弘美. The text is based on eclectic Bible passages, and the melody is similar to a popular song, but without an indelible melodic progression. Songs of this type might be suitable for song leaders or vocal soloists rather than for congregational singing together at worship services.

Clay Music

Clay Music 泥土音樂 is a music ministry organization established in California in 2004 by Amy Sand 盛曉玫. The name of the music ministry was inspired by the text from Jer 18:4–6, as mentioned in her testimony. The group has produced CDs, and they often give concerts and sing at churches in North America, Taiwan, and Southeast Asia, with Sand as the lead singer.

One song, "Decision of a Lifetime" (*Yisheng de jueze* 一生的抉擇), is a song for vocal solo with instrumental accompaniment. Both the text and melody are simple and could be sung repeatedly. This song and other songs of the group are similar to contemporary Chinese popular songs with a touch of American popular music.[36]

Conclusion

The survey of hymns and songs in Chinese Christianity indicates a variety of purposes and, thus, different types of hymns and songs: those expressing the Scriptures or doctrines, enabling revival or evangelism, and/or promoting worship and praise. The influence of the Bible on Chinese hymns lies in the lyrics that are biblically based and linguistically Chinese, especially in the period of translation of foreign hymns. K. K. Yeo, a Chinese NT scholar, has worked on cross-cultural understanding of biblical interpretation and hymnic texts in the liturgical context of worship, proclamation, community formation, and social change,[37] and sees the significance of the Chinese church imitating:

> the early church [to be] a singing church, exemplified by Jesus and his disciples, who sang a hymn before going out from the Last Supper (Matt 26:30; Mark 14:26). The early Christians used the OT as Scripture, and there is no doubt that they used the Psalms in their study, reading, and chanting. Besides new hymns, psalms, and songs of their own creation, the New Testament church also used the OT psalms as their hymn texts. Of all the genres in the OT, the poetic literature, especially the Psalms, became the main source of inspiration for the NT church to interpret the Messiah or the Christ.... Singing in the early church was a Christian act of worship that...gave expression to the new faith of the early believers, a worshipful response to God's salvation in Christ, and a liturgical call for the faithful to glorify God and serve one another.[38]

The history of Chinese Christian hymns and songs "reflects to one degree or another where the church is and where it is moving."[39] The development of Chinese Christian hymns and songs has followed a long path, from translating foreign hymns, contextualizing and writing Chinese hymns, to writing contemporary Chinese hymns and songs. The rich repertoire of congregational songs for twenty-first-century Chinese churches connects Chinese Christians with Christians of the South and West and all continents, while Chinese Christians continue to sing the hymns and songs that represent the unique heritage of the global church.

Notes

1. See Fang-Lan Hsieh, *A History of Chinese Christian Hymnody: From Its Missionary Origins to Contemporary Indigenous Productions* (Lewiston, NY: Edwin Mellen Press, 2009); John Julian, *Dictionary of Hymnology* (London: J. Murray, 1908; repr., Grand Rapids: Kregel Publications, 1985); David Sheng, "A Study of the Indigenous Elements in Chinese Christian Hymnody" (D.M.A. diss., University of Southern California, 1964).
2. For the English translation of the hymn text, see the revised edition of *Hymns of the Universal Praise* (Hong Kong: Chinese Christian Literature Council Ltd., 2006), no. A 1, pp. 1880–1881.

3. Yushan Wu was a famous painter, poet, calligrapher, and a musician. He joined the Jesuits in 1682. After training at a Jesuit seminary in Macao, he was ordained and became a Jesuit priest in 1688. Wu ministered at churches in Shanghai and the surrounding area for thirty years.
4. *Yayue* 雅樂, the elegant and pure music, is an ancient traditional instrumental court music. Emperors used this style of music for celebration and worshipping the heavens and the earth. Chinese scholars also use *yayue* for celebration at the Confucius temple.
5. This English text is taken from the 1981 English edition of the *Hymns of Universal Praise*, no. 680.
6. See 1981 English edition of the *Hymns of Universal Praise*, no. 680.
7. This translated text is taken from the 1981 English edition of the *Hymns of Universal Praise*, no. 170.
8. The hymnal was compiled by Henry Blodget 白漢理 (1825–1903) and Chauncey Goodrich 富善 (1836–1925).
9. John Julian, *Dictionary of Hymnology* (London: J. Murray, 1908; repr. Grand Rapids: Kregel Publications, 1985), 743.
10. C. S. Champness, "Hymnology in the Chinese Church," in *The China Mission Year Book*, 2nd ed., ed. G. H. Bondfield (Shanghai: Christian Literature Society for China, 1912), 249.
11. My English translation is based on the Chinese text found in Champness, "Hymnology in the Chinese Church," 249.
12. Francesca French, *The Songs of Pastor Hsi* (London: Morgan & Scott, 1920).
13. French, *The Songs of Pastor Hsi* (London: Morgan & Scott, 1920), 22–23.
14. Sheng, "A Study of the Indigenous Elements in Chinese Christian Hymnody," 527.
15. The text has been translated by Bettie A. Ricketson and Warren Yang 楊敏. It is collected in the *New Songs of Praise* (*Songzhu xinge* 頌主新歌, 1973) with a tune written by Ji-fang Liang 梁季芳 in 1934.
16. The *Revival Hymns and Choruses* was edited by Timothy Sianghui Tow 杜祥輝 (1920–2009) and published by the Bible-Presbyterian Church of Singapore in 1970.
17. *Chinese Praise* (*Huaren shengsong* 華人聖頌) (Hong Kong: Christian Communications Ltd., 1992).
18. Fifteen of Margaret Emma Barber's hymn texts, most of them in Chinese, were indexed in http://hymnary.org (all websites in this essay accessed September 1, 2020).
19. *The Hymnary* (*Shengtu shige* 聖徒詩歌) (Rosemead, CA: Testimony Publications, 1984).
20. The English text is found in *Hymns by Witness Lee & Watchman Nee*, no. 626 (http://www.lsm.org). Used with permission.
21. The English and Chinese texts of this hymn are found in *Hymns by Witness Lee & Watchman Nee*, no. 626 (http://www.lsm.org). Used with permission.
22. In 1998, Su selected two hundred hymns previously issued and fifty others from his *Heavenly People Choruses* 天人短歌, with several new ones added to the collection. It was published under the new title, *Heavenly People Hymnal: 250 Pieces*.
23. Shen-yin Wang, *Companion to The New Hymnal* (*Zanmeishi xinbian shihua* 讚美詩新編史話) (Shanghai: Chinese Christian Council, 1992), 372 (in Chinese).
24. T. C. Chao, "The Chinese Church Realized Itself," *The Chinese Recorder* 58 (May–June 1927): 305.
25. All Martin Rinkart's hymns are available in the public domain: https://library.timelesstruths.org/music/Now_Thank_We_All_Our_God/. For T. C. Chao's Chinese translation, see *Christian Fellowship Hymns* [in Chinese] (Beijing: Yenching University Press, 1931), no. 19.

26. The Church of Christ in China 中華基督教會 was a coalition of churches in China established in 1927.
27. The denominations involved were the Church of Christ in China, the Chung Hwa Sheng Kung Hwei, the East China Baptist Convention, the Methodist Episcopal Church North (MEN), the Methodist Episcopal Church South (MES), and the North China Kung Li Hui (i.e., Congregational Church).
28. Walter N. Lacy, *A Hundred Years of China Methodism* (New York: Abingdon-Cokesbury Press, 1948), 304.
29. Yuangguan 陽關 was located at the Western terminus of the Great Wall of China.
30. The text was translated by missionary Frank W. Price 畢範宇 (1895–1974) in 1953, see *Hymns of Universal Praise* (*Putian songzan*) (Shanghai: Christian Literature Society, 1981), 20.
31. See *The New Hymnal*, English-Chinese bilingual edition (Shanghai: China Christian Council, 1999), no. 177.
32. See *The New Hymnal*, English-Chinese bilingual edition, no. 125.
33. http://www.heavenlymelody.com.tw/en/. Permission granted by Heavenly Melody to use this hymn.
34. http://www.heavenlymelody.com.tw/en/. Permission granted by Heavenly Melody to use this hymn.
35. http://www.sop.org/home/home.aspx.
36. The contemporary Christian songs composed and promoted by Chinese Christian singers and music groups in Taiwan, North America, and other places probably have to stand the test of time in order to become part of the Chinese church music heritage.
37. K. K. Yeo, *Musing with Confucius and Paul: Toward a Chinese Christian Theology* (Eugene, OR: Cascade Books, 2008), 231–240.
38. Ibid. 234.
39. Beth Bergeron Folkemer, "Reflections on the Hymnody in *ELW*," *Dialog: A Journal of Theology* 47 (Summer 2008): 178.

Primary Sources

Chao, T. C. and Bliss Wiant. *Christian Fellowship Hymns* [in Chinese] *Tuanqi shengge ji* 團契聖歌集. Beijing: Yenching University Press, 1931.

Chao, T. C. and Bliss Wiant. *Hymns for the People* [in Chinese] *Minzhong shengge ji* 民眾聖歌集. Beijing: Yenching University Press, 1931.

Chinese Praise [in Chinese] *Huaren shengsong* 華人聖頌. Hong Kong: Christian Communications Ltd., 1992.

French, Francesca. *The Songs of Pastor Hsi* [in Chinese] *Xishengmo shige* 席勝魔詩歌. London: Morgan & Scott, 1920.

Heavenly Melody 天韻合唱團: http://www.heavenlymelody.com.tw/en/.

Hymns by Witness Lee & Watchman Nee. www.witness-lee-hymns.org.

Hymns of Praise [in Chinese] *Zanmei shi* 讚美詩. Singapore: Christian Nationals' Evangelism Commission, 1978.

Hymns of Universal Praise [English-Chinese bi-lingual edition] *Putian songzan* 普天頌讚. Shanghai: Christian Literature Society, 1936. Kowloon, Hong Kong: Chinese Christian Literature Council Ltd., 1981. New revised edition, 2006.

The Hymnary [in Chinese] *Shengtu shige* 聖徒詩歌. Rosemead, CA: Testimony Publications, 1984.

The New Hymnal [in Chinese] *Zanmeishi xinbian* 讚美詩新編. Shanghai: China Christian Council, 1983. English-Chinese bi-lingual edition, 1999.

The New Hymnal Supplement [in Chinese] *Zanmeishi xinbian buchongben* 讚美詩新編補充本. Shanghai: China Christian Council, 2009. Online version: http://www.zanmeishi.com/songbook/37.html

Lü, Xiaomin. *Canaan Hymns* [in Chinese] 迦南詩歌 *Jianan shige*. Online version: https://www.zanmeishi.com/songbook/canaan-hymns.html.

Lü, Xiaomin. "At Five O'clock in the Morning in China" [in Chinese] 中國的早晨五點鐘. https://www.youtube.com/watch?v=hfsp42Ij9uU.

New Songs of Praise [in Chinese] *Songzhu xinge* 頌主新歌. Kowloon, Hong Kong: Baptist Press, 1973. English edition, 1976.

Seng-Si 聖詩 (*Hymns*). Tainan: Gong Bao She, 1964.

Seng-Si 聖詩 (*Hymns*). Taipei: The Church Music Committee, the General Assembly of the Presbyterian Church in Taiwan, 2009.

Songzhu shige 頌主詩歌. Edited by Henry Blodget and Chauncey Goodrich. Yokohama, Japan, 1912.

Stream of Praise 讚美之泉: http://www.sop.org/home/home.aspx.

Su, John E. *Heavenly People Choruses* [in Chinese] *Tianren duange* 天人短歌. Hong Kong: Heavenly People Depot, 2003.

Su, John E. *Heavenly People Hymnal* [in Chinese] *Tianren shengge* 天人聖歌. Hong Kong: Heavenly People Depot, 1998.

CHAPTER 44

THE BIBLE AND CALLIGRAPHY IN CHINA

JEREMIAH ZHU SHUAI

Introduction

Calligraphy has played an important role in Christianity since the beginning of its mission in China. When Catholic Jesuit missionaries came to China in the Ming dynasty, Matteo Ricci and others carried out "adaptive" missionary strategies. Calligraphy, as the quintessence of Chinese culture, was respected and immediately used by missionaries for the sake of the gospel mission. When Protestantism came to China, it advocated the "indigenization" missionary route, and again calligraphy was used in the process. This is most evident in the translation and publication of the Chinese Union Version (CUV) Bible in the past hundred years. At present, the China Christian Council and the National Committee of Three-Self Patriotic Movement of the Protestant Church in China (CCC and TSPM 中國基督教兩會) are promoting the development of "Sinification of Christianity" (*jidujiao zhongguohua* 基督教中國化), and the story of biblical calligraphy and Chinese Christianity continues even today.[1]

Nestorian Calligraphy in the Tang Dynasty

The Nestorian church of the Tang dynasty is rarely recorded in Chinese literatures. Nowadays most scholars understand Nestorianism of the Tang dynasty basically based on excavated tablets and excavated texts, which allows them to study Nestorian calligraphy. The Nestorian excavated texts in the past four hundred years can be divided into stone carving inscriptions and writing scrolls according to the media of the scripts.

Among the historical materials unearthed, the stone carving inscriptions are: (1) *Daqin Jingjiao Liuxing Zhongguo Bei* 大秦景教流行中國碑 (also called Jingjiao Stele 景教碑); (2) *Daqin Jingjiao Xuanyuan Zhiben Jing* 大秦景教宣元至本經 (the content of which is roughly the same as the writing scroll of *Daqin Jingjiao Xuanyuan Ben Jing* 大秦景教宣元本經); and (3) some Nestorian epitaphs, mainly *Huaxian Epitaph* 花獻墓誌. The writing scrolls mainly include: (1) *Daqin Jingjiao Sanwei Mengdu Zan* 大秦景教三威蒙度讚; (2) *Zun Jing* 尊經; (3) *Yishen lun* 一神論; (4) *Xuting Mishisuo Jing* 序聽彌詩所經; (5) *Daqin Jingjiao Xuanyuan Ben Jing* 大秦景教宣元本經; (6) *Zhixuan Anle Jing* 志玄安樂經; (7) *Daqin Jingjiao Dasheng Tongzhen Guifa Zan* 大秦景教大聖通真歸法讚 (also known as Kojima Documents A [小島文書 A], lost, only photos remain); and (8) *Daqin Jingjiao Xuanyuan Zhiben Jing* 大秦景教宣元至本經 (also known as Kojima Documents B [小島文書 B], the content is not the same as the stone carving document of the *Daqin Jingjiao Xuanyuan Zhiben Jing* above), and other documents.

All the above were unearthed in the Dunhuang Scriptures' cave. However, the authenticity of the last two documents is still under discussion. At present, the stone carving historical materials in Nestorian excavated texts are still preserved in mainland China, while the related written documents are preserved in France, Japan, and other countries.[2]

Jingjiao Stele is the most comprehensive record of the spread of Nestorianism in the Tang dynasty. The tablet mentions that a large Nestorian temple was built in the Tang dynasty, with twenty-one Nestorian monks, and claimed Nestorianism as "benefiting people from material gains, it is suitable for the world" (濟物利人, 宜行天下). In the past, it was generally believed that, from the perspective of calligraphy, Lü Xiuyan 呂秀巖, the writer of inscriptions on tablets, was not well known in the history of calligraphy and had little influence on calligraphy. But in terms of historical research, one can conclude that *Daqin Jingjiao Liuxing Zhongguo Bei* (Jingjiao Stele) is the most important stele at the Beilin (Steles) Museum in Xi'an. Recent studies have pointed out that Jingjiao Stele is likely to be unique in the history of calligraphy as well. Zhu Donghua 朱東華 points out that the stele calligraphy "acquires the main vein of the two Wangs (二王, namely Wang Xizhi 王羲之 and Wang Xianzhi 王獻之)," "inherits the three legal systems of the early Tang dynasty," and "has the vigorous atmosphere of the flourishing Tang dynasty." He writes:

> Lü Xiuyan's calligraphy mostly used the method of two Wangs, and slightly contains the dangerousness of the Ouyang Xun's 歐陽詢 calligraphy, the calmness of Yu Shinan's 虞世南 calligraphy, the elegance and ease of Chu Suiliang's 褚遂良 calligraphy, while Yan Zhenqing's 顏真卿 calligraphy was also involved in the style of the seal script, which was vigorous and upright. Therefore, Lü Xiuyan's calligraphy did not fall into the "stereotype" of the new style of Yan Zhenqing at that time, but a self-contained style.[3]

These evaluations are certainly insightful. Although the colorful Tang stele calligraphy has different features in the expression of regular script called "*Kai Shu* 楷書," the most important works in this script can have paradigmatic significance upon generations.

The regular script of Jingjiao Stele is distinctive, but its influence in the history of calligraphy at that time cannot be compared with those of Ouyang Xun, Yan Zhenqing, and Liu Gongquan 柳公權, all of whom shifted the paradigm of Chinese calligraphy. Compared with these three calligraphers in the early Tang dynasty, the calligraphy of Jingjiao Stele belongs to "development" (流) rather than "origin" (源).[4] The fact that Nestorian texts are transmitted and preserved in certain scripts speaks to the seriousness of the Nestorian Chinese in appreciating both the "Scripture" and the Chinese aesthetic culture of calligraphy.

At the beginning of the twentieth century, the discovery of the Dunhuang Scriptures' cave added many new materials to our understanding of the spread of Christianity in China and calligraphy in the Tang dynasty. Dunhuang Scriptures' cave is most likely a closed Buddhist library that has a small collection of Scriptures of other religions. Most of the writers of Dunhuang Nestorian Scriptures were anonymous professional Scripture writers, but it is unclear whether they were Nestorian or not. Since the twentieth century, some Chinese calligraphy scholars have called the classical style of Dunhuang Scriptures "*Jingsheng Ti* 經生體" or "*Xiejing Ti* 寫經體." Although their handwriting has different styles, they do share "family similarity," especially the writing style of sharp-starting and heavily-pressing at the end of the brush. This classical style of calligraphy was once favored and practiced by Liu Bannong 劉半農 and Qian Xuantong 錢玄同, two famous Peking University scholars and calligraphers of the first half of the twentieth century. At that time, people generally did not regard the writers of classical Scriptures as calligraphers, nor did they copy their daily writing to be used as calligraphy models. One often finds the natural beauty that classical calligraphy has, which stele inscriptions do not possess in the daily writing of these Scriptures. By analyzing the calligraphic styles of several classical scrolls, we can categorize them into four types. Because it's very difficult to study the early handwritten Chinese Bible, perhaps we can look at these Nestorian documents in light of their partial translations of the Bible and of the calligraphic styles used.

The first type is represented by *Daqin Jingjiao Sanwei Mengdu Zan* and *Zun Jing*. Its character style is not modified and is close to the state of natural writing. Overall, these two works cannot be a representation of the *Jingsheng Ti*, nor are they like the *Ling Fei Jing* 靈飛經 or some script so dynamic and swiftly written; they are closer to others more grainy, and some characters are secular words such as "無／无" (*wu*) "禮／礼" (*li*), similar to the ancient style which avoids the flattering and mellow nature in some *Jingsheng Ti* scrolls. As to the composition, the works of *Daqin Jingjiao Sanwei Mengdu Zan*, *Zun Jing*, and the attached texts, with different sizes and spacing of characters, are written on a piece of paper with no boundary.

The second type, represented by *Yishen Lun* and *Xuting Mishisuo Jing*, deliberately carves and shapes the strokes' form, with rounded and beautiful characters, and feature a lot of modifications of what the Chinese customarily describe as "silkworm head and swallow tail 蠶頭燕尾" and "striking one snag after another 一波三折." The calligrapher is a more skilled and experienced scholar than the copier of *Daqin Jingjiao Sanwei Mengdu Zan* and *Zun Jing*. Through the subtle changes of font and brushwork from the beginning to the end, it can be seen that he is in conscious pursuit of the beauty of font and brushwork. Researchers have long observed the calligraphy of *Xuting Mishisuo Jing* to be the best one among the known Nestorian Scriptures.[5]

The third style, represented by *Xuanyuan Ben Jing* and *Zhixuan Anle Jing*, exaggerates the contrast of the strokes and embodies the meaning of ancient script called *Wei Bei* 魏碑. The two classics are both old collections of Li Shengduo 李盛鐸; both are now collected in Japan and are written on paper with boundaries. Audiences today may view these two classics as not as beautiful as *Yishen Lun* and *Xuting Mishisuo Jing*, and the reason is that the two classics retain a lot of *Wei Bei* strokes. If we compare the style of "Stele School (*Bei Xue* 碑學)" and "Engraving School (*Tie Xue* 帖學)," which emerged in the history of calligraphy in the late Qing dynasty, we can say that *Yishen Lun* and *Xuting Mishisuo Jing* are closer to "*Tie Xue*," while *Xuanyuan Ben Jing* and *Zhixuan Anle Jing* retain more of the color of "*Bei Xue*."

The fourth style is represented by *Daqin Jingjiao Dasheng Tongzhen Guifa Zan* and *Daqin Jingjiao Xuanyuan Zhiben Jing*. These two documents also have been recognized as "Kojima Documents." Among them, *Daqin Jingjiao Dasheng Tongzhen Guifa Zan* (Kojima Document A) is not in extant except in photos. These two Kojima Documents seem to be closer to the regular scripts of later generations, but some strokes are embodying the meaning of so-called "slave scripts" (*Li Shu* 隸書), which are different from regular scripts (*Kai Shu*).

The two Kojima Documents have similar inscriptions of "signature" in calligraphy after the Yuan and Ming dynasties and even signed the names of the writers or patrons. This kind of writing is not unique in the Tang dynasty but is really rare. All of these seem to show that the Kojima Documents were forged by later generations, though this is not conclusive due to the lack of high-definition pictures and careful examination of the original scroll. Additionally, Lin Wushu pointed out that:

> ... when we look up the existing Nestorian scriptures in Dunhuang in Tang dynasty, all the Jing scriptures are made in ignorance, that is, the upper part '口' and the lower part '京.' The same is true of the *Jingjiao Bei* in Xi'an. This word seems to be a special character chosen by Nestorian Church in Tang dynasty. If the stone inscription were forged after the 1990s, ... without the direct involvement of experts and scholars familiar with this field, it is inconceivable.[6]

The theory seems to apply to the two Kojima Documents as well. According to the photographs, the documents look to be "a counterfeit" as the word "景" is comprised of the word "口" in the upper and "京" in the lower. Therefore, before accumulating more evidence to prove the authenticity of the Kojima Documents, we could regard them as the fourth type of calligraphy style of writing Nestorian Scriptures.

In addition to the documentary historical materials, the cultural relics of Nestorianism in the Tang dynasty has continued to be unearthed in recent years. There are many significant discoveries, adding numerous fresh materials for our study of Nestorianism. The image of stone carving historical materials is important, but more important is the text content, since this stone-carving calligraphy is the object of research interest. Among them, the front Scriptures of *Daqin Jingjiao Xuanyuan Zhiben Jing* are regular scripts similar to Yan Zhenqing's style of flourishing in the Tang dynasty, which are only slightly less precise and standardized than those of the Tang steles. Moreover, all the words such as "口" and "日" or their radicals are written in the form of square rather than the inverted trapezoids of modern-style regular scripts, so the ending of the scripts shows a trend of "square and upright." The inscriptions on the back of *Jingchuang Ji* 經幢記 are slightly poorer in engraving, so that they embody some meanings similar to *Wei Bei*, which could be interpreted as the result of bad engraving.

In the known Nestorian stone inscriptions, the worst carving may be the Huaxian Epitaph. This is a Nestorian epitaph, which contains an epitaph in regular script and an epitaph cover in seal script (*Zhuan Shu* 篆書). Seal scripts on the epitaph cover were not skillfully written, showing that it was not done by well-known calligraphers at that time. The epitaph part is similar to Yan Zhenqing's style of Guo Xuji Epitaph 郭虛己墓誌 or Duobaota Stele 多寶塔碑 in the same period from the aspect of character structure, but the rough and overstaffed strokes are obviously the result of rough engraving. If we divide the Huaxian Epitaph into three sections from top to bottom, the middle section can still be known as "calligraphy," and the engraving at both ends is particularly poor, so that only the character at the bottom can be recognized while the charm of the calligraphy is lost. This level of engraving also has interfered greatly with the spread of calligraphy.[7] In general, the more important a person is, the more elegant his epitaph is. This suggests inviting famous calligraphers to write and engrave. In this way, "Huaxian Epitaph" at least shows that the identity and social status of the owner of the epitaph was not high enough at that time.

Catholicism and Calligraphy in the Ming and Qing Dynasties

During the Ming dynasty, Catholicism came to China through Jesuit missionary work. The relationship between Catholicism and art is obviously more self-conscious than it was for the early Nestorians. Not only did the foreign Catholic Church make contributions to the history of human art in architecture and painting, but the Chinese Catholic Church also inherited rich artistic practices. At one time, Shanghai Tou-Se-We Art Studio 土山灣畫館, a special institution for Catholic art education, was established. Although the studio does not directly engage in calligraphy education and creation, it is almost futile to separate calligraphy from other plastic arts in China. In 1932, when discussing "Catholic art in China," Celso Benigno Luigi Cardinal Costantini, then the cardinal bishop of the Catholic Chinese diocese, wrote:

> Chinese writing itself is an art; because Chinese people value calligraphy, calligraphy has become an art of both refined and popular appreciation. Chinese calligraphy is the cornerstone of China's brilliant art development. This also explains why inscriptions

are necessary in Chinese works of art. Only after inscriptions can the art show a glorious, meticulous and one-stop beautiful special nature.[8]

Matteo Ricci, the key figure of the Jesuit missionary mission in China, found that there were many cultural barriers to the transmission of Christianity to the Chinese people, so he advocated for a missionary strategy adapted to the Chinese culture, which was recognized by the Chinese upper class. In Matteo Ricci's *The China That Was*, his impression of Chinese characters and calligraphy is recorded. In the fifth chapter of the book, "On the Application of Humanities, Natural Science and Degrees in China," Chinese calligraphy is mentioned at the beginning:

> First of all, I would like to talk about some common Chinese calligraphy. The glyphs they used are very similar to the ancient Egyptian hieroglyphs. In terms of style and structure, their written language is quite different from the language used in daily conversation. No book is suitable for oral writing. Writing a book in a style close to spoken language will be regarded as putting himself and his books at the level of ordinary people. Perhaps no one in the whole country has mastered all the symbols or has complete knowledge of the Chinese language. Many symbols have the same pronunciation, but they are written differently and have different meanings. So as a result, Chinese may be ambiguous in all languages.[9]

We can be sure that Matteo Ricci wrote Chinese characters in person during his stay in China, but we have not seen his calligraphy works today. During the missionary process of the Jesuits in China, Xu Guangqi 徐光啟 (Hsu Kuang-ch'i), Li Zhizao 李之藻 (Li Chi'h-tsao) and Yang Tingyun 楊廷筠 (Yang T'ing-yun) were baptized as Catholics. They are known as the "Three Pillars of the Catholic Church." The reason for this is not only that they were the most senior Catholics in early China but also that they contributed to different degrees to cultural exchanges and academic fields between China and foreign countries. As officials of the Ming dynasty, the three men also were good at calligraphy, though not famous for it, and they also were well trained as literati doctors. Yang Tingyun was a calligraphy collector. Although works of the three men directly writing Catholic content are rare, they all have paved the way for missionaries' works, and their handwriting also has been preserved in the form of block-engraving calligraphy, such as Xu Guangqi's *Preface to Elements with Comments Engraving Version* 刻幾何原本序 and Li Zhizao's *Preface to Ten Pieces of Abnormal Person Engraving Version* 刻畸人十篇序. In addition to these engraved calligraphy works, the style of calligraphy can be examined through their other ink works (墨跡作品). The calligraphy style of the early "Three Pillars of the Catholic Church" belongs to the typical "two Wangs" style, inheriting the Song dynasty "Academic style (*Yuan Ti* 院體)" of calligraphy, but it also has the lateral influence of Dong Qichang 董其昌 and other contemporaries, which belongs to the "*Tie Xue*" tradition.

The interaction between Matteo Ricci and other Jesuit missionaries and Chinese calligraphers at that time can be seen from some historical documents. It was the custom of the late Ming dynasty to give poetry, paintings, and fans to the missionaries, such as Matteo Ricci, Johann Adam Schall von Bell, and Giulio Aleni, reflecting the exchange between Chinese and Western cultures at the time. Some of these poems were collected in *Xichao Chongzheng Ji* 熙朝崇正集.[10] It is worth noting that many or all of the people who presented poetry to missionaries were famous calligraphers, and there were countless literati who were good at both calligraphy and literature, such as Li Zhi. Zhu Shilu, a famous calligrapher in the Wanli period (1573–1620), had close contact with Matteo Ricci and wrote a poem entitled *Giving Matteo Ricci*. Yet another famous calligrapher in the late Ming dynasty, Zhang Ruitu 張瑞圖, who is famous for his square brush and stele-style handwriting, recalls his early contacts with Matteo Ricci in a poem dedicated to missionary Giulio Aleni.

It is regrettable that the poems presented to missionaries by Zhu Shilu 祝士祿, Zhang Ruitu, and other calligraphers have not been preserved in the form of manuscripts or calligraphic works but only in texts; otherwise, we would be able to see a few classic works of Christian calligraphy with an excellent combination of poems and books. However, Wang Duo's 王鐸 *Poetry to Johann Adam Schall von Bell* 贈湯若望詩稿, which is included in *Zengyan Heke* 贈言合刻, is not only an important document of Catholicism in the late Ming dynasty, but also a masterpiece in the history of Chinese calligraphy. Besides eight seven-character poems, the poem also contains several inscriptions, such as the title of "visiting Mr. Johann Adam Schall von Bell, visiting the pavilion, hearing the overseas wonders" and the signature piece:

> When my two children play in front of the book, their voice is chaotic and some characters are missing, such as '*Long Xing Wan He* 龍形萬壑.' Painting and calligraphy should be spread in the mountains and in the clouds of the pine tree. It ought to be a pleasure to enjoy it! *Wangduo Manshi* (書時，二稚子戲於前，嘰啼聲亂，遂落數數，如龍形萬壑等字，亦可噱也。書畫事，須深山中，松濤雲影中揮灑，乃為愉快，安可得乎？王鐸漫識).
>
> Mr. Dao Wei 道未 (Johann Adam Schall von Bell) learn to connect with heaven and human beings, cultivate mystery, and convince him that he is also the Dragon elephant among human beings. Once gave him one scroll work, but it was stolen, so I wrote again, now mounted, and then to redeem the guilt of loss, knowing that the master will laugh. Wang Duo of Henan sought straightforward rectification (道未先生學通天人，養多玄秘，心服其為人中龍象也。予曾書壹卷，被盜竊去，因再書此，今裱成，再奉以贖遺失之愆，知道翁必大笑也。河南王鐸具草求正之).
>
> Monthly sickness, strive to encourage books, when absolute food, several books sold, get five buckets of millet, buy ink, ink is not good, what can I do (月來病，力疾勉書，時絕糧，書數條賣之，得五斗粟，買墨，墨不嘉耳，奈何)!

Four of the eight seven-character poems, titled "One to Four," were written by Wang Duo to Johann Adam Schall von Bell, while the following four poems were written by Wang Duo and had nothing to do with Johann Adam Schall von Bell's content. Wang

Duo wrote other poems and presented them to Johann Adam Schall von Bell in the form of calligraphy.

Unlike Xu Guangqi's and Li Zhizao's styles, Wang Duo's calligraphy has a more vigorous and bold style. Compared with Dong Qichang, Xu Guangqi, Li Zhizao, and others who merely imitated the *Tie Xue* tradition of the two Jin dynasties, Wang Duo also referred to the calligraphers from the Song dynasty to the Ming dynasty, such as Mi Fu 米芾, and even contemporaries. Therefore, compared with Dong's style of sticking to *Chun Hua Ge Tie* 淳化閣帖, Wang Duo adds many contemporary factors of his time to his works. This has something to do with the tools and materials used in Wang Duo's calligraphy. In Wang Duo's era, the paper used in calligraphy was quite different from that before the Tang dynasty; various paper-making technologies have matured, and the size of paper-making has been increasing. Many of Wang Duo's works are written on eight-foot-long (*Zhang Er* 丈二) strips and the middle hall, which were unique before the Tang and Song dynasties. Therefore, his calligraphy won with momentum rather than subtle brushwork. Relatively speaking, although the *Poetry to Johann Adam Schall von Bell* was written on slightly smaller pages, the poems are excellent and meticulous in Wang Duo's handed down calligraphy works.

Jesuit missionaries also contributed to stone-carved calligraphy; even in the tombstones of Jesuit missionaries, there are many masterpieces of calligraphy. Today, the cemeteries of Jesuit missionaries in Beijing are located mainly in the courtyard of Chegongzhuang Beijing Administrative College and the Beijing Stone Carving Museum of Five Towers Temple (五塔寺). The former has the tombstones of Matteo Ricci, Ferdinand Verbiest, Johann Adam Schall von Bell, and other famous Jesuit missionaries, while the latter includes the cemeteries of other Catholic missionaries and some Chinese Catholics besides the Jesuits. The inscriptions on the tombstones often are relatively simple. In addition to the large-character headstones, they are often bilingual, in Chinese and Latin, including the year of birth and death, the time of arrival in China, the year of new birth and the month of being in the Church (Jesuit, etc.), and so on. Some of the Chinese parts of these characters are written by calligraphers (their names are extremely rare), while others use the printed font style used for engraving directly. Besides, there are many stone-carved calligraphy works in Xu Guangqi Cemetery in Xuhui District, Shanghai.

Many calligraphy works also can be found in Catholic paintings. Some of them are signatures of the Jesuit authors, such as Giuseppe Castiglione 郎世寧. However, the signatures often are simple so they cannot be seen as calligraphy arts. One more significant kind of Catholic calligraphy in paintings is calligraphy as decoration in the background. During the Ming and Qing dynasties, a kind of image type of Xu Guangqi and Matteo Ricci began to appear with great frequency. This kind of image adopts the realistic technique, showing the scene of Matteo Ricci and Xu Guangqi standing and talking. The portraits of Xu Guangqi and Matteo Ricci include both Chinese paintings and woodcut or copperplate prints, but they all adopt Western realistic techniques. Generally speaking, Xu Guangqi and Matteo Ricci in the foreground of the picture have not changed much either in position or in action, but the background is creatively developed by different artists. In some works, there are elements such as the image of Jesus, the cross, and so on, including seal calligraphy of the word "Jesus." But in other works, there are portraits of the Virgin and the Son and couplet calligraphy. Undoubtedly, the latter can better reflect the artistic expression of the localization of Catholicism after its entry into China. From it, we also can see the general situation of Chinese room decoration in the Ming and Qing dynasties, that is, the combination of painting and calligraphy in the middle hall is an important element of room decoration. These couplets often were written in line scripts, regular scripts, or official scripts, with dignified and square fonts describing the Catholic praise of Jesus. Although these couplets are not written directly in the Bible, their contents also can be regarded as a summary and refinement of Catholic doctrines recorded in the Bible.

In addition, before the outbreak of the "Ritual/Etiquette Debate," Emperor Kangxi also took a friendly attitude towards Catholicism, inscribing plaques for the Catholic Church such as "All That Is True 萬有真原." To this day, many Catholic churches still can see this inscription signed "Kangxi." Although the original ink-marks of the four words inscribed by Emperor Kangxi are nowhere to be found, from the inscribed plaques, Kangxi's calligraphy shows the consistent elegant and noble style characteristics of royal calligraphy. Since the Qing dynasty, there have been many couplets of Catholic themes, which are also said to have originated from the couplets of Catholic themes written by Kangxi for the Catholic Church. Generally speaking, since there was no complete translation of the Bible at that time, until the time of the Jesuit missionary period in China, there were still few calligraphic works directly writing the Bible Scriptures. This situation did not change until the Protestant Church came to China.

Calligraphy of Protestantism in China

Compared with Catholicism, Protestantism pays more attention to the work of texts and printing, so Protestantism has a closer relationship with writing and calligraphy, especially in the translation, publication, and font design of the Bible in the Chinese version. The first Protestant missionary, Robert Morrison, came to China in 1807. Morrison was the editor of the first *English-Chinese Dictionary* in New China and founder of the earliest Chinese newspaper, *The Monthly Biography of the Secular Inspection* 察世俗每月統記傳. From the beginning of Morrison's work in China, Protestant missions started translation of the Bible. Until 1919, translations of Bible scrolls in various Chinese languages (including deep literary 深文理, shallow literary 淺文理, Mandarin 官話, dialect 方言, etc.) had been published in succession in China, and special Bible publishing institutions such as Hong Kong Anglo-Chinese Academy (香港英華書院) and Shanghai Huamei Academy (上海華美書院) had emerged.

Throughout the nineteenth century, the translation and publication of Protestant Bibles in China became popular. During this period, most of the Bible publishing and printing still took the form of traditional Chinese ancient books, most of which were engraved, including a very small number of movable-type printers. In 1863, Elijah Coleman Bridgman 裨治文 and Michael Simpson Culbertson's 克陛存 deep-literary translation, published by the Meihua Library in Huyi (滬邑美華書館), Jiangsu province, were printed in movable wood.[11] In 1919, the translation and publication of CUV became a milestone in the translation of the Chinese Bible. The CUV is also the most widely circulated and widely used translation of the Chinese Bible in church worship in China. However, no matter if it was engraving or movable type, the script fonts printed in this period did not use brush handwriting, but they were more in line with print media standards (印刷標準字體). Most of the fonts used in the printing of the Bible are *Song Ti* 宋體, which is consistent with the most common fonts in ancient Chinese books. This kind of font, named after the engraved font of the Song dynasty in China, originated from Yan Zhenqing's regular script (*Kai Shu*), which was standardized and decorated. It is thick and vertical, and has an obvious decorative angle, which is similar to the Western Roman font. However, a small number of Bibles are printed in a regular script called *Kai Ti*. For example, in 1838 and 1840, Karl Friedrich August Gürtzlaff 郭實臘 translated and published deep literary and scientific translations of the New Testament and the Old Testament, which are more similar to the natural writing of calligraphy.[12]

If the relationship between Christianity and calligraphy in ancient society is only an unavoidable encounter, the Chinese church can view the relationship between Christianity and calligraphy in terms of: (1) the formal beauty of the art of calligraphy in relation to the word of God; (2) the modern printing technology, fonts, and layout design of Chinese books brought about by Christianity and in dissemination of the biblical message—greatly different from contemporary Chinese people using hypertext and internet communication styles. The publication of the Bible uses a large number of traditional Chinese line bindings and engraving printing, but it also uses the Western modern printing technology brought by missionaries who made an important contribution to China's press and publishing industry.

Not only the Chinese character typographic design, but also the publication of the Bible in this period, is closely related to calligraphy itself. The titles appearing on the cover and title pages of these Bibles, such as the "Bible," "New Testament," and "Old Testament," often are written and engraved in calligraphy. The writers of the calligraphy often do not have signatures and usually use regular script or seal script. There are also individual Bibles and related books printed in engraved calligraphy. This printing method is characterized by first asking the calligrapher to write the contents of the publication (which can be written directly on the board, or on paper and then copied to the board), and then carving according to the marks of writing. For example, the National Library of Australia has a collection of Guangxu sixteenth year, *Gospel Rhymes* 福音韻語, which is engraved calligraphy. The character style is close to the other cover character of the Bible. It is a popular and standardized model book at that time.[13] This kind of engraved calligraphy book allows readers to not only read its content but also to appreciate or learn its calligraphy. There also are some Bible chapters or verses that are disseminated in manuscripts. Overall, it can be said that since the nineteenth century, a great number of publications of the Bible have greatly enriched the forms of font and layout design of ancient Chinese books.

In addition to the literary ministry, the work of early Protestant missionaries in the social gospel also was related to calligraphy. Among them, Protestant church schools and church hospitals often used the form of calligraphy to inscribe names. For example, the former Yenching University, where Peking University is now located, was once a Protestant church school. Cai Yuanpei 蔡元培 wrote the plaque on the west gate of Yanyuan in the period of the Republic of China as "Yenching University." These four characters are dignified and solemn in style and have the spirit of being upright. Wu Leichuan, a former president of Yenching University, was a Christian calligrapher. He wrote titles for various campus journals of Yenching University, taking the tablets of the *Wei Bei* 魏碑 and the *Han Li* 漢隸 as examples. In 1952, Yenching University was abolished, and Peking University moved from the inner city of Beijing to Yanyuan 燕園 of Yenching University. The four characters of Mao Zedong's handwriting, "Peking University," we see now has replaced the former plaque. Another example is the site of the Protestant University of Politics and Law in East China, the old campus of St. John's University in Shanghai, which has a Chinese archway with the name of the university, "St. John's University," and the motto "Light and Truth." It also has several couplets, such as "Song River cherishes the spirits and elites are educated, and Nishan Mountain assumes its mission and its reputation spread wildly" (淞水鍾靈英才樂育，尼山知命聲教覃敷), "Three sides of the lake are equally divided in the environment, and the tree has been half a hundred years of meritorious service" (環境平分三面水，樹人已半百年功), all of which are excellent calligraphy works in the similar style as *Wei Bei*, especially the meaning of the Zheng WenGong Stele 鄭文公碑. In addition, an observant person today can still notice the calligraphy of the names of, say, Catholic Fujen University, Protestant Hujiang University (University of Shanghai), and campus building plaques. Each of these calligraphy remains has its own Christian story and merits.

In the Republic era of China, teachers in church schools were not all Christians, nor were they aiming to train missionaries. The subjects taught were more comprehensive, which often negated calligraphy education. Chinese scholars themselves then often were not professional calligraphers, though their calligraphy often had a kind of "literary spirit" still, which was tasteful and interpretable. In the first half of the twentieth century, Chinese Protestantism advocated for "indigenization 本色化," and calligraphy was valued as a form of cultural expression. Therefore, within Protestant churches, there are many senior Christian pastors and parishioners who are receiving good education and are immersed in Chinese high culture, such as Zhao Zichen 趙紫宸, Wu Leichuan 吳雷川, Yang Yinliu 楊蔭瀏. Their style of calligraphy is not stereotypical but admirable.

Many church buildings in China adopted the Chinese style to value the indigenization movement. The use of calligraphy in Protestant church decoration also was common. For example, St. Paul's Protestant Church, located at the junction of Taiping South Road and Baixia Road in Nanjing, is an old church with a century-old history. The pillar style inside the church is a traditional colonial European style, but the top is engraved with the Gospel of Matthew's "Eight Blessings." It is written in a classical Chinese translation, regular script, with no signature, but its style is stable and strong and represents good Christian calligraphy. Sicheng Church 思澄堂 in Hangzhou is also a Protestant church with a history of nearly one hundred years. The name itself used by this North Presbyterian Church has Chinese characteristics. In addition to the three characters written in Li Shu script, "*Sicheng Tang*," with Yi Bingshou's 伊秉綬 calligraphy style, there are also scattered in the courtyard such Christian calligraphic stone carvings as "*Bing Xiang Xia Ling* 並享遐齡" and "*Wan Shi Pan Shi* 萬世磐石." An inscription made in 1887—inscribed with three characters of "*Mu Er Tang*" in the regular script—can still be seen in the courtyard of the Mu Er Church in Shanghai, known as "Mu Er Church 慕爾堂" in the Guangxu period of the Qing dynasty. Calligraphy has become one of the important functions and decorative elements of Chinese Christian church buildings. For Christians, calligraphy as an art form is also a form of viewing the manifestation of God's glory. Therefore, apart from the author's signature, Lü Xiuyan on the Jingjiao Stele, many important Christian calligraphy works have not survived with the author's name, and some cannot be verified. It is a Chinese Christian spirit of dedication to identify calligraphy and the name of the author himself, perhaps to show God's attributes and message in artistic words.

Today, Christian arts, including calligraphy, are very attractive in China. Some folk artists have held many Chinese Christian art exhibitions, attracting domestic and international attention. One of the most influential exhibitions was the "First China Religious Art Exhibition," held by the Institute of Religious Culture of Peking University and the Library of Peking University in September 2014 on the campus of Peking University. Although it included the works of the five major religious artists in China, the Bible-themed calligraphy by Christian artists attracted special attention. To this day, behind the platform of many Protestant churches in China, there are biblical sentences such as "神愛世人 *shen ai shi ren*" ("God loves the world") and "以馬內利 *yi ma nei li*" (Emmanuel) written with brushes.[14]

In recent years, the publication of the handwritten Bible in the Chinese church also has become popular. On the one hand, some Christian calligraphers have published handwritten Bible volumes in the form of internal publications, such as Proverbs (handwritten version) written by Han Xingguang 韓興光 in brush, which circulate among Christian calligraphy enthusiasts.[15] On the other hand, some Christian associations have organized believers to copy the Bible with ball-point pens. For example, in 2017, the Tianjin Christian Church Council and the Tianjin TSPM organized a large-scale handwritten Bible-copying activity with the theme of "putting down mobile phones and focusing on Holy words." A total of 1,189 Christians in the churches from Tianjin TSPM copied 1,189 chapters of the Bible (CUV) and finally published the New Testament Manual Version by the CCC and TSPM in 2017.[16] Although the handwriting levels shown in these publications are not as skillful as well-trained calligraphers, they can be seen as the expression of Chinese Christians' enthusiasm for calligraphy today.

Conclusion

The Bible, as believed to be God's Word, is recorded and handed down in handwriting. To the Chinese however, Chinese scripts or characters include "meaning," "sound," and "shape." Therefore, the Bible has content, voice/utterance, and artistic visual form of various styles in the Chinese vernacular. Chinese calligraphy is a visual manifestation of language that embodies and expresses meaning in and through the calligrapher's creation of the world via brushstrokes.[17] To Christians, the Chinese people's aesthetic pursuit of handwriting means that beautiful writing itself reveals and witnesses to God's glory. Calligraphy in China has become an important element of Christian art and gospel proclamation of the Christian localization movement. The Chinese believe that "Seeing a person's words is like seeing that person 見字如面 *jian zi ru mian*" and the "words of a person are like him 字如其人 *zi ru qi ren*." Since "holy words" have transcendental characteristics in Christianity, and the Chinese language itself is combined with its visual form, so the holy words in the Bible expressed by Chinese calligraphy have an ontological meaning of "incarnation." Christian calligraphy will certainly have a broader role and purpose to play for the Chinese church.

Notes

1. See K. K. Yeo 楊克勤, *Confucius and Paul* [in Chinese] 孔子與保羅 (Shanghai: East China Normal University Press, 2010), 42–49, 404–413, on Chinese language and Chinese Christian theology; also Wang Zhixin 王治心, *History of Christianity in China* [in Chinese] 中國基督教史 (Shanghai: Shanghai Classics Publishing House, 2004); Gao Shining 高師寧, *Christianity and Christians in Contemporary Beijing* [in Chinese] 當代北京的基督教與基督徒 (Hong Kong: Logos & Pneuma Press, 2005).
2. See Zhu Qianzhi 朱謙之, *Chinese Nestorian* [in Chinese] 中國景教 (Beijing: People's Publishing House, 1998); Weng Shaojun 翁紹軍, *Interpretation of Chinese Nestorian Texts* [in Chinese] 漢語景教文本詮釋 (Beijing: SDX Joint Publishing Company, 1996); Rong Xinjiang 榮新江, *Eighteen Lectures on Dunhuang Studies* [in Chinese] 敦煌學十八講 (Beijing: Peking University Press, 2001).
3. Zhu Donghua, "A Study on the Calligraphy of the Daqin Jingjiao Liuxing Zhongguo Bei" [in Chinese] 大秦景教流行中國碑書法考論, *Logos & Pneuma* 34 (2011): 244–245.
4. In the history of Chinese calligraphy, the early calligraphers in the development stage of calligraphy are often regarded as "origin," while the late calligraphers who learn these early calligraphers and form their own style on the basis of them are often regarded as "development." It is generally believed that the artistic achievement of "origin" is higher than that of "development."
5. Chen Yuan 陳垣, "History of Christianity Came to China" [in Chinese] 基督教入華史, in Chen Yuan's *Collection of Academic Essays* 陳垣學術論文集 (Beijing: Zhonghua Book Company, 1980), 1:98, here taken from Lin Wushu 林悟殊, "Question on the Saeki's Text of the Nestorian *Zhixuan Anle Jing* Dunhuang Version" [in Chinese] 敦煌本景教<志玄安樂經>佐伯錄文質疑, *Zhongshan daxue xuebao* (中山大學學報: 社科版) 4 (2001): 1–7.

6. Lin Wushu 林悟殊, "Supplementary Notes: On the Identification of the Nestorian Stone Carving Inscriptions" [in Chinese] 補記：關於經幢真偽的鑒定, in *Nestorian Heritage: A Study of the New Excavated Nestorian Stone Carving Inscriptions in Tang Dynasty in Luoyang* 景教遺珍—洛陽新出唐代景教經幢研究, ed. Ge Chengyong (葛承雍) (Beijing: Cultural Relics Publishing House, 2009), 88.
7. Sha Menghai 沙孟海, "Writing and Carving Style of Calligraphy in Two Jin Dynasties: A Key Issue in the Debate of *Lantingxu*" [in Chinese] 兩晉南北朝書跡的寫體與刻體—蘭亭帖爭論的關鍵問題, *New Arts* (新美術) 3 (1990): 11–12.
8. Celso Benigno Luigi Cardinal Costantini 剛恒毅 et al., *Catholic Arts in China* [in Chinese] 中國天主教美術, trans. Sun Maoxue 孫茂學 (Taichung: Kuangchi Cultural Group, 1968), 7.
9. Matteo Ricci and Nicolas Trigault, *The China That Was* [in Chinese] 利瑪竇中國劄記, trans. He Gaoji 何高濟, Wang Zunzhong 王遵仲, and Li Shen 李申 (Beijing: Zhonghua Book Company, 1983), 27–43.
10. Han Qi 韓琦 and Wu Min 吳旻, eds., *Xichao Chongzheng Ji, Xichao Ding'an and Three Other Texts* [in Chinese] 熙朝崇正集 熙朝定案(外三種) (Beijing: Zhonghua Book Company, 2006).
11. Elijah Coleman Bridgman and Michael Simpson Culbertson, trs., *Old Testament, New Testament* [in Chinese] 江蘇滬邑美華書館活字版 (Shanghai: The American Presbyterian Mission Press, 1863).
12. Karl Friedrich August Gützlaff, tr., *Old Testament New Testament Literary Chinese Version* [in Chinese] 舊遺詔聖書, 新遺詔聖書: 深文理譯本 (Shanghai: American Bible Society, 1838, 1840).
13. Mrs. Arnold Foster, *Gospel Rhymes* [in Chinese] 福音韻語 (Hankou: Christian Bookstore, 1886).
14. A Bible-themed calligraphy exhibition was held in May 2019 on the first floor of Beijing Chaoyang Protestant Church. Among the works, there were not only long Scriptures, but also classical and sentence calligraphy works such as "Emmanuel" and "God loves the world."
15. Han Xingguang 韓興光, *Proverbs Handwritten Version* [in Chinese] 聖經箴言手寫卷 (Internal publication).
16. *New Testament Manual Version* [in Chinese] 新約聖經手抄本 (Shanghai: China Christian Council, 2017).
17. Yeo, *Confucius and Paul*, 42–49; Yeo, *Classical Rhetoric*, 1–5, 117–248.

Primary Sources

Bible: Chinese Union Version [in Chinese] 聖經(和合本). Shanghai: China Christian Council, 2006.

"Faith, Hope, Love: Rare Edition Bible Collection Digital Retrieval System" [in Chinese] 信望愛：珍本聖經數位典藏查詢系統). https://bible.fhl.net/gbdoc/ob/index.html.

"Tang Daqin Jingjiao Liuxing Zhongguobei" [in Chinese] 唐大秦景教流行中國碑. Xi'an: Shanxi People's Publishing House, 2006.

Wangduo Zeng Tangruowang Shice [in Chinese] 王鐸贈湯若望詩冊. Jinan: Shandong Pictorial Publishing House, 2016.

CHAPTER 45

BIBLICAL PRESENCE IN CHINESE CONTEMPORARY FILMS

JINGHAN XU

Introduction

Photographic images inclusive of forms such as films, TV programs, and still photography play an increasingly important role in our world of mass media today. Besides depending on traditional media forms like texts, paintings, and music, artists pay attention to the use of contemporary visual media in order to disseminate the Christian faith to a larger audience and/or to use biblical metaphor and message to extend the rhetorical power of the gospel[1] in explaining or transforming Chinese society. This essay looks at the exploration of the Christian faith by means of Chinese contemporary photographic images through categorizing Christianity-related image artwork in China over recent years.

The scope of this essay is limited in terms of the "film" genre and the artists. First, it mainly reviews the genre of Chinese contemporary films and documentaries. In terms of territories, it focuses primarily on works produced in the Chinese mainland, but also mentions some works from Hong Kong and Taiwan because of the influence of these works reaching China.

Visual artwork related to Christianity in China may be reflected in two ways: through the use of Christian symbols or through the embodiment of biblical teachings. Since church architecture, the Christian cross, the image of Jesus Christ, clergy or priests, Christian music, and other biblical symbols are not common in indigenous Chinese culture, and because of the government restriction against using these symbols in film production, the above symbols are intentionally inserted into movies by the producers, and they play the role of nuancing or promoting the development of plots.

Visual artwork embodied with Christian messages cannot be recognized as easily as those with Christian symbols, and they are even more controversial. The controversy involves questions about how religious faith is blended into mass culture, and how religious faith breaks through various limitations and expresses itself. The most recognizable Christian theologies or doctrines include "sin," "redemption," and "sacrificial love." Artwork that reflects Christian theology is reviewed in this essay.

Second, in terms of artists, they include both Christian and non-Christian Chinese artists, though some do not disclose their religious beliefs; this essay surveys any artwork that reflects Christian symbols or theology without discriminating whether or not the artists are Christian. The study of the history of art in China shows the self-awareness of artists to be important, as they consciously embody Christian symbols or theology in the works. Some works magnify strong Christian theology, but other artists may have no definite intention to express them (or at times it is impossible to know whether they have such intentions or not).

The task here is to discuss films and documentary films embedded with Christian symbols and theology in contemporary China (2000 to 2018). Works produced by official or folk religious institutions for missionary purposes, preaching, or witnessing are not included in the discussion.

Films under the influence of Christianity can be divided roughly into three categories:

1. Bible films: stories in the *Bible* that are reproduced in films, such as in the examples of foreign films: *The Gospel According to St. Matthew* (馬太福音, 1964), *The Prince of Egypt* (埃及王子, 1998), etc.
2. Christianity-themed films: contents touch on the topics of the church, disciples, nuns and friars, and the "end time" (eschatology), such as in the examples of foreign films: *The Mission* (教會, 1986), *Dead Man Walking* (死囚漫步, 1995), etc.
3. Films under the influence of Christian values, which are more diversified. In the examples of foreign films, the themes of some contemporary Hollywood films include conservative values found in the Bible, or the derivations of these values, the theme of sin and redemption (*The Shawshank Redemption*, 肖申克的救贖, 1994), exploration of truth (*The Matrix*, 黑客帝國, 1999), and essence of love (*Frozen*, 冰雪奇缘, 2013), etc.

Art Films and Experimental Films

Now we look at a few directors' works in art films and experimental films that have affinities with Christianity motifs.

Gan Xiao'er

Gan Xiao'er 甘小二 could be seen as the first director who focuses on the theme of Christianity in the film industry of mainland China. He founded "The Seventh Seal Film

Workshop" in 2000. He wishes to finish seven films related to Christianity. Currently, works including *The Only Sons* (山清水秀, 2002), *Raised from Dust* (舉自塵土, 2007), *Waiting for God* (在期待之中, 2012), and *Church Cinema* (教堂電影院, 2008) have been completed.

Under the political ecology and the specific cultural background of China mainland, Gan pays attention to Christianity-related topics. In China, there are 800 million farmers, and they are marginalized in their political and cultural identity. Farmers who are Christians are marginalized even more than others because of their religious identity. Gan pays close attention to Christians in rural areas with his camera and attempts to present their spiritual world through their daily lives.

The Only Sons, released in 2002, is the first feature film produced by Gan, and is also the first attempt to shoot a Christianity-themed film in mainland China. This film tells a tragic story about Ah Shui, who sold his son and wife in order to bail out his younger brother. Despite this sacrifice, his brother was executed by shooting, his wife committed suicide, and he died of AIDS. Against the backdrop of the beautiful and tranquil scenery, the miserable plots unfold themselves gradually, intertwined with the knots of human sins. Ah Shui is not only a victim but also a perpetrator, living at the bottom of society. It is exactly his behavior of selling his wife and son that brings about family destruction in the film.

In this film, Christianity functions more as background for the story to unfold. Ah Shui did not believe in Christianity, but the preacher in his village was concerned about his struggles in life and thus tried to preach to him. Ah Shui began to reflect on the issue of faith with a sense of guilt. Various Christian symbols can be found in the film, such as the boat with a cross, the woman holding a child in the boat, the cross-shaped pendant, and the music, "Amazing Grace," etc. These symbols appear a little stiff in the film, but they strengthen the theme of redemption and hope in the insolubly tragic atmosphere.

If the Christianity in *The Only Sons* is only setting for the story, *Raised from Dust* and *Waiting for God* give a direct description of the status quo of Christianity in rural China. Close attention is paid to how farmer Christians face their hard life, while love and care among them is demonstrated. For example, *Raised from Dust* represents the hard family life of rural woman Xiao Li and her service in the church choir. Although her life was beset with difficulties, Xiao Li was resilient and hopeful with life through her Christian faith. *Waiting for God* tells the story of Jiang Xiaoyang, a female church leader, who got pregnant by her boyfriend, who made his living engraving idols before marriage and thus suffered from a sense of guilt. The significance of this film lies in its direct confrontation with the existing problems in the church (crimes committed by Christians, dogmatism existing in some churches, etc.), and how Christians face and overcome their own sense of guilt.

Such details as the Christian cross, church life, prayer, and hymnals are especially displayed in Gan's films, which not only reflect the actual living conditions of Christians but also function to highlight emotions and further advance the plot development. They also reflect the theme of Christians seeking hope amidst suffering and guilt. These three feature films shift their focus from the integration of Christian elements in the story to the presentation of Christian life, and then to the exploration of Christianity's core belief; thus, demonstrating the increasingly mature filming process of Gan.

Documentary *Church Cinema* is also a meaningful work. It records the situation when Gan played his film *Raised from Dust* in Qiliying Church—one of the filming locations. This documentary records farmers' understanding of the Christian faith, plus their opinions and suggestions for the film *Raised from Dust*. This work has a certain cognitive understanding of Christian ecology in Chinese rural areas. From the perspective of media research, the value of this work is that it enables a farmer audience to express their opinions of Christianity-themed films. How to deal with the relationship between the profundity of the film motifs and the reception of the film becomes a goal that Gan needs to further explore.

Wang Chao

As a "sixth-generation"[2] director in China, Wang Chao 王超 confesses that his works find inspiration from Christianity. His main works are *Orphan of Anyang* (安陽嬰兒, 2001), *Night and Day* (日日夜夜, 2004), *Luxury Car* (江城夏日, 2006), *Looking for Rohmer* (尋找羅麥, 2018), and others.

In 1996, a book titled *Truth on the Way to the Cross* (走向十字架上的真), wherein the author Liu Xiaofeng 劉小楓 reviews Western theological thought in the contemporary age, had a profound influence on Wang Chao and thus became a turning point for his works. Liu writes: "The God came down and suffered on the Cross, not to actually relieve human sufferings, but to bring love to those who are suffered and to acknowledge their suffering... provide a meaning for people's suffering."[3] Wang believes, as a Chinese film director, that he should directly confront and undertake contemporary reality in China, rather than escape or sugarcoat it.

As Dietrich Bonhoeffer has said:

> Confront the life, including all of its responsibilities and confusions, its successes and failures, and its experience and loneliness. Only in this kind of life, can we... share the suffering and bitterness of God, and, along with Christ on the Mount Olive, bear the suffering of this life and stay up all night to safeguard the human world.[4]

In his early works, such as *Orphan of Anyang*, *Night and Day*, and *Luxury Car*, Wang focuses on life for the unprivileged population in China, and he is excellent at demonstrating themes like suffering, depth of sins, etc. in his works, while placing that hope of redemption within them. The image of an infant, which represents hope, appears repeatedly in his films, but there is no explicit presentation of Christian symbols. From the film *Love Reclaimed* (重來), released in 2009, Wang gradually turns his attention to living conditions for the urban middle class, as he shows his care for their spiritual world and employs more and more surrealistic images in his works.

Looking for Rohmer, released in 2018, represents Wang's latest achievement in faith exploration. Rohmer, a French youth, killed a man by accident, so he set foot on a journey to Tibet to free himself. Unfortunately, he lost his life in a snowstorm. His homosexual lover, Zhao Jie, rushed to Tibet to make arrangements for Rohmer's funeral and then went to Europe to inform and comfort Rohmer's family. On the two journeys, Zhao Jie experienced the rituals of Tibetan Buddhism and Christianity and finally found the meaning of his life in the spirit of Tibetan dance and Tibetan locales.

Wang reveals his religious thinking in the film without necessarily having a clarity about the purpose of life himself. He most likely thinks that, in terms of the effect of redemption, different religions arrive at the same end by different means. Yet, Wang's works, such as *Looking for Rohmer*, represents the view of a Chinese intellectual who has no explicit religious faith but seeks to explore the meaning of life and personal redemption.

Hu Jie

Hu Jie 胡杰 is a documentary film director and a professional painter. Hu started producing documentaries independently in 1995, and so far, he has produced ten of them. His works focus on the reality of the underclass as well as historical subjects in the age of Mao Zedong 毛澤東. Topics like suffering and the struggles of the weak are depicted in his works. His main works include *Searching for Lin Zhao's Soul* (尋找林昭的靈魂, 2004), *Though I Am Gone* (我雖死去, 2007), *Spark* (星火, 2013), and *The Song of Mai Di Chong* (麥地沖的歌聲, 2016).

Hu was born in 1958 at the start of the Cultural Revolution, which he experienced during his boyhood and youth and made a deep imprint in his works. The Cultural Revolution has been a forbidden zone in Chinese literature and art, but Hu's identity outside the official media system enables him to express this history from his personal perspective.

Searching for Lin Zhao's Soul, released in 2004, is an important early work of Hu Jie. He puts forward a question in this film: "How we enter history and make it into a memory?" At first, Hu wondered how the character Lin Zhao, faced with oppression, could keep her faith in a hopeless situation of loneliness and suffering. After understanding Lin Zhao's Christian faith, Hu was deeply moved.

The Song of Mai Di Chong, released in 2016, pays attention to Christian themes against the backdrop of the Cultural Revolution. Hu interviewed four descendants of martyred priest Wang Zhiming 王志明 in the mountainous Miao-populated areas in Yunnan. He also recorded the religious life of local Christians and their encomiastic singing. Meanwhile, Hu presented the impact of material enjoyment and modern recreation on people's faith. The persecution of characters in the film during the Cultural Revolution fills the film with a harsh and desolate atmosphere, but the melodious chanting breaks through the darkness and horror of history and brings about happiness and bright hope to the people.

Besides documentary films, Hu Jie has a great number of print works, among which are some that revolve on Christian themes and some that center on the history of Cultural Revolution. These two themes echo each other, connecting people's sufferings with their dynamic faith.

Hu is moved by Lin Zhao and the Christian faith of many common people, but he seems to believe that, although Christians have faith, they cannot avoid committing crimes. His viewpoint here, representative of many intellectuals in China, seems to neglect an important doctrine of Christianity, viz., "justification by faith," God's grace that accepts people as they are and, in a process of sanctification, the same grace that gradually shapes them to be Christlike. Hu was baptized at the end of 2018.

Commercial Films and Popular Films

The works of a few Chinese directors of commercial and popular films often use Christianity motifs, even though sometimes with their own intentions and biases.

Zhang Yimou

Zhang Yimou 張藝謀 is one of the most famous directors in China and has won many international film awards. In 2011, he produced *The Flowers of War* (金陵十三釵) painstakingly as an attempt to win an Academy Award. It tells a story set during the Sino-Japanese War in 1937, in a church in the occupied area of Nanjing, where a group of prostitutes took refuge and sacrificed their lives to protect students in the church. Probably to cater to the tastes of Western audience, the story is set in a church and many Christian elements such as a priest, a Christian cross, hymn singing, and self-sacrificial love are depicted in the film.

The production of this film is excellent, and the use of Christian elements is also to the point. Besides overall national interests, Yu Mo, John Miller, and George Chen together demonstrate the theme of self-sacrifice in the film. However, some reviewers are of the opinion that erotic and violent plots are rendered in this film deliberately so as to meet the "voyeuristic" psychology of the audience, thus raising the debate about whether such technique shows real respect for the characters. Scholar Shi Hengtan 石衡潭 writes: "Zhang Yimou has been walking between the elegant and the vulgar, the affection and the desire."[5] *The Flowers of War* can be seen as a reflection of the essential conflict of Zhang's works, for there is a huge misplacement and breakage between the elegant and the vulgar. Such a portrayal is different from the biblical portrayal of love in the Song of Songs and Revelation, which uphold and celebrate the purity of love.

Different from *The Flowers of War*, Zhang released *Coming Home* (歸來) in 2014, as he returned to the subject of local history. The work turned out to be a great success in film art. This film contains some Christian values. The story takes place during the Cultural Revolution, when people "placed [Chinese notion of] righteousness above family loyalty for the sake of politics"—that is, the Chinese understanding that "*da yi mie qing* 大義滅親" (great righteousness destroys family/relatives). The daughter prevented her mother from meeting her father, who fled home after he was required to take part in labor training in the countryside and the mother was upset. When the Cultural Revolution ended, the father returned home. He forgave and accepted his daughter and patiently looked after his wife who, after a long separation and trauma, had amnesia and was unable to recognize him. There the "father" is no longer the authoritative image in the Chinese tradition, but a tolerant and self-giving image. The father forgave the daughter who once betrayed him, a reminder of the image of Jesus and the father in the "prodigal son" story (Luke 15:11–32). Here the mother never gave up waiting for her husband to return to her side, a reminder of the scenario of the Jews waiting for the Messiah. The father accompanied the mother patiently, a reminder of Jesus patiently waiting for sinners to recognize him and repent. Compared with Feng Xiaogang's work, *Youth* (芳華, 2017), which also portrays the Cultural Revolution, *Coming Home* echoes the biblical theme of courage in the face of a harsh reality, as well as the themes of love and hope.

It should be noted that art film awards represented by three major European film festivals usually reflect a variety of values, while the commercial film awards represented by the Academy Awards has long been influenced by Western mainstream values (mainly the conservative values of Christianity, although there have been some special cases in recent years). Therefore, to obtain the favor of the Academy, besides learning the narrative mode of Hollywood films, it also is necessary to acknowledge and integrate Western mainstream, and sometimes Christian, values in the films.

Feng Xiaogang

Feng Xiaogang 馮小剛 is one of the most successful commercial film directors in China. His "Feng's Comedy"[6] has great box-office appeal. Feng knows that "New Year films" pursue box office and profits, but they cannot be produced hastily. Instead, they must be treated seriously and adapted to the narrative system and production mode of commercial films. Therefore, he takes the Hollywood commercial films as his learning objective. Similarly, some films produced by Feng in recent years also draw lessons from this mode, such as the theme of "self-identity verification" in *The Assembly* (集結號, 2007), the theme of "meaning of love" in *If You Are the One* (非誠勿擾, 2008), the theme of "reconciliation and forgiveness" in *Aftershock* (唐山大地震, 2010) and the theme of "face the sufferings" in *Back to 1942* (一九四二, 2012).

When Feng learns from Hollywood commercial films, he also, consciously or unconsciously, comes into contact with Christian or biblical motifs. In 2008, a church and a priest appear in the film, *If You Are the One.* There, the presentation of Christian elements is to serve the development of the plot: first, the story is set in Western countries; second, they can create a comical dramatic effect of a conflicting encounter between East and West. Many wealthy Chinese people today in Western society are facing similar distress and difficulty in their spiritual lives, and they do not feel comfortable when encountering Western culture.

By depicting a group of characters, *Back to 1942*, which was released in 2012, portrays the terrible drought in Chinese history. Although it still contains humorous elements, the image of a priest and his serious reflection on Christianity is described in the film. Father Sim migrated along with people who fled the famine, and he preached his religious faith along the way. His understanding of Christianity was rather dogmatic. For example, he declared to the public: "Why do you flee from famine? Because you are heretics." But after witnessing a series of deaths, Father Sim began to question his own faith. He asked his predecessor, Bishop Megan: "Does God know these sufferings? Why doesn't He do something?" "If God can't defeat the demon, why should I believe in Him?" Bishop Megan replied: "Everything happened in the world is the will of God," and "You can't question God." Perhaps, the confusion of Father Sim and Bishop Megan represents the filmmakers' doubt about Christianity. Indeed, "the cause and meaning of suffering" and "God's position and behaviors in the history" are both significant theological themes.

Another meaningful scenario in the film occurs when Chiang Kai Shek 蔣介石 came to the church to pray alone and shed tears after learning about the truth of the drought in Henan province. This scene, to some extent, represents the worldly utilitarian judgment of Christianity by the public. That is, if the Christian faith of the civilians and ruling class could not save themselves and their country, what is the use of this Christian faith?

In the sad and depressive atmosphere, the end of the film uses "*The River of Life*," which is recomposed from a Christian song of Xiaomin[7] as the theme music, adding bright color to the film. The filmmaker seems to feel the redemption quality and breath-taking power possessed by Christianity, but due to a lack of in-depth understanding of some fundamental doctrines of the Christian faith, his expression and employment of Christian theology is superficial.

Peter Chan

Peter Chan 陳可辛 is a famous Hong Kong film director with many films. Christian elements are frequently used in many Hong Kong films because of its Western cultural background. For example, in movies directed by John Woo 吳宇森, churches and pigeons become classic images of his violence aesthetics. It's impossible to ascertain the faith of Peter Chan, but in some of his films, we can find Christian elements. Yet, when compared to John Woo, Peter Chan is more skillful in his employment of these elements and is more profound in his interpretations.

The Warlords (投名狀) released in 2007 tells a story about three "blood" brothers (Pang Qingyun, Zhao Erhu, Jiang Wuyang) during the period of imperial court in the late Qing dynasty who were exterminated by the Taiping Army. There existed a background of Christian "faith" of the Taiping Heavenly Kingdom, so it is very reasonable and credible that the cross-shaped pendant and the story of Jesus "feeding 5,000 men with 5 loaves and 2 fish" appear in the film. Huang Wenqing, leader of the Taiping Army in Soochow City, sacrificed his life willingly to save the people in the city. His chivalrous deed that imitated the self-sacrificing spirit of Jesus was in sharp contrast with the Chinese culture that was inundated with the "rule of the jungle" (survival of the fittest), mutual suspicions, and deceptions. Huang was like a breath of fresh air and greatly shocked Zhao Erhu, the second elder brother. The Christian faith failed to save Huang Wenqing, the five thousand soldiers in Soochow City and Zhao Erhu's life, but it protected all residents in Soochow City. The Christian faith moved and changed Zhao Erhu for the better and lightened dark historical events with the spiritual power of "laying down one's life for a just cause." This spiritual dimension of abandoning the present and pursuing the eternal is absent from Chinese culture, which is heavy with pragmatism. *The Warlords* gives a good interpretation of Christian theology in the Chinese cultural background, but, regrettably, its value is covered up by superficial power struggles and entanglements among the three brothers in the film.

Dearest (親愛的), released in 2014, tells a story about recovering kidnapped children. Different from the "black or white" routine story, this film adds a lot of elements about human nature to traditionally negative characters. This film also contains the theme of "understanding and tolerance" among people. The film does not blend in many Christian elements, but the documentary footage at the end of the film shows the audience that Gao Yongxia, the prototype of Li Hongqin in real life, converted to Christianity through a cross on the wall. The core footage of this film disclosed many Christian messages.

Li Hongqin, wife of the human trafficker, should have been hated by everyone in real life, but in this film, she is presented positively, and the filmmaker also shows deep sympathy for her. I think the film's bold ideas, that everyone is a sinner and that there is no difference between perpetrators and victims, do reflect Paul's theology in Romans 3 that "all have sinned and fall short of the glory of God" (3:23; NRSV throughout this essay). The story in the film *Dearest* is about "seeking lost relatives," but its core narrative contains something much deeper. The theme in the film of searching for lost ones reveals the deep structure of mutual understanding and forgiveness in human relationship, and this message comes closer to the biblical message of "love your enemies" (Matt 5:44). The film's promotional words read: "There are thousands of roads to leave the home, but only one road to return." Director Peter Chan also said: "*Dearest* lays a way home about losing and seeking for the audience."[8] It embodies the metaphorical meaning of "the return of the prodigal son" in the Gospel of Luke.

In real life, Gao Yongxia, the prototype of Li Hongqin, lived alone and helplessly—her husband died of an illness, and her two adopted children also left her. At the end of *Dearest*, documentary footage shows that Peng Gaofeng (the prototype of Tian Wenjun) and his families went to the village to visit Gao Yongxia and reconciled with her. We see that actors of this film also watched this documentary, and the real characters came to the filming site and embraced the actors warmly, which pushes the emotions of the audience to a new high and also deepens the theme of "reconciliation and tolerance." This multi-media "reunion" ending across time and space is deliberately created by the filmmaker, but the great emotional strength is real. Real life is incomplete, while this happy and positive atmosphere of "reunion" becomes, in a sense, the foreboding of the final reunion in the biblical vision of paradise.

As an administrative region that implements the policy of "one nation, two systems," Hong Kong and its well-developed film industry once had a far-reaching influence on the mainland. Now as the mainland and Hong Kong cooperate more frequently in the film industry, the pattern of "co-productions" is bringing more mature opportunities for both sides. We also hope that more integration and identification at the level of values can be achieved.

A Rhetorical Hermeneutic of Re-reading Christian Elements in Chinese Films

Though the "textuality" and genre of film and the Bible are different, yet in hermeneutics, we can re-read the rhetorical persuasion of the gospel and Christian elements in Chinese films. Based on the "cross-cultural and rhetorical hermeneutics" work of K. K. Yeo, this re-reading can be explained as an attempt to discover the "interpretive understanding (hermeneutic) and communicative understanding of that interpretation (rhetoric) between"[9] films and the Bible. The "rhetorical hermeneutic" of watching a movie and reading a biblical text are not exactly the same, but they do share in at least two ways: (1) the viewer or interpreter's interaction with the film or the Bible respectively; (2) a triangular interactive relationship exists among the motion-picture (parallel to utterance of the biblical text), the characters in the films (parallel to biblical characters and the plot), and the directors (parallel to the biblical authors or rhetors).[10] There are two results of this rhetorical-hermeneutical re-reading: (1) the "textuality" of a film (much like that of the biblical text) represents the "goadings of mystery" (Kenneth Burke) that "invites the audience to be confronted or transformed in the transactional process"[11] in the movie-watching experience; (2) the "intent and process of a rhetorical enterprise is not to stop at the historical meaning" of what the film portrayed "but to allow fusion of horizon taking place in a reader [viewer and interpreter] who is not in the historical situation of the first audience."[12] Film, as an art form, offers much more creativity and aesthetic power than any vernacular script could. It evokes imagination to translate and interpret and extend and, therefore, to embody and relive, the biblical story of divine presence despite the appearance of evil, sin, and hopelessness.

Christian Symbols

The Image of Priest/Clergy

As preachers of the gospel, priests or clergy play a significant role in Christianity. The priest images in contemporary Chinese films reflect Chinese viewers' negative attitude toward priests. In the film, *If You Are the One*, the priest was put in an extremely awkward position by Qin Fen's trivial confession that lasted for hours and eventually had to show him the door. In Jiang Wen's film, *Let the Bullets Fly* (讓子彈飛, 2010), the priest in the funeral made his memorial speech without paying any attention to the incident of a hostage being kidnapped. In the above two films, the priest is presented as an object to be mocked and ridiculed, much like "the Pharisees" are profiled for biblical readers as the "bad guys" (cf. Matt 12:1–8).

In *Back to 1942*, Father Sim and Bishop Megan fulfilled their duty as priests, but due to their partial understanding of the gospel, they began to question their faith. In *The Flowers of War*, John Miller was a mortician who disguised himself as a priest. He did something just and self-giving, though he is not a real priest and could not lead his congregations spiritually. Here we see the nuancing of a "bad guy" (cf. Luke 5:17; Matt 5:20).

Priest Liu, in *Dying to Survive* (我不是藥神) released in 2018, is a character worthy of attention. It is a contemporary Christian figure that has rarely appeared in Chinese movies in recent years. Director Wen Muye 文牧野 always has been interested in religious and spiritual subjects. *Dying to Survive* is inclined to Buddhism in terms of its overall tone, and Cheng Yong is portrayed as a bodhisattva image of "divine intervention" (普渡眾生) or "the savior." In the film, Priest Liu represents the face of Christianity. What he does is sometimes against orthodox Christianity, and he also receives little spiritual exploration from the director in this film. However, his act of throwing himself forward for the benefit of the patients serves to show the biblical teaching to serve rather than stand aloof from worldly affairs—representing the Jesus figure, perhaps? The film also has raised propositions worth pondering over, such as "which is greater, law or human sentiment" (corresponding to the Christian "legalism," cf. Matt 9:13, 12:7) and "should Christianity be mundane or transcendental?"

The answer, of course, is not a binary answer, but the Mid-Eastern and oriental understanding of "in and not of the world" (John 15:19, 17:14–16; Rom 12:2)—that is, not to befriend the world values but actively care for the needs of the peoples in the world (James 1:27, 4:4. The above three characters can be categorized as priests who have secular identity without spiritual meaning. Perhaps they have the priest's identity and do the work of a priest, even some self-sacrificial deeds (Mark 9:40 "he who is not against us is for us"), though they lack the qualities of spiritual leaders and cannot feed the congregation well.

Compared with other directors, Gan Xiao'er presents the priests in his films quite positively and objectively, including the priest in *The Only Sons*, who cared about the salvation of the underprivileged population and the rigid and dogmatic priest in *Waiting for God*.

Church Space

Church buildings or church space also are commonly used elements in films related to Christianity. *Before Born* (結果), released in 2006 by Zhang Ming 章明, is a film with modernist characteristics and in the style of "waiting for Godot," which fills the film with strong biblical metaphors and themes. In this movie, two men and one woman kept looking for Li Chonggao (Li Noble) but failed. Li Chonggao is synonymous with God. He was mysterious and did not show his face in the whole film, but he got two women pregnant (odd implication that God impregnated virgins), and that was very irresponsible.

The characters went to look for Li Chonggao in the Christian church twice but did not find him there. However, in this footage, the shot focused on the Madonna hung up in the church, indicating the absence of God. There the church became a very strong symbol of Christian culture and was taken as the dwelling of God/Li Chonggao. The keynote of this film is despair—God abandoned human beings and hid himself from them, while human beings also were caught in an awkward situation where they kept looking for God but never succeeded in finding God and the meaning of life—similar to the biblical narrative of Job, or even Jesus' cry of forsakenness in Mark 15:34 (but see Psalm 22:1, 29–31).

City of Life and Death (南京! 南京!), released in 2009 by Lu Chuan 陸川, tells a story that happened in Nanjing when the Japanese army invaded China. In this film, we can also find church space. When the church appeared for the first time in the film, thousands of Chinese people were taking refuge here, but they were all discovered and captured by a team made up of a dozen Japanese soldiers. When the church appeared for the second time, one hundred Chinese women in the crowd volunteered to be women whose role is to comfort and save more people from being hurt. Regardless of the director's understanding of Christianity, there the church has a profound meaning and even conveys the biblical teaching of the "church" in essence, that it is neither about a physical space nor merely bodily redemption (though it might have this function in history, just as the film *The Flowers of War* has represented), but more so a spiritual space (and soul-filled body as temple of the Holy Spirit, 1 Cor 6:19–20) used to worship God and motivate people to serve others sacrificially so as to follow God faithfully (Romans 12–14).

Similarly, the cross is not an amulet. For example, in the film *The Warlords*, Lian Sheng, the wife of the second elder brother, was killed by Jiang Wuyang when she was wearing a cross-shaped pendant. The cross, as a symbol that Jesus sacrificed himself to save humanity (John 3:16; Gal 6:1–2; Heb 13:1–3), reminds people to follow God, which is what Zhao Erhu realized when he entered Soochow City wearing the same cross pendant.

Christian teaching focuses on the salvation of the soul-filled body beyond gains and losses in this lifetime—this wholly and spiritual characteristic (Revelation 20–21) is extremely different from the pragmatic attitude that Chinese people hold for religions—Chinese people "embrace Buddha's feet only in their hour of need." It requires Chinese artists to understand and represent this difference carefully in films.

Christian Music

Compared with churches, priests, and other physical elements, the use of Christian music seems to be more restrained in films. Yet, because music can touch and move people, it is worth our analysis.

At present, besides some sacred music like that of Bach that was used occasionally in Chinese films, *Amazing Grace* is the Christian song used most frequently in films, such as *The Only Sons*, *Wolf Warriors 2* (戰狼 2), *Forever Young* (無問西東).

As a representation of "nationalism" (cf. Gal 3:28 "in Christ there is neither Jews nor gentiles, neither slaves nor free, no male and females") in Chinese films in recent years, *Wolf Warriors 2*, released in 2017, tells a story about Leng Feng, a Chinese veteran going deep into Africa to save Chinese compatriots and black workers who were hijacked by scoundrels. In the decisive battle, when Leng Feng was in danger, the music of *Amazing Grace* rang out, which filled the audience with a common hatred for the enemy in the film. Eventually Leng Feng defeated the male white scoundrel. *Amazing Grace* is a Christian song that originally expressed the biblical salvation of God's grace and Christians' praise of God. Later, it became universalized as a symbol representing people's pursuit of peace. In *Wolf Warriors 2*, the indiscriminate love for enemies, originally taught by Jesus in the Bible (Matt 5:44; Luke 6:27–36), is replaced by "love for the country and families and hatred for enemies," while the "internationalized" core of this song is hijacked by "nationalist" intentions.

The music of *Amazing Grace* also is used several times in the film, *Forever Young*, released in 2018. Probably because of its involvement with Tsinghua University[13] and director Li Fangfang's study in the United States, the implication of *Amazing Grace* in this film does reflect its original meaning. *Forever Young* is produced in honor of the one-hundredth birthday of Tsinghua University. With youth and election as the mega themes, this film consists of four stories. The filmmakers' suggestion, through audio and visual language as well as the motivation of characters acting out of love, can be found in the footage when the Western missionary taught poor children to sing *Amazing Grace*. *Amazing Grace* runs through the plots of the four stories, which deepens the theme of "inheritance of grace and love." Perhaps in order to avoid the government's control over religion, religious elements in the lyrics of *Amazing Grace* are removed from this film, and the film also possesses humanist tones such as "gain success in individual struggle," but the positive power of faith in this song still infects the audience beyond time and space and life and death.

In short, the employment of Christian symbols can make some movies more universal and grant them a sense of holiness and transcendence, despite the fact that some of these films may not conform to Christian values or that some of them even may be anti-Christian (e.g., films produced by Cui Zi'en 崔子恩). For the Christian symbols to be used positively and accurately in reflecting the Christian meanings, it requires Chinese filmmakers to have a profound theological knowledge while producing films with integrity under the audio-visual rules and expectation of the industry.

Christian Values

Besides the direct use of Christian symbols in films, another approach is to integrate biblical values into films. Compared with tangible symbols, it takes skill to communicate intangible Christian values.

The Theme of "Sin"

Due to the Confucianist teaching that "man's nature is good at birth," Chinese culture turned a blind eye to the subject of "sin" for years. Even if numerous "bad guys" have been portrayed in movies, the concept of "sin" that is hidden deep in everyone's nature has been neglected constantly in Chinese films.

In recent years, some Chinese films have represented themes of "sin" or "the evil of human nature," such as *Blind Shaft* (盲井, 2003) produced by Li Yang 李楊, *No Man's Land* (無人區, 2013) produced by Ning Hao 寧浩. In these films, what we see is no longer the confrontation between positive and negative characters in traditional Chinese movies, but a world decided by the rule of the jungle and a world in which everyone is "sinful" in nature.

After realizing people's "brokenness" and "sin," finding a way out is the next step. Regrettably, most Chinese films do not give the answers. There are films that portray people's helplessness in the midst of "sin," as well as the "sin and punishment" theme, but rarely do we see the theme of "sin and redemption" (as pervasive in the Bible) in Chinese movies. Redemption in Chinese movies, if at all present, it is still about "self-striving" methods. Exposing the darkness of human nature is inadequate to the way of redemption, for redemption is not self-saving by one's own efforts or knowledge (Eph 2:8–10), but the centrality of "Christ's redemptive work" (Rom 4:25).

Released in 2013 by Jia Zhangke 賈樟柯, *A Touch of Sin* (天注定), a film adapted from three criminal cases in contemporary China, attempted to solve humanity's problem. This film not only presented the causes and consequences of the cases and analyzed the characters' motivation but also paid attention to the spiritual world of Chinese people. Viewers can notice various religious objects and imagery in the film. To some extent, it exposes to the audience the reality that people today have many possessions yet homeless souls. The film suggests that the anomie of the society usually is caused by the disorder of the public's spiritual life (confusion of faith and values), leading the audience to have a serious reflection on faith.

The Theme of "Self-Sacrifice"

"Self-sacrifice" is a significant theme related to biblical values. The quality of God's love is called "*agapē*" in Greek, and it is a word used in early Christianity to also refer to the Love Feast (Communion). It may have some affinity with the value of "laying down one's life for a just cause," advocated by conventional Chinese morality, but they have qualitative differences. Rom 5:7–8 reads: "Very rarely will anyone die for a righteous man, though for a good man someone might possibly dare to die. But God demonstrates his own love for us in this: While we were still sinners, Christ died for us." The teachings of "dying for sinners" and "loving enemies" are very rare in Chinese culture. Therefore, although we see the chivalrous deeds that represent the call to "sacrifice oneself" for friends in such films as *The Flowers of War*, *City of Life and Death*, *Forever Young*, such deeds were mocked by the national audience of *Wolf Warriors 2* in China, for they believe that "anyone who offends China will be punished no matter how far the target is."

Silent Witness (全民目擊), released in 2013, by Fei Xing 非行 is a unique case, bearing a hint of the biblical teaching of "sacrificial love" and "redemption." In order to exempt the daughter who had committed murder from criminal penalty, the father, Lin Tai, willingly falsified evidence so as to take the penalty for her. Because of the "sacrificial love" of her father, the obstinate daughter finally recognized her own sins. At the end of the film, there is a scene showing the daughter stretching her arms in the heavy rain, which on the one hand pays tribute to the American film, *The Shawshank Redemption* (肖申克的救贖, 1994, which has the same footage, in order to express the joy of freedom of the character), and on the other hand, points to the biblical meaning of redemption.

We have mentioned before that, different from the authoritative father image in Chinese traditional culture, some contemporary Chinese films also begin to shape the tolerant and self-giving father image (cf. Luke 15), such as the father in the film, *Coming Home*. The father in *Silent Witness* not only was a loving father for his daughter but also was endowed with the spiritual quality of "dying for sinners," by which he persuaded the sinner to shun evil and do good.

Conclusion

We have analyzed the biblical symbols and theology in Chinese films. For filmmakers, they experience much difficulty with one main question: Should they display explicitly Christian symbols in movies or obscurely demonstrate the biblical values? The former tends to make the audience feel that there is a missionary purpose and therefore disapprove of it; while the latter can hardly convey Christian meanings accurately due to the absence of Christian symbols. Indeed, it will take wisdom to solve this dilemma, but there is no doubt that the spiritual dimension of the film is important. In 2015, the Chinese film, *The Dead End* (烈日灼心) produced by Cao Baoping 曹保平, used the story pattern of the American film, *Dead Man Walking* (死囚漫步, 1995) to some extent, which weakened the motivation of character transformation and the power of moving people.

Due to the cultural and socio-political differences between China and foreign countries, it remains a challenge to reproduce the biblical symbols and theology in Chinese films. Restricted by political constraints, it is still possible to make Bible-themed films, such as the stories of missionaries coming to China in early years, the anti-Christianity movement, massacres from history, or contemporary China church history. Chinese films have bright prospects in terms of the films under the influence of Christian values.

The essay has shown, however, the potential benefits of imitating the biblical rhetorical hermeneutics in film production and appreciation. It has the potential to allow directors to see themselves as having the sacred task of re-interpreting the biblical worldview and theology of knots and resolutions in complex life experiences, which writing scripts alone could have expressed neither fully nor richly. "Rhetorical-hermeneutical criticism is a process that does not 'freeze' a text,"[14] be that the Scripture or a story any film that makes it onto the big screen. The mystery of God and the biblical faith will inspire more Chinese films to pursue "visible divinity" and thus eventually may be able to free the biblical script of its own textuality.

NOTES

1. See K. K. Yeo, *Classical Rhetoric: Greco-Roman Culture and Biblical Hermeneutic* [in Chinese] 古修辭學：希羅文化與聖經詮釋 (Hong Kong: Logos & Pneuma, 2002).
2. Most of the "sixth-generation" directors were born in the 1960s and 1970s. They entered the Beijing Film Academy in the 1980s. After the 1990s, they began to direct their films. Many of them focused on realistic subjects.
3. Liu Xiaofeng, *Truth on the Way to the Cross* [in Chinese] (Shanghai: SDX Joint Publishing Company, 1995), 139.
4. Taken from ibid. 150.
5. Shi Hengtan, *Faith, Hope, Love in the Movies* [in Chinese] 光影中的信望爱 (Beijing: Beijing World Publishing Corporation, 2013), 17.
6. Feng Xiaogang is famous for making comedy movies that generate great box-office returns. These movies were called "Feng's Comedy."
7. Xiaomin, whose real name is Lv Xiaomin, is a Christian songwriter of China. She was born in the countryside of Henan and never studied in a music school. But she has written 1,600 songs in her collection entitled "Canaan Hymns."
8. "There are thousands of roads to leave the home, but only one road to return." https://movie.douban.com/review/7104765/.
9. K. K. Yeo, *Rhetorical Interaction in 1 Corinthians 8 and 10: A Formal Analysis with Implications for a Cross-Cultural, Chinese Hermeneutic* (Leiden: E. J. Brill, 1995), 15–75 (15); K. K. Yeo, *Classical Rhetoric*; K. K. Yeo, ed. and tr., *Handbook for Biblical Studies* [in Chinese] 聖經研究手冊 (Shanghai: China Christian Council, 2002).
10. Yeo, *Rhetorical Interaction in 1 Corinthians*, 16–17.
11. Ibid. 17.
12. Ibid.
13. Tsinghua University is a major research university in China. Its former part called Tsinghua College, was established in 1911 to serve as a preparatory school for students the government planned to send to study in the United States.
14. Yeo, *Rhetorical Interaction in 1 Corinthians*, 20.

PRIMARY SOURCES

Chinese films only:

The Only Sons (山清水秀, 2002), directed by Gan Xiao'er 甘小二.
Raised from Dust (舉自塵土, 2007), directed by Gan Xiao'er.
Waiting for God (在期待之中, 2012), directed by Gan Xiao'er.
Church Cinema (教堂電影院, documentary, 2008), directed by Gan Xiao'er.
Orphan of Anyang (安陽嬰兒, 2001), directed by Wang Chao 王超.
Night and Day (日日夜夜, 2004), directed by Wang Chao.
Luxury Car (江城夏日, 2006), directed by Wang Chao.
Love Reclaimed (重來, 2009), directed by Wang Chao.
Looking for Rohmer (尋找羅麥, 2018), directed by Wang Chao.
Searching for Lin Zhao's Soul (尋找林昭的靈魂, documentary, 2004), directed by Hu Jie 胡杰.
The Song of Mai Di Chong (麥地沖的歌聲, documentary, 2016), directed by Hu Jie.
The Flowers of War (金陵十三釵, 2011), directed by Zhang Yimou 張藝謀.

Coming Home (歸來, 2014), directed by Zhang Yimou.
If You Are the One (非誠勿擾, 2008), directed by Feng Xiaogang 馮小剛.
Back to 1942 (一九四二, 2012), directed by Feng Xiaogang.
The Warlords (投名狀, 2007), directed by Peter Chan 陳可辛.
Dearest (親愛的, 2014), directed by Peter Chan.
Let the Bullets Fly (讓子彈飛, 2010), directed by Jiang Wen 姜文.
Dying to Survive (我不是藥神, 2018), directed by Wen Muye 文牧野.
Before Born (結果, 2006), directed by Zhang Ming 章明.
City of Life and Death (南京! 南京!, 2009), directed by Lu Chuan 陸川.
Wolf Warriors 2 (戰狼 2, 2017), directed by Wu Jing 吳京.
Forever Young (無問西東, 2018), directed by Li Fangfang 李芳芳.
Blind Shaft (盲井, 2003), directed by Li Yang 李楊.
No Man's Land (無人區, 2013), directed by Ning Hao 寧浩.
A Touch of Sin (天注定, 2013), directed by Jia Zhangke 賈樟柯.
Silent Witness (全民目擊, 2013), directed by Fei Xing 非行.
The Dead End (烈日灼心, 2015), directed by Cao Baoping 曹保平.

CHAPTER 46

CHINESE CONTEMPORARY CHRISTIAN ARTS AND THE BIBLE

CLOVER XUESONG ZHOU

Introduction

Since the emergence of modern art, Christian communities have, by and large, lamented the secularization of art. However, recent trends in contemporary art have begun to reintegrate religion into art via philosophy, spirituality, and cultural dialogue. Meanwhile, in concert with the advent of globalization, Western art is de-secularizing as it increasingly branches out into an open field of different beliefs.[1] This has resulted in a seemingly contradictory, de-Christianized, and yet increasingly de-secularized field. Contemporary Christian artists join this trend of de-secularization, but their resistance to the vestiges of modernist de-Christianization retains something of an "underground" quality. In general, contemporary Christian artists avoid overt, classical Christian narratives, images, or symbols, favoring instead a more subtle or hidden expression of Christian faith.

Regarding *Chinese* contemporary Christian art, the current situation is more complex. Globalization introduced both modern and contemporary art as well as large-scale Christianity to China within a single century. Positioned between the contemporary art scene and classic Christian theology, Chinese contemporary Christian artists strive to find the common ground. Meanwhile, in light of the rapid transformations of contemporary Chinese society, these artists also struggle to express Chinese cultural identity in their works of art. Each Chinese contemporary Christian artist blazes a unique trail in navigating these tensions, evincing different perspectives on the relationship between Christian faith and creativity, between Christian culture and contemporary art, and between their cultural and religious identities. These conditions contribute to a unique creativity that distinguishes Chinese contemporary Christian art from the wider contemporary art scene.

Chinese Contemporary Art and Christianity

Chinese Christian contemporary artists are split between three sociological realms: Chinese culture/identity, Christianity, and contemporary art. The fact that some individuals even exist at this intersection is extraordinary since these three sociological realms tend to be mutually exclusive.

The Mutual Exclusivity between Chinese Culture, Christianity, and Contemporary Art

Contemporary art grew out of modern art. Modern art is frequently associated with the goal of developing art that is independent of religion, politics, etc. As modern art developed, Christianity was gradually marginalized in the discourse of the field of art. In contrast to the non-conceptual and abstract emphasis of modern art, the postmodern orientation of contemporary art now emphasizes conceptual and philosophical perspectives. Despite the return from abstraction, contemporary art still remains largely estranged from Christianity.

In contrast to the mostly linear progression from modern to contemporary art in the West, Chinese modern and contemporary art are far more hybridized. Gao Minglu 高名潞 observes that, compared with Euro-American modernity, Chinese society—like the cultures of many other developing countries—has not experienced a conceptually logical historical line of progression from premodern, to modern, to postmodern development. Instead, premodern, modern, postmodern all persist in a hybridized state. Gao Minglu describes this dynamic: "Third World societies have been obliged to merge characteristics of all these periods, adopting them in hybrid forms, and often using incompatible elements at the same time."[2] This hybridization is both socioeconomic and cultural. For example, in the 1980s, Chinese art and culture circles were exposed suddenly to Western contemporary theory. They received cutting-edge postmodern theories, but the society they were in was still largely premodern. As a result, Gao Minglu explains, "postmodernity was considered mostly as a set of concepts that served as the first step in a search for modernity."[3] Without experiencing regular modernization, Chinese contemporary artists sought to develop a social and cultural model based on Chinese translations of publications from the Western intellectual stream of thought. They derived from many postmodern publications a vague impression of the future they were pursuing. However, China was still in the process of developing from a premodern to a modern society. Thus, early Chinese contemporary artists synthesized postmodern theory with the semi-modern reality of China.

However, in the 1980s and 1990s, Chinese contemporary artists were fiercely countercultural. The dawn of Chinese contemporary art is generally thought to mark the end of the Cultural Revolution. "Scar Art" (傷痕美術) in the late 1970s and 1980s famously employed a critical realistic (批判現實主義) approach to narrate, reflect on, and critique the past decade of the Cultural Revolution. At the same time, as Western intellectual traditions gained popularity in China, many Chinese artists and intellectuals began to adopt modern Western and even postmodern theories as the theoretical foundation of their art. This adoption of Western concepts compounded the tension between Chinese contemporary art and Chinese authorities. Notwithstanding, these artists inevitably inherited from the Cultural Revolution in which they grew up a certain tendency to reject the past. The Cultural Revolution targeted what is called the "Four Olds," comprising "old ideas, old culture, old customs, and old habits of the exploiting classes, which have corrupted the people for thousands of years." In place of the "Four Olds," the Revolution sought "to create and construct the proletarian new idea, new culture, new customs and new habits among the masses."[4]

In like fashion, contemporary artists in the 1980s used Western theories as tools to create experimental art that was inimical toward Chinese traditional culture and aesthetics.[5] The exhibition of Chinese Modern Art at the China National Gallery in 1989 is considered the high-water mark of Chinese contemporary art in 1980s. The event featured prominent banners of "no U-turn" symbols that represented their firm stance in favor of embracing modern progress and their refusal to revert to traditional naivete. This exhibition manifested as chaos, however, as many of the artists' experiments breached the boundaries of socio-ethical taboos. On its raucous opening day, the exhibition was permanently shut down by the police. These events inaugurated a ten-year conflict between Chinese contemporary artists and Chinese government authorities, during which time Chinese contemporary art was forced underground, while Chinese contemporary artists, most of whom were not employed, were seen as vagabonds by the wider society.

The contentious relationship between Chinese authorities and Chinese contemporary art has a parallel in the relationship between Chinese authorities and the Chinese family church. That story has a longer history dating to the beginning of the People's Republic of China. In 1950, Protestant leaders led by Y. T. Wu met with Premier Zhou Enlai, who encouraged them to form the Three-Self Patriotic Movement. A document from this movement entitled "Direction of Endeavor for Chinese Christianity in the Construction of New China" was issued and circulated to churches all around the country for Christians to sign expressing their devotion to the new government. Progressive pastors held an optimistic attitude towards the government-friendly Three-Self Patriotic Movement in light of what they perceived as government-driven, positive social progress. Fundamentalist pastors, however, such as Wang Mingdao, agreed that Christians *as individuals* can confess their patriotism but maintained that it was beyond the purview of the church to sign such a document. This resulted in a schism between "Three-Self" churches and family churches in China.[6] In the following years, family churches were gradually forced underground while many of their leaders and ministers were persecuted and jailed. The tension between Chinese authorities and Christians has ebbed and flowed at various times, but it has never truly ceased. In 2017, after forty years of relative tolerance, the Chinese government formally outlawed family churches.

Christianity and Chinese nationalism had a history of conflict, however, long before the Cultural Revolution. Since foreign missionaries arrived in concert with the exploitations of colonialism, it was inevitable that many Chinese nationalists arrived at a negative perception of foreign missionaries and the religion they were associated with.[7] Although foreign missionaries in the late nineteenth and early twentieth centuries took on roles as leaders, teachers, or philanthropists in general to minister to the Chinese people, oftentimes they had little respect for, or personal interest in, Chinese culture. This imposition naturally engendered Chinese resentment towards Christianity.

In terms of Chinese contemporary artists' attitudes toward Christianity, rejection is still the mainstream—just as it is in the Western art world due to echoes of modern secularization. On the one hand, Chinese artists and intellectuals subconsciously inherited the anti-religious legacy of the Cultural Revolution. On the other hand, however, quite a few artists and intellectuals still remember the traumatic consequences of the national enchantment with Maoism, and they associate religious devotion with that dangerous fervor. These perspectives, combined with their knowledge of historical, religiously motivated warfare, help to account for the fact that many Chinese contemporary artists and intellectuals have a less-than-positive outlook toward Christianity.

Integration Happens within Conflicts

Thus, it is in spite of mainstream antagonism between Chinese culture, Christianity, and contemporary art that some individuals have begun to integrate these three spheres. First of all, some recent trends have made increasingly possible the integration of contemporary art and Christianity. Contemporary art in the United States has witnessed the return of religion. Not only have artists felt more free to involve religious elements but also artistic scholarship has shown a renewed interest in religion. In 2003, Yale art historian Sally Promey published the essay "The 'Return' of Religion in the Scholarship of American Art." "Western intellectual and social history," she argues, "tend to ensure that religious significance was misconstrued, marginalized, and underestimated when it came to constructing the canonical academic narrative of American art history and criticism."[8] The forceful swing of the pendulum that was the modern intellectual negation of religion is now, in the United States, settling into a more neutral position as modernist fervor subsides.

Jonathan A. Anderson and William A. Dyrness also comment on this phenomenon in their *Modern Art and the Life of a Culture: The Religious Impulses of Modernism*:

> ... there is a growing sense that art history and criticism cannot adequately account for the depth and complexity of how art "means" in a given cultural context without accounting, even if only on a strictly sociological level, for the religious backgrounds and dynamics in that society.[9]

Even though the secularization of Western society has been an inevitable trend since modernization, Christian history is still an indelible cultural influence. Similarly, as Anderson and Dyrness also note, although church congregations are dwindling in recent years, religion is making a return on personal and philosophical levels. Meanwhile, even many self-identified secular art historians and theoreticians are announcing their "disenchantment with modern disenchantment."[10] The trend is a reversal of dry, modernist rationalism that looks instead toward the spiritual possibilities of art that is what Jeffrey Kosky calls "full of charm."[11] This trend is converging with another converse trend, as Christian contemporary artists display their personal Christian faith and spirituality in increasingly subtle ways that are more palatable to a tentatively de-secularized art world.

While the history of enmity between Christianity and the American art world is taking a more amicable turn, there are also some seeds of reconciliation and synthesis in the conflicts between Christianity, Chinese culture, and Chinese contemporary art. Christianity is booming in China. Despite the exercise of political control over Chinese churches, between the early 1980s and 2010, the number of Chinese Christians has increased from 6 million to over 23 million.[12] Meanwhile, since early 2000, Chinese authorities have lifted the prohibition on exhibiting Chinese contemporary art. In fact, ever since a sensational auction of some Chinese contemporary artists' works at Sotheby's New York in 2007, the government has begun actively supporting contemporary art as a signature Chinese export.

All the while, university campus ministries have been the crucible for the integration of contemporary art, Christianity, and Chinese culture. Because of certain policy changes to the Hu Kou registration system, the center of momentum of Chinese Christianity shifted from rural areas in the 1980s to urban areas in the 1990s.[13] Simultaneously, Deng Xiaoping's economic and education reforms in the 1990s significantly altered the complexion of Chinese universities and markets. Chinese universities began to admit large numbers of unsubsidized, tuition-paying students, leading to a high demand for educators. With the increase in opportunities for international trade, university English teachers were in particularly high demand. These conditions allowed foreign missionaries to come to China under the guise of secular careers as English-language educators. The end result was a widespread dissemination of the Bible and its message among urban university students. Many Chinese culture elites, reeling from the violent suppression of the 1989 Tiananmen Square protests, had given up their faith in the project of a political-social utopia. As a result, they were more open to the spiritual orientation of Christianity. Campus ministries at Chinese universities have advanced rapidly since that time. Meanwhile, the influx of people from developed countries that accompanied China's economic reforms included art collectors and other members of arts circles who catalyzed the advance of Chinese contemporary artists into the international art scene.

As previously mentioned, in 2007, Chinese contemporary artists set new records, selling millions of dollars of art at Sotheby's auction houses. This, in turn, stimulated the growth of the Chinese art market and encouraged greater numbers of Chinese students to major in art.

Some of these young students in art academies heard the Bible and became followers of Christ through Christian fellowships and small groups on campus. Later on, these Christian art teachers and students became the driving force behind the proclamation of Christianity in the art industry, and some of them specialized in contemporary art. The latter individuals, however, were placed in a challenging position in that they, along with mainstream contemporary art, hold values that are quite different from or even hostile to traditional Christian values while, conversely, most Chinese churches have not developed theological responses to contemporary art. Some of these individuals, however, have been pioneering an intersection of contemporary art and Christianity within a Chinese context.

Chinese Christian Artists' Contemporary Art Practice

Chinese Christian contemporary artists exhibit a number of sundry conceptions of the relationship between art and faith. Art can be a medium for worship or for evangelizing. It can be a tool for generating cultural dialogue. It can be a means of pursuing truth, or it can be an exercise in visual hermeneutics. Most Chinese Christian artists present a blend of these aspects. Yet, each artist has a different emphasis. This section introduces three Chinese Christian contemporary artists who are representative of three trends within the field.

Feng Chun Lan: Art as a Way to Worship and Evangelize

Feng Chun Lan 馮君藍 is a Taiwanese pastor and photographer. It might be controversial to list a Taiwanese man among Chinese Christian artists, but it makes sense to include him given that Taiwan and China share the same cultural roots. Moreover, since 2015, Feng Chun Lan's art has been very influential in mainland China, even more so than in Taiwan.

Feng Chun Lan was born in Hong Kong in 1961. At 3 years old, Feng Chun Lan moved with his family, when his father was sent to Taiwan as a Methodist missionary. He studied art and design in college and began producing photographs in the early 1980s. He held his first photography exhibition in 1988. After college, besides pursuing photography, Feng Chun Lan mainly worked as an advertisement designer. However, it was only after 2008, when Feng Chun Lan was ordained a pastor, that he began to create his most well-known series of photographs, "Dust Icon" (微塵聖像).[14]

For this ongoing series, Feng Chun Lan invites Christian friends from church to be his models. According to each of their personalities, Feng lets them pose either as characters from the Bible or in any way that implies an image of one of Jesus' followers. He usually frames them in a simple, dark, and old-fashioned setting. These models mostly dress in traditional Chinese garments such as a *qi pao* 旗袍 or a Chinese tunic suit. Their expressions are often inscrutable. They do not smile, laugh, or weep. Only the occasional negative figures will do some inappropriate expression, such as rage on the face of Cain (Genesis 4). For the most part, their expressions are characterized by stillness. Their eyes seem to stare into some distant place—as far as eternity. Their timeless expressions in a vintage setting seem to transcend time and space, evoking deep reflection on what it means to be human through a powerful exhibition of the spirit of contemporary Taiwanese believers.

Although Feng Chun Lan employs a classical aesthetic style in his photography, his art exhibits both postmodern and Christian artistic theory. His photographs are reminiscent of medieval icons that were—and in many cases still are—considered to convey the presence of saints. By employing ordinary Taiwanese Christians in this iconographic role, these photographs present the inner selves and the divine potential of ordinary people. Yet, they also create a diversion of classic symbol and narrative—a popular, postmodern methodology used in the contemporary art world. By casting ordinary Christians as biblical figures and entitling the series *Dust Icon*, Feng Chun Lan strikes an interesting balance and tension between iconophile and iconoclasm: to Christians or anyone familiar with the biblical narrative, these images are not mundane but rather point to a divine narrative and perspective. Yet, the ordinary quality of the photographs reminds us that even biblical figures or saints are ordinary human beings. Thus, depending upon the semiotic ideology of the interpreter, the images either supernaturally convey the presence of both the subject and the biblical figure, they negate the unrealistic sacralization of those figures, or they do both of those things simultaneously![15]

Feng Chun Lan has close relationships with his models, most of whom are from his church congregation. Even though, as a pastor, Feng Chun Lan usually has very little time for photography—usually only one day per month—because of his close relationships, he is able quickly capture the spiritual presence of his subjects. One of Feng's favorites among his photographs, for instance, is a portrait of Taiwanese gospel singer Guo Xiaowen 郭曉雯. Guo Xiaowen was diagnosed with rectal cancer in the early stage of her pregnancy. Her doctor recommended that she opt to induce abortion in order to receive treatment for her cancer, but she refused to do so. She suffered a lot in order to give birth to the baby while sacrificing the best opportunity for her to receive treatment. She passed away when the baby was 3. Six days before her passing, she asked Feng Chun Lan to photograph her as a memorial for her husband and daughter and also as a confession of her identity as a Christian on the mother earth. During the shoot, Feng Chun Lan worried that her extreme physical weakness could send her toppling from the chair he had set her in. However, Guo Xiaowen encouraged him not to be nervous. She cherished her last chance to be photographed in this way, and insisted that he shoot until he was satisfied. Both of them were deeply touched as Feng Chun Lan captured the beauty of the last moment of her life on earth. He named it "The Lord's Handmaiden" (主的使女).[16] This is but one of the encounters that Feng Chun Lan felt were divine, experienced through his photography. Because he believes he encounters God's glory in his subjects—humans, who are made from and will return to dust and yet share God's image and likeness—Feng Chun Lan gave the series the title of *Dust Icon*.

The encounter between Feng Chun Lan and his subjects is a mutual experience. Transcendental face-to-face experience underlying Feng Chun Lan's photography recalls a well-known piece of contemporary performance art enacted by a Serbian writer, performance and film artist, Marina Abramović: *The Artist Is Present*. During this performance at The Museum of Modern Art in New York City, Abramović's audience had an opportunity to sit one-on-one across from her at a table for however long they wished. Well-known art historian and critic Arthur Danto reflected on the performance "To sit together is to share one another's presence.... It was a moment of spiritual exchange."[17] Likewise, Feng Chun Lan's photography is intended to capture a spiritual exchange of presence. As a pastor, his presence to the model is believed to be a kind of divine grace, while, conversely, a model's presence to the photographer is also believed to be an embodiment of divine grace—commonly presented in the incarnational theology of Jesus in the Gospel of John as Christ has a face-to-face encounter with Nicodemus, the Samaritan woman, Mary Magdalene, Simon Peter, and others. This exchange of presence (and specifically, this mutual appreciation and mutual respect for each other as God's divine creation that is thought to be exchanged through Holy Spirit) underlies Feng Chun Lan's photography. As such, Feng Chun Lan's photography constitutes a communal worship event in the artistic realm.

Feng Chun Lan spent almost ten years working on this series. He saw that displaying his artwork to the public was an opportunity for the purpose of mission. Through exhibition guides, lectures, and interviews, Feng sought to bring the gospel message to art lovers—a great number of whom are non-believers. His evangelism employs his otherwise serene art in order to attract and provoke his audience to action. Even though the government has increasingly limited the family church since 2017, the comparably free hand the government now gives to contemporary art provides Christian artists an opportunity to share the Bible with some Chinese artists who otherwise are unable to learn it from a church.

Li Ran: Art as a Means of Cultural Dialogue

Li Ran 李然 is a contemporary artist who specializes in video art. He was born in 1986 in Hu Bei. He became a Christian when he was studying in Sichuan Fine Art Academy in 2008. He was one of the art academy Christians who became Christian through the aforementioned campus ministries set up by foreign missionary teachers. After graduation, he began his career as a contemporary artist, and by 2014, he developed a special interest in incorporating his art with subtle evangelism.

His 2014 video, *Escape from the Scene-The Land of Mystery*, in 2014 was his first attempt intentionally integrating Christianity into his artwork.[18] In this video, Li Ran dubbed footage of friends from church playing through an escape room with a voiceover of testimonies narrated by of a young female Christian. Her testimonies centered around the exorcism of evil spirits. The escape room functions as a metaphor of salvation that parallels the testimonies of deliverance (cf. Mark 5).

After *Escape from the Scene—The Land of Mystery*, it would be three years before Li Ran released another Christian work of art. This time, however, he overtly announced his Christian identity. In 2017, Li Ran's explicitly Christian solo exhibition titled *Life of the Pilgrim* debuted at Shanghart Beijing. The title of the exhibition, "Life of the Pilgrim," shares its name with the exhibition's central piece video art. The video features hundreds of old photographs of sheep that were shepherded by a group of military construction workers in Xinjiang, China in 1954.[19] Li Ran employs the sheep as a symbol for Christians, weaving together in the photographs in order to tell a story of Protestant church history. Simultaneously, the same story—told through the same footage of sheep photographs—conveys the past sixty years of Chinese political history.

The video begins with the sound of a train as the title appears on the black screen. The title then fades to the old, black-and-white photographs. In the first photo, a group of soldiers stand in a wild terrain. The artist's voice-over begins the narrative: "In the early spring, Kantumans and iron shovels broke into the frozen earth." As the narrative progresses, oblique references to toponyms from Xinjiang, such as "Bogell Peak," divulge the geography of the literal story.[20] However, the narrative weaves that geographical information with images from Protestant church history, especially drawing on themes related to the Puritan American Pilgrims. Li Ran skillfully weaves these narratives together; for example, Li Ran narrates, "Confronted with the same cold, staying warm is a necessity."[21] The cryptic phrase "same cold" (共同的寒冷) is laden with poetic implications. The "cold" refers both to the climate and to the new immigrants' isolation. However, the "same" cold hints to the listener that there is more than one story being told. The sheep and the construction-worker immigrants in Xinjiang, the American pilgrims, and perhaps the viewers themselves all face the "same cold"—akin to the biblical story of early church gatherings in catacombs or homes for fellowship. Meanwhile, in Chinese culture, "staying warm" (取暖) is a social metaphor that refers to conquering loneliness or difficulties by staying together as a group. Thus staying warm is both literal and metaphorical, that is, physical and social necessity for the sheep, for the immigrant-construction workers, and for the Puritans alike, the narratives of which comprise the three layers of *The Life of Pilgrim*.

The Protestant history storyline eventually proceeds all the way to the Pentecostal movement. The voiceover recounts visions Pentecostal Christians had in their dreams. These visions are interwoven with images of the sheep and verses from the Bible, such as "You are the sons of light, the sons of daylight. We do not belong to the night, neither to darkness" (1 Thess 5:5). From this ethereal moment, the narrative abruptly turns to the situation of the immigrants in Xinjiang and metaphorically depicts their perception of the local shamanism: "At the foot of Tianshan in 1954, those are ancient scriptures from the secret religions of Babylon. Those sexual symbols, masculine and feminine, the silver moon and the blazing sun, appearing elusively in pairs,"[22] These words accompany pictures of performances (from a different time and place) by military artists, mostly *pas de deux* ballet depicting Chinese historical legends.

On the one hand, much of this indicates the influence of shamanism in Xinjiang. On the other hand, the images bring to mind the historical event known as "The Eight Thousand Hunan Women on Tianshan Mountain." The all-male military construction workers in Xinjiang were kept as bachelors while serving there. The local women were mostly minorities who, because the government wanted to protect their own culture, were not allowed to marry People's Liberation Army soldiers. Thus, in 1954, in order to help the military construction worker bachelors in Xinjiang, the military recruited 8,000 educated, female soldiers from Human province. While the extent to which these women understood their assignment is unclear, it is likely some of them had such love for Chinese communism that they were glad to sacrifice for the benefit of the nation. Meanwhile, some of them were likely attracted to the idea of marrying a soldier who had a relatively stable and good-paying job.

With this history in mind, Li Ran's voiceover, "those are ancient scriptures from the secret religions of Babylon. Those sexual symbols, masculine and feminine," recalls the semi-religious devotion to Marxism that drove the sexual decision-making in the story of the soldiers in Xinjiang. The comparison to Babylon then would cast the spiritual and material offer of communism in a somewhat negative light, recalling the biblical exhortations for the Judahites to resist cultural assimilation during the Babylonian exile (Ezra and Nehemiah). Thus, as is typical throughout of *Life of the Pilgrim*, this section conjures and weaves together impressions of types of pilgrimage and religious or semi-religious fervor.

Throughout the video, Li Ran maintains his strategy of juxtaposing a central storyline of Protestant church history with metaphorically connected images of the sheep and the history of the Xinjiang construction-worker soldiers. However, near the end of the video, he breaks with this strategy, presenting, instead of sheep, the familiar contemporary scene of crowded Beijing subways. This quickly gives way to photos of the Xinjiang construction-worker soldiers who were introduced at the beginning of the video. Silent subtitles quickly review the history of the soldiers' work in Xinjiang, explaining how they shepherded the sheep and ultimately slaughtered them. In a cruel tone, Li Rain concludes that these "fuzzy things you see," although fed and cared for, were finally killed and sold. The lives of "the slaughterers"—the construction-worker soldiers—were also less than ideal. The conclusion recounts their return to the city in 1964 "to wait for the next movement that will fundamentally reform them." This particular "reformation" refers to the miserable ten years of the Cultural Revolution (or "Cultural Destruction" in hindsight[23]). For Li Ran, this ending expressed the dissonance he feels, particularly as a Christian artist, between reality and faith. Although personal, Li Ran's self-expression in *Life of the Pilgrim* proceeds from the intersection of theology and sociology, ultimately constituting a testimony to dynamics of the interplay between society and faith.

Similarly, the reception of *Life of the Pilgrim* constituted a useful reflection of these socio-theological dynamics. The reception was representative of the current state of the interplay between the realms of Chinese culture, contemporary art, and Christianity. The exhibition's debut in December of 2017 happened to coincide with the beginning in Beijing of China's campaign to evict "low-end population" from major cities. Millions of migrant workers were driven out of the city in a rather unhumanitarian fashion. In the context of these mass evictions, Li Ran's *The Life of Pilgrim* generated a lot of discussion about how migrant workers contributed to the cities' development only to be eventually evicted. It also triggered some of the older generations to reflect on Chinese political history, resonating with their feeling that their utopian communist dreams were eventually rudely awakened by a harsh reality.

For Chinese Christians, the overtly Christian theme was attractive. However, the largely fundamentalist sensibilities of the mainstream Chinese church translated into reservations about the video's juxtapositions: in paralleling the criticism of Chinese political history, it is not hard to perceive a cynical criticism of Protestant church history as well. While that is a reasonable conclusion, it is also possible, however, to more charitably interpret the slaughtered sheep as a symbol of Christians' suffering, as pervasive symbolism also in the book of Revelation (5:6, 12, 7:9, 14, 12:11, 13:8) and other biblical books (Isa 53:7, 66:3; Jer 11:19; Mark 14:12; Luke 22:7; Acts 8:32; 1 Cor 5:7).[24]

During the subsequent seminars and publications related to *Life of the Pilgrim*, most secular art professionals and intellectuals mainly focused on the popular philosophical approach in contemporary art such as "fiction in the archives" and "cultural reproduction" to interpret Li Ran's work, avoiding direct discussion of its Christian themes. As of yet, few people have found the language for integrating contemporary art, philosophy, and Christianity in the Chinese contemporary art scene. However, Li Ran's art already has begun to establish a bridge, but the success of that bridge depends on people's willingness to make use of it—to venture out in the pursuit of dialogue between traditionally separate realms.

Gao Lei: Biblical Hermeneutics in the Visual Arts

Like Li Ran, Gao Lei 高磊 is a full-time contemporary artist who is active in the art field. He was born in 1980 in Hunan, China. He first became Christian while he was in high school at the Fine Art School Affiliated with the China Central Academy of Fine Arts, and he became an ardent Christian while he continued his study in college at the China Central Academy of Fine Arts. He joins a Methodist family church set up by Taiwanese missionaries. Like Li Ran, Gao Lei is another fruit of foreign missionaries' campus ministries in China.

Gao Lei specializes in installation art. He prefers simple materials and visual languages that can obscure the meaning of his art. As such, in the contemporary art field, most people interpret his art as a reflection of contemporary social reality. However, below the surface of viable, secular sociological interpretation, Gao Lei's core themes are drawn from Christian eschatology. The theological underpinnings are usually hidden. Only a few of his works of art are explicitly theological.

In 2011, Gao Lei contributed an installation work of art called *NS24* to the group exhibition "Almost Tangible" (觸摸) in the Arario Beijing Gallery.[25] From a sociological perspective, this work of art resonates with communist values and aesthetics. The installation presents two rooms of the same size and of similar settings. On the left, a goat in excellent condition is lying comfortably in a bathtub full of white fleece. Above the goat's face, a bundle of microphones are suspended by a white thread connecting them to a speaker in the other room. Directly below the speaker, a human skeleton with the skull of a ram is lying totally shorn, as it were, jaw slacked open in a barber chair. White fleece, like that in the tub of the goat, litters the floor around the skeletal remains. The speaker, barber chair, and bathtub are all of a Soviet style, a reminder for Chinese people that Chinese industry and culture was once greatly influenced by the Soviet Union. The juxtaposition of the goat lounging comfortably in the fleece of the skeletally shorn sheep is a powerful illustration of exploitation. The exploiter has all of the power in discourse while the exploited can only listen and obey. Meanwhile, it is important to note that taking a bath and going to the barber are fairly mundane and commonplace activities. Thus, the dramatic scene is a poignant critique not only of exploitation but also of the fact that it is so ubiquitous in both space and time. In fact, "NS" is an abbreviation for the north and south poles, while twenty-four represents the twenty-four time zones or the twenty-four hours in a day. This title implies that the scene is a microcosm of the entire globe.

On a theological level, meanwhile, the installation alludes to Matt 25:31–46, a passage in which Jesus employs the language of Ezek 34:17 to explain that the Lord will separate people one from another, placing the so-called "sheep" on his right side but the "goats" on the left. The Lord will judge them according to their deeds in the world. *NS24* does not depict this eschatological scene. Rather, it portrays the deeds and circumstances of the goats and the sheep—still on the viewer's left and right, however—during their lives on the earth. *NS24* also relates to Luke 16's comparison of Lazarus and the rich man. Samuel Pagán from Evangelical Seminary of Puerto Rico writes in his essay "Poor and Poverty: Social Distance and Bible Translation" that, in the Bible, the term "the rich" does not only imply an economically privileged status but that it also carries some social and moral connotation: "It meant having the power or capacity to take something from someone weaker," Pagan writes.[26] In Gao Lei's installation, the goat gratuitously robs the sheep of its protective fleece. Similarly, Pagan suggests that the term "the poor" in the Bible connotes people who are not able to "maintain their inherited 'honor' standing in society due to misfortune or because [of] the injustices of other people."[27] In the context of *NS24*, the poor sheep suffers from the oppression of the rich goat. Gao Lei himself gives a provocative interpretation: the poor sheep is a martyr who pursues righteousness at the cost of self-sacrifice. The sheep's open gesture and the vague smile on the skeletal face is meant to portray the joy of making a righteous sacrifice, even in circumstances of utter deprivation. Forsaking even necessity, the sheep joyfully gives of itself to the point of death. The Lord says to it: "For I was hungry and you gave me food; I was thirsty and you gave me drink; I was a stranger and you took me too; I was naked and you clothed me; I was sick and you visited me; I was in prison and you came to me." (Matt 25:35–36) *NS24* works as a visual sermon, illustrating biblical principles in a contemporary setting. It testifies against modern and yet timeless situations of exploitation, prophesying eternal judgment while highlighting saintly self-sacrifice and its eternal reward.

Later on, Gao Lei's biblically themed works of art became more abstract. In 2016, he created a mixed-media composition called *Screen—The Saw of Manasseh* (瑪拿西之鋸).[28] The overall form of the composition is that of a four-paneled screen painting akin to those produced throughout the church's first several centuries. Yet, its minimalistic steel frame and overall style are distinctly modern. Within the frame, Gao Lei has traced the outline of a hacksaw in thin steel strips placed perpendicular to the surface of the panels. Most of the saw is abstract and low on detail except for the blade, which consists of hundreds of braided, small steep strips.

The limited visual information of the composition means that the title becomes a key hermeneutical detail. "The Saw of Manasseh" refers to the death of the biblical prophet Isaiah, as imagined by the Rabbinic Jewish Talmudic passage, Yevamot 49b. The passage states that, at the time of King Manasseh, the king judged Isaiah as a false witness for having contradicted Moses in the Torah. Isaiah knew that King Manasseh would kill him even if he did explain himself on the basis of Torah, so, rather than making Manasseh into an "intentional transgressor," Isaiah escaped into a cedar tree. Manasseh's servant brought the tree and sawed through it in order to kill him. Because, in the biblical tradition, upon seeing God, Isaiah exclaimed, "Woe is me! For I am lost; for I am a man of unclean lips, and I dwell in the midst of a people of unclean lips" (Isa 6:5a ESV), Yevamot 49b asserts that Isaiah died at the moment the saw touched his lips: "He was punished for referring to the Jewish people in a derogatory manner." Although the tradition that Isaiah was sawn to death is not explicitly attested to in the biblical canon, the reference in Heb 11:37 "they were sawn" likely alludes to the death of Isaiah. Similarly, many church fathers, such as Tertullian, Origen, and Jerome, refer to this tradition in their sermons and writings.

Gao Lei appropriates the tradition to address contemporary social reality. The saw can be understood as a metaphor for structural evil in modern society. Modern theologian Cynthia Moe-Lobeda develops the term "structural evil" from earlier thinkers such as Jean-Jacques Rousseau, explaining that structural evils are of the "chains that bind us into systemic exploitation of others and of the Earth."[29] They are usually both hidden and complex, qualities which are crucial to facilitating broad complicity. In *Screen—The Saw of Manasseh,* the braid-like blade is comprised of numerous small blades representing the multitudes being naive to their involvement in a structural evil—just as Manasseh's servant may have trusted the unjust sentence that their master, Manasseh, passed on Isaiah. The hacksaw in this composition is overtly industrial in contrast to any sort of saw that Manasseh's servants might have used, pointing to a modern context. The complexity of modern society facilitates widespread, passive involvement in systemic evils akin to the king's murder of the prophet. Especially in China, the saw is a metaphor for the unjust treatment of dissidents who champion the people's need. They are, in a sense, modern prophets, and they share the sufferings resulting from challenging systemic evil that was experienced by the ancient prophets.

Thus, Gao Lei's art is clandestine biblical commentary in the form of contemporary visual art. Its theological value has yet to be noticed by either Chinese or by Western Christian scholars. Yet, Gao Lei almost certainly will generate future inspiration for the integration of Chinese culture, Christianity, and contemporary art with a subtle emphasis on biblical social justice.

Conclusion

Chinese contemporary Christian art is, as yet, a small and tender sprout taking root in newly emerging cracks in the long-standing barriers between biblical Christianity, Chinese culture and government, and contemporary art. The increasingly open attitudes toward spirituality among contemporary art circles allow more opportunities for Christian artists, along with artists of other religions, to create art that pertains to faith. Regarding the relationship between Chinese culture/authority and biblical faith, even though political regulation has been tightening again in recent years, the explosion of the Christian population in China seems to have reached an unstoppable critical mass. It is almost certain that the Bible will continue to make headway in its integration with Chinese culture. Meanwhile, after two decades of conflict with Chinese culture/authority, as Chinese contemporary art has gained esteem in the international art scene, Chinese authorities have reversed their attitudes, even subsidizing its development these days. These sea changes are providing a new opportunity for Chinese Christians to integrate their culture and faith in the production of contemporary art.

For Feng Chun Lan, photography is a practice of worship and evangelism. He has spent ten years on his *Dust Icon* series, inviting friends from his congregation to pose as biblical figures rendering the unique result of contemporary, photographical icons. However, the often early modern apparel and Asian features of the subjects distance the photographs from traditional iconography in a typically postmodern diversion of classic symbol and narrative. Even though his models are not the historical saints, Feng Chun Lan present their divine character as created according to the image and likeness of God. Meanwhile, the artistic process entails a mutual, divine encounter between the two Christians through face-to-face, mutual appreciation and mutual respect for each other as God's divine creation.

For video artist Li Ran, contemporary art can be a tapestry of church experience, church history, and Chinese culture woven together into in parallel to create a semi-fictional, narrative expression of personal, Christian experience. His courageously explicit *The Life of Pilgrim* used hundreds of old photographs of sheep that were shepherded by military construction workers as a symbol for Christians in a telling of Protestant church history. The video sometimes exhibits contradictory judgments reflecting the complex reality of human hopes and disappointments. His emphasis on generating cultural dialogue has a great potential to bring the sundry fields of contemporary art, philosophy, history, and Christianity into meaningful conversation.

Finally, Gao Lei employs contemporary art in a subtle interpretation and application of biblical themes. His installation, *NS24*, makes an explicit allusion to Matt 25:31–46, bringing the eschatological passage to bear on present times by depicting the lives of the "goats" and the "sheep" on the earth and presenting them as exploitative but empty and self-sacrificing yet joyful respectively. His mixed media composition, *Screen—The Saw of Manasseh*, alludes to Isaiah's death according to Jewish tradition in a symbolic critique of systemic injustice. Both of these works relate biblical narrative with contemporary social reality with special relevance to China. In this sense, Gao Lei's art is a like a nearly subliminal contemporary biblical commentary with an eye toward social justice.

These three artists' practices represent three prototypical approaches that Christian artists take to contemporary art creation in China. Unlike the Taiwanese Feng Chun Lan, Li Ran and Gao Lei have yet to make Christianity their primary or most explicit theme. However, their Christian and, therefore, countercultural orientations contribute to the uniqueness of their art, which has great potential to generate dialogue between Christianity, contemporary art, and its accompanying disciplines.

Despite the challenges, the intersection of Christianity, contemporary art, and Chinese culture affords some rare opportunities. First, unlike Western modern and contemporary art, Chinese contemporary art never has experienced a period of disenchantment with Christianity since Christianity has never been mainstream in Chinese culture. The artistic expression of Christianity in Chinese context is comparably new. Meanwhile, as Chinese intellectuals and artists have been afforded abundant opportunities with secular Western thought, they have gradually developed a sense of disenchantment with Western theories. In stark contrast to Western-style secularism, Christian contemporary art in a Chinese context could have a refreshing appeal. Meanwhile, influenced by the increasingly global "disenchantment with modern disenchantment," the Chinese contemporary art field is increasingly disarmed against religion in general. Finally, Chinese Christianity and contemporary art share common ground in pursuing freedom under the threat of the despotic potential of the Chinese government. In this sense, Chinese Christianity wins some respect from the contemporary art field. Thus, even though the field seems fraught with obstacles, the nascence of Chinese Christian contemporary art is nonetheless filled with promise. The likes of Jung Fenlan, Li Ran, and Gao Lei are quietly breaking new ground, and their work paves the way for future artists to integrate these three important facets of Chinese society.

APPENDIX

FIGURE 46.1 Feng Chun Lan, *David, the Shepherd Boy*, copyright: the artist.

FIGURE 46.2 Feng Chun Lan, *The Lord's Handmaiden*, copyright: M Art Center and the artist.

FIGURE 46.3 Feng Chun Lan, *Hannah*, copyright: the artist.

FIGURE 46.4 Li Ran, *Life of the Pilgrims*, copyright: the artist.

FIGURE 46.5 Li Ran, *Life of the Pilgrims*, copyright: the artist.

FIGURE 46.6 Li Ran, *Life of the Pilgrims*, copyright: the artist.

FIGURE 46.7 Gao Lei, *NS24*, copyright: Arario Beijing Gallery and the artist.

FIGURE 46.8 Gao Lei, *NS24*, copyright: Arario Beijing Gallery and the artist.

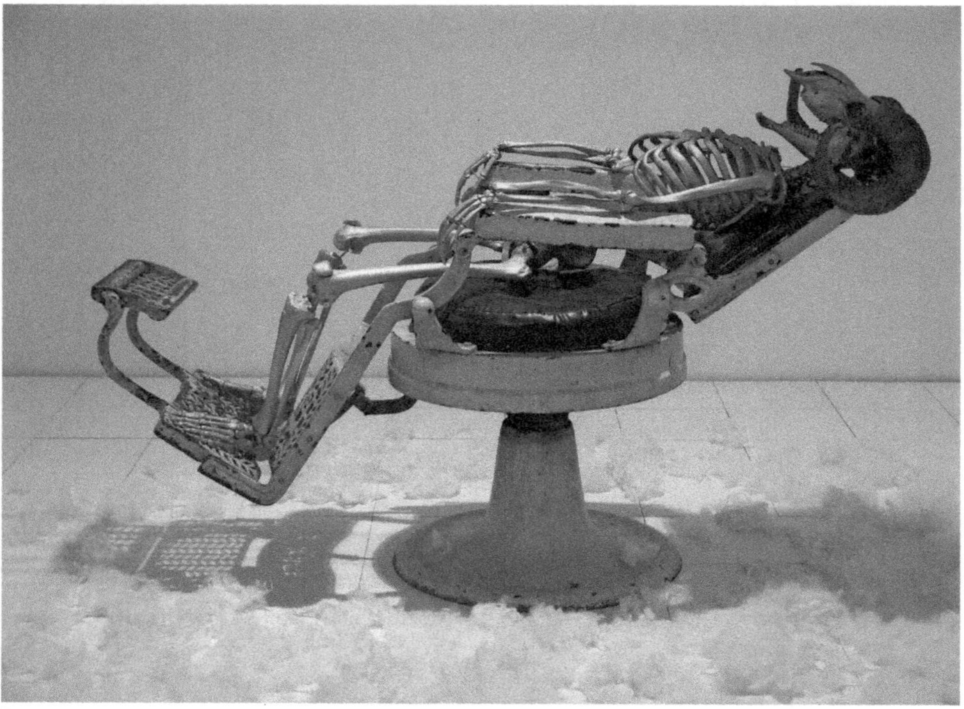

FIGURE 46.9 Gao Lei, *NS24*, copyright: Arario Beijing Gallery and the artist.

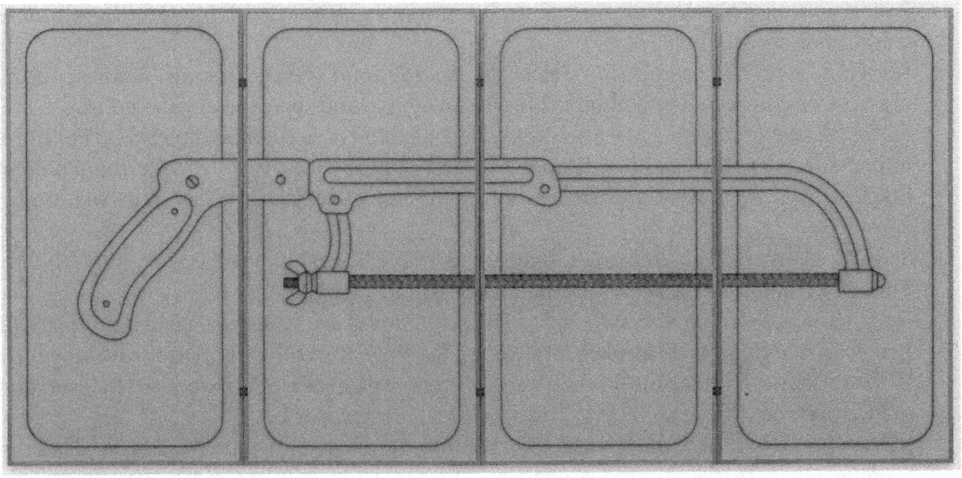

FIGURE 46.10 Gao Lei, *Screen—The Saw of Manasseh*, copyright: Whitespace Gallery and the artist.

NOTES

1. Although the term "Western" is used inaccurately as a reductionist designation, it is used in this essay to reference a particular stream of artistic and intellectual tradition. "Western" cultural phenomena are the artifacts of cultures that claim long-term involvement in a progressive history of mostly "Western European" (North Atlantic region) and "North American" (excluding indigenous and new immigrants) periods—from classical to Renaissance to neoclassical to modern and postmodern. This cultural stream originated in Western Europe but has expanded through colonization and, subsequently, globalization. The geographical areas traditionally associated with the non-Western traditions include former colonies that came to have a predominantly European heritage, whereas Western-influenced regions that trace most of their heritage to a different stream of traditions qualify as "non-Western." Thus, while hard and precise geographical boundaries of "Western" culture are not always forthcoming, it is nonetheless a useful term for referencing that particular stream of artistic and intellectual tradition.
2. Minglu Gao, *Total Modernity and the Avant-Garde in Twentieth-Century Chinese Art* (Cambridge, MA: MIT Press, 2011), 2.
3. Ibid. 3.
4. Jiang Jiehong, *Burden or Legacy: From the Chinese Cultural Revolution to Contemporary Art* (Hong Kong: Hong Kong University Press, 2007), 2.
5. These artists, although intending to resist the Cultural Revolution, inevitably inherited some its anti-traditional polemic. The Cultural Revolution itself was influenced greatly by statist Soviet ideology. Although Russia and the Soviet Union always have been on the periphery of the Western intellectual traditions, Soviet influence in the twentieth century, especially after the rise of Stalin, was antithetical to the Western, liberal-democratic intellectual tradition. Thus, while the anti-traditional activities of Chinese contemporary artists in the 1980s inevitably also reflect Soviet influence via the Cultural

Revolution, the Western intellectual tradition was the primary driving force for Chinese contemporary artists.

6. See K. K. Yeo, *Chairman Mao Meets the Apostle Paul* (Grand Rapids: Brazos, 2002), 139–190, on Three-Self and family churches in China, and their theological politics.
7. Some missionaries were involved actively in the exploitative colonial diplomacy. For more information see, for example, Daniel H. Bays, *A New History of Christianity in China*, Blackwell Guides to Global Christianity (Chichester, West Sussex: Wiley-Blackwell, 2012), 64.
8. Sally M. Promey, "The 'Return' of Religion in the Scholarship of American Art," *The Art Bulletin* 85.3 (October): 581, http://dx.doi.org/10.2307/3177387.
9. Jonathan A. Anderson and William A. Dyrness, *Modern Art and the Life of a Culture: The Religious Impulses of Modernism*, Studies in Theology and the Arts (Downers Grove, IL: IVP Academic, and imprint of InterVarsity Press, 2016), part 1: *Introduction: Religion and the Discourse of Modernism*, MLA (Modern Language Assoc).
10. Jeffrey L. Kosky, *Arts of Wonder: Enchanting Secularity—Walter De Maria, Diller + Scofidio, James Turrell, Andy Goldsworthy* (Chicago: University of Chicago Press, 2013), 21; see also Anderson and Dyrness, *Modern Art*.
11. Kosky, *Arts of Wonder*, 22.
12. Eleanor Albert, "Christianity in China," *Council on Foreign Relations*, https://www.cfr.org/backgrounder/christianity-china, last updated October 11, 2018; Ma Li, "How Many Christians Are in China—A Blue Book of Religion in 2010," Chinese national newspaper, 2010, issue 006, 1.
13. As soon as the Cultural Revolution ended, family churches exploded in countryside areas. In 1979, Deng Xiaoping launched the first step of economic reform, initiating a temporary reprieve from the limitations placed on culture and religion. Meanwhile, the Hu Kou system, a household registration policy that limits residents from relocating between cities, was not yet established in rural areas. The combination of these two factors meant that family churches and church missionaries were relatively free to move around the countryside preaching the gospel. However, the churches in the cities were still recovering from the persecution of the revolution, and government restrictions on urban churches were still quite strict. The restrictions of the Hu Kou system slowed down urban evangelism, limiting the development of churches in the cities. Chinese contemporary artists living in the cities were exposed to secular Western modern and postmodern theories, but they rarely had a chance to hear about the gospel.
14. Feng Chun Lan, *Dust Icon* series, 2009, in Elsa Art Gallery (室清藝術中心), Taipei.
15. Semiotic ideology refers to one's (usually latent) presuppositions about representation—that is, what things constitute semiotic forms and what those semiotic forms convey. For a specific treatment of semiotic ideology in the context of religion, see Matthew Engelke, "Material Religion," in *The Cambridge Companion to Religious Studies*, ed. Robert Orsi, Cambridge Companions to Religion (Cambridge: Cambridge University Press, 2011), 221–229.
16. Feng Chun Lan, *The Lord's Servantress*, 2012, M Art Center, Shanghai.
17. Arthur C. Danto, "On Art, Action and Meaning," *New York Times*, https://opinionator.blogs.nytimes.com/2010/06/03/on-art-action-and-meaning/.
18. Li Ran, *Escape from the Scene—The Land of Mystery*, 2014, OCT contemporary art terminal (OCT Shanghai).
19. Li Ran, *Life of the Pilgrim*, 2017, Shanghart Beijing.

20. Bogell Peak is a well-known peak among the Eastern Tianshan Mountains in Xinjiang, China. Li Ran, *Life of the Pilgrim*, in his solo exhibition "Life of the Pilgrim" in Shanhart Beijing, 2017, 33:00.
21. Ibid.
22. Ibid.
23. Yeo, *Chairman Mao Meets the Apostle Paul*, 160.
24. See K. K. Yeo, *What Has Jerusalem to Do with Beijing* (Eugene, OR: Pickwick, 2018), 197–240.
25. Gao Lei, *NS24*, 2011, Arario Beijing Gallery, Beijing.
26. Samuel Pagán, "Poor and Poverty: Social Distance and Bible Translation" in *Semeia* 76 (1996), 75; see a similar view but applying Isaiah and Amos to Chinese society: Yeo, *What Has Jerusalem to Do with Beijing*, 112–135, 242–267.
27. Pagán, "Poor and Poverty," 75.
28. Gao Lei, *Screen—The Saw of Manasseh*, 2016, Whitespace (空白空間), Beijing.
29. Cynthia D. Moe-Lobeda, *Resisting Structural Evil: Love as Ecological and Economic Vocation* (Minneapolis, MN: Fortress Press, 2013), 2.

Primary Sources

Feng Chun Lan 馮君藍, *Dust Icon*, 2009, two-fold solo exhibition at Elsa Art Gallery (雲清藝術中心), Taipei, 2009, solo exhibition at M Art Center (M 藝術中心), Shanghai, 2017.

Li Ran 李然, *Escape from the Scene—The Land of Mystery*, 2014, joined group exhibition of "1st OCAT & Pierre Huber Prize Annual Exhibition of Emerging Media Artist," OCT contemporary art terminal (OCT Shanghai), "Biennale of Movie Image," Centre d'Art Contemporain Geneve, Geneva, Switzerland, 2014.

Li Ran, solo exhibition "Life of the Pilgrim," Shanhart Beijing Gallery, 2017.

Gao Lei 高磊, *NS24*, 2011, joined "Almost Tangible" (觸摸), Arario Beijing Gallery, Beijing, 2011.

Gao Lei, *Screen-The Saw of Manasseh* in his solo exhibition "Wilderness (狂野)," Whitespace Gallery (空白空間), Beijing, 2016.

CHAPTER 47

SACRED IMAGES AND SPACE OF THE JESUIT CHURCHES IN BEIJING

LIANMING WANG

INTRODUCTION

To the visitors who traveled to Beijing in the seventeenth and eighteenth centuries, three Catholic churches owned by Portuguese and French Jesuit missionaries were fruitful sites of transcultural encounters in urban contexts. Besides the wonders performed by European scientific instruments, what impressed visitors most was the wealth of Christian iconographies mirrored in exquisitely painted altarpieces and *trompe l'oeil* murals. These painted decorations depicting Christ and the saints, as well as biblical themes, were both considered persuasive means of catechesis to non-Christian visitors and a correlative way of internalizing the salvation of Christ.

Following the successful careers of early missionaries, such as Matteo Ricci S.J. (1552–1602), the Jesuit mission prospered in seventeenth-century Beijing, and two European-style churches were established first under the protection of the Portuguese Padroado: (1) the church of Xitang residence 西堂 (West residence), dedicated to the St. Savior; and (2) the church of Dongtang residence 東堂 (East residence), rebuilt and renamed St. Joseph's Church after 1721.[1] By the end of the seventeenth century, the French Jesuits also had built their own church within the imperial city. This essay first looks at the way these Christian themes and biblical narratives were placed and told in space, in conversation with seventeenth-century woodblock prints and catechetical pamphlets of similar themes.

Placing the Images in Context: Icons and Narrative Altarpieces

A virtual tour should be made first of the church of Xitang residence, renamed Nantang 南堂 (South residence) after 1723. Serving as the ecclesiastical headquarters of the Portuguese mission, a large, three-aisled church building laid out in the shape of a Latin cross occupied a huge tract of land given by the Qing court; it was built in 1650 next to the residence purchased by Ricci in Beijing.[2] This is considered the first public ecclesiastical building in the history of early modern Christianity in China. Although no pictorial source has survived, it is known that the interior of the Xitang church was adorned with five altarpieces, as stated by its founder Johann Adam Schall von Bell s.j. (1591–1666):

> On the main altar, the Savior was seated, holding the globe with one hand and blessing the people with the other, surrounded by the masses of angels and the apostles kneeling around him. The altars between the columns displayed the depictions of the patriarchs Ignatius [Loyola] and Francisco Xavier. Another altar on the left was dedicated to the Blessed Virgin with the surname of the Mary Major, another on the right-hand side, which is of minor rank in China, was dedicated to the St. Michael and other angels.[3]

Beside the icons placed on altars, there also were biblical texts and Christian catechesis—including the lives of Christ and the Virgin Mary, the legends of the angel, the *Ten Commandments* (Exodus 19), Christ's *Beatitudes* (Matt 5:3–12) and works of mercy—displayed on gilded panels that "shimmered from every side" as they hung on the wall, functioning as secondary references to the oral teachings and icons on the altarpieces.[4] In this case, the worship of Christian sacred images and the practices of catechetical education were brought into a new entity, reinforcing the internalization of the doctrines. In the Dongtang church, which was rebuilt in the eighteenth century, for instance, the iconic "image of the Lord of Heaven with dense hair flanked by two standing figures" on the main altar also was enriched by narratives from the life of Christ.[5]

The appearance of the icons of Christ and the "Mary Major" (Virgin Mary) mentioned by Schall were associated with the Gospels of the New Testament and claimed a great importance in the painted decorations of church interiors. Although Christ's image was placed on the main altar of the Xitang church, its scenic and even narrative character, as indicated by the "masses of angels" and the "kneeling apostles," is notably different from its iconic depiction from the early seventeenth century.

During Ricci's time, three types of altarpieces copied after European paintings were displayed in the Jesuit interiors in Beijing. They are a large triptych with the depiction of the Virgin Mary with the infant Jesus and John the Baptist,[6] a small, but "very well painted" image of Christ from Rome,[7] and a copy of the *Salus Populi Romani* from the Santa Maria Maggiore in Rome, known as the "Luke Madonna."[8] The triptych, which was painted with tempera on wood and described as an image of "rare delicacy of the lively colors and figures,"[9] was commissioned in Spain and brought via New Spain to Macao along the trading routes. According to the Gospel of St. Luke (Luke 1:36, 76–77), John the Baptist was both the cousin and precursor of Jesus. In Giulio Aleni's SJ (1582–1649) illustrated book on Christ's life, known as *Tianzhu jiangsheng chuxiang jingjie* 天主降生出相經解 (*Illustrated Explanation of the Incarnation of the Lord of Heaven*, 1637), the announcement of the birth of John the Baptist (Luke 1:5–25) was therefore the first scene of Christ's biography.[10]

While the copy of this triptych was displayed only occasionally in Beijing, such as on the feast of St. John (June 24) and was not seen after 1605, the icons of Christ and the Luke Madonna were used mainly as altarpieces.[11] Most likely, however, these two icons were not placed in the same space after the "Zhaoqing incident" in 1583, in which the image of the Virgin Mary was banned from the main altar to avoid the impression that the Christian god was a woman.[12] The same impression was stated constantly in the contemporary writings of the Chinese literati, who were the major recipients of the Christian images, including an official named Xie Zhaozhe (1567–1624), who falsely assumed in 1609 after seeing a copy of the Luke Madonna in Beijing that the "Lord of Heaven" (Jesus Christ) was female.[13]

Bearing this in mind, it is reasonable to suggest the separate placement of the two icons in Ricci's church, which was built earlier on the same plot. Compared to the previous chapel, this church was a more elaborate free-standing building with a triangular layout; the main altar with the image of Christ was placed on an elevated dais with three steps, as the name of the church reveals—the "Hall of the Lord of Heaven." (*Tianzhu tang* 天主堂)[14] Although the church building had not been used for years because of Christian persecution, the images of Christ and the Luke Madonna continued to be displayed until the 1630s, as witnessed by a Chinese visitor named Liu Tong (1593–1636):

> On the main altar, a portrait of Christ was worshipped.... He was in the guise of a man of about 30, holding a world atlas [probably a globe] in his left hand. The crossed fingers of his right hand were directed as if pointing at what he was saying. His beard and raised eyebrows gave the impression of him being furious but happy at the same time... on the right-hand side there was a chapel of the Holy Mother. The Mother was in the form of a young girl holding a child in her arms, which was Jesus.[15]

Liu's account is revealing, as it provides an insightful clue about their separate placement in the interior: while Christ's image was worshipped on the main altar, the Luke Madonna was placed in a women's chapel founded by Ricci and dedicated to the Congregation of the Holy Mother, known as the *Shengmu hui* 聖母會.[16] An engraving (Fig. 47.1) from Athanasius Kircher's S.J. (1602–1680) *China illustrata*[17] depicts the image of the Luke Madonna placed on the altar behind the curtains as the backdrop of Ricci's encounter with Xu Guangqi 徐光啟 (1562–1633), who became Christian afterwards. Heavily relying on correspondence with the Beijing Jesuits, Kircher's engraving suggests the separate use of the image of the Virgin Mary in the space of congregational community, instead of being placed on the church's main altar.

In all known cases, including the other two Jesuit churches in Beijing, the adoration of the Virgin Mary was secondary in the church interior, as the icon of Christ was always placed on the main altar. Images of Mary were primarily featured in feminine sacred spaces.[18] As a matter of fact, the Luke Madonna was the protagonist of Marian devotion, and there was a reason for the Jesuit preference of this image. Its prototype (Fig. 47.2), in which the Holy Mother wears a dark blue cloak bordered with gold over a crimson tunic and holds the Jesus child, was an ancient Byzantine icon brought to Rome in 590 CE. Against the background of the increased significance of Marian devotion stressed by Jesuit spirituality, the Luke Madonna, which was considered "the face of universal, post-Tridentine Catholicism,"[19] was chosen for duplication. With the permission of Pope Pius V (r. 1566–1572), it was reproduced massively and distributed globally, both as painted replicas and prints.[20]

As proven by its multiple copies, the predominance of the Lukan Madonna in early Jesuit spaces in China was beyond question. Although the style, format, and quality of such copies varied, their "validity... was dependent on a *believed* association with the original in Rome"[21] and charged with the Pope's authoritative power as well as the mysticism of St. Luke's narrative. Toward the end of this century, it was recorded that a large painting of the Virgin Mary by Jacob De Nijis (1650–?), the court painter to the Duke of Mantua, had arrived in Beijing.[22] Coincidentally, a separate women's chapel, known as *Lingbao tang* 領報堂 (Hall of the Annunciation), was erected on the grounds of the Xitang residence, reserved for women and other congregational activities.[23]

Unlike Jesuit settlements in South America, where a variety of biblical themes were favored for making altarpieces, including the Circumcision and Crucifixion, the icon of Christ claimed a great importance in China. Known as *Salvator Mundi*, associated with an eschatological undertone, this type of image represents Christ's dominion over the world, paralleled with Jesuit ambitions for global expansion. It had been invented in the late Middle Ages but gained importance during the Reformation, first through the engravings of the Wierix brothers who commercially engaged in the global circulation of Christian images. In the aforementioned book illustration commissioned by Aleni, which was partially based on the *Evangelicae historiae imagines* (1593),[24] the four Gospels were stated clearly as the sources of Christ's hagiographical narratives.[25]

Given the fact that the Chinese copy of the Roman Savior image was painted with oils on a small copperplate, it is reasonable to suggest that its Roman model was probably in line with those circulated in Japan, as evidenced by a well-known Japanese example (Fig. 47.3) copied from an engraving by Hieronymus Wierix (1553–1619) with slight modifications. In this view, the figure of Christ appears as a half-figured, middle-aged man with shoulder-length hair and a beard. Holding up his right hand as a blessing, his left hand rests on a ball embedded with astronomic implications of the heliocentric worldview promoted by the Jesuits. This standardized representation of a three-quarter profile departed from the frontal view common in the fifteenth century, as in Leonardo da Vinci's (1452–1519) famous *Salvator Mundi*, and was widely circulated in Asia, especially in Beijing.

By the mid-seventeenth century, the previous iconic altarpieces notably were replaced by a new set of scenic and narrative iconographies copied from European prints. The painted decoration of Schall's Xitang church, as noted earlier, provides such an example. This significant turn in the interior paralleled the Chinese copying of European prints, as evidenced by Schall's illustrated book on the life of Christ presented to the Chinese emperor, known as *Jingcheng shuxiang* 進呈書相 (*The Explanatory Illustrations, Presented to His Majesty*).[26] As in the Xitang church's main altarpiece, Christ (Fig. 47.4) is presented floating in the clouds sideways, surrounded by countless *putti*, who either playfully hide in his robe or in the clouds.[27]

Besides the main altar, the other four altarpieces were placed in the lateral chapels of the Xitang church. As a counterpart to the Luke Madonna in the left-hand chapel next to the main altar, an image of St. Michael the Archangel stood in the right chapel. The portrayal of St. Michael from the New Testament, who appeared in the guise of an armed knight, gained an increased importance among the Jesuits due to his symbolic significance as conqueror of the devil and leader of the heavenly kingdom. In the early catechistic practices, for instance in Ningbo, Zhejiang province, the narrative on the Fall of the Angels (Rev 12:7–10) also was included.[28] The devil, or Satan, who was defeated by St. Michael, often was represented as a dragon in European prints and now gained a new meaning in China, the dragon's kingdom.

Like the Salvator Mundi, the image of St. Michael was associated with a strong sense of eschatological meanings, and its emergence in sacred space reveals Christ's salvation and moreover, stressed the close ties to Jesuit spirituality as well. In Loyola's spiritual exercises, which led the Christian believers to the path of personal knowledge of God via themed mediation, the fifth exercise of the first week of meditation was conceived with the contemplation of hell.[29] It is probable that the image of St. Michael was incorporated into both the Xitang church's later period and two other Jesuit churches in Beijing as well.[30]

The iconographic program of the Xitang church's interior strongly resembled that in Macao. In addition to St. Michael, the images of Jesuit saints St. Xavier and St. Ignatius, both canonized in 1622, also were placed in chapels. Their involvement in the interior's iconographic program conveyed a strong sense of a consolidated Jesuit identity in the iconography, which could be traced back to the hierarchical system of Christian carvings on the façade of Macao's St. Paul church, finished in 1637.[31] Known as the "Bible carved in stone," four Jesuit saints, including St. Francis Borgia (1510–1572) and St. Gonzaga (1568–1591), early pioneers of the Jesuit global mission, formed a solid basis of the framework of biblical narrative carved on St. Paul's façade, in which Christ is placed above the Virgin Mary and below the Holy Spirit.

Stimulated by the increased number of European prints arriving in China, such as the portrait of St. Michael and biblical scenes like the War in Heaven (Rev 12:7–17),[32] this iconographic turn achieved by the mid-seventeenth century had a lasting impact, including Xitang's baroque building erected between 1703 and 1711. Following the Il-Gesù scheme, the new building presented itself as a single, wide-nave hall church with an enlarged chancel and two transepts connecting to the lateral rows of chapels (Fig. 47.5). In the exterior view, the nave and transepts formed a Latin cross, which evoked Christ's crucifixion in a symbolic way. This unique single-nave structure, on one hand, took advantage of the acoustic results for conducting sermons and other liturgical activities, and, on the other hand emphasized the sacramental symbolism in church architecture.[33]

In a letter sent from Beijing in 1711, an image of St. Joseph, the earthly father of Jesus and member of the Holy Family, was placed in the transept as the counterpart to the Luke Madonna, and an altarpiece dedicated to the guardian angel was added, in addition to the Jesuit saints and St. Michael; as before, the image of Christ was placed on the main altarpiece.[34] Most remarkably, as suggested by a drawing (Fig. 47.6) kept in the Historical Overseas Archive in Lisbon, the main altarpiece later was placed on a monumental baroque altar for the Eucharist adoration.

A large-sized documentary painting (Fig. 47.7), now kept in the Bibliothèque nationale de France, presents us an exceptional example of how the presence of Christ was celebrated in the eighteenth-century Beitang church.[35] In line with the contemporary written account, the Feast of Sacred Heart was captured as a ceremonial moment with a musical performance dedicated to the Holy Wounds of Christ (John 19:34, 20:24–29), represented by five devotional tablets positioned in front of the church façade. When prayers were done, a holy mass was celebrated afterwards in the Chapel of St. Sacrament, and the blessed sacrament was then accompanied by a solemn procession and placed in front of the main altar, celebrating Christ's presence in the Eucharist.

Religious Experience, Illusionism, and Transcultural Encounters

By 1700, when the French mission became independent from the Portuguese Padroado, the frescoed interior of the Beitang church presented a highly competitive project to other Jesuit interiors, in particular the Xitang church. This major shift was inseparable from both the Jesuit success of their frescoed spaces in Rome and positive Chinese reactions to Christian altarpieces in seventeenth-century Beijing.

In general, the religious experience and, therewith, the theological-pedagogic purpose of sacred images like the Luke Madonna and Salvador Mundi, did not receive too much attention in the case of spontaneous visitors in Beijing—as opposed to their underlying painterly value. This emphasized superiority of European oil painting, achieved through the volumetric effect of the oil and tempera colors, impressed the Chinese visitors the most.[36] Hence, it is not surprising that the interests of and reactions from visitors first focused more on the volumetric, partly illusionistic effects, than on its iconography and related biblical narratives.

Bearing these in mind, the interpretation of Christian images seemed completely disconnected from the European context of religious painting. In his influential *Painting and Experience in Fifteenth-Century Italy*, Michael Baxandall informed us that three functions were given priority in the making of religious painting: the mediation of the sacraments and the faith in pictorial form for the laity; the visualization of the history of Christian salvation and passion in view of the unreliability of human memory; and finally, the evocation of sentiments and piety.[37] We must be aware of the fact that the sacred images displayed on altars were primarily religious paintings, based on the iconography of existing holy Scriptures and biblical chapters; they were subordinated to a fully developed system of theological interpretations and were placed in the center of the liturgical-meditative activities as well as a more complex system of image worship in an ecclesiastical context.

With that said, it is worth emphasizing that Chinese perceptions about Christian iconography were anchored primarily in the aesthetic and mastery of painting techniques, instead of iconography or biblical themes. In other words, the catechetical experience in the early seventeenth century was rooted first in the field of a transcultural, painterly encounter and was not primarily religious. In the eyes of the Chinese, the altarpieces and murals were primarily painterly masterpieces, intended for viewing, appreciating, and contemplating, but not for worship or meditation of the sacraments.

In the case of seventeenth-century spontaneous visitors, the altarpieces placed in sacred spaces did not seem to fully accomplish the tasks of establishing an existential connection between the viewer and the iconography depicted, including the narratives of the salvation and the passion that had been internalized behind all of these iconic images.

The religious experience and understanding of Christian iconography require culture-specific prior knowledge and, further, a catechetical education, which was unknown to spontaneous visitors. A report from Beijing in 1605 gave us a well-known example of this issue: The protagonist was a Chinese visitor with Jewish roots named Ai Tian 艾田 (1598–1645) from Kaifeng, Henan province. After being shown a copy of the aforementioned triptych (with depiction of the Virgin Mary with the infant Jesus and John the Baptist), he was confused, as he recognized its subject as Rebecca with Jacob and Esau.[38] Even though early Jesuit agents put great emphasis on the explanation of Christian iconography—even composing a poem for Chinese Buddhist devotees to understand it[39]—the imparting of pictorial content was limited due to their placement in a new cultural surrounding, even though they were placed in a Christian sacred space.

The problems outlined here lead us to an important point in the discussions that follow. The lack of preexisting thought patterns and categories, the shortage of practices in a series of conventions of visual representation, as well as the experience deducted from the surroundings,[40] finally led to an almost pre-iconographic perception of form and color and an accentuation of the material aspect of the Christian images.

The painterly illusionism was admired greatly by visitors to Beijing. Stimulated by the splendid murals in the Beitang church, a Jesuit lay brother named Giuseppe Castiglione (1688–1766) was called to Beijing with the primary task of decorating the interior of the new Xitang church finished in 1711. In the time after his arrival, apart from his engagement in the imperial workshop, Castiglione dedicated himself to the making of altarpieces and *trompe l'oeil* murals.[41] In 1721, a Korean visitor named Lee Gi-ji 李器之 (1690–1722) thoroughly described the altarpieces during his visit and identified the iconography of the main altar as a person dressed in red and floating in clouds, accompanied by six men, suggesting its iconography as the transfiguration of Jesus (Matt 17:1–8; Mark 9:2–8; Luke 9:28–36).[42] In seventeenth-century China, this iconography was known as "Jesus, the Lord of heaven, reveals his appearance" (*Tianzhu Yesu xian shengrong xiang* 天主耶穌顯聖容像) in Schall's illustrated book.[43]

According to Lee's description, the main altarpiece depicted Jesus drawing aside the disciples Peter, Jacob, and John and leading them onto a hill, surrounded by dense clouds; above him, the Holy Spirit appeared in the shape of an old man in the glory of light, who, according to Lee, "hid in the clouds and looked out" (Fig. 47.8).[44] This iconography is, however, different from the Salvador Mundi on the main altar of 1711. Also, iconographies of altarpieces in the newly decorated Xitang church were stated clearly in contemporary sources. There is less dispute about the identity of the "winged God of heaven, who kills the demons with the spear" on an altar[45] as St. Michael. Given textural explanations of the aforementioned Lisbon drawing, the iconographies of the other altarpieces made by Castiglione could be specified as the annunciation (Luke 1:26–26, 38:26), St. Joseph, St. Ignatius, St. Xavier, and the guardian angel (Fig. 47.9).

In a later, separate passage following the description of the ceiling painting, Lee mentioned another iconography related to Christ, in which he was "lying in the clouds" and holding a "blue, translucent ball about the size of a human's head."[46] In the ceiling of the Beitang church, a depiction of Christ "seated in the clouds on a group of Angels and holding the Globe of the World in his hand"[47] also was included. In the Dongtang church, a fresco cycle including the adoration of the Magi (Matt 2:11) and the resurrection of Jesus (Matt 28:16; Mark 16:14–18; Luke 24: 44–49) was added, in addition to the image of Christ.[48]

The main emphasis behind Castiglione's painterly renewal was the effectiveness of the ecclesiastical interior and a visually more suggestive system of persuasion in front of the eyes of visitors. After a significant change from scenic and narrative depiction to an illusionistic moment, the frescoed interiors in both the Xitang and Dongtang churches presented an affect-evoking space of synesthetic experience to the visitors for touching and playing, in addition to the admirable plasticity of the altarpieces. One of Lee's contemporaries named Han Deok-hoo 韓德厚 (1732–?) was so taken by the painterly illusion, he grasped the painting with his hands: "... they [the figures] moved, as if they were living human beings; but it was hard to identify whether they were real or painted humans.... I touched them with my hands, then I realized after all that they were painted."[49]

Han was not the only one who transferred his viewing experience to the tactile sense. Another Korean visitor named Hong Dae-yong 洪大容 (1731–1783), who was aware of the mathematic-geometric origin of illusionary space, did so as well. Hong finally concluded that "the secrets of European painting" were derived from mathematics, and the genre of painterly work constituted an independent branch of science.[50]

Through the use of illusionistic murals, eighteenth-century Jesuit interiors transformed from sites with an abundance of painterly pieces and curiosities into spaces of aesthetically playful experience, in which the narration of Christ's salvation was perceived by a synesthetic experience of illusion that lured numerous visitors. It is worth mentioning, however, that none of the altarpieces and illusionistic murals by Castiglione survived the fire of 1775, and the main altarpiece was, by the time of its reconstruction, replaced by a large-sized painting of *Immaculate*.[51]

By the end of the eighteenth century, the scenes of the Nativity of Christ (Matt 1:18–25; Luke 2:1–7), the Annunciation, the War in Heaven and the Descent from the Cross (John 19:38–42) were still mentioned by visitors as altarpieces in its side chapels.[52]

Conclusion

In seventeenth- and eighteenth-century Beijing, the wealth of Christian sacred images presented in Jesuit church interiors were the primary objects of correlative, partly synesthetic ways of seeing for many visitors. Meanwhile, those sacred images achieved a notable transformation from the icons via scenic and narrative to illusionistic moments for worshippers and some visitors. Medieval icons were used first as altarpieces. Their typologies were, however, greatly conditioned by the availability of their painterly copies from Europe. Although these copies in early Jesuit spaces formed a typological and iconographical coherence, a hierarchy in their spatial displacement was highly visible. For example, while the image of Christ was placed constantly as the main altarpiece, the image of the Virgin Mary was downgraded mainly to a secondary role in the church interior and was engaged mostly in the congregational and feminine sacred spaces.

After an abundance of European prints flooded China, the iconic images soon were replaced by coherent iconographic programs enriched by Jesuit saints and scenes from the New Testament. This significant turn had a persistent impact on the painted decorations found in later ecclesiastical buildings, including Schall's church of the Xitang residence and its later enlargement. In response to the painterly illusionism exhibited in the French Beitang church, the new Xitang church (later renamed Nantang) successfully transformed from a site with an abundance of painterly pieces into an aesthetically playful space of experience of touching and playing that greatly shaped the way non-Christian visitors perceived Christianity in eighteenth-century Beijing.

APPENDIX

FIGURE 47.1 Matteo Ricci with Xu Guangqi, engraving, in Athanasius Kircher, *China illustrata*... (Amsterdam: Meurs, 1667), 118.

FIGURE 47.2 *Salus Populi Romani*, known as the "Luke Madonna," 117 x 79 cm, color on wooden plate, Basilica of Santa Maria Maggiore, Rome.

FIGURE 47.3 *Salvador mundi*, unknown Japanese painter, oil on small-sized copperplate, dated 1597, University of Tokyo General Library.

FIGURE 47.4 Folio "Image of the one Lord to whom all heaven and earth belong" (*Tiandi zonggui yizhu xiang*), in *Explanatory Illustrations, Presented to His Majesty*, woodblock prints, commissioned by Johann Adam Schall von Bell, 1640, Beijing, Austrian National Library.

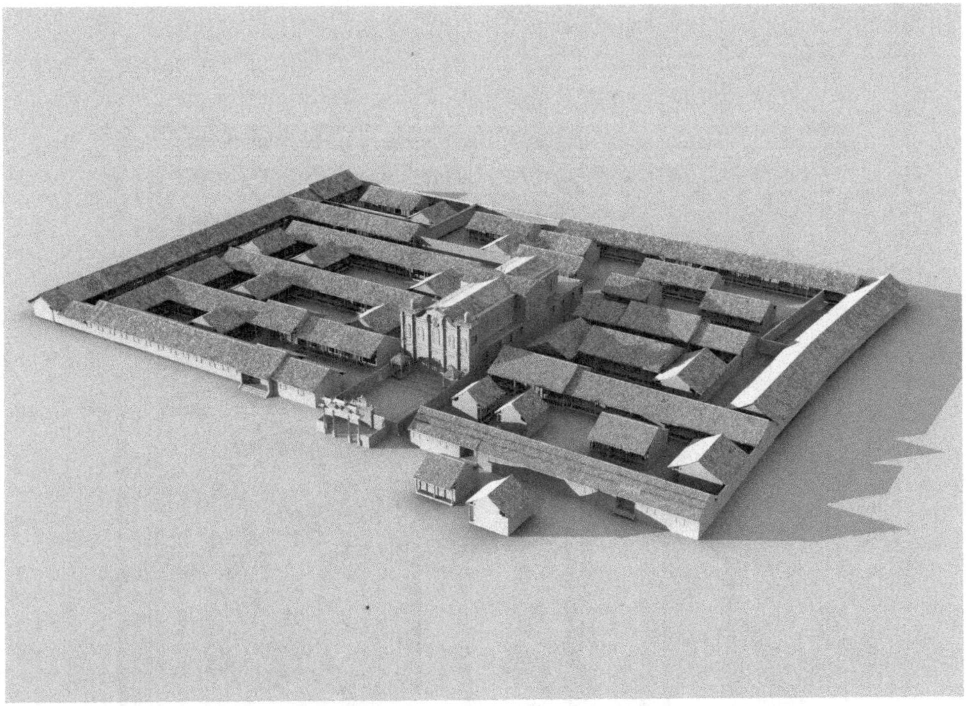

FIGURE 47.5 Reconstruction of the eighteenth-century Xitang (Nantang) church in Beijing and its compound.

FIGURE 47.6 Interior of the Xitang (Nantang) church in Beijing, ink and light color on paper, 55.5 x 50.5 cm, ca. 1730, Arquivo Histórico Ultramarino, Lisbon.

FIGURE 47.7 Anonymous, a documentary painting showing a solemn procession in front of the Beitang church, color on silk, 185.7 x 130 cm, after 1786 (?), Bibliothèque nationale de France, Paris.

FIGURE 47.8 Reconstruction of the view of the main altarpiece in the eighteenth-century Xitang (Nantang) church.

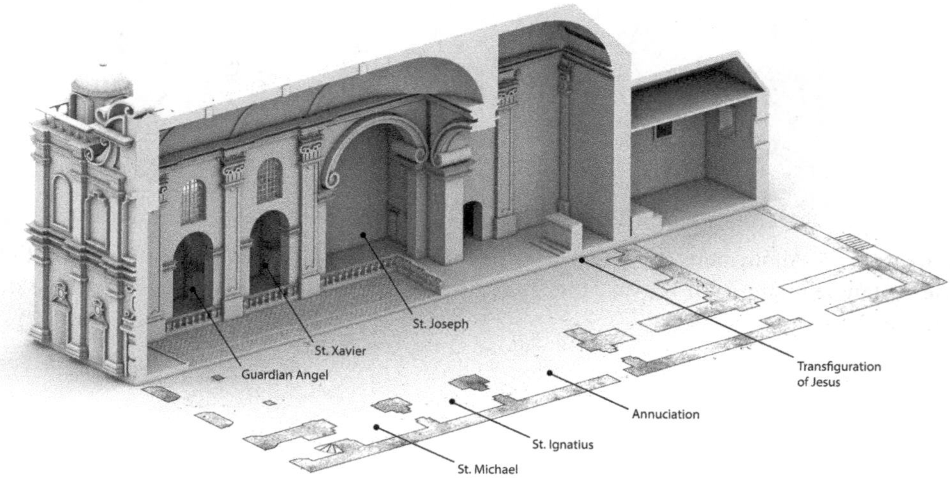

FIGURE 47.9 Reconstruction of the iconographic program of the Xitang (Nantang) church after 1719.

NOTES

1. For a brief history of the Jesuit churches in Beijing, see Walter Devine, *The Four Churches of Peking* (London: Oates & Washbourne, 1930), 17–47.
2. Johann Adam Schall von Bell and Ignaz Schumann von Mannsegg, eds., *Geschichte der chinesischen Mission unter der Leitung des Pater Johann Adam Schall, Priester aus der Gesellschaft Jesu* (Vienna: Mechitaristen-Congregationsbuchhandlung, 1834), 353–355; see also Matteo Ricci and Pietro Tacchi Venturi, eds., *Opere storiche del P. Matteo Ricci. Con prolegomeni note e tavole dal P. Pietro Tacchi Venturi S.J.* Macerata: Premiato stab. tip. F. Giorgetti, 1911–1913), 1:397; Matteo Ricci, Pasquale d'Elia, ed., *Fonti Ricciane: Storia dell'introduzione del cristianesimo in Cina* (Rome: Roma Libreria dello Stato, 1942–1949), 2:352.
3. Schall, *Geschichte der chinesischen Mission*, 356–357; Alfons Väth, *Johann Adam Schall von Bell S.J.: Missionar in China, kaiserlicher Astronom und Ratgeber am Hofe von Peking 1592–1666* (Nettetal: Steyler, 1991), 167.
4. Ibid.
5. Kim Soon-hyup, *Yeonhengrok* 燕行錄 (1729), in *Yeonhaengnok chonjip* 燕行錄全集 (Seoul: Tongguk Taehakkyo Ch'ulp'anbu, 2001), 38:357; Huang Shijian, "Chaoxian yanxinglu suoji de Beijing tianzhutang 朝鮮燕行錄所記的北京天主堂," in *Hanguoxue lunwenji* 韓國學論文集 (Beijing: Shehui kexueyuan wenxian chubanshe, 1999), 158–159.
6. Venturi, *Opere storiche*, 1:125–126, 157–158.
7. D'Elia, *Fonti Ricciane*, 1:230–231; 2:4.
8. Ibid. 2:89–91; see also Pasquale d'Elia, "La Prima Diffusione nel Mondo dell'Imagine di Maria *Salus Populi Romani*," *Fede e Arte* 10 (1954): 1–11.
9. Venturi, *Opere storiche*, 1:125–126, 157–158; Gauvin A. Bailey, *Art on the Jesuit Missions in Asia and Latin America 1542–1773* (Toronto: University of Toronto Press, 2013), 91.
10. Qu Yi, "Konfuzianische Convenevolezza in chinesischen christlichen Illustrationen. Das Tianzhu jiangsheng chuxiang jingjie von 1637," *Asiatische Studien* 4 (2012): 1005–1008.
11. Venturi, *Opere storiche*, 1:468–469; 2:291–293; D'Elia, *Fonti Ricciane*, 2:316–317.
12. D'Elia, *Fonti Ricciane*, 1:194, 231; Henri Bernard-Maître, *Le père Matthieu Ricci et la société chinoise de son temps (1552–1610)* (Tianjin: A la Procure de la Mission, 1937), 134.
13. Xie Zhaozhe, Fu Cheng, ed., *Wuzazu* 五雜組 (after 1613), repr. (Shanghai: Shanghai guji chubanshe, 2012), 76.
14. D'Elia, *Fonti Ricciane*, 2:257.
15. Liu Tong and Yu Yizheng, *Dijing jingwu lüe* 帝京景物略 (1635), repr. (Beijing: Beijing guji chubanshe, 1980), 153. For an English translation, see Gail King, "Note on a Late Ming Dynasty Chinese Description of 'Ricci's Church' in Beijing," *Sino-Western Cultural Relations Journal* 20 (1998): 49–51.
16. Venturi, *Opere storiche*, 1:591; Liam Matthew Brockey, *Journey to the East: The Jesuit Mission to China 1579–1724* (Cambridge, MA: Harvard University Press, 2007), 333–364. More on the Marian congregation in China, see Jeremy Clarke, "Our Lady of China: Marian Devotion and the Jesuits," *Studies in the Spirituality of Jesuits* 41.3 (2009): 40–42.
17. Athanasius Kircher, *China monumentis, qua sacris qua profanis, nec non variis naturae et artis spectaculis, aliarumque rerum memorabilium argumentis illustrata* (Antwerp: Meurs, 1667).
18. Matteo Ripa and Fortunato Prandi, eds., *Memoirs of Father Ripa, during Thirteen Years' Residence at the Court of Peking in the Service of the Emperor of China* (London: J. Murray,

1844), 167; Paul Bornet, "Les anciennes églises de Pékin. Notes et histoire," *Bulletin catholique de Pékin* 375 (1944): 535–539; Devine, *Four Churches*, 7; Brockey, *Journey to the East*, 364.
19. Mia M. Mochizuki, "Sacred Art in an Age of Mechanical Reproduction: The *Salus Populi Romani* Madonna in the World," *Kyoto Studies in Art History* 1 (2016): 131.
20. On the reproduction and circulation of this icon, see Guido Anichini, "*La 'Mater Dei Dignissima' di S. Maria Maggiore*," in *L'illustrazione vaticana* 2.15 (1931): 22–26; Kirstin Noreen, "The Icon of Santa Maria Maggiore, Rome: An Image and Its Afterlife," *Renaissance Studies* 19.5 (2005): 664–666.
21. Cf. Norren, "The Icon of Sant Maria Maggiore," 666.
22. Noël Golvers, *Libraries of Western Learning for China: Formation of Jesuit Libraries* (Leuven: Leuven University Press, 2013), 2:9.
23. Paul Bornet, "Les anciennes églises de Pékin. Nant'tang," *Bulletin catholique de Pékin* 377 (1945): 29.
24. Gerónimo Nadal et al., *Evangelicae historiae imagines: ex ordine euangeliorum, quae toto anno in missae sacrificio recitantur, in ordinem temporis vitae Christi digestae* (Antwerp 1593).
25. Nicolas Standaert, *An Illustrated Life of Christ Presented to the Chinese Emperor: The History of Jincheng Shuxiang (1640)* (Nettetal: Steyler 2007), 112–118.
26. Ibid. 13–15, 120–121.
27. A nearly identical European model did not seem to have been discovered, but a colored miniature drawing made by the Mughal court stood in close alliance to a copper engraving by the Wierix brothers, which was used as the model for its Chinese copy. See more in Bailey, *Art on Jesuit Missions*, 30–31.
28. Junhyoung Michael Shin, "The Jesuits and the Portrait of God in Late Ming China," *Harvard Theological Review* 107.2 (2014): 202.
29. Alfred Feder, *Ignatius von Loyola. Geistliche Übungen* (Regensburg: G.J. Manz, 1922), 50–52.
30. Elisabetta Corsi, "Pozzo's Treatise as a Workshop for the Construction of a Sacred Catholic Space in Beijing," in *Artifizi della metafora. Saggi su Andrea Pozzo*, ed. Richard Bösel and Lydia Salviucci Insolera (Rome: Artemide, 2011), 241–242.
31. Manuel Teixeira, *The Church of St. Paul in Macau* (Lisboa: Centro de Estudos Históricos Ultramarinos da Junta de Investigações Científicas do Ultramar, 1979), 72–75.
32. These prints were arrived in Beijing between 1691 and 1694, see Noël Golvers, *Building Humanistic Libraries in Late Imperial China: Circulation of Books, Prints and Letters between Europe and China (XVII–XVIII cent.) in the Framework of the Jesuit Mission* (Rome: Roma Nuova Cultura, 2011), 140.
33. Coris, "Pozzo's Treatise as a Workshop," 237–239.
34. Anttónio Vasconcelos de Saldanha, ed., *De Kangxi para o Papa pela via de Portugal: memtória e documentos relativos à intervenção de Portugal e da Companhia de Jesus na questão dos ritos chineses e nas relações entre o imperados Kangxi e a Santa Sé* (Macao: Instituto Português do Oriente, 2002), 181.
35. For an overview of this painting, see Lianming Wang, "Church, A 'Sacred Event' and the Visual Perspective of an 'Etic Viewer': An 18th-Century Western-Style Chinese Painting Held in the Bibliothèque nationale de France," in *Face to Face: The Transcendence of the Arts in China and Beyond*, ed. Rui O. Lopes (Lisbon: University of Lisbon, 2014), 1:182–213.
36. Johannes Bettray, *Die Akkommodationsmethode des P. Matteo Ricci S.I. in China* (Rome: Apud aedes Universitatis Gregorianae, 1955), 55.
37. Michael Baxandall, *Painting and Experience in Fifteenth-Century Italy: A Primer in the Social History of Pictorial Style* (Oxford: Oxford University Press), 40–46.

38. Paul Pelliot, "Le juif Ngai: informateur du P. Mathieu Ricci," *T'oung pao* 20.1 (1920–1921): 32–39.
39. Albert Chan, "Michele Ruggieri SJ (1543–1667) and His Chinese Poems," *Monumenta Serica* 41 (1993): 168.
40. Baxandall, *Painting and Experience in Fifteenth Century Italy*, 55.
41. George Loehr, "Missionary Artists at the Manchu Court," *Transactions of the Oriental Ceramic Society* 34 (1962–1963): 51–67; Cécile Beurdeley, *Castiglione, peintre jésuite à la coeur de Chine* (Fribourg: Office du Livre, 1971), 11, 92; Howard Rogers, "For the Love of God: Castiglione at the Qing Imperial Court," in *Chinese Painting under the Qianlong Emperor*, ed. Chou Ju-hsi, Claudia Brown (Phoenix: Arizona State University, 1988), 142; Wang Jia-ji, *Giuseppe Castiglione and the Early Qing Court Painting*, MA thesis (Chinese Culture University, Taipei, 1986), 92–99.
42. Lee Gi-ji, *Iramgi* 一庵集 (1720), vol. 2, fol. 290; see more in Shin Ik-Cheol, "The Experiences of Visiting Catholic Churches in Peking and the Recognition of Western Learning Reflected in the Journals of Travel to Beijing," *The Review of Korean Studies* 9 (2006): 11–31; Lianming Wang, "Europerie und Macht. Akteure und Publika der transkulturellen Bilderbauten aus der Regierungszeit des Kaisers Qianlong," in *Wechselblicke. Zwischen China und Europa 1669–1907*, ed. Matthias Weiß, Eva-Maria Troelenberg, and Joachim Brand (Berlin: Imhof, 2017), 59.
43. Standaert, *An Illustrated Life of Christ*, 202.
44. Lee, *Iramgi*, fol. 291.
45. Ibid.
46. Ibid. fol. 230.
47. Kristina Kleutghen, *Imperial Illusions: Crossing Pictorial Boundaries in the Qing Palaces* (Seattle: University of Washington Press, 2015), 81.
48. Huang, "Chaoxian yanxinglu," 158–159.
49. Han Deok-hoo, *Yeonheng iirok* 燕行日錄 (1732), in *Yonhaengnok sonjip* 燕行錄選集, ed. Sungkyunkwan University (Seoul: Soongyun'gwan Taehakkyo Taedong Munhwa Yoon'guwoon, 1962), 2:376.
50. Huang, "Chaoxian yanxinglu," 158–159.
51. Louis Pfister, *Notices biographiques et bibliographiques sur les jésuites de l'ancienne mission de Chine, 1552–1773* (Shanghai: Shanghai Mission Catholique, 1932–1934), 2:972.
52. Huang, "Chaoxian yanxinglu," 157.

Primary Sources

Ai Rulüe (Giulio Aleni). *Tianzhu jiangsheng chuxiang jingjie* 天主降生出像經解 (*Illustrated Explanation of the Incarnation of the Lord of Heaven*), woodcut, Jinjiang (Fujian) 1637. Bibliothèque nationale de France, Chinois 6750.

Gerónimo Nadal et al. *Evangelicae historiae imagines: ex ordine euangeliorum, quae toto anno in missae sacrificio recitantur, in ordinem temporis vitae Christi digestae*. Antwerp 1593.

Tang Ruowang (Johann Adam Schall von Bell). *Jingcheng shuxiang* 進呈書像 (*The Explanatory Illustrations, Presented to His Majesty*), woodcut. Beijing, 1640. Biblioteca Nazionale Centrale Vittorio Emanuele II, Rome, VE 72 B. 299.

Index of Ancient Texts [IAT]

Note: Tables are indicated by an italic "*t*".

For the benefit of digital users, indexed terms that span two pages (e.g., 52–53) may, on occasion, appear on only one of those pages.

Chinese Classical Texts

Index of Names and Subjects

Note: *Cross-reference with* Index of Ancient Texts, *abbreviated as* IAT

Tables and figures are indicated by an italic "*t*" and "*f*", respectively, following the page number.

For the benefit of digital users, indexed terms that span two pages (e.g., 52–53) may, on occasion, appear on only one of those pages.